ROGET'S THESAURUS

Existence

Ens, entity, being, existence | Nonentity, nullity, nihility
Essence, quintessence, quiddity | nonexistence, nothing, nought
Nature, thing, substance, course, world, frame, position, constitution | void, zero, cypher, blank, empty
Reality, (v. Truth) actual existence — fact, course of things, under ye sun, extant, present | Unreal, ideal, imaginary, unsubstantial, visionary, fabulous, fictitious, supposititious, absent, shadow, dream, phantom, phantasm
Positive, affirmative, absolute, intrinsic, substantive, inherent | Negative, virtual, extrinsic, potential, adjective

To be, exist, obtain, stand
pass, subsist, prevail, lie
— on foot, on ye tapis
to constitute, form, compose, to consist of
State, mode of existence, condition, nature, constitution, habit, scope, habitude, temperament
Affection, predicament, situation, position, posture, place, contingency
Circumstance, case, plight, trim, tune, — point, degree
juncture, conjuncture, pass, emergency, exigency.

— Mode, manner, style, cast, fashion, form, shape
strain, way, degree. — tenure, terms, tenor
footing, character, capacity
Relation, relationship, affinity, alliance, analogy, filiation, (v. Connection)
Reference, about, respect, regard, concerning, touching
in point of, as to, — pertaining to, belonging, applicable to
relatively, according to
Comparable, commensurate, correspondent, account, -able | incompatible, incommensurate, -ble, irreconcilable, discordant.

Facsimile of the first page of the MS. classified catalogue of words completed
by Dr. P. M. Roget in 1805, which was the germ of the Thesaurus.

THESAURUS
OF ENGLISH WORDS AND PHRASES

CLASSIFIED AND ARRANGED
SO AS TO FACILITATE THE EXPRESSION OF IDEAS
AND TO ASSIST IN LITERARY COMPOSITION

BY

PETER MARK ROGET, M.D., F.R.S.

ENLARGED BY

JOHN LEWIS ROGET, M.A.

THIS CLASSIC AMERICAN EDITION WAS ORIGINALLY
REVISED AND ENLARGED BY

SAMUEL ROMILLY ROGET, M.A.

AVENEL BOOKS
New York

Library of Congress Catalog Card Number: 76-48411
This edition is published by Avenel Books
a division of Barre Publishing Inc.
f g h
Manufactured in the United States of America

FOREWORD

TO THE

AUTHORIZED AMERICAN EDITION

It is fitting that a new American edition of Roget's Thesaurus, issued by the American Company of its original London publishers, should have some account of its origin and progress.

Early in the nineteenth century the idea of the utility of a list of words classified according to the ideas that they express occurred to Dr. Peter Mark Roget, and his first draft was completed in 1805. It was added to from time to time, but it was not until Dr. Roget was over seventy years of age and had retired from the active secretaryship of the Royal Society that he was able to devote three or four years to the work of expansion.

It was first published in London by Longman, Brown, Green and Longmans in 1852, and went into a second edition in 1853. Two years later the "third and cheaper edition enlarged and improved" appeared, and was followed by the fourth edition in the same year. The fifth edition was issued in 1857, and since then edition has followed edition almost every year, and occasionally two or three times in one year, until seventy-seven printings have been called for, totalling more than two hundred thousand books.

The merits of the Thesaurus, its scholarship and erudition, were appreciated from the first, and successive improvements and enlargements by the author, the author's son and grandson, have caused it to maintain its great reputation.

In the course of years there have been several competing editions printed in America, all based on the London editions, but from none of these did the author or his representatives derive any pecuniary advantage.

The present edition, edited and revised by Willard Jerome Heggen, is the first one to be issued in America with the sanction and approval of Samuel Romilly Roget, the author's grandson, and holder of the existing British copyright.

It is worthy of note that it took three generations of the Roget family to compile and perfect this Thesaurus, and that after eighty years it is still published in London by the same firm, and from the same address in Paternoster Row, as when issued originally.

June 1933

PREFACE

Since the preface of March 17, 1879, was written, Mr. John L. Roget continued to revise periodical reprints of the Thesaurus until his death in 1908. It then devolved upon the undersigned, his son, to carry on this task, and it has been his endeavour to follow the same lines in making such additions that have seemed suitable from time to time. The opportunity has now, however, presented itself for a rather more complete revision, owing to the necessity of resetting the entire work, and in the edition that is now presented not only have a few hitherto unnoticed errors been corrected but some hundreds of new words and phrases have been added throughout the book, some of which have only recently become a part of the language as the result of progress in the various arts of peace and the unfortunate necessities of war. Many additional entries of words already represented have also been made, where the meanings have widened out or where for other reasons it has been thought advisable, but in practically no case has a word been removed, as archaic and even obsolete words are often sought for by authors. A few examples of alternative and obsolete spelling have been removed, but no alteration whatever has been made with the general arrangement and classification of the categories.

The editor would at all times welcome practical suggestions from users of the Thesaurus, and would take this opportunity of expressing his thanks for much kind help already afforded in this direction.

S. R. Roget

July 1925

PREFACE

TO

THE FIRST EDITION

(1852)

It is now nearly fifty years since I first projected a system of verbal classification similar to that on which the present Work is founded. Conceiving that such a compilation might help to supply my own deficiencies, I had, in the year 1805, completed a classed catalogue of words on a small scale, but on the same principle, and nearly in the same form, as the Thesaurus now published.* I had often during that long interval found this little collection, scanty and imperfect as it was, of much use to me in literary composition, and often contemplated its extension and improvement; but a sense of the magnitude of the task, amidst a multitude of other avocations, deterred me from the attempt. Since my retirement from the duties of Secretary of the Royal Society, however, finding myself possessed of more leisure, and believing that a repertory of which I had myself experienced the advantage might, when amplified, prove useful to others, I resolved to embark in an undertaking which, for the last three or four years, has given me incessant occupation, and has, indeed, imposed upon me an amount of labour very much greater than I had anticipated. Notwithstanding all the pains I have bestowed on its execution, I am fully aware of its numerous deficiencies and imperfections, and of its falling far short of the degree of excellence that might be attained. But, in a Work of this nature, where perfection is placed at so great a distance, I have thought it best to limit my ambition to that moderate share of merit which it may claim in its present form; trusting to the indulgence of those for whose benefit it is intended, and to the candour of critics who, while they find it easy to detect faults, can at the same time duly appreciate difficulties.

P. M. Roget

April 29th, 1852

* A facsimile of the first page of this little manuscript book which is the original form of the Thesaurus is given in the frontispiece.

EDITOR'S PREFACE

(1879)

(Slightly Abridged)

THE FIRST EDITION of Dr. Roget's Thesaurus was published in the year 1852, and a second in the ensuing spring. On the issue of the third, in 1855, the volume was stereotyped. Since that time until now, the work has been reprinted in the same form and with little alteration, in rapidly succeeding editions, the printing of which has worn out the original plates.

During the last years of the author's life, which closed, at a very advanced age, in the month of September, 1869, he was engaged in the task of collecting additional words and phrases, for an enlarged edition which he had long projected. This he did not live to complete, and it became my duty, as his son, to attempt to carry the design into execution.

The result of the author's labours was embodied in a copy of the Thesaurus, in which the margins and spaces about the letterpress were closely covered with written words and phrases, without any very precise indication of the places in the text where additions or alterations were intended to be made. On a careful examination of these *addenda*, I came to the conclusion that, in order to introduce them with advantage, it would be necessary to make some slight changes; without, however, interfering at all with the framework of the book, and but little with the details of its system. In this proceeding my course has been mainly determined by the following considerations.

Any attempt at a philosophical arrangement under categories of the words of our language must reveal the fact that it is impossible to separate and circumscribe the several groups by absolutely distinct boundary lines. Many words, originally employed to express simple conceptions, are found to be capable, with perhaps a very slight modification of meaning, of being applied in many varied associations. Connecting links, thus formed, induce an approach between the categories; and a danger arises that the outlines of our classification may, by their means, become confused and eventually merged. Were we to disengage these interwoven ramifications, and seek to confine every word to its main or original import, we should find some secondary meaning has become so firmly associated with many words and phrases, that to sever the alliance would be to deprive our language of the richness due to an infinity of natural adaptations.

Were we, on the other hand, to attempt to include, in each category of the Thesaurus, every word and phrase which could by any possibility

be appropriately used in relation to the leading idea for which that
category was designed, we should impair, if not destroy, the whole use and
value of the book. For, in the endeavour to enrich our treasury of
expression, we might easily allow ourselves to be led imperceptibly onward
by the natural association of one word with another, and to add word
after word, until group after group would successively be absorbed under
some single heading, and the fundamental divisions of the system be
effaced. The small cluster of nearly synonymous words, which had formed
the nucleus of a category, would be lost in a sea of phrases, and it would
become difficult to recognize those which were peculiarly adapted to
express the leading ideas.

These considerations were material in dealing with the new and multitudinous store of words and phrases which the author had accumulated.
Many of these were altogether new to the Thesaurus. Many were merely
repetitions in new places of words already included in its pages. With
reference to cases similar to the latter, the author had declared it to have
been a general rule with him 'to place words and phrases which appertain
more especially to one head, also under other heads to which they have
a relation,' whenever it appeared to him 'that this repetition would suit
the convenience of the inquirer and spare him the trouble of turning to
other parts of the work.' But, with the now increased mass of words, it
became a question, in many cases, whether such repetition would still
prove convenient. Where categories might by that course be unduly
swollen, or where they might, by reason of their being separated from
each other by subtile distinctions or faint lines of demarcation, be thereby
too nearly assimilated, I thought it would often be better to confine words
of the kind referred to to their primary headings. The necessity of keeping the book within reasonable dimensions had also to be borne in mind.

Under these circumstances, the best method of ensuring the ready
accessibility of the multitude of words now to be dealt with, and at the
same time preserving unimpaired the unity of the several categories,
appeared to me to lie in the copious use of references from one place in
the book to another. Relying on this contrivance as a means of opening
more widely the resources of the collection, by making the groups of
words mutually suggestive, and thereby leading not only to more varied
forms of expression, but to kindred ideas, I have added largely to the
references already inserted by the author. I have also ventured occasionally to substitute a reference for a group of words, when the identical
group existed in another place, and could thus be made immediately
available.

In order, at the same time, to make the value of the references more
appreciable, I have (whenever it has appeared to me to be necessary)
inserted, in a parenthesis, a word indicating the nature of the group or
category referred to. Any one using the book will thereby be enabled
to judge whether it will be worth his while to turn to the place in question.

The cross references may also be looked upon as indicating in some degree the natural points of connection between the categories, and the ramification of the ideas which they embody. As would be the case under any classification of language, a large proportion of the expressions, to find which recourse is had to the Thesaurus, lie on an ill-defined border land between one category and another; and it is not always easy, even with the aid of a carefully compiled index, to determine under which of several allied headings they should be sought. In the present edition, when the inquirer has once started on his voyage of discovery, the references enable him to pass freely from one division to another without recurring to the Index.

Many new words have also been inserted which were not contained in the author's manuscript.

Except in a very few cases, where distinct ideas were obviously united under one head, I have not had the presumption to meddle with the author's division into categories; but, within each category, I have endeavoured to carry somewhat further the sorting of words according to the ideas which they convey.

With these objects in view, I have supplied the work with a new and elaborate Index, much more complete than that which was appended to the previous editions. Although, in the original design of his work, the author appears to have conceived the process of search for a required expression as one in which the system of classification would be first consulted, and the Index afterwards called in aid if necessary, I believe that almost everyone who uses the book finds it more convenient to have recourse to the Index first.

From the peculiar nature and use of the Thesaurus, its Index will be found to differ, in some of its essential functions, from an alphabetical table of contents. The present Index does not merely afford an indication of the place where every given word or topic occurs or is dealt with in the text; but it is intended as a guide to other expressions which may be found there. The word we look out in this Index is not that which we require, but that which we wish to avoid. It is, therefore, not necessary that every word there given should be a repetition of one in the text. It may even happen that the word selected as a guide, though suggestive of the group wanted, is wholly unfit to be comprised within it.

The new Index contains not only all the *words* in the book (without needless repetition of conjugate forms), but likewise the *phrases,* all of which had been excluded from the Index to the previous editions. It is hoped that these additions, although they increase the bulk of the book, will have the effect of extending its usefulness in at least a corresponding degree.

Some changes of detail have also been made, where the form of the work seemed susceptible of improvement, and there was no reason to suppose that the author would have disapproved of the alteration. In the previous editions, the *phrases* were in general placed in separate paragraphs, under the heading **Phr.**, in each of the subdivisions assigned to the different grammatical parts of speech. In the present edition, *words* and *phrases* are placed together, and the heading **Phr.** is only employed in the case of phrases which have no convenient place in such an arrangement. Much space has been saved, and many repetitions have been avoided, by the use of lines and hyphens, where words or phrases in the same group have syllables or parts in common, and by references from one part of speech to another. These abbreviations may be best explained by examples, of which the following are a few:—

'with -relation, – reference, – respect, – regard- to'; is meant to include the phrases 'with relation to,' 'with reference to,' 'with respect to,' 'with regard to.'

'root –, weed –, grub –, rake- -up, – out;' includes 'root up,' 'root out,' 'weed up,' 'weed out,' 'grub up,' 'grub out,' 'rake up,' 'rake out.'

'away from –, foreign to –, beside- the -purpose, – question, – transaction, – point;' includes 'away from the purpose,' 'foreign to the purpose,' 'beside the purpose,' 'away from the question,' 'foreign to the question,' 'foreign to the transaction,' 'beside the question,' 'away from the point,' 'beside the transaction,' 'foreign to the point,' 'away from the transaction,' 'beside the point.'

'raze – to the ground'; includes 'raze,' and 'raze to the ground.'

'campan-iform, -ulate, -iliform;' includes 'campaniform,' 'campanulate,' and 'campaniliform.'

'goodness &c. *adj.*'; 'badly &c. *adj.*'; 'hindred &c. *v.*'; include all words similarly formed from synonyms of 'good,' 'bad,' and 'hinder,' respectively, given under the headings **Adj.** and **V.** in the same categories where the abbreviations occur.

The participle 'to' before a verb has in all cases been rejected, the heading **V.** being thought sufficiently distinctive; the use of capitals for the initial letters of the first words of paragraphs has been abandoned, as giving those words undue importance; and the title of each category has been kept distinct from the collection of words under its heading.

I should be ungrateful were I not to acknowledge the assistance derived, both by my father and myself, from various suggestions made by well-wishers to the work, some of whom have been personally unknown to either of us; and also to record my thanks to several kind friends, and to Messrs. Spottiswoode and Co.'s careful reader, for valuable aid during the passage of the sheets through the press.

JOHN L. ROGET

March 17th, 1879.

INTRODUCTION

[*Notes within brackets are by the editors.*]

THE present Work is intended to supply, with respect to the English language, a desideratum hitherto unsupplied in any language; namely, a collection of the words it contains and of the idiomatic combinations peculiar to it, arranged, not in alphabetical order as they are in a Dictionary, but according to the *ideas* which they express.* The purpose of an ordinary dictionary is simply to explain the meaning of the words; and the problem of which it professes to furnish the solution may be stated thus:—The word being given, to find its signification, or the idea it is intended to convey. The object aimed at in the present undertaking is exactly the converse of this: namely,—The idea being given, to find the word, or words, by which that idea may be most fitly and aptly expressed. For this purpose, the words and phrases of the language are here classed, not according to their sound or their orthography, but strictly according to their *signification*.

The communication of our thoughts by means of language, whether spoken or written, like every other object of mental exertion, constitutes a peculiar art, which, like other arts, cannot be acquired in any perfection but by long and continued practice. Some, indeed, there are more highly gifted than others with a facility of expression, and naturally endowed with the power of eloquence; but to none is it at all times an easy process to embody, in exact and appropriate language, the various trains of ideas that are passing through the mind, or to depict in their true colours and proportions, the diversified and nicer shades of feeling which accompany them. To those who are unpractised in the art of composition, or unused to extempore speaking, these difficulties present themselves in their most formidable aspect. However distinct may be our views, however vivid our conceptions, or however fervent our emotions, we cannot but be often conscious that the phraseology we have at our command is inadequate to do them justice. We seek in vain the words we need, and strive ineffectually to devise forms of expression which shall faithfully portray our thoughts and sentiments. The appropriate terms, notwithstanding our utmost efforts, cannot be conjured up at will. Like 'spirits from the vasty deep,' they come not when we call; and we are driven to the employment of a set of words and phrases either too general or too

* See note in p. xxi.

limited, too strong or too feeble, which suit not the occasion, which hit not the mark we aim at; and the result of our prolonged exertion is a style at once laboured and obscure, vapid and redundant, or vitiated by the still graver faults of affectation or ambiguity.

It is to those who are thus painfully groping their way and struggling with the difficulties of composition, that this Work professes to hold out a helping hand. The assistance it gives is that of furnishing on every topic a copious store of words and phrases, adapted to express all the recognizable shades and modifications of the general idea under which those words and phrases are arranged. The inquirer can readily select, out of the ample collection spread out before his eyes in the following pages, those expressions which are best suited to his purpose, and which might not have occurred to him without such assistance. In order to make this selection, he scarcely ever need engage in any critical or elaborate study of the subtle distinction existing between synonymous terms; for if the materials set before him be sufficiently abundant, an instinctive tact will rarely fail to lead him to the proper choice. Even while glancing over the columns of this Work, his eye may chance to light upon a particular term, which may save the cost of a clumsy paraphrase, or spare the labour of a tortuous circumlocution. Some felicitous turn of expression thus introduced will frequently open to the mind of the reader a whole vista of collateral ideas, which could not, without an extended and obtrusive episode, have been unfolded to his view; and often will the judicious insertion of a happy epithet, like a beam of sunshine in a landscape, illumine and adorn the subject which it touches, imparting new grace and giving life and spirit to the picture.

Every workman in the exercise of his art should be provided with proper implements. For the fabrication of complicated and curious pieces of mechanism, the artisan requires a corresponding assortment of various tools and instruments. For giving proper effect to the fictions of the drama, the actor should have at his disposal a well-furnished wardrobe, supplying the costumes best suited to the personages he is to represent. For the perfect delineation of the beauties of nature, the painter should have within reach of his pencil every variety and combination of hues and tints. Now, the writer, as well as the orator, employs for the accomplishment of his purposes the instrumentality of words; it is in words that he clothes his thoughts; it is by means of words that he depicts his feelings. It is therefore essential to his success that he be provided with a copious vocabulary, and that he possess an entire command of all the resources and appliances of his language. To the acquisition of this power no procedure appears more directly conducive than the study of a methodized system such as that now offered to his use.

The utility of the present Work will be appreciated more especially by those who are engaged in the arduous process of translating into English a work written in another language. Simple as the operation may appear, on a superficial view, of rendering into English each of its sentences, the task of transfusing, with perfect exactness, the sense of the original, preserving at the same time the style and character of its composition, and reflecting with fidelity the mind and the spirit of the author, is a task of extreme difficulty. The cultivation of this useful department of literature was in ancient times strongly recommended both by Cicero and by Quintilian, as essential to the formation of a good writer and accomplished orator. Regarded simply as a mental exercise, the practice of translation is the best training for the attainment of that mastery of language and felicity of diction, which are the sources of the highest oratory, and are requisite for the possession of a graceful and persuasive eloquence. By rendering ourselves the faithful interpreters of the thoughts and feelings of others, we are rewarded with the acquisition of greater readiness and facility in correctly expressing our own; as he who has best learned to execute the orders of a commander, becomes himself best qualified to command.

In the earliest periods of civilization, translators have been the agents for propagating knowledge from nation to nation, and the value of their labours has been inestimable; but, in the present age, when so many different languages have become the depositories of the vast treasures of literature and of science which have been accumulating for centuries, the utility of accurate translations has greatly increased, and it has become a more important object to attain perfection in the art.

The use of language is not confined to its being the medium through which we communicate our ideas to one another; it fulfils a no less important function as an *instrument of thought*; not being merely its vehicle, but giving it wings for flight. Metaphysicians are agreed that scarcely any of our intellectual operations could be carried on to any considerable extent, without the agency of words. None but those who are conversant with the philosophy of mental phenomena, can be aware of the immense influence that is exercised by language in promoting the development of our ideas, in fixing them in the mind, and in detaining them for steady contemplation. Into every process of reasoning, language enters as an essential element. Words are the instruments by which we form all our abstractions, by which we fashion and embody our ideas, and by which we are enabled to glide along a series of premises and conclusions with a rapidity so great as to leave in the memory no trace of the successive steps of the process; and we remain unconscious how much we owe to this potent auxiliary of the reasoning faculty. It is on this ground, also, that the present Work founds a claim to utility. The review of a catalogue of words of analogous signification, will often suggest by association other trains of thought, which, presenting the subject under new and varied aspects, will vastly expand the sphere of our mental vision. Amidst the many objects thus brought within the range of our contemplation, some striking similitude or appropriate image, some excursive flight or brilliant conception, may flash on the mind, giving point and force to our arguments, awakening a responsive chord in the imagination or sensibility of the reader, and procuring for our reasonings a more ready access both to his understanding and to his heart.

It is of the utmost consequence that strict accuracy should regulate our use of language, and that every one should acquire the power and the habit of expressing his thoughts with perspicuity and correctness. Few, indeed, can appreciate the real extent and importance of that influence which language has always exercised on human affairs, or can be aware how often these are determined by causes much slighter than are apparent to a superficial observer. False logic, disguised under specious phraseology, too often gains the assent of the unthinking multitude, disseminating far and wide the seeds of prejudice and error. Truisms pass current, and wear the semblance of profound wisdom, when dressed up in the tinsel garb of antithetical phrases, or set off by an imposing pomp of paradox. By a confused jargon of involved and mystical sentences, the imagination is easily inveigled into a transcendental region of clouds, and the understanding beguiled into the belief that it is acquiring knowledge and approaching truth. A misapplied or misapprehended term is sufficient to give rise to fierce and interminable disputes; a misnomer has turned the tide of popular opinion; a verbal sophism has decided a party question; an artful watchword, thrown among combustible materials, has kindled the flame of deadly warfare, and changed the destiny of an empire.

In constructing the following system of classification of the ideas which are expressible by language, my chief aim has been to obtain the greatest amount of practical utility. I have accordingly adopted such principles of arrangement as appeared to me to be the simplest and most natural, and which would not require, either for their comprehension or application, any disciplined acumen, or depth of metaphysical or antiquarian lore. Eschewing all needless refinements and subtleties, I have taken as my guide the more obvious characters of the ideas for which expressions were to be tabulated, arranging them under such classes and categories as reflection and experience had taught me would conduct the inquirer most readily and quickly to the object of his search. Commencing with the ideas expressing abstract relations, I proceeded to those which relate to space and to the phenomena of the material world, and lastly to those in which the mind is concerned, and which comprehend intellect, volition, and feeling; thus establishing six primary Classes of Categories.

1. The first of these classes comprehends ideas derived from the more general and ABSTRACT RELATIONS among things, such as *Existence, Resemblance, Quantity, Order, Number, Time, Power.*

2. The second class refers to SPACE and its various relations, including *Motion,* or change of place.

3. The third class includes all ideas that relate to the MATERIAL WORLD; namely, the *Properties of Matter,* such as *Solidity, Fluidity, Heat, Sound, Light,* and the *Phenomena* they present, as well as the simple *Perceptions* to which they give rise.

4. The fourth class embraces all ideas of phenomena relating to the INTELLECT and its operations; comprising the *Acquisition,* the *Retention,* and the *Communication of Ideas.*

5. The fifth class includes the ideas derived from the exercise of VOLITION; embracing the phenomena and results of our *Voluntary and Active Powers*; such as *Choice, Intention, Utility, Action, Antagonism, Authority, Compact, Property,* &c.

6. The sixth and last class comprehends all ideas derived from the operation of our SENTIENT AND MORAL POWERS; including our *Feelings, Emotions, Passions,* and *Moral and Religious Sentiments.**

The further subdivisions and minuter details will be best understood from an inspection of the Tabular Synopsis of Categories prefixed to the Work, in which are specified the several *topics* or *heads of signification,* under which the words have been arranged. By the aid of this table the reader will, with a little practice, readily discover the place which the particular topic he is in search of occupies in the series; and on turning to the page in the body of the Work which contains it, he will find the group of expressions he requires, out of which he may cull those that are most appropriate to his purpose. For the convenience of reference, I have designated each separate group or heading by a particular number; so that if, during the search, any doubt or difficulty should occur, recourse may be had to the copious alphabetical Index of words at the end of the volume, which will at once indicate the number of the required group.†

---

* It must necessarily happen in every system of classification framed with this view, that ideas and expressions arranged under one class must include also ideas relating to another class; for the operations of the *Intellect* generally involve also those of the *Will,* and *vice versâ;* and our *Affections* and *Emotions,* in like manner, generally imply the agency both of the *Intellect* and of the *Will.* All that can be effected, therefore, is to arrange the words according to the principal or dominant idea they convey. *Teaching,* for example, although a Voluntary act, relates primarily to the Communication of Ideas, and is accordingly placed at No. 537, under Class IV Division (II). On the other hand, *Choice, Conduct, Skill,* &c., although implying the co-operation of Voluntary with Intellectual acts, relate principally to the former, and are therefore arranged under Class V.

† It often happens that the same word admits of various applications, or may be used in different senses. In consulting the Index the reader will be guided to the number of the heading under which that word, in each particular acceptation, will be found, by means of *supplementary words* printed in Italics; which words, however, are not to be understood as explaining the meaning of the word to which they are annexed, but only as assisting in the required reference. I have also, for shortness' sake, generally omitted words immediately derived from the primary one inserted, which sufficiently represents the whole group of correlative words referable to the same heading. Thus the number affixed to *Beauty* applies to all its derivatives, such as *Beautiful, Beauteous, Beautifulness, Beautifully,* &c., the insertion of which was therefore needless. [In compiling the new Index the editor has adopted this principle as a general rule, from which, however, he has not scrupled to depart where he has deemed it expedient to do so.]

The object I have proposed to myself in this Work would have been put imperfectly attained if I had confined myself to a mere catalogue of words, and had omitted the numerous phrases and forms of expression composed of several words, which are of such frequent use as to entitle them to rank among the constituent parts of the language.* Very few of these verbal combinations, so essential to the knowledge of our native tongue, and so profusely abounding in its daily use, are to be met with in ordinary dictionaries. These phrases and forms of expression I have endeavoured diligently to collect and to insert in their proper places, under the general ideas that they are designed to convey. Some of these conventional forms, indeed, partake of the nature of proverbial expressions; but actual proverbs, as such, being wholly of a didactic character, do not come within the scope of the present Work; and the reader must therefore not expect to find them here inserted.†

For the purpose of exhibiting with greater distinctness the relations between words expressing opposite and correlative ideas, I have, whenever the subject admitted of such an arrangement, placed them in two parallel columns in the same page, so that each group of expressions may be readily contrasted with those which occupy the adjacent column, and constitute their antithesis. By carrying the eye from the one to the other, the inquirer may often discover forms of expression, of which he may avail himself advantageously, to diversify and infuse vigour into his phraseology. Rhetoricians, indeed, are well aware of the power derived from the skilful introduction of antitheses in giving point to an argument, and imparting force and brilliancy to the diction. A too frequent and indiscreet employment of this figure of rhetoric may, it is true, give rise to a vicious and affected style; but it is unreasonable to condemn indiscriminately the occasional and moderate use of a practice on account of its possible abuse.

The study of correlative terms existing in a particular language, may often throw valuable light on the manners and customs of the nations using it. Thus, Hume has drawn important inferences with regard to the state of society among the ancient Romans, from certain deficiencies which he remarked in the Latin language.‡

---

* For example:—To take time by the forelock;—to turn over a new leaf;—to show the white feather;—to have a finger in the pie;—to let the cat out of the bag;—to take care of number one;—to kill two birds with one stone, &c., &c.

† See Trench, *On the Lessons in Proverbs*.

‡ 'It is an universal observation,' he remarks, 'which we may form upon language, that where two related parts of a whole bear any proportion to each other, in numbers, rank, or consideration, there are always correlative terms invented which answer to both the parts, and express their mutual relation. If they bear no proportion to each other, the term is only invented for the less, and marks its distinction from the whole. Thus, *man* and *woman, master* and *servant, father* and *son, prince* and *subject, stranger* and *citizen,* are correlative terms. But the words *seaman, carpenter, smith, tailor,* &c., have no correspondent terms, which express those who are no seamen, no carpenters, &c. Languages differ very much with regard to the particular words where this distinction obtains; and may thence afford very strong inferences concerning the manners and customs of different nations. The military government of the

In many cases, two ideas which are completely opposed to each other, admit of an intermediate or neutral idea, equidistant from both; all these being expressible by corresponding definite terms. Thus, in the following examples, the words in the first and third columns, which express opposite ideas, admit of the intermediate terms contained in the middle column, having a neutral sense with reference to the former.

Identity	*Difference*	*Contrariety*
Beginning	*Middle*	*End*
Past	*Present*	*Future*

In other cases, the intermediate word is simply the negative to each of two opposite positions; as, for example—

Convexity	*Flatness*	*Concavity*
Desire	*Indifference*	*Aversion*

Sometimes the intermediate word is properly the standard with which each of the extremes is compared; as in the case of

Insufficiency	*Sufficiency*	*Redundance*

for here the middle term, *Sufficiency*, is equally opposed, on the one hand to *Insufficiency*, and on the other to *Redundance*.*

These forms of correlative expressions would suggest the use of triple, instead of double, columns, for tabulating this threefold order of words; but the practical inconvenience attending such an arrangement would probably overbalance its advantages.

It often happens that the same word has several correlative terms, according to the different relations in which it is considered. Thus, to the word *Giving* are opposed both *Receiving* and *Taking*; the former

Roman emperors had exalted the soldiery so high that they balanced all the other orders of the state: hence *miles* and *paganus* became relative terms; a thing, till then, unknown to ancient, and still so to modern languages.'—'The term for a slave, born and bred in the family, was *verna*. As *servus* was the name of the genius, and *verna* of the species without any correlative, this forms a strong presumption that the latter were by far the least numerous: and from the same principles I infer that if the number of slaves brought by the Romans from foreign countries had not extremely exceeded those which were bred at home, *verna* would have had a correlative, which would have expressed the former species of slaves. But these, it would seem, composed the main body of the ancient slaves, and the latter were but a few exceptions'.—HUME, *Essay on the Populousness of Ancient Nations.*

The warlike propensity of the same nation may, in like manner, be inferred from the use of the word *hostis* to denote both *a foreigner* and *an enemy.*

* [In the following cases, the intermediate word signifies an imperfect degree of each of the qualities set in opposition—

Light	*Dimness*	*Darkness*
Transparency	*Semitransparency*	*Opacity*
Vision	*Dimsightedness*	*Blindness*]

correlation having reference to the *persons* concerned in the transfer, while the latter relates to the *mode* of transfer. *Old* has for opposite both *New* and *Young*, according as it is applied to *things* or to *living things*. *Attack* and *Defence* are correlative terms; as are also *Attack* and *Resistance*. *Resistance*, again, has for its other correlative *Submission*. *Truth in the abstract* is opposed to *Error*; but the opposite of *Truth communicated* is *Falsehood*. *Acquisition* is contrasted both with *Deprivation* and with *Loss*. *Refusal* is the counterpart both of *Offer* and of *Consent*. *Disuse* and *Misuse* may either of them be considered as the correlative of *Use*. *Teaching* with reference to what is taught, is opposed to *Misteaching*; but with reference to the act itself, its proper reciprocal is *Learning*.

Words contrasted in form do not always bear the same contrast in their meaning. The word *Malefactor*, for example, would, from its derivation, appear to be exactly the opposite of *Benefactor*: but the ideas attached to these two words are far from being directly opposed; for while the latter expresses one who confers a benefit, the former denotes one who has violated the laws.

Independently of the immediate practical uses derivable from the arrangement of words in double columns, many considerations, interesting in a philosophical point of view, are presented by the study of correlative expressions. It will be found, on strict examination, that there seldom exists an exact opposition between two words which may at first sight appear to be the counterparts of one another; for in general, the one will be found to possess in reality more force or extent of meaning than the other with which it is contrasted. The correlative term sometimes assumes the form of a mere negative, although it is really endowed with a considerable positive force. Thus *Disrespect* is not merely the absence of *Respect*; its signification trenches on the opposite idea, namely, *Contempt*. In like manner, *Untruth* is not merely the negative of *Truth*; it involves a degree of *Falsehood*. *Irreligion*, which is properly *the want of Religion*, is understood as being nearly synonymous with *Impiety*. For these reasons, the reader must not expect that all the words which stand side by side in the two columns shall be the precise correlatives of each other; for the nature of the subject, as well as the imperfections of language, renders it impossible always to preserve such an exactness of correlation.

There exist comparatively few words of a general character to which no correlative term, either of negation or of opposition, can be assigned, and which therefore require no corresponding second column. The correlative idea, especially that which constitutes a sense negative to the primary one, may, indeed, be formed or conceived; but, from its occurring rarely, no word has been framed to represent it; for, in language, as in other matters, the supply fails when there is no probability of a demand. Occasionally we find this deficiency provided for by the contrivance of prefixing the syllable *non*; as, for instance, the negatives of *existence, performance, payment*, &c., are expressed by the compound words, *non-existence, non-performance, non-payment*, &c. Functions of a similar kind are performed by the prefixes *dis-*, anti-, contra-, mis-, in-,* and *un-*.† With respect to all these, and especially the last, great latitude is allowed according to the necessities of the case; a latitude which is limited only by the taste and discretion of the writer.

On the other hand, it is hardly possible to find two words having in all respects the same meaning, and being therefore interchangeable; that is, admitting of being employed indiscriminately, the one or the other, in all their applications. The investigation of the distinctions to be drawn between words apparently synonymous, forms a separate branch of inquiry, which I have not presumed here to enter upon; for the subject has already occupied the attention of much abler critics than myself, and its complete exhaustion would require the devotion of a whole life. The purpose of this Work, it must be borne in mind, is, not to explain the signification of words, but simply to classify and arrange them according to the sense in which they are now used, and which I presume to be already known to the reader. I enter into no inquiry into the changes of meaning they may have undergone in the course of time.‡ I am content to accept them at the value of their present currency, and have no concern with their etymologies, or with the history of their transformations; far less do I venture to thrid the mazes of the vast labyrinth into which I should be led by any attempt at a general discrimination of synonyms. The difficulties I have had to contend with have already been sufficiently great, without this addition to my labours.

The most cursory glance over the pages of a Dictionary will show that a great number of words are used in various senses, sometimes distinguished by slight shades of difference, but often diverging widely from their primary signification, and even, in some cases, bearing to it no perceptible relation. It may even happen that the very same word has two significations quite opposite to one another. This is the case with the verb *to cleave*, which means *to adhere tenaciously*, and also *to separate by a blow*. *To propugn* sometimes expressed *to attack*; at other times *to defend*. *To let* is *to hinder*, as well as *to permit*. *To*

---

* The words *disannul* and *dissever*, however, have the same meaning as *annul* and *sever; to unloose* is the same as *to loose*, and *inebriety* is synonymous with *ebriety*.

† In the case of adjectives, the addition to a substantive of the terminal syllable *less*, gives it a negative meaning: as *taste, tasteless; care, careless; hope, hopeless; friend, friendless; fault, faultless;* &c.

‡ Such changes are innumerable: for instance, the words *tyrant, parasite, sophist, churl, knave, villain*, anciently conveyed no opprobrious meaning. *Impertinent* merely expressed *irrelative*, and implied neither *rudeness* nor *intrusion*, as it does at present. *Indifferent* originally meant *impartial; extravagant* was simply *digressive;* and *to prevent* was properly *to precede* and *assist*. The old translations of the Scriptures furnish many striking examples of the alterations which time has brought in the signification of words. Much curious information on this subject is contained in Trench's *Lectures on the Study of Words*.

ravel means both *to entangle* and *to disentangle*. *Shameful* and *shameless* are nearly synonymous. *Priceless* may either mean *invaluable* or *of no value*. *Nervous* is used sometimes for *strong*, at other times for *weak*. The alphabetical Index at the end of this Work sufficiently shows the multiplicity of uses to which, by the elasticity of language, the meaning of words has been stretched, so as to adapt them to a great variety of modified significations in subservience to the nicer shades of thought, which, under peculiarity of circumstances, require corresponding expression. Words thus admitting of different meanings have therefore to be arranged under each of the respective heads corresponding to these various acceptations. There are many words, again, which express ideas compounded of two elementary ideas belonging to different classes. It is therefore necessary to place these words respectively under each of the generic heads to which they relate. The necessity of these repetitions is increased by the circumstance, that ideas included under one class are often connected by relations of the same kind as the ideas which belong to another class. Thus we find the same relations of *order* and of *quantity* existing among the ideas of *Time* as well as those of *Space*. Sequence in the one is denoted by the same terms as sequence in the other; and the measures of time also express the measures of space. The cause and the effect are often designated by the same word. The word *Sound*, for instance, denotes both the impression made upon the ear by sonorous vibrations, and also the vibrations themselves, which are the cause or source of that impression. *Mixture* is used for the act of mixing, as well as for the product of that operation. *Taste* and *Smell* express both the sensations and the qualities of material bodies giving rise to them. *Thought* is the act of thinking; but the same word denotes also the idea resulting from that act. *Judgment* is the act of deciding, and also the decision come to. *Purchase* is the acquisition of a thing by payment, as well as the thing itself so acquired. *Speech* is both the act of speaking and the words spoken; and so on with regard to an endless multiplicity of words. Mind is essentially distinct from Matter; and yet, in all languages, the attributes of the one are metaphorically transferred to those of the other. Matter, in all its forms, is endowed by the figurative genius of every language with the functions which pertain to intellect; and we perpetually talk of its phenomena and of its powers, as if they resulted from the voluntary influence of one body on another, acting and reacting, impelling and being impelled, controlling and being controlled, as if animated by spontaneous energies and guided by specific intentions. On the other hand, expressions, of which the primary signification refers exclusively to the properties and actions of matter, are metaphorically applied to the phenomena of thought and volition, and even to the feelings and passions of the soul; and in speaking of a *ray of hope*, a *shade of doubt*, a *flight of fancy*, a *flash of wit*, the *warmth of emotion*,

or the *ebullitions of anger*, we are scarcely conscious that we are employ-
ing metaphors which have this material origin.

As a general rule, I have deemed it incumbent on me to place words
and phrases which appertain more especially to one head, also under
the other heads to which they have a relation, whenever it appeared to
me that this repetition would suit the convenience of the inquirer, and
spare him the trouble of turning to other parts of the work; for I have
always preferred to subject myself to the imputation of redundance,
rather than incur the reproach of insufficiency.* When, however, the
divergence of the associated from the primary idea is sufficiently marked,
I have contented myself with making a reference to the place where
the modified signification will be found.† But in order to prevent needless extension, I have, in general, omitted *conjugate words*, ‡ which are
so obviously derivable from those that are given in the same place, that
the reader may safely be left to form them for himself. This is the case
with adverbs derived from adjectives by the simple addition of the
terminal syllable -*ly*; such as *closely, carefully, safely*, &c., from *close,
careful, safe*, &c., and also with adjectives or participles immediately derived from the verbs which are already given. In all such cases, an '&c.'
indicates that reference is understood to be made to these roots.§ I have
observed the same rule in compiling the Index; retaining only the primary or more simple word, and omitting the conjugate words obviously
derived from them. Thus I assume the word *short* as the representative
of its immediate derivatives *shortness, shorten, shortening, shortened,
shorter, shortly*, which would have had the same references, and which
the reader can readily supply. ||

The same verb is frequently used indiscriminately either in the active
or transitive, or in the neuter or intransitive sense. In these cases, I have
generally not thought it worth while to increase the bulk of the Work
by the needless repetition of that word; for the reader, whom I suppose

---

* Frequent repetitions of the same series of expressions, accordingly, will be met
with under various headings. For example, the word *Relinquishment* with its synonyms, occurs as a heading at No. 624, where it applies to *intention*, and also at
No. 782, where it refers to *property*. The word *Chance* has two significations, distinct
from one another: the one implying the *absence of an assignable cause;* in which case
it comes under the category of the relation of Causation, and occupies the No. 156:
the other, the *absence of design*, in which latter sense it ranks under the operations of
the Will, and has assigned to it the place No. 621. I have, in like manner, distinguished *Sensibility, Pleasure, Pain, Taste*, &c., according as they relate to *Physical*,
or to *Moral Affections;* the fomer being found at Nos. 375, 377, 378, 390, &c., and the
latter at Nos. 822, 827, 828, 850, &c.

† [See Editor's Preface, p. x.]

‡ By '*conjugate* or *paronymous* words is meant, correctly speaking, different parts
of speech from the same root, which exactly corresponds in point of meaning.'—
A Selection of English Synonyms, edited by Archbishop Whately.

§ [The author's practice, in this respect, has been followed in the present edition,
and a reference to the group of adjectives, verbs, or other roots, has been added,
where such suggestion has been thought expedient.]

|| [See note in p. xvii.]

to understand the use of the words, must also be presumed to be competent to apply them correctly.

There are a multitude of words of a specific character which, although they properly occupy places in the columns of a dictionary, yet, having no relation to general ideas, do not come within the scope of this compilation, and are consequently omitted.* The names of objects in Natural History, and technical terms belonging exclusively to Science or to Art, or relating to particular operations, and of which the signification is restricted to those specific objects, come under this category. Exceptions must, however, be made in favor of such words as admit of metaphorical application to general subjects, with which custom has associated them, and of which they may be cited as being typical or illustrative. Thus, the word *Lion* will find a place under the head of *Courage*, of which it is regarded as the type. *Anchor*, being emblematic of *Hope*, is introduced among the words expressing that emotion; and in like manner, *butterfly* and *weathercock*, which are suggestive of fickleness, are included in the category of *Irresolution*.

With regard to the admission of many words and expressions, which the classical reader might be disposed to condemn as vulgarisms, or which he, perhaps, might stigmatize as pertaining rather to the slang than to the legitimate language of the day, I would beg to observe, that, having due regard to the uses to which this Work was to be adapted, I did not feel myself justified in excluding them solely on that ground, if they possessed an acknowledged currency in general intercourse. It is obvious that, with respect to degrees of conventionality, I could not have attempted to draw any strict lines of demarcation; and far less could I have presumed to erect any absolute standard of purity. My object, be it remembered, is not to regulate the use of words, but simply to supply and to suggest such as may be wanted on occasion, leaving the proper selection entirely to the discretion and taste of the employer.† If a novelist or a dramatist, for example, proposed to delineate some vulgar personage, he would wish to have the power of putting into the mouth of the speaker expressions that would accord with his character; just as the actor, to revert to a former comparison, who had to personate a peasant, would choose for his attire the most homely garb, and would have just reason to complain if the theatrical wardrobe furnished him with no suitable costume.

Words which have, in process of time, become obsolete, are of course

---

* [The author did not in all cases rigidly adhere to this rule; and the editors have thought themselves justified both in retaining and in adding some words of the specific character here mentioned, which may be occasionally in request by general writers, although in categories of this nature no attempt at completeness has been made.]

† [It may be added that the Thesaurus is an aid not only in the choice of appropriate forms of expression, but in the rejection of those which are unfit; and that a vulgar phrase may often furnish a convenient clue to the group of classic synonyms among which it is placed. Moreover, the slang expressions admitted into the work bear but a small proportion to those in constant use by English writers and speakers.]

rejected from this collection.* On the other hand, I have admitted a considerable number of words and phrases borrowed from other languages, chiefly the French and Latin, some of which may be considered as already naturalized; while others, though avowedly foreign, are frequently employed in English composition, particularly in familiar style, on account of their being peculiarly expressive, and because we have no corresponding words of equal force in our own language.† The rapid advances which are being made in scientific knowledge, and consequent improvement in all the arts of life, and the extension of those arts and sciences to so many new purposes and objects, create a continual demand for the formation of new terms to express new agencies, new wants, and new combinations. Such terms, from being at first merely technical, are rendered, by more general use, familiar to the multitude, and having a well-defined acceptation, are eventually incorporated into the language, which they contribute to enlarge and to enrich. *Neologies* of this kind are perfectly legitimate, and highly advantageous; and they necessarily introduce those gradual and progressive changes which every language is destined to undergo.‡ Some modern writers, however, have indulged in a habit of arbitrarily fabricating new words and a new-fangled phraseology, without any necessity, and with manifest injury to the purity of the language. This vicious practice, the offspring of indolence or conceit, implies an ignorance or neglect of the riches in which the English language already abounds, and which would have supplied them with words of recognized legitimacy, conveying precisely the same meaning as those they so recklessly coin in the illegal mint of their own fancy.

A work constructed on the plan of classification I have proposed might, if ably executed, be of great value, in tending to limit the fluctuations to which language has always been subject, by establishing an authoritative standard for its regulation. Future historians, philologists, and lexicographers, when investigating the period when new words were introduced, or discussing the import given at the present time to the old, might find their labours lightened by being enabled to appeal to such a standard, instead of having to search for data among the scattered writings of the

---

* [A few apparently obsolete words have nevertheless found their way into the Thesaurus. In justification of their admission, it may be contended that well-known words, though no longer current, give occasional point by an archaic form of expression, and are of value to the novelist or dramatist who has to depict a bygone age.]

† All these words and phrases are printed in Italics. [A few of these expressions, although widely used by writers of English, are of a form which is really incorrect or unusual in their own language, in some more extreme cases of this kind, the more widely used or incorrect form has been given.]

‡ Thus, in framing the present classification, I have frequently felt the want of substantive terms corresponding to abstract qualities or ideas denoted by certain adjectives, and have been often tempted to invent words that might express these abstractions; but I have yielded to this temptation only in the four following instances, having framed from the adjectives *irrelative, amorphous, sinistral,* and *gaseous,* the abstract nouns *irrelation, amorphism, sinistrality,* and *gaseity.* I have ventured also to introduce the adjective *intersocial* to express the active voluntary relations between man and man.

age. Nor would its utility be confined to a single language; for the principles of its construction are universally applicable to all languages, whether living or dead. On the same plan of classification there might be formed a French, a German, a Latin, or a Greek Thesaurus, possessing, in their respective spheres, the same advantages as those of the English model.* Still more useful would be a conjunction of these methodized compilations in two languages, the French and English, for instance; the columns of each being placed in parallel juxtaposition. No means yet devised would so greatly facilitate the acquisition of the one language, by those who are acquainted with the other: none would afford such ample assistance to the translator in either language; and none would supply such ready and effectual means of instituting an accurate comparison between them, and of fairly appreciating their respective merits and defects. In a still higher degree would all those advantages be combined and multiplied in a *Polyglot Lexicon* constructed on this system.

Metaphysicians engaged in the more profound investigation of the Philosophy of Language will be materially assisted by having the ground thus prepared for them, in a previous analysis and classification of our ideas; for such classification of ideas is the true basis on which words, which are their symbols, should be classified.† It is by such analysis alone that we can arrive at a clear perception of the relation which these

* [This suggestion has been followed, in French, in a '*Dictionnaire Idéologique*' by T. Robertson (Paris, 1859); and, in German, in a '*Deutscher Sprachschatz*' by D. Sanders (Hamburg, 1878), and '*Deutscher Wortschatz oder Der passende Ausdruck*' by A. Schelling (Stuttgart, 1829).]

† The principle by which I have been guided in framing my verbal classification is the same as that which is employed in the various departments of Natural History. Thus the sectional divisions I have formed, correspond to Natural Families in Botany and Zoology, and the filiation of words presents a network analogous to the natural filiation of plants or animals.

The following are the only publications that have come to my knowledge in which any attempt has been made to construct a systematic arrangement of ideas with a view to their expression. The earliest of these, supposed to be at least nine hundred years old, is the Amera Cósha, or *Vocabulary of the Sanscrit Language*, by Amera Sinha, of which an English translation, by the late Henry T. Colebrooke, was printed at Serampoor, in the year 1808. The classification of words is there, as might be expected, exceedingly imperfect and confused, especially in all that relates to abstract ideas or mental operations. This will be apparent from the very title of the first section, which comprehends '*Heaven, Gods, Demons, Fire, Air, Velocity, Eternity, Much:*' while *Sin, Virtue, Happiness, Destiny, Cause, Nature, Intellect, Reasoning, Knowledge, Senses, Tastes, Odours, Colours*, are all included and jumbled together in the fourth section. A more logical order, however, pervades the sections relating to natural objects, such as *Seas, Earth, Towns, Plants*, and *Animals*, which form separate classes; exhibiting a remarkable effort at analysis at so remote a period of Indian literature.

The well-known work of Bishop Wilkins entitled '*An Essay towards a Real Character and a Philosophical Language*,' published in 1668, had for its object the formation of a system of symbols which might serve as a universal language. It professed to be founded on a 'scheme of analysis of the things or notions to which names were to be assigned'; but notwithstanding the immense labour and ingenuity expended in the construction of this system, it was soon found to be far too abstruse and recondite for practical application.

In the year 1797, there appeared in Paris an anonymous work, entitled 'Pasigraphie, *ou Premiers Eléments du nouvel Art-Science d'écrire et d'imprimer une langue*

symbols bear to their corresponding ideas, or can obtain a correct knowledge of the elements which enter into the formation of compound ideas, and of the exclusions by which we arrive at the abstractions so perpetually resorted to in the process of reasoning, and in the communication of our thoughts.

Lastly, such analysis alone can determine the principles on which a strictly *Philosophical Language* might be constructed. The probable result of the construction of such a language would be its eventual adoption by every civilized nation; thus realizing that splendid aspiration of philanthropists—the establishment of a Universal Language. However utopian such a project may appear to the present generation, and however abortive may have been the former endeavours of Bishop Wilkins and others to realize it,* its accomplishment is surely not beset with greater difficulties than have impeded the progress to many other beneficial objects, which in former times appeared to be no less visionary, and which yet were successfully achieved, in later ages, by the continued and persevering exertions of the human intellect. Is there at the present day, then, any ground for despair, that at some future stage of that higher civilization to which we trust the world is gradually tending, some new and bolder effort of genius towards the solution of this great problem may be crowned with success, and compass an object of such vast and paramount utility? Nothing, indeed, would conduce more directly to bring about a golden age of union and harmony among the several nations and races of mankind than the removal of that barrier to the interchange of thought and mutual good understanding between man and man, which is now interposed by the diversity of their respective languages.

de maniere a etre lu et entendu dans toute autre langue sans traduction,' of which an edition in German was also published. It contains a great number of tabular schemes of categories; all of which appear to be excessively arbitrary and artificial, and extremely difficult of application, as well as of apprehension. [Systems of grouping with relation to ideas are also adopted in an *'Analytical Dictionary of the English Language'* by David Booth (London, 1835), a *'Dictionnaire Analogique de la Langue Française'* by P. Boissière (Paris), and a *'Dictionnaire Logique de la Langue Française'* by L'Abbé Elie Blanc (Paris, 1882).]

* 'The Languages,' observes Horne Tooke, 'which are commonly used throughout the world, are much more simple and easy, convenient and philosophical, than Wilkins' scheme for a *real character;* or than any other scheme that has been at any other time imagined or proposed for the purpose.'—'Επεα Πτερόεντα, p. 125.

PLAN OF CLASSIFICATION

TABULAR SYNOPSIS OF CATEGORIES

Class I. ABSTRACT RELATIONS

I. EXISTENCE

1°. ABSTRACT..........	1. Existence.	2. Inexistence.
2°. CONCRETE..........	3. Substantiality.	4. Unsubstantiality.
3°. FORMAL............ {	*Internal.*	*External.*
	5. Intrinsicality.	6. Extrinsicality.
4°. MODAL............ {	*Absolute.*	*Relative.*
	7. State.	8. Circumstance.

II. RELATION

	9. Relation.	10. Irrelation.
	11. Consanguinity.	
1°. ABSOLUTE......... {	12. Correlation.	
	13. Identity.	14. Contrariety.
	15. Difference.	
2°. CONTINUOUS.......	16. Uniformity.	16a. Non-uniformity.
	17. Similarity.	18. Dissimilarity.
	19. Imitation.	20. Non-imitation.
3°. PARTIAL........... {	20a. Variation.	
	21. Copy.	22. Prototype.
4°. GENERAL..........	23. Agreement.	24. Disagreement.

III. QUANTITY

	Absolute.	*Relative.*
1°. SIMPLE............	25. Quantity.	26. Degree.
	27. Equality.	28. Inequality.
	29. Mean.	
	30. Compensation.	
	By Comparison with a Standard.	
2°. COMPARATIVE...... {	31. Greatness.	32. Smallness.
	By Comparison with a similar Object.	
	33. Superiority.	34. Inferiority.
	Changes in Quantity.	
	35. Increase.	36. Decrease.
	37. Addition.	38. { Non-addition. / Subduction.
	39. Adjunct.	40. Remainder.
		40a. Decrement.
3°. CONJUNCTIVE...... {	41. Mixture.	42. Simpleness.
	43. Junction.	44. Disjunction.
	45. Vinculum.	
	46. Coherence.	47. Incoherence.
	48. Combination.	49. Decomposition.

4°. CONCRETE . . . .
{
50. Whole.	51. Part.
52. Completeness.	53. Incompleteness.
54. Composition.	55. Exclusion.
56. Component.	57. Extraneous.

IV. ORDER

1°. GENERAL . . . .
{
58. Order.	59. Disorder.
60. Arrangement.	61. Derangement.
62. Precedence.	63. Sequence.
64. Precursor.	65. Sequel.

2°. CONSECUTIVE . . . .
{
66. Beginning.	67. End.
68. Middle.	
69. Continuity.	70. Discontinuity.
71. Term.	

3°. COLLECTIVE . . . .
{
| 72. Assemblage. | 73. {Non-assemblage. Dispersion. |
| 74. Focus. | |

4°. DISTRIBUTIVE . . . .
{
75. Class.	
76. Inclusion.	77. Exclusion.
78. Generality.	79. Speciality.

5°. CATEGORICAL . . . .
{
| 80. Rule. | 81. Multiformity. |
| 82. Conformity. | 83. Unconformity. |

V. NUMBER

1°. ABSTRACT . . . .
{
84. Number.	
85. Numeration.	
86. List.	

2°. DETERMINATE . . . .
{
87. Unity.	88. Accompaniment.
89. Duality.	
90. Duplication.	91. Bisection.
92. Triality.	
93. Triplication.	96. Trisection.
94. Quadruplication.	
95. Quaternity.	97. Quadrisection.
98. Five, &c.	99. Quinquesection, &c.
100. Plurality.	100a. Fraction.

3°. INDETERMINATE . . . . .
{
101. Zero.	
102. Multitude.	103. Fewness.
104. Repetition.	
105. Infinity.	

VI. TIME

1°. ABSOLUTE . . . .
{
106. Time.	107. Neverness.
Definite.	*Indefinite.*
108. Period.	109. Course.
108a. Contingent Duration.	
110. Diuturnity.	111. Transientness.
112. Perpetuity.	113. Instantaneity.
114. Chronometry.	115. Anachronism.

2°. REL- ATIVE
{
1. *to Succession*
{
116. Priority.	117. Posteriority.
118. Present time.	119. Different time.
120. Synchronism.	

2. *to a Period*
{
121. Futurity.	122. Preterition.
123. Newness.	124. Oldness.
125. Morning.	126. Evening.
127. Youth.	128. Age.
129. Infant.	130. Veteran.
131. Adolescence.	

3. *to an Effect or purpose*
{
| 132. Earliness. | 133. Lateness. |
| 134. Occasion. | 135. Intempestivity. |

3°. RECURRENT . . . .
{
| 136. Frequency. | 137. Infrequency. |
| 138. Periodicity. | 139. Irregularity. |

VII. CHANGE

VIII. CAUSATION

CLASS II. SPACE

I. SPACE IN GENERAL

II. DIMENSIONS

2°. Linear—*continued*...

210. Summit.	211. Base.
212. Verticality.	213. Horizontality.
214. Pendency.	215. Support.
216. Parallelism.	217. Obliquity.
218. Inversion.	
219. Crossing.	

3°. Centri-cal

1. *General*

220. Exteriority.	221. Interiority.
222. Centrality.	
223. Covering.	224. Lining.
225. Investment.	226. Divestment.
227. Circumjacence.	228. Interjacence.
229. Circumscription.	
230. Outline.	
231. Edge.	
232. Inclosure.	
233. Limit.	

2. *Special*

234. Front	235. Rear.
236. Laterality.	237. Contraposition.
238. Dextrality.	239. Sinistrality.

III. FORM

1°. General..........

240. Form.	241. Amorphism.
242. Symmetry.	243. Distortion.
244. Angularity.	

2°. Special............

245. Curvature.	246. Straightness.
247. Circularity.	248. Convolution.
249. Rotundity.	
250. Convexity.	252. Concavity.
251. Flatness.	

3°. Superficial........

253. Sharpness.	254. Bluntness.
255. Smoothness.	256. Roughness.
257. Notch.	
258. Fold.	
259. Furrow.	
260. Opening.	261. Closure.
262. Perforator.	263. Stopper.

IV. MOTION

1°. Motion in General

264. Motion.	265. Quiescence.
266. Journey.	267. Navigation.
268. Traveller.	269. Mariner.
270. Transference.	
271. Carrier.	
272. Vehicle.	273. Ship.

2°. Degrees of Motion

274. Velocity.	275. Slowness.

3°. Conjoined with Force............

276. Impulse.	277. Recoil.

4°. With Reference to Direction.....

278. Direction.	279. Deviation.
280. Precession.	281. Sequence.
282. Progression.	283. Regression.
284. Propulsion.	285. Traction.
286. Approach.	287. Recession.
288. Attraction.	289. Repulsion.
290. Convergence.	291. Divergence.
292. Arrival.	293. Departure.
294. Ingress.	295. Egress.
296. Reception.	297. Ejection.
298. Food.	299. Excretion.
300. Insertion.	301. Extraction.
302. Passage.	
303. Overstep.	304. Shortcoming.

2°. SENSATION

(1) General

375. Sensibility.	376. Insensibility.
377. Pleasure.	378. Pain.

(2) Special

1. Touch

379. Touch.	
380. { Sensations of Touch.	381. Numbness.

2. Heat

382. Heat.	383. Cold.
384. Calefaction.	385. Refrigeration.
386. Furnace.	387. Refrigeratory.
388. Fuel.	
389. Thermometer.	

3. Taste

390. Taste.	391. Insipidity.
392. Pungency.	
393. Condiment.	
394. Savouriness.	395. Unsavouriness.
396. Sweetness.	397. Sourness.

4. Odour

398. Odour.	399. Inodorousness.
400. Fragrance.	401. Fœtor.

5. Sound

(i.) *Sound in General.*

402. Sound.	403. Silence.
404. Loudness.	405. Faintness.

(ii.) *Specific Sounds.*

406. Snap.	407. Roll.
408. Resonance.	408a. Non-resonance.
	409. Sibilation.
410. Stridor.	
411. Cry.	412. Ululation.

(iii.) *Musical Sounds.*

413. { Melody. Concord.	414. Discord.
415. Music.	
416. Musician.	
417. Musical Instruments.	

(iv.) *Perception of Sound.*

418. Hearing.	419. Deafness.

6. Light

(i.) *Light in General.*

420. Light.	421. Darkness.
422. Dimness.	
423. Luminary.	424. Shade.
425. Transparency.	426. Opacity.
427. Semitransparency.	

(ii.) *Specific Light.*

428. Colour.	429. Achromatism.
430. Whiteness.	431. Blackness.
432. Gray.	433. Brown.
434. Redness.	435. Greenness.
436. Yellowness.	437. Purple.
438. Blueness.	439. Orange.
440. Variegation.	

(iii.) *Perceptions of Light.*

441. Vision.	442. Blindness.
443. Dimsightedness.	
444. Spectator.	
445. Optical Instruments.	
446. Visibility.	447. Invisibility.
448. Appearance.	449. Disappearance.

Class IV. INTELLECT

Division (I.). FORMATION OF IDEAS

I. OPERATIONS OF INTELLECT IN GENERAL.....

450. Intellect.	450a. Absence of Intellect.
451. Thought.	452. Incogitancy.
453. Idea.	454. Topic.
455. Curiosity.	456. Incuriosity.
457. Attention.	458. Inattention.
459. Care.	460. Neglect.

II. PRECURSORY CONDITIONS AND OPERATIONS......

461. Inquiry.	462. Answer.
463. Experiment.	
464. Comparison.	
465. Discrimination.	465a. Indiscrimination.
466. Measurement.	
467. Evidence.	468. Counter-evidence.

469. Qualification.

III. MATERIALS FOR REASONING..........

Degrees of Evidence.

470. Possibility.	471. Impossibility.
472. Probability.	473. Improbability.
474. Certainty.	475. Uncertainty.

IV. REASONING PROCESSES .

476. Reasoning.	477. { Intuition. / Sophistry.
478. Demonstration.	479. Confutation.
480. Judgement.	481. Misjudgement.
480a. Discovery.	
482. Over-estimation.	483. Under-estimation.
484. Belief.	485. { Unbelief. / Doubt.
486. Credulity.	487. Incredulity.
488. Assent.	489. Dissent.

V. RESULTS OF REASONING .

490. Knowledge.	491. Ignorance.
492. Scholar.	493. Ignoramus.
494. Truth.	495. Error.
496. Maxim.	497. Absurdity.

Faculties.

498. { Intelligence. / Wisdom.	499. { Imbecility. / Folly.
500. Sage.	501. Fool.
502. Sanity.	503. Insanity.
	504. Madman.

VI. EXTENSION OF THOUGHT

1°. *To the Past...*

505. Memory.	506. Oblivion.
507. Expectation.	508. Inexpectation.
	509. Disappointment.

2°. *To the Future.*

510. Foresight.	
511. Prediction.	
512. Omen.	
513. Oracle.	

VII. CREATIVE THOUGHT... { 514. Supposition. / 515. Imagination.

Division (II.). Communication of Ideas

Class V. VOLITION

Division (I.). Individual Volition

II. PROSPEC-TIVE VOLI-TION—cont.	3°. Precursory Measures	673. Preparation.	674. Non-preparation.
		675. Essay.	
		676. Undertaking.	
		677. Use.	678. Disuse.
			679. Misuse.

III. ACTION	1°. Simple...	680. Action.	681. Inaction.
		682. Activity.	683. Inactivity.
		684. Haste.	685. Leisure.
		686. Exertion.	687. Repose.
		688. Fatigue.	689. Refreshment.
		690. Agent.	
		691. Workshop.	
	2°. Complex .	692. Conduct.	
		693. Direction.	
		694. Director.	
		695. Advice.	
		696. Council.	
		697. Precept.	
		698. Skill.	699. Unskilfulness.
		700. Proficient.	701. Bungler.
		702. Cunning.	703. Artlessness.

IV. ANTAGONISM	1°. Conditional....	704. Difficulty.	705. Facility.
	2°. Active....	706. Hindrance.	707. Aid.
		708. Opposition.	709. Co-operation.
		710. Opponent.	711. Auxiliary.
		712. Party.	
		713. Discord.	714. Concord.
		715. Defiance.	
		716. Attack.	717. Defence.
		718. Retaliation.	719. Resistance.
		720. Contention.	721. Peace.
		722. Warfare.	723. Pacification.
		724. Meditation.	
		725. Submission.	
		726. Combatant.	
		727. Arms.	
		728. Arena.	

V. RESULTS OF ACTION.....	729. Completion.	730. Non-completion.
	731. Success.	732. Failure.
	733. Trophy.	
	734. Prosperity.	735. Adversity.
	736. Mediocrity.	

Division (II.). INTERSOCIAL VOLITION

I. GENERAL..............	737. Authority.	738. Laxity.
	739. Severity.	740. Lenity.
	741. Command.	
	742. Disobedience.	743. Obedience.
	744. Compulsion.	
	745. Master.	746. Servant.
	747. Sceptre.	
	748. Freedom.	749. Subjection.
	750. Liberation.	751. Restraint.
		752. Prison.
	753. Keeper.	754. Prisoner.
	755. Commission.	756. Abrogation.
		757. Resignation.
	758. Consignee.	
	759. Deputy.	

	760. Permission.	761. Prohibition.
	762. Consent.	
II. SPECIAL..............	763. Offer.	764. Refusal.
	765. Request.	766. Depreciation;
	767. Petitioner.	
	768. Promise.	768a. Release;
	769. Compact.	
III. CONDITIONAL.........	770. Conditions.	
	771. Security.	
	772. Observance.	773. Non-observance.
	774. Compromise.	

IV. POSSESSIVE RELATIONS

	775. Acquisition.	776. Loss.
	777. Possession.	777a. Exemption;
1°. *Property in General*	778. Participation.	
	779. Possessor.	
	780. Property.	
	781. Retention.	782. Relinquishment;
	783. Transfer.	
	784. Giving.	785. Receiving.
	786. Apportionment.	
2°. *Transfer of Property*	787. Lending.	788. Borrowing.
	789. Taking.	790. Restitution.
	791. Stealing.	
	792. Thief.	
	793. Booty.	
	794. Barter.	
	795. Purchase.	796. Sale.
3°. *Interchange of Property*........	797. Merchant.	
	798. Merchandise.	
	799. Mart.	
	800. Money.	
	801. Treasurer.	
	802. Treasury.	
	803. Wealth.	804. Poverty.
	805. Credit.	806. Debt.
4°. *Monetary Relations*..	807. Payment.	808. Non-payment.
	809. Expenditure.	810. Receipt.
	811. Accounts.	
	812. Price.	813. Discount.
	814. Dearness.	815. Cheapness.
	816. Liberality.	817. Economy.
	818. Prodigality.	819. Parsimony.

CLASS VI. AFFECTIONS

	820. Affections.	
I. AFFECTIONS GENERALLY........	821. Feeling.	
	822. Sensibility.	823. Insensibility;
	824. Excitation.	
	825. Excitability.	826. Inexcitability.

II. PERSONAL

1°. PASSIVE

827. Pleasure.	828. Pain.
829. Pleasureableness.	830. Painfulness.
831. Content.	832. Discontent.
	833. Regret.
834. Relief.	835. Aggravation.
836. Cheerfulness.	837. Dejection.
838. Rejoicing.	839. Lamentation.
840. Amusement.	841. Weariness.
842. Wit.	843. Dulness.
844. Humorist.	

2°. DISCRIMINATIVE

845. Beauty.	846. Ugliness.
847. Ornament.	848. Blemish.
	849. Simplicity.
850. Taste.	851. Vulgarity.
852. Fashion.	
	853. Ridiculousness.
	854. Fop.
	855. Affection.
	856. Ridicule.
	857. Laughing-stock.

3°. PROSPECTIVE

858. Hope.	859. Hopelessness.
	860. Fear.
861. Courage.	862. Cowardice.
863. Rashness.	864. Caution.
865. Desire.	867. Dislike.
866. Indifference.	
	868. Fastidiousness.
	869. Satiety.

4°. CONTEMPLATIVE

870. Wonder.	871. Expectance.
872. Prodigy.	

5°. EXTRINSIC

873. Repute.	874. Disrepute.
875. Nobility.	876. Commonalty.
877. Title.	
878. Pride.	879. Humility.
880. Vanity.	881. Modesty.
882. Ostentation.	
883. Celebration.	
884. Boasting.	
885. Insolence.	886. Servility.
887. Blusterer.	

III. SYMPATHETIC

1°. SOCIAL

888. Friendship.	889. Enmity.
890. Friend.	891. Enemy.
892. Sociality.	893. Seclusion.
894. Courtesy.	895. Discourtesy.
896. Congratulation.	
897. Love.	898. Hate.
899. Favourite.	
	900. Resentment.
	901. Irascibility.
	901a. Sullenness.
902. Endearment.	
903. Marriage.	904. Celibacy.
	905. Divorce.

2°. DIFFUSIVE........ 906. Benevolence. 907. Malevolence.
908. Malediction.
909. Threat.
910. Philanthropy. 911. Misanthropy.
912. Benefactor. 913. Evil doer.

3°. SPECIAL.......... 914. Pity. 914a. Pitilessness.
915. Condolence.
916. Gratitude. 917. Ingratitude.
918. Forgiveness. 919. Revenge.

4°. RETROSPECTIVE.... 920. Jealousy.
921. Envy.

IV. MORAL

1°. OBLIGATIONS....... 922. Right. 923. Wrong.
924. Dueness. 925. Undueness.
926. Duty. {927. Dereliction.
{927a. Exemption.
928. Respect. 929. Disrespect.
930. Contempt.

2°. SENTIMENTS........ 931. Approbation. 932. Disapprobation.
933. Flattery. 934. Detraction.
935. Flatterer. 936. Detractor.
937. Vindication. 938. Accusation.
939. Probity. 940. Improbity.
941. Knave.
942. Disinterestedness. 943. Selfishness.

3°. CONDITIONS........ 944. Virtue. 945. Vice.
946. Innocence. 947. Guilt.
948. Good Man. 949. Bad Man.
950. Penitence. 951. Impenitence.
952. Atonement.
953. Temperance. 954. Intemperance.
954a. Sensualist.

4°. PRACTICE.......... 955. Asceticism.
956. Fasting. 957. Gluttony.
958. Sobriety. 959. Drunkenness.
960. Purity. 961. Impurity.
962. Libertine.

963. Legality. 964. Illegality.
965. Jurisprudence.
966. Tribunal.
967. Judge.
968. Lawyer.

5°. INSTITUTIONS...... 969. Lawsuit.
970. Acquittal. 971. Condemnation.
{972. Punishment.
973. Reward. {974. Penalty.
975. Scourge.

V. RELIGIOUS

1°. SUPERHUMAN BE-
INGS AND REGIONS.. 976. Deity.
977. Angel. 978. Satan.
979. Jupiter. 980. Demon.
981. Heaven. 982. Hell.

2°. DOCTRINES........ 983. Theology.
983a. Orthodoxy. 984. Heterodoxy.
985. Revelation. 986. Pseudo-revelation.

3°. SENTIMENTS........ 987. Piety. 988. Impiety.
989. Irreligion.

4°. ACTS..............
- 990. Worship.
  - 991. Idolatry
  - 992. Sorcery.
  - 993. Spell.
  - 994. Sorcerer.

5°. INSTITUTIONS......
- 995. Churchdom.
- 996. Clergy.　　997. Laity.
- 998. Rite.
- 999. Canonicals.
- 1000. Temple.

ABBREVIATIONS, &c.

Adj.	*adj.*	Adjectives, Participles, and Words having the power of Adjectives.
Adv.	*adv.*	Adverbs and Adverbial Expressions.
Int.	*int.*	Interjections.
Phr.	*phr.*	Phrases.
V.	*v.*	Verbs.

The numbers are those of the headings, or Categories.

Words in italics within parentheses are not intended to explain the meanings of the words which precede them, but to indicate the nature of allied group of words under the numbers which follow them.

See also the Editor's Preface, p. xi.

CLASS I

Words expressing ABSTRACT RELATIONS

THESAURUS

OF

ENGLISH WORDS AND PHRASES

CLASS I

WORDS EXPRESSING ABSTRACT RELATIONS

SECTION I. EXISTENCE

1°. BEING, IN THE ABSTRACT

1. Existence.—N. existence, being, entity, *ens, esse,* subsistence, quiddity.

reality, realness, actuality; positiveness &c. *adj.*; fact, matter of fact, sober reality; truth &c. 494; actual existence.

presence &c. (*existence in space*) 186; coexistence &c. 120.

stubborn fact; not a -dream &c. 515; no joke.

substance, essence, prime constituent, hypostatis.

[Science of existence], ontology.

V. exist, be; have -being &c. *n.*; subsist, live, breathe, stand, obtain, be the case; occur &c. (*event*) 151; have place, rank, prevail; find oneself, pass the time, vegetate.

consist in, lie in, reside in, inhere in.

come into -existence &c. *n.*; arise &c. (*begin*) 66; come forth &c. (*appear*) 446.

become &c. (*be converted*) 144; bring into existence &c. 161; coexist, preexist, endure &c. 141.

Adj. existing &c. *v.*; existent, subsistent, under the sun; in -existence &c. *n.*; extant; afloat, on foot, current, prevalent, rife, in force, -vogue; undestroyed.

real, actual, positive, absolute; true &c. 494; substan-tial, -tive; self-existing, -ent.

2. Inexistence.—N. inexistence; non-existence, -subsistence; nonentity, *nil*; negativeness &c. *adj.*; nullity; nihil-ity, -ism; *tabula rasa,* blank; abeyance; absence &c. 187; no such thing &c. 4; nothingness, oblivion, *non esse.*

annihilation; extinction &c. (*destruction*) 162.

V. not -exist &c. 1; have no -existence &c. 1; be null and void; cease to -exist &c. 1; pass away, perish; be –, become- extinct &c. *adj.*; die out; disappear &c. 449; melt away, dissolve, leave not a rack behind, leave no trace; go, be no more; die &c. 360.

annihilate, render null, nullify; abrogate &c. 756; destroy &c. 162; take away; remove &c. (*displace*) 185.

Adj. inexistent, non-existent &c. 1; negative, blank, null and void; missing, omitted; absent &c. 187; visionary &c. 515.

unreal, potential, virtual; baseless, *in nubibus*; unsubstantial &c. 4; vain.

un-born, -created, -begotten, -conceived, -produced, -made.

perished, annihilated &c. *v.*; extinct, exhausted, gone, lost, departed; defunct &c. (*dead*) 360; *spurlos versenkt.*

fabulous, ideal &c. (*imaginary*) 515; supposititious &c. 514.

Adv. negatively, virtually, &c. *adj.*

well-founded, -grounded; un-ideal, -imagined; not -potential &c. 2.

Adv. actually &c. *adj.*; in -fact, – point of fact, – reality; indeed; *de –*, *ipso-facto*.

2°. Being, in the Concrete

3. Substantiality.—N. substantiality, *hypostasis*; person, thing, object, article; something, a being, an existence; creature, body, substance, flesh and blood, stuff, *substratum*; matter &c. 316; physical nature.

[Totality of existences], world &c. 318; *plenum*.

Adj. substan-tive, -tial, concrete; hypostatic; personal, bodily; tangible &c. (*material*) 316; real, corporeal, evident.

Adv. substantially &c. *adj.*; bodily, essentially.

———

4. Unsubstantiality.—N. un-, in-substantiality; nothingness, nihility.

nothing, naught, *nil*, nullity, zero, cipher, no one, nobody; never –, ne'er -a one; no such thing, none in the world; nothing -whatever, – at all, – on earth; not a -particle &c. (*smallness*) 32; all -talk, – moonshine, – stuff and nonsense, matter of no import.

thing of naught, man of straw, John Doe and Richard Roe; *nominis umbra*, nonentity, figurehead, lay figure; flash in the pan, *vox et præterea nihil*.

shadow; phantasm, phantom &c. (*fallacy of vision*) 443; dream &c. (*imagination*) 515; *ignis fatuus* &c. (luminary) 423; 'such stuff as dreams are made of'; air, thin air; bubble &c. 353; 'baseless fabric of a vision'; mockery.

hollowness, blank; vacuity, void &c. (*absence*) 187.

inanity, fool's paradise, fatuity, stupidity, emptiness of mind.

V. vanish, evaporate, fade, sink, fly –, die –, melt- away, dissolve, disappear &c. 449, become extinct, become invisible.

Adj. unsubstantial; fleeting; base-, ground-less; ungrounded; without –, having no- foundation.

visionary &c. (*imaginary*) 515; immaterial &c. 317; spectral &c. 980; dreamy; shadowy; ethereal, airy, imponderable, tenuous, vague.

vacant, vacuous; empty &c. 187; eviscerated; blank, hollow; nominal; null; inane.

Phr. there's nothing in it.

3°. Formal Existence

Internal conditions

5. Intrinsicality.—N. intrinsicality, inbeing, inherence, inhesion, immanence; subjectiveness; *ego*; essence; essentialness &c. *adj.*; essential part, essential stuff, substance, quintessence, incarnation, quiddity, gist, pith, core, kernel, marrow, sap, life-blood, backbone, heart, soul, life, flower; important part &c. (*importance*) 642.

principle, nature, constitution, character, ethos, type, quality, crasis, *diathesis*.

habit; temper, -ament; spirit, humour, grain, disposition, streak, tendency &c. 176.

External conditions

6. Extrinsicality.—N. extrinsicality, objectiveness, *non ego*; extraneousness &c. 57; accident; letter of the law.

Adj. derived from without; objective; extrin-sic, -sical; extraneous &c. (*foreign*) 57; modal, adventitious, additional, supervenient, fortuitous; a-, ad-scititious; incidental, casual, accidental, unessential, non-essential, accessory.

implanted, ingrafted, instilled, inculcated.

outward &c. (*external*) 220.

Adv. extrinsically &c. *adj.*

———

endowment, capacity; capability &c. (*power*) 157; moods, de-
clensions, features, aspects; peculiarities &c. (*specialty*) 79; idiosyncrasy; idiocrasy; diagnostics.

V. be -, run- in the blood; be born so; be -intrinsic &c. *adj.*

Adj. derived from within, subjective; idiocratic, idiosyncratic,
intrin-sic, -sical; fundamental, cardinal, normal; inherent, essential,
natural; in-nate, -born, -bred, -dwelling, -grained, -wrought; radical, incarnate, thoroughbred, hereditary, inherited, immanent;
congen-ital, -ite; connate, running in the blood; coeval with birth,
genetic, ingenerate, -genite; indigenous; in the -grain &c. *n.*; bred
in the bone, instinctive; inward, internal &c. 221; to the manner
born; virtual.

characteristic &c. (*special*) 79, (*indicative*) 550; invariable, incurable, ineradicable, fixed, settled, constant, unchanging.

Adv. intrinsically &c. *adj.*; at bottom, in the main, in effect,
essentially, practically, virtually, substantially, *au fond*; fairly.

4°. MODAL EXISTENCE

Absolute

7. State.—N. state, condition, category, estate, lot, case, trim, mood,
pickle, plight &c. 704; temper; aspect
&c. (*appearance*) 448.

constitution, habitude, *diathesis*;
frame, fabric &c. 329; stamp, set, fit,
mould.

mode, modality, schesis; fettle; form
&c. (*shape*) 240.

tone, tenor, turn; trim, guise, fashion, light, complexion, style, character.

V. be in -, possess -, enjoy -, labour
under- a -state &c. *n.*; be on a footing,
do, fare; come to pass.

Adj. conditional, modal, formal;
structural, organic.

Adv. conditionally &c. *adj.*; as -the
matter stands, - things are; such being
the case &c. 8.

Relative

8. Circumstance.—N. circumstance,
situation, phase, position, posture,
attitude, place, point; terms; *régime*;
footing, standing, status.

occasion, juncture, conjuncture; contingency &c. (*event*) 151.

predicament; emergen-ce, -cy; exigency, crisis, pinch, pass, push; turning
point; crossroads.

bearings, how the land lies.

Adj. circumstantial; given, conditional, provisional; critical; modal;
contingent, incidental; adventitious
&c. (*extrinsic*) 6.

Adv. in the circumstances &c. *n.*,
under the conditions &c. 7; thus, in
such wise.

accordingly; that -, such- being the
case; that being so, since, seeing that.
as matters stand; as -things, - times-
go.

conditionally, provided, if, in case; if -so, - so be, - it be so;
if it so -happen, - turn out; in the event of; in such a -contingency,
- case, - event; provisionally, unless, without.

according to -circumstances, - the occasion; as it may -happen,
- turn out, - be; as the -case may be, - wind blows; *pro re natâ*.

SECTION II. RELATION

1°. ABSOLUTE RELATION

9. Relation.—N. relation, bearing,
reference, connection, apposition, interconnection, concern, cognation; applicability, appositeness; correlation

10. [Want, or absence of relation.]
Irrelation.—N. irrelation, dissociation;
inapplicability; inconnection; multifariousness; disconnection &c. (*dis-*

&c. 12; analogy; similarity &c. 17; affinity, intimacy, friendship; homology, alliance, homogeneity, association, rapport; approximation &c. (*nearness*) 197; filiation &c. (*consanguinity*) 11; interest; relevancy &c. 23; relationship, relative position; relativity; interrelation &c. 12.

comparison &c. 464; ratio, proportion.

link, tie, bond, bond of union.

V. be-related &c. *adj.*; have a relation &c. *n.*; relate –, refer- to; bear upon, regard, concern, touch, affect, have to do with; pertain –, belong –, appertain- to; have respect to; answer to; interest.

bring -into relation with, – to bear upon; connect, associate, draw a parallel; link &c. 43.

Adj. relative; correlative &c. 12; cognate; relating to &c. *v.*; relative to, in relation with, referable *or* referrible to; belonging to &c. *v.*; appurtenant to, in common with.

related, connected; implicated, associated, affiliated, akin, allied to; collateral, cognate, congenial, kindred, affinitive, *en rapport*, in touch with.

approxima-tive, -ting; approaching; proportion-al, -ate, -able; allusive, comparable.

in the same -category &c. 75; like &c. 17; relevant &c. (*apt*) 23.

Adv. relatively &c. *adj.*; pertinently &c. 23.

thereof; as -to, – for, – respects, – regards; about; concerning &c. *v.*; anent; relating –, as relates- to; with -relation, – reference, – respect, – regard- to; in respect of; while speaking –, *à propos*- of; in connection with; by the -way, – by; whereas; for –, in -as much as; in point of, as far as; on the -part, – score- of; *quoad hoc*; *pro re natâ*; under the -head &c. (*class*) **75-** of; in the matter of, *in re.*

Phr. 'thereby hangs a tale.'

junction) 44; inconsequence, independence; incommensurability; irreconcilableness &c. (*disagreement*) 24; heterogeneity; unconformity &c. 83; irrelevancy, impertinence, *nihil ad rem*; intrusion &c. 24.

V. have no -relation &c. 9 to, – bearing upon, – concern &c. 9 with, – business with; not -concern &c. 9; have -nothing to do with, – no business there; intrude, &c. 24.

bring –, drag –, haul –, lug- in head and shoulders.

Adj. irrelative, irrespective, unrelated, irrelated; arbitrary; independent, unallied; un-, dis-connected; adrift, isolated, insular; extraneous, strange, alien, foreign, outlandish, exotic.

not comparable, incommensurable, heterogeneous; unconformable &c. 83.

irrelevant; rambling &c. 279; inapplicable; not -pertinent, – to the purpose; impertinent, inapposite, beside the mark, *à propos de bottes*; away from –, foreign to –, beside- the -purpose, – question, – transaction, – point; misplaced &c. (*intrusive*) 24.

remote, far fetched, out of the way, forced, neither here nor there, quite another thing; detached, segregated, segregate.

multifarious; discordant &c. 24.

incidental, parenthetical, *obiter dictum*, episodic.

Adv. parenthetically &c. *adj.*; by the -way, – by; *en passant*, incidentally; irrespectively &c. *adj.*; without reference, – regard- to; in the abstract &c. 87; *a se.*

---

11. [Relations of kindred.] **Consanguinity.**—**N.** consanguinity, relationship, kindred, blood; parentage &c. (*paternity*) 166; filiation, affiliation; lineage, agnation, connection, cognation, alliance; family -connection, – tie; ties of blood; blood relationship; nepotism.

kins-man, -folk; people; kith and kin; rela-tion, -tive; connection; sib; next of kin; uncle, aunt, nephew, niece; cousin, -german; first –, second- cousin; cousin -once, – twice &c.- removed; near –, distant- relation; brother, sister, one's own flesh and blood.

[4]

family, patriarch, matriarch; fraternity; brother-, sister-, cousin-hood.

race, stock, generation; sept &c. 166; stirps, side; strain; breed, clan, tribe.

V. be -related &c. *adj.* – to; claim -relationship &c. *n.*- with.

Adj. related, akin, consanguineous, matrilinear, patrilineal, of the blood, family, allied, collateral; cog-, ag-, con-nate; kindred; affiliated, affine; fraternal, avuncular.

intimately –, nearly –, closely –, remotely –, distantly- related, – allied; german.

12. [Double or reciprocal relation.] **Correlation.—N.** reciprocalness &c. *adj.*; recipro-city, -cality, -cation; mutuality, correlation, correspondence, interdependence; interchange &c. 148; exchange, barter; interrelation, interconnection; alternation, see-saw.

V. reciprocate, alternate; interchange &c. 148; exchange; counterchange; interact, correspond, mutualize, give and take.

Adj. reciprocal, mutual, commutual, correlative; alternate; interchangeable; international; correspondent, complementary, analogous.

Adv. *mutatis mutandis*; *vice versâ*; each other; by turns &c. 148; reciprocally &c. *adj.*; to and fro &c. 314.

13. Identity.—N. identity, sameness, oneness, ditto, homogeneity; unity, coincidence, coalescence; convertibility; equality &c. 27; selfness, self, oneself; identification.

monotony, tautology &c. (*repetition*) 104.

synonym.

fac-simile &c. (*copy*) 21; *alter ego* &c. (*similar*) 17; *ipsissima verba* &c. (*exactness*) 494; same; self -, very -, one and the- same; very -, actual-thing; no other.

V. be -identical &c. *adj.*; match, coincide, coalesce.

treat as -, render- -the same, –identical; identify; recognize the identity of.

Adj. identical; self, ilk; the -same &c. *n.*; self same; synonymous; one and the same.

coincid-, coalesc-ent, -ing; indistinguishable; one; equivalent &c. (*equal*) 27; much -the same, – of a muchness; unaltered.

Adv. identically &c. *adj.*; on all fours; *ibid-, -em.*

14. [Non-coincidence.] **Contrariety.—N.** contrariety, contrast, foil, antithesis, oppositeness; counterpole; contradiction; antagonism &c. (*opposition*) 708; counteraction &c. 179.

inversion &c. 218; the -opposite, – reverse, – inverse, – converse, – antipodes, – other extreme &c. 237.

antonym.

V. be -contrary &c. *adj.*; contrast with, oppose; differ *toto cœlo*.

invert, reverse, turn the tables &c. 218.

contra-dict, -vene; antagonize &c. 708.

Adj. contrar-y, -ious, -iant; opposite, counter, dead against; ad-, con-, reverse; opposed, antithetical, contrasted, antipodean, antagonistic, opposing; conflicting, inconsistent, contradictory, at cross purposes; negative; hostile &c. 708.

differing *toto cœlo*; diametrically opposite; as opposite as -black and white, – light and darkness, – fire and water, – the poles, as different as chalk from cheese; 'Hyperion to a satyr'; quite the -contrary, – reverse; no such thing, just the other way, *tout au contraire.*

Adv. contrarily &c. *adj.*; *contra*, contrariwise, *per contra*, on the contrary, nay rather; topsy-turvy; *vice versâ*; on the other hand &c. (*in compensation*) 30.

15. Difference.—N. difference, unlikeness; heterogeneity; vari-ance, -ation, -ety; diversity, dissimilarity &c. 18; disagreement &c. 24; disparity &c. (*inequality*) 28; distinction, contradistinction; distinctness; discrepancy, divergence, contrast &c. 18; nonconformity, incompatibility, antithesis.

discord &c. 713.

modification, moods and tenses.

nice –, fine –, delicate –, subtle- distinction; shade of difference, *nuance;* discrimination &c. 465; *differentia.*

different thing, something else, variant, apple off another tree, horse of another colour, another pair of shoes; this that or the other.

V. be -different &c. *adj.*; differ, vary, ablude, mismatch, contrast; diverge –, depart –, deviate- -from; divaricate; differ -*toto cœlo*, – *longo intervallo.*

disagree &c. 713.

vary, modify &c. (*change*) 140.

discriminate &c. 465.

Adj. differing &c. *v.*; different, diverse, divided, heterogeneous; distinguishable; varied, modified; divergent, incongruous, diversified, various; discrepant, dissentient, differential; divers, all manner of; variform &c. 81; discordant &c. 713.

other, another, not the same; unequal &c. 28; unmatched; widely apart.

distinctive, characteristic; discriminative; distinguishing.

Adv. differently &c. *adj.*

Phr. *il y a fagots et fagots; tot nomines tot sententiæ*; one man's meat is another man's poison.

2°. Continuous Relation

16. Uniformity. — N. uniformity; homogene-ity, -ousness; continuity, stability, consistency; connatural-ity, -ness; homology; accordance; conformity &c. 82; agreement &c. 23.

regularity, constancy, even tenor, routine; monotony, evenness, sameness, dead level; steadiness, equability, unity.

V. be -uniform &c. *adj.*; accord with &c. 23; run through.

become -uniform &c. *adj.*; conform to &c. 82.

render uniform &c. *adj.*; assimilate, level, smooth, dress.

16a. [Absence or want of uniformity.] **Non-uniformity.—N.** diversity irregularity, unevenness; multiformity &c. 81; unconformity &c. 83; roughness &c. 256; heterogeneity, heteromorphism.

Adj. diversified, varied, irregular, uneven, rough &c. 256; multifarious; multiform &c. 81; of various kinds; all -manner, – sorts, – kinds- of.

Adv. in all manner of ways, here there and everywhere.

Adj. uniform; homo-geneous, -logous; of a piece, consistent, steady; connatural; monotonous, changeless, dreary, even, invariable, equable, level, regular, stereotyped, unchanged, unvarying; methodical &c. 60; habitual &c. 613.

Adv. uniformly &c. *adj.*; uniformly with &c. (*conformably*) 82; in harmony with &c. (*agreeing*) 23; in a -rut, – groove.

always, ever &c. 112; invariably, without exception, never otherwise; by clock-work; endlessly &c. 112.

Phr. *ab uno disce omnes.*

3°. Partial Relation

17. Similarity.—N. similarity, resemblance, likeness, similitude, sem-

18. Dissimilarity.—N. dissimil-arity, -itude; unlikeness, diversity, disparity,

blance; affinity, approximation, parallelism; parity; agreement &c. 23; ana-logy, -logicalness; correspondence, equality &c.

connatural-ness, -ity; brotherhood, family likeness.

alliteration, rhyme, pun.

repetition &c. 104; sameness &c. (*identity*) 13; uniformity &c. 16.

analogue; the like; match, *pendant*, fellow, companion, pair, mate, twin, double, counterpart, brother, sister; one's second self, *alter ego*, chip of the old block, *par nobile fratrum, Arcades ambo*, birds of a feather, *et hoc genus omne*.

parallel; simile; type &c. (*metaphor*) 521; image &c. (*representation*) 554; photograph; close –, striking –, speaking –, faithful &c. *adj.* – likeness, – resemblance.

V. be -similar &c. *adj.*; look like, resemble, bear resemblance, favour; savour –, smack- of; approximate; parallel, match, rhyme with; take after; imitate &c. 19; run in pairs.

render -similar &c. *adj.*; assimilate, approximate, bring near; connaturalize, make alike; rhyme, pun.

Adj. similar; resembling &c. *v.*; like, alike; twin.

analog-ous, -ical; parallel, of a piece; such as, so.

connatural, congeneric, allied to; corresponding, cognate; akin to &c. (*consanguineous*) 11.

approximate, much the same, near, close, something like, such like; a show of; mock, *pseudo*, simulating, representing.

exact &c. (*true*) 494; lifelike, faithful, realistic; true to -nature, – the life; the -very image – picture- of; for all the world like, *comme deux gouttes d'eau*; as like as -two peas, – it can stare; *instar omnium*, cast in the same mould, ridiculously like.

Adv. as if, so to speak; as –, as if- it were; *quasi*, just as, *veluti in speculum*.

dissemblance; divergence, inequality, difference &c. 15; novelty; variation, variety, originality, disguise.

V. be -unlike &c. *adj.*; vary &c. (*differ*) 15; bear no resemblance to, differ *toto cœlo*.

render -unlike &c. *adj.*; vary &c. (*diversify*) 140.

Adj. dissimilar, unlike, disparate; of a different kind &c. (*class*) 75; unmatched, unique; new, novel; unprecedented &c. 83; original.

nothing of the kind; no such –, quite another- thing; far from it, other than, cast in a different mould, *tertium quid*, as like a dock as a daisy, 'very like a whale'; as different as -chalk from cheese, – Macedon and Monmouth; *lucus a non lucendo*.

diversified &c. 16a.

Adv. otherwise, *alias*.

---

19. Imitation.—N. imitation; copying &c. *v.*; transcription; repetition, mimeograph, mimeotype, duplication, reduplication; quotation; reproduction.

mockery, mimicry, mime, simulation, personation; representation &c. 554; semblance, simulacrum; pretence; copy &c. 21; assimilation.

paraphrase, parody &c. 21.

ṗlagiarism; forgery &c. (*falsehood*) 544.

imitator, echo, cuckoo, parrot, ape, monkey, mocking-bird, mimic, impersonator; copyist.

V. imitate, copy, mirror, reflect, reproduce, repeat, borrow; do like, echo, re-echo, catch; transcribe; match, parallel.

20. Non-Imitation.—N. no imitation, genuineness, originality; creativeness.

Adj. unimitated, uncopied; unmatched, unparalleled; inimitable &c. 33; *unique*, original, primordial, primary, pristine, underived, first-hand, archetypal, prototypal.

---

mock, take off, mimic, ape, simulate, personate, impersonate; forge; act &c. (*drama*) 599; represent &c. 554; counterfeit, duplicate; portray, parody, travesty, caricature, burlesque.

follow -, tread- in the- -steps, - footsteps, - wake- of; pattern after, take pattern by; follow -suit, - the example of; walk in the shoes of, take a leaf out of another's book, strike in with; take -, model -after; emulate.

Adj. imitated &c. *v.*; mock, mimic; counterfeit, false, pseudo; modelled after, moulded on, paraphrastic; literal; imitative, apish; second-hand; imitable; sham &c. 545.

Adv. literally, to the letter, strictly, precisely, *verbatim, literatim, sic, totidem verbis*, word for word, *mot à mot*.

Phr. like master like man.

20a. Variation.—N. variation; alteration &c. (*change*) 140.
modification, moods and tenses; modulation.
divergency &c. 291; deviation &c. 279; aberration; innovation.
V. vary &c. (*change*) 140; deviate &c. 279; diverge &c. 291.
Adj. varied &c. *v.*; modified; dissimilar &c. 18; diversified &c. 16a.

21. [Result of imitation.] **Copy.—N.** copy, fac-simile, counterpart, *effigies*, effigy, symbol, image, form, likeness, similitude, semblance, resemblance, cast, electrotype, stereotype, tracing, ectype; imitation &c. 19; model, representation, adumbration, study; counterfeit presentment, portrait &c. (*representment*) 554.

duplicate; transcript, -ion; reflex, -ion; shadow, echo; chip of the old block; reprint, reproduction, casting, engraving, replica; transfer; second edition &c. (*repetition*) 104; *réchauffé*; apograph, fair copy, revise.

22. [Thing copied.] **Prototype.—N.** prototype, original, model, pattern, founding, precedent, standard, scantling, type, arche-, anti-type; protoplast, copy-book, module, exemplar, example, ensample, specimen; paradigm; guide; templet; lay-figure.

text, copy, manuscript, MS., design; fugleman, keynote.

die, mould; matrix, engraving, last, plasm; pro-, proto-plasm; mint; seal, punch, *intaglio*, negative, stamp.

V. be -, set- an example; set a copy; standardize.

parody, caricature, cartoon, burlesque, travesty, paraphrase.
servile -copy, - imitation; counterfeit &c. (*deception*) 545; *pasticcio*.
Adj. faithful; lifelike &c. (*similar*) 17.

4°. GENERAL RELATION

23. Agreement. — N. agreement; ac-cord, -cordance; unison, harmony, syntony; concord &c. 714; concordance, concert, understanding, convention, *entente -cordiale, consortium*, consensus of opinion, pact, mutual understanding, unanimity.

conformity &c. 82; conformance; uniformity &c. 16; consonance, consentaneousness, consistency; congruity, -ence; keeping; congeniality; correspondence, concinnity, parallelism, apposition, union.

fitness, aptness &c. *adj.*; relevancy;

24. Disagreement. — N. disagreement; dis-cord, -cordance; disunion, dissonance, dissidence, discrepancy; unconformity &c. 83; incongru-ity, -ence; discongruity, *mésalliance, oxymoron*; jarring &c. *v.*; clash, collision, dissension &c. 713; conflict &c. (*opposition*) 708; controversy &c. 720; falling out, wrangle, argument.

disparity, mismatch, misfit, disproportion; disproportionateness &c. *adj.*; variance, divergence, repugnance.

unfitness &c. *adj.*; inaptitude, impropriety; inapplicability &c. *adj.*; in-

pertinen-ce, -cy; sortance; case in point; aptitude, coaptation, propriety, applicability, admissibility, commensurability, compatibility, suitability; cognation &c. (*relation*) 9.

adaptation, adjustment, arrangement, graduation, accommodation; reconcil-iation -ement; assimilation; attunement.

consent &c. (*assent*) 448; concurrence &c. 178; co-operation &c. 709.

right man in the right place, very thing; quite -, just- the thing.

V. be -accordant &c. *adj.*; agree, accord, harmonize; correspond, tally, respond; meet, suit, fit, befit, do, adapt itself to; fall in -, chime in -, square -, quadrate -, consort -, comport- with; dovetail, assimilate; fit like a glove; fit to a -tittle, − T; match &c. 17; become one.

consent &c. (*assent*) 488.

render -accordant &c. *adj.*; fit, suit, adapt, accommodate; graduate; adjust &c. (*render equal*) 27; dress, regulate, readjust; accord, harmonize, reconcile; fadge, dovetail, square.

Adj. agreeing, suiting &c. *v.*; in accord, accordant, concordant, consonant, congruous, consentaneous, correspondent, corresponding, homologous, congenial; becoming; harmonious, reconcilable, conformable; in -accordance, − harmony, − keeping, − unison, &c. *n.*- with; at one with, of one mind, of a piece; consistent, compatible, proportionate, answerable; commensurate; on all fours.

apt, apposite, pertinent, pat; to the -point, − purpose; happy, felicitous, germane, *ad rem*, in point, bearing upon, applicable, relevant, admissible.

fit, adapted, *in loco*, *à propos*, appropriate, seasonable, sortable, suitable, idoneous, deft; meet &c. (*expedient*) 646.

at home, in one's proper element.

Adv. *à propos of*; pertinently &c. *adj.*; *pro rata*.

Phr. *rem acu tetigisti*, the cap fits.

consistency, inconcinnity; irrelevancy &c. (*irrelation*) 10.

misjoin-ing, -der; syncretism, intrusion, interference; *concordia discors*.

fish out of water.

V. disagree; clash, quarrel, jar &c. (*discord*) 713; interfere, intrude, come amiss; not concern &c. 10; mismatch; *hymano capiti cervicem jungere equinam*.

Adj. disagreeing &c. *v.*; discordant, discrepant; at -variance, − war; hostile, antagonistic, repugnant, factious, contradictory, dissentious, incompatible, irreconcilable, inconsistent with; unconformable, exceptional &c. 83; intrusive, incongruous; disproportionate, -ed; unharmonious; unconsonant; divergent, repugnant to.

inapt, unapt, inappropriate, inept, infelicitous, improper; unsuit-ed, -able; inapplicable; un-fit, -fitting, -befitting; unbecoming; ill-timed, ill-adapted, unseasonable, *mal à propos*, inadmissible; inapposite &c. (*irrelevant*) 10.

uncongenial; ill-assorted, -sorted, -matched; mis-matched, -mated, -joined, -placed; unaccommodating, irreducible, uncommensurable, unsympathetic.

out of -character, − keeping, − proportion, − joint, − tune, − place, − season, − its element; at -odds, − variance with.

Adv. in -defiance, − contempt, − spite-of; discordantly &c. *adj.*; *à tort et à travers*.

<h1 style="text-align:center">Section III. QUANTITY</h1>

1°. Simple Quantity

25. [Absolute quantity.] **Quantity.—**
N. quantity, magnitude; size &c. (*dimensions*) 192; amplitude, mass,

26. [Relative quantity.] **Degree.—**
N. degree, grade, extent, measure, proportion, amount, ratio, stint, standard,

amount, *quantum*, measure, measurement, substance, strength.

[Science of quantity.] Mathematics, Mathesis.

[Definite or finite quantity] arm-, hand-, mouth-, spoon-, thimble-, capful; stock, batch, lot, dose, ration, quotum, quota, pittance, driblet, part, portion &c. 51.

Adj. quantitative, some, any, more or less.

Adv. to the tune of.

---

height, pitch; reach, amplitude, range, scope, size, calibre; gradation, shade; tenor, compass; sphere, station, rank, standing; rate, way, sort.

point, mark, step, stage &c. (*term*) 71; intensity, strength &c. (*greatness*) 31.

V. compare, graduate, calibrate, measure.

Adj. comparative; gradual, shading off, gradational; within the bounds &c. (*limit*), 233.

Adv. by degrees, gradually, inasmuch, *pro tanto*; how-ever, -soever; step by step, bit by bit, little by little, inch by inch, drop by drop, gradatim; by -inches, − slow degrees, − little and little; in some -degree, − measure; to some extent; just a bit.

2°. COMPARATIVE QUANTITY

27. [Sameness of quantity or degree.] **Equality.—N.** equality, parity, co-extension, symmetry, balance, poise; evenness, monotony, level.

equivalence; equi-pollence, -poise, -librium, -ponderance; par, quits; not a pin to choose; distinction without a difference, six of one and half a dozen of the other; identity &c. 13; similarity &c. 17; isotropism; coequality.

equalization, equation; equilibration, co-ordination, adjustment, readjustment.

drawn -game, -battle, draw, stalemate; neck and neck race; tie, dead heat.

match, peer, compeer, equal, mate, fellow, brother; equivalent.

V. be -equal &c. *adj.*; equal, match, reach, keep pace with, run abreast; come −, amount −, come up-to; be −, lie- on a level with; balance; cope with; come to the same thing; level off.

render -equal &c. *adj.*; equalize, level, dress, balance, equate, handicap, give points, trim, adjust, poise; fit, accommodate; adapt &c. (*render accordant*) 23; strike a balance; establish −, restore- equality, − equilibrium; readjust; stretch on the bed of Procrustes.

Adj. equal, even, level, monotonous, coequal, symmetrical, co-ordinate; on a -par, − level, − footing- with; up to the mark; equiparent.

equivalent, tantamount; quits; homologous; synonymous &c. 522; resolvable into, convertible, much at one, as broad as long, neither more nor less; much the same −, the same thing −, as good-as; all -one, − the same; equi-pollent, -ponderant, -ponderous, -balanced; equalized &c. *v.*; drawn; half and half; isochronous; isoperimetrical.

28. [Difference of quantity or degree.] **Inequality.—N.** inequality; dis-, im-parity; odds; difference &c. 15; ill-balanced; unevenness; inclination of the balance, partiality; shortcoming; casting − make- weight; superiority &c. 33; inferiority &c. 34.

V. be -unequal &c. *adj.*; countervail; have −, give- the advantage; turn the scale; kick the beam; topple, -over; over-match &c. 33; not come up to &c. 34.

Adj. unequal, uneven, disparate, partial; un-, over-balanced; top-heavy, lop-sided.

Adv. *haud passibus æquis.*

Adv. equally &c. *adj.*; *pari passu, ad eundem, cæteris paribus; in equilibrio*; to all intents and purposes.

Phr. it -comes, -adds up, – amounts- to the same thing.

29. Mean.—**N.** mean, medium, intermedium, average, run of the mill, normal, balance; mediocrity, generality, rule, ordinary -run, -ruck; golden mean &c. (*mid-course*) 628; middle &c. 68; compromise &c. 774; neutrality; middle point, middle course.

V. split the difference; take the -average &c. *n.*; reduce to a -mean &c. *n.*; strike a balance, pair off.

Adj. mean, intermediate; medial; middle &c. 68; average, normal, standard; neutral; middling, moderate.

médiocre, middle-class; *bourgeois*, commonplace &c. (*unimportant*) 643.

Adv. on an average, in the long run; taking -one with another, – all things together, – it for all in all; *communibus annis*, in round numbers.

30. Compensation.—**N.** compensation, equation; commutation; indemnification; compromise &c. 774; neutralization, nullification; counteraction &c. 179; reaction; measure for measure; retaliation &c. 718; equalization &c. 27; redemption, recoupment, recompense.

set-off, offset; make- casting-weight; counterpoise, equipoise, ballast; indemnity, reparation &c. 790; equivalent, *quid pro quo*; bribe, hush-money, tribute &c. 784; amends &c. (*atonement*) 952; counterclaim, counterbalance, equiponderance, countervail, cross demand.

V. make -amends, – compensation; com-pensate, -pense; indemnify; counter-act, -vail, -poise; equiponderate; balance; out-, over-, counter-balance; set off, offset, cancel; hedge, square, give and take; make up -for, – lee way; cover, fill up, neutralize, nullify; equalize &c. 27; make good; redeem &c. (*atone*) 952; recoup, pay &c. 973.

Adj. compensat-ing, -ory; amendatory, reparative, countervailing &c. *v.*; in the opposite scale; equivalent &c. (*equal*) 27.

Adv. in -return, – consideration; but, however, yet, still, notwith-standing; neverthe-, nath-less; although, though; al-, how-beit; in spite of, despite; maugre; at -all events, – any rate; be that as it may, for all that, even so, on the other hand, at the same time, *quoad minus, quand même*, however that may be; after all, – is said and done; taking one thing with another &c. (*average*) 29.

QUANTITY BY COMPARISON WITH A STANDARD

31. Greatness.—**N.** greatness &c. *adj.*; magnitude; size &c. (*dimensions*) 192; multitude &c. (*number*) 102; immensity, enormity; infinity &c. 105; might, strength, intensity, fulness; importance &c. 642; fame &c. 873.

great quantity, quantity, deal, power, sight, pot, volume, world; mass, heap &c. (*assemblage*) 72; stock &c. (*store*) 636; peck, bushel, load, cargo; cart -, wagon -, car -, truck -, ship- load; flood, spring tide; abundance &c. (*sufficiency*) 639.

principal -, chief -, main -, greater -,

32. Smallness.—**N.** smallness &c. *adj.*; littleness &c. (*small size*) 193; tenuity; paucity; fewness &c. (*small number*) 103; meanness, insignificance &c. (*unimportance*) 643; mediocrity, moderation.

small quantity, *modicum, minimum*; vanishing point; material point, electron, atom, particle, molecule, corpuscle, point, dab, fleck, speck, dot, mote, jot, iota, ace; *minutiæ*, details; look, thought, idea, *soupçon*, whit, tittle, shade, shadow; spark, *scintilla*, gleam; touch, cast; grain, scruple,

major –, best –, essential- part; bulk, mass &c. (*whole*) 50.

V. be -great &c. *adj.*; run high, soar, loom up, tower, bulk large, transcend; rise –, carry- to a great height; know no bounds; scale, overtop, ascend.

enlarge &c. (*increase*) 35, (*expand*) 194.

Adj. great; greater &c. 33; large, considerable, fair, above par; big, massive, huge &c. (*large in size*) 192; ample; abundant &c. (*enough*) 639; Herculean &c. 159; full, intense, strong, sound, passing, heavy, plenary, deep, high; signal, at its height, in the zenith.

world-wide, wide-spread, extensive; wholesale; many &c. 102.

goodly, noble, precious, mighty; sad, grave, serious; far gone, arrant, downright; utter, -most; crass, gross, arch, profound, intense, consummate; rank, unmitigated, red-hot, desperate; glaring, flagrant, stark staring; thoroughpaced, -going; roaring, thumping, thundering, strapping, whacking; extraordinary; important &c. 642; unsurpassed &c. (*supreme*) 33; complete &c. 52.

vast, immense, enormous, extreme; inordinate, excessive, extravagant, exorbitant, outrageous, preposterous, unconscionable, swinging, monstrous, over-grown; towering, stupendous, prodigious, astonishing, incredible; terrific, frightful; marvellous &c. (*wonder*) 870; grand.

unlimited &c. (*infinite*) 105; unapproachable, unutterable, indescribable, ineffable, unspeakable, inexpressible, beyond expression, fabulous.

un-diminished, -abated, -reduced, -restricted.

absolute, positive, stark, decided, unequivocal, essential, perfect, finished.

remarkable, of mark, marked, pointed, veriest; noticeable, uncommon, noteworthy, eminent &c. 873.

Adv. [in a positive degree] truly &c. (*truth*) 494; decidedly, unequivocally, purely, absolutely, seriously, essentially, fundamentally, radically, downright, in all conscience; for the most part, in the main.

[in a complete degree] entirely &c. (*completely*) 52; abundantly, &c. (*suf-*

granule, globule, minim, sup, sip, sop, spice, drop, droplet, sprinkling, dash, smack, tinge, tincture; inch, patch, scantling, dole; scrap, shred, tag, splinter, rag, tatter, cantlet, flitter, gobbet, mite, bit, morsel, crumb, seed, fritter, shive; snip, -pet; snick, snack, snatch, slip, scrag; chip, -ping; shiver, sliver, driblet, clipping, paring, shaving, hair.

nutshell; thimble-, spoon-, hand-, cap-, mouth-ful; fragment; fraction &c. (*part*) 51; drop in the ocean, drop in the bucket.

animalcule &c. 193.

trifle &c. (*unimportant thing*) 643; mere –, next to- nothing; hardly anything; just enough to swear by; the shadow of a shade.

finiteness, finite quantity.

V. be -small &c. *adj.*; lie in a nutshell.

diminish &c. (*decrease*) 36, (*contract*) 195.

Adj. small, little, tiny, weeny; diminutive &c. (*small in size*) 193; minute; minikin, fine, inconsiderable, dribbling, paltry &c. (*unimportant*) 643; faint &c. (*weak*) 160; slender, light, slight, scanty, scant, limited; meagre &c. (*insufficient*) 640; sparing; few &c. 103; low, so-so, middling, tolerable, no great shakes; below –, under- -par, – the mark; at a low ebb; half-way; moderate, modest; tender, subtle; petty, shallow, skin-deep.

inappreciable, evanescent, infinitesimal, homœopathic, very small, atomic, molecular, ultra-, -microscopic.

petty, shallow &c. 499.

mere, simple, sheer, stark, bare; near run.

Adv. [in a small degree] to a small extent, on a small scale; a -little, – wee, – tiny bit; slightly &c. *adj.*; imperceptibly; miserably, wretchedly; insufficiently &c. 640; imperfectly; faintly &c. 160; passably, pretty well, well enough.

[in a certain or limited degree] partially, in part; in –, to a certain degree; to a certain extent; comparatively; some, rather; in some -degree, -measure; some-thing, -what; simply, only, purely, merely; at –, at the- -least,

ficiently) 639; widely, far and wide.

[in a great or high degree] greatly &c. *adj.*; much, muckle, well, indeed, very, very much, a deal, no end of, most not a little; pretty, – well; enough, in a great measure, passing richly; to a -large, – great, – gigantic-extent; on a large scale; so; never –, ever- so; ever so much; by wholesale; mightily, mighty, powerfully; with a witness, *ultra*, in the extreme, extremely, exceedingly, intensely, exquisitely, acutely, indefinitely, immeasurably; beyond -compare, – comparison, – measure, – all bounds; incalculably, infinitely.

[in a supreme degree] pre-eminently, superlatively &c. (*superiority*) 33.

[in a too great degree] immoderately, unduly, monstrously, grossly, preposterously, inordinately, exorbitantly, excessively, enormously, out of all proportion, with a vengeance.

[in a marked degree] particularly, remarkably, singularly, curiously, uncommonly, unusually, peculiarly, notably, signally, strikingly, pointedly, mainly, chiefly; famously, egregiously, prominently, glaringly, emphatically, strangely, wonderfully, amazingly, surprisingly, astonishingly, incredibly, marvellously, awfully, stupendously.

[in an exceptional degree] peculiarly &c. (*unconformity*) 83.

[in a violent degree] furiously &c. (*violence*) 173; severely, desperately, tremendously, extravagantly, confoundedly, deucedly, devilishly, with a vengeance; *à* –, *à toute- outrance.*

[in a painful degree] painfully, sadly, grossly, sorely, bitterly, piteously, grievously, miserably, cruelly, woefully, lamentably, shockingly, frightfully, dreadfully, fearfully, terribly, horribly, distressingly, balefully.

– most; ever so little, as little as may be, *tant soit peu*, in ever so small a degree; thus far, *pro tanto*, within bounds, in a manner, after a fashion.

almost, nearly, well nigh, short of, not quite, all but; near –, close- upon; *peu s'en faut*, near the mark; within an -ace, – inch- of; on the brink of; scarcely, hardly, barely, only just, no more than.

[in an uncertain degree] about, thereabouts, somewhere about, nearly, say; be the same -more, – little more- or less.

[in no degree] no- ways, – wise; not -at all, – in the least, – a bit, – a bit of it, – a whit, – a jot, – a shadow; in no -wise, – respect; by no -means, – manner of means; on no account, at no hand.

QUANTITY BY COMPARISON WITH A SIMILAR OBJECT

33. Superiority.—N. supremacy, superiority, majority; greatness &c. 31; advantage, odds, pull; preponderance, -ation; predominance, vantage ground, coign of vantage, prevalence, partiality; personal superiority; sovereignty &c. 737; nobility &c. (*rank*) 875; Triton among the minnows, *primus inter pares, nulli secundus,* superman; captain &c. 475.

supremacy, pre-eminence; primacy, lead, *maximum*; record; climax, crest, top; culmination &c. (*summit*) 210; transcendence; *ne plus ultra*; lion's share, Benjamin's mess; excess; bisque,

34. Inferiority.—N. inferiority, minority, subordinancy; shortcoming, deficiency; handicap; *minimum*; smallness &c. 32; imperfection, shabbiness.

[personal inferiority] commonalty &c. 876; subordinate, substitute, sub.

V. be -inferior &c. *adj.*; fall –, come- short of; not -pass, – come up to; want.

become –, render- smaller &c. (*decrease*) 36, (*contract*) 195; hide its diminished head, retire into the shade, yield the palm, play second fiddle, take a back seat; bow.

Adj. inferior, smaller; small &c. 32;

surplus &c. (*remainder*) 40, (*redundance*) 641.

V. be -superior &c. *adj.*; exceed, excel, transcend; out-do, -balance, -weigh, -rival, -Herod, outrank, pass, surpass, surmount, get ahead of; over-top, -ride, -pass, -balance, -weigh, -match; top, o'er-top, cap, beat, win out, cut out; beat hollow; outstrip &c. 303; eclipse, throw into the shade, take the shine out of, put one's nose out of joint; have the -upper hand, – whip hand of, – advantage; turn the scale, play first fiddle &c. (*importance*) 642; preponderate, predominate, prevail; precede, take precedence, come first; come to a head, culminate; beat &c. all others, bear the palm; break the record, take the cake.

become –, render- -larger, &c. (*increase*) 35, (*expand*) 194.

Adj. superior, greater, major, higher; exceeding &c. *v.*; great &c. 31; distinguished, *ultra*; vaulting; more than a match for.

supreme, greatest, maximal, maximum, utmost, paramount, pre-eminent, foremost, crowning; first-rate &c. (*important*) 642, (*excellent*) 648; unrivalled; peer-, match-less; none such, second to none, *sans pareil*; un-paragoned, -paralleled, -equalled, -approached, -surpassed; superlative, inimitable, *facile princeps*, incomparable, sovereign, without parallel, *nulli secundus, ne plus ultra*; beyond -compare, – comparison; culminating &c. (*topmost*) 210; transcendent, -ental; *plus royaliste que le Roi*.

increased &c. (*added to*) 35; enlarged &c. (*expanded*) 194.

Adv. beyond, more, over; over –, above- the mark; above par; upwards –, in advance- of; over and above; at the top of the scale, on the crest, at its height.

[in a superior or supreme degree] eminently, egregiously, pre-eminently, surpassing, prominently, superlatively, supremely, above all, of all things, the most, to crown all, *par excellence*, principally, especially, particularly, peculiarly, *a fortiori*, even, yea, still more.

Phr. 'we shall not look upon his like again.'

minor, less, lesser, deficient, minus, lower, subordinate, secondary; second-rate &c. (*imperfect*) 651; sub, subaltern; thrown into the shade; weighed in the balance and found wanting; not fit to hold a candle to.

least, smallest &c. (*see* little, small &c. 193); lowest.

diminished &c. (*decreased*) 36; reduced &c. (*contracted*) 195; unimportant &c. 643.

Adv. less; under –, below- -the mark, – par; at -the bottom of the scale, – a low ebb, – a disadvantage; short of, under.

Changes in Quantity

35. Increase—N. increase, augmentation, addition, enlargement, extension; dilatation &c. (*expansion*) 194; multiplication; increment, accretion; accession &c. 37; production &c. 161; development, growth; aggrandizement, aggravation, intensification; rise; ascent &c. 305; anabasis; ex-aggeration, -acerbation; spread &c. (*dispersion*) 73; flood-, spring-, -tide; gain, produce, profit &c. 618; booty, plunder &c. 793.

V. increase, augment, add to, enlarge; dilate &c. (*expand*) 194; grow,

36. Non-Increase, Decrease.—N. decrease, diminution; lessening &c. *v.*; subtraction &c. 38; reduction, abatement, declension; shrinkage &c. (*contraction*) 195; coarctation; abridgment &c. (*shortening*) 201; extenuation.

subsidence, catabasis, wane, ebb-, neap-tide, decline; descent &c. 306; decrement, reflux, depreciation; erosion, wear and tear, deterioration &c. 659; anticlimax; mitigation &c. (*moderation*) 174.

V. decrease, diminish, lessen; abridge

wax, mount, swell, get ahead, gain strength; advance; run –, shoot- up; rise; ascend &c. 305; sprout &c. 194.

aggrandize; raise, exalt; deepen, heighten; lengthen; thicken; strengthen; intensify, enhance, inflate, magnify, double, redouble; multiply; aggravate, exaggerate; ex-asperate, -acerbate; add fuel to the flame, *oleum addere camino*, superadd &c. (*add*) 37; spread &c. (*disperse*) 73.

Adj. increased &c. *v.*; on the increase, undiminished; additional &c. (*added*) 37; increasing &c. *v.*; growing, crescent, intensive, cumulative.

Adv. *crescendo*, increasingly.

Phr. *vires acquirit eundo.*

&c. (*shorten*) 201; shrink &c. (*contract*) 195; drop –, fall –, tail- off; fall away, waste, wear, erode; wane, ebb, decline; descend &c. 306; subside; deliquesce, melt –, die -away; retire into the shade, hide its diminished head, fall to a low ebb, run low, languish, decay, crumble, consume away.

bate, abate, dequantitate; discount; depreciate; extenuate, lower, weaken, attenuate, fritter away; mitigate &c. (*moderate*) 174; belittle, minimize; dwarf, throw into the shade; keep down, reduce &c. 195; shorten &c. 201; subtract &c. 38.

Adj. unincreased &c. (*see* increase &c. 35); decreased &c. *v.*; decreasing &c. *v.*; on the -wane &c. *n.*; deliquescent.

Adv. *diminuendo*, *decrescendo*, decreasingly.

3°. Conjunctive Quantity

37. Addition.—**N.** addition, annexation, adjection; junction &c. 43; super-position, -addition, -junction, -fetation; accession, reinforcement; increase &c. 35; increment, supplement; accompaniment &c. 88; interposition &c. 228; insertion &c. 300; summation &c. 85; adjunct &c. 39.

V. add, annex, adject, affix, attach, superadd, subjoin, superpose; clap –, saddle- on; tack to, postfix, append, tag; ingraft; saddle with; sprinkle; introduce &c. (*interpose*) 228; insert &c. 300.

become added, accrue; ad-, supervene; add up &c. 85.

reinforce, strengthen, swell the ranks of; augment &c. 35.

Adj. added &c. *v.*; additional; supplement, -al, -ary; suppletory, subjunctive; adjec-, adsci-, asci-titious; additive, extra, spare, further, fresh, more, new, ulterior, other, auxiliary, supernumerary, accessory.

Adv. in addition, more, plus, extra; and, also, likewise, too, furthermore, further, item; and -also, – eke; else, besides, to boot, *et cætera*; &c.; and so -on, – forth; into the bargain, *cum multis aliis*, over and above, moreover.

with, withal; including, inclusive, as well as, not to mention, let

38. Non-Addition. Subduction.—**N.** sub-traction, -duction; deduction, retrenchment; removal; ab-, sub-lation; abstraction &c. (*taking*) 789; garbling &c. *v.*; mutilation, detruncation; amputation, severance; abs-, ex-, re-cision; curtailment &c. 201; minuend, subtrahend; decrease &c. 36; abrasion.

V. sub-tract, -duct; rebate, de-duct, -duce; bate, retrench; remove, withdraw; take -from, – away; detract.

garble, mutilate, amputate, sever, detruncate; cut -off, – away, – out; expurgate; abscind, excise; pare, thin, prune, decimate; abrade, scrape, file; geld, castrate, emasculate, unman, spay, caponize; eliminate.

diminish &c. 36; curtail &c. (*shorten*) 201; deprive of &c. (*take*) 789; weaken.

Adj. subtracted &c. *v.*; subtractive. tailless, acáudal.

Adv. in -deduction &c. *n.*; less; short of; minus, without, except, excepting, with the exception of, barring, bar, save, exclusive of, save and except, with a reservation.

alone; together –, along –, coupled –, in conjunction- with; conjointly; jointly &c. 43.

39. [Thing added.] **Adjunct.—N.** adjunct; addit-ion, -ament; *additum,* affix, appendage, annex; augment, -ation; increment, reinforcement, supernumerary, accessory, item; garnish, sauce; accompaniment &c. 88; adjective, *addendum,* accession, complement; supplement; continuation; extension, subscript, tag, appendix, postscript, interlineation, interpolation, insertion.

rider, codicil, off-shoot, episode, side issue, corollary; piece; flap, lapel, label, tab, strip, fold, lappet, apron, skirt, embroidery, trappings, *cortège*; tail, suffix &c. (*sequel*) 65; wing.

Adj. additional &c. 37.

Adv. in addition &c. 37.

40. [Thing remaining.] **Remainder·—N.** remainder, residue; remains, *remanet,* remnant, rest, relic, relict; leavings, heel-tap, odds and ends, cheese-parings, candle ends, orts; *residuum;* dottle, dregs &c. (*dirt*) 653; refuse &c. (*useless*) 645; stubble, result, educt; fag-end, stub; ruins, wreck, skeleton, stump; *alluvium.*

surplus, overplus, excess; balance, complement; superfluity &c. (*redundance*) 641; surviv-al, -ance; afterglow.

V. remain; be -left &c. *adj.*; exceed, survive; leave.

Adj. remaining, left; left -behind, – over; residu-al, -ary; over, odd; unconsumed, sedimentary; surviving; net; exceeding, over and above; outlying, -standing; cast off &c. 782; superfluous &c. (*redundant*) 641.

40a. [Thing deducted.] **Decrement.—N.** decrement, discount, rebate, defect, loss, deduction, eduction, tare; drawback; waste, wastage; reprise.

41. [Forming a whole without coherence.] **Mixture.—N.** mix-, admix-, commix-ture, -tion, mingling; commixion, immixture, interfusion, intermixture, alloyage, matrimony; junction &c. 43; combination &c. 48; entanglement, interlacing; miscegenation, interbreeding.

impregnation; in-, dif-, suf-, trans fusion; infiltration; seasoning, sprinkling, interlarding; interpolation &c. 228; adulteration, sophistication.

[Thing mixed] tinge, tincture, touch, dash, smack, sprinkling, spice, seasoning, infusion, *soupçon.*

[Compound resulting from mixture] alloy, brass, bronze, pewter &c.; amalgam, *magma,* blend, half-and-half, *mélange, tertium, quid,* miscellany, *ambigu,* medley, mess, hash, hotchpotch, hodgepodge, *pasticcio,* patchwork, odds and ends, all sorts; jumble &c. (*disorder*) 59; salad, sauce, mash, *omnium gatherum,* gallimaufry, ragout, *olla podrida, olio,* salmagundi, *potpourri,* Noah's ark; texture, mingled yarn; mosaic &c. (*variegation*) 440.

half-blood, -caste, -breed, Eurasian; mulatto; terc-, quart-, quinteron &c.; quad-, octo-roon; *griffo, zambo;* cross, hybrid, mongrel &c. 83.

42. [Freedom from mixture.] **Simpleness.—N.** simpleness &c. *adj.*; purity, homogeneity.

elimination; sifting &c. *v.*; purification &c. (*cleanness*) 652.

V. render -simple &c. *adj.*; simplify.

sift, winnow, bolt, eliminate; narrow down; get rid of, exclude &c. 55; clear; purify &c. (*clean*) 652; disentangle &c. (*disjoin*) 44.

Adj. simple, uniform, of a piece, homogeneous, single, pure, clear, sheer, neat; Attic.

un-mixed, -mingled, -blended, -combined, -compounded; elementary, undecomposed; un-adulterated, -sophisticated, -alloyed, -tinged, -fortified; pure and simple.

free –, exempt- from; exclusive.

Adv. simply &c. *adj.*; only.

V. mix; join &c. 43; combine &c. 48; com-, im-, inter-mix; mix up with, mingle; com-, inter-, be-mingle; shuffle &c. (*derange*) 61; pound together; hash –, stir- up; knead, brew; impregnate with; interlard &c. (*interpolate*) 228; inter-twine, -weave &c. 219; associate with, miscegenate, interbreed.

be mixed &c.; get among, be entangled with.

instil, imbue; in-, suf-, trans-fuse; infiltrate, dash, tinge, tincture, season, sprinkle, besprinkle, attemper, medicate, blend, cross; alloy, amalgamate, compound, adulterate, sophisticate, infect.

Adj. mixed &c. *v.*; implex, composite, half-and-half, linsey-wolsey, hybrid, mongrel, heterogeneous; motley &c. (*variegated*) 440; miscellaneous, promiscuous, indiscriminate; miscible.

Adv. among, amongst, amid, amidst, with; in the midst of, in the crowd.

43. Junction.—N. junction; joining &c. *v.*; joinder, union; con-nection, -junction, -jugation, compendency, annex-ion, -ation, -ment; coalition; astriction, attachment, compagination, vincture, ligation, alligation; accouplement; marriage &c. (*wedlock*) 903; infibulation, inosculation, symphysis, anastomosis, confluence, communication, concatenation; concurrence, meeting, reunion; assemblage &c. 72.

copulation, coition, intercourse.

joint, joining, juncture, chiasma, pivot, hinge, articulation, commissure, seam, suture, gusset, stitch, splice; link &c. 45; mitre, mortise.

closeness, tightness &c. *adj.*; coherence &c. 46; combination &c. 48.

V. join, unite; con-join, -nect; associate; put –, lay –, clap –, hang –, lump –, hold –, piece –, tack –, fix –, bind up- together; embody, re-embody; roll into one.

attach, fix, affix, saddle on, fasten, bind, secure, clinch, twist, make -fast &c. *adj.*; tie, pinion, string, strap, sew, lace, stitch, tack, paste, knit, button, buckle, hitch, lash, truss, bandage, braid, splice, swathe, gird, tether, moor, picket, harness, chain; fetter &c. (*restrain*) 751; lock, latch, belay, brace, hook, grapple, leash, couple, accouple, link, yoke, bracket; marry &c. (*wed*) 903; bridge over, span.

pin, nail, bolt, hasp, clasp, clamp, screw, rivet; impact, solder, braze, cement, set; weld –, fuse- together; wedge, rabbet, mortise, mitre, jam, dovetail, enchase; graft, ingraft, inosculate; en-, in-twine; inter-link, -lace,

44. Disjunction.—N. dis-junction, -connection, -unity, -union, -association, -engagement, -sociation; discontinuity &c. 70; inconnection; abstraction, -edness; isolation; insul-arity, -ation; oasis; separateness &c. *adj.*; severalty; *disjecta membra*; dispersion &c. 73; apportionment &c. 786.

separation; parting &c. *v.*; detachment, segregation; divorce, sejunction, seposition, diduction, diremption, discerption; elision; *cæsura*, division, subdivision, break, fracture, rupture; compartition; dis-memberment, -integration, -location; luxation; sever-, dis-sever-ance; scission; re-, ab-scission; circumcision; lacer-, dilacer-ation; dis-, ab-ruption; avulsion, divulsion; section, resection, cleavage; fission; separability; separatism.

fissure, breach, rent, split, rift, crack, slit, slot, incision.

dissection, anatomy; decomposition &c. 49; cutting instrument &c. (*sharpness*) 253; saw.

V. be -disjoined &c.; come –, fall--off, – to pieces; peel off; get loose.

dis-join, -connect, -engage, -unite, -sociate, -pair; divorce, part, dispart, detach, uncouple, separate, cut off, rescind, segregate; set –, keep- apart; insulate, isolate; throw out of gear; cut adrift; loose; un-loose, -do, -bind, -tie, -hitch, -chain, -lock &c. (*fix*) 43, -pack, -ravel; disentangle; set free &c. (*liberate*) 750.

sunder, divide, subdivide, sectionalize, sever, dissever, abscind; cut; segment; in-cide, -cise; circumcise; saw, snip, nib, nip, cleave, rive, rend, slit,

-twine, -twist, -weave; entangle; twine round, belay; tighten; trice –, screw-up.

be -joined &c.; hang –, hold- together; cohere &c. 46.

Adj. joined &c. *v.*; joint; con-joint, -junct; corporate, compact; hand in hand.

firm, fast, close, tight, taut, taught, tense, secure, set, intervolved; in-separable, -dissoluble, -secable, -severable.

Adv. jointly &c. *adj.*; in conjunction with &c. (*in addition to*) 37; fast, firmly &c. *adj.*; intimately.

split, splinter, chip, crack, snap, break, tear, burst; rend &c. -asunder, – in twain; wrench, rupture, shatter, shiver, cranch, crunch, craunch, chop; rip up; hack, hew, slash; whittle; haggle, hackle, discind, lacerate, scamble, mangle, gash, hash, slice.

cut up, carve, quarter, dissect, anatomize; take –, pull –, pick –, tear- to pieces; tear to tatters, – piecemeal; divellicate; skin &c. 226; dis-integrate, -member, -branch, -band; disperse &c. 73; dis-locate, -joint; break up; mince; comminute &c. (*pulverize*) 330; distribute, apportion &c. 786.

part, – company; separate, leave; alienate, estrange.

Adj. disjoined &c. *v.*; discontinuous &c. 70; bipartite, multipartite, abstract; digitate; disjunctive; isolated &c. *v.*; insular, separate, disparate, discrete, apart, asunder, far between, loose, free; unattached, -annexed, -associated, -connected; distinct; adrift; straggling; rift, reft, cleft, split.

[capable of being divided] scissile, partible, divisible, separable, severable, detachable.

Adv. separately &c. *adj.*; one by one, severally, apart; adrift, asunder, in twain; in the abstract, abstractedly.

45. [Connecting medium.] **Vinculum.—N.** vinculum, link, *nexus*; connec-tive, -tion; junction &c. 43; bond of union, copula, intermedium, hyphen; bracket; bridge, stepping-stone, isthmus.

bond, tendon, tendril; fibre; cord, -age; riband, ribbon, rope, guy, cable, line, halser, hawser, painter, moorings, wire, chain; string &c. (*filament*) 205.

fastening, tie; liga-ment, -ture; strap; bowline, halliard, tackle, lanyard, rigging, shrouds; standing –, running- rigging; traces, harness; yoke; band, -age; brace, roller, fillet; inkle; with, withe, withy; thong, braid; girder, tie-beam; girt, cinch, girth, girdle, cestus, garter, braces, suspenders, halter, noose, lasso, lariat, surcingle, knot, hitch, running knot, frog.

pin, corking pin, nail, brad, tack, skewer, staple, cleat, clamp; cramp, screw, button, buckle, clasp, hasp, hinge, hank, catch, latch, bolt, ring, latchet, pawl, tag; tooth; stud; hook, – and eye; morse, lock, holdfast, padlock, rivet; anchor, grappling-iron, drawbar, coupler, drawhead, coupling, treenail, trennel, stake, pale, pile, post, bollard.

cement, glue, gum, paste, size, wafer, solder, lute, putty, bird-lime, mortar, stucco, plaster, grout.

shackle, rein &c. (*means of restraint*) 752; suspender &c. 214; prop &c. (*support*) 215.

V. bridge over, span; connect &c. 43; hang &c. 214.

46. Coherence.—N. co-, ad-herence, -hesion, -hesiveness; concretion, accretion; con-, ag-glutination, -glomeration; aggregation; consolidation, set, cementation; sticking, soldering &c. *v.*; connection.

47. [Want of adhesion, non-adhesion, immiscibility.] **Incoherence.—N.** nonadhesion; immiscibility; incoherence; looseness &c. *adj.*; laxity; relaxation; loosening &c. *v.*; freedom; disjunction &c. 44; rope of sand.

tenacity, toughness; stickiness &c. 352; insepara-bility, -bleness; bur, remora.

conglomerate, concrete &c. (*density*) 321.

V. cohere, adhere, stick, cling, cleave, hold, take hold of, hold fast, close with, embrace, clasp, hug; grow –, hang-together; twine round &c. (*join*) 43.

stick like -a leech, – wax; stick close; cling like -ivy, – a bur; adhere like -a remora, – Dejanira's shirt.

glue; ag-, con-glutinate; cement, lute, paste, gum; solder, weld; cake, coagulate, consolidate &c. (*solidify*) 321; agglomerate.

Adj. co-, ad-hesive, -hering &c. *v.*; tenacious, tough; sticky &c. 352.

united, unseparated, sessile, inseparable, inextricable, infrangible; compact &c. (*dense*) 321.

V. make -loose &c. *adj.*; loosen slacken, relax; un-glue &c. 46; detach &c. (*disjoin*) 44.

Adj. non-adhesive, immiscible; incoherent, detached, loose, slack, baggy, lax, relaxed, flapping, streaming; dishevelled; segregated, like grains of sand; un-consolidated &c. 321, -combined &c. 48; non-cohesive.

---

48. Combination.—N. combination; mixture &c. 41; alloy; junction &c. 43; union, unification, synthesis, incorporation, amalgamation, embodiment, coalescence, crasis, fusion, blend, blending, absorption, centralization, federation.

compound, amalgam, composition, *tertium quid*; resultant, impregnation.

V. combine, unite, incorporate, alloy, intertwine &c. 41; amalgamate, embody, absorb, re-embody, blend, merge, fuse, melt into one, consolidate, coalesce, centralize, impregnate; put –, lump- together; federate, associate; fraternize; cement a union, marry, wed, couple, pair, ally.

Adj. combined &c. *v.*; conjunctive, conjugate, conjoint, allied, confederate; impregnated with, ingrained, inoculated.

49. Decomposition.—N. decomposition, analysis, diæresis, dissection, resolution, catalysis, electrolysis, hydrolysis, photolysis, dissolution; dispersion &c. 73; disjunction &c. 44; disintegration, decay, rot, putrefaction, putrescence, caries, necrosis, corruption &c. (*uncleanness*) 653.

V. decom-pose, -pound; analyze, disembody, dissolve; resolve –, separate-into its elements; electrolyze; dissect, decentralize, break up; disintegrate; disperse &c. 73; unravel &c. (*unroll*) 313; crumble into dust; decay &c. *n.*; deteriorate &c. 659.

Adj. decomposed &c. *v.*; catalytic, analytical.

4°. CONCRETE QUANTITY

50. Whole. [Principal part.]—N. whole, totality, integrity; totalness &c. *adj.*; entirety, *ensemble*, collectiveness; unity &c. 87; completeness &c. 52; indivisibility, indiscerptibility; integration, embodiment; integer, integral.

all, the whole, total, aggregate, one and all, gross amount, sum, sum-total, *tout ensemble*, length and breadth of, Alpha and Omega, 'be all and end all,' lock, stock and barrel.

bulk, mass, lump, tissue, staple, body, torso, *compages*; trunk, bole, hull, hulk, skeleton; greater –, major

51. Part.—N. part, portion; dose; item, particular; aught, any; division, ward; subdivision, section; chapter, verse; article, clause, count, paragraph, passage; phrase; number, volume, book, fascicule; sector, segment; fraction, fragment; cantle, -t; frustum; detachment, parcel, unit, class &c. 75.

piece, lump, bit; cut, -ting; chip, chunk, collop, slice, scale, shard; lamina &c. 204; moiety; small part; morsel, scrap, crumb; particle &c. (*smallness*) 32; instalment, dividend; share &c. (*allotment*) 786.

–, best –, principal –, main- part; essential part &c. (*importance*) 642; lion's share, Benjamin's mess; the long and the short; nearly –, almost- all.

V. form –, constitute- a whole; integrate, embody, amass; aggregate &c. (*assemble*) 72; amount to, come to.

Adj. whole, total, integral, entire; complete &c. 52; one, individual.

un-broken, -cut, -divided, -severed, -clipped, -cropped, -shorn; seamless; undiminished; un-demolished, -dissolved, -destroyed, -bruised.

in-divisible, -dissoluble, -dissolvable, -discerptible.

wholesale, sweeping, comprehensive.

Adv. wholly, altogether; totally &c. (*completely*) 52; entirely, all, all in all, considering all things, in a body, collectively, all put together; in the -aggregate, – lump, – mass, – gross, – main, – long run; *en masse*, on the whole, as a whole, bodily, *en bloc*, *in extenso*, throughout, every inch; substantially.

débris, odds and ends, oddments, *detritus*; *excerpta*; member, limb, lobe, lobule, arm, wing, scion, branch, bough, joint, link, offshoot, ramification, twig, stipule, tendril, bush, spray, sprig; runner; leaf, -let; stump; constituent, ingredient, component part &c. 56.

compartment; department &c. (*class*) 75; county &c. (*region*) 181.

V. part, divide, break &c. (*disjoin*) 44; partition &c. (*apportion*) 786.

Adj. fractional, fragmentary; sectional, aliquot; divided &c. *v.*; in compartments, multifid, incomplete, partial, divided &c. 44.

Adv. partly, in part, partially; piecemeal, part by part; by -instalments, – snatches, – inches, – driblets; bit by bit, inch by inch, foot by foot, drop by drop; in -detail, – lots.

---

52. Completeness.—**N.** completeness &c. *adj.*; completion &c. 729; integration; integrality.

entirety; universality; totality; perfection &c. 650; solid-ity, -arity; unity; all; *ne plus ultra*, ideal, limit.

complement, supplement, make-weight; filling up &c. *v.*

impletion; satur-ation, -ity; high water; high –, flood –, spring- tide; fill, load, bumper, bellyful; brimmer; sufficiency &c. 639.

V. be -complete &c. *adj.*; come to a head.

render -complete &c. *adj.*; complete &c. (*accomplish*) 729; fill, charge, load, replenish; make-up, – good; piece –, eke- out; supply deficiencies; fill -up, – in, – to the brim, – the measure of; saturate &c. 869.

go the whole -hog, – length, go all lengths.

Adj. complete, entire; whole &c. 50; perfect &c. 650; full, good, absolute, thorough, plenary; solid, undivided; with all its parts.

exhaustive, radical, sweeping, thorough-going; dead.

regular, consummate, unmitigated, sheer, unqualified, unconditional, free; abundant &c. (*sufficient*) 639.

53. Incompleteness.—**N.** incompleteness &c. *adj.*; deficiency, short -measure, – weight; shortcoming &c. 304; insufficiency &c. 640; imperfection &c. 651; immaturity &c. (*non-preparation*) 674; half measures.

[part wanting] defect, deficit, shortage, ullage, defalcation, omission, *caret*; interval &c. 198; break &c. (*discontinuity*) 70; non-completion &c. 730; missing link.

V. be -incomplete &c. *adj.*; fall short of &c. 304; lack &c. (*be insufficient*) 640; neglect &c. 460.

Adj. incomplete; imperfect &c. 651; unfinished; uncompleted &c. (*see complete &c. 729*); defective, deficient, wanting; failing; in -default, – arrear; short, – of; hollow, meagre, lame, half-and-half, perfunctory, sketchy; crude &c. (*unprepared*) 674.

mutilated, garbled, mangled, docked, lopped, truncated; bobtailed, cropped, bobbed, shingled.

in -progress, – hand; going on, proceeding.

Adv. incompletely &c. *adj.*; by halves.

Phr. *cætera desunt*; *caret*.

---

brimming; brim-, top-ful; chock –, choke- full; as full as -an egg
is of meat, – a vetch, – a tick; saturated, crammed; replete &c.
(*redundant*) 641; fraught, laden; full-laden, -fraught, -charged;
heavy laden.

completing &c. *v.*; supplement-al, -ary; ascititious.

Adv. completely &c. *adj.*; altogether, outright, wholly, totally,
in toto, quite; over head and ears; effectually, for good and all,
nicely, fully, through thick and thin, head and shoulders; neck and
-heel, – crop; all out; in -all respects, – every respect; at all points,
out and out, to all intents and purposes; *toto cœlo*; utterly, clean, –
as a whistle; to the -full, – utmost, – backbone; hollow, stark; heart
and soul, root and branch; down to the ground.

to the top of one's bent, as far as possible, *à outrance*.

throughout; from -first to last, – beginning to end, – end to end,
– one end to the other, – Dan to Beersheba, – head to foot, – head
to heels, – top to toe, – top to bottom; *de fond en comble*; *à fond, a
capite ad calcem, ab ovo usque ad mala*, fore and aft; every -whit, –
inch; *cap-à-pie*, to the end of the chapter; up to the -brim, – ears,
– eyes; as . . . as can be.

on all accounts; *sous tous les rapports*; with a -vengeance, – witness.

---

54. Composition.—N. composition,
constitution, crasis, synthesis; make-
up; combination &c. 48; inclusion,
admission, comprehension, reception;
embodiment, formation, conformation,
production.

compilation &c. 72; (*musical*) composition &c. 415; painting &c. 556;
writing &c. 590; typography &c. 591.

V. be -composed, – made, – formed,
– made up- of; consist of, be resolved
into.

include &c. (*in a class*) 76; subsume;
synthesize; contain, hold, comprehend,
take in, admit, embrace, embody; involve; implicate, drag into.

compose, constitute, form, make;
make –, fill –, build- up; weave, construct, fabricate; compile; write, draw;
set up (*printing*); enter into the composition of &c. (*be a component*) 56.

Adj. containing, constituting &c. *v.*

---

56. Component.—N. component;
component –, integral –, integrant-
part; element, constituent, ingredient,
leaven; part and parcel; contents;
appurtenance; feature; member &c.
(*part*) 51; personnel.

V. enter into, – the composition of;
be a -component &c. *n.*; be –, form-
part of; merge –, be merged- in; be

55. Exclusion.—N. exclusion, non-
admission, omission, exception, rejection, repudiation; exile &c. (*seclusion*)
893; preclusion, lock out, ostracism,
prohibition; disbarment, expulsion, ban.

separation, segregation, seposition,
elimination, coffer-dam.

V. be excluded from &c.

exclude, bar, ban; leave –, shut –,
thrust –, bar- out; reject, repudiate,
spurn, blackball; ostracize, boycott;
lay –, put –, set -apart, – aside; relegate,
segregate; throw overboard; strike -off,
– out; neglect &c. 460; banish &c.
(*seclude*) 893; separate &c. (*disjoin*) 44.

pass over, omit; garble; eliminate,
weed, winnow.

Adj. excluding &c. *v.*; exclusive.

excluded &c. *v.*; unrecounted, not
included in; inadmissible; preventive,
interdictive.

Adv. exclusive of, barring; except;
with the exception of; save, bating.

---

57. Extraneousness.—N. extraneousness &c. *adj.*; extrinsicality &c. 6;
exteriority &c. 220; alienism.

foreign -body, – substance, – element; alien, stranger, intruder, interloper, foreigner, tramontane, *novus
homo*, new comer, immi-, emi-grant;
creole, Afrikander; outsider, outlander,
tenderfoot.

implicated in; share in &c. (*participate*) 778; belong –, appertain- to.

form, make, constitute, compose.

Adj. forming &c. *v.*; inclusive; inherent &c. 5.

Adj. extraneous, foreign, alien, ulterior; exterior, external, outside, outlandish; oversea; tra-, ultra-montane.

excluded &c. 55; inadmissible; exceptional.

Adv. in foreign -parts, – lands; abroad, beyond seas, overseas.

Section IV. ORDER

1°. Order in General

58. Order.—N. order, regularity &c. 80; uniformity, symmetry, *lucidus ordo*; harmony, music of the spheres.

gradation, progression; series &c. (*continuity*) 69.

subordination; course, even tenor, routine; method, disposition, arrangement, array, system, economy, discipline; orderliness &c. *adj.*

rank, place, &c. (*term*) 71.

V. be –, become- in order &c. *adj.*; form, fall in, draw up; arrange –, range –, place- itself; adjust; fall into –, take- -one's place, – rank; rally round; arrange &c. 60.

Adj. orderly, regular; in -order, – trim, – apple-pie order, according to Cocker, – its proper place, neat, neat as a pin, tidy, *en règle*, well regulated, correct, methodical, uniform, symmetrical, ship-shape, business-like, systematic; habitual; unconfused &c. (*see* confuse &c. 61) arranged &c. 60.

Adv. in order; methodically &c. *adj.*; in -turn, – its turn; step by step; by regular -steps, – gradations, – stages, – intervals; *seriatim*, systematically, by clockwork, *gradatim*; at stated periods &c. (*periodically*) 138.

---

59. [Absence, or want of Order, &c.] Disorder.—N. disorder; derangement &c. 61; irregularity; anomaly &c. (*unconformity*) 83; anar-chy, -chism; want of method; dishevelment, untidiness &c. *adj.*; disunion; discord &c. 24.

confusion; confusedness &c. *adj.*; disarray, jumble, mix-up, huddle, litter, lumber; *cahotage*; farrago; mess, muss, mash, muddle, hash; hotchpotch; *imbroglio*, chaos, *omnium gatherum*, medley; mere -mixture &c. 41; fortuitous concourse of atoms, *disjecta membra*, *rudis indigestaque moles*.

complexity; complexness &c. *adj.*; com-, im-plication; intri-cacy, -cation; perplexity; network, maze, labyrinth; wilderness, jungle; involution, ravelling, entanglement; coil &c. (*convolution*) 248; sleave, tangled skein, knot, Gordian knot, kink, web; wheels within wheels.

turmoil; ferment, &c. (*agitation*) 315; to do, trouble, pudder, pother, row, disturbance, convulsion, tumult, pandemonium, uproar, riot, rumpus, stour, scramble, *fracas*, embroilment, *mêlée*, spill and pelt, rough and tumble; whirlwind &c. 349; bear garden, Babel, Saturnalia, Donnybrook Fair, confusion worse confounded, most admired disorder, *concordia discors*; Bedlam –,

hell- broke loose; bull in a china shop; all the fat in the fire, *diable à quatre*, Devil to pay; pretty kettle of fish; pretty piece of -work, – business.

slattern, slut, sloven, draggle-tail.

V. be -disorderly &c. *adj.*; ferment, play at cross purposes.

put out of order; derange &c. 61; ravel &c. 219; ruffle, rumple; bungle, botch.

Adj. disorderly, orderless; out of -order, – place, – gear, – whack; irregular, desultory; anomalous &c. (*unconformable*) 83; acephalous, disorganized, straggling; un-, im-methodical; unsymmetric; unsystematic; untidy, slovenly, bedraggled, messy; dislocated; out of sorts; promiscuous, indiscriminate; chaotic, anarchical, lawless; unarranged &c. 60; confused, tumultuous, turbulent, tempestuous; deranged &c. 61; topsy turvy &c. (*inverted*) 218; shapeless &c. 241; disjointed, out of joint.

com-plex, -plexed; intricate, complicated, perplexed, involved, ravelled, entangled, knotted, tangled, inextricable; irreducible.

troublous; riotous &c. (*violent*) 173.

Adv. irregularly &c. *adj.*; by fits and -snatches, – starts; pell-mell; higgledy-piggledy; helter-skelter, harum-scarum; in a ferment; at -sixes and sevens, – cross purposes; upside down &c. 218.

Phr. the cart before the horse, chaos is come again.

---

60. [Reduction to Order.] **Arrangement.**—**N.** arrangement; plan &c. 626; preparation &c. 673; dispos-al, -ition; col-, al-location; distribution; sorting &c. *v.*; assortment, allotment; grouping; apportionment, *taxis*, taxonomy, *syn-taxis*, graduation, organization, grading; re-organization, rationalization.

analysis, classification, division, digestion; systematism.

[Result of arrangement] order, orderliness, form, array; digest, synopsis &c. (*compendium*) 596; *syntagma*, table, atlas; register &c. (*record*) 551; score &c. 415; cosmos, organism, architecture.

[Instrument for sorting] sieve &c. 260; file, card index.

V. reduce to –, bring into- order; introduce order into; rally.

arrange, dispose, place, form; put –, set –, place- in order; straighten up, tidy up; set out, collocate, allocate, pack, marshal, range, size, rank, array, group, parcel out, allot, space, distribute, deal; cast –, assign- the parts; dispose of, assign places to; assort, sort; sift, riddle; put –, set- -to rights, – into shape, – in trim, – in array.

class, -ify; divide; file, string together, thread; register &c. (*record*) 551; list, catalogue, tabulate, index, alphabeticize, graduate, digest, grade, codify; orchestrate, score.

methodize, regulate, systematize, standardize, co-ordinate, organize, settle, fix.

unravel, disentangle, ravel, card; disembroil.

Adj. arranged &c. *v.*; embattled, in battle array; cut and dried; methodical, orderly, regular, systematic, tabular.

61. [Subversion of Order; bringing into disorder.] **Derangement.**—**N.** derangement &c. *v.*; disorder &c. 59; evection, discomposure, disturbance; dis-, de-organization; involvement; dislocation; perturbation, interruption; shuffling &c. *v.*; inversion &c. 218; corrugation &c. (*fold*) 258; insanity &c. 503.

V. derange; dis-, mis-arrange; dis-, mis-place; mislay, discompose, disorder, de-, dis-organize; embroil, unsettle, disturb, confuse, trouble, perturb, jumble, tumble; huddle, shuffle, muddle, toss, hustle, fumble, riot; bring –, put –, throw- into -disorder &c. 59; break the ranks, disconcert, convulse; break in upon.

unhinge, dislocate, put out of joint, throw out of gear.

turn topsy-turvy &c. (*invert*) 218; bedevil; complicate, involve, perplex, confound; im-, em-brangle; tangle, en-tangle, ravel, tousle, dishevel, ruffle, rumple &c. (*fold*) 258; dement.

litter, scatter; mix &c. 41.

Adj. deranged &c. *v.*; syncre-tic, -tistic.

2°. CONSECUTIVE ORDER

62. Precedence.—N. precedence; coming before &c. *v.*; the lead, *le pas*; superiority &c. 33; importance &c. 642; anteced-ence, -ency; anteriority &c. (*front*) 234; precursor &c. 64; priority &c. 116; precession &c. 280; anteposition, preference.

V. precede; come -before, – first; forerun, head, lead, take the lead; lead the -way, – dance; introduce, usher in; have the *pas*; set the fashion &c. (*influence*) 175; lead off, kick off, open the ball; take –, have- precedence; outrank; have the start &c. (*get before*) 280.

place before; prefix; premise, prelude, preface.

Adj. preceding &c. *v.*; pre-, antecedent; anterior; prior &c. 116; before; former, foregoing; before-, above-mentioned; aforesaid, said; precurs-ory, -ive; prevenient, preliminary, prefatory, introductory; prelus-ive, -ory; proemial, preparatory.

Adv. before; in advance &c. (*precession*) 280.

Phr. *seniores priores.*

64. Precursor.—N. precursor, antecedent, precedent, predecessor; forerunner, van-courier, *avant-coureur*, pioneer, prodrome, *prodromos*, outrider; leader, bell-wether; herald, harbinger; dawn.

prelude, preamble, preface, prologue, foreword, *avant-propos*, *prolasis*, prolusion, proem, *prolepsis*, *prolegomena*, prefix, introduction; lead, heading, frontispiece, groundwork; preparation &c. 673; overture, voluntary, *exordium*, symphony, *ritornello*; premises.

prefigurement &c. 511; omen &c. 512.

Adj. precursory; prelu-sive, -sory, -dious; proemial, introductory, prefatory, prodromous, inaugural, preliminary; precedent &c. (*prior*) 116.

66. Beginning.—N. beginning, commencement, opening, outset, incipience, inception, inchoation; introduction &c. (*precursor*) 64; *alpha*; initial; foundation; inauguration, *début*, *le premier pas*, embarcation, rising of the curtain; zero hour; exordium, curtain raiser; maiden speech; prelude; outbreak, onset, brunt; initiative, move, first move; gambit, narrow –, thin-

63. Sequence.—N. sequence, coming after; going after &c. (*following*) 281; consecution, succession; posteriority &c. 117.

continuation; prolongation, order of succession; successiveness; Elijah's mantle.

secondariness; subordinancy &c. (*inferiority*) 34.

V. succeed; come -after, – on, – next; follow, ensue, step into the shoes of; alternate.

place after, suffix, append.

Adj. succeeding &c. *v.*; sequent; sub-, con-sequent; sequacious, proximate, next; consecutive &c. (*continuity*) 69; alternate, amœbæan.

latter; posterior &c. 117.

Adv. after, subsequently; behind &c. (*rear*) 235.

65. Sequel.—N. sequel, suffix, successor; tail, *queue*, train, wake, trail, rear; retinue, suite; appendix, postscript, subscript; epilogue; conclusion; peroration; codicil; continuation, *sequela*; appendage &c. 39; tail –, heelpiece; tag, more last words; *colophon*.

follower, after-glow, -growth, -crop, -taste, -math.

after-part, -piece, -course, -thought, -game; *arrière pensée*, second thoughts.

67. End.—N. end, close, termination; desinence, conclusion, *finis*, *finale*, period, term, *terminus*, last, *omega*; extreme, -tremity; gable –, butt –, fagend; tip, nib, point; tail &c. (*rear*) 235; verge &c. (*edge*) 231; tag, epilogue, peroration; *bonne bouche*; bitter end, tail end; terminal; *apodosis*; appendix.

consummation, *dénouement*; finish &c. (*completion*) 729; fate; doom, -sday;

end of the wedge; fresh start, new departure; forefront.

origin &c. (*cause*) 153; source, rise; bud, germ &c. 153; egg, rudiment; genesis, birth, nativity, cradle, infancy, incunabula; start, starting-point &c. 293; dawn &c. (*morning*) 125.

title-page; head, -ing, caption; van &c. (*front*) 234.

en-trance, -try; inlet, orifice, mouth, chops, lips, porch, portal, portico, *propylon*, door; gate, -way; postern, wicket, threshold, vestibule; skirts, border &c. (*edge*) 231; tee.

first -stage, – blush, – glance, – impression, – sight.

rudiments, elements, outlines, *principia*, grammar, *protasis*; alphabet, ABC.

V. begin, commence, inchoate, rise, arise, originate, institute, conceive, initiate, open, dawn, set in, take its rise, enter upon, start; enter; set out &c. (*depart*) 293; embark in.

usher in; lead -off, – the way; take the -lead, – initiative; inaugurate, head; stand -at the head, – first, – for; lay the foundations &c. (*prepare*) 673; found &c. (*cause*) 153; set -up, – on foot, – agoing, – abroach, – the ball in motion; apply the match to a train; launch, broach; open -up, – the door to; set -about, – to work; make a -beginning, – start; handsel; take the

crack of doom, day of Judgment, fall of the curtain, wind-up; goal, destination; limit, stoppage, end all, determination; expiration, expiry; death &c. 360; end of all things; finality; eschatology.

break up, *commencement de la fin*, last stage, turning point; *coup de grâce*, death-blow; knock-out.

V. end, close, finish, terminate, conclude, be all over; expire; die &c. 360; come –, draw- to a -close &c. n.; have run its course; run out, pass away.

bring to an -end &c. n.; put an end to, make an end of; determine; get through; achieve &c. (*complete*) 729; stop &c. (*make to cease*) 142; shut up shop.

Adj. ending &c. v.; final, terminal, definitive, conclusive; crowning &c. (*completing*) 729; last, ultimate; hindermost; rear &c. 235; caudal.

contermin-ate, -ous, -able.

ended &c. v.; at an end; settled, decided, over, played out, set at rest.

penultimate; last but -one, – two, &c.

unbegun, uncommenced; fresh.

Adv. finally &c. adj.; in fine; at the last; once for all.

---

first step, lay the first stone, cut the first turf; break -ground, – the ice, – cover; pass –, cross- the Rubicon; open -fire, – the ball; ventilate, air; undertake &c. 676.

come into -existence, – the world; make one's *début*, take birth; burst forth, break out; spring –, crop- up.

begin -at the beginning, – *ab ovo*, – again, – *de novo*; start afresh, make a fresh start, shuffle the cards, resume, recommence.

Adj. beginning &c. v.; initi-al, -atory, -ative; inceptive, introductory, incipient; proemial, inaugural; incho-ate, -ative; embryonic, rudimental; primogenial; primeval &c. (*old*) 124; rudimentary, aboriginal; natal, nascent.

first, foremost, front, leading, head; maiden.

begun &c. v.; just -begun &c. v.

Adv. at –, in- the beginning &c. n.; first, in the first place, *imprimis*, first and foremost; *in limine*; in -the bud, – embryo, – its infancy; from -the beginning, – its birth; *ab -initio, – ovo, – incunabilis*, primarily, originally.

68. Middle.—N. middle, midst, mediety; mean &c. 29; medium, middle term; centre &c. 222, mid-course &c. 628; *mezzo termine*; *juste milieu* &c. 628; half-way house, nave, navel, omphalos; nucle-us, -olus.

equidistance, bisection, half-distance; equator, diaphragm, midriff; interjacence &c. 228.

Adj. middle, medial, mesial, mean, mid; middle-, mid-most; middling; mediate; intermediate &c. (*interjacent*) 228; equidistant; central &c. 222; mediterranean, equatorial.

Adv. in the middle; in the thick; mid-, half-way; midships, *in medias res.*

69. [Uninterrupted sequence.] **Continuity.**—N. continuity; consecu-tion, -tiveness &c. *adj.*; succession, round, suite, progression, series, train, chain; cat-, concat-enation; catena; scale; gradation, course, constant flow, perpetuity.

procession, column; retinue, *cortège,* cavalcade, rank and file, line of battle, array.

pedigree, genealogy, lineage, race &c. 166.

rank, file, line, row, range, tier, string, thread, team; suit; colonnade.

V. follow in –, form- a series &c. *n.*; fall in.

arrange in a -series &c. *n.*; string together, catenate, file, thread, graduate, tabulate.

Adj. continu-ous, -ed; consecutive; progressive, gradual; serial, successive; immediate, unbroken, entire; linear; in a -line, – row &c. *n.*; uninter-rupted, -mitting; unremitting; perennial, evergreen; constant.

Adv. continuously &c. *adj.*; *seriatim*; in a -line &c. *n.*; in -succession, – turn; running, gradually, step by step, *gradatim,* at a stretch; in -file, – column, – single file, – Indian file.

70. [Interrupted sequence.] **Discontinuity.**—N. discontinuity; disjunction &c. 44; anacoluthon; interruption, break, fracture, flaw, fault, split, crack, cut; gap &c. (*interval*) 198; solution of continuity, *cæsura*; broken thread; parenthesis, episode; rhapsody, patchwork; intermission; alternation &c. (*periodicity*) 138; dropping fire.

V. be -discontinuous &c. *adj.*; alternate, intermit.

discontinue, pause, interrupt; intervene; break, – in upon; interpose &c. 228; break –, snap- the thread; disconnect &c. (*disjoin*) 44.

Adj. discontinuous, unsuccessive, broken, interrupted, *décousu*; dis-, un-connected, discrete, disjunctive; fitful &c. (*irregular*) 139; spasmodic, desultory, intermit-ting &c. *v.*, -tent; alternate; recurrent &c. (*periodic*) 138; few and far between.

Adv. at intervals; by -snatches, – jerks, – skips, – catches, – fits and starts; skippingly, *per saltum*; *longo intervallo.*

71. Term.—N. term, rank, station, stage, step; degree &c. 26; scale, remove, grade, link, peg, round –, rung- of the ladder, *status*, position, place, point, mark, *pas*, period, pitch; stand, -ing; footing, range.

V. hold –, occupy –, fall into- a place &c. *n.*

3°. COLLECTIVE ORDER

72. Assemblage.—N. assemblage; col-lection, -location, -ligation; compilation, levy, gathering, ingathering, mobilization, meet, foregathering, muster, *attroupement*; con-course, -flux, -gregation, -tesseration, -vergence &c. 290; meeting, *levée, réunion,* drawing room, at home; conversazione &c. (*social gathering*) 892; assembly, congress, eisteddfod; conven-tion, -ticle;

73. Non-assemblage. Dispersion.—N. dispersion; disjunction &c. 44; divergence &c. 291; scattering &c. *v.*; dissemination, broadcasting, diffusion, dissipation, distribution; apportionment &c. 786; spread, respersion, circumfusion, interspersion, spargefaction.

waifs and estrays, flotsam and jetsam, *disjecta membra.*

V. disperse, scatter, sow, dissemi-

gemote; conclave, &c. (*council*) 696; posse, *posse comitatûs*; Noah's ark.

miscellany, *collectanea*, symposium; museum, menagerie, &c. (*store*) 636.

crowd, throng, multitude; flood, rush, deluge; rout, rabble, mob, press, crush, *cohue*, jam, horde, body, tribe; crew, gang, knot, squad, band, party; swarm, shoal, school, covey, flock, herd, drove, kennel; array, bevy, galaxy; *corps*, company, troop, *troupe*; army, force, regiment, &c. (*combatants*) 726; host &c. (*multitude*) 102; populousness.

clan, brotherhood, association &c. (*party*) 712.

volley, shower, storm, cloud.

group, cluster, Pleiades, clump, pencil; set, batch, lot, pack; budget, *dossier*, assortment, bunch; parcel; pack-et, -age; bundle, *fasciculus*, fascine, bale; ser-on, -oon; faggot, wisp, truss, tuft; shock, rick, fardel, stack, sheaf, swath, gavel, haycock, stook.

accumulation &c. (*store*) 636; congeries, heap, lump, pile, *rouleau*, tissue, mass, pyramid; drift; snow-ball, -drift; acervation, cumulation; amassment, glom-, agglom-eration; conglobation; conglomeration, -ate; coacervation, coagmentation, aggregation, concentration, congestion, *omnium gatherum*, *spicilegium*, black hole of Calcutta; quantity &c. (*greatness*) 31.

collector, gatherer; whip, -per in.

V. [be or come together] assemble, collect, muster; meet, unite, join, rejoin; cluster, flock, swarm, surge, stream, herd, crowd, throng, associate; con-gregate, -glomerate, -centrate; centre round, *rendezvous*, resort; come –, flock –, get –, pig- together; forgather; huddle; reassemble.

[get or bring together] assemble, muster, mobilize; bring –, get –, put –, draw –, scrape –, lump- together; col-lect, -locate, -ligate; get –, whip- in; gather; hold a meeting; con-vene, -voke, -vocate; rake up, dredge; heap, mass, pile; pack, put up, truss, cram; acervate; ag-glomerate, -gregate; compile; group, aggroup, concentrate, unite; collect –, bring- into a focus; amass, accumulate &c. (*store*) 636; collect in a drag-net; heap Ossa upon Pelion.

Adj. assembled &c. *v.*; closely packed, dense, serried, crowded to suffocation, teeming, swarming, populous; as thick as hops; all of a heap, fasciculated; cumulative.

Phr. the plot thickens.

74. [Place of meeting.] **Focus.**—**N.** focus; point of- convergence &c. 290; corradiation; centre &c. 222; gathering-place, resort; haunt; retreat; *venue, rendezvous*; rallying point, head-quarters, home, club; *dépôt* &c. (*store*) 636; tryst, trysting-place; place of -meeting, – resort, – assignation; *point de –, lieu de- réunion*; issue.

V. bring to- a point, – a focus, – an issue; focus.

4°. Distributive Order

75. Class.—**N.** class, category, *categorema*, head, order, sec-

nate, radiate, diffuse, shed, spread, ted, bestrew, overspread, dispense, disband, disembody, demobilize, dismember, distribute; apportion &c. 786; blow off, let out, dispel, cast forth, draught off; strew, straw, strow; spirtle, cast, sprinkle, shatter; issue, deal out, retail, utter; re-, inter-sperse; set abroach, circumfuse.

turn –, cast- adrift; scatter to the winds; sow broadcast.

spread like wildfire, disperse themselves.

Adj. unassembled &c. (*see* assemble &c. 72); dispersed &c. *v.*; sparse, dispread, broadcast, sporadic, widespread; far-flung; epidemic &c. (*general*) 78; adrift, stray; dishevelled; streaming.

Adv. *sparsim*, here and there, *passim*.

tion; division, subdivision; department, province, domain, sphere.

kind, sort, genus, species, variety, branch, family, race, tribe, caste, sept, clan, breed; *clique, coterie*; type, kit, sect, set; assortment; feather, kidney; suit; range; gender, sex, kin.

manner, description, denomination, persuasion, connection, designation, character, stamp; predicament; conviction &c. 484.

similarity &c. 17.

76. Inclusion. [Comprehension under, or reference to a class.]—**N.** inclusion, admission, incorporation, comprehension, reception.

composition &c. (*inclusion in a compound*) 54.

V. be -included in &c.; come –, fall –, range- under; belong –, pertain- to; range with; merge in.

include, compromise, comprehend, contain, admit, embrace, receive; enclose &c. (*circumscribe*) 229; incorporate, cover, embody, encircle.

reckon –, enumerate –, number- among; refer to; place –, arrange-under, – with; take into account.

Adj. includ-ed, -ing &c. *v.*; inclusive; comprehensive, all-embracing; congen-er, -erous: of the same -class &c. 75.

Phr. *et hoc genus omne,* &c.; *et cætera.*

77. Exclusion.*—N. exclusion &c. 55.

---

78. Generality. — N. general-ity, -ization; universality; catholic-ity, -ism; miscel-lany, -laneousness; drag-net.

every-one, -body; all hands, all the world and his wife; any body, N or M, all sorts; *tout le monde.*

prevalence, run.

V. be -general &c. *adj.*; prevail, obtain, be going about, stalk abroad.

render -general &c. *adj.*; generalize; spread, broadcast.

Adj. general, usual, current, generic, collective; broad, comprehensive, sweeping; encyclopedical, panoramic, widespread &c. (*dispersed*) 73.

universal; catho-lic, -lical; common, world-wide; œ-, e-cumenical; transcendental; prevalent, prevailing, rife, epidemic, besetting; all over, covered with.

every, all; indeterminate, indefinite, unspecified, impersonal.

customary &c. (*habitual*) 613.

Adv. what-ever, -soever; to a man, one and all, without exception.

generally &c. *adj.*; always, for better

79. Speciality.—N. speciality, *spécialité*; individ-uality, -uity; particularity, peculiarity; idiocrasy &c. (*tendency*) 176; personality, characteristic, mannerism, idiosyncrasy, attribute specificness &c. *adj.*; singularity &c. (*unconformity*) 83; reading, version, lection; state; *trait*; distinctive feature; technicality; *differentia.*

particulars, details, minutiæ, items, counts.

I, self, I myself, *ego*; my-, him-, her-, it-self.

V. specify, particularize, individualize, realize, specialize, designate, differentiate, determine, define, denote, indicate, itemize, detail.

descend to particulars, enter into detail, come to the point.

Adj. special, particular, individual, specific, proper, personal, intimate, original, private, respective, definite, concrete, determinate, especial, certain, esoteric, endemic, partial, party, peculiar, marked, appropriate, several, characteristic, diagnostic, exact, exclusive; singular &c. (*exceptional*) 83;

---

* The same set of words is used to express *Exclusion from a class* and *Exclusion from a compound.* Reference is therefore made to the former at 55. This identity does not occur with regard to *Inclusion,* which therefore constitutes a separate category.

for worse; in general, generally speaking; speaking generally; for the most part; in the long run &c. (*on an average*) 29.

idiomatic; typical, representative, distinctive.

this, that; yon, -der.

Adv. specially &c. *adj.*; in particular, *in propriâ personâ*; *ad hominem*; for my part.

each, apiece, one by one; severally, respectively, each to each; *seriatim*, in detail, bit by bit; *pro hac vice, – re natâ.*

namely, that is to say, *videlicet*, viz.; to wit.

5°. ORDER AS REGARDS CATEGORIES

80. Rule.—N. regularity, uniformity &c. 16; clock-work precision; punctuality &c. (*exactness*) 494; routine &c. (*custom*) 613; formula; system; rut; canon, convention, maxim; rule &c. (*form, regulation*) 697; key-note, standard, model; precedent &c. (*prototype*) 22; conformity &c. 82.

nature, principle; law; order of things; normal –, natural –, ordinary –, model- -state, – condition; standing -dish, – order; normality; Procrustean law; law of the Medes and Persians; hard and fast rule.

Adj. regular, uniform, symmetrical, constant, steady; according to rule &c. (*conformable*) 82; customary &c. 613; orderly &c. 58.

81. Multiformity.—N. multi-, omniformity; variety, diversity; multifariousness &c. *adj.*

Adj. multi-form, -fold, -farious, -generous; multiplex, variform, manifold, many-sided, multiplicate; omni-form, -genous, -farious; polymorphic; protean; heterogeneous, motley, mosaic; epicene, indiscriminate, desultory, irregular, diversified, different, divers; all manner of; of -every description, – all sorts and kinds; *et hoc genus omne*; and what not? *de omnibus rebus et quibusdam aliis.*

82. Conformity.—N. conform-ity, -ance; observance.

naturalization; conventionality &c. (*custom*) 613; agreement &c. 23.

example, instance, specimen, sample, quotation; exemplification, illustration, case in point; object lesson.

conventionalist, formalist, Philistine. pattern &c. (*prototype*) 22.

V. conform to, – rule; accommodate –, adapt- oneself to; rub off corners. be -regular &c. *adj.*; move in a groove; follow –, observe –, go by –, bend to –, obey- -rules, – precedents; comply –, tally –, chime in –, fall in- with; be -guided, – regulated- by; fall into a -custom, – usage; follow the -fashion, – multitude; pass muster, do as others do, *hurler avec les loups*; do at Rome as the Romans do; go –, swim- with the -stream, – current, – tide; tread the beaten track &c. (*habit*) 613; rubber-stamp; keep one in countenance.

exemplify, illustrate, cite, quote, put

83. Unconformity.—N. non-conformity &c. 82; un-, dis-conformity; unconventionality, informality, abnormity, anomaly; anomalousness &c. *adj.*; exception, peculiarity, &c. 79; infraction –, breach –, violation –, infringement- of -law, – custom, – usage; eccentricity, *bizarrerie*, oddity, *je ne sais quoi*, monstrosity, rarity; freak of Nature.

individuality, idiosyncrasy, singularity, originality, mannerism.

aberration; irregularity; variety; singularity; exemption; salvo &c. (*qualification*) 469.

nonconformist; nondescript, character, original, nonsuch, monster. prodigy, wonder, miracle, curiosity, missing link, flying fish, black swan, *lusus naturæ, rara avis*, queer fish; mongrel; half-caste, -blood, -breed; *métis*, cross breed, hybrid, mule, mulatto, sacatra, marabou; *tertium quid*. hermaphrodite, gynander, androgyn.

phœnix, chimera, hydra, sphinx, minotaur; griff-in, -on; centaur; hippo-

a case; produce an- instance &c. *n.*

Adj. conformable to rule, adaptable, compliant, consistent, agreeable; regular &c. 80; according to -regulation, – rule, – Cocker; *en règle, selon les règles,* well regulated, orderly; symmetric &c. 242.

conventional, commonplace &c. (*customary*) 613; of -daily, – every day-occurrence; in the natural order of things; ordinary, common, – or garden, prosaic, habitual, usual.

in the order of the day; naturalized.

typical, normal, formal; canonical, orthodox, sound, strict, rigid, positive, uncompromising, Procrustean; point device.

secundum artem, ship-shape, technical. exemplary, illustrative, in point.

Adv. conformably &c. *adj.*; by rule; agreeably to; in -conformity, – accordance, – keeping- with; according to; consistently with; as usual, *ad instar, instar omnium; more -solito,* – *majorum.*

for the sake of conformity; of –, as a matter of- course; *pro formâ,* for form's sake, by the card; according to plan.

invariably &c. (*uniformly*) 16.

for -example, – instance; *exempli gratiâ; e.g.; inter alia.*

Phr. *cela va sans dire; ex pede Herculem, noscitur a sociis.*

griff, -centaur; sagittary; kraken, cockatrice, wyvern, roc, liver, dragon, sea-serpent; mermaid; unicorn; Cyclops, 'men whose heads do grow beneath their shoulders'; Teratology.

fish out of water; neither -one thing nor another, – fish flesh nor fowl nor good red herring; one in a -way, – thousand; out-cast, -law; Ishmael, pariah; oasis.

V. be -unconformable &c. *adj.*; leave the beaten -track, – path; infringe –, break –, violate- a -law, – habit, – usage, – custom; drive a coach and six through; stretch a point; have no business there; baffle –, beggar- all description.

Adj. unconformable, exceptional; abnorm-al, -ous; anomal-ous, -istic; out of -order, – place, – keeping, – tune, – one's element; irregular, arbitrary; lawless, informal, aberrant, stray, wandering, wanton; peculiar, exclusive, unnatural, eccentric, crotchety, egregious; out of the -beaten track, – common, – common run, – pale of; misplaced; funny.

un-usual, -accustomed, -customary, -wonted, -common; rare, singular, *unique,* curious, odd, extraordinary, strange, monstrous; wonderful &c. 870; unexpected, unaccountable; *outré,* out of the way, remarkable, noteworthy; queer, quaint, nondescript, none such, *sui generis;* original, unconventional, Bohemian, unfashionable; un-described, -precedented, -paralleled, -exampled, -heard of, -familiar; fantastic, new-fangled, grotesque, *bizarre;* outlandish, exotic, *tombé des nues,* preternatural; denaturalized.

heterogeneous, heteroclite, amorphous, mongrel, amphibious, epicene, half-blood, hybrid; androgyn-ous, -al; unsymmetric &c. 243.

qualified &c. 469.

Adv. unconformably &c. *adj.*; except, unless, save, barring, beside, without, save and except, let alone.

however, yet, but.

Int. what -on earth! – in the world!

Phr. never was -seen, – heard, – known- the like.

Section V. NUMBER

1°. Number, in the Abstract

84. Number.—N. number, symbol, numeral, figure, cipher, digit, integer; counter; round number; formula; function; series.

sum, total, aggregate, difference, complement, subtrahend; product; multipli-cand, -er, -cator; coefficient, multiple; dividend, divisor, factor, quotient, sub-multiple, fraction; mixed number; numerator, denominator; decimal, circulating decimal, repetend; common measure, aliquot part; reciprocal; prime number; totitive, totient.

permutation, combination, variation; election.

ratio, proportion; progression; arithmetical –, geometrical –, harmonical- progression; percentage.

figurate –, pyramidal –, polygonal- numbers.

power, root, exponent, index, logarithm, antilogarithm; modulus. differential, integral, fluxion, fluent.

Adj. numeral, complementary, divisible, aliquot, reciprocal, prime, fractional, decimal, figurate, incommensurable.

proportional, exponential, logarithmic, logometric, differential, fluxional, integral.

positive, negative; rational, irrational; surd, radical, real, imaginary, impossible.

85. Numeration.—N. numeration; numbering &c. *v.*; pagination; tale, tally, recension, enumeration, summation, reckoning, computation, supputation; calcu-lation, -lus; algorithm, rhabdology, dactylonomy; measurement &c. 466; statistics.

arithmetic, analysis, algebra, fluxions; differential –, integral –, infinitesimal- calculus; calculus of differences.

[Statistics] dead reckoning, muster, poll, census, capitation, roll-call, recapitulation; account &c. (*list*) 86.

[Operations] notation, addition, subtraction, multiplication, division, proportion, rule of three, practice, equations, extraction of roots, reduction, involution, evolution, approximation, interpolation, differentiation, integration.

[Instruments] abacus, swan-pan, logometer, sliding –, slide- rule, tallies, Napier's bones, calculating –, adding- machine, difference engine; cash register.

arithmetician, calculator, abacist; mathematician, actuary, statistician, surveyor, geodesist.

V. number, count, tell; call –, run- over, take an account of, enumerate, call the roll, muster, poll, recite, recapitulate; sum; sum –, cast- up; tell off, score, cipher, compute, calculate, set a price, reckon, – up, estimate; suppute, add, subtract, multiply, divide, extract roots.

check, prove, demonstrate, balance, audit, overhaul, take stock; affix numbers to, page, foliate, paginate.

amount –, come- to.

Adj. numer-al, -ical; arithmetical, analytic, algebraic, statistical, numerable, computable, calculable; commensur-able, -ate; incommensur-able, -ate.

86. List.—N. list, catalogue, enumeration, inventory, schedule; register &c. (*record*) 551; account; bill, – of costs; syllabus; terrier, tally, file; almanac, calendar, index, table, atlas, contents, card index; rota, ticket; book, ledger; synopsis, *catalogue raisonné; tableau;* scroll, manifest, invoice, bill of lading; prospectus, *programme;* bill of fare, *menu, carte;* score, census, statistics, returns; Red –, Blue –, Domesday- book; *cadastre;* directory, gazetteer, dictionary, glossary, lexicon, thesaurus, gradus.

roll; check –, chequer –, bead- roll, – of honour; muster -roll, – book; roster, panel; cartulary, diptych.

V. list, enrol, schedule, register &c. *n.*; indent, post, docket; matriculate.

Adj. cadastral, listed &c. *v.*

2°. DETERMINATE NUMBER

87. Unity.—**N.** unity; oneness &c. *adj.*; individuality; solitude &c. (*seclusion*) 893; isolation &c. (*disjunction*) 44; unification &c. 48.

one, unit, ace; item; individual; solo, none else, no other, naught beside.

V. be -one, – alone &c. *adj.*; dine with Duke Humphrey.

isolate &c. (*disjoin*) 44.

render one; unite &c. (*join*) 43, (*combine*) 48.

Adj. one, sole, single, solitary, only-begotten; individual, apart, alone; kithless.

un-accompanied, -attended; *solus*, single-handed; singular, odd, unique, unrepeated, azygous, first and last; isolated &c. (*disjoined*) 44; insular; unitary.

lone; lone-ly, -some; desolate, dreary.

in-secable, -severable, -discerptible; compact, irresolvable.

Adv. singly &c. *adj.*; alone, by itself, *per se*, only, apart, in the singular number, in the abstract; one -by one, – at a time; simply; one and a half, *sesqui-*.

Phr. *natura il fece, e poi roppe la stampa.*

88. Accompaniment.—**N.** accompaniment; appurtenance, adjunct &c. 39; context.

coexistence, concomitance, company, association, companionship; part-, co-part-nership; coefficiency.

concomitant, accessory, coefficient; companion, attendant, fellow, associate, consort, spouse, colleague, *fidus Achates*; part-, co-part-ner; satellite, hanger on, shadow; escort, *entourage*, suite, *cortège*; convoy, follower &c. 65; attribute.

V. accompany, coexist, attend, convoy, chaperon; hang –, wait- on; go hand in hand with; synchronize &c. 120; bear –, keep- company; row in the same boat; bring in its train, associate –, couple- with.

Adj. accompanying &c. *v.*; concomitant, fellow, twin, joint; associated –, coupled- with; accessory, attendant, *obbligato*.

Adv. with, withal; together –, along –, in company- with; hand in hand, side by side; cheek by -jowl, – jole; arm in arm; there-, here-with; and &c. (*addition*) 37.

together, in a body, collectively.

---

89. Duality.—**N.** dual-ity, -ism; duplicity; bi-plicity, -formity; span, polarity.

two, deuce, couple, couplet, doublet, brace, pair, cheeks, twins, Castor and Pollux, *gemini*, Siamese twins; fellows; yoke, conjugation, dyad, distich.

V. [unite in pairs] pair, couple, bracket, yoke; conduplicate, mate.

Adj. two, twain; dual, -istic; binary, binomial; twin, biparous; dyadic; conduplicate; duplex &c. 90; *tête-à-tête*; paired; dihedral.

coupled &c. *v.*; conjugate.

both, – the one and the other.

90. Duplication.—**N.** duplication; doubling &c. *v.*; gemi-, ingemi-nation; reduplication; iteration &c. (*repetition*) 104; renewal.

V. double; re-double, -duplicate; geminate; repeat &c. 104; renew &c. 660; duplicate, copy &c. 21.

Adj. double; doubled &c. *v.*; bicameral, bicapital, bi-fold, -form, -lateral,

91. [Division into two parts.] **Bisection.**—**N.** bi-section, -partition; di-, subdi-chotomy; halving &c. *v.*; dimidiation; *hendiadis*.

bifurcation, forking, branching, furcation, ramification, divarication; fork, prong; fold.

half, moiety.

V. bisect, halve, divide, split, cut in

-farious, -facial; two-fold, -sided, -headed, -edged &c.; duplex; double-faced; twin, duplicate, ingeminate; second; dual &c. 29.

Adv. twice, once more; over again &c. (*repeatedly*) 104; as much again, twofold.

secondly, in the second place, again.

two, cleave, dimidiate, dichotomize, divaricate.

go halves, divide with.

separate, fork, bifurcate; branch -off, – out; ramify.

Adj. bisected &c. *v.*; cloven, cleft; bipartite, biconjugate, bicuspid, bifid; bifur-cous, -cate, -cated; semi-, demi-hemi-.

92. Triality.—N. triality, trinity,* triplicity.

three, triad, triplet, trey, trio, ternion, trinomial, leash; tierce; tri-ennium; trefoil, triangle, trident, tripod, triumvirate, *troika*.

third power, cube.

Adj. three; tri-form, -nal, -nomial; tertiary; triune.

93. Triplication.—N. tripli-cation, -city; trebleness, trine, trilogy.

V. treble, triple, triplicate, cube.

Adj. treble, triple; tern, -ary; triplex, triplicate, threefold, trilogistic; third; trinal; trihedral.

Adv. three -times, – fold; thrice, in the third place, thirdly; trebly &c. *adj.*

94. [Division into three parts.] Tri-section. — N. tri-section, -partition, -chotomy; third, – part.

V. trisect, divide into three parts, trifurcate.

Adj. trifid; trisected &c. *v.*; tri-partite, -chotomous, -sulcate.

95. Quaternity.—N. quaternity, four, tetrad, quartet, quaternion, square, quadrature, quarter, quadruplet; quadrilateral, quadrangle, quatrefoil; *quadriga*.

V. reduce to a square, square.

Adj. four; quat-ernary, -ernal; quadratic; quartile, quartic, tetractic, tetrad, tetrahedral; quadrennial; quadrivalent.

96. Quadruplication.—N. quadrupli-cation.

V. multiply by four, quadruplicate, biquadrate.

Adj. fourfold; quad-ruple, -ruplicate, -rible; quadruplex; fourth.

Adv. four times; in the fourth place, fourthly.

97. [Division into four parts.] Quad-risection.—N. quadri-section, -parti-tion; quartering &c. *v.*; fourth; quart, -er, -ern; farthing (*i.e.* fourthing); quarto.

V. quarter, divide into four parts, quadrisect.

Adj. quartered &c. *v.*; quadri-fid, -partite.

98. Five, &c.—N. five, cinque, quint, quincunx, quintuplet, quintet, penta-gon, pentameter, Pentateuch; six, half-a-dozen, sextet, hexagon, hexameter; seven, Heptarchy; eight, octet, octa-gon, octave; nine, three times three; ten, decade; eleven; twelve, dozen; thirteen; long –, baker's- dozen.

twenty, score; twenty-four, four and twenty, two dozen; twenty-five, five and twenty, quarter of a hundred; forty, two score; fifty, half a hundred; sixty, three score, sexagenarian; seventy, three score and ten, septuagenarian; eighty, four score, octogenarian; ninety, four score and ten, nonagenarian.

99. Quinquesection, &c.—N. divi-sion by -five &c. 98; quinquesection &c.; fifth &c.; decimation.

V. decimate, quinquesect.

Adj. quinque-fid, -partite; quinquar-ticular; octifid; decimal, tenth, tithe, teind; duodecimal, twelfth; sexagesi-mal, -genary; hundredth, centesimal; millesimal &c.

* *Trinity* is hardly ever used except in a theological sense; *see* Deity 976.

hundred, centenary, hecatomb, century; hundredweight, cwt.; one hundred and forty-four, gross; bicentenary, tercentenary &c.

thousand, chiliad; myriad, millennium, ten thousand; lac, lakh, one hundred thousand, plum; million; thousand million, *milliard.*

billion, trillion &c.

V. centuriate.

Adj. five, quinary, quintuple; fifth; senary, sextuple; sixth; seventh; octuple; eighth; ninefold, ninth; tenfold, decimal, denary, decuple, tenth; eleventh; duo-denary, -denal; twelfth; in one's 'teens, thirteenth.

vices-, viges-imal; twentieth; twenty-fourth &c. *n.*

cent-uple, -uplicate, -ennial, -enary, -urial; secular, hundredth; thousandth; millenary &c.

3°. INDETERMINATE NUMBER

100. [More than one.] **Plurality.—N.** plurality; a -number, – certain number; one or two, two or three &c.; a few, several; multitude &c. 102.

Adj. plural, more than one, upwards of, some, certain; not -alone &c. 87.

Adv. *et cætera,* &c., etc.

Phr. *non deficit alter.*

100a. [Less than one.] **Fraction.—N.** fraction, fractional part, fragment; part &c. 51.

Adj. fractional, fragmentary, partial.

101. Zero.—N. zero, nothing, naught, nought, duck's egg, goose egg; cipher, none, nobody; not a soul; *âme qui vive;* absence &c. 187; unsubstantiality &c. 4.

Adj. not -one, – any.

102. Multitude.—N. multitude; numerousness &c. *adj.;* numer-osity, -ality; multiplicity; profusion &c. (*plenty*) 639; legion, host; great –, large –, round –, enormous- number; a quantity, numbers, array, sight, army, sea, galaxy; scores, peck, bushel, school, shoal, swarm, draft, bevy, cloud, flock, herd, drove, flight, covey, hive, brood, litter, farrow, fry, nest; mob, crowd &c. (*assemblage*) 72; lots, loads, heaps; all the world and his wife.

[Increase of number] greater number, majority; multiplication, multiple.

V. be -numerous &c. *adj.;* swarm –, teem –, crawl –, creep -with; crowd, swarm, come thick upon; outnumber, multiply; people; swarm like -locusts, – bees.

Adj. many, several, sundry, divers, various, not a few; a -hundred, – thousand, – myriad, – million, – thousand and one; some -ten or a dozen, – forty or fifty &c.; half a -dozen, – hundred &c.; very –, full –, ever so- many; numer-ous, -ose; profuse, in profusion; manifold, multiplied, multitudinous, multiferous, multiple, multinomial, teeming, crawling, populous, peopled, crowded, thick, studded; galore.

thick coming, many more, more than one can tell, a world of; no end -of, – to; *cum multis aliis;* thick as -hops, – hail; plenty as blackberries; numerous as the -stars in the firmament, – sands on

103. Fewness.—N. fewness &c. *adj.;* paucity, small number; small quantity &c. 32; scarcity, sparsity; rarity; infrequency &c. 137; handful; maniple; minority, exiguity.

[Diminution of number] reduction; weeding &c. *v.;* elimination, sarculation, decimation.

V. be -few &c. *adj.*

render -few &c. *adj.;* reduce, diminish the number, weed, eliminate, thin, decimate.

Adj. few; scarce; scant, -y; thin, rare, thinly scattered, few and far between; exiguous; infrequent &c. 137; *rari nantes;* hardly –, scarcely-any; to be counted on one's fingers; reduced &c. *v.;* unrepeated.

Adv. here and there.

the sea-shore, – hairs on the head; and -what not, – heaven knows what; endless &c. (*infinite*) 105.

Phr. their name is 'Legion.'

104. Repetition.—N. repetition, iteration, reiteration, duplication, ding-dong, alliteration; *epistrophe*; harping, recurrence, succession, run; batto-, tauto-logy; monotony, tautophony; rhythm &c. 138; pleonasm, redundancy, diffuseness.

chimes, repetend, echo, *ritornello*, burden of a song, *refrain*; rehearsal; encore; *réchauffé*, *rifacimento*, recapitulation.

cuckoo &c. (*imitation*) 19; reverberation &c. 408; drumming &c. (*roll*) 407; renewal &c. (*restoration*) 660.

twice-told tale; old -story, – song, chestnut; second –, new- edition; reprint, new impression; return game, return match, reappearance, reproduction; periodicity &c. 138.

V. repeat, iterate, reiterate, reproduce, parrot, echo, re-echo, drum, harp upon, battologize, hammer, redouble.

recur, revert, return, reappear; renew &c. (*restore*) 660.

rehearse; do –, say- over again; ring the changes on; harp on the same string; din –, drum- in the ear; conjugate in all its moods, tenses and inflexions, begin again, go over the same ground, go the same round, never hear the last of; resume, return to, recapitulate, reword.

Adj. repeated &c. *v.*; repetition-al, -ary; recur-rent, -ring; ever recurring, thick coming; frequent, incessant, redundant, pleonastic, tautological.

monotonous, harping, iterative; mocking, chiming; retold; aforesaid, -named; above-mentioned, said; habitual &c. 613; another.

Adv. repeatedly, often, again, afresh, anew, over again, once more; ditto, *encore, de novo, bis, da capo*.

again and again; over and over, – again; many times over; time- and again, – after time; year after year; day by day &c.; many –, several –, a number of- times; many –, full many- a time; times out of number, year in and year out, morning, noon and night; frequently &c. 136.

Phr. *ecce iterum Crispinus, toujours perdrix*, cut and come again; 'tomorrow and tomorrow.'

105. Infinity.—N. infini-ty, -tude, -teness &c. *adj.*; perpetuity &c. 112.

V. be -infinite &c. *adj.*; know –, have- no -limits, – bounds; go on for ever.

Adj. infinite; immense; number-, count-, sum-, measure-less; in-numer-, immeasur-, incalcul-, illimit-, intermin-, unfathom-, unapproach-able; exhaustless, inexhaustible, indefinite; without -number, – measure, – limit, – end; incomprehensible; limit-, end-, bound-, term-less; un-told, -numbered, -measured, -bounded, -limited; illimited; perpetual &c. 112.

Adv. infinitely &c. *adj.*; *ad infinitum*.

Section VI. TIME

1°. Absolute Time

106. Time.—N. time, duration; period, term, stage, space, span, spell, season; the whole -time, – period; course &c. 109.

107. Neverness.*—N. 'neverness'; absence of time, no time; *dies non*; Tib's eve; Greek Kalends.

Adv. never; at no -time, – period;

* A term introduced by Bishop Wilkins.

[35]

intermediate time, while, *interim*, interval, bit, pendency; inter-vention, -mission, -mittence, -regnum, -lude; respite.

era, epoch, æon, cycle; time of life, age, year, date; decade &c. (*period*) 108; moment, &c. (*instant*) 113; reign &c. 737.

glass –, ravages –, whirligig –, noiseless foot- of time; scythe.

V. continue, last, endure, go on, hold out, remain, stay, persist, abide, run; intervene; elapse &c. 109.

take –, take up –, fill –, occupy- time.

pass –, pass away –, spend –, while away –, consume –, talk against –, kill- time; tide over; use –, employ- time; tarry &c. 110; seize an opportunity &c. 134; waste time &c. (*be inactive*) 683.

Adj. continuing &c. *v.*; on foot; permanent &c. (*durable*) 110.

Adv. while, whilst, during, pending; during the -time, – interval; in the course of; for the time being, day by day; in the time of, when; mean-time, -while; in the -meantime, – *interim*; *ad interim*, *pendente lite*; *de die in diem*; from -day to day, – hour to hour &c.; hourly, always; for a -time, – season; till, until, up to, yet; the whole –, all the- time; all along; throughout &c. (*completely*) 52; for good &c. (*diuturnity*) 110.

here-, there-, where-upon; then; *anno*, – *Domini*; A.D.; *ante Christum*; A.C.; before Christ; B.C.; *anno urbis conditæ*; A.U.C.; *anno regni*; A.R.; once upon a time, one fine morning.

Phr. time -runs, – runs against; *tempus fugit*.

on no occasion, never in all one's born days, nevermore, *sine die*.

---

108. [Definite duration, or portion of time.] **Period.**—**N.** period; second, minute, hour, day, week, sennight, octave, month, moon, quarter, semester, year, *lustrum*, *quinquennium*, decade, *decennium*, indiction, lifetime, generation, epoch, era, cycle.

century, age, *millennium*; *annus magnus*.

Adj. horary; hourly, annual &c. (*periodical*) 138.

108a. Contingent Duration.—**Adv.** during -pleasure, – good behaviour; *quamdiu se bene gesserit*.

Phr. *labitur et labetur*; *truditur dies die*; *fugaces labuntur anni*; 'tomorrow and tomorrow and tomorrow creeps in this petty pace from day to day.'

109. [Indefinite duration.] **Course.**—**N.** course –, progress –, process –, succession –, lapse –, flow –, flux –, effluxion, stream –, tract –, current –, sweep –, tide –, march –, step –, flight- of time; duration &c. 106.

[Indefinite time] aorist.

V. elapse, lapse, flow, run, proceed, advance, pass; roll –, wear –, press –, drag- on; flit, fly, slip, slide, glide, crawl; run -its course.

out; expire; go –, pass- by; be -past &c. 122.

Adj. elapsing &c. *v.*; aoristic; progressive, transient &c. 111.

Adv. in due -time, – season; in -course, – process, – the fulness- of time; in time.

---

110. [Long duration.] **Diuturnity.**—**N.** diuturnity; a -long –, length of- time; an age, a century, an eternity,

111. [Short duration.] **Transientness.**—**N.** transientness &c. *adj.*; evanescence, impermanence, fugacity, transi-

æons; slowness &c. 275; perpetuity &c. 112; blue moon.

dura-bleness, -bility; persistence, lastingness &c. *adj.*; continuance, assiduity, endurance, standing; permanence &c. (*stability*) 150; survi-val, -vance; longevity &c. (*age*) 128; distance of time.

protraction –, prolongation –, extension- of time; delay &c. (*lateness*) 133.

V. last, endure, stand, remain, abide, continue, brave a thousand years.

tarry &c. (*be late*) 133; drag -on, – its slow length along, – a lengthening chain; protract, prolong; spin –, eke –, draw –, lengthen- out; temporize; gain –, make –, talk against- time.

out-last, -live; survive; live to fight again.

Adj. durable; perdurable; lasting &c. *v.*; of long -duration, – standing; permanent, chronic, long-standing; intransi-ent, -tive; intransmutable, persistent; life-, live-long; longeval, long-lived, macrobiotic, diuturnal, sempervirent, evergreen, perennial; unin-, ter-, unre-mitting; perpetual &c. 112.

lingering, protracted, prolonged, spun out &c. *v.*; long-pending, -winded; slow &c. 275.

Adv. long; for -a long time, – an age, – ages, – ever so long, – many a long day; long ago &c. (*in a past time*) 122; *longo intervallo*.

all the -day long, – year round; the livelong day, as the day is long, morning, noon and night; hour after hour, day after day, &c.; for good; permanently &c. *adj.*

112. [Endless duration.] **Perpetuity.**
—N. perpetuity, eternity, timelessness; everness,* aye, sempiternity, immortality, athanasia; everlastingness &c. *adj.*; perpetuation; infinite duration.

V. last –, endure –, go on- for ever; have no end.

eternize, eternify, perpetuate, immortalize.

Adj. perpetual, eternal, eterne; everlasting, -living, -flowing; continual, constant, sempiternal; co-eternal; endless, unending; ceaseless, incessant, uninterrupted, indesinent, unceasing; interminable, having no end; unfad-

toriness, volatility, caducity, mortality, span; flash in the pan, nine days' wonder, bubble, May-fly; spurt; temporary arrangement, interregnum.

velocity &c. 274; suddenness &c. 113; changeableness &c. 149.

V. be -transient &c. *adj.*; flit, pass away, fly, gallop, vanish, fade, fleet, melt away, evaporate; pass away like a -cloud, – summer cloud, – shadow, – dream.

Adj. transi-ent, -tory, -tive; passing, evanescent, fleeting; flying &c. *v.*; fug-acious, -itive; shifting, slippery; spasmodic.

tempor-al, -ary; provis-ional, -ory; cursory, short-lived, ephemeral, deciduous; perishable, mortal, precarious; impermanent.

brief, quick, brisk; cometary, meteoric, extemporaneous, summary; pressed for time &c. (*haste*) 684; sudden, momentary &c. (*instantaneous*) 113.

Adv. temporarily &c. *adj.*; *pro tempore*; for -the moment, – a time; awhile, *en passant, in transitu*; in a short time; soon &c. (*early*) 132; briefly &c. *adj.*; at short notice; on the -point, – eve -of; *in articulo*; between cup and lip.

Phr. one's days are numbered; the time is up; here to-day and gone to-morrow; *non semper erit æstas; eheu! fugaces labuntur anni; sic transit gloria mundi.*

113. [Point of time.] **Instantaneity.**
—N. instantane-ity, -ousness; sudden-, abrupt-ness.

moment, instant, second, minute; twinkling, trice, flash, breath, crack, jiffy, *coup*, burst, flash of lightning, stroke of time.

epoch, time; time of -day, – night; hour, minute; very -minute &c., – time, – hour; present –, right –, true –, exact –, correct- time.

V. be -instantaneous &c. *adj.*; twinkle, flash.

Adj. instantaneous, momentary, extempore, sudden, instant, abrupt;

* Bishop Wilkins.

ing, evergreen, amaranthine; never-ending, -dying, -fading; deathless, immortal, undying, imperishable.

Adv. perpetually &c. *adj.*; always, ever, evermore, aye; for -ever, – aye, – evermore, – ever and a day, – ever and ever; in all ages, from age to age; without end; world –, time- without end; *in sæcula sæculorum*; to the -end of time, – crack of doom, – 'last syllable of recorded time'; till dooms-day; constantly &c. (*very frequently*) 136.

Phr. *esto perpetuum*; *labitur et labetur in omne volubilis ævum.*

subitaneous, hasty; quick as -thought,* – lightning, – a flash; rapid as electricity.

Adv. instantaneously &c. *adj.*; in –, in less than- no time; *presto, subito, instanter*, suddenly, at a stroke, like- a shot, – greased lightning; in a trice, in a moment &c. *n.*; eftsoons, in the twinkling of -an eye, – a bed post; at one jump, in the same breath, *per saltum, uno saltu*; at –, all at- once; in one's tracks; plump, slap; 'at one fell swoop'; at the same -instant &c. *n.*; immediately &c. (*early*) 132; *ex tempore*, on the -spot, – spur of the moment, – dot; just then; slap- dash &c. (*haste*) 684; before you could -turn round, – say -knife, – Jack Robinson.

Phr. touch and go; no sooner said than done.

114. [Estimation, measurement, and record of time.] **Chronometry.—N.** chrono-, horo-metry, -logy; date, epoch; style, era.

almanac, calendar, ephemeris; regis-ter, -try; chronicle, annals, journal, diary, chronogram.

[Instruments for the measurement of time] clock, watch; chrono-meter, -scope, -graph; repeater, alarum; time-keeper, -piece; dial, sun-dial, *gnomon, pendule*, horologe, pendulum, hour-glass, water clock, clepsydra.

mean –, Greenwich –, solar –, sidereal –, local –, summer- time; daylight saving.

chrono-grapher, -loger, -logist; annalist.

V. fix –, mark- the time; date, register, chronicle; measure –, beat –, mark- time; bear date.

Adj. chrono-logical, -metrical, -grammatical; isochronal.

Adv. o'clock; *a.m., p.m.*

115. [False estimate of time.] **Anachronism.—N.** ana-, meta-, para-, pro-chronism; *prolepsis*, misdate; anticipa-tion, antichronism.

disregard –, neglect –, oblivion- of time.

intempestivity &c. 135.

V. mis-, ante-, post-, over-date; anticipate; take no note of time.

Adj. misdated &c. *v.*; undated; over-due; out of date; anachronous &c. *n.*

2°. Relative Time

1. *Time with reference to Succession*

116. Priority.—N. priority, ante-cedence, anteriority, pre-existence, pre-cedence &c. 62; precession &c. 280; precursor &c. 64; the past &c. 122; premises.

V. precede, come before; forerun; antecede, go before &c. (*lead*) 280; pre-exist; dawn; premise, presage &c. 511.

be -beforehand &c. (*be early*) 132;

117. Posteriority.—N. posteriority; succession, sequence; following &c. 281; subsequence, supervention; futurity &c. 121; successor; sequel &c. 65; remainder, reversion.

V. follow &c. 281 –, come –, go-after; ensue, result; succeed, supervene; step into the shoes of.

Adj. subsequent, posterior, following, after, later, succeeding, postliminious,

* See note on 264.

steal a march upon, anticipate, forestall; have –, gain- the start.

Adj. prior, previous; preced-ing, -ent; anterior, antecedent; pre-existing, -existent; foresighted; former, foregoing; afore –, before-, above-mentioned; aforesaid, said; introductory &c. (*precursory*) 64; pre-war.

Adv. before, prior to; earlier; previously &c. *adj.*; afore, ere, theretofore, erewhile; ere –, before- -then, – now; erewhile, already, yet, beforehand; aforetime, on the eve of, in anticipation.

118. The Present Time.—**N.** the present -time, – day, – moment, – juncture, – occasion; the times, existing time, time being; twentieth century; nonce, crisis, epoch, day, hour.

age, time of life.

Adj. present, actual, instant, current, latest, existing, that is.

Adv. at this -time, – moment &c. 113; at the -present time &c. *n.*; now, at present.

at this time of day, to-day, now-a-days; already; even –, but –, just-now; on the present occasion; for the -time being, – nonce; *pro hâc vice*; on the -nail, – spot; on the spur of the -moment, – occasion.

until now; to -this, – the present day.

postnate; successive &c. 63; postdiluvial, -an; *puisné*; posthumous; post-war, future &c. 121.

Adv. subsequently, after, afterwards, since, later; at a -subsequent, – later-period; next, in the sequel, close upon, thereafter, thereupon, upon which, eftsoons; from that -time, – moment; after a -while, – time; in process of time.

postcenal, postcibal, postprandial, after-dinner.

119. [Time different from the present.] **Different Time.**—**N.** different –, other- time.

[Indefinite time] aorist.

Adj. aoristic.

Adv. at that –, at which- -time, – moment, – instant; then, on that occasion, upon.

when; when-ever, -soever; upon which, on which occasion; at -another, – a different, – some other, – any- time; at various times; some –, one- -of these days, – fine morning, – day; sooner or later; some time or other; once upon a time, once.

120. Synchronism.—**N.** synchronism; coexistence, coincidence; simultaneousness &c. *adj.*; concurrence, concomitance, unity of time, interim.

[Having equal times] isochronism, syntony.

contemporary, coetanian.

V. coexist, concur, accompany, go hand in hand, keep pace with; synchronize, isochronize.

Adj. synchron-ous, -al, -ical, -istical; simultaneous, coexisting, coincident, concomitant, concurrent; coev-al, -ous; contempora-ry, -neous; coetaneous; coterminous, coeternal; isochronous.

Adv. at the same time; simultaneously &c. *adj.*; together, in concert, during the same time; in the same breath; *pari passu*; in the interim.

at the -very moment &c. 113; just as, as soon as; meanwhile &c. (*while*) 106.

121. [Prospective time.] **Futurity.** —**N.** futur-ity, -ition; future, hereafter, time to come; approaching –, coming –, after- -time, – age, – days, – hours, – years, – ages, – life; morrow, to-morrow, by and by; millennium, doomsday, day of judgment, crack of doom, remote future.

122. [Retrospective time.] **Preterition.**—**N.** preterition; priority &c. 116; the past, past time; days –, times- -of yore, – of old, – past, – gone by; bygone days, good old days; old –, ancient –, former -times; fore time; yesterdays; the olden –, good old-time; auld lang syne; eld.

approach of time, advent, time draw-ing on, womb of time; destiny &c. 152; eventuality.

heritage, heirs, posterity, descend-ants.

prospect &c. (*expectation*) 507; fore-sight &c. 510.

V. look forwards; anticipate &c. (*ex-pect*) 507, (*foresee*) 510; forestall &c. (*be early*) 132.

come –, draw- on; draw near; ap-proach, await, threaten; impend &c. (*be destined*) 152.

Adj. future, to come; coming &c. (*impending*) 152; next, near; near –, close- at hand; eventual, ulterior; ex-pectant, prospective, in prospect &c. (*expectation*) 507.

Adv. prospectively, hereafter, on the knees of the gods, in future; to-morrow, the day after to-morrow; in -course, – process, – the fulness- of time; even-tually, ultimately, sooner or later; *proximo*; *paulo post futurum*; in after time; one of these days; after a -time, – while.

from this time; hence-forth, -for-wards; thence; thence-forth, -forward; whereupon, upon which.

soon &c. (*early*) 132; on the -eve, – point, – brink- of; about to; close upon.

---

antiquity, antiqueness, *status quo*; time immemorial; distance of time; remote -age, – time; ancient history; remote past; rust of antiquity; ancient-ness.

pale-ontology, -ography, -ology; pa-lætiology,* archæology; archaism, an-tiquarianism, mediævalism, pre-Raph-aelitism; retrospection, looking back, memory &c. 505.

laudator temporis acti; mediævalist, pre-Raphaelite; antiqu-ary, -arian; archæologist &c.; Oldbuck, Dryasdust.

ancestry &c. (*paternity*) 166.

V. be -past &c. *adj.*; have -expired &c. *adj.*, – run its course, – had its day; pass; pass –, go- -by, – away, – off; lapse, blow over.

look –, trace –, cast the eyes- back; exhume.

Adj. past, gone, gone by, over, passed away, bygone, foregone; elapsed, lapsed, preterlapsed, expired, no more, run out, blown over, that has been, whilom, extinct, never to return, exploded, forgotten, irrecover-able; obsolete &c. (*old*) 124; extinct as the dodo.

former, pristine, *quondam, ci-devant*, late; ancestral.

foregoing; last, latter; recent, over-night; past, preterite, preter-perfect, -pluperfect, past perfect.

looking back &c. *v.*; retro-spective, -active; archæological &c. *n.*

Adv. formerly; of -old, – yore; erst, whilom, erewhile, time was, ago, over; in -the olden time &c. *n.*; anciently, long -ago, – since; a long -while, – time- ago; years –, ages- ago; some time -ago, – since, – back.

yesterday, the day before yesterday; last -year, – season, – month &c.; *ultimo*; lately &c. (*newly*) 123.

retrospectively; ere –, before –, till- now; hitherto, heretofore; no longer; once, – upon a time; from time immemorial; in the memory of man; time out of mind; already, yet, up to this time; *ex post facto*.

Phr. time was; the time -has, – hath- been.

2. *Time with reference to a particular Period*

123. Newness.—N. newness &c. *adj.*; neologism, neoterism; novelty, recency; immaturity; youth &c. 127; gloss of novelty.

124. Oldness.—N. oldness &c. *adj.*; age, antiquity; cobwebs of antiquity.

maturity, ripeness; decline, decay; senility &c. 128.

* Whewell.

innovation; renovation &c. (*restoration*) 660.

modernist, neologist, neoteric.

modernism, modernity; mushroom; latest fashion, *dernier cri*.

upstart, *parvenu, nouveau riche*.

V. renew &c. (*restore*) 660; modernize.

Adj. new, novel, recent, fresh, green; young &c. 127; evergreen; raw, immature; virgin; un-tried, -handseled, -used, -trodden, -beaten; fledgling.

late, modern, neoteric; new-born, -fashioned, -fangled, -fledged; of yesterday; just out, brand –, span-new, up to date, topical; vernal, renovated; innovatory.

fresh as -a rose, – a daisy, – paint; spick and span.

Adv. newly &c. *adj.*; afresh, anew, lately, just now, only yesterday, the other day; latterly, of late.

not long –, a short time- ago.

---

seniority, eldership, primogeniture.

archaism &c. (*the past*) 122; thing –, relic- of the past; megatherium.

tradition, prescription, custom, folklore, immemorial usage, common law.

V. be -old &c. *adj.*; have -had, – seen- its day; become -old &c. *adj.*; age, fade.

Adj. old, olden, ancient, antique; of long standing, time-honoured, venerable; eld-er, -est; first-born.

prime; prim-itive, -eval, -igenous; primordi-al, -nate; aboriginal &c. (*beginning*) 66; diluvian, antediluvian; pre-historic; patriarchal, preadamite; palæocrystic; fossil, paleozoic, preglacial, ante-mundane; archaic, classic, mediæval, pre-Raphaelite, ancestral, black-letter.

immemorial, traditional, prescriptive, customary, whereof the memory of man runneth not to the contrary; inveterate, rooted.

antiquated, of other times, rococo, of the old school, after-age, obsolete; fusty, moth-eaten; out of -date, – fashion; stale, old-fashioned, behind the -age, – times; exploded; gone out, – by; *passé*, outworn, run out; disused; senile &c. 128; time-worn; crumbling &c. (*deteriorated*) 659; second-hand.

old as -the hills, – Methuselah, – Adam, – history.

Adv. since the -world was made, – year one, – days of Methuselah.

125. Morning. [Noon.]—**N.** morning, morn, matins, forenoon, *a.m.*, prime, dawn, daybreak, daylight, sun-up, peep –, break- of day; aurora, Eos; first blush –, prime- of the morning; twilight, crepuscule, sunrise, cockcrow.

spring; vernal equinox.

noon; mid-, noon-day; noontide, meridian, prime.

summer, midsummer; summer solstice.

Adj. matin, matutinal; vernal, æstival.

Adv. at -sunrise &c. *n.*; with the lark, when the morning dawns.

127. Youth.—**N.** youth; juven- -ility, -escence; juniority; infancy; baby-, child-, boy-, girl-, youth-hood; *incunabula*; minority, immaturity, nonage, teens, tender age, bloom.

cradle, nursery, leading-strings, pupilage, puberty, *pucelage*.

126. Evening. [Midnight.]—**N.** evening, eve; decline –, fall –, close- of day; eventide, evensong, vespers; candlelight; nightfall, curfew, dusk, twilight, blind man's holiday; eleventh hour; sun-set, -down; going down of the sun, cock-shut, dewy eve, gloaming, bed-time.

afternoon, *post meridiem*, *p.m.*

autumn; fall, – of the leaf; autumnal equinox, Indian summer, harvest-time.

midnight; dead –, witching time- of night; winter, – solstice.

Adj. vesperine, autumnal, nocturnal, wintry, brumal, hiemal.

128. Age.—**N.** age; oldness &c. *adj.*; old –, advanced- age; sen-ility, -escence; years, anility, grey hairs, climacteric, grand climacteric, declining years, decrepitude, hoary age, caducity, superannuation; second childhood, -ishness; dotage; vale of years,

prime -, flower -, spring-tide -, seed-time -, golden season- of life; heyday of youth, school days; rising generation, younger generation.

Adj. young, youthful, juvenile, green, callow, budding, sappy, *puisné*, beardless, unfledged, unripe, under age, in one's teens; *in statu pupillari*; younger, junior.

decline of life, 'sear and yellow leaf'; three-score years and ten; green old age, ripe old age; longevity; time of life.

seniority, eldership; elders &c. (*veteran*) 130; firstling; *doyen*, dean, father; primogeniture; nostology.

V. be -aged &c. *adj.*; grow -, get-old &c. *adj.*; age; decline, wane.

Adj. aged; old &c. 124; elderly, senile; matronly, anile; in years; ripe, mellow, run to seed, declining, waning, past one's prime; grey, -headed; hoar, -y; venerable, time-worn, antiquated, *passé*, effete, doddering, decrepit, superannuated; advanced in -life, - years; stricken in years; wrinkled, marked with the crow's foot; having one foot in the grave; doting &c. (*imbecile*) 499.

old-, eld-er, -est; senior; first-born.

turned of, years old; of a certain age, no chicken, old as Methuselah; gerontic; ancestral; patriarchal &c. (*ancient*) 124.

129. Infant.—N. infant, babe, baby; nurse-, suck-, year-, wean-ling; *papoose, bambino.*

child, bairn, little- one, - tot, - mite, chick, brat, chit, pickaninny, kid, urchin; bant-, brat-ling; elf.

youth, boy, lad, slip, sprig, stripling, youngster, cub, unlicked cub, younker, callant, whipster, whipper-snapper, schoolboy, hobbledehoy, hopeful, cadet, minor, master.

scion; sap-, seed-ling; tendril, olive-branch, nestling, chicken, duckling; larva, caterpillar, chrysalis, cocoon; tadpole, whelp, cub, pullet, fry, callow; codlin, -g; *fœtus*, calf, colt, pup, foal, kitten; lamb, -kin.

girl; lass, -ie; wench, miss, damsel, *demoiselle*, damozel; maid, -en; virgin; nymph; colleen; minx, baggage, school-girl; tomboy, flapper, hoyden.

Adj. infant-ine, -ile; puerile; boy-, girl-, child-, baby-, kitten-ish; baby; new-born, unfledged, new-fledged, callow.

in -the cradle, - swaddling clothes, - long clothes, - arms, - leading strings; at the breast; in one's teens; young &c. 127.

130. Veteran.—N. veteran, old man, seer, patriarch, greybeard, dugout, grand-father, -sire; grandam, beldam; gaffer, gammer; hag, crone; pantaloon; sexage-, octoge-, nonage-, cente-narian; old stager; dotard &c. 501.

preadamite, Methuselah, Nestor, Rip van Winkle, old Parr; elders; forefathers &c. (*paternity*) 166.

131. Adolescence.—N. adolescence, pubescence, majority; adultness &c. *adj.*; manhood, virility, maturity; flower of age; prime -, meridian- of life.

man &c. 373; woman &c. 374; adult, no chicken.

V. come -of age, - to man's estate, - to years of discretion; attain majority, assume the *toga virilis*; have -cut one's eye-teeth, - sown one's wild oats, settle down.

Adj. adolescent, pubescent, of age; of -full, - ripe- age; out of one's teens, grown up, mature, full- blown, - grown, in one's prime, in full bloom, manly, virile, adult; womanly, matronly; marriageable, nubile.

3. *Time with reference to an Effect or Purpose*

132. Earliness.—**N.** earliness &c. *adj.*; morning &c. 125.

punctuality; promptitude &c. (*activity*) 682; haste &c. (*velocity*) 274; suddenness &c. (*instantaneity*) 113.

prematurity, precocity, precipitation, anticipation; prevenience, a stitch in time.

V. be -early &c. *adj.*, – beforehand &c. *adv.*; keep time, take time by the forelock, anticipate, forestall; have –, gain- the start; steal a march upon; gain time, draw on futurity; bespeak, secure, engage, pre-engage.

accelerate; expedite &c. (*quicken*) 274; make haste &c. (*hurry*) 684.

Adj. early, prime, timely, in time, punctual, forward; prompt &c. (*active*) 682; summary.

premature, precipitate, precocious; prevenient, anticipatory; rathe.

sudden &c. (*instantaneous*) 113; unexpected &c. 508; impending, imminent; near, – at hand; immediate.

Adv. early, soon, anon, betimes, rathe; eft, -soons; ere –, before- long; punctually &c. *adj.*; to the minute; in time; in -good, – military, – pudding, – due- time; time enough.

beforehand; prematurely &c. *adj.*; precipitately &c. (*hastily*) 684; too soon; before -its, – one's- time; in anticipation; unexpectedly &c. 508.

suddenly &c. (*instantaneously*) 113; before one can say 'Jack Robinson,' at short notice, extempore; on the spur of the -moment, – occasion; at once; on the -spot, – instant; at sight; off –, out of- hand; *à vue d'œil*; straight, -way, -forth; forthwith, incontinently, summarily, instanter, immediately, briefly, shortly, quickly, speedily, apace, before the ink is dry, almost immediately, presently, at the first opportunity, in no long time, by and by, in a while, directly.

Phr. touch and go, no sooner said than done.

134. Occasion.—**N.** occasion, opportunity, opening, room, scope, field; suitable –, proper- -time, – season; high time; opportuneness &c. *adj.*; tempestivity.

133. Lateness.—**N.** lateness &c. *adj.*; tardiness &c. (*slowness*) 275.

de-lay, -lation; cunctation, procrastination; detention; deferring &c. *v.*; filibuster, postponement, adjournment, prorogation, retardation, respite, reprieve, stay; protraction, prolongation, moratorium; contango; demurrage; remand; Fabian policy, *médecine expectante*, chancery suit; leeway; high time.

V. be -late &c. *adj.*; tarry, wait, stay, bide, take time; dawdle &c. (*be inactive*) 683; linger, loiter, saunter, lag behind; bide –, take- one's time; hang -about, – around, – back, – in the balance; gain time; hang fire; stand –, lie-over.

put off, defer, delay, lay over, suspend; shift –, stave- off; waive, retard, remand, postpone, adjourn; procrastinate; dally; prolong, protract; spin –, draw –, lengthen- out; prorogue; keep back; tide over; push –, drive- to the last; let the matter stand over; reserve &c. (*store*) 636; temporize; consult one's pillow, sleep upon it.

shelve, table, lay on the table.

lose an opportunity &c. 135; be kept waiting, dance attendance; kick –, cool- one's heels; *faire antichambre*; wait impatiently; await &c. (*expect*) 507; sit up, – at night.

Adj. late, tardy, slow, behindhand, belated, postliminious, posthumous, backward, unpunctual; dilatory &c. (*slow*), overdue 275; delayed &c. *v.*; in abeyance.

Adv. late; late-, back-ward; late in the day; at -sunset, – the eleventh hour, – length, – last, – long; ultimately; after –, behind- time; too late; too late for &c. 135.

slowly, leisurely, deliberately, at one's leisure; *ex post facto*; *sine die*.

Phr. *nonum prematur in annum.*

———

135. Intempestivity.—**N.** intempestivity; unseasonableness; unsuitable –, improper-time; unreasonableness &c. *adj.*; evil hour; *contretemps*; intrusion; anachronism &c. 115.

crisis, turn, juncture, emergency, conjuncture; turning point, given time.

nick of time; golden –, well-timed –, fine –, favourable- opportunity; clear stage, fair field; *mollia tempora*; *fata Morgana*; spare time &c. (*leisure*) 685.

V. seize &c. (*take*) 789 –, use &c. 677 –, give &c. 784- an -opportunity, – occasion; improve the occasion.

suit the occasion &c. (*be expedient*) 646.

strike the iron while it is hot, *battre le fer sur l'enclume*, make hay while the sun shines, take time by the forelock, *prendre la balle au bond*.

Adj. opportune, timely, well-timed, timeous, timeful, seasonable.

providential, lucky, fortunate, happy, favourable, propitious, auspicious, critical; suitable &c. 23; *obiter dicta*.

Adv. opportunely &c. *adj.*; in -proper, – due- -time, – course, – season; for the nonce; in the -nick, – fulness- of time; all in good time; just in time, at the eleventh hour, now or never.

by the -way, – by; *en passant, à propos*; *pro -re natâ, – hac vice*; *par parenthèse*, parenthetically, by way of parenthesis; while -speaking of, – on this subject; *ex tempore*; on the spur of the -moment, – occasion; on the spot &c. (*early*) 132.

Phr. *carpe diem*; *occasionem cognosce*; one's hour is come, the time is up; that reminds me.

V. be -ill timed &c. *adj.*; mistime, intrude, come amiss, break in upon; have other fish to fry; be -busy, – engaged, – tied up, – occupied.

lose –, throw away –, waste –, neglect &c. 460- an opportunity; allow –, suffer- the -opportunity, – occasion- to -pass, - slip, – go by, – escape, – lapse; waste time &c. (*be inactive*) 683; let slip through the fingers, lock the stable door when the steed is stolen.

Adj. ill-, mis-timed; untimely, intrusive, unseasonable; out of -date, – season; inopportune, timeless, untoward, *mal à propos*, unlucky, inauspicious, unpropitious, unfortunate, unfavourable; unsuited &c. 24; inexpedient &c. 647.

unpunctual &c. (*late*) 133; too late for; premature &c. (*early*) 132; too soon for; wise after the event.

Adv. inopportunely &c. *adj.*; as ill luck would have it, in an evil hour, the time having gone by, a day after the fair.

Phr. after meat mustard, after death the doctor.

3°. Recurrent Time

136. Frequency.—N. frequency, oftness; repetition, &c. 104.

V. recur &c. 104; do nothing but; keep, – on.

Adj. frequent, many times, not rare, thickcoming, incessant, perpetual, continual, constant, recurrent, repeated &c. 104; habitual &c. 613; hourly, &c. 138.

Adv. often, often to be met with, oft; oft-, often-times; frequently; repeatedly &c. 104; unseldom, not unfrequently; in -quick, – rapid- succession; many a time and oft; daily, hourly &c.; every -day, – hour, – moment &c.

perpetually, continually, constantly, incessantly, without ceasing, at all times, daily and hourly, night and day,

137. Infrequency.—N. infrequency, infrequence, rareness, rarity; fewness &c. 103; seldomness, uncommonness.

V. be -rare &c. adj.

Adj. un-, in-frequent; uncommon, sporadic, rare, – as a blue diamond; few &c. 103; scarce; almost unheard of, unprecedented, which has not occurred within the memory of the oldest inhabitant, not within one's previous experience.

Adv. seldom, rarely, scarcely, hardly; not often, unfrequently, infrequently, unoften; scarcely –, hardly- ever; once in a blue moon.

once; once -for all, – in a way; *pro hac vice*; like angels' visits, few and far between.

day and night, day after day, morning noon and night, ever and anon.

most often; commonly &c. (*habitually*) 613.

sometimes, occasionally, at times, now and then, from time to time, there being times when, *toties quoties*, often enough, again and again &c. 104.

138. Regularity of recurrence. **Periodicity.**—**N.** periodicity, intermittence; beat; oscillation &c. 314; pulse, pulsation; rhythm; alter-nation, -nateness, -nativeness, -nity.

bout, round, revolution, rotation, turn.

anniversary, birthday, jubilee, centenary, bi-, ter-centenary.

[Regularity of return] rota, cycle, period, stated time, routine; days of the week; Sunday, Monday &c.; months of the year; January &c.; feast, fast, saint's day &c.; Christmas, Easter, New Year's Day &c. 998; quarter-, Lady-, Midsummer-, Michaelmas-day; May Day, the King's Birthday; leap year; seasons.

punctuality, regularity, steadiness.

V. recur in regular -order, – succession; return, revolve, rotate; come -again, – in its turn; come round, – again; beat, pulsate; alternate; intermit.

Adj. periodic, -al; serial, recurrent, cyclic-, -al, rhythmic-, -al, even; recurring &c. *v.*; inter-, re-mittent; alternate, every other.

hourly; diurnal, daily; quotidian, tertian, weekly; hebdomad-al, -ary; bi-weekly, fortnightly; monthly, menstrual, catamenial; yearly, annual; biennial, triennial, &c.; bissextile; centennial, secular; paschal, lenten, &c.

regular, steady, punctual, constant, methodical, regular as clockwork.

Adv. periodically &c. *adj.*; at -regular intervals, – stated times; at -fixed, – established- periods; punctually &c. *adj.*; *de die in diem*; from day to day, day by day.

by turns; in -turn, – rotation; alternately, every other day, off and on, ride and tie, round and round.

139. Irregularity of recurrence.—**N.** irregularity, uncertainty, unpunctuality; fitfulness &c. *adj.*

Adj. irregular, uneven, uncertain, unpunctual, capricious, erratic, desultory, fitful, flickering; rambling, rhapsodical; spasmodic, unsystematic, unequal, variable, halting.

Adv. irregularly &c. *adj.*; by fits and starts &c. (*discontinuously*) 70.

Section VII. CHANGE

1°. Simple Change

140. [Difference at different times.] **Change.**—**N.** change, alteration, mutation, permutation, variation, modification, modulation, inflexion, mood, qualification, innovation, *metastasis*, deviation, shift, turn; diversion; break.

transformation, transfiguration; metamorphosis; metabolism; transmutation; transubstantiation; metagenesis, transanimation, transmigration, me-

141. [Absence of change.] **Permanence.**—**N.** stability &c. 150; quiescence &c. 265; obstinacy &c. 606.

permanence, -cy, persistence, fixity, fixity of purpose, endurance, durability; standing, *status quo*; maintenance, preservation, conservation; conservatism; *laissez-faire*; law of the Medes and Persians; standing dish.

V. let -alone, – be; persist, remain,

tempsychosis; version; metathesis; transmogrification; catalysis; *avatar*; alterative.

conversion &c. (*gradual change*) 144; revolution &c. (*sudden or radical change*) 146; inversion &c. (*reversal*) 218; displacement &c. 185; transference &c. 270.

changeableness &c. 149; tergiversation &c. (*change of mind*) 607.

V. change, alter, vary, wax and wane; modulate, diversify, qualify, tamper with; turn, shift, veer, jibe, tack, chop, shuffle, swerve, dodge, warp, deviate, turn aside, evert, intervert; pass to, take a turn, turn the corner, resume.

work a change, modify, vamp, revamp, superinduce; trans-form, –mute, -ume, -figure &c. *n.*; metamorphose, ring the changes; convert, resolve; revolutionize; chop and change; patch, re-shape.

innovate, introduce new blood, shuffle the cards, spin the wheel; give a -turn, – colour- to; influence, turn the scale; shift the scene, turn over a new leaf.

recast &c. 146; reverse &c. 218; disturb &c. 61; convert into &c. 144.

Adj. changed &c. *v.*; new-fangled; changeable &c. 149; transitional; modifiable; alterative.

Adv. *mutatis mutandis.*

Int. *quantum mutatus!*

Phr. 'a change came o'er the spirit of my dream'; *nous avons changé tout cela; tempora mutantur et nos mutamur in illis; non sum qualis eram.*

stay, tarry, rest; hold, – on; last, endure, bide, abide, aby, dwell, maintain, keep; stand, – still, – fast; subsist, live, outlive, survive; hold –, keep- one's -ground, – footing; hold good.

Adj. stable &c. 150; persisting &c. *v.*; permanent; established, fixed; durable; unchanged &c. (change &c. 140); unrenewed; intact, inviolate; persistent; monotonous, uncheckered; unfailing.

un-destroyed, -repealed, -suppressed; conservative, *qualis ab incepto*; prescriptive &c. (*old*) 124; stationary &c. 265.

Adv. *in statu quo*; for good, finally; at a stand, -still; *uti possidetis*; without a shadow of turning.

Phr. as you were!; *j'y suis j'y reste; esto perpetua; nolumus leges Angliæ mutari*; let sleeping dogs lie.

---

142. [Change from action to rest.] **Cessation.—N.** cessation, discontinuance, desistance, desinence.

inter-, re-mission; sus-pense, -pension; interruption, hitch; hartal; stop; stopping &c. *v.*; closure, stoppage, halt; arrival &c. 292.

pause, rest, lull, respite, truce, armistice, drop; interregnum, abeyance.

closure &c. 261.

dead -stop, – stand, – lock; checkmate; comma, colon, semicolon, period, full stop; end &c. 67; death &c. 360; *cæsura.*

V. cease, discontinue, desist, stay; break –, leave- off; hold, stop, pull up, stall, stop short, check; stick, deadlock, hang fire; halt; pause, rest.

have done with, give over, surcease,

143. Continuance in action.—**N.** continu-ance, -ation; run; extension, prolongation; maintenance, perpetuation; persistence &c. (*perseverance*) 604a; repetition &c. 104.

V. continue, persist; go –, jog –, keep –, carry –, run – hold- on; abide, keep, pursue, stick to; endure; take –, maintain- its course; keep up.

sustain, uphold, hold up, keep on foot; follow up, perpetuate, prolong; maintain; preserve &c. 604a; harp upon &c. (*repeat*) 104.

keep -going, – alive, – at it, – the pot boiling, – the ball rolling, – up the ball; plod-, plug- along; slog on; die in harness; hold on –, pursue- the even tenor of one's way.

let be; *stare super antiquas vias;*

shut up shop; give up &c. (*relinquish*) 624.

hold –, stay- one's hand; rest on one's oars, repose on one's laurels.

come to a -stand, – standstill, – dead lock, – full stop; arrive &c. 292; go out, die away, peter out; wear -away, – off; pass away &c. (*be past*) 122; be at an end.

intromit, interrupt, suspend, interpel; inter-, re-mit; put -an end, – a stop, – a period- to; bring to a stand, -still; stop, cut out, cut short, arrest, avast; stem the -tide, – torrent; pull the check string; switch off.

Int. halt! hold! stop! enough! avast! have done! a truce to! soft! leave off! shut up! give over! chuck it!

quieta non movere; let things take their course.

Adj. continuing &c. *v.*; uninterrupted, unintermitting, unremitting, unvarying, unshifting; unreversed, unstopped, unrevoked, unvaried; sustained; undying &c. (*perpetual*) 112; inconvertible.

follow-up.

Int. carry on! right away!

Phr. *vestigia nulla retrorsum*; *labitur et labetur*.

---

144. [Gradual change to something different.] **Conversion.**—**N.** conversion, reduction, transmutation, transformation, development, resolution, assimilation; assumption; naturalization.

chemistry, alchemy; progress, growth, lapse, flux.

passage; transit, -ion; transmigration, shifting &c. *v.*; conjugation; convertibility.

crucible, alembic, caldron, retort, test tube &c.

convert, neophyte, proselyte, pervert, renegade, deserter, apostate, turncoat.

V. be converted into; become, get, wax; come –, turn- -to, – into; turn out, lapse, shift; run –, fall –, pass –, slide –, glide –, grow –, ripen –, open –, resolve itself –, settle –, merge- into; melt, grow, come round to, mature, mellow; assume the -form, – shape, – state, – nature, – character- of; illapse; assume a new phase, undergo a change.

convert –, resolve- into; make, render; mould, form &c. 240; remodel, new model, refound, reform, reorganize; assimilate –, bring –, reduce- to; transform.

Adj. converted into &c. *v.*; convertible, resolvable into; transitional; naturalized.

Adv. gradually &c. (*slowly*) 275; *in transitu* &c. (*transference*) 270.

145. Reversion.—**N.** reversion, return; revulsion; reaction.

turning point, turn of the tide; *status quo ante bellum*; calm before a storm.

alternation &c. (*periodicity*) 138; inversion &c. 219; recoil &c. 277; regression &c. 283; restoration &c. 660; relapse &c. 661; vicinism, atavism, throwback.

V. revert, turn back, return; relapse &c. 661; recoil &c. 277; retreat &c. 283; restore &c. 660; undo, unmake; turn the -tide, – scale; escheat.

Adj. reverting &c. *v.*; revulsive, reactionary.

Adv. *à rebours*, wrong side out.

146. [Sudden or violent change.] **Revolution.**—**N.** revolution, *bouleversement*, subversion, break up; destruction &c. 162; sudden –, radical –, sweeping –, organic- change; clean sweep, *coup d'état*, overthrow, *débâcle*; counter-revolution, rebellion &c. 742.

transilience, jump, leap, plunge, jerk, start; explosion; spasm, convulsion, throe, revulsion; storm, earthquake, eruption, upheaval, cataclysm.

legerdemain &c. (*trick*) 545.

V. revolutionize; new model, remodel, recast; strike out something new, break with the past; change the face of, unsex; revert &c. 742.

Adj. unrecognizable.

Revolutionary, Bolshevik &c. 742.

147. [Change of one thing for another.] **Substitution.**—**N.** substitution, subrogation, commutation; supplanting &c. *v.*, supersession, metonymy &c. (*figure of speech*) 521.

[Thing substituted] substitute, *succedaneum*, make-shift, temporary expedient, shift, *pis aller*, stop-gap, jury-mast, *locum tenens*, warming-pan, dummy, goat, scape-goat; double; changeling; *quid pro quo*, alternative; remount; representative &c. (*deputy*) 759; palimpsest.

price, purchase-money, consideration, equivalent.

V. substitute, put in the place of, change for; make way for, give place to; supply –, take- the place of; supplant, supersede, replace, cut out, serve as a substitute; step into –, stand in- the shoes of; make a shift –, put up- with; borrow of Peter to pay Paul; commute, redeem, compound for.

Adj. substituted &c. *v.*; vicarious, subdititious; substitutional.

Adv. instead; in -place, – lieu, – the stead, – the room- of; *faute de mieux*.

148. [Double or mutual change.] **Interchange.**—**N.** inter-, ex-change; com-, per-, inter-mutation; reciprocation, transposal, transposition, shuffling; reciprocity, castling [at chess]; hocus-pocus.

interchange-ableness, -ability.

barter &c. 794; tit for tat &c. (*retaliation*) 718; cross fire, battledore and shuttlecock; *quid pro quo.*

V. inter-, ex-, counter-change; bandy, transpose, shuffle, change hands, swap, trade, permute, reciprocate, commute; give and take, return the compliment; play at -puss in the corner, – battledore and shuttlecock; retaliate &c. 718; barter &c. 794.

Adj. interchanged &c. *v.*; reciprocal, mutual, commutative, interchanged &c. *v.*; interchangeable, intercurrent.

Adv. in exchange, *vice versâ, mutatis mutandis*, backwards and forwards, by turns, turn and turn about, turn about; each –, every one- in his turn.

2°. COMPLEX CHANGE

149. Changeableness.—**N.** changeableness &c. *adj.*; mutability, inconstancy; versatility, mobility; instability, unstable equilibrium; vacillation &c. (*irresolution*) 605; fluctuation, vicissitude; alternation &c. (*oscillation*) 314.

restlessness &c. *adj.*; fidgets, disquiet; dis-, in-quietude; unrest; agitation &c. 315.

moon, Proteus, chameleon, kaleidoscope, quicksilver, shifting sands, weathercock, harlequin, Cynthia of the minute, April showers; wheel of Fortune; transientness &c. 111.

V. fluctuate, vary, waver, flounder, flicker, flitter, flit, flutter, shift, shuffle, shake, totter, tremble, vacillate, wamble, turn and turn about, ring the changes; sway –, shift- to and fro; change and change about; oscillate

150. Stability.—**N.** stability; immutability &c. *adj.*; unchangeableness &c. *adj.*; constancy; stable equilibrium, immobility, soundness, vitality, stabiliment, stabilization, stiffness, ankylosis, solidity, *aplomb.*

establishment, fixture; rock, pillar, tower, foundation, leopard's spots, Ethiopian's skin, law of the Medes and Persians.

stabilimeter, stabilisator.

permanence &c. 141; obstinacy &c. 606.

V. be -firm &c. *adj.*; stick fast; stand –, keep –, remain- firm; weather the storm.

settle, establish, stablish, ascertain, fix, set, stabilitate, stabilize; retain, stet, keep hold; make -good, – sure; fasten &c. (*join*) 43; set on its legs, float; perpetuate.

&c. 314; vibrate –, oscillate- between two extremes; alternate; have as many phases as the moon.

Adj. change-able, -ful; changing &c. 140; mutable, variable, checkered, ever changing, kaleidoscopic, prote-an, -iform; versatile.

unstaid, inconstant; un-steady, -stable, -fixed, -settled; fluctuating &c. *v.*; restless; mercurial; agitated &c. 315; erratic, fickle; irresolute &c. 605; capricious &c. 608; touch-and-go; inconsonant, fitful, spasmodic; vibratory; vagrant, wayward, wavering; desultory; afloat; alternating; alterable, plastic, mobile; fleeting, transient &c. 111.

Adv. see-saw &c. (*oscillation*) 314; off and on.

---

settle down; strike –, take- root; take up one's abode &c. 184; build one's house on a rock.

Adj. unchangeable, immutable; un-alter-ed, -able; not to be changed, constant; permanent &c. 141; invariable, undeviating; stable, durable; perennial &c. (*diuturnal*) 110.

fixed, steadfast, firm, fast, steady, balanced; confirmed, valid, fiducial, immovable, irremovable, riveted, rooted; settled, established &c. *v.*; vested; incontrovertible, stereotyped, indeclinable.

tethered, anchored, moored, at anchor, on a rock, firm as a rock; firmly -seated, – established &c. *v.*; deeprooted, ineradicable; inveterate; obstinate &c. 606.

transfixed, stuck fast, aground, high and dry, stranded.

indefeasible, irretrievable, intransmutable, incommutable, irresoluble, irrevocable, irreversible, reverseless, inextinguishable, irreducible; indissol-uble, -vable; indestructible, undying, imperishable, indelible, indeciduous; insusceptible, – of change.

Int. *stet.*

Present Events

151. Eventuality.—N. eventuality, event, occurrence, incident, affair, transaction, proceeding, fact; matter of –, naked- fact; phenomenon; advent.

business, concern; circumstance, particular, casualty, happening, accident, adventure, passage, crisis, pass, emergency, contingency, consequence &c. 154.

the world, life, things, doings, affairs, matters; things –, affairs- in general; the times, state of affairs, order of the day; course –, tide –, stream –, current –, run –, march- of -things, – events; ups and downs of life; chapter of accidents &c. (*chance*) 156; situation &c. (*circumstances*) 8.

V. happen, occur; take -place, – effect; come, become of; come -off, – about, – round, – into existence, – forth, – to pass, – on; pass, present itself; fall; fall –, turn- out; run, be on foot, fall in; be-fall, -tide, -chance; prove, eventuate, draw on; turn –, crop –, spring –, cast- up; super-, sur-vene; issue, emanate, arrive, ensue,

Future Events

152. Destiny.—N. destiny &c. (*necessity*) 601; hereafter, future –, postexistence; future state, next world, world to come, after life; futurity &c. 121; everlasting -life, – death; prospect &c. (*expectation*) 507.

V. impend; hang –, lie –, hoverover; threaten, loom, await, come on, approach, stare one in the face; fore-, pre-ordain; predestine, doom, foredoom, foreshadow, have in store for.

Adj. impending &c. *v.*; destined; about to -be, – happen; coming, in store, to come, going to happen, instant, at hand, near; near –, close- at hand; overhanging, hanging over one's head, imminent; brewing, preparing, forthcoming; in the wind, on the cards, in reserve; that -will, – is to- be; in prospect &c. (*expected*) 507; looming in the -distance, – horizon, – future; unborn, in embryo; in the womb of -time; – futurity; on the knees of the gods; pregnant &c. (*producing*) 161.

Adv. in -time, – the long run; all in good time; eventually &c. 151; what-

arise, start, hold, take its course; pass off &c. (*be past*) 122.

meet with; experience; fall to the lot of; be one's -chance, – fortune, – lot; find; encounter, undergo; pass –, go-through; endure &c. (*feel*) 821.

Adj. happening &c. *v.*; going on, doing, current; in the wind, afloat; on -foot, – the *tapis*; at issue, in question; incidental.

eventful, momentous, signal; stirring, bustling, full of incident.

Adv. eventually, ultimately, in -the event of, – case; in the course of things; in the -natural, – ordinary- course of things; as -things, – times- go; as the world -goes, – wags; as the -tree falls, – cat jumps; as it may -turn out, – happen.

Phr. the plot thickens.

ever may happen &c. (*certainly*) 474; as -chance &c. 156- would have it.

SECTION VIII.   CAUSATION

1°. CONSTANCY OF SEQUENCE IN EVENTS

153. [Constant antecedent.] **Cause.** —**N.** cause, origin, source, principle, element; occasioner, prime mover, engine, turbine, motor, *primum mobile*; *vera causa*; author &c. (*producer*) 164; main-spring, agent; dynamo, generator, battery (electric); leaven; groundwork, foundation &c. (*support*) 215.

spring, fountain, well, font; fountain –, spring- head; *fons et origo*, genesis; descent &c. (*paternity*) 166; remote cause; influence.

pivot, hinge, turning-point, lever; key; kernel, core; proximate cause, *causa causans*; last straw that breaks the camel's back.

ground; reason, – why; why and wherefore, rationale, occasion, deriva-tion; final cause &c. (*intention*) 620; *le dessous des cartes*; undercurrents.

rudiment, egg, germ, embryo, fœtus bud, root, *radix*, radical, etymon, nucleus, seed, stem, stalk, stock, *stirps*, trunk, tap-root; latent organism.

nest, cradle, nursery, womb, *nidus*, birth-, breeding-place, hot-bed.

caus-ality, -ation; origination; pro-duction &c. 161.

V. be the -cause &c. *n.*- of; originate; give -origin, – rise, – occasion- to; cause, occasion, sow the seeds of, kindle, suscitate; bring -on, – to pass, – about; produce; create &c. 161; set -up, – afloat, – on foot; found, broach,

154. [Constant sequent.] **Effect.**—**N.** effect, consequence, sequela; deriva-tive, -tion; result; result-ant, -ance; upshot, issue, *dénouement*; outcome; termination, end &c. 67; development, outgrowth, fruit, crop, harvest, prod-uct, bud, blossom, florescence, ear.

production, produce, product, fin-ished product, work, handiwork, fabric, performance; creature, creation; off-spring, -shoot; first-fruits, -lings; *prémices*.

V. be the -effect &c. *n.*- of; be -due, – owing- to; originate -in, – from; rise –, arise –, take its rise –, spring –, proceed –, emanate –, come –, grow –, bud –, sprout –, germinate –, issue –, flow –, result –, follow –, derive its origin –, accrue- from; come -to, – of, – out of; depend –, hang –, hinge –, turn- upon.

take the consequences, sow the wind and reap the whirlwind.

Adj. owing to; resulting from &c. *v.*; resultant; derivable from; due to; caused &c. by, 153; dependent upon; derived –, evolved- from; derivative; hereditary.

Adv. of course, it follows that, natu-rally, consequently; as a –, in- con-sequence; through all, all along of, necessarily, eventually.

Phr. *cela va sans dire*, thereby hangs a tale.

institute, lay the foundation of, inaugurate; lie at the root of.

procure, induce, draw down, open the door to, superinduce, evoke, entail, operate; elicit, provoke.

conduce to &c. (*tend to*) 176; contribute; promote; have a -hand in, – finger in- the pie; determine, decide, turn the scale, give the casting vote; have a common origin; derive its origin &c. (*effect*) 154.

Adj. caused &c. *v.*; causal, original; prim-ary, -itive, -ordial; aboriginal; radical; inceptive, embry-onic, -otic; in -embryo, – ovo; seminal, germinal; formative, productive &c. 168; at the bottom of; connate, having a common origin.

Adv. because &c. 155; behind the scenes.

155. [Assignment of cause.] **Attribu-tion.—N.** attribution, theory, etiology, ascription, reference to, rationale; accounting for &c. *v.*; palætiology,* imputation, derivation from.

fil-, affil-iation; pedigree &c. (*pater-nity*) 166.

explanation &c. (*interpretation*) 522; reason why &c. (*cause*) 153.

V. attribute –, ascribe –, impute –, refer –, lay –, point –, trace –, bring home- to; put –, set- down- to; charge –, ground- on; invest with, assign as cause, charge with, blame, lay at the door of, father upon; saddle with; affiliate; account for, derive from, point out the -reason &c. 153; theorize; tell how it comes; put the saddle on the right horse.

Adj. attributed &c. *v.*; attributable &c. *v.*; refer-able, -rible; due to, deri-vable from; owing to &c. (*effect*) 154; putative.

Adv. hence, thence, therefore, for, since, on account of, because, owing to; on that account; from -this, – that- cause; thanks to, forasmuch as; whence, *propter hoc.*

why? wherefore? whence? how -comes, – is, – happens- it? how does it happen?

in -some, – some such- way; some-how, – or other.

Phr. that is why; *hinc illæ lachrymæ; cherchez la femme.*

156. [Absence of assignable cause.] **Chance.†—N.** chance, indetermination, accident, fortune, hazard, hap, hap-hazard, chance-medley, random, luck, *raccroc*, casualty, fortuity, contingence, coincidence, adventure, hit; fate &c. (*necessity*) 601; equal chance; lottery, raffle, tombola, sweepstake; toss up &c. 621; turn of the -table, – cards; hazard of the die, chapter of accidents; cast –, throw- of the dice; heads or tails, wheel of Fortune, whirligig of chance; *sortes, – Virgilianæ.*

probability, possibility, contingency, odds, long odds, run of luck; main-chance.

theory of -probabilities, – chances; book-making; assurance; speculation, gamble, gaming &c. 621.

V. chance, hap, turn up; fall to one's lot; be one's -fate &c. 601; stumble on, light –, blunder –, hit- upon; take one's chance &c. 621.

Adj. casual, fortuitous, accidental, haphazard, random, stray, adventi-tious, adventive, causeless, incidental. contingent, uncaused, undetermined, indeterminate; possible &c. 470; unin-tentional &c. 621.

Adv. by -chance, – accident; casually; perchance &c. (*possibly*) 470; for aught one knows; as -good, – bad, – ill-luck &c. *n.*- would have it; as it may -be, – chance, – turn up, – happen; as the case may be.

2°. CONNECTION BETWEEN CAUSE AND EFFECT

157. Power.—N. power; poten-cy, -tiality; puissance, might, force; energy &c. 171; dint; right -hand, – arm;

158. Impotence.—N. impotence; in-, dis-ability; disablement, impuissance, imbecility, caducity; incapa-city,

* Whewell, 'History of the Inductive Sciences,' book xviii, vol. iii., p. 397 (3rd edit.).

† The word *Chance* has two distinct meanings: the first, the absence of assignable *cause*, as above; and the second, the absence of *design*—for the latter see 621.

ascendency, sway, control; pre-potency, -pollence; almightiness, omnipotence; authority &c. 737; strength &c. 159.

ability; ableness &c. *adj.*; competency; effi-ciency, -cacy; validity, cogency; enablement; vantage ground; influence &c. 175; horse power; dynamometer.

pressure; elasticity; gravity, electricity, magnetism, galvanism, voltaic electricity, voltaism, electro-magnetism, electrostatics, electrification, electric current &c.; attraction, repulsion; *vis -inertiæ*, – *mortua*, – *viva*; potential –, dynamic –, kinetic –, electrical –, chemical –, atomic- energy; friction, suction.

capability, capacity; *quid valeant humeri quid ferre recusent*; faculty, quality, attribute, endowment, virtue, gift, property, qualification, susceptibility.

V. be -powerful &c. *adj.*; gain -power &c. *n.*

belong –, pertain- to; lie –, be- in one's power; can.

give –, confer –, exercise- power &c. *n.*; empower, enable, invest; in-, en-due; endow, arm; strengthen &c. 159; compel &c. 744.

Adj. powerful, puissant; potent, -ial; capable, able; equal –, up- to; cogent, valid; effect-ive, -ual; efficient, efficacious, adequate, competent; multi-, pleni-, omni-, armi- potent; mighty, ascendent; almighty.

electric, electrical &c.

forcible &c. *adj.* (*energetic*) 171; influential &c. 175; productive &c. 168.

Adv. powerfully &c. *adj.*; by -virtue, – dint- of.

-bility; inapt-, inept-itude; indocility; invalidity, inefficiency, incompetence, disqualification.

telum imbelle, brutum fulmen, blank cartridge, flash in the pan, *vox et præterea nihil,* dead letter, bit of waste paper, dummy; scrap of paper.

inefficacy &c. (*inutility*) 645; failure &c. 732.

helplessness &c. *adj.*; prostration, paralysis, palsy, ataxia, apoplexy, syncope, sideration, *deliquium,* collapse, exhaustion, softening of the brain, emasculation, inanition, senility &c. 128; castrato, eunuch.

cripple, old woman, muff, mollycoddle, milksop.

V. be -impotent &c. *adj.*; not have a leg to stand on.

vouloir -rompre l'anguille au genou, – prendre la lune avec les dents.

collapse, faint, swoon, fall into a swoon, drop; go by the board; end in smoke &c. (*fail*) 732.

render -powerless &c. *adj.*; deprive of power; decontrol; dis-able, -enable; disarm, incapacitate, disqualify, unfit, invalidate, undermine, deaden, cramp, tie the hands; double up, prostrate, paralyze, muzzle, cripple, becripple, maim, lame, hamstring, draw the teeth of; throttle, strangle, *garrotte*; ratten, silence, sprain, clip the wings of, render *hors de combat,* spike the guns; take the wind out of one's sails, scotch the snake, put a spoke in one's wheel; break the -neck, – back; un-hinge, -fit; put out of gear.

unman, unnerve, devitalize, attenuate, enervate; emasculate, spay, caponize, castrate, geld; effeminize.

shatter, exhaust; weaken &c. 160.

Adj. powerless, impotent, unable, incapable, incompetent; ineff-icient, -ective; inept; un-fit, -fitted; un-, dis-qualified; unendowed; in-, un-apt; crippled, decrepit, disabled &c. *v.*; armless.

harmless, unarmed, weaponless, defenceless, *sine ictu,* unfortified, indefensible, vincible, pregnable, untenable.

para-lytic, -lyzed; palsied, imbecile; nerve-, sinew-, marrow-, pith-, lust-less; emasculate, disjointed; out of -joint, – gear; un--nerved, -hinged; water-logged, on one's beam ends, rudderless; laid on one's back; done up, dead beat, exhausted, shattered, demoralized; gravelled &c. (*in difficulty*) 704; helpless, unfriended, fatherless; without a leg to stand on, *hors de combat,* laid on the shelf.

null and void, nugatory, inoperative, good for nothing; dud; invertebrate; ineffectual &c. (*failing*) 732; inadequate &c. 640; inefficacious &c. (*useless*) 645.

159. [Degree of power.] **Strength.** —**N.** strength; power &c. 157; energy &c. 171; vigour, force; main -, physical -, brute- force; spring, elasticity, tone; tension, tonicity.

stoutness &c. *adj*; lustihood, stamina, nerve, muscle, sinew, thews and sinews, *physique*; pith, -iness; virility, vitality.

athlet-ics, -icism; gymnastics, feats of strength.

adamant, steel, iron, oak, heart of oak; iron grip; grit, bone.

athlete, gymnast, tumbler, acrobat; Atlas, Hercules, Antæus, Samson, Cyclops, Goliath, Titan; tower of strength; giant refreshed.

strengthening &c. *v.*; invigoration, refreshment, refocillation.

[Science of forces] dynamics, statics.

V. be -strong &c. *adj.*, - stronger; overmatch.

render -strong &c. *adj.*; give -strength &c. *n.*; strengthen, invigorate, brace, nerve, fortify, buttress, sustain, harden, case-harden, steel; gird; screw -, wind -, set- up; gird -, brace- up one's loins; recruit, set on one's legs; vivify; refresh &c. 689; refect; reinforce &c. (*restore*) 660.

Adj. strong, mighty, vigorous, forcible, hard, adamantine, stout, robust, sturdy, hardy, powerful, potent, puissant, valid.

resistless, irresistible, invincible, proof against, impregnable, unconquerable, indomitable, inextinguishable, unquenchable; incontestable; more than a match for; over-powering, -whelming; all-powerful; sovereign.

able-bodied; athletic, gymnastic; Herculean, Cyclopean, Atlantean; muscular, husky, brawny, wiry, well-knit, broad-shouldered, sinewy, strapping, stalwart, gigantic.

man-ly, -like, -ful; masculine, male, virile, in the prime of manhood.

un-weakened, -allayed, -withered, -shaken, -worn, -exhausted; in full -force, - swing; in the plenitude of power.

160. Weakness.—N. weakness &c. *adj.*; debility, atony, relaxation, languor, enervation; impotence &c. 158; infirmity; effeminacy, feminality; fragility, flaccidity; inactivity &c. 683.

declension -, loss -, failure- of strength; delicacy, invalidation, decrepitude, asthenia, adynamy, cachexy, *cachexia*, anæmia, bloodlessness, sprain, strain.

reed, thread, rope of sand, broken reed, house -of cards, - built on sand.

soft-, weak-ling; infant &c. 129; youth &c. 127.

V. be -weak &c. *adj.*; drop, crumble, give way, totter, tremble, shake, halt, limp, fade, languish, decline, flag, fail, have one foot in the grave.

render -weak &c. *adj.*; weaken, enfeeble, debilitate, shake, deprive of strength, relax, enervate; un-brace, -nerve; cripple, unman, &c. (*render powerless*) 158; cramp, reduce, sprain, strain, blunt the edge of; dilute, impoverish; decimate; extenuate; reduce -in strength, - the strength of; invalidate; *mettre de l'eau dans son vin.*

Adj. weak, feeble, debile; impotent &c. 158; relaxed, unnerved &c. *v.*; sap-, strength-, power-less; weakly, unstrung, flaccid, adynamic, asthenic; nervous.

soft, effeminate, feminate, womanish.

frail, fragile, shattery, frangible, brittle &c. 328; flimsy, unsubstantial, gimcrack, gingerbread; rickety, cranky; creachy; drooping, tottering &c. *v.*; broken, lame, halt, game, withered, shattered, shaken, crazy, shaky, tumble-down; palsied &c. 158; decrepit; C3.

languid, poor, poorly, infirm; faint, -ish; sickly &c. (*disease*) 655; dull, slack, evanid, spent, short-winded, effete; weatherbeaten; decayed, rotten, worn, seedy, languishing, wasted, washy, wishy-washy, laid low, pulled down, the worse for wear.

un-strengthened &c. 159, -supported, -aided, -assisted; aidless, defenceless &c. 158.

stubborn, thick-ribbed, made of iron, deep-rooted; strong as -a lion, – a horse, – brandy; sound as a roach; in -fine, – high- feather; in fine fettle; like a giant refreshed.

Adv. strongly &c. *adj.*; by -force &c. *n.*; by main force &c. (*by compulsion*) 744.

Phr. 'our withers are unwrung.'

on its last legs; weak as a -child, – baby, – chicken, – cat, – rat; weak as -water, – water gruel, – gingerbread, – milk and water; colourless &c. 429.

Phr. *non sum qualis eram.*

3°. Power in Operation

161. Production.—N. production, creation, construction, formation, fabrication, manufacture; building, architecture, erection, edification; coinage; organization; *nisus formativus*; putting together &c. *v.*; establishment; workmanship, performance; achievement &c. (*completion*) 729; effect &c. 154.

flowering, fructification, fruition.

bringing forth &c. *v.*; parturition, birth, birth-throe, child-birth, delivery, confinement, *accouchement*, travail, labour, midwifery, obstetrics; geniture; gestation &c. (*maturation*) 673; evolution, development, growth; genesis, fertilization, breeding, conception, germination, generation, *epigenesis*, pro-creation, -generation, -pagation; fecundation, impregnation; spontaneous generation; *arche-genesis*, *-biosis*; *bio-*, *abio-*, *homo-*, *xeno-genesis.**

authorship, publication; works, *œuvre*, *opus*.

edifice, building, structure, fabric, erection, pile, tower, flower, fruit.

V. produce, perform, operate, do, make, gar, form, construct, fabricate, frame, contrive, manufacture; weave, forge, coin, carve, chisel; build, raise, edify, rear, erect, put together; set –, run- up; establish, constitute, compose, organize, institute, get up; achieve, accomplish &c. (*complete*) 729.

flower, sprout, blossom, burgeon, bear fruit, fructify, spawn, teem, ean, yean, farrow, drop, calf, pup, whelp, kitten, kindle, bear, lay, bring forth, give birth to, lie in, be brought to bed of, evolve, pullulate, usher into the world.

make productive &c. 168; create; beget, conceive, get, generate, fecun-

162. [Non-production.] Destruction. —N. destruction; waste, dissolution, breaking up; di-, dis-ruption; consumption; disorganization.

fall, downfall, ruin, perdition, crash, smash, havoc, *délabrement*, *débâcle*; break -down, – up; prostration; desolation, *bouleversement*, wreck, crack-up, crash, wrack, shipwreck, cataclysm; Caudine Forks, Sedan.

extinction, annihilation; destruction of life &c. 361; knock-out, knock-down blow; doom, crack of doom.

destroying &c. *v.*; demo-lition, -lishment; biblioclasm; overthrow, subversion, suppression; abolition &c. (*abrogation*) 756; sacrifice; ravage, devastation, *sabotage*, *razzia*; incendiarism; revolution &c. 146; extirpation &c. (*extraction*) 301; *commencement de la fin*, road to ruin; dilapidation &c. (*deterioration*) 659.

V. be -destroyed &c.; perish; fall, – to the ground; tumble, topple; go –, fall- to pieces; break up; crumble, – to dust; go to -the dogs, – the wall, – smash, – shivers, – wreck, – pot, – wrack and ruin; go -by the board, – all to smash, – to pieces, – under; be all -over, – up- with; totter to its fall.

destroy; do –, make- away with; nullify; annul &c. 756; sacrifice, demolish; tear up; over-turn, -throw, -whelm; upset, subvert, put an end to; seal the doom of, do for, dish, undo; break -, cut- up; break –, cut –, pull –, mow –, blow –, beat- down; suppress, quash, put down; cut short, take off, blot out; dispel, dissipate, dissolve; consume.

smash, – to smithereens, quell, squash, squelch, crumple up, shatter,

* Huxley.

date, impregnate; pro-create, -generate, -pagate; engender; bring –, call- into -being, – existence; breed, hatch, develop, bring up.

induce, superinduce; suscitate; cause &c. 153; acquire &c. 775.

Adj. produc-ed, -ing &c. *v.*; productive of; prolific &c. 168; creative; formative; gen-etic, -ial, -ital; fertile, pregnant; *enceinte*, big –, fraught-with; with child, in the family way, teeming, parturient, in the straw, brought to bed of; puerper-al, -ous.

architectonic; constructive.

---

shiver; batter; tear –, crush –, cut –, shake –, pull –, pick- to pieces; nip; tear to -rags, – tatters; crush –, knock-to atoms; pulverize; ruin; strike out; throw –, knock- -down, – over; lay by the heels; fell, sink, swamp, scuttle, wreck, crash, shipwreck, engulf, submerge; lay in -ashes, – ruins; sweep away, erase, expunge, strike out, delete, efface, raze; level, – with the -ground, – dust.

deal destruction, lay waste, ravage, gut; disorganize; dismantle &c. (*render useless*) 645; devour, swallow up, desolate, devastate, sap, mine, blast, confound; exterminate, extinguish, quench, annihilate; snuff –, put –, stamp –, trample- out; lay –, trample- in the dust; prostrate; tread –, crush –, trample- under foot; lay the axe to the root of; make -short work, – a clean sweep, – mince-meat- of; cut up root and branch; fling –, scatter- to the winds; throw overboard; strike at the root of, sap the foundations of, spring a mine, blow up; ravage with fire and sword; cast to the dogs; eradicate &c. 301.

Adj. destroyed &c. *v.*; perishing &c. *v.*; trembling –, nodding –, tottering- to its fall; in course of -destruction &c. *n.*; extinct.

destructive, subversive, ruinous, incendiary, deletory; destroying &c. *v.*; suicidal; deadly &c. (*killing*) 361.

Adv. with -crushing effect, – a sledge-hammer.

Phr. *delenda est Carthago.*

---

163. Reproduction.—**N.** reproduction, renovation; restoration &c. 660; renewal; new edition, reprint &c. 21; revival, regeneration, palingenesia, revivification; apotheosis; resuscitation, reanimation, resurrection, resurgence, reappearance, atavism; Phœnix; reincarnation.

generation &c. (*production*) 161; multiplication.

V. reproduce; restore &c. 660; revive, renovate, renew, regenerate, revivify, resuscitate, reanimate, refashion, stir the embers, put into the crucible; multiply, repeat, resurge.

crop up, spring up like mushrooms.

Adj. reproduced &c. *v.*; renascent, reappearing; reproductive; resurgent; progenitive; Hydra-headed.

---

164. Producer.—**N.** producer, creator, deviser, designer, originator, inventor, author, founder, generator, mover, architect; grower, constructor, maker &c. (*agent*) 690.

166. Paternity.—**N.** paternity; parentage; fatherhood; consanguinity &c. 11.

parent, father, sire, dad, daddy, papa, governor, *pater*, *paterfamilias*, *abba*; genitor, progenitor, procreator, begetter; ancestor; grand-sire, -father; great-grandfather.

165. Destroyer.—**N.** destroyer &c. (destroy &c. 162); cankerworm &c. (*bane*) 663; iconoclast; assassin &c. (*killer*) 361; executioner &c. (*punish*) 975; Hun, Vandal, nihilist, anarchist.

167. Posterity.—**N.** posterity, progeny, breed, issue, offspring, brood, litter, seed, farrow, spawn, spat; family, children, grandchildren, heirs; great-grandchild.

child, son, daughter; kid; infant &c. 129; bantling, scion; shoot, sprout, olive branch, sprit, branch; off-shoot,

house, stem, trunk, tree, stock, *stirps*, pedigree, lineage, line, family, tribe, sept, race, clan; genealogy, descent, extraction, birth, ancestry; forefathers, forbears, patriarchs.

motherhood, maternity; mother, dam, mamma, *materfamilias*; grandmother; matriarch.

Adj. paternal, parental; maternal; matrilinear, patrilineal, patriarchal.

-set; ramification; descendant; heir, -ess; heir -apparent, – presumptive; chip of the old block; heredity; rising generation.

straight descent, sonship, line, lineage, filiation, primogeniture.

Adj. filial.

___

family, ancestral, linear,

168. Productiveness.—N. productiveness &c. *adj.*; fecundity, fertility, luxuriance, uberty.

pregnancy, pullulation, fructification, multiplication, propagation, procreation; superfetation.

milch cow, rabbit, hydra, warren, seed-plot, land flowing with milk and honey; second crop, after-crop, -growth, -math; fertilization.

V. make -productive &c. *adj.*; fructify; procreate, generate, fertilize, spermatize, impregnate; fecund-ate, -ify; teem, pullulate, multiply; produce &c. 161; conceive.

Adj. productive, prolific; teem-ing, -ful; fertile, fruitful, frugiferous, fruit-bearing; fructiferous; fecund, luxuriant; pregnant, uberous.

procre-ant, -ative; generative, life-giving, spermatic; originative; multiparous; omnific; propagable.

parturient &c. (*producing*) 161; profitable &c. (*useful*) 644.

169. Unproductiveness.—N. unproductiveness &c. *adj.*; infertility, sterility, infecundity; impotence &c. 158-unprofitableness &c. (*inutility*) 645.

waste, desert, Sahara, wild, wilderness, howling wilderness.

V. be -unproductive &c. *adj.*; hang fire, flash in the pan, come to nothing.

Adj. unproductive, inoperative, barren, addle, unfertile, unprolific, arid, sterile, unfruitful, acarpous, infecund; *sine prole*; fallow; teem-, issue-, fruitless; unprofitable &c. (*useless*) 645; null and void, of no effect.

___

170. Agency.—N. agency, operation, force, working, strain, function, office, maintenance, exercise, work, swing, play; inter-working, -action, procuration, procurement.

causation &c. 153; instrumentality &c. 631; influence &c. 175; action &c. (*voluntary*) 680; *modus operandi* &c. 627.

quickening –, maintaining- power; home stroke.

V. be -in action &c. *adj.*; operate, work; act, – upon; perform, play, support, sustain, strain, maintain, take effect, quicken, strike.

come –, bring- into -operation, – play; have -play, – free play; bring to bear upon.

Adj. operative, efficient, efficacious, practical, effectual.

at work, on foot; acting &c. (*doing*) 680; in -operation, – force, – action, – play, – exercise; acted –, wrought- upon.

Adv. by the -agency &c. *n.*- of; through &c. (*instrumentality*) 631; by means of &c. 632.

171. Physical Energy.—N. energy, physical energy, force; keenness &c. *adj.*; intensity, vigour, strength, elasticity; go; pep, live wire, high pressure; backbone, mettle, fire, vim.

acri-mony, -tude, -dity; causticity,

172. Physical Inertness.—N. inertness, dulness &c. *adj.*; inertia, *vis inertiæ*, inertion, inactivity, torpor, languor; dormancy, quiescence &c. 265; latency, inaction, passivity.

mental inertness; sloth &c. (*inac-*

virulence, poignancy; harshness &c. *adj.*; severity, edge, point; pungency &c. 392.

cantharides; Spanish fly; seasoning &c. (*condiment*) 393, stimulant, excitant.

activity, agitation, effervescence; ferment, -ation; ebullition, splutter, perturbation, stir, bustle; voluntary energy &c. 682; quicksilver.

resolution &c. (*mental energy*) 604; exertion &c. (*effort*) 686; excitation &c. (*mental*) 824.

V. give -energy &c. *n.*; energize, stimulate, kindle, excite, activate, exert; sharpen, pep up, intensify; inflame &c. (*render violent*) 173; wind up &c. (*strengthen*) 159.

strike, – into, – hard, – home; make an impression.

Adj. strong, energetic, forcible, active; strenuous, forceful, mettlesome, enterprising, go ahead; intense, deep-dyed, severe, keen, vivid, sharp, acute, incisive, trenchant, brisk, vigorous, live.

rousing, irritating; poignant; virulent, caustic, corrosive, mordant, harsh, stringent; double-edged, – shotted, – distilled; drastic, escharotic; racy &c. (*pungent*) 392; sarcastic &c. 932.

potent &c. (*powerful*) 157; radio-active.

Adv. strongly &c. *adj.*; *fortiter in re*; with telling effect.

Phr. the steam is up; *vires acquirit eundo*.

173. Violence.—**N.** violence, inclemency, vehemence, might, impetuosity; boisterousness &c. *adj.*; effervescence, ebullition; turbulence, bluster; uproar, riot, row, rumpus, *le diable à quatre*, devil to pay, all the fat in the fire.

severity &c. 739; ferocity, rage, berserk, fury; exacerbation, exasperation, malignity; fit, paroxysm, orgasm; force, brute force; outrage; *coup de main*; strain, shock, shog; spasm, convulsion, throe; hysterics, passion &c. (*state of excitability*) 825.

out-break, -burst; burst, bounce, dissilience, discharge, volley, explosion, blow up, blast, detonation, rush, eruption, displosion, torrent.

turmoil &c. (*disorder*) 59; ferment &c. (*agitation*) 315; storm, tempest, rough weather; squall &c. (*wind*) 349; earthquake, volcano, thunderstorm.

fury, dragon, demon, tiger, beldame, Tisiphone, Megæra, Alecto, madcap, wild beast; fire-eater &c. (*blusterer*) 887.

V. be -violent &c. *adj.*; run high; ferment, effervesce; romp, rampage; run -wild, – riot; break the peace;

tivity) 683; inexcitability &c. 826; irresolution &c. 605; obstinacy &c. 606; permanence &c. 141.

V. be -inert &c. *adj.*; hang fire, smoulder.

Adj. inert, inactive, passive, pacific; torpid &c. 683; sluggish, stagnant, dull, heavy, flat, slack, tame, slow, blunt; lifeless, dead, uninfluential.

latent, dormant, smouldering, unexerted.

Adv. inactively &c. *adj.*; in -suspense, -abeyance.

——————

174. Moderation.—**N.** moderation; lenity &c. 740; temperance, temperateness, gentleness &c. *adj.*; sobriety; quiet; mental calmness &c. (*inexcitability*) 826.

moderating &c. *v.*; relaxation, remission, mitigation &c. 834; tranquillization, alleviation, assuagement, appeasement, contemporation, pacification.

measure, *juste milieu*, golden mean &c. 29.

moderator; lullaby, sedative, lenitive, demulcent, rose-water, balm, soothing syrup, poppy, opiate, anodyne, milk, opium, laudanum, 'poppy or mandragora'; wet blanket; palliative, calmative.

V. be -moderate &c. *adj.*; keep within -bounds, – compass; sober –, settle-down; keep the peace, remit, relent; take in sail.

moderate, soften, mitigate, temper, accoy; at-, con-temper; mollify, lenify, dull, take off the edge, blunt, obtund, sheathe, subdue, chasten; sober –, tone –, smooth- down; censor, blue-

rush, tear; rush head-long, -foremost; run amuck, raise a storm, make a riot; make –, kick up- a row, – a fuss; bluster, rage, roar, riot, storm; boil, – over; fume, foam, come in like a lion, wreak, bear down, ride rough-shod, out-Herod Herod; spread like wildfire.

break –, fly –, burst- out; bounce, shock, strain; break-, pry-, force-, prize- open.

render -violent &c. *adj.*; sharpen, stir up, quicken, excite, incite, urge, lash, stimulate; irritate, inflame, exacerbate, kindle, suscitate, foment; accelerate, aggravate, exasperate, convulse, infuriate, madden, lash into fury; fan –, add fuel to- the flame; *oleum addere camino.*

explode, go off, displode, fly, detonate, thunder, blow up, flash, flare, erupt, burst; let -off, – fly; discharge, detonize, fulminate.

Adj. violent, vehement, forcible; warm; acute, sharp; rough, rude, ungentle, bluff, boisterous, wild, vicious; brusque, abrupt, waspish; impetuous; rampant.

turbulent; disorderly; blustering, raging &c. *v.*; troublous, riotous; tumultu-ary, -ous; obstreperous, uproarious; extravagant, unmitigated; ravening, tameless; frenzied &c. (*insane*) 503; desperate &c. (*rash*) 863; infuriate, towering, furious, outrageous, frantic, hysteric, in hysterics.

fiery, flaming, scorching, hot, red-hot, ebullient.

savage, fierce, ferocious, fierce as a tiger.

excited &c. *v.*; un-quelled, -quenched, -extinguished, -repressed, -bridled, -ruly; headstrong; un-governable, -appeasable, -mitigable; un-, in-controllable; insup-, irre-pressible.

spasmodic, convulsive, explosive; detonating &c. *v.*; volcanic, meteoric; stormy &c. (*wind*) 349.

Adv. violently &c. *adj.*; amain; by -storm, – force, – main force; with might and main; tooth and nail, *vi et armis*, at the point of the -sword, – bayonet; at one fell swoop; with a high hand, through thick and thin; in desperation, with a vengeance; *à –, à toute-outrance*; head-long, -foremost, -first; like a bull at a gate.

pencil, weaken &c. 160; lessen &c. (*decrease*) 36; check; palliate.

tranquillize, assuage, appease, dulcify, swage, lull, soothe, compose, still, calm, cool, quiet, hush, quell, sober, pacify, tame, damp, lay, allay, rebate, slacken, smooth, alleviate, rock to sleep, deaden, smother; throw -cold water on, – a wet blanket over; slake; curb &c. (*restrain*) 751; tame &c. (*subjugate*) 749; smooth over; pour oil on the -waves, – troubled waters; pour balm into, *mettre de l'eau dans son vin.*

go out like a lamb, 'roar you as gently as any sucking dove.'

Adj. moderate; lenient &c. 740; gentle, mild; cool, sober, temperate, reasonable, measured; tempered &c. *v.*; calm, unruffled, quiet, tranquil, still; slow, smooth, untroubled; tame; peaceful, -able; pacific, halcyon.

un-exciting, -irritating; soft, bland, oily, demulcent, lenitive, anodyne; hypnotic &c. 683; sedative; assuaging.

mild as mother's milk; milk and water; gentle as a lamb.

Adv. moderately &c. *adj.*; gingerly; *piano*; under easy sail, at half speed; within -bounds, – compass; in reason.

Phr. *est modus in rebus.*

4°. INDIRECT POWER

175. Influence.—N. influence; importance &c. 642; weight, pressure, preponderance, prevalence, sway, pull; predomi-nance, -nancy; ascendency; control, dominance, reign; authority

175a. Absence of Influence.—N. impotence &c. 158; inertness &c. 172; irrelevancy &c. 10.

V. have no -influence &c. 175.

Adj. uninfluential; unconduc-ing,

&c. 737; capability &c. (*power*) 157; interest; spell, magic, magnetism.

footing; purchase &c. (*support*) 215; play, leverage, vantage ground.

tower of strength, host in himself; protection, patronage, auspices.

V. have -influence &c. *n.*; be -influential &c. *adj.*; carry weight, actuate, sway, bias, weigh, tell; have a hold upon, magnetize, bear upon, gain a footing, work upon; take -root, – hold; strike root in.

run through, pervade; prevail, dominate, predominate, subject; out-, over-weigh; over-ride, -bear, – come; gain head; rage; be -rife &c. *adj.*; spread like wildfire; have –, get –, gain- -the upper hand, – full play.

be -recognized, – listened to; make one's voice heard, gain a hearing; play a -part, – leading part- in; lead, control, rule, master; get the mastery over; make one's influence felt, cut ice with; take the lead, pull the strings; turn –, throw one's weight into- the scale; set the fashion, lead the dance.

Adj. influential; important &c. 642; weighty; prevailing &c. *v.*; prevalent, rife, rampant, dominant, regnant, predominant, in the ascendant, hegemonical; authoritative, recognized, telling, with authority.

Adv. with telling effect.

176. Tendency.—N. tendency; apt-ness, -itude; proneness, proclivity, bent, turn, tone, bias, set, warp, leaning to, predisposition, inclination, conatus, propensity, susceptibility; liability &c. 177; quality, nature, temperament; characteristic, idio-crasy, -syncrasy; cast, vein, grain; humour, mood; drift &c. (*direction*) 278; con-duciveness, -ducement; applicability &c. (*utility*) 644; subservience &c. (*instrumentality*) 631.

V. tend, contribute, conduce, lead, dispose, incline, verge, bend to, warp, turn, trend, affect, carry, redound to, bid fair to, gravitate towards; promote &c. (*aid*) 707.

Adj. tending &c. *v.*; conducive, working towards, in a fair way to, calculated to; liable &c. 177; subservient &c. (*instrumental*) 631; useful &c. 644; subsidiary &c. (*helping*) 707.

Adv. for, whither.

177. Liability.—N. lia-bility, -bleness; possibility, contingency; suscepti-vity, -bility.

V. be -liable &c. *adj.*; incur, lay oneself open to; run the –, stand a- chance; lie under, expose oneself to, open a door to.

Adj. liable, subject; in danger &c. 665; open –, exposed –, obnoxious- to; answerable, responsible, accountable, amenable; unexempt from; apt to; dependent on; incident to.

contingent, incidental, possible, on the cards, within range of, at the mercy of.

5°. COMBINATIONS OF CAUSES

178. Concurrence.—N. concurrence, cooperation, coagency; coincidence, consilience; union; agreement &c. 23; consent &c. (*assent*) 488; alliance; concert &c. 709; partnership &c. 712; collaboration, conformity.

V. con-cur, -duce, -spire, -tribute;

179. Counteraction.—N. counteraction, opposition; contrariety &c. 14; antagonism, polarity; clashing &c. *v.*; collision, interference, resistance, renitency, friction; reaction; retroaction; repercussion &c. (*recoil*) 277; counterblast; neutralization &c. (*compensa-*

-ive, -ting to; powerless &c. 158; irrelevant &c. 10.

agree, unite, harmonize; hang –, pull-together &c. (*co-operate*) 709; help to &c. (*aid*) 707.

keep pace with, run parallel to; go –, go along –, go hand in hand- with.

Adj. concurring &c. *v.*; concurrent, conformable, joint, co-operative, concordant, coincident, concomitant, harmonious; in alliance with, banded together, of one mind, at one with; parallel.

Adv. with one consent.

tion) 30; *vis inertiæ*; check &c. (*hindrance*) 706.

voluntary -opposition &c. 708, – resistance &c. 719; repression &c. (*restraint*) 751.

V. counteract; run counter, clash, cross; interfere –, conflict- with; jostle; go –, run –, beat –, militate- against; stultify; antagonize, frustrate, oppose &c. 708; withstand &c. (*resist*) 719; hinder &c. 706; repress &c. (*restrain*) 751; react &c. (*recoil*) 277.

undo, neutralize, cancel; counterpoise &c. (*compensate*) 30; overpoise.

Adj. counteracting &c. *v.*; antagonistic, conflicting, retroactive, renitent, reactionary; contrary &c. 14.

Adv. although &c. 30; in spite of &c. 708; *malgré*; against.

CLASS II

Words Relating to SPACE

CLASS II

WORDS RELATING TO SPACE

SECTION I. SPACE IN GENERAL

1°. ABSTRACT SPACE

180. [Indefinite space.] **Space.—N.** space, extension, extent, superficial extent, expanse, stretch; capacity, room, accommodation, scope, range, latitude, field, way, expansion, compass, sweep, play, swing, spread.

spare –, elbow –, house- room; stowage, roomage, margin; opening, sphere, arena; lee-, sea-, head-way.

open –, free- space; wide open spaces; void &c. (*absence*) 187; waste; wild-, wilder-ness; up-, bottom-, moor -land; *campagna, veldt,* prairie, steppe.

abyss &c. (*interval*) 198; unlimited space; infinity &c. 105; world, wide world; ubiquity &c. (*presence*) 186; length and breadth of the land.

proportions, acreage; acres, – roods and perches; square -inches, – yards &c.

Adj. spacious, roomy, extensive, expansive, capacious, ample; wide-spread, vast, world-wide, uncircumscribed; boundless &c. (*infinite*) 105; shore-, track-, path-less; large &c. 192.

Adv. extensively &c. *adj.*; wherever; everywhere; far and -near, – wide; right and left, all over, all the world over; throughout the -world, – length and breadth of the land; under the sun, in every quarter; in all -quarters, – lands; here, there and everywhere; from -pole to pole, – China to Peru, – Indus to the pole, – Dan to Beersheba, – end to end; on the face of the earth, in the wide world, from all points of the compass; to the -four winds, – uttermost parts of the earth.

180a. Inextension.—N. in-, nonextension; point; atom &c. (*smallness*) 32; pinprick; limitation &c. 229.

181. [Definite space.] **Region.—N.** region, sphere, sphere of influence, corridor, ground, soil, area, realm, hemisphere, quarter district, beat, orb, circuit, circle; pale &c. (*limit*) 233; com-, de-partment; domain, tract, territory, terrain, country, canton, county, shire, province, *arrondissement,* diocese, parish, township, borough, constituency, *commune,* ward, wapentake, hundred, riding, lathe, garth, soke, tithing, bailiwick; empire, kingdom, principality, duchy, grand –, arch- duchy, palatinate; republic, commonwealth, dominion, colony, state, island.

arena, precincts, *enceinte,* walk, march; patch, plot, enclosure, &c. 232; close, *enclave,* field, court; street &c. (*abode*) 189.

clime, climate, zone, meridian, latitude.

Adj. territorial, local, parochial, provincial, insular.

182. [Limited space.] **Place.—N.** place, lieu, spot, point, dot; niche, nook, &c. (*corner*) 244; hole; pigeonhole &c. (*receptacle*) 191; compartment; premises, precinct, station, confine; area, court, yard, quadrangle, square, compound; abode &c. 189; locality &c. (*situation*) 183.

ins and outs; every hole and corner.

Adv. somewhere, in some place, wherever it may be, here and there, in various places, *passim.*

2°. Relative Space

183. Situation.—N. situation, position, locality, *locale*, *status*, latitude and longitude; footing, standing, standpoint, post; stage; aspect, attitude, posture, *pose*.

place, site, base, station, seat, *venue*, whereabouts, environment, neighbourhood; bearings &c. (*direction*) 278; spot &c. (*limited space*) 182.

top-, ge-, chor-ography; map &c. 554.

V. be -situated, – situate; lie; have its seat in.

Adj. situ-ate, -ated; local, topical, topographical &c. *n.*

Adv. *in -situ*, – *loco*; here and there, *passim*; here-, there-, whereabouts; in place, here, there.

in –, amidst- such and such- -surroundings, – *environs*, – *entourage*.

184. Location.—N. loca-tion, -liza-tion; lodgment; de-, re-position; stow-, pack-age; collocation; packing, lading; establishment, settlement, installation; fixation; insertion &c. 300.

anchorage, roadstead, mooring, mooring mast, encampment, camp, bivouac.

plantation, colony, settlement, cantonment, encampment, reservation; colonization, domestication, situation; habitation &c. (*abode*) 189; cohabitation; 'a local habitation and a name'; indenization, naturalization.

V. place, situate, locate, localize, make a place for, put, lay, set, seat, station, lodge, quarter, post, install; storehouse, stow; establish, fix, pin, root; graft; plant &c. (*insert*) 300; shelve, pitch, camp, lay down, deposit, reposit; cradle; moor, tether, picket; pack, tuck in; embed; vest, invest in.

billet on, quarter upon, saddle with; load, lade, freight; pocket, put up, bag.

inhabit &c. (*be present*) 186; domesticate, colonize, populate, people; take –, strike- root; anchor; cast –, come to an- anchor; sit –, settle-down; settle; take up one's -abode, – quarters; plant –, establish –, locate- oneself; squat, perch, hive, *se nicher*, bivouac, burrow, get a footing; encamp, pitch one's tent; put up -at, – one's horses at; keep house.

indenizen, naturalize, adopt.

put back, replace &c. (*restore*) 660.

Adj. placed &c. *v.*; situate, posited, ensconced, embedded, embosomed, rooted; domesticated; vested in, unremoved.

moored &c. *v.*; at anchor.

185. Displacement.—N. displacement, elocation, transposition.

ejectment &c. 297; exile &c. (*banishment*) 893; removal &c. (*transference*) 270; unshipment.

misplacement, dislocation &c. 61; fish out of water.

V. dis-place, -plant, -lodge, -nest, -establish; misplace, unseat, disturb; exile &c. (*seclude*) 893; ablegate, set aside, remove; take –, cart- away; take –, draft- off; lade &c. 184, unship.

unload, empty &c. (*eject*) 297; transfer &c. 270; dispel.

vacate; depart &c. 293.

Adj. displaced &c. *v.*; un-placed, -housed, -harboured, -established, -settled; house-, home-less; out of -place, – a situation.

misplaced, out of its element.

3°. Existence in Space

186. Presence.—N. presence; occupancy, -ation; attendance; whereness.

permeation, pervasion; diffusion &c. (*dispersion*) 73.

187. [Nullibiety.*] **Absence. — N.** absence; inexistence &c. 2; non-residence, absenteeism; non-attendance, *alibi.*

* Bishop Wilkins.

ubi-ety, -quity, -quitariness; omni-presence.

bystander &c. (*spectator*) 444.

V. exist in space, be -present &c. *adj.*; assist at; make one -of, − at; look on, attend, remain; find −, present- oneself; show one's face; fall in the way of, occur in a place; lie, stand; occupy.

people; inhabit, dwell, reside, stay, sojourn, live, room, abide, bunk, lodge, nestle, roost, perch; take up one's abode &c. (*be located*) 184; tenant, occupy.

resort to, frequent, haunt; revisit.

fill, pervade, permeate; be -diffused, − disseminated- through; over-spread, -run; run through; meet one at every turn.

Adj. present; occupying, inhabiting &c. *v.*; moored &c. 184; residential, resi-ant, -dent, -dentiary; domiciled.

ubiquit-ous, -ary; omnipresent.

peopled, populous, full of people, inhabited.

Adv. here, there, where, everywhere, aboard, on board, at home, afield; on the spot; here, there and everywhere &c. (*space*) 180; in presence of, before; under the -eyes, − nose- of; in the face of; *in propriâ personâ.*

emptiness &c. *adj.*; void, *vacuum*; vac-uity, -ancy; *tabula rasa*; exemption; *hiatus* &c. (*interval*) 198; no man's land.

truant, absentee.

nobody; nobody -present, − on earth; no one; not a soul; *âme qui vive.*

V. be -absent &c. *adj.*; keep -away, − out of the way; play truant, absent oneself, stay away.

withdraw, make oneself scarce, vacate; go away, slip out, slip away, retreat &c. 293.

Adj. absent, not present, away, non-resident, gone, from home; missing; lost; wanted, wanting; omitted; nowhere to be found; inexistent &c. 2.

empty, void; blank, vac-ant, -uous; untenanted, -occupied, -inhabited; tenantless; desert, -ed; devoid; un-, uninhabitable.

exempt from, not having.

Adv. without, *minus*, nowhere; elsewhere; neither here nor there; in default of; *sans*; behind one's back.

Phr. the bird has flown, *non est inventus.*

---

188. Inhabitant. — N. inhabitant; habitant, resident, -iary; dweller, indweller; occup-ier, -ant, farmer, planter; householder, lodger, boarder, paying guest; inmate, tenant, renter, incumbent, sojourner, *locum tenens*, commorant; settler, squatter, backwoodsman, colonist; islander; denizen, citizen; burgher, oppidan, cockney, cit, townsman, burgess; villager; cot-tager, -tier, -ter; compatriot.

native, indigene, aboriginal, aborigines, autochthones; Briton, Englishman, John Bull; new comer &c. (*stranger*) 57.

garrison, crew; population; people &c. (*mankind*) 372; colony, settlement; household.

V. inhabit &c. (*be present*) 186; in-denizen &c. (*locate oneself*) 184.

Adj. indigenous; enchorial; national, nat-ive, -al; autochthonous; British, English; colonial; domestic; domicil-

189. [Place of habitation, or resort.] **Abode.—N.** abode, dwelling, lodging, -s; diggings, domicile, residence, address, habitation, where one's lot is cast, local habitation, berth, seat, lap, sojourn, housing, quarters, headquarters, resiance, tabernacle, throne, ark.

home, fatherland, mother country, country &c. 181; home-stead, -stall; fireside, chimney corner; hearth, − stone; household gods, *lares et penates*, roof, household, housing, *dulce domum*, paternal domicile; native -soil, − land, blighty.

nest, *nidus*, snuggery; arbour, bower &c. 191; lair, den, cave, hole, hiding-place, cell, *sanctum sanctorum*, aerie, eyry, rookery, hive; *habitat*, haunt, covert, resort, retreat, perch, roost; nidification.

bivouac, camp, encampment, cantonment, castrametation; barrack, casemate, casern.

iated, -ed; naturalized, vernacular, domesticated; domiciliary.

in the occupation of; garrisoned –, occupied- by.

_____

tent &c. (*covering*) 223; building &c. (*construction*) 161; chamber &c. (*receptacle*) 191.

tenement, messuage, farm, farm-house, grange, *hacienda*.

cot, cabin, log cabin, shack, hut, *châlet*, croft, shed, booth, stall, hovel, bothy, shanty, igloo, tepee, wigwam; pen &c. (*inclosure*) 232; barn, bawn; kennel, sty, dog-hole, cote, coop, hutch, byre; cow-house, -shed; stable, dove-cote, shippen.

house, mansion, place, villa, cottage, box, lodge, hermitage, *rus in urbe*, folly, rotunda, tower, *château*, castle, pavilion, hotel, court, manor-house, capital messuage, hall, palace, alcazar; country seat; kiosk, bungalow; temple &c. 1000; home of rest, alms-, poor-, work-house, asylum; boarding-, lodging-house; flat, maisonette, duplex, penthouse, suite of rooms, apartments, rooms, room, building &c. 161; Mansion House, town hall, Capitol.

assembly-room, auditorium, coliseum, meeting-house, pump-room, spa, health resort, watering-place; club; theatre &c. 840; drill hall, gymnasium, church &c. 1000; Houses of Parliament &c. 696; school &c. 542; inn; hostel, -ry; hotel, tavern, caravansary, khan, hospice; public-, ale-, pot-, mug-house; gin-palace, gin mill; coffee-, eating-house; canteen, *restaurant*, *rôtisserie*, cafeteria, grill-room, *buffet*, *café*, *estaminet*, *posada*, *bodega*; bar; saloon, speakeasy, shebeen.

hamlet, village, thorp, dorp, ham, kraal; borough, burgh, town, county-seat, – town, city, capital, metropolis; suburb, quarter, parish &c. 181; ghetto; province, country.

street, place, terrace, parade, esplanade, promenade, pier, embankment, road, villas, row, walk, lane, alley, court, quadrangle, quad, wynd, close, yard, passage, rents, mansions, buildings, mews.

square, polygon, circus, crescent, mall, *piazza*, arcade, colonnade, peristyle, cloister; gardens, grove, residences; block of buildings, market-place, *place*.

anchorage, roadstead, roads; dock, basin, wharf, quay, port, harbour; dry-, graving-, floating-dock.

garden, park, pleasure-ground, pleasance, demesne.

V. take up one's abode &c. (*locate oneself*) 184; inhabit &c. (*be present*) 186.

Adj. urban, oppidan, metropolitan; suburban; provincial, rural, rustic; countrified; regional, parochial, domestic; cosmopolitan; palatial.

190. [Things contained.] **Contents.—N.** contents; cargo, lading, freight, shipment, load, bale, burden; cart-, ship-load; cup –, basket –, &c. (*receptacle*) 191- of; inside &c. 221; stuffing, ullage.

V. load, lade, ship, charge, fill, stuff.

191. Receptacle.—N. receptacle, container; inclosure &c. 232; recipient, receiver, reservatory.

compartment; cell, -ule; follicle; hole, corner, niche, recess, nook; crypt, stall, pigeon-hole, cove, oriel; cave &c. (*concavity*) 252.

capsule, vesicle, cyst, pod, calyx, *cancelli*, utricle, bladder, udder.

stomach, paunch, *venter*, abdomen, ventricle, crop, craw, ingluvies, maw, gizzard, bread-basket, belly, little Mary; mouth.

pocket, pouch, fob, sheath, scabbard, socket, bag, vanity bag, compact, sac, sack, saccule, despatch –, attaché-, tachy- case, wallet, scrip, card-, note- case, billfold, poke, knit, knap-, haver-, ruck-sack, sachel, satchel, reticule, budget, net; ditty-, -box, -bag, kitbag; portfolio; saddlebags, holster; quiver &c. (*magazine*) 636.

chest, box, coffer, caddy, case, casket, pyx, pix, *caisson*, desk, *bureau*, reliquary, shrine; trunk, portmanteau, band-box, *valise*, suitcase, hand-, traveling-, overnight-, Gladstone-, carpet-bag, brief case; boot, imperial; *vache*; cage, manger, rack.

vessel, vase, bushel, barrel; canister, jar; pottle, basket, punnet, pannier, buck-basket, hopper, maund, creel, cran, crate, cradle, bassinet, wisket, whisket, *jardinière*, *corbeille*, hamper, wastepaper basket, dosser, dorser, tray, hod, scuttle, utensil, spittoon, cuspidor.

[For liquids] cistern &c. (*store*) 636; vat, caldron, barrel, cask, puncheon, keg, rundlet, tun, butt, firkin, hogshead, kilderkin, carboy, amphora, ampulla, bottle, jar, leather bottle, decanter, ewer, cruse, carafe, crock, kit, canteen, flagon; demijohn; flask, -et; stoup, noggin, vial, phial, ampoulé, cruet, caster; gourd; urn, *épergne*, salver, *patella*, *tazza*, *patera*; pig-, big-gin; tea-, coffee-pot, percolator, *samovar*; tyg, nipperkin, pocket-pistol; tub, bucket, pail, skeel, pot, tankard, jug, pitcher, toby, mug, pipkin; gal-, gall-ipot, pannikin; matrass, receiver, retort, alembic, bolthead, can, kettle; bowl, basin, jorum, punch-bowl, cup, goblet, chalice, tumbler, glass, wineglass, rummer, beaker, tass, horn, saucepan, skillet, posnet, tureen, terrine, *casserole*, sauce-, gravy-boat.

plate, platter, paten, dish, vegetable –, *entrée*- dish, trencher, calabash, porringer, potager, saucer, pan, crucible.

shovel, trowel, spoon; table-, dessert-, tea-, egg-, salt-spoon; spatula, ladle; dipper; baler; watch-glass, thimble.

closet, commode, cupboard, cellaret, *chiffonnière*, locker, bin, bunker, *buffet*, press, safe, sideboard, drawer, chest of drawers, till, *scrutoire*, *secrétaire*, *écritoire*, davenport, book-case, cabinet, canterbury; corner cupboard, wardrobe.

chamber, apartment, room, cabin; office, court, hall, atrium; suite of rooms, flat, story; saloon, *salon*, parlour; presence-chamber; sitting-, drawing-, reception-, state-, living-, work-room; gallery, cabinet, closet, cubicle; pew, box; *boudoir*; *adytum, sanctum*; bed-room, dormitory, dressing-room; refectory, dining-room, *salle-à-manger*; nursery, school-room; library, study; *studio*; billiard-, bath-, smoking-room; den, canteen, mess, officers' mess; gun-, ward-, mess-room.

attic, loft, garret, cockloft, clerestory; cellar, vault, hold, cockpit; *entre-sol*; mezzanine floor; ground-floor, *rez-de-chaussée*; basement, kitchen, cook-house, galley, pantry, scullery, offices; store-room &c. (*depository*) 636; lumber-room; dust-hole, -bin; dairy, laundry, coach-house; *garage*; *hangar*; out-, pent-house; lean-to.

portico, porch, piazza, verandah, lobby, court, hall, vestibule, corridor, passage; ante-room, -chamber; lounge; *foyer, loggia*.

conservatory, green-house, glass-house, vinery, bower, arbour, summer-house, alcove, grotto, hermitage, pergola.

lodging &c. (*abode*) 189; bed &c. (*support*) 215; carriage &c. (*vehicle*) 272.

Adj. capsular; saccu-lar, -lated; recipient; ventricular, cystic, vascular, vesicular, cellular, camerated, locular, multilocular, poly-gastric; marsupial; siliqu-ose, -ous.

Section II.   DIMENSIONS

1°. General Dimensions

192. Size.—**N.** size, magnitude, dimension, bulk, volume; largeness &c. *adj.*; greatness &c. (*of quantity*) 31; expanse &c. (*space*) 180; amplitude, mass; proportions.

capacity; ton-, tun-nage; calibre, scantling.

turgidity &c. (*expansion*) 194; corpulence, obesity; plumpness, &c. *adj.*; *embonpoint*, corporation, flesh and blood, lustihood.

hugeness &c. *adj.*; enormity, immensity, monstrosity.

giant, Brobdingnagian, Antæus, Goliath, Gog and Magog, Gargantua, monster, mammoth, Cyclops; whale, porpoise, behemoth, leviathan, elephant, hippopotamus; colossus; tun, lump, bulk, block, loaf, mass, clod, nugget, bushel, thumper, whopper, spanker, strapper; Triton among the minnows.

mountain, mound; heap &c. (*assemblage*) 72.

largest portion &c. 50; full-, life-size.

V. ve- large &c. *adj.*; become -large &c. (*expand*) 194.

Adj. large, big; great &c. (*in quantity*) 31; considerable, bulky, voluminous, ample, massive, massy; capacious, comprehensive; spacious &c. 180; mighty, towering, fine, magnificent.

corpulent, stout, fat, plump, squab, full, lusty, strapping, bouncing; portly, burly, well-fed, full-grown; stalwart, brawny, fleshy; goodly; in good -case, – condition; in condition; chopping, jolly; chub-, chubby-faced.

lubberly, hulky, unwieldy, lumpish, gaunt, spanking, whacking, whopping, thumping, thundering, hulking; overgrown; puffy &c. (*swollen*) 194.

huge, immense, enormous, mighty; vast, -y; amplitudinous, stupendous; monst-er, -rous; gigantic, elephantine;

193. Littleness.—**N.** littleness &c. *adj.*; smallness &c. (*of quantity*) 32; exiguity, inextension; parvi-tude, -ty; duodecimo; Elzevir edition, epitome, microcosm; rudiment; vanishing point; thinness &c. 203.

dwarf, pigmy, atomy, Liliputian, midget, chit, pigwidgeon, urchin, elf; doll, puppet; Tom Thumb, Hop-o'-my thumb, Humpty-dumpty; man-. mannikin; *homunculus*, dapperling, fingerling, dandiprat, cock-sparrow, scalawag.

animalcule, monad, mite, insect, emmet, fly, midge, gnat, shrimp, minnow, worm, maggot, entozoon; *bacillus*, microbe, micro-organism, *bacteria*; *infusoria*; microbe; grub; tit, tomtit, runt, mouse, small fry; millet-, mustard-seed; barley-corn; pebble, grain of sand; mole-hill, button, bubble.

point; atom &c. (*small quantity*) 32; fragment &c. (*small part*) 51; powder &c. 330; point of a pin, mathematical point; *minutiæ* &c. (*unimportance*) 643.

micro-graphy, -meter, -scope; vernier; scale.

V. be -little &c. *adj.*; lie in a nutshell; become small &c. (*decrease*) 36, (*contract*) 195.

Adj. little; small &c. (*in quantity*) 32; minute, diminutive, microscopic; inconsiderable &c. (*unimportant*) 643; exiguous, puny, tiny, wee, petty, minikin, miniature, pigmy, elfin; under sized; dwarf, -ed, -ish; spare, stunted, limited; cramp, -ed; pollard, Liliputian, dapper, pocket; port-ative, -able; duodecimo; dumpy, squat; compact, handy; short &c. 201.

impalpable, intangible, evanescent, imperceptible, invisible, inappreciable, infinitesimal, homœopathic; atomic, corpuscular, molecular; rudiment-ary, -al; embryonic.

weazen, scant, scraggy, scrubby;

giant, -like; colossal, Cyclopean, Brobdingnagian, Gargantuan, Titanic; infinite &c. 105.

large as life; plump as a -dumpling,
– partridge; fat as -a pig, – a quail,
– butter, – brawn, – bacon.

194. Expansion. — N. expansion;
increase &c. 35 -of size; enlargement,
extension, augmentation; ampli-fica-
tion, -ation; aggrandizement, spread,
increment, growth, development, pullulation, swell, dilation, dilatation, rarefaction; turg-escence, -idness, -idity;
obesity &c. (*size*) 192; dropsy, tume-
faction, intumescence, swelling, tumour, *diastole*, distension; puff-ing,
-iness; inflation; pandiculation.

dilatability, expansibility.

germination, growth, upgrowth; accretion &c. 35.

over-growth, -distension; hypertrophy, tympany.

bulb &c. (*convexity*) 250; plumper;
superiority of size.

V. become -larger &c. (large &c. 192);
expand, widen, enlarge, extend, grow,
increase, incrassate, swell, gather; fill
out; deploy, take open order, dilate,
stretch, spread; mantle, wax; grow –,
spring- up; bud, bourgeon, shoot,
sprout, germinate, put forth, vegetate,
pullulate, open, burst forth, flower,
blow &c. 734; gain –, gather- flesh;
outgrow; spread like wildfire, overrun.

be larger than; surpass &c. (*be superior*) 33.

render -larger &c. (large &c. 192);
expand, spread, extend, aggrandize,
distend, develop, amplify, spread out,
widen, magnify, rarefy, inflate, puff,
puff out, blow up, stuff, pad, cram;
exaggerate; fatten.

Adj. expanded &c. *v.*; larger &c.
(large &c. 192); swollen; expansive;
wide-open, -spread; fan-shaped; flabelliform; overgrown, exaggerated,
bloated, fat, turgid, tumid, hyper-
trophied, dropsical; pot-, swag-bellied;
œdematous, obese, puffy, pursy,
blowzy, distended; patulous; bulbous &c. (*convex*) 250; full-blown,
-grown, -formed; big &c. 192.

196. Distance.—N. distance; space
&c. 180; remoteness, farness; far- cry

thin &c. (*narrow*) 203; granular &c.
(*powdery*) 330; shrunk &c. 195.

Adv. in a -small compass, – nutshell;
on a small scale.

---

195. Contraction.—N. contraction,
reduction, diminution; decrease &c. 36-
of size; defalcation, decrement; lessening, shrinkage; collapse, emaciation,
attenuation, tabefaction, consumption,
marasmus, atrophy; systole, neck,
hour-glass.

condensation, compression, constraint, compactness; compendium &c.
596; squeezing &c. *v.*; strangulation;
corrugation; astringency, constrin-
gency; astringents, sclerotics; contractility, compressibility; coarctation.

inferiority in size.

V. become -small, – smaller; lessen,
decrease &c. 36; grow less, dwindle,
shrink, contract, narrow, shrivel, collapse, wither, lose flesh, wizen, fall
away, waste, wane, ebb; decay &c.
(*deteriorate*) 659.

be smaller than, fall short of; not
come up to &c. (*be inferior*) 34.

render smaller, lessen, diminish, contract, draw in, narrow, coarctate; constrict, constringe; condense, compress,
boil down, deflate, exhaust, empty;
squeeze, corrugate, crush, crumple up,
warp, purse up, pack, stow; pinch,
tighten, strangle; cramp; dwarf, bedwarf; shorten &c. 201; circumscribe
&c. 229; restrain &c. 751; fold &c. 258.

pare, reduce, attenuate, rub down,
scrape, file, grind, chip, shave, shear.

Adj. contracting &c. *v.*; astringent;
shrunk, contracted &c. *v.*; strangulated,
tabid, wizened, stunted; tabescent;
marasmic; waning &c. *v.*; neap; compact.

unexpanded &c. (expand &c. 194);
inswept; contractile; compressible;
smaller &c. (small &c. 193).

---

197. Nearness.—N. nearness &c.
adj.; proximity, propinquity; vicinity,

to; longinquity, elongation; offing, background; removedness; parallax; reach, span, stride; drift.

out-post, -skirt; horizon, sky-line; aphelion; foreign parts, *ultima Thule*, *ne plus ultra*, antipodes; long range, giant's stride.

dispersion &c. 73.

V. be -distant &c. *adj.*; extend –, stretch –, reach –, spread –, go –, get –, stretch away- to; range, outrange, outreach.

remain at a distance; keep –, stand- -away, – off, – aloof, – clear of.

Adj. distant; far -off, – away; remote, telescopic, distal, wide of; stretching to &c. *v.*; yon, -der; ulterior; trans-marine, -pontine, -atlantic, -alpine; tramontane; ultra-montane, -mundane; hyperborean, antipodean; inaccessible, out of the way; unapproach-ed, -able; incontiguous.

Adv. far -off, – away; afar, -off; off; away; a -long, – great, – good- way off; wide away, aloof; wide –, clear- of; out of -the way, – reach; abroad, yonder, farther, further, beyond; *outre mer*, over the border, far and wide, over the hills and far away; from pole to pole &c. (*over great space*) 180; to the -uttermost parts, – ends- of the earth; out of -hearing, – range, nobody knows where, *à perte de vue*, out of the sphere of, wide of the mark; a far cry to.

apart, asunder; wide -apart, – asunder; *longo intervallo*; at arm's length.

-age; neighbourhood, adjacency; contiguity &c. 199.

short -distance, – step, – cut; earshot, close quarters, stone's throw; bow –, gun –, pistol- shot; hair's breadth, span; close-up.

purlieus, neighbourhood, vicinage, *environs*, *alentours*, suburbs, confines, *banlieue*, borderland; whereabouts.

bystander; neighbour, borderer.

approach &c. 286; convergence &c. 290; perihelion.

V. be -near &c. *adj.*; adjoin, hang about, trench on; border –, verge upon; stand by, approximate, tread on the heels of, cling to, clasp, hug; cuddle, huddle; hang upon the skirts of, hover over; burn; abut.

bring –, draw- -near &c. 286; converge &c. 290; crowd &c. 72; place -side by side &c. *adv.*

Adj. near, nigh; close –, near- at hand; close, neighbouring, propinquent, bordering upon; adjacent, adjoining, limitrophe; proxim-ate, -al; at hand, handy; near the mark, near run; home, intimate.

Adv. near, nigh; hard –, fast- by; close -to, – upon, – up; at the point of; next door to; within -reach, – call, – hearing, – earshot, – range; within an ace of; but a step, not far from, at no great distance; on the -verge, – brink, – skirts- of; in the -environs &c. *n.*; at one's -door, – feet, – elbow, – finger's end, – side; on the tip of one's tongue; under one's nose; within a -stone's throw &c. *n.*; in -sight, – presence- of; at close quarters; cheek by -jole, – jowl; beside, alongside, side by side, *tête-à-tête*; in juxtaposition &c. (*touching*) 199; yard-arm to yard-arm; at the heels of; on the confines of, at the threshold, bordering upon, verging to; in the way.

about; here-, there-abouts; roughly, in round numbers; approxim- -ately, -atively; as good as, well nigh.

198. Interval.—**N.** interval, interspace; separation &c. 44; break, gap, opening; hole &c. 260; chasm, *hiatus*, cæsura; inter-ruption, -regnum; interstice, *lacuna*, cleft, mesh, crevice, chink, rime, creek, cranny, crack, chap, slit, slot, fissure, scissure, rift, flaw, breach, fracture, rent, gash, cut, leak, dike, ha-ha.

199. Contiguity. — N. contiguity, contact, proximity, apposition, juxtaposition, touching &c. *v.*; abutment, osculation; meeting, appulse, appulsion, *rencontre*, rencounter, syzygy, coincidence, conjunction, coexistence; adhesion &c. 46.

border-land; frontier &c. (*limit*) 233; tangent.

gorge, defile, ravine, cañon, *crevasse*, abyss, abysm; gulf; inlet, frith, strait, gully, gulch, nullah; pass; notch; furrow &c. 259; yawning gulf; *hiatus -maxime, – valde- deflendus*; parenthesis &c. (*interjacence*) 228; void &c. (*absence*) 187; incompleteness &c. 530.

V. gape &c. (*open*) 260.

Adj. with an interval, far between.

Adv. at intervals &c. (*discontinuously*) 70; *longo intervallo*.

V. be -contiguous &c. *adj.*; join, adjoin, abut on, march with, border; tick, graze, touch, meet, osculate, kiss, come in contact, coincide; coexist; adhere &c. 46.

Adj. contiguous; touching &c. *v.*; in -contact &c. *n.*; conterminous, end to end, osculatory; pertingent; tangential.

hand to hand; close to &c. (*near*) 197; with no -interval &c. 198.

2°. LINEAR DIMENSIONS

200. Length.—**N.** length, longitude, span, extent, mileage.

line, bar, rule, stripe, streak, spoke, radius.

lengthening &c. *v.*; pro-longation, -duction, -traction; ten-sion, -sure; extension.

[Measures of length] line, nail, inch, hand, palm, foot, cubit, yard, ell, fathom, rod, pole, perch, furlong, mile, league; chain, metre, kilo-, centi-, milli- &c. -metre.

pedometer, perambulator, odometer, odograph, speedometer, cyclometer, log, telemeter, range finder; scale &c. (*measurement*) 466.

V. be -long &c. *adj.*; stretch out, sprawl; extend –, reach –, stretch- to; make a long arm, 'drag its slow length along.'

render -long &c. *adj.*; lengthen, extend, elongate; stretch; pro-long, -duce, -tract; let –, pay –, draw –, spin- out; drawl.

enfilade, look along, view in perspective.

Adj. long, -some; lengthy, lank, wire-drawn, outstretched; lengthened &c. *v.*; sesquipedalian &c. (*words*) 577; interminable, no end of.

line-ar, -al; longitudinal, oblong.

as long as -my arm, – to-day and to-morrow; unshortened &c. (shorten &c. 201).

Adv. lengthwise, at length, longitudinally, endlong, along; *tandem*; in a line &c. (*continuously*) 69; in perspective.

from -end to end, – stem to stern, – head to foot, – the crown of the head to the sole of the foot, – top to toe, – head to heels; fore and aft.

201. Shortness.—**N.** shortness &c. *adj.*; brevity; littleness &c. 193; a span.

shortening &c. *v.*; abbrevia-tion, -ture; abridgment, concision, retrenchment, curtailment, decurtation; reduction &c. (*contraction*) 195; epitome &c. (*compendium*) 596.

abridger, abstractor, epitomiser.

elision, ellipsis; conciseness &c. (*in style*) 572.

V. be -short &c. *adj.*; render -short &c. *adj.*; shorten, curtail, abridge, abbreviate, take in, reduce; compress &c. (*contract*) 195; epitomize &c. 596.

retrench, cut short, obtruncate; scrimp, cut, chop up, hack, hew; cut –, pare- down; clip, snip, dock, lop, prune; shear, shave, mow, reap, crop; snub; truncate, pollard, stunt, nip, nip in the bud, check the growth of; [in drawing] foreshorten.

Adj. short, brief, curt; compendious, compact; stubby, scrimp; shorn, stubbed; stumpy, thickset, podgy, stocky, pug; squab, -by; squat, dumpy; little &c. 193; curtailed of its fair proportions; short by; oblate; concise &c. 572; summary.

Adv. shortly &c. *adj.*; in short &c. (*concisely*) 572.

202. Breadth. Thickness.—N.

breadth, width, latitude, amplitude; diameter, bore, calibre, radius; superficial extent &c. (*space*) 180.

thickness, crassitude; corpulence &c. (*size*) 192; dilatation &c. (*expansion*) 194.

V. be -broad &c. *adj.*; become –, render- -broad &c. *adj.*; expand &c. 194; thicken, widen.

Adj. broad, wide, ample, extended; discous;fan-like;out-spread,-stretched; wide as a church-door.

thick, dumpy, squab, squat, thickset, tubby; thick as a rope, stubby &c. 201.

203. Narrowness. Thinness. —N.

narrowness &c. *adj.*; closeness, exility; exiguity &c. (*little*) 193.

line; hair's –, finger's -breadth; strip, streak, vein.

thinness &c. *adj.*; tenuity; emaciation, macilency, *marcor*.

shaving, slip &c. (*filament*) 205; threadpaper, skeleton, shadow, scrag, anatomy, spindle-shanks, barebones, lantern jaws, mere skin and bone.

middle constriction, stricture, neck, waist, isthmus, wasp, hour-glass; ridge, *ghaut*, pass; ravine &c. 198.

narrowing, coarctation, angustation, tapering; contraction &c. 195.

V. be -narrow &c. *adj.*; narrow, taper, contract &c. 195; render -narrow &c. *adj.*

Adj. narrow, close; slender, thin, fine; *svelte*; thread-like &c. (*filament*) 205; finespun, taper, slim, gracile, slight, slight-made; scant, -y; spare, delicate, incapacious; contracted &c. 195; unexpanded &c. (expand &c. 194); slender as a thread, capillary.

emaciated, lean, meagre, gaunt, macilent; lank, -y; weedy, skinny, scrawny, scraggy; starv-ed, -eling; attenuated, shrivelled, wizened, pinched, peaky, skeletal, spindling, spindle- -legged, -shanked; extenuated, tabid, marcid, bare-bone, raw-boned; herring-gutted; worn to a shadow, lean as a rake; thin as a -lath, – whipping post, – wafer; hatchet-faced; lantern-jawed.

204. Layer.—N.

layer, stratum, course, bed, zone, *substratum*, floor, flag, stage, story, tier, slab, escarpment, table, tablet, panel, plaque; board, plank; trencher, platter.

plate; lam-ina, -ella; sheet, flake, foil, wafer, scale, coat, peel, pellicle, ply, thickness, membrane, film, leaf, slice, shive, cut, rasher, shaving, integument &c. (*covering*) 223.

stratification, lamination, scaliness, nest of boxes, coats of an onion.

V. slice, shave, pare, peel; plate, coat, veneer; cover &c. 223.

Adj. lamell-ar, -ated, -iform; laminated, -iferous; micaceous; schist-ose, -ous; scaly, filmy, membranous, flaky, squamous; folia-ted, -ceous; stratified, -form; tabular, discoid, spathic.

205. Filament.—N.

filament, line; fibre, fibril; funicle, vein, hair, capillament, *cilium*, tendril, gossamer; hairstroke; harl.

wire, string, thread, packthread, cotton, sewing-silk, twine, twist, whipcord, cord, rope, cable, yarn, hemp, oakum, jute, wool, worsted.

strip, shred, slip, spill, list, band, fillet, *fascia*, ribbon, riband, tape, roll, lath, slat, strake, splinter, shiver, shaving.

beard &c. (*roughness*) 256; ramification; strand.

Adj. fil-amentous, -aceous, -iform; fibr-ous, -illous; thread-like, wiry, stringy, ropy; capill-ary, -iform; funicular, wire-drawn; anguilliform; flagelliform; hairy &c. (*rough*) 256; ligulate.

206. Height.—N.

height, altitude, elevation, ceiling; eminence. pitch; loftiness &c. *adj.*; sublimity.

tallness &c. *adj.*; stature, procerity; prominence &c. 250.

207. Lowness.—N.

lowness &c. *adj.*; debasement, depression; prostration &c. (*horizontal*) 213; depression &c. (*concave*) 252.

molehill; lowlands; bottomlands;

colossus &c. (*size*) 192; giant, grenadier, giraffe.

mount, -ain; hill, butte, monticle, fell, knap; cape; head-, fore-land; promontory; ridge, hog's back, dune; rising -, vantage- ground; down; moor, -land; Alp; up-, high-lands; heights &c. (*summit*) 210; knoll, hummock, hillock, barrow, mound, mole, *kopje*; steeps, bluff, cliff, craig, tor, peak, pike, clough; escarpment, edge, ledge, brae; dizzy height.

tower, pillar, column, pylon, obelisk, monument, steeple, spire, minaret, *campanile*, belfry, turret, roof, dome, cupola, pagoda, pyramid; sky scraper; Eiffel tower.

pole, pikestaff, maypole, flagstaff; mast, top -, topgallant- mast.

ceiling &c. (*covering*) 223.

high water; high -, flood -, spring- tide.

altimetry &c. (*angle*) 244; altimeter, height-finder, hypsometer, barograph.

V. be -high &c. *adj.*; tower, soar, command; hover; cap, culminate; overhang, hang over, impend, beetle; bestride, ride, mount; perch, surmount; cover &c. 233; overtop &c. (*be superior*) 33; stand on tiptoe.

become -high &c. *adj.*; grow, - higher, - taller; upgrow; rise &c. (*ascend*) 305.

render -high &c. *adj.*; heighten &c. (*elevate*) 307.

Adj. high, elevated, eminent, exalted, lofty, supernal; tall; gigantic &c. (*big*) 192; Patagonian; towering, beetling, soaring, hanging [gardens]; elevated &c. 307; upper; highest &c. (*topmost*) 210; monticolous, perching, hill-dwelling.

up-, moor-land; hilly, mountainous, alpine, sub-alpine, heaven-kissing; cloud-topt, -capt, -touching; aerial.

overhanging &c. *v.*; incumbent, overlying; super-incumbent, -natant, -imposed; prominent &c. 250.

tall as a -maypole, - poplar, - steeple; lanky &c. (*thin*) 203.

Adv. on high, high up, aloft, up, above, aloof, overhead; up -, above- stairs; in the clouds; on -tiptoe, - stilts, - the shoulders of; over head and ears; breast high.

over, upwards; from top to bottom &c. (*completely*) 52.

basement- ground-floor; *rez de chaussée* &c. 211; hold; feet, heels.

low water; low -, ebb -, neap -, spring- tide.

V. be -low &c. *adj.*; lie -low, - flat; underlie; crouch, slouch, wallow, grovel; lower &c. (*depress*) 308.

Adj. low, neap, debased; nether, -most; flat, level with the ground; lying low &c. *v.*; crouched, subjacent, squat, prostrate &c. (*horizontal*) 213.

Adv. under; be-, under-neath; below; down, -wards; adown, at the foot of; under-foot, -ground; down -, below-stairs; at a low ebb; below par.

---

208. Depth.—N. depth; deepness &c. *adj.*; profundity, depression &c. (*concavity*) 252.

hollow, pit, shaft, well, crater, abyss; gulf &c. 198; bowels of the earth, bottomless pit, hell.

soundings, depth of water, water, draught, submersion; plummet, sound, line, - machine; lead; submarine, diving bell, bathysphere; diver.

V. be -deep &c. *adj.*; render -deep &c. *adj.*; deepen.

plunge &c. 310; sound, heave the lead, take soundings; dig &c. (*excavate*) 252.

209. Shallowness.—N. shallowness &c. *adj.*; shoals; mere scratch.

Adj. shallow, superficial; skin -, ankle -, knee- deep; just enough to wet one's feet; shoal, -y

probe; sounding -rod, -

Adj. deep, -seated; profound, sunk, buried; submerged &c. 310; sub-aqueous, -marine, -terranean, -terrene; underground.

bottom-, sound-, fathom-less; unfathom-ed, -able; abysmal; deep as a well, deep-sea.

knee-, ankle-deep.

Adv. beyond –, out of- one's depth; over head and ears, over one's head.

210. Summit.—**N.** summit, -y; top, vertex, apex, zenith, pinnacle, acme, acropolis, culmination, meridian, utmost height, *ne plus ultra*, height, pitch, maximum, climax, apogee; culminating –, crowning –, turning- point; turn of the tide, fountain head; water-shed, -parting; sky, pole.

tip, -top; crest, crow's nest, cap, truck, peak, nib; end &c. 67; crown, brow; head, nob, noddle, pate.

high places, heights.

top-, top-gallant mast, sky scraper; quarter –, hurricane- deck.

architrave, frieze, cornice, coping, coping-stone, zoophorus, capital, headpiece, capstone, epistyle, sconce, pediment, entablature; tympanum; ceiling &c. (*covering*) 223.

attic, loft, garret, house-top, upper story, roof.

V. culminate, cap, crown, top; overtop &c. (*be superior to*) 33.

Adj. highest &c. (high &c. 206); top; top-, upper-most; tip-top; culminating &c. *v.*; meridi-an, -onal; capital, head, polar, supreme, supernal, top-gallant.

Adv. a-top, at the top of – the tree, – the heap.

211. Base.—**N.** base, -ment; plinth, dado, wainscot, baseboard; foundation &c. (*support*) 215; substructure, *substratum*, sump, ground, earth, pavement, floor, paving, flag, carpet, ground-floor, deck; footing, groundwork, basis; hold, bilge, orlop deck.

bottom, nadir, foot, sole, toe, hoof, keel, kelson, root.

Adj. bottom; under-, nether-most; fundamental; founded –, based –, grounded –, built- on.

212. Verticality. — **N.** verticality; erectness &c. *adj.*; perpendicularity; right angle, normal; azimuth circle.

wall, palisade, precipice, cliff, steep, bluff.

elevation, erection; square, plumb-line, plummet.

V. be -vertical &c. *adj.*; stand -up, – on end, – erect, – upright; stick –, cock-up.

render -vertical &c. *adj.*; set –, stick –, raise –, cock- up; erect, rear, raise, pitch, raise on its legs.

Adj. vertical, upright, erect, perpendicular, normal, plumb, straight, bolt upright; rampant; straight –, standing-up &c. *v.*; rectangular, orthogonal.

Adv. vertically &c. *adj.*; up, on end; up –, right- on end; *à plomb*, endwise; on one's legs; at right angles.

213. Horizontality.—**N.** horizontality; flatness; level, plane; stratum &c. 204; dead -level, – flat; level plane.

recumbency; lying down &c. *v.*; reclination, decumbence; de-, discumbency; proneness &c. *adj.*; accubation, supination, resupination, prostration; azimuth.

plain, floor, platform, bowling-green; cricket-ground; court; gridiron; baseball diamond; hockey rink; tennis-, croquet-ground, – lawn; billiard table; terrace, estrade, esplanade, *parterre*, table-land, *plateau*, ledge.

spirit-, level; T-square.

V. be -horizontal &c. *adj.*; lie, recline, couch; lie -down, – flat, – prostrate; sprawl, loll; sit down.

render -horizontal &c. *adj.*; lay, – down, – out; level, flatten, even, raze, equalize, smooth, align; prostrate, knock down, floor, fell, ground.

Adj. horizontal, level, even, plane;

flat &c. 251; flat as a -billiard table, − bowling green; alluvial; calm, − as a mill-pond; smooth, − as glass.

re-, de-, pro-, ac-cumbent; lying &c. *v.*; prone, supine, couchant, jacent, prostrate.

Adv. horizontally &c. *adj.*; on -one's back, − all fours, − its beam ends.

214. Pendency.—N. pend-, dependency; suspension, hanging &c. *v.*

pendant, drop, tippet, tassel, lobe, tail, train, flap, lappet, skirt, pig-tail, queue, pendulum.

peg, knob, button, hook, nail, stud, ring, staple, tenterhook; davit; fastening &c. 45; spar, horse.

chande-, gase-, electro-lier.

V. be -pendent &c. *adj.*; hang, depend, swing, dangle, droop, sag; swag; daggle, flap, trail, flow.

suspend, hang, sling, hook up, hitch, fasten to, append.

Adj. pend-ent, -ulous; pensile; hanging &c. *v.*; dependent; suspended &c. *v.*; lowering, overhanging, beetling, decumbent; loose, flowing.

having a -peduncle &c. *n.*; pedunculate, tailed, caudate.

---

215. Support.—N. support, ground, foundation, base, basis; *terra firma*; bearing, fulcrum, *point d'appui*, caudex, purchase, footing, hold, -*locus standi*; landing, − stage, − place; stage, platform; block; rest, resting-place; groundwork, *substratum*, sustentation, subvention; floor &c. (*basement*) 211.

supporter; aid &c. 707; prop, stand, anvil, fulciment; hod, stay, shore, skid, rib, sprag, truss, bandage; sleeper; stirrup, stilts, shoe, sole, heel, splint, lap; bar, rod, boom, sprit, outrigger.

staff, stick, crutch, alpenstock, bourdon; *bâton*, maulstick, colstaff, cowlstaff, staddle; stalk, ped-icel, -icle, − uncle.

post, pillar, shaft, column, pilaster; pediment, pedestal; plinth, shank, leg, socle, zocle; buttress, jamb, mullion, abutment; pile, baluster, banister, stanchion, king post; balustrade.

frame, -work, body, *chassis, fuselage*; scaffold, skeleton, beam, rafter, girder, lintel, joist, cantilever, travis, trave, corner-stone. summer, transom; rung, round, step, sill.

columella, back-bone; key-stone; axle, -tree; axis; arch, ogive, mainstay.

trunnion, pivot, rowlock; peg &c. (*pendency*) 214; tie-beam &c. (*fastening*) 45; thole pin.

board, ledge, shelf, hob, bracket, trevet, trivet, arbor, rack, hatrack; mantel, -piece, -shelf; slab, console; counter, dresser; flange, corbel; table, trestle, teapoy; shoulder; perch; horse; easel, desk; retable, predella.

seat, throne, dais; divan, musnud; chair, bench, form, stool, camp-stool, sofa, settee, davenport, stall, miserere, arm −, easy −, elbow −, rocking- chair; couch, day bed, *fauteuil*, woolsack, ottoman, settle, squab, bench, box, dicky; saddle, pannel, pillion; side −, pack- saddle; pommel.

bed, berth, pallet, tester, crib, cot, bassinet, hammock, shakedown, camp bed, bunk, truckle-bed, cradle, litter, stretcher, bedstead; four-poster, French bed; bedding, mattress, *paillasse*; pillow, bolster; mat, rug, cushion.

stool, footstool, hassock, faldstool, *prie-dieu*; tabouret; tripod. Atlas, Persides, Atlantes, Caryatides, Hercules.

V. be -supported &c.; lie −, sit −, recline −, lean −, loll −, rest −, stand −, step −, repose −, abut −, beat −, be based &c.- on; have at one's back; be-stride, -straddle.

support, bear, carry, hold, sustain, shoulder; hold −, back −, bolster –, shore- up; up-hold, -bear; prop; under-prop, -pin, -set; bandage, &c. 43; brace, truss; cradle, pillow.

give –, furnish –, afford –, supply –, lend- -support, – foundations; bottom, found, base, ground, embed.

maintain, keep on foot; aid &c. 707.

Adj. support-ing, -ed, &c. *v.*; atlantean, columellar; sustentative, fundamental, basal.

Adv. astride on, astraddle; pick-a-back.

216. Parallelism.—N. parallelism; coextension, concentricity, collimation.

V. be –, lie- parallel to; collimate.

Adj. parallel; coextensive, collateral, concentric, concurrent.

Adv. alongside, abreast &c. (*laterally*) 236.

217. Obliquity.—N. obliquity, inclination, skew, slope, slant; crookedness &c. *adj.*; slopeness; leaning &c. *v.*; bevel, bezel, ramp, tilt; bias, list, twist, swag, cant, lurch; distortion &c. 243; bend &c. (*curve*) 245; tower of Pisa.

acclivity, rise, ascent, grade, gradient, *glacis*, rising ground, hill, bank, declivity, downhill, dip, fall, devexity; gentle –, rapid- slope; easy -ascent, – descent; shelving beach; *talus; montagne Russe; facilis descensus Averni.*

steepness &c. *adj.*; cliff, precipice &c. (*vertical*) 212; escarpment, scarp.

[Measure of inclination] clinometer, theodolite, level, sextant, quadrant, protractor; angle, sine, cosine, tangent &c. hypothenuse.

diagonal; zigzag, chevron.

V. be -oblique &c. *adj.*; slope, slant, lean, incline, shelve, stoop, decline, descend, bend, heel, careen, sag, swag, seel, slouch, cant, sidle.

render -oblique &c. *adj.*; sway, bias; slope, slant; incline, bend, crook; cant, tilt; distort &c. 243.

Adj. oblique, inclined; sloping &c. *v.*; tilted &c. *v.*; recumbent, clinal, skew, askew, slant, aslant, bias, plagiedral, indirect, wry, awry, ajee, crooked; knock-kneed &c. (*distorted*) 243; bevel, out of the perpendicular.

uphill, rising, ascending, acclivous; downhill, falling, descending; declining, declivous, devex, anticlinal; steep, abrupt, precipitous, breakneck.

diagonal; trans-verse, -versal; athwart, antiparallel; curved &c. 245.

Adv. obliquely &c. *adj.*; on –, all on- one side; askew, askant, askance, aslope, asquint, edgewise, at an angle; side-long, -ways; slope-, slant-wise; by a side wind.

218. Inversion.—N. in-, e-, sub-, re-, retro-, intro-version; contraposition &c. 237; contrariety &c. 14; reversal; turn of the tide.

overturn; somer-sault, -set; summerset; *culbute*; revulsion; *pirouette.*

transposition, transposal, anastrophy, *metastasis, hyperbaton, anastrophe, hysteron-proteron,* hypallage, *synchysis, tmesis,* parenthesis; *metathesis;* palindrome; Spoonerism.

pronation and supination.

V. be -inverted &c.; turn –, go –, wheel- -round, – about, – to the right about; turn –, go –, tilt –, topple-over; capsize, turn turtle.

in-, sub-, retro-, intro-vert; reverse; up-, over-turn, -set; turn -topsy turvy &c. *adj.*; *culbuter;* transpose, put the cart before the horse, turn the tables.

Adj. inverted &c. *v.*; wrong side -out, – up; inside out, upside down; bottom –, keel- upwards; supine, on one's head, topsy turvy, *sens dessus sens dessous.*

inverse; reverse &c. (*contrary*) 14; opposite &c. 237.

topheavy, unstable.

Adv. inversely &c. *adj.*; hirdie-girdie; heels over head, head over heels.

219. Crossing.—N. crossing &c. *v.*; inter-section, – lacement, – twinement, -digitation; decussation, transversion; convolution &c. 248.

reticulation, meshwork, network; inosculation, anastomosis, intertexture, mortise.

net, *plexus*, web, mesh, twill, skein, sleeve, felt, lace; wicker; mat, -ting; plait, trellis, wattle, lattice, grating, *grille*, gridiron, tracery, fretwork, filigree, reticle; tissue, netting, mokes.

cross, crucifix, rood, crisscross, crux; chain, wreath, braid, cat's cradle, knot; entanglement &c. (*disorder*) 59.

[woven fabrics] cloth, linen, muslin, cambric, drill, homespun, tweed, broadcloth &c.

V. cross, decussate; inter-sect, -lace, -twine, -twist, -weave, -digitate, -link.

twine, entwine, weave, inweave, twist, wreathe; anastomose, inosculate, dovetail, splice, link.

mat, plait, plat, braid, felt, twill; tangle, entangle, ravel; net, knot; dishevel, raddle.

Adj. crossing &c. *v.*; crossed, matted &c. *v.*; transverse.

cross, cruciform, crucial; reti-form, -cular, -culated; areolar, cancellated, mullioned, latticed, grated, barred, streaked; textile, secant, plexal; interfretted.

Adv. across, thwart, athwart, transversely, crosswise.

3°. Centrical Dimensions*

1. *General*

220. Exteriority. — N. exteriority; outside, exterior; surface, superficies; skin &c. (*covering*) 223; *superstratum*; disk, disc; face, facet.

excentricity; circumjacence &c. 227.

V. be -exterior &c. *adj.*; lie around &c. 227.

place -exteriorly, – outwardly, – outside; put –, turn- out.

Adj. exter-ior, -nal; extraneous, outer, -most; out-ward, -lying, -side, -door; round about &c. 227; extramural.

superficial, skin-deep; frontal, discoid.

extraregarding; eccentric; outstanding; extrinsic &c. 6.

Adv. externally &c. *adj.*; out, without, over, outwards, *ab extra*, out of doors; *extra muros.*

221. Interiority.—N. interiority; inside, interior, endocrine; interspace, subsoil, *substratum.*

contents &c. 190; substance, pith, marrow; backbone &c. (*centre*) 222; heart, bosom, breast, abdomen; vitals, viscera, entrails, bowels, belly, intestines, guts, chitterlings, womb, lap; gland, cell; internal organs, *penetralia*, recesses, innermost recesses; cave &c. (*concavity*) 252.

inhabitant &c. 188.

V. be -inside &c. *adj.*, – within &c. *adv.*

place –, keep- within; enclose &c. (*circumscribe*) 229; intern; embed &c. (*insert*) 300.

Adj. inter-ior, -nal; inner, inside, intimate, inward, intraregarding; in-, inner-most; deep-seated; visceral, intes-

* That is, Dimensions having reference to a centre.

in the open air; *sub -Jove, – dio*; *à la belle étoile, al fresco*.

———————

tine, -tinal; inland; subcutaneous; interstitial &c. (*interjacent*) 228; inwrought &c. (*intrinsic*) 5; enclosed &c. *v.*

home, domestic, indoor, intramural, vernacular; endemic.

Adv. internally &c. *adj.*; inwards, within, in, inly; here-, there-, where-in; *ab intra*, withinside; in –, within- doors; at home, in the bosom of one's family.

222. Centrality.—N. centrality, centricalness, centre; middle &c. 68; focus &c. 74.

core, kernel; nucleus, nucleolus; heart, pole, axis, pivot, fulcrum, bull's eye; hub, nave, navel; *umbilicus*, spine, backbone, marrow, pith; hot-bed; concentration &c. (*convergence*) 290; centralization; symmetry.

centre of -gravity, – pressure, – percussion, – oscillation, – buoyancy &c. metacentre.

V. be -central &c. *adj.*; converge &c. 290.

render central, centralize, concentrate; bring to a focus.

Adj. centr-al, -ical; middle &c. 68; axial, pivotal, focal, umbilical, concentric; middlemost, nuclear, centric, centraidal; spinal, vertebral.

Adv. middle; midst; centrally &c. *adj.*

223. Covering.—N. covering, cover; canopy, tilt, awning, baldachin, tent, marquee, *tente d'abri*, umbrella, parasol, sunshade; veil (*shade*) 424; shield &c. (*defence*) 717; hall.

roof, dome, cupola, mansard roof; ceiling; thatch, tile; pan-, pen-tile; tiling, shingles, slates, slating, leads; shed &c. (*abode*) 189.

224. Lining.—N. lining, inner coating; coating &c. (*covering*) 223; stalactite, -agmite.

filling, stuffing, wadding, padding, bushing.

wainscot, *parietes*, wall, brattice.

V. line, stuff, incrust, wad, pad, fill.

Adj. lined &c. *v.*

———————

top, lid, covercle, door, *operculum*, eyelid, blind, curtain.

bandage, plaster, lint, wrapping, dossil, finger stall.

coverlet, counterpane, sheet, quilt, comforter, eiderdown; tarpaulin, blanket, rug, drugget, linoleum, oilcloth; housing.

in-, tegument; skin, pellicle, fleece, fell, fur, ermine, miniver, sable, sealskin &c.; fabrikoid; leather, morocco, calf, pigskin, elk, kid, cowhide &c.; shagreen, hide; pelt, -ry; cuticle, *dermis*, scarfskin, *epidermis*.

clothing &c. 225; mask &c. (*concealment*) 530.

peel, crust, bark, rind, *cortex*, husk, shell, coat.

capsule; ferrule; sheath, -ing; pod, cod; casing, case, theca; *elytron*; *involucrum*; wrapp-ing, -er, cellophane; envelope, vesicle; dermatology, conchology.

armour, -plate, armouring; veneer, facing; pavement; scale &c. (*layer*) 204; coating, paint, stain; varnish &c. (*resin*) 356a; anointing &c. *v.*; inunction; incrustation, superposition, obduction, ground, enamel, whitewash, plaster, stucco, rough cast, pebble dash, compo; rendering; cerement; ointment &c. (*grease*) 356.

V. cover; super-pose, -impose; over-lay, -spread; wrap &c. 225; incase; face, case, veneer, pave, paper; tip, cap, bind, revet.

coat, paint, varnish, pay, incrust, stucco, cement, dab, plaster, tar; wash; be-, smear; be-, daub; anoint, do over; gild, plate, electroplate, japan, lacquer, lacker, enamel, whitewash; lay it on thick.

over-lie, -arch; conceal &c. 528.

Adj. covering &c. *v.*; cutaneous, dermal, cortical, cuticular, tegumentary, skinny, scaly, squamous; covered &c. *v.*; imbricated, loricated, armour-plated, iron-clad; under cover, hooded, cloaked, cowled.

225. Investment.—N. investment; covering &c. 223; dress, clothing, raiment, drapery, costume, attire, guise, toilet, *toilette*, trim; habiliment; vesture, -ment; garment, garb, palliament, apparel, wardrobe, wearing apparel, clothes, things.

array; tailoring, millinery; best bib and tucker; finery &c. (*ornament*) 847; full dress &c. (*show*) 882; garniture; theatrical properties.

outfit, equipment, *trousseau*; uniform, khaki, regimentals; academicals, canonicals &c. 999; livery, gear, harness, turn out, accoutrement, caparison, suit, rigging, trappings, traps, slops, togs, toggery; masquerade.

dishabille, morning dress, lounge suit, tea-gown, *kimono, négligé*, dressing-gown, *peignoir*, wrapper, undress; shooting-coat; smoking-jacket, mufti; rags, tatters, old clothes; mourning, weeds; duds; slippers.

robe, tunic, dolman, *paletot*, habit, gown, coat, coatee, frock, blouse, *pelisse*, middy, sagum, *toga*, smock-frock; frock-, dress-, morning-, tail-coat; dress-suit, – clothes, swallow-tail coat, dinner-, Eton-jacket.

cloak, pall; mantle, mantlet, mantua, shawl, *pelisse*, veil, yashmak; cape, tippet, kirtle, plaid, muffler, comforter,

226. Divestment.—N. divestment; taking off &c. *v.*

nudity; bareness &c. *adj.*; undress; dishabille &c. 225, altogether; nu-, denu-dation; decortication, depilation, excoriation, desquamation; moulting; exfoliation.

baldness, alopecia, acomia.

V. divest; uncover &c. (*cover* &c. 223); denude, bare, strip; undress, unclothe, disrobe &c. (dress, enrobe, &c. 225); uncoif; dismantle; uncase; put –, take –, cast- off; shed, doff; husk, peel, pare, decorticate, desquamate, excoriate, skin, scalp, flay, bark, expose, lay open; exfoliate, moult, mew; cast the skin.

Adj. divested &c. *v.*; bare, naked, nude; un-dressed, -draped, -clad, -clothed, -appareled; exposed; in dishabille; *décolleté*; bald, threadbare, ragged, callow, roofless.

in -a state of nature, – nature's garb, – buff, – native buff, – birthday suit; *in puris naturalibus*; with nothing on, stark naked; bald as a coot, bare as the back of one's hand; out at elbows; barefoot; bareback; leaf-, nap-, hairless, shaved, clean shaven, tonsured, beardless, bald-headed, acomous.

Balaclava helmet, haik, huke, chlamys, mantilla, tabard, housing, horse-cloth, burnous, *roquelaure; houppelande*; sur-, top-, over-, great-coat; *surtout*, spencer, cardigan, sweater, blazer; mackintosh, waterproof, slicker, raincoat, oilskin, trench coat, ulster, monkey-, pea-, pilot-jacket, redingote; wraprascal, poncho, cardinal, pelerine, talma.

jacket, jumper, vest, jerkin, waistcoat, doublet, *camisole*, gabardine; stays, *corsage*, corset, corselet, bodice; stomacher; skirt, petticoat, slip, farthingale, kilt, jupe, crinoline, bustle, hobble skirt, *panier*, apron, pinafore; loin cloth.

trousers; breeches, trews, pantaloons, unmentionables, inexpressibles, overalls, pyjamas, smalls, small-clothes; tights, pants, shorts, drawers; knickerbockers, knickers, plus fours, bloomers, divided skirt; phil-, fill-ibeg.

head-dress, -gear; cap, *béret*, tam o' shanter, glengarry, topee,
sombrero; hat; cocked –, high –, tall –, top –, silk –, opera –, crush
-hat, *gibus*, beaver, castor, bonnet, tile, wideawake, billy-cock;
bowler; soft felt –, straw –, leghorn -hat, panama; toque; wimple;
night-, mob-, skull-cap, biretta; hood, cowl, coif; capote, calach;
scull-cap; kerchief, snood; head, *coiffure*; crown &c. (*circle*) 247;
chignon, pelt, wig, front, peruke, periwig; caftan, turban, fez, *tarboosh*, taj, shako, csako, busby; *képi*, forage cap, bearskin; helmet
&c. 717; mask, domino.

body clothes; linen; shirt, sark, smock, shift, *chemise, lingerie*;
night-gown, -shirt; bed-gown, *sac de nuit*; jersey, guernsey; underclothing, -waistcoat.

neck-erchief, -cloth; tie, ruff, collar, cravat, stock, handkerchief,
bandana, scarf; bib, tucker; dicky; boa; girdle &c. (*circle*) 247;
cummerbund.

shoe, pump, brogue, boot, slipper, sandal, galoche, goloshes,
arctics, rubber boots, overshoes, patten, clog, sabot; high-low;
Blucher –, Wellington –, Hessian –, jack –, top- boot; Balmoral;
legging, puttee, buskin, greave, galligaskin, moccasin, *gamache*,
gambado, gaiter, spatter-dash, spat, antigropeles; stocking, hose,
gaskins, trunk-hose, sock, hosiery.

glove, gauntlet, mitten, cuff, muffettee, wristband, sleeve.
swaddling cloth, baby-linen, *layette*; pocket-handkerchief.
shroud &c. 363.

clothier, tailor, milliner, *costumier*, sempstress, seamstress, snip;
dress-, habit-, breeches-, shoe-maker; cordwainer, cobbler, Crispin,
hosier, hatter; draper, linendraper, haberdasher, mercer.

V. invest; cover &c. 223; envelop, lap, involve; in-, en-wrap;
wrap; fold –, wrap –, lap –, muffle- up; overlap; sheathe, swathe,
swaddle, roll up in, shroud, circumvest.

vest, clothe, array, dress, dight, drape, robe, enrobe, attire, tire,
garb, habilitate, apparel, accoutre, rig, fit out; bedizen, deck &c.
(*ornament*) 847; perk; equip, harness, caparison; dress up.

wear; don; put –, huddle –, slip- on; mantle.

Adj. invested &c. *v.*; habited; dight, -ed; clad, *costumé*, shod,
chaussé; *en grande tenue* &c. (*show*) 882.

sartorial.

---

227. Circumjacence.—N. circumjacence, -ambience; environment, en-
compassment; atmosphere, medium;
surroundings, *entourage*.

outpost; border &c. (*edge*) 231; girdle
&c. (*circumference*) 230; outskirts,
boulevards, suburbs, purlieus, precincts,
faubourgs, *environs*, *banlieue*, neighbourhood, vicinity.

V. lie -around &c. *adv.*; surround,
beset, compass, encompass, environ,
inclose, enclose, encircle, circle, embrace, circumvent, lap, gird; begird,
girdle, engird; skirt, twine round; hem
in &c. (*circumscribe*) 229; besiege,
invest, blockade.

Adj. circum-jacent, -ambient, -fluent;

228. Interjacence.—N. inter-jacence,
-currence, -venience, -location, -digita-
tion, -penetration; permeation.

inter-jection, -polation, -lineation,
-spersion, -calation; embolism.

inter-vention, -ference, -position; in-,
ob-trusion; insinuation; insertion &c.
300; dovetailing; infiltration; intromission.

intermedi-um, -ary; go-between,
agent, middleman, medium, bodkin,
intruder, interloper; parenthesis, episode; fly-leaf.

partition, *septum*, diaphragm, midriff; party-wall, panel, vail, bulkhead,
brattice, *cloison*; half-way house.

V. lie –, come –, get- between; inter-

ambient; surrounding &c. *v.*; circumferential, surburban.

Adv. around, about; without; on
-every side, – all sides; right and left,
all round, round about; in the neighbourhood.

vene, slide in, interpenetrate, permeate.

put between, introduce, intromit,
import; throw –, wedge –, edge –,
jam –, worm –, foist –, run –, plough –,
work- in; inter-pose, -ject, -calate,
-polate, -line, -leave, -sperse, -weave,
-lard, -digitate; let in, dovetail, splice,
mortise; insinuate, smuggle; infiltrate,
ingrain.

interfere, put in an oar, thrust one's nose in; intrude, obtrude;
have a finger in the pie; introduce the thin end of the wedge; thrust
in &c. (*insert*) 300.

Adj. inter-jacent, -current, -venient, -vening &c. *v.*, -mediate,
-mediary, -calary, -stitial, -costal, -mural, -planetary, -stellar;
embolismal.

parenthetical, episodic; mediterranean; intrusive; embosomed;
merged, mean, middle, medium, median.

Adv. between, betwixt; 'twixt; among, -st; amid, -st; 'mid, -st;
in the thick of; betwixt and between; sandwich-wise; parenthetically,
obiter dictum.

229. Circumscription.—N. circumscription, limitation, inclosure;
confinement &c. (*restraint*) 751; circumvallation, encincture; envelope
&c. 232.

V. circumscribe, limit, bound, confine, enclose; surround &c. 227;
compass about; imprison &c. (*restrain*) 751; hedge –, wall –, rail- in;
fence –, hedge- round; embar; picket, corral.

enfold, bury, incase, pack up, enshrine, inclasp; wrap up &c. (*invest*)
225; embosom.

Adj. circumscribed &c. *v.*; begirt, lapt; circumambient; buried –,
immersed- in; embosomed, in the bosom of, imbedded, encysted,
mewed up; imprisoned &c. 751; land-locked, in a ring fence.

230. Outline.—N. outline, circumference; peri-meter, -phery; ambit,
circuit, lines, *tournure, contour*, profile, *silhouette*, lineaments; bounds,
coastline.

zone, belt, girth, band, baldric, zodiac, girdle, tire, cingle, clasp,
girt; *cordon* &c. (*inclosure*) 232; circlet &c. 247.

V. outline, delineate, *silhouette*, circumscribe &c. 229; profile, block
out.

Adj. outlined &c. *v.*; circumferential, perimetric, peripheral.

231. Edge.—N. edge, verge, brink, brow, brim, margin, border, confines, skirt, rim, felloe, felly, flange, side, mouth; jaws, chops, chaps,
fauces; lip, muzzle.

threshold, door, porch; portal &c. (*opening*) 260; coast, shore, strand,
beach, bank, wharf, quay, dock.

frame, fringe, flounce, frill, list, trimming, edging, skirting, hem,
selvedge, welt; furbelow, valance, exergue.

Adj. border, marginal, skirting; labial, labiated, marginated.

232. Inclosure.—N. inclosure, enclosure, envelope; case &c. (*receptacle*) 191; wrapper; girdle &c. 230.

pen, fold, croft, sty; pen-, in-, sheep-fold; paddock, pound, corral,
kraal; yard, compound; net, seine net.

wall; hedge, -row; *espalier*; fence &c. (*defence*) 717; pale, paling, balustrade, rail, railing, gunwale; quickset hedge, park paling, circumvallation, *enceinte*, ring fence.

barrier, barricade; gate, -way; door, hatch, *cordon*; prison &c. 752.

dike, dyke, ditch, fosse, moat, trench.

V. inclose; circumscribe &c. 229.

233. Limit.—N. limit, boundary, bounds, confine, *enclave*, term, bourn, verge, kerb-stone, curbstone, but, pale; termin-ation, -us; stint, frontier, precinct, marches.

boundary line, landmark; line of -demarcation, – circumvallation; pillars of Hercules; Rubicon, turning-point; *ne plus ultra*; sluice, flood-gate.

V. limit, bound, confine, define, circumscribe, demarcate, delimit, encompass.

Adj. definite; contermin-ate, -able, terminable, limitable; terminal, frontier, border, bordering, boundary.

Adv. thus far, – and no further.

2. *Special*

234. Front.—N. front; fore, – part; foreground; forefront, face, disk, disc, frontage, *façade*, *proscenium*, facia, frontispiece; priority, anteriority; obverse [of a medal].

fore –, front- rank, first line; van, -guard; advanced guard; outpost, scout.

brow, forehead, visage, physiognomy, phiz, features, countenance; map, mug; rostrum, beak, bow, stem, prow, prore, jib, bowsprit; forecastle.

pioneer &c. (*precursor*) 64; metoposcopy.

V. be –, stand- in front &c. *adj.*; front, face, confront, breast, brave; bend forwards; come to the -front, – fore.

Adj. fore, forward, anterior, front, frontal.

Adv. before; in -front, – the van, – advance; ahead, right ahead; fore-, head-most; in the foreground; before one's -face, – eyes; face to face, *vis-à-vis*.

235. Rear.—N. rear, back, posteriority; rear -rank, – guard; background, *hinterland*.

occiput, nape, scruff, chine; heels; tail, rump, croup, buttock, posteriors, bottom, seat, backside, scut, breech, *dorsum*, loin; dorsal –, lumbar- region; hind quarters.

stern, poop, after-part, counter; postern, heel-, tail-piece, crupper.

wake; train &c. (*sequence*) 281.

reverse; other side of the shield.

V. be -behind &c. *adv.*; fall astern; bend backwards; bring up the rear; follow &c. 622; tail, shadow.

Adj. back, rear; hind, -er, -most, -ermost; post-ern, -erior; dorsal, after; caudal, lumbar; mizzen.

Adv. behind; in the -rear, – ruck, – back-ground; behind one's back; at the -heels, – tail, – back- of; back to back.

after, -most, aft, abaft, astern, sternmost, aback, rear-, hind-, back-ward.

---

236. Laterality.—N. laterality; side, flank, beam, quarter, lee; hand; cheek, jowl, jole, wing; profile; temple, *parietes*, loin, haunch, hip.

gable, -end; broadside; lee side.

points of the compass; East, Orient, Levant; West, occident; orientation.

V. be -on one side &c. *adv.*; flank, outflank; sidle; skirt, border.

Adj. lateral, sidelong; collateral;

237. Contraposition.—N. contraposition, opposition; polarity; inversion &c. 218; opposite side; antithesis; reverse, inverse; counterpart; antipodes; opposite poles, North and South.

V. be -opposite &c. *adj.*; subtend.

Adj. opposite; reverse, inverse; antipodal, subcontrary; fronting, facing, diametrically opposite.

Northern, Septentrional, Boreal, arc-

parietal, flanking, skirting; flanked; sideling.

many-sided; multi-, bi-, tri-, quadrilateral.

East-ern, -ward, -erly; orient, -al, auroral, Levantine; West-ern, -ward, -erly; occidental, Hesperian; equatorial.

Adv. side-ways, -long; broadside on; on one side, abreast, abeam, alongside, beside, aside; by, – the side of; side by side; cheek by jowl &c. (*near*) 197; to -windward, – leeward; laterally &c. *adj.*; right and left; on her beam ends.

238. Dextrality. — N. dextrality; right, – hand; dexter, offside, starboard.

Adj. dextral, right-handed; ambidextral, dexterous, dextrorsal &c.

tic; Southern, Austral, antarctic, polar.

Adv. over, – the way, – against; against; face to face, *vis-à-vis*; as poles asunder.

———

239. Sinistrality.—N. sinistrality; left, – hand; *sinister*, nearside, larboard, port.

Adj. sinistral, sinister, sinistrorsal &c., left-handed, sinistromanual, sinistrous.

SECTION III. FORM

1°. GENERAL FORM

240. Form.—N. form, figure, shape; con-formation, -figuration; make, formation, frame, construction, design, cut, set, build, trim, cut of one's jib; stamp, type, cast, mould; fashion; contour &c. (*outline*) 230; structure &c. 329.

feature, lineament, outline, turn; phase &c. (*aspect*) 448; posture, attitude, *pose*.

[Science of form] morphology.

[Similarity of form] isomorphism.

forming &c. *v.*; form-, figur-, efformation; sculpture.

V. form, shape, figure, fashion, efform, carve, cut, chisel, hew, cast; rough-hew, -cast; sketch; block –, hammer- out; trim; lick –, put- into shape; model, knead, work up into, set, mould, sculpture; cast, stamp; built &c. (*construct*) 161.

Adj. formed &c. *v.*

[Receiving form] plastic, fictile, full-fashioned &c.

[Giving form] plasmic &c.

[Similar in form] isomorphous &c.

241. [Absence of form.] Amorphism. —N. amorphism, informity, uncouthness; unlicked cub, rough diamond; *rudis indigestaque moles*; disorder &c. 59; deformity &c. 243.

disfigure-, deface-ment, deformation; mutilation.

V. [Destroy form] deface, disfigure, deform, mutilate, truncate; derange &c. 61.

Adj. shapeless, amorphous, malformed, formless; un-formed, -hewn, -fashioned, -shapen; rough, rude, Gothic, barbarous, rugged, in the rough; misshapen &c. 243.

———

242. [Regularity of form.] Symmetry. —N. symmetry, shapeliness, finish; beauty &c. 845; proportion, eurythmy, eurythmic, uniformity, parallelism; bi-, tri-, multi-lateral symmetry; centrality &c. 222.

243. [Irregularity of form.] Distortion.—N. dis-, de-, con-tortion; knot, mop, warp, buckle, screw, twist; crookedness &c. (*obliquity*) 217; grimace; deformity; mal-, malcon-formation; monstrosity, misproportion, want

arborescence, branching, ramification.

Adj. symmetrical, shapely, well set, finished; beautiful &c. 845; classic, chaste, severe.

regular, uniform, balanced; equal &c. 27; parallel, coextensive.

arbor-escent, -iform; dendr-iform, -oid; branching; ramous, ramose.

of symmetry, *anamorphosis*; ugliness &c. 846; teratology.

V. distort, contort, twist, warp &c. *n.*; wrest, writhe, make faces, deform, misshape.

Adj. distorted &c. *v.*; out of shape, irregular, unsymmetric, awry, wry, askew, crooked, sinuous; anamorphous; not -true, – straight; on one side, crump, deformed; mis-shapen, -begotten; mis-, ill-proportioned; ill-made; grotesque, crooked as a ram's horn; hump-, hunch-, bunch-, crook-backed; bandy; bandy-, bow-legged; bow-, knock-kneed; splay-, club-footed; taliped; round-shouldered; snub-nosed; curtailed of one's fair proportions; scalene, stumpy &c. (*short*) 201; gaunt &c. (*thin*) 203; bloated &c. 194.

Adv. all manner of ways.

2°. Special Form

244. Angularity.—N. angular-ity, -ness; aduncity; angle, cusp, bend; fold &c. 258; notch &c. 257; fork, bifurcation.

elbow, knee, knuckle, ankle, groin, crotch, crutch, crane, fluke, scythe, sickle, zigzag, kimbo.

corner, nook, recess, niche, oriel.

right angle &c. (*perpendicular*) 212; obliquity &c. 217; angle of 45°, mitre; acute –, obtuse –, salient –, re-entrant –, spherical –, solid –, dihedral- angle.

angular -measurement, – elevation, – distance, – velocity; trigon-, goni-ometry; altimetry; clin-, graph-, goni-ometer; theodolite; transit circle; sextant, quadrant; dichotomy.

triangle, trigon, wedge; rectangle, square, lozenge, diamond; rhomb, -us; quadr-angle, -ilateral; parallelogram; quadrature; poly-, penta-, hexa-, hepta-, octa-, deca-gon.

Platonic bodies; cube, rhomboid; tetra-, penta-, hexa-, octa-, dodeca-, icosa-hedron; prism, pyramid; parallelopiped.

V. bend, fork, bifurcate, crinkle, divaricate, branch, ramify.

Adj. angular, bent, crooked, aduncous, uncinated, aquiline, jagged, serrated; falc-iform, -ated; furcular, furcated, forked, bifurcate, crotched; zigzag; dovetailed; knock-kneed, crinkled, akimbo, kimbo, geniculated; oblique &c. 217.

fusiform, wedge-shaped, cuneiform; tri-angular, -gonal, -lateral; quadr-angular, -ilateral; rectangular, square, foursquare, multilateral; polygonal &c. *n.*; cubical, rhomboidal, pyramidal.

245. Curvature.—N. curv-ature, -ity, -ation; incurv-ity, -ation; bend; flex-ure, -ion; conflexure; crook, hook, bought, bending; de-, inflexion; arcuation, devexity, turn; deviation, *détour*, sweep; curl, -ing; bough; recurv-ity, -ation; sinuosity &c. 248; aduncity.

curve, arc, arch, arcade, vault, dome, bow, crescent, *meniscus*, half-moon, lunule, horse-shoe, loop, crane-neck;

246. Straightness.—N. straightness, rectilinearity, directness; inflexibility &c. (*stiffness*) 323; straight –, right –, direct-, bee- line; short cut.

V. be -straight &c. *adj.*; have no turning; not -incline, – bend, – turn, – deviate- to either side; go straight; steer for &c. (*direction*) 278.

render straight, straighten, rectify; set –, put- straight; un-bend, -fold,

para-, hyper-bola; catenary, festoon; conch-, cardi-oid; caustic, instep; tracery.

V. be -curved &c. *adj.*; sweep, swag, sag; deviate &c. 279; turn; re-enter.

render -curved &c. *adj.*; bend, curve, incurvate; de-, in-flect; crook; turn, round, arch, arcuate, arch over, loop the loop, concamerate; bow, coil, curl, recurve, frizzle.

Adj. curved &c. *v.*; curvi-form, -lineal, -linear; devex, devious; recurv-ed, -ous; *retroussé*; crump; bowed &c. *v.*; vaulted; hooked; falc-iform, -ated; semicircular, crescentic; lun-iform, -ular; semi-lunar, meniscal; conchoidal; cord-iform, -ated; cardioid; heart-, bell-, pear-, fig-shaped; reniform; lenti-form, -cular; bow-legged &c. (*distorted*) 243; oblique &c. 217; circular &c. 247.

-curl &c. 248, -ravel &c. 219, -wrap.

Adj. straight; rectiline-ar, -al; direct, even, right, true, in a line; unbent &c. *v.*; un-deviating, -turned, -distorted, -swerving; straight as an arrow &c. (*direct*) 278; inflexible &c. 323.

---

247. [Simple circularity.] **Circularity.** —**N.** circularity, roundness; rotundity &c. 249.

circle, circlet, ring, washer, areola, hoop, roundlet, *annulus*, annulet, bracelet, armlet, armilla; ringlet; eye, loop, wheel; cycle, orb, orbit, rundle, zone, belt, *cordon*, band; sash, girdle, cestus, cincture, baldric, fillet, *fascia*, wreath, garland; crown, corona, coronet, chaplet, snood, necklace, collar; noose, lasso, lariat.

ellipse, oval, ovule; ellipsoid, cycloid; epi-cycloid, -cycle; semi-circle; quadrant, sextant, sector.

V. make -round &c. *adj.*; round.

go round; encircle &c. 227; describe -a circle &c. 311.

Adj. round, rounded, circular, annular, orbicular; oval, ovate; elliptic, -al; ovoid, egg-shaped; pear-shaped &c. 245; cycloidal &c. *n.*; spherical &c. 249.

---

248. [Complex circularity.] **Convolution.**—**N.** winding &c. *v.*; con-, in-, circum-volution; wave, undulation, tortuosity, anfractuosity; sinu-osity, -ation, sinuousness; meandering, circuit, circumbendibus, twist, twirl, windings and turnings, *ambages*; torsion; inosculation; reticulation &c. (*crossing*) 219.

coil, roll, curl, buckle, spire, spiral, helix, corkscrew, worm, volute, whorl, rundle; tendril; scollop, scallop, escalop; kink.

serpent, snake, eel, maze, labyrinth.

V. be -convoluted &c. *adj.*; wind, twine, turn and twist, twirl; wave, undulate, meander; inosculate; entwine, intwine; twist, coil, roll; wrinkle, curl, crisp, twill; frizz, -le; crimp, crape, indent, scollop, scallop; wring, intort; contort; wreathe &c. (*cross*) 219.

Adj. convoluted; winding, twisted &c. *v.*; tortile, tortive; wavy; und-ated, -ulatory; circling, snaky, snake-like, serpentine; serpent-, anguill-, verm-iform; vermicular; mazy, tortuous, anfractuous, sinuous, flexuous, wavy, sigmoidal.

involved, intricate, complicated, perplexed; labyrinth-ic, -ian, -ine; circuitous; peristaltic; dædalian, curly.

wreathy, frizzly, *crêpé*, buckled; ravelled &c. (*in disorder*) 59.

spiral, coiled, helical, turbinated.

Adv. in and out, round and round.

---

249. Rotundity.—**N.** rotundity; roundness &c. *adj.*; cylindricity; spher-icity, -oidity; globosity.

cylin-der, -droid; barrel, drum; roll, -er; *rouleau*, column, rolling-pin, rundle; chimney-pot, drain-pipe.

cone, conoid; pear-, egg-, bell-shape.

sphere, globe, ball, boulder, bowlder; spher-, ellips-, ge-, glob-oid, oblong –, oblate- spheroid; drop, spherule, globule, vesicle, bulb, bullet, pellet, *pelote*, clew, pill, marble, pea, knob, pommel, knot.

V. render -spherical &c. *adj.*; form into a sphere, sphere, roll into a ball; give -rotundity &c. *n.*; round.

Adj. rotund; round &c. (*circular*) 247; cylindr-ic, -ical, -oid; columnar, lumbriciform; conic, -al; spher-ical, -oidal; glob-ular, -ated, -ous, -ose; egg-, bell-, pear-shaped; ov-oid, -iform; gibbous; campaniform, -ulate, -iliform; fungiform, bead-like, moniliform, pyriform, bulbous; *teres atque rotundus*; round as -an orange, – an apple, – a ball, – a billiard ball, – a cannon ball.

3°. Superficial Form

250. Convexity. — N. convexity, prominence, projection, swelling, gibbosity, bilge, bulge, protuberance, protrusion; excrescency, camber.

intumescence; tumour, tumor; tubercle, -osity; excrescence; hump, hunch, bunch, gnarl.

tooth, knob, elbow, process, *apophysis*, condyle, bulb, node, nodule, nodosity, tongue, *dorsum*, boss, embossment, bump, clump; sugar-loaf &c. (*sharpness*) 253; bow; mamelon.

pimple, wen, wheal, *papula*, postule, pock, proud flesh, growth, goitre, *sarcoma*, caruncle, corn, bunion, wart, furnuncle, polypus, adenoid, fungus, fungosity, *exostosis*, bleb, blister, blain; boil &c. (*disease*) 655; bubble, blob.

papilla, nipple, teat, pap, breast, dug, mammilla; proboscis, nose, neb, beak, snout, nozzle, snozzle; Adam's apple; belly, paunch, corporation; withers, back, shoulder, lip, flange.

peg, button, stud, ridge, rib, jutty, trunnion, snag.

cupola, dome, bee-hive; arch, balcony, eaves; pilaster.

relief, relievo, *cameo*; *basso-*, *mezzo-*, *alto-rilievo*; low-, bas-, high-relief.

hill &c. (*height*) 206; cape, promontory, mull; fore-, head-land; point of land, naze, ness, mole, jetty, hummock, ledge, spur.

V. be -prominent &c. *adj.*; project, bulge, protrude, bag, belly, pout, bouge, bunch; jut –, stand –, stick –, poke- out; stick –, bristle –, start –, cock –, shoot- up; swell –, hang –, bend- over; beetle.

render -prominent &c. *adj.*; raise 307; emboss, chase.

251. Flatness.—N. flatness &c. *adj.*; smoothness &c. 255.

plane; level &c. 213; plate, platter, table, tablet, slab.

V. render flat, flatten, squash; level &c. 213.

Adj. flat, plane, even, flush, scutiform, discoid; level &c. (*horizontal*) 213; smooth; flat as -a pancake, – a fluke, – a flounder, – a board, – my hand.

252. Concavity.—N. concavity, depression, dip; hollow, -ness; indentation, *intaglio*, cavity, antrum, dent, dint, dimple, follicle, pit, *sinus*, *alveolus*, *lacuna*; excavation, trench, sap, mine, tunnel, burrow; trough &c. (*furrow*) 259; honeycomb.

cup, basin, crater, punch-bowl; cell &c. (*receptacle*) 191; socket, faucet.

valley, vale, dale, dell, gap, dingle, combe, bottom, slade, strath, glade, grove, glen, cave, cavern, cove; grot, -to; alcove, *cul-de-sac*, blind alley; gully &c. 198; arch &c. (*curve*) 245; bay &c. (*of the sea*) 343.

excavator, sapper, miner.

V. be -concave &c. *adj.*; retire, cave in.

render -concave &c. *adj.*; depress, hollow; scoop, – out; gouge, dig, delve, excavate, dent, dint, mine, sap, undermine, burrow, tunnel, stave in.

Adj. depressed &c. *v.*; concave, hollow, stove in; dished; spoon-like; retiring; retreating; cavernous; porous &c. (*with holes*) 260; cellular, spongy, spongious; honeycombed, alveolar; infundibul-ar, -iform; funnel-, bell-shaped; campaniform, capsular; vaulted, arched.

Adj. convex, prominent, protuberant, underhung, undershot; projecting &c. *v.*; bossed, bossy, nodular, bunchy; clav-ate, -ated; hummocky, *moutonné*, mammiform; papul-ous, -ose; hemispheric, bulbous; bowed, arched; bold; bellied; tuber-ous, -culous; tumorous; cornute, knobby, odontoid; lenti-form, -cular; gibbous.

salient, in relief, raised, *repoussé*; bloated &c. (*expanded*) 194.

---

253. Sharpness.—N. sharpness &c. *adj.*; acuity, acumination; spinosity.

point, spike, spine, *spiculum*, tine; needle, pin; tack, nail; prick, -le; spur, rowel, barb; spit, cusp; horn, antler; snag; tag; thorn, bristle.

nib, tooth, incisor, tusk; spoke, cog, ratchet.

crag, crest, *arête*, cone, peak, sugar-loaf, pike, *aiguille*; spire, pyramid, steeple.

beard, *chevaux de frise*, porcupine, hedgehog, brier, bramble, thistle; comb, awn, bur.

wedge; knife-, cutting- edge; blade, edge-tool, cutlery, knife, penknife, whittle, razor; scalpel, bistoury, lancet; chisel; plough-share, coulter; hatchet, axe, pick-axe, mattock, pick, adze, bill; bill-hook, cleaver, cutter; skiver; scythe, sickle, scissors, shears; sword &c. (*arms*) 727; bodkin &c. (*perforator*) 262.

sharpener, hone, strop; grind-, whet-stone; steel, emery.

V. be -sharp &c. *adj.*; taper to a point; bristle with.

render -sharp &c. *adj.*; sharpen, point, aculeate, acuminate, whet, barb, spiculate, set, strop, grind.

cut &c. (*sunder*) 44.

Adj. sharp, keen; acute; aci-cular, -form; acu-leated, -minated; pointed; tapering; conical, pyramidal; mucron-ate, -ated; spindle-, needle-shaped; spiked, spiky, ensiform, peaked, salient, cusp-ed; -idate, -idated; corn-ute, -uted, -iculate; prickly; spiny, spinous; thorny, bristling, muricated, pectinated, studded, thistly, briery; craggy &c. (*rough*) 256; snaggy; digitated, two-edged, fusiform; denti-form, -culated; toothed; odontoid; star-like; stell-ated, -iform; arrow-headed; arrowy, barbed, spurred, sagittal; spear-shaped, hastate; horned; conical.

cutting; sharp-, knife-edged; sharp -, keen- as a razor; sharp as a needle; sharpened &c. *v.*; set.

254. Bluntness.—N. bluntness &c. *adj.*

V. be -, render- blunt &c. *adj.*; obtund, dull; take off the -point, - edge; turn.

Adj. blunt, obtuse, dull, bluff.

---

255. Smoothness.—N. smoothness &c. *adj.*; polish, gloss; lubric-ity, -ation.

down, velvet, silk, satin; slide; bowling green &c. (*level*) 213; glass, ice; asphalt, pavement, flags.

roller, steam-roller; iron, flat-iron, tailor's goose; sand-, emery-paper; burnisher, turpentine and bees-wax.

V. smooth, -en; plane; file; mow, shave; level, roll; macadamize; polish, burnish, planish, levigate, calender, glaze; iron, hot-press, mangle; lubricate &c. (*oil*) 332.

256. Roughness.—N. roughness &c. *adj.*; tooth, grain, texture, ripple; asperity, rugosity, salebrosity, corrugation, nodosity; arborescence &c. 242.

brush, hair, beard, shag, mane, whisker, mutton-chops, *moustache*, *mustachio*, imperial, Van Dyke, tress, lock, curl, ringlet, *fimbriæ*, *cilia*, *villi*; eyelashes, eye-brows, love-lock.

plum-age, -osity; plume, *panache*, crest; feather, tuft, tussock, fringe, toupee.

wool, velvet, plush, nap, pile, floss,

Adj. smooth; polished &c. *v.*; even; level &c. 213; plane &c. (*flat*) 251; sleek, glossy; silken, silky; lanate, downy, velvety; glabrous, slippery, glassy, lubricous, oily, soft; unwrinkled; smooth as -glass, – ice, – velvet, – oil; slippery as an eel; woolly &c. (*feathery*) 256.

fluff, fur, down; byssus, moss, bur.

V. be -rough &c. *adj.*; go against the grain.

render -rough &c. *adj.*; roughen, rough cast, knurl; ruffle, crisp, crumple, crinkle, corrugate, engrail; set on edge, stroke –, rub- the wrong way, rumple.

Adj. rough, uneven; scabrous, knotted; nodular; rug-ged, -ose, -ous; asperous, crisp, salebrous, gnarled, unpolished, unsmooth, rough-hewn; knurled, cross-grained, crag-gy, -ged; crankling, scraggy, jagged, unkempt, prickly &c. (*sharp*) 253; arborescent &c. 242; leafy, well-wooded; feathery; plum-ose, -igerous; tufted, fimbriated, hairy, bristly, ciliated, filamentous, hirsute; crin-ose, -ite; bushy, hispid, villous, pappous, bearded, pilous, shaggy, shagged; fringed, befringed; set-ous, -ose, -aceous; 'like quills upon the fretful porcupine'; rough as a -nutmeg grater, – bear.

downy, velvety, flocculent, woolly; lan-ate, -ated; lanugin-ous. -ose; tomentous.

Adv. against the grain, in the rough, on edge.

257. Notch.—**N.** notch, dent, nick, cut; indent, -ation; serration; dimple.

embrasure, battlement, machicolation; saw, tooth, crenelle, scallop, scollop, vandyke.

V. notch, nick, cut, pink, mill, score, dent, indent, jag, scarify, scotch, crimp, scollop, crenulate, vandyke.

Adj. notched &c. *v.*; crenate, -d; dentate, -d; denticulate, -d; toothed, palmated, serrated.

258. Fold.—**N.** fold, plicature, pleat, plait, ply, crease; tuck, gather; flexion, flexure, joint, elbow, doubling, duplicature, wrinkle, rimple, crinkle, crankle, crumple, rumple, rivel, ruck, ruffle, dog's ear, corrugation, frounce, flounce, lapel; pucker, crow's feet.

V. fold, double, plicate, pleat, plait, crease, wrinkle, crinkle, crankle, curl, smock, cockle up, crocker, rimple, rumple, frizzle, frounce, rivel, twill, corrugate, ruffle, crimple, crumple, pucker; turn –, double- -down, – under; tuck, ruck, hem, gather.

Adj. folded &c. *v.*

259. Furrow.—**N.** furrow, groove, rut, *sulcus*, scratch, streak, *striæ*, crack, score, incision, slit; chamfer, fluting.

channel, gutter, trench, ditch, dike, dyke, moat, fosse, trough, kennel; ravine &c. (*interval*) 198.

V. furrow &c. *n.*; flute, groove, carve, corrugate, plough; incise, chase, enchase, grave, engrave, etch, bite in, cross-hatch.

Adj. furrowed &c. *v.*; ribbed, striated, sulcated, fluted, canaliculated; bisulc-ous, -ate; trisulcate; corduroy.

260. Opening.—**N.** hole, foramen; puncture, blow-out, perforation; pin-, key-, loop-, port-, peep-, mouse-, pigeon-hole; eye, – of a needle; eyelet; slot.

opening; apert-ure, -ness; hiation,

261. Closure.—**N.** closure, occlusion. blockade; shutting up &c. *v.*; obstruction &c. (*hindrance*) 706; gag; embolism; contraction &c. 195; infarction; con-, ob-stipation; blind -alley, – corner; *cul-de-sac*, *cæcum*; imper-foration,

yawning, oscitancy, dehiscence, patefaction, pandiculation; gap, chasm &c.
(*interval*) 198.

embrasure, window, casement, light;
sky-, fan-light; lattice; bay-, bow-
window; oriel; dormer, lantern.

out-, in-let; vent, vomitory; *embouchure*; orifice, mouth, sucker, muzzle,
throat, gullet, placket, weasand, wizen,
nozzle, *æsophagus*.

portal, porch, gate, ostiary, postern,
wicket, trap-door, hatch, door; arcade;
gate-, door-, hatch-, gang-way; lych-
gate.

way, path &c. 627; thoroughfare;
channel, passage, tube, pipe; water-
pipe &c. 350; air-pipe &c. 351; vessel,
tubule, canal, gut, fistula; adjutage,
ajutage; chimney, smoke stack, flue,
tap, funnel, gully, tunnel, main; mine,
pit, adit, shaft; gallery.

alley, aisle, glade, lane, vista.

bore, calibre; pore; blind orifice.

por-ousness, -osity; sieve, cullender, colander; grater, shredder;
cribble, riddle, screen; honeycomb.

apertion, perforation; piercing &c. *v.*; terebration, empalement,
pertusion, puncture, acupuncture, penetration.

opener, key, master-key, *passe-partout*.

V. open, ope, gape, dehisce, yawn, bilge; fly open.

perforate, pierce, empierce, tap, bore, drill; mine &c. (*scoop out*)
252; tunnel; trans-pierce, -fix; enfilade, impale, spike, spear, gore,
spit, stab, pink, puncture, lance, trepan, trephine, stick, prick,
riddle, punch; stave in.

cut a passage through; make -way, - room- for.

un-cover, -close, -rip; lay -, cut -, rip -, throw- open.

Adj. open; perforated &c. *v.*; perforate; wide open, agape, ajar;
un-closed, -stopped; oscitant, gaping, yawning; patent.

tubular, cannular, fistulous; per-vious, -meable; foraminous;
vesi-, vas-cular; porous, follicular, cribriform, honeycombed, in-
fundibular, riddled; tubul-ous, -ated, piped.

opening &c. *v.*; aperient.

Int. *open sesame!*

262. Perforator. — N. perforator,
piercer, borer, auger, gimlet, stylet,
drill, wimble, awl, bradawl, scoop,
terrier, corkscrew, dibble, trocar, tre-
pan, trephine, probe, bodkin, needle,
stiletto, broach, reamer, rimer, warder,
lancet; punch, -eon; spikebit, gouge;
spear &c. (*weapon*) 727.

-viousness &c. *adj.*, -meability; stopper
&c. 263; *operculum*.

V. close, occlude, plug; block -,
stop -, fill -, bung -, cork -, button -,
stuff -, shut -, dam- up, obturate;
blockade; obstruct &c. (*hinder*) 706;
bar, bolt, stop, seal, plumb; choke,
throttle; ram down, tamp, dam, cram;
trap, clinch; put to -, shut- the door;
batten down the hatches.

Adj. closed &c. *v.*; shut, operculated;
unopened.

unpierced, imporous, cæcal; imperforate, -vious, -meable; impenetrable;
un-, im-passable; invious; path-, way-
less; untrodden.

unventilated; air-, water-tight; hermetically sealed; tight, snug.

---

263. Stopper.—N. stopper, stopple;
plug, cork, bung, spike, spill, stop-cock,
tap; rammer; ram, -rod; piston; stop-
gap; wadding, stuffing, padding, stopping, dossil, pledget, tompion, tourniquet, obturator; wad.

cover &c. 223; valve, slide valve;
vent-peg, spigot.

janitor, door -, gate- keeper, porter,
commissionaire, *concierge*, warder,
beadle, Cerberus, usher, guard, sentry,
sentinel; ostiary.

Section IV. MOTION

1°. Motion in General

264. [Successive change of place.*] **Motion.**—**N.** motion, movement, move; motivity, motility, going &c. *v.*; unrest.

stream, current, flow, flux, run, course, stir; conduction, evolution; kinematics.

step, rate, pace, tread, stride, gait, clip, port, footfall, cadence, carriage, velocity, angular velocity; progress, locomotion; journey &c. 266; voyage &c. 267; transit &c. 270.

restlessness &c. (*changeableness*) 149; mobility; movableness, motive power; laws of motion; mobilization.

V. be -in motion &c. *adj.*; move, go, hie, gang, budge, stir, pass, flit; hover -round, – about; shift, slide, slither, glide; roll, – on; flow, stream, run, drift, sweep along; wander &c. (*deviate*) 279; walk &c. 266; change -, shift- one's -place, – quarters; dodge; keep -going, – moving.

put -, set- in motion; move; impel &c. 276; propel &c. 284; render movable, mobilize.

Adj. moving &c. *v.*; in motion; motile, transitional; motory, motive; shifting, movable, mobile, mercurial, unquiet; restless &c. (*changeable*) 149; nomadic &c. 266; erratic &c. 279.

Adv. under way; on the -move, – wing, – tramp, – march.

---

265. Quiescence.—**N.** rest; stillness &c. *adj.*; quiescence; stag-nation, -nancy; fixity, immobility, catalepsy; indisturbance; quietism.

quiet, tranquillity, calm; repose &c. 687; peace; dead calm, anticyclone; statue-like repose; silence &c. 403; not a -breath of air, – mouse stirring; sleep &c. (*inactivity*) 683.

pause, lull &c. (*cessation*) 142; stand, – still; standing still &c. *v.*; lock; dead -lock, – stop, – stand; full stop; fix; embargo.

resting-place; bivouac; home &c. (*abode*) 189; pillow &c. (*support*) 215; haven &c. (*refuge*) 666; goal &c. (*arrival*) 292.

V. be -quiescent &c. *adj.*; stand -, lie- still; keep quiet, repose, hold the breath.

remain, stay; stand, lie to, ride at anchor, remain *in situ*, mark time, tarry; bring -, heave -, lay- to; pull -, draw- up; hold, halt; stop, – short; rest, pause, anchor; cast -, come to an- anchor; rest on one's oars; repose on one's laurels, take breath; stop &c. (*discontinue*) 142.

stagnate, vegetate; *quieta non movere*; let -alone, – well alone; abide, rest and be thankful; keep within doors, stay at home, go to bed.

dwell &c. (*be present*) 186; settle &c. (*be located*) 184; alight &c. (*arrive*) 292.

stick, – fast; stand, – like a post; not stir a -peg, – step; be at a -stand &c. *n.*

quell, becalm, hush, stay, lull to sleep, lay an embargo on; put the brake on.

Adj. quiescent, still; motion-, move-less; fixed; stationary; at -rest, – a stand, – a stand-still, – anchor; stock-still; immotile; standing still &c. *v.*; sedentary, untravelled, stay-at-home; becalmed, stagnant, quiet; un-moved, -disturbed, -ruffled; calm, restful; cataleptic; immovable &c. (*stable*) 150; sleeping &c. (*inactive*) 683; silent &c. 403; still as -a statue, – a post, – a mouse, – death.

Adv. at a stand &c. *adj.*; *tout court*; at the halt.

Int. stop! stay! avast! halt! hold, – hard! whoa!

Phr. *requiescat in pace.*

---

* A thing cannot be said to *move* from one place to another, unless it passes in succession through every intermediate place; hence motion is only such a change of place as is *successive*. 'Rapid, swift, &c., as thought' are therefore incorrect expressions.

266. [Locomotion by land.] **Journey.**
—**N.** travel; travelling &c. *v.*; wayfaring, campaigning.

journey, excursion, expedition, tour, trip, grand tour, circuit, peregrination, discursion, ramble, pilgrimage, *trek*, course, ambulation, march, walk, hike, promenade, constitutional, stroll, saunter, tramp, jog-trot, turn, stalk, perambulation; noctambulation; somnambulism, sleep walking; outing, ride, drive, airing, jaunt.

equitation, horsemanship, riding, *manège*, ride and tie.

roving, vagrancy, pererration; marching and countermarching; nomadism; vagabond-ism, -age; gadding; flit, -ting; migration; e-, im-, de-, inter-migration.

plan, itinerary, guide; hand-, road-book; Baedeker, Murray, Bradshaw, time table.

procession, parade, cavalcade, caravan, file, *cortège*, column.

[Organs and instruments of locomotion] vehicle &c. 272; locomotive &c. 271; legs, feet, pegs, pins, trotters.

traveller &c. 268.

V. travel, journey, course; tour; take -, go- a journey; take -, go out for- -a walk &c. *n.*; have a run; take the air.

flit, take wing; migrate, emigrate, *trek*; rove, prowl, roam, range, patrol, pace up and down, traverse; scour -, traverse- the country; peragrate; per-, circum-ambulate; nomadize, wander, ramble, stroll, saunter, hover, go one's rounds, straggle; gad, - about; expatiate.

walk, march, step, tread, pace, plod, wend; promenade; trudge, tramp; stalk, stride, straddle, strut, foot it, stump, bundle, bowl along, toddle; paddle; tread -, follow -, pursue- a path.

take horse, ride, drive, trot, amble, canter, prance, fisk, frisk, *caracoler*; gallop &c. (*move quickly*) 274; motor, cycle, taxi; go by -car, - train, - tram, - bus, - plane.

peg -, jog -, wag -, shuffle- on; stir one's stumps; bend one's -steps, - course; make -, find -, wend -, pick -, thread -, plough-one's way; coast, slide, glide, skim, skate, ski; march in procession, file off, defile.

go -, repair -, resort -, hie -, betake oneself- to.

Adj. travelling &c. *v.*; ambulatory, itinerant, peripatetic, peram-

267. [Locomotion by water, or air.] **Navigation.**—**N.** navigation; aquatics; boating, cruising, yachting; ship &c. 273; oar, scull, sweep, punt pole, paddle, - wheel, screw, propeller, stern wheel, sail, canvas.

natation, swimming; fin, flipper-fish's tail.

aerial navigation, air service, airways, airmanship, aero-donetics, -dynamics, -mechanics, -station, -statics, -nautics; ballooning, balloonry; balloon &c. 273; flying, flight, aviation, volitation; wing, pinion, *aileron*.

voyage, sail, cruise, passage, circumnavigation, *periplus*; head-, stern-, lee-way.

mariner, aeronaut &c. 269.

V. sail; put to sea &c. (*depart*) 293; take ship, get under way; spread -sail, - canvas; gather way, have way on; make -, carry- sail; plough the -waves, - deep, - main, - ocean; walk the waters.

navigate, warp, luff, scud, boom, kedge; drift, course, cruise, coast; hug the -shore, - land; circumnavigate.

ply the oar, row, paddle, pull, scull, punt, steam.

swim, float; buffet the waves, ride the storm, skim, *effleurer*, dive, wade.

fly, aviate, be wafted, hover, soar, drift, glide, plane, sideslip, *volplane*, pique, dive, spin, roll, loop, flutter; take -wing, - a flight; wing one's -flight, - way.

Adj. sailing &c. *v.*; seafaring, nautical, maritime, naval; sea-going, coasting; afloat; navigable, aquatic, natatory.

volitant, volant, aerostatic, aerial, aeronautic; alar, alate, pennate.

Adv. under -way, - sail, - canvas, - steam; on the wing.

———

bulatory, roving, rambling, gadding, discursive, vagrant, migratory, nomadic; circumforane-an, -ous; somnambular, nocti-, mundi-vagant; locomotive, automotive, self-moving.

way-faring, -worn; travel-stained.

Adv. on -foot, – horseback, – Shanks's mare; by the Marrowbone stage; *in transitu* &c. 270; *en route* &c. 282.

Int. come along!

268. Traveller.—N. traveller, way-farer, voyager, itinerant, passenger.

tourist, excursionist, globe-trotter; explorer, adventurer, mountaineer, Alpine Club; peregrinator, wanderer, rover, straggler, rambler; bird of passage; gad-about, -ling; vagrant, scatterling, landloper, waifs and estrays, wastrel, stray; loafer; tramp, -er, hobo, beachcomber, vagabond, nomad, Bohemian, gipsy, Arab, Wandering Jew, Hadji, pilgrim, palmer; peripatetic; somnambulist, sleep walker, noctambulist; emigrant, fugitive, refugee, *émigré*.

runner, courier, King's messenger; Mercury, Iris, Ariel, comet.

269. Mariner.—N. sailor, mariner, navigator, argonaut; sea-man, -farer, -faring man; yachtsman; tar, jack tar, salt, gob, sea-dog, shellback, able seaman, A.B.; man-of-war's man, bluejacket, marine, jolly; midshipman, middy, reefer; captain, commander, master mariner, skipper, mate; ship-, boat-, ferry-, water-, lighter-, barge-, longshore- man, hoveller; bargee, gondolier; oar-, -sman; rower; boat-, cock-swain; coxswain; steersman, helmsman, pilot; crew; lascar.

aerial navigator, aeronaut, balloonist, Icarus, aviator, pilot, observer, flyer, airman.

pedestrian, walker, foot-passenger; cyclist; wheelman.

rider, horseman, equestrian, cavalier, jockey, rough rider, trainer, breaker, huntsman.

driver, coachman, whip, Jehu, charioteer, postilion, post-boy, carter, wagoner, drayman, truckman; cab-man, -driver; *voiturier*, *vetturino*, *condottiere*; engine-driver; stoker, fireman, guard, brake-man, conductor; chauffeur, automobilist, motorist, motor –, truck --, taxi- driver.

270. Transference.—N. transfer, -ence; trans-, e-location; displacement; *meta-stasis, -thesis*; removal; re-, a-motion; relegation; de-, as-portation; extradition, conveyance, draft; carrying, carriage; convection, -duction, -tagion, infection; transfusion; transfer &c. (*of property*) 783.

transit, transition; passage, ferry, gestation; portage, porterage, carting, cartage; shovelling &c. *v.*; vect-ion, -ure, -itation; shipment, freight, wafture; trans-mission, -port, -portation, -umption, -plantation, -lation; shift-, dodg-ing; dispersion &c. 73; transposition &c. (*interchange*) 148; traction &c. 285.

[Thing transferred] drift, alluvium, detritus, *moraine*; gift, legacy, bequest, lease; freight, mails, cargo, luggage, baggage, goods.

V. trans-fer, -mit, -port, -place, -plant; convey, assign, carry, bear, fetch and carry; carry –, ferry- over; hand, pass, forward; shift; conduct, convoy, bring, fetch, reach.

send, delegate, consign, mail, post, relegate, turn over to, pass the buck, deliver; ship, embark; waft; switch, shunt; transpose &c. (*interchange*) 148; displace &c. 185; throw &c. 284; drag &c. 285.

shovel, lade, dip, ladle, bale, decant, draft off, transfuse.

Adj. transferred &c. *v.*; drifted; movable; port-able, -ative; conductive; contagious, infectious.

transferable, assignable, conveyable, devisable, negotiable, transmissible.

Adv. from -hand to hand, – pillar to post.

on –, by- the way; on the -road, – wing; as one goes; *in transitu, en route, chemin faisant, en passant*, in mid-progress.

271. Carrier.—N. carrier, porter, red cap, bearer, messenger, postman, tranter, conveyer; stevedore; coolie; conductor, locomotive, tractor, caterpillar tractor, motor.

beast of burden, cattle, horse, steed, nag, palfrey, Arab, blood horse, thorough-bred, galloway, charger, courser, racer, hunter, jument, pony, filly, colt, foal, barb, roan, jade, hack, *bidet,* pad, cob, tit, punch, roadster, goer; race-, pack-, draft-, cart-, dray-, post-horse, mount; Shetland pony, sheltie; garran; jennet, genet, bayard, mare, stallion, gelding; stud.

Pegasus, Bucephalus, Rozinante.

ass, donkey, jackass, mule, hinny; sumpter -horse, – mule; reindeer; camel, dromedary, mehari, llama, elephant; carrier pigeon.

carriage &c. (*vehicle*) 272; ship &c. 273.

Adj. equine, asinine.

272. Vehicle.—N. vehicle, conveyance, carriage, car, caravan, van, furniture van, pantechnicon; wagon, wain, dray, cart, lorry.

carriole; sledge, sled, sleigh, bob-sleigh, toboggan, *luge,* truck, tram; limber, tumbrel, pontoon; barrow; wheel-, hand- -barrow, – cart, trolley; perambulator; Bath –, wheel –, sedan-chair, jinriksha, rickshaw; ekka; chaise; palan-keen, -quin; litter, horse-litter, brancard, crate, hurdle, stretcher, ambulance; velocipede, hobby-horse, coaster, scooter, go-cart; cycle; bi-, tri-, quadri-cycle; tandem, safety; skate, roller skate; ski, snow-shoe.

equipage, turn-out; coach, chariot, *quadriga,* chaise, phaëton, break, brake, mail-phaëton, wagonette, drag, curricle, tilbury, whisky, landau, *barouche,* victoria, brougham, clarence, calash, *calèche,* britzska, *araba,* kibitka; berlin; sulky, *désobligeant,* sociable, *vis-à-vis, dormeuse;* jaunting –, outside- car; *tarantass;* runabout; shay.

post-chaise; diligence, stage; stage –, mail –, hackney –, glass- coach; stage-wagon; car, omnibus, bus, fly, *cabriolet,* cab, hansom, shofle, four-wheeler, growler, *droshki,* drosky.

dog-cart, trap, gig, whitechapel, buggy, four-in-hand, unicorn, random, tandem; shandredhan, *char-à-banc.*

automobile, motor-, auto-, touring-, racing-, cycle-, side-, steam-, electric-

273. Ship.—N. ship, vessel, sail; craft, bottom.

navy, marine, fleet, flotilla, squadron; shipping.

man of war &c. (*combatant*) 726; transport, tender, store-ship; merchant ship, merchantman; packet, liner; whaler, slaver, collier, coaster, tanker, freighter, freight steamer, cargo boat, lighter; fishing-, pilot- boat; trawler, drifter; cable ship; hulk; yacht; floating palace, ocean greyhound.

ship, bark, barque, brig, snow, hermaphrodite brig; brigantine, barquentine; schooner; topsail –, fore and aft –, three masted- schooner; *chasse-marée;* sloop, cutter, corvette, clipper, foist, yawl, dandy, ketch, smack, lugger, barge, hoy, cat-, -boat, buss; sail-er, -ing vessel, wind jammer; steam-er, -boat, -ship; mail –, paddle –, screw –, sternwheel- steamer; tug; train-ferry; line of steamers &c.

boat, pinnace, launch, motor-boat, picket-boat; hydroplane; life-, long-, jolly-, bum-, fly-, cock-, ferry-, canal-boat, dory, dugout, galliot; shallop, gig, funny, skiff, dingy, scow, cockle-shell, wherry, coble, punt, cog, lerret; eight-, four-, pair- oar; randan; outrigger; float, raft, pontoon; prame, ice-yacht.

state barge, bucentaur.

catamaran, coracle, gondola, carvel, caravel; felucca, caique, canoe; trireme;

car; motor-, -omnibus, – bus, – cab, – cycle; limousine, landaulette, cabriolet, *coupé*, *voiturette*, runabout, electromobile, taxi, -cab.

train; passenger –, express –, freight –, subway –, special –, corridor –, parliamentary –, luggage –, goods-train, *train de luxe*; 1st-, 2nd-, 3rd-class- -train, – carriage, – compartment; Pullman –, sleeping-, club-, observation-, dining-, restaurant-car; mail-, luggage-, brake-van, coach, car, carriage; rolling stock; horse-box, cattle-truck.

tramcar, trolley-omnibus, trackless trolley.

shovel, spoon, spatula, ladle, hod, hoe; spade, spaddle, loy; spud; pitch-fork.

Adj. vehicular.

---

galley, – foist; bilander, dogger, hooker, howker; argosy, carack; galliass, galleon; galliot, polacca, polacre, corsair, tartane, junk, lorcha, praam, proa, prahu, saick, sampan, xebec, dhow; dahabeah; nuggar, cayak, piroque; trireme.

submarine, submersible.

aircraft (*combatant*) &c. 726; flying machine, air mail, aero-, air-, mono-, bi-, tri-, hydro aero-plane, plane, cabin plane, transport plane, *avion*, flying boat, glider, *aviette*, helicopter; balloon, air-, fire-, gas-, Mongolfier-, pilot-, captive-, free-, kite-, dirigible- balloon, air-ship, *Zeppelin*, blimp; kite, parachute.

nacelle, car, gondola, aileron; hangar, airport, landing field, airdrome; catwalk, controls, rudder, tail.

Adj. marine, maritime, naval, nautical, seafaring, sea-, ocean-going, seaworthy.

aerial, aeronautical, air-worthy, flying &c. *n.*
Adv. afloat, aboard; on -board, – ship board, – board ship.

2°. DEGREES OF MOTION

274. Velocity.—**N.** velocity, speed, celerity; swiftness &c. *adj.*; rapidity, eagle speed; expedition &c. (*activity*) 682; pernicity; acceleration; haste &c. 684.

spurt, rush, dash, race, steeplechase; smart –, lively –, swift &c. *adj.* –, rattling –, spanking –, strapping- -rate, – pace; round pace; flying, flight.

gallop, canter, trot, round trot, run, scamper; hand –, full- gallop; swoop.

lightning, light, electricity, wind; cannon-ball, rocket, arrow, dart, quicksilver; telegraph, express train; torrent; swallow flight.

eagle, antelope, courser, race-horse, gazelle, greyhound, hare, doe, squirrel.

Mercury, Ariel, Camilla, Harlequin.

[Measurement of velocity] speed-ometer, log, -line, tachometer.

V. move quickly, trip, fisk; speed, hie, hasten, sprint, spurt, post, spank, scuttle; scud, -dle, scurry; scour, – the plain; scamper; run, – like mad; fly, race, run a race, cut away, cut and run, shoot, tear, whisk, whiz, sweep, skim, brush; cut –, bowl- along; rush

---

275. Slowness.—**N.** slowness &c. *adj.*; languor &c. (*inactivity*) 683; drawl; creeping &c. *v.*, lentor.

retardation; slackening &c. *v.*; delay &c. (*lateness*) 133; claudication.

jog-, dog-trot, walk; mincing steps; slow -march, – time.

slow -goer, – coach, – back; lingerer, loiterer, sluggard, tortoise, snail; dawdle &c. (*inactive*) 683.

V. move -slowly, &c. *adv.*; creep, crawl, lag, slug, walk, drawl, linger, loiter, saunter; plod, trudge, stump along, lumber; trail; drag; dawdle &c. (*be inactive*) 683; grovel, worm one's way, steal along; jog –, rub –, bundle-on; toddle, waddle, wabble, slug; traipse, slouch, shuffle, halt, hobble, limp, claudicate, shamble; flag, falter, totter, stagger; mince, step short; march in -slow time, – funeral procession; take one's time; hang fire &c. (*be late*) 133.

retard, relax; slacken, check, moderate, rein in, curb; reef; strike –, shorten –, take in- sail; put on the drag, apply the brake; clip the wings; reduce the

&c. (*be violent*) 173; dash -on, – off, – forward; bolt; trot, gallop, bound, flit, spring, dart, boom; march in -quick, – double-time; ride hard, get over the ground, scorch.

hurry &c. (*hasten*) 684; accelerate, put on; quicken; quicken –, mend- one's pace; clap spurs to one's horse; make -haste, – rapid strides, – forced marches, – the best of one's way; put one's best leg foremost, stir one's stumps, wing one's way, set off at a score; carry –, crowd- sail; go off like a shot, go ahead, gain ground; outstrip the wind, fly on the wings of the wind.

keep -up, – pace- with; outstrip &c. 303.

Adj. fast, speedy, swift, rapid, quick, fleet; nimble, agile, expeditious; ex- press; active &c. 682; flying, galloping &c. *v.*; light-, nimble-footed; winged, eagle-winged, mercurial, electric, tele- graphic; light-legged, light of heel; swift

as -an arrow &c. *n.*; quick as -lightning &c. *n.*, – thought.*

Adv. swiftly &c. *adj.*; with -speed &c. *n.*; apace; at -a great rate, – full speed, – railway speed; full -drive, – gallop; post-haste, in full sail, tantivy; trippingly; instantaneously &c. 113; like a shot.

under press of -sail, – canvas, – sail and steam; *velis et remis*, on eagle's wing, in double quick time; with -rapid, – giant- strides; *à pas de géant*; in seven league boots; whip and spur; *ventre à terre*; as fast as one's -legs, – heels- will carry one; as fast as one can lay feet to the ground, at the top of one's speed; by leaps and bounds; with haste &c. 684; in- high – gear, – speed.

Phr. *vires acquirit eundo.*

speed, decelerate; slacken -speed, – one's pace, lose ground; back -water, – pedal, put the engines astern, throttle down.

Adj. slow, slack; tardy; dilatory &c. (*inactive*) 683; gentle, easy; leisurely; deliberate, gradual; insensible, imper- ceptible; languid, sluggish, apathetic, phlegmatic, slow-paced, tardigrade, snail-like; creeping &c. *v.*

Adv. slowly &c. *adj.*; leisurely; *piano, adagio*; *largo, larghetto*; at half speed, under easy sail; at a -foot's, – snail's, – funeral- pace; slower than molasses in January; in slow time; with -mincing steps, – clipped wings; *haud passibus æquis*; in- low –, gear, – speed.

gradually &c. *adj.*; *gradatim*; by -degrees, – slow degrees, – inches, – little and little; step by step; inch by inch, bit by bit, little by little, *seriatim*; consecutively.

3°. Motion Conjoined with Force

276. Impulse.—**N.** impulse, impul- sion, impetus; momentum; push, pulsion, thrust, shove, jog, jolt, brunt, booming, boost, throw; explosion &c. (*violence*) 173; propulsion &c. 284.

percussion, concussion, collision, oc- cursion, clash, encounter, cannon, *carambole*, appulse, shock, crash, bump; impact; *élan*; charge &c. (*attack*) 716; beating &c. (*punishment*) 972.

blow, dint, stroke, knock, tap, rap, slap, smack, pat, dab; fillip; slam, bang; hit, whack, thwack, clout; cuff &c. 972; squash, dowse, whap, swap, punch, thump, swipe, jab, pelt, kick, punce, calcitration; *ruade*; arietation; cut, thrust, lunge, yerk.

277. Recoil.—**N.** recoil; re-, retro- action; revulsion; rebound, *ricochet*; re-percussion, -calcitration; kick, *contre- coup*; springing back &c. *v.*; elasticity &c. 325; reflexion, reflex, reflux; rever- beration &c. (*resonance*) 408; rebuff, repulse; return.

ducks and drakes; boomerang; spring; reactionist, reactionary.

V. recoil, resile, react; spring –, fly –, bound- back; rebound, reverberate, repercuss, recalcitrate, echo, *ricochet*.

Adj. recoiling &c. *v.*; re-fluent, -percussive, -calcitrant, -actionary; retroactive.

Adv. on the -recoil &c. *n.*

* See note on 264.

hammer, sledge-hammer, mall, maul, mallet, flail; ram, -mer; bat-tering-ram, monkey, pile-driver, punch, bat, tamper, tamping iron; cudgel &c. (*weapon*) 727; axe &c. (*sharp*) 253.

[Science of mechanical forces] mechanics, dynamics &c.

V. give an -impetus &c. *n.*; impel, push; start, give a start to, set going; drive, urge, boom; thrust, prod, foin; cant; elbow, shoulder, jostle, justle, hustle, hurtle, shove, jog, jolt, bean, encounter; run -, bump -, butt- against; knock -, run- one's head against; impinge.

strike, knock, hit, bash, tap, rap, bat, slap, flap, dab, pat, thump, beat, bang, slam, dash; punch, thwack, whack; hit -, strike- hard; swap, batter, dowse, baste; pelt, patter, skelter, buffet, belabour, tamp; fetch one a blow, swat; poke at, pink, lunge, yerk; kick, calcitrate; butt; strike at &c. (*attack*) 716; whip &c. (*punish*) 972; propel &c. 284.

come -, enter- into collision; collide; foul; fall -, run- foul of. throw &c. (*propel*) 284.

Adj. impelling &c. *v.*; im-pulsive, -pellent; booming; dynamic, -al; impelled &c. *v.*

4°. Motion with Reference to Direction

278. Direction.—N. direction, bear-ing, course, set, drift, tenor; tendency &c. 176; incidence; bending, trending &c. *v.*; dip, tack, aim, collimation; steer-ing, -age.

point of the compass, cardinal -, half -, quarter- points; North, East, South, West; N by E, ENE, NE by N, NE &c.; rhumb, azimuth, line of collimation.

line, path, road, range, quarter, line of march; a-, al-lignment; straight shot, bee-line.

V. tend -, bend -, point- towards; conduct -, go- to; point -to, - at; bend, trend, verge, incline, dip, determine.

steer -, make- -for, - towards; aim -, level- at; take aim; keep -, hold- a course; be bound for; bend one's steps towards; direct -, steer -, bend -, shape- one's course; align -, allign- one's march; go straight, - to the point; march -on, - on a point.

ascertain one's -direction &c. *n.*; *s'orienter*, see which way the wind blows; box the compass.

Adj. directed &c. *v.*, - towards; pointing towards &c. *v.*; bound for; aligned -, alligned- with; direct, straight; un-deviating, -swerving; straightforward; North, -ern, -erly, &c. *n.*

directable &c. *v.*

Adv. towards; on the -road, - high

279. Deviation. — N. deviation; swerving &c. *v.*; obliquation, warp, refraction; flection, flexion; sweep; de-flection, -flexure; declination.

diversion, digression, departure from, aberration, drift, sheer; divergence &c. 291; zigzag; *détour* &c. (*circuit*) 629.

[Desultory motion] wandering &c. *v.*; vagrancy, evagation; by-paths and crooked ways.

[Motion sideways, oblique motion] sidling &c. *v.*; *échelon*, leeway; knight's move (at chess).

V. alter one's course, deviate, depart from, turn, trend; bend, curve &c. 245; swerve, heel, bear off.

intervert; deflect; divert, - from its course; put on a new scent, shift, shunt, switch, wear, draw aside, crook, warp, short circuit.

stray, straggle; sidle, edge; diverge &c. 291; tralineate, digress, divagate, wander; wind, twist, meander, meander around Robin Hood's barn; veer, tack, sheer; turn -aside, - a corner, - away from; wheel, steer clear of; ramble, rove, drift; go -astray, - adrift; yaw, dodge; step aside, ease off, make way for, shy.

fly off at a tangent; glance off; turn, wheel -, face- about; turn -, face- to the right about; wabble &c. (*oscillate*) 314; go out of one's way &c. (*perform a circuit*) 629; lose one's way.

road- to; *versus*, to; hither, thither, whither; directly; straight, – forwards, – as an arrow; point blank; in a -direct, – straight- line -to, – for, – with; in a line with; full tilt at, as the crow flies.

before –, near –, close to –, against- the wind; windwards, in the wind's eye.

through, *via*, by way of; in all -directions, – manner of ways; *quaquaversum*, from the four winds.

280. [Going before.] **Precession.—N.** precession, leading, heading; precedence &c. 62; priority &c. 116; the lead, *le pas*; van &c. (*front*) 234; precursor &c. 64.

V. go -before, – ahead, – in the van, – in advance; precede, forerun; usher in, introduce, herald, head, take the lead; lead, – the way, – the dance; get –, have- the start; steal a march; get -before, – ahead, – in front of; outstrip &c. 303; take precedence &c. (*first in order*) 62.

Adj. foremost, first, leading &c. *v.*

Adv. in advance, before, ahead, in the van; fore-, head-most; in front.

Phr. *seniores priores.*

---

282. [Motion forwards; progressive motion.] **Progression.—N.** progress, -ion, -iveness; advancing &c. *v.*; advance, -ment; ongoing; flood-tide, headway; march &c. 266; rise; improvement &c. 658.

V. advance; proceed, progress; get -on, – along, – over the ground; gain ground; jog –, rub –, wag- on; go with the stream; keep –, hold on- one's course; go –, move –, come –, get –, pass –, push –, press- -on, – forward, – forwards, – ahead; press onwards, step forward; make –, work –, carve –, push –, force –, edge –, elbow- one's way; make -progress, – head, – way, – headway, – advances, – strides, – rapid strides &c. (*velocity*) 274; go –, shoot- ahead; distance; make up leeway.

Adj. advancing &c. *v.*; pro-gressive, -fluent; advanced.

Adj. deviating &c. *v.*; aberrant, errant; ex-, dis-cursive; devious, desultory, loose; rambling; stray, erratic, vagrant, undirected; circuitous, indirect, zigzag; crab-like.

Adv. astray from, round about, wide of the mark; to the right about; all manner of ways; circuitously &c. 629.

obliquely, sideling, like the move of the knight on a chessboard.

---

281. [Going after.] **Sequence.—N.** sequence, run; coming after &c. (*order*) 63; (*time*) 117; following; pursuit &c. 622.

follower, attendant, satellite, shadow, dangler, train.

V. follow; pursue &c. 622; go –, fly- after.

attend, beset, dance attendance on, dog, be-dog; tread -in the steps of, – close upon; be –, go –, follow- in the -wake, – trail, – rear- of; trail, follow as a shadow, hang on the skirts of; tread –, follow- on the heels of, tag after.

lag, get behind.

Adj. following &c. *v.*

Adv. behind; in the -rear &c. 235, – train of, wake of; after &c. (*order*) 63, (*time*) 117.

---

283. [Motion backwards.] **Regression.—N.** regress, -ion; retro-cession, -gression, -gradation, -action; *reculade*; retreat, withdrawal, retirement, re-migration; recession &c. (*motion from*) 287; recess; crab-like motion.

re-fluence, -flux; backwater, regurgitation, ebb, return; resilience; re-flexion (*recoil*) 277; *volte-face*.

counter -motion, – movement, – march; veering, tergiversation, re-cidivation, backsliding, fall, relapse; deterioration &c. 659.

turning-point &c. (*reversion*) 145.

V. re-cede, -grade, -turn, -vert, -treat, -tire; retro-grade, -cede; back, – down, – out, crawl; withdraw; rebound &c. 277; go –, come –, turn –, hark –, draw –, fall –, get –, put –, run- back; lose ground; fall –, drop- astern; back water, put about; veer, – round; double,

Adv. forward, onward; forth, on ahead, under way, *en route* for, on -one's way, – the way, – the road, – the high road- to; in -progress, – mid progress; *in transitu* &c. 270.

Phr. *vestigia nulla retrorsum.*

---

wheel, counter-march; ebb, regurgitate; jib, shrink, shy.

turn -tail, – round, – upon one's heel, – one's back upon; retrace one's steps, dance the back step; sound –, beat- a retreat; go home.

Adj. receding &c. *v.*; retro-grade, -gressive; re-gressive, -fluent, -flex, -cidivous, -silient; crab-like; reactionary &c. 277; counter-clockwise.

Adv. back, -wards; reflexively, to the right about; *à reculons, à rebours.*

Phr. *revenons à nos moutons,* as you were.

284. [Motion given to an object situated in front.] **Propulsion.—N.** pro-pulsion, -jection; *vis a tergo*; push &c. (*impulse*) 276; e-, jaculation; ejection &c. 297; throw, fling, toss, shot, discharge, shy.

[Science of propulsion] gunnery, ballistics, archery.

missile, projectile, ball, *discus*, javelin, hammer, quoit, brickbat, shot, bullet; arrow, shaft, gun &c. (*arms*) 727.

shooter, shot; gunner, gun-layer; archer, toxophilite; bow-, rifle-, marksman; good –, crack- shot; sharpshooter &c. (*combatant*) 726.

V. propel, project, throw, fling, cast, pitch, chuck, toss, jerk, heave, shy, hurl; flirt, fillip.

dart, lance, tilt; e-, jaculate; fulminate, bolt, drive, sling, pitchfork.

send; send –, let –, fire- off; discharge, shoot; launch, send forth, let fly; dash.

put –, set- in motion; set agoing, start; give -a start, – an impulse-to; push, impel &c. 276; trundle &c. (*set in rotation*) 312; expel &c. 297.

carry one off one's legs; put to flight.

Adj. propelled &c. *v.*; propelling &c. *v.*; pro-pulsive, -jectile.

285. [Motion given to an object situated behind.] **Traction.—N.** traction; drawing &c. *v.*; draught, pull, haul; rake; 'a long pull, a strong pull and a pull all together'; towage, haulage.

V. draw, pull, haul, lug, rake, drag, draggle, tug, tow, trail, trawl, train; take in tow.

wrench, jerk, twitch.

Adj. drawing &c. *v.*; tractive, tractile; ductile.

286. [Motion towards.] **Approach.—N.** approach, approximation, appropinquation; access; appulse; afflux, -ion; advent &c. (*approach of time*) 121; pursuit &c. 622; convergence &c. 290.

V. approach, approximate; near; get –, go –, draw- near; come, – near, – to close quarters; move –, set in-towards; drift; make up to; gain upon; pursue &c. 622; tread on the heels of; bear up; make the land; hug the -shore, – land.

Adj. approaching &c. *v.*; approximative; convergent; affluent; impending, imminent &c. (*destined*) 152.

287. [Motion from.] **Recession.—N.** recession, retirement, withdrawal; retreat; retrocession &c. 283; departure &c. 293; recoil &c. 277; flight &c. (*avoidance*) 623.

V. recede, go, move from, retire, ebb, withdraw, shrink; come –, move –, go –, get –, drift- away; depart &c. 293; retreat &c. 283; move –, stand –, sheer- off; swerve from; fall back, stand aside; run away &c. (*avoid*) 623.

remove, shunt, side track, switch off.

Adj. receding &c. *v.*

Adv. on the road.

Int. come hither! approach! here! come! come near!

288. [Motion towards, actively.] **Attraction.**—**N.** attract-ion, -iveness; pull; drawing to, pulling towards, adduction, magnetism, gravity, attraction of gravitation; lure, bait, decoy.

lode-stone, -star; magnet, siderite, magnetite.

V. attract; draw –, pull –, drag- towards; adduce.

lure, bait, decoy.

Adj. attracting &c. *v.*; attrahent, attractive, adducent, adductive.

289. [Motion from, actively.] **Repulsion.**—**N.** repulsion; driving from &c. *v.*; repulse; abduction.

V. repel; push –, drive – &c. 276. from; chase, dispel; retrude; abduce, abduct; send away, repulse, dismiss.

keep at arm's length, turn one's back upon, give the cold shoulder; send packing; send -off, – away- with a flea in one's ear, – about one's business.

Adj. repelling &c. *v.*; repellant, repulsive; abducent, abductive.

290. [Motion nearer to.] **Convergence.** —**N.** con-vergence, -fluence, -course, -flux, -gress, -currence, -centration; appulse, meeting; corradiation.

assemblage &c. 72; resort &c. (*focus*) 74; asymptote.

V. converge, concur; come together, unite, meet, fall in with; close -with, – in upon; centre -round, – in; enter in; pour in.

gather together, unite, concentrate, bring into a focus.

Adj. converging &c. *v.*; con-vergent, -fluent, -current; centripetal; asymptotical.

291. [Motion further off.] **Divergence.** —**N.** diverg-ence, -ency; divarication, ramification, radiation; separation &c. (*disjunction*) 44; dispersion &c. 73; deviation &c. 279; aberration, declination.

V. diverge, divaricate, radiate; ramify; branch –, glance –, file- off; fly off, – at a tangent; spread, scatter, disperse &c. 73; deviate &c. 279; part &c. (*separate*) 44; splay apart.

Adj. diverging &c. *v.*; divergent, radiant, centrifugal; aberrant.

292. [Terminal motion at.] **Arrival.** —**N.** arrival, advent; landing; de-, disem-barkation; reception, welcome, *vin d'honneur.*

home, goal, bourn; landing-place, -stage; resting –, stopping -place; destination, harbour, haven, port; terminal, terminus, railway station, depot, airport; halt, halting -place, – ground; anchorage &c. (*refuge*) 666.

return, recursion, remigration; meeting; ren-, en-counter.

completion &c. 729.

V. arrive; get to, come to; come; reach, attain; come up, – with, – to; overtake; make, fetch; complete &c. 729; join, rejoin.

light, alight, dismount; land, go ashore; debark, disembark; put -in, – into; visit, cast anchor, pitch one's tent; sit down &c. (*be located*) 184; get to one's journey's end; make the

293. [Initial motion from.] **Departure.**—**N.** departure, decession, decampment; embarkation; take-off; outset, start; removal; exit &c. (*egress*) 295; exodus, Hejira, flight.

leave-taking, *congé*, valediction, valedictory, adieu, farewell, good-bye, stirrup-cup.

starting -point, – post; point –, place- of -departure, – embarkation; port of embarkation.

V. depart; go, – away; take one's departure, set out; set –, march –, put –, start –, be –, move –, get –, whip –, pack –, go –, take oneself- off; start, issue, march out, debouch; go –, sally- forth; sally, set forward; be gone.

leave a place, quit, vacate, evacuate, abandon; go off the stage, make ones' exit; retire, withdraw, remove; go -one's way, – along, – from home; take -flight, – wing; spring, fly, flit, wing

land; be in at the death; come –, get- -back, – home; return; come in &c. (*ingress*) 294; make one's appearance &c. (*appear*) 446; drop in; detrain; outspan.

come to hand; come -at, – across; hit; come –, light –, pop –, bounce –, plump –, burst –, pitch- upon; meet; en- ren-counter; come in contact.

Adj. arriving &c. *v.*; homeward-bound; terminal.

Adv. here, hither.

Int. welcome! hail! all hail! good-day, – morrow; greetings! hullo! well!

one's flight; fly –, whip- away; take off, hop off; embark; go -on board, – aboard; set sail; put –, go- to sea; sail, take ship; hoist blue Peter; get under way, weigh anchor; strike tents, break camp, decamp; walk one's chalks, make tracks, cut one's stick; cut and run; take leave; say –, bid- -good-bye &c. *n.*; disappear &c. 449; abscond &c. (*avoid*) 623; entrain, embus, emplane; saddle –, harness –, hitch- up; inspan.

Adj. departing &c. *v.*; valedictory; outward bound.

Adv. whence, hence, thence; with a foot in the stirrup; on the -wing, – move.

Int. begone! &c. (*ejection*) 297; to horse! all aboard! farewell! adieu! good-bye, – day! *au revoir! auf wiedersehen!* fare you well! so long! God -bless you, – speed! *bon voyage!*

---

294. [Motion into.] **Ingress.—N.** ingress; entrance, entry; introgression; influx; intrusion, inroad, incursion, invasion, irruption; pene-, interpenetration; illapse, import, importation, infiltration; immigration; admission &c. (*reception*) 296; insinuation &c. (*interjacence*) 228; insertion &c. 300.

inlet; way in; mouth, door &c. (*opening*) 260; path &c. (*way*) 627; conduit &c. 350; immigrant, visitor, incomer, newcomer, colonist.

V. have the *entrée*; enter; go –, come –, pour –, flow –, creep –, slip –, pop –, break –, burst- -into, – in; set foot on; burst –, break- in upon; invade, intrude, butt in, horn in, crash; insinuate itself; inter-, penetrate; infiltrate; find one's way –, wriggle –, worm oneself- into.

give entrance to &c. (*receive*) 296; insert &c. 300.

Adj. incoming, ingressive &c. *n.*; inward bound.

Adv. inward.

295. [Motion out of.] **Egress.—N.** egress, exit, issue; emer-sion, -gence; disemboguement; out-break, -burst; e-, pro-ruption; emanation; evacuation; ex-, trans-udation; extravasation, per-spiration, sweating, leakage, percolation, distillation, oozing; gush &c. (*water in motion*) 348; outpour, -ing; effluence, effusion; efflux, -ion; drain; dribbling &c. *v.*; defluxion; drainage; out-come, -put; discharge &c. (*excretion*) 299.

export; expatriation; e-, re-migration; *débouche*; exodus &c. (*departure*) 293; emigrant, migrant, *émigré*, colonist.

outlet, vent, spout, tap, sluice, flood-gate; pore; vomitory, out-gate, sally-port; way out; mouth, door &c. (*opening*) 260; path &c. (*way*) 627; conduit &c. 350; air-pipe &c. 351.

V. emerge, emanate, issue; go –, come –, move –, pass –, pour –, flow-out of; pass off, evacuate; migrate.

ex-, trans-ude; leak; run, – out, – through; per-, trans-colate; seep; strain, distil; perspire, sweat, drain, ooze; filter, filtrate; dribble, gush, spout, flow out; well, – out; pour, trickle &c. (*water in motion*) 348; effuse, extravasate, disembogue, discharge itself, debouch; come –, break- forth; burst- out, – through; find vent, escape &c. 671.

Adj. effused &c. *v.*; outgoing, outward bound.

Adv. outward.

296. [Motion into, actively.] **Reception.**—**N.** reception; admission, admittance, *entrée*, importation; initiation; intro-duction, -mission, -ception; immission, ingestion, imbibition, absorption, ingurgitation, inhalation; suction, sucking; eating, drinking &c. (*food*) 298; insertion &c. 300; interjection &c. 228.

V. give -entrance to, – admittance to, – the *entrée*; intro-duce, -mit; usher, admit, receive, import, initiate, bring in, open the door to, throw open, ingest, absorb, imbibe, inhale, infiltrate; let –, take –, suck- in; re-admit, -sorb, -absorb; snuff up; swallow, ingurgitate; engulf, engorge; gulp; eat, drink &c. (*food*) 298.

Adj. admit-ting &c. *v.*, -ted &c. *v.*; admissible; absorbent; introductory, introceptive, intromittent, initiatory.

297. [Motion out of, actively.] **Ejection.**—**N.** ejection, emission, effusion, rejection, expulsion, eviction, extrusion, trajection; discharge.

egestion, evacuation, vomition, disgorgement, voidance, eruption, eruptiveness; ruc-, eruc-tation, blood-letting, venesection, phlebotomy, paracentesis; tapping, drainage; clear-ance, -age, voidance; vomiting, excretion &c. 299.

deportation; banishment &c. (*punishment*) 972; rogue's march; relegation, extradition; dislodgment.

V. give -exit, – vent- to; let –, give –, pour –, send- out; des-, dis-patch; exhale, excern, excrete, disembogue, secrete, secern; extravasate, shed, void, evacuate, egest, emit; open the -sluices, – floodgates; turn on the tap; extrude, detrude; effuse, spend, expend; pour forth; squirt, spirt, spill, slop; perspire &c. (*exude*) 295; breathe, blow &c. (*wind*) 349.

tap, draw off; bale –, lade- out; let blood, broach.

eject, reject; expel, discard; cut, send to Coventry, boycott, ostracize; *chasser*; banish &c. (*punish*) 972; throw &c. 284 -out, – up, – off, – away, – aside; push &c. 276 -out, – off, – away, – aside; shovel –, sweep- -out, – away; brush –, whisk –, turn –, send- -off, – away; discharge; send –, turn –, cast- adrift; turn –, bundle- out; throw overboard; give the sack to; send -packing, – about one's business, – to the right about; strike off the roll &c. (*abrogate*) 756; turn out- neck and heels, – head and shoulders, – neck and crop; pack off; send away with a flea in the ear; send to Jericho; bow out, show the door to, dismiss, fire, sack.

turn out of -doors, – house and home; evict, oust; exorcise, un-house, -kennel; dislodge; un-, dis-people; depopulate; relegate, deport.

empty; drain, – to the dregs; sweep off; clear, – off, – out, – away; suck, draw off, extract; clean out, make a clean sweep of, clear decks, purge.

em-, dis-, disem-bowel; eviscerate, gut; unearth, root -out, – up; averruncate; weed –, get out; eliminate, get rid of, do away with, shake off; exenterate.

vomit, spew, puke, keck, retch; belch, – out, eruct, eructate; cast –, bring- up; disgorge; expectorate, salivate, clear the throat, hawk, spit, sputter, splutter, slobber, drool, drivel, slaver, slabber.

unpack, unlade, unload, unship; break bulk.

be let out; ooze &c. (*emerge*) 295.

Adj. emitt-ing, -ed &c. *v.*

begone! get you gone! get –, go- -away, – along, – along with you! go your way! away, – with! off with you! go, – about your business! be off! avaunt! aroynt! get out!

298. [Eating.] Food.—N. eating &c.
v.; deglutition, gulp, epulation, masti-
cation, manducation, rumination, gastronomy, gastrology; panto-, hippo-,
ichthyo-phagy &c.; gluttony &c. 957;
carnivorousness, vegetarianism.

mouth, jaws, mandible, mazard,
chops.

drinking &c. *v.*; potation, draught,
libation; carousal &c. (*amusement*) 840;
drunkenness &c. 959.

food, *pabulum*; aliment, nourishment, nutriment; susten-ance, -tation;
nurture, subsistence, provender, feed,
fodder, provision, ration, keep, commons, board; commissariat &c. (*provision*) 637; prey, forage, pasture,
pasturage; fare, cheer; diet, -ary;
regimen; belly timber, staff of life;
bread, -and cheese; proteins, carbohydrates, vitamines.

comestibles, eatables, victuals, edibles, *ingesta*; grub, prog, tack,
hard tack, meat; bread, -stuffs; cereals; viands, cates, delicacy,
dainty, creature comforts, contents of the larder, flesh-pots; festal
board; ambrosia; good -cheer, – living.

hors-d'œuvre; soup, pottage, *potage*, broth, *bouillon*, *consommé*,
purée, *borsch*, stock, skilly, gumbo; fish, – cakes, – pie; joint, *rôti*,
pièce de résistance, *relevé*, hash, *réchauffé*, stew, *ragoût*, fricassee,
mince, *salim*, *goulash*, *bouillabaisse*, remove, *entrée*, croquette, *rissole*,
sausage, curry, bubble and squeak; haggis, collops, giblets; poultry,
game &c.; biscuit, bun, scone, rusk, pancake, pie, pastry, pasty,
patty, *patisserie*, tart, turnover, *vol-au-vent*, *soufflé*, dumpling, pudding, duff, *compote*, fritters, cake, napoleon, *blancmange*, custard,
jelly, jam, sweets &c. 396; *entremet*; oatmeal, porridge, hasty pudding, gruel; eggs, omelet, cheese, matzoon, savoury; vegetable,
salad, *mayonnaise*, fruit; sauce, condiment &c. 393; kickshaws.

table, *cuisine*, bill of fare, *menu*, *table d'hôte*, ordinary, *à la carte*;
cover.

meal, repast, feed, spread; mess; dish, plate, course, side dish;
regale; regale-, refresh-, entertain-ment; refection, collation, picnic,
feast, banquet, junket; breakfast; lunch, -eon; *déjeuner*, bever,
tiffin, tea, dinner, supper, snack, whet, bait, dessert; pot-luck,
table d'hôte, *déjeuner à la fourchette*; hearty –, square –, substantial
–, full- -meal; blow out; light refreshment; pemmican.

mouthful, bolus, gobbet, tit-bit, morsel, sop, sippet.

drink, beverage, liquor, broth, soup; potion, dram, draught,
drench, swill; nip, peg, sip, sup, gulp.

wine, champagne, spirits, *liqueur*, beer, porter, stout, ale, malt
liquor, julep, Sir John Barleycorn, stingo, heavy wet, bitter, lager-
beer, cider; grog, toddy, flip, purl, punch, negus, cup, bishop,
posset, wassail; bitters, *apéritif*, high-ball, cocktail; whisky, rum,
absinthe; gin &c. (*intoxicating liquor*) 959; coffee, chocolate, cocoa,
tea, *maté*, the cup that cheers but not inebriates.

eating-house &c. 189.

299. Excretion.—N. excretion, discharge, emanation; ejection &c. 297;
exhalation, exudation, extrusion, secretion, effusion, extravasation, *ecchymosis*, evacuation, cacation, defecation,
dysentery, dejection, *fæces*, excrement;
perspiration, sweat; sub-, exud-ation;
diaphoresis; sewage.

saliva, spittle, rheum; ptyalism,
salivation, catarrh, distemper; diarrhœa; *ejecta*, *egesta*, *sputum*, *sputa*;
excreta; lava; *exuviæ* &c. (*uncleanness*)
653.

hemorrhage, bleeding; catamenia,
menses; outpouring &c. (*egress*) 295;
leucorrhea.

V. excrete &c. (*eject*) 297; emanate
&c. (*come out*) 295.

Adj. excretory, fæcal, secretory;
ejective, eliminant.

V. eat, feed, fare, devour, swallow, take; gulp, bolt, snap; fall to; despatch, dispatch; discuss; take -, get -, gulp-down; lay -, tuck- in; lick, pick, peck; gormandize &c. 957; bite, champ, munch, cranch, craunch, crunch, chew, masticate, nibble, gnaw, mumble.

live on; feed -, batten -, fatten -, feast- upon; browse, graze, crop, regale; carouse &c. (*make merry*) 840; eat heartily, do justice to, play a good knife and fork, banquet.

break -bread, - one's fast; breakfast, lunch, dine, take tea, sup.

drink, - in, - up, - one's fill; quaff, sip, sup; suck, - up; lap; swig; swill, tipple &c. (*be drunken*) 959; empty one's glass, drain the cup; toss -off, - one's glass; wash down, crack a bottle, wet one's whistle.

cater, purvey &c. 637.

Adj. eatable, edible, esculent, comestible, alimentary; cereal, cibarious; dietetic; culinary; nutri-tive, -tious; succulent; drinkable, pot-able, -ulent; bibulous.

omn-, carn-, herb-, frug-, gran-, gramin-, phyt-ivorus; ichthyoph-agous.

prandial.

300. [Forcible ingress.] **Insertion.**— **N.** insertion, implantation, intercalation, embolism, introduction; interpolation, insinuation &c. (*intervention*) 228; planting &c. *v.*; injection, inoculation, importation, infusion; forcible -ingress &c. 294; immersion; submersion, -gence; dip, plunge; bath &c. (*water*) 337; interment &c. 363.

V. insert; intro-duce, -mit; put -, run- into; import; inject; interject &c. 228; infuse, instil, inoculate, impregnate, imbue, imbrue.

graft, ingraft, bud, plant, implant; dovetail.

obtrude; thrust -, stick -, ram -, stuff -, tuck -, press -, drive -, pop -, whip -, drop -, put- in; impact; empierce &c. (*make a hole*) 260.

embed; immerse, immerge, merge; bathe, soak &c. (*water*) 337; dip, plunge &c. 310.

bury &c. (*inter*) 363.

insert &c.- itself; plunge *in medias res.*

Adj. inserted &c. *v.*

301. [Forcible egress.] **Extraction.**— **N.** extraction; extracting &c. *v.*; removal, elimination, extrication, eradication, evolution.

evulsion, avulsion; wrench; expression, squeezing; extirpation, extermination; ejection &c. 297; export &c. (*egress*) 295; distillation.

extractor, corkscrew, forceps, pliers.

V. extract, draw, pit; take -, draw -, pull -, tear -, pluck -, pick -, get- out; wring from, wrench; extort; root -, weed -, grub -, rake- up, - out; eradicate; pull -, pluck- up by the roots; averruncate; unroot; uproot, pull up, extirpate, dredge.

remove; educe, elicit; evolve, extricate; eliminate &c. (*eject*) 297; eviscerate &c. 297.

express, squeeze -, press- out; distil.

Adj. extracted &c. *v.*

---

302. [Motion through.] **Passage.—N.** passage, transmission; permeation; pene-, interpene-tration; transudation, infiltration; *osmosis,* osmose, endos-, exos-mose; intercurrence; ingress &c. 294; egress &c. 295; path &c. 627; conduit &c. 350; opening &c. 260; journey &c. 266; voyage &c. 267.

V. pass, - through; perforate &c. (*hole*) 260; penetrate, permeate, thread, thrid, enfilade; go -through, - across; go -, pass- over; cut across; ford, cross; pass and repass, work; make -, thread -, worm -, force- one's way; make -, force- a passage; cut one's way through;

find its -way, – vent; transmit, make way, clear the course; traverse, go over the ground.

Adj. passing &c. *v.*; intercurrent; osmotic &c. *n.*

Adv. *en passant* &c. (*transit*) 270.

303. [Motion beyond.] **Overstep.**—
N. trans-cursion, -ilience, -gression; infraction, intrusion; trespass; en-croach-, infringe-ment; extravagation, transcendence; redundance &c. 641; ingress &c. 294.

V. transgress, surpass, pass; go- beyond, – by; show in –, come to the-front; shoot ahead of; steal a march –, gain- upon.

over-step, -pass, -reach, -go, -ride, -leap, -jump, -skip, -lap, -shoot the mark; out-strip, -leap, -jump, -go, -step, -run, -ride, -rival, -do; beat, – hollow; distance; leave in the -lurch, – rear; go one better, throw into the shade; exceed, transcend, surmount; soar &c. (*rise*) 305.

encroach, intrude, trespass, infringe, invade, trench upon, intrench on; strain; stretch –, strain- a point; pass the Rubicon.

Adj. surpassing &c. *v.*

Adv. beyond the mark, ahead.

304. [Motion short of.] **Shortcoming.**
—**N.** shortcoming, failure; delinquency; falling short &c. *v.*; de-fault, -falcation; leeway; labour in vain, no go.

incompleteness &c. 53; imperfection &c. 651; insufficiency &c. 640; non-completion &c. 730; failure &c. 732.

V. come –, fall –, stop- -short, – short of; not reach; want; keep within -bounds, – the mark, – compass.

break down, stick in the mud, col-lapse, come to nothing; fall -through, – to the ground, – down; cave in, end in smoke, fizzle out, miss the mark, fail; lose ground; miss stays, slump.

Adj. unreached; deficient; short, – of; *minus*; out of depth; perfunctory &c. (*neglect*) 460.

Adv. within -the mark, – compass, – bounds; behindhand; *re infectâ*; to no purpose; far from it.

Phr. the bubble burst.

---

305. [Motion upwards.] **Ascent.**—**N.** ascent, ascension; rising &c. *v.*; rise, upgrowth; leap &c. 309; acclivity, hill &c. 217; stair, stairs, stair-case, -way, flight of -steps, – stairs; ladder, com-panion, – way; lift, elevator &c. 307.

rocket, lark; sky-rocket, -lark; Alpine Club.

V. ascend, rise, mount, arise, uprise; go –, get –, work one's way –, start –, spring –, shoot- up; zoom; aspire.

climb, clamber, ramp, scramble, swarm, *escalade*, surmount; scale, – the heights.

tower, soar, hover, spire, plane, swim, float, surge; leap &c. 309.

Adj. rising &c. *v.*; scandent, buoyant; super-natant, -fluitant; excelsior.

Adv. uphill.

---

306. [Motion downwards.] **Descent.**
—**N.** descent, descension, declension, declination; fall; falling &c. *v.*; drop, cadence; subsidence, lapse; come-down, downfall, tumble, slip, tilt, trip, lurch, cropper, *culbute*; titubation, stumble; fate of Icarus; dive, nose-dive, *volplané*.

avalanche, *débâcle*, landslip, slide.

declivity, dip, hill; decline, drop.

V. descend; go –, drop –, come-down; fall, gravitate, drop, slip, slide, glissade, dive, plunge, settle; decline, slump, set, sink, droop, come down a peg.

dismount, alight, light, get down; swoop; stoop &c. 308; fall prostrate, precipitate oneself; let fall &c. 308.

tumble, trip, stumble, titubate, lurch, pitch, swag, topple; topple –, tumble- -down, – over; tilt, sprawl, plump down, come a cropper.

Adj. descending &c. *v.*; descendent, declivitous; downcast; decur-rent, sive; labent, deciduous; nodding to its fall.

Adv. down, -hill, -wards.

307. Elevation.—N. elevation; raising &c. *v.*; erection, lift; sublevation, upheaval; sublimation, exaltation; prominence &c. (*convexity*) 250.

lever &c. 633; crane, derrick, windlass, capstan, winch, dredger, lift, elevator, escalator, dumb waiter.

V. heighten, elevate, raise, lift, erect; set –, stick –, perch –, perk –, tilt- up; rear, hoist, heave; up-lift, -raise, -rear, -bear, -cast, -hoist, -heave; buoy, weigh, mount, give a lift; exalt, sublimate; place –, set- on a pedestal.

take –, drag –, fish- up; dredge.

stand –, rise –, get –, jump- up; spring to one's feet; hold -oneself, – one's head- up; draw oneself up to his full height.

Adj. elevated &c. *v.*; standing up; stilted, attollent, rampant.

Adv. on -stilts, – the shoulders of, – one's legs, – one's hind legs.

---

309. Leap.—N. leap, jump, hop, spring, bound, vault, saltation.

dance, caper, gambol; curvet, caracole; *gam-bade, -bado*; capriole, demi-volt; buck, – jump; hop, skip and jump.

kangaroo, jerboa, chamois, goat, frog, grasshopper, flea.

V. leap; jump -up, – over the moon; hop, spring, bound, vault, ramp, cut capers, gambol, trip, skip, dance, caper; curvet, *caracole*; foot it, bob, bounce, flounce, start, frisk &c. (*amusement*) 840; jump about &c. (*agitation*) 315; trip it on the light fantastic toe, dance oneself off one's legs.

Adj. leaping &c. *v.*; saltatory, frisky.
Adv. on the light fantastic toe.

308. Depression.—N. lowering &c. *v.*; depression; dip &c. (*concavity*) 252; abasement; detrusion; reduction.

over-throw, -set, -turn; upset; prostration, subversion, precipitation.

bow; courtesy, curtsy; genuflexion, *kowtow*, obeisance, *salaam*.

V. depress, lower; let –, take- -down, – down a peg; cast; let -drop, – fall; sink, debase, bring low, abase, slash, reduce, detrude, pitch, precipitate.

over-throw, -turn, -set; upset, subvert, prostrate, level, fell; cast –, take –, throw –, fling –, dash –, pull –, cut –, knock –, hew- down; raze, – to the ground; humiliate, trample in the dust, pull about one's ears.

sit, – down; couch, squat, crouch, stoop, bend, bow, courtsey, curtsy; bob, duck, dip, genuflect, kneel; *kowtow*, *salaam*, make obeisance, prostrate oneself; bend, bow- the -head, – knee; incline the head; bow down; cower; recline &c. (*be horizontal*) 213.

Adj. depressed &c. *v.*; at a low ebb; prostrate &c. (*horizontal*) 213; detrusive.

310. Plunge.—N. plunge, dip, dive, header; ducking &c. *v.*; submergence, immersion, diver.

V. plunge, dip, souse, duck; dive, plump; take a -plunge, – header, make a plunge; bathe &c. (*water*) 337.

sub-merge, -merse; immerse, douse, sink, engulf, send to -the bottom, – Davy Jones' locker.

get out of one's depth; go -to the bottom, – down like a stone; founder, welter, wallow.

---

311. [Curvilinear motion.] **Circuition.—N.** circuition, circulation; turn, curvet; excursion; circum-vention, -navigation, -ambulation; north-west passage; ambit, gyre, lap, circuit &c. 629.

turning &c. *v.*; wrench; evolution; coil, helix, spiral; corkscrew.

V. turn, bend, wheel; go –, put- about; heel; go –, turn -round, – to the right about; turn on one's heel; make –, describe- a -circle, – complete circle; encircle; go –, pass- through -180°, – 360°.

circum-navigate, -aviate, -ambulate, -vent; put a girdle round the earth, go the round, make the round of.

turn –, round- a corner; double a point.

wind, circulate, meander; whisk, twirl; twist &c. (*convolution*) 248; make a *détour* &c. (*circuit*) 629.

Adj. turning &c. *v.*; circuitous; circum-foraneous, -fluent; devious, roundabout, circum-ambient, -flex, -navigable.

Adv. round about.

312. [Motion in a continued circle.] **Rotation.**—**N.** rotation, revolution, gyration, circulation, roll; circum-rotation, -volution, -gyration; volutation, circination, turbination, *pirouette*, convolution.

verticity; whir, whirl, swirl, eddy, vortex, whirlpool, gurge; cyclone, tornado; surge; *vertigo*, dizzy round; Maelstrom, Charybdis; Ixion; wheel of Fortune.

313. [Motion in a reverse circle.] **Evolution.**—**N.** evolution, unfolding, development; eversion &c. (*inversion*) 218.

V. evolve; un-fold, -roll, -wind, -coil, -twist, -furl, -twine, -ravel; disentangle; develop.

Adj. evolving &c. *v.*; evolved &c. *v.*

wheel, screw, propeller, whirligig, rolling stone, windmill; top, teetotum, merry-go-round; roller; cog-, fly-wheel, spit; jack; caster.

axis, axle, spindle, spool, pivot, pin, hinge, pole, swivel, gimbals, arbor, bobbin, mandrel, shaft.

[Science of rotatory motion] trochilics, gyrostatics.

V. rotate; roll, – along; revolve, spin; turn, – round; circumvolve; circulate, gyre, gyrate, wheel, whirl, swirl, twirl, trundle, troll, bowl; slew round.

roll up, furl; wallow, welter; box the compass; spin like a -top, – teetotum.

Adj. rotating &c. *v.*; rota-tory, -ry; circumrotatory, trochilic, vertiginous, gyratory; vortic-al, -ose.

Adv. head over heels, round and round, like a horse in a mill.

314. [Reciprocating motion, motion to and fro.] **Oscillation.**—**N.** oscillation; vibration, libration; motion of a pendulum; nutation; undulation; pulsation; pulse; throb; seismic disturbance.

alternation; coming and going &c. *v.*; ebb and flow, flux and reflux, ups and downs; wave, vibratiuncle, swing, beat, shake, wag, see-saw, dance, lurch, dodge; fluctuation; vacillation &c. (*irresolution*) 605.

seismometer, vibroscope, seismograph.

V. oscillate; vi-, li-brate; alternate, undulate, wave; sway, rock, swing; pulsate, beat; wag, -gle; nod, bob, courtesy, curtsy; tick; play; chatter, wamble, wabble; teeter, dangle, swag.

fluctuate, dance, curvet, reel, quake; quiver, quaver, shake, flicker; wriggle; roll, toss, pitch; flounder, stagger, totter, waddle; move –, bob- up and down &c. *adv.*; pass and repass, ebb and flow, come and go, shuttle; vacillate &c. 605.

brandish, shake, flourish.

Adj. oscillating &c. *v.*; oscill-, undul-, puls-, libr-atory; vibrat-ory, -ile; pendulous, shutterwise, seismic.

Adv. to and fro, up and down, backwards and forwards, see-saw, zigzag, wibble-wabble, in and out, from side to side, like buckets in a well.

315. [Irregular motion.] **Agitation.**—**N.** agitation, stir, tremor, shake, ripple, jog, jolt, jar, jerk, shock, succussion, trepidation, quiver, quaver, dance; jactit-ation, -ance; shuffling &c. *v.*; twitter, flicker, flutter.

disquiet, perturbation, commotion, turmoil, turbulence; tumult, -uation; hubbub, rout, bustle, fuss, racket, *subsultus*, staggers, megrims, epilepsy, fits, twitching, vellication, St. Vitus' dance.

spasm, throe, throb, palpitation, convulsion, paroxysm; tetanus.

disturbance &c. (*disorder*) 59; restlessness &c. (*changeableness*) 149.

ferment, -ation; ebullition, effervescence, hurly burly, *cahotage;* tempest, storm, ground swell, heavy sea, whirlpool, vortex &c. 312; whirlwind &c. (*wind*) 349.

V. be -agitated &c.; shake; tremble, – like an aspen leaf; quiver, quaver, quake, shiver, twitter, twire, dither, dodder; twitch, writhe, toss, shuffle, tumble, stagger, bob, reel, sway; wag, -gle, wiggle; wriggle, – like an eel; squirm; dance, stumble, shamble, flounder, totter, flounce, flop, curvet, prance.

throb, pulsate, beat, palpitate, go pit-a-pat; flutter, flitter, flicker, bicker; bustle.

ferment, effervesce, foam; boil, – over; bubble, – up; simmer.

toss –, jump- about; jump like a parched pea; shake like an aspen leaf; shake to its -centre, – foundations; be the sport of the winds and waves; reel to and fro like a drunken man; move –, drive- from post to pillar and from pillar to post; keep between hawk and buzzard.

agitate, shake, convulse, toss, tumble, bandy, wield, brandish, flap, flourish, whisk, jerk, hitch, jolt; jog, -gle; jostle, buffet, hustle, disturb, stir, shake up, churn, jounce, wallop, whip, vellicate.

Adj. shaking &c. *v.;* agitated, tremulous; de-, sub-sultory; shambling; giddy-paced, saltatory, convulsive, jerky, unquiet, restless, all of a twitter.

Adv. by fits and starts; subsultorily &c. *adj.; per saltum;* hop, skip and jump; in -convulsions, – fits, pit-a-pat.

CLASS III

Words relating to MATTER

Section I.   MATTER IN GENERAL

316. Materiality.—N. material-ity, -ness; materialization; corpor-eity, -ality; substantiality, material existence, incarnation, flesh and blood, *plenum*; physical condition.

matter, body, substance, brute matter, stuff, element, principle, protoplasm, plasma, *parenchyma*, material, *substratum*, hyle, *corpus*, *pabulum*; frame.

object, article, thing, something; still life; stocks and stones; materials &c. 635.

[Science of matter] physics; somatology, -ics; natural –, experimental-philosophy; physical science, *philosophie positive*, materialism, hylism; materialist, physicist.

V. materialize, incorporate, incarnate, substantiate, embody.

Adj. material, bodily; corpor-eal, -al; physical; somat-ic, -oscopic; sensible, tangible, ponderable, palpable, substantial; fleshly, incarnate.

objective, impersonal, neuter, unspiritual, materialistic.

317. Immateriality.—N. immateriality, -ness; incorporeity, dematerialization, unsubstantiality, spirituality; inextension; astral plane.

personality; I, myself, me; *ego*, spirit &c. (*soul*) 450; astral body; immaterialism; spiritual-ism, -ist; subliminal –, subconscious- self.

V. disembody, spiritualize, dematerialize.

Adj. immateri-al, -ate; incorpor-eal, -al; asomatous, unextended; un-, disembodied; extramundane, supersensible, unearthly; pneumatoscopic; spiritual &c. (*psychical*) 450; aery.

personal, subjective.

---

318. World.—N. world, creation, nature, universe; earth, globe, wide world; *cosmos*; terraqueous globe, sphere; macro-, mega-cosm; music of the spheres.

heavens, sky, welkin, empyrean; starry -heaven, – host; firmament; vault –, canopy- of heaven; celestial spaces.

heavenly bodies, stars, luminaries, nebulæ; galaxy, milky way, galactic circle, *via lactea*.

sun, orb of day, Apollo, Phœbus; photo-, chromo-sphere; solar system; planet, -oid, asteroid; comet; satellite; moon, orb of night, Diana, Luna; aerolite, meteor; falling –, shooting- star; meteorite.

constellation, zodiac, signs of the zodiac, Charles's wain, Great Bear, Southern Cross, Orion's belt, Cassiopeia's chair, Pleiades &c.

colures, equator, ecliptic, orbit.

[Science of heavenly bodies] astronomy; urano-graphy, -logy; cosmo-logy, -graphy, -gony; *eidouranion*, orrery; geography; geodesy

&c. (*measurement*) 466; star-gazing, -gazer; astronomer; cosmogonist, geodesist, geographer; observatory.

Adj. cosmic, cosmical, mundane; terr-estrial, -estrious, -aqueous, -ene, -eous; telluric, earthly, geotic, geodetic, cosmogonal, under the sun; sub-lunary, -astral.

solar, heliacal; lunar; celestial, heavenly, empyreal, sphery; starry, stellar; sider-eal, -al; astral; nebular.

Adv. in all creation, on the face of the globe, here below, under the sun.

319. Gravity.—N. gravi-ty, -tation; weight; heaviness &c. *adj.*; specific gravity; ponderosity, pressure, load; bur-den, -then; ballast, counterpoise; lump –, mass –, weight- of.

lead, millstone, mountain, Ossa on Pelion.

weighing, ponderation, trutination; weights; avoirdupois –, troy –, apothecaries'- weight; grain, scruple, drachm, ounce, pound, lb., load, stone, hundred-weight, cwt., ton, quintal, carat, penny-weight, tod, gramme, kilogramme &c.

[Weighing instrument] balance, scales, steelyard, beam, weighbridge, spring balance, weighing machine.

[Science of gravity] statics.

V. be -heavy &c. *adj.*; gravitate, weigh, press, cumber, load.

[Measure the weight of] weigh, poise.

Adj. weighty; weighing &c. *v.*; heavy, – as lead; ponder-ous, -able; lump-ish, -y; cumber-, burden-some; cumbrous, unwieldy, massive.

in-, superin-cumbent.

320. Levity.—N. levity; lightness &c. *adj.*; imponderability, imponderables, buoyancy, volatility.

feather, dust, mote, down, thistle-down, flue, cobweb, gossamer, straw, cork, bubble; float, buoy; ether, air.

leaven, ferment, barm, yeast, enzyme.

V. be -light &c. *adj.*; float, swim, be buoyed up.

render -light &c. *adj.*; lighten, levitate; leaven.

Adj. light, subtile, subtle, airy; im-ponder-ous, -able; astatic, weightless, ethereal, sublimated; uncompressed, volatile; buoyant, floating &c. *v.*; barmy, frothy; portable.

light as -a feather, – thistle down, – air.

fermenting &c. *n.*

Section II. INORGANIC MATTER

1°. Solid Matter

321. Density.—N. density, solidity; solidness &c. *adj.*; impenetra-, im-permea-bility; incompressibility; im-porosity; cohesion &c. 46; constipation, consistence, spissitude.

specific gravity; hydro-, areo-meter.

condensation; solid-ation, -ification; consolidation; concretion, caseation, coagulation; petrifaction &c. (*hardening*) 323; crystallization, precipitation; deposit, precipitate, silt; inspissation; thickening &c. *v.*

indivisibility, indiscerptibility, in-dissolvableness.

solid body, mass, block, knot, lump; con-cretion, -crete, -glomerate; cake,

322. Rarity.—N. rarity; tenuity; absence of -solidity &c. 321; subtility; sponginess, compressibility.

rarefaction, expansion, dilatation, inflation, subtilization.

ether &c. (*gas*) 334.

V. rarefy, expand, dilate, subtilize, attenuate, thin.

Adj. rare, subtile, thin, fine, tenuous, compressible, flimsy, slight; light &c. 320; cavernous, spongy &c. (*hollow*) 252.

rarefied &c. *v.*; unsubstantial; un-com-pact, -pressed.

clot, stone, curd, coagulum, grume; bone, gristle, cartilage.

V. be -dense &c. *adj.*; become –, render- solid &c. *adj.*; solid-ify, -ate; concrete, set, take a set, consolidate, congeal, coagulate; curd, -le; fix, clot, cake, candy, precipitate, deposit, cohere, crystallize; petrify &c. (*harden*) 323.

condense, thicken, inspissate, incrassate; compress, squeeze, ram down, constipate.

Adj. dense, solid; solidified &c. *v.*; cohe-rent, -sive &c. 46; compact, close, serried, thickset; substantial, massive, lumpish; impenetrable, impermeable, imporous; incompressible; constipated; concrete &c. (*hard*) 323; knot-ted, -ty; gnarled; crystal-line, -lizable; thick, grumous, stuffy.

un-dissolved, -melted, -liquefied, -thawed.

in-divisible, -discerptible, -frangible, -dissolvable, -dissoluble, -soluble, -fusible.

323. Hardness.—N. hardness &c. *adj.*; rigidity, renitence, inflexibility, temper, callosity, durity.

induration, petrifaction; lapid-ifica-tion, -escence; vitri-, ossi-, corni-fica-tion; crystallization.

stone, pebble, flint, marble, rock, fossil, crag, crystal, quartz, granite, adamant; bone, cartilage; heart of oak, block, board, deal board; iron, steel; cast –, wrought- iron; nail; brick, concrete; cement.

V. render -hard &c. *adj.*; harden, stiffen, indurate, petrify, temper, ossify, vitrify.

Adj. hard, rigid, stubborn, stiff, firm; starch, -ed; stark, unbending, unlimber, unyielding; inflexible, tense; indurate, -d; gritty, proof.

adamant-ine, -ean; concrete, stony, rocky, lithic, granitic, vitreous; crystalline; horny, corneous; bony; oss-eous, -ific; cartilaginous; hard as a -stone &c. *n.*; stiff as -buckram, – a poker.

325. Elasticity. — N. elasticity, springiness, spring, resilience, renitency, buoyancy.

india-rubber, caoutchouc, gutta-percha, whalebone, gum elastic.

V. be -elastic &c. *adj.*; spring back &c. (*recoil*) 277.

Adj. elastic, tensile, springy, ductile, resilient, renitent, buoyant.

327. Tenacity.—N. tenacity, toughness, strength; cohesion &c. 46; sequacity; stubbornness &c. (*obstinacy*) 606; viscidity &c. 352.

leather; gristle, cartilage.

324. Softness.—N. softness, pliable-ness &c. *adj.*; flexibility; pli-ancy, -ability; sequacity, malleability; flabbiness; duct-, tract-ility; extend-, extensibility; plasticity; inelasticity, flaccidity, laxity.

clay, wax, butter, dough, pudding; cushion, pillow, feather-bed, pad, down, padding, wadding.

mollification; softening &c. *v.*

V. render -soft &c. *adj.*; soften, mollify, mellow, relax, temper; mash, knead, squash, *massage.*

bend, yield, relent, relax, give.

Adj. soft, tender, supple; pli-ant, -able; flex-ible, -ile; lithe, -some; lissom, limber, plastic; ductile; tract-ile, -able; malleable, extensile, sequacious, inelastic, mollient.

yielding &c. *v.*; flabby, limp, flimsy.

flaccid, flocculent, downy; spongy, œdematous, medullary, doughy, argillaceous, mellow.

soft as -butter, – down, – silk; yielding as wax; tender as a chicken.

326. Inelasticity.—N. want of –, absence of- elasticity &c. 325; inelasticity &c. (*softness*) 324.

Adj. inelastic &c. (*soft*) 324.

328. Brittleness.—N. brittleness &c. *adj.*; frag-, friab-, frangib-, fiss-ility; frailty; house of -cards, – glass.

V. be -brittle &c. *adj.*; live in a glass house.

V. be -tenacious &c. *adj.*; resist fracture.

Adj. tenacious, tough, cohesive, adhesive, strong, resisting, sequacious, stringy, gristly, cartilaginous, leathery, coriaceous, tough as whit-leather; stubborn &c. (*obstinate*) 606.

break, crack, snap, split, shiver, splinter, crumble, break short, burst, fly, give way; fall to pieces; crumble -to, – into- dust.

Adj. breakable, brittle, frangible, fragile, frail, friable, delicate, gimcrack, shivery, fissile; splitting &c. *v.*; lacerable, splintery, crisp, crimp, short, brittle as glass.

---

329. [Structure.] **Texture.—N.** structure, organization, anatomy, frame, mould, fabric, construction; frame-work, carcass, architecture; stratification, cleavage.

substance, stuff, *compages*, *parenchyma*; constitution, staple, organism.

[Science of structures] organ-, oste-, my-, splanchn-, neur-, angi-, aden-ology; angi-, aden-ography.

texture; inter-, con-texture; tissue, grain, web, surface; warp and -woof, – weft; tooth, nap &c. (*roughness*) 256; fineness –, coarseness- of grain.

[Science of textures] histology.

Adj. structural, organic; anatomic, -al.

text-ural, -ile; fine-, coarse-grained; fine, delicate, subtile, gossamery, filmy; coarse; home-spun; linsey-woolsey.

330. Pulverulence.—N. [State of powder.] pulverulence; sandiness &c. *adj.*; efflorescence; friability.

powder, dust, sand, shingle; sawdust; grit; attrition; meal, bran, flour, *farina*, spore, sporule; crumb, seed, grain; particle &c. (*smallness*) 32; thermion; limature, filings, *débris*, *detritus*, scobs, magistery, fine powder; *flocculi*.

smoke; cloud of -dust, – sand, – smoke; puff –, volume -of smoke; sand –, dust- storm.

[Reduction to powder] pulverization, comminution, attenuation, granulation, disintegration, subaction, contusion, trituration, levigation, abrasion, detrition, multure; limation; filing &c. *v.*

[Instruments for pulverization] mill, millstone, grater, rasp, file, pestle and mortar, nutmeg grater, teeth, molar, grinder, chopper, grindstone, kern, quern, muller.

V. come to dust; be -disintegrated, – reduced to powder &c.

reduce –, grind- to powder; pulverize, comminute, granulate, triturate, levigate; scrape, file, abrade, rub down, grind, grate, rasp, pound, bray, bruise; con-tuse, -tund; beat, crush, cranch, craunch, crunch, muller, scranch, crumble, disintegrate; attenuate &c. 195.

Adj. powdery, pulverulent, granular, mealy, floury, farinaceous, branny, furfuraceous, flocculent, dusty, sandy, sabulous; aren-ose, -arious, -aceous; gritty; efflorescent, impalpable.

pulverizable; friable, crumbly, shivery; pulverized &c. *v.*; attrite; in pieces.

331. Friction.—N. friction, attrition; rubbing &c. *v.*; erasure; con-frication, -trition; affriction, abrasion, arrosion, limature, frication, rub; elbow-grease; rosin; *massage*.

V. rub, scratch, abrade, scrape, scrub,

332. [Absence of friction. Prevention of friction.] **Lubrication.—N.** smoothness &c. 255; unctuousness &c. 355.

lubri-cation, -fication; anointment; oiling &c. *v.*

fray, rasp, graze, curry, scour, polish, rub out, erase, gnaw; file, grind &c. (*reduce to powder*) 330; *massage.*

set one's teeth on edge; rosin.

Adj. anatriptic, abrasive.

synovia; lubricant, graphite, glycerine, oil &c. 356; saliva; lather.

V. lubri-cate, -citate; oil, grease; lather, soap; wax.

Adj. lubricated &c. *v.*

2°. FLUID MATTER

1. *Fluids in General*

333. Fluidity.—N. fluidity, liquidity; liquidness &c. *adj.*; gaseity &c. 334; liquefaction &c. 334.

fluid, inelastic fluid; liquid, liquor; lymph, humour, juice, sap, serum, blood, serosity, gravy, rheum, ichor, sanies.

solu-bility, -bleness.

[Science of liquids] hydro-logy, -statics, -dynamics, hydraulics &c.

V. be -fluid &c. *adj.*; flow &c. (*water in motion*) 348; liquefy &c. 335.

Adj. liquid, fluid, serous, juicy, succulent, sappy; fluent &c. (*flowing*) 348.

liquefied &c. 335; uncongealed; soluble, hydrostatic &c. *n.*

334. Gaseity.—N. gaseity, gaseousness; vapourousness &c. *adj.*; flatulence, -lency; volatility, aeration, gasification.

elastic fluid, gas, air, vapour, ether, steam, fume, reek, *effluvium, flatus*; cloud &c. 353.

[Science of elastic fluids] pneumat-ics, -ostatics; aero-statics, -dynamics &c.

gas-, gaso-meter.

V. gassify, aerate, aerify; emit vapour &c. 336.

Adj. gaseous, aeriform, ethereal, aerial, airy, vaporous, volatile, evaporable; flatulent; aerostatic &c. *n.*

335. Liquefaction.—N. liquefaction; liquescen-ce, -cy, deliquescence; melting &c. (*heat*) 384; colliqu-ation, -efaction; thaw; de-, liquation; lixiviation, dissolution.

solution, apozem, lixivium, infusion, decoction, flux.

solvent, diluent, menstruum, alkahest, *aqua fortis.*

V. render -liquid &c. 333; liquefy, run, deliquesce; melt &c. (*heat*) 384; solve; dissolve, resolve; liquate; hold in solution; leach, lixiviate.

Adj. lique-fied &c. *v.*, -scent, -fiable; deliquescent, soluble, colliquative; solvent.

336. Vaporization. — N. vapor-, volatil-ization; gasification; e-, vaporation; distillation, cohobation, sublimation, exhalation; volatility.

vaporizer, still, retort, spray, atomizer; fumigation, steaming.

V. render -gaseous &c. 334; vaporize, volatilize; distil, sublime; evaporate, exhale, smoke, transpire, emit vapour, fume, reek, steam, fumigate.

Adj. volatilized &c. *v.*; reeking &c. *v.*; volatile; evaporable, vaporizable.

----

2. *Specific Fluids*

337. Water.—N. water; serum, serosity; lymph; rheum; diluent.

dilution, maceration, lotion; washing &c. *v.*; im-, mersion; humectation, infiltration, spargefaction, affusion, irrigation, *douche*, balneation, bath.

deluge &c. (*water in motion*) 348; high water, flood-, spring-tide.

338. Air.—N. air &c. (*gas*) 334; common –, atmospheric- air; atmosphere, stratosphere, isothermal layer, troposphere, Heaviside layer.

open, – air; sky, welkin; blue, – sky; cloud &c. 353.

weather, climate, rise and fall of the barometer, isobar.

V. be -watery &c. *adj.*; reek.

add water, water, wet; moisten &c. 339; dilute, dip, immerse; merge; im-, sub-merge; plunge, souse, duck, drown; soak, steep, macerate, pickle, wash, sprinkle, sparge, lave, bathe, affuse, splash, swash, douse, slosh, drench; dabble, slop, slobber, irrigate, inundate, deluge; syringe, inject, gargle; infiltrate, percolate.

Adj. watery, aqueous, aquatic, lymphatic; balneal, diluent; drenching &c. *v.*; diluted &c. *v.*; weak; wet &c. (*moist*) 339.

Phr. the waters are out.

339. Moisture.—N. moisture; moistness &c. *adj.*; hum-idity, -ectation; madefaction, dew; *serein*; marsh &c. 345; Hygromet-ry, -er.

V. moisten, wet; humect, -ate; sponge, damp, dampen, bedew; imbue, imbrue, infiltrate, saturate; seethe, sop; soak, drench &c. (*water*) 337.

be -moist &c. *adj.*; not have a dry thread; perspire &c. (*exude*) 295.

Adj. moist, damp; watery &c. 337; undried, humid, wet, dank, muggy, dewy; roric; roscid; juicy.

wringing wet; wet -through, – to the skin; saturated &c. *v.*

swashy, soggy, dabbled; reeking, seething, dripping, soaking, soft, sodden, sloppy, muddy; swampy &c. (*marshy*) 345; irriguous.

341. Ocean.—N. sea, ocean, main, deep, brine, salt water, waters, waves, billows, high seas, offing, great waters, watery waste, 'vasty deep,' briny ocean, herring pond, steamer track, the seven seas; wave, tide &c. (*water in motion*) 348.

hydrograph-y, -er, oceanography; Neptune, Thetis, Triton, Naiad, Nereid; sea-nymph, Siren, mer-maid, -man; trident, dolphin.

Adj. oceanic; mar-ine, -itime; pleagic, -ian; sea-going, -worthy; hydrographic.

Adv. at -, on- sea; afloat, on the high seas.

[Science of air] pneumatics, aero-logy, -scopy, -graphy; meteorology, climatology; eudio-, baro-, aero-meter; aneroid, baro-graph, -scope; weather-gauge, -glass, -cock.

exposure to the -air, – weather; ventilation; aero-station, -nautics, -naut &c. 265 and 269.

V. air, ventilate; fan &c. (*wind*) 349.

Adj. containing air, flatulent, effervescent; windy &c. 349.

atmospheric, airy; aeri-al, -form; pneumatic; meteorological; weatherwise.

Adv. in the open air, out of doors, *à la belle étoile, al fresco; sub -Jove, – dio.*

340. Dryness.—N. dryness &c. *adj.*; siccity, aridity, drought, ebb-, neaptide, low water.

drying, ex-, de-siccation; evaporation; dehydration; arefaction, dephlegmation, drainage.

drier, desiccator.

V. be -dry &c. *adj.*; render -dry &c. *adj.*; dry; dry –, soak- up; sponge, swab, wipe; ex-, de-siccate, dehydrate, anhydrate; drain, parch.

be fine, hold up.

Adj. dry, anhydrous, arid, waterless; dried &c. *v.*; undamped; juice-, sapless; sear; husky; rainless, without rain, fine; dry as -a bone, – dust, – a stick, – a mummy, – a biscuit; desiccated; dehydrated; water-proof, -tight.

---

342. Land.—N. land, earth, ground, dry land, *terra firma.*

continent, mainland, peninsula, delta; tongue –, neck- of land; isthmus; oasis; promontory &c. (*projection*) 250; highland &c. (*height*) 206.

coast, shore, scar, strand, beach; bank, lea; sea- board, -side, -shore, -bank, -coast, -beach; rock-, ironbound coast; loom of the land; derelict; innings; *alluvium*, alluvion.

soil, glebe, clay, loam, marl, cledge, chalk, gravel, mould, subsoil, clod, clot; rock, crag, cliff.

acres; real estate &c. (*property*) 780; landsman, land-lubber, farmer.

geography &c. 318; agriculture &c. 371.

V. land, come to land; set foot on -the soil, – dry land; come –, go- ashore.

Adj. earthy; continental, midland; littoral, riparian, ripuarian; alluvial; terrene &c. (*world*) 318; landed, predial, territorial.

Adv. ashore; on -shore, – land.

343. Gulf. Lake.—N. land covered with water, gulf, gulph, bay, inlet, bight, estuary, arm of the sea, fiord, armlet; frith, firth, ostiary, mouth; lagune, lagoon; indraught; cove, creek; natural harbour; roads; strait, narrows; Euripus; sound, belt, gut, kyles.

lake, loch, lough, mere, tarn, plash, broad, pond, pool, lin, puddle, well, artesian well, tank, sump; standing –, dead –, sheet of- water; fish –, mill-pond; race; ditch, dike, dyke, dam; reservoir &c. (*store*) 636.

Adj. lacustrine; land locked.

344. Plain.—N. plain, table land, mesa, face of the country; open –, champaign-country; basin, downs, waste, weary waste, desert, tundra, wild, steppe, pampas, savanna, prairie, champaign, heath, common, wold, veld; moor, -land, uplands, fell; bush; *plateau* &c. (*level*) 213; *campagna.*

meadow, mead, haugh, pasturage, park, field, lawn, green, plat, plot, grass-plat, greensward, sward, grass, turf, sod, heather; lea, ley, lay; grounds.

Adj. campestrian, champaign, alluvial.

345. Marsh.—N. marsh, swamp, morass, marish, moss, fen, bog, quagmire, slough, sump, wash; mud, squash, slush.

Adj. marsh, -y; swampy, boggy, plashy, poachy, quaggy, soft; muddy, sloppy, squashy, spongy; paludal; moor-ish, -y; fenny.

346. Island.—N. island, isle, islet, eyot, ait, holm, reef, atoll, breaker; archipelago; islander.

Adj. insular, sea-girt.

---

3. *Fluids in Motion*

347. [Fluid in motion.] **Stream.—N.** stream &c. (*of water*) 348, (*of air*) 349.

V. flow &c. 348; blow &c. 349.

348. [Water in motion.] **River.—N.** running water.

jet, spirt, squirt, spout, splash, swash, rush, gush, *jet d'eau*; sluice, chute.

water-spout, -fall; fall, cascade, force, foss; lin, -n; ghyll, Niagara; cata-ract, -dupe, -clysm; *débâcle*, inundation, deluge.

rain, -fall; *serein*; shower, scud; downpour, cloud burst; driving –, pouring –, drenching- rain; hyeto-logy, -graphy; rainy season, monsoon; predominance of Aquarius, reign of St. Swithin; mizzle, drizzle, *stillicidium*, plash; dropping &c. v.

stream, course, flux, flow, profluence; effluence &c. (*egress*) 295; defluxion; flowing &c. v.; current, tide, race.

spring; fount, -ain; rill, rivulet, gill,

349. [Air in motion.] **Wind.—N.** wind, draught, *flatus, afflatus,* air; breath, – of air; puff, whiff, zephyr; blow, drift; *aura*; stream, current; under-current.

gust, blast, breeze, squall, gale, half a gale, storm, tempest, hurricane, whirlwind, tornado, samiel, cyclone, typhoon; simoon; harmattan, monsoon, trade wind, sirocco, *mistral, bise, föhn,* tramontane, levanter; capful of wind; fresh –, stiff- breeze; keen blast; blizzard.

windiness &c. *adj.*; ventosity; rough –, dirty –, ugly –, stress of- weather; dirty-, windy-, mackerel- sky; mare's tail; thick –, black –, white- squall.

anemography, aerodynamics; wind-gauge, anemometer, weather-cock, vane.

gullet, rillet; stream-, brook-let; runnel, sike, burn, beck, brook, stream, river; reach; tributary.

body of water, torrent, rapids, flush, flood, swash, spate; spring –, high –, full-tide; bore; eagre, *hygre*; fresh, -et; undertow, indraught, reflux, under-current, eddy, vortex, gurge, whirlpool, Maelström, regurgitation, overflow; confluence, corrivation.

wave, billow, surge, swell, ripple; roller, ground swell, surf, breaker, white horses; comber, beach-comber; rough –, heavy –, cross –, long –, short –, chopping –, choppy- sea, choppiness; tidal wave.

[Science of fluids in motion] Hydro-dynamics; Hydraul-ics &c.; rain-gauge &c.

water-bearer, – carrier, Aquarius.

irrigation &c. (*water*) 337; pump; watering-pot, – cart; hydrant, stand-pipe, hose, sprinkler, drencher; fire-engine, squirt, syringe.

V. flow, run; meander; gush, pour, spout, roll, jet, well, issue; drop, drip, dribble, plash, squirt, spurt, spirtle, trill, trickle, distil, percolate; stream, overflow, inundate, deluge, flow over, splash, swash; guggle, murmur, babble, bubble, purl, gurgle, sputter, regurgitate; ooze, flow out &c. (*egress*) 295.

rain, – hard, – in torrents, – cats and dogs, – pitchforks; come down in sheets; pour with rain, drizzle, mizzle, spit, sprinkle, set in.

flow –, fall –, open –, drain- into; discharge itself, disembogue.

[Cause a flow] pour; pour out &c. (*discharge*) 297; shower down; irrigate, drench &c. (*wet*) 337; spill, splash.

[Stop a flow] stanch; dam, -up &c. (*close*) 261; obstruct &c. 706.

Adj. fluent; dif-, pro-, af-fluent; tidal; flowing &c. *v.*; meand-ering, -ry, -rous; fluvi-al, -atile; streamy, showery, rainy, drizzly, drizzling, pluvial, pluviose, stillicidous.

suf-, insuf-, per-, in-, af-flation; blowing, fanning &c. *v.*; ventilation.

sneezing &c. *v.*; sternutation; hic-cup, -cough; catching of the breath; breathing &c.

Eolus, Eurus, Boreas, Zephyr, cave of Eolus.

air-pump, lungs, bellows, blow-pipe, fan, blower; pulmotor, ventilator, punkah, aspirator, exhauster, ejector.

V. blow, waft; blow -hard, – great guns, – a hurricane &c. *n.*; whistle, roar, howl, ring in the shrouds; stream, issue.

respire, breathe, in-, ex-hale, puff; whif, -fle; gasp, wheeze; snuff, -le; sniff, -le; sneeze, cough, belch.

fan, ventilate; in-, per-flate; blow –, pump- up.

Adj. blowing &c. *v.*; windy, airy, æolian, flatulent; breezy, gusty, squally; stormy, tempestuous, blustering; bois-terous &c. (*violent*) 173.

pulmon-ic, -ary.

---

350. [Channel for the passage of water.] **Conduit.**—**N.** conduit, channel, duct, watercourse, race; head –, tail-race; adit, aqueduct, canal, trough, flume, gutter, pantile; dike, canyon, ravine, gorge, hollow, main, gully, moat, ditch, drain, sewer, culvert, *cloaca*, sough, kennel, siphon, *piscina*; pipe &c. (*tube*) 260; funnel; tunnel &c. (*passage*) 627; water –, waste- pipe; emunctory, gully-hole, artery, aorta, vein, blood vessel; lymphatic; throat, alimentary canal, intestine; pore, spout, scupper; ad-, a-jutage;

351. [Channel for the passage of air.] **Air-pipe.**—**N.** air-pipe, – shaft, – way, – passage, – tube; shaft, flue, chimney, funnel, vent, blow-hole, nostril, nozzle, throat, weasand, *trachea*; *bronch-us, -ia*; larynx, tonsils, wind-pipe, spiracle; venti-duct, -lator; louvre, Venetian blinds; blow-pipe &c. (*wind*) 349; pipe &c. (*tube*) 260.

---

hose; gar-, gur-goyle; penstock, weir; flood-, water-gate; sluice, lock, valve; rose; waterworks.

Adj. vascular &c. (*with holes*) 260.

3°. Imperfect Fluids

352. Semiliquidity.—N. semiliquidity; stickiness &c. *adj.*; visc-idity, -osity; gumm-, glutin-, muc-osity; spiss-, crass-itude; lentor; adhesiveness &c. (*cohesion*) 46.

inspiss-, incrass-ation; thickening, coagulation.

jelly, aspic, mucilage, gelatin, isinglass; colloid, mucus, phlegm; pituite, lava; glair, starch, gluten, albumen, milk, cream, protein; syrup, treacle; gum, size, glue, paste; wax, bee's-wax; emulsoid, emulsion, soup; squash, mud, slush, slime, ooze; moisture &c. 339; marsh &c. 345.

V. inspiss-, incrass-ate; coagulate, gelatinize, gelatinify, gel, jell, emulsify, thicken; mash, squash, churn, beat up.

Adj. semi-fluid, -liquid; half-melted, -frozen; milky, muddy &c. *n.*; lact-eal, -ean, -eous, -escent, -iferous; emulsive, curdled, thick, succulent, uliginous.

gelat-, album-, mucilag-, glut-inous; gelatine, mastic, amylaceous, ropy, clammy, clotted; vis-cid, -cous; sticky, tacky; slab, -by; lentous, pituitous; mu-cid, -culent, -cous.

354. Pulpiness.—N. pulpiness &c. *adj.*; pulp, paste, dough, sponge, curd, pap, rob, jam, pudding, mush, fool, poultice, grume.

Adj. pulpy &c. *n.*; pultaceous, grumous.

V. pulp, pulpify, mash.

353. [Mixture of air and water.] Bubble. [Cloud.]—N. bubble; foam, froth, head, fume, spume, lather, suds, spray, surf, yeast, barm, spindrift.

cloud, vapour, fog, mist, haze, steam; scud, rack, *nimbus*; *cumulus*, woolpack, *cirrus, stratus; cirro-, cumulostratus; cirro-cumulus*; mackerel sky, mare's tail, dirty sky.

[Science of clouds] nephelognosy, nephology.

effervescence, fermentation; bubbling &c. *v.*

nebula; cloudiness &c. (*opacity*) 426; nebulosity &c. (*dimness*) 422.

V. bubble, boil, foam, froth, spume, mantle, sparkle, guggle, gurgle; effervesce, ferment, fizzle; aerate; cloud, overcast, befog.

Adj. bubbling &c. *v.*; frothy, nappy, effervescent, sparkling, *mousseux*, up, fizzy, with a head on.

cloudy &c. *n.*; vaporous, nebulous, overcast; nubiferous, nephological; foggy, brumous.

355. Unctuousness.—N. unctuousness &c. *adj.*; unctuosity, lubricity; ointment &c. (*oil*) 356; anointment; lubrication &c. 332.

V. oil &c. (*lubricate*) 332.

Adj. unctuous, oily, oleaginous, adipose, sebaceous; fat, -ty; greasy; waxy, butyraceous, soapy, saponaceous, pinguid, lardaceous; slippery.

---

356. Oil.—N. oil, fat, butter, cream, grease, tallow, suet, lard, dripping, margarine, oleomargarine, exunge, blubber; glycerine, stearine, elaine, oleagine; soap; soft soap, wax, cerement; paraffin, spermaceti, adipocere; petroleum, mineral –, rock –, crystal- oil, kerosene, vegetable –, colza –, olive –, linseed –, cotton seed –, rape –, nut –, fusel- oil; animal –, neat's foot –, signal –, train- oil; ointment, unguent, liniment, salve, pomade, pomatum, brilliantine, spike –, nard.

356a. Resin.—N. resin, rosin, colophony; gum; lac, shellac, sealing-wax; amber, -gris; bitumen, pitch, tar, asphalt, -e, -um; varnish, copal, mastic, magilp, lacquer, japan.

V. varnish &c. (*overlay*) 223.

Adj. resinous, bituminous, pitchy, tarry.

Section III. ORGANIC MATTER

1°. Vitality

1. *Vitality in general*

357. Organization.—N. organized -world, – nature; living –, animated-nature; living beings; organic remains, organism; fossils; animal and vegetable kingdom, *fauna* and *flora*, biota.

prot-oplasm, -ein; albumen; structure &c. 329; organ-ization, -ism.

[Science of living beings] biology; natural history,* organic –, bio-chemistry, anatomy, physiology, embryology, morphology, evolution, Darwinism, Lamarkism, zoology &c. 368; botany &c. 369; naturalist, biologist &c.

Adj. organ-ic, -ized.

359. Life.—N. life; vi-tality, -ability; animation; vital -spark, – flame, – force.

respiration, wind; breath -of life, – of one's nostrils; life-blood; Archeus; existence &c. 1.

vivification, vitalization; revivification &c. 163; Prometheus; life to come &c. (*destiny*) 152.

[Science of life] physiology, etiology, embryology, biology; animal economy.

nourishment, staff of life &c. (*food*) 298.

V. be -alive &c. *adj.*; live, breathe, respire; subsist &c. (*exist*) 1; walk the earth; strut and fret one's hour upon a stage; be spared.

see the light, be born, come into the world; fetch –, draw- -breath, – the breath of life; quicken; revive; come to, – life.

give birth to &c. (*produce*) 161; bring to life, put into life, vitalize; vivi-fy, -ficate; reanimate &c. (*restore*) 660; keep -alive, – body and soul together, – the wolf from the door; support life.

have nine lives like a cat.

358. Inorganization. — N. mineral -world, – kingdom; unorganized –, inorganic –, brute –, inanimate- matter.

[Science of the mineral kingdom] mineralogy; geo-logy, -gnosy, -scopy; metall-urgy, -ography; lithology; orycto-logy, -graphy.

V. turn to dust, pulverize.

Adj. in-organic, -animate; unorganized; azoic; mineral.

---

360. Death.—N. death, dying &c. *v.*; de-cease, -mise; dissolution, departure, *obit*, release, rest, *quietus*, fall; loss, bereavement.

end &c. 67 –, cessation &c. 142 –, loss –, extinction –, ebb- of -life &c. 359.

death-warrant, -watch, -rattle, -bed; stroke –, agonies –, shades –, valley of the shadow –, jaws –, hand- of death; last -breath, – gasp, – agonies; dying -day, – breath, – agonies; swan song, *chant du cygne*; *rigor mortis*; Stygian shore; crossing the bar, the great adventure.

King -of terrors, – Death; Death, Angel of Death; mortality; doom &c. (*necessity*) 601.

euthanasia; happy release; break up of the system; natural -death, – decay; sudden –, violent- death; untimely end, watery grave; suffocation, *asphyxia*; heart failure; fatal disease &c. (*disease*) 655; death-blow &c. (*killing*) 361.

necrology, bills of mortality, obituary; death-song &c. (*lamentation*) 839.

V. die, expire, perish; meet one's -death, – end; pass away, be taken; yield –, resign- one's breath; resign

---

* The term *Natural History* is also used as relating to all the objects in Nature whether organic or inorganic, and including therefore *Mineralogy, Geology, Meteorology*, &c.

Adj. living, alive; in -life, – the flesh, – the land of the living; on this side of the grave, above ground, breathing, quick, animated, viable; lively &c. (*active*) 682; alive and kicking; tenacious of life.

vital; vivi-fying, -fied &c. *v.*; Promethean.

Adv. *vivendi causâ.*

one's -being, – life; end one's -days, – life, – earthly career; breathe one's last; cease to -live, – breathe; depart this life; be -no more &c. *adj.*; go –, drop –, pop -off; lose –, lay down –, relinquish –, surrender- one's life; drop –, sink- into the grave; close one's eyes; fall –, drop- dead, – down dead; break one's neck; give –, yield- up the ghost; be all over with one.

pay the debt to nature, shuffle off this mortal coil, take one's last sleep; go the way of all flesh; join the -greater number, – majority, – choir invisible, to life immortal awake; come –, turn- to dust; cross the Stygian ferry; go to -one's long account, – one's last home, – Davy Jones's locker, – the wall; receive one's death warrant, make one's will, die a natural death, go out like the snuff of a candle; come to an untimely end; catch one's death; go off the hooks, kick the bucket, peg out; go West; hop the twig, turn up one's toes; die a violent death &c. (*be killed*) 361; make the supreme sacrifice.

Adj. dead, lifeless; deceased, demised, departed, defunct; late, gone, no more; ex-, in-animate; out of the world, taken off, released; departed this life &c. *v.*; dead and gone; bereft of life, stone dead, dead as -a door nail, – a door post, – mutton, – a herring, – nits; launched into eternity, gathered to one's fathers, numbered with the dead, gone to a better land, behind the veil, beyond the grave, – mortal ken.

dying &c. *v.*; mori-bund, -ent, Acherontic; hippocratic; *in -articulo, – extremis*; in the -jaws, – agony- of death; going, – off; *aux abois*; on one's -last legs, – death bed; at -the point of death, – death's door, – the last gasp; near one's end, given over, booked, fey; with one foot in –, tottering on the brink of- the grave.

still-born; mortuary; deadly &c. (*killing*) 361.

Adv. *post -obit, – mortem.*

Phr. life -ebbs, – fails, – hangs by a thread; one's -days are numbered, – hour is come, – race is run, – doom is sealed; Death -knocks at the door, – stares one in the face; the breath is out of the body; the grave closes over one; *sic itur ad astra.*

361. [Destruction of life; violent death.] **Killing.—N.** killing &c. *v.*; homicide, manslaughter, murder, assassination, trucidation, occision; lynching, effusion of blood; blood, -shed; gore, slaughter, carnage, butchery; *battue*, gladiatorial combat.

massacre; *fusillade, noyade, pogrom*; thuggism; racketeering.

death blow, finishing stroke, *coup de grâce, quietus*; execution &c. (*capital punishment*) 972; judicial murder; martyrdom.

butcher, slayer, murderer, Cain, assassin, cut-throat, garrotter, *bravo*, thug, racketeer, gunman, mobster, gangster, Moloch, *matador, sabreur; guet-à-pens*; gallows, executioner &c. (*punishment*) 975; man-eater.

regicide, parricide, fratricide, infanticide, aborticide &c.

suicide, *felo de se, suttee, hara kiri*, Juggernaut; immolation, holocaust.

suffocation, strangulation, *garrotte*; hanging &c. *v.*

deadly weapon &c. (*arms*) 727; Aceldama; the potter's field, the field of blood.

fatal accident, violent death, casualty.

[Destruction of animals] slaughtering; phthiozoics;* sport, -ing; the chase, venery; hunting, coursing, shooting, fishing; pig-sticking; sports-, hunts-, fisher-man; hunter, Nimrod; slaughterer, knacker, slaughter-house, shambles, *abattoir.*

V. kill, put to death, slay, shed blood; murder, assassinate, butcher, slaughter; victimize, immolate; massacre; take away –, deprive of-life; make away with, put an end to; despatch, dispatch; burke settle, do, – to death, – for.

strangle, garrotte, hang, lynch, throttle, choke, stifle, suffocate, stop the breath, smother, asphyxiate, drown.

sabre; cut -down, – to pieces, – the throat; jugulate; stab, run through the body, bayonet; put to the -sword, – edge of the sword.

shoot, – dead; blow one's brains out; brain, knock on the head; stone, lapidate; give –, deal- a death blow; give a *-quietus, – coup de grâce.*

behead, bowstring &c. (*execute*) 972.

hunt, shoot &c. *n.*

cut off, nip in the bud, launch into eternity, send to one's last account, bump off, rub out, sign one's death warrant, strike the death knell of.

give no quarter, pour out blood like water; decimate; run amuck, wade knee-deep –, imbrue one's hands- in blood.

die a violent death, welter in one's blood; dash –, blow- out one's brains; commit suicide; kill –, -make away with –, put an end to- oneself.

Adj. killing &c. *v.*; murd-, slaught-erous; sanguin-ary, -olent; blood-stained, -thirsty; homicidal, red-handed; bloody, -minded; ensanguined, gory, sanguineous.

mortal, fatal, lethal; dead-, death-ly; mort-, leth-iferous; unhealthy &c. 657; internecine; suicidal.

sporting; piscator-ial, -y.

Adv. in at the death.

362. Corpse.—N. corpse, corse, carcass, bones, skeleton, dry-bones; defunct, relics, *relinquiæ*, remains, mortal remains, dust, ashes, earth, clay; mummy; carrion; food for- worms, – fishes; tenement of clay, this mortal coil.

shade, ghost, *manes*, apparition &c. 980.

organic remains, fossils.

Adj. cadaverous, corpse-like; unburied &c. 363.

363. Interment.—N. interment, burial, inhumation, sepulture, en-tombment; in-, humation; obs-, ex-equies; funeral, wake, pyre, funeral pile; cremation.

funeral -rite, – solemnity; knell, passing bell, tolling; dirge &c. (*lamentation*) 839; cypress; *obit*, dead march, muffled drum; coroner, mortician, undertaker, mute, mourner, professional mourner, pall-bearer; elegy; funeral -oration, – sermon; epitaph.

grave clothes, shroud, winding-sheet, cere-cloth; cerement.

coffin, shell, sarcophagus, urn, pall, bier, hearse, catafalque, cinerary urn.

grave, pit, sepulchre, tomb, vault, crypt, catacomb, mausoleum, *Gol-gotha*, house of death, narrow house, long home; cemetery, necropolis, boneyard; burial-place, -ground; grave-, church-yard; God's acre; mortuary, tope, cromlech, dolmen, menhir, barrow, tumulus, cairn;

* Bentham, 'Chrestomathia.'

ossuary; bone-, charnel-, dead-house; *Morgue*; lich-gate; crematorium.
sexton, grave-digger.

monument, memorial, cenotaph, shrine; grave-, head-, tomb-stone; *memento mori*; hatchment, stone, cross.

exhumation, disinterment; necropsy, autopsy, *post-mortem* examination.

V. inter, bury; lay in –, consign to- the -grave, – tomb; en-, in-tomb; inhume; lay out, prepare for burial, embalm, mummify; conduct a funeral, hold services; toll the knell; put to bed with a shovel.

exhume, disinter, unearth.

Adj. buried &c. *v.*; burial; fune-real, -brial; mortuary, sepulchral, cinerary; elegiac; necroscopic.

Adv. *in memoriam*; *post-obit, -mortem*; beneath –, under- the sod.

Phr. *hic jacet, ci-git, requiescat in pace.*

2. *Special Vitality*

364. Animality.—N. animal life; anima-tion, -lity, -lization; breath.

flesh, – and blood; corporeal nature; *physique*; strength &c. 159.

V. animalize, incorporate.

Adj. fleshly, incarnate, carnal, corporeal, human.

366. Animal.*—N. animal, – kingdom; *fauna*; brute creation.

beast, brute, creature, created being; creeping –, living- thing; dumb -animal, – creature.

flocks and herds, live stock; domestic –, wild- animals; game, *feræ naturæ*; beasts of the field, fowls of the air, denizens of the day.

vertebrate, bi-, quadru-ped, mammal, marsupial, bird, reptile, batrachian, amphibian, fish, crustacean, shell fish, articulate, mollusc, worm, insect, zoophyte; protozoon, animalcule &c. 193.

horse &c. (*beast of burden*) 271; cattle, kine, ox; bull, -ock; steer, stot; cow, milch-cow, calf, heifer, shorthorn; sheep; lamb, -kin; ewe –, pet- lamb; ewe, ram, tup; pig, swine, boar, hog, shoat, sow; tag, teg, wether.

dog, bitch, hound; pup, -py; whelp, cur, mutt, mongrel; house-, watch-, sheep-, shepherd's-, sporting-, fancy-, lap-, toy-, bull-, badger-dog; mastiff; blood-, grey-, stag-, deer-, fox-, otter-hound; harrier, beagle, spaniel, pointer,

365. Vegetability.—N. vegetable life; vegeta-tion, -bility; herbage.

V. vegetate, germinate, sprout, shoot; cultivate.

Adj. vegetable &c. 367; rank, lush.

367. Vegetable.*— N. vegetable – kingdom; *flora*, verdure.

plant; tree, shrub, bush; creeper; vine; herb, -age; grass.

annual; per-, bi-, tri-ennial; exotic.

timber; primeval –, virgin- forest; wood, -lands; hurst, frith, holt, weald, park, chase, greenwood, brake, grove, copse, coppice, *bocage, tope*, clump of trees, thicket, spinet, spinney; under-. brush-wood; boscage, scrub; the oak and the ash and the bonny ivy tree.

bush, jungle, prairie; heath, -er; fern, bracken; furze, gorse, whin broom; grass, turf, grassland, greensward, green, lawn, meadow; pas-ture, -turage; turbary; sedge, rush, weed; fungus, mushroom, toadstool; lichen, moss, conferva, mould; seaweed &c.; growth, crop.

foliage, leafage, branch, bough, ramage; spray &c. 51; leaf, frond, flag, petal, shoot, tendril.

flower, blossom, bud, bloom, bine; flowering plant; tree, sapling, pollard; timber-, fruit-tree; palm-, gum-tree; pulse, legume.

* Extended lists of names of specific varieties of animals, vegetables, &c., are beyond the scope of this work; see Introduction, p. xxv.

setter, retriever; Newfoundland; water
-dog, – spaniel; pug, poodle; dachshund;
Pinscher; turnspit; terrier; fox –, Skye-
terrier; Dandie Dinmont; colley.

cat; puss, -y; kitten; grimalkin; gib-,
tom-cat; mouser; fox, Reynard, vixen,
stag, deer, hart, buck, doe, roe, antelope.

bird; poultry, fowl, cock, hen,
chicken, chanticleer, partlet, rooster,
dunghill cock, barn-door fowl; feathered -tribes, – songster; singing –, dicky- bird; canary; finch; auk, dodo, moa, roc, phœnix.

snake, serpent, viper, adder; newt, eft; asp, vermin.

Adj. animal, zoological.

equine, bovine, vaccine, canine, feline; fishy; piscator-y, -ial;
molluscous, vermicular.

Adj. veget-able, -ous; herb-aceous,
-al; botanic; sylvan, silvan; arbor- ary,
-eous, -escent, -ical; dendritic, dendriform; woody, grassy; ver-dant, -durous;
floral, mossy; lign-ous, -eous; wooden,
leguminous; end-, ex-ogenous.

----

368. [The science of animals.] **Zoology.—N.** zoo-logy, -nomy, -graphy,
-tomy; anatomy; comparative anatomy; animal –, comparative- physiology; morphology.

anthrop-, ornith-, ichthy-, herpet-,
ophi-, malac-, helminth-, entom-, oryct-,
paleont-ology; ichthy- &c. -otomy;
taxidermy.

zo- &c. -ologist.

Adj. zoological &c. *n.*

370. [The economy or management
of animals.] **Cicuration.—N.** taming &c.
v.; cicuration, zoohygiantics; domestication, -ity; *manège*; veterinary art;
breeding, pisciculture, apiculture &c.

menagery, vivarium, zoological garden, zoo; bear-pit; aviary, apiary, hive;
aquarium, fishery, fish hatchery; duck-,
fish-pond; stud-farm; stock farm, dairy.

[Destruction of animals] phthisozoics* &c. (*killing*) 361.

neat-, cow-, shep-herd, shepherdess;
grazier, drover, cowboy, cowkeeper;
trainer, breeder, groom, ostler &c. 746;
veterinary surgeon, vet, horse doctor;
farrier; keeper; game keeper.

cage &c. (*prison*) 752; hen-coop,
bird-cage, cauf; sheep-fold &c. (*inclosure*) 232.

V. tame, domesticate, acclimatize,
breed, tend, break in, train, corral,
round up; cage, bridle &c. (*restrain*)
751; ride &c. 266.

drive, yoke, harness, hitch; groom,

369. [The science of plants.] **Botany.
—N.** botany; phyto-graphy, -logy,
-tomy; vegetable physiology, herbori-
zation, dendr-, myc-, fung-, alg-ology;
flora, pomona; botanist &c.; botanic
garden &c. (*garden*) 371; *hortus siccus,
herbarium*, herbal.

herb-ist, -arist, -alist, -orist, -arian
&c.

V. botanize, herborize.

Adj. botanical &c. *n.*

371. [The economy or management
of plants.] **Agriculture.—N.** agriculture, cultivation, husbandry, farming;
georgics, geoponics; tillage, tilth, agronomy, gardening, spade husbandry,
vintage; hort-, arbor-, silv-, citr-, vit-,
flor-iculture; intensive culture; landscape gardening; forestry, afforestation.

husbandman, horticulturist, citri-
culturist, gardener, florist; agricult-or,
-urist; yeoman, farmer, cultivator,
tiller of the soil, ploughman, sower,
reaper; woodcutter, backwoodsman,
forester; vine grower, vintager; Boer;
Triptolemus.

field, meadow, garden; botanic –,
winter –, ornamental –, flower –, kitchen –, truck –, market –, hop- garden;
nursery; green-, hot-, glass-house;
conservatory, cucumber frame, *cloche*,
bed, border, seed-plot; grass-plat,
lawn; park &c. (*pleasure ground*) 840;
parterre, shrubbery, plantation, avenue,

----

* Bentham.

curry-comb; milk; shear; hatch; incubate.

Adj. pastoral, bucolic; tame, domestic, domesticated, broken in, gentle, docile.

---

arboretum, pinery, *pinetum*, orchard; vineyard, vinery; orangery; farm &c. (*abode*) 189.

V. cultivate; till, – the soil; farm, garden; sow, plant; reap, mow, cut; manure, dress the ground, dig, delve, dibble, hoe, plough, plow, harrow, rake, weed, lop and top, force, transplant, thin out, bed out, prune, graft.

Adj. agr-icultural, -arian, -estic.

arable; predial, rural, rustic, country, bucolic, Bœotian; horticultural.

---

372. Mankind.—N. man, -kind; human -race, – species, – nature; humanity, mortality, flesh, generation.

[Science of man] anthropo-logy, -graphy, -sophy; ethno-logy, -graphy; humanitarianism.

human being; person, -age; individual, creature, fellow creature, mortal, body, somebody, one; such a –, some- one; soul, living soul; earthling; party, head, hand; *dramatis personæ*.

people, persons, folk, public, society, world; community, – at large; general public; nation, -ality; state, realm; common-weal, -wealth; republic, body politic; million &c. (*commonalty*) 876; population &c. (*inhabitant*) 188.

cosmopolite; lords of the creation; ourselves.

Adj. human, mortal, personal, individual, national, civic, public, cosmopolitan; anthropoid.

---

373. Man.—N. man, male, he; manhood &c. (*adolescence*) 131; gentleman, sir, master; yeoman, wight, swain, fellow, guy, blade, *beau*, chap, gaffer, good man; husband &c. (*married man*) 903; Mr., mister, *monsieur, sahib, Herr, señor, signor*; boy &c. (*youth*) 129; Adonis.

[Male animal] cock, drake, gander, dog, boar, stag, hart, buck, horse, entire horse, stallion; gib-, tom-cat; he-, Billy-goat; ram, tup; bull, -ock; capon, ox, gelding; steer, stot.

Adj. male, he, masculine; manly, virile; un-womanly, -feminine.

---

374. Woman.—N. woman, she, female, petticoat, skirt, moll, broad.

feminality, feminity, muliebrity; womanhood &c. (*adolescence*) 131; feminism; gynecology, gyniatrics, gynics.

womankind; the -sex, – fair; fair –, softer- sex; weaker vessel; the distaff side.

dame, madam, *madame*, mistress, Mrs., lady, *mem-sahib, Frau, señora, signora, donna, belle*, matron, dowager, goody, gammer; good -woman, – wife; squaw; wife &c. (*marriage*) 903; matron-age, -hood.

Venus, nymph, wench, *grisette*; little bit of fluff; girl &c. (*youth*) 129.

inamorata (love) &c. 897; courtesan &c. 962.

spinster, old maid, virgin, bachelor girl, new woman, amazon.

[Female animal] hen, slut, bitch, sow, doe, roe, mare; she-, Nanny-goat; ewe, cow; lioness, tigress; vixen.

gynecæum, harem, *seraglio, zenana, purdah*.

Adj. female, she; feminine, womanly, ladylike, matronly, maidenly; womanish, effeminate unmanly, gynecic.

2°. SENSATION

(1.) *Sensation in general*

375. Physical Sensibility.—N. sensibility; sensitiveness &c. *adj.*; physical sensibility, feeling, perceptivity, anaphylaxis, susceptibility, æsthetics; moral sensibility &c. 822.

sensation, impression, effect; consciousness &c. (*knowledge*) 490.

external senses.

V. be -sensible &c. *adj.* -of; feel, perceive.

render, -sensible &c. *adj.*; excite, stir, sharpen, cultivate, tutor.

cause sensation, impress; excite -, produce- an impression.

Adj. sens-ible, -itive, -uous; æsthetic, perceptive, sentient; conscious &c. (*aware*) 490; impressionable, responsive, alive to.

acute, sharp, keen, vivid, lively, impressive, thin-skinned.

Adv. to the quick.

377. Physical Pleasure.—N. pleasure; physical -, sensual -, sensuous-pleasure; bodily enjoyment, animal gratification, sensuality; hedonism, luxuriousness &c. *adj.*; dissipation, round of pleasure; titillation, *gusto*, creature comforts, comfort, ease; pillow &c. (*support*) 215; luxury, lap of luxury; purple and fine linen; bed of -down, - roses; velvet, clover; cup of Circe &c. (*intemperance*) 954.

treat; diversion, divertisement, entertainment; refreshment, regale; feast; *délice*; dainty &c. 394; *bonne bouche*.

source of pleasure &c. 829; happiness &c. (*mental enjoyment*) 827.

V. feel -, experience -, receive-pleasure; enjoy, relish; luxuriate -, revel -, riot -, bask -, swim -, wallow-in; feast on; gloat -over, - on; smack the lips.

live -on the fat of the land, - in comfort &c. *adv.*; bask in the sunshine, *faire ses choux gras*.

give pleasure &c. 829.

376. Physical Insensibility.—N. insensibility, physical insensibility; obtuseness &c. *adj.*; palsy, paralysis, *anæsthesia, analgesia, narcosis, hypnosis,* twilight sleep, stupor, coma, trance, catalepsy; sleep &c. (*inactivity*) 683; moral insensibility &c. 823; numbness &c. 381.

anæsthetic agent, general -, local-anæsthetic, opium, ether, chloroform, cocaine, novocaine, chloral; nitrous oxide, laughing gas; refrigeration.

V. be -insensible &c. *adj.*; have a -thick skin, - rhinoceros hide.

render -insensible &c. *adj.*; blunt, pall, obtund, benumb, deaden, paralyze; anæsthetize, drug, dope; put under the influence of -chloroform &c. *n.*; hypnotize; stupefy, stun, narcotize.

Adj. insensible, unfeeling, senseless, comatose, dazed, impercipient, callous, thick-skinned, pachydermatous; hard, -ened; case-hardened; proof; obtuse, dull; anæsthetic; paralytic, palsied, numb, dead.

378. Physical Pain.—N. pain; suffering, -ance; bodily - physical- -pain, - suffering; mental suffering &c. 828; dolour, ache; aching &c. *v.*; smart; shoot, -ing; twinge, twitch, gripe, head-, ear-, tooth-ache; *migraine*, neuralgia, neuritis, lumbago, gout, sciatica; hurt, cut; sore, -ness; discomfort, *malaise*; *tic douloureux*.

spasm, cramp; nightmare, *ephialtes*; crick, stitch, kink; thrill, convulsion, throe; throb &c. (*agitation*) 315; pang.

sharp -, piercing -, throbbing -, shooting -, gnawing -, burning- pain; anguish, agony.

torment, torture; rack; cruci-ation, -fixion; martyrdom; martyr, toad under a harrow, vivisection.

V. feel -, experience -, suffer -, undergo- pain &c. *n.*; suffer, ache, smart, bleed; tingle, shoot; twinge, twitch, lancinate; writhe, wince, make a wry face; sit on -thorns, - pins and needles.

give -, inflict- pain; pain, hurt, chafe, sting, bite, gnaw, gripe, stab, grind;

Adj. enjoying &c. *v.*; luxurious, voluptuous, sensual, hedonistic, comfortable, cosy, snug, in comfort, at ease.

agreeable &c. 829; grateful, refreshing, comforting, cordial, genial; sensuous; palatable &c. 394; sweet &c. (*sugar*) 396; fragrant &c. 400; melodious &c. 413; lovely &c. (*beautiful*) 845.

Adv. in -comfort &c. *n.*; on -a bed of roses &c. *n.*; at one's ease.

pinch, tweak; grate, gall, fret, prick, pierce, wring, convulse; torment, torture; rack, agonize; crucify; ex-, cruciate; break on the wheel, put to the rack; flag &c. (*punish*) 972; grate on the ear &c. (*harsh sound*) 410.

Adj. in -pain &c. *n.*, – a state of pain; pained &c. *v.*

painful; aching &c. *v.*; biting, poignant; sore, raw, tender, with exposed nerve.

(2.) *Special Sensation*

1. *Touch*

379. [Sensation of pressure.] **Touch.**—**N.** touch; tact, -ion, -ility; feeling; palp-ation, -ability; manipulation; brush, tick, graze, contact &c. 199.

[Organ of touch] hand, finger, fore-finger, thumb, paw, feeler, *antenna*.

V. touch, feel, handle, finger, thumb, paw, fumble, grope, grabble; twiddle, tweedle; pass -, run- the fingers over, massage, rub, knead; palpate, stroke, manipulate, wield; throw out a feeler.

Adj. tact-ual, -ile; tangible, palpable; lambent.

380. Sensations of Touch.—**N.** itching &c. *v.*; titillation, formication, *aura*.

V. itch, tingle, creep, thrill, sting; prick, -le; tickle, titillate.

Adj. itching &c. *v.*

381. [Insensibility to touch.] **Numbness.**—**N.** numbness &c. (*physical insensibility*) 376; pins and needles.

local anæsthetic, cocaine, novocaine &c.; morphia.

V. benumb &c. 376; freeze, dull, deaden.

Adj. numb; benumbed &c. *v.*; intangible, impalpable.

---

2. *Heat*

382. Heat.—**N.** heat, caloric; temperature, warmth, fervour, calidity; incal-, incand-, recal-, decal-escence; glow, flush, blush; fever, hectic.

phlogiston; fire, spark, scintillation, flash, flame, blaze; arc; bonfire; firework, pyrotechny; wild-fire; sheet of fire, lambent flame; devouring element; conflagration.

summer, dog-days, canicule; baking &c. 384 -, white -, tropical -, Afric -, Bengal -, summer -, blood- heat; heat wave, sirocco, simoon; broiling sun; isolation; warming &c. 384.

sun &c. (*luminary*) 423; fire worshipper &c. 991; furnace &c. 386.

geyser, hot spring, volcano.

[Science of heat] pyrology; therm-

383. Cold.—**N.** cold, -ness &c. *adj.*; frigidity, gelidity, algidity, inclemency, *fresco*.

winter; depth of -, hard- winter; Siberia, Nova Zembla; Ant-, arctic, North -, South- Pole.

ice; snow, - flake, - crystal, - drift; sleet; hail, -stone; rime, frost; hoar -, white -, hard -, sharp- frost; icicle, thick-ribbed ice; fall of snow, snow storm, heavy fall, *avalanche*; ice-berg, -floe; floe, berg; *glacier*; *nevée, serac*.

[Sensation of cold] chilliness &c. *adj.*; chill; shivering &c. *v.*; gooseskin, -flesh; *rigor*, horripilation, chattering of teeth; frostbite, chilblain.

V. be -cold &c. *adj.*; shiver, starve, quake, shake, tremble, shudder, didder,

ology, -otics; thermometer &c. 389.

V. be -hot &c. *adj.*; glow, incandesce, flush, sweat, swelter, bask, smoke, reek, stew, simmer, seethe, boil, burn, singe, scorch, scald, grill, broil, blaze, flame; smoulder; parch, fume, pant.

heat &c. (*make hot*) 384; thaw, fuse, melt, give.

Adj. hot, heated, warm, mild, genial, tepid, lukewarm, unfrozen; therm-al, -ic; calorific; ferv-ent, -id; ardent; aglow.

sunny, torrid, tropical, estival, cani-cular; close, sultry, stifling, stuffy, suffocating, oppressive; reeking &c. *v.*; baking &c. 384.

red –, white –, smoking –, burning &c. *v.* –, piping- hot; like -a furnace, – an oven; hot as -fire, – pepper; hot enough to roast an ox.

fiery; incand-, incal-escent; candent, ebullient, glowing, smoking; on fire; blazing &c. *v.*; in -flames, – a blaze; alight, afire, ablaze; un-quenched, -extinguished; smouldering; in a -heat, – glow, – fever, – perspiration, – sweat; sudorific; swelter-ing, -ed; blood-hot, -warm; warm as -a toast, – wool; recalescent, thermo-genic, pyrotechnic, feverish, febrile, inflamed.

volcanic, plutonic, igneous; isother-mal, -mic, -al.

Phr. Not a breath of air.

384. Calefaction.—N. increase of temperature; heating &c. *v.*; cale-, tepe-, torre-faction; melting, fusion; liquefaction &c. 335; burning &c. *v.*; kindling, combustion; in-, ac-cension; con-, cremation; scorification; cauter-y, -ization; ustulation, calcination; in-, cineration; cupellation; carbonization.

ignition, inflammation, adustion, flagration; de-, con-flagration; em-pyrosis, incendiarism; arson; *auto da fé*; suttee.

boiling &c. *v.*; coction, ebullition, estuation, elixation, decoction.

furnace &c. 386; blanket, flannel, fur, muffler, wrap; wadding &c. (*lining*) 224; clothing &c. 225.

match &c. (*fuel*) 388; incendiary, pyromaniac; *pétroleur*, *pétroleuse*; cau-terant, caustic, lunar caustic, apozem, moxa.

sunstroke, *coup de soleil*; insolation, sunburn.

pottery, ceramics, crockery, porce-lain, china; earthen-, stone-ware; pot,

quiver; perish with cold; chill &c. (*render cold*) 385.

Adj. cold, cool; chill, -y; gelid, frigid, algid; fresh, keen, bleak, raw, inclem-ent, bitter, biting, niveous, cutting, nipping, piercing, pinching; clay-cold; starved &c. (*made cold*) 385; shivering &c. *v.*; aguish, *transi de froid*; frost-bitten, -bound, -nipped.

cold as -a stone, – marble, – lead, – iron, – a frog, – charity, – Christmas; cool as -a cucumber, – custard.

icy, glacial, frosty, freezing, wintry, brumal, hibernal, boreal, arctic, ant-arctic, polar, Siberian, hyemal; hyper-bore-an, -al; ice-bound; frozen out.

un-warmed, -thawed, -heated; iso-cheimal, -chimenal.

Adv. coldly, bitterly &c. *adj.*; *à pierre fendre.*

---

385. Refrigeration.—N. refrigera-tion, infrigidation, reduction of tem-perature; cooling &c. *v.*; con-gelation, -glaciation; ice &c. 383; solidification &c. (*density*) 321; refrigerator &c. 387.

extincteur; fire, – engine, – extin-guisher, – annihilator, – brigade, – man; sprinkler, hose, hydrant, standpipe.

incombusti-bility, -bleness &c. *adj.*

V. cool, fan, refrigerate, refresh, ice; congeal, freeze, glaciate; benumb, starve, pinch, chill, petrify, chill to the marrow, nip, cut, pierce, bite, make one's teeth chatter; damp, slack; quench; put –, stamp- out; extinguish.

go –, burn- out.

Adj. cooled &c. *v.*; frozen out; cooling &c. *v.*; frigorific.

incombustible; un-, unin-flammable; fire-proof.

mug, *terra-cotta*, brick, clinker; cinder, ash, *scoriæ*; embers, dress, slag, products of combustion, coke, carbon, charcoal.

inflamma-, combusti-bility.

[Transmission of heat] diathermancy, transcalency.

V. heat, warm, chafe, stive, foment; make -hot &c. 382; sun oneself, bask in the sun.

fire; set -fire to, – on fire; kindle, enkindle, light, ignite, strike a light; apply the -match, – torch- to; re-kindle, -lume; fan –, add fuel to- the flame; poke –, stir –, blow- the fire; make a bonfire of; burn at the stake.

melt, thaw, fuse; liquefy &c. 335.

burn, inflame, roast, toast, fry, grill, singe, parch, bake, torrefy, scorch; brand, cauterize, sear, burn in; corrode, char, carbonize, calcine, incinerate; smelt, cupel, scorify; reduce to ashes; burn to a cinder; commit –, consign- to the flames.

boil, digest, stew, cook, seethe, scald, parboil, simmer; do to rags.

take –, catch- fire; blaze &c. (*flame*) 382.

Adj. heated &c. *v.*; molten, sodden; *réchauffé*; heating &c. *v.*

inflammable, burnable, inflammatory, combustible; diatherm-al -anous; burnt &c. *v.*; volcanic.

386. Furnace.—N. furnace, blast furnace, fire-box, stove, incinerator, destructor, crematorium, crematory, kiln, oven, oast-house; hot-, bake-, wash-house; laundry; conservatory; hearth, focus; athanor, hypocaust, reverberatory; volcano; forge, fiery furnace; *tuyère*, brasier, salamander, heater, warming-pan, foot-warmer, hot-water bottle; radiator; boiler, geyser, caldron, seething caldron, pot; urn, kettle; chafing-dish; retort, crucible, alembic, still; saggar.

fire-place, -dog, -irons; hearth, ingle, grate, range, kitchener; kitchen range; oil-, gas-, electric, -cooker, -stove; fireless cooker; fire; galley; ca-, cam-boose; poker, tongs, shovel, hob, trivet; and-, grid-iron; frying-, stew-pan &c.

hot –, Turkish –, Russian –, vapour –, shower –, warm- bath; *calidarium, tepidarium, sudatorium,* sudatory; *hammam.*

387. Refrigerator.—N. refrigerator, -y; *frigidarium*; cold storage; refrigerating-plant, – machine; ice-house, -pail, -bag, -chest, -pack; cooler, damper; wine-cooler, freezing mixture.

388. Fuel.—N. fuel, firing, combustible, coal, wallsend, anthracite, bituminous coal, slack, culm, cannel coal, lignite, briquette, coke, carbon, charcoal; turf, peat, fire-wood, bobbing, faggot, log, yule log, ember, cinder &c. (*products of combustion*) 384; kindling wood, tinder, touch-wood; fumigator, sulphur, brimstone; incense; port-fire; fire-barrel, -ball, -brand.

fuel oil, gas, gasoline, electricity.

brand, torch, fuse; wick; spill, match, safety match, light, lucifer, congreve, vesuvian, vesta, fusee, locofoco; linstock; illuminant.

candle &c. (*luminary*) 423; oil &c. (*grease*), 356; petrol, gasoline, methylated –, spirit; gas, acetylene.

Adj. carbonaceous; combustible, inflammable.

V. stoke, fire, feed, add fuel to the flames.

389. Thermometer.—N. thermo-meter, -scope, -stat, -pile, differential thermometer; pyro-, calori-meter; radio micrometer &c.

3. *Taste*

390. Taste.—N. taste, flavour, gust, *gusto*, relish, savour; sapor, sapidity; twang, smack, smatch; after-taste, tang.

tasting; de-, gustation.

palate, tongue, tooth, stomach.

V. taste, savour, smatch, smack, flavour, twang; tickle the palate &c. (*savoury*) 394; smack the lips.

Adj. sapid, saporific; gusta-ble, -tory; strong; flavoured, spiced, savoury; palatable &c. 394.

391. Insipidity.—N. insipidity; taste-lessness &c. *adj.*

V. be -tasteless &c. *adj.*

Adj. void of -taste &c. 390; insipid; jejune; taste-, gust-, savour-less; in-gustible, mawkish, milk and water, weak, stale, flat, vapid, *fade*, wishy-washy, mild; untasted.

---

392. Pungency.—N. pungency, piquancy, poignancy, *haut-goût*, strong taste, twang, race, tang.

sharpness &c. *adj.*; acrimony, acridity; roughness &c. (*sour*) 397; unsavouriness &c. 395.

nitre, saltpetre; mustard, cayenne, caviare; seasoning &c. (*condiment*) 393; brine.

dram, cordial, nip, pick-me-up, bracer, potion.

nicotine, tobacco, snuff, quid; segar; cigar, -ette, gasper, fag; cheroot; weed; fragrant –, Indian- weed; pipe, clay pipe, churchwarden, brier, meerschaum, hookah, hubble-bubble.

V. be -pungent &c. *adj.*; bite the tongue.

render -pungent &c. *adj.*; season, spice, salt, pepper, pickle, brine, devil, curry.

smoke, chew, take snuff.

Adj. pungent, strong; high-, full-flavoured; high-tasted, -seasoned; gamy; sharp, stinging, rough, *piquant*, racy; biting, mordant; spicy; seasoned &c. *v.*; hot, – as pepper; peppery, vellicating, escharotic, meracious; acrid, acrimonious, bitter; rough &c. (*sour*) 397; unsavoury &c. 395.

salt, saline, brackish, briny; salt as -brine, – a herring, – Lot's wife.

393. Condiment.—N. condiment, flavouring, salt, mustard, pepper, cayenne, curry, seasoning, sauce, spice, cinnamon, chillies, relish, *sauce piquante*, caviare, pot-herbs, onion, garlic, pickle, chutney, nutmeg &c.

V. season &c. (*render pungent*) 392.

---

394. Savouriness.—N. savouriness &c. *adj.*; relish, zest.

tit-bit, dainty, delicacy, ambrosia, nectar, *bonne bouche*; game, turtle, venison.

V. taste good, be -savoury &c. *adj.*; tickle the -palate, – appetite; flatter the palate.

render -palatable &c. *adj.*

relish, like, smack the lips.

Adj. savoury, well-tasted, to one's taste, tasty, good, palatable, nice, dainty, delectable; tooth-ful, -some;

395. Unsavouriness.—N. unsavouri-ness &c. *adj.*; amaritude; acri-mony, -tude; roughness &c. (*sour*) 397; acerb-ity, austerity; gall and worm-wood, rue, quassia, aloes; sickener.

V. be -unpalatable &c. *adj.*; sicken, disgust, nauseate, pall, turn the stomach.

Adj. un-savoury, -palatable, -sweet; ill-flavoured, un-appetizing, -eatable, inedible; bitter, – as gall; acrid, acri-monious; rough.

offensive, repulsive, nasty; sickening

gustful, appetizing, lickerish, delicate, delicious, exquisite, rich, luscious, ambrosial.

Adv. *per amusare la bocca.*

Phr. *cela se laisse manger.*

&c. *v.*; nauseous; loath-, ful-some; unpleasant &c. 830.

---

396. Sweetness.—N. sweetness, dulcitude, saccharinity.

sugar, cane-, beet-sugar; saccharine, glucose, syrup, treacle, molasses, honey, manna; confection, -ary; sweets, grocery, conserve, preserve, *confiture,* jam, marmalade, julep; sugar-candy, -plum; licorice, liquorice, plum, lollipop, *bon bon, jujube,* comfit, sweetmeat, caramel, toffee, butterscotch.

nectar; hydromel, mead, metheglin, honeysuckle, *liqueur,* sweet wine.

pastry, pie, tart, puff, pudding, cake.

dulc-ification, -oration.

V. be -sweet &c. *adj.*

render -sweet &c. *adj.*; sugar, saccharize, sweeten; edulcorate; dulc-orate, -ify; candy; mull.

Adj. sweet, sugary; sacchar-ine, -iferous; dulcet, honied, candied, luscious, nectarious, melliferous; sweetened &c. *v.*

sweet as -a nut, – sugar, – honey.

397. Sourness.—N. sourness &c. *adj.*; acid, -ity; acetous fermentation; acerbity.

vinegar, verjuice, crab, alum.

V. be –, turn- -sour &c. *adj.*; set the teeth on edge.

render -sour &c. *adj.*; acid-ify, -ulate.

Adj. sour; acid, -ulous, -ulated; acerb; tart, crabbed; acet-ous, -ose; sour as vinegar, sourish, acescent, sub-acid; styptic, hard, rough; unripe, green.

---

4. *Odour*

398. Odour.—N. odour, smell, odorament, scent, effluvium; eman-, exhal-ation; fume, essence, trail, nidor, redolence.

sense of smell; scent; act of -smelling &c. *v.*

V. have an -odour &c. *n.*; smell, – of, – strong of; exhale; give out a -smell &c. *n.*; scent.

smell, scent; snuff, – up; sniff, nose, inhale.

Adj. odor-ous, -iferous; smelling, strong-scented; redolent, graveolent, nidorous, pungent.

[Relating to the sense of smell] olfactory, quick-scented.

399. Inodorousness.—N. inodorousness; absence –, want- of smell.

V. be -inodorous &c. *adj.*; not smell. deodorize.

Adj. inodor-ous, -ate; scentless; without –, wanting- smell &c. 398.

deodoriz-ed, -ing.

---

400. Fragrance. — N. fragrance, aroma, redolence, perfume, *bouquet;* sweet smell, aromatic perfume.

perfumery; incense; musk, frankincense; pastil, -le; myrrh, perfumes of Arabia, chypre; otto, ottar, attar; bergamot, balm, civet, *pot-pourri,* pulvil; nosegay, *boutonnière;* scent, -bag; *sachet,* scent-bottle, smelling bottle, *vinaigrette;* toilet water, *eau de Cologne;* thurible, censer, thurification.

perfumer; incense bearer.

401. Fetor.—N. fetor, fetidness; bad &c. *adj.*; -smell, – odour; stench, stink; mephitis, foul –, mal- odour; *empyreuma;* mustiness &c. *adj.*; rancidity; foulness &c. (*uncleanness*) 653.

stoat, polecat, skunk; assafœtida; fungus, garlic; stink-pot, -bomb.

V. have a -bad smell &c. *n.*; smell, stink, – in the nostrils, – like a polecat; smell -strong &c. *adj.*, – offensively.

Adj. fetid; strong-smelling; high, bad, strong, fulsome, offensive, noisome, rank, rancid, reasty, tainted, musty,

V. be -fragrant &c. *adj.*; have a -perfume &c. *n.*; smell sweet, scent, perfume, thurify, embalm.

Adj. fragrant, aromatic, redolent, spicy, balmy, scented; sweet-smelling, -scented; perfum-ed, -atory; thuriferous; fragrant as a rose, muscadine, ambrosial.

fusty, frouzy; olid, -ous; nidorous; smelling, stinking; putrid &c. 653; suffocating, mephitic; empyreumatic.

---

5. *Sound*

(i.) Sound in General

402. Sound.—N. sound, noise, strain; accent, twang, intonation, tone, tune; cadence; sonority, sonorousness &c. *adj.*; audibility; resonance &c. 408; voice &c. 580.

[Science of sound] acou-, acu-stics; catacoustics, cataphonics; phon-ics, -etics, -ology, -ography; dia-coustics, -phonics.

telephone, phonograph &c. 418.

V. produce sound; sound, make a noise; give out -, emit- sound; phonetize, phonate; resound &c. 408.

Adj. sounding; soniferous; sonorific; resonant, audible, acoustic, auditory, distinct; stertorous; phonic, sonant; phonetic.

---

403. Silence.—N. silence; stillness &c. (*quiet*) 265; peace, hush, lull, rest; muteness &c. 581; solemn -, awful -, dead -, deathlike- silence.

V. be -silent &c. *adj.*; hold one's tongue &c. (*not speak*) 585.

render -silent &c. *adj.*; silence, still, hush; stifle, muffle, gag, stop; muzzle, put to silence &c. (*render mute*) 581.

Adj. silent; still, -y; calm, quiet; noise-, sound-, speech-less; hushed &c. *v.*; mute &c. 581; aphonic.

soft, solemn, awful, deathlike, silent as the grave; inaudible &c. (*faint*) 405.

Adv. silently &c. *adj.*; *sub silentio*; in perfect silence.

Int. hush! 'sh! silence! soft! whist! tush! chut! tut! *pax!* mum's the word! hold your tongue! shut up! be silent! be quiet! stop that noise! hold your row! dry up! peace, be still!

Phr. one might hear a -feather, - pin- drop.

---

404. Loudness.—N. loudness, power; loud noise, din; clang, -or; clatter, noise, bombilation, roar, uproar, racket, static, grinders, hubbub, *fracas*, *charivari*, trumpet blast, blare, flourish of trumpets, fanfare, *tintamarre*, peal, swell, blast, alarum, boom; resonance &c. 408.

vociferation; pandemonium, hullaballoo &c. 411; lungs; Stentor; megaphone; siren.

artillery, cannon, gunfire, shellburst, bomb; thunder.

V. be -loud &c. *adj.*; peal, swell, clang, boom, thunder, fulminate, roar; resound &c. 408; speak up, shout &c. (*vociferate*) 411; bellow &c. (*cry as an animal*) 412; give tongue.

rend the -air, - skies; fill the air; din -, ring -, thunder- in the ear;

---

405. Faintness.—N. faintness &c. *adj.*; faint sound, whisper, breath; under-tone, -breath; murmur, hum, rustle, buzz, purr; plash; sough, moan, sigh, susurration; tinkle; 'still small voice.'

hoarseness &c. *adj.*; raucity.

silencer, soft pedal, damper, mute, *sourdine*.

V. whisper, breathe, murmur, purl, hum, gurgle, ripple, babble, flow; tinkle; mutter &c. (*speak imperfectly*) 583.

steal on the ear; melt in -, float on- the air.

muffle, mute, deaden, damp, stifle.

Adj. inaudible; scarcely -, just-audible; low, dull; stifled, muffled; hoarse, husky; gentle, soft, faint; floating; purling, flowing &c. *v.*;

pierce –, split –, rend- the -ears, – head; deafen, stun; *faire le diable à quatre;* make one's windows shake; awaken –, startle- the echoes; make the welkin ring.

Adj. loud, sonorous; high-, big-sounding; blatant; deep, full, powerful, noisy, clangorous, multisonous, *fortissimo;* thundering, deafening &c. *v.;* trumpet-tongued; ear-splitting, -rending, -deafening; piercing; obstreperous, rackety, uproarious; enough to wake the -dead, – seven sleepers.

shrill &c. 410; clamorous &c. (*vociferous*) 411; stentor-ian, -ophonic.

Adv. loudly &c. *adj.;* aloud; at the top of one's voice, lustily, in full cry.

Phr. the air rings with.

whispered &c. *v.;* liquid; soothing; dulcet &c. (*melodious*) 413.

Adv. in a whisper, with bated breath, *sotto voce,* between the teeth, aside; *pian-o, -issimo; à la sourdine; con sordine;* out of earshot, inaudibly &c. *adj.*

(ii.) Specific Sounds*

406. [Sudden and violent sounds.] **Snap.—N.** snap &c. *v.;* rapping &c. *v.;* de-, crepitation; smack, clap, report; thud; burst, explosion, discharge, detonation, blow-out, back-fire, firing, salvo, volley, pistol-shot.

squib, cracker, gun, rifle, pop-gun.

V. rap, snap, tap, knock; click; clash; crack, -le; crash; pop; slam, bang, clap, thump, plump; toot; back-fire, explode, burst on the ear.

Adj. rapping &c. *v.*

Int. crash! bang!

407. [Repeated and protracted sounds.] **Roll.—N.** roll &c. *v.;* drumming &c. *v.;* tattoo; ding-dong; tantara; rataplan; whirr; rat-a-tat; rub-a-dub; pit-a-pat; quaver, clutter, *charivari,* racket; cuckoo; repetition &c. 104; peal of bells, devil's tattoo; reverberation &c. 408.

drumfire, barrage.

machine gun.

V. roll, drum, rumble, rattle, clatter, rustle, roar, drone, patter, clack.

hum, trill, shake; chime, peal, toll; tick, beat.

drum –, din- in the ear.

Adj. rolling &c. *v.;* monotonous &c. (*repeated*), 104; like a bee in a bottle.

---

408. Resonance.—N. resonance; ring &c. *v.;* ringing &c. *v.;* tintinnabulation; reflection, reverberation, clangor.

low –, base –, bass –, flat –, grave –, deep –, pedal- note; bass; *basso, – profondo;* bari-, bary-tone; *contralto.*

V. re-sound, -verberate, -echo; ring, ding, sing, jingle, gingle, chink, clink; tink, -le; chime; gurgle &c. 405; plash, guggle, echo, ring in the ear.

Adj. resounding &c. *v.;* resonant, tinnient, tintinnabulary; deep-toned, -sounding, -mouthed; hollow, sepulchral; gruff &c. (*harsh*) 410.

408a. Non-resonance. — N. thud, thump, dead sound; non-resonance; muffled drums, cracked bell; silencer, damper; mute, *sourdine.*

V. sound dead; stop –, damp- the -sound, – reverberations; deaden, muffle.

Adj. non-resonant, dead, muted. muffled.

---

409. [Hissing sounds.] **Sibilation.—N.** sibilation; hiss &c. *v.;* sternutation; high note &c. 410.

goose, serpent, snake.

* [The author's classification of sounds has been retained, though it does not entirely accord with the theories of modern science.—Ed.]

V. hiss, buzz, whiz, rustle; fizz, -le, sizzle, swish; wheeze, whistle, snuffle; squash; sneeze.

Adj. sibilant; hissing &c. *v.*; wheezy.

410. [Harsh sounds.] **Stridor.**—**N.** creak &c. *v.*; creaking &c. *v.*; discord &c. 414; stridor; harshness, roughness, sharpness &c. *adj.*; cacophony.

acute –, high- note; *soprano*, treble, tenor, *alto*, falsetto, *voce di testa*; shriek, cry &c. 411.

piccolo, fife, penny -whistle, – trumpet.

V. creak, grate, jar, burr, pipe, twang, jangle, clank, clink; scream &c. (*cry*) 411; yelp &c. (*animal sound*) 412; buzz &c. (*hiss*) 409.

set the teeth on edge, *écorcher les oreilles*; pierce –, split- the -ears, – head; offend –, grate upon –, jar upon- the ear.

Adj. creaking &c. *v.*; strident, stridulous, harsh, coarse, hoarse, horrisonous, raucous, metallic, rough, gruff, grum, sepulchral.

sharp, high, acute, shrill, high-pitched; trumpet-toned; piercing, ear-piercing; cracked; discordant &c. 414; cacophonous.

---

411. Cry.—**N.** cry &c. *v.*; voice &c. (*human*) 580; bark &c. (*animal*) 412.

vociferation, outcry, hullaballoo, chorus, clamour, hue and cry, plaint; lungs; stentor.

V. cry, roar, shout, bawl, brawl, halloo, halloa, hail, hoop, whoop, yell, bellow, howl, scream, screech, screak, shriek, shrill, squeak, squeal, squall, whine, whinny, pule, pipe, yaup.

cheer, hurrah; hoot; grumble, moan, groan.

snore, snort; grunt &c. (*animal sounds*) 412.

vociferate; raise –, lift up- the voice; call –, sing –, cry- out; exclaim; rend the air; thunder –, shout- at the -top of one's voice, – pitch of one's breath; *s'égosiller*; strain the -throat, – voice, – lungs; give a -cry &c.

Adj. crying &c. *v.*; clam-ant, -orous; vociferous; stentorian &c. (*loud*) 404; open-mouthed.

412. [Animal sounds.] **Ululation.**—**N.** cry &c. *v.*; crying &c. *v.*; ululation, latration, belling; reboation; call, note; bark, howl, yelp; twittering, woodnote; insect cry, fritinancy, drone; screech; cuckoo.

V. cry, ululate, howl, roar, bellow, blare, rebellow, bark, yelp; bay, – the moon; yap, growl, yarr, yawl, snarl, howl; grunt, -le; snort, squeak; neigh, bray; mew, mewl; purr, caterwaul, pule; bleat, low, moo; troat, croak, crow, screech, caw, coo, gobble, quack, cackle, gaggle, guggle; chuck, -le; cluck; clack; cheep, chirp, chirrup, twitter, sing, cuckoo; pout, wail, hum, buzz; hiss, blatter; hoot.

Adj. crying &c. *v.*; blatant, latrant; re-, mugient; deep-, full-mouthed.

Adv. in full cry.

(iii.) MUSICAL SOUNDS

413. Melody. Concord.—**N.** melody, rhythm, measure; rhyme &c. (*poetry*) 597.

pitch, *timbre*, intonation, tone, over-tone.

scale, gamut; diapason; diatonic –, chromatic –, enharmonic- scale; key, clef, chords,

modulation, temperament, syncope, syncopation, preparation, suspension, resolution.

414. Discord.—**N.** discord, -ance; dissonance, cacophony, caterwauling; harshness &c. 410; consecutive fifths.

[Confused sounds] Babel, pande-monium; Dutch –, cat's- concert; marrow-bones and cleavers.

V. be -discordant &c. *adj.*; jar &c. (*sound harshly*) 410.

Adj. discordant; dis-, ab-sonant; out of tune, tuneless; un-musical, -tunable; un-, im-melodious; un-, in-harmonious;

staff, stave, line, space, brace; bar, rest; *appogia-to, -tura; acciaccatura,* shake, *arpeggio.*

note, musical note, notes of a scale; sharp, flat, natural; high note &c. (*shrillness*) 410; low note &c. 408; interval; semitone; second, third, fourth &c.; diatessaron.

breve, semibreve, minim, crotchet, quaver; semi-, demisemi-quaver; sustained note, drone, burden.

tonic; key-, leading-, fundamental- note; supertonic, mediant, dominant; sub-mediant, -dominant, organ-, pedal-point; octave, tetrachord; major –, minor- -mode, – scale, – key; Doric mode, passage, phrase.

concord, harmony; unison, -ance; chime, homophony; euphon-y, -ism; tonality; consonance; concent; part.

orchestration, harmonization, – phrasing.

[Science of harmony] harmon-y, -ics; thorough-, fundamental-bass; counterpoint; faburden.

piece of music &c. 415; composer, harmonist, contrapuntist.

V. be -harmonious &c. *adj.*; harmonize, chime, symphonize, transpose; put in tune, tune, accord, string; score, arrange, orchestrate.

Adj. harmoni-ous, -cal; in -concord &c. *n.*, – tune, – concert; unisonant, concentual, symphonizing, isotonic, homophonous, assonant, consonant.

measured, rhythmical, diatonic, chromatic, enharmonic.

melodious, musical; tuneful, tunable; sweet, dulcet, canorous; mell-ow, -ifluous; soft; clear, – as a bell; silvery; euphon-ious, -ic, -ical; symphonious; enchanting &c. (*pleasure-giving*) 829; fine-, full-, silver-toned.

Adv. harmoniously &c. *adj.*

sing-song; cacophonous; jarring, harsh &c. 410.

---

415. Music.—**N.** music, classical –, modern –, descriptive- music; concert, recital; strain, tune, air, *motif*; melody &c. 413; *aria, arietta*; piece of music, *sonata; rond-o, -eau; pastorale, cavatina,* roulade, *fantasia, toccata, concerto,* overture, symphony, symphonic poem, tone poem, prelude, voluntary, *intermezzo,* variations, *cadenza*; cadence; fugue, canon, serenade, *nocturne, notturno,* rhapsody, romance, *aubade,* dithyramb; opera, operetta; oratorio; composition, movement; stave.

instrumental music; full-, orchestral- score; minstrelsy, tweedle-dum and tweedledee, band, orchestra &c. 416; concerted piece, *pot-pourri,* medley, *capriccio,* incidental music; improvisation; peal.

vocal music, vocalism; chaunt, chant; psalm, -ody; hymn; song &c. (*poem*) 597; canticle, canzonet, *cantata, bravura, coloratura*; lay, ballad, ditty, carol, barcarolle, pastoral, recitative, *recitativo, solfeggio,* tonic sol-fa.

Lydian measures; slow -music, – movement; *adagio* &c. *adv.*; minuet; siren strains, soft music, lullaby; *berceuse,* cradle song, dump; dirge &c. (*lament*) 839; pibroch; martial music, march, funeral-, dead- march; dance music; waltz &c. (*dance*) 840; rag-time, syncopation, jazz.

solo, duet, *duo,* trio; quartet; quintet, sextet, septet; part song, descant, glee, madrigal, catch, round, chorus, *chorale*; antiphon, -y; accompaniment, second –, alto –, tenor –, bass- part; score, thorough bass; counterpoint.

composer &c. 413; musician &c. 416.

V. compose, perform &c. 416; attune.

Adj. musical; instrumental, orchestral, vocal, choral, lyric, operatic; harmonious &c. 413.

Adv. *adagio*; *largo, larghetto, andan-te, -tino*; *alla capella*; *maestoso, moderato*; *allegr-o, -etto*; *spiritoso, vivace, veloce*; *prest-o, -issimo*; *pian-o, -issimo, fort-e, -issimo, sforzando*; *con brio*; *capriccioso*; *scherz-o, -ando*; *legato, sostenuto, staccato, crescendo, diminuendo, rallentando, affettuoso, arioso*; *parlante, cantabile*; *obbligato*; *pizzicato, tremolo, vibrato*.

416. Musician. [Performance of Music.]—**N.** musician, *artiste, virtuoso*, performer, player, minstrel; bard &c. (*poet*) 597; instrumental-, organ-, accompan-, pian-, violin-, flaut-, harp-ist; harper, fiddler, fifer, trumpeter, piper, drummer; catgut scraper.

band, orchestra, waits.

vocal-, melod-ist; singer, warbler; songst-, chaunt-er, -ress; *diva, cantatrice*, coloratura, soprano, mezzo-soprano, alto, contralto, tenor, baritone, bass, *basso, -profondo*.

choir, quire, chorister; chorus, – singer; choral society, festival, *eisteddfod*.

nightingale, philomel, thrush; siren; Orpheus, Apollo, the Muses, Erato, Euterpe, Terpsichore; tuneful -nine, – quire.

composer &c. 413.

performance, virtuosity, execution, touch, expression, solmization.

V. play, pipe, strike –, tune- up, sweep the chords, tickle –, paw- the ivories, vamp, tweedle, fiddle; strike the lyre, beat the drum; blow –, sound –, wind- the horn; grind the organ; touch the -guitar &c. (*instruments*) 417; thrum, strum, twang, drum, beat –, keep- time, conduct.

execute, perform; accompany; sing –, play- a second; compose, write music, set to music, arrange, harmonize, orchestrate.

sing, chaunt, chant, hum, warble, carol, chirp, chirrup, lilt, purl, quaver, trill, shake, twitter, whistle; sol-fa; intone.

have -an ear for music, – a musical ear, – a correct ear, – absolute pitch.

Adj. playing &c. *v.*; musical, lyric.

Adv. *adagio, andante* &c. (*music*) 415.

417. Musical Instruments.—**N.** musical instruments; band; string-, brass-, drum and fife-, military-, bugle-, German-, dance-, jazz-band; orchestra, string quartet; orchestrion, orchestrelle.

[Stringed instruments] mono-, poly-chord; harp, lyre, lute, archlute, thearbo; mandol-a, -in, -ine; guitar; *ukulele*; psaltery, zither; bandore, cither, -n; gittern, rebeck, *bandurria*, banjo, zither banjo, *balalaika, samisen*; plectrum.

viol, -in, Cremona, Stradivarius; fiddle, kit; *vielle, viola, – d'amore, – di gamba*; tenor, *violoncello*, cello; bass, bass-, base-viol; double-bass, *contrabasso, violone*, hurdy-gurdy; strings, catgut; bow, fiddlestick.

piano, -forte; grand –, concert grand –, baby –, upright –, cottage-piano; pianino, pianette; harpsi-, clavi-, clari-, mani-chord; *clavier*, spinet, virginals; dulcimer, *cymbalo*; Eolian harp; piano-organ, -player, electric piano, player-piano, pianola.

[Wind instruments] organ, church –, pipe –, American- organ; harmoni-um, -phon; accordion, seraphina, concertina; melodeon; barrel-organ; humming top.

flute, fife, piccolo, flageolet, penny-whistle, reed instrument; clari-net, -onet; bass clarionet; saxophone; basset horn, *corno di bassetto*; musette, shawm, oboe, hautboy, *cor Anglais*, *corno Inglese*, bassoon, double bassoon, *contrafagotto*; bag-, union-pipes; ocarina, Pandean pipes; calliope; sirene, pipe, pitch-pipe; sourdet; whistle, catcall.

horn, bugle, key bugle, cornet, *cornet-à-pistons*, cornopean, clarion, trumpet, trombone, ophicleide, serpent; English-, French-, bugle-, sax-, flugel-, alt-, helicon-, post-horn; sackbut, euphonium, bombardon, tuba, bass tuba.

[Vibrating surfaces] cymbal, bell, gong, peal of bells, *carillon*; tambour, -ine; drum, tom-tom, tab-or, -ret, -ourine, -orin; *sistrum*; *grand caisse*, bass-, big-, side-, kettle-drum; *tympani*; war drums; tymbal, timbrel, castanet, bones; musical-glasses, -stones; harmonica, sounding-board, rattle; gramophone, phonograph.

[Vibrating bars] reed, tuning-fork, triangle, Jew's harp, musical box, harmonicon, xylophone, marimba, *celeste*.

sord-ine, -et; *sourd-ine, -et*; mute.

(iv.) PERCEPTION OF SOUND

418. [Sense of sound.] **Hearing.—N.** hearing &c. *v.*; audition, auscultation; eavesdropping; audibility; acoustics &c. 402.

acute –, nice –, delicate –, quick –, sharp –, correct –, musical -ear; ear for music.

ear, auricle, lug, acoustic organs, auditory apparatus, ear-drum, tympanum; ear-, speaking-trumpet, megaphone; telephone, radiophone, stethoscope, phonograph, gramophone, microphone.

hearer, auditor, listener, eavesdropper; audi-tory, -ence.

V. hear, overhear; hark, -en; list, -en; give –, lend –, bend- an ear; give attention; catch a sound, prick up one's ears; give -a hearing, – audience- to.

hang upon the lips of, be all ear, listen with both ears, monitor.

become audible; meet –, fall upon –, catch –, reach- the ear; be heard; ring in the ear &c. (*resound*) 408.

Adj. hearing &c. *v.*; auditory, auricular, aural, auditive, acoustic.
Adv. *arrectis auribus.*
Int. hark, – ye! hear! list, -en! *Oyez!* attention! lend me your ears!

419. Deafness.—N. deafness, hardness of hearing, surdity; inaudibility.

V. be -deaf &c. *adj.*; have no ear; shut –, stop –, close- one's ears; turn a deaf ear to.

render deaf, stun, deafen.

Adj. deaf, earless, surd; hard –, dull- of hearing; deaf-mute, stunned, deafened; stone deaf; deaf as -a post, – an adder, – a beetle, – a trunk-maker.

inaudible &c. 405; out of hearing.

6. *Light*

(i.) LIGHT IN GENERAL

420. Light.—N. light, ray, beam, stream, gleam, streak, pencil; sun-, moon-beam; dawn, aurora.

day; sunshine; light of -day, – heaven; sun &c. (*luminary*) 432, day-, broad day-, noontide- light; noon-tide, -day; glare.

421. Darkness.—N. darkness &c. *adj.*; blackness &c. (*dark colour*) 431; obscurity, gloom, murk; dusk &c. (*dimness*) 422; tenebrosity, umbrageousness.

Cimmerian –, Stygian –, Egyptian-darkness; night; midnight; dead of –,

glow &c. *v.*; afterglow, sunset; glimmering &c. *v.*; glint; play –, flood- of light; phosphorescence, lambent flame.

flush, halo, glory, nimbus, aureole, *aureola*.

spark, *scintilla*; *facula*; sparkling &c. *v.*; emication, scintillation, flash, blaze, coruscation, fulguration; flame &c. (*fire*) 382; lightning, *ignis fatuus*, &c. (*luminary*) 423, radio-activity.

lustre, sheen, shimmer, reflection; gloss, tinsel, spangle, brightness, brilliancy, splendour; ef-, re-fulgence; ful-gor, -gidity; dazzlement, resplendence, transplendency; luminousness &c. *adj.*; luminosity; lucidity; renitency; radi-ance, -ation; irradiation, illumination, phosphorescence, luminescence.

radiation, radiant heat, infra-red rays, visible radiation, ultra-violet –, actinic- rays, actinism; X –, Roentgen-rays; phot-, heli-ography; optical instruments &c. 445.

[Science of light] optics; photo-logy, -metry; di-, cat-optrics.

[Distribution of light] *chiaroscuro*, *clair-obscur*, clear obscure, breadth, light and shade, black and white, tonality, half-tone, mezzotint.

reflection, refraction, dispersion, double refraction, polarization, diffraction, interference.

illuminant &c. 423.

V. shine, glow, glitter, phosphoresce; glis-ter, -ten; twinkle, gleam; flare, – up; glare, beam, shimmer, glimmer, flicker, sparkle, scintillate, coruscate, flash, fulgurate, blaze; be -bright &c. *adj.*; reflect light, daze, dazzle, bedazzle, radiate, shoot out beams.

clear up, brighten.

lighten, enlighten; light, – up; irradiate, shine upon; give –, hang out- a light; cast –, throw –, shed- -lustre, – light- upon; illum-e, -ine, -inate; relume, strike a light; kindle &c. (*set fire to*) 384.

Adj. shining &c. *v.*; lumin-ous, -iferous; luc-id, -ent, -ulent, -ific, -iferous; illuminating, light, -some; bright, vivid, splendent, nitid, lustrous, shiny, brilliant, beamy, scintillant, radiant, lambent; sheen, -y; glossy,

witching time of- night; blind man's holiday; darkness -visible, – that can be felt; palpable, obscure; Erebus.

shade, shadow, umbra, penumbra; sciagraphy; *silhouette*; radiograph, skiagraph.

obscuration; ad-, ob-umbration; obtenebration, offuscation, caligation; extinction; eclipse, total eclipse; gathering of the clouds.

shading; distribution of shade; *chiaroscuro* &c. (*light*) 420.

noctivagation, noctograph, noctuary. obscurantist.

V. be -dark &c. *adj.*

darken, obscure, shade; dim; tone down, lower; over-cast, -shadow; cloud, eclipse; ob-, of-fuscate; ob-, ad-umbrate, cast into the shade; be-cloud, -dim, -darken; cast –, throw –, spread- a -shade, – shadow, – gloom.

extinguish; put –, blow –, snuff- out; doubt.

Adj. dark, -some, -ling; obscure, tenebrous, tenebrious, sombrous, pitch dark, pitchy; caliginous; black &c. (*in colour*) 431.

sunless, lightless &c. (*see* sun, light, &c. 423); sombre, dusky; unilluminated &c. (*see* illuminate &c. 420); nocturnal; dingy, lurid, gloomy; murk-y, -some; shady, umbrageous; overcast &c. (*dim*) 422; cloudy &c. (*opaque*) 426; darkened &c. *n.*

dark as -pitch, – a pit, – Erebus.

benighted; noctivag-ant, -ous.

Adv. in the -dark, – shade; at night.

422. Dimness.—N. dimness &c. *adj.*; darkness &c. 421; paleness &c. (*light colour*) 429.

half-light, *demi-jour*; partial -shadow, – eclipse; shadow of a shade; glimmer, -ing; nebulosity; cloud &c. 353; eclipse.

aurora, dusk, twilight, gloaming, blind man's holiday, shades of evening, crepuscule, cockshut time; break of day, daybreak, dawn.

moon-light, -beam, -shine; star-, owl's-, candle-, rush-, fire-light; farthing candle.

V. be –, grow- -dim &c. *adj.*; flicker, twinkle, glimmer; loom, lower; fade; darken; pale, – its ineffectual fire.

burnished, glassy, sunny, orient, meridian; noon-day, -tide; cloudless, clear; un-clouded, -obscured.

garish; re-, tran-splendent; re-, effulgent; ful-gid, -gent; relucent, splendid, blazing, in a blaze, ablaze, rutilant, meteoric, phosphorescent; aglow.

bright as silver; light –, bright- as -day, – noonday, – the sun at noonday.

optical, actinic; photo-genic, -graphic; heliographic, radioactive.

423. [Source of light &c.] **Luminary.**
—**N.** luminary; light &c. 420; flame &c. (*fire*) 382.

spark, *scintilla*; phosphorescence.

sun, orb of day, day star, Phœbus, Apollo, Helios, Phaethon, Hyperion, Ra, Aurora; star, orb, meteor; falling –, shooting- star; blazing –, dog- star; Sirius, canicula, Aldebaran; morning star, Lucifer, Phosphor, evening star; Hesperus, Venus, planet, moon &c. 318; constellation, galaxy; northern light, *aurora -borealis*, – *australis*, zodiacal light; mock sun, parhelion.

lightning; fork –, sheet –, summer- lightning, St. Elmo's fire; phosphorus; *ignis fatuus*; Jack o' –, Friar's- lantern; Will o' the wisp, fire-drake, *Fata Morgana*.

glow-worm, fire-fly.

radium, luminous paint.

[Artificial light] gas; gas –, lime –, electric –, head –, search –, spot –, flash –, flood –, foot-light; lamp, oil –, gas –, arc –, incandescent- lamp; flare; lant-ern, -horn; dark lantern, bull's eye, projector; candle, *bougie*, tallow –, wax- candle; dip, farthing dip; taper, rush-light; oil &c. (*grease*) 356; wick, burner; Argand, moderator, duplex; torch, *flambeau*, link, brand; cresset; gase-, chande-, electro-lier; candelabrum, *girandole*, sconce, lustre, candle-stick.

firework, fizgig; pyrotechnics; Roman candle, Véry light, star shell, parachute light; rocket, lighthouse &c. (*signal*) 550.

V. illuminate &c. (*light*) 420.

Adj. self-luminous, incandescent; phosphor-ic, -escent; luminescent, fluorescent, radiant &c. (*light*) 420.

425. Transparency. — **N.** transparen-ce, -cy; translucen-ce, -cy; diaphaneity; luc-, pelluc-, limp-idity.

transparent medium, glass, crystal, mica; lymph, water.

V. be -transparent &c. *adj.*; transmit light.

Adj. transparent, pellucid, lucid, diaphanous; trans-, tra-lucent; limpid, clear, serene, crystalline, clear as crys-

render -dim &c. *adj.*; dim, bedim, obscure.

Adj. dim, dull, lack-lustre, dingy, darkish, shorn of its beams; dark 421.

faint, shadowed forth; glassy; bleary; cloudy; misty &c. (*opaque*) 426; muggy, fuliginous; nebul-ous, -ar; obnubilated, overcast, crepuscular, twilight, muddy, lurid, leaden, dun, dirty; looming &c. *v.*

pale &c. (*colourless*) 429; confused &c. (*invisible*) 447.

424. Shade.—**N.** shade; awning &c. (*cover*) 223; parasol, sunshade, umbrella; screen, curtain, shutter, blind, gauze, veil, mantle, mask; cloud, mist, gathering of clouds; smoke screen; smoked glasses, coloured spectacles; blinkers, blinders.

umbrage, glade; shadow &c. 421.

V. draw a curtain; put up –, close- a shutter; veil &c. *v.*; cast a shadow &c. (*darken*) 421; screen, obstruct the view.

Adj. shady, umbrageous, bowery.

426. Opacity.—**N.** opacity; opaqueness &c. *adj.*

film; cloud &c. 353.

V. be -opaque &c. *adj.*; obstruct the passage of light; ob-, of-fuscate.

Adj. opaque, impervious to light.

dim &c. 422; turbid, thick, muddy, opacous, obfuscated, fuliginous, cloudy, hazy, foggy, vaporous, nubiferous, muggy.

tal, vitreous, transpicuous, glassy, hyaline.

smoky, fumid, murky, dirty.

427. Semitransparency.—N. semi-transparency, opalescence, milkiness, pearliness; gauze, muslin; film; mist &c. (*cloud*) 353; frosted glass.

Adj. semi-transparent, -pellucid, -diaphanous, -opacous, -opaque; opal-escent, -ine; pearly, milky, frosted, mat; misty.

(ii.) SPECIFIC LIGHT

428. Colour.—N. colour, hue, tint, tinge, dye, complexion, shade, tincture, cast, livery, coloration, chromatism, glow, flush; tone, key.

pure –, positive –, primary –, primitive –, complementary- colour; three primaries; spectrum, chromatic dispersion; broken –, secondary –, tertiary-colour.

local colour, colouring, keeping, tone, value, aerial perspective.

[Science of colour] chromatics, spectrum analysis; prism, spectroscope.

pigment, colouring matter, paint, dye, wash, distemper, stain; medium; mordant; oil-paint &c. (*painting*) 556.

V. colour, dye, tinge, stain, tint, tinct, tone, paint, wash, ingrain, grain, illuminate, emblazon, imbue; paint &c. (*fine art*) 556; daub.

Adj. coloured &c. *v.*; colorific, tingent, tinctorial; chromatic, prismatic; full-, high-, deep-coloured; doubly-dyed; polychromatic.

bright, vivid, intense, deep; fresh, unfaded; rich, gorgeous; highly coloured; gay; variegated &c. 440.

gaudy, florid; garish; showy, flaunting, flashy; raw, crude; glaring, flaring; discordant, inharmonious.

mellow, harmonious, pearly, sweet, delicate, tender, refined.

429. [Absence of colour.] Achromatism.—N. achromatism; de-, discoloration; pall-or, -idity; paleness &c. *adj.*; etiolation; neutral tint, monochrome, black-and-white.

V. lose -colour &c. 428; fade, fly, go; become -colourless &c. *adj.*; turn pale, pale, whiten.

deprive of colour, decolorize, bleach, tarnish, achromatize, blanch, etiolate, wash out, tone down.

Adj. uncoloured &c. (*see* colour &c. 428); colourless, achromatic, hueless, pale, pallid; pale-, tallow-faced; faint, dull, cold, muddy, leaden, dun, wan, sallow, dead, dingy, ashy, ashen, ghastly, cadaverous, glassy, lack-lustre; discoloured &c. *v.*

light-coloured, fair, *blond*; white &c. 430.

pale as -death, – ashes, – a witch, – a ghost, – a corpse.

430. Whiteness.—N. whiteness &c. *adj.*; argent.

albification, albescence, albinism, etiolation.

snow, paper, chalk, milk, lily, ivory, silver, alabaster; white lead, chinese –, flake –, ivory –, zinc- white, white-wash, -ning, whiting.

V. be -white &c. *adj.*

render -white &c. *adj.*; whiten-bleach, blanch, etiolate, whitewash, silver, frost.

Adj. white; milky, milk-, snow-white; snowy, niveous, candid, chalky; hoar,

431. Blackness.—N. blackness &c. *adj.*; darkness &c. (*want of light*) 421; swarthness, lividity, dark colour, tone, colour; *chiaroscuro* &c. 420.

nigrification, infuscation, denigration.

jet, ink, ebony, coal, pitch, soot, smudge, charcoal, sloe, raven, crow; negro, blackamoor, man of colour, nigger, darky, Ethiopian, black.

[Pigments] lamp –, ivory –, blue-black; writing –, printing –, printer's –, Indian- ink.

V. be -black &c. *adj.*

-y; frosted, silvery; argent, -ine; canescent.

whitish, creamy, pearly, ivory, fair, *blond*, ash-blond, platinum blond; blanched &c. *v.*; high in tone, light.

white as -a sheet, – driven snow, – a lily, – silver; like -ivory &c. *n.*

black as -jet &c. *n.*, – my hat, – a shoe, – a tinker's pot, – November, – thunder, – midnight; nocturnal &c. (*dark*) 421; nigrescent; gray &c. 432; obscure &c. 421.

Adv. in mourning.

432. Gray.—N. gray &c. *adj.*; neutral tint, silver, pepper and salt, *chiaroscuro, grisaille*, grayness.

[Pigments] Payne's gray; black &c. 431.

Adj. gray, grey; steel –, iron- gray, dun, drab, dingy, leaden, livid, sombre, sad, pearly; silver, -y, -ed; ash-en, -y; ciner-eous, -itious; grizzl-y, -ed; dove-, slate-, stone-, mouse-, ash-coloured; mole; cool.

render -black &c. *adj.*; blacken, infuscate, denigrate; blot, -ch; smutch; smirch; darken &c. 421.

Adj. black, sable, swarthy, sombre, dark, inky, ebon, atramentous, jetty; coal-, jet-black; fuliginous, pitchy, sooty, swart, dusky, dingy, murky, Ethiopic; low-toned, low in tone; of the deepest dye.

433. Brown.—N. brown &c. *adj.*

[Pigments] bistre, ochre, sepia, Vandyke brown.

Adj. brown, adust, bay, dapple, auburn, chestnut, nutbrown, cinnamon, hazel, fawn, puce, *écru*, russet, tawny, fuscous, chocolate, maroon, foxy, tan, brunette, whitey-brown; snuff-, liver-coloured; brown as -a berry, – mahogany; reddish brown; copper-, rust- coloured; henna, bronze, khaki; russet, roan, sorrel.

sun-burnt; tanned &c. *v.*

V. render -brown &c. *adj.*; tan, embrown, bronze.

Primitive Colours*

434. Redness.—N. red, scarlet, vermilion, cardinal, Post Office, red, carmine, crimson, pink, lake, *cerise*, cherry red, maroon, carnation, *couleur de rose, rose du Barry*; magenta, damask; flesh -colour; – tint; colour; fresh –, high-colour; warmth; gules.

ruby, garnet, carbuncle; rose; rust, iron-mould.

[Dyes and pigments] cinnabar, cochineal; fuchsine; ruddle, madder, red-lead; Indian –, light –, Venetian- red; red ink, annotto.

redness &c. *adj.*; rub-escence, -icundity, -ification; erubescence, blush.

V. be –, become- -red &c. *adj.*; blush, flush, colour up, mantle, redden.

render -red &c. *adj.*; redden, rouge; rub-ify, -ricate; incarnadine; ruddle.

Adj. red &c. *n.*, -dish; rufous, ruddy, florid, incarnadine, sanguine, bloody, gory; ros-y, -eate; blowz-y, -ed; brunt; rubi-cund, -form;

Complementary Colours

435. Greenness.—N. green &c. *adj.*; blue and yellow; vert.

emerald, verd antique, verdigris, malachite, beryl, aquamarine, reseda.

[Pigments] *terre verte*, verditer, bice, chlorophyl.

greenness, verdure, verdancy; virid-ity, -escence.

Adj. green, verdant; glaucous, olive; porraceous; green as grass.

emerald –, pea –, grass –, apple –, sea –, olive –, bottle –, leaf- green.

greenish; vir-ent, -escent.

* The author's classification of colours has been retained, though it does not entirely accord with the theories of modern science: Complete lists of shades or pigments are beyond the scope of this work.

lurid, stammel, blood-red; russet, murrey, carroty, sorrel, lateritious.

rose-, ruby-, cherry-, claret-, wine-, plum-, flame-, flesh-, peach-, salmon-, brick-, brickdust-coloured, reddish brown &c. 433.

blushing &c. *v.*; erubescent; reddened &c. *v.*

red as -fire, – blood, – scarlet, – a turkeycock, – a lobster; warm, hot; foxy.

436. Yellowness.—N. yellow &c. *adj.*; or.

[Pigments] gamboge; cadmium –, chrome –, Indian –, lemon- yellow; orpiment, yellow ochre, Claude tint, aureolin.

crocus, saffron, topaz, gold.

jaundice; London fog; yellowness &c. *adj.*

Adj. yellow, aureate, gold, golden, gilt, gilded, flavous, citrine, fallow; fulv-ous, -id; sallow, luteous, fawny, creamy, sandy; xanth-ic, -ous; jaundiced.

gold-, citron-, saffron-, lemon-, sulphur-, amber-, straw-, primrose-, cream-coloured; flaxen, yellowish, buff.

yellow as a -quince, – guinea, – crow's foot.

437. Purple.—N. purple &c. *adj.*; blue and red, bishop's purple; aniline dyes, gridelin, amethyst; purpure.

livid-ness, -ity.

V. empurple.

Adj. purple, violet, plum-coloured, lavender, lilac, puce, *mauve*; livid.

---

438. Blueness.—N. blue &c. *adj.*; garter-blue; watchet.

[Pigments] ultramarine, smalt, cobalt, cyanogen; Prussian –, syenite-blue; bice, indigo, woad.

lapis lazuli, sapphire, turquoise.

blue-, bluish-ness; bloom.

Adj. blue, azure, cerulean; sky-blue, -coloured, -dyed; navy-blue, aquamarine, electric blue, royal blue, cyanic; bluish; atmospheric, retiring; cold.

439. Orange.—N. orange, red and yellow; gold; or; flame &c. colour, *adj.*

[Pigments] ochre, Mars orange, cadmium.

V. gild, warm.

Adj. orange; ochreous; orange-, gold-, flame-, copper-, brass-, apricot-coloured; warm, hot, glowing.

---

440. Variegation.—N. variegation; di-, tri-chroism; iridescence, irisation, play of colours, polychrome, maculation, spottiness, striæ.

spectrum, rainbow, iris, tulip, peacock, chameleon, butterfly, tortoise-shell; mackerel, – sky; zebra, leopard, mother-of-pearl, nacre, opal, marble, batik.

check, plaid, tartan, patchwork; mar-, par-quetry; mosaic, *tesseræ*, tesselation, chess-board, checkers, chequers; harlequin; Joseph's coat; tricolour; patches, bands, stripes, spots &c. of colour.

V. be -variegated &c. *adj.*; variegate, stripe, streak, checker, chequer; be-, speckle, fleck; be-, sprinkle; stipple, maculate, dot, bespot; tattoo, inlay, tesselate, damascene; embroider, braid, quilt.

Adj. variegated &c. *v.*; many-coloured, -hued; divers-, parti-coloured; di-, poly-chromatic; bi-, tri-, versi-colour; of all -the colours of the rainbow, – manner of colours; kaleidoscopic.

iridescent; opal-ine, -escent; prismatic, nacreous, pearly, shot, *gorge de pigeon, chatoyant*, irisated.

pied, piebald, skewbald; motley; mottled, marbled; pepper and salt, paned, dappled, clouded, cymophanous.

mosaic, tesselated, chequered, plaid; tortoiseshell &c. *n.*

spott-ed, -y; punctated, powdered; speckled &c. *v.*; freckled, flea-bitten, studded; fleck-ed, -ered; striated, barred, veined; brind-ed, -led; tabby; watered; grizzled; listed; embroidered &c. *v.*; dædal.

(iii.) PERCEPTIONS OF LIGHT

441. Vision.—N. vision, sight, optics, eye-sight.

view, look, espial, glance, ken, *coup d'œil*; glimpse, peep, glint; gaze, stare, leer; perlustration, contemplation; conspect-ion, -uity; regard, survey; in-, intro-spection; *reconnaissance*, speculation, watch, espionage, *espionnage*, autopsy; ocular -inspection, – demonstration; sight-seeing.

macrography, micrography.

point of view; view-, stand-point; gazebo, loop-hole, *belvedere*, watch-tower.

field of view; theatre, amphitheatre, arena, vista, horizon; commanding –, bird's eye –, panoramic- view; periscope.

visual organ, organ of vision; eye; naked –, unassisted- eye; eye-ball, retina, pupil, iris, cornea, white; optics, orbs; saucer –, goggle –, gooseberry-eyes.

short sight &c. 443; clear –, sharp –, quick –, eagle –, piercing –, penetrating--sight, – glance, – eye; perspicacity, discernment; catopsis.

eagle, hawk; cat, lynx; Argus.

evil eye; basilisk, cockatrice.

spectacles, telescope &c. 445.

V. see, behold, discern, perceive, have in sight, descry, sight, make out, discover, distinguish, recognize, spy, espy, ken; get –, have –, catch- a -sight, – glimpse- of; command a view of; witness, contemplate, speculate; cast –, set- the eyes on; be a -spectator &c. 444- of; look on &c. (*be present*) 186; see sights &c. (*curiosity*) 455; see at a glance &c. (*intelligence*) 498.

look, view, eye; lift up the eyes, open one's eye; look -at, – on, – upon, – over, – about one, – round; survey, scan, inspect; run the eye -over, – through; reconnoitre, glance -round, – on, – over; turn –, bend- one's looks upon; direct the eyes to, turn the eyes on, cast a glance, make eyes at.

observe &c. (*attend to*) 457; watch &c. (*care*) 459; see with one's own eyes; watch for &c. (*expect*) 507; peek, peep, peer, pry, take a peep; play at bo-peep.

look -full in the face, – hard at, – intently; strain one's eyes; fix –, rivet- the eyes upon; stare, gaze; pore over, gloat -over, – on; leer, ogle, glare; goggle; cock the eye, squint, gloat, look askance; give the glad eye.

Adj. seeing &c. *v.*; visual, ocular, -al; ophthalmic.

far-, clear-sighted &c. *n.*; eagle-, hawk-, lynx-, keen-, Argus-eyed.

visible &c. 446.

442. Blindness.—N. blindness, anopsia, cecity, excecation, *amaurosis*, cataract, ablepsy, prestriction; dim-sightedness &c. 443.

V. be -blind &c. *adj.*; not see; lose sight of; have the eyes bandaged; grope in the dark.

not look; close –, shut –, turn away –, avert- the eyes; look another way; wink &c. (*limited vision*) 443; shut the eyes –, be blind- to; wink –, blink- at.

render -blind &c. *adj.*; blind, -fold; hoodwink, dazzle; put one's eyes out; throw dust into one's eyes; *jeter de la poudre aux yeux*; screen from sight &c. (*hide*) 528.

Adj. blind; eye-, sight-, vision-less; dark; stone-, sand-, stark-blind; undiscerning; dim-sighted &c. 443.

blind as -a bat, – a buzzard, – a beetle, – a mole, – an owl; wall-eyed.

blinded &c. *v.*

Adv. blind-ly, -fold; darkly.

Adv. visibly &c. 446; in sight of, with one's eyes open.

at -sight, − first sight, − a glance, − the first blush; *primâ facie*.

Int. look! &c. (*attention*) 457.

Phr. the scales falling from one's eyes.

443. [Imperfect vision.] **Dim-sightedness.** [Fallacies of vision.]—**N.** dim −, dull −, half −, short −, near −, long −, double −, astigmatic −, failing- sight; dim &c. -sightedness; snow blindness; purblindness, lippitude; my-, presby-opia; confusion of vision; astigmatism, nystagmus; colour-blindness, dichromism, chromato-pseudo-blepsis, Daltonism; nyctalopy; *strabismus*, strabism, squint, cast in the eye, swivel eye, goggle eyes; obliquity of vision.

winking &c. *v.*; nictitation; blinkard, albino.

dizziness, swimming, scotomy; cataract; ophthalmia.

[Limitation of vision] eye shade, blinker, blinder; screen &c. (*hider*) 530.

[Fallacies of vision] *deceptio visûs*; refraction, distortion, illusion, false light, *anamorphosis*, virtual image, *spectrum, mirage*, looming, phasma; phant-asm, -asma, -om; vision; spectre, apparition, ghost; *ignis fatuus* &c. (*luminary*) 423; spectre of the Brocken; magic mirror; magic lantern &c. (*show*) 448; mirror, lens &c. (*instrument*) 445.

V. be -dim-sighted &c. *n.*; see double; have a -mote in the eye, − mist before the eyes, − film over the eyes; see through a -prism, − glass darkly; wink, blink, nictitate; squint; look ask-ant, -ance; screw up the eyes, glare, glower.

dazzle, glare, blur, swim, loom.

Adj. dim-sighted &c. *n.*; my-, presby-opic; astigmatic; moon-, mope-, blear-, goggle-, gooseberry-, one-eyed; blind of one eye, monoculous; half-, pur-, colour-blind; dichromatic.

blind as a bat &c. (*blind*) 442; winking &c. *v.*

444. Spectator.—**N.** spectator, beholder, observer, inspector, viewer, looker-on, onlooker, witness, eye-witness, bystander, passer by; sight-seer.

spy, scout; sentinel &c. (*warning*) 668.

V. witness, behold &c. (*see*) 441; look on &c. (*be present*) 186.

445. Optical Instruments.—**N.** optical instruments; lens, meniscus, magnifier, reading −, burning- glass; micro-, mega-, teino-scope; spectacles, glasses, barnacles, goggles, giglamps, eyeglass, *pince-nez*, monocle; periscopic lens; telescope, glass, lorgnette, binocular; spy-, opera-, field-glass, periscope, range finder.

mirror, reflector, speculum; looking-, pier-, cheval-, hand-glass.

prism; camera, *camera-lucida*, *-obscura*; projector, stereopticon, magic lantern &c. (*show*) 448; chro-, thau-matrope; stereo-, pseudo-, poly-, kaleido-scope.

photo-, opto-, erio-, actino-, luci-, radio-, spectro-meter; polari-, polemo-, spectro-scope, diffraction grating.

optics, optician, optometry, optometrist; microscop-y, -ist; photometry, photography; photographer.

446. Visibility.—**N.** visibility, perceptibility; conspicuousness, distinctness &c. *adj.*; conspicuity; appearance &c. 448; exposure; manifestation &c. 525; ocular -proof, − evidence, − demonstration; field of view &c. (*vision*) 441.

447. Invisibility.—**N.** invisibility, non-appearance, imperceptibility; indistinctness &c. *adj.*; mystery, delitescence.

concealment &c. 528; latency &c. 526.

V. be –, become- -visible &c. *adj.*; appear, emerge, open to the view; meet –, catch- the eye; present –, show –, manifest –, produce –, discover –, reveal –, expose –, betray-itself; stand -forth, – out; show; arise; peep –, peer –, crop- out; start –, spring –, show –, turn –, crop- up; glimmer, glitter, glow, loom; glare; burst forth, scintillate; burst upon the -view, – sight; heave in sight; come -in sight, – into view, – out, – forth, – forward; see the light of day; break through the clouds; make its appear-ance, show its face, materialize, appear to one's eyes, come upon the stage, enter; float before the eyes, speak for itself &c. (*manifest*) 525; attract the attention &c. 457; reappear; live in a glass house.

expose to view &c. 525.

Adj. visible, perceptible, perceivable, discernible, apparent; in -view, – full view, – sight; exposed to view, *en évidence*; unclouded.

obvious &c. (*manifest*) 525; plain, clear, distinct, definite; well-defined, -marked; in focus; recognizable, palpable, autoptical; glaring, staring, conspicuous; stereoscopic; in -bold, – strong, – high- relief.

periscopic, panoramic.

before –, under- one's eyes; before one, *à vue d'œil*, in one's eye, *oculis subjecta fidelibus*.

Adv. visibly &c. *adj.*; in sight of; before one's eyes &c. *adj.*; *veluti in speculum*.

V. be -invisible &c. *adj.*; be hidden &c. (*hide*) 528; lurk &c. (*lie hidden*) 526; escape notice.

render -invisible &c. *adj.*; conceal &c. 528; put out of sight.

not see &c. (*be blind*) 442; lose sight of.

Adj. invisible, imperceptible; un-, in-discernible; un-, non-apparent; out of –, not in- sight; *à perte de vue*; be-hind the -scenes, – curtain; view-, sight-less; in-, un-conspicuous; unseen &c. (*see* see &c. 441); covert &c. (*latent*) 526; eclipsed, under an eclipse.

dim &c. (*faint*) 422; mysterious, dark, obscure, confused; indistin-ct, -guishable; shadowy, indefinite, unde-fined; ill-defined, -marked; blurred, fuzzy, out of focus; misty &c. (*opaque*) 426; veiled &c. (*concealed*) 528; de-litescent.

---

448. Appearance.—N. appearance, phenomenon, sight, spectacle, show, premonstration, scene, species, view, *coup d'œil*; look-out, out-look, prospect, vista, perspective, bird's-eye view, scenery, landscape, picture, *tableau*; display, exposure, *mise en scène*; scenery, *décor*; rising of the curtain.

phant-asm, -om &c. (*fallacy of vision*) 443.

pageant, *spectacle*; peep-, raree-, gal-lanty-show; *ombres chinoises*; projector, optical –, magic- lantern, phantasma-goria, dissolving views; cinema, -tograph; bio-scope, -graph; moving pictures, movies, film, screen &c.; pan-, di-, cosm-, ge-orama; *coup –, jeu- de théâtre*; pageantry &c. (*ostentation*) 882; insignia &c. (*indication*) 550.

aspect, phase, *phasis*, seeming; shape &c. (*form*) 240; guise, look,

449. Disappearance.—N. disappear-ance, evanescence, eclipse, occultation.

departure &c. 293; exit, vanishing point; dissolving views.

V. disappear, vanish, dissolve, fade, melt away, pass, go, avaunt; be -gone &c. *adj.*; leave -no trace, – 'not a rack behind'; go off the stage &c. (*depart*) 293; suffer –, undergo- an eclipse; be lost to –, retire from- -sight, – view.

lose sight of.

efface &c. 552.

Adj. disappearing &c. *v.*; evanescent; missing, lost; lost to -sight, – view; gone; *spurlos versenkt*.

Int. vanish! disappear! avaunt! &c. (*ejection*) 297.

---

complexion, colour, image, mien, air, cast, carriage, port, demeanour; presence, expression, first blush, face of the thing; point of view, light.

lineament, feature, trait, lines; out-line, -side; contour, *silhouette*, face, countenance, physiognomy, visage, phiz, mug, cast of countenance, profile, *tournure*, cut of one's jib, metoposcopy; outside &c. 220.

V. appear; be –, become- visible &c. 446; seem, look, show; present –, wear –, carry –, have –, bear –, exhibit –, take –, take on –, assume- the -appearance, – semblance- of; look like; cut a figure, figure; present to the view; show &c. (*make manifest*) 525.

Adj. apparent, seeming, ostensible; on view.

Adv. apparently; to all -seeming, – appearance; ostensibly, seemingly, as it seems, on the face of it, *primâ facie*; at the first blush, at first sight; in the eyes of; to the eye.

CLASS IV

Words relating to the INTELLECTUAL FACULTIES

CLASS IV

WORDS RELATING TO THE INTELLECTUAL FACULTIES

DIVISION (I.) FORMATION OF IDEAS

Section I. OPERATIONS OF INTELLECT IN GENERAL

450. Intellect.—N. intellect, mind, understanding, reason, thinking principle; rationality; cogitative –, cognitive –, intellectual- faculties; faculties, senses, consciousness, observation, percipience, apperception, mentality, intelligence, intellection, intuition, association of ideas, instinct, flair, conception, judgment, wits, parts, capacity, intellectuality, reasoning power, brains, genius; wit &c. 498; ability &c. (*skill*) 698; wisdom &c. 498.

soul, spirit, ghost, inner man, heart, breast, bosom, *penetralia mentis, divina particula auræ,* heart's core; ego, psyche, pneuma, subconsciousness, subconscious, subliminal self; dual personality.

organ –, seat- of thought; *sensorium,* sensory, brain, gray matter; head, -piece; pate, noddle, skull, scull, *pericranium, cerebrum, cranium,* brain-pan, -box; sconce, upper story.

[Science of mind] metaphysics; psychics, psycho-logy, -metry, -genesis, -analysis, -physics, psychi-atry, -cal research, thought reading &c. 992; ideology; mental –, moral- philosophy; philosophy of the mind; pneumat-, phren-ology; no –, cranio-logy, -scopy.

ideal-ity, -ism; transcendental-, spiritual-ism; immateriality &c. 317.

metaphysician, psychologist &c.

V. note, notice, mark; take -notice, – cognizance- of; be -aware, – conscious- of; realize; appreciate; ruminate &c. (*think*) 451; fancy &c. (*imagine*) 515; conceive, reason, understand.

Adj. [Relating to intellect] intellectual, mental, rational, subjective, metaphysical, nooscopic, spiritual; ghostly; psych-ical, -ological; cerebral.

immaterial &c. 317; endowed with reason.

Adv. *in petto.*

450a. Absence or want of Intellect.—N. absence –, want- of -intellect &c. 450; imbecility &c. 499; brutality; brute -instinct, – force.

Adj. unendowed with reason.

---

451. Thought.—N. thought; exercitation –, exercise- of the intellect; reflection, cogitation, consideration, meditation, study, lucubration, speculation, deliberation, pondering; head-,

452. [Absence or want of thought.] Incogitancy.—N. incogitancy, vacancy, inunderstanding; inanity, fatuity &c. 499; thoughtlessness &c. (*inattention*) 458.

brain-work; cerebration; mentation, deep reflection; close study, application &c. (*attention*) 457.

abstract thought, abstraction, contemplation, musing; brown study &c. (*inattention*) 458; reverie, Platonism; depth of thought, workings of the mind, thoughts, inmost thoughts; self-counsel, -communing, -consultation.

association –, succession –, flow –, train –, current- of -thought, – ideas.

after –, mature- thought; reconsideration, second thoughts; retrospection &c. (*memory*) 505; excogitation; examination &c. (*inquiry*) 461; invention &c. (*imagination*) 515.

thoughtfulness &c. *adj.*

V. think, reflect, reason, cogitate, excogitate, consider, deliberate; bestow -thought, – consideration- upon; speculate, contemplate, meditate, ponder, muse, dream, ruminate; brood –, con- over; animadvert, study; bend –, apply- the mind &c. (*attend*) 457; digest, discuss, hammer at, weigh, perpend; realize, appreciate; fancy &c. (*imagine*) 515; trow.

take into consideration; take counsel &c. (*be advised*) 695; commune with –, bethink- oneself; collect one's thoughts; revolve –, turn over –, run over- in the mind; chew the cud –, sleep- upon; take counsel of –, advise with- one's pillow.

rack –, ransack –, crack –, beat –, cudgel- one's brains; set one's -brain, – wits- to work.

harbour –, entertain –, cherish –, nurture- an -idea &c. 453; take into one's head; bear in mind; reconsider.

occur; present –, suggest- itself; come –, get- into one's head; strike one, flit across the view, come uppermost, run in one's head; enter –, pass in –, cross –, flash on –, flash across –, float in –, fasten itself on –, be uppermost in –, occupy- the mind; have in one's mind.

make an impression; sink –, penetrate- into the mind; engross the thoughts.

Adj. thinking &c. *v.*; thoughtful, pensive, meditative, reflective, cogitative, museful, wistful, contemplative, speculative, deliberative, studious, sedate, introspective, Platonic, philosophical.

lost –, engrossed –, rapt –, absorbed- in thought &c. (*inattentive*) 458; deep musing &c. (*intent*) 457.

in the mind, under consideration, in contemplation.

Adv. all things considered; taking everything into account.

Phr. the mind being on the stretch; the -mind, – head- -turning, – running- upon.

V. not -think &c. 451; not think of; dismiss from the -mind, – thoughts &c. 451.

indulge in reverie &c. (*be inattentive*) 458.

put away thought; unbend –, relax –, divert- the mind.

Adj. vacant, unintellectual, unideal, unoccupied, unthinking, inconsiderate, thoughtless; absent &c. (*inattentive*) 458; diverted; irrational &c. 499; narrow-minded &c. 481.

un-thought of, -dreamt of, -considered; off one's mind; incogitable, not to be thought of, inconceivable.

---

453. [Object of thought.] **Idea.—N.** idea, notion, conception, thought, apprehension, impression, perception, image, sentiment, reflection, observation, consideration; abstract idea, principle; archetype.

view &c. (*opinion*) 484; theory &c.

454. [Subject of thought.] **Topic.—N.** subject of –, material for- thought; food for the mind, mental *pabulum*.

subject, -matter; matter, theme, topic, what it is about, *thesis*, text, business, affair, matter in hand, argument; motion, resolution; head, chap-

514; conceit, fancy; phantasy &c. (*imagination*) 515.

point of view &c. (*aspect*) 448; field of view.

___

ter; case, point; proposition, theorem; field of inquiry; moot point, problem, &c. (*question*) 461.

V. float –, pass- in the mind &c. 451.

Adj. thought of; uppermost in the mind; *in petto.*

Adv. under -discussion, – consideration, – advisement; in -question, – the mind; on -foot, – the carpet, – the *tapis*; before the house, relative to &c. 9.

___

Section II. Precursory Conditions and Operations

455. [The desire of knowledge.] **Curiosity.** — **N.** interest, thirst for knowledge; curi-osity, -ousness; inquiring mind; inquisitiveness.

sight-seer, quidnunc, newsmonger, Paul Pry, peeping Tom, eavesdropper; gossip &c. (*news*) 532; questioner, *enfant terrible.*

V. be -curious &c. *adj.*; take an interest in, stare, gape; prick up the ears, see sights, lionize; pry, speer; dig up.

Adj. curious, inquisitive, burning with curiosity, overcurious, nosey; inquiring &c. 461; prying; inquisitorial; agape &c. (*expectant*) 507; attentive &c. 457.

Phr. what's the matter? what next?

456. [Absence of curiosity.] **Incuriosity.**—**N.** incuriosity; incuriousness &c. *adj.*; *insouciance* &c. 866; indifference, apathy.

V. be -incurious &c. *adj.*; have no -curiosity &c. 455; take no interest in &c. 823; mind one's own business.

Adj. incurious, uninquisitive, uninterested, indifferent, bored; impassive &c. 823.

___

457. Attention.—**N.** attention; mindfulness &c. *adj.*; intent-ness, -iveness; thought &c. 451; adverten-ce, -cy; observ-ance, -ation; consideration, reflection, perpension; heed; particularity; notice, regard &c. *v.*; circumspection &c. (*care*) 459; study, scrutiny, once-over; in-, intro-spection; revision, -al.

active –, diligent –, exclusive –, minute –, close –, intense –, deep –, profound –, abstract –, laboured –, deliberate- -thought, – attention, – application, – study.

minuteness, attention to detail &c. 459.

absorption of mind &c. (*abstraction*) 458.

indication, calling attention to &c. *v.*

V. be -attentive &c. *adj.*; attend, advert to, observe, look, see, view, remark, notice, regard, take notice, mark; give –, pay- -attention, – heed- to; listen in, incline –, lend- an ear to; trouble one's head about; give a

458. Inattention.—**N.** in-attention, -consideration; inconsiderateness &c. *adj.*; oversight; inadverten-ce, -cy; non-observance, disregard.

supineness &c. (*inactivity*) 683; *étourderie*; want of thought; heedlessness &c. (*neglect*) 460; *insouciance* &c. (*indifference*) 866.

abstraction; absence –, absorption- of mind; preoccupation, distraction, reverie, brown study, deep musing, fit of abstraction, woolgathering.

V. be -inattentive &c. *adj.*; overlook, disregard; pass by &c. (*neglect*) 460; not -observe &c. 457; think little of.

close –, shut- one's eyes to; wink at; pay no attention to; dismiss –, discard –, discharge- from one's -thoughts, – mind; drop the subject, think no more of; set –, turn –, put- aside; turn -away from, – one's attention from, – a deaf ear to; – one's back upon.

abstract oneself, dream, indulge in reverie.

escape -notice, – attention; come in

thought –, animadvert- to; occupy oneself with; contemplate &c. (*think of*) 451; look -at, – to, – after, – into, – over; see to; turn –, bend –, apply –, direct –, give- the -mind, – eye, – attention- to; have -an eye to, – in one's eye; bear in mind; take into -account, – consideration; keep in -sight, – view; have regard to, heed, mind, take cognizance of, be engaged in, entertain, recognize; make –, take- note of; note.

examine cursorily; glance -at, – upon, – over; cast –, pass- the eyes over; run over, turn over the leaves, dip into, perstringe; skim &c. (*neglect*) 460; take a cursory view of.

examine, – closely, – intently; scan, scrutinize, consider; give –, bend- one's mind to; overhaul, revise, pore over; inspect, review, pass under review; take stock of; fix –, rivet –, focus –, devote- the -eye, – mind, – thoughts, – attention- on *or* to; hear –, think- out; mind one's business.

revert –, hark back- to; watch &c. (*expect*) 507, (*take care of*) 459; hearken –, listen- to; prick up the ears; have –, keep- the eyes open; come to the point.

meet with attention; fall under one's -notice, – observation; be -under consideration &c. (*topic*) 454.

catch –, strike- the eye; attract notice; catch –, awaken –, wake –, invite –, solicit –, attract –, claim –, excite –, engage –, occupy –, strike –, arrest –, fix –, engross –, absorb –, rivet- the- attention, – mind, – thoughts; be -present to, – uppermost in- the mind.

bring under one's notice; point -out, – to, – at, – the finger at; lay the finger on, indigitate, indicate; direct –, call- attention to; show; put a -mark &c. (*sign*) 550- upon; call soldiers to 'attention'; bring forward &c. (*make manifest*) 525.

Adj. attentive, mindful, heedful, observant, regardful; alive –, awake- to, alert; observing &c. *v.*; taken up –, occupied- with; engaged –, engrossed –, interested –, wrapped- in; absorbed, rapt; breathless; pre-occupied &c. (*inattentive*) 458; watchful &c. (*careful*) 459; intent on, open-eyed, breathless, undistracted, upon the stretch; on the watch &c. (*expectant*) 507 steadfast.

Int. see! look, – here, – out, – alive, – you, – to it! mark! lo!

at one ear and go out at the other; forget &c. (*have no remembrance*) 506.

call off –, draw off –, call away –, divert –, distract- the -attention, – thoughts, – mind; put out of one's head; dis-concert, -compose; put out, confuse, perplex, bewilder, moider, fluster, muddle, dazzle; throw a sop to Cerberus.

Adj. inattentive; un-observant, -mindful, -heeding, -discerning; inadvertent; mind-, regard-, respect-less; listless &c. (*indifferent*) 866; blind, deaf; flighty, hand over head; cur-, percur-sory; giddy-, scatter-, hare-brained; unreflecting, écervelé, inconsiderate, off-hand, thoughtless, dizzy, muzzy, brainsick; giddy, – as a goose; wild, harum-scarum, rantipole, high-flying; heed-, care-less &c. (*neglectful*) 460.

absent, absent-minded, abstracted, *distrait*; lost; lost –, wrapped- in thought, woolgathering; rapt, in the clouds, bemused; dreaming –, musing- on other things; pre-occupied; en-grossed &c. (*attentive*) 457; in a -reverie &c. *n.*; off one's guard &c. (*inexpectant*) 508; napping; dreamy.

disconcerted, put out &c. *v.*; rattled.

Adv. inattentively, inadvertently &c. *adj.*; *per incuriam, sub silentio.*

Int. stand -at ease, – easy!

Phr. the attention wanders; one's wits gone a -woolgathering, – bird's nesting; it never entered into one's head; the mind running on other things; one's thoughts being elsewhere; had it been a bear it would have bitten you.

――――――

behold! soho! hark, – ye! mind! halloo! observe! lo and behold!
attention! *nota bene*; N.B.; *, †; I'd have you to know; notice!
take notice! O yes! *Oyez!*

Phr. this is –, these are- to give notice.

459. Care. [Vigilance.]—**N.** care,
solicitude, heed; heedfulness &c. *adj.*;
scruple &c. (*conscientiousness*) 939.

watchfulness &c. *adj.*; vigilance,
surveillance, eyes of Argus, watch, vigil,
look out, watch and ward, *l'œil du
maître.*

alertness &c. (*activity*) 682; attention &c. 457; prudence &c., circumspection &c. (*caution*) 864; forethought
&c. 510; precaution &c. (*preparation*)
673; tidiness &c. (*order*) 58, (*cleanli-
ness*) 652; accuracy &c. (*exactness*) 494;
minuteness, attention to detail; meticu-
lousness, nicety, circumstantiality.

V. be -careful &c. *adj.*; reck; take
care &c. (*be cautious*) 864; pay attention to &c. 457; take care of; look –,
see- -to, – after; keep -an eye, – a
sharp eye- upon; keep -watch, – watch
and ward; mount guard, set watch,
watch; keep in -sight, – view; chaperon,
play gooseberry; mind, – one's business.

look -sharp, – about one; look with
one's own eyes; keep a -good, – sharp-
look-out; have all one's -wits, – eyes-
about one; watch for &c. (*expect*) 507;
stand to; keep one's eyes –, have the
eyes –, sleep with one eye- open.

take precautions &c. 673; protect
&c. (*render safe*) 664.

do one's best &c. 682; mind one's
Ps and Qs, speak by the card, pick
one's steps.

Adj. care-, regard-, heed-ful; taking
care &c. *v.*; particular; prudent &c.
(*cautious*) 864; considerate; thoughtful &c. (*deliberative*) 451; provident
&c. (*prepared*) 673; alert &c. (*active*)
682; sure-footed.

guarded, on one's guard; on the
-*qui vive*, – alert, – watch, – look-out;
awake, broad awake, vigilant; watch-,
wake-, wist-ful; Argus-, lynx- eyed;
wide awake &c. (*intelligent*) 498;
on the watch for &c. (*expectant*)
507.

tidy &c. (*orderly*) 58, (*clean*) 652;
accurate &c. (*exact*) 494; scrupulous

460. Neglect.—**N.** neglect; carelessness &c. *adj.*; trifling &c. *v.*; negligence;
omission, laches, default; remissness,
slackness, procrastination; supineness
&c. (*inactivity*) 683; inattention &c.
458; *nonchalance* &c. (*insensibility*) 822;
imprudence, recklessness &c. 863;
slovenliness &c. (*disorder*) 59, (*dirt*)
653; improvidence &c. 674; non-completion &c. 730; inexactness &c. (*error*)
495.

paraleipsis [in rhetoric].

trifler, slacker, waster, waiter on
Providence; Micawber.

V. be -negligent &c. *adj.*; take no
care of &c. (take care of &c. 459);
neglect; let -slip, – go; lay –, set –,
cast –, put- aside; keep –, leave- out of
sight; lose sight of.

overlook, disregard; pass -over, – by;
let pass; blink; wink –, connive- at;
gloss over; take no -note, – notice, –
thought, – account- of; pay no regard
to; *laisser aller*; allow to lie on the
table.

scamp; trifle, fribble; do by halves;
skimp; cut; slight &c. (*despise*) 930;
play –, trifle- with; slur; skim, – the
surface; *effleurer*; take a cursory view
of &c. 457.

slur –, slip –, skip –, jump- over;
pretermit, miss, skip, jump, omit, give
the go-by to, push aside, throw into
the background, shelve, sink; ignore,
shut one's eyes to, refuse to hear, turn
a deaf ear to; leave out of one's calculation; not -attend to &c. 457, – mind;
not trouble -oneself, – one's head-
-with, –about; forget &c. 506; be caught
napping &c. (*not expect*) 508; leave a
loose thread; let the grass grow under
one's feet.

render -neglectful &c. *adj.*; put –,
throw- off one's guard.

Adj. neglecting &c. *v.*; unmindful,
negligent, neglectful; heedless, careless,
thoughtless; perfunctory, remiss,
slack.

inconsiderate; un-, in-circumspect;

&c. (*conscientious*) 939; *cavendo tutus* &c. (*safe*) 664.

Adv. carefully &c. *adj.*; with care, gingerly.

Phr. *quis custodiet ipsos custodes?*

---

off one's guard; un-wary, -watchful, -guarded; offhand.

supine &c. (*inactive*) 683; inattentive &c. 458; *insouciant* &c. (*indifferent*) 823; imprudent, reckless &c. 863; slovenly &c. (*disorderly*) 59, (*dirty*) 653; inexact &c. (*erroneous*) 495; improvident &c. 674.

neglected &c. *v.*; un-heeded, -cared for, -perceived, -seen, -observed, -noticed, -noted, -marked, -attended to, -thought of, -regarded, -remarked, -missed; shunted, shelved.

un-examined, -studied, -searched, -scanned, -weighed, -sifted, -explored.

abandoned; buried in a napkin, hid under a bushel.

Adv. negligently &c. *adj.*; hand over head, anyhow; in an unguarded moment &c. (*unexpectedly*) 508; *per incuriam.*

Int. never mind, no matter, let it pass; it will be all the same a hundred years hence.

---

461. Inquiry. [Subject of Inquiry. Question.]—**N.** inquiry; request &c. 765; search, research, quest; pursuit &c. 622.

examination, review, scrutiny, investigation, indagation; per-quisition, -scrutation, -vestigation; inqu-est, -isition; exploration; *exploitation*, ventilation.

sifting; calculation, analysis, dissection, resolution, induction; Baconian method.

strict –, close –, searching –, exhaustive- inquiry; narrow –, strict-search; study &c. (*consideration*) 451. *scire facias, ad referendum*; trial.

questioning &c. *v.*; interroga-tion, -tory; third degree; interpellation; challenge, examination, cross-examination, catechism; feeler, Socratic method, zetetic philosophy; leading question; discussion &c. (*reasoning*) 476; questionnaire, questionary.

reconnoitering, *reconnaissance*; prying &c. *v.*; espionage, *espionnage*; domiciliary visit, peep behind the curtain; lantern of Diogenes.

question, query, problem, *desideratum*, point to be solved, porism; subject –, field- of -inquiry, – controversy; point –, matter- in dispute; moot-point; issue, question at issue; bone of contention &c. (*discord*) 713; plain –, fair –, open- question; enigma &c. (*secret*) 533; knotty point &c. (*difficulty*) 704; *quod-libet*; threshold of an inquiry.

inquirer, investigator, experimenter, inquisitor, inspector, querist,

462. Answer.—N. answer, response, reply, replication, *riposte*, rejoinder, surrejoinder, rebutter, surrebutter, counter-evidence &c. 468, counter-charge, defence, plea; retort, repartee; contradiction &c. 536; rescript, -ion; antiphon, -y; acknowledgment; pass word; echo.

discovery &c. 480a; solution &c. (*explanation*) 522; rationale &c. (*cause*) 153; clue &c. (*indication*) 550.

Œdipus; oracle &c. 513; return &c. (*record*) 551.

V. answer, respond, reply, rebut, retort, rejoin; give –, return for- answer; acknowledge, echo.

explain &c. (*interpret*) 522; solve &c. (*unriddle*) 522; discover &c. 480a; fathom, hunt out &c. (*inquire*) 461; satisfy, set at rest, determine.

Adj. answering &c. *v.*; respon-sive, -dent; oracular; antiphonal; conclusive.

Adv. because &c. (*cause*) 153; on the -scent, – right scent.

Int. *eureka!*

---

examiner, catechist; scrut-ator, -ineer; analyst; quidnunc &c. (*curiosity*) 455.

V. make -inquiry &c. *n.*; inquire, seek, search, frisk, speer, look -for, – about for, – out for; scan, reconnoitre, explore, sound, rummage, ransack, pry, peer, look round; look –, go- -over, – through; spy, over-haul.

scratch the head, slap the forehead.

look –, peer –, pry- into every hole and corner; look behind the scenes; trace up; hunt –, fish –, dig –, ferret- out; unearth; leave no stone unturned.

seek a -clue, – clew; hunt, track, trail, shadow, mouse, dodge, trace; follow the -trail, – scent; pursue &c. 622; beat up one's quarters; fish for; feel for &c. (*experiment*) 463.

investigate; take up –, institute –, pursue –, follow up –, con-duct –, carry on –, prosecute- -an inquiry &c. *n.*; look -at, – into; pre-examine; discuss, canvass, agitate.

examine, study, consider, calculate; dip –, dive –, delve –, go deep- into; make sure of, probe, sound, fathom; probe to the -bottom, – quick; scrutinize, analyze, anatomize, dissect, parse, resolve, sift, winnow; view –, try- in all its phases; thresh out.

bring in question, subject to examination; put to the proof &c. (*experiment*) 463; audit, tax, pass in review; take into consideration &c. (*think over*) 451; take counsel &c. 695.

ask, question, demand; put –, pop –, propose –, propound –, moot –, start –, raise –, stir –, suggest –, put forth –, ventilate –, grapple with –, go into- a question.

put to the question, interrogate, catechize, pump, grill; cross-question, -examine; dodge; require an answer; pick –, suck- the brains of; feel the pulse.

be -in question &c. *adj.*; undergo examination.

Adj. inquiry &c. *v.*; inquisitive &c. (*curious*) 455; requisit-ive, -ory; catechetical, inquisitorial, analytic; in -search, – quest- of; on the look-out for, interrogative, zetetic; all-searching.

un-determined, -tried, -decided; in -question, – dispute, – issue, – course of inquiry; under -discussion, – consideration, – investiga-tion &c. *n.*, *sub judice*, moot, proposed; doubtful &c. (*uncertain*) 475.

Adv. what? why? wherefore? whence? whither? where? *quære?* how -comes, – happens, – is- it? what is the reason? what's -the matter, – up, – in the wind? what on earth? when? who?

463. Experiment.—**N.** experiment; essay &c. (*attempt*) 675; research &c. (*investigation*) 461; trial, tentative method, *tâtonnement*.

verification, probation, *experimentum crucis*, proof, criterion, diag-nostic, test, tryout, crucial test, acid test.

crucible, reagent, check, touchstone, pix; assay, ordeal; ring.

empiricism, rule of thumb.

feeler; pilot –, messenger- balloon, *ballon d'essai*; pilot engine; scout; straw to show the wind.

speculation, random shot, leap in the dark.

analy-zer, -st; adventurer, explorer, sourdough, prospector; experi-ment-er, -ist, -alist; assayer.

V. experiment; essay &c. (*endeavour*) 675; try, assay, sample; make -an experiment, – trial of; give a trial to; put upon –, subject to- trial; experiment upon; rehearse; put –, bring –, submit- to the -test, – proof; prove, verify, test, touch, practise upon, try one's strength.

grope; feel –, grope- -for, – one's way; fumble; *tâtonner, aller à tâtons*; put –, throw- out a feeler; send up a pilot balloon; see how the -land lies, – wind blows; consult the barometer; feel the pulse; fish –, bob- for; cast –, beat- about for; angle, trawl, cast one's net, beat the bushes.

venture, try one's fortune &c. (*adventure*) 675; explore &c. (*inquire*) 461.

Adj. experimental; probat-ive, -ory, -ionary; analytic, docimastic; tentative; empirical; speculative, tentative.

under probation, on one's trial, on trial, on approval.

464. Comparison.—N. comparison, collation, contrast; identification. sim-ile, -ilitude; allegory &c. (*metaphor*) 521.

V. compare -to, – with; collate, confront; place side by side &c. (*near*) 197; set –, pit- against one another; contrast, balance.

identify, draw a parallel, parallel.

compare notes; institute a comparison; *parva componere magnis*.

Adj. comparative, relative; metaphorical &c. 521.

compared with &c. *v.*; comparable.

Adv. relatively &c. (*relation*) 9; as compared with &c. *v.*

465. Discrimination.—N. discrimination, distinction, differentiation, diagnosis, diorism; nice perception; perception –, appreciation- of difference; acuteness; estimation &c. 466; nicety, refinement; taste &c. 850; *critique*, judgement, tact; insight, discernment &c. (*intelligence*) 498; *nuances*.

V. discriminate, distinguish, differentiate, severalize; separate; draw the line, sift; separate –, winnow- the chaff from the wheat; split hairs.

estimate &c. (*measure*) 466; know -which is which, – one's stuff, – one's way about, – what is what, – 'a hawk from a handsaw.'

take into -account, – consideration; give –, allow- due weight to; weigh carefully.

Adj. discriminating &c. *v.*; dioristic, discriminative, critical, distinctive; nice.

Phr. *il y a fagots et fagots; rem acu tetigisti.*

465a. Indiscrimination.—N. indiscrimination; promiscuity; indistinctness, -ion; uncertainty &c. (*doubt*) 475; obtuseness.

V. not -indiscriminate &c. 465; overlook &c. (*neglect*) 460- a distinction; con-found, -fuse, jumble; swallow whole.

Adj. indiscriminate, undiscriminating, promiscuous; undistinguish-ed, -able, -ing; unmeasured.

466. Measurement.—N. measurement, admeasurement, mensuration, survey, valuation, appraisement, assessment, assize; estim-ate, -ation; dead reckoning; reckoning &c. (*numeration*) 85; gauging &c. *v.*

metrology, weights and measures, compound arithmetic.

measure, yard measure, standard, rule, foot-rule, chain, tape, staff, compass, callipers; dividers; gage, gauge, planimeter; meter, line, rod, check.

volt, kilowatt, ampere, candle power; horse power; axle load; foot pound.

flood –, high water- mark; Plimsoll mark; index &c. 550.

scale; gradu-ation, -ated scale; nonius; vernier &c. (*minuteness*) 193; pedo (*length*)- 200, sounding line &c. (*depth*) 208, thermo (*heat* &c. 389)-, baro (*air* &c. 338)-, dynamo (*power*)- 276, anemo (*wind* 349)-, gonio (*angle* 244)- meter; landmark &c. (*limit*) 233; balance &c. (*weight*) 310; optical instruments &c. 445.

co-ordinates, ordinate and abscissa, polar co-ordinates, latitude and longitude, declination and right ascension, altitude and azimuth.

geo-, stereo-, hypso-metry; metage; surveying, land surveying; geo-desy, -detics, -desia; ortho-, alti-metry; *cadastre*.

astrolabe, armillary sphere.

land, -surveyor; geometer, topographer, cartographer, hydrographer.

V. measure, meter, mete; value, assess, rate, appraise, estimate, form an estimate, set a value on; appreciate; standardize.

span, pace, step; apply the -compass &c. *n*.; gauge, plumb, probe, calliper, sound, fathom &c. 208; heave the -log, – lead; weigh &c. 319; survey.

take an average &c. 29; graduate.

Adj. measuring &c. *v*.; metric, -al; measurable; geodetical, cadastral, topographical.

Section III. Materials for Reasoning

467. Evidence [on one side.]—**N.** evidence; facts, premises, *data*, *præcognita*, grounds.

indication &c. 550; criterion &c. (*test*) 463.

testi-mony, -fication; attestation; deposition &c. (*affirmation*) 535; examination.

admission &c. (*assent*) 488; authority, warrant, credential, diploma, voucher, certificate, docket; record &c. 551; document, muniments; *pièce justificative*; deed, warranty &c. (*security*) 771; signature, seal &c. (*identification*) 550; exhibit, citation, reference.

witness, indicator; eye-, ear-witness; deponent; sponsor.

oral –, documentary –, hearsay –, external –, extrinsic –, internal –, intrinsic –, circumstantial –, cumulative –, *ex parte* –, presumptive –, collateral –, constructive- evidence; proof &c. (*demonstration*) 478; evidence in chief; finger prints, dactylogram.

secondary evidence; confirmation, corroboration, adminicle, support; ratification &c. (*assent*) 488; authentication, verification; compurgation, wager of law, comprobation.

citation, reference.

V. be -evidence &c. *n*.; evince, show, betoken, tell of; indicate &c. (*denote*) 550; imply, involve, argue, bespeak, breathe.

have –, carry- weight; tell, speak

468. [Evidence on the other side, on the other hand.] **Counter-evidence.**—**N.** counter-evidence; evidence on the other -side, – hand; disproof; refutation &c. 479; negation &c. 536; conflicting evidence.

plea &c. 617; vindication &c. 937; counter-protest; *tu quoque* argument; other side –, reverse- of the shield.

V. countervail, oppose; run counter; rebut &c. (*refute*) 479; subvert &c. (*destroy*) 162; check, weaken; contravene; contradict &c. (*deny*) 536; tell another story, turn the -tables, – scale; alter the case; cut both ways; prove a negative.

audire alteram partem.

Adj. countervailing &c. *v*.; contradictory, in rebuttal.

un-attested, -authenticated, -supported by evidence; supposititious, trumped up.

Adv. *per contra*, conversely, on the other hand.

469. Qualification.—**N.** qualification, limitation, modification, colouring.

allowance, grains of allowance, consideration, extenuating circumstances.

condition, proviso, exception; exemption; salvo, saving clause; discount &c. 813.

V. qualify, limit, modify, affect, temper, leaven, give a colour to, introduce new conditions.

allow –, make allowance- for; ad-

volumes; speak for itself &c. (*manifest*) 525.

rest –, depend- upon; repose on.

bear -witness &c. *n.*; give -evidence &c. *n.*; testify, depose, witness, vouch for; sign, seal, undersign, set one's hand and seal, sign and seal, deliver as one's act and deed, certify, attest; acknowledge &c. (*assent*) 488.

make absolute, confirm, ratify, corroborate, endorse, countersign, support, bear out, vindicate, uphold, warrant.

adduce, attest, cite, quote; refer –, appeal- to; call, – to witness; bring -forward, – into court; allege, plead; produce –, confront- witnesses; collect –, bring together –, rake up- evidence.

have –, make out- a case; establish, circumstantiate, authenticate, substantiate, verify, make good, quote chapter and verse; bring -home to, – to book.

Adj. showing &c. *v.*; evidential, indica-tive, -tory; deducible &c. 478; grounded –, founded –, based- on; first hand, authentic, verifiable; corroborative, confirmatory; significant, conclusive.

Adv. by inference; according to, witness, *a fortiori*; still -more, – less; *raison de plus*; in corroboration &c. *n.* of; *valeat quantum*; under -seal, – one's hand and seal.

mit exceptions, take into account. take exception, object.

Adj. qualifying &c. *v.*; conditional; extenuatory; exceptional &c. (*unconformable*) 83.

hypothetical &c. (*supposed*) 514; contingent &c. (*uncertain*) 475.

Adv. provided, – always; if, unless, but, yet; according as; conditionally, admitting, supposing; on the supposition of &c. (*theoretically*) 514; with the understanding, even, although, though, for all that, after all, at all events.

with grains of allowance, *cum grano salis*; *exceptis excipiendis*; wind and weather permitting; if possible &c. 470.

subject to; with this -proviso &c. *n.*

Degrees of Evidence

470. Possibility.—N. possibility, potentiality; what -may be, – is possible &c. *adj.*; compatibility &c. (*agreement*) 23.

practicability, feasibility; practicableness &c. *adj.*

contingency, chance &c. 156.

V. be -possible &c. *adj.*; stand a chance, have a leg to stand on; admit of, bear.

render -possible &c. *adj.*; put in the way of.

Adj. possible; on the -cards, – dice; *in posse*, within the bounds of possibility, conceivable, credible, imaginable; compatible &c. 23.

practicable, feasible, workable, performable, achievable; within -reach, – measurable distance; accessible, superable, surmountable; at-, ob-tainable; contingent &c. (*doubtful*) 475.

Adv. possibly, by possibility; perhaps, -chance, -adventure; may be, haply, mayhap.

471. Impossibility.—N. impossibility &c. *adj.*; what -cannot, – can never- be; sour grapes; infeasibility, impracticability, hopelessness &c. 859.

V. be -impossible &c. *adj.*; have no chance whatever.

attempt impossibilities; square the circle; discover the -philosopher's stone, – elixir of life, – secret of perpetual motion; wash a blackamoor white; skin a flint; make -a silk purse out of a sow's ear, – bricks without straw; have nothing to go upon; weave a rope of sand, build castles in the air, *prendre la lune avec les dents*, extract sunbeams from cucumbers, set the Thames on fire, milk a he-goat into a sieve, catch a weasel asleep, *rompre l'anguille au genou*, be in two places at once.

Adj. impossible; not -possible &c. 470; absurd, contrary to reason; unlikely, at variance with facts; unreasonable &c. 477; incredible &c. 485; beyond the bounds of -reason, – possi-

if possible, wind and weather permitting, God willing, *Deo volente*, D.V.

---

impracticable, unachievable; un-, in-feasible; insuperable; un-,
in-surmountable; unat-, unob-tainable; out of -reach, – the question;
not to be -had, – thought of; beyond control; desperate &c. (*hopeless*)
859; incompatible &c. 24; inaccessible, uncomeatable, impassable
impervious, innavigable, inextricable.

out of –, beyond- one's -power, – depth, – reach, – grasp; too
much for; *ultra crepidam*.

Phr. the grapes are sour; *non possumus*; *non nostrum tantas
componere lites*.

bility; from which reason recoils;
visionary; inconceivable &c. (*improbable*) 473; prodigious &c. (*wonderful*)
870; un-, in-imaginable, unthinkable,
not a Chinaman's chance.

472. Probability.—N. probability,
likelihood; likeliness &c. *adj.*

vraisemblance, verisimilitude, plausi-
bility; colour, semblance, show of;
presumption; presumptive –, circum-
stantial- evidence; credibility.

reasonable –, fair –, good –, favour-
able- -chance, – prospect; prospect,
well-grounded hope; chance &c. 156.

V. be -probable &c. *adj.*; give –,
lend- colour to; point to; imply &c.
(*evidence*) 467; bid fair &c. (*promise*)
511; stand fair for; stand –, run- a
good chance.

presume, infer, suppose, take for
granted.

think likely, dare say, flatter oneself;
expect &c. 507; count upon &c. (*believe*)
484.

Adj. probable, likely, hopeful, to be expected, in a fair way.

plausible, specious, ostensible, colourable, *ben trovato*, well-
founded, reasonable, credible, easy of belief, presumable, presumptive, apparent.

Adv. probably &c. *adj.*; belike; in all -probability, – likelihood;
very –, most- likely; as likely as not; like enough; ten &c. to one;
apparently, seemingly, according to every reasonable expectation;
primâ facie; to all appearance &c. (*to the eye*) 448.

Phr. the -chances, – odds- are; appearances –, chances- are in
favour of; there is reason to -believe, – think, – expect; I dare say;
all Lombard Street to a China orange.

473. Improbability.—N. improbability, unlikelihood; unfavourable –,
bad –, little –, small –, poor –, scarcely
any –, no –, not a ghost of a- chance;
bare possibility; long odds; incredi-
bility &c. 485.

V. be -improbable &c. *adj.*; have a
-small chance &c. *n.*

Adj. improbable, unlikely, contrary
to all reasonable expectation, implau-
sible.

rare &c. (*infrequent*) 137; unheard of,
inconceivable; un-, in-imaginable; incredible &c. 485; more than doubtful.

Int. not likely! no fear!

Phr. the chances are against.

---

474. Certainty.—N. certainty; necessity &c. 601; certitude, certainness,
surety, assurance, sureness; dead –,
moral- certainty; infallibleness &c. *adj.*;
infallibility, reliability.

gospel, scripture, church, pope, court
of final appeal; *res judicata, ultimatum.*

positiveness; dogmat-ism, -ist, -izer;
doctrinaire, know-all, bigot, -ry; opin-

475. Uncertainty.—N. uncertainty,
incertitude, doubt; doubtfulness &c.
adj.; dubi-ety, -tation, -tancy, -ousness.

hesitation, suspense; perplexity, embarrassment, dilemma, quandary, Morton's fork, bewilderment; timidity &c.
(*fear*) 860; indecision, vacillation &c.
605; *diaporesis*, indetermination.

vagueness &c. *adj.*; haze, fog; ob-

ionist, Sir Oracle; *ipse dixit*; zealot.

fact; positive –, matter of- fact; *fait accompli*.

V. be -certain &c. *adj.*; stand to reason.

render -certain &c. *adj.*; in-, en-, assure; clinch, make sure; determine, decide, set at rest, 'make assurance double sure'; know &c. (*believe*) 484; dismiss all doubt.

dogmatize, lay down the law.

Adj. certain, sure; assured &c. *v.*; solid, well-founded.

unqualified, absolute, positive, determinate, definite, clear, unequivocal, categorical, unmistakable, decisive, decided, ascertained.

inevitable, unavoidable, ineluctable, avoidless.

unerring, infallible; unchangeable &c. 150; to be depended on, trustworthy, reliable, bound.

un-impeachable, -deniable, -questionable; in-disputable, -contestable, -controvertible, -defeasible, -dubitable; irrefutable &c. (*proven*) 478; conclusive, without power of appeal, final.

indubious; without –, beyond a –, without a shade or shadow of- -doubt – question; past dispute; beyond all -question, – dispute; un-doubted, -contested, -questioned, -disputed; question-, doubt-less.

bigoted, fanatical, dogmatic, opinionat-ed, -ive, *doctrinaire*.

authoritative, authentic, official.

sure as -fate, – death and taxes, – a gun.

evident, self-evident, axiomatic; clear, – as day, – as the sun at noonday; obvious.

Adv. certainly &c. *adj.*; for certain, certes, sure, no doubt, doubtless, and no mistake, *flagrante delicto*, sure enough, to be sure, of course, as a matter of course, *à coup sur*, to a certainty, undoubtedly; in truth &c. (*truly*) 494; at -any rate, – all events; without fail; *coûte que coûte*; whatever may happen, if the worst come to the worst; come –, happen- what -may, – will; sink or swim; rain or shine.

Phr. *cela va sans dire*; there is -no question, – not a shadow of doubt;

scurity &c. (*darkness*) 421; ambiguity &c. (*double meaning*) 520; contingency, double contingency, possibility upon a possibility; conjecture; open question &c. (*question*) 461; *onus probandi*; blind bargain, pig in a poke, leap in the dark, something or other; needle in a bottle of hay; roving commission.

fallibility, unreliability, untrustworthiness, precariousness.

V. be -uncertain &c. *adj.*; wonder whether.

lose the -clue, – clew, – scent; miss one's way.

not know -what to make of &c. (*unintelligibility*) 519, – which way to turn, – whether one stands on one's head or one's heels; float in a sea of doubt, hesitate, flounder; lose -oneself, – one's head, – one's way, wander aimlessly; muddle one's brains.

render -uncertain &c. *adj.*; put out, pose, puzzle, perplex, embarrass; confuse, -found; bewilder, mystify, bother, moider, nonplus, addle the wits, throw off the scent; *ambiguas in vulgus spargere voces*; keep in suspense.

doubt &c. (*disbelieve*) 485; hang –, tremble- in the balance; depend.

Adj. uncertain; casual; random &c. (*aimless*) 621; changeable &c. 149.

doubtful, dubious; indecisive; unsettled, -decided, -determined; in suspense, open to discussion; controvertible; in question &c. (*inquiry*) 461; insecure, unstable.

vague; in-determinate, -definite; ambiguous, equivocal; undefin-ed, -able; confused &c. (*indistinct*) 447; mystic, mysterious, veiled, obscure, cryptic, oracular.

perplexing &c. *v.*; enigmatic, paradoxical, apocryphal, problematical, hypothetical; experimental &c. 463.

fallible, questionable, precarious, slippery, ticklish, debatable, disputable; un-reliable, -trustworthy.

contingent, – on, dependent on; subject to; dependent on circumstances; occasional; provisional.

unauth-entic, -enticated, -oritative; un-ascertained, -confirmed; undemonstrated; un-told, -counted.

in a -state of uncertainty, – cloud,

the die is cast &c. (*necessity*) 601.

_____

– maze; ignorant &c. 491; on the horns of a dilemma; afraid to say; out of one's reckoning, astray, adrift; at -sea,

– fault, – a loss, – one's wit's end, – a *nonplus*; puzzled &c. *v.*; lost, abroad, *désorienté*; dis-tracted, -traught.

Adv. *pendente lite*; *sub spe rati*.

Phr. Heaven knows; who can tell? who shall decide when doctors disagree?

Section IV. Reasoning Processes

476. Reasoning. — N. reasoning; ratio-cination, -nalism; dialectics, in-duction, generalization.

discussion, comment; ventilation; inquiry &c. 461.

argumentation, controversy, debate; polemics, wrangling; contention &c. 720; logomachy; dis-putation, -cepta-tion; paper war.

art of reasoning, logic.

process –, train –, chain- of reason-ing; de-, in-duction; synthesis, analysis.

argument; case, plea, *plaidoyer*, opening; *lemma*, proposition, terms, premises, postulate, *data*, starting point, principle; inference &c. (*judg-ment*) 480.

pro-, syllogism; enthymeme, sorites, dilemma, *perilepsis*, *a priori* reasoning, *reductio ad absurdum*, horns of a di-lemma, *argumentum ad hominem*, com-prehensive argument.

reasoner, logician, dialectician; dis-putant; controver-sialist, -tist; wrang-ler, arguer, debater, polemic, casuist, rationalist; scientist.

logical sequence; good case; correct –, just –, sound –, valid –, cogent –, logical –, forcible –, persuasive –, per-suasory –, consectary –, conclusive &c. 478 –, subtle- reasoning; force of argu-ment; strong -point, – argument.

arguments, reasons, pros and cons.

V. reason, argue, discuss, debate, dispute, wrangle; bandy -words, – arguments; chop logic; hold –, carry on- an argument; controvert &c. (*deny*) 536; canvass; comment –, moralize-upon; consider &c. (*examine*) 461.

open a -discussion, – case; join –, be at- issue; moot; come to the point; stir –, agitate –, ventilate –, torture- a question; try conclusions; take up a -side, – case.

477. [The absence of reasoning.] **Intuition.** [False or vicious reasoning; show of reason.] **Sophistry.—N.** intui-tion, instinct, association; presenti-ment; rule of thumb.

sophistry, paralogy, perversion, casu-istry, jesuitry, equivocation, evasion, mental reservation; chicane, -ry; quid-dit, quiddity; mystification; special pleading; speciousness &c. *adj.*; non-sense &c. 497; word-, tongue-fence.

false –, vicious- reasoning; *petitio principii, ignoratio elenchi; post hoc ergo propter hoc; non sequitur, ignotum per ignotius.*

misjudgment &c. 481; false teaching &c. 538.

sophism, solecism, paralogism; quib-ble, quirk, *elenchus*, elench, fallacy, *quodlibet*, subterfuge, subtlety, quillet; inconsistency, antilogy; 'a mockery, a delusion and a snare'; claptrap, mere words; 'lame and impotent conclusion.'

meshes –, cobwebs- of sophistry; flaw in an argument; weak point, bad case.

over-refinement; hair-splitting &c. *v.*

sophist, casuist, paralogist.

V. judge -intuitively, – by intuition; hazard a proposition, talk at random.

reason -ill, – falsely &c. *adj.*; paralo-gize; misjudge &c. 481.

pervert, quibble; equivocate, mysti-fy, evade, elude; gloss over, varnish; misteach &c. 538; mislead &c. (*error*) 495; cavil, refine, subtilize, split hairs; misrepresent &c. (*lie*) 544.

beg the question, reason in a circle, cut blocks with a razor, beat about the bush, play fast and loose, blow hot and cold, prove that black is white and white black, travel out of the record, *parler à tort et à travers*, put oneself out of court, not have a leg to stand on.

Adj. intuitive, instinctive, impulsive;

contend, take one's stand upon, insist, lay stress on; infer &c. 480.

follow from &c. (*demonstration*) 478.

Adj. rational; reasoning &c. *v.*; rationalistic; argumentative, controversial, dialectic, polemical; discursory, -ive; disputatious.

debatable, controvertible.

logical; in-, de-ductive; synthetic, analytic; relevant &c. 23.

Adv. for, because, hence, whence, seeing that, since, sith, then, thence, so; for -that, – this, – which- reason; for-, inasmuch as; whereas, *ex concesso*, considering, in consideration of; there-, where-fore; consequently, *ergo*, thus, accordingly; *a fortiori*.

in -conclusion, – fine; finally, after all, *au bout du compte*, on the whole, taking one thing with another.

rationally &c. *adj.*

---

478. Demonstration.—N. demonstration, proof; conclusiveness &c. *adj.*; *apodixis*, probation, comprobation.

logic of facts &c. (*evidence*) 467; *experimentum crucis* &c. (*test*) 463; argument &c. 476; irrefragability.

V. demonstrate, prove, establish, make good; show; evince &c. (*be evidence of*) 467; verify &c. 467; settle the question, reduce to demonstration, set the question at rest.

make out, – a case; prove one's point, have the best of the argument; draw a conclusion &c. (*judge*) 480.

follow, – of course; stand to reason; hold -good, – water.

Adj. demonstra-ting &c. *v.*, -tive, -ble; probative, unanswerable, conclusive; apodictic, -al; irre-sistible, -futable, -fragable, undeniable.

categorical, decisive, crucial.

demonstrated &c. *v.*; proven; un-confuted, -answered, -refuted; evident &c. 474.

deducible, consequential, consectary, inferential, following.

Adv. of course, in consequence, consequently, as a matter of course.

Phr. *probatum est*; there is nothing more to be said, Q.E.D., it must follow.

independent of –, anterior to- reason; gratuitous, hazarded; unconnected.

unreasonable, illogical, false, unsound, invalid; unwarranted, not following; inconsequent, -ial; inconsistent, incongruous; abson-ous, -ant; unscientific; untenable, inconclusive, incorrect; fall-acious, -ible; groundless, unproved.

deceptive, sophistical, sophisticated, casuistical, jesuitical; illus-ive, -ory; specious, hollow, plausible, *ad captandum*, evasive; irrelevant &c. 10.

weak, feeble, poor, flimsy, loose, vague, irrational; nonsensical &c. (*absurd*) 497; foolish &c. (*imbecile*) 499; frivolous, pettifogging, quibbling; fine-spun, over-refined.

at the end of one's tether, *au bout de son latin*.

Adv. intuitively &c. *adj.*; by intuition; illogically &c. *adj.*

Phr. *non constat*; that goes for nothing.

---

479. Confutation.—N. con-, re-futation; answer, complete answer; disproof, conviction, redargution, invalidation; expos-ure, -ition; clincher; retort; *reductio ad absurdum*; knock down –, *tu quoque*- argument.

V. con-, re-fute; parry, negative, disprove, redargue, expose, show the fallacy of, rebut, defeat; demolish &c. (*destroy*) 162; over-throw, -turn; scatter to the winds, explode, invalidate; silence; put –, reduce- to silence; clinch -an argument, – a question; give one a set down, stop the mouth, shut up; have, – on the hip; get the better of; confound, convince.

not leave a leg to stand on, cut the ground from under one's feet.

be confuted &c.; fail; expose –, show- one's weak point.

Adj. confut-ing, -ed &c. *v.*; capable of refutation; re-, con-futable.

condemned -on one's own showing, – out of one's own mouth.

Phr. the argument falls to the ground, *cadit quæstio*, it does not hold water, '*suo sibi gladio hunc jugulo.*'

Section V. Results of Reasoning

480. Judgment. [Conclusion.]—N.

result, conclusion, upshot; deduction, inference, ergotism, illation; corollary, porism; moral.

estimation, valuation, appreciation, judication; di-, ad-judication; arbitrament, -ement, -ation; assessment, ponderation.

award, estimate; review, criticism, *critique*, notice, report.

decision, determination, judgment, finding, verdict, sentence, decree, – nisi, – absolute, – interlocutory; dictum; *res judicata*.

plébiscite, referendum, voice, casting vote; vote &c. (*choice*) 609; opinion &c. (*belief*) 484; good judgment &c. (*wisdom*) 498.

judge, jurist, umpire; arbi-ter, -trator; assessor, referee; censor, reviewer, critic; *connoisseur*; commentator &c. 524; inspector, inspecting officer.

V. judge, conclude; come to –, draw –, arrive at- a conclusion; ascertain, determine, make up one's mind.

deduce, derive, gather, collect, draw an inference, make a deduction, weet, ween.

form an estimate, estimate, size up, appreciate, value, count, assess, rate, rank, account; regard, consider, think of; look upon &c. (*believe*) 484.

settle; pass –, give- an opinion; decide, try, pronounce, rule; pass -judgment, – sentence; sentence, doom; find; give –, deliver- judgment; adjud-ge, -icate; arbitrate, award, report; bring in a verdict; make absolute, set a question at rest; confirm &c. (*assent*) 488.

comment, criticize; review, pass under review &c. (*examine*) 457; investigate &c. (*inquire*) 461.

hold the scales, sit in judgment; try –, hear- a cause.

Adj. judging &c. *v.*; judicious &c. (*wise*) 498; determinate, conclusive, censorious, critical &c. 932.

Adv. on the whole, all things considered.

481. Misjudgment. — N.

misjudgment, obliquity of –, warped- judgment; mis-calculation, -computation, -conception &c. (*error*) 495; hasty conclusion.

prejud-gment, -ication, -ice; foregone conclusion; pre-notion, -vention, -conception, -dilection, -possession, -apprehension, -sumption, -sentiment; fixed –, preconceived- idea; *idée fixe*; *mentis gratissimus error*; fool's paradise.

esprit de corps, party spirit, race –, class- prejudice, partisanship, clannishness, *prestige*.

bias, warp, twist; hobby, fad, whim, craze, quirk, crotchet, partiality, infatuation, blind side, mote in the eye.

one-sided –, partial –, narrow –, confined –, superficial- -views, – ideas, – conceptions, – notions; narrow mind; bigotry &c. (*obstinacy*) 606; *odium theologicum*; pedantry; hypercriticism.

doctrinaire &c. (*positive*) 474.

V. mis-judge, -estimate, -think, -conjecture, -conceive &c. (*error*) 495; fly in the face of facts; mis-calculate, -reckon, -compute.

overestimate &c. 482; underestimate &c. 483.

pre-, fore-judge; pre-suppose, -sume, -judicate; dogmatize; have a -bias &c. *n.*; have only one idea; *jurare in verba magistri*, run away with the notion; jump –, rush- to a conclusion; look only at one side of the shield; view -with jaundiced eye, – through distorting spectacles; not see beyond one's nose; *dare pondus fumo*; get the wrong sow by the ear &c. (*blunder*) 699.

give a -bias, – twist; bias, warp, twist; pre-judice, -possess.

Adj. misjudging &c. *v.*; ill-judging, wrong-headed; prejudiced, prejudicial, &c. *v.*; jaundiced; short-sighted, purblind; partial, one-sided, superficial.

narrow-minded; confined, insular, provincial, parochial, illiberal, intolerant, narrow, besotted, infatuated, fanatical, cracked, warped, *entêté,* positive, dogmatic, dictatorial; conceited; opin-, opini-ative; opinion-ed, -ate, -ative, -ated; self-opinioned, wedded to an opinion, *opiniâtre*; bigoted &c. (*obstinate*) 606; crotchety, fussy, impracticable; unreason-able, -ing; stupid &c. 499; credulous &c. 486.

misjudged &c. *v.*

Adv. *ex parte.*

Phr. nothing like leather; the wish the father to the thought.

480a. [Result of search or inquiry.] **Discovery.—N.** discovery, invention, detection, disenchantment, disclosure, find, ascertainment, revelation.

trover &c. 775.

V. discover, find, determine, evolve; fix upon; find –, trace –, make –, hunt –, fish –, worm –, ferret –, root- out; fathom; bring –, draw- out; educe, elicit, bring to light, invent; dig –, grub –, fish- up; unearth, disinter.

solve, resolve; un-riddle, -ravel, -lock; pick –, open- the lock; find a -clue, – clew- to; interpret &c. 522; disclose &c. 529.

trace, get at; hit it, have it; lay one's -finger, – hands- upon; spot; get –, arrive- at the -truth &c. 494; put the saddle on the right horse, hit the right nail on the head.

be near the truth, burn; smoke, scent, sniff, smell a rat.

open the eyes to; see -through, – daylight, – in its true colours, – the cloven foot; detect; catch, – tripping.

pitch –, fall –, light –, hit –, stumble –, pop- upon; come across; meet –, fall in- with.

recognize, realize, verify, make certain of, identify.

Int. *eureka!*

482. Overestimation.—N. overestimation &c. *v.*; exaggeration &c. 549; vanity &c. 880; optim-, pessim-ism, -ist; megalomania.

much -cry and little wool, – ado about nothing; storm in a teacup; fine talking, rodomontade, gush, hot air, gas, bombast.

egotism &c. 880; boasting &c. 884.

V. over-estimate, -rate, -value, -prize, -weigh, -reckon, -strain, -praise; estimate too highly, attach too much importance to, make mountains of molehills, catch at straws; strain, magnify; exaggerate &c. 549; set too high a value upon; think –, make- -much, – too much- of; outreckon.

extol, – to the skies; make the -most, – best, – worst- of, eulogize, panegyrize, gush, puff, boost; make two bites of a cherry.

have too high an opinion of oneself &c. (*vanity*) 880.

Adj. overestimated &c. *v.*; oversensitive &c. (*sensibility*) 822; inflated, puffed up, exaggerated &c. 549.

Phr. all his geese are swans; *parturiunt montes.*

483. Underestimation.—N. underestimation; depreciation &c. (*detraction*) 934; pessim-ism, -ist; under-valuing &c. *v.*; modesty &c. 881.

V. under-rate, -estimate, -value, -reckon; depreciate; disparage &c. (*detract*) 934; not do justice to; mis-, dis-prize; ridicule &c. 856; slight &c. (*despise*) 930; neglect &c. 460; slur over, under-state.

make -light, – little, – nothing, – no account- of; minimize, belittle, run down, think nothing of; set -no store by, – at naught; shake off as dewdrops from the lion's mane.

Adj. depreciat-ing, -ed, -ive, -ory, &c. *v.*; un-appreciated, -valued, -prized; pejorative.

484. Belief.—N. belief; credence; credit; assurance; faith, trust, troth, confidence, presumption, sanguine expectation &c. (*hope*) 858; dependence on, reliance on.

persuasion, conviction, convincement, plerophory, self-conviction; certainty &c. 474; opinion, mind, view; conception, thinking; impression &c. (*idea*) 453; surmise &c. 514; conclusion &c. (*judgment*) 480.

tenet, dogma, principle, way of thinking; popular belief &c. (*assent*) 488.

firm -, implicit -, settled -, fixed -, rooted -, deep-rooted -, staunch -, unshaken -, steadfast -, inveterate -, calm -, sober -, dispassionate -, impartial -, well-founded- -belief, - opinion &c.; *uberrima fides*.

system of opinions, school, doctrine, articles, canons; declaration -, profession- of faith; tenets, *credenda*, creed; thirty-nine articles &c. (*orthodoxy*) 983*a*; catechism; assent &c. 488; *propaganda* &c. (*teaching*) 537.

credibility &c. (*probability*) 472.

V. believe, credit; give -faith, - credit, - credence- to; see, realize; assume, receive; set down -, take- for; have -, take- it; consider, esteem, presume.

count -, depend -, calculate -, pin one's faith -, reckon -, lean -, build -, rely -, rest- upon; lay one's account for; make sure of.

make oneself easy -about, - on that score; take on -trust, - credit; take for -granted, -gospel; allow -, attach- some weight to.

know, - for certain; have -, make- no doubt; doubt not; be - rest- -assured &c. *adj.*; persuade -, assure -, satisfy- oneself; make up one's mind.

give one credit for; confide -, believe -, put one's trust- in; place -, repose- implicit confidence in; take -one's word for, - at one's word; place reliance on, rely upon, swear by, regard to.

think, hold; take, - it; opine, be of opinion, conceive, trow, ween, fancy, apprehend; have -, hold -, possess -, entertain -, adopt -, imbibe -, embrace

485. Unbelief. Doubt.—N. un-, dis-, mis-belief; discredit, miscreance; infidelity &c. (*irreligion*) 989; dissent &c. 489; change of -opinion &c. 484; retraction &c. 607.

doubt &c. (*uncertainty*) 475; skepticism, misgiving, demur; dis-, mis-trust; misdoubt, suspicion, jealousy, scruple, qualm; *onus probandi*.

incredib-ility, -leness; incredulity; unbeliever &c. 487.

V. dis-believe, -credit; not -believe &c. 484; misbelieve; refuse to admit &c. (*dissent*) 489; refuse to believe &c. (*incredulity*) 487.

doubt; be -doubtful &c. (*uncertain*) 475; doubt the truth of; be -skeptical as to &c. *adj.*; diffide; dis-, mis-trust; suspect, smoke, scent, smell a rat; have -, harbour -, entertain- -doubts, - suspicions; have one's doubts.

demur, stick at, pause, hesitate, scruple, waver, stop and consider.

hang in -suspense, - doubt.

throw doubt upon, raise a question; bring -, call- in question; question, challenge, query; dispute; deny &c. 536; cavil; cause -, raise -, start -, suggest -, awake- a -doubt, - suspicion; ergotize.

startle, stagger; shake -, stagger- one's faith, - belief.

Adj. unbelieving; incredulous -, skeptical- as to; distrustful -, shy -, suspicious- of; doubting &c. *v.*

doubtful &c. (*uncertain*) 475; disputable; unworthy -, undeserving- of -belief &c. 484; questionable; sus-pect, -picious; open to -suspicion, - doubt; staggering, hard to believe, incredible, not to be believed, inconceivable.

fallible &c. (*uncertain*) 475; undemonstrable; controvertible &c. (*untrue*) 495.

Adv. *cum grano salis.*

Phr. *fronti nulla fides; nimium ne crede colori; 'timeo Danaos et dona ferentes'; credat Judæus Apella;* let those believe who may.

–, get hold of –, hazard –, foster –, nurture –, cherish- -a belief,
– an opinion &c. *n.*

view –, consider –, take –, hold –, conceive –, regard –, esteem –,
deem –, look upon –, account –, set down- as; surmise &c. 514.

get –, take- it into one's head; come round to an opinion; swallow
&c. (*credulity*) 486.

cause to -be believed &c. *v.*; satisfy, persuade, have the ear of,
gain the confidence of, assure; con-vince, -vict, -vert; put across,
sell; wean, bring round; bring –, put –, win- over; indoctrinate &c.
(*teach*) 537; cram down the throat; produce –, carry- conviction;
bring –, drive- home to.

go down, find credence, pass current; be -received &c. *v.*, – current
&c. *adj.*; possess –, take hold of –, take possession of- the mind.

Adj. believing &c. *v.*; certain, sure, assured, positive, cocksure,
satisfied, confident, unhesitating, convinced, secure.

under the impression; impressed –, imbued –, penetrated- with.

confiding, trustful, suspectless; unsusp-ecting, -icious; void of
suspicion; credulous &c. 486; wedded to.

believed &c. *v.*; accredited, putative; unsuspected.

worthy of –, deserving of –, commanding- -belief, – confidence;
credible, reliable, trusted, trustworthy, to be depended on, un-
doubted; satisfactory; probable &c. 472; fiduci-al, -ary; persuasive,
impressive.

relating to belief, doctrinal.

Adv. in the -opinion, – – eyes- of; *me judice*; me-seems, -thinks;
to the best of one's belief; I -dare say, – doubt not, – have no
doubt, – am sure; in my opinion; sure enough &c. (*certainty*) 474;
depend –, rely- upon it; be –, rest- assured; I'll warrant you &c.
(*affirmation*) 535.

---

486. Credulity.—N. credul-ity, -ous-
ness &c. *adj.*; gull-, cull-ibility; gross
credulity, infatuation; self-delusion,
-deception; blind reasoning; superstition; one's blind side; bigotry &c.
(*obstinacy*) 606; hyper-orthodoxy &c.
984; misjudgment &c. 481.

credulous person &c. (*dupe*) 547.

V. be -credulous &c. *adj.*; *jurare in
verba magistri*; follow implicitly; swallow, – whole, gulp down; take on trust;
take for -granted, – gospel; run away
with -a notion, – an idea; jump –,
rush- to a conclusion; think the moon
is made of green cheese; take –, grasp-
the shadow for the substance; catch at
straws.

impose upon &c. (*deceive*) 545.

Adj. credulous, gullible; easily -de-
ceived &c. 545; simple, green, soft,
childish, silly, stupid; over-credulous,
-confident; infatuated, superstitious; confiding &c. (*believing*) 484.

Phr. the wish the father to the thought; *credo quia impossibile.*

487. Incredulity.—N. incredul-ous-
ness, -ity; skepticism, pyrrhonism;
want of faith &c. (*irreligion*) 989.

suspiciousness &c. *adj.*; scrupulosity;
suspicion &c. (*unbelief*) 485; dissent
&c. 489.

unbeliever, skeptic, aporetic; atheist,
agnostic, infidel, disbeliever, misbeliever, pyrrhonist &c. 989; heretic &c.
(*heterodox*) 984.

V. be -incredulous &c. *adj.*; distrust
&c. (*disbelieve*) 485; refuse to believe;
shut one's -eyes, – ears- to; turn a deaf
ear to; hold aloof; ignore; *nullis jurare
in verba magistri.*

Adj. incredulous, skeptical, unbelieving, inconvincible; hard –, shy- of
belief; suspicious, scrupulous, distrustful, heterodox &c. 984.

488. Assent.—N. assent, -ment; acquiescence, admission; nod; ac-, con-cord, -cordance; agreement &c. 23; affirm-ance, -ation; recognition, acknowledgment, avowal; confession, – of faith.

unanimity, common consent, *consensus*, acclamation, chorus, *vox populi*; popular –, current- -belief, – opinion; public opinion; concurrence &c. (*of causes*) 178; co-operation &c. (*voluntary*) 709.

ratification, confirmation, corroboration, approval, acceptance, *visa*; indorsement &c. (*record*) 551.

consent &c. (*compliance*) 762.

affirmant, consenter, covenantor, subscriber, endorser, upholder.

V. assent; give –, yield –, nod- assent; acquiesce; agree &c. 23; receive, accept, accede, accord, concur, lend oneself to, consent, coincide, reciprocate, go with; be -at one with &c. *adj.*; go along –, chime in –, strike in –, close- with; echo, enter into one's views, agree in opinion; vote –, give one's voice- for; recognize; subscribe –, conform –, defer- to; say -yes, – ditto, – amen, – aye- to.

acknowledge, own, admit, allow, avow, confess; concede &c. (*yield*) 762; come round to; abide by; permit &c. 760.

come to –, arrive at- -an understanding, – terms, – an agreement.

con-, af-firm; ratify, approve, endorse, countersign; visa; corroborate &c. 467.

go –, swim- with the stream, float with the current; be in the fashion, join in the chorus; be in every mouth.

Adj. assenting &c. *v.*; of one -accord, – mind; of the same mind, at one with, agreed, acquiescent, content; willing &c. 602.

un-contradicted, -challenged, -questioned, -controverted.

carried –, agreed- -*nem. con.* &c. *adv.*; unanimous; agreed on all hands, carried by acclamation.

affirmative &c. 535.

Adv. yes, yea, ay, aye, true; good; well; very -well, – true; well and good; granted; *placet*; even –, just- so; to be sure, surely, 'thou hast said'; truly, exactly, precisely,

489. Dissent.—N. dissent; discordance &c. (*disagreement*) 24; difference –, diversity- of opinion.

non-conformity &c. (*heterodoxy*) 984; protestantism, recusancy, schism; disaffection; secession &c. 624; recantation &c. 607.

dissension &c. (*discord*) 713; discontent &c. 832; cavilling.

protest; contradiction &c. (*denial*) 536; non-compliance &c. (*rejection*) 764; disapprobation &c. 932; hartal.

dissent-ient, -er; non-juror, -content; recusant, sectary, schismatic, protestant, non-conformist, separatist, non-co-operator, conscientious objector, passive resister.

V. dissent, demur; call in question &c. (*doubt*) 485; differ in opinion, disagree; say -no &c. 536; refuse -assent, – to admit; cavil, protest, raise one's voice against, make bold to differ; repudiate; contradict &c. (*deny*) 536; agree to differ.

have no notion of, differ *toto cœlo*; revolt -at, – from the idea.

shake the head, shrug the shoulders; look -askance, – askant.

secede; recant &c. 607.

Adj. dissenting &c. *v.*; negative &c. 536; diss-ident, -entient; unconsenting &c. (*refusing*) 764; non-content, -juring; protestant, recusant; uncon-vinced, -verted.

unavowed, unacknowledged; out of the question.

discontented &c. 832; unwilling &c. 603; extorted.

sectarian, denominational, schismatic, heterodox, intolerant.

Adv. no &c. 536; at -variance, – issue- with; under protest; *non placet*.

Int. God forbid! not for the world; not on your life; I beg to differ; I'll be hanged if; never tell me; your humble servant, pardon me; tell that to the marines.

Phr. many men many minds; *quot homines tot sententiæ*; *tant s'en faut*; *il s'en faut bien*.

that's just it, indeed, certainly, certes, *ex concesso*; of course, un-questionably, assuredly, no doubt, doubtless, undoubtedly.

be it so; so -be it, – let it be, so mote it be; amen; with all my heart; willingly &c. 602.

affirmatively, in the affirmative.

with one -consent, – voice, – accord; unanimously, *unâ voce*, by common consent, in chorus, to a man, *nem. con.*; *nemine -contradi-cente*, – *dissentiente*; without a dissentient voice; as one man, one and all, on all hands.

---

490. Knowledge.—N. knowledge; cogn-izance, -ition, -oscence; acquaint-ance, experience, ken, privity, insight, familiarity; com-, ap-prehension; re-cognition; appreciation &c. (*judgment*) 480; intuition; consci-ence, -ousness; perception, precognition; acroamatics.

light, enlightenment; glimpse, ink-ling; side light; glimmer, -ing; dawn; scent, suspicion; impression &c. (*idea*) 453; discovery &c. 480a.

system –, body- of knowledge; science, philosophy, pansophy; theory, Etiology; circle of the sciences; pan-dect, doctrine, body of doctrine; cy-, ency-clopædia; school &c. (*system of opinions*) 484.

tree of knowledge; republic of letters &c. (*language*) 560.

erudition, learning, lore, scholarship, reading, letters; literature; book-learning, bookishness; biblio-mania, -latry; information, general informa-tion; store of -knowledge &c.; educa-tion &c. (*teaching*) 537; culture, attain-ments; acqui-rements, -sitions; ac-complishments, proficiency; practical knowledge &c. (*skill*) 698; higher edu-cation, liberal education; dilettantism; rudiments &c. (*beginning*) 66.

deep –, profound –, solid –, accurate –, acroatic –, acroamatic –, vast –, ex-tensive –, encyclopædical- -knowledge, – learning; omniscience, pantology.

march of intellect; progress –, ad-vance- of -science, – learning; school-master abroad.

V. know, ken, scan, wot; wot –, be aware &c. *adj.*- of; ween, weet, trow, have, possess.

conceive; ap-, com-prehend; take, realize, understand, appreciate; fathom, make out; recognize, discern, perceive, see, get a sight of, experience.

491. Ignorance. — N. ignorance, nescience, *tabula rasa*, crass ignorance, *ignorance crasse*; unacquaintance; un-consciousness &c. *adj.*; dark-, blind-ness; incomprehension, inexperience, simplicity.

unknown quantities, x, y, z.

sealed book, *terra incognita*, virgin soil, unexplored ground; dark ages.

[Imperfect knowledge] smattering, superficiality, half-learning, sciolism, glimmering; bewilderment &c. (*uncer-tainty*) 475; incapacity.

[Affectation of knowledge] pedantry; charlatan-ry, -ism.

V. be -ignorant &c. *adj.*; not -know &c. 490; know -not, – not what, – no-thing of; have no -idea, – notion, – conception; not have the remotest idea; not know chalk from cheese.

ignore, be blind to; keep in ignorance &c. (*conceal*) 528.

see through a glass darkly; have a -film over the eyes, – glimmering &c. *n.*; wonder whether; not know what to make of &c. (*unintelligibility*) 519; not pretend –, not take upon oneself-to say.

Adj. ignorant, nescient; un-knowing, -aware, -acquainted, -apprized, -wit-ting, -weeting, -conscious; wit-, weet-less; a stranger to; unconversant.

un-informed, -cultivated, -versed, -instructed, -taught, -initiated, -tu-tored, -schooled, -guided, -enlightened; Philistine; behind the age.

shallow, superficial, green, rude, empty, half-learned, illiterate; un-read, -informed, -educated, -learned, -let-tered, -bookish; empty-headed; low-brow; pedantic.

in the dark; be-nighted, -lated; blind-ed, -fold; hoodwinked; misin-formed; *au bout de son latin*, at the

know full well; have –, possess- some knowledge of; be -*au courant* &c. *adj.*; have -in one's head, – at one's fingers' ends; know by -heart, – rote; be master of; *connaître le dessous des cartes*, know what's what &c. 698.

see one's way; learn, discover &c. 480*a*.

come to one's knowledge &c. (*information*) 527.

Adj. knowing &c. *v.*; cognitive; acroamatic.

aware –, cognizant –, conscious- of; acquainted –, made acquainted- with; privy –, no stranger- to; *au -fait*, – *courant*; in the secret; up –, alive- to; sensible of; behind the -scenes, – curtain; let into; apprized –, informed- of; undeceived.

proficient –, versed –, read –, forward –, strong –, at home- in; conversant –, familiar- with.

erudite, instructed, learned, lettered, educated; high-brow; well-conned, -informed, -read, -grounded, -educated; enlightened, shrewd, insightful, *savant*, blue, bookish, scholastic, solid, profound, deep-read, book-learned; accomplished &c. (*skilful*) 698; omniscient; self-taught, -educated.

known &c. *v.*; ascertained, well-known, recognized, received, notorious, noted; proverbial; familiar, – as household words, to every schoolboy; hackneyed, trite, commonplace.

knowable, cogn-oscible, -izable.

Adv. to –, to the best of- one's knowledge.

Phr. one's eyes being opened &c. (*disclosure*) 529.

end of his tether; at fault; at sea &c. (*uncertain*) 475; caught tripping.

un-known, -apprehended, -explained, -ascertained, -investigated, -explored, -heard of, -perceived; concealed &c. 528; novel.

Adv. ignorantly &c. *adj.*; unawares; for -anything, – aught- one knows; not that one knows.

Int. God –, Heaven –, the Lord –, nobody- knows.

Phr. a little learning is a dangerous thing.

---

492. Scholar—N. scholar, *connoisseur*, *savant*, pundit, schoolman, professor, graduate, wrangler, moonshee; academ-ician, -ist; fellow, don, post graduate, advanced student; master –, bachelor- of arts; doctor, licentiate, gownsman; philo-sopher, -math; scientist, clerk; soph, -ist, -ister; linguist, classicist; glosso-, etymo-, philologist; philologer; lexico-, glosso-grapher; scholiast, commentator, annotator, grammarian; *littérateur*, *literati*, *dilettanti*, *illuminati*; Mezzofanti, admirable Crichton, Mæcenas.

book-worm, *helluo librorum*, biblio-phile, -maniac; blue-stocking, *bas-bleu*; big-wig, learned Theban.

learned –, literary- man; *homo multarum literarum*; man of -learning, – letters, – education; high-brow, intelligentsia.

antiquar-ian, -y; archæologist; sage &c. (*wise man*) 500.

pedant, *doctrinaire*; pedagogue, Dr. Pangloss; pantologist.

teacher &c. 540; schoolboy &c. (*learner*) 541.

Adj. learned &c. 490; brought up at the feet of Gamaliel.

493. Ignoramus.—N. ignoramus, illiterate, moron, dunce, numskull; wooden spoon; no scholar.

sciolist, smatterer, dabbler, half-scholar; *charlatan*; wiseacre.

novice, griffin; greenhorn &c. (*dupe*) 547; tyro &c. (*learner*) 541.

lubber &c. (*bungler*) 701; fool &c. 501; pedant &c. 492.

Adj. bookless, shallow, simple, dense, dumb, thick, dull, ignorant &c. 491.

---

494. [Object of knowledge.] **Truth.**
—**N.** fact, reality &c. (*existence*) 1;
plain matter of fact; nature &c. (*principle*) 5; truth, verity; gospel; orthodoxy &c. 983*a*; authenticity; veracity &c. 543.

accuracy, exactitude; exact-, precise-ness &c. *adj.*; precision, delicacy; rigour, mathematical precision, punctuality; clockwork precision &c. (*regularity*) 80.

orthology; *ipsissima verba*; letter of the law, realism.

plain -, honest -, sober -, naked -, unalloyed -, unqualified -, stern -, exact -, intrinsic- truth; *nuda veritas*; the very thing; not an -illusion &c. 495; real Simon Pure; unvarnished tale; the truth, the whole truth and nothing but the truth; just the thing.

V. be -true &c. *adj.*, - the case; stand the test; have the true ring; hold -good, - true, - water; conform to rule.

render -, prove- -true &c. *adj.*; substantiate &c. (*evidence*) 467.

get at the truth &c. (*discover*) 480*a*.

Adj. real, actual &c. (*existing*) 1; veritable, true; certain &c. 474; substantially -, categorically- true &c.; true -to the letter, - to life, - to scale, - the facts, - as gospel; unimpeachable; veracious &c. 543; unre-, uncon-futed; un-ideal, -imagined; realistic.

exact, accurate, definite, precise, well defined, just, right, correct, strict, severe; close &c. (*similar*) 17; literal; rigid, rigorous; scrupulous &c. (*conscientious*) 939; religiously exact, punctual, mathematical, scientific; faithful, constant, unerring; curious, particular, punctilious, meticulous, nice, delicate, fine.

genuine, authentic, legitimate, pukka; orthodox &c. 983*a*; official, *ex officio*.

pure, natural, sound, sterling; unsophisticated, -adulterated, -varnished, -coloured; in its true colours.

well-grounded, -founded; solid, substantial, tangible, valid; undis-torted, -guised; un-affected, -exaggerated, -romantic, -flattering.

Adv. truly &c. *adj.*; verily, indeed, in reality; as a matter of fact; beyond

495. Error.—**N.** error, fallacy; misconception, -apprehension, -understanding; inexactness &c. *adj.*; laxity; misconstruction &c. (*misinterpretation*) 523; miscomputation &c. (*misjudgment*) 481; *non-sequitur* &c. 477; misstatement, -report; anachronism; malapropism.

mistake; miss, fault, blunder, boner, bloomer, howler, *quid pro quo*, cross purposes, oversight, misprint, *erratum, corrigendum*, slip, blot, flaw, loose thread; trip, stumble &c. (*failure*) 732; botchery &c. (*want of skill*) 699; slip of the -tongue, - pen; *lapsus -linguæ, - calami*, clerical error; bull &c. (*absurdity*) 497.

il-, de-lusion; false -impression, - idea; bubble; self-deceit, -deception; warped notion; mists of error; superstition, exploded notion.

heresy &c. (*heterodoxy*) 984; hallucination &c. (*insanity*) 503; false light &c. (*fallacy of vision*) 443; dream &c. (*fancy*) 515; fable &c. (*untruth*) 546; bias &c. (*misjudgment*) 481; misleading &c. *v.*

V. be -erroneous &c. *adj.*

cause error; mis-lead, -guide; lead -astray, - into error; beguile, misinform &c. (*misteach*) 538; delude; give a false -impression, - idea; falsify, garble, misstate; deceive &c. 545; lie &c. 544.

err; be -in error &c. *adj.*, - mistaken &c. *v.*; be deceived &c. (*duped*) 547; mistake, receive a false impression, deceive oneself; fall into -, lie under -, labour under- -an error &c. *n.*; be in the wrong, blunder; mis-apprehend, -conceive, -understand, -reckon, -count, -calculate &c. (*misjudge*) 481.

play -, be- at cross purposes &c. (*misinterpret*) 523.

trip, stumble; lose oneself &c. (*uncertainty*) 475; go astray; fail &c. 732; take the wrong sow by the ear &c. (*mismanage*) 699; put the saddle on the wrong horse; reckon without one's host; take the shadow for the substance &c. (*credulity*) 486; dream &c. (*imagine*) 515.

Adj. erroneous, untrue, false, devoid of truth, fallacious, faulty, apocryphal,

-doubt, – question; with truth &c. (*veracity*) 543; certainly &c. (*certain*) 474; actually &c. (*existence*) 1; in effect &c. (*intrinsically*) 5.

exactly &c. *adj.*; *ad amussim*; *verbatim*, – *et literatim*; word for word, literally, *literatim, totidem verbis, sic*, to the letter, chapter and verse, *ipsissimis verbis*; *ad unguem*; to an inch; to a -nicety, – hair, – tittle, – turn, – T; *au pied de la lettre*; neither more nor less; in -every respect, – all respects; *sous tous les rapports*; at -any rate, – all events; strictly speaking.

Phr. the -truth, – fact- is; *rem acu tetigisti*.

unreal, ungrounded, groundless; unsubstantial &c. 4; heretical &c. (*heterodox*) 984; unsound; illogical &c. 477; wrong.

in-, un-exact; in-accurate, -correct; indefinite &c. (*uncertain*) 475.

illus-ive, -ory; delusive; mock; ideal &c. (*imaginary*) 515; spurious &c. 545; deceitful &c. 544; perverted.

controvertible, unsustain-able, -ed; unauthenticated, untrustworthy.

exploded, refuted, discarded.

in –, under an- error &c. *n.*; mistaken &c. *v.*; tripping &c. *v.*; out, – in one's reckoning; aberrant; beside –, wide of the- -mark, – truth; astray &c. (*at fault*) 475; on -a false, – the wrong-scent; in the wrong box; at cross purposes, all in the wrong, all abroad, at sea.

Adv. more or less.

---

496. Maxim.—N. maxim, aphorism; apo-, apoph-thegm; *dictum*, saying, gnome, adage, saw, proverb, epigram; sentence, *mot*, motto, word, by-word, precept, moral, phylactery, *protasis*, brocard.

axiom, postulate, theorem, *scholium*, truism.

reflection &c. (*idea*) 453; conclusion &c. (*judgment*) 480; golden rule &c. (*precept*) 697; principle, *principia*; profession of faith &c. (*belief*) 484; formula.

wise –, sage –, received –, admitted –, recognized- maxim &c.; true –, common –, hackneyed –, trite –, common-place- saying &c.

Adj. aphoristic, proverbial, phylacteric; axiomatic, gnomic.

Adv. as -the saying is, – they say.

497. Absurdity.—N. absurd-ity, -ness &c. *adj.*; imbecility &c. 499; alogy, nonsense, paradox, inconsistency; stultiloqu-y, -ence, futility.

blunder, muddle, bull; Irish-, Hibernic-ism; slip-slop; anticlimax, bathos; sophism &c. 477.

farce, burlesque, *galimatias, amphigouri*, rhapsody; farrago &c. (*disorder*) 59; extravagance, romance; sciomachy.

joke, catch, sell, pun, verbal quibble, macaronic.

jargon, fustian, twaddle &c. (*no meaning*) 517; exaggeration &c. 549; moonshine, stuff; mare's nest.

vagary, tomfoolery, mummery, monkey trick, practical joke, *boutade, escapade*.

V. play the fool &c. 499; stultify, blunder, muddle; joke; talk nonsense, *parler à tort et à travers*; *battre la campagne*; be -absurd &c. *adj.*

Adj. absurd, nonsensical, preposterous, egregious, senseless, farcical, inconsistent, ridiculous, extravagant, quibbling, futile; macaronic, punning, paradoxical.

foolish &c. 499; sophistical &c. 477; unmeaning &c. 517; without rhyme or reason; fantastic.

Int. fiddle-de-dee! pish! pish and tush! pho! stuff and nonsense! rubbish! rot! bosh! in the name of the Prophet—figs!

Phr. *credat Judæus Apella*; tell it to the marines.

Faculties

498. Intelligence. Wisdom.—N. intelligence, capacity, comprehension,

499. Imbecility. Folly.—N. want of -intelligence &c. 498, – intellect &c.

understanding; intellect &c. 450; nous, parts, sagacity, mother wit, wit, *esprit*, gumption, quick parts, grasp of intellect; acuteness &c. *adj.*; acumen, subtlety, penetration; perspica-cy, -city; discernment, long-headedness, due sense of, good judgment; discrimination &c. 465; craftiness, cunning &c. 702; refinement &c. (*taste*) 850.

head, brains, gray matter, headpiece, upper story, long head; eagle -eye, – glance; eye of a -lynx, – hawk.

wisdom, sapience, sense; good –, common –, plain –, horse- sense; clear thinking; rationality, reason; reasonableness &c. *adj.*; judgment; solidity, depth, profundity, calibre; enlarged views; reach –, compass- of thought; enlargement of mind.

genius, inspiration, *geist*, fire of genius, heaven-born genius, soul; talent &c. (*aptitude*) 698.

[Wisdom in action] prudence &c. 864; vigilance &c. 459; tact &c. 698; foresight &c. 510; sobriety, self-possession, *aplomb*, ballast, mental -poise, – balance.

a bright thought, inspiration, brainwave, not a bad idea.

V. be -intelligent &c. *adj.*; have all one's wits about one; understand &c. (*intelligible*) 518; catch –, take in- an idea; take a -joke, – hint.

see -through, – at a glance, – with half an eye, – far into, – through a millstone; penetrate; discern &c. (*descry*) 441; foresee &c. 510.

discriminate &c. 465; know what's what &c. 698; listen to reason.

Adj. [Applied to persons] intelligent, quick of apprehension, keen, acute, alive, brainy, awake, bright, quick, sharp; quick-, keen-, clear-, sharp--eyed, -sighted, -witted; wide awake; canny, shrewd, astute; clear-headed; far-sighted &c. 510; discerning, perspicacious, penetrating, piercing; argute; nimble-, needle-witted; sharp as a needle; alive to &c. (*cognizant*) 490; clever &c. (*apt*) 698; arch &c. (*cunning*) 702; *pas si bête*; acute &c. 682.

wise, sage, sapient, sagacious, reasonable, rational, sound, in one's right

450; shallow-, silli-, foolish-ness &c. *adj.*; imbecility, incapacity, vacancy of mind, poverty of intellect, clouded perception, poor head, apartments to let; stup-, stol-idity; hebetude, dull understanding, meanest capacity; short-sightedness; incompetence &c. (*unskilfulness*) 699.

one's weak side; bias &c. 481; infatuation &c. (*insanity*) 503.

simplicity, puerility, babyhood; dotage, anility, second childishness, senile dementia, fatuity; idio-cy, -tism; drivelling.

folly, frivolity, desipience, irrationality, trifling, ineptitude, nugacity, inconsistency, lip-wisdom, conceit; sophistry &c. 477; giddiness &c. (*inattention*) 458; eccentricity &c. 503; extravagance &c. (*absurdity*) 497; rashness &c. 863.

act of folly &c. 699.

V. be -imbecile &c. *adj.*; have no -brains, – sense &c. 498.

trifle, drivel, *radoter*, dote; ramble &c. (*madness*) 503; play the -fool, – monkey, – goat, take leave of one's senses; not see an inch beyond one's nose; stultify oneself &c. 699; talk nonsense &c. 497.

Adj. [Applied to persons] un-intelligent, -intellectual, -reasoning; mind-, wit-, reason-, brain-less; having no -head &c. 498; not -bright &c. 498; inapprehensible.

weak-, addle-, puzzle-, blunder-, muddle-, muddy-, pig-, beetle-, maggoty-, gross-headed; beef-, fat- -witted, -headed.

weak-, feeble-minded; dull-, shallow-, rattle-, lack-brained; half-, nit-, short-, dull-, blunt-witted; shallow-, clod-, addle-pated; dim-, short-sighted; thick-skulled; weak in the upper story.

shallow, *borné*, weak, wanting, soft, nutty, sappy, spoony; dull, – as a beetle; stupid, heavy, insulse, obtuse, blunt, stolid, doltish, asinine; inapt &c. 699; prosaic &c. 843.

child-ish, -like; infant-ine, -ile; baby-, bab-ish; puerile, anile; simple &c. (*credulous*) 486.

fatuous, idiotic, imbecile, moronic,

mind, sensible, *abnormis sapiens*, judicious, strong-minded.

un-prejudiced, -biassed, -bigoted, -prepossessed; un-dazzled, -perplexed; of unwarped judgment, impartial, equitable, fair, broad-minded.

cool; cool-, long-, hard-, strong-headed; long-sighted, calculating, thoughtful, reflecting; solid, deep, profound.

oracular; heaven-directed, -born.

prudent &c. (*cautious*) 864; sober, staid, solid; considerate, politic, wise in one's generation; watchful &c. 459; provident &c. (*prepared*) 673; in advance of one's age; wise as -a serpent, – Solomon, – Solon.

[Applied to actions] wise, sensible, reasonable, judicious; well-judged, -advised; prudent, politic; expedient &c. 646.

---

drivelling; blatant, babbling; vacant; sottish; bewildered &c. 475.

blockish, unteachable; Bœot-ian, -ic; bovine; un-gifted, -discerning, -enlightened, -wise, -philosophical; apish.

foolish, silly, senseless, irrational, insensate, nonsensical, inept; maudlin.

narrow-minded &c. 481; bigoted &c. (*obstinate*) 606; giddy &c. (*thoughtless*) 458; rash &c. 863; eccentric &c. (*crazed*) 503.

[Applied to actions] foolish, unwise, indiscreet, injudicious, improper, unreasonable, without reason, ridiculous, silly, stupid, asinine; ill-imagined, -advised, -judged, -devised; inconsistent, irrational, unphilosophical; extravagant &c. (*nonsensical*) 497; sleeveless, idle; useless &c. 645; inexpedient &c. 647; frivolous &c. (*trivial*) 643; absurd &c. 497.

Phr. *Davis sum non Œdipus.*

---

500. Sage.—N. sage, wise man; pundit; master -mind, – spirit of the age; longhead, thinker, philosopher.

authority, oracle, mentor, luminary, shining light, *esprit fort, magnus Apollo*, Solon, Solomon, Nestor, Magi, 'second Daniel.'

man of learning &c. 492; expert &c. 700; wizard &c. 994.

[Ironically] wiseacre, bigwig.

Adj. wise, learned; authoritative, oracular; erudite &c. 490; venerable, reverenced, revered, *emeritus*.

---

501. Fool.—N. fool, idiot, tomfool, wiseacre, simpleton, Simple Simon, nit-wit, witling, dizzard, donkey, ass; ninny, -hammer; moron, dolt, booby, Tom Noddy, looby, hoddy-doddy, noddy, nonny, noodle, nizy, owl; goose, -cap; *imbécile*; gaby, *radoteur*, nincompoop, *badaud*, zany; trifler, babbler; pretty fellow; natural, *niais*.

child, baby, infant, innocent, milksop, sop.

oaf, lout, loon, lown, dullard, doodle, calf, colt, buzzard, block, put, stick, stock, numps, tony.

bull-, dunder-, addle-, block-, dull-, logger-, jolt-, jolter-, beetle-, gross-, thick-, giddy-head; num-, thick-skull; lack-, shallow-brain; half-, lack-wit; dunder-pate; fat-head, poor stick.

sawney, gowk; clod, -hopper; clod-, clot-poll, -pate; bull-calf; men of Bœotia, wise men of Gotham.

un sot à triple étage, sot; jobbernowl, changeling, mooncalf, *gobemouche*.

dotard, driveller; old -fogey, – woman; crone, grandmother.

greenhorn &c. (*dupe*) 547; dunce &c. (*ignoramus*) 493; lubber &c. (*bungler*) 701; madman &c. 504.

one who -will not set the Thames on fire, – did not invent gunpowder; *qui n'a pas inventé la poudre*; no conjuror.

---

502. Sanity.—N. sanity; soundness &c. *adj.*; rationality, normality, sobriety, lucidity, lucid interval; senses, sober senses, sound mind, *mens sana*.

---

503. Insanity.—N. disordered -reason, – intellect; diseased –, unsound –, abnormal- mind; derangement, unsoundness.

V. be -sane &c. *adj.*; retain one's senses, – reason.

become -sane &c. *adj.*; come to one's senses, sober down.

render -sane &c. *adj.*; bring to one's senses, sober.

Adj. sane, rational, reasonable, *compos mentis*, of sound mind; sound, -minded.

self-possessed; sober, -minded.

in one's -sober senses, – right mind; in possession of one's faculties.

Adv. sanely &c. *adj.*

---

insanity, lunacy; madness &c. *adj.*; mania, *rabies*, *furor*, mental alienation, paranoia, aberration; *amentia*, dementation, -tia, -cy; *dementia præcox*; *morosis*, idiocy, phrenitis, frenzy, raving, incoherence, wandering, delirium, calenture of the brain, delusion, hallucination; lycanthropy, brain storm, *delirium tremens*, D.T.'s.

vertigo, dizziness, swimming; sunstroke, *coup de soleil*, siriasis.

fanaticism, infatuation, craze; oddity, eccentricity, twist, monomania; klepto-, dipso-mania; hypochondriasis &c. (*low spirits*) 837; *melancholia*, hysteria.

screw –, tile –, slate- loose; bee in one's bonnet, rats in the upper story.

dotage &c. (*imbecility*) 499.

V. be –, become- -insane &c. *adj.*; lose one's senses, – reason, – faculties, – wits; go –, run- mad, run amuck; rave, dote, ramble, wander; drivel &c. (*be imbecile*) 499; have a -screw loose &c. *n.*, – devil; *avoir le diable au corps*; lose one's head &c. (*be uncertain*) 475.

derange, render –, drive- -mad &c. *adj.*; madden, dementate, addle the wits, derange the head, infatuate, befool; turn -the brain, – one's head.

Adj. insane, mad, lunatic; crazy, crazed, *aliéné, non compos mentis*; not right, cracked, touched; bereft of reason; unhinged, deranged, unsettled in one's mind; insensate, reasonless, beside oneself, demented, daft; phren-, fren-zied, -etic; possessed, – with a devil; far gone, maddened, moonstruck; shatterpated; barmy; mad-, scatter-, shatter-, crack-brained; off one's head; bug-house, *loco*.

maniacal; manic, manic-depressive; delirious, light-headed, incoherent, rambling, doting, wandering; frantic, raving, stark staring mad, amok, amuck.

corybantic, dithyrambic; rabid, giddy, vertiginous, dizzy, wild, haggard, mazed; flighty; distr-acted, -aught; bewildered &c. (*uncertain*) 475.

mad as a -March hare, – hatter; of -unsound mind &c. *n.*; touched –, wrong –, not right- in one's -head, – mind, – wits, – upper story; out of one's -mind, – senses, – wits; not in one's right mind.

fanatical, infatuated, odd, eccentric; hypp-ed, -ish.

imbecile, silly &c. 499.

Adv. like one possessed.

Phr. the mind having lost its balance; the reason under a cloud; *tête -exaltée, -montée.*

---

504. Madman.—N. madman, lunatic, maniac, bedlamite, candidate for Bedlam, raver, madcap; energumen; paranoiac; auto-, mono-, pyro-, megalo-, dipso-, klepto-maniac; hypochondriac &c. (*low spirits*) 837.

dreamer &c. 515; rhapsodist, seer, high-flier, enthusiast, crank, eccentric, nut, fanatic, *fanatico*; *exalté*; knight errant, Don Quixote.

idiot &c. 501.

Section VI. Extension of Thought

1°. *To the Past*

505. Memory.—**N.** memory, remembrance; reten-tion, -tiveness; tenacity; *veteris vestigia flammæ*; tablets of the memory; readiness.

reminiscence, recognition, recurrence, recollection, rememoration; retrospect, -ion; after-thought.

suggestion &c. (*information*) 527; prompting &c. *v.*; hint, reminder, token of remembrance, *memento*, *souvenir*, keepsake, relic, *memorandum*; remembrancer, flapper; memorial &c. (*record*) 551; commemoration &c. (*celebration*) 883.

things to be remembered, *memorabilia*.

art of –, artificial- memory; *memoria technica*; mnemo-nics, -technics; phrenotypics; Mnemosyne; memorandum-, note-, engagement-, prompt-book.

retentive –, tenacious –, green –, trustworthy –, capacious –, faithful –, correct –, exact –, ready –, prompt-memory.

V. remember, mind; retain the -memory, – remembrance- of; keep in view.

have –, hold –, bear –, carry –, keep –, retain- in *or* in the -thoughts, – mind, – memory, – remembrance; be in –, live in –, remain in –, dwell in –, haunt –, impress- one's -memory, – thoughts, – mind.

sink in the mind; run in the head; not be able to get it out of one's head; be deeply impressed with; rankle &c. (*revenge*) 919.

506. Oblivion.—**N.** oblivion; forgetfulness &c. *adj.*; obliteration &c. 552, of –, insensibility &c. 823 to- the past.

short –, treacherous –, loose –, slippery –, failing- memory; decay –, failure –, lapse- of memory; memory like a sieve; waters of -Lethe, – oblivion, *amnesia*.

pardon, acquittal, amnesty, oblivion; absolution.

V. forget; be -forgetful &c. *adj.*; fall –, sink- into oblivion; have -a short memory &c. *n.*, – no head.

forget one's own name, have on the tip of one's tongue, come in at one ear and go out at the other.

slip –, escape –, fade from –, die away from- the memory; lose, – sight of.

unlearn; efface &c. 552 –, discharge- from the memory; consign to -oblivion, – the tomb of the Capulets; think no more of &c. (*turn the attention from*) 458; cast behind one's back, wean one's thoughts from; let bygones be bygones &c. (*forgive*) 918.

Adj. forgotten &c. *v.*; unremembered, past recollection, bygone, out of mind; buried –, sunk- in oblivion; clean forgotten; gone out of one's -head, – recollection.

forgetful, oblivious, mindless, heedless, Lethean; insensible &c. 823- to the past.

Phr. *non mi ricordo*; the memory -failing, – deserting one, – being at (*or* in) fault.

---

recur to the mind; flash -on the mind, – across the memory.

recognize, recollect, bethink oneself, recall, call up, conjure up, retrace; look –, trace- -back, – backwards; think –, look back- upon; review; call –, recall –, bring- to mind; remembrance; carry one's thoughts back; rake up the past.

suggest &c. (*inform*) 527; prompt; put –, keep- in mind; remind; fan the embers; call –, summon –, rip- up; renew; *infandum renovare dolorem*; task –, tax –, jog –, flap –, refresh –, rub up –, awaken- the memory; pull by the sleeve; bring back to the memory, put in remembrance, memorialize.

get –, have –, learn –, know –, say –, repeat- by -heart – rote; drive –, get- into -one's head; say one's lesson; repeat, – as a parrot; have at one's fingers' ends.

commit to memory; memorize; con, – over; fix –, rivet –, imprint –, impress –, stamp –, grave –, engrave –, store –, treasure up –, bottle up –, embalm –, enshrine- in the memory; load –, store –, stuff –, burden- the memory with.

redeem from oblivion; keep the memory -alive, – green; *tangere ulcus*; keep up the memory of; commemorate &c. (*celebrate*) 883.

make a note of &c. (*record*) 551.

Adj. remember-ing, -ed &c. *v.*; mindful, reminiscential; retained in the memory &c. *v.*; pent up in one's memory; fresh; green, – in remembrance, still vivid; unforgotten, present to the mind; within one's -memory &c. *n.*; indelible; not to be forgotten, unforgettable, enduring; uppermost in one's thoughts; memorable &c. (*important*) 642.

Adv. by -heart, – rote; without book, *memoriter*.

in memory of; *in memoriam*; suggestive.

Phr. *manet altâ mente repostum*; *forsan et hæc olim meminisse juvabit.*

2°. *To the Future*

507. Expectation.—N. expect-ation, -ance, -ancy; anticipation, reckoning, calculation; contingency; foresight &c. 510.

contemplation, prospection, look out; prospect, perspective, horizon, vista; destiny &c. 152.

suspense, waiting, abeyance: curiosity &c. 455; anxious –, ardent –, eager –, breathless –, sanguine- expectation; torment of Tantalus.

presumption, hope &c. 858; trust &c. (*belief*) 484; prognostication, auspices &c. (*prediction*) 511.

V. expect; look -for, – out for, – forward to; hope for, anticipate; have in -prospect, – contemplation; keep in view; contemplate, promise oneself; not -wonder &c. 870 -at, – if.

wait –, tarry –, lie in wait –, watch –, bargain- for; keep a -good, – sharp- look-out for; await; stand at 'attention,' abide, bide one's –, mark- time, watch.

foresee &c. 510; prepare for &c. 673; forestall &c. (*be early*) 132; count upon &c. (*believe in*) 484; think likely &c. (*probability*) 472; make one's mouth water.

lead one to expect &c. (*predict*) 511; have in store for &c. (*destiny*) 152.

prick up one's ears, hold one's breath.

Adj. expectant; expecting &c. *v.*; in -expectation &c. *n.*; on the watch &c. (*vigilant*) 459; open -eyed, -mouthed;

508. Inexpectation.—N. in-, non-expectation; false expectation &c. (*disappointment*) 509; miscalculation &c. 481; unforeseen contingency, the unforeseen, the unexpected.

surprise, sudden burst, thunderclap, blow, shock; bolt out of the blue; eye-opener; wonder &c. 870.

V. not -expect &c. 507; be taken by surprise; start; miscalculate &c. 481; not bargain for; come –, fall- upon.

be -unexpected &c. *adj.*; come -unawares &c. *adv.*; turn up, pop, drop from the clouds; come –, burst –, flash –, bounce –, steal –, creep- upon one; come –, burst- like a thunderclap, -bolt; take –, catch- -by surprise, – unawares, – napping.

pounce –, spring a mine- upon.

surprise, startle, take aback, electrify, stun, stagger, take away one's breath, throw off one's guard; astonish &c. (*strike with wonder*) 870.

Adj. non-expectant; surprised &c. *v.*; un-warned, -aware; off one's guard; inattentive &c. 458.

un-expected, -anticipated, -prepared for, -looked for, -foreseen, -hoped for; dropped from the clouds; beyond –, contrary to –, against- expectation; out of one's reckoning; unheard of &c. (*exceptional*) 83; startling; sudden &c. (*instantaneous*) 113.

Adv. abruptly, unexpectedly, plump, pop, *à l'improviste*, unawares; without

agape, gaping, all agog; on -tenter-
hooks, – tiptoe, – the tiptoe of expectation; *aux aguets*; ready; curious &c.
455; looking forward to; prepared for;
on the rack.

expected &c. *v.*; long expected, foreseen; in prospect &c. *n.*; prospective;
in -one's eye, – view, – the horizon;
impending &c. (*destiny*) 152.

Adv. expectantly; in the event of; on the watch &c. *adj.*; with
-breathless expectation &c. *n.*, – bated breath, – eyes, – ears strained;
arrectis auribus; on edge.

Phr. we shall see; *nous verrons*.

-notice, – warning, – saying 'by your
leave'; like a -thief in the night, –
thunderbolt; in an unguarded moment;
suddenly &c. (*instantaneously*) 113.

Int. heyday! &c. (*wonder*) 870.

Phr. little did one -think, – expect;
nobody would ever -suppose, – think,
– expect; who would have thought?

---

509. [Failure of expectation.] **Disappointment.—N.** disappointment,
disillusionment; blighted hope, balk; blow; slip 'twixt cup and lip;
non-fulfilment of one's hopes; sad -, bitter- disappointment; trick of
fortune; afterclap; false -, vain- expectation; miscalculation &c. 481;
fool's paradise; much cry and little wool.

V. be disappointed; look -blank, – blue; look -, stand- -aghast &c.
(*wonder*) 870; find to one's cost; laugh on the wrong side of one's
mouth; find one a false prophet.

disappoint; crush -, dash -, balk -, disappoint -, blight -, falsify -,
defeat -, not realize- one's -hope, – expectation; balk, jilt, bilk; play one
-false, – a trick; dash the cup from the lips; tantalize; dumb-found,
-founder; disillusion, -ize; dissatisfy, disgruntle.

Adj. disappointed &c. *v.*; disconcerted, aghast; out of one's reckoning; disgruntled.

Phr. the mountain brought forth a mouse; *nascitur ridiculus mus*;
parturiunt montes; *diis aliter visum*, the bubble burst; one's countenance
falling.

510. Foresight.—N. foresight, prospicience, prevision, longsighted-
ness; anticipation; providence &c. (*preparation*) 673.

fore-thought, -cast; pre-deliberation, -surmise; foregone conclusion
&c. (*prejudgment*) 481; prudence &c. (*caution*) 864.

foreknowledge; *prognosis*; pre-cognition, -science, -notion, -sentiment;
second sight; sagacity &c. (*intelligence*) 498.

prospect &c. (*expectation*) 507; foretaste; prospectus &c. (*plan*) 626.

V. foresee; look -forwards to, – ahead, – beyond; scent from afar;
feel in one's bones; look -, pry -, peep- into the future.

see one's way; see how the -land lies, – wind blows, – cat jumps.

anticipate; expect &c. 507; be beforehand &c. (*early*) 132; predict
&c. 511; fore-know, -judge, -cast; surmise; have an eye to the -future,
– main chance; *respicere finem*; keep a sharp look-out &c. (*vigilance*)
459; forewarn &c. 668.

Adj. foreseeing &c. *v.*; prescient; anticipatory; far-seeing, -sighted;
sagacious &c. (*intelligent*) 498; weather-wise; provident &c. (*prepared*)
673; prospective &c. 507.

Adv. against the time when.

511. Prediction.—N. prediction, announcement; program, programme
&c. (*plan*) 626; premonition &c. (*warning*) 668; *prognosis*, prophecy,
vaticination, Mantology, prognostication, premonstration, augur-y,
-ation; a-, ha-riolation; fore-, a-boding; bode-, abode-ment; omin-ation,

-ousness; auspices, forecast; sign, presage, prognostic; omen &c. 512; horoscope, nativity; sooth, -saying; fortune-telling; divination; crystal gazing, necromancy &c. 992; prophet &c. 512.

[Divination by the stars] astrology, horoscopy, astromancy, judicial astrology.*

[Place of prediction] *adytum.*

prefigur-ation, -ement; prototype, type.

V. predict, prognosticate, prophesy, vaticinate, divine, foretell, sooth-say, augurate, tell fortunes; cast a -horoscope, – nativity; advise; forewarn &c. 668.

presage, augur, bode; a-, fore-bode, -cast; fore-, be-token; pre-figure, -show; portend; fore-show, -shadow, shadow forth, typify, ominate, signify, point to, precurse.

usher in, herald, premise, announce; lower.

hold out –, raise –, excite- -expectation, – hope; bid fair, promise, lead one to expect; be the -precursor &c. 64.

Adj. predicting &c. *v.*; predictive, prophetic, fatidical, vaticinal, oracular, Sibylline, haruspical, weatherwise.

ominous, presageful, portentous; augur-ous, -al, -ial; auspici-al, -ous; prescious, monitory, extispicious, premonitory, precusory, significant of, pregnant with, big with the fate of.

Phr. 'coming events cast their shadows before.'

512. Omen.—N. omen, portent, presage, prognostic, augury, auspice; sign &c. (*indication*) 550; herald, forerunner, harbinger &c. (*precursor*) 64.

bird of ill omen; signs of the times; gathering clouds; warning &c. 668.

prefigurement &c. 511.

513. Oracle.—N. oracle; prophet, -ess; seer, soothsayer, augur, fortune-teller, palmist, medium, clairvoyant, crystal gazer, witch, geomancer, *aruspex*; a-, ha-ruspice; Sibyl; Python, -ess; Pythia; Pythian –, Delphian- oracle; Monitor, Sphinx, Tiresias, Cassandra, Sibylline leaves; Zadkiel, Old Moore; sorcerer &c. 994; interpreter &c. 524.

Section VII. Creative Thought

514. Supposition.—N. supposition, assumption, postulation, condi-tion, pre-supposition, hypothesis, postulate, *postulatum,* theory, *data*; pro-, position; *thesis,* theorem; proposal &c. (*plan*) 626.

* The following terms, expressive of different forms of divination, have been col-lected from various sources, and are here given as a curious illustration of bygone superstitions:

Divination *by oracles,* Theomancy; *by the Bible,* Bibliomancy; *by ghosts,* Psycho-mancy; *by spirits seen in a magic lens,* Cristallomantia; *by shadows or manes,* Scio-mancy; *by appearances in the air,* Aeromancy, Chaomancy; *by the stars at birth,* Genethliacs; *by meteors,* Meteoromancy; *by winds,* Austromancy; *by sacrificial ap-pearances,* Aruspicy (*or* Haruspicy), Hieromancy, Hieroscopy; *by the entrails of animals sacrificed,* Hieromancy; *by the entrails of a human sacrifice,* Anthropomancy; *by the entrails of fishes,* Ichthyomancy; *by sacrificial fire,* Pyromancy; *by red-hot iron,* Sidero-mancy; *by smoke from the altar,* Capnomancy; *by mice,* Myomancy; *by birds,* Orniscopy, Ornithomancy; *by a cock picking up grains,* Alectryomancy (*or* Alectoromancy); *by fishes,* Ophiomancy; *by herbs,* Botanomancy; *by water,* Hydromancy; *by fountains*

bare –, vague –, loose- -supposition, – suggestion; conceit; conjecture; guess, – work; rough guess, shot; conjecturality; surmise, suspicion, inkling, suggestion, suggestiveness, association of ideas, hint; presumption &c. (*belief*) 484; divination, speculation.

theorist, speculator, doctrinarian, hypothesist.

V. suppose, conjecture, surmise, suspect, guess, divine; theorize; pre-sume, -surmise, -suppose; assume, fancy, wis, take it; give a guess, speculate, believe, dare say, take it into one's head, take for granted.

put forth; pro-pound, -pose; moot; hypothesize; start, put a case, submit, move, make a motion; hazard –, throw out –, put forward- a - suggestion, – conjecture.

allude to, suggest, hint, put it into one's head.

suggest itself &c. (*thought*) 451; run in the head &c. (*memory*) 505; marvel –, wonder- -if, – whether.

Adj. supposing &c. *v.*; given, mooted, postulatory; assumed &c. *v.* supposit-ive, -itious; gratuitous, speculative, conjectural, hypothetical, suppositional, theoretical, academic, supposable, presumptive, putative.

suggestive, allusive, stimulating.

Adv. if, – so be; an; on the -supposition &c. *n.*; *ex hypothesi*; in -case, – the event of; *quasi*, as if, provided; perhaps &c. (*by possibility*) 470; for aught one knows.

515. Imagination.—N. imagination; originality; invention; fancy; inspiration; *verve*; empathy.

warm –, heated –, excited –, sanguine –, ardent –, fiery –, boiling –, wild –, bold –, daring –, playful –, lively –, fertile- -imagination, – fancy. 'mind's eye'; 'such stuff as dreams are made of.'

ideal-ity, -ism; romanticism, utopianism, castle-building; dreaming; frenzy; ecs-, ex-tasy; calenture &c. (*delirium*) 503; reverie, brown study, trance; somnambulism.

conception, *vorstellung*, excogitation, 'a fine frenzy,' poetic frenzy, divine afflatus; cloud-, dream-land; flight –, fumes- of fancy; 'thick-coming fancies'; creation –, coinage- of the brain; imagery, word painting.

conceit, maggot, figment, myth, dream, vision, shadow, chimera; phan-tasm, -tasy; fantasy, fancy; whim, -sey; vagary, rhapsody, romance, *extravaganza*; air-drawn dagger, bugbear, nightmare; flying Dutchman, great sea-serpent, man in the moon, castle in the air, *château en Espagne*; Utopia, Atlantis, happy valley, millennium, fairy land; land of Prester John, kingdom of Micomicon; work of fiction &c. (*novel*) 594; poetry &c. 597; drama &c. 599; Arabian nights; *le pot au lait*; dream of Alnaschar &c. (*hope*) 858; day –, golden- dream.

illusion &c. (*error*) 495; phantom &c. (*fallacy of vision*) 443; *Fata*

Pegomancy; *by a wand*, Rhabdomancy; *by dough of cakes*, Crithomancy; *by meal*, Aleuromancy, Alphitomancy; *by salt*, Halomancy; *by dice*, Cleromancy; *by arrows*, Belomancy; *by a balanced hatchet*, Axinomancy; *by a balanced sieve*, Coscinomancy; *by a suspended ring*, Dactyliomancy; *by dots made at random on paper*, Geomancy; *by precious stones*, Lithomancy; *by pebbles*, Pessomancy; *by pebbles drawn from a heap*, Psephomancy; *by mirrors*, Catoptromancy; *by writings in ashes*, Tephramancy; *by dreams*, Oneiromancy; *by the hand*, Palmistry, Chiromancy; *by nails reflecting the sun's rays*, Onychomancy; *by finger rings*, Dactylomancy; *by numbers*, Arithmancy; *by drawing lots*, Sortilege; *by passages in books*, Stichomancy; *by the letters forming the name of the person*, Onomancy, Nomancy; *by the features*, Anthroposcopy; *by the mode of laughing*, Geloscopy; *by ventriloquism*, Gastromancy; *by walking in a circle*, Gyromancy; *by dropping melted wax into water*, Ceromancy; *by currents*, Bletonism.

Morgana &c. (*ignis fatuus*) 423; vapour &c. (*cloud*) 353; stretch of the imagination &c. (*exaggeration*) 549.

idealist, romanticist, visionary; mopus; romancer, dreamer; somnambulist; rhapsodist &c. (*fanatic*) 504.

V. imagine, fancy, conceive; ideal-, real-ize; dream, – of; 'give to airy nothing a local habitation and a name.'

create, originate, devise, invent, coin, fabricate; improvise, strike out something new.

set one's wits to work; strain –, crack- one's invention; rack –, ransack –, cudgel- one's brains; excogitate.

give -play, – the reins, – a loose- to the -imagination, – fancy; empathize; indulge in reverie.

conjure up a vision; fancy –, represent –, picture –, figure- to oneself; envisage.

float in the mind; suggest itself &c. (*thought*) 451.

Adj. imagined &c. *v.*; *ben trovato*; air-drawn, -built.

imagin-ing &c. *v.*, -ative; original, inventive, creative, fertile, productive; ingenious.

romantic, high-flown, flighty, extravagant, fanatic, enthusiastic, Utopian, Quixotic; preposterous, rhapsodical.

ideal, unreal; in the clouds, *in nubibus*; unsubstantial &c. 4; illusory &c. (*fallacious*) 495; fictitious, theoretical, hypothetical.

fabulous, legendary; myth-ic, -ological; chimerical; imagin-, visionary; notional; fan-cy, -ciful, -tastic, -tastical; whimsical; fairy, -like.

dreamy, entranced, vaporous.

Division (II.) COMMUNICATION OF IDEAS
Section I. Nature of Ideas Communicated

516. [Idea to be conveyed.] **Meaning.** [Thing signified.]—**N.** meaning; signific-ation, -ance; sense, expression; im-, pur-port; drift, tenor, implication, connotation, essence, force, spirit bearing, colouring; scope.

matter; subject, -matter; argument, text, sum and substance; gist &c. 5.

general –, broad –, substantial –, colloquial –, literal –, plain –, simple –, accepted –, natural –, unstrained –, true &c. (*exact*) 494 –, honest &c. 543 –, *primâ facie* &c. (*manifest*) 525- meaning.

literality; literal interpretation; after acceptation; allusion &c. (*latency*) 526; suggestion &c. (*information*) 527; synonym; figure of speech &c. 521; acceptation &c. (*interpretation*) 522.

V. mean, signify, express, connote, denote; im-, pur-port; convey, imply, breathe, indicate, bespeak, bear a sense; tell –, speak- of; touch on; point –, allude- to; drive at; involve &c. (*latency*) 526; declare &c. (*affirm*) 535.

517. [Absence of meaning.] **Unmeaningness.**—**N.** unmeaningness &c. *adj.*; scrabble, scribble, scrawl, daub, (*painting*), strumming (*music*).

empty sound, dead letter, *vox et præterea nihil*; 'a tale told by an idiot, full of sound and fury, signifying nothing'; 'sounding brass and a tinkling cymbal.'

nonsense, jargon, gibberish, jabber, mere words, hocus-pocus, fustian, rant, bombast, balderdash, palaver, patter, flummery, *verbiage*, babble, *bavardage*, *baragouin*, platitude, *niaiserie*; inanity; rigmarole, rodomontade; truism; *nugæ canoræ*; twaddle, twattle, fudge, trash; stuff, – and nonsense; bosh, rubbish, rot, drivel, moonshine, wish-wash, fiddle-faddle, flapdoodle; absurdity &c. 497; vagueness &c. (*unintelligibility*) 519.

V. mean nothing; be -unmeaning &c. *adj.*; twaddle, quibble, rant, gabble, scrabble &c. *n.*

Adj. unmeaning; meaning-, sense-less;

understand by &c. (*interpret*) 522.

Adj. meaning &c. *v.*; expressive, suggestive, meaningful, allusive; signific-ant, -ative, -atory; pithy; full of –, pregnant with- meaning.

declaratory &c. 535; intelligible &c. 518; literal, metaphrastic; synonymous; tantamount &c. (*equivalent*) 27; implied &c. (*latent*) 526; explicit &c. 525; literal &c. 562.

Adv. to that effect; that is to say &c. (*being interpreted*) 522.

literally; evidently, from the context.

518. Intelligibility.—N. intelligibility, clearness, clarity, explicitness &c. *adj.*; lucidity, perspicuity; legibility, plain speaking &c. (*manifestation*) 525; precision &c. 494; a word to the wise.

V. be -intelligible &c. *adj.*; speak -for itself, – volumes; tell its own tale, lie on the surface.

render -intelligible &c. *adj.*; popularize, simplify, clear up; elucidate &c. (*explain*) 522.

understand, comprehend; take, – in; catch, grasp, recognize, follow, collect, master, make out; see -with half an eye, – daylight, – one's way; enter into the ideas of; come to an understanding.

Adj. intelligible; clear, – as -day, – crystal, – noonday; lucid; per-, transpicuous; luminous, transparent; comprehensible.

easily understood, easy to understand, for the million, intelligible to the meanest capacity, popularized.

plain, distinct, explicit, clear-cut; positive; definite &c. (*precise*) 494.

graphic, vivid, telling; expressive &c. (*meaning*) 516; illustrative &c. (*explanatory*) 522.

un-ambiguous, -equivocal, -mistakable &c. (*manifest*) 525, -confused; legible, recognizable; obvious &c. 525.

Adv. in plain -terms, – words, – English.

Phr. he that runs may read &c. (*manifest*) 525.

---

nonsensical; void of -sense &c. 516.

in-, un-expressive; vacant, fatuous; not significant; insignificant.

trashy, washy, inane, vague, trumpery, trivial, fiddle-faddle, twaddling, quibbling.

unmeant, not expressed; tacit &c. (*latent*) 526.

inexpressible, undefinable, incommunicable.

Int. rubbish! &c. 497.

---

519. Unintelligibility.—N. unintelligibility, incomprehensibility, imperspicuity; inconceivableness, vagueness &c. *adj.*; obscurity; ambiguity &c. 520; doubtful meaning; uncertainty &c. 475; perplexity &c. (*confusion*) 59; spinosity; *obscurum per obscurius*; mystification &c. (*concealment*) 528; latency &c. 526; transcendentalism.

paradox; enigma, riddle &c. (*secret*) 533; *dignus vindice nodus*; sealed book; steganography, freemasonry.

pons asinorum, asses' bridge; double –, high- Dutch, Greek, Hebrew; jargon &c. (*unmeaning*) 517.

obscurantist.

V. be -unintelligible &c. *adj.*; require -explanation &c. 522; have a doubtful meaning, pass comprehension.

render -unintelligible &c. *adj.*; conceal &c. 528; darken &c. 421; confuse &c. (*derange*) 61; perplex &c. (*bewilder*) 475.

not -understand &c. 518; lose, – the clue; miss; not know what to make of, be able to make nothing of, give it up; not be able to -account for, – make either head or tail of; be at sea &c. (*uncertain*) 475; wonder &c. 870; see through a glass darkly &c. (*ignorance*) 491.

not understand one another; play at cross purposes &c. (*misinterpret*) 523.

Adj. un-intelligible, -accountable, -decipherable, -discoverable, -knowable, -fathomable; in-cognizable, -explicable, -scrutable; inap-, incomprehensible; insol-vable, -uble; impenetrable.

illegible, indecipherable, as Greek to one, unexplained, paradoxical; enigmatic, -al; puzzling, baffling.

obscure, dark, muddy, clear as mud, seen through a mist, dim, nebulous, shrouded in mystery; undiscernible &c. (*invisible*) 447; misty &c. (*opaque*) 426; hidden &c. 528; latent &c. 526.

indefinite &c. (*indistinct*) 447; perplexed &c. (*confused*) 59; undetermined, vague, loose, ambiguous; mysterious; mystic, -al; transcendental; occult, recondite, esoteric, abstruse, crabbed.

incon-ceivable, -ceptible; searchless; above –, beyond –, past-comprehension; beyond one's depth; unconceived.

inexpressible, undefinable, incommunicable, unutterable, ineffable, unpronounceable.

520. [Having a double sense.] **Equivocalness.—N.** equivocalness &c. *adj.*; double -meaning &c. 516; ambiguity, *double entendre*, pun, para-gram, *calembour*, quibble, *équivoque*, anagram; conundrum &c. (*riddle*) 533; word-play &c. (*wit*) 842; homonym, -y; amphibo-ly, -logy; ambiloquy.

Sphinx, Delphic oracle.

equivocation &c. (*duplicity*) 544; white lie, mental reservation &c. (*concealment*) 528.

V. be -equivocal &c. *adj.*; have two -meanings &c. 516; equivocate &c. (*palter*) 544.

Adj. equivocal, ambiguous, amphibolous, homonymous; double-tongued &c. (*lying*) 544.

521. Metaphor.—N. figure of speech; *façon de parler*, way of speaking, colloquialism.

phrase &c. 566; figure, trope, metaphor, tralatition, metonymy, enallage, *catachresis, synecdoche, autonomasia*; irony, satire, figurative-ness &c. *adj.*; image, -ry; *metalepsis*, type, anagoge, simile, personifica-tion, *prosopopœia*, allegory, apologue, parable, fable; allusion, adum-bration; application; euphemism; euphuism.

V. employ -metaphor &c. *n.*; personify, allegorize, adumbrate, shadow forth, apply, allude –, refer- to.

Adj. metaphorical &c. *n.*; figurative, catachrestical, typical, tralati-tious, parabolic, allegorical, allusive, anagogical; ironical; colloquial.

Adv. so to -speak, – say, – express oneself; as it were.

Phr. *mutato nomine de te fabula narratur.*

522. Interpretation.—N. interpreta-tion, definition; explan-, explic-ation; solution, answer; rationale; plain –, simple –, strict- interpretation; mean-ing &c. 516.

translation; rend-ering, -ition; red-dition; literal –, free- translation; key, crib; secret; clew &c. (*indication*) 550; Rosetta stone.

exegesis; ex-pounding, -position; Hermeneutics; comment, -ary; infer-ence &c. (*deduction*) 480; illustration, exemplification; gloss, annotation, *scholium*, note; e-, di-lucidation, enucle-ation; *éclaircissement, mot de l'énigme.*

symptomat-, semei-ology; metopo-scopy, physiognomy; diagnosis, prog-

523. Misinterpretation. — N. mis-interpretation, -apprehension, -under-standing, -acceptation, -construction, -application; *catachresis*; cross -read-ing, – purposes; mistake &c. 495.

misrepresentation, perversion, exag-geration &c. 549; false -colouring, – construction; abuse of terms; parody, travesty; falsification &c. (*lying*) 544.

V. mis-interpret, -apprehend, -under-stand, -conceive, -judge, -doubt, -spell, -translate, -construe, -apply; mistake &c. 495.

misrepresent, pervert; garble &c. (*falsify*) 544; distort, detort; travesty, play upon words; stretch –, strain –, wrest- the -sense, – meaning; explain

nosis; paleography &c. (*philology*) 560.

accept-ion, -ation, -ance; light, reading, lection, construction, version.

equivalent, – meaning &c. 516; synonym; para-, meta-phrase; convertible terms, apposition; dictionary &c. 562; polyglot.

V. interpret, explain, define, construe, translate, render; do –, turn-into; transfuse the sense of.

find out &c. 480a- -the meaning &c. 516- of; read; spell –, figure –, make- out; decipher, decode, unravel, disentangle, puzzle out; find the key of, enucleate, resolve, solve; read between the lines.

account for; find –, tell- the cause &c. 153- of; throw –, shed--light, – new light, – a fresh light- upon; clear up, elucidate.

illustrate, exemplify; unfold, expound, comment upon, annotate; popularize &c. (*render intelligible*) 518.

take –, understand –, receive –, accept- in a particular sense; understand by, put a construction on, be given to understand.

Adj. explanatory, expository; explica-tive, -tory; exegetical; hermeneutic, interpretive, illustrative, elucidative, annotative, scholiastic.

polyglot; literal; para-, meta-phrastic; cosignificative, synonymous; equivalent &c. 27.

Adv. in -explanation &c. *n.*; that is to say, *id est, videlicet*, to wit, namely, in other words.

literally, strictly speaking; in -plain, – plainer- -terms, – words, – English; more simply.

away; put a -bad, – false- construction on; give a false colouring, look through -rose coloured –, – dark – spectacles.

be –, play- at cross purposes.

Adj. misinterpreted &c. *v.*; untranslat-ed, -able.

Adv. at cross purposes.

---

524. Interpreter.—N. interpreter, translator, ex-positor, -pounder, -ponent, -plainer; demonstrator.

scholiast, commentator, annotator; meta-, para-phrast.

spokesman, speaker, mouthpiece, prolocutor; diplomat &c. 758.

guide, courier, dragoman, *valet de place, cicerone*, showman; oneiro-critic; Œdipus; oracle &c. 513.

Section II. Modes of Communication

525. Manifestation.—N. manifestation; unfolding; plainness &c. *adj.*; plain speaking; expression; showing &c. *v.*; exposition, demonstration, *séance*; exhibition, production; display, showing off &c. 882, premonstration. [Thing shown] exhibit, show.

indication &c. (*calling attention to*) 457; publicity &c. 531; disclosure &c. 529; openness &c. (*honesty*) 543, (*artlessness*) 703; *épanchement*, prominence.

V. make -, render- -manifest &c. *adj.*; bring -forth, – forward, – to the front, – into view; give notice; express; represent, set forth, exhibit; show, – up; expose; produce; hold up –, expose- to view; set –, place –, lay-

526. Latency.—N. latency, inexpression; hidden –, occult- meaning; occultness, occultism, mysticism, mystery, cabala, symbolism, anagoge; silence &c. (*taciturnity*) 585; concealment &c. 528; more than meets the -eye, – ear; Delphic oracle; *le dessous des cartes*, undercurrent.

allusion, insinuation, implication; innuendo &c. 527; adumbration; 'something rotten in the state of Denmark.'

snake in the grass &c. (*pitfall*) 667; secret &c. 533.

darkness, invisibility, imperceptibility.

latent influence, power behind the throne; friend at court, wire puller.

before -one, – one's eyes; tell to one's face; trot out, put through one's paces, unfold, show off, show forth, unveil, bring to light, display, demonstrate, unroll; lay open; draw –, bring- out; bring out in strong relief; call –, bring- into notice; hold up the mirror; wear one's heart upon his sleeve; show one's -face, – colours; manifest oneself; speak out; make no -mystery, – secret- of; unfurl the flag; proclaim &c. (*publish*) 531.

indicate &c. (*direct attention to*) 457; disclose &c. 529; elicit &c. 480a; interpret &c. 522.

be -manifest &c. *adj.*; appear &c. (*be visible*) 446; transpire &c. (*be disclosed*) 529; speak for itself, stand to reason; stare one in the face; loom large, appear on the horizon, rear its head; give -token, – sign, – indication of; tell its own tale &c. (*intelligible*) 518; go without saying.

Adj. manifest, apparent; salient, striking, demonstrative, prominent, in the foreground, notable, pronounced.

flagrant; notorious &c. (*public*) 531; arrant; stark staring; unshaded, glaring.

defin-ed, -ite; distinct, conspicuous &c. (*visible*) 446; obvious, evident, incontestable, unmistakable, not to be mistaken, plain, clear, palpable, self-evident, autoptical; intelligible &c. 518; clear as -day, – daylight, – noonday; plain as -a pikestaff, – the sun at noonday, – the nose on one's face, – the way to the parish church.

ostensible; open, – as day; overt, patent, express, explicit; naked, bare, literal, downright, undisguised, ex-oteric.

V. be -latent &c. *adj.*; lurk, smoulder, underlie, make no sign; escape -observation, – detection, – recognition; lie hid &c. 528.

laugh in one's sleeve; keep back &c. (*conceal*) 528.

involve, imply, implicate, connote, import, understand, allude to, infer, leave an inference; symbolize; whisper &c. (*conceal*) 528.

Adj. latent; lurking &c. *v.*; secret &c. 528; occult, symbolic, mystic; implied &c. *v.*; dormant.

un-apparent, -known, -seen &c. 441; in the background; invisible &c. 447; indiscoverable, dark; impenetrable &c. (*unintelligible*) 519; un-spied, -suspected.

un - said, - written, - published, -breathed, -talked of, -told &c. 527, -sung, -exposed, -proclaimed, -disclosed &c. 529, -pronounced, -mentioned, -expressed; not expressed, tacit.

un-developed, -solved, -explained, -traced, -discovered &c. 480a, -tracked, -explored, -invented.

indirect, crooked, inferential; by -inference, – implication; implicit; constructive; allusive, covert, muffled; steganographic; under-stood, -hand, -ground; concealed &c. 528; delitescent.

Adv. by a side wind; *sub silentio*; in the background; behind -the scenes, – one's back, – the veil; below the surface; on the tip of one's tongue; secretly &c. 528; between the lines; by a mutual understanding.

Phr. 'thereby hangs a tale.' 'that is another story.'

---

unreserved; frank, plain spoken &c. (*artless*) 703; barefaced, brazen, bold, shameless, daring, flaunting, loud.

manifested &c. *v.*; disclosed &c. 529; expressible, capable of being shown, producible; in-, un-concealable.

Adv. manifestly, openly &c. *adj.*; before one's eyes, under one's nose, to one's face, face to face, above board, *cartes sur table*, on the stage, in plain sight, in open court, in the open, – streets; at the cross roads; in market overt; in the face of -day, – heaven; in -broad –, open- daylight; without reserve; at first blush, *primâ facie*, on the face of; in set terms.

Phr. *cela saute aux yeux*; he that runs may read; you can see it with half an eye; it needs no ghost to tell us; the meaning lies on the surface; *cela va sans dire*; *res ipsa loquitur*.

527. Information.—N. information, enlightenment, acquaintance, knowledge &c. 490; publicity &c. 531.

communication, intimation; not-ice, -ification; e-, an-nunciation; announcement; representation, round robin, presentment.

case, estimate, specification, report, advice, monition; news &c. 532; return &c. (*record*) 551; account &c. (*description*) 594; statement &c. (*affirmation*) 535.

mention; acquainting &c. *v.*; instruction &c. (*teaching*) 537; outpouring; intercommunication, communicativeness.

informant, authority, teller, announcer, annunciator, harbinger, herald, intelligencer, commentator, columnist, reporter, exponent, mouthpiece; informer, keek, eavesdropper, delator, detective, sleuth; *mouchard*, spy, stool pigeon, newsmonger; messenger &c. 534; *amicus curiæ*.

valet de place, cicerone, pilot, guide; guide-, hand-book; *vade mecum*; manual; map, plan, chart, gazetteer; itinerary &c. (*journey*) 266.

hint, suggestion, wrinkle, innuendo, inkling, whisper, passing word, word in the ear, subaudition, cue, by-play; gesture &c. (*indication*) 550; gentle −broad- hint; *verbum sapienti*; word to the wise; insinuation &c. (*latency*) 526.

V. tell; inform, − of; acquaint, − with; impart, − to; make acquainted with, bring to the ears of, apprise, advise, enlighten, awaken.

let fall, mention, express, intimate, represent, communicate, make known; publish &c. 531; notify, signify, specify, convey the knowledge of.

let one −, have one to- know; serve notice, give one to understand; give notice; set −, lay −, put- before; point out, put into one's head; put one in possession of; instruct &c. (*teach*) 537; direct the attention to &c. 457.

an-nounce, -nunciate; report, − progress; bring −, send −, leave −, write- word; tele-graph, -phone; ring −, call- up; wire; retail, render an account; give an account &c. (*describe*) 594; state &c. (*affirm*) 535.

528. Concealment.—N. concealment; hiding &c. *v.*; occultation, mystification.

seal of secrecy; screen &c. 530; disguise &c. 530; masquerade; masked battery; hiding place &c. 530; cipher, code, crypt-, stegan-ography; invisible −, sympathetic- ink; palimpsest; freemasonry.

stealth, -iness; obreption; slyness &c. (*cunning*) 702.

latit-ancy, -ation; seclusion &c. 893; privacy, secrecy, secretness; *incognita*.

reticence; reserve; mental −, reservation, aside; *arrière pensée*, suppression, evasion, white lie, misprision; silence &c. (*taciturnity*) 585; suppression of truth &c. 544; underhand dealing; close-, secretive-ness &c. *adj.*; mystery.

latency &c. 526; snake in the grass; secret &c. 533.

V. conceal, hide, secrete, stow away, put out of sight; lock −, seal −, bottle- up.

cover, screen, cloak, veil, shroud; screen from -sight, − observation; draw the veil; draw −, close- the curtain; curtain, shade, eclipse, throw a veil over; be-cloud, -fog, -mask; mask, disguise; ensconce, muffle, smother; whisper.

keep -from, − back, − to oneself; keep -snug, − close, − secret, − dark; bury; sink, suppress; keep -from, − out of- -view, − sight; keep in −, throw into- the -shade, − background; cover up one's tracks; stifle, hush up, withhold, reserve; fence with a question; ignore &c. 460.

code, codify, use a cipher.

keep -a secret, − one's own counsel; hold one's tongue &c. (*silence*) 585; make no sign, not let it go further; not breathe a -word, − syllable- about; not let the right hand know what the left is doing; hide one's light under a bushel, bury one's talent in a napkin.

keep −, leave- in -the dark, − ignorance; blind, − the eyes; blindfold, hoodwink, mystify; puzzle &c. (*render uncertain*) 475; bamboozle &c. (*deceive*) 545.

be -concealed &c. *v.*; suffer an eclipse;

disclose &c. 529; show cause; explain &c. (*interpret*) 522.

hint; give an inkling of; **give –**, drop –, throw out- a hint; insinuate; allude –, make allusion- to; glance at; tip off, tip the wink &c. (*indicate*) 550; suggest, prompt, give the cue, breathe; whisper, – in the ear.

give a bit of one's mind; tell one plainly, – once for all; speak volumes.

un-deceive, -beguile; set right, correct, open the eyes of, disabuse.

be -informed of &c.; know &c. 490; learn &c. 539; get scent of, gather from; awaken –, open one's eyes- to; become -alive, – awake- to; keep posted; hear, overhear, understand.

come to one's -ears, – knowledge; reach one's ears.

Adj. informed &c. *v.*; *communiqué*; reported &c. *v.*; published &c. 531; advisory.

expressive &c. 516; explicit &c. (*open*) 525, (*clear*) 518; plain-spoken &c. (*artless*) 703.

declara-, nuncupa-, exposi-tory; declarative, enunciative, communicat-ive, -ory; oral.

Adv. from information received; according to -rumour, – report; in the air; from what one can gather.

Phr. a little bird told me.

———

retire from sight, couch; hide oneself; lie -hid, – in ambush, – low, – *perdu*, – snug, – close; seclude oneself &c. 893; lurk, sneak, skulk, slink, pussy-foot, prowl; steal -into, – out of, – by, – along; play at -bopeep, – hide and seek; hide in holes and corners.

Adj. concealed &c. *v.*; hidden; veiled, secret, recondite, mystic, cabalistic, occult, dark; cryptic, -al; private, privy, *in petto*, auricular, clandestine, close, inviolate.

behind a -screen &c. 530; under -cover, – an eclipse; in -ambush, – hiding, – disguise; in a -cloud, – fog, – mist, – haze, – dark corner; in the -shade, – dark; clouded, wrapt in clouds; invisible &c. 447; buried, underground, *perdu*; incommunicado; secluded &c. 893.

un-disclosed &c. 529, -told &c. 527; covert &c. (*latent*) 526; mysterious &c. (*unintelligible*) 519.

irrevealable, inviolable; confidential; esoteric; not to be spoken of.

obreptitious, furtive, stealthy, feline; skulking &c. *v.*; surreptitious, underhand, hole and corner; sly &c. (*cunning*) 702; secretive, evasive, noncommittal, reserved, reticent, uncommunicative, buttoned up; close, – as wax; taciturn &c. 585.

Adv. secretly &c. *adj.*; in -secret, – private, – one's sleeve, – holes and corners; in the dark &c. *adj.*

januis clausis, with closed doors, *à huis clos*; hugger-mugger, *à la dérobée*; under the -cloak of, – rose, – table; *sub rosâ, en tapinois*, in the background, aside, on the sly, with bated breath, *sotto voce*, in a whisper, without beat of drum, *à la sourdine*.

in –, strict- confidence; confidentially &c. *adj.*; between -ourselves, – you and me; *entre nous, inter nos*, under the seal of secrecy; in -code, – cipher.

underhand, by stealth, like a thief in the night; stealthily &c. *adj.*; behind -the scenes, – the curtain, – one's back, – a screen &c. 530; *incognito; in camerâ*.

Phr. it -must, – will- go no further; 'tell it not in Gath,' nobody the wiser.

529. Disclosure.—N. disclosure; retection; unveiling &c. *v.*; deterration, revealment, revelation; divulgence; expos-ition, -ure; *exposé*; whole truth; tell-tale &c. (*news*) 532.

acknowledgment, avowal; confession, -al; shrift.

530. Ambush. [Means of concealment.]—**N.** hiding-place; secret -place, – drawer; recess, hole, funk hole, holes and corners; closet, crypt, *adytum*, abditory, *oubliette*, safe, – deposit.

am-bush, -buscade; stalking horse; lurking-hole, -place; secret path,

bursting of a bubble; *dénouement*.

V. dis-close, -cover, -mask; draw –, draw aside –, lift –, raise –, lift up –, remove –, tear- the -veil, – curtain; un-mask, -veil, -fold, -cover, -seal, -kennel; take off –, break- the seal; lay -open, – bare; expose; open, – up; bare, bring to light; evidence; make - clear, – evident, – manifest; evince.

divulge, reveal, break; let into the secret; reveal the secrets of the prison-house; tell &c. (*inform*) 527; breathe, utter, blab, peach; let -out, – fall, – drop, – the cat out of the bag; betray; tell tales, – out of school; come out with; give -vent, – utterance- to; open the lips, blurt out, vent, whisper about; speak out &c. (*make manifest*) 525; make public &c. 531; unriddle &c. (*find out*) 480a; split; blow the gaff; break the news.

acknowledge, allow, concede, grant, admit, own, confess, avow, throw off all disguise, turn inside out, make a clean breast; show one's -hand, – cards; unburden –, disburden- one's -mind, – conscience, – heart; open –, lay bare –, tell a piece of- one's mind; unbosom oneself, own to the soft impeachment; say –, speak- the truth; turn -King's, –Queen's, –State's- evidence.

raise –, drop –, lift –, remove –, throw off- the mask; expose; debunk; lay open; un-deceive, -beguile; disabuse, set right, correct, open the eyes of; *désillusionner*.

be -disclosed &c.; transpire, come to light; come in sight &c. (*be visible*) 446; become known, escape the lips; come –, ooze –, creep –, leak –, peep –, crop- out; show its -face, – colours; discover &c. itself; break through the clouds, flash on the mind.

Adj. disclosed &c. *v.*

Int. out with it!

Phr. the murder is out; a light breaks in upon one; the scales fall from one's eyes; the eyes are opened.

backstairs; retreat &c. (*refuge*) 666.

screen, cover, shade, blinker; veil, curtain, blind, *purdah*, cloak, cloud.

mask, vizor, visor, disguise, masquerade dress, domino; *camouflage*.

pitfall &c. (*source of danger*) 667; trap &c. (*snare*) 545.

V. ambush, ambuscade, lie in ambush &c. (*hide oneself*) 528; lie in wait for; set a trap for &c. (*deceive*) 545.

Adv. *aux aguets*.

---

531. Publication.—**N.** publication; public -announcement &c. 527; promulgation, propagation, proclamation, pronouncement, encyclical, *pronunciamento*; circulation, indiction, edition, imprint, impression, printing; hue and cry.

publicity, notoriety, currency, flagrancy, cry, *bruit*; *vox populi*; report &c. (*news*) 532.

the Press, fourth estate, public press, newspaper, periodical, journal, gazette; house organ, trade publication, tabloid; daily, weekly, monthly, quarterly, annual, magazine, monograph, book; review; news sheet, special edition, supplement, feature, rotogravure, comic strips; leaflet, pamphlet; telegraphy; publisher &c. *v.*

circular, – letter; manifesto, advertisement, puff, placard, bill, *affiche*, broadside, poster; notice &c. 527; programme.

V. publish; make -public, – known &c. (*information*) 527; speak –, talk- of; broach, utter; put forward; circulate, propagate, promulgate; spread –, abroad; rumour, diffuse, disseminate, evulgate; put –, give –, send- forth; emit, edit, get out; issue; cover, report; bring –, lay –, drag- before the public; give -out, – to the world; put –, bandy –, hawk –, buzz –, whisper –, bruit –, blaze- about; drag into the -open day, – limelight; voice.

proclaim, herald, blazon; blaze –, noise- abroad; sound a trumpet; trumpet –, thunder- forth; give tongue; announce with -beat of drum, – flourish of trumpets; proclaim -from the housetops, – at Charing Cross, at the cross roads; declare, declaim.

advertise, placard; post, – up; *afficher*, publish in the Gazette, send round the crier.

raise a -cry, – hue and cry, – report; set news afloat.

telegraph, cable, wireless, broadcast.

be -published &c.; be –, become- public &c. *adj.*; come out; go –, fly –, buzz –, blow- about; get -about, – abroad, – afloat, – wind; find vent; see the light; go forth, take air, acquire currency, pass current; go -the rounds, – the round of the newspapers, – through the length and breadth of the land; *virum volitare per ora*; pass from mouth to mouth; spread; run –, spread- like wildfire.

Adj. published &c. *v.*; current &c. (*news*) 532; in circulation, public; notorious; flagrant, arrant; open &c. 525; trumpet-tongued; encyclical, promulgatory; exoteric.

Adv. publicly &c. *adj.*; in open court, with open doors; in the limelight.

Int. *Oyez!* O yes! notice!

Phr. notice is hereby given; this is –, these are- to give notice.

---

532. News.—N. news; information &c. 527; piece –, budget- of -news, – information; report, story, yarn, copy, filler, intelligence, tidings; stop press news.

word, advice, *aviso*, message; dis-, des-patch; radio, telegram, cable, wireless telegram, radio-gram, marconi-gram, communication, errand, embassy; *bulletin.*

rumour, hearsay, *on dit*, flying rumour, news stirring, cry, buzz, *bruit*, fame; talk, *oui-dire*, scandal, eaves-dropping; town –, table- talk; tittle-tattle; *canard*, topic of the day, idea afloat.

fresh –, stirring –, old –, stale- news; glad tidings; old –, stale- story.

narrator &c. (*describe*) 594; news-, scandal-monger; tale-bearer; tell-tale, gossip, tattler, busy-body, chatterer; informer.

V. transpire &c. (*be disclosed*) 529; rumour &c. (*publish*) 531.

Adj. many-tongued; rumoured; publicly –, currently- -rumoured, – reported; rife, current, floating, afloat, going about, in circulation, in everyone's mouth, all over the town.

Adv. as the story -goes, – runs; as they say, it is said.

533. Secret.—N. secret; dead –, profound- secret; *arcanum*, mystery; latency &c. 526; Asian mystery; sealed book, secrets of the prison-house; *le dessous des cartes.*

enigma, riddle, puzzle, nut to crack, conundrum, charade, rebus, logograph; mono-, ana-gram; acrostic, cross-word puzzle; Sphinx; *crux criticorum.*

maze, labyrinth, Hyrcynian wood.

problem &c. (*question*) 461; paradox &c. (*difficulty*) 704; unintelligibility &c. 519; *terra incognita* &c. (*ignorance*) 491.

Adj. secret &c. (*concealed*) 528.

---

534. Messenger.—N. messenger, envoy, emissary, legate; nuncio, internuncio; intermediary; ambassador &c. (*diplomatist*) 758.

marshal, flag-bearer, herald, crier, trumpeter, bellman, pursuivant, *parlementaire, apparitor.*

courier, runner, dawk, *estafette*; Hermes, Mercury, Iris, Ariel.

postman, letter carrier, telegraph boy, messenger boy, district messenger; despatch rider, commissionaire, errand-boy.

mail; post, -office; letter-bag; mail -boat, – train, – coach, – van, aerial mail; tele-graph, -phone; cable, wire; carrier-pigeon; wireless tele-graph, -phone; radiotele-graph, -phone.

journalist, newspaperman, reporter; gentleman –, representative- of the press; sob sister; penny-a-liner; special –, war –, own- correspond-ent; spy, scout; informer &c. 527.

535. Affirmation.—N. affirm-ance, -ation; statement, allegation, assertion, predication, declaration, word, aver-ment.

asseveration, adjuration, swearing, oath, affidavit; deposition &c. (*record*) 551; avouchment, assurance; protest, -ation; profession; acknowledgment &c. (*assent*) 488; pledge.

vote, voice, suffrage, ballot.

remark, observation; position &c. (*proposition*) 514; saying, *dictum*, sen-tence, *ipse dixit*.

emphasis, positiveness, peremptori-ness; dogmatism &c. (*certainty*) 474; dogmatist &c. 887.

V. assert; make -an assertion &c. *n.*; have one's say; say, affirm, predicate, declare, state, represent; protest, pro-fess.

put -forth, – forward; advance, allege, propose, propound, enunciate, enounce, broach, set forth, hold out, maintain, contend, pronounce, pretend.

depose, depone, aver, avow, avouch, asseverate, swear; make –, take one's-oath; make –, swear –, put in- an affidavit; take one's Bible oath, kiss the book, vow, *vitam impendere vero*; swear till -one is black in the face, – all's blue; be sworn, call Heaven to witness; vouch, warrant, certify, assure, swear by bell, book and candle.

swear by &c. (*believe*) 484; insist –, take one's stand- upon; emphasize, lay stress on; assert -roundly, – positively; lay down, – the law; raise one's voice, dogmatize, have the last word; rap out; repeat; re-assert, -affirm.

announce &c. (*information*) 527; ac-knowledge &c. (*assent*) 488; attest &c. (*evidence*) 467; adjure &c. (*put to one's oath*) 768.

Adj. asserting &c. *v.*; declaratory, predicatory, pronunciative, affirmative, *soi-disant*; positive; certain &c. 474; express, explicit &c. (*patent*) 525; absolute, emphatic, flat, broad, round, pointed, marked, distinct, decided, confident, assertive, insistent, trenchant, dogmatic, definitive, formal, solemn, categorical, peremptory; un-retracted; predicable, affirmable.

536. Negation.—N. ne-, abne-gation; denial; dis-avowal, -claimer; abjura-tion; contra-diction, -vention; recu-sation, protest; rebuttal; recusancy &c. (*dissent*) 489; flat –, emphatic- -con-tradiction, – denial; *démenti*.

qualification &c. 469; repudiation &c. 610; retractation &c. 607; confuta-tion &c. 479; refusal &c. 764; prohibi-tion &c. 761.

V. deny; contra-dict, -vene; contro-vert, give denial to, gainsay, negative, shake the head.

dis-own, -affirm, -claim, -avow; re-cant &c. 607; revoke &c. (*abrogate*) 756.

dispute, impugn, traverse, rebut, join issue upon; bring –, call- in question &c. (*doubt*) 485.

deny -flatly, – peremptorily, – em-phatically, – absolutely, – wholly, – en-tirely; give the lie to, belie.

repudiate &c. 610; set aside, ignore &c. 460; rebut &c. (*confute*) 479; qualify &c. 469; refuse &c. 764.

Adj. denying &c. *v.*; denied &c. *v.*; contradictory; negat-ive, -ory; revoca-tory; recusant &c. (*dissenting*) 489; at issue upon.

Adv. no, nay, not, nowise; not a -bit, – whit, – jot; not -at all, – in the least, – so; no such thing; nothing of the -kind, – sort; quite the contrary, *tout au contraire*, far from it; *tant s'en faut*; on no account, in no respect; by -no, – no manner of- means; negatively.

Phr. there never was a greater mis-take; I know better; *non hæc in fœdera*.

Adv. affirmatively &c. *adj.*; in the affirmative.

with emphasis, *ex cathedrâ*, without fear of contradiction.

I must say, indeed, i' faith, let me tell you, why, give me leave to say, marry, you may be sure, I'd have you to know; upon my -word, – honour; by my troth, egad, I assure you; by -jingo, – Jove, – George, – &c.; troth, seriously, sadly; in –, in sober- -sadness, – truth, – earnest; of a truth, truly, pardi, perdy; in all conscience, upon oath; be assured &c. (*belief*) 484; yes &c. (*assent*) 488; I'll -warrant, – warrant you, – engage, – answer for it, – be bound, – venture to say, – take my oath; in fact, as a matter of fact, forsooth, joking apart; so help me God; not to mince the matter.

Phr. quoth he; *dixi*.

537. Teaching.—N. teaching &c. *v.*; instruction; edification; education; pedagogy; tuition; tutor-, tutel-age; direction, guidance.

qualification, preparation; train-, school-ing &c. *v.*; discipline; exer-cise, -citation; drill, practice.

persuasion, proselytism, propagand-ism, *propaganda*; in-doctrination, -cul-cation, -oculation.

explanation &c. (*interpretation*) 522; lesson, lecture, sermon, homily; apo-logue, parable; discourse, prelection, preachment, disquisition.

exercise, task; *curriculum*; course, – of study; grammar, three R's, initi-ation, A. B. C. &c. (*beginning*) 66.

elementary –, primary –, secondary –, grammar school –, high school –, college –, university –, technical –, liberal –, classical –, religious –, de-nominational –, moral –, secular- edu-cation; technical –, vocational- train-ing; university extension lectures; propædeutics, moral tuition; evening classes, correspondence course.

physical education, gymnastics, calis-thenics, eurythmics; *sloyd*.

V. teach, instruct, edify, school, tutor; cram, prime, coach; enlighten &c. (*inform*) 527.

in-culcate, -doctrinate, -oculate, -fuse, -stil, -fix, -graft, -filtrate; im-bue, -pregnate, -plant; graft, sow the seeds of, disseminate, propagandize.

give an idea of; put -up to, – in the way of; set right.

sharpen the wits, enlarge the mind; give new ideas, open the eyes, bring forward, 'teach the young idea how to shoot'; improve &c. 658.

538. Misteaching.—N. mis-teaching, -information, -intelligence, -guidance, -direction, -persuasion, -instruction, -leading &c. *v.*; perversion, false teach-ing; sophistry &c. 477; college of Laputa; the blind leading the blind.

V. mis-inform, -teach, -direct, -guide, -instruct, -correct; pervert; put on a false –, throw off the- scent; deceive &c. 545; mislead &c. (*error*) 495; mis-represent; lie &c. 544; *ambiguas in vulgum spargere voces*, preach to the wise, teach one's grandmother to suck eggs.

render unintelligible &c. 519; bewil-der &c. (*uncertainty*) 475; mystify &c. (*conceal*) 528; unteach.

Adj. misteaching &c. *v.*; unedifying.

Phr. *piscem natare doces*.

539. Learning.—N. learning; acqui-sition of -knowledge &c. 490, – skill &c. 698; acquirement, attainment; edification, scholarship, erudition; lore; information; self-instruction; study, reading, perusal; inquiry &c. 461.

ap-, prenticeship; pupil-age, -arity; tutelage, novitiate, matriculation.

docility &c. (*willingness*) 602; apti-tude &c. 698.

V. learn; acquire –, gain –, receive –, take in –, drink in –, imbibe –, pick up –, gather –, get –, obtain –, collect –, glean- -knowledge, – information, – learning.

acquaint oneself with, master; make oneself -master of, – acquainted with; grind, cram; get –, coach- up; learn by -heart, – rote.

read, spell, peruse; con –, pore –, thumb- over; wade through; dip into;

expound &c. (*interpret*) 522; lecture; prelect; read –, give- a -lesson, – lecture, – sermon, – discourse; hold forth, preach; sermon-, moral-ize; point a moral.

train, discipline; bring up, – to; educate, form, ground, prepare, qualify, drill, exercise, practice, habituate, familiarize with, nurture, dry-nurse, breed, rear, take in hand; break, – in; tame; pre-instruct; initiate; inure &c. (*habituate*) 613.

put to nurse, send to school.

direct, guide; direct attention to &c. (*attention*) 457; impress upon the -mind, – memory; beat into, – the head; convince &c. (*belief*) 484.

Adj. teaching &c. *v.*; taught &c. *v.*; educational; scholastic, academic, doctrinal; disciplinal; instructive, didactic, hortative, pedagogic, tutorial.

Phr. the schoolmaster abroad.

540. Teacher.—**N.** teacher, trainer, instructor, institutor, master, tutor, don, director, Corypheus, dry nurse, coach, grinder, crammer; governor, bear-leader; governess, duenna; disciplinarian.

professor, lecturer, reader, prelector, prolocutor, preacher; Boanerges; pastor &c. (*clergy*) 996; schoolmaster, dominie, usher, pedagogue, abecedarian; schoolmistress, dame, monitor, proctor, pupil-teacher.

expositor &c. 524; preceptor, guide; mentor &c. (*adviser*) 695; pioneer, apostle, missionary, propagandist, moonshee; example &c. (*model for imitation*) 22.

professorship &c. (*school*) 542.

tutelage &c. (*teaching*) 537.

Adj. professorial, tutorial &c. 537.

run the eye -over, – through; turn over the leaves.

study; be -studious &c. *adj.*; consume the midnight oil, mind cne's book.

go to -school, – college, – the university; serve -an (*or* one's) apprenticeship, – one's time; learn one's trade; be -informed &c. 527; be -taught &c. 537.

Adj. studious; schol-astic, -arly; teachable; docile &c. (*willing*) 602; apt &c. 698, industrious &c. 682; learned, erudite.

Adv. at one's books; *in statu pupillari* &c. (*learner*) 541.

541. Learner.—**N.** learner, scholar, student, *alumnus*, *élève*, pupil; ap-, prentice; articled clerk; school-boy, -girl, beginner, tyro, abecedarian, alphabetarian.

recruit, novice, neophyte, tenderfoot, inceptor, *débutant*, catechumen, probationer; undergraduate; freshman, frosh; sophomore, junior, senior; junior –, senior- soph; sophister, questionist, fellow-, commoner, pensioner, exhibitioner, sizar, scholar, fellow, advanced –, post graduate –, research- student.

class, form, grade, standard, remove; pupilage &c. (*learning*) 539.

disciple, follower, apostle, proselyte; fellow student, school-mate, -fellow, class mate, condisciple.

Adj. *in statu pupillari*, in leading strings, sophomoric.

542. School.—**N.** school, academy, university, *alma mater*, college, seminary, Lyceum; instit-ute, -ution, *conservatoire*; *palæstra*, *gymnasium*.

day -. boarding –, public –, preparatory –, elementary –, primary –, infant –, dame's –, grammar –, middle class –, Board –, County –, Council –, parochial –, denominational –, Sunday –, National –, British and Foreign –, collegiate –, secondary –, continuation –, night –, correspondence –, secretarial –, military –, law –, medical –, business –, technical- school; technical –, training- college; Polytechnic; training ship; *Kindergarten*, nursery, *crèche*, reformatory.

pulpit, desk, reading desk, ambo, class-, lecture-room, theatre, amphitheatre, forum, stage, rostrum, platform, hustings, tribune.

school –, horn –, text- book; grammar, primer, abecedary, rudiments, manual, *vade mecum*, Lindley Murray, Cocker.

professor-, lecture-, reader-ship; chair; schoolmaster &c. 540.

School Board, Council of Education; *propaganda*.

Adj. scholastic, academic, collegiate; educational.

Adv. *ex cathedrâ.*

---

543. Veracity.—N. veracity; truthfulness, frankness &c. *adj.*; truth, sooth, sincerity, candour, honesty, fidelity; plain dealing, *bona fides*; love of truth; probity &c. 939; ingenuousness &c. (*artlessness*) 703.

the truth the whole truth and nothing but the truth; honest –, sober-truth &c. (*fact*) 494; unvarnished tale; light of truth.

V. speak –, tell- the truth; speak by the card; paint in its –, show oneself in one's-true colours; make a clean breast &c. (*disclose*) 529; speak one's mind &c. (*be blunt*) 703; not -lie &c. 544, – deceive &c. 545.

Adj. truthful, true; ver-acious, -edical; scrupulous &c. (*honourable*) 939; sincere, candid, frank, open, straightforward, unreserved; open-, true-, simple- hearted; honest, trustworthy; undissembling &c. (dissemble &c. 544); guileless, pure; unperjured, true blue, as good as one's word; unaffected, unfeigned, *bonâ fide*; outspoken, ingenuous &c. (*artless*) 703; undisguised &c. (*real*) 494.

Adv. truly &c. (*really*) 494; on oath; in plain words &c. 703; in –, with –, of a –, in good –, very- truth; as the -dial to the sun, – needle to the pole; honour bright; troth; in good -sooth, – earnest; unfeignedly, with no nonsense, in sooth, sooth to say, *bonâ fide*, *in foro conscientiæ*; without equivocation; *cartes sur table*, from the bottom of one's heart; by my troth &c. (*affirmation*) 535.

---

544. Falsehood. — N. false-hood, -ness; fals-ity, -ification; misrepresentation; deception &c. 545; untruth &c. 546; guile; bad faith; lying &c. *v.*; misrepresentation; mendacity, perjury, false swearing; forgery, invention, fabrication; subreption; covin.

perversion –, suppression- of truth; *suppressio veri*; perversion, distortion, false colouring; exaggeration &c. 549; prevarication, equivocation, shuffling, fencing, evasion, fraud; *suggestio falsi* &c. (*lie*) 546; mystification &c. (*concealment*) 528; simulation &c. (*imitation*) 19; dis-simulation, -sembling; deceit.

sham; pretence, pretending, malingering.

lip -homage, – service; mouth honour; hollowness; mere -show, – outside, eye-wash, window dressing; duplicity, double dealing, insincerity, hypocrisy, cant, humbug, casuistry; jesuit-ism, -ry; pharisaism; Machiavelism, 'organized hypocrisy'; crocodile tears, mealy-mouthedness, quackery; charlatan-ism, -ry; gammon; bun-kum, -come; flam, bam, flim-flam, cajolery, flattery; Judas kiss; perfidy &c. (*bad faith*) 940; *il volto sciolto i pensieri stretti.*

unfairness &c. (*dishonesty*) 940; artfulness &c. (*cunning*) 702; misstatement &c. (*error*) 495.

V. be -false &c. *adj.*, – a liar &c. 548; speak -falsely &c. *adv.*; tell -a lie &c. 546; lie, fib; lie like a trooper; swear falsely, forswear, perjure oneself, bear false witness.

mis-state, -quote, -cite, -report, -represent; belie, falsify, pervert, distort; put a false construction upon &c. (*misinterpret*) 523.

prevaricate, equivocate, quibble; palter, – to the understanding; *répondre en Normand*; trim, shuffle, fence, mince the truth, beat about the bush, blow hot and cold, play fast and loose.

garble, gloss over, disguise, give a colour to; give –, put- a -gloss, – false colouring- upon; colour, varnish, cook, dress up, embroider: varnish right and puzzle wrong, exaggerate &c. 549.

invent, fabricate; trump –, get- up; forge, hatch, concoct; romance &c. (*imagine*) 515; cry 'wolf!'

dis-semble, -simulate; feign, assume, put on, pretend, make believe; play -false, – a double game; coquet; act –, play- a part; affect &c. 855; simulate, pass off for; counterfeit, fake, sham, make a show of; malinger; swing the lead; say the grapes are sour.

cant, play the hypocrite, sham Abraham, *faire pattes de velours*, put on the mask, clean the outside of the platter, lie like a conjuror; hang out –, hold out –, sail under- false colours; 'commend the poisoned chalice to the lips'; *ambiguas in vulgus spargere voces*; deceive &c. 545.

Adj. false, deceitful, mendacious, unveracious, fraudulent, untruthful, dishonest; faith-, truth-, troth-less; un-fair, -candid; evasive; un-, dis-ingenuous; hollow, insincere, *Parthis mendacior*; forsworn.

canting; hypocrit-, jesuit-, pharisa-ical; tartuffish; Machiavelian; double-tongued, -faced, -handed, -minded, -hearted, -dealing; two-faced, bare-faced; Janus-faced; smooth-faced, -spoken, -tongued; plausible; mealy-mouthed; affected &c. 855.

collus-ive, -ory; artful &c. (*cunning*) 702; perfidious &c. 940, spurious &c. (*deceptive*) 545; untrue &c. 546; falsified &c. *v.*; covinous.

Adv. falsely &c. *adj.*; *à la Tartufe*, with a double tongue; out of whole cloth; slily &c. (*cunning*) 702.

545. Deception.—N. deception; falseness &c. 544; untruth &c. 546; impos-ition, -ture; fraud, deceit, guile; fraudulen-ce, -cy; covin; knavery &c. (*cunning*) 702; misrepresentation &c. (*falsehood*) 544.

delusion, gullery, bluff, spoof, *blague*; juggl-ing, -ery; sleight of hand, legerdemain; presti-giation, -digitation; magic &c. 992; conjur-ing, -ation; hocus pocus, jockeyship; trickery, coggery, hanky-panky, chicanery, pettifogging, sharp practice; *supercherie*, cozenage, circumvention, ingannation, collusion; treachery &c. 940; practical joke.

trick, cheat, wile, ruse, blind, feint, plant, bubble, fetch, catch, chicane, juggle, reach, hocus, bite; thimble-rig, card-sharping, artful dodge, machination, swindle, hoax; tricks upon travellers; confidence trick; stratagem &c. (*artifice*) 702; theft &c. 791.

snare, trap, pitfall, decoy, gin; sprin-ge, -gle; noose, hook; bait, decoy-duck, tub to the whale, baited trap, *guet-à-pens*; cobweb, net, meshes, toils, mouse-trap, bird-lime; ambush &c. 530; trap-door, sliding panel, false bottom; spring-net, -gun; mask, -ed battery; mine; booby trap.

Cornish hug; wolf in sheep's clothing &c. (*deceiver*) 548; disguise, -ment; false colours, masquerade, mummery, borrowed plumes; *pattes de velours*.

mockery &c. (*imitation*) 19; copy &c. 21; counterfeit, sham, brummagem, make-believe, forgery, fraud, fake; lie &c. 546; 'a mockery, a delusion, and a snare,' hollow mockery.

whited –, painted- sepulchre; tinsel, paste, false jewellery, scagliola, ormolu, German silver, Britannia metal, paint; jerry building; man of straw.

illusion &c. (*error*) 495; *ignis fatuus* &c. 423; *mirage* &c. 443.

V. deceive, take in; defraud, cheat, jockey, do, cozen, diddle, nab, gyp, chouse, double cross, play one false, bilk, cully, jilt, bite, pluck, swindle, victimize; abuse; mystify; blind one's eyes; blindfold, hoodwink, spoof, bluff; throw dust into the eyes, 'keep the word of promise to the ear and break it to the hope,' 'draw a herring across the trail.'

impose -, practise -, play -, put -, palm -, foist- upon; snatch a verdict.

circumvent, overreach; out-reach, -wit, -manœuvre; steal a march upon, give the go-by to, leave in the lurch.

set -, lay- a -trap, - snare- for; bait the hook, forelay, spread the toils, lime; decoy, waylay, lure, beguile, delude, inveigle; tra-, tre-pan; kidnap; let-, hook-in; trick; en-, in-trap, -snare, entoil, benet; nick, springe; catch, - in a trap; sniggle, entangle, illaqueate, hocus, practise on one's credulity, dupe, gull, hoax, fool, befool, bamboozle; hum, -bug; gammon, stuff up, dope, sell; play a -trick, - practical joke- upon one; balk, trip up, throw a tub to a whale; fool to the top of one's bent, send on -a wild goose chase, - a fool's errand; make -game, - a fool, - an April fool, - an ass- of; trifle with, cajole, flatter; come over &c. (*influence*) 615; gild the pill, make things pleasant, divert, put a good face upon; dissemble &c. 544.

cog, - the dice, play with marked cards; live by one's wits, play at hide and seek; obtain money under false pretences &c. (*steal*) 791; conjure, juggle, practise chicanery; gerrymander.

play -, palm -, foist -, fob- off.

lie &c. 544; misinform &c. 538; mislead &c. (*error*) 495; betray &c. 940; be -deceived &c. 547.

Adj. deceived &c. *v.*; deceiving &c. *v.*; cunning &c. 702; prestigi-ous, -atory; decept-ive, -ious; deceitful, covinous; delus-ive, -ory; illus-ive, -ory; elusive, insidious, *ad captandum vulgus.*

untrue &c. 546; mock, sham, make-believe, counterfeit, faked, pseudo, spurious, so-called, pretended, feigned, trumped up, bogus, scamped, fraudulent, tricky, factitious, artificial, bastard; surreptitious, illegitimate, contraband, adulterated, sophisticated; unsound, rotten at the core; colourable; disguised; meretricious; tinsel, pinchbeck, plated; catch-penny; Brummagem; simulated &c. 544.

Adv. under -false colours, - the garb of, - cover of; over the left.

Phr. *fronti nulla fides.*

546. Untruth.—N. untruth, falsehood, lie, story, thing that is not, fib, bounce, crammer, taradiddle, whopper.

forgery, fabrication, invention; mis-statement, -representation; per-version, falsification, gloss, *suggestio falsi*; exaggeration &c. 549.

fiction; fable, nursery tale; romance &c. (*imagination*) 515; untrue -, false -, trumped up- -story, - statement; thing devised by the enemy; *canard*; shave, sell, hum, yarn, traveller's tale, Canterbury tale, cock and bull story, fairy tale, clap-trap.

myth, moonshine, bosh, all my eye, -and Betty Martin, mare's nest, farce.

irony; half truth, white lie, pious fraud; mental reservation &c. (*concealment*) 528.

pretence, pretext; false -plea &c. 617; subterfuge, evasion, shift, shuffle, make-believe; sham &c. (*deception*) 545.

profession, empty words; Judas kiss &c. (*hypocrisy*) 544; disguise &c. (*mask*) 530.

V. have a false meaning; not ring true.

pretend, sham, feign, counterfeit, make believe.

Adj. untrue, false, trumped up; void of -, without- foundation; far from the truth, false as dicer's oaths; unfounded, *ben trovato*, invented, fabulous, fabricated, forged; fict-, fact-, supposit-, surrept-itious; e-, il-lusory; ironical; satirical; evasive; *soi-disant* &c. (*misnamed*) 565.

Phr. *se non e vero e ben trovato.*

547. Dupe.—N. dupe, gull, gudgeon, *gobemouche*, cull, cully, victim, sucker, pigeon, April fool; laughing stock &c. 857; Cyclops, simple Simon, flat, mug, greenhorn; fool &c. 501; puppet, cat's paw.

V. be -deceived &c. 545, – the dupe of; fall into a trap; swallow –, nibble at- the bait; bite; catch a Tartar.

Adj. credulous &c. 486; mistaken &c. (*error*) 495.

548. Deceiver.—N. deceiver &c. (deceive &c. 545); dissembler, hypo-crite; sophist, Pharisee, Jesuit, Maw-worm, Pecksniff, Joseph Surface, Tar-tufe, Janus; serpent, snake in the grass, cockatrice, Judas, wolf in sheep's clothing; Molly Maguire; jilt; shuffler.

liar &c. (lie &c. 544); story-teller, perjurer, false-witness, *menteur à triple étage*, Scapin.

impostor, pretender, capper, decoy, fraud, *soi-disant*, humbug; adventurer; Cagliostro, Fernam Mendez Pinto; ass in lion's skin &c. (*bungler*) 701; actor &c. (*stage player*) 599.

quack, *charlatan*, mountebank, saltimbanco, *saltimbanque*, em-piric, quacksalver, medicaster.

conjuror, juggler, magician, necromancer, trickster, prestidigita-tor, medium, jockey; crimp; decoy-duck, stool pigeon; rogue, knave, cheat; swindler &c. (*thief*) 792; jobber.

549. Exaggeration.—N. exaggeration; expansion &c. 194; hyperbole, stretch, strain, colouring; high colouring, caricature, *caricatura*; extrav-agance &c. (*nonsense*) 497; Baron Munchausen; men in buckram, yarn, fringe, embroidery, traveller's tale; Pelion upon Ossa.

storm in a teacup; much ado about nothing &c. (*over-estimation*) 482; puffery &c. (*boasting*) 884; rant &c. (*turgescence*) 577.

figure of speech, *façon de parler*; stretch of -fancy, – the imagination; flight of fancy &c. (*imagination*) 515.

false colouring &c. (*falsehood*) 544; aggravation &c. 835.

V. exaggerate, magnify, pile up, aggravate; amplify &c. (*expand*) 194; overestimate &c. 482; hyperbolize; over-charge, -state, -draw, -lay, -shoot the mark, -praise; make -much, – the most- of; strain, – a point; stretch, – a point; go great lengths; spin a long yarn; draw –, shoot with- a long-bow; deal in the marvellous.

out-Herod Herod, run riot, talk at random.

heighten, overcolour; colour -highly, – too highly; embroider, *broder*; flourish; colour &c. (*misrepresent*) 544; puff &c. (*boast*) 884.

Adj. exaggerated &c. *v.*; overwrought; bombastic &c. (*magniloquent*) 577; hyperbolical, on stilts; fabulous, extravagant, preposterous, egre-gious, *outré*, high-flying.

Adv. hyperbolically &c. *adj.*

Section III. MEANS OF COMMUNICATING IDEAS
1.° *Natural Means*

550. Indication.—N. indication; symbol-ism, -ization; semeio-logy, -tics; sign of the times.

lineament, feature, *trait*, characteristic, trick, diagnostic; divining-rod; cloven hoof; footfall; means of recognition; earmark.

sign, symbol; ind-ex, -ice, -icator; point, -er; marker; exponent, note, token, symptom.

type, figure, emblem, cipher, device; representation &c. 554; epigraph, motto, posy.

gest-ure, -iculation; pantomime; wink, glance, leer; nod, shrug, beck; touch, nudge; grip; dactylo-logy, -nomy; freemasonry, telegraphy, chirology, by-play, dumb-show; cue; hint &c. 527; clue, clew, key, scent, track &c. 551.

signal, -post; rocket, blue light; watch-fire, -tower; telegraph, semaphore, flag-staff; cresset, fiery cross; calumet; heliograph, signal-, flash-lamp.

mark, line, stroke, dash, score, stripe, streak, scratch, tick, dot, point, notch, nick, blaze; asterisk, red letter, Italics, heavy type, inverted commas, quotation marks, sublineation, underlining, jotting; print; impr-int, -ess, -ession; note, annotation, mark of exclamation.

[For identification] badge, criterion; counter-check, -mark, -sign, -foil; duplicate, tally; label, tab, ticket, stub, billet, letter, counter, *tessera*, card, bill, check; witness, voucher; stamp; *cachet*; trade –, Hall- mark; broad arrow; signature; address –, visiting- card; *carte de visite*; credentials &c. (*evidence*) 467; passport, identity book; attestation; hand, – writing, sign-manual; cipher; monogram, – mark, seal, sigil, signet; autograph, -y; paraph, brand; superscription; in-, endorsement; title, heading, rubric, docket; *mot -de passe, – du guet*; *passe-parole*; shibboleth; watch-, catch-, pass-word; open *sesame*.

insignia; banner, -et, -ol; bandrol; flag, colours, streamer, standard, eagle, labarum, oriflamb, *oriflamme*; figure-head; ensign; pen-non, -nant, -dant; burgee, blue Peter, jack, ancient, gonfalon, union-jack; tricolour, stars and stripes; bunting.

heraldry, crest; coat of –, arms; armorial bearings, hatchment; e-, scutcheon; shield, supporters; livery, uniform; cockade, *epaulette*, brassard, chevron; garland, chaplet, love-knot, fillet, favour.

[Of locality] beacon, cairn, post, staff, flagstaff, hand, pointer, vane, cock, weathercock; guide-, hand-, finger-, directing-, sign-post; pillars of Hercules, pharos, signal fire; land-, sea-mark; lighthouse, balize; pole-, load-, lode-star; cynosure, guide; address, direction, name; sign, -board.

[Of the future] warning &c. 668; omen &c. 512; prefigurement &c. 511. [Of the past] trace record &c. 551. [Of danger] warning &c. 668; alarm &c. 669. [Of authority] sceptre &c. 747. [Of triumph] trophy &c. 733. [Of quantity] gauge &c. 466. [Of distance] mile-stone, -post. [Of disgrace] brand, fool's cap, stigma, mark of Cain. [For detection] check, tell-tale; test &c. (*experiment*) 463.

notification &c. (*information*) 527; advertisement &c. (*publication*) 531.

word of command, call; bugle-, trumpet-call; reveille, taps; bell, alarum, cry; battle –, rallying- cry.

church, bell, angelus, sacring bell; muezzin.

exposition &c. (*explanation*) 522; proof &c. (*evidence*) 463; pattern &c. (*prototype*) 22.

V. indicate; be the -sign &c. *n.-* of; denote, betoken; argue, testify &c. (*evidence*) 467; bear the -impress &c. *n.-* of; con-note, -notate.

represent, stand for; typify &c. (*prefigure*) 511; symbolize.

put -an indication, – a mark, – &c. *n.*; note, mark, tick, blaze, stamp, earmark; set one's seal upon; label, ticket, docket; dot, spot, score, dash, trace, chalk; print; im-print, -press, surprint; engrave, stereotype, electrotype.

make a -sign &c. *n.*; signalize; give –, hang out- a signal; beck, -on; gesture; nod; wink, glance, leer, nudge, shrug, tip the wink; gesticulate; raise –, hold up- the -finger, – hand; saw the air, suit the action to the word.

wave –, unfurl –, hoist –, hang out- a banner &c. *n.*; wave -the hand, – a kerchief; give the cue &c. (*inform*) 527; show one's colours; give –, sound- an alarm; beat the drum, sound the trumpets, raise a cry.

sign, seal, attest &c. (*evidence*) 467; underline &c. (*give importance to*) 642; call attention to &c. (*attention*) 457; give notice &c. (*inform*) 527.

Adj. indicat-ing &c. *v.*, -ive, -ory; de-, con-notative; diacritical, representative, typical, symbolic, pantomimic, pathognomonic, symptomatic, ominous, characteristic, demonstrative, diagnostic, exponential, emblematic, armorial; individual &c. (*special*) 79.

known –, recognizable- by; indicated &c. *v.*; pointed, marked.
[Capable of being denoted] denotable; indelible.

Adv. in token of; symbolically &c. *adj.*; in dumb show.

Phr. *ecce signum*; *ex ungue leonem, ex pede Herculem.*

---

551. Record.—**N.** trace, vestige, relic, remains; scar, *cicatrix*; foot-step, -mark, -print; track, mark, wake, trail, spoor, scent, *piste.*

monument, hatchment, escutcheon, slab, tablet, trophy, achievement; obelisk, pillar, column, monolith, cromlech, dolmen; memorial; *memento* &c. (*memory*) 505; testimonial, medal, ribbon, order; commemoration &c. (*celebration*) 883.

record, note, minute; *dossier*; register, -try; census, roll &c. (*list*) 86; cartulary, diptych, Domesday book; entry, memorandum, indorsement, inscription, copy, duplicate, docket; notch &c. (*mark*) 550; muniment, deed &c. (*security*) 771; document; deposition, *procès-verbal*; affidavit; certificate &c. (*evidence*) 467.

552. [Suppression of sign.] Obliteration.—**N.** obliteration; erasure, rasure; effacement; cancel, -lation; cassation; circumduction; deletion, blot; *tabula rasa.*

V. efface, obliterate, erase, rase, expunge, cancel; blot –, take –, rub –, scratch –, strike –, wipe –, wash –, sponge- out; wipe –, rub- off; wipe away; deface, render illegible; draw the pen through, apply the sponge.

be -effaced &c.; leave no -trace &c. 449; 'leave not a rack behind.'

Adj. obliterated &c. *v.*; out of print; printless; leaving no trace; intestate; un-recorded, -registered, -written.

Int. *dele*; out with it!

---

note-, memorandum-, pocket-, commonplace-book; portfolio; scoring-board, -sheet; bulletin board; card index, file; pigeon-holes, *excerpta, adversaria,* jottings, dottings.

gazette, -er; newspaper, magazine &c. 531; alman-ac, -ack; calendar, ephemeris, noctuary, diary, log, journal, account-, cash-, day-book, ledger.

archive, scroll, state-paper, Congressional Record, return, blue-book; statistics &c. 86; *compte rendu*; Acts –, Transactions –, Proceedings- of; Hansard's Debates; chronicle, annals; legend; history, biography &c. 594.

registration; en-, in-rolment; tabulation; entry, booking; signature &c. (*identification*) 550; recorder &c. 553; journalism.

drawing, photograph &c. 554; phonograph –, gramophone-record; music roll.

V. record; put –, place- upon record; go on record; chronicle, calendar, hand down to posterity; keep up the memory of &c. (*remember*) 505; commemorate &c. (*celebrate*) 883; report &c. (*inform*) 527; commit to –, reduce to- writing; put –, set down- -in writing, – in black and white; put –, jot –, take –, write –, note –, set- down; note, minute, put on paper; take –, make- a -note, – minute, – memorandum; make a return.

mark &c. (*indicate*) 550; sign &c. (*attest*) 467.

enter, book; post, – up; insert, make an entry of; mark –, tick- off; register, list, docket, enroll, inscroll; file &c. (*store*) 636.

Adv. on record.

553. Recorder.—**N.** recorder, notary, clerk; regis-trar, -trary, -ter; prothonotary; amanuensis, secretary, scribe, stenographer, remem- brancer, book-keeper, *custos rotulorum*, Master of the Rolls.

annalist; histori-an, -ographer; chronicler, journalist, reporter, col- umnist; biographer &c. (*narrator*) 594; antiquary &c. (*antiquity*) 122; memorialist.

draughtsman &c. 559; engraver 558; photographer, cinematographer, camera man.

Recording instrument, recorder, camera, phonograph, gramophone, dictaphone, telegraphone, telautograph, printing telegraph, tape ma- chine, ticker, time recorder, cash register, turnstile, speedometer, voting machine, seismograph, photostat.

554. Representation.—**N.** represent- -ation, -ment; imitation &c. 19; illus- tration, delineation, depictment, por- trayal; imagery, portraiture, iconog- raphy; design, -ing; art, fine arts; painting &c. 556; sculpture &c. 557; engraving &c. 558; photography, radi- ography, skiagraphy.

person-ation, -ification; impersona- tion; drama &c. 599.

picture, drawing, sketch, draught, draft; tracing; copy &c. 21; photo-, helio-graph; daguerreo-, talbo-, calo-, helio-type; cabinet, *carte-de-visite*, snapshot; X-ray photo- graph; radio-gram, -graph, skia-graph, -gram.

image, likeness, icon, portrait; striking –, speaking- likeness; very image; effigy, fac-simile.

figure, – head; puppet, doll, *figurine*, aglet, manikin, lay-figure, model, *marionnette*, *fantoccini*, bust; waxwork, statue, -tte, auto- maton, Robot.

hieroglyphic, anaglyph; dia-, mono-gram, -graph.

map, plan, chart; ground plan, projection, elevation; ichno-, carto-graphy; atlas; outline, scheme; view &c. (*painting*) 556.

artist, draughtsman &c. 559.

V. represent, delineate; depict, -ure; portray; picture; take –, catch- a likeness &c. *n.*; hit off, photograph, daguerreotype; figure; shadow -forth, – out; adumbrate; body forth; describe &c. 594; trace, copy; mould.

dress up; illustrate, symbolize.

paint &c. 556; carve &c. 557; engrave &c. 558.

person-ate, -ify; impersonate; assume a character; pose as; act;

555. Misrepresentation.—**N.** mis- representation, distortion, exaggera- tion; daubing &c. *v.*; bad likeness, daub, sign-painting; scratch, carica- ture; *anamorphosis*.

V. misrepresent, distort, overdraw, travesty, parody, burlesque, exagger- ate, caricature, daub.

Adj. misrepresented &c. *v.*

play &c. (*drama*) 599; mimic &c. (*imitate*) 19; hold the mirror up to nature.

Adj. represent-ing &c. *v.*, -ative; illustrative; represented &c. *v.*; imitative, figurative.

like &c. 17; graphic &c. (*descriptive*) 594.

556. Painting.—N. painting; depicting; drawing &c. *v.*; design; perspective, skiagraphy; *chiaroscuro* &c. (*light*) 420; composition; treatment, values, atmosphere, tone, technique.

historical –, portrait –, miniature –, landscape –, marine –, flower –, scene- painting; scenography.

school, style; the grand style, high art, *genre*, portraiture; ornamental art &c. 847.

mono-, poly-chrome; *grisaille*.

pallet, palette; easel; brush, pencil, stump; blacklead, charcoal, crayons, chalk, pastel; paint &c. (*colouring matter*) 428; water-, body-, oil-colour; oils, oil-paint; varnish &c. 356*a*; *gouache*, tempera, distemper, fresco, water-glass; enamel; encaustic painting; *graffito*, *gesso*; mosaic; tapestry.

picture, painting, piece, *tableau*, canvas; oil &c.- painting; fresco, cartoon; easel –, cabinet- picture; drawing, draught, draft; pencil &c. –, watercolour- drawing; sketch, outline; study.

portrait &c. (*representation*) 554; whole –, full –, half- length; kitcat, head; miniature; shade, *silhouette*; profile.

landscape, sea-piece, -scape; view, scene, prospect; interior; bird's-eye view; pan-, di-orama; still life.

picture –, art- gallery; *studio, atelier*.

V. paint, design, limn, draw, sketch, pencil, scratch, shade, stipple, hatch, dash off, chalk out, square up; colour, dead-colour, wash, varnish; draw in -pencil &c. *n.*; paint in -oils &c. *n.*; stencil; depict &c. (*represent*) 554.

Adj. painted &c. *v.*; pictorial, graphic, picturesque, decorative; classical, romantic, pre-Raphaelite, modern, cubist, futurist, vorticist.

pencil, oil &c. *n.*

Adv. in -pencil &c. *n.*

Phr. *fecit, delineavit.*

557. Sculpture.—N. sculpture, insculpture; carving &c. *v.*; statuary ceramics, plastic arts.

high –, low –, bas- relief; relievo; *basso-, alto-, mezzo-relievo; intaglio* anaglyph; medal, -lion; *cameo*.

marble, bronze, *terra cotta*; ceramic ware, pottery, porcelain, china, earthenware, faïence, enamel; *cloisonné*.

statue &c. (*image*) 554; cast &c. (*copy*) 21; glyptotheca.

V. sculpture, carve, cut, chisel, model, mould; cast.

Adj. sculptured &c. *v.*; in relief, anaglyptic, ceroplastic, ceramic; parian; marble &c. *n.*

558. Engraving.—N. engraving, chalcography; line –, mezzotint –, stipple –, chalk- engraving; dry-point, bur; etching, aquatinta; plate –, copper-plate –, steel –, wood-, process-, photo-engraving; xylo-, ligno-, glypto-, cero-, litho-, chromolitho-, photolitho-, zinco-, glypho- -graphy, -graph.

impression, print, engraving, plate; steel-, copper-plate; etching; mezzo-, aqua-, litho-tint; cut, woodcut, block; stereo-, grapho-, auto-, helio-type; half-tone; *photogravure, rotogravure*.

graver, *burin*, etching-point, style; plate, stone, wood-block, negative; die, punch, stamp.

printing; plate –, copper-plate –, intaglio –, anastatic –, lithographic –, colour –, three colour- printing; type-printing &c. 591.

illustr-, illumin-ation; *vignette*, initial letter, *cul de lampe*, tail-piece.

V. engrave, grave, stipple, scrape, etch; bite, – in; lithograph &c. *n.*; print.

Adj. insculptured; engraved &c. *v.*

Phr. *sculpsit, imprimit.*

559. Artist.—N. artist; painter, limner, drawer, sketcher, delineator; cartoon-, caricatur-ist, designer, engraver; draughtsman; copyist; enamel-ler, -list.

historical –, landscape –, genre –, marine –, flower –, portrait –, miniature –, scene –, sign- painter; engraver; Apelles; sculptor, carver, chaser, modeller, lapidary, *figuriste*, statuary; Phidias, Praxiteles; Royal Academician.

photographer, retoucher.

2°. *Conventional Means*

1. *Language generally*

560. Language.—N. language; phraseology &c. 569; speech &c. 582; tongue, lingo, vernacular, slang; mother –, vulgar –, native- tongue; household words; King's *or* Queen's English; idiom; dialect &c. 563.

volapuk, esperanto, ido, occidental, Ro.

confusion of tongues, Babel, *pasigraphie*; pantomime &c. (*signs*) 550; *onomatopœia.*

phil-, gloss-, glott-ology; linguistics, chrestomathy; paleo-logy; -graphy; comparative grammar.

literature, letters, polite literature, *belles lettres*, muses, humanities, *literæ humaniores*, republic of letters, dead languages, classics; genius of a language; scholarship &c. (*knowledge*) 490.

linguist &c. (*scholar*) 492.

V. speak, say, express by words &c. 566.

Adj. lingu-al, -istic; dialectic; vernacular, current, colloquial, slangy; bilingual, polyglot; literary.

561. Letter.—N. letter; character; hieroglyphic &c. (*writing*) 590; type &c. (*printing*) 591; capitals; majus-, minus-cule; alphabet, ABC, abecedary, Christ-cross-row.

consonant, vowel, diphthong; mute, surd; sonant, liquid, labial, dental, palatal, guttural.

syllable; mono-, dis-, poly-syllable; affix, prefix, suffix.

spelling, orthography; phon-ography, -etic spelling; ana-, meta-grammatism.

cipher, monogram, anagram; double –, acrostic.

V. spell.

Adj. literal; alphabetical, abecedarian; syllabic; uncial &c. (*writing*) 590; phonetic, voiced, mute &c. *n.*

562. Word.—N. word, term, vocable; name &c. 564; phrase &c. 566; root, etymon; derivative; part of speech &c. (*grammar*) 567.

dictionary, vocabulary, word book,

563. Neology.—N. neolo-gy, -gism; new-fangled expression; barbarism; caconym; archaism, black letter, monkish Latin; corruption; missaying, antiphrasis.

lexicon, index, glossary, thesaurus, *gradus, delectus,* concordance.

etymology, lexicology, derivation; phonology, orthoepy; gloss-, termin-, orism-ology; paleology &c. (*philology*) 560; comparative philology.

lexicograph-er, -y; glossographer &c. (*scholar*) 492; etymologist; logolept.

verbosity, verbiage, loquacity &c. 584.

Adj. verbal, literal; titular, nominal. [Similarly derived] conjugate, parony-mous; derivative.

Adv. verbally &c. *adj.*; *verbatim* &c. (*exactly*) 494.

paronomasia, play upon words; word-play &c. (*wit*) 842; *double-entente* &c. (*ambiguity*) 520; palindrome, paragram, clinch; abuse of -language, – terms.

dialect, brogue, *patois,* provincialism, broken English, *lingua franca*; Brit-, Gall-, Scott-, Hibern-icism; American-ism; Gipsy lingo, Romany, pidgin English.

dog Latin, macaronics, gibberish, confusion of tongues, Babel; jargon.

colloquialism &c. (*figure of speech*) 521; by-word; technicality, lingo, slang, cant, *argot,* St. Giles's Greek, thieves' Latin, peddler's French, flash tongue, Billingsgate, Wall Street slang.

pseudonym &c. (*misnomer*) 565; Mr. So-and-so; what d'ye call 'em, what's his name; thingum-my, -bob; *je ne sais quoi.*

neologist, coiner of words.

V. coin words.

Adj. neologic, -al; rare; archaic; obsolete &c. (*old*) 124; colloquial, dialectic, slang, cant.

---

564. Nomenclature. — N. nomen-clature; naming &c. *v.*; nuncupation, nomination, baptism; orismology; *onomatopœia*; antonomasia.

name; appella-tion, -tive; designa-tion; title; head, -ing, caption; denomi-nation; by-name, epithet.

style, proper name; præ-, ag-, cog-nomen; patronymic, surname; cog-nomination; compellation, description; empty -title, – name; handle to one's name; namesake, eponym.

synonym, antonym.

term, expression, noun; by-word; convertible terms &c. 522; technical term; cant &c. 563.

V. name, call, term, denominate, designate, style, entitle, intitule, clepe, dub, christen, baptize, nickname, char-acterize, specify, define, distinguish by the name of; label &c. (*mark*) 550.

be -called &c. *v.*; take –, bear –, go (*or* be known) by –, go (*or* pass) under –, rejoice in- the name of.

Adj. named &c. *v.*; hight, yclept, known as; what one may -well, – fairly, – properly, – fitly- call.

nuncupa-tory, -tive; cognominal, titular, nominal; orismological.

565. Misnomer.—N. misnomer; *lucus a non lucendo*; Mrs. Malaprop; what d'ye call 'em &c. (*neologism*) 563.

nickname, *sobriquet,* by-name, han-dle, moniker; assumed -name, – title; *alias*; *nom de -guerre, – plume, – théâtre*; pseudonym, pen name, stage name.

V. mis-name, -call, -term; nick-name; assume -a name, – an alias.

Adj. misnamed &c. *v.*; pseudony-mous; *soi-disant*; self-called, -styled, -christened; so-called.

nameless, anonymous; without a –, having no- name; innominate, un-named.

Adv. in no sense.

---

566. Phrase.—N. phrase, expression, set phrase; sentence, paragraph; figure of speech &c. 521; idi-om, -otism; turn of expression.

paraphrase &c. (*synonym*) 522; periphrase &c. (*circumlocution*) 573; motto &c. (*proverb*) 496.

phraseology &c. 569.

V. express, phrase; word, – it; give -words, – expression- to; voice; arrange in –, clothe in –, put into –, express by- words; couch in terms; find words to express; speak by the card.

Adj. expressed &c. *v.*; idiomatic.

Adv. in -round, – set, – good, set- terms; in set phrases.

567. Grammar.—N. grammar, accidence, syntax, *praxis*, analysis, paradigm, punctuation; parts of speech; inflexion, case, declension, conjugation; *jus et norma loquendi*; Lindley Murray &c. (*school-book*) 542; correct style; philology &c. (*language*) 560.

V. parse, analyze; decline, conjugate; punctuate.

Adj. grammatical; syntactic; inflexional.

568. Solecism.—N. solecism; bad --, false –, faulty- grammar; slip, error; slip of the -pen, – tongue; *lapsus calami-, – linguæ; faux pas*; slip-slop; bull.

V. use -bad, – faulty- grammar; solecize, commit a solecism; murder the -King's, – Queen's- English; break Priscian's head.

Adj. ungrammatical; in-correct, -accurate; faulty, improper, incongruous, abnormal.

569. Style.—N. style, diction, phraseology, wording; manner, strain; composition; mode of expression, choice of words, literary power, ready pen, pen of a ready writer; command of language &c. (*eloquence*) 582; authorship; *la morgue littéraire.*

V. express by words &c. 566; write.

Various Qualities of Style

570. Perspicuity.—N. perspicuity &c. (*intelligibility*) 518; plain speaking &c. (*manifestation*) 525; defin-iteness, -ition; exactness &c. 494; perspicuousness, logical acuteness.

Adj. lucid &c. (*intelligible*) 518; explicit &c. (*manifest*) 525; exact &c. 494.

571. Obscurity.—N. obscurity &c. (*unintelligibility*) 519; involution; hard words; ambiguity &c. 520; vagueness &c. 475, inexactness &c. 495; what d'ye call 'em &c. (*neologism*) 563; cloudiness, confusion.

Adj. obscure &c. *n.*; crabbed, involved, confused.

572. Conciseness.—N. conciseness &c. *adj.*; brevity, 'the soul of wit,' laconism; Tacitus; ellipsis; syncope; abridgment &c. (*shortening*) 201; compression &c. 195; epitome &c. 596; monostich; portmanteau word, telescope word, protogram.

V. be -concise &c. *adj.*; condense &c. 195; abridge &c. 201; abstract &c. 596; come to the point.

Adj. concise, brief, short, terse, close; to the point, exact; neat, compact, condensed, pointed; laconic, curt, pithy, trenchant, summary; pregnant; compendious &c. (*compendium*) 596; succinct; elliptical, epigrammatic, crisp, sententious.

Adv. concisely &c. *adj.*; briefly,

573. Diffuseness.—N. diffuseness &c. *adj.*; amplification &c. *v.*; dilating &c. *v.*; verbosity, *verbiage*, wordiness, cloud of words, *copia verborum*; flow of words &c. (*loquacity*) 584.

poly-, tauto-, batto-, perisso-logy; pleonasm, exuberance, redundance; thrice-told tale; prolixity; circumlocution, *ambages*; periphra-se, -sis; roundabout phrases; episode; expletive; penny-a-lining; padding, drivel, twaddle, rigmarole; richness &c. 577.

V. be -diffuse &c. *adj.*; run out on, descant, expatiate, enlarge, dilate, amplify, expand, inflate, pad; launch –, branch- out; rant.

maunder, prose; harp upon &c. (*repeat*) 104; dwell on, insist upon.

summarily; in -brief, – short, – a word, – few words, – a nutshell; for shortness sake; to -come to the point, – make a long story short, – cut the matter short, – be brief; it comes to this, the long and the short of it is.

digress, ramble, *battre la campagne*, beat about the bush, perorate, spin a long yarn, protract; spin –, swell –, draw- out, drivel.

Adj. dif-, pro-fuse; wordy, verbose, largiloquent, copious, exuberant, effusive, pleonastic, lengthy; long, -some, -winded, -spun, -drawn out; diffusive, spun out, protracted, prolix, prosing, maundering; circumlocutory, periphrastic, ambagious, roundabout; digressive; dis-, ex-cursive; rambling, episodic; flatulent, frothy.

Adv. diffusely &c. *adj.*; at large, *in extenso*; about it and about it.

574. Vigour.—N. vigour, power, force; boldness, raciness &c. *adj.*; spirit, point, antithesis, piquancy; *verve*, glow, fire, warmth, ardour, enthusiasm; 'thoughts that breathe and words that burn'; strong language; punch; gravity, sententiousness; elevation, loftiness, sublimity.

eloquence; command of -words, – language.

Adj. vigorous, nervous, powerful, forcible, trenchant, mordant, biting, incisive, impressive; sensational.

spirited, lively, glowing, sparkling, racy, bold, slashing; pungent, *piquant*, full of point, pointed, pithy, antithetical; sententious.

lofty, elevated, sublime, grand, weighty, ponderous; eloquent; vehement, petulant, impassioned; poetic.

Adv. in -glowing, – good set, – no measured- terms.

575. Feebleness.—N. feebleness &c. *adj.*

Adj. feeble, bald, tame, meagre, insipid, nerveless, jejune, vapid, trashy, cold, frigid, poor, dull, dry, languid; pros-ing, -y, -aic; unvaried, monotonous, weak, frail, washy, wishy-washy, sloppy; sketchy, slight; careless, slovenly, loose, lax; slip-shod, -slop; inexact; dis-jointed, -connected; puerile, childish; flatulent; rambling &c. (*diffuse*) 573.

576. Plainness.—N. plainness &c. *adj.*; simplicity, severity; plain -terms, – English; Saxon English; household words.

V. speak plainly; call a spade 'a spade'; plunge *in medias res*; come to the point.

Adj. plain, simple; un-ornamented, -adorned, -varnished; home-ly, -spun; neat; severe, chaste, pure, Saxon; commonplace, matter of fact, natural, prosaic, sober, unimaginative.

dry, unvaried, monotonous &c. 575.

Adv. in plain -terms, – words, – English, – common parlance; point blank.

577. Ornament. — N. ornament; floridness &c. *adj.*; turg-idity, -escence; altiloquence &c. *adj.*; orotundity; declamation, teratology; well-rounded periods; elegance &c. 578.

inversion, antithesis, alliteration, *paronomasia*; figurativeness &c. (*metaphor*) 521.

flourish; flowers of -speech, – rhetoric; euph-uism, -emism.

big-, high-sounding words; macrology, *sesquipedalia verba*, sesquipedalianism; Alexandrine; inflation, pretension; rant, bombast, fustian, bunkum, balderdash, prose run mad; fine writing; Minerva press.

phrasemonger; euph-uist, -emist.

V. ornament, overlay with ornament, overcharge; smell of the lamp.

Adj. ornamented &c. *v.*; beautified &c. 847; ornate, florid, rich, flowery; euph-uistic, -emistic; sonorous; high-, big-sounding; inflated, swelling, tumid; turg-id, -escent; pedantic, pompous, stilted;

high-flown, -flowing; sententious, rhetorical, declamatory; grandiose; grand-, magn-, alt-iloquent; sesquipedal, -ian; Johnsonian, mouthy; bombastic; fustian; frothy, flashy, flaming, flamboyant.

antithetical, alliterative; figurative &c. 521; artificial &c. (*inelegant*) 579.

Adv. *ore rotundo*; with rounded phrase.

578. Elegance.—N. elegance, purity, grace, ease, felicity, distinction, gracefulness, refinement, readiness &c. *adj.*; concinnity, euphony, numerosity, balance, rhythm, symmetry, proportion; restraint; good taste, propriety.

well rounded –, well turned –, flowing- periods; the right word in the right place; antithesis &c. 577.

purist, stylist.

V. point an antithesis, round a period.

Adj. elegant, polished, classical, Attic, correct, Ciceronian, artistic; chaste, pure, Saxon, academical.

graceful, easy, readable, fluent, flowing, tripping; unaffected, natural, unlaboured; mellifluous; euph-onious, -emistic; rhythmical, balanced, symmetrical.

felicitous, happy, neat; well –, neatly- -put, – expressed.

579. Inelegance. — N. inelegance; vulgarity, bad taste; stiffness &c. *adj.*; unlettered Muse; barbarism; slang &c. 563; solecism &c. 568; mannerism &c. (*affectation*) 855; euphuism; fustian &c. 577; cacophony; want of balance; words that -break the teeth, – dislocate the jaw.

V. be -inelegant &c. *adj.*

Adj. inelegant, graceless, ungraceful, unpolished; harsh, abrupt; dry, stiff, cramped, formal, *guindé*; forced, laboured, awkward; artificial, mannered, ponderous; turgid &c. 577; affected, euphuistic; barbarous, uncouth, grotesque, rude, crude, halting; vulgar, offensive to ears polite.

---

2. *Spoken Language*

580. Voice.—N. voice; vocality; organ, lungs, bellows; good –, fine –, powerful &c. (*loud*) 404 –, musical &c. 413- voice; intonation; tone &c. (*sound*) 402- of voice.

vocalization; cry &c. 411; strain, utterance, prolation; exclam-, ejacul-, vocifer-ation; enunci-, articul-ation; articulate sound, distinctness; clearness, – of articulation; stage whisper; delivery; attack.

accent, -uation; emphasis, stress; broad –, strong –, pure –, native –, foreign- accent; pronunciation.

[Word similarly pronounced] homonym.

orthoepy; euphony &c. (*melody*) 413.

gastri-, ventri-loquism; ventriloquist; polyphon-ism, -ist.

[Science of voice] phonology &c. (*sound*) 402.

V. sing, speak, utter, breathe, voice; give -utterance, – tongue; cry &c.

581. Aphony.—N. aphony, *aphonia*; dumbness &c. *adj.*; obmutescence; absence –, want- of voice; dysphony; silence &c. (*taciturnity*) 585; raucity; harsh &c. 410 –, unmusical &c. 414- voice; *falsetto*, 'childish treble'; mute, dummy, deaf mute.

V. keep silence &c. 585; speak -low, – softly; whisper &c. (*faintness*) 405.

silence; render -mute, – silent &c. 403; muzzle, muffle, suppress, smother, gag, strike dumb, dumb-found, -founder; drown the voice, put to silence, stop one's mouth, cut one short.

stick in the throat.

Adj. aphon-ous, -ic, dumb, mute; deaf-mute, – and dumb; mum; tongue-tied; breath-, tongue-, voice-, speech-, word-less; mute as a -fish, – stockfish, – mackerel; silent &c. (*taciturn*) 585; muzzled; in-articulate, -audible.

croaking, raucous, hoarse, husky,

(*shout*) 411; ejaculate, rap out; vocalize, prolate, articulate, enunciate, enounce, pronounce, accentuate, aspirate, deliver, mouth; emit, murmur, whisper, – in the ear, croon, yodel.

Adj. vocal, phonetic, oral; ejaculatory, articulate, distinct, stertorous; enunciative; accentuated, aspirated; euphonious &c. (*melodious*) 413.

dry, hollow, sepulchral, hoarse as a raven.

Adv. with -bated breath, – the finger on the lips; *sotto voce*; in a -low tone, – cracked voice, – broken voice; in an aside.

Phr. *vox faucibus hæsit.*

------

582. Speech.—N. speech, faculty of speech; locution, talk, parlance, verbal intercourse, prolation, oral communication, word of mouth, *parole*, palaver, prattle; effusion.

oration, recitation, delivery, say, address, speech, lecture, harangue, sermon, *tirade*, screed, formal speech, salutatory, peroration; prelection; speechifying; soliloquy &c. 589; allocution &c. 586; interlocution &c. 588.

oratory; elo-cution, -quence; rhetoric, declamation; grandi-, multiloquence; burst of eloquence; facundity; talkativeness; flow –, command- of -words, – language; *copia verborum*; power of speech, gift of the gab; *usus loquendi.*

speaker &c. *v.*; spokesman; pro-, inter-locutor; mouthpiece, Hermes; ora-tor, -trix, -tress; Demosthenes, Cicero; rhetorician; stump –, platform-orator, tub-thumper; elocutionist; speech-maker, patterer, *improvisatore.*

V. speak, – of; say, utter, pronounce, deliver, give utterance to; utter –, pour- forth; breathe, let fall, come out with; rap –, blurt- out; have on one's lips; have at the -end, – tip- of one's tongue.

break silence; open one's -lips, – mouth; lift –, raise- one's voice; give –, wag the- tongue; talk, outspeak; put in a word or two.

hold forth; make –, deliver- -a speech &c. *n.*; speechify, harangue, declaim, stump, flourish, spout, rant, recite, lecture, preach, sermonize, discourse, be on one's legs; have –, say- one's say; expatiate &c. (*speak at length*) 573; speak one's mind.

soliloquize &c. 589; tell &c. (*inform*) 527; speak to &c. 586; talk together &c. 588.

be -eloquent &c. *adj.*; have -a tongue in one's head, – the gift of the gab &c. *n.*

pass –, escape- one's lips; fall from the -lips, – mouth.

Adj. speaking &c., spoken &c. *v.*; oral, lingual, phonetic, not written, unwritten, outspoken; elo-quent, -cutionary; orat-, rhet-orical; declamatory; grandiloquent &c. 577; talkative &c. 584.

583. [Imperfect Speech.] **Stammering.—N.** inarticulateness; stammering &c. *v.*; hesitation &c. *v.*; impediment in one's speech; aphasia, titubancy, traulism; whisper &c. (*faint sound*) 405; lisp, drawl, tardiloquence; nasal -tone, – accent; twang; *falsetto* &c. (*want of voice*) 581; broken -voice, – accents, – sentences.

brogue &c. 563; slip of the tongue, *lapsus linguæ.*

V. stammer, stutter, hesitate, falter, hammer; balbu-tiate, -cinate; haw, hum and haw, be unable to put two words together.

mumble, mutter; maund, -er; whisper &c. 405; mince, lisp; jabber, gabble, gibber; sp-, spl-utter; muffle, mump; drawl, mouth; croak; speak -thick, – through the nose; snuffle, clip one's words; murder the -language, – King's (*or* Queen's) English; mis-pronounce, -say.

Adj. stammering &c. *v.*; inarticulate, guttural, nasal; tremulous.

Adv. *sotto voce* &c. (*faintly*) 405.

Adv. orally &c. *adj.*; by word of mouth, *vivâ voce*, from the lips of.

Phr. quoth –, said- he &c.

---

584. Loquacity. — N. loquac-ity, -iousness; talkativeness &c. *adj.*; garrulity; multiloquence, much speaking, effusion, wordiness.

jaw; gab, -ble; jabber, chatter; prate, prattle, cackle, clack; twaddle, twattle, rattle; *caquet, -terie*; blabber, *bavardage*, bibble-babble, gibble-gabble; small talk &c. (*converse*) 588.

fluency, flippancy, volubility, flowing tongue; flow, – of words; *flux de -bouche, – mots, – paroles; copia verborum, cacoëthes loquendi*; verbosity &c. (*diffuseness*) 573; gift of the gab &c. (*eloquence*) 582.

talker; chatter-er, -box; babbler &c. *v.*; rattle; ranter; sermonizer, proser, driveller; wind bag; gossip &c. (*converse*) 588; magpie, jay, parrot, poll, Babel; *moulin à paroles*.

V. be -loquacious &c. *adj.*; talk glibly, pour forth, patter; prate, palaver, prose, chatter, prattle, clack, jabber, jaw; rattle, – on; twaddle, twattle; babble, gabble; out-talk; talk oneself -out of breath, – hoarse; maunder, gush, blatter; talk a donkey's hind leg off; expatiate &c. (*speak at length*) 573; gossip &c. (*converse*) 588; din in the ears &c. (*repeat*) 104; talk -at random, – nonsense &c. 497; be hoarse with talking.

Adj. loquacious, talkative, conversational, garrulous, linguacious, multiloquous; chattering &c. *v.*; chatty &c. (*sociable*) 892; declamatory &c. 582; open-mouthed.

fluent, voluble, glib, flippant; long-tongued, -winded &c. (*diffuse*) 573.

Adv. trippingly on the tongue; glibly &c. *adj.*

Phr. the tongue running -fast, – loose, – on wheels.

---

585. Taciturnity.—N. silence, muteness, obmutescence; taciturnity, pauciloquy, costiveness, curtness; reserve, reticence &c. (*concealment*) 528; *aposiopesis*.

man of few words.

V. be -silent &c. *adj.*; keep silence; hold one's -tongue, – peace, – jaw; not speak &c. 582; say nothing; seal –, close –, put a padlock on- the -lips, – mouth; put a bridle on one's tongue; keep one's tongue between one's teeth; make no sign, not let a word escape one; keep a secret &c. 528; not have a word to say; lay –, place- the finger on the lips; render mute &c. 581.

stick in one's throat.

Adj. silent, mute, mum; silent as -a post, – a stone, – the grave &c. (*still*) 403; dumb &c. 581.

taciturn, sparing of words; close, – mouthed, – tongued; laconic, costive, inconversable, curt; reserved; reticent &c. (*concealing*) 528.

Int. tush! silence! mum! hush! *chut!* hist! tut! &c. 403.

---

586. Allocution. — N. allocution, alloquy, address; speech &c. 582; apostrophe, interpellation, appeal, invocation, salutation; word in the ear.

[Feigned dialogue] dialogism.

platform &c. 542; audience &c. (*interview*) 588.

V. speak to, address, accost, make up to, apostrophize, appeal to, invoke; hail, salute; call to, halloo.

take -aside, – by the button, button-hole; talk to in private.

lecture &c. (*make a speech*) 582.

Int. soho! halloo! hey! hist! hi!

---

587. Response &c., *see* Answer 462;

---

588. Interlocution.—N. interlocution; collocution, colloquy, converse, conversation, confabulation, talk, discourse, verbal intercourse; communion, oral communication, commerce; dia-, duo-, tria-logue.

causerie, chat, chit-chat; small –, table –, teatable –, town –, village –, idle- talk; tattle, gossip, tittle-tattle; babble, -ment; *tripotage*, cackle, prittle-prattle, *on dit*; talk of the -town, – village.

conference, parley, interview, audience, *pourparler*; *tête-à-tête*; reception, *conversazione*; congress &c. (*council*) 696; pow-wow.

hall of audience, *durbar*, coliseum, assembly hall, auditorium.

palaver, debate, logomachy, war of words, controversy.

talker, gossip, tattler; Paul Pry; tabby; chatterer &c. (*loquacity*) 584; interlocutor &c. (*spokesman*) 582; conversation-ist, -alist; dialogist.

'the feast of reason and the flow of soul'; *mollia tempora fandi*.

V. talk together, converse, confabulate; hold –, carry on –, join in –, engage in- a conversation; put in a word; shine in conversation; bandy words; parley; palaver; chat, gossip, tattle; prate &c. (*loquacity*) 584.

discourse –, confer –, commune –, commerce- with; hold -converse, – conference, – intercourse; talk it over; be closeted with; talk with one -in private, – *tête-à-tête*.

Adj. conversing &c. *v.*; interlocutory; convers-ational, -able; discursive, -çoursive; chatty &c. (*sociable*) 892; colloquial, *tête-à-tête*, confabulatory.

589. Soliloquy.—N. soliloquy, monologue, apostrophe.

solilo-quist, -quizer, monologist.

V. soliloquize; say –, talk- to oneself; say aside, think aloud, apostrophize.

Adj. soliloquizing &c. *v.*

Adv. aside.

---

3. *Written Language*

590. Writing.—N. writing &c. *v.*; chiro-, stelo-, cero-graphy, graphology; stylography; pen-craft, -script, -manship; quill-driving; typewriting.

writing, manuscript, MS., *literæ scriptæ*; these presents.

stroke –, dash- of the pen; *coup de plume*; line; pen and ink.

letter &c. 561; uncial writing, cuneiform character, arrow-head, Ogham, Runes, futhorc; hieroglyphic, hieratic, demotic; script; contraction.

short-hand; steno-, brachy-, tachy-graphy; secret writing, writing in cipher; crypt-, stegan-ography; phono-, pasi-, poly-, logo-graphy.

copy; tran-, re-script; draft, rough –, fair- copy; handwriting; signature, sign-manual; auto-, mono-, holo-graph; hand, fist; mark.

calligraphy; good –, running –,

591. Printing.—N. printing; block –, type- printing, lino-, mono-type; plate printing &c. (*engraving*) 558; the press &c. (*publication*) 531; composition.

print, letterpress, text, matter, standing type; context, note, page, column; over-running; head-, foot-line, title.

typography; stereo-, electro-, aprotype; type, black letter, heavy type, font, fount; pi, pie; capitals &c. (*letters*) 561; diamond, pearl, nonpareil, minion, brevier, bourgeois, long primer, small pica, pica, english, great primer.

folio &c. (*book*) 593; copy, impression, pull, proof, galley –, author's –, page- proof, revise.

printer, compositor, reader; printer's devil.

V. print; compose; put –, go- to press; pass –, see- through the press;

flowing –, cursive –, legible –, copper-plate –, round –, bold- hand.

cacography, *griffonage*, *barbouillage*; bad –, cramped –, crabbed –, illegible-hand; scribble &c. *v.*; *pattes de mouche*; ill-formed letters; pot-hooks and hangers.

stationery; pen, quill, goose-quill, reed; stylographic-, fountain-pen; pencil, style, stylus; paper, foolscap, parchment, vellum, papyrus, pad, tablet, block, note book, slate, marble, pillar, table, black board.

ink-bottle, -pot, -stand, -well, -horn; typewriter.

transcription &c. (*copy*) 21; inscription &c. (*record*) 551; super-scription &c. (*indication*) 550.

composition, authorship; *cacoethes scribendi*.

writer, scribe, amanuensis, scrivener, secretary, clerk, penman, copyist, transcriber, quill-driver; writer for the press &c. (*author*) 593.

shorthand writer, stenographer; typewriter, typist.

V. write, pen; copy, engross; write out, – fair; transcribe; scribble, scrawl, scrabble, scratch; interline; stain paper; write down &c. (*record*) 551; sign &c. (*attest*) 467; take down, – in shorthand; typewrite, type.

compose, indite, draw up, redact, draft, formulate; dictate; in-scribe, throw on paper, dash off; concoct.

take -up the pen, – pen in hand; shed –, spill –, dip one's pen in- ink.

Adj. writing &c. *v.*; written &c. *v.*; in -writing, – black and white; under one's hand.

uncial, Runic, cuneiform, hieroglyphical &c. *n.*

Adv. *currente calamo*; pen in hand.

publish &c. 531; bring out; appear in –, rush into- print.

Adj. printed &c. *v.*; in type; typo-graphical &c. *n.*

---

592. Correspondence. — N. corre-spondence, letter, epistle, note, *billet*, post-, letter-card, missive, circular, form letter; favour, *billet-doux*; des-, dis-patch; *bulletin*, communication &c. 532; these presents; rescript, -ion; post &c. (*messenger*) 534; letter writer, correspondent.

V. correspond, – with; write –, send a letter- to; keep up a correspondence; drop a line to; despatch; communicate with; circularize.

Adj. epistolary.

---

593. Book.—N. book, -let; writing, work, volume, tome, opuscule; tract, -ate; *livret*; *brochure*, *libretto*, hand-book, treatise, text-book, codex, man-ual, pamphlet, monograph, enchiridion, circular, publication; book of poems; novel; chap-book.

part, issue, number, *livraison*; album, portfolio; periodical, serial, magazine, *ephemeris*, annual, journal.

paper, bill, sheet, broadsheet, screed; leaf, -let; fly-leaf, page; quire, ream.

chapter, section, head, article, para-graph, passage, clause, supplement, appendix; *feuilleton*.

folio, quarto, octavo; duo-, sexto-, octo-decimo.

en-, cyclopædia, dictionary, lexicon, thesaurus, concordance, anthology, bibliography; compilation, compendium, catalogue &c. 86; library, bibliotheca; the press &c. (*publication*) 531.

writer, author, *littérateur*, essayist, journalist, publicist; scribe, penman, war –, special –, correspondent; pen, scribbler, the scrib-bling race; ghost, hack, literary hack, Grub-street writer; writer for –, gentleman of –, representative of- the press; reporter, penny-a-liner; editor, sub-editor; playwright &c. 599; poet &c. 597.

bookseller, publisher; biblio-pole, -polist, -grapher; librarian; book -collector, – worm.

book -shop, – club, circulating –, lending –, public- library; publishing house.

knowledge of books, bibliography; book-learning &c. (*knowledge*) 490.

594. Description.—N. description, account, statement, report; *exposé* &c. (*disclosure*) 529; specification, particulars, scenario, plot; state –, summary- of facts; brief &c. (*abstract*) 596; return &c. (*record*) 551; *catalogue raisonné* &c. (*list*) 86; guide-book &c. (*information*) 527.

delineation &c. (*representation*) 554; sketch, vignette; monograph; minute –, detailed –, particular –, circumstantial –, graphic- account; narration, recital, rehearsal, relation.

histori-, chron-ography; historic Muse, Clio; history; bi-, autobi-ography; necrology, obituary.

narrative, history; memoir, memorials; annals &c. (*chronicle*) 551; tradition, legend, saga, epic, epos, story, tale, historiette; personal narrative, journal, letters, life, adventures, fortunes, experiences, confessions; anecdote, ana, *trait*.

work of fiction, short story, novelette, novel, romance, penny dreadful, shilling shocker, Minerva press; fairy –, nursery- tale; fable, allegory, parable, apologue.

relator &c. *v.*; *raconteur*; historian &c. (*recorder*) 553; biographer, fabulist, novelist, story teller, romancer, teller of tales, spinner of yarns, anecdotist.

V. describe; set forth &c. (*state*) 535; draw a picture, picture; portray &c. (*represent*) 554; characterize, particularize; narrate, relate, recite, recount, sum up, run over, recapitulate, rehearse, fight one's battles over again.

unfold &c. (*disclose*) 529- a tale; tell; give –, render- an account of; report, make a report, draw up a statement.

detail; enter into –, descend to- -particulars, – details.

Adj. descriptive, graphic, narrative, epic, suggestive, well-drawn; historic; auto-, biographical, realistic, expository, tradition-al, -ary; legendary; fabulous, mythical; anecdotic, storied; described &c. *v.*

595. Dissertation.—N. dissertation, treatise, essay; *thesis*, theme; tract, -ate, -ation, excursus; discourse, memoir, disquisition, lecture, sermon, homily, pandect.

commentary, review, *critique*, criticism, article; lead-er, -ing article, editorial; argument, running commentary.

investigation &c. (*inquiry*) 461; study &c. (*consideration*) 451; discussion &c. (*reasoning*) 476; exposition &c. (*explanation*) 522.

commentator, critic, essayist, pamphleteer; publicist, reviewer, leader writer, editor, annotator.

V. dissert –, descant –, write –, touch- upon a subject; dissertate; treat of –, take up –, ventilate –, discuss –, deal with –, go into –, canvass –, handle –, do justice to- a subject; comment, criticize, interpret &c. 522.

Adj. dis-cursive, -coursive; disquisitional, disquisitionary; expository, critical.

596. Compendium.—N. compend, -ium; abstract, *précis*, epitome, *multum in parvo*, analysis, pandect, digest, sum and substance, brief, abridgment, summary, *aperçu*, draft, minute, note; synopsis, text-book, *conspectus*, outlines, syllabus, contents, heads, prospectus.

album; scrap –, note –, memorandum –, commonplace- book; extracts, *excerpta*, cuttings; fugitive -pieces, – writings; *spicilegium*, flowers, anthology, miscellany, *collectanea, analecta*; compilation.

recapitulation, *résumé*, review.

abbrevia-tion, -ture; contraction; shortening &c. 201; compression &c. 195.

V. abridge, abstract, epitomize, summarize; make –, prepare –, draw –, compile- an abstract &c. *n.*

recapitulate, review, skim, run over, sum up.

abbreviate &c. (*shorten*) 201; condense &c. (*compress*) 195; compile &c. (*collect*) 72; edit, blue pencil.

Adj. compendious, synoptic, analectic, analytical; abridged &c. *v.*

Adv. in -short, – epitome, – substance, – few words.

Phr. it lies in a nutshell.

---

597. Poetry.—N. poetry, poetics, poesy, Muse, Calliope, tuneful Nine, Parnassus, Helicon, Pierides, Pierian spring, afflatus, inspiration.

versification, rhyming, making verses; prosody, scansion, orthometry.

poem; epic, – poem; epopee, *epopæa*, ode, epode, idyl, lyric, eclogue, pastoral, bucolic, georgic, dithyramb, anacreontic, sonnet, roundelay, *rondel, rondoletto, rondeau, rondo,* triolet; madrigal, canzonet, *cento*, monody, elegy, palinode; rhapsody.

dramatic –, lyric- poetry; opera; posy, anthology.

song, ballad, lay; love –, drinking –, war –, folk –, sea- song; lullaby; music &c. 415; nursery rhymes.

[Bad poetry] doggerel, Hudibrastic verse, prose run mad; macaronics; macaronic –, leonine- verse; runes.

canto, stanza, distich, verse, line, couplet, triplet, quatrain, sestet; *strophe, antistrophe*, refrain, chorus, burden.

verse, rhyme, assonance, crambo, metre, measure, foot, numbers, strain, rhythm; accentuation &c. (*voice*) 580; iambus, dactyl, spondee, trochee, anapæst &c.; hex-, pent-ameter; Alexandrine; blank verse, alliteration.

elegiacs &c. *adj.*; elegiac &c. *adj.* -verse, – metre, – poetry.

poet, – laureate; laureate; minor poet, bard, lyrist, scald, troubadour, *trouvère*; minstrel; minne-, meister-singer; *improvisatore*; versifier, sonneteer; ballad monger; rhym-er, -ist, -ester; poetaster.

V. poetize, sing, versify, make verses, rhyme, scan.

Adj. poetic, -al; lyric, -al; tuneful; epic; dithyrambic &c. *n.*; metrical; a-, catalectic; elegiac, iambic, trochaic, spondaic, anapæstic; Ionic, Sapphic, Alcaic, Pindaric.

598. Prose.—N. prose, – writer, pros-aism, -aist, -er.

V. prose, write prose.

write -prose, – in prose.

Adj. pros-y, -aic; unpoetical.

rhymeless, unrhymed, in prose, not in verse.

---

599. The Drama.—N. the -drama, – stage, – theatre, – play; theatricals, dramaturgy, histrionic art, buskin, sock, *cothurnus*, Melpomene and Thalia, Thespis.

play, drama, stage-play, piece, five-act play, tragedy, comedy, opera, comic opera, *vaudeville, comedietta, lever de rideau*, curtain raiser, interlude, afterpiece, exode, farce, *divertissement, extravaganza*, burletta, harlequinade, pantomime, mimodrama, burlesque, *opéra bouffe*, musical comedy, review, revue, intimate revue, variety, cabaret entertainment, *ballet, spectacle*, masque, *drame, comédie drame*; melo-drama, -drame; *comédie larmoyante*, emotional drama, sensation drama, tragi-, farcical-comedy; mono-drame, -logue; duologue; trilogy; charade, *proverbe*; mystery, miracle –, morality- play.

act, scene, *tableau*; in-, intro-duction; pro-, epi-logue, curtain; *libretto*, book, script.

performance, representation, show, *mise en scène*, stagery, *jeu de théâtre*, stage-craft; acting; gesture &c. 550; impersonation &c. 554; stage business, gag, patter, buffoonery.

theatre; play-, opera-house; house; music hall; *cabaret*; amphi-theatre, circus, hippodrome; puppet-show, *fantoccini*; *marionnettes*, Punch and Judy.

cinema, -tograph-, picture –, theatre, the pictures, the movies, the talkies.

auditory, *auditorium*, front of the house, stalls, boxes, balcony, dress –, upper- -circle, – boxes, amphitheatre, pit, gallery; *foyer*; green-room; dressing rooms, *coulisses*.

flat; drop, – scene; wing, screen, side-scene; transformation scene, curtain, act-drop, safety –, fire- curtain; *proscenium*, forestage.

stage, revolving stage, scene, the boards; star –, grave –, trap, mezzanine floor; flies; gridiron, floats, battens, footlights; lime –, spot –, flood –, bunch-lights; scenery, set, *décor*; orchestra;

theatrical -costume, – properties, props.

part, *rôle*, character, cast, *dramatis personæ*; *répertoire*.

actor, player; stage –, strolling- player; old –, stager, performer; mime, -r; *artiste*; com-, trag-edian, straight man; *tragédienne*, Thespian, Roscius, star.

pantomimist, clown, harlequin, *buffo*, buffoon, *farceur, grimacier*, pantaloon, columbine; *Pierrot, Pierrette*; punch, -inello; *pulcinell-o*, -a; mute, *figurante*, general utility; super, -numerary, extra.

mummer, guiser, guisard, gysart, masque.

mountebank, Jack Pudding; tumbler, posture-master, acrobat, equilibrist, juggler, contortionist; *danseuse, ballerina*, ballet -dancer, – girl, *coryphée*; *bayadère, geisha*; chorus -singer, – girl.

company; first tragedian, *prima donna*, lead, leading lady, pro-tagonist; *jeune premier*; juvenile lead, *débutant, -e*; light –, genteel –, low- -comedy, – comedian; *soubrette*, walking gentleman, *amoroso*, heavy, heavy father, *ingénue, jeune veuve, commère, compère*.

property man, *costumier*, machinist, stage hand, electrician, prompter, call-boy; director, manager; stage –, acting –, business- manager; *entrepreneur, impresario*, producer, press agent.

dramatic -author, – writer; play-writer, -wright; dramatist, mimo-grapher; dramatic critic.

V. act, play, perform; stage, produce, put on the stage; personate &c. 554; mimic &c. (*imitate*) 19; enact; play –, act –, go through –, perform- a part; rehearse, spout, gag, rant; 'strut and fret one's hour upon a stage'; tread the -stage, – boards; come out; star.

Adj. dramatic; theatric, -al; scenic, histrionic, anctorial, comic, tragic, buskined, farcical, tragi-comic, melodramatic, operatic; stagey spec-tacular; stagestruck.

Adv. on the -stage, – boards; before -the floats, – an audience; in the limelight, behind the footlights; behind the scenes.

CLASS V

Words relating to THE VOLUNTARY POWERS*

CLASS V

Words relating to THE VOLUNTARY POWERS*

Division (I.) INDIVIDUAL VOLITION

Section I. Volition in General

1°. *Acts of Volition*

600. Will.—N. will, volition, co-nation†, velleity; will and pleasure, free-will; freedom &c. 748; discretion; choice, inclination, intent, purpose, option &c. (*choice*) 609; voluntariness; spontane-ity, -ousness; originality.

pleasure, wish, desire, mind; frame of mind &c. (*inclination*) 602; intention &c. 620; predetermination &c. 611; self-control &c. determination &c. (*resolution*) 604; will-power.

V. will, list; see –, think- fit; determine &c. (*resolve*) 604; settle &c. (*choose*) 609; volunteer.

have a will of one's own; do what one chooses &c. (*freedom*) 748; have it all one's own way; have one's -will, – own way.

use –, exercise- one's discretion; take -upon oneself, – one's own course, – the law into one's own hands; do -of one's own accord, – upon one's own -responsibility, – authority; take the bit between one's teeth; take responsibility; originate &c. (*cause*) 153.

Adj. voluntary, volitive, volitional, wilful; free &c. 748; optional; discretion-al, -ary; volitient; dictatorial.

minded &c. (*willing*) 602; prepense &c. (*predetermined*) 611; intended &c. 620; autocratic; unbidden &c. (bid &c. 741); spontaneous; original &c. (*causal*) 153.

Adv. voluntarily &c. *adj.*; at -will, – pleasure; *à -volonté, – discrétion; al piacere; ad -libitum, – arbitrium*; as -one thinks proper, – it seems good to.

* Conative powers or faculties (Hamilton).

601. Necessity.—N. involuntariness; instinct, blind –, natural- impulse; inborn –, innate- proclivity; the force of circumstances.

necessi-ty, -tation, necessarianism; obligation; compulsion &c. 744; sub-jection &c. 749; stern –, hard –, dire –, imperious –, inexorable –, iron –, ad-verse- -necessity, – fate; what must be.

desti-ny, -nation; fatality, fate, *kis-met*, doom, foredoom, election, pre-destination; pre-, fore-ordination; lot, fortune; fatalism, determinism; in-evitableness &c. *adj.*; spell &c. 993.

star, -s; planet, -s; astral influence; sky, Fates, Norns, *Parcæ*, Sisters three, Clotho, Lachesis, Atropos; book of fate; God's will, will of Heaven; wheel of Fortune, Ides of March, Hobson's choice.

last -shift, – resort; *dernier ressort*; *pis aller* &c. (*substitute*) 147; necessaries &c. (*requirement*) 630.

necess-arian, -itarian; fatalist, deter-minist; automaton.

V. lie under a necessity; be -fated, – doomed, – destined &c., – in for, – under the necessity of; have no -choice, – alternative; be- obliged –, forced –, driven –, one's -fate &c. *n.*-to; be -pushed to the wall, – driven into a corner, – unable to help, – drawn irresistibly.

destine, doom, foredoom, devote; pre-destine, -ordain; cast a spell &c. 992; necessitate; compel &c. 744.

†Hamilton.

of one's own -accord, – free will; *proprio –, suo –, ex mero- motu*; out of one's own head; by choice &c. 609; purposely &c. (*intentionally*) 620; deliberately &c. 611.

Phr. *stet pro ratione voluntas; sic volo sic jubeo.*

Adj. necessary; needful &c. (*requisite*) 630.

fated; destined &c. *v.*; fateful; elect; spell-bound.

compulsory &c. (*compel*) 744; uncontrollable, inevitable, unavoidable, irresistible, irrevocable, inexorable, binding; avoid-, resist-less; written in the book of fate.

involuntary, instinctive, automatic, blind, mechanical; un-conscious, -witting, -thinking; unintentional &c. (*undesigned*) 621; impulsive &c. 612.

Adv. necessarily &c. *adv.*; of -necessity, – course; *ex necessitate rei*; needs must; perforce &c. 744; *nolens volens*; will he nil he, willy nilly, *bon gré mal gré*, willing or unwilling, *coûte que coûte*, forcefully. *faute de mieux*; by stress of; if need be.

Phr. it cannot be helped; there is no- help for, – helping- it; it -will, – must, – must needs- be, – be so, – have its way; the die is cast; *jacta est alea*; *che sarà sarà*; 'it is written'; one's- days are numbered, – fate is sealed; *Fata obstant; diis aliter visum.*

---

602. Willingness.—N. willingness, voluntariness &c. *adj.*; willing mind, heart.

disposition, inclination, leaning, *animus*; frame of mind, humour, mood, vein; bent &c. (*turn of mind*) 820; *penchant* &c. (*desire*) 865; aptitude &c. 698.

doc-ility, -ibleness, tractability; persuasi-bleness, -bility; pliability &c. (*softness*) 324.

geniality, cordiality; goodwill; alacrity, readiness, earnestness, forwardness, enthusiasm; zeal, eagerness &c. (*desire*) 865.

assent &c. 488; compliance &c. 762; pleasure &c. (*will*) 600.

labour of love, self-appointed task; volunteer, -ing, gratuitous service; unpaid worker, amateur.

V. be -willing &c. *adj.*; incline, lean to, mind, propend; had as lief; lend –, give –, turn- a willing ear; have -a, – half a, – a great- mind to; hold –, cling- to; desire &c. 865.

see –, think- -good, – fit, – proper; acquiescence &c. (*assent*) 488; comply with &c. 762.

swallow –, nibble at- the bait; gorge the hook; swallow hook, line and sinker; have –, make- no scruple of; make no bones of; jump –, catch- at; meet half way; volunteer, offer oneself &c. 763.

603. Unwillingness.—N. unwillingness &c. *adj.*; indispos-ition, -edness; disinclination, aversation, aversion; nolleity, nolition; renitence; reluctance; indifference &c. 866; backwardness &c. *adj.*; slowness &c. 275; want of -alacrity, – readiness; indocility &c. (*obstinacy*) 606.

scrupul-ousness, -osity; qualms of conscience, delicacy, demur, scruple, qualm, shrinking, recoil; hesitation &c. (*irresolution*) 605; fastidiousness &c. 868.

averseness &c. (*dislike*) 867; dissent &c. 489; refusal &c. 764.

slacker, scrimshanker, *embusqué*, unwilling worker, forced labor.

V. be -unwilling &c. *adj.*; nill; dislike &c. 867; grudge, begrudge; not be able to find it in one's heart to, not have the stomach to.

demur, stick at, scruple, stickle; hang fire, run rusty, slack, shirk, scamp, give up, fight shy of, not pull fair; recoil, shrink, swerve; hesitate &c. 605; avoid &c. 623.

oppose &c. 708; dissent &c. 489; refuse &c. 764.

Adj. unwilling; not in the vein, loth, shy of, disinclined, indisposed, averse, reluctant, not content; adverse &c. (*opposed*) 708; laggard, backward, remiss, slack, slow to; renitent; indifferent &c. 866; scrupulous; squeamish

Adj. willing, minded, fain, disposed, inclined, favourable; favourably-minded, -inclined, -disposed; nothing loth; in the -vein, – mood, – humour, – mind.

ready, forward, enthusiastic, earnest, eager; bent upon &c. (*desirous*) 865; predisposed, propense.

docile; persua-dable, -sible; suasible, easily persuaded, facile, easy-going; amenable; tractable &c. (*pliant*) 324; genial, gracious, cordial, hearty; content &c. (*assenting*) 488.

voluntary, gratuitous, spontaneous; unasked &c. (ask &c. 765); unforced &c. (*free*) 748.

Adv. willingly &c. *adj.*; fain, freely, as lief, heart and soul; with -pleasure, – all one's heart, – open arms; with -good, – right good- will; *de bonne volonté, ex animo*; *con amore*, heart in hand, nothing loth, without reluctance, of one's own accord, graciously, with a good grace, without demur.

à la bonne heure; by all -means, – manner of means; to one's heart's content; yes &c. (*assent*) 488.

Int. sure, -ly! of course!

&c. (*fastidious*) 868; repugnant &c. (*dislike*) 867; rest-iff, -ive; demurring &c. *v.*; unconsenting &c. (*refusing*) 764; involuntary &c. 601; grudging, irreconcilable.

Adv. unwillingly &c. *adj.*; grudgingly, with a heavy heart; with -a bad, – an ill- grace; against –, sore against- -one's wishes, – one's will, – the grain; *invitâ Minervâ*; *à contre cœur*; *malgré soi*; in spite of -one's teeth, – oneself; *nolens volens* &c. (*necessity*) 601; perforce &c. 744; under protest; no &c. 536; not for the world, far be it from me; not if I can help it; if I must I must.

---

604. Resolution.—N. determination, will; iron –, unconquerable- will; will of one's own, decision, resolution, backbone, grit; strength of -mind, – will; resolve &c. (*intent*) 620; *intransigeance*; firmness &c. (*stability*) 150; energy, manliness, vigour; game, pluck; resoluteness &c. (*courage*) 861; zeal &c. 682; *aplomb*; desperation; devot-ion, -edness.

mastery over self; self-control, -command, -mastery, -possession, -reliance, -government, -restraint, -conquest, -denial; moral -courage, – strength, – fibre; perseverance &c. 604a; tenacity; obstinacy &c. 606; bull-dog; British lion.

V. have -determination &c. *n.*; know one's own mind; be -resolved &c. *adj.*; make up one's mind, will, resolve, determine; decide &c. (*judgment*) 480; form –, come to- a -determination, – resolution, – resolve; conclude, fix, seal, determine once for all, bring to a crisis, drive matters to an extremity; take a decisive step &c. (*choice*) 609; take upon oneself &c. (*undertake*) 676.

devote oneself –, give oneself up- to; throw away the scabbard, kick down

605. Irresolution.—N. irresolution, infirmity of purpose, indecision; in-, un-determination, loss of will power; unsettlement; uncertainty &c. 475; demur, suspense; hesi-tating &c. *v.*, -tation, -tancy; vacillation; ambivalence; changeableness &c. 149; fluctuation; alternation &c. (*oscillation*) 314; caprice &c. 608; lukewarmness.

fickleness, levity, *légèreté*; pliancy &c. (*softness*) 324; weakness; timidity &c. 860; cowardice &c. 862; half measures.

waverer, ass between two bundles of hay; shuttlecock, butterfly; time-server, opportunist, turn coat.

V. be -irresolute &c. *adj.*; hang –, keep- in suspense; leave 'ad referendum'; think twice about, pause; dawdle &c. (*inactivity*) 683; remain neuter; dilly dally, hesitate, boggle, hover, wobble, shilly-shally, hum and haw, demur, not know one's own mind; debate, balance; dally –, coquet- with; will and will not, *chasser-balancer*; go half-way, compromise, make a compromise; be thrown off one's balance, stagger like a drunken man; be afraid &c. 860; let 'I dare not' wait upon 'I would'; falter, waver.

the ladder, nail one's colours to the mast, set one's back against the wall, set one's teeth, put one's foot down, burn one's bridges, take one's stand; stand firm &c. (*stability*) 150; steel oneself; stand no nonsense, not listen to the voice of the charmer.

buckle to; put –, lay –, set- one's shoulder to the wheel; put one's heart into; run the gantlet, make a dash at, take the bull by the horns; beard the lion in his den; rush –, plunge- *in medias res*; go in for; insist upon, make a point of; set one's heart, – mind- upon.

stick at nothing; make short work of &c. (*activity*) 682; not stick at trifles; go -all lengths, – the whole hog; persist &c. (*persevere*) 604a; go down with colours flying, die game; go through fire and water, ride in the whirlwind and direct the storm.

Adj. resolved &c. *v.*; determined; strong-willed, -minded; resolute &c. (*brave*) 861; self-possessed, plucky, tenacious; decided, definitive, peremptory; un-hesitating, -flinching, -shrinking; firm, cast iron, indomitable, game to the backbone; inexorable, relentless, not to be -shaken, – put down; *tenax propositi*; inflexible &c. (*hard*) 323; obstinate &c. 606; steady &c. (*persevering*) 604a; unbending, unyielding, irrevocable; firm as a rock; grim.

earnest, serious; set –, bent –, intent- upon.

steeled –, proof- against; *in utrumque paratus*.

Adv. resolutely &c. *adj.*; in –, in good- earnest; seriously, joking apart, earnestly, heart and soul; on one's metal; manfully, like a man, with a high hand; with a strong hand &c. (*exertion*) 686.

at any -rate, – risk, – hazard, – price, – cost, – sacrifice; at all -hazards, – risks, – events; cost what it may; *coûte que coûte*; *à tort et à travers*; once for all; neck or nothing; rain or shine; with colours nailed to the mast.

Phr. *spes sibi quisque.*

vacillate &c. 149; change &c. 140; retract &c. 607; fluctuate; alternate &c. (*oscillate*) 314; keep off and on, play fast and loose; blow hot and cold &c. (*caprice*) 608.

shuffle, palter, blink; trim.

Adj. irresolute, infirm of purpose, double-minded, half-hearted; un-decided, -resolved, -determined; drifting; shilly-shally; fidgety, tremulous; wobbly; hesitating &c. *v.*; off one's balance; at a loss &c. (*uncertain*) 475.

vacillating &c. *v.*; unsteady &c. (*changeable*) 149; unsteadfast, fickle, unreliable, irresponsible, unstable, without ballast; capricious &c. 608; volatile, frothy; light, -some, -minded; giddy; fast and loose.

weak, feeble-minded, frail; timid &c. 860; cowardly &c. 862; facile; pliant &c. (*soft*) 324; unable to say 'no,' easy-going.

revocable, reversible.

Adv. irresolutely &c. *adj.*; irresolvedly; in faltering accents; off and on; from pillar to post; see-saw &c. 314.

Int. 'how happy could I be with either!'

604a. Perseverance.—**N.** perseverance; continuance &c. (*inaction*) 143; permanence &c. (*absence of change*) 141; firmness &c. (*stability*) 150.

constancy, steadiness; singleness –, tenacity- of purpose; persistence, plodding, patience; sedulity &c. (*industry*) 682; pertina-cy, -city, -ciousness; iteration &c. 104.

bottom, game, pluck, stamina, backbone, grit; indefatiga-bility, bleness; bulldog courage.

V. persevere, persist; hold -on, – out; die in the last ditch, be in at the death; stick –, cling –, adhere- to; stick to one's text, keep on; keep to –, maintain- one's -course, – ground; bear –, keep –, hold-up; plod; stick to work &c. (*work*) 686; continue &c. 143; follow up; die -in harness, – at one's post.

Adj. persevering, constant; stead-y, -fast; un-deviating, -wavering, -faltering, -swerving, -flinching, -sleeping, -flagging, -drooping; steady as time; uninter-, un-remitting; plodding; industrious &c. 682; strenuous &c. 686; pertinacious; persist-ing, -ent.

solid, sturdy, staunch, stanch, true to oneself; unchangeable &c. 150; unconquerable &c. (*strong*) 159; indomitable, game to the last, indefatigable, untiring, unwearied, never tiring.

Adv. through -evil report and good report, – thick and thin, – fire and water; *per fas et nefas*; without fail, sink or swim, at any price, *vogue la galère*; in sickness and in health.

Phr. never say die; *vestigia nulla retrorsum*.

606. Obstinacy.—N. obstinateness &c. *adj.*; obstinacy, tenacity; perseverance &c. 604a; immovability; old school; inflexibility &c. (*hardness*) 323; obdur-acy, -ation; dogged resolution; resolution &c. 604; ruling passion; blind side.

self-will, contumacy, perversity; pervica-cy, -city; indocility.

bigotry, intolerance, dogmatism; opinia-try, -tiveness; fixed idea &c.; intractability, incorrigibility; (*prejudgment*) 481; fanaticism, zealotry, infatuation, monomania, opinionativeness.

mule; opin-ionist, -ionatist, -iator, -ator; stickler, dogmatist, die-hard, bitter-ender; bigot; zealot, enthusiast, fanatic.

V. be -obstinate &c. *adj.*; stickle, take no denial, fly in the face of facts; opinionate, be wedded to an opinion, hug a belief; have one's own way &c. (*will*) 600; persist &c. (*persevere*) 604a; have –, insist on having- the last word.

die -hard, – fighting, fight -against destiny, – to the last ditch; not yield an inch, stand out.

Adj. obstinate, tenacious, stubborn, obdurate, case-hardened; inflexible &c. (*hard*) 323; immovable, not to be moved; inert &c. 172; unchangeable &c. 150; inexorable &c. (*determined*) 604; mulish, obstinate as a mule, pig-headed.

dogged; sullen, sulky; un-moved, -influenced, -affected.

wilful, self-willed, perverse; res-ty, -tive, -tiff; pervicacious, wayward, refractory, unruly; head-y, -strong; *entêté*; contumacious; cross-grained.

607. Tergiversation.—N. change of -mind, – intention, – purpose; afterthought.

tergiversation, recantation; palin-ode, -ody; renunciation; abjur-ation, -ement; defection &c. (*relinquishment*) 624; going over &c. *v.*; apostasy; retract-ion, -ation; withdrawal, disavowal &c. (*negation*) 536; revo-cation, -kement; reversal; repentance &c. 950; *redintegratio amoris*.

coquetry, flirtation; vacillation &c. 605; back-sliding, recidivation.

turn-coat, -tippet; rat, apostate, renegade, mugwump; con-, per-vert; proselyte, deserter; backslider, recidivist; black leg.

time-server, -pleaser; timist, Vicar of Bray, trimmer, ambidexter; weathercock &c. (*changeable*) 149; Janus.

V. change one's -mind, – intention, – purpose, – note; abjure, renounce; withdraw from &c. (*relinquish*) 624; wheel –, turn –, veer- round; turn a *pirouette*; go over –, pass –, change –, skip- from one side to another; go to the right about; box the compass, shift one's ground, go upon another tack; back down, crawl, crawfish.

apostatize, change sides, go over, rat; recant, retract; revoke; rescind &c. (*abrogate*) 756; recall, forswear, abjure, unsay; come -over, – round- to an opinion.

draw in one's horns, eat one's words; eat –, swallow- the leek; swerve, flinch, back out of, retrace one's steps, think better of it; come back –, return- to one's first love; turn over a new leaf &c. (*repent*) 950.

arbitrary, dogmatic, opinionated, positive, bigoted; prejudiced &c. 481; prepossessed, infatuated; stiff-backed, -necked, -hearted; hard-mouthed, hidebound; unyielding; im-pervious, -practicable, -persuasible; unpersuadable; in-, un-tractable; incorrigible, deaf to advice, impervious to reason; crotchety &c. 608.

Adv. obstinately &c. adj.

Phr. non possumus; no surrender.

trim, shuffle, play fast and loose, blow hot and cold, coquet, flirt, hold with the hare but run with the hounds; straddle; nager entre deux eaux; wait to see how the -cat jumps, – wind blows.

Adj. changeful &c. 149; irresolute &c. 605; ductile, slippery as an eel, trimming, ambidextrous, timeserving; coquetting &c. v.

revocatory, reactionary.

Phr. 'a change came o'er the spirit of my dream.'

---

608. Caprice.—N. caprice, fancy, humour; whim, -sey, -wham; crotchet, capriccio, quirk, freak, maggot, fad, vagary, prank, fit, flimflam, escapade, boutade, wild-goose chase; capriciousness &c. adj.; kink.

V. be -capricious &c. adj.; have a maggot in the brain; take it into one's head, strain at a gnat and swallow a camel; blow hot and cold; play -fast and loose, – fantastic tricks.

Adj. capricious; erratic, eccentric, fitful, hysterical; full of -whims &c. n.; maggoty; inconsistent, fanciful, fantastic, whimsical, crotchety, particular, humoursome, freakish, skittish, wanton, wayward; contrary; captious; arbitrary; unrestrained, undisciplined; not amenable to reason; uncomfortable &c. 83; penny wise and pound foolish; fickle &c. (irresolute) 605; frivolous, sleeveless, giddy, volatile.

Adv. by fits and starts, without rhyme or reason, at one's own sweet will.

Phr. nil fuit unquam sic impar sibi; the deuce is in him.

---

609. Choice.—N. choice, option; discretion &c. (volition) 600; preoption; alternative; dilemma; embarras de choix; adoption, co-optation; novation; decision &c. (judgment) 480.

election, poll, ballot, vote, voice, suffrage, plumper, cumulative vote; plebiscitum, plébiscite, vox populi; referendum, electioneering; voting &c. v.; franchise; ballot box; slate; ticket.

selection, excerption, gleaning, eclecticism; excerpta, gleanings, cuttings; scissors and paste; pick &c. (best) 650.

preference, prelation; predilection &c. (desire) 865.

V. offer for one's choice, set before; hold out –, present –, offer- the alternative; put to the vote.

use –, exercise –, one's- -discretion, – option; adopt, take up, embrace, espouse; choose, elect, co-opt; take –, make- one's choice; make choice of, fix upon.

vote, poll, hold up one's hand; divide.

settle; decide &c. (adjudge) 480; list

609a. Absence of Choice.—N. no –, Hobson's- choice; first come, first served; necessity &c. 601; not a pin to choose &c. (equality) 27; any, the first that comes.

neutrality, indifference; indecision &c. (irresolution) 605.

V. be -neutral &c. adj.; have no choice; waive, not vote; abstain –, refrain- from voting; leave undecided; make a virtue of necessity.

Adj. neu-tral, -ter; indifferent; undecided &c. (irresolute) 605.

Adv. either &c. (choice) 609.

610. Rejection.—N. rejection, repudiation, exclusion; declination; refusal &c. 764.

V. reject; set –, lay- aside; give up; decline &c. (refuse) 764; exclude, except, eliminate; pluck, spin; cast.

repudiate, scout, set at naught; fling –, cast –, thrown –, toss- -to the winds, – to the dogs, – overboard, – away; send to the right about; dis-

&c. (*will*) 600; make up one's mind &c. (*resolve*) 604.

select; pick, – and choose; pick –, single- out, excerpt; cull, glean, winnow; sift –, separate –, winnow- the chaff from the wheat; pick up, pitch upon; pick one's way; indulge one's fancy.

set apart, reserve, mark out for; mark &c. 550.

prefer; have -rather, – as lief; fancy &c. (*desire*) 865; be persuaded &c. 615.

take a -decided, – decisive- step; commit oneself to a course; pass –, cross- the Rubicon; cast in one's lot with; take for better or for worse.

Adj. optional; co-optative; discretional &c. (*voluntary*) 600; on approval.

eclectic; choosing &c. *v.*; preferential; chosen &c. *v.*; choice &c. (*good*) 648.

Adv. optionally &c. *adj.*; at pleasure &c. (*will*) 600; either, – the one or the other; or; at the option of; whether or not; once for all; for one's money.

by -choice, – preference; in preference; rather, before.

claim &c. (*deny*) 536; discard &c. (*eject*) 297, (*have done with*) 678.

Adj. rejected &c. *v.*; reject-aneous, -itious; not -chosen &c. 609, – to be thought of; out of the question.

Adv. neither, – the one nor the other; no &c. 536.

Phr. *non hæc in fœdera.*

---

611. Predetermination. — N. premeditation, -deliberation, -determination, -destination; foreordination; foregone conclusion; *parti pris*; resolve, propendency; intention &c. 620; project &c. 626.

V. pre-determine, -destine, -meditate, -resolve, -concert; foreordain; resolve beforehand.

Adj. pre-pense, -meditated &c. *v.*, -designed; advised, studied, designed, calculated; aforethought; intended &c. 620; foregone.

well-laid, -devised, -weighed; maturely considered; cut and dried; cunning.

Adv. advisedly &c. *adj.*; with premeditation, deliberately, all things considered, with eyes open, in cold blood; intentionally &c. 620.

612. Impulse.—N. impulse, sudden thought; *impromptu*, improvisation; inspiration, hunch, flash, spurt.

improvisatore, improvisatrice, improviser, extemporizer; creature of impulse.

V. flash on the mind.

say what comes uppermost; improvise, extemporize; rise to the occasion; spurt.

Adj. extemporaneous, impulsive, indeliberate; improvis-ed, -ate, -atory; un-, unpre-meditated; *improvisé*; unprompted, -guided; natural, unguarded; spontaneous &c. (*voluntary*) 600; instinctive &c. 601.

Adv. extem-pore, -poraneously; offhand, *impromptu, à l'improviste*; improviso; on the spur of the -moment, – occasion.

613. Habit.—N. habit, -ude; assuetude, -faction; wont; run, way.

common –, general –, natural –, ordinary –, habitual- -course, – run, – state- of things; matter of course; beaten -path, – track, – ground.

prescription, custom, use, usage, immemorial usage, practice; tradition; prevalence, observance; conventional-

614. Desuetude.—N. desuetude, disusage; disuse &c. 678; want of -habit, – practice; inusitation; newness to; new brooms.

infraction of usage &c. (*unconformity*) 83; non-prevalence; 'a custom more honoured in the breach than the observance.'

V. be -unaccustomed &c. *adj.*; leave

ism, -ity; mode, fashion, vogue; *etiquette*
&c. (*gentility*) 852; order of the day,
cry; conformity &c. 82.

habitué, addict.

one's old way, old school, consuetude, *veteris vestigia flammæ; laudator
temporis acti.*

rule, standing order, precedent,
routine; red-tape, -tapism; pipe-clay;
rut, groove.

cacoëthes; bad –, confirmed –, inveterate –, intrinsic &c. 5- habit;
addiction, trick.

training &c. (*education*) 537; seasoning, hardening, inurement; radication;
second nature, acclimatization; knack
&c. (*skill*) 698.

V. be -wont &c. *adj.*

fall into a custom &c. (*conform to*) 82; tread –, follow- the beaten
-track, – path; *stare super antiquas vias*; move in a rut, run on in a
groove, go round like a horse in a mill, go on in the old jog-trot way.

habituate, inure, harden, season, caseharden; accustom, familiarize; naturalize, acclimatize; keep one's hand in; train &c. (*educate*)
537.

get into the -way, – knack- of; learn &c. 539; cling –, adhere- to;
repeat &c. 104; acquire –, contract –, fall into- a -habit, – trick;
addict oneself –, take- to; accustom oneself to.

be -habitual &c. *adj.*; prevail; come into use, become a habit,
take root; gain –, grow- upon one.

Adj. habitual; ac-, customary; prescriptive; accustomed &c. *v.*;
traditional; of -daily, – every-day- occurrence; wonted, usual, general, ordinary, common, frequent, every-day, household, jog-trot;
well-trodden, -known; familiar, vernacular, trite, commonplace,
banal, bromidic, conventional, regular, set, stock, officinal, established, stereotyped; pre-vailing, -valent; current, received, acknowledged, recognized, accredited; of course, admitted, understood.

conformable &c. 82; according to -use, – custom, – routine; in
-vogue, – fashion; fashionable &c. (*genteel*) 852.

wont; used – given – addicted –, attuned –, habituated &c. *v.*- to;
in the habit of; *habitué*; at home in &c. (*skilful*) 698; seasoned; per-
meated –, imbued- with; devoted –, wedded- to; never free from.

hackneyed, fixed, rooted, deep-rooted, ingrafted, permanent, inveterate, besetting; naturalized; ingrained &c. (*intrinsic*) 5.

Adv. habitually &c. *adj.*; always &c. (*uniformly*) 16.

as -usual, – is one's wont, – things go, – the world goes, – the
sparks fly upwards; *more -suo, – solito.*

as a rule, for the most part; generally &c. *adj.*; most often, – frequently.

Phr. *cela s'entend.*

off –, cast off –, break off –, wean oneself of –, violate –, break through –,
infringe- -a habit, – a custom, – a usage;
break one's fetters; disuse &c. 678;
wear off.

Adj. un-accustomed, -used, -wonted,
-seasoned, -inured, -habituated, -train-
ed; new; green &c. (*unskilled*) 699;
fresh, original, unhackneyed.

unusual &c. (*unconformable*) 83; unconventional, non-observant; disused
&c. 678.

Adv. just for once.

2°. *Causes of Volition*

615. Motive.—N. motive, springs of
action.

reason, ground, call, principle; main-

615a. Absence of Motive.—N. absence of motive; caprice &c. 608;
chance &c. (*absence of design*) 621.

spring, *primum mobile*, key-stone; the why and the wherefore; *pro* and *con*, reason why; secret –, ulterior- motive, *arrière-pensée*; intention &c. 620.

inducement, consideration; attraction &c. 288; loadstone; magnet, -ism, -ic force; allect-ation, -ive; temptation, enticement, *agacerie*, allurement, witchery; bewitch-ment, -ery; charm; spell &c. 993; fascination, blandishment, cajolery; seduc-tion, -ement; honeyed words, voice of the tempter, son of the Sirens; forbidden fruit, golden apple.

persuasi-bility, -bleness; attractability; impress-, suscept-ibility; softness; persuas-, attract-iveness; tantalization.

influence, prompting, dictate, instance; impuls-e, -ion; incit-ement, -ation; press, instigation; provocation &c. (*excitation of feeling*) 824; inspiration; per-, suasion; encouragement, advocacy; exhortation, advice &c. 695; solicitation &c. (*request*) 765; lobbying.

incentive, stimulus, spur, fillip, whip, goad, rowel, provocative, whet, dram.

bribe, lure; decoy, – duck; bait, trail of a red herring; bribery and corruption; sop, – for Cerberus.

prompter, tempter; seduc-er, -tor; suggester, coaxer, wheedler; instigator, firebrand, incendiary; Siren, Circe; *agent provocateur*; lobbyist.

V. induce, move; draw, – on; bring in its train, give an -impulse &c. *n.*- to; inspire; put up to, prompt, call up; attract, beckon.

stimulate &c. (*excite*) 824; spirit up, inspirit; a-, rouse; ecphorize; animate, incite, provoke, instigate, set on, actuate; act –, work –, operate- upon; encourage; pat –, clap- on the -back, – shoulder.

influence, weigh with, bias, sway, incline, dispose, predispose, turn the scale, inoculate; lead, – by the nose; have –, exercise-influence- -with, – over, – upon; go –, come- round one; turn the head, magnetize.

persuade; prevail -with, – upon; overcome, carry; bring -round, – to one's senses; draw –, win –, gain –, come –, talk- over; procure, enlist, engage; invite, court.

tempt, seduce, overpersuade, entice, allure, captivate, fascinate, intrigue, bewitch, carry away, charm, conciliate, wheedle, coax, lure, suggest; inveigle; tantalize; cajole &c. (*deceive*) 545.

tamper with, bribe, suborn, grease the palm, bait with a silver hook, gild the pill, make things pleasant, put a sop into the pan, throw a sop to, bait the hook.

V. have no motive; scruple &c. (*be unwilling*) 603.

Adj. without rhyme or reason; aimless &c. (*chance*) 621.

Adv. capriciously; out of mere caprice.

616. Dissuasion.—**N.** dissuasion, dehortation, expostulation, remonstrance; deprecation &c. 766.

discouragement, damper, wet blanket; warning.

cohibition &c. (*restraint*) 751; curb &c. (*means of restraint*) 752; check &c. (*hindrance*) 706.

reluctance &c. (*unwillingness*) 603; contraindication.

V. dissuade, dehort, cry out against, remonstrate, expostulate, warn, contraindicate.

disincline, indispose, shake, stagger; dispirit; dis-courage, -hearten, -enchant; deter; hold –, keep- back &c. (*restrain*) 751; render -averse &c. 603; repel; turn aside &c. (*deviation*) 279; wean from; act as a drag &c. (*hinder*) 706; throw cold water on, damp, cool, chill, blunt, calm, quiet, quench; deprecate &c. 766.

Adj. dissuading &c. *v.*; dissuasive; dehortatory, expostulatory; monit-ive, -ory.

dissuaded &c. *v.*; uninduced &c. (induce &c. 615); unpersuadable &c. (*obstinate*) 606; averse &c. (*unwilling*) 603; repugnant &c. (*dislike*) 867.

---

enforce, force; impel &c. (*push*) 276; propel &c. 284; whip, lash, goad, spur, prick, urge; egg –, hound –, hurry- on; drag &c. 285; exhort; advise &c. 695; call upon &c., press &c. (*request*) 765; advocate.

set -an example, – the fashion; keep in countenance; back up.

be -persuaded &c.; yield to temptation, come round; concede &c. (*consent*) 762; obey a call; follow -advice, – the bent, – the dictates of; act on principle.

Adj. impulsive, motive; suas-, persuas-, hortat-ive, -ory; protreptical; inviting, tempting &c. *v.*; seductive, attractive, irresistible; fascinating &c. (*pleasing*) 829; provocative &c. (*exciting*) 824.

induced &c. *v.*; disposed; persuadable &c. (*docile*) 602; spellbound; instinct –, smitten- with; inspired &c. *v.*- by.

Adv. because, therefore &c. (*cause*) 155; from -this, – that- motive; for -this, – that- reason; for; by reason –, for the sake –, on the score –, on account- of; out of, from, as, forasmuch as.

for all the world; on principle.

617. [Ostensible motive, ground, or reason assigned.] **Plea.—N.** plea, pretext; allegation, advocation; ostensible -motive, – ground, – reason; excuse &c. (*vindication*) 937; colour; gloss, guise.

loop-, starting-hole; how to creep out of, salvo, come off.

handle, peg to hang on, room, *locus standi*; stalking-horse, *cheval de bataille*, cue.

pretence &c. (*untruth*) 546; put off, subterfuge, dust thrown in the eyes; blind; moonshine; mere –, shallow- pretext; lame -excuse, – apology; tub to a whale; false plea, sour grapes; makeshift, shift, white lie; special pleading &c. (*sophistry*) 477; soft sawder &c. (*flattery*) 933.

V. plead, allege; shelter oneself under the plea of; excuse &c. (*vindicate*) 937; gloss over; lend a colour to; furnish a -handle &c. *n.*; make a -pretext, – handle- of; use as a plea &c. *n.*; take one's stand upon, make capital out of; pretend &c. (*lie*) 544.

Adj. ostensible &c. (*manifest*) 525; excusing; alleged, apologetic; pretended &c. 545.

Adv. ostensibly; under -colour, – the plea, – the pretence- of.

3°. *Objects of Volition*

618. Good.—N. good, benefit, advantage; improvement &c. 658; interest, service, behoof, behalf; weal; main chance, *summum bonum*, common weal; 'consummation devoutly to be wished'; gain, boot; profit, harvest.

boon &c. (*gift*) 784; good turn; blessing, benison; world of good; piece of good -luck, – fortune; nuts, prize, windfall, godsend, waif, treasure trove.

good fortune &c. (*prosperity*) 734; happiness &c. 827.

[Source of good] goodness &c. 648; utility &c. 644; remedy &c. 662; pleasure-giving &c. 829.

Adj. commendable &c. 931; useful &c. 644; good &c., beneficial &c. 648.

619. Evil.—N. evil, ill, harm, hurt, mischief, nuisance; machinations of the devil, Pandora's box, ills that flesh is heir to.

blow, buffet, stroke, scratch, bruise, wound, gash, mutilation; mortal -blow, – wound; *immedicabile vulnus*; damage, loss &c. (*deterioration*) 659.

disadvantage, prejudice, drawback.

disaster, accident, casualty; mishap &c. (*misfortune*) 735; bad job, devil to pay; calamity, bale, woe, catastrophe, tragedy; ruin &c. (*destruction*) 162; adversity &c. 735.

mental suffering &c. 828. [Evil spirit] demon &c. 980. [Cause of evil] bane &c. 663. [Production of evil]

V. benefit, profit, advantage, serve, help, avail; do good to, gain, prosper, flourish.

Adv. well, aright, satisfactorily, favourably, not amiss; all for the best; to one's -advantage &c. *n.*; in one's -favour, – interest &c. *n.*

Phr. so far so good.

badness &c. 649; painfulness &c. 830; evil doer &c. 913.

outrage, wrong, injury, foul play; bad -, ill- turn; disservice; spoliation &c. 791; grievance, crying evil.

V. be in trouble &c. (*adversity*) 735; harm, injure, hurt, do disservice to.

Adj. disastrous, bad &c. 649; awry, out of joint; disadvantageous, injurious, harmful.

Adv. amiss, wrong, ill, to one's cost.

Section II. Prospective Volition*

1°. *Conceptional Volition*

620. Intention.—N. intent, -ion, -ionality; purpose; *quo animo*; project &c. 626; undertaking &c. 676; predetermination &c. 611; design, ambition.

contemplation, mind, *animus*, view, purview, proposal; study; look out.

final cause; *raison d'être*; *cui bono*; object, aim, end; 'the be all and the end all'; drift &c. (*meaning*) 516; tendency &c. 176; destination, mark, point, butt, goal, target, bull's-eye, quintain; prey, quarry, game.

decision, determination, resolve; set -, settled- purpose; *ultimatum*; resolution &c. 604; wish &c. 865; *arrière-pensée*; motive &c. 615.

[Study of final causes] teleology.

V. intend, purpose, design, mean; have to; propose to oneself; harbour a design; have in -view, – contemplation, – one's eye, – *petto*; have an eye to.

bid -, labour- for; be -, aspire -, endeavour- after; be -, aim -, drive -, point-, level - at; take aim; set before oneself; study to.

take upon oneself &c (*undertake*) 676; take into one's head; meditate, contemplate; think – dream -, talk- of; premeditate &c. 611; compass, calculate; dest-ine, -inate; propose.

project &c. (*plan*) 626; have a mind to &c. (*be willing*) 602; desire &c. 865; pursue &c. 622.

Adj. intended &c. *v.*; intentional, advised, express, determinate; prepense &c. 611; bound for; intending &c. *v.*; minded, disposed, inclined;

621. [Absence of purpose in the succession of events.] **Chance.†—N.** chance &c. 156; lot, fate &c. (*necessity*) 601; luck; good luck &c. (*good*) 618; bad luck &c. 735; wheel of fortune; mascot; swastika.

speculation, venture, stake, flutter, flier, gamble, game of chance; mere -, random- shot; blind bargain, leap in the dark; pig in a poke &c. (*uncertainty*) 475; fluke, pot-luck.

drawing lots; sorti-legy, -tion; *sortes, – Virgilianæ*; *rouge et noir*, hazard, *roulette*, pitch and toss, chuck-farthing, cup-tossing, heads or tails, cross and pile, wager; bet, -ting; risk, stake, plunge; gambling; the turf.

stock exchange, bourse, board of trade, curb exchange.

gaming-, gambling-, betting-house; hell; betting ring, totalisator; dice, – box; dicer; gam-bler, -ester, plunger, stock operator, manipulator, punter; man of the turf; adventurer, speculator; bookmaker, layer, backer.

V. chance &c. (*hap*) 156; stand a chance &c. (*be possible*) 470.

toss up; cast -, draw- lots; leave -, trust- -to chance, – to the chapter of accidents; tempt fortune; chance it, take one's chance; run -, incur -, encounter- the -risk, – chance; stand the hazard of the die.

speculate, try one's luck, set on a cast, raffle, put into a lottery, buy a pig in a poke, shuffle the cards.

risk, venture, hazard, stake; lay, – a wager; make a bet, wager, bet, gamble,

* That is, volition having reference to a future object.   † See note on 156.

bent upon &c. (*earnest*) 604; at stake, on the -anvil, – *tapis*; in -view; – prospect, – the breast of; *in petto*; teleological.

Adv. intentionally &c. *adj.*; advisedly, wittingly, knowingly, designedly, purposely, on purpose, by design, studiously, pointedly; with -intent &c. *n.*; deliberately &c. (*with premeditation*) 611; with one's eyes open, in cold blood.

for; with -a view, – an eye- to; in order -to, – that; to the end –, with the intent- that; for the purpose –, with the view –, in contemplation –, on account- of.

in pursuance of, pursuant to; *quo animo*; to all intents and purposes.

game, play for; play at chuck-**farthing**.

Adj. fortuitous &c. 156; unintentional, -ded; accidental; not meant; un-designed, -purposed; unpremeditated &c. 612; never thought of.

indiscriminate, promiscuous; undirected, random; aim-, drift-, design-, purpose-, cause-less; without purpose. possible &c. 470.

Adv. casually &c. 156; unintentionally &c. *adj.*; unwittingly.

en passant, by the way, incidentally; as it may happen; at -random, – a venture, – haphazard; as luck would have it, by -chance, – good fortune; un-, -luckily.

---

622. [Purpose in action.] **Pursuit.**— N. pursuit; pursuing &c. *v.*; prosecution; pursuance; enterprise &c. (*undertaking*) 676; business &c. 625; adventure &c. (*essay*) 675; quest &c. (*search*) 461; scramble, hue and cry, game; hobby.

chase, hunt, *battue*, race, steeplechase, hunting, coursing; ven-ation, -ery; fox-chase; sport, -ing; shooting, angling, fishing, hawking.

pursuer; hunt-er, -sman; sportsman, Nimrod, the field; hound &c. 366.

V. pursue, prosecute, follow; run –, make –, be –, hunt –, prowl- after; shadow; carry on &c. (*do*) 680; engage in &c. (*undertake*) 676; set about &c. (*begin*) 66; endeavour &c. 675; court &c. (*request*) 765; seek &c. (*search*) 461; aim at &c. (*intention*) 620; follow the trail &c. (*trace*) 461; fish for &c. (*experiment*) 463; press on &c. (*haste*) 684; run a race &c. (*velocity*) 274.

chase, give chase, course, dog, hunt, hound, stalk; tread –, follow- on the heels of &c. (*sequence*) 281.

rush upon; rush headlong &c. (*violence*) 173; ride –, run- full tilt at; make a leap –, jump –, snatch- at; run down; start game.

tread a path; take –, hold- a course; shape –, direct –, bend- one's -steps, – course; play a game; fight –, elbow- one's way; follow up; take -to, – up; go in for; ride one's hobby.

Adj. pursuing &c. *v.*; in quest of &c.

623. [Absence of pursuit.] **Avoidance.** —N. abst-ention, -inence; forbearance; refraining &c. *v.*; inaction &c. 681; neutrality.

avoidance, evasion, elusion; seclusion &c. 893.

avolation, flight; escape &c. 671; retreat &c. 287; recoil &c. 277; departure &c. 293; rejection &c. 610.

shirker &c. *v.*; slacker; truant; fugitive, refugee; runa-way, -gate; renegade; deserter.

V. abstain, refrain, spare, not attempt; not do &c. 681; maintain the even tenor of one's way.

eschew, keep from, let alone, have nothing to do with; keep –, stand –, hold- -aloof, – off; take no part in, have no hand in.

avoid, shun; steer –, keep- clear of; fight shy of; keep -one's, – at a respectful- distance; keep –, get- out of the way; evade, elude, turn away from; set one's face against &c. (*oppose*) 708; deny oneself.

shrink; hang –, hold –, draw- back; recoil &c. 277; retire &c. (*recede*) 287; flinch, blink, blench, shy, shirk, dodge, parry, make way for, give place to.

beat a retreat; turn -tail, – one's back; take to one's heels; run, -away, – for one's life; cut and run; be off, – like a shot; fly, flee; fly –, flee –, run away- from; take –, take to- flight; desert, elope; make –, scamper –, sneak –, shuffle –, sheer- off; break –,

(*inquiry*) 461; in -pursuit, – full cry, – hot pursuit; on the scent.

Adv. in pursuance of &c. (*intention*) 620; after.

Int. tally-ho! yoicks! so-ho!

———

burst –, tear oneself –, slip –, slink –, steal- -away, – away from; slip cable, part company, turn on one's heel; sneak out of, play truant, give one the go by, give leg bail, take French leave, slope, decamp, flit, bolt, abscond, levant, skedaddle, absquatulate, cut one's stick, walk one's chalks, show a light pair of heels, make oneself scarce; escape &c. 671; go away &c. (*depart*) 293; abandon &c. 624; reject &c. 610.

lead one a -dance, – a merry chase, – pretty dance; throw off the scent, play at hide and seek.

Adj. unsought, unattempted; avoiding &c. *v.*; neutral; shy of &c. (*unwilling*) 603; elusive, evasive, distant; fugitive, runaway; shy, wild.

Adj. lest, in order to avoid.

Int. forbear! keep –, hands- off! *sauve qui peut!* devil take the hindmost!

624. Relinquishment.—N. relinquish-, abandon-ment; desertion, defection, secession, withdrawal; cave of Adullam; *nolle prosequi.*

discontinuance &c. (*cessation*) 142; renunciation &c. (*recantation*) 607; abrogation &c. 756; resignation &c. (*retirement*) 757; desuetude &c. 614; cession &c. (*of property*) 782.

V. relinquish, give up, abandon, desert, forsake, leave in the lurch; depart –, secede –, withdraw- from; back – out of, – down from, leave, go back on one's word, quit, take leave of, bid a long farewell; vacate &c. (*resign*) 757.

renounce &c. (*abjure*) 607; forego, have done with, drop; write off; disuse &c. 678; discard &c. 782; wash one's hands of; drop all idea of; *nolle-pros.*; lose interest in.

break –, leave- off; desist; stop &c. (*cease*) 142; hold –, stay- one's hand; quit one's hold; give over, shut up shop.

throw up the -game, – cards; give up the -point, – argument; pass to the order of the day, move the previous question, table the motion.

Adj. unpursued; relinquished &c. *v.*; relinquishing &c. *v.*

Int. avast &c.! (*stop*) 142.

625. Business.—N. business, occupation, employment; pursuit &c. 622; what one is doing-, – about; affair, concern, matter, case, undertaking.

matter in hand, irons in the fire; thing to do, *agendum*, task, work, job, chore, errand, transaction, commission, mission, charge, care; duty &c. 926.

part, *rôle*, cue; province, function, look-out, department, capacity, sphere, orb, field, line; walk, – of life; beat, round, routine; race, career.

office, place, post, incumbency, living; situation, appointment, billet, berth, employ; service &c. (*servitude*) 749; engagement; undertaking &c. 676.

vocation, calling, profession, *métier*, cloth, faculty; industry, art; industrial arts; craft, mystery, handicraft; trade &c. (*commerce*) 794.

exercise; work &c. (*action*) 680; avocation; press of business &c. (*activity*) 682.

V. pass –, employ –, spend- one's time in; employ oneself -in, – upon;

occupy −, concern- oneself with; make it one's -business &c. *n.*; undertake &c. 676; enter a profession; betake oneself to, turn one's hand to; have to do with &c. (*do*) 680.

drive a trade; carry on −, do −, transact- -business, − a trade &c. *n.*; keep a shop; ply one's task, − trade; labour in one's vocation; pursue the even tenor of one's way; attend to -business, − one's work.

officiate, serve, act; act −, play- one's part; do duty; serve −, discharge −, perform- the -office, − duties, − functions- of; hold −, fill- -an office, − a place, − a situation; hold a portfolio.

be -about, − doing, − engaged in, − employed in, − occupied with, − at work on; have one's hands in, have in hand; have on one's -hands, − shoulders; bear the burden; have one's hands full &c. (*activity*) 682.

be -in the hands of, − on the stocks, − on the anvil; pass through one's hands.

Adj. business-like; work-a-day; professional; official, functional; busy &c. (*actively employed*) 682; on −, in- -hand, − one's hands; afoot; on -foot, − the anvil; going on; acting.

Adv. in the course of business, all in a day's work; professionally &c. *adj.*

626. Plan.—**N.** plan, scheme, design, project; propos-al, -ition; suggestion; resolution, motion; precaution &c. (*provision*) 673; deep-laid &c. (*premeditated*) 611- plan &c.; racket.

system &c. (order) 58; organization &c. (*arrangement*) 60; germ &c. (*cause*) 153; Five Year Plan.

sketch, skeleton, outline, draught, draft, *ébauche*, *brouillon*; rough -cast, − draft, − draught, − copy; copy; proof, revise.

forecast, *programme*, prospectus, scenario; *carte du pays*; card; bill, protocol; order of the day, list of agenda, *memorandum*; bill of fare &c. (*food*) 298; base of operations; platform, plank.

rôle; policy &c. (*line of conduct*) 692.

contrivance, invention, expedient, receipt, nostrum, artifice, device, gadget; stratagem &c. (*cunning*) 702; trick &c. (*deception*) 545; alternative, loophole, shift &c. (*substitute*) 147; last shift &c. (*necessity*) 601.

measure, step; stroke, − of policy; master stroke; trump-, court-card; *cheval de bataille*, great gun; *coup*, − *d'état*; clever −, bold −, good- -move, − hit, − stroke; bright -thought, − idea, great idea.

intrigue, cabal, plot, frame-up, conspiracy, complot, machination; under-, counter-plot.

schem-ist, -atist; strategist, machinator, schemer; projector, author, builder, artist, promoter, designer &c. *v.*; conspirator; *intrigant* &c. (*cunning*) 702.

V. plan, scheme, design, frame, contrive, project, forecast, sketch; conceive, devise, invent &c. (*imagine*) 515; set one's wits to work &c. 515; spring a project; fall −, hit- upon; strike −, chalk −, cut −, lay −, map-out; lay down a plan; shape −, mark- out a course; predetermine &c. 611; concert, preconcert, preestablish; prepare &c. 673; hatch, − a plot; concoct; take -steps, − measures.

cast, recast, systematize, organize; arrange &c. 60; digest, mature.

plot; counter-plot, -mine; dig a mine; lay a train; intrigue &c. (*cunning*) 702.

Adj. planned &c. *v.*; strategic, -al; planning &c. *v.*; in course of preparation &c. 673; under consideration; on the -*tapis*, − carpet, − table.

627. Method. [Path.]—**N.** method, way, manner, wise, gait, form, mole, fashion, tone, guise; *modus operandi*; procedure &c. (*line of conduct*) 692.

path, road, route, course; line of -way, – road; trajectory, orbit, track, beat, tack.

steps; stair, -case; flight of stairs, ladder, stile.

bridge, viaduct, gauntry, pontoon, stepping stone, plank, gangway, catwalk, drawbridge; pass, ford, ferry, tunnel, subway, elevated; pipe &c. 260.

door; gateway &c. (*opening*) 260; channel, passage, avenue, means of access, approach, perron, adit, entrance; artery, lane, alley, aisle, lobby, corridor, cloister; back- door, -stairs; secret passage; covert-way.

road-, path-, stair-way; thoroughfare; highway, pike, turnpike, trail, parkway, *boulevard*; turnpike –, royal –, coach- road; broad –, King's –, Queen's- highway; beaten -track, – path; horse –, bridle- road, – track, – path; pathway; walk, *trottoir*, foot-path, pavement, flags, side-walk; by –, cross- -road, – path, – way; cut; short -cut &c. (*mid-course*) 628; *carrefour*; private –, occupation- road; highways and byways; rail-, tram-road, -way; funicular, ropeway, causeway; defile, cutting; canal &c. (*conduit*) 350; street &c. (*abode*) 189.

Adv. how; in what -way, – manner; by what mode; so, in this way, after this fashion, on these lines.

one way or another, anyhow; somehow or other &c. (*instrumentality*) 631; by way of; *viâ*; *in transitu* &c. 270; on the high road to.

Phr. *hæ tibi erunt artes.*

628. Mid-course.—**N.** middle-, mid-course; moderation, mean &c. 29; middle &c. 68; *juste milieu*, *mezzo termine*, golden mean, *aurea mediocritas*.

straight &c. (*direct*) 278 -course, – path; short –, cross- cut; short-circuit; great circle sailing.

neutrality; half –, half and half-measures; compromise.

V. keep in –, steer –, preserve- -a middle, – an even- course; go straight &c. (*direct*) 278.

go half way, compromise, make a compromise.

Adj. neutral, average, even, impartial, moderate, straight &c. (*direct*) 278.

629. Circuit.—**N.** circuit, round-about way, digression, divagation, *détour*, circum-ambience, -ambulation, bendibus, *ambages*, loop; winding &c. (*circuition*) 311; zigzag &c. (*deviation*) 279.

V. perform –, make- a circuit; go -round about, – out of one's way; make a *détour*; meander &c. (*deviate*) 27; circumambulate.

lead a pretty dance; beat about, – the bush; make two bites of a cherry.

Adj. circuitous, indirect, round-about; zig-zag &c. (*deviating*) 279; circum-ambient, -ambulatory.

Adv. by -a side wind, – an indirect course; in a roundabout way; from pillar to post.

630. Requirement.—**N.** requirement, need, wants, necessities; neces-saries, – of life; stress, exigency, pinch, *sine quâ non*, matter of necessity; case of -need, – life or death.

needfulness, essentiality, necessity, indispensability, urgency, pre-requisite.

requisition &c. (*request*) 765, (*exaction*) 741; run upon; demand –, call- for.

desideratum &c. (*desire*) 865; want &c. (*deficiency*) 640.

charge, claim, command, injunction, requisition, mandate, order, *ultimatum*.

V. require, need, want, have occasion for, entail; not be able to -do without, – dispense with; prerequire.

render necessary, necessitate, create a necessity for, call for, put in requisition; make a requisition &c. (*ask for*) 765, (*demand*) 741.

stand in need of; lack &c. 640; desiderate; desire &c. 865; be -necessary &c. *adj.*

Adj. required &c. *v.*; requisite, needful, necessary, imperative, essential, indispensable, prerequisite; called for; in -demand, – request.

urgent, exigent, pressing, instant, crying, absorbing.

in want of; destitute of &c. 640.

Adv. *ex necessitate rei* &c. (*necessarily*) 601; of –, out of stern- necessity; at a pinch.

Phr. there is no time to lose; it cannot be -spared, – dispensed with.

2° *Subservience to Ends*

1. *Actual Subservience*

631. Instrumentality.—N. instrumentality; aid &c. 707; subservien-ce, -cy; mediation, inter-vention, -mediacy, medium, inter-medium, -mediary, vehicle, hand; agency &c. 170.

minister, handmaid, servant, slave, maid, valet; midwife, *accoucheur,* obstetrician; go-between; cat's paw; stepping-stone.

key; master –, pass –, latch- key; 'open sesame'; passport, *passe partout,* safe-conduct; influence.

instrument &c. 633; expedient &c. (*plan*) 626; means &c. 632.

V. subserve, minister, tend, mediate, intervene; come –, go- between, interpose; pull the strings; be -instrumental &c. *adj.*; pander to.

Adj. instrumental; useful &c. 644; ministerial, subservient, mediatorial; inter-mediate, -vening; conducive.

Adv. through, by, *per*; where-, there-, here-by; by the -agency &c. 170- of; by dint of; by –, in- virtue of; through the -medium &c. *n.-* of; along with; on the shoulders of; by means of &c. 632; by –, with--the aid &c. (*assistance*) 707- of.

per fas et nefas, by fair means or foul; somehow, – or other; by hook or by crook.

632. Means.—N. means, resources, revenue, wherewithal, ways and means, income; capital &c. (*money*) 800; stock in trade &c. 636; provision &c. 637; a shot in the locker; appliances &c. (*machinery*) 633; means and appliances; conveniences; cards to play; expedients &c. (*measures*) 626; two strings to one's bow; sheet anchor &c. (*safety*) 666; aid &c. 707; medium &c. 631.

V. find –, have –, possess- means &c. *n.*; provide the wherewithal.

Adj. instrumental &c. 631; mechanical &c. 633.

Adv. by means of, with; by -what, – all, – any, – some- means; where-, here-, there-with; wherewithal.

how &c. (*in what manner*) 627; through &c. (*by the instrumentality of*) 631; with –, by- the aid &c. (*assistance*) 707- of; by the -agency &c. 170- of.

633. Instrument.—N. machinery, mechanism, engineering.

instrument, organ, tool, implement, utensil, contrivance, machine, motor, engine, lathe, gin, mill, pump.

gear; tack-le, -ling, trice, rigging, gear, apparatus, appliances; plant, *matériel;* harness, trappings, fittings, accoutrements; equip-ment, -age;

appointments, furniture, upholstery; chattels; paraphernalia &c. (*belongings*) 780; *impedimenta*.

mechanical powers; lever, -age; mechanical advantage; crow, -bar; handspike, gavelock, jemmy, arm, limb, wing; oar, paddle; pulley, sheave; parbuckle; wheel and axle; wheel-, clock-work; wheels within wheels; pinion, gear wheel, spur –, bevel- gearing, chains, belting, crank, winch, capstan, windlass, crane, derrick, hoist, lift &c. 307; cam; pedal; wheel &c. (*rotation*) 312; inclined plane; wedge; screw; jack; spring, mainspring.

handle, hilt, haft, shaft, heft, shank, blade, trigger, tiller, helm, treadle, key; turnscrew, screwdriver, spanner, wrench.

hammer &c. (*impulse*) 276; edge tool &c. (*cut*) 253; borer &c. 262; vice, teeth &c. (*hold*) 781; nail, rope &c. (*join*) 45; peg &c. (*hang*) 214; support &c. 215; spoon &c. (*vehicle*) 272; arms &c. 727; oar &c. (*navigation*) 267.

Adj. instrumental &c. 631; mechanical, machinal, automatic, self-acting; brachial.

634. Substitute.—**N.** substitute &c. 147; deputy &c. 759; proxy, alternative, understudy.

635. Materials.—**N.** material, raw material, stuff, stock, staple; building materials, bricks and mortar; metal; stone; clay, brick; crockery &c. 384; compo, -sition; reinforced –, ferro-, concrete; cement; wood, ore, timber; gravel, cobbles, macadam, asphalt, tarmac.

materials; supplies, munition, fuel, grist, household stuff; *pabulum* &c. (*food*) 298; ammunition &c. (*arms*) 727; contingents; relay, reinforcement; baggage &c. (*personal property*) 780; means &c. 632.

Adj. raw &c. (*unprepared*) 674; wooden &c. *n.*

636. Store.—**N.** stock, fund, mine, vein, lode, quarry; spring; fount, -ain; well, -spring; milch-cow.

stock in trade, supply; heap &c. (*collection*) 72; treasure; reserve, *corps de réserve*, reserve fund, nest-egg, savings, *bonne bouche*.

crop, harvest, mow, vintage; yield, product, gleanings.

store, accumulation, hoard, rick, stack; lumber; relay &c. (*provision*) 637.

store-house, -room, -closet; depository, *dépôt*, *cache*, safe deposit, vault, pantechnicon, re-pository, -servatory, -pertory; *repertorium*; promptuary, warehouse, *entrepôt*, magazine, dump, buttery, larder, pantry, panary, lanary, still-room, spence; crib, garner, granary, silo, barn; bunker; thesaurus; bank &c. (*treasury*) 802; armoury; arsenal; dock; gallery, museum, library, conservatory, hot-house; menag-ery, -erie, aquarium, zoological gardens.

reservoir, cistern, tank, sump, pond, mill-pond; gasometer.

budget, quiver, bandolier, portfolio; coffer &c. (*receptacle*) 191.

conservation; storing &c. *v.*; storage.

dictionary &c. 562; list &c. 86.

V. store; put –, lay –, set- by; stow away; set –, lay- apart; store –, hoard –, treasure –, lay –, heap –, put –, garner –, save- up; *cache*; accumulate, amass, hoard, fund, garner, save, bank.

conserve, reserve; keep –, hold- back; husband, – one's resources.

deposit; stow, stack, load, dump; harvest; heap, collect &c. 72; lay -in, – down, – by, store &c. *adj.*; keep, file [papers]; lay in &c. (*provide*) 637; preserve &c. 670; put by for a rainy day.

Adj. stored &c. *v.*; in -store, – reserve, – ordinary; spare, super-numerary.

637. Provision.—N. provision, sup-ply; grist, – to the mill; subvention &c. (*aid*) 707; resources &c. (*means*) 632.

providing &c. *v.*; purveyance; rein-forcement; commissary, commissariat.

rations; iron –, emergency- rations; provender &c. (*food*) 298; *viaticum*; ensilage.

caterer, purveyor, commissary, quar-termaster, steward, housekeeper, man-ciple, feeder, batman, victualler, store-keeper, grocer, provision merchant, green-, grocer, *comprador, restaurateur*; sutler &c. (*merchant*) 797; innkeeper, publican, confectioner, baker, butcher, wine merchant, vintner.

V. provide; make -provision, – due provision for; lay in, – a stock, – a store.

sup-ply, -peditate; furnish; find, – one in; arm.

cater, victual, provision, purvey, for-age; beat up for; stock, – with; make good, replenish; fill, – up; recruit, feed, ration.

have in -store, – reserve; keep, – by one, – on foot; have to fall back upon; store &c. 636; provide against a rainy day &c. (*economy*) 817.

638. Waste.—N. consumption, ex-penditure, exhaustion; dispersion &c. 73; ebb; leakage &c. (*exudation*) 295; loss &c. 776; wear and tear; waste; prodigality &c. 818; misuse &c. 679; wasting &c. *v.*; rubbish &c. (*useless*) 645.

mountain in labour.

V. spend, expend, use, consume, swallow up, exhaust, deplete; impov-erish; spill, drain, empty; disperse &c. 73.

cast –, throw –, fling –, fritter- away; burn the candle at both ends, waste; squander &c. 818.

'waste its sweetness on the desert air'; cast -one's bread upon the waters, – pearls before swine; employ a steam engine to crack a nut, waste powder and shot, break a butterfly on a wheel; labour in vain &c. (*useless*) 645; cut a whetstone with a razor, pour water into a sieve; tilt at windmills.

leak &c. (*run out*) 295; run to waste; ebb; melt away, run dry, dry up.

Adj. wasted &c. *v.*; at a low ebb.

wasteful &c. (*prodigal*) 818; penny wise and pound foolish.

Phr. *magno conatu magnas nugas; le jeu n'en vaut pas la chandelle.*

639. Sufficiency.—N. sufficiency, adequacy, enough, withal, *quantum sufficit*, satisfaction, competence; no less.

mediocrity &c. (*average*) 29.

fill; fulness &c. (*completeness*) 52; plen-itude, -ty; abundance; copiousness &c. *adj.*; amplitude, galore, lots, pro-fusion; full measure; 'good measure pressed down, shaken together and running over.'

luxuriance &c. (*fertility*) 168; afflu-ence &c. (*wealth*) 803; fat of the land; 'a land flowing with milk and honey'; cornucopia; horn of -plenty, – Amal-thæa; mine &c. (*stock*) 636.

outpouring; flood &c. (*great quantity*) 31; tide &c. (*river*) 348; repletion &c. (*redundance*) 641; satiety &c. 869; rich man &c. 803.

640. Insufficiency.—N. insufficiency; inadequa-cy, -teness; incompetence &c. (*impotence*) 158; deficiency &c. (*incom-pleteness*) 53; imperfection &c. 651; shortcoming &c. 304; paucity; stint; scantiness &c. (*smallness*) 32; none to spare; bare subsistence.

scarcity, dearth; want, need, lack, poverty, exigency; inanition, starva-tion, famine, drought.

dole, pittance, mite; short -allow-ance, – commons; half-rations; ban-yan –, fast- day, Lent.

emptiness, poorness &c. *adj.*; deple-tion, vacancy, flaccidity; ebb-tide; low water; 'a beggarly account of empty boxes'; indigence &c. (*poverty*) 804; insolvency &c. (*non-payment*) 808; poor man &c. 804; bankrupt &c. 808.

V. be -insufficient &c. *adj.*; not -suf-

V. be -sufficient &c. *adj.*; suffice, do, just do, satisfy, pass muster; have -enough &c. *n.*; eat –, drink –, have-one's fill; roll –, swim- in; wallow in &c. (*superabundance*) 641.

abound, exuberate, teem, flow, stream, rain, shower down; pour, – in; swarm; bristle with.

render -sufficient &c. *adj.*; replenish &c. (*fill*) 52.

Adj. sufficient, enough, adequate, up to the mark, commensurate, competent, satisfactory, valid, tangible.

measured; moderate &c. (*temperate*) 953.

full &c. (*complete*) 52; ample; plen-ty, -tiful, -teous; plenty as blackberries; copious, abundant; abounding &c. *v.*; replete, enough and to spare, flush; choke-full; well-stocked, -provided; liberal; unstint-ed, -ing; stintless; without stint; un-sparing, -measured; lavish &c. 641; wholesale.

rich; luxuriant &c. (*fertile*) 168; affluent &c. (*wealthy*) 803; wantless; big with &c. (*pregnant*) 161.

un-exhausted, -wasted; exhaustless, inexhaustible.

Adv. sufficiently, amply &c. *adj.*; full; in -abundance &c. *n.*; with no sparing hand; to one's heart's content, *ad libitum*, without stint.

Phr. cut and come again.

fice &c. 639; come short of &c. 304; run dry.

want, lack, need, require; *caret*; be in want &c. (*poor*) 804; live from hand to mouth.

render- insufficient &c. *adj.*; drain of resources; impoverish &c. (*waste*) 638; stint &c. (*begrudge*) 819; put on short -commons, – allowance.

do -insufficiently &c. *adv.*; scotch the snake.

Adj. insufficient, inadequate; too -little &c. 32; not -enough &c. 639; unequal to; incompetent &c. (*impotent*) 158; 'weighed in the balance and found wanting'; perfunctory &c. (*neglect*) 460; deficient &c. (*incomplete*) 53; wanting &c. *v.*; imperfect &c. 651; ill-furnished, -provided, -stored, -off.

slack, at a low ebb; empty, vacant, bare; short –, out –, destitute –, devoid –, bereft &c. 789 –, denuded- of; dry, drained.

un -provided, -supplied, -furnished; un-replenished, -fed; un-stored, -treasured; empty-handed.

meagre, poor, thin, scrimp, sparing, spare, stinted, stunted; skimpy; starv-ed, -eling; half-starved, emaciated, famine-stricken, famished, underfed, undernourished; jejune.

scant &c. (*small*) 32; scarce; not to be had, – for love or money, – at any price; scurvy; stingy &c. 819; at the end of one's tether; without -resources &c. 632; in want &c. (*poor*) 804; in debt &c. 806.

Adv. insufficiently &c. *adj.*; in default –, for want- of; failing.

641. Redundance.—N. redundance; too -much, – many; super-abundance, -fluity, -fluence, -saturation; nimiety, transcendency, exuberance, profuseness; profusion &c. (*plenty*) 639; repletion, enough in all conscience, *satis superque*, lion's share; more than -enough &c. 639; plethora, engorgement, congestion, load, surfeit, sickener; turgescence &c. (*expansion*) 194; over-dose, -measure, -supply, -flow; inundation &c. (*water*) 348; avalanche.

accumulation &c. (*store*) 636; heap &c. 72; drug, – in the market; glut; crowd; burden.

excess; sur-, over-plus, epact; margin; remainder &c. 40; duplicate; surplusage, expletive; work of –, supererogation; *bonus, bonanza*.

luxury; intemperance &c. 954; extravagance &c. (*prodigality*) 818; exorbitance, lavishment.

pleonasm &c. (*diffuseness*) 573; too many irons in the fire; embarrassment of riches; money to burn.

V. super-, over-abound; know no bounds, swarm; meet one at every turn; creep –, bristle- with; overflow; run –, flow –, well –, brim-over; run riot; over-run, -stock, -lay, -charge, -dose, -feed, -burden, -load, -do, -whelm, -shoot the mark &c. (*go beyond*) 303; surcharge, supersaturate, gorge, glut, load, drench, whelm, inundate, deluge, flood; drug, – the market.

choke, cloy, accloy, suffocate; pile up, lay it on, – with a trowel, lay on thick; impregnate with; lavish &c. (*squander*) 818.

send –, carry- coals to Newcastle, – owls to Athens; teach one's grandmother to suck eggs; *pisces natare docere*; kill the slain, 'gild refined gold,' 'paint the lily'; butter one's bread on both sides, put butter upon bacon; employ a steam-engine to crack a nut &c. (*waste*) 638.

exaggerate &c. 549; wallow in; roll in &c. (*plenty*) 639; remain on one's hands, hang heavy on hand, go a begging.

Adj. redundant; too -much, – many; exuberant, inordinate, super-abundant, excessive, overmuch, replete, profuse, lavish; prodigal &c. 818; exorbitant; overweening; extravagant; overcharged &c. *v.*; super-saturated, drenched, overflowing; running -over, – to waste, – down.

crammed –, filled- to overflowing; gorged, stuffed, ready to burst; dropsical, turgid, plethoric, full-blooded; obese &c. 194; voluminous.

superfluous, unnecessary, needless, supervacaneous, uncalled for, to spare, in excess; over and above &c. (*remainder*) 40; *de trop*; adscititious &c. (*additional*) 37; supernumerary &c. (*reserve*) 636; on one's hands, spare, duplicate, supererogatory, expletive; *un peu fort*.

Adv. over, too, over and above; over –, too- much; too far; without –, beyond –, out of- measure; with . . . to spare; over head and ears; up to one's -eyes, – ears; *extra*; beyond the mark &c. (*transcursion*) 303; over one's head.

Phr. it never rains but it pours.

2. *Degree of Subservience*

642. Importance.—N. importance, consequence, moment, prominence, consideration, mark, materialness.

import, significance, concern; emphasis, interest.

greatness &c. 31; superiority &c. 33; notability &c. (*repute*) 873; weight &c. (*influence*) 175; value &c. (*goodness*) 648; usefulness &c. 644.

gravity, seriousness, solemnity; no -joke, – laughing matter; pressure, urgency, stress; matter of life and death.

memorabilia, *notabilia*, great doings; red-letter day.

great -thing, – point; main chance, 'the be all and end all,' cardinal point, outstanding feature; substance, gist &c. (*essence*) 5; sum and substance, *gravamen*, head and front; important –, principal –, prominent –, essential-part; half the battle; *sine quâ non*; breath of one's nostrils &c. (*life*) 359; cream, salt, core, kernel, heart, nucleus;

643. Unimportance.—N. unimportance, insignificance, nothingness, immateriality.

triviality, trivia, fribble, levity, frivolity; paltriness &c. *adj.*; poverty; smallness &c. 32; vanity &c. (*uselessness*) 645; matter of -indifference &c. 866; no object; side issue.

nothing, – to signify, – worth speaking of, – particular, – to boast of, – to speak of; small –, no great –, trifling &c. *adj.* -matter; mere -joke, – nothing; hardly –, scarcely- anything; nonentity, cipher, figurehead; no great shakes, *peu de chose*; child's play; small beer.

toy, plaything, popgun, paper pellet, gimcrack, gewgaw, bauble, trinket, *bagatelle*, kickshaw, knicknack, whim-wham, trifle, 'trifles light as air.'

trumpery, trash, rubbish, stuff, *fatras*, frippery; 'leather or prunello'; chaff, drug, froth, bubble, smoke, cob-

key, -note, -stone; corner stone; trump-card &c. (*device*) 626; salient points.

top-sawyer, first fiddle, *prima donna*, chief, big-wig; triton among the minnows.

V. be -important &c. *adj.*, – somebody, – something; import, signify, matter, be an object; carry weight &c. (*influence*) 175; make a figure &c. (*repute*) 873; be in the ascendant, come to the front, lead the way, take the lead, play first fiddle, throw all else into the shade; lie at the root of; deserve –, merit –, be worthy- -of notice, – regard, – consideration.

attach –, ascribe –, give- importance &c. *n.*- to; value, care for; set store -upon, – by; mark &c. 550; mark with a white stone, underline; write –, put –, print- in -italics, – capitals, – large letters, – large type, – letters of gold; accentuate, emphasize, lay stress on.

make -a fuss, – a stir, – a piece of work, – much ado- about; make -of, – much of.

Adj. important; of -importance &c. *n.*; momentous, material; to the point; not to be -overlooked, – despised, – sneezed at; egregious; weighty &c. (*influential*) 175; of note &c. (*repute*) 873; notable, prominent, salient, signal; memorable, remarkable; worthy of -remark, – notice; never to be forgotten; stirring, eventful.

grave, serious, earnest, noble, grand, solemn, impressive, commanding, imposing.

urgent, pressing, critical, instant.

paramount, essential, vital, all-absorbing, radical, cardinal, chief, main, prime, primary, principal, leading, capital, foremost, overruling; of vital &c. importance.

in the front rank, first-rate, A1; superior &c. 33; considerable &c. (*great*) 31; marked &c. *v.*; rare &c. 137.

significant, telling, trenchant, emphatic, pregnant; *tanti*.

Adv. materially &c. *adj.*; in the main; above all, *par excellence*, to crown all.

---

web; weed; refuse &c. (*inutility*) 645; scum &c. (*dirt*) 653.

joke, jest, snap of the fingers; fudge &c. (*unmeaning*) 517; fiddlestick, – end; pack of nonsense, mere farce.

straw, pin, fig, continental, button, rush; bulrush, feather, halfpenny, farthing, brass farthing, doit, peppercorn, jot, rap, pinch of snuff, old song.

minutiæ, details, minor details, small fry; dust in the balance, feather in the scale, drop in the ocean, flea-bite, molehill; fingle-fangle.

nine days' wonder, *ridiculus mus*; flash in the pan &c. (*impotence*) 158; much ado about nothing &c. (*overestimation*) 482; storm in a teacup.

V. be -unimportant &c. *adj.*; not -matter &c. 642; go for –, matter –, signify- -little, – nothing, – little or nothing; not matter a -straw &c. *n.*

make light of &c. (*underestimate*) 483; catch at straws &c. (*overestimate*) 482.

Adj. unimportant; of -little, – small, – no- -account, – importance &c. 642; immaterial; un-, non-essential; not vital; irrelevant, incidental, indifferent.

subordinate &c. (*inferior*) 34; *médiocre* &c. (*average*) 29; passable, fair, respectable, tolerable, commonplace; uneventful, mere, common; ordinary &c. (*habitual*) 613; inconsiderable, so-so, insignificant, inappreciable, nugatory.

trifling, trivial; slight, slender, light, flimsy, frothy, idle; puerile &c. (*foolish*) 499; airy, shallow; weak &c. 160; powerless &c. 158; frivolous, petty, niggling; pid-, ped-dling; fribble, inane, ridiculous, farcical; fini-cal, -kin; fiddle-faddle, namby-pamby, wishy-washy, milk and water.

poor, paltry, pitiful; contemptible &c. (*contempt*) 930; sorry, mean, meagre, shabby, miserable, wretched, vile, scrubby, scrannel, weedy, niggardly, scurvy, putid, beggarly, worthless, twopenny-halfpenny, cheap, trashy, catchpenny, gimcrack, trumpery, one-horse; toy.

not worth -the pains, – while, – mentioning, – speaking of, – a thought, – a curse, – a straw, – rap &c. *n.*; beneath –, unworthy of- -notice, – regard, – consideration, – contempt; *de lanâ caprinâ;* vain &c. (*useless*) 645.

Adv. slightly &c. *adj.;* rather, somewhat, pretty well, fairly well, tolerably.

for aught one cares.

Int. no matter! pish! tush! tut! pshaw! pugh! pooh, -pooh! fudge! bosh! humbug! fiddle-stick, – end! fiddlededee! never mind! *n'importe!* what -signifies, – matter, – boots it, – of that, –'s the odds! a fig for! stuff! nonsense! stuff and nonsense!

Phr. *magno conatu magnas nugas; le jeu n'en vaut pas la chandelle;* it -matters not, – does not signify; it is of no -consequence, – importance.

644. Utility.—N. utility; usefulness &c. *adj.;* efficacy, efficiency, adequacy; service, use, stead, avail; help &c. (*aid*) 707; applicability &c. *adj.;* subservience &c. (*instrumentality*) 631; function &c. (*business*) 625; value; worth &c. (*goodness*) 648; money's worth; productiveness &c. 168; *cui bono* &c. (*intention*) 620; utilization &c. (*use*) 677; step in the right direction.

common weal, public good; utilitarianism &c. (*philanthropy*) 910.

V. be -useful &c. *adj.;* avail, serve; subserve &c. (*be instrumental to*) 631; conduce &c. (*tend*) 176; answer –, serve- -one's turn, – a purpose.

act a part &c. (*action*) 680; perform –, discharge- -a function &c. 625; do –, render- -a service, – good service, – yeoman's service; bestead, stand one in good stead; be the making of; help &c. 707.

bear fruit &c. (*produce*) 161; bring grist to the mill; profit, remunerate; benefit &c. (*do good*) 648.

find one's -account, – advantage- in; reap the benefit of &c. (*be better for*) 658.

render useful &c. (*use*) 677.

Adj. useful; of -use &c. *n.;* serviceable, usable, proficuous, good for; subservient &c. (*instrumental*) 631; conducive &c. (*tending*) 176; subsidiary &c. (*helping*) 707.

advantageous &c. (*beneficial*) 648; profitable, gainful, remunerative, worth one's salt; in-, valuable; prolific &c. (*productive*) 168.

adequate; ef-ficient, -ficacious; effect-ive, -ual; practicable, expedient &c. 646.

645. Inutility.—N. inutility; uselessness &c. *adj.;* inefficacy, futility; inep-, inap-titude; unsubservience; inadequacy &c. (*insufficiency*) 640; inefficiency &c. (*incompetence*) 158; unskilfulness &c. 699; disservice; unfruitfulness &c. (*unproductiveness*) 169; labour -in vain, – lost, – of Sisyphus; lost -trouble, – labour; work of Penelope; sleeveless errand, wild goose chase, mere farce.

tautology &c. (*repetition*) 104; supererogation &c. (*redundance*) 641.

vanitas vanitatum, vanity, inanity, worthlessness, nugacity; triviality &c. (*unimportance*) 643.

caput mortuum, waste paper, dead letter; blunt tool.

litter, rubbish, lumber, odds and ends, cast-off clothes; button-top; shoddy; rags, orts, trash, refuse, sweepings, scourings, off-scourings, dross, slag, waste, rubble, dottle, drast, *débris;* stubble, leavings; broken meat; dregs &c. (*dirt*) 653; weeds, tares; rubbish heap, dust hole; *rudera,* deads.

fruges consumere natus &c. (*drone*) 683.

V. be -useless &c. *adj.;* go a begging &c. (*redundant*) 641; fail &c. 732.

seek –, strive- after impossibilities; use vain efforts, labour in vain, roll the stone of Sisyphus, beat the air, lash the waves, *battre l'eau avec un bâton, donner un coup d'épée dans l'eau,* fish in the air, milk the ram, drop a bucket into an empty well, sow the sand; bay the moon; preach –, speak- to the winds; whistle jigs to a milestone; kick against the pricks, *se battre contre des moulins;* lock the stable door

applicable, available, ready, handy, at hand, tangible; commodious, adaptable; of all work.

Adv. usefully &c. *adj.*; *pro bono publico.*

when the steed is stolen &c. (*too late*) 135; hold a farthing candle to the sun; cast pearls before swine &c. (*waste*) 638; carry coals to Newcastle &c. (*redundance*) 641; wash a blackamoor white &c. (*impossible*) 471.

render -useless &c. *adj.*; dis-mantle, -mast, -mount, -qualify, -able; unrig; cripple, lame &c. (*injure*) 659; spike guns, clip the wings; put out of gear.

Adj. useless, inutile, inefficacious, futile, unavailing, bootless; inoperative &c. 158; inadequate &c. (*insufficient*) 640; in-, un-sub-servient; inept, inefficient &c. (*impotent*) 158; of no -avail &c. (*use*) 644; ineffectual &c. (*failure*) 732; incompetent &c. (*unskilful*) 699; 'stale, flat and unprofitable'; superfluous &c. (*redundant*) 641; dispensable; thrown away &c. (*wasted*) 638; abortive &c. (*immature*) 674.

worth-, value-less; unsaleable; not worth a straw &c. (*trifling*) 643; dear at any price.

vain, empty, inane; gain-, profit-, fruit-less; un-serviceable, -profitable; ill-spent; unproductive &c. 169; *hors de combat*; barren, sterile, impotent, unproductive; effete, past work &c. (*impaired*) 659; obsolete &c. (*old*) 124; fit for the -dust-hole, – wastepaper basket; good for nothing; of no earthly use; not worth -having, – powder and shot; leading to no end, uncalled for; un-necessary, -needed, superfluous.

Adv. uselessly &c. *adj.*; to -little, – no, – little or no- purpose.

Int. *cui bono?* what's the good!

---

646. [Specific subservience.] **Expedience.**—**N.** expedien-ce, -cy; desirableness, -bility &c. *adj.*; fitness &c. (*agreement*) 23; utility &c. 644; propriety; advantage; opportunism, pragmatism.

high time &c. (*occasion*) 134.

V. be -expedient &c. *adj.*; suit &c. (*agree*) 23; befit; suit –, befit- the -time, – season, – occasion.

conform &c. 82.

Adj. expedient; desir-, advis-, acceptable; convenient; worth while, meet; fit, -ting; due, proper, eligible, seemly, becoming; befitting &c. *v.*; opportune &c. (*in season*) 134; *in loco*; suitable &c. (*accordant*) 23; applicable &c. (*useful*) 644; practical, effective, pragmatical; suitable, handy.

Adv. in the right place; conveniently &c. *adj.*; in the nick of time.

Phr. *operæ pretium est.*

647. Inexpedience.—**N.** inexpedien-ce, -cy; undesira-bleness, -bility &c. *adj.*; discommodity, impropriety; unfitness &c. (*disagreement*) 24; inutility &c. 645; inconvenience, inadvisability; disadvantage.

V. be -inexpedient &c. *adj.*; come amiss &c. (*disagree*) 24; embarrass &c. (*hinder*) 706; put to inconvenience; pay too dear for one's whistle.

Adj. inexpedient, undesirable; un-, in-advisable; objectionable; troublesome, in-apt, -eligible, -admissible, -convenient; in-, dis-commodious; disadvantageous; inappropriate, unsuitable, unfit &c. (*inconsonant*) 24.

ill-contrived, -advised; unsatisfactory; unprofitable &c., unsubservient &c. (*useless*) 645; inopportune &c. (*unseasonable*) 135; out of –, in the wrong-place; improper, unseemly.

clumsy, awkward; cum-brous, -bersome; lumbering, unwieldy, hulky; un-

manageable &c. (*impracticable*) 704; impedient &c. (*in the way*) 706. unnecessary &c. (*redundant*) 641.

Phr. it will never do.

648. [Capability of producing good. Good qualities.] **Goodness.**—**N.** goodness &c. *adj.*; excellence, merit; virtue &c. 944; value, worth, price.

super-excellence, -eminence; superiority &c. 33; perfection &c. 650; *coup de maître*; master-piece, *chef d'œuvre*, prime, flower, cream, *élite*, pick, A1, none such, *nonpareil*, *crème de la crème*, flower of the flock, cock of the roost, salt of the earth; champion.

tid-bit; gem, – of the first water; *bijou*, precious stone, jewel, pearl, diamond, ruby, brilliant, treasure; good thing; *rara avis*, one in a thousand.

beneficence &c. 906; good man &c. 948.

V. be -beneficial &c. *adj.*; produce –, do- -good &c. 618; profit &c. (*be of use*) 644; benefit; confer a -benefit &c. 618.

be the making of, do a world of good, make a man of.

produce a good effect; do a good turn, confer an obligation; improve &c. 658.

do no harm, break no bones.

be -good &c. *adj.*; excel, transcend &c. (*be superior*) 33; bear away the bell.

stand the -proof, – test; pass -muster, – an examination.

challenge comparison, vie, emulate, rival.

Adj. harm-, hurt-less; unobnoxious; in-nocuous, -nocent, -offensive.

beneficial, valuable, of value; serviceable &c. (*useful*) 644; advantageous, profitable, edifying; salutary &c. (*healthful*) 656.

favourable; propitious &c. (*hope-giving*) 858; fair.

good, – as gold; excellent; better; superior &c. 33; above par; nice, fine; genuine &c. (*true*) 494.

best, choice, select, picked, elect, eximious, *recherché*, rare, priceless; unpara-goned, -lleled &c. (*supreme*) 33; superlatively &c. 33- good; super-fine, -excellent; bonzer; of the first water; first-rate, -class; high-wrought; exquisite, very best, crack, prime, tip-top, gilt-edged, capital, cardinal; standard &c. (*perfect*) 650; inimitable.

admirable, estimable; praiseworthy &c. (*approve*) 931; pleasing &c. 829; *couleur de rose*, precious, of great price;

649. [Capability of producing evil. Bad qualities.] **Badness.**—**N.** hurtfulness &c. *adj.*; virulence.

evil doer &c. 913; bane &c. 663; plague-spot &c. (*insalubrity*) 657; evil star, ill wind; snake in the grass, skeleton in the closet; *amari aliquid*, thorn in the side; Jonah, jinx, hoodoo.

malignity; malevolence &c. 907; tender mercies [ironically].

ill-treatment, annoyance, molestation, abuse, oppression, persecution, outrage; misusage &c. 679; injury &c. (*damage*) 659.

badness &c. *adj.*; peccancy, abomination; painfulness &c. 830; pestilence &c. (*disease*) 655; guilt &c. 947; depravity &c. 945.

V. be -hurtful &c. *adj.*; cause –, produce –, inflict –, work –, do- evil &c. 619; damnify, endamage, hurt, harm, scathe; injure &c. (*damage*) 659; pain &c. 830.

wrong, aggrieve, oppress, persecute; trample –, tread –, bear hard –, put-upon; overburden; weigh -down, – heavy on; victimize; run down; molest &c. 830.

maltreat, abuse; ill-use, -treat; thwart, buffet, bruise, scratch, maul; smite &c. (*scourge*) 972; do -violence, – harm, – a mischief; stab, pierce, outrage.

do –, make- mischief; bring –, get-into trouble.

destroy &c. 162.

Adj. hurt-, harm-, scath-, bane-, baleful; injurious, deleterious, detrimental, noxious, pernicious, mischievous, full of mischief, mischief-making, malefic, malignant, nocuous, noisome; prejudicial; dis-serviceable, -advantageous; wide-wasting.

unlucky, sinister; obnoxious, untoward, disastrous.

oppressive, burdensome, onerous; malign &c. (*malevolent*) 907.

corrupting &c. (corrupt &c. 659); virulent, venomous, envenomed, corrosive; poisonous &c. (*morbific*) 657; deadly &c. (*killing*) 361; destructive &c. (*destroying*) 162; inauspicious &c. 859.

bad, ill, arrant, as bad as bad can be, dreadful; hor-rid, -rible; dire; rank,

costly &c. (*dear*) 814; worth -its weight in gold, – a Jew's eye, – a king's ransom; matchless, peerless, invaluable, inestimable, precious as the apple of the eye.

tolerable &c. (*not very good*) 651; up to the mark, un-exceptionable, -objectionable; satisfactory, tidy.

in -good, – fair- condition; fresh; unspoiled; sound &c. (*perfect*) 650.

Adv. beneficially &c. *adj.*; well &c. 618.

———

peccant, foul, fulsome; rotten, – at the core.

vile, base, villainous; mean &c. (*paltry*) 643; injured &c., deteriorated &c. 659; unsatisfactory, exception, -able, indifferent; below par &c. (*imperfect*) 651; ill-contrived, -conditioned; wretched, sad, grievous, deplorable, lamentable; piti-ful, -able, woeful &c. (*painful*) 830.

evil, wrong; depraved &c. 945; shocking; reprehensible &c. (*disapprove*) 932.

hateful, – as a toad; abominable, detestable, execrable, cursed, accursed, confounded; damn-ed, -able; infernal; diabolic &c. (*malevolent*) 907.

inadvisable &c. (*inexpedient*) 647; unprofitable &c. (*useless*) 645; incompetent &c. (*unskilful*) 699; irremediable &c. (*hopeless*) 859.

Adv. badly &c. *adj.*; wrong, ill; to one's cost; where the shoe pinches.

Phr. bad is the best; the worst come to the worst.

650. Perfection. — N. perfection; perfectness &c. *adj.*; indefectibility; impecc-ancy, -ability.

pink, *beau idéal*, phœnix, paragon; pink –, acme- of perfection; *ne plus ultra*; summit &c. 210.

cygne noir; philosopher's stone; chrysolite, Koh-i-noor, black tulip.

model, standard, pattern, mirror, admirable Crichton; trump; very prince of.

master-piece, -stroke, super-excellence &c. (*goodness*) 648; transcendence &c. (*superiority*) 33.

V. be -perfect &c. *adj.*; transcend &c. (*be supreme*) 33.

bring to perfection, perfect, ripen, mature; consummate, complete &c. 729; put in trim &c. (*prepare*) 673; put the finishing touch to.

Adj. perfect, faultless, ideal; indefective, -ficient, -fectible; immaculate, spotless, impeccable; free from -imperfection &c. 651; un-blemished, -injured &c. 659; sound, – as a roach; in perfect condition; scathless, intact, harmless; seaworthy &c. (*safe*) 644; right as a trivet; *in seipso totus teres atque rotundus*; consummate &c. (*complete*) 52; finished &c. 729; complete in itself.

best &c. (*good*) 648; model, standard; inimitable, unparagoned, unparalleled &c. (*supreme*) 33; superhuman, divine;

651. Imperfection.—N. imperfection; imperfectness &c. *adj.*; deficiency; inadequacy &c. (*insufficiency*) 640; peccancy &c. (*badness*) 649; immaturity &c. 674.

fault, defect, weak point; screw loose; rift within the lute; fly in the ointment; flaw &c. (*break*) 70; gap &c. 198; twist &c. 243; taint, attainder; bar sinister, hole in one's coat; blemish &c. 848; weakness &c. 160; half-blood, touch of the tar brush; shortcoming &c. 304; drawback; seamy side.

mediocrity; no great -shakes, – catch; not much to boast of.

V. be -imperfect &c. *adj.*; have a -defect &c. *n.*; lie under a disadvantage; spring a leak.

not –, barely- pass muster; fall short &c. 304.

Adj. imperfect; not -perfect &c. 650; de-ficient, -fective; faulty, unsound, mutilated, tainted; out of -order, – tune; cracked, leaky; sprung; warped &c. (*distort*) 243; lame; injured &c. (*deteriorated*) 659; peccant &c. (*bad*) 649; frail &c. (*weak*) 160; inadequate &c. (*insufficient*) 640; crude &c. (*unprepared*) 674; incomplete &c. 53; found wanting; below par; short-handed; below –, under- its full -strength, – complement.

indifferent, middling, ordinary, medi-

beyond all praise &c. (*approbation*) 931; *sans peur et sans reproche*.

Adv. to perfection, to the limit; perfectly &c. *adj.*; *ad unguem*; clean, – as a whistle.

———

ocre; average &c. 29; so-so; *così-così*, milk and water; tolerable, fair, passable; pretty -well, – good; rather –, moderately- good; good –, well- enough; decent; not -bad, – amiss; inobjectionable, admissible, bearable, only better than nothing.

secondary, inferior; second-rate, -best, one-horse.

Adv. almost &c.; to a limited extent, rather &c. 32; pretty, moderately; only; considering, all things considered, enough.

Phr. *surgit amari aliquid.*

———

652. Cleanness.—N. cleanness &c. *adj.*; purity; cleaning &c. *v.*; purification, defecation &c. *v.*; purgation, lustration; de-, abs-tersion; epuration, mundation, ablution, lavation, colature; disinfection &c. *v.*; drain-, sewerage.

lavatory, bath, -room; swimming pool, natatorium; public baths; hot –, cold –, Turkish –, Swedish –, Russian –, vapour- bath; *hammam*, laundry, washhouse; washerwoman, laundress, laundryman; scavenger, cleaner, sweeper, goodie; crossing sweeper, white wings, dustman, sweep.

brush; broom, besom, carpet-sweeper, vacuum-cleaner, mop, squilgee, rake, shovel, sieve, riddle, screen, filter; scraper, strigil.

napkin, *serviette*, cloth, table-, carving-cloth, table-linen, napery, maukin, handkerchief, towel, sudary; doyley, doily, duster, sponge, mop, swab.

cover, drugget, mat, doormat.

soap, wash, lotion, detergent, cathartic, purgative; purifier &c. *v.*; dentifrice, tooth-powder, -paste; mouth wash; disinfectant.

V. be –, render- clean &c. *adj.*

clean, -se; mundify, rinse, wring, flush, full, wipe, mop, sponge, scour, swab, scrub, holystone, brush up.

wash, shampoo, lave, launder, buck; abs-, de-terge; clear, purify; de-purate, -spumate, -fecate; purge, expurgate; Bowdlerize; elutriate, lixiviate, edulcorate, clarify, refine, rack; fil-ter, -trate; drain, strain.

disinfect, sterilize, pasteurize, fumigate, ventilate, deodorize; whitewash.

sift, winnow, screen, riddle, pick, weed, comb, rake, brush, sweep.

653. Uncleanness.—N. uncleanness &c. *adj.*; impurity; immundi-ty, -city; impurity &c. [of mind] 961.

defilement, contamination &c. *v.*; defœdation; soil-ure, -iness; abomination; leaven; taint, -ure; fetor &c. 401.

decay; putre-scence, -faction; corruption; mould, must, mildew, dry-rot, *mucor*, rubigo, caries.

slovenry; slovenliness &c. *adj.*; squalor.

dowdy, drab, slut, malkin, slattern, sloven, slammerkin, scrub, draggletail, mudlark, dustman, sweep; beast.

dirt, filth, soil, slop; dust, cobweb, flue; smoke, soot, smudge, smut, grime, raff.

sordes, dregs, grounds, lees; sedi-, settle-ment; heel-tap; dross, -iness; mother, precipitate, *scoriæ*, ashes, cinders, recrement, slag; scum, froth.

hog-wash, swill, ditch-, dish-, bilgewater; rinsings, cheese-parings; sweepings &c. (*useless refuse*) 645; off-, outscourings; off-scum; *caput mortuum*, *residuum*, sprue, feculence, clinker, draff; scurf, -iness; *exuviæ*, morphew; fur, -fur; dandruff; tartar.

riffraff; vermin, louse, cootie, flea, bug.

mud, mire, quagmire, *alluvium*, silt, sludge, slime, slush, slosh.

spawn, offal, garbage, carrion; *excreta* &c. 299; slough, peccant humour, pus, matter, suppuration, *lienteria*; *fæces*, excrement, ordure, dung; sew-, sewer-age; muck, coprolite; guano, manure, compost.

dunghill, *coluvies*, mixen, midden, bog, laystall, sink, w.c., water-, earth-closet, latrine, privy, jakes, John's; cess, -pool; sump, sough, *cloaca*, drain,

rout –, clear –, sweep &c.- out; make a clean sweep of.

Adj. clean, -ly; pure; immaculate; spot-, stain-, taint-less; without a stain, un-stained, -spotted, -soiled, -sullied, -tainted, -infected, -adulterated; aseptic; sweet, – as a nut.

neat, spruce, tidy, trim, gimp, clean as a new penny, like a cat in pattens; cleaned &c. *v.*; kempt.

Adv. neatly &c. *adj.*; clean as a whistle.

sewer, common sewer; Cloacina; dust-hole.

sty, pig-sty, lair, den, Augean stable, sink of corruption; slum, rookery.

V. be –, become- unclean &c. *adj.*; rot, putrefy, fester, rankle, reek; stink &c. 401; mould, -er; go -bad &c. *adj.*

render -unclean &c. *adj.*; dirt, -y; soil, smoke, tarnish, slaver, spot, smear, daub, blot, blur, smudge, smutch, smirch; d-, dr-abble, -aggle; spatter, slubber; be-smear &c., -mire, -slime, -grime, -foul; splash, stain, distain, maculate, sully, pollute, defile, debase, corrupt &c. (*injure*) 659; cover with -dust &c. *n.*; drabble in the mud.

contaminate, taint, leaven; wallow in the mire; slob-, slab-ber.

Adj. unclean, dirty, filthy, grimy; soiled &c. *v.*; not to be handled with kid gloves; dusty, snuffy, smutty, sooty, smoky; thick, turbid, dreggy; slimy.

uncleanly, slovenly, untidy, sluttish, dowdy, slatternly, draggle-tailed; un-combed, -kempt, -scoured, -swept, -wiped, -washed, -strained, -purified; squalid.

nasty, coarse, foul, impure, offensive, abominable, beastly, reeky, reechy; fetid &c. 401.

mouldy, lentiginous, musty, mildewed, rusty, moth-eaten, mucid, rancid, bad, gone bad, touched, fusty, reasty, rotten, corrupt, tainted, high, fly-blown, maggoty; putr-id, -escent, -efied; purulent, carious, peccant, fec-al, -ulent; stercoraceous, excrementitious; scurfy, impetiginous; gory, bloody; rotting &c. *v.*; rotten as -a pear, – cheese.

crapulous &c. (*intemperate*) 954; gross &c. (*impure in mind*) 961.

---

654. Health.—N. health, sanity; soundness &c. *adj.*; vigour; good –, perfect –, excellent –, rude –, robust-health; bloom, *mens sana in corpore sano*; Hygeia; incorrupti-on, -bility; good state –, clean bill- of health, eupepsia.

V. be in health &c. *adj.*; bloom, flourish.

keep -body and soul together, – on one's legs; enjoy -good, – a good state of- health; have a clean bill of health.

return to health; recover &c. 660; get better &c. (*improve*) 658; take a -new, – fresh- lease of life; convalesce, be convalescent, recruit; restore to health; cure &c. (*restore*) 660.

Adj. health-y, -ful; in -health &c. *n.*; well, sound, strong, fit, hearty, hale, fresh, blooming, green, whole; florid, flush, hardy, stanch, staunch,

655. Disease.*—N. disease; illness, sickness &c. *adj.*; ailing &c. *v.*; 'the ills that flesh is heir to'; morb-idity, -osity; infirmity, ailment, indisposition; complaint, disorder, malady; distemper, -ature.

visitation, attack, seizure, stroke, fit, epilepsy, apoplexy, shock, shell-shock.

delicacy, loss of health, valetudinarianism, invalidism, cachexy; *cachexia*, atrophy, *marasmus*; indigestion, *dyspepsia*; decay &c. (*deterioration*) 659; malnutrition, decline, consumption, palsy, paralysis, prostration; occupational diseases.

taint, pollution, infection, contagion, septicity, septicæmia, blood poisoning, pyæmia, epi-, en-demic; murrain, plague, pestilence, virus, pox.

sore, ulcer, abscess, fester, boil; pimple &c. (*swelling*) 250; carbuncle,

* Extended lists of different diseases are beyond the scope of this work.

brave, robust, vigorous, weather-proof; convalescent.

un-scathed, -injured, -maimed, -marred, -tainted; sound of wind and limb, safe and sound; without a scratch.

on one's legs; sound as a -roach, – bell; fresh as -a daisy, – a rose, – April; picture of health; bursting with health; fit as a fiddle; hearty as a buck; in -fine, – high- feather; in -good case, – full bloom; in fine fettle; pretty bobbish, tolerably well, as well as can be expected.

sanitary &c. (*health-giving*) 656; sanatory &c. (*remedial*) 662.

___

gathering, whitlow, imposthume, peccant humour, issue; rot, canker, cancer, *carcinoma*, *caries*, mortification, corruption, gangrene, *sphacelus*, leprosy, eruption, rash, breaking out, venereal disease.

fever, calenture; inflammation.

fatal &c. (*hopeless*) 859- -disease &c.; dangerous illness, galloping consumption, churchyard cough; general breaking up, break up of the system.

[Disease of mind] neurasthenia; idiocy &c. 499; insanity &c. 503.

martyr to disease; cripple; 'the halt, the lame and the blind'; valetudinar-y, -ian; invalid, patient, case; sick-room, -chamber, hospital &c. 662.

[Science of disease] path-, eti-, nos-ology, therapeutics, diagnosis, prognosis.

V. be -ill &c. *adj.*; ail, suffer, labour under, be affected with, complain of; droop, flag, languish, halt; sicken, peak, pine, waste away, fail, lose strength; gasp.

keep one's bed; feign sickness &c. (*falsehood*) 544, malinger.

lay -by, – up; take –, catch- -a disease &c. *n.*, – an infection; be stricken by; break out.

Adj. diseased; ailing &c. *v.*; ill, – of; taken ill, seized with; indisposed, unwell, sick, squeamish, poorly, seedy; affected –, afflicted- with illness; laid up, confined, bed-ridden, invalided, in hospital, on the sick list; out of -health, – sorts; valetudinary.

un-sound, -healthy; sickly, morbose, healthless, infirm, chlorotic, unbraced, drooping, flagging, lame, halt, crippled, halting.

morbid, tainted, vitiated, peccant, contaminated, poisoned, septic, tabid, mangy, leprous, cankered; rotten, – to, – at- the core; withered, palsied, paralytic, tuberculous; dyspeptic.

touched in the wind, broken-winded, spavined, gasping; *hors de combat* &c. (*useless*) 645.

weak-ly, -ened &c. (*weak*) 160; decrepit; decayed &c. (*deteriorated*) 659; incurable &c. (*hopeless*) 859; in declining health; cranky; in a bad way, in danger, prostrate; moribund &c. (*death*) 360.

morbific, epidemic &c. 657.

___

656. Salubrity.—N. salubrity, salubriousness; healthiness &c. *adj.*

fine -air, – climate; eudiometer.

[Preservation of health] *hygiène*; valetudinarian, -ism, preventorium, sanitarian; *sanitarium, sanitorium*, immunity.

V. be -salubrious &c. *adj.*; agree with, be good for; assimilate &c. 23.

Adj. salu-brious, -tary, -tiferous, wholesome; health-y, -ful; sanitary, prophylactic, benign, bracing, tonic,

657. Insalubrity.—N. insalubrity; unhealthiness &c. *adj.*; non-naturals; plague spot; malaria &c. (*poison*) 663; death in the pot, contagion.

Adj. insalubrious; un-healthy, -wholesome; noxious, noisome, foul; morbi-fic, -ferous; mephitic, septic, azotic, deleterious; pesti-lent, -ferous, -lential; virulent, venomous, envenomed, poisonous, toxic, narcotic.

contagious, infectious, catching, taking, communicable, epidemic, zymotic;

invigorating, good for, nutritious, hyg-eian, -ienic.

in-noxious, -nocuous, -nocent; harmless, uninjurious, uninfectious; immune.

sanative &c. (*remedial*) 662; restorative &c. (*reinstate*) 660; useful &c. 644.

658. Improvement.—N. improvement; a-, melioration; betterment; mend, amendment, emendation; mending &c. *v.*; advancement; advance &c. (*progress*) 282; ascent &c. 305; promotion, preferment; elevation &c. 307; increase &c. 35.

cultiv-, civiliz-ation; menticulture, culture, march of intellect; eugenics, euthenics, meliorism, telesis.

reform, -ation; revision, radical reform; second thoughts, correction, *limæ labor*, refinement, elaboration; purification &c. 652; repair &c. (*restoration*) 660; recovery &c. 660.

revise; revised –, new- edition.

reformer, radical, progressive.

V. improve; be –, become –, getbetter; mend, amend.

advance &c. (*progress*) 282; ascend &c. 305; increase &c. 35; fructify, ripen, mature; pick up, come about, rally, take a favourable turn; turn -over a new leaf, – the corner; raise one's head, sow one's wild oats; recover &c. 660.

be -better &c. *adj.*, – improved by; turn to -right, – good, – best- account; profit by, reap the benefit of; make -good use of, – capital out of; place to good account; take advantage of.

render better, improve, emend, make over, better; a-, meliorate; correct.

improve –, refine- upon; rectify; enrich, mellow, elaborate, fatten.

promote, cultivate, advance, forward, enhance; bring -forward, – on; foster &c. 707; invigorate &c. (*strengthen*) 159.

touch –, rub –, brush –, furbish –, bolster –, vamp –, brighten –, warmup; polish, cook, make the most of, set off to advantage; prune; repair &c. (*restore*) 660; put in order &c. (*arrange*) 60.

review, revise, edit, redact; make -corrections, – improvements &c. *n.*; doctor &c. (*remedy*) 662; purify &c. 652.

sporadic, endemic, pandemic, epizoötic.

innutritious, indigestible, ungenial; uncongenial &c. (*disagreeing*) 24.

deadly &c. (*killing*) 361.

---

659. Deterioration.—N. deterioration, debasement; want, ebb; recession &c. 287; retrogradation &c. 283; decrease &c. 36.

degenera-cy, -tion, -teness; degradation; deprav-ation, -ement; depravity &c. 945; demoralization, retrogression.

impairment, inquination, injury, damage, loss, detriment, delaceration, outrage, havoc, inroad, ravage, scath; perversion, prostitution, vitiation, discoloration, oxidation, pollution, defœdation, poisoning, venenation, leaven, contamination, canker, corruption, adulteration, alloy.

decl-ine, -ension, -ination; decadence, -cy; falling off &c. *v.*; caducity, decrepitude, senility.

decay, dilapidation, ravages of time, wear and tear; cor-, e-rosion; mouldi-, rotten-ness; moth and rust, dry-rot, blight, marasmus, atrophy, collapse; disorganization; *délabrement* &c. (*destruction*) 162.

wreck, mere wreck, honeycomb, *magni nominis umbra*.

V. be –, become--worse,–deteriorated &c. *adj.*; have seen better days, deteriorate, degenerate, fall off; wane &c. (*decrease*) 36; ebb; retrograde &c. 283; decline, droop; go down &c. (*sink*) 306; go -downhill, – on from bad to worse, – farther and fare worse; jump out of the frying pan into the fire.

run to -seed, – waste; swale, sweal; lapse, be the worse for; break, – down; spring a leak, crack, start; shrivel &c. (*contract*) 195; fade, go off, wither, moulder, rot, rankle, decay, go bad; go to –, fall into- decay; 'fall into the sear and yellow leaf,' rust, crumble, shake; totter, – to its fall; perish &c. 162; die &c. 360.

[Render less good] deteriorate; weaken &c. 160; put back; taint, infect, contaminate, poison, empoison,

relieve, refresh, revive, infuse new blood into, recruit, re-invigorate, re-new, revivify, freshen, build -afresh, – anew; uplift, inspire.

re-form, -model, -organise; new model, civilize.

view in a new light, think better of, appeal from Philip drunk to Philip sober.

palliate, mitigate; lessen &c. 36- an evil.

Adj. improving &c. *v.*; progressive, improved &c. *v.*; better, – off, – for; all the better for; better advised.

reform-, emend-atory; reparatory &c. (*restorative*) 660; remedial &c. 662.

corrigible, improvable, curable, ac-cultural.

Adv. on -consideration, – reconsider-ation, – second thoughts, – better advice; *ad melius inquirendum*; on the -mend, – up grade.

---

envenom, canker, corrupt, exulcerate, pollute, vitiate, inquinate; de-, em-base; denaturalize, leaven; de-flower, -bauch, -file, -prave, -grade; stain &c. (*dirt*) 653; discolour; alloy, adulterate, sophisticate, tamper with, prejudice.

pervert, prostitute, demoralize, bru-talize; render vicious &c. 945; compro-mise.

embitter, ex-, acerbate, aggravate.

injure, impair, labefy, damage, harm, hurt, shend, scathe, spoil, mar, despoil, dilapidate, waste; overrun; ravage; pillage &c. 791.

wound, stab, pierce, maim, lame, surbate, cripple, hough, hamstring, hit between wind and water, scotch, mangle, mutilate, disfigure, blemish, deface, warp.

blight, rot; cor-, e-rode, eat away; wear -away, – out; gnaw, – at the root of; sap, mine, undermine, shake, sap the foundations of, break up; dis-organ-ize, -mantle, -mast; destroy &c. 162.

damnify &c. (*aggrieve*) 649; do one's worst; knock down; deal a blow to; play -havoc, – sad havoc, – the mischief, – the deuce, – the very devil- -with, – among; decimate.

Adj. unimproved &c. (improve &c. 658); deteriorated &c. *v.*; altered, – for the worse; injured &c. *v.*; sprung; withering, spoiling, &c. *v.*; on the -wane, – decline; tabid; degenerate; worse; the –, all the- worse for; out of -repair, – tune; imperfect &c. 651; the worse for wear; battered; weather-ed, -beaten; stale, *passé*, shaken, dilapidated, frayed, faded, wilted, shabby, second-hand, second-rate, threadbare; worn, – to- -a thread, – a shadow, – the stump, rags; reduced, – to a skeleton, skeletonized; far gone.

decayed &c. *v.*; moth-, worm-eaten; mildewed, rusty, mouldy, spotted, seedy, time-worn, moss-grown; discoloured; effete, wasted, crumbling, mouldering, rotten, cankered, blighted, tainted; depraved &c. (*vicious*) 945; decrep-id, -it; broken down; done, – for, – up; worn out, used up; fit for the -dust-hole, – wastepaper basket; past work &c. (*useless*) 645.

at a low ebb, in a bad way, on one's last legs, washed -up, – out; undermined, deciduous; nodding to its fall &c. (*destruction*) 162; tottering &c. (*dangerous*) 665; past cure &c. (*hopeless*) 859; fatigued &c. 688; backward, retrograde &c. (*retrogressive*) 283; deleterious &c. 649; behind the times.

Adv. on the down grade; beyond hope.

Phr. out of the frying pan into the fire; *ægrescit medendo*.

---

660. Restoration.—N. restor-ation, -al; re-instatement, -placement, -habil-itation, -establishment, -construction; reproduction &c. 163; re-novation, -newal; reviv-al, -escence; refreshment

661. Relapse.—N. relapse, lapse; falling back &c. *v.*; retrogradation &c. (*retrogression*) 283; deterioration &c. 659.

[Return to, or recurrence of a bad

&c. 689; re-suscitation, -animation, -vivification, -viction; Phœnix; reorganization.

renaissance, renascence, rebirth, second youth, rejuvenation, rejuvenescence, new birth; regenera-tion, -cy, -teness; palingenesis, reconversion, resurgence, resurrection.

redress, retrieval, reclamation, recovery; convalescence; resumption, *résumption.*

recurrence &c. (*repetition*) 104; *réchauffé, rifacimento.*

cure, recure, sanation; healing &c. *v.*; redintegration; rectification, instauration.

repair, reparation, mending; recruiting &c. *v.*; cicatrization; disinfection; tinkering.

reaction; redemption &c. (*deliverance*) 672; restitution &c. 790; relief &c. 834.

mender, repairer, renewer; tinker, cobbler; doctor &c. 662; *vis medicatrix* &c. (*remedy*) 662.

curableness.

V. return to the original state; recover, rally, revive; come -to, – round, – to oneself; pull through, weather the storm, be oneself again; get -well, – round, – the better of, – over, – about; rise from -one's ashes, – the grave; resurge, resurrect; survive &c. (*outlive*) 110; resume, reappear; come to, – life again; live –, rise- again; relive.

heal, skin over, cicatrize; right itself.

restore, put back, place *in statu quo*; re-instate, -place, -seat, -habilitate, -establish, -estate, -install.

re-construct, -build, -organize, -constitute; reconvert; re-new, -novate; recondition; regenerate; rejuvenate.

re-deem, -claim, -cover, -trieve; rescue &c. (*deliver*) 672.

redress, recure; cure, heal, remedy, doctor, physic, medicate; break of; bring round, set on one's legs.

re-suscitate, -vive, -animate, -vivify, -call to life; reproduce &c. 163; warm up; reinvigorate, refresh &c. 689.

redintegrate, make whole; recoup &c. 790; make -good, – all square; rectify; put –, set- -right, – to rights, – straight; set up, correct; put in order &c. (*arrange*) 60; refit, recruit; fill up, – the ranks; reinforce.

repair, mend; put in -repair, – thorough repair, – complete repair; retouch, botch, vamp, tinker, doctor, cobble; do –, patch –, plaster –, vamp- up; darn, fine-draw, heel-piece; stop a gap, stanch, staunch, caulk, calk, careen, splice, bind up wounds.

Adj. restored &c. *v.*; *redivivus,* convalescent; in a fair way; none the worse; rejuvenated, renascent.

restoring &c. *v.*; restorative, recuperative; sana-, repara-tive, -tory; curative, remedial.

restor-, recover-, san-, remedi-, retriev-, cur-able.

Adv. *in statu quo*; as you were.

Phr. *revenons à nos moutons.*

state] backsliding, recidivation, recrudescence.

V. relapse, lapse; fall –, slide –, sink-back; have a relapse; return; retrograde &c. 283; recidivate; fall off &c. 659- again.

---

662. Remedy.—N. remedy, help, redress; antidote, anti-toxin, anti-,

663. Bane.—N. bane, curse, thorn in the -side, -flesh, bugbear, *bête noire*;

counter-poison, prophylactic, antiseptic, germicide, bactericide, corrective, restorative, stimulant, pick-me-up, tonic; sedative &c. 174; palliative; febrifuge; alter-ant, -ative; specific; emetic, carminative; narcotic &c. *adj.*; Nepenthe, Mithridate.

cure; radical –, perfect –, certain-cure; sovereign remedy.

physic, medicine, patent medicine, Galenicals, simples, drug, potion, draught, dose, pill, bolus, lozenge, tablet, tabloid, capsule; electuary; linct-us, -ure; medicament.

nostrum, receipt, recipe, prescription; catholicon, panacea, elixir, *elixir vitæ*, philosopher's stone; balm, balsam, cordial, theriac, ptisan.

salve, ointment, cerate, oil, lenitive, lotion, cosmetic; plaster; epithem, embrocation, liniment, cataplasm, sinapism, arquebusade, traumatic, vulnerary, pepastic, poultice, collyrium, depilatory.

compress, pledget; bandage &c. (*support*) 215.

treatment, medical treatment, regimen; diet-ary, -etics; *vis medicatrix*, – *naturæ*; *médecine expectante*; seton, blood-letting, bleeding, venesection, phlebotomy, cupping, leeches; operation, surgical operation; tonsillectomy, appendectomy; injection, electrolysis, massage.

pharma-cy, -cology, -ceutics; acology; materia medica, pharmacopœia, therapeutics, therapy, posology, pathology &c. 655; homœ-, hetero-, all-, hydr-opathy; cold water –, open air- cure; dietetics; sur-, chirur-gery, osteopathy; healing art, leechcraft, practice of medicine; ortho-pædy, -praxy; dentistry, midwifery, obstetrics, gynæcology.

faith -cure, – healing, Christian science; psycho-therapy, -analysis, psychiatry.

hospital, infirmary, clinic; pest-, lazar-house; lazaretto, lazaret; lock hospital; *maison de santé*; *ambulance*; dispensary; *sanatorium*, *sanitarium*, spa, baths, pump-room, well; *hospice*; Red Cross; nursing home; asylum.

doctor, physician, surgeon; medical –, general- practitioner, consultant, specialist; medical attendant; medical student, medico; chemist, apothecary, pharmacopolist, druggist; leech; Æsculapius, Hippocrates, Galen; *accoucheur*, gynæcologist, midwife, oculist, aurist, dentist; operator; osteopath, bonesetter; nurse, monthly nurse, sister; dresser; *masseur, masseuse.*

V. apply a -remedy &c. *n.*; doctor, dose, physic, nurse, minister to, attend, dress the wounds, plaster, bandage, poultice; heal, cure, work a cure, kill or cure, remedy, stay (disease), snatch from the jaws of death; prevent &c. 706; relieve &c. 834; palliate &c. 658;

evil &c. 619; hurtfulness &c. (*badness*) 649; painfulness &c. (*cause of pain*) 830; scourge &c. (*punishment*) 975; *damnosa hereditas*; white elephant.

sting, fang, thorn, tang, bramble, briar, nettle.

poison, leaven, virus, venom; intoxicant; arsenic, Prussic acid, antimony, tartar emetic, strychnine, nicotine, cyanide of potassium, corrosive sublimate; curare; hyoscine &c.; poison-, mustard-, tear-gas; carbon di-, monoxide; ptomaine poisoning, botulism; miasm, mephitis, malaria, azote, sewer gas; pest, stench &c. 401.

rust, worm, moth, moth and rust, fungus, mildew; dry-rot; canker, -worm; cancer; torpedo; viper &c. (*evil-doer*) 913; demon &c. 980.

hemlock, hellebore, nightshade, *belladonna*, henbane, aconite; Upas tree.

drugs, dope, opium, morphia, morphine, cocaine, heroin, hashish, bhang.

[Science of poisons] Toxicology.

Adj. baneful &c. (*bad*) 649; poisonous &c. (*unwholesome*) 657.

---

restore &c. 660; drench with physic; consult, operate, extract, de-liver; bleed, cup, let blood, transfuse; electrolyse; psycho-analyse.

Adj. remedial; restorative &c. 660; corrective, palliative, healing; sana-tory, -tive; prophylactic; salutiferous &c. (*salutary*) 656; medic-al, -inal; therapeutic, surgical, chirurgical, orthopedic, epu-lotic, paregoric, tonic, corroborant, analeptic, balsamic, anodyne, hypnotic, neurotic, narcotic, sedative, lenitive, demulcent, emollient; depuratory; deter-sive, -gent; abstersive, disinfectant, febrifugal, alternative; traumatic, vulnerary.

dietetic, alimentary; nutrit-ious, -ive; peptic; alexi-pharmic, -teric; remedi-, cur-able.

3. *Contingent Subservience*

664. Safety.—N. safety, security, impregnability; invulnera-bility, -ble-ness &c. *adj.*; danger -past, – over; storm blown over; coast clear; escape &c. 671; means of escape, safety-valve; safeguard, palladium, sheet anchor, rock, tower of strength.

guardian-, ward-, warden-ship; tu-telage, custody, safe keeping; preser-vation &c. 670; protection, auspices.

safe-conduct, escort, convoy; guard, shield &c. (*defence*) 717; guardian angel, tutelary -god, – deity, – saint; *genius loci*.

protector, guardian; ward-en, -er; preserver, custodian, *duenna, chaperon,* third person.

watch-, ban-dog; Cerberus; watch-, patrol-, police-man, constable, peeler, bobby, copper, cop, bull, flat-foot, de-tective, armed guard; sentinel, sentry, scout &c. (*warning*) 668; garrison; guard-ship.

[Means of safety] refuge &c., anchor &c. 666; precaution &c. (*preparation*) 673; quarantine, *cordon sanitaire.* [Sense of security] confidence &c. 858.

V. be -safe &c. *adj.*; keep one's head above water, tide over, save one's bacon; ride out –, weather- the storm; light upon one's feet; bear a charmed life; escape &c. 671; possess nine lives.

make –, render- -safe &c. *adj.*; pro-tect, watch over; take care of &c. (*care*) 459; preserve &c. 670; cover, screen, shelter, shroud, flank, ward; guard &c. (*defend*) 717; secure &c. (*restrain*) 751; intrench, fence round &c. (*circumscribe*) 229; house, nestle, ensconce; take charge of.

665. Danger.—N. danger, peril, in-security, jeopardy, risk, hazard, ven-ture, precariousness, slipperiness; in-stability &c. 149; defencelessness &c. *adj.*

exposure &c. (*liability*) 177; vulner-ability; vulnerable point, heel of Achilles; forlorn hope &c. (*hopeless-ness*) 859.

[Dangerous course] leap in the dark &c. (*rashness*) 863; road to ruin, *facilis descensus Averni,* hair-breadth escape.

cause for alarm; source of danger &c. 667. [Approach of danger] rock –, breakers- ahead; storm brewing; clouds -in the horizon, – gathering; warning &c. 668; alarm &c. 669. [Sense of danger] apprehension &c. 860.

V. be -in danger &c. *adj.*; be exposed to –, run into –, incur –, encounter- -danger &c. *n.*; run a risk; lay oneself open to &c. (*liability*) 177; lean on –, trust to- a broken reed; feel the ground sliding from under one, have to run for it; have the -chances, – odds- against one.

hang by a thread, totter; tremble on the -verge, – brink; sleep –, stand -on a volcano; sit on a barrel of gunpowder, live in a glass house.

bring –, place –, put- in -danger &c. *n.*; endanger, expose to danger, im-peril; jeopard, -ize, compromise; sail too near the wind &c. (*rash*) 863; put one's head in the lion's mouth.

adventure, risk, hazard, venture, stake, set at hazard; run the gauntlet &c. (*dare*) 861; engage in a forlorn hope.

threaten &c. 909- danger; run one

escort, convoy; garrison; watch, mount guard, patrol, scout, spy.

make assurance double sure &c. (*caution*) 864; take up a loose thread; take precautions &c. (*prepare for*) 673; take in a reef; double reef topsails.

seek safety; take –, find- shelter &c. 666; run into port.

Adj. safe, secure, sure; in -safety, – security; have an anchor to windward; on the safe side; under the -shield of, – shade of, – wing of, – shadow of one's wing; under -cover, – lock and key; out of -danger, – the meshes, – harm's way; in -harbour, – port; on sure ground, at anchor, high and dry, above water, on *terra firma*; un-threatened, -molested; protected &c. *v.*; *cavendo tutus*; panoplied &c. (*defended*) 717.

snug, sea-, air-worthy; weather-, water-, fire-, bomb-proof.

defensible, tenable, proof against, in-vulnerable; un-assailable, -attackable; im-pregnable, -perdible; founded on a rock; inexpugnable.

safe and sound &c. (*preserved*) 670; harmless; scathless &c. (*perfect*) 650; unhazarded; not -dangerous &c. 665.

protecting &c. *v.*; guardian, tutelary; preservative &c. 670; trustworthy &c. 939.

Adv. *ex abundanti cautelâ*; with im-punity.

Phr. all's well; all clear; *salva res est*; *suave mari magno*; safety first.

---

hard; lay a trap for &c. (*deceive*) 545.

Adj. in -danger &c. *n.*; endangered &c. *v.*; fraught with danger; danger-, hazard-, peril-, parl-, pericul-ous; un-safe, unprotected &c. (safe, protect &c. 664); insecure, untrustworthy, un-reliable; built upon sand, on a sandy basis.

defence-, fence-, guard-, harbour-less; unshielded; vulnerable, expugn-able, unsheltered, exposed; open to &c. (*liable*) 177.

aux abois, at bay; on -the wrong side of the wall, – a lee shore, – the rocks.

at stake, in question; precarious, aleatory, critical, ticklish; slip-pery, -py; hanging by a thread &c. *v.*; with a halter round one's neck; between -the hammer and the anvil, – Scylla and Charybdis, – two fires; on the -edge, – brink, – verge of a- -precipice, – volcano; in the lion's den, on slippery ground, under fire; not out of the wood.

un-warned, -admonished, -advised; unprepared &c. 674; off one's guard &c. (*inexpectant*) 508.

tottering; un-stable, -steady; shaky, top-heavy, tumble-down, ramshackle, crumbling, waterlogged; help-, guide-less; in a bad way; reduced to –, at the last extremity; trembling in the balance; nodding to its fall &c. (*destruction*) 162.

threatening &c. 909; ominous, ill-omened; alarming &c. (*fear*) 860; ex-plosive; poisonous &c. 657.

adventurous &c. (*rash*) 863, (*bold*) 861.

Int. stop! look out! beware! take care!

Phr. *incidit in Scyllam qui vult vitare Charybdim; nam tua res agitur paries dum proximus ardet.*

---

666. [Means of safety.] **Refuge.—N.** refuge, sanctuary, retreat, fastness; stronghold, keep, last resort; ward; prison &c. 752; asylum, ark, home, almshouse, refuge for the destitute; hiding-place &c. (*ambush*) 530; *sanctum sanctorum* &c. (*privacy*) 893.

roadstead, anchorage; breakwater, mole, port, haven; harbour, – of refuge; sea-port; pier, jetty, embankment, quay.

667. [Source of danger.] **Pitfall.—N.** rocks, reefs, coral reef, sunken rocks, snags; sands, quicksands, Goodwin sands, sandy foundation; slippery ground; breakers, shoals, shallows, bank, shelf, flat, lee shore, iron-bound coast; rock –, breakers- ahead; derelict.

precipice; abyss, chasm, pit, cre-vasse; maelstrom, whirlpool, eddy, vortex, rapids, current, bore, tidal wave; storm, squall, hurricane, whirl-

covert, shelter, abri, screen, lee-wall, wing, shield, umbrella; splash-, dash-board, mudguard.

wall &c. (*inclosure*) 232; fort &c. (*defence*) 717.

anchor, kedge; grap-nel, -pling iron; sheet-, mushroom-anchor, main-stay; support &c. 215; check &c. 706; ballast.

jury-mast; vent-peg; safety -valve, – lamp; lightning conductor.

means of escape &c. (*escape*) 671; life-boat, swimming belt, cork jacket; life preserver, breeches buoy; parachute, plank, stepping-stone. safeguard &c. (*protection*) 664.

V. seek –, take –, find- refuge &c. *n.*; seek –, find- safety &c. 664; throw oneself into the arms of; claim sanctuary; take to the -hills, – woods; make port, reach shelter, bar –, bolt –, lock -the door, – gate; let the portcullis down; raise the drawbridge.

wind; volcano; ambush &c. 530; pit-fall, trap-door; trap &c. (*snare*) 545.

sword of Damocles; wolf at the door, snake in the grass, viper in one's bosom, death in the pot; latency &c. 526.

ugly customer, dangerous person, *le chat qui dort*; firebrand, hornet's nest.

Phr. *latet anguis in herbâ*; *proximus ardet Ucalegon.*

---

668. Warning.—N. warning, caution, *caveat*; notice &c. (*information*) 527; premoni-tion, -shment; prediction &c. 511; contraindication; symptom; lesson, dehortation; admonition, monition; alarm &c. 669.

handwriting on the wall, *tekel upharsin*, yellow flag; fog-signal, -horn; siren; monitor, warning voice, Cassandra, signs of the times, Mother Carey's chickens, stormy petrel, bird of ill omen, gathering clouds, clouds in the horizon, cloud no bigger than a man's hand, death-watch.

watch-tower, beacon, signal-post; light-house &c. (*indication of locality*) 550.

sent-inel, -ry; watch, -man; watch and ward; watch-, ban-, house-dog; patrol, vedette, picket, bivouac, scout, spy, spial; advanced –, rear-guard, lookout, flagman.

cautiousness &c. 864.

V. warn, caution; fore-, pre-warn; ad-, pre-monish; give -notice, – warning; menace &c. (*threaten*) 909; put on one's guard; sound the alarm &c. 669; croak.

beware, ware; take -warning, – heed at one's peril; watch out for; keep watch and ward &c. (*care*) 459.

Adj. warning &c. *v.*; premonitory, monitory, cautionary; admoni-tory, -tive; ominous, threatening, lowering, minatory, symptomatic.

warned &c. *v.*; on one's guard &c. (*careful*) 459, (*cautious*) 864.

Adv. *in terrorem* &c. (*threat*) 909.

Int. beware! ware! take care! mind –, take care-what you are about; mind! look out!

Phr. *ne reveillez pas le chat qui dort*; *fœnum habet in cornu.*

669. [Indication of danger.] Alarm.—N. alarm; alarum, larum, alarm bell, tocsin, *alerte*, beat of drum, sound of trumpet, note of alarm, hue and cry, signal of distress, S.O.S.; blue-lights; war-cry, -whoop; warning &c. 668; fog-signal, -horn; siren; yellow flag; danger signal; red -light, – flag; fire -bell, – alarm; burglar alarm, police whistle, watchman's rattle.

false alarm, cry of wolf; bug-bear, -aboo.

V. give –, raise –, sound –, beat- the *or* an -alarm &c. *n.*; alarm; warn &c. 668; ring the tocsin; *battre la générale*; cry wolf.

Adj. alarming &c. *v.*

Int. *sauve qui peut! qui vive?* who goes there?

670. Preservation.—N. preservation; safe keeping; conservation &c. (*storage*) 636; maintenance, upkeep, support, sustentation, conservatism; *vis conservatrix*; salvation &c. (*deliverance*) 672; drying &c. *v.*

[Means of preservation] prophylaxis; preserv-er, -ative; canned goods; cold pack; hygi-astics, -antics; cover, drugget; *cordon sanitaire.*

[Superstitious remedies] charm &c. 993.

V. preserve, maintain, keep, sustain, support; keep -up, – alive; not willingly let die; shore –, bank- up; nurse; save, rescue; be –, make- -safe &c. 664; take care of &c. (*care*) 459; guard &c. (*defend*) 717.

stare super antiquas vias; hold one's own; hold –, stand- -one's ground &c. (*resist*) 719.

embalm, dry, cure, smoke, salt, pickle, season, kyanize, bottle, pot, tin, can; husband &c. (*store*) 636.

Adj. preserving &c. *v.*; conservative; prophylactic; preserva-tory, -tive; hygienic.

preserved &c. *v.*; un-impaired, -broken, -injured, -hurt, -singed, -marred; safe, – and sound; intact, with a whole skin, without a scratch.

Phr. *nolumus leges Angliæ mutari.*

671. Escape.—N. escape, scape; avolation, elopement, flight, get-away; evasion &c. (*avoidance*) 623; retreat; narrow –, hairbreadth-escape; close –, near- shave; come off, impunity.

[Means of escape] loophole &c. (*opening*) 260; path &c. 627; secret -door, – passage; refuge &c. 666; vent, – peg; safety-valve; draw-bridge, fire-escape.

reprieve &c. (*deliverance*) 672; liberation &c. 750.

refugee &c. (*fugitive*) 623.

V. escape, scape; make –, effect –, make good- one's escape, make a get-away; get -off, – clear off, – well out of; *échapper belle*, save one's bacon; weather the storm &c. (*safe*) 664; escape scot-free.

elude &c., make off &c. (*avoid*) 623; march off &c. (*go away*) 293; give one the slip; slip through the -hands, – fingers; slip the collar, wriggle out of; break -loose, – from prison; break –, slip –, get- away; find -vent, – a hole to creep out of.

Adj. escap-ing, -ed &c. *v.*; stolen away, fled.

Phr. the bird has flown.

672. Deliverance.—N. deliverance, extrication, rescue; repriev-e, -al; respite; ransom; liberation &c. 750; truce, armistice; redemption, salvation; riddance; gaol delivery; exemption, day of grace; redeemableness.

V. deliver, extricate, rescue, save, redeem, ransom, free, liberate, release, set free, redeem, emancipate; bring -off, – through; *tirer d'affaire*, get the wheel out of the rut; snatch from the jaws of death, come to the rescue; rid; retrieve &c. (*restore*) 660; be –, get- rid of.

Adj. saved &c. *v.*; extric-, redeem-, rescu-able.

Phr. to the rescue!

3°. *Precursory Measures*

673. Preparation.—N. preparation; providing &c. *v.*; provi-sion, -dence; anticipation &c. (*foresight*) 510; pre-caution, -concertation, -disposition;

674. Non-Preparation. — N. non-, absence of –, want of- preparation; un-preparedness; inculture, inconcoction, improvidence.

forecast &c. (*plan*) 626; rehearsal, note of preparation.

[Putting in order] arrangement &c. 60; clearance; adjustment &c. 23; tuning; equipment, outfit, accoutrement, armament, array.

ripening &c. *v.*; maturation, evolution; elaboration, concoction, digestion; gestation, hatching, incubation, sitting.

groundwork, datum, first stone, cradle, stepping-stone; foundation, scaffold &c. (*support*) 215; scaffolding, *échafaudage*.

[Preparation -of men] training &c. (*education*) 537; inurement &c. (*habit*) 613; novitiate; [– of food] cook-ing, -ery; brewing, culinary art; [– of the soil] till-, plough-, sow-ing; semination, cultivation.

[State of being prepared] prepared-, readi-, ripe-, mellow-ness; maturity; *un impromptu fait à loisir*.

[Preparer] preparer, teacher, coach, trainer, pioneer; *avant-courrier*, *·coureur*; sappers and miners, paviour, navvy; packer, stevedore; warming-pan; precursor &c. 64.

V. prepare; get -, make- ready; make preparations, settle preliminaries, get up, sound the note of preparation; address oneself to.

set -, put- in order &c. (*arrange*) 60; forecast &c. (*plan*) 626; prepare -, plough -, dress- the ground; till -, cultivate- the soil; predispose, sow the seed, lay a train, dig a mine; lay -, fix- the -foundations, - basis, -groundwork; dig the foundations, erect the scaffolding; lay the first stone &c. (*begin*) 66.

rough-hew; cut out work; block -, hammer- out; lick into shape &c. (*form*) 240.

elaborate, mature, ripen, mellow, season, bring to maturity; nurture &c.

(*aid*) 707; hatch, cook, brew; temper; anneal, smelt; dry, cure &c. 670.

equip, arm, man; fit-out, -up; furnish, rig, dress, garnish, betrim, accoutre, array, fettle, fledge; dress -, furbish -, brush -, vamp- up; refurbish; sharpen one's tools, trim one's foils, set, prime, attune; whet the -knife, - sword; wind -, screw- up; adjust &c. (*fit*) 27; put in -trim, - train, - gear, - working order, - tune, - a groove for, - harness; pack, stow away, store.

immaturity, crudity; rawness &c. *adj.*; abortion; disqualification.

[Absence of art] nature, state of nature; virgin soil, unweeded garden; rough diamond, neglect &c. 460.

rough copy &c. (*plan*) 626; germ &c. 153; raw material &c. 635.

improvisation &c. (*impulse*) 612.

V. be -unprepared &c. *adj.*; want -, lack- preparation; lie fallow; *s'embarquer sans biscuits*; live from hand to mouth.

[Render unprepared] dismantle &c. (*render useless*) 645; undress &c. 226.

extemporize, improvise.

surprise, pay a surprise visit, take by surprise, drop in upon, take unawares; take pot-luck.

Adj. un-prepared &c. [prepare &c. 673]; without -preparation &c. 673; incomplete &c. 53; rudimental, embryonic, abortive; immature, unripe, raw, green, crude; coarse; rough, -cast, -hewn; in the rough; un-hewn, -formed, -fashioned, -wrought, -laboured, -blown, -cooked, -boiled, -concocted, -cut, -polished.

callow, un-hatched, -fledged, -nurtured, -licked, -taught, -educated, -cultivated, -trained, -tutored, -drilled, -exercised; precocious, premature; un-, in-digested; un-mellowed, -seasoned, -leavened.

fallow; un-sown, -tilled; natural, in a state of nature; undressed; in dishabille, *en déshabille, en négligé*.

un-, dis-qualified; unfitted; ill-digested; un-begun, -ready, -arranged, -organized, -furnished, -provided, -equipped, -trimmed; out of -gear, - order; dismantled &c. *v.*

shiftless, improvident, unthrifty, thoughtless, unguarded; happy-go-lucky; caught napping &c. (*inexpectant*) 508; unpremeditated &c. 612.

Adv. extempore &c. 612.

---

train &c. (*teach*) 537; inure &c. (*habituate*) 613; breed; prepare &c.- for; rehearse; make provision for; take -steps, – measures, – precautions; provide, – against; beat up for recruits; open the door to &c. (*facilitate*) 705.

set one's house in order, make all snug; clear -decks, – for action; close one's ranks; shuffle the cards.

prepare oneself; serve an apprenticeship &c. (*learn*) 539; lay oneself out for, get into harness, gird up one's loins, buckle on one's armour, *reculer pour mieux sauter*, prime and load, shoulder arms, get the steam up, put the horses to.

guard –, make sure- against; forearm, make sure, prepare for the evil day, have a rod in pickle, provide against a rainy day, feather one's nest; lay in provisions &c. 637; make investments; keep on foot.

be -prepared, – ready &c. *adj.*; hold oneself in readiness, watch and pray, keep one's powder dry; lie in wait for &c. (*expect*) 507; anticipate &c. (*foresee*) 510; *principiis obstare*; *veniente occurrere morbo*.

Adj. preparing &c. *v.*; in -preparation, – course of preparation, – agitation, – embryo, – hand, – train; afoot, afloat; on -foot, – the stocks, – the anvil; under consideration &c. (*plan*) 626; brewing, hatching, forthcoming, brooding; in -store for, – reserve.

precautionary, provident; prepara-tive, -tory; provisional, in-choate, under revision; preliminary &c. (*precedent*) 62.

prepared &c. *v.*; in readiness; ready, – to one's hand, – made, cut and dried; ready for use, reach me down; made to one's hand, handy, on the table, made to order; in gear; in working -order, – gear; snug; in practice.

ripe, mature, mellow; practised &c. (*skilled*) 698; laboured, elab-orate, highly-wrought, smelling of the lamp, worked up.

in -full feather, – best bib and tucker; in –, at- harness; in – the saddle, – arms, – battle array, – war paint; up in arms; armed -at all points, – to the teeth, – *cap-à-pie*; sword in hand; booted and spurred.

in utrumque –, semper- paratus; on the alert &c. (*vigilant*) 459; at one's post.

Adv. in -preparation, – anticipation of; afoot, astir, abroad; abroach.

675. Essay.—N. essay, trial, endeavour, aim, attempt; venture, ad-venture, speculation, *coup d'essai*, *début*; probation &c. (*experiment*) 463.

V. try, essay; experiment &c. 463; endeavour, strive; tempt, tackle, take on, attempt, make an attempt; venture, adventure, speculate, take one's chance, tempt fortune; try one's -fortune, – luck, – hand; use one's endeavour; feel –, grope –, pick- one's way.

try hard, push, make a bold push, use one's best endeavour; do one's best &c. (*exertion*) 686.

Adj. essaying &c. *v.*; experimental &c. 463; tentative, empirical, probationary.

Adv. experimentally &c. *adj.*; on trial, at a venture; by rule of thumb. if one may be so bold.

676. Undertaking.—N. undertaking; compact &c. 769; engagement &c. (*promise*) 768; enter-, em-prise; venture &c. 675; pilgrimage; mat-ter in hand &c. (*business*) 625; move; first move &c. (*beginning*) 66.

V. undertake; engage –, embark- in; launch –, plunge- into; volunteer; apprentice oneself to; engage &c. (*promise*) 768; contract &c. 769; take upon -oneself, – one's shoulders; devote oneself to &c. (*determination*) 604.

take -up, – in hand; tackle; set –, go- about; set –, fall- -to, – to work; launch forth; set up shop; put in -hand, – execution; set forward; break the neck of a business, be in for; put one's hand to; betake oneself to, turn one's hand to, go to do; begin &c. 66; broach, institute, &c. (*originate*) 153; put –, lay- one's -hand to the plough, – shoulder to the wheel.

have in hand &c. (*business*) 625; have many irons in the fire &c. (*activity*) 682.

Adj. undertaking &c. *v.*; on the anvil &c. 625; adventurous, venturesome.

Int. here goes!

677. Use.—N. use; employ, -ment; exer-cise, -citation; appli-cation, -ance; adhibition, disposal; consumption; agency &c. (*physical*) 170; usufruct; usefulness &c. 644; recourse, resort, avail, pragmatism.

[Conversion to use] utilization, service, wear.

[Way of using] usage.

V. use, make use of, employ, put to use; apply, put in -action, – operation, – practice; set -in motion, – to work.

ply, work, wield, handle, manipulate; play, – off; exert, exercise, practise, avail oneself of, profit by; resort –, have recourse –, recur –, take –, betake oneself- to; take -up with, – advantage of; lay one's hands on, try.

render useful &c. 644; mould; turn to -account, – use; convert to use, utilize, administer; work up; call –, bring- into play; put into requisition; call –, draw- forth; press –, enlist- into the service; bring to bear upon, devote, dedicate, consecrate, apply, adhibit, dispose of; make a -handle, – cat's paw- of.

fall back upon, make a shift with; make the -most, – best- of.

use –, swallow- up; consume, absorb, expend; tax, task, wear, put to task.

Adj. in use; used &c. *v.*; well-worn, -trodden.

useful &c. 644; subservient &c. (*instrumental*) 631; utilitarian; pragmatical.

678. Disuse.—N. forbearance, abstinence; disuse; relinquishment &c. 782; desuetude &c. (*want of habit*) 614.

V. not use; do without, dispense with, let alone, not touch, forbear, abstain, spare, waive, neglect; keep back, reserve.

lay -up, – by, – on the shelf, – up in a napkin; shelve; set –, put –, lay-aside; disuse, leave off, have done with; supersede; discard &c. (*eject*) 297; dismiss, give warning.

throw aside &c. (*relinquish*) 782; make away with &c. (*destroy*) 162; cast –, heave –, throw- overboard; cast to the -dogs, – winds; dismantle &c. (*render useless*) 645.

lie –, remain- unemployed &c. *adj.*

Adj. not used &c. *v.*; un-employed, -applied, -disposed of, -spent, -exercised, -touched, -trodden, -essayed, -gathered, -culled; uncalled for, not required.

disused &c. *v.*; done with; run down, used up, cast off.

679. Misuse.—N. mis-use, -usage, -employment, -application, -appropriation.

abuse, profanation, prostitution, desecration; waste &c. 638.

V. mis-use, -employ, -apply, -appropriate.

desecrate, abuse, profane, prostitute; waste &c. 638; over-task, -tax, -work; squander &c. 818.

cut a whetstone with a razor, employ a steam-engine to crack a nut; catch at a straw.

Adj. misused &c. *v.*

Section III. Voluntary Action

1°. *Simple Voluntary Action*

680. Action.—N. action, performance; doing &c. *v.*; perpetration; exercise, -citation; movement, operation, evolution, work; labour &c. (*exertion*) 686; *praxis*, execution; procedure &c. (*conduct*) 692; handicraft; business &c. 625; agency &c. (*power at work*) 170.

deed, act, overt act, stitch, touch, gest; transaction, job, doings, dealings, proceeding, measure, step, manœuvre, bout, passage, move, stroke, blow; *coup, – de main, – d'état; tour de force* &c. (*display*) 882; feat, exploit, stunt; achievement &c. (*completion*) 729; handiwork, workmanship, craftsmanship; manufacture; stroke of policy &c. (*plan*) 626.

actor &c. (*doer*) 690.

V. do, perform, execute; achieve &c. (*complete*) 729; transact, enact; commit, perpetrate, inflict; exercise, prosecute, carry on, work, practise, play.

employ oneself, ply one's task; officiate, have in hand &c. (*business*) 625; labour &c. 686; be at work; pursue a course; shape one's course &c. (*conduct*) 692.

act, operate; take -action, – steps; strike a blow, lift a finger, stretch forth one's hand; take in hand &c. (*undertake*) 676; put oneself in motion; put in practice; carry into execution &c. (*complete*) 729; act upon.

be -an actor &c. 690; take –, act –, play –, perform- a part in; participate in; have a -hand in, – finger in the pie; have to do with; be a -party to, – participator in; bear –, lend- a hand; pull an oar, run in a race; mix oneself up with &c. (*meddle*) 682.

be in action; come into operation &c. (*power at work*) 170.

Adj. doing &c. *v.*; acting; in action; in harness; on duty; at work; in operation &c. 170; up to one's ears in work, in the midst of things.

Adv. in the -act, – midst of, – thick of; red-handed, *in flagrante delicto*; while one's hand is in.

681. Inaction.—N. inaction, passiveness, abstinence from action; non-interference; Fabian –, conservative-policy; neglect &c. 460; stagnation, vegetation; loafing.

inactivity &c. 683; rest &c. (*repose*) 687; quiescence &c. 265; want of –, in- occupation; unemployment; idle hours, time hanging on one's hands, *dolce far niente*; sinecure.

V. not -do, – act, – attempt; be -inactive &c. 683; abstain from doing, do nothing, hold, spare; not -stir, – move, – lift- a -finger, – foot, – peg; fold one's -arms, – hands; leave –, let- alone; let -be, – pass, – things take their course, – it have its way, – well alone; *quieta non movere; stare super antiquas vias*; rest and be thankful, live and let live; lie –, rest- upon one's oars; *laisser -aller, – faire*; stand aloof; refrain &c. (*avoid*) 623; keep oneself from doing; remit –, relax- one's efforts; desist &c. (*relinquish*) 624; stop &c. (*cease*) 142; pause &c. (*be quiet*) 265.

wait, lie in wait, bide one's time, take time, tide it over.

cool –, kick- one's heels; loaf, while away the -time, – tedious hours; pass –, fill up –, beguile- the time; talk against time; waste time &c. (*inactive*) 683.

lie -by, – on the shelf, – in ordinary, – idle, – to, – fallow; keep quiet, slug; have nothing to do, whistle for want of thought; twiddle one's thumbs.

undo, do away with; take -down, – to pieces; destroy &c. 162.

Adj. not doing &c. *v.*; not done &c. *v.*; undone; passive; un-occupied, -employed; out of -employ, – work, – a job; fallow; *désœuvré*.

Adv. *re infectâ*, at a stand, *les bras croisés*, with folded arms; with the hands -in the pockets, – behind one's back; *pour passer le temps*.

Int. so let it be! stop! &c. 142; hands off!

Phr. nothing doing; *cunctando restituit rem*.

682. Activity.—N. activity; brisk-ness, liveliness &c. *adj.*; animation, life, vivacity, spirit, verve, dash, energy, go.

nimbleness, agility; smartness, quick-ness &c. *adj.*; velocity &c. 274; alacrity, promptitude; des-, dis-patch; expedi-tion; haste &c. 684; punctuality &c. (*early*) 132.

eagerness, zeal, ardour, *perfervidum ingenium, empressement*, earnestness, intentness; *abandon*; vigour &c. (*physi-cal energy*) 171; devotion &c. (*resolu-tion*) 604; exertion &c. 686.

industry, assiduity; assiduousness &c. *adj.*; sedulity; laboriousness; drudg-ery &c. (*labour*) 686; painstaking, diligence; perseverance &c. 604a; in-defatigation; habits of business.

vigilance &c. 459; wakefulness; sleep-, rest-lessness; *pervigilium, in-somnia*; racketing.

movement, bustle, hustle, stir, fuss, ado, bother, pottering; fidget, -iness; flurry &c. (*haste*) 684.

officiousness; dabbling, meddling; inter-ference, -position, -meddling, but-ting in, intrusiveness; tampering with, intrigue.

press of business, no sinecure, plenty to do, many irons in the fire, great doings, busy hum of men, battle of life, thick of -things, – the action; the mad-ding crowd.

housewife, busy bee; new brooms; sharp fellow, blade; hustler, devotee, enthusiast, fan, zealot, fanatic; med-dler, intermeddler, intriguer, busybody, kibitzer, pickthank.

V. be -active &c. *adj.*; busy oneself in; stir, -about, – one's stumps; bestir –, rouse- oneself; speed, hasten, peg away, lay about one, bustle, fuss; raise –, kick up- a dust; push; make a -push, – fuss, – stir; go ahead, push forward; flight –, elbow- one's way; make prog-ress &c. 282; toil &c. (*labour*) 686; drudge, plod, persist &c. (*persevere*) 604a; keep -up the ball, – the pot boiling.

look sharp; have all one's eyes about one &c. (*vigilance*) 459; rise, arouse oneself, get up early, hustle, push; be about, keep moving, steal a march, kill two birds with one stone; seize the opportunity &c. 134; lose no time, not

683. Inactivity.—N. inactivity; in-action &c. 681; inertness &c. 172; obstinacy &c. 606.

lull &c. (*cessation*) 142; quiescence &c. 265; rust, -iness.

idle-, remiss-ness &c. *adj.*; sloth, indolence, indiligence; otiosity, daw-dling &c. *v.*

dullness &c. *adj.*; languor; segni-ty, -tude; lentor; sluggishness &c. (*slow-ness*) 275; procrastination &c. (*delay*) 133; torp-or, -idity, -escence; stupor &c. (*insensibility*) 823; somnolence; drowsiness &c. *adj.*; nodding &c. *v.*; oscit-ation, -ancy; pandiculation, hyp-notism, lethargy; heaviness, heavy eye-lids, sand in the eyes.

sleep, slumber; sound –, heavy –, balmy- sleep; Morpheus, dreamland; coma, trance, catalepsy, hypnosis, ecstasis, dream, hibernation, nap, doze, snooze, *siesta*, wink of sleep, forty winks, snore; Hypnology.

dull work; pottering; relaxation &c. (*loosening*) 47; Castle of Indolence.

[Cause of inactivity] lullaby, *ber-ceuse*; anæsthetic, sedative &c. 174; torpedo.

idler, drone, droil, dawdle, mopus; do-little, *fainéant*, dummy, sleeping partner; afternoon farmer; truant &c. (*runaway*) 623; lounger, *lazzarone*, floater, loafer, tramp, beggar, cadger; lub-ber, -bard; slow-coach &c. (*slow*) 275; opium –, lotus- eater; slug; lag-, slug-gard, lie-abed; slumberer, dor-mouse, marmot; waiter on Providence, *fruges consumere natus.*

V. be -inactive &c. *adj.*; do nothing &c. 681; move slowly &c. 275; let the grass grow under one's feet; take one's time, dawdle, poke, drawl, droil, lag, hang back, slouch; loll, -op; lounge, loaf, loiter; go to sleep over; sleep at one's post, *ne battre que d'une aile.*

take -it easy, – things as they come; lead an easy life, vegetate, swim with the stream, eat the bread of idleness; loll in the lap of -luxury, – indolence; waste –, consume –, kill –, lose- time; burn daylight, waste the precious hours.

idle –, trifle –, fritter –, fool- away time; spend –, take- time in; ped-, pid-dle; potter, putter, dabble, faddle,

lose a moment, make the most of one's time, not suffer the grass to grow under one's feet, improve the shining hour, make short work of; dash off; make haste &c. 684; do one's best, take pains &c. (*exert oneself*) 686; do –, work- wonders.

have -many irons in the fire, – one's hands full, – much on one's hands; have other -things to do, – fish to fry; be busy; not have a moment -to spare, – that one can call one's own.

have one's fling, run the round of; go all lengths, stick at nothing, run riot.

outdo; over-do, -act, -lay, -shoot the mark; make a toil of a pleasure.

have a hand in &c. (*act in*) 680; take an active part, put in one's oar, have a finger in the pie, mix oneself up with, trouble one's head about, intrigue; agitate.

tamper with, meddle, moil; inter-meddle, -fere, -pose; obtrude; poke –, thrust- one's nose in, butt in.

Adj. active; brisk, – as a lark, – as a bee; lively, animated, vivacious; alive, – and kicking; frisky, spirited, stirring.

nimble, – as a squirrel; agile; light-, nimble-footed; featly, tripping.

quick, prompt, yare, instant, ready, alert, spry, sharp, smart, slick, go-ahead; fast &c. (*swift*) 274; quick as a lamplighter, expeditious; awake, broad awake; wide awake &c. (*intelligent*) 498.

forward, eager, ardent, strenuous, zealous, enterprising, pushing, in earnest; resolute &c. 604.

industrious, assiduous, diligent, sedulous, notable, painstaking; intent &c. (*attention*) 457; indefatigable &c. (*persevering*) 604a; unwearied; unsleeping, sleepless, never tired; plodding, hardworking &c. 686; business-like, workaday.

bustling; restless, – as a hyæna; fussy, fidgety, pottering; busy, – as a hen with one chicken.

working, labouring, at work, on duty, in harness; up in arms; on one's legs, at call; up and -doing, – stirring.

busy, occupied; hard at -work, – it; up to one's ears in, full of business, busy as a bee.

meddling &c. *v.*; meddlesome, pushing, officious, overofficious, *intrigant*.

astir, stirring; a-going, -foot; on foot; in full swing; eventful; on the alert &c. (*vigilant*) 459.

fribble, fiddle-faddle; dally, dilly-dally.

sleep, slumber, be asleep; hibernate; oversleep; sleep like a -top, – log, – dormouse; sleep -soundly, – heavily; doze, drowze, snooze, nap; take a -nap &c. *n.*; dream; snore; settle –, go –, go off- to sleep; drop off; fall –, drop-asleep; close –, seal up- -the -eyes, – eyelids; weigh down the eyelids; get sleepy, nod, yawn; go to bed, turn in.

languish, expend itself, flag, hang fire; relax.

render -idle &c. *adj.*; sluggardize; mitigate &c. 174.

Adj. inactive; motionless &c. 265; unoccupied &c: (*doing nothing*) 681.

indolent, lazy, slothful, idle, otiose, lusk, remiss, slack, inert, torpid, sluggish, languid, supine, heavy, dull, leaden, lumpish; exanimate, soulless; listless; dron-y, -ish; lazy as Ludlam's dog.

dilatory, laggard; lagging &c. *v.*; slow &c. 275; rusty, flagging; lackadaisical, maudlin, fiddle-faddle; pottering &c. *v.*; shilly-shally &c. (*irresolute*) 605.

sleeping &c. *v.*; asleep; fast –, dead –, sound- asleep; in a sound sleep; sound as a top, dormant, comatose; in the -arms, – lap- of Morpheus.

sleep-y, -ful; dozy, drowsy, somnolent, torpescent; lethargic, -al; heavy, – with sleep; napping; somni-fic, -ferous; sopor-ous, -ific, -iferous; hypnotic; balmy, dreamy; un-, una-wakened.

sedative &c. 174.

Adv. inactively &c. *adj.*; at leisure &c. 685.

Phr. the eyes begin to draw straws.

Adv. actively &c. *adj.*; with -life and spirit, – might and main &c. 686, – haste &c. 684, – wings; full tilt, *in mediis rebus.*

Int. be –, look- -alive, – sharp! move –, push- on! keep moving! go ahead! stir your stumps! *age quod agis!*

Phr. *carpe diem* &c. (*opportunity*) 134; *nulla dies sine lineâ*; *nec mora nec requies*; no sooner said than done &c. (*early*) 132; catch a weasel asleep.

---

684. Haste.—N. haste, urgency; des-, dis-patch; acceleration, spurt, spirt, forced march, rush, dash; velocity &c. 274; precipit-ancy, -ation, -ousness &c. *adj.*; impetuosity; *brusquerie*; hurry, scurry, scuttle, drive, scramble, push, hustle, bustle, fuss, fidget, flurry, flutter, splutter.

V. haste, hasten; make -haste, – a dash &c. *n.*; hurry –, dash –, whip –, push –, press- -on, – forward; hurry, skurry, scuttle along, bundle on, dart to and fro, bustle, flutter, scramble; plunge, – headlong; run, race, speed; dash off; rush &c. (*violence*) 173.

bestir oneself &c. (*be active*) 682; lose -no time, – not a moment, – not an instant; make short work of; make the best of one's -time, – way.

be -precipitate &c. *adj.*; jump at; be in -haste, – a hurry &c. *n.*; have -no time, – not a moment- -to lose, – to spare; work -under pressure, – against time.

quicken &c. 274; accelerate, expedite, put on, precipitate, urge, whip, spur, flog, goad.

Adj. hasty, hurried, *brusque*; scrambling, cursory, precipitate, headlong, furious, boisterous, impetuous, hot-headed; feverish, fussy; pushing.

in -haste, – a hurry &c. *n.*; in -hot, – all- haste; breathless, pressed for time, hard pressed, urgent.

Adv. with -haste, – all haste, – breathless speed; in haste &c. *adj.*; apace &c. (*swiftly*) 274; amain; all at once &c. (*instantaneously*) 113; at short notice &c., immediately &c. (*early*) 132; posthaste; by -express, – telegraph, – wire, – wireless, – air mail.

hastily, precipitately &c. *adj.*; helter-skelter, hurry-skurry, holus-bolus; slap-dash, -bang; full-tilt, -drive; heels over head, head and shoulders, headlong, *à corps perdu.*

by -fits and starts, – spurts; hop, skip and jump.

Phr. *sauve qui peut*, devil take the hindmost, no time to be lost; no sooner said than done &c. (*early*) 132; a word and a blow.

Int. hurry up! look alive! get a move on! buck up! double march! rush! urgent!

685. Leisure.—N. leisure; spare -time, – hours, – moments; vacant hour; time, – to spare, – on one's hands; holiday &c. (*rest*) 687; *otium cum dignitate*, ease.

V. have -leisure &c. *n.*; take one's -time, – leisure, – ease; repose &c. 687; move slowly &c. 275; while away the time &c. (*inaction*) 681; be -master of one's time, – an idle man; *desipere in loco.*

Adj. leisurely; slow &c. 275; deliber-ate, quiet, calm, undisturbed; at -leisure, – one's ease, – a loose end.

Phr. time hanging heavy on one's hands.

---

686. Exertion.—N. exertion, effort, strain, tug, pull, stress, force, pressure, throw, stretch, struggle, spell, spurt, spirt; stroke –, stitch- of work.

687. Repose.—N. repose, rest, silken repose; sleep &c. 683.

relaxation, breathing time; halt, pause &c. (*cessation*) 142; respite.

'a strong pull, a long pull and a pull all together'; dead lift; heft; gymnastics, sports; exer-cise, -citation; wear and tear; ado; toil and trouble; uphill –, hard –, warm- work; harvest time.

labour, work, toil, travail, manual labour, sweat of one's brow, swink, operoseness, drudgery, slavery, fagging, hammering; *limæ labor*.

trouble, pains, duty; resolution &c. 604; energy &c. (*physical*) 171.

V. exert oneself; exert –, tax- one's energies; use exertion.

labour, work, toil, moil, sweat, fag, drudge, slave, drag a lengthened chain, wade through, strive, strain; make –, stretch- a long arm; pull, tug, ply; ply –, tug at- the oar; do the work; take the labouring oar.

bestir oneself (*be active*) 682; take trouble, trouble oneself.

work hard; rough it; put forth -one's strength, – a strong arm; fall to work, bend the bow; buckle to, set one's shoulder to the wheel &c. (*resolution*) 604; work like a -Briton, – horse, – carthorse, – galley-slave, – coalheaver; labour –, work- day and night; redouble one's efforts; do double duty; work double -hours, – tides; sit up, burn the -midnight oil, – candle at both ends; stick to &c. (*persevere*) 604a; work –, fight- one's way; lay about one, hammer at.

take pains; do one's -best, – level best, – utmost; do -the best one can, – all one can, – all in one's power, – as much as in one lies, – what lies in one's power; use one's -best, – utmost- endeavour; try one's -best, – utmost; play one's best card; put one's -best, – right- leg foremost; have one's whole soul in one's work, put all one's strength into, strain every nerve; spare no -efforts, – pains; go all lengths; go through fire and water &c. (*resolution*) 604; move heaven and earth, leave no stone unturned.

Adj. labouring &c. *v.*

laborious, operose, elaborate; strained; toil-, trouble-, burden-, weari-some; uphill; herculean, gymnastic, athletic, palestric.

hardworking, painstaking, strenuous, energetic.

hard at work, on the stretch.

Adv. laboriously &c. *adj.*; lustily; with -might and main, – all one's might, – a strong hand, – sledge-hammer, – much ado; to the best of one's abilities, *totis viribus, vi et armis, manibus pedibusque*, tooth and nail, *unguibus et rostro*, hammer and tongs, heart and soul; through thick and thin &c. (*perseverance*) 604a.

by the sweat of one's brow, *suo Marte*.

day of rest, *dies non*, Sabbath, Lord's day, holiday, red-letter day, vacation, recess.

V. repose; rest, – and be thankful; take -rest, – one's ease.

relax, unbend, slacken; take breath &c. (*refresh*) 689; rest upon one's oars; pause &c. (*cease*) 142; stay one's hand.

lie down; recline, – on a bed of down, – on an easy chair; go to -rest, – bed, – sleep &c. 683.

take a holiday, shut up shop; lie fallow &c. (*inaction*) 681.

Adj. reposing &c. *v.*; unstrained.

Adv. at rest.

---

688. Fatigue.—**N.** fatigue; weariness &c. 841; yawning, drowsiness &c. 683; lassitude, tiredness, fatigation, exhaustion; sweat.

anhelation, shortness of breath, panting; faintness; collapse, prostration,

689. Refreshment.—**N.** bracing &c. *v.*; recovery of -strength &c. 159; restoration, revival &c. 660; repair, refection, refocillation, refreshment, regalement, bait; relief &c. 834.

V. brace &c. (*strengthen*) 159; rein-

swoon, fainting, *deliquium,* syncope, lipothymy.

V. be -fatigued &c. *adj.*; yawn &c. (*get sleepy*) 683; droop, sink, flag; lose -breath, – wind; gasp, pant, puff, blow, drop, swoon, faint, succumb.

fatigue, tire, weary, bore, irk, fag, jade, harass, exhaust, knock up, wear out, prostrate.

tax, task, strain; over-task, -work, -burden, -tax, -strain.

Adj. fatigued &c. *v.*; weary &c. 841; drowsy &c. 683; drooping &c. *v.*; haggard; toil-, way-worn; footsore, surbated, weatherbeaten; faint; done -, used -, knocked- up; exhausted, prostrate, spent; over-tired, -spent, -fatigued; forspent; unre-freshed, -stored.

worn, – out; battered, shattered, pulled down, seedy, altered.

breath-, wind-less; short of –, out of -breath, – wind; blown, puffing and blowing; short-breathed; anhelous; broken-, short-winded.

ready to drop, more dead than alive, dog -tired, – weary, walked off one's legs, tired to death, on one's last legs, played out, *hors de combat.*

fatiguing &c. *v.*; tire-, irk-, weari-some; weary; trying.

vigorate; air, freshen up, refresh, recruit; repair &c. (*restore*) 660; fan, refocillate.

breathe, respire; draw –, take –, gather –, take a long –, regain –, recover- breath; get better, raise one's head; recover –, regain –, renew- one's strength &c. 159; perk up.

come to oneself &c. (*revive*) 660; feel like a giant refreshed.

Adj. refreshing &c. *v.*; recuperative &c. 660.

refreshed &c. *v.*; un-tired, -wearied.

---

690. Agent.—N. doer, actor, agent, performer, perpetrator, operator; execu-tor, -trix; practitioner, worker, stager.

bee, ant, working bee, labouring oar, shaft horse, servant –, maid-of all work, general servant, factotum.

workman, artisan; crafts-, handicrafts-man; mechanic, operative; working –, labouring- man; hewers of wood and drawers of water, labourer, navvy; hand, man, day labourer, journeyman, hack; mere -tool &c. 633; porter, docker, stevedore, beast of burden, drudge, fag.

maker, artificer, artist, wright, manufacturer, architect, contractor, builder, mason, bricklayer, smith, forger, Vulcan; black-, tin-smith; carpenter; ganger, platelayer.

machinist, mechanician, engineer, electrician, plumber, gasfitter &c.

semp-, sem-, seam-stress; needle-, char-, work-woman; tailor, cord-wainer.

minister &c. (*instrument*) 631; servant &c. 746; representative &c. (*commissioner*) 758, (*deputy*) 759.

co-worker, fellow-worker, party to, participator in, co-operator, colleague, associate, collaborator, *particeps criminis, dramatis personæ; personnel.*

Phr. '*quorum pars magna fui.*'

---

691. Workshop.—N. work-shop, -house; laboratory; manufactory, mill, factory, armoury, arsenal, mint, forge, loom; cabinet, *studio, bureau, atelier;* hive, – of industry; nursery; hot-house, -bed; kitchen, kitchenette; dock, -yard; slip, yard, wharf; found-ry, -ery; furnace; vineyard, orchard, farm, kitchen garden.

melting pot, crucible, alembic, caldron, mortar, *matrix.*

2°. *Complex Voluntary Action*

692. Conduct.—N. dealing, transaction &c. (*action*) 680; business &c. 625.

tactics, game, policy, polity; general-, statesman-, seaman-ship; strate-gy, -gics; plan &c. 626.

husbandry; house-keeping, -wifery; stewardship; *ménage*; regimen, *régime*; econom-y, -ics; political economy; management; government &c. (*direction*) 693.

execution, manipulation, treatment, campaign, career, life, course, walk, race.

conduct; behaviour; de-, com-portment; carriage, *maintien*, demeanour, guise, bearing, manner, mien, air, observance.

course -, line- of -conduct, - action, - proceeding; *rôle*; process, ways, practice, procedure, *modus operandi*; method &c., path &c. 627.

V. transact, execute; des-, dis-patch; proceed with, discharge; carry -on, - through, - out, - into effect; work out; go -, get- through; enact; put into practice; officiate &c. 625.

behave -, comport -, demean -, carry -, bear -, conduct -, acquit-oneself.

run a race, lead a life, play a game; take -, adopt- a course; steer -, shape- one's course; play one's- -part, - cards; shift for oneself; paddle one's own canoe.

conduct; manage &c. (*direct*) 693.

deal -, have to do- with; treat, handle a case; take -steps, - measures.

Adj. conducting &c. *v.*; strategical, business-like, practical, economic, executive.

693. Direction.—N. direction; manage-ment, -ry; government, gubernation, conduct, legislation, regulation, guidance; steer-, pilot-age; reins, - of government; helm, rudder, controls, joy stick, needle, compass, binnacle; guiding -, load -, lode -, pole- star; cynosure.

super-vision, -intendence; *surveillance*, oversight; eye of the master; control, charge, auspices; board of control &c. (*council*) 696; command &c. (*authority*) 737.

premier-, senator-ship; director &c. 694; chair, seat, portfolio.

statesmanship; state-, king-craft.

minis-try, -tration; administration; steward-, proctor-ship; agency.

V. direct, manage, govern, conduct; order, prescribe, cut out work for; head, lead; lead -, show- the way; take the lead, lead on; regulate, guide, steer, pilot; take -, be at- the helm; have -, handle -, hold -, take- the reins, handle the ribbons; drive, tool; tackle.

super-intend, -vise; overlook, control, keep in order, look after, see to, oversee, legislate for; administer, ministrate; patronize; have the -care, - charge- of; have -, take- the direction; pull the -strings, - wires; rule &c. (*command*) 737; have -, hold- -office, - the portfolio; preside, - at the board; take -, occupy -, be in- the chair; pull the stroke oar.

Adj. directing &c. *v.*; executive, supervisory, hegemonic.

Adv. at the -helm, - head of, in charge of; under the auspices of.

694. Director.—N. director, manager, governor, rector, comptroller; super-intendent, -visor; intendant; over-seer, -looker; foreman, boss, straw boss; supercargo, husband, inspector, visitor, ranger, surveyor, ædile, moderator, monitor, taskmaster; master &c. 745; leader, ring-leader, demagogue, corypheus, conductor, fugleman, precentor, bell-wether, agitator.

guiding star &c. (*guidance*) 693; adviser &c. 695; guide &c. (*information*) 527; pilot; helmsman; steers-man, -mate; man at the wheel; wire-puller.

driver, whip, Jehu, charioteer; coach-, car-, cab-man, jarvey; postilion, *vetturino*, muleteer, teamster; whipper in; engineer, engine driver, motorman, *chauffeur*.

head, – man; principal, president, speaker; chair, -man; captain &c. (*master*) 745; superior; dean; mayor &c. (*civil authority*) 745; vice-president, prime minister, premier, vizier, grand vizier; dictator.

officer, functionary, minister, official, red-tapist, bureaucrat; man –, Jack- in office; office-bearer; person in authority &c. 745.

statesman, strategist, legislator, lawgiver, politician, administrator, statist, statemonger; Minos, Draco; arbiter &c. (*judge*) 967; king maker, power behind the throne.

board &c. (*council*) 696.

secretary, – of state; Reis Effendi; vicar &c. (*deputy*) 759; steward, factor; agent &c. 758; bailiff, middleman; ganger, clerk of works; landreeve; factotum, major-domo, seneschal, housekeeper, shepherd, *croupier*; proctor, procurator, curator, librarian.

Adv. *ex officio.*

695. Advice.—N. advice, counsel, adhortation; word to the wise; suggestion, submonition, recommendation, advocacy, consultation.

exhortation &c. (*persuasion*) 615; expostulation &c. (*dissuasion*) 616; admonition &c. (*warning*) 668; guidance &c. (*direction*) 693.

instruction, charge, injunction.

adviser, prompter; counsel, -lor; monitor, mentor, Nestor, *magnus Apollo*, senator; teacher &c. 540.

guide, manual, chart &c. (*information*) 527.

physician, leech, archiater; arbiter &c. (*judge*) 967.

refer-ence, -ment; consultation, conference, parley, *pourparler* &c. 696.

V. advise, counsel; give -advice, – counsel, – a piece of advice; suggest, prompt, submonish, recommend, prescribe, advocate; exhort &c. (*persuade*) 615.

enjoin, enforce, charge, instruct, call; call upon &c. (*request*) 765; dictate.

expostulate &c. (*dissuade*) 616; admonish &c. (*warn*) 668.

advise with; lay heads –, consult- together; compare notes; hold a council, deliberate, be closeted with.

confer, consult, refer to, call in; take –, follow- advice; follow implicitly; be advised by, have at one's elbow, take one's cue from.

Adj. recommendatory; hortative &c. (*persuasive*) 615; dehortatory &c. (*dissuasive*) 616; admonitory &c. (*warning*) 668; consultative.

Int. go to!

696. Council.—N. council, committee, subcommittee, *comitia*, court, chamber, cabinet, board, bench, staff; consultation.

senate, *senatus*, parliament, house, – of Lords, – Peers, – Commons, legislature, legislative assembly, federal council, chamber of deputies, directory, *reichsrath*, *rigsdag*, *cortes*, storthing, witenagemote, *junta*, divan, *musnud*, *sanhedrim*, Amphictyonic council; *duma*, *zemstvo*, *soviet*, *cheka*, *ogpu*; *Dail Eireann*; caput, consistory, chapter, syndicate; court of appeal &c. (*tribunal*) 966; board of -control, – works; vestry; county –, borough –, district –, parish –, town- council, local board.

cabinet –, privy- council, royal commission; cockpit, convocation, synod, congress, congregation, convention, diet, states-general, aulic council.

League of Nations, assembly, *caucus*, conclave, *clique*, conventicle; meeting, sitting, *séance*, conference, session, hearing, palaver, *pourparler*, *durbar*, pow-wow, house; *quorum*.

senator; member, – of parliament; councillor, M.P., representative of the people.

Adj. senatorial, curule, parliamentary.

697. Precept.—N. precept, direction, instruction, charge; prescript, -ion; *recipe*, receipt; golden rule; maxim &c. 496.

commandment, rule, ruling, canon, law, code, *corpus juris*, *lex scripta*, common –, unwritten –, canon-law; the Ten Commandments; act, statute, convention, rubric, stage direction, regulation; form, -ula, -ulary; technicality; nice point.

order &c. (*command*) 741.

698. Skill.—N. skill, skilfulness, address; dexter-ity, -ousness; adroitness, expertness &c. *adj.*; proficiency, competence, craft, callidity, facility, knack, trick, sleight; master-y, -ship; excellence, panurgy; ambidext-erity, -rousness; sleight of hand &c. (*deception*) 545.

sea-, air-, marks-, horse-manship; tight-, rope-dancing.

accomplish-, acquire-, attain-ment; art, science; techn-icality, -ology, -ique; practical –, technical- knowledge; technocracy; finish, technic.

knowledge of the world, world wisdom, *savoir-faire*; tact; mother wit &c. (*sagacity*) 498; discretion &c. (*caution*) 864; *finesse*; craftiness &c. (*cunning*) 702; management &c. (*conduct*) 692; *ars celare artem*; self-help.

cleverness, talent, ability, ingenuity, capacity, parts, talents, faculty, endowment, *forte*, turn, gift, genius, flair, feeling; intelligence &c. 498; sharpness, readiness &c. (*activity*) 682; invention &c. 515; apt-ness, -itude; turn –, capacity –, genius- for; felicity, capability, *curiosa felicitas*, qualification, habilitation.

proficient &c. 700.

masterpiece, *coup de maître*, *chef-d'œuvre*, *tour de force*; good stroke &c. (*plan*) 626.

V. be -skilful &c. *adj.*; excel in, be master of; have -a turn for &c. *n.*

know -what's what, – a hawk from a handsaw, – what one is about, – on

699. Unskilfulness.—N. unskilfulness &c. *adj.*; want of -skill &c. 698; incompeten-ce, -cy; in-ability, -felicity, -dexterity, -experience; clumsiness; disqualification, unproficiency; quackery.

folly, stupidity &c. 499; indiscretion &c. (*rashness*) 863; thoughtlessness &c. (*inattention*) 458, (*neglect*) 460.

mis-management, -conduct; impolicy; maladministration; mis-rule, -government, -application, -direction, -feasance.

absence of rule, rule of thumb; bungling &c. *v.*; failure &c. 732; screw loose; too many cooks.

blunder &c. (*mistake*) 495; *étourderie*, *gaucherie*, act of folly, *balourdise*; botch, -ery; bad job, sad work.

sprat sent out to catch a whale, much ado about nothing, wildgoose chase.

bungler &c. 701; fool &c. 501.

layman, amateur.

V. be -unskilful &c. *adj.*; not see an inch beyond one's nose; blunder, bungle, boggle, fumble, muff, botch, bitch, flounder, loppet, stumble, trip; hobble &c. 275; put one's foot in it; make a -mess, – hash, – sad work- of; overshoot the mark.

play -tricks with, – Puck; mis-manage, -conduct, -direct, -apply, -send.

stultify –, make a fool of –, commit-oneself; act foolishly; play the fool; put oneself out of court; lose one's -head, – cunning.

begin at the wrong end; do things

which side one's bread is buttered, – what's o'clock, – a thing or two; have cut one's -eye, – wisdom- teeth.

see -one's way, – where the wind lies, – which way the wind blows; have -all one's wits about one, – one's hand in; *savoir vivre*; *scire quid valeant humeri quid ferre recusent*.

look after the main chance; cut one's coat according to one's cloth; live by one's wits; exercise one's discretion, feather the oar, sail near the wind; stoop to conquer &c. (*cunning*) 702; play one's -cards well, – best card; hit the right nail on the head, put the saddle on the right horse.

take advantage of, make the most of; profit by &c. (*use*) 677; make a hit &c. (*succeed*) 731; make a virtue of necessity; make hay while the sun shines &c. (*occasion*) 134.

Adj. skilful, dexterous, adroit, expert, apt, slick, handy, quick, deft, ready, resourceful, gain; smart &c. (*active*) 682; proficient, good at, up to, at home in, master of, a good hand at, *au fait*, thoroughbred, masterly, crack, accomplished; conversant &c. (*knowing*) 490.

experienced, practised, skilled; up –, well up- in; in -practice, – proper cue; competent, efficient, qualified, capable, fitted, fit for, up to the mark, trained, initiated, prepared, primed, finished.

clever, able, ingenious, felicitous, gifted, talented, endowed, cute, inventive &c. 515; shrewd, sharp &c. (*intelligent*) 498; cunning &c. 702; alive to, up to snuff, not to be caught with chaff; discreet.

neat-handed, fine-fingered, ambidextrous, sure-footed; cut out –, fitted- for.

technical, artistic, scientific, dædalian, shipshape; workman-, business-, statesman-like.

Adv. skillfully &c. *adj.*; well &c. 618; artistically; with -skill, – consummate skill; *secundum artem, suo Marte*; to the best of one's abilities &c. (*exertion*) 686; like a machine.

by halves &c. (*not complete*) 730; make two bites of a cherry; play at cross purposes; strain at a gnat and swallow a camel &c. (*caprice*) 608; put the cart before the horse; lock the stable door when the horse is stolen &c. (*too late*) 135.

not know -what one is about, – one's own interest, – on which side one's bread is buttered; stand in one's own light, quarrel with one's bread and butter, throw a stone in one's own garden, kill the goose which lays the golden eggs, pay dear for one's whistle, cut one's own throat, burn one's fingers; knock –, run- one's head against a stone wall; fall into a trap, catch a Tartar, bring the house about one's ears; have too many -eggs in one basket (*imprudent*) 863, – irons in the fire.

mistake &c. 495; take the shadow for the substance &c. (*credulity*) 486; be in the wrong box, aim at a pigeon and kill a crow; take –, get- the wrong sow by the ear, – the dirty end of the stick; put -the saddle on the wrong horse, – a square peg into a round hole, – new wine into old bottles.

cut a whetstone with a razor; hold a farthing candle to the sun &c. (*useless*) 645; fight with –, grasp at- a shadow; catch at straws, lean on a broken reed, reckon without one's host, pursue a wildgoose chase; go on a fool's –, sleeveless- errand; go further and fare worse; loose –, miss- one's way; fail &c. 732.

Adj. un-skilful &c. 698; unskilled, inexpert; bungling &c. *v.*; awkward, clumsy, unhandy, lubberly, *gauche*, *maladroit*; left-, heavy-handed; slovenly, slatternly; gawky.

adrift, at fault.

in-, un-apt; inhabile; un-tractable, -teachable; giddy &c. (*inattentive*) 458; inconsiderate &c. (*neglectful*) 460; stupid &c. 499; inactive &c. 683; incompetent; un-, dis-, ill-qualified; unfit; quackish; raw, green, inexperienced, rusty, out of practice.

un-accustomed, -used, -trained &c. 537, -initiated, -conversant &c. (*ignorant*) 491; shiftless; unbusinesslike, unpractical; unstatesmanlike.

un-, ill-, mis-advised; ill-devised, -imagined, -judged, -contrived, -conducted; un-, mis-guided; misconducted, foolish, wild; infelicitous; penny wise and pound foolish &c. (*inconsistent*) 608.

Phr. one's fingers being all thumbs; the right hand forgets its cunning.

il se noyerait dans une goutte d'eau.

incidit in Scyllam qui vult vitare Charybdim; out of the frying pan into the fire.

700. Proficient.—**N.** proficient, expert, adept, dab; *connoisseur* &c. (*scholar*) 492; master, -hand; top-sawyer, *prima donna*, first fiddle, *chef de cuisine*; protagonist; past master; profess-or, -ional, specialist.

picked man; medallist, prizeman.

veteran; old -stager, – campaigner, – soldier, – file, – hand; man of -business, – the world.

nice –, good –, clean- hand; practised –, experienced- -eye, – hand; marksman; good –, dead –, crack- shot; rope-dancer, funambulist, acrobat, contortionist; cunning man; conjuror &c. (*deceiver*) 548; wizard &c. 994.

genius; master-mind, – head, – spirit; cunning –, sharp -blade, – fellow; jobber; cracksman &c. (*thief*) 792; politician, tactician, diplomat, -ist, strategist.

pantologist, admirable Crichton, Jack of all trades; prodigy of learning; walking encyclopædia; mine of information.

701. Bungler.—**N.** bungler; blunderer, -head; marplot, fumbler, lubber, lout, oaf, duffer, stick, clown; bad –, poor- -hand, – shot; butter-fingers.

no conjuror, flat, muff, slow coach, looby, lubber, swab; clod, yokel, hick, awkward squad, novice, greenhorn, jaywalker, *blanc-bec*.

land lubber; fresh water –, fair weather- sailor; horse-marine; fish out of water, ass in lion's skin, jackdaw in peacock's feathers; quack &c. (*deceiver*) 548; Lord of Misrule.

sloven, slattern, trapes.

Phr. *il n'a pas inventé la poudre*; he will never set the Thames on fire.

702. Cunning.—**N.** cunning, craft; cunningness, craftiness &c. *adj.*; subtlety, artificiality; manœuvring &c. *v.*; temporization; circumvention.

chicane, -ry; sharp practice, knavery, jugglery; concealment &c. 528; nigger in the woodpile; guile, duplicity &c. (*falsehood*) 544; foul play.

diplomacy, politics; Machiavellism; jobbery, back-stairs influence, gerrymandering.

art, -ifice; device, machination; plot &c. (*plan*) 626; manœuvre, stratagem, dodge, artful dodge, wile; trick, -ery &c. (*deception*) 545; *ruse*, – *de guerre*; *finesse*, side-blow, thin end of the wedge, shift, go by, subterfuge, evasion; white lie &c. (*untruth*) 546; juggle, *tour de force*; tricks -of the trade, – upon travellers; imposture, deception; *espièglerie*; net, trap &c. 545.

Ulysses, Machiavel, sly boots, fox,

703. Artlessness.—**N.** artlessness &c. *adj.*; nature, simplicity; innocence &c. 946; *bonhomie, naïveté, abandon*, candour, sincerity; singleness of -purpose, – heart; honesty &c. 939; plain speaking; *épanchement*.

rough diamond, matter of fact man; *le palais de vérité; enfant terrible*.

V. be -artless &c. *adj.*; look one in the face; wear one's heart upon his sleeves for daws to peck at; think aloud; speak -out, – one's mind; be free with one, call a spade a spade.

Adj. artless, natural, pure, native, simple, plain, inartificial, untutored, unsophisticated, *ingénu*, unaffected, *naïve*; sincere, frank; open, – as day; candid, ingenuous, guileless, unsuspicious, childlike; honest &c. 939; innocent &c. 946; Arcadian; undesigning, straightforward, unreserved, unvarnished, above-board; simple-, single-

reynard; Scotch-, Yorkshire-man; Jew, Yankee; intriguer, *intrigant,* schemer, trickster.

V. be -cunning &c. *adj.*; have cut one's eye-teeth; contrive &c. (*plan*) 626; live by one's wits; manœuvre; intrigue, gerrymander, *finesse,* double, temporize, stoop to conquer, *reculer pour mieux sauter,* circumvent, steal a march upon; overreach &c. 545; throw off one's guard; surprise &c. 508; out-do, get the better of, snatch from under one's nose; snatch a verdict; waylay, undermine, introduce the thin end of the wedge; play -a deep game, – tricks with; have an axe to grind; *ambiguas in vulgum spargere voces*; flatter, make things pleasant.

Adj. cunning, crafty, artful; skilful &c. 698; subtle, feline, vulpine; cunning as a -fox, – serpent; deep, – laid; profound; designing, contriving; intriguing &c. *v.*; strategic, diplomatic, politic, Machia-vellian, time-serving; artificial; trick-y, -sy; wily, sly, slim, insidious, stealthy, foxy; underhand &c. (*hidden*) 528; subdolous; deceitful &c. 545; double-tongued, -faced; shifty; crooked; arch, pawky, shrewd, acute; sharp, – as a needle; canny, astute, leery, knowing, up to snuff, too clever by half, not to be caught with chaff.

Adv. cunningly &c. *adj.*; slily, on the sly, by a side wind.

Phr. diamond cut diamond.

minded; frank-, open-, single-, simple-hearted; open and above-board.

free-, plain-, out-spoken; blunt, downright, direct, matter of fact, un-poetical; unflattering.

Adv. in plain -words, – English; without mincing the matter; not to mince the matter &c. (*affirmation*) 535.

Phr. *Davus sum non Œdipus; liberavi animam meam.*

Section IV. ANTAGONISM

1°. *Conditional Antagonism*

704. Difficulty.—**N.** difficulty; hard-ness &c. *adj.*; impracticability &c. (*impossibility*) 471; tough -, hard -, uphill- work; hard -, Herculean -, Augean- task; task of Sisyphus, Sisy-phean labour, tough job, teaser, rasper, dead lift.

dilemma, embarrassment; perplexity &c. (*uncertainty*) 475; involvement; in-tricacy; entanglement &c. 59; cross fire; awkwardness, delicacy, ticklish card to play, deadlock, knot, Gordian knot, *dignus vindice nodus,* net, meshes, maze; coil &c. (*convolution*) 248; crooked path.

nice -, delicate -, subtle -, knotty-point; vexed question, *vexata quæstio,* poser; puzzle &c. (*riddle*) 533; para-dox; hard -, nut to crack; bone to pick, *crux, pons asinorum,* where the shoe pinches.

nonplus, quandary, strait, pass, pinch, pretty pass, stress, brunt; criti-

705. Facility. — **N.** facility, ease; easiness &c. *adj.*; capability; feasibility &c. (*practicability*) 470; flexibility, pli-ancy &c. 324; smoothness &c. 255; convenience.

plain -, smooth -, straight- sailing; mere child's play, holiday task.

smooth water, fair wind; smooth – royal- road; clear -coast, – stage; *tabula rasa; full play* &c. (*freedom*) 748.

disen-cumbrance, -tanglement; de-oppilation; permission &c. 760.

V. be -easy &c. *adj.*; go on -, run-smoothly; have -full play &c. *n.*; go -, run- on all fours; obey the helm, work well.

flow -, swim -, drift -, go- with the--stream, – tide; see one's way; have -it all one's own way, – the game in one's own hands; walk over the course, win -at a canter, – hands down; make -light of, – nothing of; be at home in &c. (*skilful*) 698.

cal situation, crisis; trial, rub, emergency, exigency, scramble.

scrape, hobble, slough, quagmire, hot water, hornet's nest; sea –, peck- of troubles; pretty kettle of fish; pickle, stew, *imbroglio*, mess, muddle, botch, fuss, bustle, ado; false position; set fast, stand; dead -lock, – set; fix, horns of a dilemma, *cul de sac*; hitch; stumbling block &c. (*hindrance*) 706.

V. be -difficult &c. *adj.*; run one hard, go against the grain, try one's patience, put one out; put to one's -shifts, – wit's end; go hard with –, try- one; pose, perplex &c. (*uncertain*) 475; bother, nonplus, gravel, bring to a dead lock; be -impossible &c. 471; be in the way of &c. (*hinder*) 706.

meet with –, labour under –, get into –, plunge into –, struggle with –, contend with –, grapple with- difficulties; labour under a disadvantage; be -in difficulty &c. *adj.*

fish in troubled waters, buffet the waves, swim against the stream, scud under bare poles.

have -much ado with, – a hard time of it; come to the -push, – pinch; bear the brunt.

grope in the dark, lose one's way, weave a tangled web, walk among eggs.

get into a -scrape &c. *n.*; bring a hornet's nest about one's ears; be put to one's shifts; flounder, boggle, struggle; not know which way to turn &c. (*uncertain*) 475; get -tangled up, – wound up; *perdre son latin*; stick - at, – in the mud, – fast; come to a -stand, – dead lock; hold the wolf by the ears.

render -difficult &c. *adj.*; encumber, embarrass, ravel, entangle; put a spoke in the wheel &c. (*hinder*) 706; lead a pretty dance.

Adj. difficult, not easy, hard, tough; trouble-, toil-, irk-some; operose, laborious, onerous, arduous, Herculean, formidable; sooner –, more easily- said than done; difficult –, hard- to deal with; ill-conditioned, crabbed; not -to be handled with kid gloves, – made with rosewater.

awkward, unwieldy, unmanageable; intractable, stubborn &c. (*obstinate*) 606; perverse, refractory, plaguy, trying, thorny, rugged; knot-ted, -ty; invious; path-, track-less; labyrinthine &c. (*convoluted*) 248; intricate, complicated &c. (*tangled*) 59; impracticable &c. (*impossible*) 471; not -feasible &c. 470; desperate &c. (*hopeless*) 859.

embarrassing, perplexing &c. (*uncertain*) 475; delicate, ticklish,

render -easy &c. *adj.*; facilitate, smooth, ease; popularize; lighten, – the labour; free, clear; dis-encumber, -embarrass, -entangle, -engage; deobstruct, unclog, extricate, unravel; untie –, cut- the knot; disburden, unload, exonerate, emancipate, free from, deoppilate; humour &c. (*aid*) 707; lubricate &c. 332; relieve &c. 834.

leave -a hole to creep out of, – a loophole, – the matter open; give -the reins to, – full play, – full swing; make way for; open the -door to, – way; prepare –, smooth –, clear- the -ground, – way, – path, – road; pave the way, bridge over; permit &c. 760.

Adj. easy, facile; feasible &c. (*practicable*) 470; easily -managed, – accomplished; within reach, accessible, easy of access, for the million, open to.

manageable, wieldy; towardly, tractable; submissive; yielding, ductile; pliant &c. (*soft*) 324; glib, slippery; smooth &c. 255; on -friction wheels, – velvet; convenient.

un-, dis-burdened, -encumbered, -embarrassed; exonerated; un-loaded, -obstructed, -trammelled, - impeded, -restrained &c. (*free*) 748; at ease, light.

at –, quite at- home; in -one's element, – smooth water.

Adv. easily &c. *adj.*; readily, smoothly, swimmingly, *ad lib.*, on easy terms, single-handed.

Phr. touch and go.

Int. all clear!

critical; beset with –, full of –, surrounded by –, entangled by –, encompassed with- difficulties.

under a difficulty; in -difficulty, – hot water, – the suds, – a cleft stick, – a fix, – the wrong box, – a scrape &c. *n.*, – deep water, – a fine pickle; *in extremis*; between -two stools, – Scylla and Charybdis; surrounded by -shoals, – breakers, – quicksands; at cross purposes; not out of the wood.

reduced to straits; hard –, sorely- pressed; run hard; pinched, put to it, straitened; hard -up, – put to it, – set; put to one's shifts; puzzled, at a loss &c. (*uncertain*) 475; at -the end of one's tether, – one's wit's end, – a nonplus, – a standstill; gravelled, nonplussed, stranded, aground; stuck –, set- fast; up a tree, at bay, *aux abois*, driven -into a corner, – from post to pillar, – to extremity, – to one's wit's end, – to the wall; *au bout de son latin*; out of one's -depth, – reckoning; put –, thrown -out.

accomplished with difficulty; hard-fought, -earned.

Adv. with -difficulty, – much ado; hardly &c. *adj.*; uphill; against the -stream, – grain; *à rebours*; *invitâ Minervâ*; in the teeth of; at –, upon- a pinch; at long odds.

Phr. ay there's the rub; *hic labor hoc opus*; things are come to a pretty pass.

2°. *Active Antagonism*

706. Hindrance. — **N.** prevention, preclusion, obstruction, stoppage; prohibition; inter-ruption, -ception, -clusion; hindrance, impedition; retardment, -ation; constriction; embarrassment, oppilation; coarctation, stricture, restriction; anchor &c. 666; restraint &c. 751 & 752; inhibition &c. 761; blockade &c. (*closure*) 261; picketing.

inter-ference, -position; obtrusion; dis-couragement, -countenance, -approval, -approbation; opposition &c. 708.

impediment, let, obstacle, obstruction, knot, knag; check, hitch, *contretemps*, *impasse*, screw loose, grit in the oil.

bar, stile, barrier; turn-stile, -pike; gate, portcullis; bulwark, parapet, barricade &c. (*defence*) 717; wall, dead wall, breakwater, groyne; bulkhead, block, buffer; stopper &c. 263; boom, dam, weir, burrock.

drawback, objection; stumbling-block, -stone; lion in the path; snag; snags and sawyers.

en-, in-cumbrance; clog, skid, shoe, spoke; brake, drag, – chain, – weight; stay, stop; preventive, prophylactic; contraception; load, burden, fardel,

707. Aid.—**N.** aid, -ance; assistance, help, opitulation, succour; support, lift, advance, furtherance, promotion; coadjuvancy &c. (*co-operation*) 709.

patronage, championship, countenance, favour, interest, advocacy, auspices.

sustentation, subvention, subsidy, bounty, alimentation, nutrition, nourishment, maintenance; manna in the wilderness; food &c. 298; means &c. 632.

ministr-y, -ation; subministration; accommodation.

relief, rescue; help at a dead lift; supernatural aid; *deus ex machinâ*.

supplies, reinforcements, succours, contingents, recruits; support &c. (*physical*) 215; adjunct, ally &c. (*helper*) 711.

V. aid, assist, help, succour, lend one's aid; come to the aid &c. *n.*- of; contribute, subscribe to; bring –, give –, furnish –, afford –, supply- -aid &c. *n.*; render assistance; give –, stretch –, lend –, bear –, hold out- a -hand, – helping hand; give one a -lift, – cast, – turn; take -by the hand, – in tow; help a lame dog over a stile, lend wings to.

onus, millstone round one's neck, *impedimenta*; dead weight; lumber, pack; nightmare, Ephialtes, incubus, old man of the sea; remora.

difficulty &c. 704; insuperable &c. 471- obstacle; estoppel; ill wind; head wind &c. (*opposition*) 708; trammel, tether &c. (*means of restraint*) 752; hold back, counterpoise; damper, wet blanket, hinderer, marplot, kill-joy, dog in the manger, interloper; trail of a red herring; opponent &c. 710.

V. hinder, impede, impedite, embarrass.

keep -, stave -, ward- off; picket; obviate; a-, ante-vert; turn aside, draw off, prevent, forefend, nip in the bud; retard, slacken, check, let; counter-act, -check; preclude, debar, foreclose, estop; inhibit &c. 761; shackle &c. (*restrain*) 751; restrict, restrain, cohibit.

obstruct, filibuster, stop, stay, bar, bolt, lock; block, - up; belay, barricade; block -, stop- the way; dam up &c. (*close*) 261; put on the -brake &c. *n.*; scotch -, lock -, put a spoke in- the wheel; put a stop to &c. 142; traverse, contravene; inter-rupt, -cept; oppose &c. 708; hedge -in, - round; cut off; interclude.

inter-pose, -fere, -meddle &c. 682.

cramp, hamper; clog, - the wheels; cumber; en-, in-cumber; handicap; choke; saddle -, load- with; overload, lay; lumber, trammel, tie one's hands, put to inconvenience; in-, discommode; discompose; hustle, drive into a corner; choke off.

run -, fall- foul of; cross the path of, break in upon.

thwart, frustrate, disconcert, balk, foil, baffle, snub, override, circumvent; defeat &c. 731; spike guns &c. (*render useless*) 645; spoil, mar, clip the wings of; cripple &c. (*injure*) 659; put an extinguisher on; damp; dishearten &c. (*dissuade*) 616; discountenance, throw cold water on, spoil sport; lay -, throw- a wet blanket on; cut the ground from under one, take the wind out of one's sails, undermine; be -, stand- in the way of; act as a drag; hang like a millstone round one's neck.

relieve, rescue; set -up, - agoing, - on one's legs; bear -, pull- through; give new life to, be the making of; reinforce, recruit; set -, put -, push-forward; give -a lift, - a shove, - an impulse- to; promote, further, forward, advance; speed, expedite, quicken, hasten.

support, sustain, uphold, prop, hold up, bolster.

cradle, nourish; nurture, nurse, dry nurse, suckle, put out to nurse; manure, cultivate, force; foster, cherish, foment; feed -, fan- the flame.

serve; do service to, tender to, pander to; ad-, sub-, minister to; tend, attend, wait on; take care of &c. 459; entertain; smooth the bed of death.

oblige, accommodate, consult the wishes of; humour, cheer, encourage.

second, stand by; back, - up; pay the pipe*r*, abet; work -, make interest -, stick up -, take up the cudgels- for; take up -, espouse -, adopt- the cause of; advocate, beat up for recruits, press into the service; squire, give moral support to, keep in countenance, countenance, patronize; lend -oneself, - one's countenance- to; smile -, shine-upon; favour, befriend, take up, take in hand, enlist under the banners of; side with &c. (*co-operate*) 709.

be of use to; subserve &c. (*instrument*) 631; benefit &c. 648; render a service &c. (*utility*) 644; conduce &c. (*tend*) 176.

Adj. aiding &c. *v.*; auxiliary, adjuvant, helpful; coadjuvant &c. 709; subservient, ministrant, ancillary, accessory, subsidiary.

at one's beck; friendly, amicable, favourable, propitious, well-disposed; neighbourly; obliging &c. (*benevolent*) 906.

Adv. with -, by- -the aid &c. *n.*- of; on -, in- behalf of; in -aid, - the service, - the name, - favour, - furtherance-of; on account of; for the sake of, on the part of; *non obstante*.

Int. help! save us! to the rescue! S.O.S.!

Adj. hindering &c. *v.*; obstr-uctive, -uent; impedi-tive, -ent; intercipient; prophylactic &c. (*remedial*) 662.

in the way of, unfavourable; onerous, burdensome; cumb-rous, -ersome; obtrusive.

hindered &c. *v.*; wind-bound, water-logged, heavy laden; hard pressed.

unassisted &c. (*see* assist &c. 707); single-handed, alone; deserted &c. 624.

708. Opposition.—N. opposition, antagonism; oppug-nancy, -nation; impugnation; contravention; counteraction &c. 179; counterplot.

cross-fire, under-current, head-wind.

clashing, collision, conflict, lack of harmony, contest.

competition, two of a trade, rivalry, emulation, race; war to the knife.

absence of -aid &c. 707; resistance &c. 719; restraint &c. 751; hindrance &c. 706.

V. oppose, counteract, run counter to; withstand &c. (*resist*) 719; control &c. (*restrain*) 751; hinder &c. 706; antagonize, oppugn, fly in the face of, go dead against, kick against, fall foul of; set -, pit- against; face, confront, cope with; make a -stand, - dead set- against; set -oneself, one's face- against; protest -, vote -, raise one's voice- against; disfavour, turn one's back upon; set at naught, slap in the face, slam the door in one's face.

be -, play- at cross purposes; counter-work, -mine; thwart, overthwart.

stem, breast, encounter; stem -, breast- the -tide, - current, - flood; buffet the waves; beat up -, make head- against; grapple with; kick against the pricks &c. (*resist*) 719; contend &c. 720 -, do battle &c. (*warfare*) 722- -with, - against.

contra-dict, -vene; belie; go -, run -, beat -, militate- against; come in conflict with.

emulate &c. (*compete*) 720; rival, spoil one's trade.

Adj. oppos-ing, -ed &c. *v.*; adverse, antagonistic; ambivalent; contrary &c. 14; at variance &c. 24; at issue, at war with; in opposition; 'agin the Government.'

un-favourable, -friendly; hostile, inimical, cross, unpropitious.

709. Co-operation.—N. co-operation; coadju-vancy, -tancy; coagency, co-efficiency; concert, concurrence, complicity, participation; union &c. 43; amalgamation, combination &c. 48; collusion.

association, alliance, colleagueship, jointstock, copartnership, trust, cartel, pool, ring, combine, interlocking directorate; confederation &c. (*party*) 712; federation, coalition, fusion; a long pull, a strong pull and a pull all together; log-rolling, freemasonry.

unanimity &c. (*assent*) 488; *esprit de corps*, party spirit; clan-, partisan-ship; reciprocity, concord &c. 714.

V. co-operate, co-adjute, concur; conduce &c. 178; combine, cartelize, unite one's efforts; keep -, draw -, pull -, club -, hang -, hold -, league -, band -, be banded- together; stand -, put-shoulder to shoulder; act in concert, join forces, fraternize, cling to one another, conspire, concert, lay one's heads together; confederate, be in league with; collude, understand one another, play into the hands of, hunt in couples.

side -, take side -, go along -, go hand in hand -, join hands -, make common cause -, strike in -, unite -, join -, mix oneself up -, take part -, play along -, cast in one's lot- with; join -, enter into- partnership with; rally round, follow the lead of; come to, pass over to, come into the views of; be -, row -, sail- in the same boat; sail on the same tack.

be a party to, lend oneself to; participate; have a -hand in, - finger in the pie; take -, bear- part in; second &c. (*aid*) 707; take the part of, play the game of; espouse a -cause, - quarrel.

Adj. co-operating &c. *v.*; in -co-operation &c. *n.*, - league &c. (*party*) 712;

in hostile array, front to front, with crossed bayonets, at daggers drawn; up in arms; resistant &c. 719.

competitive, emulous.

Adv. against, *versus*, counter to, in conflict with, at cross purposes.

against the -grain, – current, – stream, – wind, – tide; with a head-wind; with the wind -ahead, – in one's teeth.

in spite, in despite, in defiance; in the -way, – teeth, – face- of; across; a-, over-thwart; where the shoe pinches.

though &c. 30; even; *quand même*; *per contra*.

Phr. *nitor in adversum*.

coadju-vant, -tant; hand and glove with.

favourable &c. 707- to; un-opposed &c. 708.

Adv. as one man &c. (*unanimously*) 488; shoulder to shoulder; in co-operation with.

———

710. Opponent.—N. opponent, antagonist, adversary; adverse party, opposition; enemy &c. 891; assailant.

oppositionist, obstructive; obscurantist; brawler, wrangler, brangler, disputant, extremist, irreconcilable, die-hard, bitter-ender.

malcontent; Jacobin, Fenian &c. 742; demagogue, reactionist.

passive resister, conscientious objector.

rival, competitor, contestant.

———

711. Auxiliary.—N. auxiliary; recruit; assistant; adju-vant, -tant; adjunct; help, -er, -mate, -ing hand; midwife; colleague, partner, mate, *confrère*, co-operator; coadju-tor, -trix; collaborator.

ally; friend &c. 890, confidant, *fidus Achates*, pal, chum, buddy, *alter ego*.

confederate; ac-, complice; accessory, – after the fact; *particeps criminis*.

aide-de-camp, secretary, clerk, associate, marshal; right-hand; candle-, bottle-holder; hand-maid; servant &c. 746; puppet, cat's-paw, stooge, dependent, creature, jackal; tool, *âme damnée*; satellite, adherent, parasite.

votary, disciple; secta-rian, -ry; seconder, backer, upholder, supporter, abettor, advocate, partisan, champion, patron, friend at court, mediator.

friend in need, Jack at a pinch, *deus ex machinâ*, guardian angel, fairy godmother; special providence, tutelary genius.

712. Party.—N. party, faction, side, denomination, class, communion, set, crowd, crew, band, horde, posse, phalanx; regiment &c. 726; family, clan &c. 166.

Tories, Conservatives, Unionists, Whigs, Liberals, Radicals, Labour party, Socialists, Communists &c.; Republicans, Democrats, Farmer-Labor; *Fascisti*, Revolutionaries &c. 742.

community, body, fellowship, sodality, solidarity; con-, fraternity; sorority; brother-, sister-hood.

Freemasons, Knights Templars, Odd Fellows, Ku Klux Klan &c.

knot, gang, *clique*, ring, circle; *coterie*, club, *casino*.

corporation, corporate body, guild; establishment, company; co-partnership; firm, house; joint concern, joint-stock company, trust, investment trust, combine &c. 709.

society, association; instit-ute, -ution; union; trade-union; league, syndicate, alliance, *Verein, Bund, Zollverein*, combination; league -, alliance- offensive and defensive; coalition; federation; confedera -tion, -cy; junto, cabal, *camarilla, camorra, brigue*; freemasonry; party spirit &c. (*co-operation*) 709.

staff; cast, *dramatis personæ.*

V. unite, join; club together &c. (*co-operate*) 709; cement –, form- a party &c. *n.*; associate &c. (*assemble*) 72.

Adj. in -league, – partnership, – alliance &c. *n.*

bonded –, banded –, linked &c. (*joined*) 43- together; embattled; confederated, federative, joint, corporate, leagued, fraternal, masonic, cliquish.

Adv. hand in hand, side by side, shoulder to shoulder, *en masse*, in the same boat.

---

713. Discord.—N. disagreement &c. 24; dis-cord, -accord, -sidence, -sonance; jar, clash, shock; jarring, jostling &c. *v.*; screw loose.

variance, difference, dissension, misunderstanding, cross purposes, odds, *brouillerie*; division, split, rupture, disruption, division in the camp, house divided against itself, rift within the lute; disunion, breach; schism &c. (*dissent*) 489; feud, faction.

quarrel, dispute, rippet, spat, tiff, *tracasserie*, squabble, altercation, words, high words; wrangling &c. *v.*; jangle, brabble, cross questions and crooked answers, snip-snap; family jars.

polemics; litigation; strife &c. (*contention*) 720; warfare &c. 722; outbreak, open rupture; breaking off of negotiations, recall of ambassadors; declaration of war.

broil, brawl, row, racket, hubbub, rixation; embroilment, embranglement, *imbroglio, fracas*, breach of the peace, piece of work, scrimmage, rumpus; breeze, squall; riot, disturbance &c. (*disorder*) 59; commotion &c. (*agitation*) 315; bear garden, Donnybrook Fair.

subject of dispute, ground of quarrel, battle ground, disputed point; bone -of contention, – to pick; apple of discord, *casus belli*; question at issue &c. (*subject of inquiry*) 461; vexed question, *vexata quæstio*, brand of discord.

troublous times; cat-and-dog life; contentiousness &c. *adj.*; enmity &c. 889; hate &c. 898; Kilkenny cats; disputant &c. 710; strange bedfellows.

V. be -discordant &c. *adj.*; disagree, come amiss &c. 24; clash, jar, jostle, pull different ways, conflict, have no measures with, misunderstand one another; live like cat and dog; differ; dissent &c. 489; have a -bone to pick, – crow to pluck- with.

fall out, quarrel, dispute; litigate; controvert &c. (*deny*) 536;

714. Concord.—N. concord, accord, harmony, symphony, homology; agreement &c. 23; sympathy &c. (*love*) 897; response; union, unison, unity; bonds of harmony; peace &c. 721; unanimity &c. (*assent*) 488; league &c. 712; happy family.

rapprochement; réunion; amity &c. (*friendship*) 888; reciprocity; alliance, *entente cordiale*, good understanding, conciliation, arbitration, peacemaker &c. 724.

V. agree &c. 23; accord, harmonize with; fraternize; be -concordant &c. *adj.*; go hand in hand; blend –, tone in- with; run parallel &c. (*concur*) 178; understand one another; pull together &c. (*co-operate*) 709; put up one's horses together, sing in chorus.

side –, sympathize –, go –, chime in –, fall in- with; come round; be pacified &c. 723; assent &c. 488; enter into the -ideas, – feelings- of; reciprocate.

hurler avec les loups; go –, swim- with the stream.

pour oil on troubled waters, keep in good humour, render accordant, put in tune; come to an understanding, meet half-way; keep the –, remain at- peace.

Adj. concordant, congenial; agreeing &c. *v.*; in- accord &c. *n.*; harmonious, united, cemented; banded together &c. 712; allied; friendly &c. 888; fraternal; conciliatory; at one with; of one mind &c. (*assent*) 488.

at peace, in still water; tranquil &c. (*pacific*) 721.

Adv. with one voice &c. (*assent*) 488; in concert with, hand in hand; on one's side, unanimously.

---

squabble, wrangle, jangle, brangle, bicker, nag; spar &c. (*contend*) 720; have -words &c. *n.* with; fall foul of.

split; break -, break squares -, part company- with; declare war, try conclusions; join -, put in- issue; pick a quarrel, fasten a quarrel on; sow -, stir up- -dissension &c. *n.*; embroil, estrange, entangle, disunite, widen the breach; set -at odds, - together by the ears; set -, pit- against; rub up the wrong way.

get into hot water, fish in troubled waters, brawl; kick up a -row, - dust; turn the house out of window.

Adj. discordant; disagreeing &c. *v.*; out of tune, dissonant, in-harmonious, harsh, grating, jangling, ajar, on bad terms; dissentient &c. 489; inconsistent, contradictory, incongruous, discrepant; un--reconciled, -pacified.

quarrelsome, unpacific; gladiatorial, controversial, polemic, dis-putatious; factious; liti-gious, -gant; pettifogging.

at odds, at loggerheads, at daggers drawn, at variance, at issue, at cross purposes, at sixes and sevens, at feud, at high words; up in arms, together by the ears, in hot water, embroiled.

torn, disunited.

Phr. *quot homines tot sententiæ*; no love lost between them, *non nostrum tantas componere lites.*

715. Defiance.—N. defiance; daring &c. *v.*; dare, challenge, *cartel*; threat &c. 909; war-cry, -whoop.

V. defy, dare, beard; brave &c. (*courage*) 861; bid defiance to; set at -defiance, - naught; hurl defiance at; dance the war dance; snap the fingers at, laugh to scorn; disobey &c. 742.

show -fight, - one's teeth, - a bold front; bluster, look big, stand akimbo; double -, shake- the fist; threaten &c. 909.

challenge, call out; throw -, fling- down the -gauntlet, - gage, - glove.

Adj. defiant; defying &c. *v.*; with arms akimbo; rebellious, insolent; reckless, greatly daring.

Adv. in -defiance, - the teeth- of; under one's very nose.

Int. do your worst! come if you dare! come on! marry come up! hoity toity!

Phr. *noli me tangere; nemo me impune lacessit.*

716. Attack.—N. attack; assault, - and battery; onset, onslaught, charge.

aggression, drive, offence; incursion, inroad, invasion; irruption; outbreak; *estrapade, ruade; coup de main*, sally, *sortie, camisade*, raid, foray; run -at, - against; dead set at.

storm, -ing; boarding, *escalade;* siege, investment, obsession, bombardment, cannonade; air raid.

fire, volley; platoon -, file -, rapid-fire; *fusillade*; sharp-shooting, sniping; broadside; raking -, cross -, machine gun- fire; volley of grapeshot, *feu d'enfer*; salvo.

cut, thrust, lunge, pass, *passado, carte* and *tierce*, home thrust; *coup de pied*; kick, punch &c. (*impulse*) 276.

717. Defence.—N. defence, protec-tion, guard, ward; shielding &c. *v.*; propugnation; preservation &c. 670; guardianship.

self-defence, -preservation; resistance &c. 719.

safeguard &c. (*safety*) 664; screen &c. (*shelter*) 666, (*concealment*) 530; barrage; fortification; muni-tion, -ment; bulwark, fosse, moat, ditch, intrench-ment, trench, dugout, gas mask; dike, dyke; parapet, parados, sunk fence, embankment, mound, mole, bank; earth- field-work, gabions; fence, wall, dead wall, contravallation; paling &c. (*inclosure*) 232; palisade, haha, stock-ade, *stoccado, laager, sangar*; barri-er, -cade; boom; portcullis, *chevaux de*

battue, razzia, Jacquerie, dragonnade; devastation &c. 162.

assailant, aggressor, invader.

base of operations, point of attack.

V. attack, assault, assail; set –, fall-upon; charge, impugn, break a lance with, enter the lists.

assume –, take- the offensive; be –, become- the aggressor; strike the first blow, fire the first shot, throw the first stone at; lift a hand –, draw the sword-against; take up the cudgels; advance –, march- against; march upon, invade, harry; come on, show fight.

strike at, poke at, thrust at; aim –, deal- a blow at; give –, fetch- one a -blow, – kick; have a -cut, – shot, – fling, – shy- at; be down –, pounce-upon; fall foul of, pitch into, launch out against; bait, slap on the face; make a -thrust, – pass, – set, – dead set- at; dunt; bear down upon.

close with, come to close quarters, bring to bay.

ride full tilt against; let fly at, dash at, run a tilt at, rush at, tilt at, run at, fly at, hawk at, have at, let out at; make a -dash, – rush at; attack tooth and nail; strike home; drive –, press- one hard; be hard upon, run down, strike at the root of.

lay about one, run amuck.

fire -upon, – at, – a shot at; shoot at, pop at, level at, let off a gun at; open fire, pepper, bombard, shell, pour a broadside into; fire -a volley, – red-hot shot; spring a mine.

throw -a stone, – stones- at; stone, lapidate, pelt; hurl -at, – against, – at the head of.

beset, besiege, beleaguer; lay siege to, invest, open the trenches, plant a battery, sap, mine; storm, board, scale the walls.

cut and thrust, bayonet, butt; kick, strike &c. (*impulse*) 276; whip &c. (*punish*) 972.

Adj. attacking &c. *v.*; aggressive, offensive, obsidional.

up in arms; on the warpath; over the top.

Adv. on the offensive.

Int. 'up and at them!'

———

frise; aba-, abat-, abba-tis; *vallum*, circumvallation, battlement, rampart, scarp; e-, counter-scarp; glacis, case-mate.

mine, countermine.

buttress, abutment; shore &c. (*support*) 215.

breastwork, *banquette*, curtain, mant-let, bastion, demilune, redan, ravelin; advanced –, horn –, out- work, lunette; barb-acan, -ican; redoubt; fort-elage, -alice; lines; coast defence.

loop-hole, machicolation; sally-port, postern gate.

hold, stronghold, fastness; asylum &c. (*refuge*) 666; keep, donjon, fort-ress, citadel; capitol, castle; tower, – of strength; fort, barracoon, pah, sconce, martello tower, peel-house, block-house, rath; wooden walls; turret, barbette.

buffer, corner-stone, fender, apron, mask, gauntlet, thimble, carapace, armour, shield, buckler; target, targe, ægis, breastplate, cuirass, plastron, habergeon, mail, coat of mail, brigan-dine, hauberk, lorication, helmet, helm, basinet, sallet, salade, heaume, morion, murrion, armet, cabaset, vizor, cas-quetel, siege-cap, head-piece, casque, steel helmet, tin hat; *pickelhaube*, csako; shako &c. (*dress*) 225; bearskin; panoply; truncheon &c. (*weapon*) 727.

garrison, picket, piquet; defender, protector; guardian &c. (*safety*) 664; trabant, body guard, champion; knight-errant, Paladin; propugner.

V. defend, forfend, fend; shield, screen, shroud; fence round &c. (*cir-cumscribe*) 229; fence, intrench; guard &c. (*keep safe*) 664; guard against; take care of &c. (*vigilance*) 459; bear harm-less; keep –, ward –, beat- off; hinder &c. 706.

parry, repel, propugn, put to flight; give a warm reception to [*ironical*]; hold –, keep- at -bay, – arm's length.

stand –, act- on the defensive; show fight; maintain –, stand- one's ground; stand by; hold one's own; bear –, stand- the brunt; fall back upon, hold, stand in the gap.

Adj. defending &c. *v.*; defensive; mural; armed, – at all points, – *cap-à-pie*, – to the teeth; panoplied, accoutred, harnessed; iron-plated, -clad; loop-holed, castellated, machicolated, casemated; defended &c. *v.*; proof against, bomb-, bullet-proof; protective.

Adv. defensively; on the -defence, – defensive; in defence; at bay, *pro aris et focis.*

Int. no surrender! *il ne passeront pas!*

Phr. defence not defiance.

718. Retaliation. — N. retaliation, reprisal, retort; counter-stroke, -blast, -plot, -project; retribution, *lex talionis*; reciprocation &c. (*reciprocity*) 12.

requital, desert, tit for tat, give and take, blow for blow, *quid pro quo*, a Roland for an Oliver, measure for measure, an eye for an eye, diamond cut diamond, the biter bit, a game at which two can play; boomerang.

recrimination &c. (*accusation*) 938; revenge &c. 919; compensation &c. 30; reaction &c. (*recoil*) 277.

V. retaliate, retort, turn upon; pay -off, – back; pay in -one's own, – the same- coin; cap; reciprocate &c. 148; turn the tables upon, return the compliment; give -a *quid pro quo* &c. *n.*, – as much as one takes; give and take, exchange -blows, – fisticuffs; be -quits, – even- with; pay off old scores.

serve one right, be hoist on one's own petard, throw a stone in one's own garden, catch a Tartar.

Adj. retaliating &c. *v.*; retalia-tory, -tive; retributive, recriminatory, reciprocal.

Adv. in retaliation; *en revanche.*

Phr. *mutato nomine de te fabula narratur; par pari refero; tu quoque;* you're another; *suo sibi gladio hunc jugulo.*

719. Resistance. — N. resistance, stand, front, oppugnation; opposition &c. 708; renitence, reluctation, recalcitration, recalcitrance; repugnance; kicking &c. *v.*

repulse, rebuff.

insurrection &c. (*disobedience*) 742; strike; turn –, lock –, barring- out; *levée en masse, Jacquerie*; riot &c. (*disorder*) 59.

V. resist; not -submit &c. 725; repugn, reluctate, withstand; stand up –, strive –, bear up –, be proof –, make head- against; stand, – firm, – one's ground, – the brunt of, – out; hold -one's ground, – one's own, – out.

breast the -wave, – current; stem the -tide, – torrent; face, confront, grapple with; show a bold front &c. (*courage*) 861; present a front; make a –, take one's- stand.

kick, – against; recalcitrate, kick against the pricks; oppose &c. 708; fly in the face of; lift the hand against &c. (*attack*) 716; rise up in arms &c. (*war*) 722; strike, turn out; draw up a round robin &c. (*remonstrate*) 932; revolt &c. (*disobey*) 742; make a riot.

prendre le mors aux dents; take the bit between the teeth; sell one's life dearly, die hard, keep at bay; repel, repulse.

Adj. resisting &c. *v.*; resist-ive, -ant; refractory &c. (*disobedient*) 742; recalcitrant, re-nitent, -pulsive, -pellant; up in arms.

proof against; unconquerable &c. (*strong*) 159; stubborn, unconquered; indomitable &c. (*persevering*) 604a; unyielding &c. (*obstinate*) 606.

Int. hands off! keep off!

720. Contention. — N. contention, strife; contest, -ation; struggle; belligerency; opposition &c. 708.

controversy, polemics; debate &c. (*discussion*) 476; war of words, logomachy, litigation; paper war, ink slinging; high words &c. (*quarrel*) 713; sparring &c. *v.*

721. Peace.—N. peace; amity &c. (*friendship*) 888; harmony &c. (*concord*) 714; tranquillity &c. (*quiescence*) 265; truce &c. (*pacification*) 723; pacificism; pipe –, calumet- of peace.

piping time of peace, quiet life; neutrality.

V. be at peace; keep the peace &c.

competition, rivalry; corrival-ry, -ship; agonism, *concours*, match, race, horse-racing, heat, steeple chase, point-to-point race, handicap; boat race, regatta; field-day; sham fight, Derby day; turf, sporting, bull-fight, tauro-machy, *gymkhana*, rodeo, Olympiad.

wrestling, *ju-jitsu*, pugilism, boxing, fisticuffs, spar, mill, set-to, scrap, round, bout, event; prize-fighting; quarter-staff, single stick; gladiatorship, gymnastics; athletic-s, – sports; games of skill &c. 840.

shindy; *fracas* &c. (*discord*) 713; clash of arms; tussle, scuffle, broil, fray; affray, -ment; velitation; col-, luctation; brabble, *brigue*, scramble, *mêlée*, scrimmage, stramash, bush-fighting.

free –, stand up –, hand to hand –, running- fight.

conflict, skirmish; ren-, en-counter; *rencontre*, collision, affair, brush, fight; battle, – royal; combat, action, engagement, joust, tournament; tilt, -ing; tourney, list; pitched battle, guerilla warfare.

death-struggle, struggle for life or death, Armageddon; hard knocks, sharp contest, tug of war.

naval -engagement, – battle; *naumachia*, sea-fight.

duel, -lo; single combat, monomachy, satisfaction, *passage d'armes*, passage of arms, affair of honour; triangular duel; hostile meeting, digladiation; appeal to arms &c. (*warfare*) 722.

deeds –, feats- of arms; pugnacity; combativeness &c. *adj.*; bone of contention &c. 713.

V. contend; contest, strive, struggle, scramble, wrestle; spar, square; exchange -blows, – fisticuffs; scrap, mix with, fib, justle, tussle, tilt, box, stave, fence; skirmish; fight &c. (*war*) 722; wrangle &c. (*quarrel*) 713.

contend &c. –, grapple –, engage –, close –, buckle –, bandy –, try conclusions –, have a brush &c. *n.* –, tilt- with; encounter, fall foul of, pitch into, clapperclaw, run a tilt at; oppose &c. 708; reluct.

join issue, come to blows, be at loggerheads, set-to, come to the scratch, exchange shots, measure swords, meet hand to hand; take up the -cudgels, – glove, – gauntlet; enter the lists; couch one's lance; give satisfaction; appeal to arms &c. (*warfare*) 722.

lay about one; break the peace.

compete –, cope –, vie –, race- with; outvie, emulate, rival; run a race; contend &c. –, stipulate –, stickle- for; insist upon, make a point of.

Adj. contending &c. *v.*; together by the ears, at loggerheads, at war, at issue.

competitive, rival; belligerent; contentious, combative, bellicose, unpeaceful; warlike &c. 722; quarrelsome &c. 901; pugnacious; pugilistic, gladiatorial; palestric, -al.

Phr. *a verbis ad verbera*; a word and a blow.

---

722. Warfare.—N. warfare; fighting &c. *v.*; hostilities; war, arms, the sword; Mars, Bellona, grim visaged war, *horrida bella*, Armageddon.

appeal to -arms, – the sword; ordeal

(*concord*) 714; make peace &c. 723.

Adj. pacific; peace-able, -ful; calm, tranquil, untroubled, halcyon; blood-less; neutral.

Phr. the storm blown over; the lion lies down with the lamb.

---

723. Pacification.—N. pacification, conciliation; reconcil-iation, -ement; shaking of hands, accommodation, arrangement, adjustment; terms, compromise; amnesty, deed of release.

–, wager- of battle; *ultima ratio regum*, arbitrament of the sword.

battle array, campaign, crusade, expedition; mobilization; state of siege; battle-field &c. (*arena*) 728; warpath.

art of war, tactics, strategy, castrametation; general-, soldier-ship; aerial–, submarine –, naval –, chemical- warfare; military evolutions, ballistics, gunnery; chivalry; poison gas; gunpowder, shot, – and shell.

battle, tug of war &c. (*contention*) 720; service, campaigning, active service, tented field; fiery cross, trumpet, clarion, bugle, pibroch, slogan; war-cry, -whoop; battle cry, beat of drum, rappel, tom-tom; word of command; pass-, watch-word.

war to the -death, – knife; *guerre à -mort, – outrance*; open –, internecine –, civil- war.

V. arm; raise –, mobilize- troops; raise up in arms; take up the cudgels &c. 720; take up –, fly to –, appeal to- -arms, – the sword; draw –, unsheathe- the sword; dig up the hatchet; go to –, declare –, wage –, let slip the dogs of- war; cry havoc; kindle –, light- the torch of war; raise one's banner, send round the fiery cross; hoist the black flag; throw –, fling- away the scabbard; enrol, enlist, join up; take the field; take the law into one's own hands; do –, give –, join –, engage in –, go to- battle; flesh one's sword; set to, fall to, engage, measure swords with, draw the trigger, cross swords; come to -blows, – close quarters; fight; combat; contend &c. 720; battle –, break a lance- with.

serve; see –, be on- -service, – active service; campaign; wield the sword, shoulder a musket, smell powder, be under the fire; spill –, imbrue the hands in- blood; be on the warpath.

carry on -war, – hostilities; keep the field; fight the good fight; go over the top; cut one's way through; fight -it out, – like devils, – one's way, – hand to hand; sell one's life dearly.

Adj. conten-ding, -tious &c. 720; armed, – to the teeth, – cap-à-pie; sword in hand; in –, under –, up in- arms; at war with; bristling with arms; in -battle array, – open arms, – the field; embattled.

unpacific, unpeaceful; belligerent, combative, armigerous, bellicose, martial, warlike; mili-tary, -tant; soldier-like, -ly; chivalrous; strategical, internecine.

Adv. *flagrante bello*, in the -thick of the fray, – cannon's mouth; at the -sword's point, – point of the bayonet.

Int. *væ victis!* to arms! to your tents O Israel!

Phr. the battle rages.

peace-offering; olive-branch; overtures; pipe –, calumet –, preliminaries- of peace.

truce, armistice; suspension of -arms, – hostilities; breathing-time; convention; *modus vivendi*; flag of truce, white flag, *parlementaire, cartel*.

hollow truce, *pax in bello*; drawn battle.

V. pacify, tranquillize, compose; allay &c. (*moderate*) 174; reconcile, propitiate, placate, conciliate, meet half-way, hold out the olive-branch, heal the breach, make peace, restore harmony, bring to terms.

settle –, arrange –, accommodate- -matters, – differences; set straight; make up a quarrel, *tantas componere lites*; come to -an understanding, – terms; bridge over, hush up; make -it, – matters- up; shake hands.

raise a siege; put up –, sheathe- the sword; bury the hatchet, lay down one's arms, turn swords into ploughshares; smoke the calumet of peace, close the temple of Janus; keep the peace &c. (*concord*) 714; be -pacified &c.; come round.

Adj. conciliatory, pacificatory; composing &c. *v.*; pacified &c. *v.*

Phr. *requiescat in pace.*

————

724. Mediation.—N. media-tion, -torship, -tization; inter-vention, -position, -ference, -meddling, -cession; parley, negotiation, arbitration; flag of truce &c. 723; good offices, peace-offering; diploma-tics, -cy; compromise &c. 774.

mediator, intercessor, peacemaker, make-peace, negotiator, go-between; diplomatist &c. (*consignee*) 758; moderator, propitiator, umpire, arbitrator.

V. media-te, -tize; inter-cede, -pose, -fere, -vene; step in, negotiate; meet half-way; arbitrate; *magnas componere lites.*

Adj. mediatory, propitiatory, diplomatic.

725. Submission.—N. submission, yielding, acquiescence, compliance; non-resistance; obedience &c. 743; submissiveness, deference.

surrender, cession, capitulation, resignation.

obeisance, homage, kneeling, genuflexion, courtesy, curtsy, *salaam*, *kowtow*, prostration.

V. succumb, submit, yield, bend, resign, defer to, accede.

lay down –, deliver up- one's arms; hand over one's sword; lower –, haul down –, strike- one's flag, – colours; deliver the keys of the city.

surrender, – at discretion; cede, capitulate, come to terms, retreat, beat a retreat; draw in one's horns &c. (*humility*) 879; give -way, – ground, – in, – up; cave in; suffer judgment by default; bend, – to one's yoke, – before the storm; reel back; bend –, knuckle- -down, – to, – under; knock under.

humble oneself; eat -dirt, – the leek, – humble pie; bite –, lick- the dust; be –, fall- at one's feet; craven; crouch before, throw oneself at the feet of; swallow the -leek, – pill; kiss the rod; turn the other cheek; *avaler des couleuvres*, gulp down.

obey &c. 743; kneel to, bow to, pay homage to, cringe to, truckle to; bend the -neck, – knee; kneel, fall on one's knees, bow submission, courtesy, curtsy, *kowtow*; make obeisance.

pocket the affront; make -the best of, – a virtue of necessity; grin and abide, shrug the shoulders, resign oneself; submit with a good grace &c. (*bear with*) 826.

Adj. surrendering &c. *v.*; submissive, resigned, crouching; down-trodden; down on one's marrow bones; on one's bended knee; weak-kneed, un-, non-resisting; pliant &c. (*soft*) 324; undefended.

untenable, indefensible; humble &c. 879.

Phr. have it your own way; it can't be helped; amen &c. (*assent*) 488.

726. Combatant.—N. combatant; disputant, controversialist, polemic, litigant, belligerent; competitor, rival, corrival; fighter, assailant, aggressor; champion, Paladin; moss-trooper, swashbuckler, fire-eater, duellist, bully, bludgeon-man, rough, fighter, fighting-man, prize-fighter, pugilist, pug, boxer, bruiser, the fancy, gladiator, athlete, wrestler; fighting-, game-cock; swordsman, *sabreur.*

warrior, soldier, Amazon, man-at-arms, armigerent; campaigner, veteran; red-coat, military man, *rajpoot*, brave.

armed force, troops, soldiery, military, forces, sabaoth, the army, standing army, regulars, the line, troops of the line, militia, territorials, yeomanry, volunteers, trainband, fencible; auxiliary –, reserve- forces; reserves, *posse comitatus*, national guard, *gendarme*, beefeater; guards, -man; yeoman of the guard, life guards, household troops.

janissary; myrmidon; Mama-, Mame-luke; spahee, *spahi*, Cossack,

Croat, Pandour; irregular, free lance, *franc-tireur, bashi-bazouk, guerilla, condottiere*; mercenary.

levy, draught, commando; *Land-wehr, -sturm*; conscript, recruit, rookie, cadet, raw levies.

private, – soldier; Tommy Atkins, rank and file, peon, trooper, doughboy, sepoy, *askari, légionnaire*, legionary, food for powder, cannon fodder; officer &c. (*commander*) 745; subaltern, ensign, shave-tail, standard bearer, non-com; spear-, pike-man; halberdier, lancer; musketeer, carabineer, rifleman, sharpshooter, yager, skirmisher; grenadier, fusileer; archer, bowman.

horse and foot; horse –, foot- soldier; cavalry, horse, artillery, horse –, field –, heavy –, mountain- artillery, infantry, light horse, *voltigeur, Uhlan*, mounted rifles, dragoon, hussar, trooper; light –, heavy-dragoon; heavy; *cuirassier*; gunner, cannoneer, bombardier, artilleryman, matross; sapper, – and miner; engineer; light infantry, rifles, *chasseur, zouave*; military train, supply and transport, coolie.

army, – corps, *corps d'armée*, host, division, column, wing, detachment, *escadrille*, garrison, flying column, brigade, regiment, *corps*, battalion, squadron, company, platoon, battery, subdivision, section, squad; piquet, picket, guard, rank, file; legion, phalanx, cohort; cloud of skirmishers; impi.

war-horse, charger, *destrier*.

armoured -train, – car; tank.

marine, man of war's man &c. (*sailor*) 269; navy, first line of defence, wooden walls; naval forces, fleet, flotilla, armada, squadron.

man-of-war, warship; H.M.S., U.S.S.; capital ship; line-of-battle ship, battle ship; super-, dreadnought, battle –, armoured –, protected – light- cruiser; scout, flotilla leader; destroyer, torpedo boat; submarine, submersible, U-boat; submarine chaser, eagle boat, mystery ship, Q-boat; mine-layer, -sweeper; ship of the line, iron-clad, turret-ship, ram, Monitor, floating battery; first-rate, frigate, sloop of war, corvette, gunboat, bomb-vessel, fire-boat; flag ship, guard ship, cruiser; airplane carrier; privateer; tender; depôt –, parent- ship; store –, troop- ship; transport, catamaran.

aircraft &c. 273, air force, scout, fighter, bomber, troop carrier, aerial patrol, seaplane, flying boat, torpedo plane; airship, Zeppelin; rigid –, semi-rigid –, non-rigid- airship; dirigible –, free –, captive –, kite –, observation- balloon.

anti-aircraft guns, searchlights, sound locators; catapult.

727. Arms.—N. arm, -s; weapon, deadly weapon; arma-ment, -ture; panoply, stand of arms; armour &c. (*defence*) 717; armoury &c. (*store*) 636.

ammunition; powder, – and shot; explosive; propellant; gun-powder, -cotton; dynam-, melin-, cord-, lydd-ite; trinitrotoluene, T.N.T., ammonal; cartridge; ball cartridge, *cartouche*, fire-ball; dud, black Maria; 'villainous saltpetre'; poison –, mustard –, lachrymatory –, tear- gas.

sword, sabre, broadsword, cutlass, falchion, scimitar, cimeter, brand, whinyard, bilbo, glaive, glave, rapier, skean, Toledo, Ferrara, tuck, claymore, creese, kris, *kukri*, dagger, dirk, hanger, poniard, stiletto, stylet, dudgeon, bayonet; sword-bayonet, -stick; side arms, foil, blade, steel; axe, bill; pole-, battle-axe; gisarm, halberd, partisan, tomahawk, bowie-knife; at-, att-, yat-aghan; yatachan; good –, trusty –, naked-sword; cold –, naked- steel.

club, mace, truncheon, staff, bludgeon, cudgel, life-preserver, shillelagh, sprig; hand-, quarter-staff; bat, cane, stick, knuckle-duster, sand bag.

gun, piece; fire-arms; artillery, ordnance; siege –, battering-train; park, battery; cannon, gun of position, heavy –, siege –, field –, mountain –, anti-aircraft –, breech loading –, quick firing- gun; field piece, mortar, trench mortar, mine thrower, howitzer, carronade, culverin, basilisk; falconet, jingal, swivel, *pederero, bouche à feu*; smooth bore, rifled cannon; Armstrong –, Lancaster –, Paixhan –, Whitworth –, Parrott –, Krupp –, Gatling –, Maxim –, Vickers –, Hotchkiss –, Lewis –, machine- gun; tommy gun, Thompson's submachine gun; *mitrailleu-r, -se*; pompom; blow pipe.

small arms; musket, -ry, firelock, flintlock, fowling-piece, shot gun, rifle, *fusil*, caliver, carbine, blunderbuss, musketoon, Brown Bess, matchlock, harquebuss, *arquebuse*, haguebut; petronel; smallbore; breech-, muzzle-loader; Miniè –, Enfield –, Westley Richards –, Snider –, Springfield –, Martini-Henry –, Lee-Metford –, Lee-Enfield –, Mauser –, Männlicher –, magazine –, repeating- rifle; needle-gun, *chassepot*; pistol, -et; revolver, automatic pistol, automatic; wind-, air-gun; flame –, gas-projector.

bow, cross-bow, arbalest, balister, catapult, sling; battering-ram &c. (*impulse*) 276; gunnery; ballistics &c. (*propulsion*) 284.

missile, bolt, projectile, shot, pellet, ball; grape; grape –, canister –, bar –, cannon –, langrel –, langrage –, round –, chain- shot; explosive; incendiary –, expanding –, soft-nosed –, dum-dum- bullet; slug, stone, brickbat; hand –, rifle- grenade; high explosive –, incendiary –, star –, gas- shell; depth –, gas –, incendiary –, stink- bomb; petard, torpedo, carcass, rocket; congreve, – rocket; shrapnel, *mitraille*; thunderbolt; mine, land mine, infernal machine.

pike, lance, spear, spontoon, javelin, assagai, throwing stick, dart, djerrid, arrow, reed, shaft, bolt, boomerang, harpoon, gaff.

728. Arena.—**N.** arena, field, platform; scene of action, theatre; walk, course; hustings; stage, boards &c. (*playhouse*) 599; amphitheatre; Coli-, Colos-seum; Flavian amphitheatre, hippodrome, circus, race-course, track, *stadium, corso*, turf, cockpit, bear-garden, playground, playing fields, *gymnasium, palæstra*, ring, lists; tilt-yard, -ing ground; *Campus Martius, Champ de Mars*; aerodrome, airport, air base, flying field.

theatre –, seat- of war; battle-field, -ground; field of -battle, – slaughter; no man's land; Aceldama, camp; the enemy's camp; trysting-place &c. (*place of meeting*) 74.

Section V. Results of Voluntary Action

729. Completion.—**N.** completion; accomplish-, achieve-, fulfil-ment; performance, execution; des-, dis-patch; consummation, culmination, climax; finish, conclusion, effectuation; close &c. (*end*) 67; terminus &c. (*arrival*) 292; winding up; *finale, dénouement*, catastrophe, issue, upshot, result; final –, last –, crowning –, finishing- -touch, – stroke; last finish, *coup de grâce*;

730. Non-Completion.—**N.** non-completion, -fulfilment; shortcoming &c. 304; incompleteness &c. 53; drawn -battle, – game; work of Penelope, task of Sisyphus.

non-performance, inexecution; neglect &c. 460.

V. not -complete &c. 729; leave -unfinished &c. *adj.*, – undone; neglect &c. 460; let -alone, – slip; lose sight of.

crowning of the edifice; coping-, keystone; missing link &c. 53; superstructure, *ne plus ultra*, work done, *fait accompli*.

elaboration; finality; completeness &c. 52.

V. effect, -uate; accomplish, achieve, compass, consummate, hammer out; bring to -maturity, – perfection; perfect, complete; elaborate.

do, execute, make; go –, get- through; work out, enact; bring -about, – to bear, – to pass, – through, – to a head.

des-, dis-patch; knock –, finish –, polish- off; make short work of; dispose of, set at rest; perform, discharge, fulfil, realize; put in -practice, – force; carry -out, – into effect, – into execution; make good; be as good as one's word.

do thoroughly, not do by halves, go the whole hog; drive home; be in at the death &c. (*persevere*) 604a; carry through, play out, exhaust, deliver the goods, fill the bill.

finish, bring to a close &c. (*end*) 67; wind up, stamp, clinch, seal, set the seal on, put the seal to; give the -final touch &c. *n.* to; put the -last, – finishing- hand to; crown, – all; cap.

ripen, culminate; come to a -head, – crisis; come to its end; die -a natural death, – of old age; run -its course, – one's race; touch –, reach –, attain- the goal; reach &c. (*arrive*) 292; get in the harvest.

Adj. completing, final; conclu-ding, -sive; crowning &c. *v.*; exhaustive, complete, mature, perfect, consummate.

done, completed &c. *v.*; done for, sped, wrought out; highly wrought &c. (*preparation*) 673; thorough &c. 52; ripe &c. (*ready*) 673.

Adv. completely &c. (*thoroughly*) 52; to crown all, out of hand.

Phr. the race is run; *actum est*; *finis coronat opus*; *consummatum est*; *c'en est fait*; it is all over; the game is played out, the bubble has burst.

fall short of &c. 304; do things by halves; scotch the snake, not kill it; hang fire; be slow to; collapse &c. 304.

Adj. not completed &c. *v.*; incomplete &c. 53; uncompleted, unfinished, unaccomplished, unperformed, unexecuted; sketchy, addle.

in progress, in hand; going on, proceeding; on one's hands; on the fire; on the stocks; in preparation; lacking the finishing touch.

Adv. *re infectâ*.

---

731. Success.—N. success, -fulness; speed; advance &c. (*progress*) 282.

trump card; hit, stroke; lucky –, fortunate –, good- -hit, – stroke; bold –, master- stroke; *coup de maître*, checkmate; half the battle, prize; profit &c. (*acquisition*) 775; best seller.

continued success; good fortune &c. (*prosperity*) 734; time well spent.

advantage over; edge; upper-, whip-hand; ascendancy, mastery; expugnation, conquest, victory, subdual; subjugation &c. (*subjection*) 749.

triumph &c. (*exultation*) 884; proficiency &c. (*skill*) 698; conqueror, victor, winner, champion; master of the -situation, – position.

V. succeed; be -successful &c. *adj.*;

732. Failure. — N. failure; non-success, -fulfilment; dead failure, successlessness; abortion, miscarriage; *brutum fulmen* &c. 158; labour in vain &c. (*inutility*) 645; no go; inefficacy; inefficaciousness &c. *adj.*; vain –, ineffectual –, abortive- -attempt, – efforts; flash in the pan, 'lame and impotent conclusion'; frustration; slip 'twixt cup and lip &c. (*disappointment*) 509.

blunder &c. (*mistake*) 495; fault, omission, miss, oversight, slip, trip, stumble, claudication, footfall; false –, wrong- step; *faux pas*, titubation, *bévue, faute*, lurch; botchery &c. (*want of skill*) 699; scrape, jam, mess, muddle, foozle, *fiasco*, breakdown.

mishap &c. (*misfortune*) 735; split,

gain one's -end, - ends; crown with success.

gain -, attain -, carry -, secure -, win- -a point, - an object; put over; make a go of; manage to, contrive to; accomplish &c. (*effect, complete*) 729; do -, work- wonders.

come off -well, - successfully, - with flying colours; make short work of; take -, carry- by storm; bear away the bell; win -one's spurs, - the battle; win -, carry -, gain- the -day, - prize, - palm; climb on the bandwagon; have -the best of it, - it all one's own way, - the game in one's own hands, - the ball at one's feet, - one on the hip; walk over the course; carry all before one, remain in possession of the field; score a success, win hands down.

speed; make progress &c. (*advance*) 282; win -, make -, work -, find- one's way; strive to some purpose; prosper &c. 734; drive a roaring trade; make profit &c. (*acquire*) 775; reap -, gather- the -fruits, - benefit of, - harvest; make one's fortune, get in the harvest, turn to good account; turn to account &c. (*use*) 677.

triumph, be triumphant; gain -, obtain- -a victory, - an advantage; chain victory to one's car.

surmount -, overcome -, get over- -a difficulty, - an obstacle &c. 706; *se tirer d'affaire*; make head against; stem the -torrent, - tide, - current; weather -the storm, - a point; turn a corner, keep one's head above water, tide over; master; get -, have -, gain- the -better of, - best of, - upper hand, - ascendancy, - whip hand, - start of; distance; surpass &c. (*superiority*) 33.

defeat, conquer, vanquish, discomfit; over-come, ·throw, -power, -master, -match, -set, -ride, -reach; out-wit, -do, -flank, -manœuvre, -general, -vote; take the wind out of one's adversary's sails; beat, - hollow; rout, lick, drub, floor, worst; put -down, - to flight, - to the rout, - *hors de combat*, - out of court.

silence, quell, nonsuit, checkmate, upset, confound, nonplus, trump; baffle &c. (*hinder*) 706; circumvent, elude; trip up, - the heels of; drive

collapse, smash, blow, explosion.

repulse, rebuff, defeat, rout, over-throw, discomfiture; beating, drubbing; *quietus*, nonsuit, subjugation; check-, fool's-mate.

fall, downfall, ruin, perdition; wreck &c. (*destruction*) 162; death-blow; bankruptcy &c. (*non-payment*) 808.

losing game, *affaire flambée*.

victim, prey; bankrupt.

V. fail; be -unsuccessful &c. *adj.*; not -succeed &c. 731; make -vain efforts &c. *n.*; do -, labour -, toil- in vain; lose one's labour, take nothing by one's motion; bring to naught, make nothing of; wash a blackamoor white &c. (*impossible*) 471; roll the stone of Sisyphus &c. (*useless*) 645; do by halves &c. (*not complete*) 730; lose ground &c. (*recede*) 283; flunk; fall short of &c. 304.

miss, - one's aim, - the mark, - one's footing, - stays; slip, trip, stumble; make a -slip &c. *n.*, - blunder &c. 495, - mess of, - botch of; bitch it, mis-carry, abort, go up like a rocket and come down like the stick, reckon with-out one's host; get the wrong sow by the ear &c. (*blunder, mismanage*) 699.

limp, halt, hobble, titubate; fall, tumble; lose one's balance; fall -to the ground, - between two stools; flounder, falter, stick in the mud, run aground, split upon a rock; run -, knock -, dash-one's head against a stone wall; break one's back; break down, sink, drown, founder, have the ground cut from under one; get into -trouble, - a mess, - a scrape; come to grief &c. (*adversity*) 735; go to -the wall, - the dogs, - pot; lick -, bite- the dust; be -defeated &c. 731; have the worst of it, lose the day, come off second best, lose; fall a prey to; succumb &c. (*submit*) 725; not have a leg to stand on.

come to nothing, end in smoke; fall -to the ground, - through, - dead, - still-born, - flat; slip through one's fingers; hang -, miss- fire; flash in the pan, collapse; topple down &c. (*descent*) 305; go to wrack and ruin &c. (*destruction*) 162.

go amiss, go wrong, go cross, go hard with, go on a wrong tack; go on -,

-into a corner, – to the wall; run hard, put one's nose out of joint.

settle, do for; break the -neck of, – back of; capsize, sink, shipwreck, drown, swamp; subdue; subjugate &c. (*subject*) 749; reduce; make the enemy bite the dust; victimize, roll in the dust, trample under foot, put an extinguisher upon.

answer, – the purpose; avail, prevail, take effect, do, turn out well, work well, take, tell, bear fruit; hit -it, – the mark, – the right nail on the head; nick it; turn up trumps, make a hit; find one's account in.

Adj. succeeding &c. *v.*; successful; prosperous &c. 734; triumphant; flushed –, crowned- with success; victorious; set up; in the ascendant; unbeaten &c. (*see* beat &c. *v.*); well-spent; felicitous, effective, in full swing.

Adv. successfully &c. *adj.*; with flying colours, in triumph, swimmingly; *à merveille*, beyond all hope; to some –, good- purpose; to one's heart's content.

Phr. *veni vidi vici*, the day being one's own, one's star in the ascendant; *omne tulit punctum.*

come off –, turn out –, work- ill; take -a wrong, – an ugly- turn; gang agley.

be all -over with, – up with; explode; dash one's hopes &c. (*disappoint*) 509; defeat the purpose; upset the apple cart; sow the wind and reap the whirlwind, jump out of the frying pan into the fire.

Adj. unsuccessful, successless; failing, tripping &c. *v.*; at fault; unfortunate &c. 735.

abortive, addle, still-born; fruitless, sterile, bootless; ineffect-ual, -ive; inefficient &c. (*impotent*) 158; inefficacious; lame, hobbling, *décousu*; insufficient &c. 640; unavailing &c. (*useless*) 645; of no effect.

aground, grounded, swamped, stranded, cast away, wrecked, foundered, capsized, shipwrecked, non-suited; foiled; defeated &c. 731; struck –, borne –, broken- down; down-trodden; over-borne, -whelmed; all up with; beaten to a frazzle.

lost, undone, ruined, broken; bankrupt &c. (*not paying*) 808; played out; done -up, – for; dead beat, ruined root and branch, *flambé*, knocked on the head; destroyed &c. 162.

frustrated, thwarted, crossed, unhinged, disconcerted, dashed; thrown -off one's balance, – on one's back, – on one's beam ends; unhorsed, in a sorry plight; hard hit.

stultified, befooled, dished, hoist on one's own petard; victimized, sacrificed.

wide of the mark &c. (*error*) 495; out of one's reckoning &c. (*inexpectation*) 508; left in the lurch; thrown away &c. (*wasted*) 638; unattained; uncompleted &c. 730.

Adv. unsuccessfully &c. *adj.*; to little or no purpose, in vain, *re infectâ.*

Phr. the bubble has burst, the game is up, all is lost; the devil to pay; *parturiunt montes* &c. (*disappointment*) 509.

733. Trophy.—**N.** trophy; medal, prize, palm; ribbon, blue ribbon, *cordon bleu*; citation; cup; laurel, -s; bays, crown, chaplet, wreath, civic crown; Victoria Cross, V.C., *Croix de Guerre*, Iron Cross; Distinguished Service Cross, Medal of Honor, Congressional Medal; insignia &c. 550; feather in one's cap &c. (*honour*) 873; decoration &c. 877; garland, triumphal arch.

triumph &c. (*celebration*) 883; flying colours &c. (*show*) 882. *monumentum ære perennius.*

734. Prosperity.—**N.** prosperity, welfare, well-being; affluence &c. (*wealth*) 803; success &c. 731; thrift, roaring

735. Adversity.—**N.** adversity, evil &c. 619; failure &c. 732; bad –, ill –, evil –, adverse –, hard- -fortune, – hap,

trade; chicken in every pot, the full dinner pail; good –, smiles of- fortune; blessings, godsend.

luck; good –, run of- luck; sunshine; fair -weather, – wind; palmy –, bright –, halcyon- days; piping times, tide, flood, high tide.

Saturnia regna, Saturnian age; golden -time, – age; bed of roses; fat of the land, milk and honey, loaves and fishes, fleshpots of Egypt.

made man, lucky dog, *enfant gâté*, spoiled child of fortune.

upstart, *parvenu*, *nouveau riche*, profiteer, skipjack, mushroom.

V. prosper, thrive, flourish; be -prosperous &c. *adj.*; drive a roaring trade; go on -well, – smoothly, – swimmingly; sail before the wind, swim with the tide; run -smooth, – smoothly, – on all fours.

rise –, get on- in the world; work –, make- one's way; look up; lift –, raise- one's head, make one's -fortune, – pile, feather one's nest.

flower, blow, blossom, bloom, fructify, bear fruit, fatten, batten.

keep oneself afloat; keep –, hold- one's head above water; light –, fall- on one's -legs, – feet; drop into a good thing; bear a charmed life; bask in the sunshine; have a -good, – fine- time of it; have a run, – of luck; have the -good fortune &c. *n.* to; take a favourable turn; live -on the fat of the land, – in clover.

Adj. prosperous; thriving &c. *v.*; in a fair way, buoyant; well -off, – to do, – to do in the world; set up, at one's ease; rich &c. 803; in good case; in -full, – high- feather; fortunate, lucky, in luck; born -with a silver spoon in one's mouth, – under a lucky star; on the sunny side of the hedge.

auspicious, propitious, providential.

palmy, halcyon; agreeable &c. 829; *couleur de rose*.

Adv. prosperously &c. *adj.*; swimmingly; as good luck would have it; beyond all -expectation, – hope, – one's wildest dreams.

Phr. one's star in the ascendant, all for the best, one's course runs smooth.

–––––––

– luck, – lot; frowns of fortune; evil -dispensation, – star, – genius; ups and downs of life, broken fortunes; hard -case, – lines, – life; sea –, peck- of troubles; hell upon earth; slough of despond; jinx.

trouble, humiliation, hardship, curse, blight, blast, load, pressure.

pressure of the times, iron age, evil day, time out of joint; hard –, bad –, sad- times; rainy day, cloud, dark cloud, gathering clouds, ill wind; visitation, infliction; affliction &c. (*painfulness*) 830; bitter -pill, – cup; care, trial; the sport of fortune.

mis-hap, -chance, -adventure, -fortune; disaster, calamity, catastrophe; accident, casualty, cross, reverse, check, *contretemps*, rub, pinch, setback.

losing game; falling &c. *v.*; fall, down-fall, come-down; ruin-ation, -ousness; undoing; extremity; ruin &c. (*destruction*) 162.

V. be -ill off &c. *adj.*; go hard with; fall on evil, – days; go on ill; not -prosper &c. 734.

go -downhill, – to rack and ruin &c. (*destruction*) 162, – to the dogs; fall, – from one's high estate; decay, sink, decline, go down in the world; have seen better days; bring down one's grey hairs with sorrow to the grave; come to grief; be all -over, – up- with; bring a -wasp's, – hornet's- nest about one's ears.

Adj. unfortunate, unblest, unhappy, unlucky; im-, un-prosperous; luck-, hap-less; out of luck; in trouble, in a bad way, in an evil plight; under a cloud; clouded; ill -, badly- off; in adverse circumstances; poor &c. 804; behindhand, down in the world, decayed, undone; on the road to ruin, on its last legs, on the wane; in one's utmost need.

planet-struck, devoted; born -under an evil star, – with a wooden ladle in one's mouth; ill-fated, -starred, -omened; inconspicuous, ominous, doomed, unpropitious.

adverse, untoward; disastrous, calamitous, ruinous, dire, deplorable.

Adv. if the worst come to the worst, as ill luck would have it, from bad to worse, out of the frying pan into the fire.

Phr. one's star is on the wane; one's luck -turns, – fails; the game is up, one's doom is sealed, the ground crumbles under one's feet, *sic transit gloria mundi, tant va la cruche à l'eau qu'à la fin elle se casse.*

736. Mediocrity.—N. moderate –, average- circumstances; respectability; middle classes, *bourgeoisie*; mediocrity; golden mean &c. (*midcourse*) 628, (*moderation*) 174.

V. jog on; go –, get on- -fairly, – quietly, – peaceably, – tolerably, – respectably; steer a middle course &c. 628.

Adj. middling, so-so, fair, medium, moderate, mediocre, second-, third- &c. -rate.

Division (II). INTERSOCIAL VOLITION*

Section I. General Intersocial Volition

737. Authority.—N. authority; influence, patronage, power, preponderance, credit, *prestige*, prerogative, jurisdiction; right &c. (*title*) 924.

divine right, dynastic rights, authoritativeness; absolut-eness, -ism; despotism, tyranny; *jus nocendi.*

command, empire, sway, rule; domin-ion, -ation; sovereignty, supremacy, suzerainty; lord-, head-ship; chiefdom; seignior-y, -ity, hegemony, patriarchate, patriarchy; master-y, -ship, -dom; government &c. (*direction*) 693; dictation, control.

hold, grasp; grip, -e; reach; iron sway &c. (*severity*) 739; fangs, clutches, talons; rod of empire &c. (*sceptre*) 747.

reign, regnancy, *régime*, dynasty; director-, dictator-ship; protector-ate, -ship; caliphate, pashalic, electorate; presiden-cy, -tship; administration; pro-, consulship; prefecture; seneschalship; magistra-ture, -cy; raj.

empire; monarchy; king-hood, -ship; royalty, regality, autocracy, monocracy, arist-archy, -ocracy; oligarchy, democracy, demogogy; republic, -anism, federalism; socialism, collectivism; communism, bolshevism, syndicalism; mob law, mobocracy, ochlocracy, ergatocracy; *vox populi, imperium in imperio*; bureaucracy; beadle-, bumble-dom; stratocracy; martial law, military -power, – government; feodality, feudal system, feudalism.

Thearchy, diarchy; du-, tri-, heter-archy; du-, tri-umvirate; auto-cracy, -nomy; limited monarchy; constitutional -government, – monarchy; home rule, autonomy; self-government, -determination; representative government; Soviet government.

738. [Absence of authority.] **Laxity. —N.** laxity; lax-, loose-, slack-ness; toleration &c. (*lenity*) 740; freedom &c. 748.

anarchy, interregnum; relaxation; loosening &c. *v.*; remission; dead letter, *brutum fulmen*, misrule; licence, licentiousness; insubordination &c. (*disobedience*) 742; lynch law &c. (*illegality*) 964; nihilism.

[Deprivation of power] dethronement, deposition, usurpation, abdication.

V. be -lax &c. *adj.*; *laisser -faire, – aller*; hold a loose rein; give -the reins to, – rope enough, – a loose to; tolerate; relax; misrule.

go beyond the length of one's tether; have one's -swing, – fling; act without -instructions, – authority; act on one's own responsibility, usurp authority.

dethrone, depose; abdicate.

Adj. lax, loose; slack; remiss &c. (*careless*) 460; weak.

relaxed; licensed; reinless, unbridled; anarchical; unauthorized &c. (*unwarranted*) 925.

---

* Implying the action of the will of one mind over the will of another.

[274]

gyn-archy, -ocracy, -æocracy; petticoat government, matri-archate, matriarchy.

[Vicarious authority] commission &c. 755; deputy &c. 759; permission &c. 760.

country, state, realm, commonwealth, canton, constituency, toparchy, municipality, polity, body politic, *posse comitatus.*

person in authority &c. (*master*) 745; judicature &c. 965; cabinet &c. (*council*) 696; usurper; seat of -government, – authority; head-quarters.

[Acquisition of authority] accession; installation &c. 755; usurpation.

V. authorize &c. (*permit*) 760; warrant &c. (*right*) 924; dictate &c. (*order*) 741; have –, hold –, possess –, exercise –, exert –, wield- -authority &c. *n.*

be -at the head of &c. *adj.*; hold –, be in –, fill an- office; hold –, occupy- a post; be -master &c. 745.

rule, sway, command, control, administer; govern &c. (*direct*) 693; lead, preside over, reign; possess –, be seated on –, occupy- the throne; sway –, wield- the sceptre; wear the crown.

have –, get- the -upper, – whip- hand; gain a hold upon, preponderate, dominate, boss, rule the roost; over-ride, -rule, -awe; lord it over, hold in hand, keep under, make a puppet of, lead by the nose, hold in the hollow of one's hand, turn round one's little finger, bend to one's will, hold one's own, wear the breeches; have -the ball at one's feet, – it all one's own way, – the game in one's own hand, – on the hip, – under one's thumb; be master of the situation; take the lead, play first fiddle, set the fashion; give the law to; carry with a high hand; lay down the law; 'ride in the whirl-wind and direct the storm'; rule with a rod of iron &c. (*severity*) 739.

ascend –, mount- the throne, take the reins, – into one's hand; assume -authority &c. *n.*, – the reins of government; take –, assume the- command.

be -governed by, – in the power of; be under -the rule of, – the domination of.

Adj. ruling &c. *v.*; regnant, at the head, dominant, paramount, supreme, predominant, preponderant, in the ascendant, influential; gubernatorial; imperious; authoritative, executive, administrative, clothed with authority, official, *ex officio*, ministerial, bureaucratic, departmental, imperative, peremptory, overruling, absolute; hegemonic, -al; arbitrary; compulsory &c. 744; stringent.

regal, sovereign; royal, -ist; monarchical, kingly; imperial, -istic; princely; feudal; aristo-, auto-cratic; oligarchic &c. *n.*; democratic, republican, dynastic.

at one's command; in one's -power, – grasp; under control; authorized &c. (*due*) 924.

Adv. in the name of, by the authority of, *de par le Roi*, in virtue of; under the auspices of, in the hands of.

at one's pleasure; by a -dash, – stroke- of the pen; *ex mero motu*; *ex cathedrâ.*

Phr. the grey mare the better horse; 'every inch a king.'

---

739. Severity.—N. severity; strict-ness, formalism, harshness &c. *adj.*; rigour, stringency, austerity; inclem-

740. Lenity. — N. leni-ty, -ence, -ency; moderation &c. 174; toler-ance, -ation; mildness, gentleness; favour;

ency &c. (*pitilessness*) 914*a*; arrogance &c. 885.

arbitrary power; absolut-, despotism; dictatorship, autocracy, tyranny, domineering, oppression; assumption, usurpation; inquisition, reign of terror, martial law; iron -heel, – rule, – hand, – sway; tight grasp; brute -force, – strength; coercion &c. 744; strong –, tight- hand.

hard -lines, – measure; tender mercies [ironical]; sharp practice; bureaucracy, red tape; pipe-clay, officialism.

tyrant, disciplinarian, martinet, stickler, formalist, bashaw, despot, hard master, Draco, oppressor, inquisitor, extortioner, harpy, vulture, bird of prey.

V. be -severe &c. *adj.*

assume, usurp, arrogate, take liberties; domineer, bully &c. 885; tyrannize, inflict, wreak, stretch a point, put on the screw; be hard upon; bear –, lay- a heavy hand on; be –, come- down upon; illtreat; deal -hardly with, – hard measure to; rule with a rod of iron, chastise with scorpions; dye with blood; oppress, override; trample –, tread- -down, – upon, – under foot; crush under an iron heel, ride roughshod over; rivet the yoke; hold –, keep- a tight hand; force down the throat; coerce &c. 744; give no quarter &c. (*pitiless*) 914*a*.

Adj. severe; strict, hard, harsh, dour, rigid, stiff, stern, rigorous, uncompromising, exacting, exigent, *exigeant*, inexorable, inflexible, obdurate, austere, relentless, Spartan, Draconian, stringent, straitlaced, puritanical, prudish, searching, unsparing, ironhanded, hardheaded, peremptory, absolute, positive, arbitrary, imperative; coercive &c. 744; tyrannical, despotic, masterful, extortionate, grinding, withering, oppressive, inquisitorial; inclement &c. (*ruthless*) 914*a*; cruel &c. (*malevolent*) 907; haughty, arrogant &c. 885.

Adv. severely &c. *adj.*; with a -high, – strong, – tight, – heavy-hand.

at the point of the -sword, – bayonet.

Phr. *Delirant reges plectuntur Achivi.*

indulgen-ce, -cy; clemency, mercy, forbearance, quarter; compassion &c. 914.

V. be -lenient &c. *adj.*; tolerate, bear with; *parcere subjectis*, give quarter.

indulge, allow one to have his own way, spoil.

Adj. lenient; mild, – as milk; gentle, soft; tolerant, indulgent, easy-going; clement &c. (*compassionate*) 914; forbearing; complaisant, long-suffering.

---

741. Command.—N. command, order, ordinance, act, *fiat*, bidding, *dictum*, hest, behest, call, beck, nod.

des-, dis-patch; message, direction, injunction, charge, instructions; appointment, fixture.

demand, exaction, imposition, requisition, claim, reclamation, revendication; *ultimatum* &c. (*terms*) 770; request &c. 765; requirement.

dictation; dict-, mand-ate; *caveat*, decree, decree -nisi, – absolute, *senatus consultum*; precept; pre-, re-script; writ, ordination, bull, edict, decretal, dispensation, prescription, brevet, placet, ukase, *firman*, hattisheriff, warrant, passport, *mittimus, mandamus*, summons, subpœna, *nisi prius*, interpellation, citation; word, – of command; *mot d'ordre*; bugle –, trumpet- call; beat of drum, tattoo; order of the day; enactment &c. (*law*) 963; *plébiscite* &c. (*choice*) 609.

V. command, order, decree, enact, ordain, dictate, direct, give orders.

prescribe, set, appoint, mark out; set –, prescribe –, impose- a task; set to work, put in requisition &c. 926.

bid, enjoin, charge, call upon, instruct; require, – at the hands of; exact, impose, tax, task; demand; insist on &c. (*compel*) 744.

claim, lay claim to, revendicate, reclaim.

cite, summon; call –, send- for; subpœna; beckon.

issue a command; make –, issue –, promulgate- -a requisition, – a decree, – an order &c. *n*.; give the -word of command, – word, – signal; call to order; give –, lay down- the law; assume the command &c. (*authority*) 737; remand.

be -ordered &c.; receive an order &c. *n*.

Adj. commanding &c. *v*.; authoritative &c. 737; decret-ory, -ive, -al; imperative, jussive, decisive, final.

Adv. in a commanding tone; by a -stroke, – dash- of the pen; by order, at beat of drum, on the first summons; at the word of command.

Phr. the decree is gone forth; *sic volo sic jubeo*; *le Roi le veut*.

---

742. Disobedience.—N. disobedience, insubordination, contumacy; infraction, -fringement; violation, non-compliance; non-observance &c. 773.

revolt, rebellion, mutiny, outbreak, rising, uprising, putsch, insurrection, *émeute*; riot, tumult &c. (*disorder*) 59; strike &c. (*resistance*) 719; barring out; defiance &c. 715.

mutinousness &c. *adj*.; mutineering; sedition, treason; high –, petty –, misprision of- treason; *premunire*; *lèse-majesté*; violation of law &c. 964; defection, secession, revolution, *sabotage*, bolshevism, *Sinn Fein*.

insurgent, mutineer, rebel, revolter, rioter, traitor, *carbonaro*, *sansculottes*, red republican, communist, Fenian, chartist, *frondeur*; seceder, runagate, brawler, anarchist, demagogue; suffragette; Spartacus, Masaniello, Wat Tyler, Jack Cade; bolshevist, bolshevik, maximalist, ringleader.

V. disobey, violate, infringe; shirk; set at defiance &c. (*defy*) 715; set authority at naught, run riot, fly in the face of, bolt, take the law into one's own hands; kick over the traces.

turn –, run- restive; champ the bit; strike &c. (*resist*) 719; rise, – in arms; secede; mutiny, rebel.

Adj. disobedient; uncompl-ying, -iant; unsubmissive, unruly, ungovernable; insubordinate, impatient of control; rest-iff, -ive; refractory, contumacious; recusant &c. (*refuse*) 764; recalcitrant; resisting &c. 719; lawless, mutinous, seditious, insurgent, riotous, revolutionary.

disobeyed, unobeyed; unbidden.

743. Obedience.—N. obedience; observance &c. 772; compliance; submission &c. 725; subjection &c. 749; non-resistance; passiveness, passivity, resignation.

allegiance, loyalty, fealty, homage, deference, devotion, fidelity, constancy.

submiss-ness, -iveness; ductility &c. (*softness*) 324; obsequiousness &c. (*servility*) 886.

V. be -obedient &c. *adj*.; obey, bear obedience to; submit &c. 725; comply, answer the helm, come at one's call; do -one's bidding, – what one is told, – suit and service; attend to orders, serve -devotedly, – loyally, – faithfully.

follow, – the lead of, – to the world's end; serve &c. 746; play second fiddle.

Adj. obedient; compl-ying, -iant; law-abiding, loyal, faithful, leal, devoted; at one's -call, – command, – orders, – beck and call; under -beck and call, – control.

restrainable; resigned, passive; submissive &c. 725; henpecked; pliant &c. (*soft*) 324.

unresist-ed, -ing.

Adv. obediently &c. *adj*.; in compliance with, in obedience to.

Phr. to hear is to obey; as –, if- you please; at your service.

744. Compulsion.—N. compulsion, coercion, coaction, constraint, eminent domain, duress, enforcement, press, conscription.

force; brute –, main –, physical- force; the sword, *ultima ratio*; club –, mob –, lynch- law; *argumentum baculinum, le droit du plus fort*, martial law.

restraint &c. 751; necessity &c. 601; *force majeure*; Hobson's choice; the spur of necessity.

V. compel, force, make, drive, coerce, constrain, enforce, necessitate, oblige.

force upon, press; cram –, thrust –, force- down the throat; say it must be done, make a point of, insist upon, take no denial; put down, dragoon.

extort, wring from; put –, turn- on the screw; drag into; bind, – over; pin –, tie- down; require, tax, put in force; commandeer; restrain &c. 751.

Adj. compelling &c. *v.*; coercive, coactive; inexorable &c. 739; compuls-ory, -atory; obligatory, stringent, peremptory, binding.

forcible, not to be trifled with; irresistible &c. 601; compelled &c. *v.*; fain to.

Adv. by -force &c. *n.*, – force of arms; on compulsion, perforce; *vi et armis*, under the lash; at the point of the -sword, – bayonet; forcibly; by a strong arm.

under protest, in spite of one's teeth; against one's will &c. 603; *nolens volens* &c. (*of necessity*) 601; by stress of -circumstances, – weather; under press of; *de rigueur*.

---

745. Master.—N. master, *padrone*; lord, – paramount; command-er, -ant; captain; chief, -tain; *sahib*, sirdar, sachem, sheik, head, senior, governor, *duce*, ruler, dictator; leader &c. (*director*) 694.

lord of the ascendant; cock of the -walk, – roost; grey mare; mistress.

potentate; liege, – lord; suzerain, sovereign, monarch, autocrat, despot, tyrant, oligarch, overlord.

crowned head, emperor, king, anointed king, majesty, *imperator*, protector, president, stadtholder, judge.

cæsar, kaiser, czar, sultan, grand Turk, caliph, imaum, shah, padishah, sophi, mogul, great mogul, khan, cham; lama, tycoon, mikado, inca, cazique; domn; vaivode; wai-, way-wode; landamman; seyyid, cacique.

prince, duke &c. (*nobility*) 875; archduke, doge, elector; seignior; mar-, land-grave; rajah, emir, nizam, nawab, negus.

empress, queen, sultana, czarina, princess, infanta, duchess, margravine, begum, maharani.

regent, viceroy, exarch, palatine,

746. Servant.—N. subject, liegeman; servant, retainer, follower, henchman, servitor, domestic, menial, help, lady help, *employé, attaché*; official.

retinue, suite, *cortège*, staff, court.

attendant, squire, usher, page, buttons, donzel, footboy; dog robber; train-, cup-bearer; waiter, busboy, tapster, butler, livery servant, lackey, footman, flunkey, valet, *valet de chambre*; boots; scout, gyp; equerry, groom; jockey, hostler, ostler, tiger, orderly, messenger, cad, gillie, caddie; *wallah*; journeyman, herdsman, swineherd.

bailiff, castellan, seneschal, chamberlain, *major-domo*, groom of the chambers.

secretary; under –, assistant- secretary; clerk; clerical staff, stenographer, subsidiary; agent &c. 758; subaltern; under-ling, -strapper; man.

maid, -servant, waitress; handmaid; *confidente*, lady's maid, abigail, *soubrette*; nurse, *bonne, ayah*; nurse-, nursery-, house-, parlour-, waiting-, chamber-, kitchen-, scullery-, between –, laundry –, dairy-maid; *femme –, fille-de chambre; camarista*; chef de cuisine,

khedive, hospodar, beglerbeg, three-tailed bashaw, pasha, pashaw, bashaw, bey, beg, dey, scherif, tetrarch, satrap, mandarin, subhadar, nabob, maharajah; burgrave; laird &c. (*proprietor*) 779; High Commissioner.

the -authorities, – powers that be, – government; staff, *état major*, aga, official, man in office, person in authority.

[Naval authorities] admiral, -ty, – of the fleet; rear-, vice-, port-admiral; senior-, naval officer, S.N.O., commodore, captain, commander, lieutenant-commander, lieutenant, sub-lieutenant, midshipman, warrant –, petty- officer, leading seaman; skipper, mate, master.

[Military authorities] marshal, field-marshal, *maréchal*; general, -issimo; commander-in-chief, *seraskier, hetman*; lieutenant-, major-general; commandant; colonel, lieutenant-colonel, major, captain, centurion, skipper, lieutenant, second-lieutenant, officer, staff-officer, *aide de camp*, brigadier, brigade-major, adjutant, *jemidar*, ensign, cornet, cadet, subaltern, warrant officer, quartermaster, noncommissioned officer, N.C.O.; sergeant, -major; top-sergeant, colour sergeant; corporal, -major; lance-, acting-corporal; drum major; shavetail.

[Air authorities] air -marshal, – commodore; group captain, squadron leader, wing commander, flight lieutenant, flying –, pilot-officer.

[Civil authorities] judge &c. 967; mayor, -alty; prefect, chancellor, archon, provost, magistrate, syndic; alcalde, alcaid; burgomaster, *corregidor*, seneschal, alderman, warden, constable, portreeve; lord mayor, sheriff; officer &c. (*executive*) 965.

cordon bleu, cook, scullion, Cinderella; maid –, servant- of all work, tweeny, general servant, girl, slavey; laundress, bed-maker, goodie, char-woman &c. (*worker*) 690.

serf, vassal, slave, negro, helot; bondsman, -woman; bondslave; *âme damnée, odalisque,* ryot, *adscriptus glebæ*; vill-ain, -ein; bead-, bede-sman; sizar; pension-er, -ary; client; dependant, -ent; hanger on, stooge, satellite; parasite &c. (*servility*) 886; led captain; *protégé,* ward, hireling, mercenary, puppet, creature.

badge of slavery; bonds &c. 752.

V. serve; minister to, wait –, attend –, dance attendance –, pin oneself-upon; squire, tend, hang on the sleeve of, char, do for; fag; valet.

Adj. in the train of; in one's -pay, – employ; at one's call &c. (*obedient*) 743; in bonds.

---

747. [Insignia of authority.] **Sceptre.**—**N.** sceptre, regalia, rod of empire, sword of state, mace, *fasces*, wand; staff, – of office; *bâton*, truncheon; flag &c. (*insignia*) 550; ensign –, emblem –, badge –, insignia- of authority, rank marks, brassard, badge, sash; cocked –, brass- hat.

epaulette, aiguilette, crown, star, eagle, bar, double bar, pip, stripe, chevron, curl, ring, anchor, shoulder-strap, tab.

throne, chair, musnud, divan, dais, woolsack.

toga, pall, mantle, robes of state, ermine, purple.

crown, coronet, diadem, tiara, triple crown, mitre, crozier, cardinal's hat &c.; cap of maintenance; decoration; title &c. 877; portfolio.

key, signet, seals, talisman; helm; reins &c. (*means of restraint*) 752.

---

748. Freedom.—**N.** freedom, liberty, independence; licence &c. (*permission*) 760; facility &c. 705.

scope, range, latitude, play; free –, full- -play, – scope; free stage and no

749. Subjection. — **N.** subjection; depend-ence, -ance, -ency; subordination; thrall, thraldom, enthralment, subjugation, bondage, serfdom; feudal--ism, -ity; vassalage, villenage; slavery,

favour; swing, full swing, elbow-room, margin, rope, wide berth; Liberty Hall.

franchise, denization; free –, freed-, livery- man; denizen.

autonomy, self-government, home-rule, self-determination, liberalism, free trade; non-interference &c. 706.

immunity, exemption; emancipation &c. (*liberation*) 750; en-, af-franchise-ment; rights, privileges.

free land, freehold; allodium; frank-almoigne, mortmain.

independent, free-lance, -thinker, -trader.

V. be -free &c. *adj.*; have -scope &c. *n.*, – the run of, – one's own way, – a will of one's own, – one's fling; do what one -likes, – wishes, – pleases, – chooses; go at large, feel at home, paddle one's own canoe; stand on one's -legs, – rights; shift for oneself.

take a liberty; make -free with, – oneself quite at home; use a freedom; take -leave, – French leave.

set free &c. (*liberate*) 750; give the reins to &c. (*permit*) 760; allow –, give-scope &c. *n.* to; give a horse his head.

make free of; give the -freedom of, – franchise; en-, af-franchise.

laisser -faire, – aller; live and let live; leave to oneself; leave –, let- alone; mind one's own business.

Adj. free, – as air; out of harness, independent, at large, loose, scot free; left -alone, – to oneself.

in full swing; uncaught, uncon-strained, unbuttoned, unconfined, un-restrained, unchecked, unprevented, unhindered, unobstructed, unbound, uncontrolled, untrammelled.

unsubject, ungoverned, unenslaved, unenthralled, unchained, unshackled, unfettered, unreined, unbridled, un-curbed, unmuzzled, unimpeded.

unrestricted, unlimited, unconditional; absolute; discretionary &c. (*optional*) 600.

unassailed, unforced, uncompelled.

unbiassed, unprejudiced, uninfluenced, spontaneous.

free and easy; at –, at one's- ease; *dégagé*, quite at home; wanton, rampant, irrepressible, unvanquished.

exempt; freed &c. 750; freeborn; autonomous, freehold, allodial; *gratis* &c. 815.

unclaimed, going a begging.

Adv. freely &c. *adj.*; *ad libitum* &c. (*at will*) 600.

enslavement, involuntary servitude.

service; servi-tude, -torship; ten-dence, employ, tutelage, clientship; liability &c. 177; constraint &c. 751; oppression &c. (*severity*) 739; yoke &c. (*means of restraint*) 752; submission &c. 725; obedience &c. 743.

V. be -subject &c. *adj.*; be –, lie- at the mercy of; depend –, lean –, hang-upon; fall -a prey to, – under; play second fiddle.

be a -mere machine, – puppet, – foot-ball; not dare to say one's soul is his own; drag a chain.

serve &c. 746; obey &c. 743; submit &c. 725.

break in, tame; subject, subjugate; master &c. 731; tread -down, – under foot; weigh down; drag at one's chariot wheels; reduce to -subjection, – slavery; en-, in-, be-thral; enslave, lead captive; take into custody &c. (*restrain*) 751; rule &c. 737; drive into a corner, hold at the sword's point; keep under; hold in -bondage, – leading strings, – swad-dling clothes.

Adj. subject, dependent, subordi-nate; feud-al, -atory; in subjection to, under control; in -leading strings, – harness; subjected, enslaved &c. *v.*; constrained &c. 751; subservient, ser-vile, fawning, slavish, obsequious, cringing; down-trodden; over-borne, -whelmed; under the lash, on the hip, led by the nose, henpecked; the -pup-pet, – sport, – plaything- of; under one's -orders, – command, – thumb; like dirt under one's feet; a slave to; at the mercy of; in the -power, – hands, – clutches- of; at the feet of; at one's beck and call &c. (*obedient*) 743; liable &c. 177; parasitical; stipendiary.

Adv. under.

_____

750. Liberation.—**N.** liberation, disengagement, release, disenthrallment, enlargement, emancipation; af-, enfranchisement; manumission; discharge, dismissal.

deliverance &c. 672; redemption, extrication, acquittance, absolution; acquittal &c. 970; escape &c. 671.

V. liberate, free; set -free, – clear, – at liberty; render free, emancipate, release; en-, af-franchise; manumit; enlarge; dis-band, -charge, -miss, -enthral; let -go, – loose, – out, – slip; cast –, turn- adrift; deliver &c. 672; absolve &c. (*acquit*) 970; reprieve.

unfetter &c. 751; untie &c. 44; loose &c. (*disjoin*) 44; loosen, relax; un-bolt, -bar, -close, -cork, -clog, -hand, -bind, -latch, -chain, -harness; dis-engage, -entangle; clear, extricate, unloose.

gain –, obtain –, acquire- one's -liberty &c. 748; get -rid, – clear- of; deliver oneself from; shake off the yoke, slip the collar; break -loose, – prison; tear asunder one's bonds, cast off trammels; escape &c. 671.

Adj. at -liberty, – large, free, liberated &c. *v.*; out of harness &c. 748; adrift.

Int. unhand me! let me go!

---

751. Restraint.—**N.** restraint; hindrance &c. 706; coercion &c. (*compulsion*) 744; cohibition, constraint, repression; discipline, control, self-restraint &c. 604.

confinement; durance, duress; im-, prisonment; incarceration, coarctation, entombment, mancipation, durance vile, thrall, -dom, limbo, captivity; blockade; quarantine; detention.

arrest, -ation; custody, keep, care, charge, ward, restringency.

curb &c. (*means of restraint*) 752; *lettres de cachet*.

limitation, restriction, protection, monopoly; prohibition &c. 761; economic pressure.

prisoner &c. 754.

V. restrain, check; put –, lay- under restraint; en-, in-, be-thral; restrict; debar &c. (*hinder*) 706; constrain; coerce &c. (*compel*) 744; curb, control; hold –, keep- -back, – from, – in, – in check, – within bounds; hold in -leash, – leading strings; withhold.

keep under; repress, suppress; smother; pull in, rein in; hold, – fast; keep a tight hand on; prohibit &c. 761; in-, co-hibit.

enchain; fasten &c. (*join*) 43; fetter, shackle; en-, trammel; bridle, muzzle, gag, pinion, manacle, handcuff, tie one's hands, hobble, bind hand and foot; swathe, swaddle; pin –, peg- down; tether, picket; tie, – up, – down; secure; forge fetters.

confine; shut –, clap –, lock –, box –, mew –, bottle –, cork –, seal –, button- up; shut –, hem –, bolt –, wall –, rail- in; impound, pen, coop; enclose &c. (*circumscribe*) 229; cage; in-, en-cage; close the door upon, cloister; imprison, immure; incarcerate, entomb; clap –, lay- under hatches; put in -irons, – a strait waistcoat; throw –, cast- into prison; put into bilboes.

arrest; take -up, – charge of, – into custody; take –, make- -prisoner, – captive; captivate; lead -captive, – into captivity; send –, commit- to prison; commit; give in -charge, – custody; subjugate &c. 749.

Adj. re-, con-strained; imprisoned &c. *v.*; pent up; jammed in, wedged in; under -restraint, – lock and key, – hatches; serving –, doing- time; in swaddling clothes; on *parole*; in custody &c. (*prisoner*) 754; cohibitive; coactive &c. (*compulsory*) 744.

stiff, restringent, straitlaced, hide-bound.

ice-, wind-, weather-bound; 'cabined, cribbed, confined'; in Lob's pound, laid by the heels.

Adv. in captivity, under arrest, behind the bars, in -prison, – jail, – durance vile.

752. [Means of restraint.] Prison.—**N.** prison, -house; jail, gaol, cage, coop, den, death house, condemned –, cell; stronghold, fortress, keep, donjon, dungeon, *Bastille, oubliette*, bridewell, house of correction, hulks, toll-booth, panopticon, penitentiary, guard-room, clink, can, stir, tronk, jug, lock-up, hold; round –, watch –, station –, sponging-house; station; house of detention, black hole, pen, fold, pound; enclosure &c. 232; penal settlement; chain gang; debtors' prison; reformatory; federal penitentiary, state prison; criminal lunatic asylum; bilboes, stocks, limbo, quod.

Dartmoor, Newgate, Fleet, Marshalsea; King's (*or* Queen's) Bench; Sing Sing, Dannemora.

bond; strap, bandage, splint, tourniquet; irons, pinion, gyve, fetter, shackle, trammel, manacle, handcuff, bracelets, darbies, strait waistcoat, strait-jacket.

yoke, collar, halter, harness; muzzle, gag, bit, brake, curb, snaffle, bridle; rein, -s; ribbons, lines, bearing-rein; martingale, leading string; tether, picket, band, guy, chain; cord &c. (*fastening*) 45.

bolt, bar, lock, padlock, rail, wall; paling, palisade; fence; barrier, barricade.

brake, drag &c. (*hindrance*) 706.

753. Keeper.—**N.** keeper, custodian, *custos*, ranger, warder, jailer, gaoler, turnkey, castellan, guard; watch, -dog, -man; Charley; sen-try, -tinel; watch and ward; *concierge*, coast-guard, *guarda costa*, gamekeeper.

escort, body guard, convoy.

protector, governor, duenna; guardian; governess &c. (*teacher*) 540; nurse, *bonne, ayah, amah.*

754. Prisoner.—**N.** prisoner, captive, *détenu*, close prisoner.

jail-bird, ticket-of-leave man.

V. stand committed; be -imprisoned &c. 751.

Adj. imprisoned &c. 751; in -prison, – quod, – durance vile, – limbo, – custody, – charge, – chains; under -lock and key, – hatches; on *parole*; detained at his Majesty's pleasure.

755. [Vicarious authority.] Commission.—**N.** commission, delegation; con-, as-signment; procuration; deputation, legation, mission, embassy; agency, agentship; power of attorney, proxy; clerkship.

errand, charge, *brevet*, diploma, *exequatur*, permit &c. (*permission*) 760.

appointment, nomination, return; charter; ordination; installation, inauguration, investiture; accession, coronation, enthronement.

vicegerency; regency, regentship.

viceroy &c. 745; consignee &c. 758; deputy &c. 759.

V. commission, delegate, depute; consign, assign; charge; in-, en-trust; turn over to; commit, – to the hands of; authorize &c. (*permit*) 760.

put in commission, accredit, engage, hire, bespeak, appoint, name, nominate, return, ordain; install, induct,

756. Abrogation.—**N.** abrogation, annulment, nullification; cancelling &c. *v.*; cancel; revo-cation, -kement; repeal, rescission, defeasance.

dismissal, *congé*, demission; depos-al, -ition; sack, dethronement; disestablish-, disendow-ment; deconsecration.

aboli-tion, -shment; dissolution.

counter-order, -mand; repudiation, retractation; recantation &c. (*tergiversation*) 607.

V. abrogate, annul, cancel; destroy &c. 162; abolish; revoke, repeal, rescind, reverse, retract, recall; over-rule, -ride; set aside; disannul, dissolve, quash, nullify, declare null and void; dis-establish, -endow; deconsecrate.

disclaim &c. (*deny*) 536; ignore, repudiate; recant &c. 607; divest oneself, break off.

counter-mand, -order; do away with; sweep –, brush- away; throw -over-

inaugurate, invest, crown; en-roll, -list.

employ, empower; give power of attorney to; set –, place- over; send out.

be commissioned, be accredited; represent, stand for; stand in the -stead, – place, – shoes- of.

Adj. commissioned &c. *v.*

Adv. *per procuratione.*

board, – to the dogs; scatter to the winds, cast behind.

dismiss, discard; cast –, turn- -off, – out, – adrift, – out of doors, – aside, – away; send -off, – away, – about one's business; discharge, get rid of, fire out, fire &c. (*eject*) 297; jilt.

cashier; break; oust; set down, unseat, -saddle; un-, de-, disen-throne; depose, uncrown; unfrock, strike off the roll; dis-bar, -bench.

be -abrogated &c.; receive its quietus.

·**Adj.** abrogated &c. *v.*; *functus officio.*

Int. get along with you! begone! go about your business! away with!

---

757. Resignation.—N. resignation, retirement, abdication, renunciation, abjuration, disclaimer, abandonment, relinquishment.

V. resign; give –, throw- up; lay down, throw up the cards, wash one's hands of, abjure, renounce, forego, disclaim, abandon, relinquish, retract, demit; deny &c. 536.

abrogate &c. 756; desert &c. (*relinquish*) 624; get rid of &c. 782.

abdicate; vacate, – one's seat; accept the stewardship of the Chiltern Hundreds; retire; tender –, send in –, hand in- one's resignation.

Adj. abdicant, renunciatory &c. *v.*

Phr. 'Othello's occupation's gone.'

---

758. Consignee.—N. consignee, trustee, nominee, committee.

delegate; commiss-ary, -ioner; emissary, envoy, commissionaire; messenger &c. 534.

diplomatist, diplomat, *corps diplomatique*, embassy; am-, em-bassador; representative, resident, consul, legate, nuncio, internuncio, *chargé d'affaires, attaché.*

vicegerent &c. (*deputy*) 759; plenipotentiary.

functionary, placeman, curator; treasurer &c. 801; agent, factor, bailiff, steward, clerk, secretary, attorney, solicitor, proctor, broker, underwriter, commission agent, auctioneer, one's man of business; factotum &c. (*director*) 694; caretaker.

negotiator, go between; middleman; under agent, *employé*; servant &c. 746.

salesman; commercial, – traveller; bagman, *commis-voyageur*, touter.

newspaper –, own –, war –, special- correspondent; reporter.

---

759. Deputy.—N. deputy, substitute, vice, proxy, *locum tenens*, delegate, representative, next friend, surrogate, secondary.

regent, vicegerent, vizier, minister, vicar; premier &c. (*director*) 694; chancellor, prefect, provost, warden, lieutenant, archon, consul, proconsul; viceroy &c. (*governor*) 745; commissioner &c. 758; plenipotentiary, *alter ego.*

team, eight, eleven; champion.

V. be -deputy &c. *n.*; stand –, appear –, hold a brief –, answer- for; represent; stand –, walk- in the shoes of; stand in the stead of.

substitute, ablegate, accredit; commission, empower, delegate &c. 755.

Adj. acting; vice, -regal; accredited to.

Adv. in behalf of, by proxy.

Section II. Special Intersocial Volition

760. Permission.—N. permission, leave; allow-, suffer-ance; toler-ance, -ation; liberty, law, licence, concession, grace; indulgence &c. (*lenity*) 740; favour, dispensation, exemption, release; connivance; vouchsafement.

authorization, warranty, accordance, admission.

permit, warrant, *brevet*, precept, sanction, authority, *firman*; pass, -port; furlough, licence, *carte blanche*, ticket of leave; grant, charter, patent.

V. permit; give -permission &c. *n.*, – power; let, allow, admit; suffer, bear with, tolerate, recognize; concede &c. 762; accord, vouchsafe, favour, humour, gratify, indulge, stretch a point; wink at, connive at; shut one's eyes to.

grant, empower, charter, enfranchise, privilege, confer a privilege, license, authorize, warrant; sanction; entrust &c. (*commission*) 755.

give -*carte blanche*, – the reins to, – scope to &c. (*freedom*) 748; leave -alone, – it to one, – the door open; open the -door to, – floodgates; give a loose to.

let off; absolve &c. (*acquit*) 970; release, exonerate, dispense with.

ask –, beg –, request- -leave, – permission.

761. Prohibition.—N. pro-, in-hibition; *veto*, disallowance; interdict, -ion; injunction; embargo, ban, *verboten*, taboo, proscription; *index expurgatorius*; restriction &c. (*restraint*) 751; hindrance &c. 706; forbidden fruit.

V. pro-, in-hibit; forbid, put one's *veto* upon, disallow; bar; debar &c. (*hinder*) 706, forefend.

keep -in, – within bounds; restrain &c. 751; cohibit, withhold, limit, circumscribe, clip the wings of, restrict, narrow; interdict, taboo; put –, place-under -an interdiction, – the ban; proscribe, censor; exclude, shut out; shut –, bolt –, show- the door; warn off; dash the cup from one's lips; forbid the banns.

Adj. prohibit-ive, -ory; interdictive; proscriptive; restrictive, exclusive; forbidding &c. *v.*

prohibited &c. *v.*; not -permitted &c. 760; unlicensed, contraband, under the ban of; illegal &c. 964; unauthorized, not to be thought of.

Adv. on no account &c. (*no*) 536.

Int. forbid it heaven! &c. (*deprecation*) 766.

hands –, keep- off! hold! stop! avast!

Phr. that will never do.

Adj. permitting &c. *v.*; permissive, indulgent; permitted &c. *v.*; patent, chartered, permissible, allowable, lawful, legitimate, legal; legalized &c. (*law*) 963; licit; unforbid, -den; unconditional.

Adv. permissibly; by –, with –, on- -leave &c. *n.*; *speciali gratiâ*; under favour of; *pace*; *ad libitum* &c. (*freely*) 748, (*at will*) 600; by all means &c. (*willingly*) 602; yes &c. (*assent*) 488.

---

762. Consent.—N. consent; assent &c. 488; acquiescence; approval &c. 931; compliance, agreement, concession; yield-ance, -ingness; accession, acknowledgment, acceptance, agnition.

settlement, ratification, confirmation, adjustment.

permit &c. (*permission*) 760; promise &c. 768.

V. consent; assent &c. 488; yield assent, admit, allow, concede, grant, yield; come -over, – round; give in to, acknowledge, agnize, give consent, comply with, acquiesce, agree to, fall in with, accede, accept, embrace an offer, close with, take at one's word, have no objection.

satisfy, meet one's wishes, settle, come to terms &c. 488; not -refuse &c. 764; turn a willing ear &c. (*willingness*) 602; jump at; deign, vouchsafe; promise &c. 768.

Adj. consenting &c. *v.*; agreeable, compliant; agreed &c. (*assent*) 488; unconditional.

Adv. yes &c. (*assent*) 488; by all means &c. (*willingly*) 602; if –, as-you please; be it so, so be it, well and good, of course.

763. Offer.—N. offer, proffer, pre-sentation, tender, bid, overture; pro-pos-al, -ition; motion, invitation; can-didature; offering &c. (*gift*) 784.

V. offer, proffer, present, tender; bid; propose, move; make -a motion, – advances; start; invite, hold out, place- at one's disposal, – in one's way, put forward.

hawk about; offer for sale &c. 796; press &c. (*request*) 765; lay at one's feet.

offer –, present- oneself; volunteer, come forward, be a candidate; stand –, bid- for; seek; be at one's service; go a begging; bribe &c. (*give*) 784.

Adj. offer-ing, -ed &c. *v.*; in the market, for sale, to let, disengaged, on hire.

764. Refusal.—N. refusal, rejection; non-, in-compliance; denial; declining &c. *v.*; declension; peremptory –, flat –, point blank- refusal; repulse, rebuff; discountenance.

recusancy, renunciation, abnegation, negation, protest, disclaimer; dissent &c. 489; revocation &c. 756.

V. refuse, reject, deny, decline; nill, negative; refuse –, withhold- one's assent; shake the head; close the -hand, – purse; grudge, begrudge, be slow to, hang fire.

be deaf to; turn -a deaf ear to, – one's back upon; set one's face against, discountenance, not hear of, have nothing to do with, wash one's hands of, stand aloof, forswear, set aside, cast behind one; not yield an inch &c. (*obstinacy*) 606.

resist, cross; not -grant &c. 762; repel, repulse; shut –, slam- the door in one's face; rebuff; send -back, – to the right about, – away with a flea in the ear; deny oneself, not be at home to; discard &c. (*repudiate*) 610; rescind &c. (*revoke*) 756; disclaim, protest; dissent &c. 489.

Adj. refusing &c. *v.*; rest-ive, -iff; recusant; uncomplying, non-compliant, unconsenting, uncomplaisant, protestant; not willing to hear of, deaf to.

refused &c. *v.*; ungranted, out of the question, not to be thought of, impossible.

Adv. no &c. 536; on no account, not for the world; no thank you.

Phr. *non possumus*; [ironically] your humble servant; *bien obligé*.

765. Request.—N. requ-est, -isition; claim &c. (*demand*) 741; petition, suit, prayer; begging letter, round-robin.

motion, overture, application, can-vass, address, appeal, apostrophe; im-precation; rogation; proposal, propo-sition.

orison &c. (*worship*) 990; incanta-tion &c. (*spell*) 993.

mendicancy; asking, panhandling, begging &c. *v.*; postulation, solicita-tion, invitation, entreaty, importunity, supplication, instance, impetration, imploration, obsecration, obtestation, invocation, interpellation.

V. request, ask; beg, crave, sue, pray, petition, solicit, invite, pop the question, make bold to ask; beg -leave, – a boon; apply to, call to, put to; call -upon, – for; make –, address –, prefer –, put up- a -request, – prayer, – petition;

766. [Negative request.] **Depreca-tion.—N.** deprecation, expostulation; remonstrance; intercession, mediation.

V. deprecate, protest, expostulate, enter a protest, intercede for.

Adj. deprecatory, expostulatory, in-tercessory, mediatorial.

deprecated, protested.

un-, unbe-sought; unasked &c. (*see* ask &c. 765).

Int. cry you mercy! God forbid! forbid it Heaven! Heaven -forefend, – forbid! far be it from! hands off! &c. (*prohibition*) 761.

make -application, – a requisition; ask –, trouble- one for; claim &c. (*demand*) 741; offer up prayers &c. (*worship*) 990; whistle for.

beg hard, entreat, beseech, plead, supplicate, implore, apostrophize; conjure, adjure; obtest; cry to, kneel to, appeal to; invoke, evoke; impetrate, imprecate, ply, press, urge, beset, importune, dun, tax, clamour for; cry -aloud, – for help; fall on one's knees; throw oneself at the feet of; come down on one's marrow-bones.

beg from door to door, send the hat round, go a begging; mendicate, mump, cadge, panhandle, beg one's bread.

dance attendance on, besiege, knock at the door.

bespeak, canvass, tout, make interest, court; seek, bid for &c. (*offer*) 763; publish the banns.

Adj. requesting &c. *v.*; precatory; suppli-ant, -cant, -catory; invoc-, imprec-, rog-atory; postulant, mendicant.

importunate, clamorous, urgent; solicitous; cap in hand; on one's -knees, – bended knees, – marrow-bones.

Adv. prithee, do, please, pray; be so good as, be good enough; have the goodness, vouchsafe, will you, I pray thee, if you please.

Int. for -God's, – heaven's, – goodness', – mercy's- sake.

767. Petitioner.—**N.** petitioner, solicitor, applicant; suppli-ant, -cant; suitor, candidate, claimant, postulant, aspirant, competitor, bidder; place –, pot- hunter; prizer.

beggar, mendicant, mumper, sturdy beggar, cadger, panhandler.

canvasser, barker, touter &c. 768.

sycophant, parasite &c. 886.

Section III. Conditional Intersocial Volition

768. Promise.—**N.** promise, undertaking, word, troth, plight, pledge, *parole*, word of honour, vow; oath &c. (*affirmation*) 535; profession, assurance, warranty, guarantee, insurance, obligation; contract &c. 769.

engagement, pre-engagement: affiance; betroth, -al, -ment; marriage -compact, – vow.

V. promise; give a -promise &c. *n.*; undertake, engage; make –, form- an engagement; enter -into, – on- an engagement; bind –, tie –, pledge –, commit –, take upon- oneself; vow; swear &c. (*affirm*) 535, give –, pass –, pledge –, plight- one's -word, – honour, – credit, – troth; betroth, plight faith; take the vows.

assure, warrant, guarantee, vouch for, avouch, covenant &c. 769; attest &c. (*bear witness*) 467.

hold out an expectation; contract an obligation; become -bound to, – sponsor for; answer –, be answerable- for; secure; give security &c. 771; underwrite.

adjure, administer an oath, put to one's oath, swear a witness.

Adj. promising &c. *v.*; promissory; votive; under hand and seal; upon -oath, – affirmation.

promised &c. *v.*; affianced, pledged, bound; committed, compromised; in for it.

Adv. as one's head shall answer for; upon my honour.

Phr. in for a penny, in for a pound.

768a. Release from engagement.— **N.** release &c. (*liberation*) 750.

Adj. absolute; unconditional &c. (*free*) 748.

769. Compact.—N. compact, contract, agreement, bargain, deal, transaction; affidation; pact, -ion; bond, covenant, indenture.

stipulation, settlement, convention; compromise, *cartel*.

protocol, treaty, *concordat, Zollverein, Sonderbund*, charter, *Magna Charta*, Pragmatic Sanction.

negotiation &c. (*bargaining*) 794; diplomacy &c. (*mediation*) 724; negotiator &c. (*agent*) 758.

ratification, completion, signature, seal, sigil, signet.

V. contract, covenant, agree for, engage &c. (*promise*) 768.

treat, negotiate, stipulate, make terms; bargain &c. (*barter*) 794.

make –, strike- a bargain; come to -terms, – an understanding; compromise &c. 774; set at rest; close, – with; conclude, complete, settle; confirm, ratify, clench, subscribe, underwrite; en-, in-dorse; put the seal to; sign, seal &c. (*attest*) 467; indent.

take one at one's word, bargain by inch of candle.

Adj. contractual, agreed &c. *v.*; conventional; under hand and seal; signed, sealed and delivered.

Phr. *caveat emptor.*

770. Conditions.—N. conditions, terms; articles, – of agreement.

clauses, provisions; proviso &c. (*qualification*) 469; covenant, stipulation, obligation, *ultimatum, sine quâ non; casus fœderis*.

V. make –, come to- -terms &c. (*contract*) 769; make it a condition, stipulate, insist upon, make a point of; bind, tie up.

Adj. conditional, provisional, guarded, fenced, hedged in.

Adv. conditionally &c. (*with qualification*) 469; provisionally, *pro re natâ*; on condition; with a reservation.

771. Security.—N. security; guaran-ty, -tee; gage, warranty, bond, tie, pledge, plight, mortgage, debenture, hypothecation, bill of sale, lien, pignus, pawn, pignoration; real security; bottomry; collateral, vadium.

stake, deposit, earnest, handsel, caution.

promissory note; bill, – of exchange; I.O.U.; personal security, covenant, specialty; *parole* &c. (*promise*) 768.

acceptance, indorsement, signature, execution, stamp, seal.

spon-sor, -sion, -sorship; surety, bail; mainpernor, hostage.

recognizance; deed –, covenant- of indemnity.

authentication, verification, warrant, certificate, voucher, docket, doquet; record &c. 551; probate, attested copy.

receipt; ac-, quittance; discharge, release.

muniment, title-deed, instrument; deed, – poll; assurance, insurance, indenture; charter &c. (*compact*) 769; charter-poll; paper, parchment, settlement, will, testament, last will and testament, codicil.

V. give -security, – bail, – substantial bail; go bail; pawn, impawn, hock, spout, mortgage, hypothecate, impignorate.

guarantee, warrant, assure; accept, indorse, underwrite, insure.

execute, stamp; sign, seal &c. (*evidence*) 467.

let, sett; grant –, take –, hold- a lease; hold in pledge; lend on security &c. 787.

Adj. secure, -ed; pledged &c. *v.*; in pawn, on deposit.

772. Observance.—N. observance, performance, compliance; obedience

773. Non-observance. — N. non-observance &c. 772; evasion, inob-

&c. 743; fulfilment, satisfaction, discharge; acquit-tance, -tal.

adhesion, acknowledgment; fidelity &c. (*probity*) 939; exact &c. 494- observance.

V. observe, comply with, respect, acknowledge, abide by; cling to, adhere to, be faithful to, act up to; meet, fulfil; carry -out, - into execution; execute, perform, keep, satisfy, discharge; do one's office.

perform -, fulfill -, discharge -, acquit oneself of- an obligation; make good; make good -, keep- one's -word, - promise; redeem one's pledge; keep faith with, stand to one's engagement.

Adj. observant, faithful, true, loyal; honourable &c. 939; true as the -dial to the sun, - needle to the pole; punct-ual, -ilious; meticulous; literal &c. (*exact*) 494; as good as one's word.

Adv. faithfully &c. *adj.*

servance, failure, omission, neglect, laches, laxity, informality.

infringement, infraction; violation, transgression.

retractation, repudiation, nullification; protest; forfeiture.

lawlessness; disobedience &c. 742; bad faith &c. 940.

V. fail, neglect, omit, elude, evade, give the go by to, cut, set aside, ignore; shut -, close- one's eyes to, avoid.

infringe, transgress, pirate, violate, break, trample under foot, do violence to, drive a coach and six through.

discard, protest, repudiate, fling to the winds, set at naught, nullify, declare null and void; cancel &c. (*wipe off*) 552.

retract, go back from, be off, forfeit, go from one's word, palter; stretch -, strain- a point.

Adj. violating &c. *v.*; lawless, transgressive; elusive, evasive; lax, casual; non-observant.

unfulfilled &c. (*see* fulfil &c. 772).

---

774. Compromise.—N. com-promise, -mutation, -position; middle term, *mezzo termine*; compensation &c. 30; adjustment, mutual concession.

V. com-promise, -mute, -pound; take the mean; split the difference, meet one half way, give and take; come to terms &c. (*contract*) 769; submit to -, abide by- arbitration; patch up, bridge over, fix up, arrange; adjust, - differences; agree; make -the best of, - a virtue of necessity; take the will for the deed.

Section IV. Possessive Relations*

1°. *Property in general*

775. Acquisition.—N. acquisition; gaining &c. *v.*; obtainment; procuration, -ement; purchase, descent, inheritance; gift &c. 784.

recovery, retrieval, revendication, replevin; redemption, salvage, trover; find, *trouvaille*, foundling.

gain, thrift; money-making, -grubbing; lucre, filthy lucre, loaves and fishes, the main chance, pelf; emolument &c. 973; wealth &c. 803.

profit, earnings, winnings, innings, clean-up, pickings, perquisite, net profit; income &c. (*receipt*) 810; proceeds, -duce, -duct; out-come, -put;

776. Loss.—N. loss; de-, perdition; forfeiture, lapse.

privation, bereavement; deprivation &c. (*dispossession*) 789; riddance.

V. lose; incur -, experience -, meet with- a loss; miss; mislay, let slip, allow to slip through the fingers, squander; be without &c. (*exempt*) 777a; forfeit.

get rid of &c. 782; waste &c. 638.

be lost, lapse.

Adj. losing &c. *v.*; not having &c. 777a.

shorn of, deprived of; denuded, bereaved, bereft, *minus*, cut off; dispos-

* That is, relations which concern property.

return, fruit, crop, harvest, tilth; second crop, aftermath; benefit &c. (*good*) 618.

sweepstakes, trick, prize, pool.

[Fraudulent acquisition] subreption·
theft, stealing &c. 791.

V. acquire, get, gain, win, earn, obtain, procure, gather, annex; collect &c. 72; pick, – up; glean, take &c. 789.

find; come –, pitch –, light- upon; scrape -up, – together; get in, reap and carry, net, bag, sack, bring home, secure, come across, derive, draw, get in the harvest.

profit; make –, draw- profit; turn to -profit, – account; make -capital out of, – money by; obtain a return, reap the fruits of; reap –, gain- an advantage; turn -a penny, – an honest penny; make the pot boil, bring grist to the mill; make –, coin –, raise- money; raise -funds, – the wind; fill one's pocket &c. (*wealth*) 803.

treasure up &c. (*store*) 636; realize, clear; produce &c. 161; take &c. 789.

get back, recover, regain, retrieve, revendicate, replevy, redeem, come by one's own.

come -by, – in for; receive &c. 785; inherit; step into, – a fortune, – the shoes of; succeed to.

get -hold of, – between one's finger and thumb, – into one's hand, – at; take –, come into –, enter into- possession.

be -profitable &c. *adj.*; pay, answer.

accrue &c. (*be received*) 785.

Adj. acquir-ing, -ed &c. *v.*; acquisitive; productive, profitable, advantageous, gainful, remunerative, paying, lucrative.

sessed &c. 789; rid of, quit of; out of pocket.

lost &c. *v.*; long lost; irretrievable &c. (*hopeless*) 859; irredentist; off one's hands.

Int. farewell to! adieu to! good riddance!

---

777. Possession.—N. possession, seisin; ownership &c. 780; occupancy; hold, -ing; tenure, tenancy, feodality, dependency; villenage; socage, chivalry, knight service.

exclusive possession, impropriation, monopoly, corner; retention &c. 781; pre-possession, -occupancy; nine points of the law.

future possession, heritage, inheritance, heirship, reversion, fee, seigniority, feud, fief.

bird in hand, *uti possidetis*, *chose* in possession.

V. possess, have, hold, occupy, enjoy; be -possessed of &c. *adj.*; have -in hand &c. *adj.*; own &c. 780; command.

inherit; come -to, – in for.

engross, monopolize, forestall, regrate, impropriate, have all to oneself, corner; have a firm hold of &c. (*retain*) 781; get into one's hand &c. (*acquire*) 775.

belong to, appertain to, pertain to; be -in one's possession &c. *adj.*; vest in.

Adj. possessing &c. *v.*; worth; possessed of, seized of, master of, in possession of; endowed –, blest –, instinct –, fraught –, laden –, charged –, instilled –, with.

possessed &c. *v.*; on hand, by one; in hand, in store, in stock; in one's -hands, – grasp, – possession; at one's -command, – disposal; one's own &c. (*property*) 780.

unsold; unshared.

777a. Exemption.—N. exemption; exception, immunity, privilege, release &c. 927*a*; absence &c. 187.

V. not -have &c. 777; be -without &c. *adj.*

Adj. exempt from, devoid of, without, unpossessed of, unblest with, immune from.

not -having &c. 777; unpossessed; untenanted &c. (*vacant*) 187; without an owner.

unobtained, unacquired.

778. [Joint possession.] Participation.—N. participation; co-, joint-tenancy; possession –, tenancy- in common; joint –, common- stock; co-, partnership; communion; community of -possessions, – goods; communalism, communism, socialism, collectivism; co-operation &c. 709; profit sharing.

snacks, co-portion, picnic, hotchpotch; co-heirship, -parceny, -parcenary; gavelkind.

participator, sharer; co-, partner; shareholder; co-, joint-tenant; tenants in common; co-heir, -parcener.

communist, socialist.

V. par-ticipate, -take; share, – in; come in for a share; go -shares, – snacks, – halves; share and share alike.

have –, possess –, be seized- -in common, – as joint tenants &c. *n.* join in; have a hand in &c. (*co-operate*) 709.

Adj. partaking &c. *v.*; communistic, socialistic, co-operative, profit sharing.

Adv. share and share alike.

779. Possessor.—N. possessor, holder; occup-ant, -ier; tenant; person –, man- -in possession &c. 777; renter, lodger, lessee, under-lessee; zemindar, ryot; tenant -on sufferance, – at will, – from year to year, – for years, – for life.

owner; propriet-or, -ress, -ary; impropriator, master, mistress, lord.

land-holder, -owner, -lord, -lady; lord -of the manor, – paramount; heritor, laird, vavasour, landed gentry, mesne lord.

cestui-que-trust, beneficiary, mortgagor.

grantee, feoffee, relessee, devisee; legat-ee, -ary.

trustee; holder &c.- of the legal estate; mortgagee.

right –, rightful- owner.

[Future possessor] heir, – apparent; – presumptive; heiress; inherit-or, -ress, -rix; reversioner, remainder-man.

780. Property.—N. property, possession, *suum cuique, meum et tuum.*

owner-, proprietor-, lord-ship; seignority; empire &c. (*dominion*) 737.

interest, stake, estate, right, title, claim, demand, holding; tenure &c. (*possession*) 777; vested –, contingent –, beneficial –, equitable-interest; use, trust, benefit; legal –, equitable- estate; seisin.

absolute interest, paramount estate, freehold; fee, – simple, – tail; estate -in fee, – in tail, – tail; estate in tail -male, – female, – general.

limitation, term, lease, settlement, strict settlement, particular estate; estate -for life, – for years, – *pur autre vie*; remainder, reversion, expectancy, possibility.

dower, dowry, *dot*, jointure, marriage portion, appanage, inheritance, heritage, patrimony, alimony; legacy &c. (*gift*) 784.

assets, belongings, means, resources, circumstances; wealth &c. 803; money &c. 800; what one -is worth, – will cut up for; estate and effects.

landed –, real- -estate, – property; realty; land, -s; subdivision; plot, site; tenements; hereditaments; corporeal –, incorporeal- hereditaments; acres; ground &c. (*earth*) 342; acquest; messuage.

territory, state, kingdom, principality, realm, empire, protectorate, margravate, dependancy, colony, sphere of influence, mandate.

manor, honour, domain, demesne; farm, ranch, plantation, *hacienda*; allodium &c. (*free*) 748; fieff, feoff, feud, zemindary, dependency.

free-, copy-, lease-holds; chattels real; fixtures, plant, heirloom easement; folkland; right of -common, – user.

personal -property, – estate, – effects; personalty, chattels, goods, effects, movables; stock, – in trade; things, traps, rattle-traps, paraphernalia; equipage &c. 633.

parcels, appurtenances.

impedimenta; lug-, bag-gage; bag and baggage; pelf; cargo, lading.

rent-roll; income &c. (*receipts*) 810.

patent, copyright; *chose* in action; credit &c. 805; debt &c. 806.

V. possess &c. 777; be the -possessor &c. 779- of· own; have for one's own, – very own; come in for, inherit; enfeoff.

savour of the realty.

be one's -property &c. *n.*; belong to; ap-, pertain to.

Adj. one's own; landed, predial, manorial, allodial, seigniorial; free-, copy-, lease-hold; feu-, feo-dal; hereditary, entailed, personal.

Adv. to one's -credit, – account; to the good.

to one and -his heirs for ever, – the heirs of his body, – his heirs and assigns, – his executors, administrators and assigns.

---

781. Retention.—N. retention; retaining &c. *v.*; keep, detention, custody; tenacity, firm hold, grasp, gripe, grip, iron grip.

fangs, teeth, claws, talons, nail, hook, tentacle, *tenaculum*; bond &c. (*vinculum*) 45.

clutches, tongs, forceps, pincers, nippers, pliers, tweezers, vise.

paw, hand, finger, wrist, fist, neaf, neif.

bird in hand; captive &c. 754.

V. retain, keep; hold, – fast, – tight, – one's own, – one's ground; clinch, clench, clutch, grasp, gripe, hug, have a firm hold of.

secure, withold, detain; hold –, keep-back; keep close; husband &c. (*store*) 636; reserve; have –, keep- in stock &c. (*possess*) 777; entail, tie up, settle.

Adj. retaining &c. *v.*; retentive, tenacious.

unforfeited, undeprived, undisposed, uncommunicated.

incommunicable, inalienable; in mortmain; in strict settlement.

Phr. *uti possidetis.*

---

782. Relinquishment. — N. relinquishment, abandonment &c. (*of a course*) 624; renunciation, expropriation, dereliction; cession, surrender, dispensation; resignation &c. 757; riddance.

derelict &c. *adj.*; jetsam; waif, foundling, orphan.

V. relinquish, give up, surrender, yield, cede; let -go, – slip; spare, drop, resign, forego, renounce, abjure, abandon, expropriate, give away, dispose of, part with; lay -aside, – apart, – down, – on the shelf &c. (*disuse*) 678; set –, put- aside; make away with, cast behind; discard, cast off, dismiss; maroon.

give -notice to quit, – warning; supersede; be –, get- -rid of, – quit of; eject &c. 297.

rid –, disburden –, divest –, dispossess- oneself of; wash one's hands of; divorce, desert; disinherit, cut off.

cast –, throw –, pitch –, fling- -away, – aside, – overboard, – to the dogs; cast –, throw –, sweep- to the winds; put –, turn –, sweep- away; jettison. quit one's hold.

Adj. relinquished &c. *v.*; cast off, derelict; unowned, unappropriated, unculled; left &c. (*residuary*) 40; divorced; disinherited.

Int. away with!

2°. *Transfer of Property*

783. Transfer.—N. transfer, conveyance, assignment, alienation, abalienation; demise, limitation; conveyancing; transmission &c. (*transference*) 270; enfeoffment, bargain and sale, lease and release; exchange &c. (*interchange*) 148; barter &c. 794; substitution &c. 147.

succession, reversion; shifting -use, – trust; devolution.

V. transfer, convey; alien, -ate; assign; grant &c. (*confer*) 784; consign; make –, hand- over; pass, hand, transmit, negotiate; hand down; exchange &c. (*interchange*) 148.

change -hands, – from one to another; devolve, succeed; come into possession &c. (*acquire*) 775; take over.

abalienate; disinherit; dispossess &c. 789; substitute &c. 147.

Adj. alienable, negotiable, transferable, reversional.

Phr. estate coming into possession.

784. Giving.—N. giving &c. *v.*; bestowal, donation; present-ation, -ment; accordance; con-, cession; delivery, consignment, dispensation, communication, endowment; invest-ment, -iture; award.

almsgiving, charity, liberality, generosity; philanthropy &c. 910.

[Thing given] gift, donation, present, *cadeau*; fairing; free gift, boon, favour, benefaction, grant, offering, oblation, sacrifice, immolation.

grace, act of grace, *bonus, bonanza*.

allowance, contribution, subscription, subsidy, tribute, subvention.

bequest, legacy, devise, will, dotation, appanage; dowry; voluntary -settlement, – conveyance &c. 783; amortization.

alms, largess, bounty, dole, sportule, donative, help, oblation, offertory, Peter's pence, *honorarium*, gratuity, Maundy money, Christmas box, Easter offering, vail, tip, *douceur*, drink money, *pourboire, trinkgeld, backsheesh*; fee &c. (*recompense*) 973; consideration.

bribe, bait, ground-bait; peace-offering, handsel.

785. Receiving.—N. receiving &c. *v.*; acquisition &c. 775; reception &c. (*introduction*) 296; suscipiency, acceptance, admission.

re-, ac-cipient; assignee, devisee; lega-tee, -tary; grantee, feoffee, donee, relessee, lessee.

sportulary, stipendiary; beneficiary; pension-er, -ary; almsman.

income &c. (*receipt*) 810.

V. receive; take &c. 789; acquire &c. 775; admit.

take in, catch, touch; pocket; put into one's -pocket, – purse; accept; take off one's hands.

be received; come -in, – to hand; pass –, fall- into one's hand; go into one's pocket; fall to one's -lot, – share; come –, fall- to one; accrue; have -given &c. 784 to one.

Adj. receiving &c. *v.*; re-, suscipient.

received &c. *v.*; given &c. 784; second-hand.

not given, unbestowed &c. (*see* give, bestow &c. 784).

giver, grantor &c. *v.*; donor, feoffer, settlor; almoner; testator; investor, subscriber, contributor; fairy godmother; Santa Claus, benefactor &c. 816.

V. deliver, hand, pass, put into the hands of; hand –, make –, deliver –, pass –, turn- over.

present, give away, dispense, dispose of; give –, deal –, dole –, mete –, fork –, shell –, squeeze- out.

pay &c. 807; render, impart, communicate.

concede, cede, yield, part with, shed cast; spend &c. 809.

give, bestow, confer, grant, accord, award, assign.

entrust, consign, vest in.

make a present; allow, contribute, subscribe, donate, furnish its quota.

invest, endow, settle upon; bequeath, leave, devise.

furnish, supply, help; ad-, minister to; afford, spare; accommodate –, indulge –, favour- with; shower down upon; lavish, pour on, thrust upon; tip, bribe; tickle –, grease- the palm; offer &c. 763; sacrifice, immolate.

Adj. giving &c. *v.*; given &c. *v.*; allow-ed, -able; concessional; communicable; charitable, eleemosynary, sportulary, tributary; *gratis* &c. 815.

786. Apportionment.—N. apportion-, allot-, consign-, assign-, appointment; appropriation; dis-pensation, -tribution; allocation, division, deal; repartition; administration.

dividend, portion, contingent, share, allotment, lot, cut, split, measure, dose; dole, meed, pittance; *quantum*, ration; ratio, proportion, quota, *modicum*, mess, allowance.

V. apportion, divide; cut, split, divvy; distribute, administer, dispense; billet, allot, detail, cast, share, mete; portion –, parcel –, dole- out; deal, carve.

partition, assign, appropriate, appoint.

come in for one's share &c. (*participate*) 778.

Adj. apportioning &c. *v.*; respective.

Adv. respectively, each to each.

787. Lending.—N. lending &c. *v.*; loan, advance, accommodation, feneration; mortgage &c. (*security*) 771; investment.

mont de piété, pawnshop, hock shop, spout, my uncle's.

lender, pawnbroker, money lender, usurer, Jew, Shylock.

V. lend, advance, loan, accommodate with; lend on security; pawn &c. (*security*) 771.

intrust, invest; place –, put- out to interest; sink, risk.

let, demise, lease, sett, under-, sub-let.

Adj. lending &c. *v.*; lent &c. *v.*; un-borrowed &c. (*see* borrowed &c. 788).

Adv. in advance; on -loan, – security.

788. Borrowing. — N. borrowing pledging, pawning.

borrowed plumes; plagiarism &c. (*thieving*) 791.

replevin.

V. borrow, desume; pawn.

hire, rent, farm; take a -lease, – demise; take –, hire- by the -hour, – mile, – year &c.

raise –, take up- money; float bonds; raise the wind; fly a kite, borrow of Peter to pay Paul; run into debt &c. (*debt*) 806.

make use of, plagiarize, pirate.

replevy.

789. Taking.—N. taking &c. *v.*; reception &c. (*taking in*) 296; deglutition &c. (*taking food*) 298; appropriation, prehension, prensation; capture, caption; ap-, de-prehension; abreption, seizure; ab-duction, -lation; subtraction &c. (*subduction*) 38; abstraction, a-demption.

790. Restitution.—N. restitution, return; ren-, red-dition; reinstatement, restoration; reinvestment, recuperation; repatriation; rehabilitation &c. (*reconstruction*) 660; reparation, atonement, indemnity, compensation, recompense.

release, replevin, redemption; recov-

dispossession; depriv-ation, -ement; bereavement; divestment; disherison; distraint, distress; sequestration, con-fiscation, attachment, execution; evic-tion &c. 297.

rapacity, extortion, vampirism, pre-dacity, blood-sucking; theft &c. 791.

resumption; repris-e, -al; recovery &c. 775.

clutch, swoop, wrench; grip &c. (*retention*) 781; haul, take, catch; scramble.

taker, captor, capturer; vampire; extortioner.

V. take, catch, hook, nab, bag, sack, pocket, put into one's pocket, scrounge; receive; accept.

reap, crop, cull, pluck; gather &c. (*get*) 775; draw.

ap-, im-propriate; assume, possess oneself of; take possession of; commandeer; lay –, clap- one's hands on; help oneself to; make free with, dip one's hands into, lay under contribution; intercept; scramble for; deprive of.

take –, carry –, bear- -away, – off; abstract; hurry off –, run away- with; abduct; steal &c. 791; ravish; seize; pounce –, spring-upon; swoop -to, – down upon; take by -storm, – assault; snatch, reave.

snap up, nip up, whip up, catch up; kidnap, crimp, capture, lay violent hands on.

get –, lay –, take –, catch –, lay fast –, take firm- hold of; lay by the heels, take prisoner; fasten upon, grip, grapple, embrace, gripe, clasp, grab, clutch, collar, throttle, take by the throat, claw, clinch, clench, make sure of.

catch at, jump at, make a grab at, snap at, snatch at; reach, make a long arm, stretch forth one's hand.

take -from, – away from; deduct &c. 38; retrench &c. (*curtail*) 201; dispossess, ease one of, snatch from one's grasp; tear –, tear away –, wrench –, wrest –, wring- from; extort; deprive of, bereave; disinherit, cut off with a shilling.

oust &c. (*eject*) 297; divest; levy, distrain, confiscate; sequest-er, -rate, accroach; usurp; despoil, strip, fleece, shear, displume, im-poverish, eat out of house and home; drain, – to the dregs; gut, dry, exhaust, swallow up; absorb &c. (*suck in*) 296; draw off; suck, – like a leech, – the blood of.

retake, resume; recover &c. 775.

Adj. taking &c. *v.*; privative, prehensile; pred-aceous, -al, -atory, -atorial; rap-acious, -torial; ravenous: parasitic; all-devouring, -engulfing.

bereft &c. 776.

Adv. at one fell swoop.

Phr. give an inch and take an ell.

ery &c. (*getting back*) 775; remitter, reversion.

V. return, restore; recondition; give –, carry –, bring- back; render, – up; give up; let go, unclutch; dis-, re-gorge; regurgitate; recoup, reimburse, repay, indemnify, reinvest, remit, rehabilitate; repair &c. (*make good*) 660.

redeem, recover &c. (*get back*) 775; take back again; revest, revert.

Adj. restoring &c. *v.*; recuperative &c. 660; in full restitution, to compen-sate for.

Phr. *suum cuique.*

———

791. Stealing.—N. stealing &c. *v.*; theft, thievery, robbery, latrociny, direption; abstraction, appropriation; plagiar-y, -ism; rape, kidnap-ping, depredation; raid, hold up.

spoliation, plunder, pillage; sack, -age; rapine, *brigandage*, highway robbery, foray, *razzia*; black-mail; piracy, privateering, buccaneering; filibuster-ing, -ism; burglary; house-breaking; cattle-stealing, -rustling, -lifting.

peculation, embezzlement; fraud &c. 545; larceny, petty larceny, pilfering, shop-lifting.

thievishness, rapacity, kleptomania, Alsatia; den of -Cacus, – thieves. licence to plunder, letters of marque.

V. steal, thieve, rob, purloin, pilfer, filch, lift, prig, bag, nim, crib, cabbage, palm; abstract; appropriate, plagiarize.

convey away, carry off, abduct, kidnap, shanghai, impress, crimp; make –, walk –, run- off with; run away with; spirit away; seize &c. (*lay violent hands on*) 789.

plunder, pillage, rifle, sack, loot, ransack, spoil, spoliate, despoil, strip, sweep, gut, forage, levy black-mail, pirate, pickeer, maraud, lift cattle, rustle, poach, smuggle, run.

stick –, hold- up.

swindle, peculate, embezzle; sponge, mulct, rook, bilk, pluck, pigeon, skin, fleece, diddle; defraud &c. 545; obtain under false pretences; live by one's wits.

rob –, borrow of- Peter to pay Paul; set a thief to catch a thief.

disregard the distinction between *meum* and *tuum*.

Adj. thieving &c. *v.*; thievish, light-fingered; fur-acious, -tive; piratical; pred-aceous, -al, -atory, -atorial; raptorial &c. (*rapacious*) 789.

stolen &c. *v.*

Phr. *sic vos non vobis.*

792. Thief.—**N.** thief, robber, *homo trium literarum*, pilferer, rifler, filcher, plagiarist.

spoiler, depredator, pillager, marauder; harpy, shark, land-shark, falcon, moss-trooper, bushranger, Bedouin, brigand, freebooter, bandit, thug, dacoit, pirate, corsair, viking, Paul Jones; buccan-eer, -ier; piqu-, pick-eerer; rover, ranger, privateer, filibuster; rapparee, wrecker, picaroon; smuggler, poacher, plunderer; racketeer.

highwayman, Dick Turpin, Claude Duval, Macheath, knight of the road, footpad, sturdy beggar; abductor, kidnapper.

cut-, pick-purse; pick-pocket, light-fingered gentry; sharper; card-, skittle-sharper; crook; thimble-rigger; rook, Greek, blackleg, leg, welsher, defaulter; Autolycus, Cacus, Barabbas, Jeremy Diddler, Robert Macaire, artful dodger, trickster; swell mob, *chevalier d'industrie*; shop-lifter.

swindler, peculator; forger, coiner, counterfeiter, shoful; fence, receiver of stolen goods, duffer; smasher.

burglar, housebreaker; cracks-, mags-man; Bill Sikes, Jack Sheppard, Jonathan Wild, Raffles, cat burglar.

793. Booty.—**N.** booty, spoil, plunder, prize, loot, graft, swag, pickings, boodle; *spolia opima*, prey; blackmail; stolen goods.

Adj. looting &c. *n.*; manubial, spoliative.

3°. *Interchange of Property*

794. Barter.—**N.** barter, exchange, scorse, truck system; interchange &c. 148.

a Roland for an Oliver; *quid pro quo*; com-mutation, -position.

trade, commerce, mercature, buying and selling, bargain and sale; traffic, business, nundination, custom, shopping; commercial enterprise, speculation, jobbing, stock-jobbing, *agiotage*, brokery, arbitrage.

dealing, transaction, negotiation, bargain.

free trade.

V. barter, exchange, truck, scorse, swop; interchange &c. 148; commutate &c. (*substitute*) 147; compound for.

trade, traffic, buy and sell, give and take, nundinate; carry on –, ply –, drive- a trade; be in -business, – the city; keep a shop, deal in, employ one's capital in.

trade –, deal –, have dealings- with; transact –, do- business with; open –, keep- an account with.

bargain; drive –, make- a bargain; negotiate, bid for; dicker, haggle, higgle; chaffer, huckster, cheapen, beat down; stickle, – for; out-, under-bid; ask, charge; strike a bargain &c. (*contract*) 769.

speculate, give a sprat to catch a herring; buy in the cheapest and sell in the dearest market; rig the market.

Adj. commercial, mercantile, trading; interchangeable, marketable, staple, in the market, for sale.

wholesale, retail.

Adv. across the counter; on 'change.

---

795. Purchase.—N. purchase, emption; buying, purchasing, shopping; pre-emption, refusal.

coemption, bribery; slave trade.

buyer, purchaser, *emptor*, vendee; patron, employer, client, customer, *clientèle*.

V. buy, purchase, invest in, procure; rent &c. (*hire*) 788; repurchase, buy in.

keep in one's pay, bribe, suborn; pay &c. 807; spend &c. 809.

make –, complete- a purchase; buy over the counter; pay cash for.

shop, market, go a shopping.

Adj. purchased &c. *v.*

Phr. *caveat emptor.*

---

796. Sale.—N. sale, vent, disposal; auction, roup, Dutch auction; custom &c. (*traffic*) 794.

vendi-bility, -bleness.

seller, salesman; peddler, smous; vender, vendor, consignor; merchant &c. 797; auctioneer.

V. sell, vend, dispose of, effect a sale; sell -over the counter, – by auction &c. *n.*; dispense, retail; deal in &c. 794; sell -off, – out; turn into money; realize; bring -to, – under- the hammer; put up to auction; auction, offer –, put up- for sale; hawk, peddle, bring to market; offer &c. 763; undersell; dump, unload.

let; mortgage &c. (*security*) 771.

Adj. under the hammer, in the market, for sale.

saleable, marketable, vendible, in demand, having a ready sale; unsaleable &c., unpurchased, unbought; on one's hands.

---

97. Merchant.—N. merchant, trader, dealer, monger, chandler, salesman; changer; regrater; shop-keeper, -man; trades-man, -people, -folk.

retailer; chapman, hawker, huckster, higgler; peddler, smous, pedlar, *colporteur*, cadger, Autolycus; sutler, *vivandière*; coster-man, -monger; market woman; cheap jack; caterer &c. 637; tallyman.

money-broker, -changer, -lender; stock-broker, -jobber; cambist, usurer, moneyer, banker.

jobber; broker &c. (*agent*) 758; buyer &c. 795; seller &c. 796.

concern; firm &c. (*partnership*) 712.

798. Merchandise. — N. merchandise, ware, commodity, effects, goods, article, stock, produce, staple commodity; stock in trade &c. (*store*) 636; cargo &c. (*contents*) 190.

799. Mart.—N. mart; market, -place, *forum*; fair, bazaar, staple; stock –, exchange; 'change, *bourse*, Wall Street, Rialto, hall, guildhall; toll-booth, custom-house; Tattersalls.

shop, stall, booth; wharf; office, chambers, counting-house, *bureau*; coun-, comp-ter.

ware-house, -room; *dépôt*, interposit, *entrepôt*, *emporium*, establishment; store &c. 636.

open market, market-overt.

4°. *Monetary Relations*

800. Money.—N. money -matters, – market; finance; accounts &c. 811; funds, treasure; capital, stock; assets &c. (*property*) 780; wealth &c. 803; supplies, ways and means, wherewithal, sinews of war, almighty dollar, needful, cash.

sum, amount; balance, -sheet; sum total; proceeds &c. (*receipts*) 810.

currency, circulating medium, specie; coin, – of the realm; piece, hard cash, dollar, sterling coin; pounds shillings and pence; £ s. d., guineas; pocket, breeches pocket, purse; money in hand; the best, ready, – money; filthy lucre, shekels, roll, jack, rhino, blunt, dust, bawbees, brass, dibs, dough, mopus, tin, salt, chink, oof, spondulics, pile, wads.

precious metals, gold, silver, copper, nickel; bullion, bar, ingot, nugget.

petty cash; pocket-, pin-money; small –, change; small coin, loose cash; doit, stiver, rap, mite, farthing, *sou*, penny, shilling, bob, tanner, tester, groat, guinea, ducat; *rouleau*; *wampum*; good –, round –, lump-sum; power –, mint –, tons- of money; plum, lac of rupees, millions, money-bags, miser's hoard, stocking, mine of wealth &c. 803.

[Science of coins] numismatics, chrysology.

paper-money; money –, postal –, Post Office- order; note, – of hand; bank –, treasury- note; Bradbury; promissory note; I O U., bond; bill, – of exchange; draft, check, order, warrant, *coupon*, debenture, exchequer bill, *assignat*, greenback, gold –, silver- certificate.

copper, nickel, dime, quarter, two bits, half a dollar, dollar, buck, simoleon, fiver, tenner, a twenty, a sawbuck, a century, a grand; eagle, double eagle.

gold standard, bimetallism, fiat money; rate of –, exchange; in-, de-flation.

remittance &c. (*payment*) 807; credit &c. 805; liability &c. 806; solvency &c. 803.

draw-er, -ee; oblig-or, -ee; moneyer, coiner, counterfeiter, forger.

false –, bad- money; base –, counterfeit- coin, flash note, slip, kite; Bank of Elegance.

argumentum ad crumenam.

V. amount to, come to, mount up to; touch the pocket; draw, – upon; endorse &c. (*security*) 771; issue, utter, circulate; discount &c. 813.

forge, counterfeit, coin, circulate –, pass- bad money.

Adj. monetary, pecuniary, crumenal, fiscal, financial, sumptuary, numismatical; sterling; solvent &c. 803.

801. Treasurer.—N. treasurer; bursar, -y; purser, purse-bearer; cash-keeper, banker; depositary; questor, receiver, steward, trustee, chartered –, accountant; Accountant-General, almoner, liquidator, paymaster, cashier, teller; cambist; money-changer &c. (*merchant*) 797.

financier, Chancellor of the Exchequer, minister of finance; Secretary of the Treasury, Director of the Budget, Controller of Currency.

802. Treasury.—N. treasury, bank, exchequer, almonry, fisc, hanaper, bursary; safe; strong-box, -hold, -room; coffer; chest &c. (*receptacle*) 191; depository &c. 636; till, -er; cash-box, -register, purse, pocket-book, wallet; money-bag, -belt, -box; *porte-monnaie*.

purse-strings; pocket, breeches pocket.

sinking fund; stocks; government –, public –, parliamentary- -stocks, – funds, – securities, bonds; gilt-edged securities; Consols, Liberty bonds, government bonds, *crédit mobilier*.

803. Wealth.—N. wealth, riches, fortune, handsome fortune, opulence, affluence; good –, easy- circumstances; independence; competence &c. (*sufficiency*) 639; solvency, soundness, solidity.

provision, livelihood, maintenance; alimony, dowry; means, resources, substance; property &c. 780; command of money.

income &c. 810; capital, money; round sum &c. (*treasure*) 800; mint of money, mine of wealth, *El Dorado*, Pactolus, Golconda, Potosi, *bonanza*; philosopher's stone.

long –, full –, well lined –, heavy-purse; purse of Fortunatus.

pelf, Mammon, lucre, filthy lucre; loaves and fishes; fleshpots of Egypt.

rich –, moneyed –, warm- man; man of substance; capitalist, millionaire, Nabob, Crœsus, Midas, Plutus, Dives, Timon of Athens; Timo-, Pluto-cracy; Danaë.

V. be -rich &c. *adj.*; roll –, wallow-in -wealth, – riches; have money to burn.

afford, well afford; command -money, – a sum; make both ends meet, hold one's head above water.

become -rich &c. *adj.*; fill one's -pocket &c. (*treasury*) 802; feather one's nest, clean up –, make- a fortune; make money &c. (*acquire*) 775.

enrich, imburse.

worship -Mammon, – the golden calf.

Adj. wealthy, rich, affluent, opulent, moneyed, monied, worth -a great deal,

804. Poverty.—N. poverty, indigence, penury, pauperism, destitution, want; need, -iness; lack, necessity, privation, distress, difficulties, wolf at the door.

bad –, poor –, needy –, embarrassed –, reduced –, straitened- circumstances; slender –, narrow- means; straits; hand to mouth existence, *res angusta domi*, low water, impecuniosity.

beggary; mendi-cancy, -city; broken –, loss of- fortune; insolvency &c. (*non-payment*) 808.

empty -purse, – pocket; light purse; beggarly account of empty boxes.

poor man, pauper, mendicant, mumper, beggar, starveling; *pauvre diable*.

V. be -poor &c. *adj.*; want, lack, starve, live from hand to mouth, have seen better days, go down in the world, be on one's uppers, come upon the parish; go to -the dogs, – wrack and ruin; not have a -penny &c. (*money*) 800, – shot in one's locker; beg one's bread; *tirer le diable par la queue*; run into debt &c. (*debt*) 806.

render -poor &c. *adj.*; impoverish; reduce, – to poverty; pauperize, fleece, ruin, bring to the parish.

Adj. poor, indigent; poverty -stricken; badly –, poorly –, ill- off; poor as -a rat, – a church mouse, – Job's turkey, – Job; fortune-, dower-, money-, penni-less; unportioned, unmoneyed; impecunious; broke, flat; out –, short-of -money, – cash; without –, not worth- a rap &c. (*money*) 800; *qui n'a pas le sou*, out of pocket, hard up; out at

– much; well -to do, – off; warm; well –, provided for.

made of money; rich as Crœsus; rolling in -riches, – wealth.

flush, – of -cash, – money, – tin; in -funds, – cash, – full feather; solvent, solid, sound, pecunious, out of debt, all straight; able to pay 20s in the £.

Phr. one's ship coming in.

-elbows, – heels; seedy, bare-footed; beggar-ly, -ed; destitute; fleeced, strapped, stripped; bereft, bereaved; reduced.

in -want &c. *n.*; needy, necessitous, distressed, pinched, straitened; put to one's -shifts, – last shifts; unable to -keep the wolf from the door, – make both ends meet; embarrassed, under hatches; involved &c. (*in debt*) 806; insolvent &c. (*not paying*) 808.

Adv. *in formâ pauperis.*

Phr. *zonam perdidit.*

---

805. Credit.—N. credit, trust, tick, score, tally, account.

letter of credit, circular note; duplicate; mortgage, lien, debenture, paper credit, floating capital; draft; securities.

creditor, lender, lessor, mortgagee; dun; usurer.

V. keep –, run up- an account with; entrust, credit, accredit.

place to one's -credit, – account; give –, take- credit; fly a kite.

Adj. credit-ing, -ed; accredited.

Adv. on -credit &c. *n.*; to the -account, – credit- of.

806. Debt.—N. debt, obligation, liability, indebtment, debit, score.

arrears, deferred payment, deficit, default; insolvency &c. (*non-payment*) 808; bad debt.

interest; usance, usury; premium; floating -debt, – capital.

debtor, debitor; mortgagor; defaulter &c. 808; borrower.

V. be -in debt &c. *adj.*; owe; incur –, contract- a debt &c. *n.*; run up -a bill, – a score, – an account; go on tick, put on the cuff; borrow &c. 788; run –, get- into debt; outrun the constable.

answer –, go bail- for; back one's note.

Adj. indebted; liable, chargeable, answerable for.

in -debt, – embarrassed circumstances, – difficulties; incumbered, involved; involved –, plunged –, deep –, over head and ears- in debt; deeply involved; fast tied up; insolvent &c. (*not paying*) 808; *minus*, out of pocket.

unpaid; unrequieted, unrewarded; owing, due, in arrear, outstanding.

---

807. Payment.—N. pay-, defrayment; discharge; ac-, quittance; settlement, clearance, liquidation, satisfaction, reckoning, arrangement.

acknowledgment, release; receipt, – in full, – in full of all demands; voucher.

repayment, reimbursement, retribution; pay &c. (*reward*) 973; money paid &c. (*expenditure*) 809.

ready money &c. (*cash*) 800; stake, remittance, instalment.

payer, liquidator &c. 801.

V. pay, defray, make payment; pay -down, – on the nail, – ready money, – at sight, – in advance; cash, honour a bill, acknowledge; redeem; pay in kind.

808. Non-payment.—N. non-payment; default, defalcation; protest, repudiation; application of the sponge; whitewashing.

insolvency, bankruptcy, failure; overdraft, overdrawn account; insufficiency &c. 640; run upon a bank.

waste paper bonds; dishonoured –, protested- bills; bogus cheque.

bankrupt, insolvent debtor, lame duck, man of straw, welsher, stag, defaulter, absconder, levanter.

V. not -pay &c. 807; fail, break, stop payment; become -insolvent, – bankrupt; be gazetted.

protest, dishonour, repudiate, nullify.

pay under protest; button up one's

pay one's -way, – shot, – footing; pay -the piper, – sauce for all, – costs; do the needful; come across; shell –, fork- out; come down with, – the dust; tickle –, grease- the palm; expend &c. 809; put –, lay- down.

discharge, settle, quit, acquit oneself of; account –, reckon –, settle –, be even –, be quits- with; strike a balance; settle –, balance –, square- accounts with; quit scores; foot the bill; wipe –, clear- off old scores; satisfy; pay in full; satisfy –, pay in full of- all demands; clear, liquidate; pay -up, – old debts.

disgorge, make repayment; repay, refund, reimburse, retribute; make compensation &c. 30.

Adj. paying &c., paid &c. *v.*; owing nothing, out of debt, all straight, clear of -debt, – encumbrance; unowed, never indebted.

Adv. to the tune of; on the nail; money –, cash- down; cash on delivery.

pockets, draw the purse strings; apply the sponge; pay over the left shoulder, get whitewashed; swindle &c. 791; run up bills, fly kites.

Adj. not paying; in debt &c. 806; behindhand, in arrear; beggared &c. (*poor*) 804; unable to make both ends meet; *minus*; worse than nothing.

insolvent, bankrupt, in the gazette, gazetted, ruined.

unpaid &c. (*outstanding*) 806; *gratis* &c. 815; unremunerated.

---

809. Expenditure.—N. expenditure, money going out; out-goings, -lay; expenses, disbursement; prime cost &c. (*price*) 812; circulation; run upon a bank.

[Money paid] payment &c. 807; pay &c. (*remuneration*) 973; bribe &c. 973; fee, footing, garnish; subsidy; tribute, Peter's pence; contingent, quota; donation &c. 784.

pay in advance, earnest, handsel, deposit, instalment.

investment; purchase &c. 795.

V. expend, spend; run –, get- through; pay, disburse; open –, loose –, untie- the purse strings; lay –, shell –, fork- out; bleed; make up a sum, invest, sink money.

fee &c. (*reward*) 973; pay one's way &c. (*pay*) 807; subscribe &c. (*give*) 784; subsidize, bribe.

Adj. expend-ing, -ed &c. *v.*; sumptuary, liberal &c. 816; open-handed, lavish &c. 818; extensive &c. 814.

810. Receipt.—N. receipt, accountable –, conditional –, binding –, return- receipt; value received, money coming in; income, incomings, innings, reve- nue, return, proceeds; gross receipts, net profit; earnings &c. (*gain*) 775.

rent, – roll; rent-al, -age; rack-rent.

premium, *bonus*; sweepstakes, ton- tine,'prize, drawing.

pension, annuity; jointure &c. (*prop- erty*) 780; alimony, pittance; emolu- ment &c. (*remuneration*) 973.

V. receive &c. 785; take money; draw –, derive- from; get, be in receipt of, acquire &c. 775; take &c. 789.

bring in, yield, afford, pay, return; accrue &c. (*be received from*) 785.

Adj. receiv-ing, -ed &c. *v.*; profitable &c. (*gainful*) 775.

---

811. Accounts.—N. accounts, accompts; commercial –, monetary- arithmetic; statistics &c. (*numeration*) 85; money matters, finance, budget, bill, score, reckoning, account.

books, account book, ledger; day –, cash –, pass- book; journal; debtor and creditor –, cash –, petty cash –, running- account; account- current; balance, – sheet; *compte rendu*, account settled.

book-keeping, audit; double –, single- entry; reckoning &c. 85.

chartered –, certified public –, accountant; auditor, actuary, book- keeper; financier &c. 801; accounting party.

V. keep accounts, enter, post, book, credit, debit, carry over; take stock; balance –, make up –, square –, settle –, wind up –, cast up –, add up –, tot up- accounts; make accounts square.

bring to book, audit, tax, surcharge and falsify.

falsify –, garble –, cook –, doctor- an account.

Adj. monetary &c. 800; account-able, -ing; statistical.

812. Price.—N. price, amount, cost, expense, prime cost, charge, figure, demand, damage, fare, hire; wages &c. (*remuneration*) 973.

dues, duty, toll, tax, impost, cess, sess, tallage, levy, capitation-, poll-, income-, sur-, sales-, super-tax; gabel, *gabelle*; gavel, *octroi*, custom, tariff, excise, assessment, taxation, benevolence, tithe, tenths, exactment, ransom, salvage; broker-, wharf-, lighter-, ton-, freight-age.

worth, rate, value, valuation, appraisement, money's worth, par value; penny &c. -worth; price current, market price, quotation; what it will -fetch &c. *v.*

bill &c. (*account*) 811; shot.

V. bear –, set –, fix- a price; appraise, assess, price, charge, demand, ask, require, exact, run up; distrain; run up a bill &c. (*debt*) 806; have one's price; liquidate.

amount to, come to, mount up to; stand one in.

fetch, sell for, cost, bring in, yield, afford.

Adj. priced &c. *v.*; to the tune of, *ad valorem*; mercenary, venal.

Phr. no penny. no paternoster; *point d'argent, point de Suisse,* no longer pipe, no longer dance, no song, no supper.

one may have it for.

813. Discount.—N. discount, abatement, concession, reduction, depreciation, allowance, qualification, set off, drawback, poundage, *agio*, percentage; rebate, -ment; backwardation, contango; salvage; tare and tret.

V. discount, bate; a-, re-bate; deduct, reduce, mark down, take off, allow, give, make allowance; tax, depreciate.

Adj. discounting &c. *v.*

Adv. at a discount, below par.

---

814. Dearness. — N. dearness &c. *adj.*; high –, famine –, fancy- price; overcharge; extravagance; exorbitance, extortion; heavy pull upon the purse; Pyrrhic victory.

V. be -dear &c. *adj.*; cost -much, – a pretty penny; rise in price, look up.

overcharge, bleed, fleece, skin, extort.

pay -too much, – through the nose, – too dear for one's whistle.

Adj. dear; high, -priced; of great price, expensive, costly, precious, worth a Jew's eye, dear bought; unreasonable, extravagant, exorbitant, extortionate.

at a premium; not to be had, – for love or money; beyond –, above- price; priceless, of priceless value.

Adv. dear, -ly; at great –, heavy-cost; *à grands frais.*

Phr. prices looking up; *le jeu ne vaut pas la chandelle.*

---

815. Cheapness.—N. cheapness, low price; depreciation; bargain; good penny &c.- worth, *bon marché.*

[Absence of charge] gratuity; free -quarters, – seats, – admission, – warren; pass, Annie Oakley; run of one's teeth; nominal price, peppercorn rent; labour of love.

drug in the market.

V. be -cheap &c. *adj.*; cost little; come down –, fall- in price.

buy for -a mere nothing, – an old song; have one's money's worth; cheapen, beat down.

Adj. cheap; low, – priced; moderate, reasonable; in-, un-expensive; well –, worth the money; *magnifique et pas cher*; good –, cheap- at the price; dirt –, dog- cheap; cheap, -as dirt, – and nasty; catchpenny.

reduced, marked down, half-price, depreciated, unsaleable.

gratuitous, *gratis*, free, for love,

– nothing; cost-, expense-less; without charge, not charged, un-taxed; scot –, shot –, rent- free; free of -cost, – expense; honor-ary, unbought, unpaid, complimentary.

Adv. for a mere song; at -cost price, – prime cost, – a reduction, – a bargain; on the cheap.

816. Liberality.—N. liberality, gener-osity, munificence; bount-y, -eousness, -ifulness; hospitality; charity &c. (*beneficence*) 906.

benefactor, free giver, Lady Bounti-ful.

V. be -liberal &c. *adj.*; spend –, bleed- freely; shower down upon; open one's purse strings &c. (*disburse*) 809; spare no expense, give -with both hands, – *carte blanche*.

Adj. liberal, free, generous; charit-able &c. (*beneficent*) 906; hospitable; bount-iful, -eous; handsome; unspar-ing, ungrudging; open-, free-, full-handed; open-, large-, free-hearted; munificent, princely, unstinting.

overpaid.

Adv. liberally, ungrudgingly, with open hand.

---

818. Prodigality.—N. prodi-gality, -gence; unthriftiness, waste, -fulness; profus-ion, -eness; extravagance; squan-dering &c. *v.*; lavishness; malversation.

prodigal; spend-, waste-thrift; losel, play-boy, spender, squanderer, locust.

V. be -prodigal &c. *adj.*; squander, lavish, sow broadcast; pour forth like water; pay through the nose &c. (*dear*) 814; spill, waste, dissipate, exhaust, drain, eat out of house and home, overdraw, outrun the constable; run -out, – through; misspend; throw -good money after bad, – the helve after the hatchet; burn the candle at both ends; make ducks and drakes of one's money; squander one's substance, spend money like water; fool –, potter –, muddle –, fritter –, throw- away one's money; pour water into a sieve, kill the goose that lays the golden eggs; *manger son blé en herbe.*

Adj. prodigal, profuse, thriftless, un-thrifty, improvident, wasteful, losel,

817. Economy.—N. economy, fru-gality; thrift, -iness; prudence, care, husbandry, good housewifery, saving-ness, retrenchment.

savings; prevention of waste, save-all; cheese parings and candle ends; parsimony &c. 819.

V. be -economical &c. *adj.*; econo-mize, save; retrench; cut- down ex-penses, – one's coat according to one's cloth, make both ends meet, keep within compass, meet one's expenses, pay one's way; keep one's head above water; husband &c. (*lay by*) 636; save –, invest- money; put out to interest; provide –, save- -for, – against- a rainy day; feather one's nest; look after the main chance.

Adj. economical, frugal, careful, thrifty, saving, chary, spare, sparing; parsimonious &c. 819.

underpaid.

Adv. sparingly &c. *adj.*; *ne quid nimis.*

819. Parsimony. — N. parsimony, parcity; parsimoniousness, stinginess &c. *adj.*; stint; illiberality, avarice, tenacity, avidity, rapacity, extortion, venality, cupidity; selfishness &c. 943; *auri sacra fames.*

miser, niggard, churl, screw, tight-wad, skinflint, crib, codger, muckworm, money-grubber, pinchfist, scrimp, lick-penny, hunks, curmudgeon, *Harpagon*, Silas Marner, harpy, extortioner, Jew, usurer.

V. be -parsimonious &c. *adj.*; grudge, begrudge, stint, skimp, pinch, gripe, screw, dole out, hold back, withhold, starve, famish, live upon nothing, skin a flint.

drive a -bargain, – hard bargain; cheapen, beat down; stop one hole in a sieve; have an itching palm, grasp, grab.

Adj. parsimonious, penurious, stingy, miserly, mean, shabby, peddling, scrubby, pennywise, near, niggardly,

extravagant, lavish, dissipated, over liberal; full-handed &c. (*liberal*) 816.

penny wise and pound foolish.

Adv. with an unsparing hand; money burning one's pocket; recklessly profuse.

Int. hang the expense!

---

frugal to excess; close; fast-, close-, strait-handed; close-, hard-, tight-fisted; tight, sparing; chary; grudging, griping &c. *v.*; illiberal, ungenerous, churlish, hidebound, sordid, mercenary, venal, covetous, usurious, avaricious, greedy, extortionate, rapacious.

Adv. with a sparing hand.

CLASS VI

Words relating to the SENTIENT and MORAL POWERS.

CLASS VI

Words relating to the SENTIENT and MORAL POWERS.

~~~~~~~~

Section I. AFFECTIONS IN GENERAL

820. Affections.—N. affections, character, qualities, disposition, nature, spirit, tone; temper, -ament; *diathesis*, idiosyncrasy; cast –, habit –, frame- of -mind, – soul; predilection, turn; natural –, turn of mind; bent, bias, predisposition, proneness, proclivity; propen-sity, -sedness, -sion, -dency; vein, humour, mood, grain, mettle; sympathy &c. (*love*) 897.

soul, heart, breast, bosom, inner man; heart's -core, – strings, – blood; heart of hearts, *penetralia mentis*; secret and inmost recesses of the –, cockles of one's- heart; inmost -heart, – soul; back-bone.

passion, pervading spirit; ruling –, master- passion; *furore*; fulness of the heart, heyday of the blood, flesh and blood, flow of soul, force of character.

V. have –, possess- -affections &c. *n.*; be of a -character &c. *n.*; be -affected &c. *adj.*; breathe.

Adj. affected, characterized, formed, moulded, cast; at-, tempered; framed; pre-, disposed; prone, inclined; having a -bias &c. *n.*; tinctured –, imbued –, penetrated –, eaten up- with.

inborn, inbred, ingrained, in the grain, congenital, inherent, bred in the bone; deep-rooted, ineffaceable, inveterate; pathoscopic.

Adv. in one's -heart &c. *n.*; at heart; heart and soul &c. 821; in the -vein, – mood.

821. Feeling.—N. feeling; suffering &c. *v.*; endurance, tolerance, sufferance, supportance, experience, response; sympathy &c. (*love*) 897; impression, inspiration, affection, sensation, emotion, pathos, deep sense.

fire, warmth, glow, unction, *gusto*, vehemence; ferv-our, -ency; heartiness, cordiality; earnestness, eagerness; *empressement*, ardour, zeal, passion, enthusiasm, *verve*, *furore*, fanaticism; excitation of feeling &c. (*disposition*) 820; passion &c. (*state of excitability*) 825; ecstasy &c. (*pleasure*) 827.

blush, suffusion, flush; hectic; tingling, thrill, kick, turn, shock; agitation &c. (*irregular motion*) 315; quiver, heaving, flutter, flurry, fluster, twitter, tremor; throb, -bing; pulsation, palpitation, painting; trepid-, perturb-ation; ruffle, hurry of spirits, pother, stew, ferment.

V. feel; receive an -impression &c. *n.*; be -impressed with &c. *adj.*; entertain –, harbour –, cherish- -feeling &c. *n.*

respond; catch the -flame, – infection; enter the spirit of.

bear, suffer, support, sustain, endure, brook, thole, aby; abide &c.

(*be composed*) 826; experience &c. (*meet with*) 151; taste, prove; labour –, smart- under; bear the brunt of, brave, stand.

swell, glow, warm, flush, blush, change colour, mantle; turn -colour, – pale, – red, – black in the face; blench, crimson, whiten, pale, tingle, thrill, heave, pant, throb, palpitate, go pit-a-pat, tremble, quiver, flutter, twitter; stagger, reel; shake &c. 315; be -agitated, – excited &c. 824; look -blue, – black; wince, draw a deep breath.

impress &c. (*excite the feelings*) 824.

Adj. feeling &c. *v.*; sentient; sensuous; sensor-ial, -y; emo-tive, -tional; of –, with- feeling &c. *n.*

warm, quick, lively, smart, strong, sharp, acute, cutting, piercing, incisive; keen, – as a razor; trenchant, pungent, racy, *piquant*, poignant, caustic.

impressive, deep, profound, indelible; deep-, home-, heart-felt; swelling, soul-stirring, deep-mouthed, heart-expanding, electric, thrilling, rapturous, ecstatic.

earnest, wistful, eager, breathless; fer-vent, -vid; gushing, passionate, warmhearted, hearty, cordial, sincere, zealous, enthusiastic, glowing, ardent, burning, red-hot, fiery, flaming; boiling, – over.

pervading, penetrating, absorbing; rabid, raving, feverish, fanatical, hysterical; impetuous &c. (*excitable*) 825; overmastering.

impressed –, moved –, touched –, affected –, penetrated –, seized –, imbued &c. 820- with; devoured by; wrought up &c. (*excited*) 824; struck all of a heap; rapt; in a -quiver &c. *n.*; enraptured &c. 829.

Adv. heart and soul, from the bottom of one's heart, *ab imo pectore, de profundis*, at heart, *con amore*, heartily, devoutly, over head and ears.

Phr. the heart -big, – full, – swelling, – beating, – pulsating, – throbbing, – thumping, – beating high, – melting, – overflowing, – bursting, – breaking.

---

822. Sensibility. — N. sensi-bility, -bleness, -tiveness; moral sensibility; impress-, affect-ibility; suscepti-ble-ness, -bility, -vity; mobility; viva-city, -ciousness; tender-, soft-ness; senti-mental-ity, -ism.

excitability &c. 825; fastidiousness &c. 868; physical sensibility &c. 375.

sore -point, – place; where the shoe pinches.

V. be -sensible &c. *adj.*; have a -tender, – warm, – sensitive- heart.

take to –, treasure up in the- heart; shrink.

'die of a rose in aromatic pain'; touch to the quick.

Adj. sensi-ble, -tive; impressi-ble, -onable; suscepti-ve, -ble; alive to, impassion-able, -ed; gushing; warm-, tender-, soft-hearted; tender –, as a chicken; soft, sentimental, romantic; enthusiastic, highflying, spirited, mettlesome, vivacious, lively, expressive, mobile, tremblingly alive; excitable

823. Insensibility.—N. insensi-bility, -bleness; moral insensibility; inertness, *inertia, vis inertiæ*; impassi-bility, -bleness; inappetency, apathy, phlegm, dulness, hebetude, supineness, luke-warmness, insusceptibility, unimpress-ibility.

cold -fit, – blood, – heart; cold-, cool-ness; frigidity, *sang-froid*; stoicism, imperturbation &c. (*inexcitability*) 826; *nonchalance*, unconcern, dry eyes; *insouciance* &c. (*indifference*) 866; recklessness &c. 863; callousness; heart of stone, stock and stone, marble, deadness.

torp-or, -idity; obstupefaction, leth-argy, coma, trance; sleep &c. 683; suspended animation; stup-or, -efaction; paralysis, palsy; numbness &c. (*physical insensibility*) 376.

neutrality; quietism, vegetation.

V. be -insensible &c. *adj.*; have a rhinoceros hide; show -insensibility &c. *n.*; not -mind, – care, – be affected

&c. 825; over-sensitive, without skin, thin-skinned; fastidious &c. 868.

Adv. sensibly &c. *adj.*; to the -quick, – inmost core.

by; have no desire for &c. 866; have –, feel –, take- no interest in; *nil admirari*; not care a -straw &c. (*unimportance*) 643 for; disregard &c. (*neglect*) 460; set at naught &c. (*make light of*) 483; turn a deaf ear to &c. (*inattention*) 458; vegetate.

render -insensible, – callous; blunt, obtund, numb, benumb, paralyze, chloroform, deaden, hebetate, stun, stupefy; brut-ify, -alize.

inure; harden, – the heart; steel, case-harden, sear.

Adj. insensible, unconscious; impassi-ve, -ble; blind to, deaf to, dead to; un-, in-susceptible; unimpress-ionable, -ible; passion-, spirit-, heart-, soul-less; unfeeling, unmoral.

apathetic; leuco-, phlegmatic; dull, frigid; cold, -blooded, -hearted; unemotional; cold as charity; flat, obtuse, inert, supine, sluggish, torpid; sleepy &c. (*inactive*) 683; languid, half-hearted, tame; numb, -ed; comatose; anæsthetic &c. 376; stupefied, chloroformed, palsy-stricken.

indifferent, lukewarm; Laodicean; careless, mindless, regardless; inattentive &c. 458; neglectful &c. 460; disregarding.

unconcerned, *nonchalant, pococurante, insouciant, sans souci*; un-ambitious &c. 866.

un-affected, -ruffled, -impressed, -inspired, -excited, -moved, -stirred, -touched, -shocked, -struck; unblushing &c. (*shameless*) 885; unanimated; vegetative.

callous, thick-skinned, pachydermatous, impervious; hard, -ened; inured, case-hardened; steeled –, proof- against; imperturbable &c. (*inexcitable*) 826; unfelt.

Adv. insensibly &c. *adj.*; *æquo animo*; without being -moved, – touched, – impressed; in cold blood; with -dry eyes, – withers unwrung.

Phr. never mind; it is of no consequence &c. (*unimportant*) 643; it cannot be helped; nothing coming amiss; it is all -the same, – one- to.

---

824. Excitation.—N. excitation of feeling; mental –, excitement; suscitation, galvanism, stimulation, piquancy, provocation, inspiration, calling forth, infection; interest, animation, agitation, perturbation; subjugation, fascination, intoxication; en-, ravishment; entrancement, high pressure.

unction, impressiveness &c. *adj.*; emotional appeal; melodrama; psychological moment, crisis; sensationalism.

trial of temper, *casus belli*; irritation &c. (*anger*) 900; passion &c. (*state of excitability*) 825; thrill &c. (*feeling*) 821; repression of feeling &c. 826.

V. excite, affect, touch, move, impress, strike, interest, intrigue, animate, inspire, impassion, smite, infect; stir –, fire –, warm- the blood; set astir; a-, wake; a-, waken; call forth; e-, pro-voke; raise up, summon up, call up, wake up, blow up, get up, light up; raise; get up steam, rouse, arouse, stir, fire, kindle, enkindle, apply the torch, set on fire, inflame, illuminate.

stimulate; ex-, suscitate; inspirit; spirit up, stir up, work up; infuse life into, give new life to; bring –, introduce- new blood; quicken;

sharpen, whet; work upon &c. (*incite*) 615; hurry on, give a fillip, put on one's mettle.

fan the -fire, – flame; blow the coals, stir the embers; fan, – into a flame; foster, heat, warm, foment, raise to a fever heat; keep -up, – the pot boiling; revive, rekindle; rake up, rip up.

stir –, play on –, come home to- the feelings; touch -a string, – a chord, – the soul, – the heart; go to one's heart, penetrate, pierce, go through one, touch to the quick, open the wound; possess –, pervade –, penetrate –, imbrue –, absorb –, affect –, disturb- the soul.

absorb, rivet the attention; sink into the -mind, – heart; prey on the mind; intoxicate; over-whelm, -power; *bouleverser*, upset, turn one's head.

fascinate; enrapture &c. (*give pleasure*) 829.

agitate, perturb, ruffle, fluster, flutter, shake, disturb, faze, startle, shock, stagger; give one a -shock, – turn; strike -dumb, – all of a heap; stun, astound, electrify, galvanize, petrify.

irritate, sting; cut, – to the -heart, – quick; try one's temper; fool to the top of one's bent, pique; infuriate, madden, make one's blood boil; lash into fury &c. (*wrath*) 900.

be -excited &c. *adj.*; flash up, flare up; catch the infection; thrill &c. (*feel*) 821; mantle; work oneself up; seethe, boil, simmer, foam, fume, flame, rage, rave; run mad &c. (*passion*) 825.

Adj. excited &c. *v.*; wrought up, on the *qui vive*, astir, sparkling; in a -quiver &c. 821, – fever, – ferment, – blaze, – state of excitement; in hysterics; black in the face, over-wrought; hot, red-hot, flushed, feverish; all -of a twitter, – of a flutter, – of a dither, – in a pucker; with -quivering lips, – tears in one's eyes.

flaming; boiling, – over; ebullient, seething; foaming, – at the mouth; fuming, raging, carried away by passion, wild, raving, frantic, mad, distracted, distraught, beside oneself, out of one's wits, amuck, ready to burst, *bouleversé*, demoniacal.

lost, *éperdu*, tempest-tossed; haggard; ready to sink.

stung to the quick, up, on one's high ropes.

exciting &c. *v.*; impressive, warm, glowing, fervid, swelling, imposing, spirit-stirring, thrilling; high-wrought; soul-stirring, -subduing; heart-swelling, -thrilling; agonizing &c. (*painful*) 830; telling, sensational, melodramatic, hysterical; over-powering, -whelming; more than flesh and blood can bear.

piquant &c. (*pungent*) 392; spicy, appetizing, provocative, *provoquant*, tantalizing.

Adv. till one is black in the face.

Phr. the heart -beating high, – going pit-a-pat, – leaping into one's mouth; the blood -being up, – boiling in one's veins; the eye -glistening, – 'in a fine frenzy rolling'; the head turned.

---

825. [Excess of sensitiveness.] **Excitability.—N.** excitability, impetuosity, vehemence; boisterousness &c. *adj.*; turbulence; impatience, intolerance, non-endurance; irritability &c. (*irascibility*) 901; itching &c. (*desire*) 865; wincing; disquiet, -ude; restlessness; fidge-ts, -tiness; agitation &c. (*irregular motion*) 315.

826. [Absence of excitability, or of excitement.] **Inexcitability.—N.** inexcit-, imperturb-, inirrit-ability; even temper, tranquil mind, dispassion; tolerance, toleration, patience.

passiveness &c. (*physical inertness*) 172; hebet-ude, -ation; impassibility &c. (*insensibility*) 823; stupefaction.

coolness, calmness &c. *adj.*; compo-

trepidation, perturbation, ruffle, hurry, -skurry, fuss, flurry; fluster, flutter; pother, stew, ferment; whirl; thrill &c. (*feeling*) 821; state -, fever- of excitement; transport.

passion, excitement, flush, heat; fever, -heat; fire, flame, fume, blood boiling; tumult; effervescence, ebullition; boiling, – over; whiff, gust, storm, tempest; scene, breaking out, burst, fit, paroxysm, explosion; out-break, -burst; agony.

violence &c. 173; fierceness &c. *adj.*; rage, fury, *furor*, *furore*, desperation, madness, distraction, raving, delirium, brain storm; frenzy, hysterics; intoxication; tearing –, raging- passion, towering rage; anger &c. 900.

fascination, infatuation, fanaticism; Quixot-ism, -ry; *tête montée*.

V. be -impatient &c. *adj.*; not be able to -bear &c. 826; bear ill, wince, chafe, champ the bit; be in a -stew &c. *n.*; be out of all patience, fidget, fuss, not have a wink of sleep; toss, – on one's pillow.

lose one's temper &c. 900; break –, burst –, fly- out; go –, fly- -off, – off the handle, – off at a tangent; explode; flare up, flame up, fire up, burst into a flame, take fire, fire, burn; boil, – over; foam, fume, rage, rave, rant, tear; go –, run- -wild, – mad; go into hysterics; run -riot, – amuck; *battre la campagne, faire le diable à quatre*, play the deuce; raise -Cain, – the devil.

Adj. excitable, easily excited, in an excitable state; highly strung; irritable &c. (*irascible*) 901; impatient, intolerant.

feverish, febrile, hysterical; delirious, mad, moody, maggoty-headed.

unquiet, mercurial, electric, galvanic, hasty, hurried, restless, fidgety, fussy; chafing &c. *v.*

startlish, mettlesome, high mettled, skittish.

vehement, demonstrative, violent, wild, furious, fierce, fiery, hot-headed, mad-cap.

over-zealous, enthusiastic, impassioned, fanatical; rabid &c. (*eager*) 865.

rampant, clamorous, uproarious, tur-

sure, placidity, indisturbance, imperturbation, *sang-froid*, tranquillity, serenity; quiet, -ude; peace of mind, mental calmness.

staidness &c. *adj.*; gravity, sobriety, Quakerism; philosophy, equanimity, stoicism, command of temper; self-possession, -control, -command, -restraint; presence of mind.

submission &c. 725; resignation; suffer-, support-, endur-, long-suffer-, forbear-ance; longanimity; fortitude; patience -of Job, – 'on a monument,' – 'sovereign o'er transmuted ill'; moderation; repression –, subjugation- of feeling; restraint &c. 751.

tranquillization &c. (*moderation*) 174.

V. be -composed &c. *adj.*

laisser -faire, – aller; take things -easily, – as they come; take it easy, run on, live and let live; take -easily, – coolly, – in good part; *æquam serva e mentem*.

bear, – well, – the brunt; go through, support, endure, brave, disregard.

tolerate, suffer, stand, bide; abide, aby; bear –, put up –, abide- with; acquiesce; submit &c. (*yield*) 725; submit with a good grace; resign –, reconcile- oneself to; brook, digest, eat, swallow, pocket, stomach; make -light of, – the best of, – a virtue of necessity; put a good face on, keep one's countenance; carry -on, – through; check &c. 751- oneself.

compose, appease &c. (*moderate*) 174; propitiate; repress &c. (*restrain*) 751; render insensible &c. 823; overcome –, allay –, repress- one's -excitability &c. 825; master one's feelings.

make -oneself, – one's mind- easy; set one's mind at -ease, – rest.

calm –, cool- down; thaw, grow cool.

be -borne, – endured; go down.

Adj. in-, un-excitable; imperturbable; unsusceptible &c. (*insensible*) 823; un-, dis-passionate; cold-blooded, inirritable; enduring &c. *v.*; stoical, Platonic, philosophic, staid, stayed; sober, – minded; grave; sober –, grave- as a judge; sedate, demure, cool-, level-headed; steady.

easy-going, peaceful, placid, calm; quiet, – as a mouse; tranquil, serene;

bulent, tempestuous, tumultuary, bois-
terous.

impulsive, impetuous, passionate;
uncontroll-ed, -able; ungovernable,
irrepressible, stanchless, inextinguishable, burning, simmering, volcanic,
ready to burst forth.

excit-ed, -ing &c. 824.

Int. pish! pshaw!

Phr. *noli me tangere.*

---

cool, – as -a cucumber, – custard; undemonstrative.

temperate &c. (*moderate*) 174; composed, collected; un-excited, -stirred,
-ruffled, -disturbed, -perturbed, -im-
passioned; unoffended; unresisting.

meek, tolerant; patient, – as Job;
submissive &c. 725; tame; content,
resigned, chastened, subdued, lamb-
like; gentle, – as a lamb; *suaviter in
modo*; mild, – as mother's milk; soft
as peppermint; armed with patience, bearing with, clement, for-
bearant, long-suffering.

Adv. 'like patience on a monument smiling at grief'; *æquo animo*,
in cold blood &c. 823; more in sorrow than in anger.

Int. patience! and shuffle the cards.

Section II. PERSONAL AFFECTIONS*

1°. Passive Affections

827. Pleasure.—N. pleasure, gratification, enjoyment, fruition; ob-, delectation; relish, zest; *gusto* &c.
(*physical pleasure*) 377; satisfaction
&c. (*content*) 831; complacency.

well-being; good &c. 618; snugness,
comfort, ease; cushion &c. 215; *sans
souci*, mind at ease.

joy, gladness, delight, glee, cheer,
sunshine; cheerfulness &c. 836.

treat, refreshment; frolic, fun, lark,
gambol, merry-making; amusement
&c. 840; luxury &c. 377; hedonism.

mens sana in corpore sano.

happiness, felicity, bliss; beati-tude,
-fication; enchantment, transport, rapture, ravishment, ecstasy; *summum
bonum*; paradise, elysium &c. (*heaven*)
981; third –, seventh- heaven; unalloyed -happiness &c.

honeymoon; palmy –, halcyon- days;
golden -age, – time; *Saturnia regna*,
Eden, Arcadia, happy valley, Agapemone; Cockaigne.

V. be pleased &c. 829; feel –, experi-
ence- pleasure &c. *n.*; joy; enjoy –,
hug- oneself; be in -clover &c. 377,
– elysium &c. 981; tread on enchanted
ground; fall –, go- into raptures.

feel at home, breathe freely, bask in
the sunshine.

be -pleased &c. 829- with; receive –,
derive- pleasure &c. *n.*- from; take
-pleasure &c. *n.*- in; delight in, rejoice

828. Pain. — N. mental suffering,
pain, dolour; suffer-ing, -ance; ache,
smart &c. (*physical pain*) 378; passion.

displeasure, dissatisfaction, discomfort, discomposure, disquiet; *malaise*;
inquietude, uneasiness, vexation of
spirit; taking; discontent &c. 832.

dejection &c. 837; weariness &c. 841.

annoyance, irritation, worry, infliction, visitation; plague, bore; bother,
-ation; stew, vexation, mortification,
chagrin, *esclandre*; *mauvais quart
d'heure.*

care, anxiety, solicitude, trouble,
trial, ordeal, fiery ordeal, shock, blow,
cark, dole, fret, burden, load.

concern, grief, sorrow, distress, affliction, woe, bitterness, gloom, heartache;
heavy –, aching –, bleeding –, broken-
heart; heavy affliction, gnawing grief.
unhappiness, infelicity, misery, trib-
ulation, wretchedness, desolation; despair &c. 859; extremity, prostration,
depth of misery.

nightmare, *ephialtes*, incubus.

anguish, agony; throe, tor-ture,
-ment; crucifixion, martyrdom; pang,
twinge, stab; the rack, the stake;
purgatory &c. (*hell*) 982.

hell upon earth; iron age, reign of
terror; slough of despond &c. (*adversity*) 735; peck –, sea- of troubles; ills
that flesh is heir to &c. (*evil*) 619;

* Or those which concern one's own state of feeling.

in, indulge in, luxuriate in; gloat over &c. (*physical pleasure*) 377; enjoy, relish, like; love &c. 897; take -to, - a fancy to; have a liking for; enter into the spirit of.

take in good part.

treat oneself to, solace oneself with.

Adj. pleased &c. 829; not sorry; glad, -some; pleased as Punch.

happy, blest, blessed, blissful, beatified; happy as -a king, - the day is long; thrice happy, *ter quaterque beatus*; enjoying &c. *v.*; joyful &c. (*in spirits*) 836; hedonic.

in -a blissful state, - paradise &c. 981, - raptures, - ecstasies, - a transport of delight.

comfortable &c. (*physical pleasure*) 377; at ease; content &c. 831; *sans souci*, in clover.

overjoyed, entranced, enchanted; enraptured; en-, ravished; transported; fascinated, captivated.

with -a joyful face, - sparkling eyes.

pleasing &c. 829; ecstatic, beat-ic, -ific; painless, unalloyed, without alloy, cloudless.

Adv. happily &c. *adj.*; with pleasure &c. (*willingly*) 60; with -glee &c. *n.*

Phr. one's heart leaping with joy.

---

miseries of human life; unkindest cut of all.

sufferer, victim, prey, martyr, object of compassion, wretch, shorn lamb.

V. feel -, suffer -, experience -, undergo -, bear -, endure- pain &c. *n.*; smart, ache &c. (*physical pain*) 378; suffer, bleed, ail; be the victim of; bear -, take up- the cross.

labour under afflictions; quaff the bitter cup, have a bad time of it; fall on evil days &c. (*adversity*) 735; go hard with, come to grief, fall a sacrifice to, drain the cup of misery to the dregs, sup full of horrors.

sit on thorns, be on pins and needles, wince, fret, chafe, worry oneself, be in a taking, fret and fume, take -on, - to heart.

grieve; mourn &c. (*lament*) 839; yearn, repine, pine, droop, languish, sink; give way; despair &c. 859; break one's heart; weigh upon the heart &c. (*inflict pain*) 830.

Adj. in -, in a state of -, full of- pain &c. *n.*; suffering &c. *v.*; pained, afflicted, worried, displeased &c. 830; aching, griped, sore &c. (*physical pain*) 378; on the rack, in limbo; between hawk and buzzard.

un-comfortable, -easy; ill at ease; in a -taking, - way; disturbed; discontented &c. 832; out of humour &c. 901*a*; weary &c. 841.

heavy laden, stricken, crushed, a prey to, victimized, ill-used.

unfortunate &c. (*hapless*) 735; to be pitied, doomed, devoted, accursed, undone, lost, stranded.

unhappy, infelicitous, poor, wretched, miserable, woe-begone; cheerless &c. (*dejected*) 837; careworn.

concerned, sorry; sorrow-ing, -ful; cut up, chagrined, horrified, horror-stricken; in -, plunged in -, a prey to- grief &c. *n.*; in tears &c. (*lamenting*) 839; steeped to the lips in misery; heart-stricken, -broken, -scalded; broken-hearted; in despair &c. 859.

Phr. 'the iron entered into our soul'; '*hæret lateri lethalis arundo*'; one's heart bleeding.

---

829. [Capability of giving pleasure; cause or source of pleasure.] **Pleasurableness.**—**N.** pleasurable-, pleasant-, agreeable-ness &c. *adj.*; pleasure giving, jocundity, delectability; amusement &c. 840.

attraction &c. (*motive*) 615; attractiveness, -ability; invitingness &c. *adj.*; charm, fascination, captivation, en-

830. [Capability of giving pain; cause or source of pain.] **Painfulness.** —**N.** painfulness &c. *adj.*; trouble, care &c. (*pain*) 828; trial; af-, in-fliction; cross, blow, stroke, burden, load, curse; bitter -pill, - draught, - cup; waters of bitterness.

annoyance, grievance, nuisance, vexation, mortification, sickener; bore,

chantment, witchery, seduction, winsomeness, winning ways, amenity, amiability, sweetness.

loveliness &c. (*beauty*) 845; sunny –, bright- side; sweets &c. (*sugar*) 396; goodness &c. 648; manna in the wilderness, land flowing with milk and honey.

treat; regale &c. (*physical pleasure*) 377; dainty; tit-, tid-bit; nuts, *sauce piquante.*

V. cause –, produce –, create –, give –, afford –, procure –, offer –, present –, yield- pleasure &c. 827.

please, charm, delight; gladden &c. (*make cheerful*) 836; take, captivate, fascinate; enchant, entrance, enrapture, transport, bewitch; en-, ravish.

bless, beatify; satisfy; gratify, – desire &c. 865; slake, satiate, quench; indulge, humour, flatter, tickle; tickle the palate &c. (*savoury*) 394; regale, refresh; enliven; treat; amuse &c. 840; take –, tickle –, hit- one's fancy; meet one's wishes; win –, gladden –, rejoice –, warm the cockles of- the heart; do one's heart good.

attract, allure &c. (*move*) 615; stimulate &c. (*excite*) 824; interest, intrigue.

make things pleasant, popularize, gild the pill, sweeten.

Adj. causing pleasure &c. *v.*; pleasure-giving; pleas-ing, -ant, -urable; agreeable, cushy; grat-eful, -ifying; leef, lief, acceptable; welcome, – as the roses in May; welcomed; favourite; to one's -taste, – mind, – liking, – heart's content; satisfactory &c. (*good*) 648.

refreshing; comfortable; cordial; genial; glad, -some; sweet, delectable, nice, dainty; delic-ate, -ious; dulcet; luscious &c. 396; palatable &c. 394; luxurious, voluptuous; sensual &c. 377.

attractive &c. 615; inviting, prepossessing, engaging; win-ning, -some; taking, fascinating, captivating, killing; seduc-ing, -tive; alluring, enticing; appetizing &c. (*exciting*) 824; cheering &c. 836; bewitching; interesting, absorbing, enchanting, entrancing, enravishing.

charming; delightful, felicitous, exquisite; lovely &c. (*beautiful*) 845;

bother, pother, hot water, sea of troubles, hornet's nest, plague, pest.

cancer, ulcer, sting, thorn; canker &c. (*bane*) 663; scorpion &c. (*evil-doer*) 913; dagger &c. (*arms*) 727; scourge &c. (*instrument of punishment*) 975; carking –, canker worm of- care.

mishap, misfortune &c. (*adversity*) 735; *désagrément, esclandre,* rub.

source of -irritation, – annoyance; wound, sore subject, skeleton in the closet; thorn in -the flesh, – one's side; where the shoe pinches, gall and wormwood.

sorry sight, heavy news, provocation; affront &c. 929; head and front of one's offending.

infestation, molestation; malignity &c. (*malevolence*) 907.

V. cause –, occasion –, give –, bring –, induce –, produce –, create –, inflict- pain &c. 828; pain, hurt, wound.

pinch, prick, gripe &c. (*physical pain*) 378; pierce, lancinate, cut.

hurt –, wound –, grate upon –, jar upon- the feelings; wring –, pierce –, lacerate –, break –, rend- the heart; make the heart bleed; tear –, rend- the heart-strings; draw tears from the eyes.

sadden; make -unhappy &c. 828; plunge into sorrow, grieve, fash, afflict, distress; cut -up, – to the heart.

displease, annoy, incommode, discommode, discompose, trouble, disquiet, disturb, thwart, cross, perplex, molest, tease, rag, tire, irk, vex, mortify, wherret, worry, plague, bother, pester, bore, pother, harass, harry, badger, heckle, bait, beset, infest, persecute, importune, be troublesome.

wring, harrow, torment, torture; put to the -rack, – question; break on the wheel, rack, scarify; cruci-ate, -fy; convulse, agonize; barb the dart; plant a -dagger in the breast, – thorn in one's side.

irritate, provoke, sting, nettle, try the patience, pique, fret, rile, tweak the nose, chafe, gall; sting –, wound –, cut- to the quick; aggrieve, affront, enchafe, enrage, ruffle, sour the temper; give offence &c. (*resentment*) 900.

ravishing, rapturous; heartfelt, thrilling, ecstatic; beat-ic, -ific; seraphic; empyrean; elysian &c. (*heavenly*) 981. palmy, halcyon, Saturnian.

Phr. *decies repetita placebit.*

maltreat, bite, snap at, assail, bully; smite &c. (*punish*) 972.

sicken, disgust, revolt, nauseate, disenchant, repel, offend, shock, stink in the nostrils; go against -, turn- the stomach; make one sick, set the teeth on edge, go against the grain, grate on the ear; stick in one's -throat, - gizzard; rankle, gnaw, corrode, horrify, appal, freeze the blood; chill the spine; make the -flesh creep, - hair stand on end; make the blood -curdle, - run cold; make one shudder.

haunt, - the memory; weigh -, prey- on the -heart, - mind, - spirits; bring one's grey hairs with sorrow to the grave; add a nail to one's coffin.

Adj. causing pain, hurting &c. *v.*; hurtful &c. (*bad*) 649; painful; dolor-ific, -ous; unpleasant; un-, dis-pleasing; disagreeable, unpalatable, bitter, distasteful; uninviting; unwelcome; undesir-able, -ed; obnoxious; unacceptable, unpopular, thankless.

unsatisfactory, untoward, unlucky, uncomfortable.

distressing; afflict-ing, -ive; joy-, cheer-, comfort-less; dismal, disheartening; depress-ing, -ive; dreary, melancholy, grievous, piteous; woeful, rueful, mournful, deplorable, pitiable, lamentable; sad, affecting, touching, pathetic.

irritating, provoking, stinging, annoying, aggravating, mortifying, galling; unaccommodating, invidious, vexatious; trouble-, tire-, irk-, weari-some; plagu-ing, -y; awkward.

importunate; teas-, pester-, bother-, harass-, worry-, torment-, cark-ing.

in-toler-, -suffer-, -support-able; un-bear-, -endur-able; past bearing; not to be -borne, - endured; more than flesh and blood can bear; enough to -drive one mad, - provoke a saint, - make a parson swear, - try the patience of Job.

shocking, terrific, grim, appalling, crushing; dreadful, fearful, frightful; thrilling, tremendous, dire; heart-breaking, -rending, -wounding, -corroding, -sickening; harrowing, rending.

odious, hateful, execrable, repulsive, repellent, abhorrent; horri-d, -ble, -fic, -fying; offensive; nause-ous, -ating; disgust-, sicken-, revolt-ing; nasty; loath-some, -ful; fulsome; vile &c. (*bad*) 649; hideous &c. 846.

sharp, acute, sore, severe, grave, hard, harsh, cruel, biting, acrimonious, caustic; cutting, corroding, consuming, racking, excruciating, searching, searing, grinding, grating, agonizing; envenomed.

ruinous, disastrous, calamitous, tragical; desolating, withering; burdensome, onerous, oppressive; cumb-rous, -ersome.

Adv. painfully &c. *adj.*; with -pain &c. 828; deuced.

Int. *hinc illæ lachrymæ!* woe is me!

Phr. *surgit amari aliquid*; the place being too hot to hold one; the iron entering into the soul.

---

831. Content.—**N.** content, -ment, -edness; complacency, satisfaction, entire satisfaction, ease, heart's ease, peace of mind; serenity &c. 826; cheer-

832. Discontent. — **N.** discontent, -ment; dissatisfaction; dissent &c. 489; labour unrest.

disappointment, mortification; cold

fulness &c. 836; ray of comfort; comfort &c. (*well-being*) 827.

re-, conciliation; resignation &c. (*patience*) 826.

waiter on Providence.

V. be -content &c. *adj.*; rest -satisfied, – and be thankful; take the good the gods provide, let well alone, feel oneself at home, hug oneself, lay the flattering unction to one's soul.

take -up with, – in good part; assent &c. 488; be reconciled to, make one's peace with; get over it; take -heart, – comfort; put up with &c. (*bear*) 826.

render -content &c. *adj.*; set at ease, comfort; set one's -heart, – mind- at -ease, – rest; speak peace; conciliate, reconcile, win over, propitiate, disarm, beguile; content, satisfy; gratify &c. 829.

be -tolerated &c. 826; go down, – with; do.

Adj. content, -ed; satisfied &c. *v.*; at -ease, – one's ease, – home; with the mind at ease, *sans souci, sine curâ*, easy-going, not particular; conciliatory; unrepining, of good comfort; resigned &c. (*patient*) 826; cheerful &c. 836.

un-afflicted, -vexed, -molested, -plagued; serene &c. 826; at rest; snug, comfortable; in one's element.

satisfactory, satisfying, ample, sufficient, adequate, tolerable.

Adv. to one's heart's content; *à la bonne heure*; all for the best.

Int. amen &c. (*assent*) 488; very well, so much the better, well and good; it –, that- will do; it cannot be helped.

Phr. nothing comes amiss.

comfort; regret &c. 833; repining, taking on &c. *v.*; inquietude, vexation of spirit, soreness; heart-burning, -grief; querulousness &c. (*lamentation*) 839; hypercriticism.

malcontent, grumbler, growler, croaker, *laudator temporis acti*; censurer, complainer, faultfinder, murmurer, Adullamite, Diehard, Bitterender.

the Opposition, cave of Adullam, indignation meeting, 'winter of our discontent.'

V. be -discontented &c. *adj.*; quarrel with one's bread and butter; repine; regret &c. 833; wish one at the bottom of the Red Sea; take -on, – to heart; shrug the shoulders; make a wry –, pull a long- face; knit one's brows; look -blue, – black, – black as thunder, – blank, – glum.

take -in bad part, – ill; fret, chafe, make a piece of work; grumble, croak, grouse; lament &c. 839.

cause -discontent &c. *n.*; dissatisfy, disappoint, mortify, put out, disconcert; cut up; dishearten.

Adj. discontented; dissatisfied &c. *v.*; unsatisfied, ungratified; dissident; dissentient &c. 489; malcontent, exigent, exacting, hypercritical.

repining &c. *v.*; regretful &c. 833; down in the mouth &c. (*dejected*) 837.

in -high dudgeon, – a fume, – the sulks, – the dumps, – bad humour; glum, sulky; sour, – as a crab; soured, sore; out of -humour, – temper.

disappointing &c. *v.*; unsatisfactory.

Int. so much the worse!

Phr. that –, it- will never do.

---

833. Regret.—**N.** regret, repining; home sickness, nostalgia; *mal –, maladie-du pays*; lamentation &c. 839, contrition, compunction, penitence &c. 950.

bitterness, heart-burning.

laudator temporis acti &c. (*discontent*) 832.

V. regret, deplore; bewail &c. (*lament*) 839; repine, cast a longing lingering look behind; rue, – the day; repent &c. 950; *infandum renovare dolorem*.

prey –, weigh –, have a weight- on the mind; leave an aching void.

Adj. regretting &c. *v.*; regretful; home-sick.

regretted &c. *v.*; much to be regretted, regrettable; lamentable &c. (*bad*) 649.

Int. what a pity! hang it!
Phr. 'tis -pity, - too true.

834. Relief.—**N.** relief; deliverance; refreshment &c. 689; easement, softening, alleviation, mitigation, palliation &c. 174; soothing, lullaby; cradle song, *berceuse.*

solace, consolation, comfort, encouragement.

lenitive, restorative &c. (*remedy*) 662; poultice &c. *v.*; cushion &c. 215; crumb of comfort, balm in Gilead; aspirin.

V. relieve, ease, alleviate, mitigate, palliate, soothe, addulce; salve; soften, - down; foment, stupe, poultice; assuage, allay.

cheer, comfort, console; encourage, bear up, pat on the back, give comfort, set at ease; enliven, gladden -, cheer-the heart.

remedy; cure &c. (*restore*) 660; refresh; pour -balm into, - oil on.
smooth the ruffled brow of care, temper the wind to the shorn lamb, lay the flattering unction to one's soul.

disburden &c. (*free*) 705; take off a load of care.
be relieved; breathe more freely, draw a long breath; take comfort; dry -, wipe- the -tears, - eyes.

Adj. relieving &c. *v.*; consolatory, soothing; assua-ging, -sive; bal-my, -samic; lenitive, palliative; anodyne &c. (*remedial*) 662; curative &c. 660.

835. Aggravation.—**N.** aggravation, heightening; exacerbation; exasperation; overestimation &c. 482; exaggeration &c. 549.

V. aggravate, render worse, heighten, embitter, sour; ex-, acerbate; exasperate, envenom; tease, provoke, enrage.

add fuel to the -fire, - flame; fan the flame &c. (*excite*) 824; go from bad to worse &c. (*deteriorate*) 659.

Adj. aggravated &c. *v.*; worse, unrelieved; aggravable; aggravating &c. *v.*

Adv. out of the frying pan into the fire, from bad to worse, worse and worse.

Int. so much the worse!

---

836. Cheerfulness.—**N.** cheerfulness &c. *adj.*; geniality, gaiety, *l'allegro*, cheer, good humour, spirits; high -, animal -, flow of- spirits; glee, high glee, light heart; sunshine of the -mind, - breast; *gaieté de cœur, bon naturel.*

liveliness &c. *adj.*; life, alacrity, vivacity, animation, *allégresse*; jocundity, joviality, jollity; levity; jocularity &c. (*wit*) 842.

mirth, merriment, hilarity, exhilaration; laughter &c. 838; merry-making &c. (*amusement*) 840; heyday, rejoicing &c. 838; marriage bells.

nepenthe, Euphrosyne.

optimism &c. (*hopefulness*) 858; self-complacency.

V. be -cheerful &c. *adj.*; have the mind at ease, smile, put a good face upon, keep up one's spirits; view -the bright side of the picture, - things *en couleur de rose; ridentem dicere verum,*

837. Dejection.—**N.** dejection; dejectedness &c. *adj.*; depression, prosternation; lowness -, depression- of spirits; weight -, oppression -, damp-on the spirits; low -, bad -, drooping -, depressed- spirits; heart sinking; heaviness -, failure- of heart.

heaviness &c. *adj.*; infestivity, gloom; weariness &c. 841; *tædium vitæ*, disgust of life; *mal du pays* &c. (*regret*) 833.

melancholy; sadness &c. *adj.; il penseroso, melancholia*, dismals, mumps, mopes, lachrymals, dumps, blues, blue devils, doldrums, vapours, megrims, spleen, horrors, hypochondriasis, pessimism; despondency, slough of Despond; disconsolateness &c. *adj.*; hope deferred, blank despondency.

prostration, - of soul; broken heart; despair &c. 859; cave of -despair, - Trophonius.

cheer up, brighten up, light up, bear up; chirp, take heart, cast away care, drive dull care away, perk up.

rejoice &c. 838; carol, chirrup, lilt; frisk, rollick, give a loose to mirth.

cheer, enliven, elate, exhilarate, gladden, inspirit, animate, raise the spirits, inspire; put in good humour; cheer -, rejoice- the heart; delight &c. (*give pleasure*) 829.

Adj. cheerful; happy &c. 827; cheery, -ly; of good cheer, smiling; blithe; in -, in good- spirits; in high -spirits, - feather; happy as -the day is long, - a king; gay, - as a lark; *allegro*; light, -some, -hearted; buoyant, *débonnaire*, bright, free and easy, airy; janty, jaunty, canty; spright-ly, -ful; spry; spirit-ed, -ful; lively; animated, breezy, vivacious; brisk, - as a bee; sparkling; sportive; full of -play, - spirit; all alive.

sunny, palmy; hopeful &c. 858.

merry, - as a -cricket, - grig, - marriage bell; joyful, joyous, jocund, jovial; jolly, - as a thrush, - as a sandboy; blithesome; glee-ful, -some; hilarious, rattling.

winsome, bonny, hearty, buxom.

play-ful, -some; *folâtre*, playful as a kitten, tricksy, frisky, frolicsome; gamesome; jocose, jocular, waggish; mirth-, laughter-loving; mirthful, rollicking.

elate, -d; exulting, jubilant, flushed; rejoicing &c. 838; cock-a-hoop.

cheering, inspiriting, exhilarating; cardiac, -al; pleasing &c. 829; flourishing, halcyon.

Adv. cheerfully &c. *adj.*

Int. never say die! come! cheer up! hurrah! &c. 838; 'hence loathed melancholy!' begone dull care! away with melancholy!

demureness &c. *adj.*; gravity, solemnity; long -, grave- face.

hypochondriac, seek-sorrow, self-tormentor, *heautontimorumenos*, *malade imaginaire*, *médecin tant pis*; croaker, pessimist; mope, mopus.

[Cause of dejection] affliction &c. 830; sorry sight; *memento mori*; damper, wet blanket, Job's comforter; death's head, skeleton at the feast.

V. be -dejected &c. *adj.*; grieve; mourn &c. (*lament*) 839; take on, give way, lose heart, despond, droop, sink.

lower, look downcast, frown, pout; hang down the head; pull -, make- a long face; laugh on the wrong side of the mouth; grin a ghastly smile; look -blue, - like a drowned man; lay -, take- to heart.

mope, brood over; fret; sulk; pine, - away; yearn; repine &c. (*regret*) 833; despair &c. 859.

refrain from laughter, keep one's countenance; be -, look- grave &c. *adj.*; repress a smile, keep a straight face.

depress; dis-courage, -hearten; dispirit; damp, dull, deject, lower, sink, dash, knock down, unman, prostrate, break one's heart; frown upon; cast a -gloom, - shade- on; sadden; damp -, dash -, wither- one's hopes; weigh -, lie heavy -, prey- on the -mind, - spirits; damp -, depress- the spirits.

Adj. cheer-, joy-, spirit-less; uncheerful, -y; unlively; unhappy &c. 828; melancholy, dismal, sombre, dark, gloomy, adust, *triste*, clouded, murky, lowering, frowning, lugubrious, Acherontic, funereal, mournful, lamentable, dreadful.

dreary, flat; dull, - as -a beetle, - ditchwater; depressing &c. *v.*

'melancholy as a gib cat'; oppressed with -, a prey to- melancholy; downcast, -hearted; down -in the mouth, - on one's luck; heavy-hearted; in the -dumps, - suds, - sulks, - doldrums; in doleful dumps, in bad humour; sullen; mumpish, dumpish; mopish, moping; moody, glum; sulky &c. (*discontented*) 832; out of -sorts, - humour, - heart, - spirits; ill at ease, low-spirited, in low spirits, a cup too low; weary &c. 841; dis-couraged, -heartened; desponding; chop-, jaw-, crest-fallen.

sad, pensive, *penseroso*, tristful; dole-some, -ful; woebegone, lachrymose, in tears, melancholic, hypped, hypochondriacal, bilious, jaundiced, atrabilious, saturnine, splenetic; lackadaisical.

serious, sedate, staid, stayed; grave, – as -a judge, – an undertaker, – a mustard pot; sober, solemn, demure; grim; grim-faced, -visaged; rueful, wan, long-faced.

disconsolate; un-, in-consolable; forlorn, comfortless, desolate, désolé, sick at heart; soul-, heart-sick; au désespoir; in despair &c. 859; lost.

overcome; broken-, borne-, bowed-down; heart-stricken &c. (*mental suffering*) 828; cut up, dashed, sunk; unnerved, unmanned; down-fallen, -trodden; broken-hearted; care-worn.

Adv. with -a long face, – tears in one's eyes; sadly &c. *adj.*

Phr. the countenance falling; the heart -failing, – sinking within-one.

838. [Expression of pleasure.] **Rejoicing.—N.** rejoicing, exultation, triumph, jubilation, heyday, flush, revelling; merry-making &c. (*amusement*) 840; jubilee &c. (*celebration*) 883; pæan, *Te Deum* &c. (*thanksgiving*) 990; congratulation &c. 896; applause &c. 971.

smile, simper, smirk, grin; broad –, sardonic- grin.

laughter, giggle, titter, crow, cheer, chuckle, snicker, snigger, shout; Homeric laughter, horse –, hearty- laugh; guffaw; burst –, fit –, shout –, roar –, peal- of laughter; cachinnation.

risibility; derision &c. 856.

Momus; Democritus the Abderite; rollicker; Laughter holding both his sides.

V. rejoice; thank –, bless- one's stars; congratulate –, hug- oneself; rub –, clap- one's hands; smack the lips, fling up one's cap; dance, skip, caleer; sing, carol, chirrup, chirp; hurrah; cry for –, leap with- joy; exult &c. (*boast*) 884; triumph; hold jubilee &c. (*celebrate*) 883; make merry &c. (*sport*) 840; sing a pæan of joy.

smile, simper, smirk; grin, – like a Cheshire cat; mock, laugh in one's sleeve; laugh, – outright; giggle, titter, snigger, crow, smicker, chuckle, snicker, cackle; burst -out, – into a fit of laughter; shout, split, roar.

shake –, split –, hold both- one's sides; roar –, die- with laughter.

raise laughter &c. (*amuse*) 840.

Adj. rejoicing &c. *v.*; jubilant, exultant, triumphant; flushed, elated; laughing &c. *v.*; risible; ready to -burst, – split, – die with laughter; convulsed with laughter.

839. [Expression of pain.] **Lamentation.—N.** lament, -ation; wail, complaint, plaint, murmur, mutter, grumble, groan, moan, whine, whimper, sob, sigh, suspiration, heaving, deep sigh.

cry &c. (*vociferation*) 411; scream, howl; outcry, wail of woe, frown, scowl.

tear; weeping &c. *v.*; flood of tears, fit of crying, lachrymation, melting mood, weeping and gnashing of teeth.

plaintiveness &c. *adj.*; languishment; condolence &c. 915.

mourning, weeds, willow, cypress, crêpe, crape, deep mourning; sackcloth and ashes; knell &c. 363; dump, death-song, dirge, coronach, keen, *nenia*, requiem, elegy, *epicedium*; threne; mon-, thren-ody; jeremiad; ululation.

mourner, professional mourner, keener; grumbler &c. (*discontent*) 832; Niobe; Heraclitus.

V. lament, mourn, deplore, grieve, weep over; be-wail, -moan; keen; condole with &c. 915; fret &c. (*suffer*) 828; wear –, go into –, put on- mourning; wear -the willow, – sackcloth and ashes; *infandum renovare dolorem* &c. (*regret*) 833; give sorrow words.

sigh; give –, heave –, fetch- a sigh; 'waft a sigh from Indus to the pole'; sigh 'like furnace'; wail.

cry, weep, sob, greet, blubber, pipe, snivel, bibber, whimper, pule; pipe one's eye; drop –, shed- -tears, – a tear; melt –, burst- into tears; *fondre en larmes*; cry -oneself blind, – one's eyes out.

scream &c. (*cry out*) 411; mew &c. (*animal sounds*) 412; groan, moan,

laughable &c. (*ludicrous*) 853.

Int. hip, hip, -hurrah! huzza! aha! hail! tolderolloll! tra-la la! Heaven be praised! *io triumphe! tant mieux!* so much the better.

Phr. the heart leaping with joy.

————

whine, yammer; roar; roar –, bellow-like a bull; cry out lustily, rend the air, yell.

frown, scowl, make a wry face, grimace, gnash one's teeth, wring one's hands, tear one's hair, beat one's breast, roll on the ground, burst with grief.

complain, murmur, mutter, grumble, growl, clamour, make a fuss about, croak, grunt, maunder; deprecate &c. (*disapprove*) 932.

cry out before one is hurt, complain without cause.

Adj. lamenting &c. *v.*; in mourning, in sackcloth and ashes; crying, sorrowing, -ful &c. (*unhappy*) 828; mourn-, tear-ful; lachrymose; plaint-ive, -ful, quer-ulous, -imonious; in the melting mood.

in tears, with tears in one's eyes; with -moistened, – watery- eyes; bathed –, dissolved- in tears; 'like Niobe all tears.'

elagiac, epicedial, threnetic.

Adv. *de profundis*; *les larmes aux yeux.*

Int. heigh-ho! alas! alack! O dear! ah –, woe is- me! lackadaisy! well –, lack –, alack- a day! well-a-way! alas the day! *O tempora! O mores!* what a pity! *miserabile dictu!* O lud lud! too true!

Phr. tears -standing in, – starting from- the eyes; eyes -suffused, – swimming, – brimming –, overflowing- with tears.

840. Amusement.—**N.** amuse-, entertain-ment; diver-sion, -tissement; reaction, relaxation, solace; pastime, *passetemps*, sport; labour of love; pleasure &c. 827.

fun, frolic, merriment, whoopee, jollity; jovial-ity, -ness; heyday; laughter &c. 838; jocos-ity, -eness; droll-, buffoon-, tomfool-ery; mummery, masquing, pleasantry; wit &c. 842; quip, quirk.

play; game, – at romps; gambol, romp, prank, antic, rig, lark, spree, skylarking, vagary, trick, monkey trick, *gambade*, *fredaine*, *escapade*, *échappée*, bout, *espièglerie*; practical joke &c. (*ridicule*) 856.

dance; round –, square –, solo –, step –, tap –, clog –, skirt –, sand –, folk –, morris- dance, *pas seul*, step, turn, *chassé*, cut, shuffle, double shuffle; hop, reel, rigadoon, saraband, hornpipe, bolero, fandango, pavan, tarantella, minuet, waltz, polka; galop, -ade; Schottische, *pas de quatre*, Boston, one-, two-step, rumba, tango, maxixe, fox-, turkey-trot, shimmy, ragtime, cakewalk, jazz, blues, Charleston; jig, breakdown, fling, strathspey; *alle-*

841. Weariness.—**N.** weariness, defatigation, boredom, *ennui*; lassitude &c. (*fatigue*) 688; drowsiness &c. 683.

disgust, nausea, loathing, sickness; satiety &c. 869; *tædium vitæ* &c. (*dejection*) 837.

wearisome-, tedious-ness &c. *adj.*; dull work, tedium, monotony, twice told tale.

bore, button-hole, proser, wet blanket; heavy hours, 'the enemy' [time].

V. weary; tire &c. (*fatigue*) 688; bore; bore –, weary –, tire- -to death, – out of one's life, – out of all patience; set –, send- to sleep.

pall, sicken, nauseate, disgust.

harp on the same string; drag its -slow, – weary- length along.

never hear the last of; be -tired &c. *adj.* -of, – with; yawn; die with *ennui*.

Adj. wearying &c. *v.*; wearing; weari-, tire-, irk-some; uninteresting, stupid, bald, devoid of interest, dry, monotonous, dull, arid, tedious, humdrum, mortal, flat; pros-y, -ing; slow; soporific, somniferous, dormitive.

disgusting &c. *v.*; unenjoyed.

weary; tired &c. *v.*; drowsy &c. (*sleepy*) 683; uninterested, flagging,

mande; gavot, -te; mazurka, morisco; quadrille, lancers, country dance, *cotillon*, polonaise, Sir Roger de Coverley, Swedish dance; *ballet* &c. (*drama*) 599; ball; *bal, – masqué, – costumé*; masquerade, fancy dress ball; *thé dansant*; Terpsichore, choreography, Russian ballet, classical dancing; eurythmics; nautch dance, *danse du ventre*, cancan.

festivity, merry-making; party &c. (*social gathering*) 892; *fête*, festival, gala, *ridotto*; revel-s, -ry, -ling; carnival, brawl, saturnalia, high jinks; feast, banquet &c. (*food*) 298; regale, *symposium*, wassail; carous-e, -al; jollification, junket, wake, pic-nic, *fête champêtre*, garden party, gymkhana, regatta, track meet, field-day, jamboree, treat.

round of pleasures, dissipation, a short life and a merry one, racketing, holiday making, high jinks.

rejoicing &c. 838; jubilee &c. (*celebration*) 883.

bonfire, fireworks, *feu-de-joie*, rocket, catherine wheel, roman candle &c.

holiday; gala –, red letter –, play- day; high days and holidays; high –, Bank- holiday; May –, Derby- day; Saint –, Easter –, Whit- Monday; King's birthday, Empire Day; *mi-carême*; *Bairam*; wayzgoose, bean feast, beano.

place of amusement, theatre &c. 599; concert-, ball-, assembly-room; music-hall, cinema, movies, talkies, vaudeville; hippodrome, circus, rodeo; *casino, kursaal*; winter garden; park, pleasance, arbour; garden &c. 371; pleasure-, play-, cricket-, football-, polo-, croquet-, archery-, hunting-ground; golf links, race course, stadium, gridiron, bowl, speedway, racing track, ring; gymnasium, swimming pool; shooting gallery; tennis-, racket-court; bowling-green, -alley; croquet-lawn, rink, skating rink; roller-coaster, roundabout, carousel, merry-go-round; swing; *montagne russe*; switchback, scenic railway &c.

game, – of -chance, – skill; athletic sports, gymnastics; fencing; archery, rifle-shooting; tournament, pugilism &c. (*contention*) 720; sporting &c. 622; horse-racing, the turf; aquatics &c. 267; skating, roller skating; ski-running, -joring, -jumping, bobsleighing, luging, tobogganing, winter sports; sliding; cricket, tennis, lawn –, table –, deck- tennis, rackets, fives, squash, ping pong, trap bat and ball, battledore and shuttlecock, badminton, *la grâce*; pall mall, tip-cat, croquet, golf, curling, hockey, basketball, soccer, football, Rugby, Association, *pallone*, polo; tent-pegging, tilting at the ring, quintain, greasy pole; quoits, *discus*; throwing the hammer, putting the -weight, – shot, tossing the caber; knurr and spell; leap-frog, hop, skip and jump; French and English, tug of war; blind man's buff, hunt the slipper, hide-and-seek, kiss in the ring; snapdragon; cross questions and crooked answers; jig-saw puzzle; rounders, base-ball, *la crosse* &c.; angling; swimming, diving, water-polo.

billiards, pool, pyramids, snooker, bagatelle; bowls, skittles, ninepins, kail, American bowls.

cards; bridge, auction, contract, whist, rubber; round game, coon-can, loo, cribbage, *bésique*, pinocle, euchre, drole, *écarté*, skat, picquet, all-fours, quadrille, ombre, reverse, Pope Joan, commit;

used up, worn out, *blasé*, life-weary, weary of life; sick of.

Adv. wearily &c. *adj.*; *usque ad nauseam.*

Phr. time hanging heavily on one's hands; *toujours perdrix; crambe repetita.*

bo-, boa-ston; *vingt-et-un*; *quinze*, thirty-one, put-and-take, speculation, connections, brag, cassino, lottery‚commerce, snip-snap-snorem,
lift smoke, blind hookey, Polish bank, poker, banker; faro; Earl of
Coventry, Napoleon, nap, patience, pairs; old maid, fright, beggar-
my-neighbour; *baccarat, chemin de fer, monté, roulette.*

chess, draughts, backgammon, dominoes, checkers, mah jong,
merelles, nine men's morris, go-bang, solitaire; game of –, fox and-
goose; loto; &c.*

morra; gambling &c. (*chance*) 621.

toy, plaything, bauble; doll &c. (*puppet*) 554; teetotum; knick-
knack &c. (*trifle*) 643; magic lantern &c. (*show*) 448; peep-, puppet-,
raree-, gallanty-show; marionettes, Punch and Judy; toy-shop;
'quips and cranks and wanton wiles, nods and becks and wreathed
smiles.'

sportsman, gamester, gambler &c. 621; reveller, master of the
-ceremonies, – revels; *arbiter elegantiarum.*

V. amuse, entertain, divert, enliven; tickle, – the fancy; titillate,
raise a smile, put in good humour; cause –, create –, occasion –,
raise –, excite –, produce –, convulse with- laughter; set the table
in a roar, be the death of one.

recreate, solace, cheer, rejoice; please &c. 829; interest; treat,
regale.

amuse oneself; game; play, – a game, – pranks, – tricks; sport,
disport, toy, wanton, revel, junket, feast, carouse, banquet, make
merry; drown care; drive dull care away; frolic, gambol, frisk,
romp; caper; dance &c. (*leap*) 309; keep up the ball; run a rig,
sow one's wild oats, have one's fling, paint the town red, take
one's pleasure; see life; *desipere in loco,* play the fool.

make –, keep- holiday; go a Maying.

while away –, beguile- the time; kill time, dally.

Adj. amusing, entertaining, diverting &c. *v.*; recreative, lusory;
pleasant &c. (*pleasing*) 829; laughable &c. (*ludicrous*) 853; witty
&c. 842; fest-ive, -al; jovial, jolly, jocund, roguish, rompish; sporting; playful, – as a kitten; sportive, ludibrious.

amused &c. *v.*; 'pleased with a feather, tickled with a straw.'

Adv. 'on the light fantastic toe,' at play, in sport.

Int. *vive la bagatelle! vogue la galère!*

Phr. *Deus nobis hæc otia fecit; dum vivimus vivamus.*

---

842. Wit.—N. wit, -tiness; attic
-wit, – salt; atticism; salt, *esprit*, point,
fancy, whim, humour, drollery, pleasantry.

farce, buffoonery, fooling, tomfoolery; harlequinade &c. 599; broad
-farce, – humour; fun, *espièglerie*; *vis
comica.*

jocularity; jocos-ity, -eness; face-
tiousness; wagg-ery, -ishness; whim-
sicality; comicality &c. 853.

smartness, ready wit, banter, *badi-*

843. Dulness.—N. dulness, heaviness, flatness; infestivity &c. 837;
stupidity &c. 499; want of originality,
dearth of ideas.

prose, matter of fact; heavy book,
conte à dormir debout; platitude.

V. be -dull &c. *adj.*; prose, plati-
tudinize, take *au sérieux*, be caught
napping.

render -dull &c. *adj.*; damp, depress,
throw cold water on, lay a wet blanket
on; fall flat upon the ear; hang fire.

---

* A curious list of games is given in Sir Thomas Urquhart's translation of Rabelais'
Life of Gargantua, book i. chapter 22.

nage, persiflage, retort, repartee, *quid pro quo*; ridicule &c. 856.

facetiæ, quips and cranks; jest, joke, capital joke; standing -jest, − joke; conceit, quip, quirk, crank, quiddity, *concetto*, *plaisanterie*, brilliant idea; merry −, bright −, happy- thought; sally; flash, − of wit, − of merriment; scintillation; *mot, − pour rire*; witticism, smart saying, *bon mot, jeu d'esprit*, epigram; jest book; dry joke, *quodlibet*, cream of the jest.

word-play, *jeu de mots*; play -of, − upon- words; pun, -ning; *double entente* &c. (*ambiguity*) 520; quibble, verbal quibble; conundrum &c. (*riddle*) 533; anagram, acrostic, double acrostic, *nugæ canoræ*, trifling, idle conceit, *turlupinade*.

old joke, Joe Miller, chestnut, hoary-headed jest.

V. joke, jest, cut jokes; crack a joke; perpetrate a -joke, − pun; make -fun of, − merry with; set the table in a roar &c. (*amuse*) 840; scintillate.

retort, flash back; banter &c. (*ridicule*) 856; *ridentem dicere verum*; joke at one's expense.

Adj. witty, attic, salty; quick-, nimble-witted; keen, clever, smart, brilliant, pungent, jocular, jocose, funny, waggish, facetious, whimsical, humorous, gilbertian; playful &c. 840; merry and wise; pleasant, sprightly, *spirituel*, sparkling, epigrammatic, full of point, *ben trovato*; comic &c. 853.

Adv. in joke, in jest, in sport, in play.

Adj. dull, − as ditch water; dry, insipid, jejune; unentertaining, uninteresting, unlively, unimaginative; heavisome, heavy-gaited; insulse; dry as dust; pros-y, -ing, -aic; matter of fact, commonplace, banal, pointless; 'weary, flat, stale and unprofitable.'

stupid, slow, flat, sluggish, ponderous, humdrum, monotonous; melancholic &c. 837; stolid &c. 499; plodding.

Phr. *Davus sum non Œdipus.*

---

844. Humorist.—N. humorist, wag, wit, reparteeist, epigrammatist, gag man, punster; *bel esprit*, life of the party; wit-snapper, -cracker, -worm; joker, jester, jokesmith, Joe Miller, *drôle de corps, gaillard*, spark, *persiffleur*, banterer.

buffoon, *farceur*, merry-andrew, mime, tumbler, acrobat, mountebank, charlatan, posturemaster, harlequin, punch, *pulcinella*, scaramouch, clown; wearer of the -cap and bells, − motley; motley fool; pantaloon, gipsy; jack -pudding, − in the green, − a dandy; zany; mad-cap, pickle-herring, witling, caricaturist, *grimacier*.

2°. Discriminate Affections

845. Beauty.—N. beauty, the beautiful, *le beau ideal*, loveliness.

[Science of the perception of beauty] Callæsthetics.*

form, elegance, grace, beauty unadorned; symmetry &c. 242; comeliness, fairness &c. *adj.*; pulchritude, polish, gloss; good -effect, − looks; *belle tournure*; bloom, brilliancy, radiance, splendour, gorgeousness, magnificence; sublimi-ty, -fication.

846. Ugliness.—N. ugliness &c. *adj.*; deformity, inelegance; disfigurement &c. (*blemish*) 848; want of symmetry, inconcinnity; distortion &c. 243; squalor &c. (*uncleanness*) 653.

forbidding countenance, vinegar aspect, hanging look, wry face, '*spretæ injuria formæ*.'

eyesore, object, figure, sight, fright, spectre, scarecrow, hag, harridan, satyr, witch, toad, baboon, monster,

* Whewell, 'Philosophy of the Inductive Sciences.'

concinnity, delicacy, . refinement; charm, *je ne sais quoi*, style, *chic*, swank.

Venus, – of Milo; Aphrodite, Hebe, the Graces, Peri, Houri, Cupid, Apollo, Hyperion, Adonis, Antinous, Narcissus; Helen of Troy.

peacock, butterfly; flower, flow'ret gay, rose, lily, asphodel; garden; flower of, pink of; *bijou*; jewel &c. (*ornament*) 847; work of art.

pleasurableness &c. 829.

beautifying; landscape gardening; decoration &c. 847; calisthenics.

V. be -beautiful &c. *adj.*; shine, beam, bloom; become one &c. (*accord*) 23; set off, grace, flatter one.

render -beautiful &c. *adj.*; beautify; polish, burnish; gild &c. (*decorate*) 847; set out.

'snatch a grace beyond the reach of art.'

Adj. beaut-iful, -eous; handsome; pretty; lovely, graceful, elegant; delicate, dainty, refined, exquisite; fair, personable, comely, seemly; bonny; good-looking; well-favoured, -made, -formed, -proportioned; proper, shapely; symmetrical &c. (*regular*) 242; harmonious &c. (*colour*) 428; sightly.

fit to be seen, passable, not amiss.

goodly, dapper, tight, jimp; gimp; janty, jaunty; natty, quaint, trim, tidy, neat, spruce, smart, tricksy.

bright, -eyed; rosy-, cherry-cheeked; rosy, ruddy; blooming, in full bloom.

brilliant, shining; beam-y, -ing; sparkling, swanky, splendid, resplendent, dazzling, glowing; glossy, sleek.

showy, specious; rich, gorgeous, superb, magnificent, grand, fine, sublime, imposing; majestic 873.

artistic, -al; æsthetic; pict-uresque, -orial; *fait à peindre*, paintable; well-composed, -grouped, -varied; curious.

enchanting &c. (*pleasure-giving*) 829; attractive &c. (*inviting*) 615; becoming &c. (*accordant*) 23; ornamental &c. 847.

undeformed, undefaced, unspotted; spotless &c. (*perfect*) 650.

Caliban, Æsop, '*monstrum horrendum informe ingens cui lumen ademptum.*'

V. be -ugly &c. *adj.*; look ill, grin horribly a ghastly smile, make faces.

render -ugly &c. *adj.*; deface; dis-, de-figure; deform, spoil, distort &c. 243; blemish &c. (*injure*) 659; soil &c. (*render unclean*) 653.

Adj. ugly, – as -sin, – a toad, – a scarecrow, – a dead monkey; plain, bald &c. 226; homely &c. (*unadorned*) 849; ordinary, unornamental, inartistic; unsightly, unseemly, uncomely, unshapely, unlovely; sightless, seemless; not fit to be seen; unbeaut-eous, -iful; beautiless; shapeless &c. (*amorphous*) 241; course; garish, over-decorated &c. 882.

mis-shapen, -proportioned; monstrous; gaunt &c. (*thin*) 203; dumpy &c. (*short*) 201; curtailed of its fair proportions; ill-made, -shaped, -proportioned; crooked &c. (*distorted*) 243; hard-featured, -visaged; ill-, hard-, evil-favoured; ill-looking; unprepossessing.

graceless, inelegant; ungraceful, ungainly, uncouth; stiff; rugged, rough, gross, rude, awkward, clumsy, slouching, rickety; gawky; lump-ing, -ish; lumbering; hulk-y, -ing; unwieldy.

squalid, haggard; grim, -faced, -visaged; grisly, ghastly; ghost-, death-like; cadaverous, gruesome.

frightful, hideous, odious, uncanny, forbidding, repellant, repulsive; horri-d, -ble; shocking &c. (*painful*) 830.

foul &c. (*dirty*) 653; dingy &c. (*colourless*) 429; gaudy &c. (*colour*) 428; disfigured &c. *v.*; discoloured (*blemished*) &c. 848.

---

847. Ornament.—N. ornament, -ation, -al art; ornat-ure, -eness; adorn-ment, decoration, embellishment; architecture.

garnish, polish, varnish, French pol-

848. Blemish.—N. blemish, disfigurement, deformity; defect &c. (*imperfection*) 651; flaw; injury &c. (*deterioration*) 659; spots on the sun; eyesore.

ish, gilding, japanning, lacquer, ormolu, enamel.

cosmetics, rouge, powder, lipstick, lip salve, mascara; manicure, nail polish; permanent –, Marcel –, finger-wave.

pattern, diaper, powdering, panelling, graining, pargeting, inlay, detail; texture &c. 329; richness; tracery, moulding, beading, reeding, fillet, listel, strapwork, *coquillage*, flourish, *fleur-de-lis*, arabesque, fret, *anthemion*; egg and -tongue, – dart; *astragal*, zigzag, *acanthus, cartouche*; pilaster &c. (*projection*) 250; cyma, ogee.

em-, broidery, needlework; knitting, crochet, tatting, brocade, *brocatelle*, beads, bugles; galloon, lace, gimp, *guipure*, fringe, trapping, border, edging, insertion, *motif*, trimming; *passementerie*; drapery, hanging, tapestry, arras; millinery, ermine.

wreath, festoon, garland, lei, chaplet, flower, nosegay, *bouquet*, posy, 'daisies pied and violets blue.'

tassel, knot; shoulder-knot, *épaulette*, epaulet, aigulet, *aiguillette*, frog; star, rosette, bow; feather, plume, *panache*, *aigrette*.

jewel, -ry, -lery; bijoutry; *bijou*, *-terie*; diadem, tiara; pendant, trinket, locket, necklace, armilla, bracelet, bangle, armlet, anklet, ear-, nose- ring, carcanet, chain, *châtelaine*, albert, brooch, torque.

gem, precious stone; diamond, brilliant, beryl, aquamarine, alexandrite, cat's eye, emerald, calcedony, chrysoprase, cornelian, jasper, bloodstone, agate, heliotrope; girasol, -e; onyx, plasma; sard, -onyx; garnet, lapis-lazuli, opal, peridot, chrysolite, sapphire, ruby; spinel, -le; balais; oriental –, topaz; turquois, -e; zircon, jacinth, hyacinth, carbuncle, amethyst; moonstone; pearl, coral.

finery, frippery, gewgaw, gimcrack, knick-knack, tinsel, spangle, sequin, *clinquant*, pinch-beck, paste; excess of ornament &c. (*vulgarity*) 851; gaud, pride, ostentation; frills and furbelows.

illustration, illumination, *vignette*; *fleuron*; head-, tail-piece; *cul-de-lampe*; flowers of rhetoric &c. 577; work of art, article of vertu, *bric-à-brac*, curio, *bibelot*.

V. ornament, embellish, enrich, decorate, adorn, beautify, adonize.

smarten, furbish, polish, gild, varnish, whitewash, enamel, japan, lacquer, paint, grain.

garnish, trim, dizen, bedizen, prink, prank; trick –, fig- out; deck, bedeck, dight, bedight, array; dress, – up, preen, spruce up,

stain, blot, slur; spot, -tiness; speck, -le; blur, freckle, mole, *macula*, patch, blotch, birthmark, blain, maculation, tarnish, smudge, smear; dirt &c. 653; bruise, black eye, scar, wem; pustule; excrescence, pimple &c. (*protuberance*) 250.

V. disfigure &c. (*injure*) 659; speckle; render ugly &c. 846.

Adj. pitted, freckled, discoloured, bloodshot, bruised, disfigured; stained &c. *n.*; imperfect &c. 651; injured &c. (*deteriorated*) 659.

849. Simplicity. — N. simplicity; plain-, homeli-ness; undress, nudity, nakedness, beauty unadorned, chastity, chasteness.

V. be -simple &c. *adj.*

render -simple &c. *adj.*; simplify, chasten, strip of ornament.

Adj. simple, plain; home-ly, -spun; ordinary, household.

natural, unaffected; free from -affectation, – ornament; *simplex munditiis*; *sans façon, en déshabillé*, nude, naked.

chaste, inornate, severe.

un-adorned, -ornamented, -decked, -garnished, -arranged, -trimmed, -varnished.

bald, flat, dull, blank.

———

titivate; spangle, bespangle, powder; embroider, work; chase, tool, emboss, fret; emblazon, blazon, illuminate; illustrate.

become &c. (*accord with*) 23.

Adj. ornamented, beautified &c. *v.*; ornate, rich, gilt, begilt, tesselated, enamelled, inlaid; festooned; topiary.

smart, gay, tricksy, flowery, glittering; new-gilt, -spangled; fine, – as -a Mayday queen, – fivepence, – a carrot fresh scraped; pranked out, bedight, well-groomed.

in full dress &c. (*fashion*) 852; *en grande -tenue, – toilette*; in best bib and tucker, in Sunday best, *endimanché*; dressed to advantage.

showy, flashy; gaudy &c. (*vulgar*) 851; garish; gorgeous.

ornamental, decorative; becoming &c. (*accordant*) 23.

---

850. [Good taste.] **Taste.**—**N.** taste; good –, refined –, cultivated- taste; delicacy, refinement, fine feeling, gust, *gusto*, tact, *finesse*; nicety &c. (*discrimination*) 465; polish, elegance, grace.

virtu; dilettanteism, virtuosity; fine art; cul-ture, -ivation.

[Science of taste] æsthetics.

man of -taste &c.; *connoisseur*, judge, critic, *conoscente, virtuoso, amateur, dilettante*, Aristarchus, Corinthian, *arbiter elegantiarum*, stagirite, euphemist.

'caviare to the general.'

V. appreciate, judge, criticize, discriminate &c. 465.

Adj. in good taste; tasteful, tasty; unaffected, pure, chaste, classical, attic; cultivated, refined; dainty; æsthetic, artistic; elegant &c. 578; euphemistic.

to one's -taste, – mind; after one's fancy; *comme il faut*; *tiré à quatre épingles*.

Adv. elegantly &c. *adj.*

Phr. *nihil tetigit quod non ornavit.*

852. Fashion.—**N.** fashion, style, *ton, bon ton*, society; good –, polite- society; drawing room, civilized life, civilization, town, *beau monde*, high life, court; world; fashionable –, gay- world; Vanity Fair; show &c. (*ostentation*) 822.

manners, breeding &c. (*politeness*) 894; air, demeanour &c. (*appearance*) 448; *savoir faire*; gentlemanliness, gentility, decorum, propriety, *bienséance*; conventions –, dictates- of society; Mrs. Grundy; convention, -ality; punctilio; form, -ality; etiquette, point of

851. [Bad taste.] **Vulgarity.**—**N.** vulgar-ity, -ism; barbar-, Vandal-, Gothic-ism; *mauvais goût*, bad taste; Babbittry; *gaucherie*, awkwardness, want of tact; ill-breeding &c. (*discourtesy*) 895; ungentlemanly behaviour.

coarseness &c. *adj.*; indecorum, misbehaviour.

low-, homeli-ness; low life, *mauvais ton*, rusticity; boorishness &c. *adj.*; brutality; rowdy-, ruffian-, blackguard-ism; ribaldry; slang &c. (*neology*) 563.

bad joke, *mauvaise plaisanterie*.

[Excess of ornament] gaudi-, tawdri-ness; false ornament; finery, frippery, trickery, tinsel, gewgaw, *clinquant*.

rough diamond, tomboy, hoyden, cub, unlicked cub; clown &c. (*commonalty*) 876; Hun, Goth, Vandal, Bœotian; vulgarian; snob, cad, bound-er, gent; *parvenu* &c. 876; frump, dowdy; slattern &c. 653.

V. be -vulgar &c. *adj.*; misbehave; talk –, smell of the- shop.

Adj. in bad taste, vulgar, unrefined, gutter.

coarse, indecorus, ribald, gross; unseemly, unbeseeming, unpresentable; *contra bonos mores*; ungraceful &c. (*ugly*) 846.

dowdy; slovenly &c. (*dirty*) 653; ungenteel, shabby genteel; low &c. (*plebeian*) 876; uncourtly; uncivil &c. (*discourteous*) 895; ill-bred, -mannered; underbred; ungentleman-ly, -like; unladylike, unfeminine; wild, – as an unbacked colt.

unkempt, uncombed, untamed, unlicked, unpolished, uncouth, plebeian;

etiquette; custom &c. 613; mode, vogue, style, go; rage &c. (*desire*) 865; prevailing taste, *dernier cri*, dress &c. 225.

man –, woman- of -fashion, – the world; height –, pink –, star –, glass –, leader- of fashion; *arbiter elegantiarum* &c. (*taste*) 850; upper ten thousand &c. (*nobility*) 875; *élite* &c. (*distinction*) 873.

V. be -fashionable &c. *adj.*, – the rage &c. *n.*; have a run, pass current.

follow –, conform to –, fall in with- the fashion &c. *n.*; go with the stream &c. (*conform*) 82; *savoir -vivre*, – *faire*; keep up appearances, behave oneself.

set the –, bring into- fashion; give a tone to –, cut a figure in- society, rub shoulders with nobility, keep one's carriage.

incondite; heavy, rude, awkward; home-ly, -spun, -bred; provincial, hick, countrified, rustic, uncultivated, fresh-water; boorish, clownish; savage, brut-ish, blackguard, rowdy, snobbish; barbar-ous, -ic; Gothic, unclassical doggerel, heathenish, tramontane, out-landish; Bohemian.

obsolete &c. (*antiquated*) 124; un-fashionable, old-fashioned, out of date; new-fangled &c. (*unfamiliar*) 83; fan-tastic, odd &c. (*ridiculous*) 853.

particular; affected &c. 855; mere-tricious; extravagant, monstrous, hor-rid; shocking &c. (*painful*) 830.

gaudy, tawdry, bedizened, tricked out, gingerbread; obtrusive, flaunting, loud, flashy, garish, showy.

Adj. fashionable; in -fashion &c. *n.*; *à la mode, comme il faut*; admitted –, admissible- in -society &c. *n.*; presentable, decorous, punctilious, conventional &c. (*customary*) 613; genteel; well-bred, -mannered, -behaved, -spoken; gentleman-like, -ly; ladylike; civil, polite &c. (*courteous*) 894.

polished, refined, thoroughbred, courtly; *distingué*, aristocratic, unembarrassed, poised, *dégagé*; ja-, jau-nty; dashing, fast, showy, high toned, toney.

modish, stylish, in the latest style, *recherché*; new-fangled &c. (*unfamiliar*) 83.

in -court, – full, – evening- dress; *en grande tenue* &c. (*ornament*) 847.

Adv. fashionably &c. *adj.*; for fashion's sake.

853. Ridiculousness.—N. ridiculousness &c. *adj.*; comical-, odd-ity &c. *adj.*; extravagance, drollery.

farce, comedy; burlesque &c. (*ridicule*) 856; buffoonery &c. (*fun*) 840; frippery; doggerel verses; Irish bull, Hibernianism, Hibernicism; Spoonerism; absurdity &c. 497; bombast &c. (*unmeaning*) 517; anti-climax, bathos; monstrosity &c. (*unconformity*) 83; laughing stock &c. 857.

V. be -ridiculous &c. *adj.*; pass from the sublime to the ridiculous; make one laugh; play the fool, make a fool of oneself, commit an absurdity.

play a joke on, make a -fool of, – sucker of, – monkey of.

Adj. ridiculous, ludicrous; comic, -al; droll, funny, laughable, *pour rire*, grotesque, farcical, odd; whimsical, – as a dancing bear; fanciful, fantastic, queer, rum, quizzical, waggish, quaint, *bizarre*; eccentric &c. (*unconformable*) 83; strange, outlandish, out of the way, *baroque*, *rocaille*, rococo; awkward &c. (*ugly*) 846.

absurd, extravagant, *outré*, monstrous, preposterous, bombastic, inflated, stilted, burlesque, mock heroic.

drollish; serio-, tragic-comic; gimcrack, contemptible &c. (*unim-portant*) 643; doggerel; ironical &c. (*derisive*) 856; risible.

Phr. *'risum teneatis amici?' rideret Heraclitus.*

854. Fop.—**N.** fop, fine gentleman; swell; dand-y, -iprat; exquisite, coxcomb, toff, beau, macaroni, blade, blood, buck, man about town, fast man; fribble, jemmy, spark, popinjay, puppy, prig, *petit maître*; jacka-napes, -dandy; man milliner; Jemmy Jessamy, carpet-knight, masher, Dundreary, Johnnie, dude.

belle, fine lady, *coquette*, flirt.

855. Affectation.—**N.** affectation; affectedness &c. *adj.*; acting a part &c. *v.*; pretence &c. (*falsehood*) 544, (*ostentation*) 882; boasting &c. 884.

charlatanism, quakery, shallow profundity, humbug, pretension, airs, pedantry, purism, precisianism, euphuism, prunes and prisms; tera-tology &c. (*altiloquence*) 577.

mannerism, *simagrée*, grimace.

conceit, foppery, dandyism, man millinery, coxcombry, puppyism.

stiffness, formality, buckram; prudery, demureness, coquetry, mock modesty, *minauderie*, sentimentalism; *mauvaise honte*, false shame.

affector, performer, actor; pedant, pedagogue, *doctrinaire*, purist, euphuist, mannerist; shoneen; *grimacier*; lump of affectation, *précieuse ridicule*, *bas bleu*, blue stocking, poetaster; prig, hypocrite; charlatan &c. (*deceiver*) 548; *petit maître* &c. (*fop*) 854; flatterer &c. 935; *coquette*, prude, puritan; precisian, formalist.

V. affect, act a part, put on; give oneself airs &c. (*arrogance*) 885; boast &c. 884; coquet; simper, mince, attitudinize, strike a pose, pose; flirt a fan; over-act, -play, -do.

Adj. affected, full of affectation, pretentious, pedantic, stilted, stagey, theatrical, big-sounding, *ad captandum*, canting, insincere.

not natural, unnatural; self-conscious; *maniéré*; artificial; over-wrought, -done, -acted; euphuistic &c. 577.

stiff, starch, formal, prim, smug, demure, *tiré à quatre épingles*, quakerish, puritanical, prudish, pragmatical, priggish, conceited, cox-comical, foppish, dandified; fini-cal, -kin, -cky, mincing, simpering, namby-pamby, sentimental, languishing.

856. Ridicule.—**N.** ridicule, derision; sardonic -smile, – grin; irrision; snigger; scoffing &c. (*disrespect*) 929; mockery, quiz, banter, irony, *persiflage*, raillery, chaff, *badinage*; quizzing &c. *v.*

squib, satire, skit, quip, quib, grin.

parody, burlesque, travesty; farce &c. (*drama*) 599; caricature, take-off.

buffoonery &c. (*fun*) 840; practical joke, horseplay.

V. ridicule, deride; laugh at, grin at, smile at; snigger; laugh in one's sleeve; banter, rally, chaff, joke, twit, quiz, poke fun at, jolly, roast, rag; fleer; play –, play tricks- upon; fool, – to the top of one's bent; show up.

satirize, parody, caricature, burlesque, travesty.

turn into ridicule; make merry with; make -fun, – game, – a fool, – an April fool- of; rally; scoff &c. (*disrespect*) 929.

raise a laugh &c. (*amuse*) 840; play the fool, make a fool of oneself. be ridiculous &c. 853.

Adj. deris-ory, -ive; mock; sarcastic, ironical, quizzical, burlesque, Hudibrastic; scurrilous &c. (*disrespectful*) 929.

Adv. in -ridicule &c. *n.*

857. [Object and cause of ridicule.] **Laughing-stock.—N.** laughing-, jesting-, gazing-stock; butt, game, fair game; April fool &c. (*dupe*) 547.

original, oddity; queer –, odd- fish; quiz, square toes; old –, fogey *or* fogy.

monkey; buffoon &c. (*jester*) 844; pantomimist &c. (*actor*) 599. jest &c. (*wit*) 842.

3°. Prospective Affections

858. Hope.—N. hope, -s; desire &c. 865; fervent hope, sanguine expectation, trust, confidence, reliance; faith &c. (*belief*) 484; affiance, assurance; secur-eness, -ity; reassurance.

good -omen, – auspices; promise, well-grounded hopes; good –, bright-prospect; clear sky.

as-, pre-sumption; anticipation &c. (*expectation*) 507.

hopefulness, buoyancy, optimism, enthusiasm, heart of grace, aspiration; optimist, utop-ian, -ist; Pollyanna.

castles in the air, *châteaux en Espagne*, hope chest, *le pot au lait*, Utopia, millennium; day –, golden-dream; dream of Alnaschar; airy hopes, fool's paradise; *mirage* &c. (*fallacies of vision*) 443; fond hope.

beam –, ray –, gleam –, glimmer –, dawn –, flash –, star- of hope; cheer; bit of blue sky, silver lining of the cloud, bottom of Pandora's box, balm in Gilead.

anchor, sheet-anchor, main-stay; staff &c. (*support*) 215; heaven &c. 981.

V. hope, trust, confide, rely on, put one's trust in, lean upon; pin one's -hope, – faith- upon &c. (*believe*) 484.

feel –, entertain –, harbour –, indulge –, cherish –, feed –, foster –, nourish –, encourage –, cling to –, live in- hope &c. *n.*; see land; feel –, rest- -assured, – confident &c. *adj.*

presume; promise oneself; expect &c. (*look forward to*) 507.

hope for &c. (*desire*) 865; anticipate.

be -hopeful &c. *adj.*; look on the bright side of, view on the sunny side, make the best of it, hope for the best; put -a good, – a bold, – the best- face upon; keep one's spirits up; take heart, – of grace; be of good -heart, – cheer; flatter oneself, lay the flattering unction to one's soul.

859. [Absence, want, or loss of hope.] **Hopelessness.—N.** hopelessness &c. *adj.*; despair, desperation; despondency &c. (*dejection*) 837; pessimism.

hope deferred, dashed hopes; vain expectation &c. (*disappointment*) 509.

airy hopes &c. 858; forlorn hope; bad -job, – business; *enfant perdu*; gloomy –, black spots in the- horizon; slough of Despond, cave of Despair.

Job's comforter; bird of -bad, – ill-omen.

V. despair; lose –, give up –, abandon –, relinquish- -all hope, – the hope of; give -up, – over; yield to despair; falter; despond &c. (*be dejected*) 837; *jeter le manche après la cognée*.

inspire –, drive to- despair &c. *n.*; disconcert; dash –, crush –, shatter –, destroy- one's hopes; hope against hope.

Adj. hopeless, desperate, despairing, in despair, *au désespoir*, forlorn; inconsolable &c. (*dejected*) 837; broken-hearted.

out of the question, not to be thought of; impracticable &c. 471; past -hope, – cure, – mending, – recall; at one's last gasp &c. (*death*) 360; given -up, – over.

incurable, cureless, immedicable, remediless, beyond remedy; incorrigible; irre-parable, -mediable, -coverable, -versible, -trievable, -claimable, -deemable, -vocable; ruined, undone; immitigable.

unpromising, unpropitious; inauspicious, ill-omened, threatening, clouded over, lowering, ominous.

Phr. '*lasciate ogni speranza voi ch' entrate*'; its days are numbered; the worst come to the worst.

860. Fear.—N. fear, timidity, diffidence, want of confidence; apprehensive-, fearful-ness &c. *adj.*; solicitude,

catch at a straw, hope against hope, count one's chickens before they are hatched.

give –, inspire –, raise –, hold out-hope &c. *n.*; raise expectations; en-courage, hearten, cheer, assure, re-assure, buoy up, embolden; promise, bid fair, augur well, be in a fair way, look up, flatter, tell a flattering tale.

Adj. hoping &c. *v.*; in -hopes &c. *n.*; hopeful, confident; secure &c. (*certain*) 484; sanguine, in good heart, buoyed up, buoyant, elated, flushed, exultant, enthusiastic; utopian.

unsus-pecting, -picious; fearless, free –, exempt from- -fear, – suspicion, – distrust, – despair; undespairing, self-reliant.

probable, on the high road to; within sight of -shore, – land; promising, propitious; of –, full of- promise; of good omen; auspicious, *de bon augure*; reassuring; encouraging, cheering, in-spiriting, looking up, bright, roseate, *couleur de rose*, rose-coloured.

Adv. hopefully &c. *adj.*

Int. God speed! good luck!

Phr. *nil desperandum*; never say die, *dum spiro spero*, *latet scintillula forsan*, all is for the best, *spero meliora*; the wish being father to the thought; 'hope told a flattering tale'; *rusticus expectat dum defluat amnis.*

anxiety, care, apprehension, misgiving; mistrust &c. (*doubt*) 485; suspicion, qualm; hesitation &c. (*irresolution*) 605.

nervous-, restless-ness &c. *adj.*; in-, dis-quietude; flutter, trepidation, fear and trembling, perturbation, tremor, quivering, shaking, trembling, throb-bing heart, palpitation, ague fit, cold sweat; abject fear &c. (*cowardice*) 862; mortal funk, heart-sinking, despond-ency; despair &c. 859.

fright; affright, -ment; alarm, pavor, dread, awe, terror, horror, dismay, consternation, panic, scare, stampede [of horses].

intimidation, terrorism, reign of terror.

[Object of fear] bug-bear, -aboo; scarecrow; hobgoblin &c. (*demon*) 980; daymare, nightmare, Gorgon, Medusa, mormo, ogre, Hurlothrumbo, raw head and bloody bones, fee faw fum, *bête noire*, *enfant terrible*.

alarmist &c. (*coward*) 862.

V. fear, stand in awe of; be -afraid &c. *adj.*; have -qualms &c. *n.*; appre-hend, sit upon thorns, eye askance; distrust &c. (*disbelieve*) 485.

hesitate &c. (*be irresolute*) 605; falter, funk, cower, crouch; skulk &c. (*coward-ice*) 862; let 'I dare not' wait upon 'I would'; take -fright, – alarm; start, wince, flinch, shy, shrink; fly &c. (*avoid*) 623.

tremble, shake; shiver, – in one's shoes; shudder, flutter; shake –, tremble- -like an aspen leaf, – all over; quake, quaver, quiver, quail; get the wind up.

grow –, turn- pale; blench, stand aghast; not dare to say one's soul is one's own.

inspire –, excite- -fear, – awe; raise apprehensions; give –, raise –, sound- an alarm; alarm, startle, scare, cry 'wolf,' disquiet, dismay; fright, -en; affright, terrify; astound; frighten from one's propriety; frighten out of one's -wits, – senses, – seven senses; awe; strike -all of a heap, – an awe into, – terror; harrow up the soul, appal, unman, petrify, horrify.

make one's -flesh creep, – hair stand on end, – blood run cold, – teeth chatter; chill one's spine; take away –, stop- one's breath; make one -tremble &c.

haunt, obsess, beset; prey –, weigh- on the mind.

put in -fear, – bodily fear; terrorize, intimidate, cow, daunt, over-awe, abash, deter, discourage; browbeat, bully; threaten &c. 909.

Adj. fearing &c. *v.*; frightened &c. *v.*; in -fear, – a fright &c. *n.*; haunted with the -fear &c. *n.*- of.

afraid, fearful; tim-id, -orous; nervous, diffident, coy, faint-hearted, tremulous, shaky, afraid of one's shadow, apprehensive, restless, fidgety; more frightened than hurt.

aghast; awe-, horror-, terror-, panic- -struck, -stricken; frightened to death, white as a sheet; pale, – as -death, – ashes, – a ghost; breathless, in hysterics.

inspiring fear &c. *v.*; alarming; formidable, redoubtable; perilous &c. (*danger*) 665; portentous; fear-ful, -some; dread, -ful; fell; dire, -ful; shocking; terri-ble, -fic; tremendous; horri-d, -ble, -fic; ghastly; awful, awe-inspiring, eerie, weird; revolting &c. (*painful*) 830.

Adv. *in terrorem.*

Int. 'angels and ministers of grace defend us!'

Phr. *ante tubam trepidat*; *horresco referens*, one's heart failing one, *obstupui steteruntque comæ et vox faucibus hæsit.*

---

861. [Absence of fear.] **Courage.—N.** courage, bravery, valour; resolute-, bold-ness &c. *adj.*; spirit, daring, gallantry, intrepidity; contempt –, defiance- of danger; derring-do; audacity; rashness &c. 863; dash; defiance &c. 715; confidence, self-reliance.

man-liness, -hood; nerve, pluck, mettle, game; heart, – of grace; spunk, gameness, grit, face, virtue, hardihood, fortitude; firmness &c. (*stability*) 150; heart of oak; bottom, backbone &c. (*perseverance*) 604a.

resolution &c. (*determination*) 604; tenacity, bull-dog courage.

prowess, heroism, chivalry.

exploit, feat, achievement; heroic -deed, – act; bold stroke.

man, – of mettle; hero, demigod, paladin, heroine, Amazon, Hector, Joan of Arc; lion, tiger, panther, bull-dog; game-, fighting-cock; bully, fire-eater &c. 863; dare-devil.

V. be -courageous &c. *adj.*; dare, venture, make bold; face –, front –, affront –, confront –, brave –, defy –, despise –, mock- danger; look in the face; look -full, – boldly, – danger- in the face; face; meet, – in front; brave, beard; defy &c. 715.

take –, muster –, summon up –, pluck up- courage; nerve oneself, take heart; take –, pluck up- heart of grace; hold up one's head, screw one's courage to the sticking place; come -to, – up to- the scratch; stand, – to one's guns, – fire, – against; bear up, – against; hold out &c. (*persevere*) 604a.

put a bold face upon; show –,

862. [Excess of fear.] **Cowardice.—N.** cowardice, pusillanimity; cowardliness &c. *adj.*; timidity, effeminacy.

poltroonery, baseness; dastard-ness, -y; abject fear, funk; Dutch courage; fear &c. 860; white feather, faint heart.

coward, poltroon, dastard, sneak, recreant; shy –, dunghill- cock; coistril, milksop, white-liver, nidget, cur, craven, one that cannot say 'Boo' to a goose; Bob Acres, Jerry Sneak.

alarm-, terror-, pessim-ist; runagate &c. (*fugitive*) 623; shirker.

V. quail &c. (*fear*) 860; be -cowardly &c. *adj.*, – a coward &c. *n.*; funk; cower, skulk, sneak; flinch, shy, fight shy, slink, turn tail; run away &c. (*avoid*) 623; show the white feather, have cold feet, show a yellow streak.

Adj. coward, -ly; fearful, shy; tim-id, -orous; skittish; poor-spirited, spirit-less, soft, effeminate.

weak-minded; infirm of purpose &c. 605; weak-, faint-, chicken-, lily-, pigeon-hearted; yellow; white-, lily-, milk-livered; milksop, smock-faced; unable to say 'Boo' to a goose.

dastard, -ly; base, craven, sneaking, dunghill, recreant; unwar-, unsoldier-like.

'in face a lion but in heart a deer.' unmanned; frightened &c. 860.

Int. *sauve qui peut!* devil take the hindmost!

Adv. in fear and trembling, in fear of one's life, in a blue funk.

Phr. *ante tubam trepidat*, one's courage oozing out.

present- a bold front, face the music; envisage; show fight.

bell the cat, take the bull by the horns, beard the lion in his den, march up to the cannon's mouth, go through fire and water, run the gauntlet, go over the top.

give –, infuse –, inspire- courage; reassure, encourage, embolden, inspirit, cheer, hearten, nerve, put upon one's mettle, rally, raise a rallying cry; pat on the back, make a man of, keep in countenance.

Adj. courageous, brave; val-iant, -orous; gallant, intrepid; spirit-ed, -ful; high-spirited, -mettled; mettlesome, game, plucky; man-ly, -ful; resolute; stout, -hearted; iron-, lion-hearted; heart of oak; Penthesilean.

bold, – spirited; daring, audacious; fear-, daunt-, dread-, awe-less; un-daunted, -appalled, -dismayed, -awed, -blenched, -abashed, -alarmed, -flinching, -shrinking, -blenching; apprehensive; confident, self-reliant; bold as -a lion, – brass.

enterprising, adventurous; ventur-ous, -esome; dashing, chivalrous; soldierly &c. (*warlike*) 722; heroic.

fierce, savage; pugnacious &c. (*bellicose*) 720.

strong-minded, hardy, doughty; firm &c. (*stable*) 150; determined &c. (*resolved*) 604; dogged, indomitable &c. (*persevering*) 604a.

up to, – the scratch; upon one's mettle; reassured &c. *v.*; un-feared, undreaded.

Phr. one's blood being up.

---

863. Rashness.—N. rashness &c. *adj.*; temerity, want of caution, imprudence, indiscretion; over-confidence, presumption, audacity.

precipit-ancy, -ation; impetuosity; levity; foolhardi-hood, -ness; heed-, thought-lessness &c. (*inattention*) 458; carelessness &c. (*neglect*) 460; desperation; Quixotism, knight-errantry; fire-eating.

gam-ing, -bling; blind bargain, leap in the dark, fool's paradise; too many eggs in one basket.

desperado, rashling, mad-cap, daredevil, Hotspur, fire-eater, bully, *bravo*, Hector, scapegrace, *enfant perdu*; Don Quixote, knight-errant, Icarus; adventurer; gam-bler, -ester; dynamitard.

V. be -rash &c. *adj.*; stick at nothing, play a desperate game; run into danger &c. 665; play with -fire, – edge tools.

carry too much sail, sail too near the wind, ride at single anchor, go out of one's depth.

take a leap in the dark, buy a pig in a poke.

donner tête baissée; knock one's head against a wall &c. (*be unskilful*) 699; rush on destruction; kick against the

864. Caution.—N. caution; cautiousness &c. *adj.*; discretion, prudence, cautel, heed, circumspection, calculation, deliberation; safety first.

foresight &c. 510; vigilance &c. 459; warning &c. 668.

coolness &c. *adj.*; self-possession, -command; presence of mind, *sang froid*; well-regulated mind; worldly wisdom, Fabian policy.

V. be -cautious &c. *adj.*; take -care, – heed, – good care; have a care; mind, – what one is about; be on one's guard &c. (*keep watch*) 459; make assurance double sure; ca' canny.

bespeak &c. (*be early*) 132.

think twice, look before one leaps, keep one's weather eye open, count the cost, look to the main chance, cut one's coat according to one's cloth; feel one's -ground, – way; see how the land lies &c. (*foresight*) 510; wait to see how the cat jumps; bridle one's tongue; *reculer pour mieux sauter* &c. (*prepare*) 673; let well alone, let sleeping dogs lie, *ne pas réveiller le chat qui dort*.

keep out of -harm's way, – troubled waters; keep at a respectful distance, stand aloof; keep –, be- on the safe side.

pricks, tempt Providence, go on a for-lorn hope.

count one's chickens before they are hatched; reckon without one's host; catch at straws; trust to –, lean on- a broken reed.

Adj. rash, incautious, indiscreet, injudicious; imprudent, improvident, temerarious; uncalculating; heedless; careless &c. (*neglectful*) 460; without ballast, heels over head; giddy &c. (*inattentive*) 458; wanton, reckless, wild, madcap; desperate, devil-may-care.

hot-blooded, -headed, -brained; head-long, -strong; break-neck; fool-hardy; harebrained; precipitate, impulsive.

over-confident, -weening; ventur-esome, -ous; adventurous, Quixotic; fire-eating, cavalier; free-and-easy.

off one's guard &c. (*inexpectant*) 508.

Adv. post haste, *à corps perdu*, hand over head, *tête baissée*, head-foremost; happen what may.

Phr. neck or nothing, the devil being in one.

husband one's resources &c. 636.

caution &c. (*warn*) 668.

Adj. cautious, wary, guarded; on one's guard &c. (*watchful*) 459; *cavendo tutus*; *in medio tutissimus*.

care-, heed-ful; cautelous, stealthy, chary, shy of, circumspect, prudent, canny, safe, non-committal, discreet, politic; sure-footed &c. (*skilful*) 698.

unenterprising, unadventurous, cool, steady, self-possessed; over-cautious.

suspicious, leery, vigilant.

Adv. cautiously, gingerly &c. *adj.*

Int. have a care! look out! *cave canem!*

Phr. *timeo Danaos; festina lente.*

---

865. Desire.—N. desire, wish, fancy, fantasy; want, need, exigency.

mind, inclination, leaning, bent, *animus*, partiality, *penchant*, predilection; propensity &c. 820; willingness &c. 602; liking, love, fondness, relish.

longing, hankering; solicitude, anxiety; yearning, coveting; aspiration, ambition, vaulting ambition; eagerness, zeal, ardour, *empressement*, breathless impatience, over-anxiety; solicitude, impetuosity &c. 825.

appet-ite, -ition, -ence, -ency; sharp appetite, keenness, hunger, stomach, twist; thirst, -iness; drouth, mouth-watering; itch, -ing; prurience, *cacoëthes*, cupidity, lust, concupiscence.

edge of -appetite, – hunger; torment of Tantalus; sweet –, lickerish- tooth; itching palm; longing –, wistful –, sheep's- eye.

avidity; greed, -iness; covetous-, ravenous-ness &c. *adj.*; grasping, craving, canine appetite, rapacity; voracity &c. (*gluttony*) 957.

passion, rage, *furore*, mania, *manie*; inextinguishable desire; dips-, klept-, mon-omania.

[Person desiring] desirer, lover, *ama-*

866. Indifference.—N. indifference, neutrality; coldness &c. *adj.*; uncon-cern, *insouciance, nonchalance*; want of -interest, – earnestness; anorexy, in-appetency; apathy &c. (*insensibility*) 823; supineness &c. (*inactivity*) 683; disdain &c. 930; recklessness &c. 863; inattention &c. 458.

V. be -indifferent &c. *adj.*; stand neuter; take no interest in &c. (*insensibility*) 823; have no -desire &c. 865, – taste, – relish- for; not care for; care nothing -for, – about; not care a -straw &c. (*unimportance*) 643 -about, – for; not mind.

set at naught &c. (*make light of*) 483; spurn &c. (*disdain*) 930.

Adj. indifferent, cold, frigid, luke-warm; cool, – as a cucumber; uncon-cerned, *insouciant*, phlegmatic, *pococu-rante*, easy-going, devil-may-care, care-less, listless, lackadaisical, feckless; half-hearted; un-ambitious, -aspiring, -desirous, -solicitous, -attracted.

un-attractive, -alluring, -desired, -de-sirable, -cared for, -wished, -valued, all one to.

insipid &c. 391; vain.

Adv. for aught one cares.

teur, votary, devotee, aspirant, solicitant, candidate; cormorant &c. 957; sycophant.

[Object of desire] *desideratum*; want &c. (*requirement*) 630; 'consummation devoutly to be wished'; attraction, magnet, allurement, fancy, temptation, seduction, lure, fascination, *prestige*, height of one's ambition, idol; whim, -sey; maggot; hobby, -horse.

Fortunatus's cap, wishing cap, love potion.

V. desire; wish, – for; be -desirous &c. *adj.*; have a -longing &c. *n.*; hope &c. 858.

care for, affect, like, list; take to, cling to, take a fancy to; fancy; prefer &c. (*choose*) 609.

have -an eye, – a mind- to; find it in one's heart &c. (*be willing*) 602; have a fancy for, set one's eyes upon; cast a sheep's eye –, look sweet- upon; take into one's head, have at heart, be bent upon; set one's -cap at, – heart upon, – mind upon; covet.

want, miss, need, lack, desiderate, feel- the want of; would fain -have, – do; would be glad of.

be -hungry &c. *adj.*; have a good appetite, play a good knife and fork; hunger –, thirst –, crave –, lust –, itch –, hanker –, run mad- after; raven –, die- for; burn to.

desiderate; sigh –, cry –, gape –, gasp –, pine –, pant –, languish –, yearn –, long –, be on thorns –, hope- for; aspire after; catch at, grasp at, jump at.

woo, court, solicit; fish –, spell –, whistle –, put up- for; ogle.

cause –, create –, raise –, excite –, provoke- desire; whet the appetite; appetize, titillate, allure, attract, take one's fancy, tempt; hold out -temptation, – allurement; tantalize, make one's mouth water, *faire venir l'eau à la bouche*.

gratify desire &c. (*give pleasure*) 829.

Adj. desirous; desiring &c. *v.*; orectic, appetitive; inclined &c. (*willing*) 602; partial to; fain, wishful, optative; anxious, wistful, curious; at a loss for, sedulous, solicitous.

craving, hungry, sharp-set, peckish,

Int. never mind.

867. Dislike.—N. dis-like, -taste, -relish, -inclination, -placency.

reluctance; backwardness &c. (*unwillingness*) 603.

repugnance, disgust, queasiness, turn, nausea, loathing; avers-eness, -ation, -ion; abomination, antipathy, abhorrence, horror; mortal –, rooted- -antipathy, – horror; hatred, detestation; hate &c. 898; animosity &c. 900; hydrophobia.

sickener; gall and wormwood &c. (*unsavoury*) 395; shuddering, cold sweat.

V. dis-, mis-like, -relish; mind, object to; have rather not, not care for; have –, conceive –, entertain –, take- -a dislike, – an aversion- to; have no -taste, – stomach- for.

shun, avoid &c. 623; eschew; withdraw –, shrink –, recoil- from; not be able to -bear, – abide, – endure; shrug the shoulders at, shudder at, turn up the nose at, look askance at; make a -mouth, – wry face, – grimace; make faces.

loathe, nauseate, abominate, detest, abhor; hate &c. 898; take amiss &c. 900; have enough of &c. (*be satiated*) 869.

cause –, excite- dislike; disincline, repel, sicken; make –, render- sick; turn one's stomach, nauseate, wamble, disgust, shock, stink in the nostrils; go against the -grain, – stomach; stick in the throat; make one's blood run cold &c. (*give pain*) 830; pall.

Adj. disliking &c. *v.*; averse to, loth, adverse; shy of, sick of, out of conceit with; disinclined; heart-, dog-sick; queasy.

disliked &c. *v.*; uncared for, unpopular; out of favour; repulsive, repugnant, repellent; abhorrent, insufferable, fulsome, nauseous; loath-some, -ful; offensive; disgusting &c. *v.*; disagreeable &c. (*painful*) 830; unsavoury &c. 395.

Adv. *usque ad nauseam.*

Int. faugh! foh! ugh!

868. Fastidiousness.—N. fastidiousness &c. *adj.*; nicety, meticulosity,

ravening, with an empty stomach, esu-rient, lickerish, thirsty, athirst, parched with thirst, pinched with hunger, fam-ished, dry, drouthy; hungry as a -hunter, – hawk, – horse, – church mouse.

greedy, – as a hog; over-eager, vora-cious; ravenous, – as a wolf; open-mouthed, covetous, rapacious, grasp-ing, extortionate, exacting, sordid, *alieni appetens*; insati-able, -ate; un-quenchable, quenchless; omnivorous.

unsatisfied, unsated, unslaked.

eager, avid, keen; burning, fervent, ardent; agog; all agog; breathless; impatient &c. (*impetuous*) 825; bent –, intent –, set- -on, – upon; mad after, *enragé*, rabid, dying for, devoured by desire.

aspiring, ambitious, vaulting, sky-aspiring.

desirable; popular; desired &c. *v.*; in demand; pleasing &c. (*giving pleasure*) 829; appeti-zing, -ble; tantalizing.

Adv. wistfully &c. *adj.*; fain.

Int. would -that, – it were! O for! *esto perpetua!* if only!

Phr. the wish being father to the thought; *sua cuique voluptas*; *hoc erat in votis*, the mouth watering, the fingers itching; *aut Cæsar aut nullus*.

hypercriticism, difficulty in being pleased, *friandise*, epicurism, *omnia suspendens naso*.

discrimination, discernment, good taste, perspicacity.

epicure, gourmet.

[Excess of delicacy] prudery, prud-ishness, primness.

V. be -fastidious &c. *adj.*; split hairs, discriminate, have a sweet tooth.

mince the matter; turn up one's nose at &c. (*disdain*) 930; look a gift horse in the mouth, see spots on the sun.

Adj. fastidious, meticulous, exacting, nice, delicate, *délicat*, finical, finicky, difficult, dainty, lickerish, squeamish, thin-skinned; s-, queasy; hard –, diffi-cult- to please; querulous, particular, over-particular, straitlaced, prudish, prim, scrupulous; censorious &c. 932; hypercritical, discriminating, discern-ing, perspicacious.

Phr. *noli me tangere*.

869. Satiety.—N. satiety, satisfac-tion, saturation, repletion, glut, sur-feit; weariness &c. 841.

spoiled child; *enfant gâté*; too much of a good thing, *toujours perdrix*; *crambe repetita*.

V. sate, satiate, satisfy, saturate; cloy, quench, slake, pall, glut, gorge, surfeit; bore &c. (*weary*) 841; tire &c. (*fatigue*) 688; spoil.

have -enough of, – quite enough of, – one's fill, – too much of; be -satiated &c. *adj.*

Adj. satiated &c. *v.*; overgorged; *blasé*, used up, sick of, heart-sick.

Int. enough! hold! *eheu jam satis!*

4°. Contemplative Affections

870. Wonder.—N. wonder, marvel; astonish-, amaze-, wonder-, bewilder-ment; amazedness &c. *adj.*; admira-tion, awe; stup-or, -efaction; stound, fascination; sensation; surprise &c. (*inexpectation*) 508; cynosure.

note of admiration; thaumaturgy &c. (*sorcery*) 992.

V. wonder, marvel, admire; be -sur-prised &c. *adj.*; start; stare; open –, rub –, turn up- one's eyes; gloar; gape, open one's mouth, hold one's breath;

871. [Absence of wonder.] **Expec-tance.—N.** expectan-ce, -cy &c. (*expec-tation*) 507; calmness, composure, tran-quillity, serenity, coolness, imperturb-ability &c. 826.

nine days' wonder.

V. expect &c. 507; not -be surprised, – wonder &c. 870; *nil admirari*, make nothing of.

Adj. expecting &c. *v.*; unamazed, astonished at nothing; *blasé* &c. (*weary*) 841; unimaginative, calm, serene, im-

look –, stand- -aghast, – agog; look blank &c. (*disappointment*) 509; *tomber des nues*; not believe one's -eyes, – ears, – senses.

not be able to account for &c. (*unintelligible*) 519; not know whether one stands on one's head or one's heels.

surprise, astonish, amaze, astound; dumbfound, -er; startle, dazzle; strike, – with -wonder, – awe; electrify; stun, stupefy, petrify, confound, bewilder, flabbergast; stagger, throw on one's beam ends, fascinate, turn the head, take away one's breath, strike dumb; make one's -hair stand on end, – tongue cleave to the roof of one's mouth; make one stare.

take by surprise &c. (*be unexpected*) 508.

be -wonderful &c. *adj.*; beggar –, baffle- description; stagger belief.

Adj. surprised &c. *v.*; aghast, all agog, breathless, agape; openmouthed; awe-, thunder-, moon-, planet-struck; spell-bound; lost in -amazement, – wonder, – astonishment; struck all of a heap, unable to believe one's senses, like a duck in thunder.

wonderful, wondrous; surprising &c. *v.*; unexpected &c. 508; unheard of; mysterious &c. (*inexplicable*) 519; miraculous; *foudroyant*.

in-describable, -expressible, -effable; un-utterable, -speakable.

monstrous, prodigious, stupendous, marvellous; in-conceivable, -credible; in-, un-imaginable; strange &c. (*uncommon*) 83; passing strange.

striking &c. *v.*; over-whelming; wonder-working.

Adv. wonderfully &c. *adj.*; fearfully; for a –, in the name of- wonder; strange to say; *mirabile -dictu*, – *visu*; to one's great surprise.

with -wonder &c. *n.*, – gaping mouth, – open eyes, – upturned eyes; eyes starting out of one's head.

Int. lo, – and behold! O! hey-day! halloo! what! indeed! really! surely! humph! hem! good -lack, – heavens, – gracious! – lord! by jove! gad so! well a day! dear me! only think! lack-a-daisy! my -stars, – goodness! gracious goodness! goodness gracious! mercy on us! heavens and earth! God bless me! bless -us, – my heart! odzookens! *O gemini!* adzooks! hoity-toity! strong! Heaven save –, bless- the mark! can such things be! zounds! 'sdeath! what -on earth, – in the world! who would have thought it! &c. (*inexpectation*) 508; fancy! did you ever? you don't say so! what do you say to that! how now! where am I? well I'm blowed! &c.

Phr. *vox faucibus hæsit*; one's hair standing on end.

perturbable &c. 826; expected &c. *v.*; foreseen.

common, ordinary &c. (*habitual*) 613.

Int. no wonder; of course; why not?

———

872. Prodigy.—**N.** prodigy, phenomenon; wonder, -ment; genius, marvel, miracle; freak, monster &c. (*unconformity*) 83; curiosity, lion, infant prodigy, sight, spectacle; *jeu* –, *coup- de théâtre*; gazing-stock; sign; portent &c. 512.

bursting of a -shell, – bomb; volcanic eruption, peal of thunder; thunder-clap, -bolt.

what no words can paint; wonders of the world; *annus mirabilis*; *dignus vindice nodus*.

5°. Intrinsic Affections*

873. Repute.—**N.** distinction, mark, name, figure; repute, reputation, char-

874. Disrepute.—**N.** disrepute, discredit; ill-, bad- -repute, -name, -odour,

* Or personal affections derived from the opinions or feelings of others.

acter; good –, high- repute; note, notability, notoriety, *éclat*, 'the bubble reputation,' vogue, celebrity; fame, famousness; renown; popularity, *aura popularis*; esteem, approval, approbation &c. 931; credit, *succès d'estime*, *prestige*, talk of the town; name to conjure with.

glory, honour; lustre &c. (*light*) 420; illustriousness &c. *adj.*

account, regard, respect; reputableness &c. *adj.*; respectability &c. (*probity*) 939; good -name, – report; fair name.

dignity; stateliness &c. *adj.*; solemnity, grandeur, splendour, nobility, majesty, sublimity.

rank, standing, brevet rank, precedence, *pas*, station, place, *status*; position, – in society; order, degree, *locus standi*, caste, condition.

greatness &c. *adj.*; eminence; height &c. 206; importance &c. 642; pre-, super-eminence; high mightiness, primacy; top of the -ladder, – tree.

elevation; ascent &c. 305; super-, ex-altation; dignification, aggrandizement.

dedication, consecration, enthronement, canonization, apotheosis, deification, celebration, enshrinement, glorification.

hero, man of mark, great card, celebrity, worthy, lion, *rara avis*, notability, somebody; man of rank &c. (*nobleman*) 875; pillar of the -state, – society, – church.

chief &c. (*master*) 745; first fiddle &c. (*proficient*) 700; scholar &c. 492; cynosure, mirror; flower, pink, pearl; paragon &c. (*perfection*) 650; choice and master spirits of the age; *élite*; star, sun, constellation, galaxy.

ornament, honour, feather in one's cap, halo, aureole, nimbus; halo –, blaze- of glory; blushing honours; laurels &c. (*trophy*) 733.

memory, posthumous fame, niche in the temple of fame; immor-tality, -tal name; *magni nominis umbra*.

V. be conscious of glory; be proud of &c. (*pride*) 878; exult &c. (*boast*) 884; be vain of &c. (*vanity*) 880.

be -distinguished &c. *adj.*; shine &c.

-favour; disapprobation &c. 932; ingloriousness, derogation; a-, de-basement; abjectness &c. *adj.*; degradation, dedecoration; 'a long farewell to all one's greatness'; odium, obloquy, opprobrium, ignominy.

dishonour, disgrace; shame, humiliation; scandal, baseness, vileness; perfidy, turpitude &c. (*improbity*) 940; infamy.

tarnish, taint, defilement, pollution.

stain, blot, spot, blur, stigma, brand, reproach, imputation, slur.

crying –, burning- shame; *scandalum magnatum*, badge of infamy, blot in one's escutcheon; bend –, bar- sinister; champain, point champain; by-word of reproach; Ichabod.

argumentum ad verecundiam; sense of shame &c. 879.

V. be -inglorious &c. *adj.*; incur -disgrace &c. *n.*; have –, earn- a bad name; put –, wear- a halter round one's neck; disgrace –, expose- oneself.

play second fiddle; lose caste; pale one's ineffectual fire; recede into the shade; fall from one's high estate; keep in the background &c. (*modesty*) 881; be conscious of disgrace &c. (*humility*) 879; look -blue, – foolish, – like a fool; cut a -poor, – sorry- figure; laugh on the wrong side of the mouth; make a sorry face, go away with a flea in one's ear, slink away.

cause -shame &c. *n.*; shame, disgrace, put to shame, dishonour; throw –, cast –, fling –, reflect- dishonour &c. *n.* upon; be a -reproach &c. *n.* to; derogate from.

tarnish, stain, blot, sully, taint; discredit; degrade, debase, defile; beggar; expel &c. (*punish*) 972.

impute shame to, brand, post, stigmatize, vilify, defame, slur, cast a slur upon, hold up to shame, send to Coventry; tread –, trample- under foot; show up, drag through the mire, heap dirt upon; reprehend &c. 932.

bring low, put down, snub; take down a peg, – lower, – or two.

obscure, eclipse, outshine, take the shine out of; throw –, cast- into the shade; overshadow; leave –, put- in the background; push into a corner,

(*light*) 420; shine forth, figure; make –, cut- a -figure, – dash, – splash.

rival, surpass; out-shine, -rival, -vie, -jump; emulate, vie with, eclipse; throw –, cast- into the shade; over-shadow.

live, flourish, glitter, scintillate, flaunt; gain –, acquire- honour &c. *n.*; play first fiddle &c. (*be of importance*) 642; bear the -palm, – bell; lead the way; take -precedence, – the wall of; gain –, win- -laurels, – spurs, – golden opinions &c. (*approbation*) 931; gradu-ate, take one's degree, pass one's exami-nation, win a -scholarship, – fellowship.

make -a, – some- -noise, – noise in the world; leave one's mark, exalt one's horn, star, have a run, be run after; enjoy popularity, come -into vogue, – to the front; raise one's head.

enthrone, signalize, immortalize, deify, exalt to the skies; hand one's name down to posterity.

consecrate; dedicate to, devote to; enshrine, inscribe, blazon, lionize, blow the trumpet, crown with laurel.

confer –, reflect- honour &c. *n.* on; shed a lustre on; redound to one's honour, ennoble.

give –, do –, pay –, render- honour to; honour, accredit, pay regard to, dignify, glorify; sing praises to &c. (*approve*) 931; look up to; exalt, aggran-dize, elevate, nobilitate.

Adj. distinguished, *distingué*, noted; of -note &c. *n.*; honoured &c. *v.*; popu-lar; fashionable &c. 852.

in good odour; in –, in high- favour; reput-, respect-, credit-able.

remarkable &c. (*important*) 642; notable, notorious; celebrated, renowned, in every one's mouth, talked of; fam-ous, -ed; far-famed; conspicuous, to the front; foremost; in the -front rank, – ascendant.

imperishable, deathless, immortal, never fading, *ære perennius*; time-honoured.

illustrious, glorious, splendid, brilliant, radiant; bright &c. 420; full-blown; honorific.

eminent, prominent; high &c. 206; in the zenith; at the -head of, – top of the tree; peerless, of the first water; superior &c. 33; super-, pre-eminent.

great, dignified, proud, noble, honourable, worshipful, lordly, grand, stately, august, princely, imposing, solemn, transcendent, majestic, sacred, sublime, heaven-born, heroic, *sans peur et sans reproche*; sacrosanct.

Int. hail! all hail! *ave! viva! vive!* long life to! glory –, honour- be to!

put one's nose out of joint; put out, – of countenance.

upset, throw off one's centre; dis-compose, disconcert; put to the blush &c. (*humble*) 879.

Adj. disgraced &c. *v.*; blown upon; shorn of -its beams, – one's glory; overcome, down-trodden; loaded with -shame &c. *n.*; in -bad repute &c. *n.*; out of -repute, – favour, – fashion, – countenance; at a discount; under -a cloud, – an eclipse; unable to show one's face; in the -shade, – back-ground; out at elbows, down in the world, down and out.

inglorious; nameless, renownless, ob-scure, unknown to fame; un-noticed, -noted, -honoured, -glorified.

shameful; dis-graceful, -creditable, -reputable; despicable; questionable; unbecoming, unworthy; derogatory; degrading, humiliating, *infra digni-tatem*, dedecorous; scandalous, infa-mous, too bad, unmentionable; ribald, opprobrious; arrant, shocking, outra-geous, notorious, shady.

ignominious, scrubby, dirty, abject, vile, beggarly, pitiful, low, mean, shabby; base &c. (*dishonourable*) 940.

Adv. to one's shame be it spoken.

Int. fie! shame! for shame! *proh pudor! O tempora! O mores!* ough! *sic transit gloria mundi!*

Phr. one's name -being in every mouth, – living for ever; *sic itur ad astra, fama volat, aut Cæsar aut nullus;* not to know him argues oneself unknown; none but himself could be his parallel, *palmam qui meruit ferat.*

875. Nobility.—N. nobility, rank, condition, distinction, optimacy, blood, *pur sang,* birth, high descent, order; quality, gentility; blue blood of Castile; *ancien régime.*

high life, *haut monde;* upper -classes, – ten thousand; *élite,* aristocracy, great folks; fashionable world &c. *(fashion)* 852; salariat.

peer, -age; house of -lords, – peers; lords, – temporal and spiritual; *noblesse;* baronage, knightage; noble, -man; lord, -ling; grandee, *magnifico, hidalgo;* don, -ship; aristocrat, swell, three-tailed bashaw; gentleman, squire, squireen, patrician, laureate.

gentry, gentlefolk; squirarchy, better sort, *magnates, primates, optimates.*

king &c. *(master)* 745; prince, crown prince, *Dauphin;* duke; marquis, -ate; earl, viscount, baron, thane, banneret; baronet, -cy; knight, -hood; count, armiger, laird; sig-, seig-nior; esquire, boyar, margrave, vavasour, sheik, emir, ameer, scherif, *pasha,* effendi, sahib.

queen &c. 745; princess, begum, duchess, marchioness; countess &c.; lady, dame.

personage –, man- of -distinction, – mark, – rank; nota-bles, -bilities; celebrity, big-wig, magnate, great man, star; *magni nominis umbra;* 'every inch a king'; grand Panjandrum.

V. be -noble &c. *adj.*

Adj. noble, exalted; of -rank &c. *n.;* princely, titled, patrician, aristocratic; high-, well-born; of gentle blood; genteel, *comme il faut,* gentlemanlike, courtly &c. *(fashionable)* 852; highly respectable.

Adv. in high quarters.

877. Title.—N. title, honour; knighthood &c. *(nobility)* 875.

royal –, serene- highness, excellency, grace; lordship, worship, Rt. Hon., rever-ence, -end; esquire, sir; madam, *madame;* master, mistress, Mr., Mrs., *signor, señor, Mein Herr, mynheer;*

876. Commonalty.—N. commonalty, democracy; obscurity; low -condition, – life, – society, – company; *bourgeoisie;* mass of -the people, – society; Brown, Jones, and Robinson; Tom, Dick, and Harry; lower –, humbler- -classes, – orders; vulgar –, common- herd; rank and file, *hoc genus omne;* the -many, – general, – crowd, – people, – popu-lace, – multitude, – million, – masses, – mobility, – peasantry; king Mob; proletariat, *fruges consumere nati,* great unwashed; man in the street.

mob; rabble, – rout; chaff, rout, horde, *canaille;* scum –, *residuum* –, dregs- of -the people, – society; swinish multitude, *fæx populi; profanum* –, *ignobile- vulgus;* vermin, riff-raff, tag-rag and bobtail; small fry.

commoner, one of the people, democrat, plebeian, republican, proletary, *prolétaire, roturier,* Mr. Snooks, *bourgeois, épicier,* Philistine, cockney; *grisette, demi-monde.*

peasant, countryman, boor, carle, churl; vill-ain, -ein; serf, kern, tyke, tike, chuff, ryot, fellah; long-shore-man; swain, clown, hind; clod, -hopper; hobnail, yokel, hick, rube, cider squeezer, bog-trotter, bumpkin; plough-man, -boy; rustic, chawbacon, tiller of the soil; hewers of wood and drawers of water, groundling; gaffer, loon, put, cub, Tony Lumpkin, looby, lout, under-ling; *gamin,* guttersnipe, street arab, mudlark; rough, rowdy, ruffian, roughneck; pot-wallopper, slubberde-gullion; vulgar –, low- fellow; cad, curmudgeon.

upstart, *parvenu, nouveau-riche,* skip-jack; nobody, – one knows; *hesterni quirites, pessoribus orti; bourgeois gentil-homme, novus homo,* snob, gent, mush-room, no one knows who, adventurer; man of straw.

beggar, panhandler, gaberlunzie, muckworm, mudlark, *sans-culotte,* raff, tatterdemalion, caitiff, ragamuffin, Pariah, outcast of society, tramp, weary Willie, bum, vagabond, *chiffon-*

your –, his- honour; handle to one's name.

decoration, laurel, palm, wreath, garland, bays, medal, ribbon, riband, blue ribbon, *cordon*, cross, crown, coronet, star, garter; feather, – in one's cap; chevron, epaulet, *épaulette*, colours, cockade; livery; order, arms, armorial bearings, shield, scutcheon, crest, reward &c. 973.

nier, rag-picker, Cinderella, cinder-wench, scrub, jade; boots, gossoon.

Goth, Vandal, Hottentot, savage, barbarian, Yahoo; unlicked cub, rough diamond.

barbar-ousness, -ism; Bœotia.

V. be -ignoble &c. *adj.*, – nobody &c. *n.*

Adj. ignoble, common, mean, low, base, vile, sorry, scrubby, beggarly, below par; no great shakes &c. (*unimportant*) 643; home-ly, -spun; vulgar, low-minded; snobbish, *parvenu*.

plebeian, proletarian; of -low, – mean- -parentage, – origin, extraction; low-, base-, earth-born, low bred; mushroom, dunghill, risen from the ranks; unknown to fame, obscure, untitled.

rustic, uncivilized; lout-, boor-, clown-, churl-, brut-, raff-ish; rude, unlicked, unpolished.

barbar-ous, -ian, -ic, -esque; cockney, born within sound of Bow bells.

underling, menial, servile, subaltern.

Adv. below the salt.

---

878. Pride.—**N.** dignity, self-respect, *mens sibi conscia recti*.

pride; haughtiness &c. *adj.*; high notions, *hauteur*; vainglory, crest; arrogance &c. (*assumption*) 885; pomposity &c. 882.

proud man, highflier; fine -gentleman, – lady; *grande dame*.

V. be -proud &c. *adj.*; put a good face on; look one in the face; stalk abroad, perk oneself up; presume, swagger, strut; rear –, lift up –, hold up- one's head; hold one's head high, look big, take the wall, 'bear like the Turk no rival near the throne,' carry with a high hand; ride the –, mount on one's- high horse; set one's back up, bridle, toss the head; give oneself airs &c. (*assume*) 885; boast &c. 884.

pride oneself on; glory in, take a pride in; pique –, plume –, hug- oneself; stand upon, be proud of; put a good face on; not -hide one's light under a bushel, – put one's talent in a napkin; not think small beer of oneself &c. (*vanity*) 880.

Adj. dignified; stately; proud, -crested; lordly, baronial; lofty-minded; high-souled, -minded, -mettled, -handed, -plumed, -flown, -toned.

879. Humility.—**N.** hum-ility, -bleness; meek-, low-ness; lowli-ness, -hood; abasement, self-abasement, -effacement; submission &c. 725; resignation.

condescension; affability &c. (*courtesy*) 894.

modesty &c. 881; verecundity, blush, suffusion, confusion; sense of -shame, – disgrace; humiliation, mortification; let –, set- down.

V. be -humble &c. *adj.*; deign, vouchsafe, condescend; humble –, demean- oneself; stoop, – to conquer; carry coals; submit &c. 725; submit with a good grace &c. (*brook*) 826; yield the palm.

lower one's -tone, – note; sing small, draw in one's horns, sober down; hide one's -face, – diminished head; not dare to show one's face, take shame to oneself, not have a word to say for oneself; feel –, be conscious of- -shame, – disgrace; drink the cup of humiliation to the dregs; eat -humble pie, – one's words, – dirt; be humiliated, receive a snub.

blush -for, – up to the eyes; redden, change colour; colour up; hang one's head, look foolish, feel small.

render humble; humble, humiliate;

haughty, paughty, insolent, lofty, high, mighty, swollen, puffed up, flushed, blown; vain-glorious; purse-proud, fine; proud as -a peacock, Lucifer; bloated with pride.

supercilious, disdainful, bumptious, magisterial, imperious; high -handed, – and mighty; overweening, consequential; arrogant &c. 885; unblushing &c. 880.

stiff, -necked; starch; perked –, stuck- up; in buckram, straitlaced; prim &c. (*affected*) 855.

on one's -high horses, – tight ropes, – high ropes; on stilts; *en grand seigneur*.

Adv. with head erect, with one's nose in the air.

Phr. *odi profanum vulgus et arceo.*

---

let –, set –, take –, tread –, frown-down; snub, abash, abase, make one sing small, strike dumb; teach one -his distance, – his place; take down a peg, – lower; throw –, cast- into the shade &c. 874; stare –, put- out of countenance; put to the blush; confuse, ashame, mortify, disgrace, crush; send away with a flea in one's ear.

get a set down.

Adj. humble, lowly, meek; modest &c. 881; humble-, sober-minded; unoffended; submissive &c. 725; servile &c. 886.

condescending; affable &c. (*courteous*) 894.

humbled &c. *v.*; bowed down, resigned; abashed, ashamed, dashed; out of countenance; down in the mouth; down on one's -knees, – marrow-bones; humbled in the dust, brow-beaten; chap-, crest-fallen; dumbfoundered, flabbergasted, struck all of a heap.

shorn of one's glory &c. (*disrepute*) 874.

Adv. with -downcast eyes, – bated breath, – bended knee; on all fours, on one's feet.

under correction, with due deference.

Phr. I am your -obedient, – very humble- servant; my service to you.

---

880. Vanity.—N. vanity; conceit, -edness; self-conceit, -complacency, -confidence, -sufficiency, -esteem, -love, -approbation, -praise, -glorification, -laudation, -gratulation, -applause, -admiration; *amour-propre*; selfishness &c. 943.

airs, pretensions, mannerism; egotism; prigg-ism, -ishness; coxcombery, gaudery, vainglory, elation; pride &c. 878; ostentation &c. 882; assurance &c. 885.

vox et præterea nihil; *cheval de bataille*.

ego-ist, -tist; peacock, coxcomb &c. 854; Sir Oracle &c. 887.

V. be -vain &c. *adj.*, – vain of; pique oneself &c. (*pride*) 878; lay the flattering unction to one's soul.

have -too high, – an overweening-opinion of -oneself, – one's talents; blind oneself as to one's own merit; not think -small beer, – *vin ordinaire*-of oneself; put oneself forward; fish

881. Modesty.—N. modesty; humility &c. 879; diffidence, timidity; retiring disposition, unobtrusiveness, bashfulness &c. *adj.*; *mauvaise honte*; blush, -ing; verecundity; self-knowledge.

reserve, constraint; demureness &c. *adj.*; blushing honours.

V. be -modest &c. *adj.*; retire, reserve oneself; give way to; draw in one's horns &c. 879; hide one's face.

keep -private, – in the background, – one's distance; pursue the noiseless tenor of one's way, 'do good by stealth and blush to find it fame,' hide one's light under a bushel, cast a sheep's eye.

Adj. modest, diffident; humble &c. 879; timid, timorous, bashful; shy, nervous, skittish, coy, sheepish, shamefaced, blushing, over-modest.

unpreten-ding, -tious; un-obtrusive, -assuming, -ostentatious, -boastful, -aspiring; poor in spirit.

for compliments; give oneself airs &c. (*assume*) 885; boast &c. 884.

render -vain &c. *adj.*; inspire with -vanity &c. *n.*; inflate, puff up, turn up, turn one's head.

Adj. vain, – as a peacock; conceited, assured, overweening, pert, forward, perky; vain-glorious, high-flown; ostentatious &c. 882; puffed up, inflated, flushed.

self-satisfied, -confident, -sufficient, -flattering, -admiring, -applauding, -glorious, -opinionated; *entêté* &c. (*wrong-headed*) 481; wise in one's own conceit, pragmatical, overwise, pretentious, priggish; egotistic, -al; *soi-disant* &c. (*boastful*) 884; arrogant &c. 885.

un-abashed, -blushing; un-constrained, -ceremonious; free and easy.

Adv. vainly &c. *adj.*

Phr. how we apples swim!

out of countenance &c. (*humbled*) 879.

reserved, constrained, demure.

Adv. humbly &c. *adj.*; quietly, privately; without -ceremony, – beat of drum; *sans façon.*

---

882. Ostentation.—N. ostentation, display, show, flourish, parade, *étalage*, pomp, array, state, solemnity; dash, splash, glitter, strut, swank, side, swagger, pomposity; preten-se, -sions; showing off; fuss.

magnificence, splendour; *coup d'œil*; grand doings.

coup de théâtre; stage -effect, – trick; clap-trap; *mise en scène*; *tour de force*; chic.

demonstration, flying colours; tomfoolery; flourish of trumpets &c. (*celebration*) 883; pageant, -ry; spectacle, exhibition, procession; turn –, set- out; grand function; *fête*, gala, field-day, review, march past, promenade, insubstantial pageant.

dress; court –, full –, evening –, ball –, fancy- dress; tailoring, millinery, man-millinery, frippery; foppery, equipage.

ceremon-y, -ial; ritual; form, -ality; etiquette; punct-o, -ilio, -iliousness; starched-, stateli-ness.

mummery, solemn mockery, mouth honour.

attitudinarian; fop &c. 854.

V. be -ostentatious &c. *adj.*; come –, put oneself- forward; attract attention, star it.

make –, cut- a -figure, – dash, – splash; strut, blow one's own trumpet; figure, – away; make a show, – display; glitter.

show -off, – one's paces; parade, march past; display, exhibit, put forward, hold up; trot –, hang- out; sport, brandish, blazon forth; dangle, – before the eyes.

cry up &c. (*praise*) 931; *prôner*, flaunt, emblazon, prink, set off, mount, have framed and glazed.

put a good, – smiling- face upon; clean the outside of the platter &c. (*disguise*) 544.

Adj. ostentatious, showy, dashing, pretentious; ja-, jau-nty; grand, pompous, palatial; high-sounding; turgid &c. (*big-sounding*) 577; garish, gorgeous; gaudy, – as a -peacock, – butterfly, – tulip; flaunting, flashing, flaming, glittering; gay &c. (*ornate*) 847; colourful.

splendid, magnificent, sumptuous.

theatrical, dramatic, spectacular, scenic, ceremonial, ritual, -istic.

solemn, stately, majestic, formal, stiff, ceremonious, punctilious, starch-ed, -y.

en grande tenue, in best bib and tucker, in Sunday best, *endimanché*.

Adv. with -flourish of trumpet, – beat of drum, – flying colours, – a brass band.

ad captandum vulgus.

883. Celebration.—N. celebration, solemnization, jubilee, diamond jubilee, commemoration, ovation, pæan, triumph, jubilation.

triumphal arch, bonfire, salute; salvo, – of artillery; *feu de joie*, flourish of trumpets, *fanfare*, colours flying, illuminations, fireworks.

inauguration, installation, presentation; *début*, coming out, birth-day anniversary, bi-, ter-, centenary; silver –, golden –, diamond-wedding, -day; coronation; Lord Mayor's show; harvest home, red letter day, festival; trophy &c. 733; *Te Deum* &c. (*thanksgiving*) 990; fête &c. 882; holiday &c. 840.

V. celebrate, keep, signalize, do honour to, commemorate, solemnize, hallow, mark with a red letter, hold high festival, maffick.

pledge, drink to, toast, hob and nob.

inaugurate, install, instate, induct, chair.

rejoice &c. 838; kill the fatted calf, hold jubilee, roast an ox, fire a salute.

Adj. celebrating &c. *v.*; commemorative, celebrated, immortal.

Adv. in -honour, – commemoration, – celebration of.

Int. hail! all hail! *io -pæan, – triumphe!* 'see the conquering hero comes!'

884. Boasting.—N. boasting &c. *v.*; boast, vaunt, crake; preten-ce, -sions; puff, -ery; flourish, *fanfaronnade*; gasconade; bluff, swank, brag, -gardism; bravado, bunkum, Buncombe; highfalutin; jact-itation, -ancy; bounce, rant, bluster; venditation, vapouring, rodomontade, bombast, fine talking, tall talk, magniloquence, teratology, heroics; jingoism, Chauvinism; exaggeration &c. 549; gas, hot air.

vanity &c. 880; *vox et præterea nihil*; much cry and little wool, *brutum fulmen*.

exultation; glorification; flourish of trumpets; triumph &c. 883.

boaster; bragg-art, -adocio; hot air merchant; Gascon, *fanfaron*, pretender, fourflusher, *soi-disant*; windbag, blowhard, bluffer; chau-vinist; blusterer &c. 887; charlatan, jack-pudding, trumpeter; puppy &c. (*fop*) 854.

V. boast, make a boast of, brag, vaunt, puff, show off, flourish, crake, crack, trumpet, strut, swagger, vapour, bluff; draw the long bow.

exult, crow over, neigh, chuckle, triumph; glory, gloat, jubilate; throw up one's cap; talk big, *se faire valoir, faire claquer son fouet*, take merit to oneself, make a merit of, sing *Io triumphe*, holloa before one is out of the wood.

Adj. boasting &c. *v.*; magniloquent, flaming, Thrasonic, stilted, gas-conading, braggart, boastful, pretentious, *soi-disant*; vain-glorious &c. (*conceited*) 880.

elate, -d; jubilant, triumphant, exultant; in high feather; flushed, – with victory; cock-a-hoop; on stilts.

vaunted &c. *v.*

Adv. vauntingly &c. *adj.*; with a brass band.

Phr. 'let the galled jade wince.'

885. [Undue assumption of superiority.] **Insolence.—N.** insolence; haughtiness &c. *adj.*; arrogance, airs; overbearance, brashness, bumptiousness, contumely, disdain; domineering &c. *v.*; tyranny &c. 739.

impertinence; cheek, nerve, sauce; sauciness &c. *adj.*; flippancy, dicacity, petulance, procacity, bluster; swagger, -ing &c. *v.*; bounce; terrorism; jingoism, chauvinism.

as-, pre-sumption; beggar on horseback; usurpation.

impudence, assurance, audacity, self-assertion, hardihood, front, face, brass; shamelessness &c. *adj.*; effrontery, hardened front, face of brass.

assumption of infallibility.

malapert, saucebox &c. (*blusterer*) 887.

V. be -insolent &c. *adj.*; bluster, vapour, swagger, swell, give oneself airs, snap one's fingers, kick up a dust; swear &c. (*affirm*) 535; rap out oaths; roister.

arrogate; as-, pre-sume; make -bold, – free; take a liberty, give an inch and take an ell.

domineer, bully, dictate, hector; lord it over, bulldoze; *traiter de haut, regarder de haut en bas*; exact; snub, huff, beard, fly in the face of; put to the blush; bear –, beat- down; browbeat, intimidate; trample –, tread- -down, – under foot; dragoon, ride roughshod over, terrorize.

out-face, -look, -stare, -brazen, -brave; stare out of countenance; brazen out; lay down the law; teach one's grandmother to suck eggs; assume a lofty bearing; talk –, look- big; put on big looks, act the *grand seigneur*; mount –, ride- the high horse; toss the head, carry with a high hand.

tempt Providence, want snuffing.

Adj. insolent, haughty, arrogant, imperious, magisterial, dictatorial, arbitrary; high-handed, high and mighty; contumelious, supercilious, overbearing, intolerant, domineering; overweening, high-flown.

flippant, pert, cavalier, saucy, forward, impertinent, fresh, malapert.

precocious, assuming, would-be, bumptious.

bluff; brazen-, browed-faced, shameless, aweless, unblushing, unabashed; bold-, bare-faced; dead –, lost- to shame.

886. Servility.—N. servility; slavery &c. (*subjection*) 749; obsequiousness &c. *adj.*; subserviency; abasement; pros-tration, -ternation; genuflexion &c. (*worship*) 990; fawning &c. *v.*; tuft-hunting, time-serving, flunkeyism; sycophancy·&c. (*flattery*) 933; humility &c. 879.

sycophant, parasite, yes-man; toad, -y, -eater; tuft-hunter; snob, flunkey, lap-dog, spaniel, lick-spittle, smell-feast, *Græculus esuriens*, hanger on, stooge, *cavaliere servente*, led captain, carpet knight; time-server, fortune-hunter, Vicar of Bray, Sir Pertinax Mac Sycophant, pick-thank; flatterer &c. 935; doer of dirty work; *âme damnée*, tool; reptile; slave &c. (*servant*) 746; courtier; sponge, jackal; truckler.

V. cringe, bow, stoop, kneel, bend the knee; fall on one's knees, prostrate oneself; worship &c. 990.

sneak, crawl, crouch, cower, truckle to, grovel, fawn, toady, lick the feet of, kiss the hem of one's garment.

pay court to; feed –, fatten –, batten- on; dance attendance on, pin oneself upon, hang on the sleeve of, *avaler des couleuvres*, keep time to, fetch and carry, do the dirty work of.

go with the stream, follow the crowd, worship the rising sun, hold with the hare and run with the hounds.

Adj. servile, obsequious; supple, – as a glove; soapy, oily, pliant, cringing, fawning, slavish, grovelling, snivelling, mealy-mouthed; beggarly, sycophantic, parasitical; abject, prostrate, down on one's marrow-bones; base, mean, sneaking; crouching &c. *v.*

Adv. hat –, cap- in hand.

_____

impudent, audacious, presumptuous, free and easy, devil-may-care, rollicking; janty, jaunty; roistering, blustering, hectoring, swaggering, vapouring; thrasonic, fire-eating, 'full of sound and fury.'

Adv. insolently, with a high hand; *ex cathedrâ*.

Phr. one's bark being worse than his bite.

887. Blusterer.—N. bluster-, swagger-, vapour-, roister-, brawl-er; brazen-face; *fanfaron*; braggart &c. (*boaster*) 884; bully, terrorist, rough, rough-neck; hooligan, hoodlum, larrikin, ruffian; Mo-hock, -hawk; drawcansir, swashbuckler, Captain Boabdil, Sir Lucius O'Trigger, Thraso, Pistol, Parolles, Bombastes Furioso, Hector, Chrononhotonthologos; jingo; desperado, dare-devil, fire-eater; fury &c. (*violent person*) 173; rowdy.

puppy &c. (*fop*) 854; prig; Sir Oracle, dogmatist, *doctrinaire*, stump orator, jack-in-office; saucebox, malapert, jackanapes, minx; bantam-cock.

Section III. SYMPATHETIC AFFECTIONS

1°. Social Affections

888. Friendship. — N. friendship, amity; friendliness &c. *adj.*; brotherhood, fraternity, sodality, confraternity, sorosis, sisterhood; harmony &c. (*concord*) 714; peace &c. 721.

firm -, staunch -, intimate -, familiar -, bosom -, cordial -, tried -, devoted -, lasting -, fast -, sincere -, warm -, ardent- friendship.

cordiality, fraternization, *entente cordiale*, good understanding, *rapprochement*, sympathy, fellow-feeling, response, welcomeness; *camaraderie*.

affection &c. (*love*) 897; favouritism; goodwill &c. (*benevolence*) 906; partiality.

acquaintance, familiarity, intimacy, intercourse, fellowship, knowledge of; introduction.

V. be -friendly &c. *adj.*, - friends &c. 890, - acquainted with &c. *adj.*; know; have the ear of; keep company with &c. (*sociality*) 892; hold communication -, have dealings -, sympathize- with; have a leaning to; bear good will &c. (*benevolence*) 906; love &c. 897; make much of; befriend &c. (*aid*) 707; introduce to.

set one's horses together; hold out -, extend- the right hand of -friendship, - fellowship; become -friendly &c. *adj.*; make -friends &c. 890 with; break the ice, be introduced to; make -, pick -, scrape- acquaintance with; get into favour, gain the friendship of.

shake hands with, fraternize, embrace; receive with open arms, throw oneself into the arms of; meet half way, take in good part.

Adj. friendly; amic-able, -al; well affected, unhostile, neighbourly, brotherly, fraternal, sisterly, sympathetic, harmonious, hearty, cordial, warm-hearted, devoted.

889. Enmity.—N. enmity, hostility; unfriendliness &c. *adj.*; discord &c. 713.

alienation, estrangement; dislike &c. 867; hate &c. 898; antagonism.

heartburning; animosity &c. 900; malevolence &c. 907.

V. be -inimical &c. *adj.*; keep -, hold- at arm's length; be at loggerheads; bear malice &c. 907; fall out; take umbrage &c. 900; harden the heart, alienate, estrange.

Adj. inimical, unfriendly, hostile; at -enmity, - variance, - swords points, - daggers drawn, - open war with; up in arms against; in bad odour with.

on bad -, not on speaking- terms; cool; cold, -hearted; estranged, alienated, disaffected, irreconcilable.

friends –, well –, at home –, hand in hand- with; on -good, – friendly, – amicable, – cordial, – familiar, – intimate- -terms, – footing; on -speaking, – visiting- terms; in one's good -graces, – books.

acquainted, familiar, intimate, thick, hand and glove, hail fellow well met, free and easy; welcome.

Adv. amicably &c. *adj.*; with open arms; *sans cérémonie*; arm in arm.

890. Friend.—N. friend, – of one's bosom, intimate acquaintance, neighbour, well-wisher; *alter ego*; best –, bosom –, fast- friend; *amicus usque ad aras*; *fidus Achates*; *persona grata*.

favourer, *fautor*, patron, backer, Mæcenas; tutelary saint, good genius, advocate, partisan, sympathiser; ally; friend in need &c. (*auxiliary*) 711.

associate, compeer, comrade, mate, companion, *confrère*, *camarade*, *confidante*, colleague; old –, crony; side-kick; chum, buddy, bunkie, roommate, pal; play-fellow, -mate; classmate, schoolfellow; bedfellow, -mate; maid of honour.

compatriot; fellow –, countryman, – townsman.

shop-, ship-, mess-mate; fellow –, boon –, pot- companion; copartner.

Arcades ambo, Pylades and Orestes, Castor and Pollux, Nisus and Euryalus, Damon and Pythias, *par nobile fratrum*.

host, Amphitryon, Boniface; guest, visitor, frequenter, *habitué*; *protégé*.

891. Enemy.—N. enemy; antagonist, foeman; open –, bitter- enemy; opponent &c. 710; back friend.

public enemy, enemy to society, traitor, anarchist &c. 743.

Phr. every hand being against one.

---

892. Sociality.—N. soci-ality, -ability, -ableness &c. *adj.*; social intercourse; consociation; inter-course, -community; consort-, companion-, fellow-, comrade-ship; clubbism; *esprit de corps*.

conviviality; good -fellowship, – company, *camaraderie*; joviality, jollity, *savoir-vivre*, festivity, festive board, merry-making; loving cup; hospitality, heartiness; cheer.

welcome, -ness; greeting; hearty –, warm –, welcome- reception; urbanity &c. (*courtesy*) 894; intimacy, familiarity.

good –, jolly- fellow, good mixer, Rotarian; *bon enfant*.

social –, family- circle; circle of acquaintance, *coterie*, society, company.

social -gathering, – *réunion*; assembly &c. (*assemblage*) 72; party, entertainment, reception, *levée*, at home, *conversazione*, *soirée*, *matinée*, evening –, morning –, afternoon –, garden –, dinner –, tea –, cocktail- party; symposium, sing-song; kettle-, drum; *partie carrée*, dish of tea, *ridotto*, rout, house-

893. Seclusion. Exclusion.—N. seclusion, privacy; retirement; concealment; reclusion, recess; snugness &c. *adj.*; delitescence; rustication, *rus in urbe*; solitude; solitariness &c. (*singleness*) 87; isolation; loneliness &c. *adj.*; estrangement from the world, anchoritism, voluntary exile; aloofness.

cell, hermitage; convent &c. 1000; *sanctum sanctorum*; study, library, den; hide-out.

depopulation, desertion, desolation; wilderness &c. (*unproductive*) 169; howling wilderness; rotten borough, Old Sarum.

exclusion, excommunication, banishment, exile, ostracism, proscription; cut, – direct; dead cut.

inhospit-ality, -ableness &c. *adj.*; un-, dis-sociability; domesticity, Darby and Joan.

recluse, hermit, eremite, cenobite; anchor-et, -ite; Simon Stylites; Troglodyte, Timon of Athens, Santon, *solitaire*, ruralist, disciple of Zimmermann, closet cynic, Diogenes; outcast, Pariah,

warming; ball, prom, hop, dance, *thé dansant*; festival &c. (*amusement*) 840; wedding breakfast; 'the feast of reason and the flow of soul.'

visit, -ing; round of visits; call, morning call; interview &c. (*interlocution*) 588; assignation; tryst, -ing place; appointment.

club &c. (*association*) 712.

V. be -sociable &c. *adj.*; know; be -acquainted &c. *adj.*; associate -, sort -, keep company -, walk hand in hand -with; eat off the same trencher, club together, consort, bear one company, join; make acquaintance with &c. (*friendship*) 888; make advances, fraternize, embrace; intercommunicate.

be -, feel -, make oneself- at home with; make free with; crack a bottle with; take pot luck with, receive hospitality, live at free quarters.

visit, pay a visit; interchange -visits, - cards; call -at, - upon; leave a card; drop in, look in; look one up, beat up one's quarters.

entertain; give a -party &c. *n.*; be at home, see one's friends, hang out, keep open house, do the honours; receive, - with open arms; welcome; give a warm reception &c. *n.* to; kill the fatted calf.

Adj. sociable, companionable, clubbable, clubby, conversable, cosy, cosey, chatty, conversational; homiletical.

convivial; fest-ive, -al; jovial, jolly, hospitable.

welcome, - as the roses in May; *fêté*, entertained.

free and easy, hail fellow well met, familiar, on visiting terms, acquainted.

social, neighbourly; international, cosmopolitan, gregarious.

Adv. *en famille*, in the family circle; *sans -façon*, - *cérémonie*, arm in arm.

castaway, outsider, pilgarlic; wastrel, foundling, orphan.

V. be -, live- secluded &c. *adj.*; keep -, stand -, hold oneself- -aloof, - in the background; keep snug; shut oneself up; deny -, seclude- oneself; creep into a corner, rusticate, *aller planter ses choux*; retire, - from the world; hermetize, take the veil; abandon &c. 624.

cut, - dead; refuse to -associate with, - acknowledge; look cool -, turn one's back -, shut the door- upon; repel, blackball, excommunicate, exclude, exile, expatriate; banish, outlaw, maroon, ostracize, proscribe, cut off from, send to Coventry, keep at arm's length, draw a cordon round; boycott, blockade, lay an embargo on, isolate.

depopulate; dis-, un-people.

Adj. secluded, sequestered, retired, delitescent, private, bye; out of the -world, -way; in a backwater; 'the world forgetting by the world forgot.'

snug, domestic, stay-at-home.

unsociable; un-, dis-social; inhospitable, cynical, inconversable, unclubbable, *sauvage*, eremetic.

solitary; lone-ly, -some; isolated, single.

excluded, estranged; unfrequented; uninhabit-able, -ed; tenantless; un-tenanted, -occupied; abandoned; deserted, - in one's utmost need; unfriended; kith-, friend-, home-less; lorn, forlorn, desolate.

un-visited, -introduced, -invited, -welcome; under a cloud, left to shift for oneself, derelict, outcast, outside the gates.

banished &c. *v.*; under an embargo.

Phr. *noli me tangere*.

---

894. Courtesy.—N. courtesy; respect &c. 928; good -manners, - behaviour, - breeding; manners; politeness &c. *adj.*; *bienséance*, urbanity, comity, gentility; gentle -, breeding; polish, presence, cultivation, culture; civili-ty, -zation; amenity, suavity; good -temper, - humour; amiability, easy temper, complacency, soft tongue,

895. Discourtesy.—N. discourtesy; ill-breeding; ill -, bad -, ungainly-manners; insuavity; grouchiness; uncourteousness &c. *adj.*, tactlessness; rusticity, inurbanity; illiberality, incivility, displacency.

disrespect &c. 929; procacity, impudence; barbar-ism, -ity; misbehaviour, brutality, blackguardism, conduct un-

mansuetude; condescension &c. (*humility*) 879; affability, complaisance, *prévenance*, amiability, gallantry, chivalry; pink of -politeness, – courtesy.

compliment; fair –, soft –, sweet-words; honeyed phrases, flattering remarks, ceremonial; salutation, reception, presentation, introduction, *accueil*, greeting, recognition; welcome, *abord*, respects, *devoir*, regards, remembrances; kind -regards, – remembrances; love, best love, duty; deference.

obeisance &c. (*reverence*) 928; bow, courtesy, curtsy, scrape, *salaam*, *kowtow*, bowing and scraping; kneeling; genuflexion &c. (*worship*) 990; obsequiousness &c. 886; capping, shaking hands &c. *v.*; grip of the hand, embrace, hug, squeeze, *accolade*, loving cup, *vin d'honneur*, pledge; love token &c. (*endearment*) 902; kiss, buss, salute.

mark of recognition, nod; 'nods and becks and wreathed smiles'; valediction &c. 293; condolence &c. 915.

V. be -courteous &c. *adj.*; show -courtesy &c. *n.*

mind one's P's and Q's, behave oneself, be all things to all men, conciliate, speak one fair, take in good part; make –, do- the amiable; look as if butter would not melt in one's mouth; mend one's manners.

receive, do the honours, usher, greet, hail, bid welcome; welcome, – with open arms; shake hands; hold out –, press –, squeeze- the hand; bid God speed; speed the parting guest; cheer, serenade.

salute; embrace &c. (*endearment*) 902; kiss, – hands; drink to, pledge, hob and nob; move to, nod to; smile upon.

uncover, cap; touch –, take off- the hat; doff the cap; pull the forelock; present arms; make way for; bow; make one's bow; scrape, curtsy, courtesy; bob a -curtsy, – courtesy; kneel; bow –, bend- the knee; salaam, *kowtow*.

visit, wait upon, present oneself, pay one's respects, pay a visit &c. (*sociability*) 892; dance attendance on &c. (*servility*) 886; pay attentions to; do homage to &c. (*respect*) 928.

becoming a gentleman, *grossièreté*, *brusquerie*; vulgarity &c. 851.

churlishness &c. *adj.*; spinosity, perversity; moroseness &c. (*sullenness*) 901*a*.

bad-, ill-temper; sternness &c. *adj.*; austerity; moodishness, captiousness &c. 901; cynicism; tartness &c. *adj.*; acrimony, acerbity, **v** rulence, asperity.

scowl, black looks, frown; short answer, rebuff; hard words, contumely; unparliamentary language, personality.

bear, bruin, brute, grouch, blackguard, beast; unlicked cub; frump, cross-patch; saucebox &c. 887.

V. be -rude &c. *adj.*; insult &c. 929; treat with discourtesy; take a name in vain; make -bold, – free- with; take a liberty; stare out of countenance, ogle, point at, put to the blush.

cut; turn -one's back upon, – on one's heel; give the cold shoulder; keep at -a distance, – arm's length; look -cool, – coldly, – black- upon; show the door to, send away with a flea in the ear.

lose one's temper &c. (*resentment*) 900; sulk &c. 901*a*; frown, scowl, glower, pout; snap, snarl, growl.

render -rude &c. *adj.*; brut-alize, -ify.

Adj. dis-, un-courteous; uncourtly; ill-bred, -mannered, -behaved, -conditioned; unbred; unmanner-ly, ed; im-, un-polite; un-polished, -civilized, -genteel; ungentleman-like, -ly; un-ladylike; blackguard; vulgar &c. 851; dedecorous; foul-mouthed, -spoken; abusive.

un-civil, -gracious, -ceremonious; cool; pert, forward, obtrusive, impudent, rude, saucy, precocious; insolent &c. 885.

repulsive; un-complaisant, -accommodating, -neighbourly, -gallant; in-affable; un-gentle, -gainly; rough, rugged, bluff, blunt, gruff; churl-, boor-, bear-ish; brutal, *brusque*; stern, harsh, austere; cavalier.

tart, sour, crabbed, sharp, short, trenchant, sarcastic, crusty, biting, caustic, virulent, bitter, acrimonious, venomous, contumelious; snarling &c, *v.*; surly, – as a bear; perverse; grim.

prostrate oneself &c. (*worship*) 990. give –, send- one's duty &c. *n.* to.

render -polite &c. *adj.*; polish, civilize, humanize.

Adj. courteous, polite, civil, mannerly, urbane; well-behaved, -mannered, -bred, -brought up, gently bred, of gentle -breeding, – manners, good-mannered, polished, civilized, cultivated; refined &c. (*taste*) 850; gentlemanlike &c. (*fashion*) 852; gallant, chivalrous, on one's good behaviour.

fine –, fair –, soft- spoken; honey-mouthed, -tongued; oily, unctuous, bland, suave; obliging, conciliatory, complaisant, complacent; obsequious &c. 886.

ingratiating, winning; gentle, mild; good-humoured, cordial, gracious, amiable, tactful, addressful, affable, genial, friendly, familiar; neighbourly.

Adv. courteously &c. *adj.*; with a good grace; with -open, – outstretched- arms; *à bras ouverts*; *suaviter in modo*, in good humour.

Int. hail! welcome! well met! *ave!* all hail! good -day, – morning &c., – morrow! God speed! *pax vobiscum!* may your shadow never be less! *chin-chin!*

sullen &c. 901*a*; peevish &c. (*irascible*) 901.

Adv. discourteously &c. *adj.*; with -discourtesy &c. *n.*, – a bad grace.

---

896. Congratulations.—N. con-, gratulation; felicitation; salute &c. 894; condolence &c. 915; compliments of the season; good –, best- wishes.

V. con-, gratulate; felicitate, compliment; give –, wish one- joy; tender –, offer- one's congratulations; wish -many happy returns of the day, – a merry Christmas and a happy new year.

congratulate oneself &c. (*rejoice*) 838.

Adj. con-, gratulatory.

---

897. Love.—N. love; fondness &c. *adj.*; liking; inclination &c. (*desire*) 865; regard, dilection, admiration, fancy.

affection, sympathy, fellow-feeling; tenderness &c. *adj.*; heart, brotherly love; benevolence &c. 906; attachment.

yearning, tender passion, *affaire de coeur, amour,* gallantry, passion, flame, devotion, fervour, enthusiasm, transport of love, rapture, enchantment, infatuation, adoration, idolatry.

narcissism, Œdipus complex, Electra complex.

Cupid, Venus, Eros; myrtle; true lover's knot; love -token, – suit, – affair, – tale, – story; the old story, plighted love; courtship &c. 902; *amourette.*

maternal love.

attractiveness, charm; popularity; favourite &c. 899.

lover, suitor, follower, admirer, adorer, wooer, amoret, beau, sweet-

898. Hate.—N. hate, hatred, vials of hate; Hymn of Hate.

dis-affection, -favour; alienation, estrangement, coolness; enmity &c. 889; animosity &c. 900.

umbrage, pique, grudge; dudgeon, spleen; bitterness, – of feeling; ill –, bad- blood; acrimony; malice &c. 907; implacability &c. (*revenge*) 919.

repugnance &c. (*dislike*) 867; odium, unpopularity; loathing, detestation, antipathy; object of -hatred, – execration; abomination, aversion, *bête noire*; enemy &c. 891; bitter pill; source of annoyance &c. 830.

V. hate, detest, abominate, abhor, loathe; recoil –, shudder- at; shrink from, view with horror, hold in abomination, revolt against, execrate; scowl &c. 895; disrelish &c. (*dislike*) 867.

owe a grudge; bear -spleen, – a grudge, – malice &c. (*malevolence*) 907; conceive an aversion to.

heart, inamorato, swain, young man, flame, love, truelove; leman, Lothario, gallant, paramour, *amoroso, cavaliere servente*, captive, *cicisbeo*; *caro sposo*, Don Juan, sheik, ladies' man, squire of dames, Knave of Hearts.

inamorata, lady-love, idol, darling, duck, Dulcinea, angel, goddess, *cara sposa*; mistress.

betrothed, affianced, *fiancée*.

flirt, *coquette*; amorette; pair of turtle doves; abode of love, *agapemone*.

V. love, like, affect, fancy, care for, take an interest in, be partial to, sympathize with; be -in love &c. *adj.*-with; have –, entertain –, harbour –, cherish- a -love &c. *n.* for; regard, revere; take to, bear love to, be wedded to; set one's affections on; make much of, feast one's eyes on; hold dear, prize, treasure; hug, cling to, cherish, pet, caress &c. 902.

burn; adore, idolize, love to distraction, *aimer eperdument*; dote -on, – upon.

take a fancy to, fall for, be stuck on, look sweet upon; become -enamoured &c. *adj.*; fall in love with, lose one's heart; desire &c. 865.

excite love; win –, gain –, secure –, engage- the -love, – affections, – heart; take the fancy of; have a place in –, wind round- the heart; attract, attach, endear, charm, fascinate, captivate, bewitch, seduce, enamour, enrapture, turn the head.

get into favour; ingratiate –, insinuate –, worm- oneself; propitiate, curry favour with, pay one's court to, make a date with, *faire l'aimable*, set one's cap at, flirt, coquet.

Adv. loving &c. *v.*; fond of; taken –, struck- with; smitten, bitten; attached to, wedded to; enamoured; charmed &c. *v.*; in love; lovesick; over head and ears in love.

affectionate, tender, sweet upon, sympathetic, loving, fond, amorous, amatory; erotic, uxurious, ardent, passionate, rapturous, devoted, motherly.

loved &c. *v.*; beloved; well –, dearly- beloved; dear, precious, darling, pet, little; favourite, popular.

congenial; to –, after- one's -mind, – taste, – fancy, – own heart.

in one's good -graces &c. (*friendly*) 888; dear as the apple of one's eye, nearest to one's heart.

lovable, adorable; lovely, sweet; attractive, seductive, winning; charming, engaging, interesting, enchanting, captivating, fascinating, intriguing, bewitching; amiable, like an angel, angelic, seraphic.

excite –, provoke- hatred &c. *n.*; be -hateful &c. *adj.*; stink in the nostrils; estrange, alienate, repel, set against, sow dissension, set by the ears, envenom, incense, irritate, rile, ruffle, vex; horrify &c. 830.

Adj. hating &c. *v.*; abhorrent; averse from &c. (*disliking*) 867; set against.

bitter &c. (*acrimonious*) 895; implacable &c. (*revengeful*) 919.

un-loved, -beloved, -lamented, -deplored, -mourned, -cared for, -endured, -valued; disliked &c. 867.

crossed in love, forsaken, rejected, love-lorn, jilted.

obnoxious, hateful, odious, abominable, repulsive, offensive, shocking; disgusting &c. (*disagreeable*) 830.

invidious, spiteful; malicious &c. 907.

insulting, irritating, provoking.

[Mutual hate] at -daggers drawn, – swords points; not on speaking terms &c. (*enmity*) 889.

Phr. no love lost between.

———

899. Favourite.—**N.** favourite, pet, cosset, minion, idol, jewel, spoiled child, *enfant gâté*; led captain; crony; fondling; apple of one's eye, man after one's own heart; *persona grata*.

love, dear, darling, duck, honey, jewel; mopsey, moppet; sweetheart &c. (*love*) 897.

general –, universal- favourite; idol of the people; matinée idol, movie –, radio- star.

900. Resentment.—N. resentment, displeasure, animosity, anger, wrath, indignation; vexation, exasperation, bitter resentment, wrathful indignation.

pique, umbrage, huff, miff, soreness, dudgeon, acerbity, virulence, bitterness, acrimony, asperity, spleen, gall; heart-burning, -swelling; rankling.

ill –, bad- -humour, – temper; irascibility &c. 901; ill blood &c. (*hate*) 898; revenge &c. 919.

excitement, irritation; warmth, bile, choler, ire, fume, pucker, dander, ferment, ebullition; towering -passion, – rage, *acharnement*, angry mood, taking, pet, tiff, passion, fit, tantrums.

burst, explosion, paroxysm, storm, rage, fury, desperation; violence &c. 173; fire and fury; vials of wrath; gnashing of teeth, hot blood, high words.

scowl &c. 895; sulks &c. 901*a*.

[Cause of umbrage] affront, provocation, offence; indignity &c. (*insult*) 929; grudge, crow to pluck, sore subject; red rag to a bull; *casus belli*.

Furies, Erinys, Eumenides, Alecto, Megæra, Tisiphone.

buffet, slap in the face, box on the ear, rap on the knuckles.

V. resent; take -amiss, – ill, – to heart, – offence, – umbrage, – huff, – exception; take in -ill part, – bad part, – dudgeon; *ne pas entendre raillerie*; breathe revenge, cut up rough.

fly –, fall –, get- into a -rage, – passion; bridle –, bristle –, froth –, fire –, flare- up; open –, pour out- the vials of one's wrath.

pout, knit the brow, frown, scowl, lower, snarl, growl, gnarl, gnash, snap; redden, colour; look -black, – black as thunder, – daggers; bite one's thumb; show –, grind- one's teeth; champ the bit.

chafe, mantle, fume, kindle, fly out, take fire; boil, – over; boil with -indignation, – rage; rage, storm, foam; vent one's -rage, – spleen; lose one's temper, stand on one's hind legs, stamp the foot, kick up a row, fly off the handle, cut up rough; stamp –, quiver –, swell –, foam- with rage; burst with anger; raise Cain, breathe fire and fury.

have a fling at; bear malice &c. (*revenge*) 919.

cause -, raise- anger; affront, offend; give -offence, – umbrage; anger; hurt the feelings; insult, discompose, fret, ruffle, nettle, heckle, huff, pique; excite &c. 824; irritate, stir the blood, stir up bile; sting, – to the quick; rile, provoke, chafe, wound, incense, inflame, enrage, aggravate, add fuel to the flame, fan into a flame, widen the breach, envenom, embitter, exasperate, infuriate, kindle wrath; stick in one's gizzard; rankle &c. 919.

put out of humour; put one's -monkey, – back- up; set –, get- one's back up; raise one's -gorge, – dander, – choler; work up into a passion; make -one's blood boil, – the ears tingle; throw into a ferment, madden, drive one mad; lash into -fury, – madness; fool to the top of one's bent; set by the ears.

bring a hornet's nest about one's ears.

Adj. angry, wrath, irate; ire-, wrath-ful; cross &c. (*irascible*) 901; sulky &c. 901*a*; bitter, virulent; acrimonious &c. (*discourteous*) &c. 895; violent &c. 173.

warm, burning; boiling, – over; fuming, raging; foaming, – at the mouth; convulsed with rage.

offended &c. *v.*; waxy, *acharné*; wrought, worked up; indignant, hurt, sore, peeved; set against.

fierce, wild, rageful, furious, mad with rage, fiery, infuriate, rabid, savage; relentless &c. 919.

flushed with -anger, – rage; in a -huff, – stew, – fume, – pucker, – passion, – rage, – fury; on one's high ropes, up in arms; in high dudgeon.

Adv. angrily &c. *adj.*; in the height of passion; in the heat of -passion, – the moment.

Int. *tantæne animis cælestibus iræ!* marry come up! zounds! 'sdeath!

Phr. one's -blood, – back, – monkey- being up; *fervens difficili bile jecur*; the gorge rising, eyes flashing fire; the blood -rising, – boiling; *hæret lateri lethalis arundo.*

901. Irascibility.—N. irascibility, temper; crossness &c. *adj.*; susceptibility, procacity, petulance, irritability, tartness, acerbity, protervity; pugnacity &c. (*contentiousness*) 720.

excitability &c. 825; bad -, fiery -, crooked -, irritable &c. *adj.*-temper; *genus irritabile*, hot blood.

ill humour &c. (*sullenness*) 901a; asperity &c., churlishness &c. (*discourtesy*) 895.

huff &c. (resentment) 900; a word and a blow.

Sir Fretful Plagiary; brabbler, Tartar; shrew, vixen, virago, termagant, dragon, scold, Xanthippe; porcupine; spit-fire; fire-eater &c. (*blusterer*) 887; fury &c. (*violent person*) 173.

V. be -irascible &c. *adj.*; have a -temper &c. *n.*, – devil in one; fire up &c. (*be angry*) 900.

Adj. irascible; bad-, ill-tempered; irritable, susceptible; excitable &c. 825; thin-skinned &c. (*sensitive*) 822; fretful, fidgety; on the fret.

hasty, over-hasty, quick, warm, hot, testy, touchy, techy, tetchy; like -touchwood, – tinder; huffy; pet-tish, -ulant; waspish, snapp-y, -ish, peppery, fiery, passionate, choleric, shrewish, 'sudden and quick in quarrel.'

querulous, captious, mood-y, -ish; quarrelsome, contentious, disputatious; pugnacious &c. (*bellicose*) 720; cantankerous, exceptious; restive &c. (*perverse*) 901a; churlish &c. (*discourteous*) 895.

cross, – as -crabs, – two sticks, – a cat, – a dog, – the tongs; like a bear with a sore head; fractious, peevish, *acariâtre*.

in a bad temper; sulky &c. 901a; angry &c. 900.

resent-ful, -ive; vindictive &c. 919.

Int. pish!

901a. Sullenness.—N. sullenness &c. *adj.*; morosity, spleen; churlishness &c. (*discourtesy*) 895; irascibility &c. 901.

moodiness &c. *adj.*; perversity; obstinacy &c. 606; torvity, spinosity; crabbedness &c. *adj.*

ill -, bad- -temper, – humour; sulks, dudgeon, mumps, doleful dumps, doldrums, fit of the sulks, *bouderie*, black looks, scowl; huff &c. (*resentment*) 900.

V. be -sullen &c. *adj.*; sulk; frown, scowl, lower, glower, grouse, grouch, crab, gloam, pout, have a hang-dog look, glout.

Adj. sullen, sulky; ill-tempered, -humoured, -affected, -disposed; in -an ill, – a bad, ·· a shocking- -temper, – humour; out of -temper, –

humour; knaggy, **torvous**, crusty, **crabbed; sore as a** boil; surly &c.: (*discourteous*) 895.

moody; spleen-ish, -ly; splenetic, cankered.

cross, -grained; perverse, wayward, humoursome; restive; cantankerous, refractory, intractable, exceptious, sinistrous, deaf to reason, unaccommodating, rusty, crust, froward.

dogged &c. (*stubborn*) 606.

grumpy, glum, grim, grum, morose, frumpish; in the -sulks &c. *n.*; out of sorts; scowl-, glower-, growl-ing.

peevish &c. (*irascible*) 901.

902. [Expression of affection or love.] **Endearment.—N.** endearment, caress; blandish-, blandi-ment; *épanchement*, fondling, billing and cooing, dalliance.

embrace, salute, kiss, buss, smack, osculation, deosculation; amorous glances; ogle, side glance, sheep's eyes.

courtship, wooing, suit, addresses, the soft impeachment; love-making; an affair; serenading; caterwauling.

flirting &c. *v.*; flirtation, gallantry; coquetry, spooning.

true lover's knot, plighted love, engagement, bethrothal; love -tale, – token, – letter; *billet-doux*, valentine.

honeymoon; Strephon and Chloe, 'Arry and 'Arriet.

V. caress, fondle, pet, dandle, nurse; pat, – on the -head, – cheek; chuck under the chin, smile upon, coax, wheedle, cosset, coddle, cocker; make -of, – much of, pamper; cherish, foster, kill with kindness.

clasp, hug, cuddle; fold –, strain- in one's arms; nestle, nuzzle, neck, embrace, kiss, buss, smack, blow a kiss; salute &c. (*courtesy*) 894.

bill and coo, spoon, toy, dally, flirt, coquet; galli-, gala-vant; philander; make love; pay one's -court, – addresses, – attentions- to; serenade; court, woo; set one's cap at; be –, look- sweet upon; ogle, cast sheep's eyes upon; *faire les yeux doux*.

fall in love with, win the affections &c. (*love*) 897; die for.

propose; make –, have- an offer; pop the question; plight one's -troth, – faith; become -engaged, – betrothed.

Adj. caressing &c. *v.*; 'sighing like furnace'; love-sick, spoony.

caressed &c. *v.*

903. Marriage.—N. marriage, matrimony, wedlock, union, intermarriage, *vinculum matrimonii*, nuptial tie, knot.

married state, coverture, bed, cohabitation.

match; betrothment &c. (*promise*) 768; wedding, nuptials, Hymen, bridal; e-, spousals; leading to the altar &c. *v.*; nuptial benediction, *epithalamium*.

torch –, temple- of Hymen; hymeneal altar; honeymoon.

bride, bridegroom; brides-maid, -man.

best –, grooms-man, page, usher.

married -man, – woman, – couple; neogamist, Benedick, partner, spouse, mate, yokemate; husband, man, con-

904. Celibacy.—N. celibacy, singleness, single blessedness; bachelor-hood, -ship; miso-gamy, -gyny.

virginity, *pucelage*; maiden-hood, -head.

unmarried man, bachelor, Cœlebs, agamist, old bachelor; miso-gamist, -gynist; celibate.

unmarried woman, spinster; maid, -en; virgin, *feme sole*, old maid; bachelor girl; nun &c.

V. live single; keep bachelor hall.

Adj. un-married, -wedded; wife-, spouse-less; single, virgin, celibate.

905. Divorce.—N. divorce, -ment; separation; judicial separation, separ-

sort, baron; old –, good- man; wife of one's bosom; help-meet, -mate, rib, better half, grey mare, old woman, good wife; feme, – coverte; squaw, lady; matron, -age, -hood; man and wife; wedded pair, Darby and Joan.

affinity, soul-mate.

mono-, bi-, di-, deutero-, tri-, poly-gamy; mormonism; poly-andry; Turk, Bluebeard.

unlawful –, left-handed –, companionate –, morganatic –, ill-assorted- marriage; *mésalliance*; *mariage de convenance*; an affair.

match-maker, marriage broker, matrimonial agent.

V. marry, wive, take to oneself a wife; be -married, – spliced; go –, pair- off; wed, espouse, lead to the hymeneal altar, take 'for better, for worse,' give one's hand to, bestow one's hand upon; remarry; intermarry.

marry, join, handfast; couple &c. (*unite*) 43; tie the nuptial knot; give -away, – in marriage; affy, affiance; betroth &c. (*promise*) 768; publish –, bid- the banns; be asked in church.

Adj. married &c. *v.*; one, – bone and one flesh.

marriageable, nubile.

engaged, betrothed, affianced.

matrimonial, marital, conjugal, connubial, wedded; nuptial, hy-meneal, spousal, bridal.

Phr. the grey mare the better horse.

ate maintenance; *separatio a -mensâ et thoro*, – *vinculo matrimonii*.

widowhood, viduage, viduity, weeds.

widow, -er; relict; dowager; *divorcée*; cuckold.

V. live -separately, – apart; separate, divorce, disespouse, put away; wear the horns.

2°. Diffusive Sympathetic Affections

906. Benevolence.—N. benevolence, Christian charity; God's -love, – grace; good-will; philanthropy &c. 910; un-selfishness &c. 942.

good -nature, – feeling, – wishes; kind-, kindli-ness &c. *adj.*; lovingkind-ness, benignity, brotherly love, charity, humanity, fellow-feeling, sympathy; goodness –, warmth- of heart; *bon-homie*; kind-heartedness; amiability, milk of human kindness, tenderness; love &c. 897; friendship &c. 888.

toleration, consideration, generosity; mercy &c. (*pity*) 914.

charitableness &c. *adj.*; bounty, alms-giving; good works, beneficence, the luxury of doing good.

acts of kindness, a good turn; good –, kind- -offices, – treatment.

good Samaritan, sympathizer, well-wisher, philanthropist, *bon enfant*; altruist.

V. be -benevolent &c. *adj.*; have one's heart in the right place, bear good will; wish -well, – God speed;

907. Malevolence.—N. malevolence; bad intent, -ion; un-, dis-kindness; ill -nature, – will, – blood; bad blood; enmity &c. 889; hate &c. 898; malig-nity; malice, – aforethought, – pre-pense; maliciousness &c. *adj.*; spite, despite; resentment &c. 900.

uncharitableness &c. *adj.*; incom-passionateness &c. 914*a*; gall, venom, rancour, rankling, virulence, mordac-ity, acerbity; churlishness &c. (*dis-courtesy*) 895.

hardness of heart, heart of stone, obduracy; cruelty; cruelness &c. *adj.*; brutality, savagery; fer-ity, -ocity; barbarity, inhumanity, immanity, truc-ulence, ruffianism; evil eye, cloven -foot, – hoof; Inquisition; torture.

ill –, bad- turn; affront &c. (*disre-spect*) 929; outrage, atrocity; ill usage; intolerance, bigotry, persecution; ten-der mercies [ironical]; 'unkindest cut of all.'

V. be -malevolent &c. *adj.*; bear –, harbour- -spleen, – a grudge, – mal-

view -, regard- with an eye of favour; take in good part; take -, feel- an interest in; be -, feel- interested- in; sympathize with, feel for; fraternize &c. (*be friendly*) 888.

enter into the feelings of others, do as you would be done by, meet half-way.

treat well; give comfort, smooth the bed of death; do -good, - a good turn; benefit &c. (*goodness*) 648; render a service, be of use; aid &c. 707.

Adj. benevolent; kind, -ly; well-meaning; amiable; obliging, accommodating, indulgent, considerate, gracious, complacent, good-humoured.

warm-, soft-, kind-, tender-, large-, broad-hearted; merciful &c. 914; philanthropic &c. 910; charitable, beneficent, humane, benign, benignant; bount-eous, -iful &c. 816.

good-, well-natured; spleenless; sympath-izing, -etic; complaisant &c. (*courteous*) 894; kindly, well-meant, -intentioned.

fatherly, motherly, brotherly, sisterly; pat-, mat-, frat-ernal; friendly &c. 888.

Adv. with -a good intention, - the best intentions.

Int. God speed! much good may it do!

---

ice; betray -, show- the cloven foot.

hurt &c. (*physical pain*) 378; annoy &c. 830; injure, harm, wrong; do -harm, - an ill office- to; outrage; disoblige, malign, plant a thorn in the breast.

molest, worry, harass, haunt, harry, bait, tease, throw stones at; play the devil with; hunt down, dragoon, hound; persecute, oppress, grind; maltreat; ill-treat, -use.

wreak one's malice on, do one's worst, break a butterfly on the wheel; dip -, imbrue- one's hands in blood; have no mercy &c. 914a.

Adj. male-, unbene-volent; unbenign; ill-disposed, -intentioned, -natured, -conditioned, -contrived; evil-minded, -disposed.

malicious; malign, -ant; rancorous; de-, spiteful; mordacious, caustic, bitter, envenomed, acrimonious, virulent; un-amiable, -charitable; maleficent, venomous, grinding, galling.

harsh, disobliging; un-kind, -friendly, -gracious; treacherous; inofficious; invidious; uncandid; churlish &c. (*uncourteous*) 895; surly, sullen &c. 901a.

cold, -blooded, -hearted; hard-, flint-, marble-, stony-hearted; hard of heart, unnatural; ruthless &c. (*unmerciful*) 914a; relentless &c. (*revengeful*) 919.

cruel; brut-al, -ish; savage, - as a -bear, - tiger; ferine, feral, ferocious; inhuman; barbarous, fell, untamed, tameless, truculent, incendiary; bloodthirsty &c. (*murderous*) 361; atrocious.

fiend-ish, -like; demoniacal; diabolic, -al; devilish, infernal, hellish, Satanic.

Adv. malevolently &c. *adj.*; with -bad intent &c. *n.*

---

908. Malediction.—N. malediction, malison, curse, imprecation, denunciation, execration, anathema, ban, proscription, excommunication, commination, thunders of the Vatican, fulmination, *maranatha*, aspersion, vilification, vituperation, scurrility.

abuse; foul -, bad -, strong -, unparliamentary- language, Limehouse; Billingsgate, sauce, evil speaking; cursing &c. *v.*; profane swearing, oath.

threat &c. 909; more bark than bite; invective &c. (*disapprobation*) 932.

V. curse, accurse, imprecate, damn, swear at; slang; curse with bell, book and candle; invoke -, call down- curses on the head of; devote to destruction.

execrate, beshrew, scold; anathematize &c. (*censure*) 932; hold up to execration, denounce, proscribe, excommunicate, fulminate, thunder against; threaten &c. 909; curse up hill and down dale.

curse and swear; swear, – like a trooper; fall a cursing, rap out an
oath, damn, cuss.

Adj. curs-ing, -ed &c. *v.*; maledictory.

Int. woe to! beshrew! *ruat cœlum!* ill –, woe- betide! confusion
seize! damn! confound! blast! curse! devil take! hang! out with! a
plague –, out- upon! aroynt! *honi soit!*

Phr. *delenda est Carthago.*

909. Threat.—N. threat, menace; defiance &c. 715; abuse, minacity,
intimidation; fulmination; commination &c. (*curse*) 908; gathering
clouds &c. (*warning*) 668.

V. threat, -en; menace; snarl, growl, gnarl, mutter, bark, bully.
defy &c. 715; intimidate &c. 860; keep –, hold up –, hold out- *in
terrorem*; shake –, double –, clinch- the fist at; thunder, talk big, fulminate, use big words, bluster, look daggers.

Adj. threatening, menacing; mina-tory, -cious; comminatory, abusive;
in terrorem; ominous &c. (*predicting*) 511; defiant &c. 715; under
the ban.

Int. *væ victis!* at your peril! do your worst!

910. Philanthropy. — N. philanthropy; altruism, humanit-y, -arian-
ism; universal benevolence; *deliciæ
humani generis*; cosmopolitanism, utilitarianism, the greatest happiness of
the greatest number, social science,
sociology.

common weal, public welfare, socialism, communism.

patriotism, civism, nationality, love
of country, *amor patriæ*, public spirit.

chivalry, knight errantry; generosity
&c. 942.

911. Misanthropy.—N. misanthropy,
incivism; egotism &c. (*selfishness*) 943;
moroseness &c. 901a; cynicism; defeat-
ism.

misanthrope, misanthropist, egotist,
cynic, man-hater, Timon, Diogenes.

woman-hater, misogynist.

Adj. misanthropic, antisocial, unpatriotic; egotistical &c. (*selfish*) 943;
morose &c. 901a.

philanthropist, altruist &c. 906; utilitarian, Benthamite, socialist,
communist, cosmopolite, citizen of the world, *amicus humani
generis*; knight errant; patriot.

Adj. philanthropic, altruistic, humanitarian, utilitarian, cosmopolitan; public-spirited, patriotic; humane, large-hearted &c.
(*benevolent*) 906; chival-ric, -rous, generous &c. 942.

Adv. *pro -bono publico, – aris et focis.*

Phr. '*humani nihil a me alienum puto.*'

912. Benefactor. — N. benefactor,
saviour, good genius, tutelary saint,
patron, guardian angel, fairy godmother, good Samaritan; *pater patriæ*;
salt of the earth &c. (*good man*) 948;
auxiliary &c. 711.

**913. [Maleficent being.] Evil-doer.
—N.** evil- -doer, – worker; wrong doer
&c. 949; mischief maker, marplot;
oppressor, tyrant; firebrand, incendiary, pyromaniac, anarchist, destroyer,
Hun, *Boche*, Vandal, iconoclast; communist; terrorist, *apache*, gunman,
gangster, racketeer.

savage, brute, ruffian, barbarian, semi-barbarian, caitiff, desperado; Mo-hock, -hawk; bludgeon man, bully, rough, hooligan,
larrikin, dangerous classes, ugly customer; thief &c. 792.

cockatrice, scorpion, hornet; viper, adder; snake, – in the grass;

serpent, cobra, asp, rattlesnake, anaconda; canker-, wire-worm; locust, Colorado beetle; torpedo; bane &c. 663.

cannibal; Anthropophag-us, -ist; bloodsucker, vampire, ogre, ghoul, gorilla; vulture; gyr-, ger-falcon.

wild beast, tiger, hyæna, butcher, hangman; cut-throat &c. (*killer*) 361; blood-, sleuth-, hell-hound.

hag, hellhag, beldam, Jezebel.

monster; fiend &c. (*demon*) 980; homicidal maniac, devil incarnate, demon in human shape; Frankenstein's monster.

harpy, siren, vampire; Furies, Eumenides &c. 900.

Attila, scourge of the human race.

Phr. *fœnum habet in cornu.*

3°. Special Sympathetic Affections

914. Pity.—**N.** pity, compassion, commiseration; bowels, – of compassion; condolence &c. 915; sympathy, fellow-feeling, tenderness, yearning, forbearance, humanity, mercy, clemency, exorability; leniency &c. (*lenity*) 740; charity, ruth, long-suffering.

melting mood; *argumentum ad misericordiam*; quarter, grace, *locus pœnitentiæ.*

sympathizer, champion, partisan.

V. pity; have –, show –, take- pity &c. *n.*; commiserate, compassionate; condole &c. 915; sympathize; feel –, be sorry –, yearn- for; weep, melt, thaw, enter into the feelings of.

forbear, relent, relax, give quarter, wipe the tears, *parcere subjectis*, give a *coup de grâce*, put out of one's misery; be cruel to be kind.

raise –, excite- pity &c. *n.*; touch, soften; melt, – the heart; appeal to one's better feelings; propitiate, disarm.

ask for -mercy &c. *n.*; supplicate &c. (*request*) 765; cry for quarter, beg one's life, kneel; deprecate.

Adj. pitying &c. *v.*; pitiful, compassionate, sympathetic, touched.

merciful, clement, ruthful; humane; humanitarian &c. (*philanthropic*) 910; tender, – hearted, – as a chicken; soft, – hearted; unhardened; lenient &c. 740; exorable, forbearing; melting &c. *v.*; weak.

Int. for pity's sake! mercy! have –, cry you- mercy! God help you! poor -thing, – dear, – fellow! woe betide! *quis talia fando temperet a lachrymis!*

Phr. one's heart bleeding for; *haud ignara mali miseris succurrere disco.*

914a. Pitilessness.—**N.** pitilessness &c. *adj.*; inclemency; inexorability, hardness of heart; inflexibility; severity &c. 739; malevolence &c. 907.

V. have no –, shut the gates of- mercy &c. 914; give no quarter.

Adj. piti-, merci-, ruth-, bowel-less; unpitying, unmerciful, inclement; in-, un-compassionate; inexorable, inflexible; harsh &c. 739; cruel &c. 907; unrelenting &c. 919.

915. Condolence.—**N.** condolence; lamentation &c. 839; sympathy, consolation.

V. condole with, console, sympathize &c. 914, share one's misery; feel for; express –, testify- pity; afford –, supply- consolation; lament &c. 839- with; send one's condolences.

4°. RETROSPECTIVE SYMPATHETIC AFFECTIONS

916. Gratitude. — N. gratitude, thankfulness, gratefulness, feeling of obligation.

acknowledgment, recognition thanksgiving, giving thanks.

thanks, praise, benediction; pæan; *Te Deum* &c. (*worship*) 990; grace, – before, – after- meat; thank-offering. requital.

V. be -grateful &c. *adj.*; thank; give –, render –, return –, offer –, tender- thanks &c. *n.*; acknowledge, requite.

feel –, be –, lie- under an obligation; *savoir gré*; not look a gift horse in the mouth; never forget, overflow with gratitude; thank –, bless- one's stars; fall on one's knees.

Adj. grateful, thankful, obliged, beholden, indebted to, under obligation.

Int. thanks! many thanks! gramercy! much obliged! thank you! thank Heaven! Heaven be praised!

917. Ingratitude.—N. ingratitude, thanklessness, oblivion of benefits; unthankfulness.

'benefits forgot'; thankless -task, – office.

V. be -ungrateful &c. *adj.*; forget benefits; look a gift horse in the mouth.

Adj. un-grateful, -mindful, -thankful; thankless, ingrate, wanting in gratitude, insensible of benefits.

forgotten; un-acknowledged, -thanked, -requited, -rewarded; ill-requited.

Int. thank you for nothing! '*et tu Brute !*'

918. Forgiveness.—N. forgiveness, pardon, condonation, grace, remission, absolution, amnesty, oblivion; indulgence; reprieve.

conciliation; reconciliation &c. (*pacification*) 723; propitiation.

excuse, exoneration, quittance, release, indemnity; bill –, act –, covenant –, deed- of indemnity; exculpation &c. (*acquittal*) 970.

longanimity, placability, forbearance; *amantium iræ*; *locus pœnitentiæ*.

V. forgive, – and forget; pardon, condone, think no more of, let bygones be bygones, shake hands; forget an injury, bury the hatchet; clean the slate.

excuse, pass over, overlook; wink at &c. (*neglect*) 460; bear with; allow –, make allowances- for; let one down easily, not be too hard upon, pocket the affront; blot out one's transgression.

let off, remit, absolve, give absolution, reprieve; acquit &c. 970.

beg –, ask –, implore- pardon &c. *n.*; conciliate, propitiate, placate; make up a quarrel &c. (*pacify*) 723; let the wound heal.

919. Revenge.—N. revenge, -ment; vengeance; avenge-ment, -ance; sweet revenge, *vendetta*, death-feud, eye for an eye, blood for blood, a Roland for an Oliver; retaliation &c. 718; day of reckoning.

rancour, vindictiveness, implacability; malevolence &c. 907; ruthlessness &c. 914a.

avenger, vindicator, Nemesis, Eumenides.

V. re-, a-venge; take –, have one's- revenge; breathe -revenge, – vengeance; wreak one's -vengeance, – anger; give no quarter.

have -accounts to settle, – a crow to pluck, – a rod in pickle; pay off old scores.

keep the wound green; harbour -revenge, – vindictive feeling; bear malice; rankle, – in the breast; have at one's mercy.

Adj. revenge-, venge-ful; vindictive, rancorous; pitiless &c. 914a; ruthless, rigorous, avenging, retaliative.

unforgiving, unrelenting; inexorable, stony-hearted, implacable; relent-, remorse-less.

æternum servans sub pectore vulnus; rankling, immitigable.

Adj. forgiving, placable, conciliatory. forgiven &c. *v.*; un-resented, -avenged, -revenged.

Adv. cry you mercy.

Phr. *veniam petimusque damusque vicissim*; more in sorrow than in anger.

920. Jealousy.—N. jealous-y, -ness; jaundiced eye, heartburning; green-eyed monster; yellows; Juno.

V. be -jealous &c. *adj.*; view with -jealousy, – a jealous eye.

Adj. jealous, – as a Barbary pigeon; jaundiced, yellow-eyed, horn-mad.

921. Envy.—N. envy; enviousness &c. *adj.*; rivalry; *jalousie de métier*.

V. envy, covet, lust after, crave, burst with envy, regard with envious eyes.

Adj. envious, invidious, covetous; *alieni appetens*.

Phr. *manet -cicatrix, – altâ mente repostum.*

revenge is sweet.

Section IV. MORAL AFFECTIONS
1°. Moral Obligations

922. Right.—N. right; what -ought to, – should- be; fitness &c. *adj.*; *summum jus.*

justice, equity; equitableness &c. *adj.*; propriety; fair play, impartiality, measure for measure, give and take, *lex talionis*, square deal.

Astræa, Nemesis, Themis.

scales of justice, even-handed justice, retributive justice, *suum cuique*; clear stage –, fair field- and no favour; Queensberry rules.

morals &c. (*duty*) 926; law &c. 963; honour &c. (*probity*) 939; virtue &c. 944.

V. be -right &c. *adj.*; stand to reason.

see -justice done, – one righted, – fair play; do justice to; recompense &c. (*reward*) 973; hold the scales even, give and take; serve one right, put the saddle on the right horse; give -every one, – the devil- his due; *audire alteram partem*.

deserve &c. (*be entitled to*) 924.

Adj. right, good; just, reasonable; fit &c. 924; equ-al, -able, -itable; even-handed, fair, – and square.

legitimate, justifiable, rightful; as it -should, – ought to- be; lawful &c. (*permitted*) 760, (*legal*) 963.

deserved &c. 924.

Adv. rightly &c. *adj.*; in -justice, – equity, – reason.

without -distinction of, – regard to, – respect to- persons; upon even terms.

Int. all right!

923. Wrong. — N. wrong; what -ought not to, – should not- be; *malum in se*; unreasonableness, grievance; shame.

injustice; unfairness &c. *adj.*; iniquity, foul play, partiality, leaning; favour, -itism; nepotism, party spirit, partisanship; undueness &c. 925; unlawfulness &c. 964.

robbing Peter to pay Paul &c. *v.*; the wolf and the lamb; vice &c. 945.

a custom more honoured in the breach than the observance.

V. be -wrong &c. *adj.*; cry to heaven for vengeance.

do -wrong &c. *n.*; be -inequitable &c. *adj.*; favour, lean towards; encroach; impose upon; reap where one has not sown; give an inch and take an ell; rob Peter to pay Paul.

Adj. wrong, -ful; bad, too bad; unjust, -fair; in-, un-equitable; unequal, partial, one-sided.

objectionable; un-reasonable, -allowable, -warrantable, -justifiable; not cricket, not playing the game; improper, unfit; unjustified &c. 925; illegal &c. 964; iniquitous, criminal; immoral &c. 945; injurious &c. 649.

in the wrong, – box.

Adv. wrongly &c. *adj.*

Phr. it will not do; this is too bad.

924. Dueness.—N. due, -ness; right, privilege, prerogative, prescription, title, claim, pretension, demand, birthright.

immunity, licence, liberty, franchise; vested -interest, – right; licitness.

sanction, authority, warranty, charter; warrant &c. (*permission*) 760; constitution &c. (*law*) 963; tenure; bond &c. (*security*) 771.

deserts, merits, dues.

claimant, appellant; plaintiff &c. 938.

V. be -due &c. *adj.* to, – the due &c. *n.* of; have -right, – title, – claim- to; be entitled to; have a claim upon; belong to &c. (*property*) 780.

deserve, merit, be worthy of, richly deserve.

demand, claim; call upon –, come upon –, appeal to- for; re-vendicate, -claim; exact; insist -on, – upon; challenge; take one's stand, make a point of, require, lay claim to, assert, assume, arrogate, make good; substantiate; vindicate a -claim, – right; make out a case.

give –, confer- a right; sanction, entitle; authorize &c. 760; sanctify, legalize, ordain, prescribe, allot.

give every one his due &c. 922; pay one's dues; have one's -due, – rights; stand upon one's rights.

use a right, assert, enforce, put in force, lay under contribution.

Adj. having a right to &c. *v.*; entitled to; claiming; deserving, meriting, worthy of.

privileged, allowed, sanctioned, warranted, authorized; ordained, prescribed, constitutional, chartered, enfranchised.

925. [Absence of right.] **Undueness —N.** undueness &c. *adj.*; *malum prohibitum*; impropriety; illegality &c. 964.

falseness &c. *adj.*; emptiness –, invalidity- of title; illegitimacy.

loss of right, disfranchisement, forfeiture.

usurpation, assumption, tort, violation, breach, encroachment, presumption, seizure, stretch, exaction, imposition, lion's share.

usurper, pretender, Carlist; impostor.

V. be -undue &c. *adj.*; not be -due &c. 924.

infringe, encroach, trench on, exact; arrogate, – to oneself; give an inch and take an ell; stretch –, strain- a point; usurp, violate, do violence to; sail under false colours.

dis-franchise, -entitle, -qualify; invalidate.

relax &c. (*be lax*) 738; misbehave &c. (*vice*) 945; misbecome.

Adj. undue; unlawful &c. (*illegal*) 964; unconstitutional, *ultra vires*; illicit; un-authorized, -warranted, -allowed, -sanctioned, -justified; un-, dis-entitled, -qualified; un-privileged, -chartered.

illegitimate, bastard, spurious, false; usurped, tortious.

un-deserved, -merited, -earned; unfulfilled.

forfeited, disfranchised.

improper; un-meet, -fit, -befitting, -seemly; un-, mis-becoming; seemless; *contra bonos mores*; not the thing, out of the question, not to be thought of; preposterous, pretentious, would- be.

---

prescriptive, presumptive; absolute, indefeasible; un-, in-alienable; imprescriptible, inviolable, unimpeachable, unchallenged; sacrosanct.

due to, merited, deserved, condign, richly deserved, *emeritus*.

allowable &c. (*permitted*) 760; lawful, licit, legitimate, legal; legalized &c. (*law*) 963.

square, unexceptionable, right; equitable &c. 922; due, *en règle*; fit, -ting; correct, proper, meet, befitting, becoming, seemly; decorous; creditable, up to the mark, right as a trivet; just –, quite- the thing; *selon les règles*.

Adv. duly, *ex officio*, *de jure*; by -right, – divine right; as is -fitting, – proper, – fitting and proper; *jure divino, Dei gratiâ*, in the name of.

Phr. *civis Romanus sum*.

926. Duty.—N. duty, what ought to be done, moral obligation, account-ableness, liability, *onus*, responsibility; bounden –, imperative- duty; call, – of duty.

allegiance, fealty, tie; engagement &c. (*promise*) 768; part; function, calling &c. (*business*) 625.

morality, morals, decalogue; case of conscience; conscientiousness &c. (*probity*) 939; conscience, inward monitor, still small voice within, sense of duty, tender conscience.

dueness &c. 924; propriety, fitness, seemliness, amenableness, decorum; the -thing, – proper thing; the -right, – proper- thing to do.

[Science of morals] eth-ics, -ology; deon-, are-tology; moral –, ethical-philosophy; casuistry, polity.

observance, fulfilment, discharge, performance, acquittal, satisfaction, redemption; good behaviour.

V. be -the duty of, – incumbent &c. *adj.* on, – responsible &c. *adj.*; behoove, become, befit, beseem; belong –, pertain- to; fall to one's lot; devolve on; lie -upon, – on one's head, – at one's door; rest -with, – on the shoulders of.

take upon oneself &c. (*promise*) 768; be –, become- -bound to, – sponsor for; be responsible for; incur a -responsibility &c. *n.*; be –, stand –, lie- under an obligation; have to answer for, owe it to oneself.

impose a -duty &c. *n.*; enjoin, require, exact; bind, – over; saddle with, prescribe, assign, call upon, look to, oblige.

enter upon –, perform –, observe –, fulfil –, discharge –, adhere to –, acquit oneself of –, satisfy- -a duty, – an obligation; act one's part, redeem one's pledge, do justice to, be at one's post; do duty; do one's duty &c. (*be virtuous*) 944.

be on one's good behaviour, mind one's P's and Q's.

Adj. obligatory, binding; imperative, peremptory; stringent &c. (*severe*) 739; behooving &c. *v.*; incumbent –, chargeable- on; under obligation; obliged –, bound –, tied- by; saddled with.

due –, beholden –, bound –, indebted- to; tied down; compromised &c. (*promised*) 768; in duty bound.

amenable, liable, accountable, responsible, answerable.

right, meet &c. (*due*) 924; moral, ethical, casuistical, conscientious, ethological.

Adv. with a safe conscience, as in duty bound, on one's own re-

927. Dereliction of Duty.—N. dereliction of duty; fault &c. (*guilt*) 947-sin &c. (*vice*) 945; non-observance, -performance, -co-operation; neglect, carelessness, laziness, incompetence, eye-service, relaxation, infraction, violation, transgression, failure, evasion, indolence; dead letter.

slacker, loafer, striker, non-co-operator.

V. violate; break, – through; infringe; set -aside, – at naught; trample -on, – under foot; slight, neglect, evade, renounce, forswear, repudiate; wash one's hands of; escape, transgress, fail.

call to account &c. (*disapprobation*) 932.

927a. Exemption.—N. exemption, freedom, irresponsibility, immunity, liberty, licence, release, exoneration, excuse, dispensation, absolution, franchise, renunciation, discharge; exculpation &c. 970; *ægrotat*.

V. be -exempt &c. *adj.*

exempt, release, acquit, discharge, quit-claim, remise, remit; free, set at liberty, let off, pass over, spare, excuse, dispense with, give dispensation, license; stretch a point; absolve &c. (*forgive*) 918; exonerate &c. (*exculpate*) 970; save the necessity.

Adj. exempt, free, immune, at liberty, scot free; released &c. *v.*; unbound, unencumbered; irresponsible, unaccountable, not answerable; excusable.

sponsibility, at one's own risk, *suo periculo*; *in foro conscientiæ*; *quamdiu se bene gesserit*; at one's post, on duty.

Phr. *dura lex sed lex.*

2°. MORAL SENTIMENTS

928. Respect.—N. respect, regard, consideration; courtesy &c. 894; attention, deference, reverence, honour, esteem, estimation, veneration, admiration; approbation &c. 931.

homage, fealty, obeisance, genuflexion, kneeling, prostration; obsequiousness &c. 886; salaam, *kowtow*, bow, presenting arms, salute.

respects, regards, duty, *devoirs, égards.*

devotion &c. (*piety*) 987.

V. respect, regard; revere, -nce; hold in reverence, honour, venerate, hallow; esteem &c. (*approve of*) 931; think much of; entertain –, bear- respect for; have a high opinion of; look up to, defer to; pay -attention, – respect &c. *n.*- to; do –, render- honour to; do the honours, hail; show courtesy &c. 894; salute, present arms; do –, pay- homage to; pay tribute to, kneel to, bow to, bend the knee to; fall down before, prostrate oneself, kiss the hem of one's garment; worship &c. 990.

keep one's distance, make room, observe due decorum, stand upon ceremony.

command –, inspire- respect; awe, impose, overawe, dazzle.

Adj. respecting &c. *v.*; respectful, deferential, decorous, reverential, obsequious, ceremonious, bare-headed, cap in hand, on one's knees; prostrate &c. (*servile*) 886.

respected &c. *v.*; in high -esteem, – estimation; time-honoured, venerable, *emeritus.*

Adv. in deference to; with -all, – due, – the highest- respect; with submission.

saving your -grace, – presence; *salva sit reverentia*; *pace tanti nominis.*

Int. hail! all hail! *esto perpetua!* may your shadow never be less!

929. Disrespect. — N. dis-respect, -esteem, -estimation, -favour, -repute; low estimation; disparagement &c. (*dispraise*) 932, (*detraction*) 934.

irreverence; slight, neglect; *spretæ injuria formæ*; superciliousness &c. (*contempt*) 930.

vilipendency, contumely, affront, dishonour, insult, indignity, outrage, discourtesy &c. 895; practical joking; scurrility, scoffing, sibilation; ir-, derision; mockery; irony &c. (*ridicule*) 856; sarcasm.

hiss, hoot, gibe, flout, jeer, scoff, gleek, taunt, sneer, quip, fling, wipe, slap in the face.

V. hold in disrespect &c. (*despise*) 930; misprize, disregard, slight, undervalue, depreciate, trifle with, set at naught, pass by, push aside, overlook, turn one's back upon, laugh in one's sleeve; be -disrespectful &c. *adj.*, – discourteous &c. 895; treat with -disrespect &c. *n.*; set down, browbeat.

dishonour, desecrate; insult, affront, outrage.

speak slightingly of; disparage &c. (*dispraise*) 932; vilipend, call names; throw –, fling- dirt; drag through the mud, point at, indulge in personalities; make -mouths, – faces; bite the thumb; take –, pluck- by the beard; toss in a blanket, tar and feather.

have –, hold- in derision; deride, scoff, sneer, laugh at, snigger, ridicule, gibe, mock, jeer, taunt, twit, niggle, gleek, gird, flout, fleer; roast, turn into ridicule; guy, burlesque &c. 856; laugh to scorn &c. (*contempt*) 930; smoke; fool; make -game, – a fool, – an April fool- of; play a practical joke; rag; lead one a dance, run the rig upon, have a fling at, scout, hiss, hoot, mob.

Adj. disrespectful; aweless, irreverent; disparaging &c. 934; insulting &c. *v.*; supercilious &c. (*scornful*) 930; rude, derisive, contemptuous, sarcastic; scurri-le, -lous; contumelious.

un-respected, -worshipped, -envied, -saluted; un-, dis-regarded.

Adv. disrespectfully &c. *adj.*

930. Contempt.—N. contempt, disdain, scorn, sovereign contempt; despi-sal, -ciency; vilipendency, contumely; slight, sneer, spurn, by-word.

contemptuousness &c. *adj.*; scornful eye; smile of contempt; derision &c. (*disrespect*) 929.

[State of being despised] despisedness.

V. despise, contemn, scorn, disdain, feel contempt for, view with a scornful eye, disregard, slight, not mind; pass by &c. (*neglect*) 460.

look down upon; hold -cheap, – in contempt, – in disrespect; think -nothing, – small beer- of; make light of; underestimate &c. 483; esteem -slightly, – of small or no account; take no account of, care nothing for; set no store by; not care a -straw &c. (*unimportance*) 643; set at naught, laugh in one's sleeve, snap one's fingers at, shrug one's shoulders, turn up one's nose at, pooh-pooh, damn with faint praise; sneeze –, whistle –, sneer- at; curl up one's lip, toss the head, *traiter de haut*; laugh at &c. (*be disrespectful*) 929.

point the finger of –, hold up to –, laugh to- scorn; scout, hoot, flout, hiss, scoff at.

turn -one's back, – a cold shoulder- upon; tread –, trample- -upon, – under foot; spurn, kick; fling to the winds &c. (*repudiate*) 610; send away with a flea in the ear.

Adj. contemptuous; disdain-, scorn-ful; withering, contumelious, supercilious, cynical, haughty, bumptious, cavalier; derisive.

contemptible, despicable; pitiable; pitiful &c. (*unimportant*) 643; despised &c. *v.*; down-trodden; unenvied.

Adv. contemptuously &c. *adj.*

Int. a fig for &c. (*unimportant*) 643; bah! never mind! away with! hang it! fiddle-de-dee!

931. Approbation.—N. approbation; approv-al, -ement; sanction, advocacy; nod of approbation; esteem, estimation, good opinion, golden opinions, admiration; love &c. 897; appreciation, regard, account, popularity, *kudos*, credit; repute &c. 873.

commendation, praise; laud, -ation; good word; meed –, tribute- of praise; encomium; eulog-y, -ium; *éloge*, panegyric; homage, hero worship; benediction, blessing, benison.

applause, plaudit, clap; clapping, – of hands; accl-aim, -amation; cheer; pæan, hosannah; shout –, peal –, chorus –, thunders- of -applause &c.; Kentish fire; Prytaneum; blurb.

V. approve; think -good, – much of, well of, – highly of; esteem, value, prize; set great store -by, – on.

do justice to, appreciate; honour, hold in esteem, look up to, admire; like &c. 897; be in favour of, wish God speed; hail, – with satisfaction.

stand –, stick- up for; uphold, hold

932. Disapprobation.—N. disapprobation, -val; improbation; dis-esteem, -valuation, -placency; odium; dislike &c. 867; dissent &c. 489.

dis-praise, -commendation; blame, censure, obloquy; detraction &c. 934; disparagement, depreciation; denunciation; condemnation &c. 971; ostracism; boycott; black-list, -ball; *index -expurgatorius, – librorum prohibitorum.*

animadversion, reflection, stricture, objection, exception, criticism; sardonic -grin, – laugh; sarcasm, insinuation, innuendo; bad –, poor –, left-handed- compliment.

satire; sneer &c. (*contempt*) 930; taunt &c. (*disrespect*) 929; cavil, carping, censoriousness; hypercriticism &c. (*fastidiousness*) 868.

reprehension, remonstrance, expostulation, reproof, reprobation, admonition, increpation, reproach; rebuke, reprimand, castigation, jobation, lecture, curtain lecture, blow up, wigging, dressing, – down; rating, scolding, trim-

up, countenance, sanction; clap –, pat-
on the back; keep in countenance, endorse, give credit, recommend; mark
with a white -mark, – stone.

commend, praise; be-, laud; compliment, pay a tribute, bepraise; clap,
– the hands; applaud, cheer, acclaim,
acclamate, encore; panegyrize, eulogize, cry up, *prôner*, puff; extol, – to
the skies; magnify, glorify, exalt, boost,
swell, make much of; flatter &c. 933;
bless, give a blessing to; have –, say- a
good word for; speak -well, – highly,
– in high terms- of; sing –, sound –,
chaunt –, resound- the praises of; sing
praises to; cheer –, applaud- to the
-echo, – very echo.

redound to the -honour, – praise, –
credit- of; do credit to; deserve -praise
&c. *n.*; recommend itself; pass muster.

be -praised &c.; receive honourable
mention; be in -favour, – high favour-
with; ring with the praises of, win
golden opinions, gain credit, find favour
with, stand well in the opinion of;
laudari a laudato viro.

Adj. approving &c. *v.*; in favour of;
lost in admiration.

commendatory, complimentary, ben-
edictory, laudatory, panegyrical, eulo-
gistic, encomiastic, acclamatory, lavish
of praise, uncritical.

approved, praised &c. *v.*; un-cen-
sured, -impeached; popular, in good
odour; in high esteem &c. (*respected*)
928; in –, in high- favour.

deserving –, worthy of- praise &c. *n.*;
praiseworthy, commendable, of estimation; good &c. 648; meritorious, estimable, creditable, plausible, unimpeachable; beyond all praise.

Adv. commendably, with credit, to
admiration; well &c. 681; with three
times three.

Int. hear, hear! well done! *brav-o! -a!
-i! bravissimo! euge! macte virtute!* so far
so good, that's right, quite right; *optime!* one cheer more; may your shadow never be less! *esto perpetua!* long
life to! *viva! evviva!* God speed! *valete
et plaudite! encore! bis!*

Phr. *probatum est.*

---

ming; correction, set down, rap on the
knuckles, *coup de bec*, rebuff; slap, – on
the face; home thrust, hit; frown, scowl,
black look.

diatribe; jeremiad; *tirade*, philippic.

clamour, outcry, hue and cry; hiss,
-ing; sibilation, cat-call; execration &c.
908.

chiding, upbraiding &c. *v.*; exprobration, abuse, vituperation, invective,
objurgation, contumely, personal remarks; hard –, cutting –, bitter- words.

evil-speaking; bad language &c. 908;
personality.

V. disapprove; dislike &c. 867; lament &c. 839; object to, take exception to; be scandalized at, think ill
of; view with -disfavour, – dark eyes,
– jaundiced eyes; *nil admirari*, disvalue, improbate.

frown upon, look grave; bend –,
knit- the brows; shake the head at,
shrug the shoulders; turn up the nose
&c. (*contempt*) 930; look -askance, –
black upon; look with an evil eye;
make a wry -face, – mouth- at; set
one's face against.

dis-praise, -commend, -parage; deprecate, speak ill of, not speak well of,
slate, condemn &c. (*find guilty*) 971.

blame; lay –, cast- blame upon;
censure, *fronder*, reproach, pass censure
on, reprobate, impugn.

remonstrate, expostulate, recriminate.

reprehend, chide, admonish; bring –,
call- -to account, – over the coals, – to
order; take to task, reprove, lecture,
bring to book; read a -lesson, – lecture-
to; rebuke, correct.

reprimand, chastise, castigate, lash,
blow up, trounce, trim, *laver la tête*,
overhaul; give it one, – finely; gibbet.

accuse &c. 938; impeach, denounce;
hold up to -reprobation, – execration;
expose, brand, gibbet, stigmatize;
show –, pull –, take- up; cry 'shame'
upon; be outspoken; raise a hue and
cry against.

execrate &c. 908; exprobrate, speak
daggers, vituperate; abuse, – like a
pickpocket; scold, rate, objurate, upbraid, fall foul of; jaw; rail, – at, – in
good set terms; bark at; anathematize,

call names; call by -hard, – ugly- names; a-, re-vile; vili-fy, -pend; bespatter; backbite; clapperclaw; rave –, thunder –, fulminate- against; load with reproaches; lash with the tongue.

exclaim –, protest –, inveigh –, declaim –, cry out –, raise one's voice- against.

decry; cry –, run –, frown- down; clamour, hiss, hoot, mob, ostracize; draw up –, sign- a round robin; black-ball, -list.

animadvert –, reflect- upon; glance at; cast -reflection, – re- proach, – a slur- upon; insinuate, damn with faint praise; 'hint a fault and hesitate dislike'; not to be able to say much for.

scoff at, point at; twit, taunt &c. (*disrespect*) 929; sneer at &c. (*despise*) 230; satirize, lampoon; defame &c. (*detract*) 934; depre- ciate, find fault with, criticize, cut up; pull –, pick- to pieces; take exception; cavil; peck –, nibble –, carp- at; be -censorious &c. *adj.*; pick -holes, – a hole, – a hole in one's coat; make a fuss about.

take –, set- down; snub, snap one up, give a rap on the knuckles; throw a stone -at, – in one's garden; have a -fling, – snap- at; have words with, pluck a crow with; give one a -wipe, – lick with the rough side of the tongue.

incur blame, excite disapprobation, scandalize, shock, revolt; get a bad name, forfeit one's good opinion, be under a cloud, come under the ferule, bring a hornet's nest about one's ears.

take blame, stand corrected; have to answer for.

Adj. disapproving &c. *v.*; scandalized.

disparaging, condemnatory, damnatory, denunciatory, reproach- ful, abusive, objurgatory, clamorous, vituperative; defamatory &c. 934.

satirical, sarcastic, sardonic, cynical, dry, sharp, cutting, biting, severe, virulent, withering, trenchant, hard upon; censorious, criti- cal, captious, carping, hypercritical; fastidious &c. 868; sparing of –, grudging- praise.

disapproved, chid &c. *v.*; in bad odour, blown upon, unapproved; unblest; at a discount, exploded; weighed in the balance and found wanting.

blameworthy, reprehensible &c. (*guilt*) 947; to –, worthy of- blame, answerable, uncommendable, exceptionable, not to be thought of, bad &c. 649; vicious &c. 945.

un-lamented, -bewailed, -pitied.

Adv. with a wry face; reproachfully &c. *adj.*

Int. it is too bad! it -won't, – will never- do! marry come up! Oh! come! 'sdeath!

forbid it Heaven! God –, Heaven- forbid! out –, fie- upon it! away with! tut! *O tempora! O mores!* shame! fie, – for shame! out on you!

tell it not in Gath!

---

933. Flattery.—N. flattery, adula- tion, gloze; bland-ishment, -iloquence; cajolery; fawning, wheedling &c. *v.*; captation, coquetry, sycophancy, ob- sequiousness, flunkeyism, toad-eating, tuft-hunting; snobbishness.

incense, honeyed words, flummery; bun-kum, -combe; blarney, *placebo*, but-

934. Detraction.—N. detraction, dis- paragement, depreciation, vilification, obloquy, scurrility, scandal, defama- tion, aspersion, traducement, slander, calumny, obtrectation, evil-speaking, backbiting, *scandalum magnatum*.

personality, libel, squib, lampoon, skit, pasquinade; *chronique scandaleuse*.

ter; soft -soap, – sawder; rose water.

voice of the charmer, mouth honour; lip-homage; euphemism; unctuousness &c. *adj.*

V. flatter, praise to the skies, puff; wheedle, cajole, glaver, coax; fawn, – upon; humour, gloze, soothe, pet, coquet, slaver, butter; be-spatter, -slubber, -plaster, -slaver; lay it on thick, overpraise; earwig, cog, collogue; truckle –, pander *or* pandar –, pay court- to; court; creep into the good graces of; curry favour with, hang on the sleeve of; fool to the top of one's bent; lick the dust.

lay the flattering unction to one's soul, gild the pill, make things pleasant.

overestimate &c. 482; exaggerate &c. 549.

Adj. flattering &c. *v.*; adulatory; mealy-, honey-mouthed; honeyed; smooth, – tongued; soapy, oily, unctuous, blandiloquent, specious; fine-, fair-spoken; plausible, servile, sycophantic, fulsome; courtier-ly, -like.

Adv. *ad captandum.*

---

935. Flatterer.—**N.** flatterer, adulator; eu-logist, -phemist; optimist, encomiast, *laudator*, whitewasher, booster.

toad-y, -eater; sycophant, courtier, pickthank, Sir Pertinax MacSycophant; *flâneur*, *prôneur*; puffer, touter, *claqueur*; claw-back, ear-wig, doer of dirty work; parasite, hanger on &c. (*servility*) 886.

---

937. Vindication.—**N.** vindication, justification, warrant; exoneration, exculpation; acquittal &c. 970; whitewashing.

extenuation; pallia-tion, -tive; softening, mitigation.

reply, defence; recrimination &c. 938.

apology, gloss, varnish; plea &c. 617; salvo; excuse, extenuating circumstances; allowance, – to be made; *locus pœnitentiæ.*

apologist, vindicator, justifier; defendant &c. 938.

justifiable charge, true bill.

sarcasm, cynicism; criticism (*disapprobation*) 932; invective &c. 932; envenomed tongue; *spretæ injuria formæ.* detractor &c. 936.

V. detract, derogate, decry, depreciate, disparage; run –, cry- down; minimize, make light of; belittle, sneer at &c. (*contemn*) 930; criticize, pull to pieces, pick a hole in one's coat, asperse, cast aspersions, blow upon, bespatter, blacken; vili-fy, -pend; avile; give a dog a bad name, brand, malign, backbite, libel, lampoon, traduce, slander, defame, calumniate, bear false witness against; speak ill of behind one's back.

'damn with faint praise, assent with civil leer; and without sneering, others teach to sneer.'

fling dirt &c. (*disrespect*) 929; anathematize &c. 932; dip the pen in gall, view in a bad light.

Adj. detracting &c. *v.*; defamatory, detractory, derogatory; disparaging, libellous; scurril-e, -ous; abusive; foul-spoken, -tongued, -mouthed; slanderous; calumni-ous, -atory; sar-castic, -donic; satirical, cynical.

---

936. Detractor.—**N.** detractor, reprover; cens-or, -urer; cynic, critic, caviller, carper, wordcatcher.

defamer, backbiter, slanderer, knocker, Sir Benjamin Backbite, lampooner, satirist, traducer, libeller, calumniator, dearest foe, dawplucker, Thersites; Zoilus; good-natured –, candid- friend [satirically]; reviler, vituperator, castigator; shrew &c. 901.

disapprover, *laudator temporis acti.*

---

938. Accusation. — **N.** accusation, charge, imputation, slur, inculpation, exprobration, delation; crimination; in-, ac-, re-crimination; *tu quoque* argument; invective &c. 932.

de-nunciation, -nouncement; libel, challenge, citation, arraignment; im-, ap-peachment; indictment, bill of indictment, true bill; lawsuit &c. 969; condemnation &c. 971.

gravamen of a charge, head and front of one's offending, *argumentum ad hominem*; scandal &c. (*detraction*) 934; *scandalum magnatum.*

V. justify, warrant; be an -excuse &c. *n.*- for; lend a colour, furnish a handle; vindicate; ex-, dis-culpate; acquit &c. 970; clear, set right, exonerate, whitewash.

extenuate, palliate, excuse, soften, apologize, varnish, slur, gloze; put a -gloss, – good face- upon; mince; gloss over, bolster up, help a lame dog over a stile.

advocate, defend, plead one's cause; stand –, stick –, speak- up for; contend –, speak- for; bear out, keep in countenance, support; plead &c. 617; say in defence; plead ignorance; confess and avoid, propugn, put in a good word for.

take the will for the deed, make allowance for, do justice to; give -one, – the Devil- his due.

make good; prove -the truth of, – one's case; be justified by the event.

Adj. vindicat-ed, -ing &c. *v.*; vindicat-ive, -ory; palliative; exculpatory; apologetic.

excusable, defensible, pardonable; veni-al, -able; specious, plausible, justifiable.

Phr. '*honi soit qui mal y pense.*'

___

accuser, prosecutor, plaintiff, complainant, petitioner; relator, informer; appellant.

accused, defendant, prisoner, panel, co-, respondent; litigant.

V. accuse, charge, tax, impute, twit, taunt with, reproach.

brand with reproach; stigmatize, slur; cast a -stone at, – slur on; incriminate; inculpate, implicate; call to account &c. (*censure*) 932; take to -blame, – task; put in the black book.

inform against, indict, denounce, arraign; im-, ap-peach; have up, show up, pull up; challenge, cite, lodge a complaint; prosecute, bring an action against &c. 969.

charge –, saddle- with; lay to one's -door, – charge; lay the blame on, bring home to; cast –, throw- in one's teeth; cast the first stone at.

have –, keep- a rod in pickle for; have a crow to pluck with.

trump up a charge.

Adj. accusing &c. *v.*; accusat-ory, -ive; imputative, denunciatory; re-, criminatory.

accused &c. *v.*; suspected; under -suspicion, – a cloud, – *surveillance*; in -custody, – detention; in the -lock up, – watch house, – house of detention.

accusable, imputable; in-defensible, -excusable; un-pardonable, -justifiable; vicious &c. 945.

Int. look at home; *tu quoque* &c. (*retaliation*) 718.

3°. MORAL CONDITIONS

939. Probity.—N. probity, integrity, rectitude; uprightness &c. *adj.*; honesty, faith; honour; good faith, *bona fides*; purity, clean hands.

fairness &c. *adj.*; fair play, justice, equity, impartiality, principle; grace.

constancy; faithfulness &c. *adj.*; fidelity, loyalty; incorrupt-ion, -ibility.

trustworthiness &c. *adj.*; truth, candour, singleness of heart; veracity &c. 543; tender conscience &c. (*sense of duty*) 926.

punctil-iousness, -io; delicacy, nicety; scrupul-osity, -ousness &c. *adj.*; scruple; point, – of honour; punctuality.

dignity &c. (*repute*) 873; respectability, -bleness &c. *adj.*; gentleman; man of -honour, – his word; *fidus*

940. Improbity. N. improbity; dishon-esty, -our; deviation from rectitude; disgrace &c. (*disrepute*) 874; fraud &c. (*deception*) 545; lying &c. 544; bad –, Punic- faith; *mala –, Punica- fides*; infidelity; faithlessness &c. *adj.*; Judas kiss, betrayal; scrap of paper.

breach of -promise, – trust, – faith; prodition, disloyalty, divided allegiance, treason, high treason; apostacy &c. (*tergiversation*) 607; non-observance &c. 773.

shabbiness &c. *adj.*; villainy; baseness &c. *adj.*; abjection, debasement, turpitude, moral turpitude, laxity, trimming, shuffling.

perfidy; perfidiousness &c. *adj.*;

Achates, preux chevalier, galantuomo; truepenny, trump, brick; true Briton, white man, sportsman.

court of honour, a fair field and no favour; *argumentum ad verecundiam.*

V. be -honourable &c. *adj.*; deal -honourably, – squarely, – impartially, – fairly; speak the truth &c. (*veracity*) 543; tell the truth and shame the devil, *vitam impendere vero*; show a proper spirit, make a point of; do one's duty &c. 944; play the game.

redeem one's pledge &c. 926; keep –, be as good as- one's -promise, – word; keep faith with, not fail.

give and take, *audire alteram partem*, give the devil his due, put the saddle on the right horse.

redound to one's honour.

Adj. upright; honest, – as daylight; veracious &c. 543; virtuous &c. 944; honourable; fair, right, just, equitable, impartial, even-handed, square; fair –, open- and aboveboard.

constant, – as the northern star; faithful, loyal, staunch; true, – blue, – to one's colours, – to the core, – as the needle to the pole; true-hearted, trust-y, -worthy; as good as one's word, to be depended on, incorruptible.

manly, straightforward &c. (*ingenuous*) 703; frank, candid, open-hearted.

conscientious, tender - conscienced, right-minded; high-principled, -minded; scrupulous, religious, strict; nice, punctilious, correct, punctual; respect-, reput-able; gentlemanlike.

inviol - able, - ate; un - violated, -broken, -betrayed; un-bought, -bribed.

innocent &c. 946; pure; stainless; un-stained, -tarnished, -sullied, -tainted, -perjured; uncorrupt, -ed; unde-filed, -praved, -bauched; *integer vitæ scelerisque purus; justus et tenax propositi.*

chivalrous, jealous of honour, *sans peur et sans reproche*; high-spirited.

supra-mundane, unworldly, over-scrupulous.

Adv. honourably &c. *adj.*; *bona fide*; on the square, in good faith, honour bright, *foro conscientiæ*, with clean hands; by fair means.

treachery, double-dealing; unfairness &c. *adj.*; knavery, roguery, rascality, foul-play; jobb-ing, -ery; Tammany, graft; venality, nepotism; corruption, job, shuffle, fishy transaction, barratry; sharp practice, heads I win, tails you lose; mouth-honour &c. (*flattery*) 933.

V. be -dishonest &c. *adj.*; play false; break one's -word, – faith, – promise; jilt, betray, forswear; shuffle &c. (*lie*) 544; live by one's wits, sail near the wind; play with marked cards.

disgrace –, dishonour –, demean –, degrade- oneself; derogate, stoop, grovel, sneak, lose caste; sell oneself, go over to the enemy; seal one's infamy.

Adj. dishon-est, -ourable; un-conscientious, -scrupulous; fraudulent &c. 545; knavish; disgraceful &c. (*disreputable*) 874; wicked &c. 945.

false-hearted, disingenuous; unfair, one-sided; double, -tongued, -faced; time-serving, crooked, tortuous, insidious, Machiavellian, dark, slippery; questionable; fishy; perfidious, treacherous, perjured.

infamous, arrant, foul, base, vile, low, ignominious, blackguard.

contemptible, abject, mean, shabby, little, paltry, dirty, scurvy, scabby, sneaking, grovelling, scrubby, rascally, pettifogging; beneath one; not cricket.

low-minded, -thoughted; base-minded.

undignified, indign; unbe-coming, -seeming, -fitting; de-rogatory, -grading; *infra dignitatem*; ungentleman-ly, -like; un-knightly, -chivalric, -manly, -handsome; recreant, inglorious.

corrupt, venal; debased, mongrel.

faithless, of bad faith, false, unfaithful, disloyal; untrustworthy; trust-, troth-less; lost to shame, dead to honour.

Adv. dishonestly &c. *adj.*; *malâ fide*, like a thief in the night, by crooked paths; by foul means.

Int. *O tempora! O mores!*

---

941. Knave.—N. knave, rogue, villain; Scapin, rascal; Lazarillo de Tormes; bad man &c. 949; blackguard &c. 949.

traitor, betrayer, arch-traitor, conspirator, stool pigeon, Judas, Catiline; reptile, serpent, snake in the grass, wolf in sheep's clothing, sneak, Jerry Sneak, tell-tale, squealer, mischief-maker, trimmer; renegade &c. (*tergiversation*) 607; truant, recreant; sycophant &c. (*servility*) 886.

942. Disinterestedness.—N. disinterestedness &c. *adj.*; generosity; liberal-ity, -ism; altruism; benevolence &c. 906; elevation, loftiness of purpose, exaltation, magnanimity; chival-ry, -rous spirit; heroism, sublimity.

self-denial, -abnegation, -effacement, -sacrifice, -immolation, -control &c. (*resolution*) 604; stoicism, devotion, martyrdom, *suttee*.

labour of love.

V. be -disinterested &c. *adj.*; make a sacrifice, lay one's head on the block; put oneself in the place of others, do as one would be done by, do unto others as we would men should do unto us.

Adj. disinterested; unselfish; self-denying, -sacrificing, -devoted; generous.

handsome, liberal, noble; noble-, high-minded; princely, great, high, elevated, lofty, exalted, spirited, stoical, magnanimous; great-, large-hearted, chivalrous, heroic, sublime.

un-bought, -bribed; uncorrupted &c. (*upright*) 939.

943. Selfishness.—N. selfishness &c. *adj.*; self-love, -indulgence, -worship, -interest; ego-tism, -ism; egocentrism, narcissism; *amour propre* &c. (*vanity*) 880; nepotism.

worldliness &c. *adj.*; world wisdom. illiberality; meanness &c. *adj.*

time-server; tuft-, fortune-hunter; self-seeker; jobber, worldling; egotist, egoist, monopolist, nepotist, profiteer; temporizer, trimmer; dog in the manger, charity that begins at home.

V. be -selfish &c. *adj.*; please –, indulge –, coddle- oneself; consult one's own -wishes, – pleasure; look after one's own interest; feather one's nest; take care of number one, have an eye to the main chance, know on which side one's bread is buttered; give an inch and take an ell; wangle.

Adj. selfish; self-seeking, -indulgent, -interested; wrapt up –, centred- in self; egotistic, -al; egoistical; egocentric.

illiberal, mean, ungenerous, narrowminded; mercenary, venal; covetous &c. 819.

unspiritual; earthly, -minded; mundane; worldly, -minded, -wise; time-serving.

interested; *alieni appetens sui profusus.*

Adv. ungenerously &c. *adj.*; to gain some private ends; from selfish –, interested- motives.

Phr. *après nous le déluge.*

944. Virtue.—N. virtue; virtuousness &c. *adj.*; morality; moral rectitude; integrity &c. (*probity*) 939; nobleness &c. 873.

morals; ethics &c. (*duty*) 926; cardinal virtues.

merit, worth, desert, excellence, credit; self-control &c. (*resolution*) 604; self-denial &c. (*temperance*) 953.

well-doing; good -actions, – behaviour; discharge –, fulfilment –, performance- of duty; well-spent life; innocence &c. 946.

V. be -virtuous &c. *adj.*; practise virtue &c. *n.*; do –, fulfil –, perform –,

945. Vice. — **N.** vice; evil -doing, – courses; wrong doing; wickedness, viciousness &c. *adj.*; iniquity, peccability, demerit; sin, Adam; old –, offending- Adam.

immorality, impropriety, indecorum, scandal, laxity, looseness of morals; want of -principle, – ballast; obliquity, backsliding, infamy, demoralization, pravity, depravity, pollution; hardness of heart; brutality &c. (*malevolence*) 907; corruption &c. (*debasement*) 659; knavery &c. (*improbity*) 940; profligacy; lust &c. 961; flagrancy, atrocity; cannibalism.

discharge- one's duty; redeem one's pledge &c. 926; act well, – one's part; fight the good fight; acquit oneself well; command –, master- one's passions; keep -straight, – in the right path.

set -an, – a good- example; be on one's -good, – best- behaviour.

Adj. virtuous, good; innocent &c. 946; meritorious, deserving, worthy, desertful, correct; dut-iful, -eous; moral; right, -eous, -minded; well-intentioned, creditable, laudable, commendable, praiseworthy; above –, beyond- all praise; excellent, admirable; sterling, pure, noble.

exemplary; match-, peer-less; saintly, -like; heaven-born, angelic, seraphic, godlike.

Adv. virtuously &c. *adj.*; *e merito.*

---

infirmity; weakness &c. *adj.*; weakness of the flesh, frailty, imperfection; error; weak side; foible; fail-ing, -ure; crying –, besetting- sin; defect, deficiency, shortcoming; cloven foot.

lowest dregs of vice, sink of iniquity, Alsatian den; *gusto picaresco.*

fault, crime; criminality &c. (*guilt*) 947.

sinner &c. 949.

V. be -vicious &c. *adj.*; sin, commit sin, do amiss, err, transgress; misdemean –, forget –, misconduct- oneself; mis-do, -behave; fall, lapse, slip, trip, offend, trespass; deviate from the -line of duty, – path of virtue &c. 944; take a wrong course, go astray; hug a -sin, – fault; sow one's wild oats.

render -vicious &c. *adj.*; demoralize, brutalize; corrupt &c. (*degrade*) 659.

Adj.* vicious; sinful; sinning &c. *v.*; wicked, iniquitous, bad, immoral, unrighteous, wrong, criminal; naughty, incorrect; undut-eous, -iful.

unprincipled, lawless, disorderly, *contra bonos mores*, indecorous, unseemly, improper; dissolute, profligate, scampish; unworthy; worth-, desert-less; disgraceful, recreant; reprehensible, blame-worthy, uncommendable; dis-creditable, -reputable.

base, sinister, scurvy, foul, gross, vile, black, grave, facinorous, felonious, nefarious, shameful, scandalous, infamous, villainous, of a deep dye, heinous; flag-rant, -itious; atrocious, incarnate, accursed.

Mephistophelian, satanic, diabolic, hellish, infernal, stygian, fiend-ish, -like, hell-born, demoniacal, devilish.

mis-created, -begotten; demoralized, corrupt, depraved.

evil-minded, -disposed; ill-conditioned; malevolent &c. 907; heart-, grace-, shame-, virtue-less; abandoned, lost to virtue; unconscionable; sunk –, lost –, deep –, steeped- in iniquity.

incorrigible, irreclaimable, obdurate, reprobate, past praying for; culpable, reprehensible &c. (*guilty*) 947.

unjustifiable; in-defensible, -excusable; inexpiable, unpardonable, irremissible.

weak, frail, lax, infirm, imperfect, indiscreet; demoralizing, degrading.

Adv. wrong; sinfully &c. *adj.*; without excuse.

Int. *O tempora! O mores!*

---

946. Innocence. — N. innocence; guiltlessness &c. *adj.*; incorruption, impeccability.

clean hands, clear conscience, *mens sibi conscia recti.*

innocent, new born babe, lamb, dove.

V. be -innocent &c. *adj.*; *nil conscire sibi nullâ pallescere culpâ.*

947. Guilt.—N. guilt, -iness; culpability; crimin-ality, -ousness; deviation from rectitude &c. (*improbity*) 940; sinfulness &c. (*vice*) 945; peccability.

mis-conduct, -behaviour, -doing, -deed; malpractice, fault, sin, error, transgression; dereliction, delinquency; indiscretion, lapse, slip, trip, *faux pas,*

---

* Most of these adjectives are applicable both to the act and to the agent.

acquit &c. 970; exculpate &c. (*vindicate*) 937.

Adj. innocent, not guilty; unguilty; guilt-, fault-, sin-, stain-, blood-, spot-less; clear, immaculate; *rectus in curiâ*; un-spotted, -blemished, -erring; undefiled &c. 939; unhardened, Saturnian; Arcadian &c. (*artless*) 703.

in-, un-culpable; unblam-ed, -able; blameless, inerrable, above suspicion; irrepr-oachable, -ovable, -ehensible; un-exceptionable, -objectionable, -impeachable; salvable; venial &c. 937.

harmless; in-offensive, -noxious, -nocuous; dove-, lamb-like; pure, harmless as doves; innocent as -a lamb, – the babe unborn; more sinned against than sinning.

virtuous &c. 944; un-reproved, -impeached, -reproached.

Adv. innocently &c. *adj.*; with clean hands; with a -clear, – safe- conscience.

948. Good Man. — N. good man, worthy.

good woman, goddess, *madonna*, virgin.

model, paragon &c. (*perfection*) 650; good example; hero, demigod, seraph, angel; innocent &c. 946; saint &c. (*piety*) 987; benefactor &c. 912; philanthropist &c. 910; Aristides.

brick, trump, rough diamond, ugly duckling.

salt of the earth; one in ten thousand; one of the best.

Phr. *si sic omnes!*

peccadillo; flaw, blot, omission; fail-ing, -ure.

offence, trespass; mis-demeanour, -feasance, -prision; tort; mal-efaction, -feasance, -versation; crime, felony.

enormity, atrocity, outrage; deadly –, mortal –, unpardonable- sin; died without a name.

corpus delicti.

Adj. guilty, to blame, culpable, peccable, in fault, censurable, reprehensible, blameworthy, uncommendable, illaudable; weighed in the balance and found wanting; exceptionable, objectionable.

Adv. *in flagrante delicto*; red-handed, in the very act.

949. Bad Man.—N. bad man, wrong-doer, worker of iniquity; evil-doer &c. 913; sinner; the -wicked &c. 945; bad example.

rascal, scoundrel, villain, miscreant, caitiff; wretch, reptile, viper, serpent, cockatrice, basilisk, urchin; tiger, monster; devil &c. (*demon*) 980; devil incarnate; demon in human shape, Nana Sahib; hell-hound, -cat; rake-hell.

bad woman, jade, Jezebel, adultress, &c. 962.

scamp, scapegrace, rip, runagate, ne'er-do-well, reprobate, *roué*, rake; limb; one who has sold himself to the devil, fallen angel, *âme damnée, vaurien,* mauvais sujet, loose fish, sad dog; lost –, black- sheep; castaway, recreant, defaulter; prodigal &c. 818; libertine &c. 962.

rough, rowdy, ugly customer, ruffian, hoodlum, bully; Jonathan Wild; hangman; incendiary; thief &c. 792; murderer &c. 361.

culprit, delinquent, criminal, malefactor, misdemeanant; felon; convict, jail-bird, ticket-of-leave man; outlaw.

blackguard, *polisson*, loafer, sneak; raps-, ras-callion; cullion, mean wretch, varlet, kern, *âme-de-boue, drôle*; cur, dog, hound, whelp, mongrel; lown, loon, runnion, outcast, vagabond; rogue &c. (*knave*) 941; scum of the earth, riff-raff; *Arcades ambo.*

Int. sirrah!

950. Penitence.—N. penitence, contrition, compunction, repentance, remorse; regret &c. 833.

self-reproach, -reproof, -accusation,

951. Impenitence.—N. impenitence, irrepentance, recusance.

hardness of heart, seared conscience, induration, obduracy.

-condemnation, -humiliation; stings –, pangs –, qualms –, prickings –, twinge –, twitch –, touch –, voice- of conscience; compunctious visitings of nature.

acknowledgment, confession &c. (*disclosure*) 529; apology &c. 952; recantation &c. 607; penance &c. 952; resipiscence.

awakened conscience, deathbed repentance, *locus pœnitentiæ*, stool of repentance, cutty stool.

penitent, Magdalen, prodigal son, returned prodigal, a sadder and a wiser man.

V. repent, be sorry for; be -penitent &c. *adj.*; rue; regret &c. 833; think better of; recant &c. 607; knock under &c. (*submit*) 725; plead guilty; sing -*miserere*, – *de profundis*; cry *peccavi*; own oneself in the wrong; acknowledge, confess &c. (*disclose*) 529; humble oneself; beg pardon &c. (*apologize*) 952; turn over a new leaf, put on the new man, turn from sin; reclaim; repent in sackcloth and ashes &c. (*do penance*) 952; learn by experience.

Adj. penitent; repenting &c. *v.*; repentant, contrite; conscience-smitten, -stricken; self-accusing, -convicted.

penitenti-al, -ary; chastened, reclaimed; not hardened; unhardened.

Adv. *meâ culpâ.*

Phr. *peccavi*; *erubuit*; *salva res est*; *vous l'avez voulu, Georges Dandin.*

V. be -impenitent &c. *adj.*; steel –, harden- the heart; die -game, – and make no sign.

Adj. impenitent, uncontrite, obdurate; hard, -ened; seared, recusant; unrepentant; relent-, remorse-, grace-, shrift-less.

lost, incorrigible, irreclaimable.

unre-claimed, -formed; unrepented, unatoned.

---

952. Atonement.—N. atonement, reparation; compromise, composition; compensation &c. 30; quittance, quits; indemni-ty, -fication; expiation, redemption, reclamation, conciliation, propitiation.

amends, apology, *amende honorable*, satisfaction; peace –, sin –, burnt- offering; scapegoat, sacrifice.

penance, fasting, maceration, sackcloth and ashes, white sheet, shrift, flagellation, lustration; purga-tion, -tory.

V. atone, – for; expiate; propitiate; make -amends, – good; reclaim, redeem, repair, ransom, absolve, purge, shrive, do penance, stand in a white sheet, repent in sackcloth and ashes.

set one's house in order, wipe off old scores, make matters up; pay the -forfeit, – penalty.

apologize, beg pardon, express regret, *faire amende honorable*, give satisfaction; come –, fall- down on one's -knees, – marrow bones.

Adj. propitiatory, expiatory; sacrific, -ial, -atory; piacul-ar, -ous.

4°. Moral Practice

953. Temperance.—N. temperance moderation, sobriety, soberness.

forbearance, abnegation; self-denial, -restraint, -control &c. (*resolution*) 604.

frugality; vegetarianism, teetotalism, total abstinence, prohibition; abst-inence, -emiousness, asceticism &c. 955; system of -Pythagoras, – Cornaro; Pythagorism, Stoicism.

954. Intemperance.—N. intemperance; sensuality, animalism, carnality; pleasure; effeminacy, silkiness; luxur-y, -iousness; lap of -pleasure, – luxury.

indulgence; high-, free- living, inabstinence, self-indulgence; voluptuousness &c. *adj.*; epicur-ism, -eanism; sybaritism.

vegetarian; Pythagorean, gymnosophist; teetotaler &c. 958; abstainer.

V. be -temperate &c. *adj.*; abstain, forbear, refrain, deny oneself, spare; know when one has had enough; take the pledge; look not upon the wine when it is red.

Adj. temperate, moderate, sober, frugal, sparing; abst-emious, -inent; within compass; measured &c. (*sufficient*) 639.

Pythagorean; vegetarian; teetotal, pussy-foot.

dissipation; licentiousness &c. *adj.*; debauchery; crapulence.

revel-s, -ry; debauch, carousal, jollification, drinking bout, wassail, Saturnalia, orgies; excess, too much; intoxication &c. 959.

Circean cup; drug habit &c. 663.

V. be -intemperate &c. *adj.*; indulge, exceed; live -well, – high, – on the fat of the land; give a loose to -indulgence &c. *n.*; dine not wisely but too well; wallow in -voluptuousness &c. *n.*; plunge into dissipation.

revel, rake, live hard, run riot, sow one's wild oats; slake one's -appetite, – thirst; swill; pamper.

Adj. intemperate, inabstinent, intoxicated &c. 958; sensual, self-indulgent; voluptuous, luxurious, licentious, wild, dissolute, rakish, fast, debauched.

brutish, crapulous, swinish, piggish, hoggish, bestial.

Paphian, Epicurean, Sybaritical; bred –, nursed- in the lap of luxury; indulged, pampered, full-fed.

954a. Sensualist.—N. Sybarite, voluptuary, Sardanapalus, man of pleasure, carpet knight; epicure, -an; *gourm-et, -and*; gormandizer, gutling, glutton, pig, hog; votary –, swine- of Epicurus; sensualist; Heliogabalus; free –, hard- liver; libertine &c. 962; hedonist.

955. Asceticism.—N. asceticism, puritanism, sabbatarianism; cynicism, austerity; total abstinence.

mortification, maceration, sackcloth and ashes, flagellation; penance &c. 952; fasting &c. 956; martyrdom.

ascetic; anchor-et, -ite; martyr; *Heautontimorumenos*; hermit &c. (*recluse*) 893; puritan, sabbatarian, cynic.

Adj. ascetic, austere, puritanical; cynical; over-religious.

956. Fasting. — N. fasting; exrophagy; famishment, starvation; banting.

fast, *jour maigre*; fast –, banyan-day; Lent, quadragesima; Rama-dan, -zan; spare –, meagre- diet; lenten -diet, – entertainment; *soupe maigre*, short -rations, – commons; Barmecide feast; hunger strike.

V. fast, starve, clem, famish, perish with hunger; dine with Duke Humphrey; make two bites of a cherry.

Adj. lenten, quadragesimal; unfed; starved &c. *v.*; half-starved; fasting &c. *v.*; hungry &c. 865.

957. Gluttony.—N. gluttony; greed; greediness &c. *adj.*; voracity.

epicurism; good –, high- living; edacity, gulosity, crapulence; gutt-, guzz-ling; over-indulgence.

good cheer, blow out; feast &c. (*food*) 298; gastronomy.

epicure, *bon vivant, gourmand*; glutton, cormorant, hog, belly-god, Apicius, gastronome, gormandizer.

V. gormandize, gorge; over-gorge, -eat- oneself; engorge, eat one's fill, cram, stuff, stodge, glut, satiate; gutt-le, guzz-le; bolt, devour, gobble up; gulp &c. (*swallow food*) 298; raven, eat out of house and home.

have the stomach of an ostrich; play a good knife and fork &c. (*appetite*) 865.

pamper, indulge.

Adj. gluttonous, greedy; gormandizing &c. *v.*; edacious, omnivorous, crapulent, swinish, voracious, devouring.

pampered; over-fed, -gorged.

958. Sobriety.—**N.** sobriety; teetotalism, temperance &c. 953.

water-drinker; teetotal-er, -ist; abstainer, Good Templar, Rechabite, band of hope; prohibitionist, pussyfoot.

V. take the pledge.

Adj. sober, – as a judge; dry, on the water wagon.

959. Drunkenness.—**N.** drunkenness &c. *adj.*; intemperance; drinking &c. *v.*; inebri-ety, -ation; ebri-ety, -osity; befuddlement; insobriety; intoxication; temulency, bibacity, wine-bibbing; com-, potation; deep potations, bacchanals, *bacchanalia*, libations.

oino-, dipso-mania; *delirium tremens*, d.t.; alcohol, -ism.

drink; alcoholic drinks, alcohol, booze; gin, blue ruin, grog, brandy, port wine; punch, -bowl; cup, rosy wine, flowing bowl; drop, – too much; dram; beer, wine, spirits &c. (*beverage*) 298; cocktail, nip, peg; stirrup cup.

drunkard, sot, toper, tippler, bibber, wine-bibber; hard –, gin –, dram- drinker; soak, soaker, sponge, tun; love-, toss-pot; thirsty soul, reveller, carouser; Bacchanal, -ian; Bacch-al, -ante; devotee to Bacchus, dipsomaniac.

V. get –, be- drunk &c. *adj.*; see double; take a -drop, – glass- too much; drink, tipple, tope, booze, bouse, guzzle, swill, soak, sot, lush, bib, swig, carouse; sacrifice at the shrine of Bacchus; take to drinking; drink -hard, – deep, – like a fish; have one's swill, drain the cup, splice the main brace, take a hair of the dog that bit you.

liquor, – up; wet one's whistle, take a whet; lift one's elbow; crack a –, pass the- bottle; toss off &c. (*drink up*) 298; go to the -ale, – public-house.

make one -drunk &c. *adj.*; inebriate, fuddle, fuzzle, get into one's head.

Adj. drunk, tipsy; intoxicated; inebri-ous, -ate, -ated; in one's cups; in a state of -intoxication &c. *n.*; temulent, -ive; fuddled, mellow, cut, boosy, fou, fresh, merry, elevated, squiffy; plastered, befuddled, sozzled; flush, -ed; flustered, disguised, groggy, beery; topheavy; potvaliant, glorious; potulent; over-come, -taken; whittled, screwed, tight, primed, oiled, corned, raddled, sewed up, lushy, nappy, muddled, muzzy, bosky, obfuscated, maudlin; crapulous, dead –, blind- drunk.

inter pocula; in –, the worse for- liquor, having had a drop too much, half seas over, three sheets in the wind; under the table, blind to the world, one over the eight.

drunk as -a piper, – a fiddler, – a lord, – Chloe, – an owl, – David's sow, – a wheelbarrow.

drunken, bibacious, bibulous, sottish; given –, addicted- to -drink, – the bottle; toping &c. *v.*; wet.

Phr. *nunc est bibendum.*

960. Purity.—**N.** purity; decency, decorum, delicacy; continence, chastity, honesty, virtue, modesty, shame; pudicity, *pucelage*, virginity.

vestal, virgin, Joseph, Hippolytus; Lucretia, Diana; prude.

961. Impurity.—**N.** impurity; uncleanness &c. (*filth*) 653; immodesty; grossness &c. *adj.*; indelicacy, indecency; impudicity; obscenity, ribaldry, smut, bawdry, *double entendre*, *équivoque*; Aretinism; pornography.

Adj. pure, undefiled, modest, delicate, decent, decorous; *virginibus puerisque*; chaste, continent, virtuous, honest, Platonic.

———

concupiscence, lust, carnality, flesh, salacity; pruriency, lechery, lasciviency, lubricity, lewdness.

incontinence, intrigue, *faux pas*; *amour*, *-ette*; gallantry; debauchery, libertinism, *libertinage*, fornication; *liaison*; wenching, venery, dissipation.

seduction; defloration, defilement, abuse, violation, rape; incest.

social evil, harlotry, stupration, whoredom, concubinage, cuckoldom, adultery, advoutry, *crim. con.*; free love.

seraglio, harem, zenana; brothel, bagnio, stew, bawdy-house, *lupanar*, house of ill fame, *bordel*, kip.

V. be -impure &c. *adj.*; intrigue; debauch, defile, assault, attack, seduce; prostitute; abuse, violate, deflower; commit -adultery &c. *n.*

Adj. impure; unclean &c. (*dirty*) 653; not to be mentioned to ears polite; immodest, shameless; in-decorous, -delicate, -decent; loose, suggestive, *risqué*, coarse, gross, broad, free, equivocal, smutty, fulsome, ribald, obscene, bawdy, pornographic.

concupiscent, prurient, lickerish, rampant, lustful; carnal, -minded; lewd, lascivious, lecherous, libidinous, erotic, ruttish, salacious; Paphian; voluptuous; incestuous.

unchaste, light, wanton, licentious, adulterous, debauched, dissolute; of -loose character, – easy virtue; frail, gay, riggish, incontinent, meretricious, rakish, gallant, dissipated; no better than she should be; on the -town, – streets, – *pavé*, – loose.

adulterous, incestuous, bestial.

962. Libertine.—**N.** libertine; voluptuary &c. 954a; rake, debauchee, loose fish, rip, rake-hell, fast man; *intrigant*, gallant, seducer, fornicator, lecher, satyr, goat, whoremonger, *paillard*, adulterer, gay deceiver, Lothario, Don Juan, Blue-beard.

adulteress, advoutress, courtesan, prostitute, strumpet, tart, hustler, chippy, broad, harlot, whore, punk, *fille de joie*; woman, – of the town; street-walker, Cyprian, miss, piece; frail sisterhood, fallen woman; demirep, wench, trollop, trull, baggage, hussy, drab, bitch, jade, skit, rig, quean, mopsy, slut, minx, harridan; woman -of easy virtue &c. (*unchaste*) 961; wanton, fornicatress; Jezebel, Messalina, Delilah, Thaïs, Phryne, Aspasia, Lais, *lorette*, *cocotte*, *petite dame*, *grisette*; *demimonde*; white slave.

concubine, mistress, fancy woman, kept woman, doxy, *chère amie*, *bona roba*.

pimp; pand-er, -ar; bawd, *conciliatrix*, procuress, mackerel; wittol.

5°. Institutions

963. Legality.—**N.** legality; legitimacy, -teness, legitimization.

legislature; law, code, *corpus juris*, constitution, pandect, charter, act, enactment, statute, rule; canon &c. (*precept*) 697; ordinance, institution; regulation; by-, bye-law, rescript; decree &c. (*order*) 741; *ordonnance*;

964. [Absence or violation of law.] **Illegality.**—**N.** lawlessness; breach –, violation- of law; disobedience &c. 742; unconformity &c. 83.

arbitrariness &c. *adj.*; antinomy, violence, brute force, despotism, outlawry.

mob –, lynch –, club –, Lydford –,

standing order; *plébiscite* &c. (*choice*) 609.

legal process; form, -ula, -ality; rite; arm of the law; *habeas corpus*.

[Science of law] jurisprudence, nomology; legislation, codification.

equity, common law; *lex* –, *lex non-scripta*, unwritten law; law of nations, international law, *jus gentium*; *jus civile*; civil –, criminal –, canon –, statute –, ecclesiastical- law; *lex mercatoria*.

constitutional-ism, -ity; justice &c. 922.

V. legalize, legitimize; enact, ordain; decree &c. (*order*) 741; pass a law; legislate; codify, formulate; authorize.

Adj. legal, legitimate; according to law; vested, constitutional, chartered, legalized; lawful &c. (*permitted*) 760; statut-able, -ory; legislat-orial, -ive.

Adv. legally &c. *adj.*; in the eye of the law; *de jure*.

---

martial –, drumhead- law; *coup d'état*; *le droit du plus fort; argumentum baculinum.*

illegality, informality, unlawfulness, illegitimacy, bar sinister.

trover and conversion; smuggling, boot-legging, rum-running, poaching; simony.

speakeasy, speakie, blind pig.

V. offend against –, violate- the law; set the law at defiance, ride rough-shod over, drive a coach and six through a statute; make the law a dead letter, take the law into one's own hands.

smuggle, run, poach.

Adj. illegal; prohibited &c. 761; not allowed, unlawful, illegitimate, illicit, contraband, actionable.

unchartered, unconstitutional; unwarrant-ed, -able; unauthorized; informal, unofficial; in-, extra-judicial.

lawless, arbitrary; despotic, -al; summary, irresponsible; un-answerable, -accountable.

null and void; a dead letter.

Adv. illegally &c. *adj.*; with a high hand, in violation of law.

965. Jurisdiction. [Executive.]—**N.** jurisdiction, judicature, administration of justice, soc; executive, commission of the peace; magistracy &c. (*authority*) 737.

judge &c. 967; tribunal &c. 966; municipality, corporation, bailiwick, shrievalty; lord lieutenant; lord –, mayor, city manager, alderman &c. 745; sheriff, bailie, shrieve, chief –, constable; police, – force; constabulary, bumbledom.

officer; proctor, high –, commissioner; bailiff, tipstaff, bum-bailiff, catchpoll, beadle; police-man, -constable, -sergeant; *sbirro, alguazil, gendarme*, kavass, *lictor*, macebearer, *huissier*, bedel.

press-gang; exciseman, gauger, custom-house officer, *douanier.*

coroner, edile, ædile, portreeve, paritor; *posse comitatus.*

V. judge, sit in judgment.

Adj. executive, administrative, municipal; inquisitorial, causidical; judic-atory, -iary, -ial; juridical.

Adv. *coram judice.*

966. Tribunal.—**N.** tribunal, court, board, bench, judicatory, curia; court of -justice, – law, – arbitration; inquisition; guild.

justice –, judgment –, mercy- seat; woolsack; bar, – of justice; dock; forum, hustings, *bureau*, drum-head; jury-, witness-box.

senate-house, town-hall, theatre; House of -Lords, – Commons.

assize, eyre; ward-, burgh-mote; superior courts of Westminster; court of -record, – oyer and terminer, – assize, – appeal, – error; High court of -Judicature, – Appeal; Judicial Committee of the Privy Council; Star-Chamber; Court of -Chancery, – King's *or* Queen's Bench, – Exchequer, – Common Pleas, – Probate, – Arches, – Admiralty, – Criminal Appeal; Lords Justices' –, Rolls –, Vice Chancellor's –,

Stannary –, Divorce –, Palatine –, ecclesiastical –, county –, police-court; sessions; quarter –, petty- sessions; court -leet, – baron, – of pie poudre, – of common council; board of green cloth.

court-martial; drum-head court-martial; *durbar,* divan; Areopagus; *rota.*

Adj. judicial &c. 965; appellate; curial.

967. Judge.—**N.** judge; justi-ce, -ciar, -ciary; chancellor; justice –, judge- of assize; recorder, common serjeant; puisne –, assistant –, county court- judge; conservator –, justice- of the peace, J.P.; court &c. (*tribunal*) 966; grand –, petty –, coroner's- jury; panel, juror, juryman; twelve men in a box; magistrate, police magistrate, stipendiary, the great unpaid, beak; his -worship, – honour, – lordship; deemster, moderator.

Lord -Chancellor, – Justice; Master of the Rolls, Vice-Chancellor; Lord Chief -Justice, – Baron; Mr. Justice; Baron, – of the Exchequer.

jurat, assessor; arbi-ter, -trator; umpire; refer-ee, -endary; revising barrister; domesman; censor &c. (*critic*) 480; official –, receiver.

archon, tribune, prætor, *ephor,* syndic, *podestà,* mullah, ulema, mufti, cadi, kadi; Rhadamanthus.

litigant &c. (*accusation*) 938.

V. adjudge &c. (*determine*) 480; try a -case, – prisoner.

Adj. judicial &c. 965.

Phr. 'a Daniel come to judgment.'

968. Lawyer.—**N.** lawyer, jurist, legist, civilian, pundit, publicist, jurisconsult, legal adviser, advocate; barrister, – at law; counsel, -lor; King's *or* Queen's counsel; K.C.; Q.C.; silk gown, leader; junior, – counsel; stuff gown, serjeant-at-law, bencher; tubman; judge &c. 967.

bar, legal profession, gentleman of the long robe; junior –, outer –, inner- bar; Inns of Court; equity draftsman, conveyancer, pleader, special pleader.

solicitor, attorney, proctor; notary, – public; scrivener, cursitor; writer, – to the signet; S.S.C.; limb of the law; pettifogger.

V. practise -at, – within- the bar; plead; call –, be called- -to, – within- the bar; take silk.

Adj. learned in the law; at the bar; forensic.

969. Lawsuit.—**N.** lawsuit, suit, action, cause, petition; litigation; dispute &c. 713.

citation, arraignment, prosecution, impeachment; accusation &c. 938; presentment, true bill, indictment.

apprehension, arrest; committal; imprisonment &c. (*restraint*) 751.

writ, summons, subpœna, *latitat, nisi prius; habeas corpus.*

pleadings; declaration, bill, claim; *procès-verbal,* bill of right, information, *corpus delicti;* affidavit, state of facts; answer, replication, plea, demurrer, rebutter, rejoinder; surre-butter, -joinder.

suitor, party to a suit; litigant &c. 938; libellant.

hearing, trial; verdict &c. (*judgment*) 480; appeal, – motion; writ of error; *certiorari.*

case, decision, precedent, ruling; decided case, reports.

V. go to –, appeal to the- law; bring to -justice, – trial, – the bar; put on trial, pull up; accuse &c. 938; prefer –, file- a claim &c. *n.;* take the law of, inform against.

serve with a writ, cite, apprehend, arraign, sue, prosecute, bring an action against, indict, impeach, attach, distrain, commit; arrest; summon, -s; give in charge &c. (*restrain*) 751.

empanel a jury, implead, join issue; close the pleadings; set down for hearing.

try, hear a cause; sit in judgment; adjudicate &c. 480.

Adj. litigious &c. (*quarrelsome*) 713; *qui tam*; *coram* –, *sub- judice*.

Adv. *pendente lite*.

Phr. *adhuc sub judice lis est.*

---

970. Acquittal. — N. acquit-tal, -ment; clearance, exculpation, exoneration; discharge &c. (*release*) 750; *quietus*, absolution, compurgation, reprieve, respite; pardon &c. (*forgiveness*) 918.

[Exemption from punishment] impunity, immunity.

V. acquit, exculpate, exonerate, clear; absolve, whitewash, assoil, discharge, release; liberate &c. 750.

reprieve, respite; pardon &c. (*forgive*) 918; let off, – scot free.

Adj. acquitted &c. *v.*; un-condemned, -punished, -chastised; recommended to mercy.

971. Condemnation.—N. condemnation, conviction, proscription, damnation; death warrant; penalty &c. 974.

attain-der, -ture, -tment.

V. condemn, convict, cast, bring home to, find guilty, damn, doom, sign the death warrant, sentence, pass sentence on, attaint, confiscate, pro-scribe, sequestrate; non-suit.

disapprove &c. 932; accuse &c. 938.

stand condemned.

Adj. condem-, dam-natory; condemned &c. *v.*; non-suited &c. (*failure*) 732; self-convicted.

Phr. *mutato nomine de te fabula narratur.*

---

972. Punishment.—N. punishment, punition; chast-isement, -ening; correction, castigation.

discipline, infliction, trial; judgment; penalty &c. 974; retribution; thunderbolt, Nemesis; requital &c. (*reward*) 973; penology; retributive justice.

lash, scaffold &c. (*instrument of punishment*) 975; imprisonment &c. (*restraint*) 751; chain gang; transportation, banishment, expulsion, deportation, exile, involuntary exile, ostracism; penal servitude, hard labour; galleys &c. 975; beating &c. *v.*; flagellation, fustigation, gantlet, *strappado*, *estrapade*, *bastinado*, *argumentum baculinum*, stick law, rap on the knuckles, box on the ear; blow &c. (*impulse*) 276; stripe, cuff, kick, buffet, pummel; slap, – in the face; wipe, douse; *coup de grâce*; torture, rack; picket, -ing; *dragonnade*; capital punishment, extreme penalty; execution; hanging &c. *v.*; de-capitation, -collation; *garrot-te, -to*; electrocution, lethal chamber; crucifixion, impalement; martyrdom, *auto-da-fé*; *noyade*; *hara-kiri*, happy despatch.

V. punish; chast-ise, -en; castigate, correct, inflict punishment, administer correction, deal retributive justice.

visit upon, pay; pay –, serve- out; settle with, get even with, get one's own back; do for; make short work of, give a lesson to, strafe, serve one right, make an example of; have a rod in pickle for; give it one.

strike &c. 276; deal a blow to, administer the lash, smite; slap, – the face; smack, cuff, box the ears, spank, thwack, thump, beat, lay on, swinge, buffet; thresh, thrash, pummel, drub, leather, trounce, baste, belabour; lace, – one's jacket; dress, give a -dressing, – down; trim, warm, wipe, tund, cob, bang, strap, comb, lash, lick, larrup, whallop, whop, flog, scourge, whip, birch, cane, give the stick, switch, flagellate, horsewhip, *bastinado*, towel, rub down with an oaken towel, rib roast, dust one's jacket, fustigate, pitch into, lay about one, beat black and blue; beat to a -mummy, – jelly; give a black eye; hit on the head; sandbag.

tar and feather; pelt, stone, lapidate; mast-head, keelhaul.

execute; bring to the -block, – gallows; behead; de-capitate, -collate; guillotine; hang, turn off, gibbet, bowstring, hang, draw and quarter; shoot; decimate; burn; electrocute; break on the wheel, crucify; em-, im-pale; flay; lynch; put to death.

torture; put -on, – to- the rack; picket.

banish, exile; trans-, de-port; expel, ostracize; rusticate; drum out; dismiss, -bar, -bench; strike off the roll, unfrock; post.

suffer, – for, – punishment; be -flogged, – hanged &c.; come to the gallows, dance upon nothing, die in one's shoes; be rightly served.

Adj. punishing &c. *v.*; penal; puni-tory, -tive; inflictive, castigatory; punished &c. *v.*

Int. *à la lanterne!*

973. Reward.—N. reward, recompense, remuneration, prize, meed, guerdon, reguerdon; indemni-ty, -fication, price; quittance; compensation; reparation, *ersatz*, assythment, redress; retribution, reckoning, acknowledgment, requital, amends, sop; atonement; consideration, return, *quid pro quo*; salvage, perquisite; vail &c. (*donation*) 784; *douceur*, bribe, bait, baksheesh, tip; hush-, smart-money; blackmail; carcelage; *solatium*.

allowance, salary, stipend, wages; pay, -ment; emolument; tribute; batta, shot, scot; premium, fee, *honorarium*; hire.

crown &c. (*decoration of honour*) 877.

V. re-ward, -compense, -pay, -quite; re-, munerate; compensate; fee, tip, bribe; pay one's footing &c. (*pay*) 807; make amends, indemnify, atone; satisfy, acknowledge.

get for one's pains, reap the fruits of.

Adj. remunerat-ive, -ory; munerary, compensatory, retributive, reparatory.

974. Penalty.—N. penalty; retribution &c. (*punishment*) 972; pain, pains and penalties; *peine forte et dure*; penance &c. (*atonement*) 952; the devil to pay.

fine, mulct, amercement; forfeit, -ure; escheat, damages, deodand, sequestration, confiscation, *premunire*.

V. penalize, fine, mulct, amerce, sconce, confiscate; sequest-rate, -er; escheat; estreat, forfeit.

975. [Instrument of punishment.] Scourge.—N. scourge, rod, cane, stick; ra-, rat-tan; birch, – rod; rod in pickle; switch, ferule, cudgel, truncheon; rubber hose.

whip, lash, strap, thong, cowhide, knout; cat, – o'-nine-tails, *sjambok*, quirt; rope's end.

pillory, stocks, whipping-post; cuck-, duck-ing stool; brank; triangle, wooden horse, maiden, thumbscrew, boot, rack, wheel, iron heel; treadmill, crank, galleys.

scaffold; block, axe, *guillotine*; stake; cross; gallows, gibbet, Tyburn tree; drop, noose, rope, halter, bowstring; electric chair, lethal chamber.

house of correction &c. (*prison*) 752.

gaol-, jail-er; executioner; hang-, heads-man; Jack Ketch; lyncher.

Section V. RELIGIOUS AFFECTIONS

1°. Superhuman Beings and Regions

976. Deity.—N. Deity, Divinity; God-head, -ship; Omnipotence, Providence.

[Quality of being divine] divin-eness, -ity.

God, Lord, Jehovah, *Deus*; The -Almighty, – Supreme Being, – First Cause; *Ens Entium*; Author –, Creator- of all things; Author of our being; The -Infinite, – Eternal; The All-powerful, -wise, -merciful, -holy; The Omni-potent, -scient.

[Attributes and perfections] infinite -power, – wisdom, – goodness, – justice, – truth, – love, – mercy; omni-potence, -science, -presence; unity, immutability, holiness, glory, majesty, sovereignty, infinity, eternity.

The -Trinity, – Holy Trinity, – Trinity in Unity, – Triune God; Three in One and One in Three.

God the Father; The -Maker, – Creator, – Preserver.

[Functions] creation, preservation, divine government; The-ocracy, -archy; providence; ways –, dealings –, dispensations –, visitations- of Providence.

God the Son, Jesus, Christ; The -Messiah, – Anointed, – Saviour, – Redeemer, – Mediator, – Intercessor, – Advocate, – Judge; The Son of -God, – Man, – David; The Only Begotten; The Lamb of God, The Word; Em-, Im-manuel; The -King of Kings and Lord of Lords, – King of Glory, – Prince of Peace, – Good Shepherd, – Way, – Truth, – Life, – Bread of Life, – Light of the World; The -Lord our, – Sun of- Righteousness.

The -Incarnation, – Hypostatic Union, – Word made Flesh.

[Functions] salvation, redemption, atonement, propitiation, mediation, intercession, judgment.

God the Holy Ghost, The Holy Spirit, Paraclete; The -Comforter, – Consoler, – Spirit of Truth, – Dove.

[Functions] inspiration, unction, regeneration, sanctification, consolation.

eon, æon, special providence, *Deus ex machinâ*; *Avatar*.

V. create, uphold, preserve, govern &c.

atone, redeem, save, propitiate, mediate &c.

predestinate, elect, call, ordain, bless, justify, sanctify, glorify &c.

Adj. almighty, holy, hallowed, sacred, divine, heavenly, celestial; messianic; sacrosanct; all-powerful, -wise, -seeing, -knowing; omni-potent, omniscient; supreme.

super-human, -natural; ghostly, spiritual, hyperphysical, unearthly; the-istic, -ocratic, deistic; anointed.

Adv. *jure divino*, by divine right; *Deo volente*, D.V.

977. [Beneficent spirits.] **Angel.—N.** angel, archangel; heavenly host, choir invisible, host of heaven, sons of God; Michael, Gabriel &c.; seraph, -im; cherub, -im; ministering spirit, morn-

978. [Maleficent spirits.] **Satan.—N.** Satan, the Devil, Lucifer, Ahrimanes, Belial; Sammael, Zamiel, Beelzebub, the Prince of the Devils; Mephisto-pheles, his satanic majesty.*

* The slang expressions 'the -deuce, – dickens, – old Gentleman; old -Nick, – Scratch, – Horny, – Harry, – Gooseberry,' have not been inserted in the text.

ing star; saint, *Madonna*; Our Lady, the Blessed Virgin, the Virgin Mary.

Adj. angelic, seraphic, cherubic.

---

the tempter; the evil -one, – spirit; the -author of evil, – wicked one, – old Serpent; the Prince of -darkness, – this world, – the power of the air; the -foul, – arch- fiend; the devil incarnate; the -common enemy, – angel of the bottomless pit; Abaddon, Apollyon, Mammon.

fallen angels, unclean spirits, devils; the -rulers, – powers- of darkness; inhabitants of Pandemonium; demon &c. 980.

diabolism; devil-ism, -ship, -dom, -ry, -worship; *diablerie*; satanism, manicheism; the cloven foot; black magic &c. 992.

Adj. satanic, diabolic, devilish, infernal, hell-born.

Heathen, Mythological and other fabulous Deities and Powers*

979. Jupiter.—**N.** god, -dess; heathen gods and goddesses; Pantheon; Jupiter, Jove, Zeus, Apollo, Mars, Mercury, Neptune, Vulcan, Bacchus, Pluto, Saturn, Cupid, Eros, Pan; Juno, Ceres, Proserpina, Dina, Minerva, Pallas, Athenae, Venus, Aphrodite, Vesta; The Fates &c. 601.

Allah, Brahma, Vishnu, Siva, Shiva, Krishna, Juggernaut, Buddha; Ra, Isis, Osiris; Belus, Bel, Baal, Asteroth &c.; Thor, Odin; Mumbo Jumbo; good –, tutelary- genius; demiurge, familiar, – spirit; Sibyl; fairy, fay; sylph, -id; Ariel, peri, nymph, nereid, dryad, oread, sea-maid, Banshee, Benshie, Ormuzd; Oberon, Titania, Mab, hamadryad, naiad, mermaid, kelpie, Ondine, nix, nixie, sprite; denizens of the air; pixy &c. (*bad spirit*) 980.

mythology; heathen –, fairy- mythology; Lemprière, folklore.

Adj. fairy-, sylph-like; sylphic.

---

980. Demon.—**N.** demon, -ry, -ism, -ology; evil genius, fiend, familiar, – spirit, devil; bad –, unclean- spirit; cacodemon, incubus, Frankenstein's monster, succubus and succuba, Titan, Shedim, Mephistopheles, Asmodeus, Moloch, Belial, Ahriman, fury, The Furies &c. 900; harpy; Friar Rush.

vampire, ghoul; af-, ef-freet; afrite; ogre, -ss; gnome, gin, djinn, imp, deev, *lamia*; bo-gie, -gle; nis, kobold, flibbertigibbet, fairy, brownie, pixy, elf, dwarf, urchin, Puck, Robin Goodfellow; lepre-, cluri-chaune; troll, dwerger, sprite, oaf, changeling, bad fairy, nixe, pigwidgeon, Will-o'-the-wisp; Erl King.

[Supernatural appearance] ghost, spectre, apparition, genie, spirit, shade, shadow, vision, phantom &c. 443; materialization (*spiritualism*) 992; hob-, goblin; wraith, spook, werwolf, boggart, banshee, *loup-garou*, *lemures*; evil eye.

nisse, necks; mer-man, -maid, -folk; siren, Lorelei; satyr, faun.

Adj. supernatural, weird, uncanny, unearthly, spectral; ghost-ly, -like; elf-in, -like; fiend-ish, -like; impish, demoniacal; haunted.

981. Heaven.—**N.** heaven; kingdom of -heaven, – God; heavenly kingdom; throne –, presence- of God; inheritance of the saints in light.

Paradise, Eden, abode of the blessed; Holy City, New Jerusalem; celestial bliss, glory.

[Mythological -heaven] Olympus; [– paradise] Elysium, Elysian fields, Arcadia, bowers of bliss, garden of the Hesperides, Islands of the Blessed;

982. Hell.—**N.** hell, bottomless pit, place of torment; habitation of fallen angels; Pandemonium, Abaddon, Domdaniel.

hell fire; everlasting -fire, – torment; lake of fire and brimstone; fire that is never quenched, worm that never dies.

purgatory, limbo, gehenna, abyss.

[Mythological hell] Tartarus, Hades, Avernus, Styx, Stygian creek, pit of Acheron, Cocytus, Phlegethon, Lethe;

* Only a selection of those best known to literature is included.

happy hunting-ground; third –, seventh- heaven; Valhalla (Scandinavian); Nirvana (Buddhist).

future state, eternity, eternal life, life after death, eternal home, resurrection, translation; resuscitation &c. 660; apotheosis, deification.

Adj. heavenly, celestial, supernal, unearthly, from on high, paradisiacal, beatific, elysian, Olympian, Arcadian.

infernal regions, *inferno*, shades below, realms of Pluto.

Pluto, Rhadamanthus, Erebus, Charon, Cerberus; Tophet.

Adj. hellish, infernal, stygian.

2°. RELIGIOUS DOCTRINES

983. [Religious Knowledge.] **Theology.**—**N.** Theology (natural and revealed); Theo-gony, -sophy; Divinity; Hagio-logy, -graphy; Caucasian mystery; monotheism; religion; religious -persuasion, – sect, – denomination; cult; creed &c. (*belief*) 484; articles –, declaration –, profession –, confession- of faith.

theolog-ue, -ian; divine, schoolman, canonist, monotheist.

Adj. theological, religious; canonical; denominational; sectarian &c. 984.

983a. Orthodoxy.—**N.** orthodoxy; strictness, soundness, religious truth, true faith; truth &c. 494.

Christian-ity, -ism; Catholic-ism, -ity; 'the faith once delivered to the saints'; hyperorthodoxy &c. 984; iconoclasm.

the Holy –, the Orthodox- Church; Catholic –, Universal –, Apostolic –, Established- Church; temple of the Holy Ghost; Church –, body –, members –, disciples –, followers- of Christ; Christian, – community; true believer; canonist &c. (*theologian*) 983; Christendom, collective body of Christians, the Church Militant.

canons &c. (*belief*) 484; thirty-nine articles; Apostles' –, Nicene –, Athanasian- Creed; Church Catechism; textuary.

Adj. orthodox, sound, literal, strict, faithful, catholic, schismless, Christian, evangelical, scriptural, divine, monotheistic; true &c. 494.

984. Heterodoxy. [Sectarianism.]—**N.** heterodoxy; error &c. 495; false doctrine, heresy, schism; schismanticism, -alness; recusancy, backsliding, apostasy; atheism &c. (*irreligion*) 989.

bigotry &c. (*obstinacy*) 606; fanaticism, iconoclasm; hyperorthodoxy, precisianism, bibliolatry, hagiolatry, sabbatarianism, puritanism; idolatry &c. 991; superstition &c. (*credulity*) 486; dissent &c. 489.

sectar-ism, -ianism; nonconformity; secularism; syncretism, religious sects; the clash of creeds.

protestant-, advent-, Arian-, Erastian-, Calvin-, quaker-, method-, anabapt-, Pusey-, tractarian-, ritual-, Origen-, Sabellian-, Socinian-, De-, The-, mon-, material-, positiv-, latitudinarian-ism &c.

High –, Low –, Broad –, Free- Church; ultramontanism; monasticism; pap-ism, -istry; papacy; Anglican-, Catholic-, Roman-ism; popery, Scarlet Lady, Church of Rome, Greek Church; Christian Science, The Church of Christ Scientist.

---

pagan-, heathen-, ethic-ism; mythology; animism; poly-, di-, tri-, pan-theism; dualism; heathendom.

Juda-, Gentil-, Mahometan-, Islam-, Turc-, Brahmin-, Hindoo-, Buddh-, Lama-, Confucian-, Shinto-, Sabian-, Gnostic-, Soofee-, Hylothe-, Mormon-ism.

Theosophy; Spiritualism, Occultism.

heretic, antichrist; pagan, heathen; pai-, pay-nim; *giaour*; gentile; pan-, poly-theist; idolator; misbeliever, apostate, backslider.

bigot &c. (*obstinacy*) 606; fanatic, dervish, abdal, iconoclast.

latitudinarian, limitarian, Deist, Theist, Unitarian; positivist, materialist; agnostic, sceptic &c. 989.

schismatic; sectar-y, -ian, -ist; seceder, separatist, recusant, dissenter; non-conformist, -juror; Huguenot, Protestant; orthodox dissenter, Congregationalist, Independent; Episcopalian, Presbyterian; Lutheran, Calvinist, Quaker, Methodist, Wesleyan; Ana-, Baptist; Dunker; Mormon, Latter-day Saint, Irvingite, Sandemanian, Glassite, Erastian; Sub-, Supra-lapsarian; Gentoo, Antinomian, Swedenborgian, Adventist, Plymouth Brother; Theosophist &c.

Catholic, Roman Catholic, Romanist, papist, ultramontane; Old Catholic, tractarian, Anglican, Puseyite, ritualist; Puritan.

Jew, Hebrew, Rabbist; Mahometan, Mohammedan, Mussulman, Moslem, Islamite, Osmanli; Brahm-in, -an; Parsee, Sofi, Soofee; Buddhist; Zoroastrian, Magi, Gymnosophist, fire-worshipper, Sabian, Gnostic, Sadducee, Rosicrucian &c.

Adj. heterodox, heretical; un-orthodox, -scriptural, -canonical; antiscriptural, apocryphal; un-, anti-christian; schismatic, recusant, iconoclastic; sectarian; dis-senting, -sident; secular &c. (*lay*) 997.

pagan; heathen, -ish; ethnic, -al; gentile, painim; pan-, polytheistic; agnostic, sceptic.

Judaical, Mohammedan, Moslem, Brahminical, Buddhist &c. *n.* Romish, Protestant &c. *n.*

bigoted &c. (*prejudiced*) 481, (*obstinate*) 606; superstitious &c. (*credulous*) 486; fanatical; idolatrous &c. 991; visionary &c. (*imaginative*) 515.

---

985. Revelation.—N. revelation, inspiration, *afflatus*.

Word, – of God; Scripture; the -Scriptures, – Bible, – Book of Books; Holy -Writ, – Scriptures; inspired writings, Gospel.

Old Testament, Septuagint, Vulgate, Pentateuch; Octateuch; the -Law, – Jewish Law, – Prophets; major –, minor- Prophets; Hagio-grapha, -logy; Hierographa; Apocrypha.

New Testament; Gospels, Evangelists, Acts, Epistles, Apocalypse, Revelations.

Talmud; Mishna, Masorah.

prophet &c. (*seer*) 513; evangelist, apostle, disciple, saint; the –, the Apostolical- fathers; Holy Men of old, inspired -writers, – penmen.

Adj. scriptural, biblical, sacred, prophetic; evangel-ical, -istic; apostolic, -al; inspired, theopneustic, apocalyptic, ecclesiastical, canonical, textuary.

986. Pseudo-Revelation.*—N. the -Koran, – Alcoran; Ly-king, Shaster, Vedas, Zendavesta, Vedidad, Purana, Edda; Go-, Gau-tama; Book of Mormon.

[False prophets and religious founders] Buddha, Zoroaster, Zerdhusht, Confucius, Mahomet.

[Idols] golden calf &c. 991; Baal, Moloch, Dagon.

---

* See note on page 378.

3°. Religious Sentiments

987. Piety.—N. piety, religion, theism, faith; religiousness, holiness &c. *adj.*; saintship; religionism; sanctimony &c. (*assumed piety*) 988; reverence &c. (*respect*) 928; humility, veneration, devotion; prostration &c. (*worship*) 990; grace, unction, edification; sancti-ty, -tude; consecration.

spiritual existence, odour of sanctity, beauty of holiness.

theopathy, beatification, adoption, regeneration, conversion, justification, sanctification, salvation, inspiration, bread of life; Body and Blood of Christ.

believer, convert, theist, Christian, devotee, pietist; the -good, – righteous, – just, – believing, – elect; Saint, *Madonna.*

the children of -God, – the kingdom, – light.

V. be -pious &c. *adj.*; have -faith &c. *n.*; believe, receive Christ; revere &c. 928; worship &c. 950; be -converted &c.

convert, edify, sanctify, hallow, keep holy, beatify, regenerate, inspire, consecrate, enshrine.

Adj. pious, religious, devout, devoted, reverent, godly, heavenly minded, humble; pure, – in heart; holy, spiritual, pietistic; saint-ly, -like; seraphic, sacred, solemn.

believing, faithful, Christian, Catholic.

elected, adopted, justified, sanctified, regenerated, inspired, consecrated, converted, unearthly, not of the earth.

988. Impiety.—N. impiety; sin &c. 945; irreverence; profan-eness &c. *adj.*, -ity, -ation; blasphemy, desecration, sacrilege; scoffing &c. *v.*

[Assumed piety] hypocrisy &c. (*falsehood*) 544; pietism, cant, pious fraud; lip-devotion, -service, -reverence; misdevotion, formalism, austerity; sanctimon-y, -iousness &c. *adj.*; pharisaism, precisianism; sabbat-ism, -arianism; *odium theologicum*, sacerdotalism; bigotry &c. (*obstinacy*) 606, (*prejudice*) 481.

hardening, backsliding, declension, perversion, reprobation apostasy, recusancy.

sinner &c. 949; scoffer, blasphemer; sacrilegist; worldling; hypocrite &c. (*dissembler*) 548; Scribes and Pharisees; Tartufe, Maw-worm.

bigot; saint [ironically]; Pharisee, sabbatarian, formalist, methodist, puritan, pietist, precisian, religionist, devotee, ranter, fanatic, wowser.

the -wicked, – evil, – unjust, – reprobate; son of -men, – Belial, – the wicked one; children of darkness.

V. be -impious &c. *adj.*; profane, desecrate, blaspheme, revile, scoff; swear &c. (*malediction*) 908; commit sacrilege.

snuffle; turn up the whites of the eyes; idolize.

Adj. impious; irreligious &c. 989; desecrating &c. *v.*; profane, irreverent, sacrilegious, blasphemous.

un-hallowed, -sanctified, -regenerate; hardened, perverted, reprobate.

hypocritical &c. (*false*) 544; canting, pietistical, sanctimonious, unctuous, pharisaical, over-righteous, righteous over much.

bigoted, fanatical &c. 481 & 606; priest-ridden.

Adv. under the -mask, cloak, – pretence, – form, – guise- of religion.

989. Irreligion.—N. irreligion, indevotion; ungodliness &c. *adj.*; laxity, quietism, apathy, indifference, passivity.

scepticism, doubt; un-, dis-belief; incredul-ity, -ousness &c. *adj.*; want of -faith, – belief; pyrrhonism; doubt &c. 485; agnosticism.

atheism, deism; hylotheism; materialism; positivism; nihilism.

infidelity, freethinking, antichristianity, rationalism.

atheist, anti-christian, sceptic, unbeliever, deist, infidel, pyrrhonist; *giaour*, heathen, alien, gentile, Nazarene; *esprit fort*, freethinker, latitudinarian, rationalist; materialist, positivist, nihilist, agnostic.

V. be -irreligious &c. *adj.*; disbelieve, lack faith; doubt, question &c. 485.

dechristianize; serve Mammon, love darkness better than light.

Adj. irreligious; in-, un-devout; devout-, god-, grace-less; ungodly, -holy, -sanctified, -hallowed; atheistic, without God.

sceptical, free-thinking; un-believing, -converted; incredulous, faithless, lacking faith; deistical; un-, anti-christian.

worldly, mundane, earthly, carnal, unspiritual; worldly &c.-minded.

Adv. irreligiously &c. *adj.*

4°. Acts of Religion

990. Worship.—N. worship, adoration, devotion, aspiration, latria, homage, service, humiliation; kneeling, genuflexion, prostration.

prayer, invocation, supplication, rogation, intercession, orison, holy breathing; petition &c. (*request*) 765; collect, litany, Lord's prayer, paternoster, *Ave Maria*, rosary; bead-roll; latria, dulia, hyperdulia, vigils; revival; cult.

thanksgiving; giving –, returning- thanks; grace, praise, glorification, benediction, doxology, hosanna; h-, allelujah; *Te Deum, non nobis Domine, nunc dimittis*; pæan.

psalm, -ody; hymn, plainsong, chant, chaunt, response, anthem, motet; antiphon, -y.

oblation, sacrifice, incense, libation; burnt –, votive –, thank-offering; offertory, collection.

discipline; self-discipline, -examination, -denial; fasting.

divine service, office, duty; morning prayer; mass, matins, evensong, vespers, compline; holy day &c. (*rites*) 998.

worshipper, congregation, communicant, celebrant.

V. worship, lift up the heart, aspire; revere &c. 928; adore, do service, pay homage; humble oneself, kneel; bow –, bend- the knee; fall -down, – on one's knees; prostrate oneself, bow down and worship, recite the rosary.

pray, invoke, supplicate; put –, offer- up -prayers, – petitions; beseech &c. (*ask*) 765; say one's prayers, tell one's beads.

return –, give- thanks; say grace, bless, praise, laud, glorify, magnify, sing praises; give benediction, lead the choir, intone, chant, sing.

propitiate, offer sacrifice, fast, deny oneself; vow, offer vows, give alms.

work out one's salvation; go to church; attend -service, – mass; communicate &c. (*rite*) 998.

Adj. worshipping &c. *v.*; devout, devotional, reverent, pure, solemn; fervid &c. (*heartfelt*) 821.

Int. h-, allelujah! hosanna! glory be to God! O Lord! pray God that! God -grant, – bless, – save, – forbid! *sursum corda*.

991. Idolatry.—N. idol-atry, -ism; demon-ism, -olatry; idol –, demon –, devil –, fire- worship; zoolatry, fetishism, Mari-, Bibli-, ecclesi-, heli-olatry.

deification, apotheosis, canonization; hero worship.

sacrifices, hecatomb, holocaust; human sacrifices, immolation, mactation, infanticide, self-immolation, *suttee*.

idol, golden calf, graven image, fetish, *avatar*, Juggernaut, joss, *lares et penates*; Baal &c. 986.

idolater &c. *n.*

V. worship -idols, – pictures, – relics; put on a pedestal, bow down to, prostrate oneself before, make sacrifice to; deify, canonize, idolize.

Adj. idolatrous.

992. Sorcery.—N. sorcery; superstition; occult -art, – sciences; black –, magic; the black art, necromancy, theurgy, thaumaturgy; demon-ology, -omy, -ship; *diablerie*, bedevilment; witch-craft, -ery; glamour; fetis-hism, -ism; ghost dance; hoodoo, voodoo; Shamanism [Esquimaux], vampirism; conjuration; bewitchery, exorcism, enchantment, incantation, obsession, possession, mysticism, second sight, mesmerism, animal magnetism; od –, odylic- force; electro-biology, *clairvoyance*; spiritualism, spirit-rapping, table-turning; thought reading, telepathy, thought transference, automatic writing, *planchette*, ouija board; crystal gazing; spirit manifestation, materialization, astral body, ectoplasm &c.

divination &c. (*prediction*) 511; sortilege, ordeal, *sortes Virgilianæ*; hocus-pocus &c. (*deception*) 545; oracle &c. 513.

V. practice -sorcery &c. *n.*; cast a -horoscope, – nativity; conjure, exorcise, charm, enchant; be-witch, -devil; overlook, look on with the evil eye; entrance, mesmerize, magnetize; fascinate &c. (*influence*) 615; taboo; wave a wand; rub the -ring, – lamp; cast a spell; call up spirits, – from the vasty deep; raise spirits from the dead; raise –, lay- ghosts; command genii.

Adj. magic, -al; mystic, weird, cabalistic, talismanic, phylacteric, incantatory; charmed &c. *v.*

993. Spell.—N. spell, charm, incantation, exorcism, weird, cabala, exsufflation, cantrap, runes, abracadabra, hocus-pocus, open *sesame*, counter-charm, Ephesian letters, bell, book and candle, Mumbo-jumbo, evil-eye, fee-faw-fum.

talisman, amulet, periapt, telesm, phylactery, philtre, wish-bone, merry-thought, mascot, scarab, swastika; fetish; *agnus Dei.*

wand, caduceus, rod, divining rod, lamp of Aladdin, magic carpet, seven-league boots; magic ring; wishing –, Fortunatus's- cap.

994. Sorcerer.—N. sorcerer, magician; thaumat-, the-urgist; conjuror, necromancer, seer, wizard, witch; fairy &c. 980; *lamia*, hag, warlock, charmer, exorcist, voodoo, mage, diviner, dowser; cunning –, medicine- man, witch doctor; Shaman, figure-flinger, ecstatica, medium, *clairvoyant*, mesmerist, hypnotist; *deus ex machinâ*; astrologer; soothsayer &c. 513.

Katerfelto, Cagliostro, Merlin, Comus, Mesmer, Rosicrucian; Hecate, Circe, Lilith, siren, weird sisters; witch of Endor.

5°. RELIGIOUS INSTITUTIONS

995. Churchdom.—N. church, -dom; ministry, apostleship, priesthood, prelacy, hierarchy, church government, christendom, pale of the church.

clerical-, sacerdotal-, episcopalian-, ultramontan-ism; Theocracy; ecclesiolog-y, -ist; priestcraft, *odium theologicum.*

monach-ism, -y; monasticism, monkhood.

[Ecclesiastical offices and dignities] pontificate, primacy, archbishopric, archiepiscopacy; prelacy; bishop-ric, -dom; episcop-ate, -acy; see, diocese; deanery, stall; canon-ry, -icate; prebend, -aryship; benefice, incumbency, glebe, advowson, living, cure, – of souls; rectorship; vicar-iate, -ship; pastor-ate, -ship; deacon-ry, -ship; -curacy; chaplain, -cy, -ship; cardinal-ate, -ship; abbacy, presbytery.

holy orders, ordination, institution, consecration, induction, reading in, preferment, translation, presentation.

popedom, papacy; the -Vatican, – apostolic see, – see of Rome; religious sects &c. 984.

council &c. 696; conclave, college of cardinals, convocation, synod, consistory, chapter, vestry, presbytery; sanhedrim, *congé d'élire*; ecclesiastical courts, consistorial court, court of Arches.

V. call, ordain, induct, prefer, translate, consecrate, present, elect, bestow.

take -orders, – the veil, – vows.

Adj. ecclesi-astical, -ological; clerical, sacerdotal, priestly, prelatical, pastoral, ministerial, capitular, theocratic; hierarchical, archiepiscopal; episcopal, -ian; canonical; mon-astic, -achal; monkish; abbati-al, -cal; pontifical, papal, apostolic; ultramontane, priest-ridden.

---

996. Clergy.—N. clergy, clericals, ministry, priesthood, presbytery, the cloth, the pulpit.

clergyman, divine, ecclesiastic, churchman, priest, presbyter, hierophant, pastor, shepherd, minister, clerk in holy orders; father, – in Christ; *padre, abbé, curé*; patriarch; reverend; black coat; confessor; sky pilot.

dignitaries of the church; ecclesi-, hier-arch; eminence, reverence, elder, primate, metropolitan, archimandrite, archbishop, bishop, prelate, diocesan, suffragan, dean, subdean, archdeacon, prebendary, canon, rural dean, rector, parson, vicar, perpetual curate, residentiary, beneficiary, incumbent, chaplain, curate, – in charge; deacon, -ess; preacher; lay reader, lecturer; capitular; missionary, propagandist, Jesuit, revivalist, field preacher.

churchwarden, sidesman; clerk, precentor, choir; almoner, *suisse*, verger, beadle, sexton, sacristan; acol-yth, -othyst, -yte; thurifer; chorister, choir boy.

[Roman Catholic priesthood] Pope, *Papa*, Holy Father, pontiff, high priest, cardinal; ancient –, flamen; confessor, penitentiary; spiritual director.

cenobite, conventual, abbot, prior, monk, friar, lay brother, beadsman, mendicant, pilgrim, palmer; canon-regular, -secular; Jesuit, Franciscan, Friars minor, Minorites; Observant, Capuchin, Dominican, Carmelite; Augustinian; Gilbertine; Austin-, Black-, White-, Grey-, Crossed-, Crutched-Friars; Bonhomme, Carthusian, Benedictine, Cistercian, Trappist, Cluniac, Premonstratensian, Maturine; Templar. Hospitaller.

997. Laity.—N. laity, flock, fold, congregation, assembly, brethren, people.

temporality, secularization.

layman, civilian; parishioner, catechumen; secularist.

V. secularize.

Adj. secular, lay, laical, civil, temporal, profane.

abb-, prior-, canon-ess; mother superior; *religieuse*, nun, sister, *beguine*, novice, postulant.

[Under the Jewish dispensation] prophet, priest, high priest, Levite; Rabbi, -n; scribe.

[Mohammedan &c.] mullah, ulema, imauam, sheik; so-fi, -phi; mufti, hadji, muezzin, dervish; fa-kir, -quir; brahmin, gooroo, druid, bonze, santon, abdal, Lama, talapoin, caloyer &c.

V. take orders &c. 995.

Adj. the –, the very –, the Right- Reverend; ordained, in orders, called to the ministry.

998. Rite.—N. rite; ceremon-y, -ial; ordinance, observance, function, duty; form, -ulary; solemnity, sacrament; incantation &c. (*spell*) 993; service, psalmody &c. (*worship*) 990; liturgies.

ministration; preach-ing, -ment; predication, sermon, homily, exhortation, lecture, discourse, pastoral.

baptism, christening, chrism, immersion; baptismal regeneration; font; circumcision.

confirmation; imposition –, laying on- of hands; churching, purification, ordination &c. (*churchdom*) 995; excommunication.

Eucharist, Lord's supper, communion; the –, the holy- sacrament; celebration, high celebration; *missa cantata*; offertory; introit; consecration; con-, tran-substantiation; real presence; elements, bread and wine; mass; high –, low –, dry- mass.

matrimony &c. 903; burial &c. 363; visitation of the sick.

seven sacraments, impanation, extreme unction, last rites, *viaticum*, invocation of saints, canonization, transfiguration, auricular confession; fasting; maceration, flagellation, sackcloth and ashes; penance &c. (*atonement*) 952; absolution; telling of beads, reciting the rosary, processional; thurification, incense, holy water, aspersion.

relics, rosary, beads, reliquary, host, cross, rood, crucifix, pax, pix, pyx, *agnus Dei*, censer, thurible, patera, urceole; chalice, patten, Holy Grail, sangrail; seven-branch candle stick, monstrance, sacring bell.

ritual, rubric, canon, ordinal; liturgy, prayer-book, book of common prayer, pietas, euchology, litany, lectionary; missal, breviary, massbook, bead-roll.

psalter; psalm –, hymn- book; hymn-al, -ology; psalmody.

ritual-, ceremonial-ism; sabbat-ism, -arianism; ritualist, sabbatarian.

holyday, feast, fast; Sabbath, Passover, Pentecost; Advent, Christmas, Noel, Epiphany, Lent, Shrove Tuesday, Ash Wednesday, Maundy Thursday; Passion –, Holy- week; Good Friday, Easter, Ascension Day, Whitsuntide; Trinity Sunday, Corpus Christi; All-Saints' –, – Souls'- Day; Candle-, Lam-, Martin-, Michael-mas; hogmanay; Rama-dan, -zan; Bairam &c. &c.

V. perform service, do duty, minister, officiate, baptize, dip, sprinkle; confirm, lay hands on; give –, administer –, take –, receive –. attend –, partake of- the -sacrament, – communion; communicate; celebrate mass; administer –, receive- extreme unction; anele, shrive, absolve, confess; do penance; genuflect; cross oneself, make the sign of the cross.

excommunicate, ban with bell, book and candle.

preach, sermonize, predicate, lecture.

Adj. ritual, -istic; ceremonial, liturgic; baptismal, eucharistical; paschal.

999. Canonicals.—N. canonicals, vestments; robe, gown, Geneva gown, frock, pallium, surplice, cassock, dalmatic, scapulary, cope. scarf, tunicle, chasuble, alb, *alba*, stole; fan-on, -nel; tonsure, cowl, hood; calo-te, -tte; bands; capouch, amice, orarium, ephod; apron, lawn sleeves, pontificals, pall; mitre, tiara, triple crown; shovel –, cardinal's-hat; biretta; crosier; pastoral staff; costume &c. 225.

1000. Temple.—**N.** place of worship; house of -God, – prayer.

temple, cathedral, minister, church, kirk, chapel, meeting-house, bethel, tabernacle, conventicle, *basilica*, fane, holy place, chantry, oratory.

synagogue; mosque; marabout; pantheon; pagoda; joss-house; dagobah, tope; kiosk.

parsonage, rectory, vicarage, manse, deanery, glebe, church house; Vatican; bishop's palace; Lambeth.

altar, shrine, sanctuary, Holy of Holies, *sanctum sanctorum*, sacrarium, -isty; communion –, holy –, Lord's- table; table of the Lord; pyx; baptistery, font; piscina, stoup; aumbry; sedile; reredos; rood -loft, – screen; jube.

chancel, quire, choir, nave, aisle, transept, lady chapel, vestry, crypt, cloisters, porch; triforum, clerestory, churchyard, *golgotha*, calvary, Easter sepulchre; stall, pew, sitting; pulpit, ambo, lectern, reading-desk, confessional, prothesis, credence, baldachin, *baldacchino*; jesse, apse, belfry; chapter-house; presbytery.

monastery, priory, abbey, friary, convent, nunnery, cloister.

Adj. claustral, cloistered; monast-ic, -erial; conventual.

INDEX

INDEX

N.B.: The numbers refer to the headings under which the words or phrases occur. When the same word or phrase may be used in various senses, the several headings under which it, or its synonyms, will be found, according to those meanings, are indicated by the words printed in Italics. These words in Italics are not intended to explain the meaning of the word or phrase to which they are annexed, but only to assist in the required reference.

When the word given in the Index is itself the title or heading of a category, the number of reference is printed in blacker type, thus: abode **189**.

come – 658
get – *public* 531
 recover 660
go – *turn* 311
going – *news* 532
not know what
 one is – 699
put –
 turn round 283
round – 311
send – one's busi-
 ness 756
set – 676
turn – *invert* 218
what it is – 454
what one is – 625
– it and about it
 573
– to 121
– to be 152
above 206
– all 33, 642
– board
 manifest 525
 artless 703
 fair 939
– comprehension
 519
– ground 359
– the mark 33
– par 31, 648
– praise 944
– price 814
– stairs 206
– suspicion 946
– water *safe* 664
above-mentioned
 preceding 62
 repeated 104
 prior 116
abracadabra 993
Abraham,
 sham – 544
abrasion
 paring 38
 filing 330, 331
abreast 216, 236
abreption 789
abri 666
– tente d' – 233
abridge *lessen* 36
 shorten 201
 - *in writing* 572,
 596
abridgment
 compendium 596
abroach 673
abroad
 extraneous 57
 distant 196
 uncertain 475

get – *public* 531
abrogation 756
abrupt *sudden* 113
 violent 173
 steep 217
 unexpected 508
 style 579
abruption 44
abscess 655
abscissa 466
abscission
 retrenchment 38
 division 44
abscond
 escape 623
 not pay 808
absence 187
– of choice 609*a*
– of influence
 175*a*
– of intellect 450*a*
– of mind 458
– of motive 615*a*
absentee 187
absinthe 298
absolute
 not relative 1
 great 31
 complete 52
 certain 474
 affirmative 535
 authoritative 737
 severe 739
 free 748
 unalienable 924
 make – 467, 480
– interest 980
absolution 978
absolutism 506, 739
absolve
 liberate 750
 forgive 918
 exempt 927*a*
 shrive 952
 acquit 970
absonant 414, 477
absorb *combine* 48
 take in 296
 consume 677
– the mind 457,
 458
– the soul 824
– ed in thought
 451
absorbing 630, 821,
 829
absquatulate 623
abstain 623
 disuse 678
 temperance 953
– from action 681

– from voting 609*a*
abstainer 953, 958
abstemious 953
absterge 652
abstersive 662
abstinence [*see*
 abstain]
 total – 953, 955
abstract
 separate 44
 abridge 596
 take 789
 steal 791
 in the – *apart* 44
 alone 87
– idea 453
– oneself
 inattention 458
– thought 451
 attention 457
abstracted
 inattentive 458
abstruse 519
absurdity
 impossible 471
 nonsense **497**
 ridiculous 853
abundant *great* 31,
 63
 enough 639
abundanti cautelâ,
 ex – 664
abuse *deceive* 545
 ill-treat 649
 misuse 679
 malediction 908
 threat 909
 upbraid 932
 violate 961
– of language 563
– of terms 523
abusive 895, 934
abut *near* 197 *touch*
 199, 215
abutment 717
aby *remain* 141
 endure 821, 826
abysmal *deep* 208
abyss *space* 180
 depth 208
 interval 198
 danger 667
 hell 982
A.C. 106
academic
 teaching 537, 542
 theory 514
academical
 style 578
academicals
 225 *robes*

academician 492
 Royal – 559
academy 542
acanthus 847
a capite ad calcem
 52
acariâtre 901
acarpous 169
acatalectic 597
acaudal 38
accede 488, 725, 762
accelerate
 early 132
 stimulate 173
 velocity 274
 hasten 684
accension 384
accent *sound* 402
 tone of voice 580
 rhythm 597
accentuate 642
accentuated 580
accept *assent* 488
 consent 762
 receive 785
 take 789
acceptable 646, 829
acceptance 771
acceptation 522
acception 522
access 286
 easy of – 705
 means of – 627
accessible 470, 705
accession
 adjunct 39
 increase 35
 addition 37
 - *to office* 737, 755
 consent 762
accessory
 extrinsic 6
 additive 37
 adjunct 39
 accompanying 88
 aid 707
 auxiliary 711
acciaccatura 413
accidence 567
accident *event* 151
 chance 156
 disaster 619
 misfortune 735
 fatal – 361
accidental
 extrinsic 6
 fortuitous 156
 undesigned 621
accidents,
 trust to the chap-
 ter of – 621

- of an obligation 772
acquittal 506, 970
acquittance 771
acres *space* 180
   land 342
   property 780
Acres, Bob 862
acrid 392, 395
acridity 171
acrimony
   physical 171
   caustic 830
   discourtesy 895
   hatred 898
   anger 900
   malevolence 907
acroamatism 490
acrobat
   strength 159
   actor 599
   proficient 700
   mountebank 844
Acropolis 210
across 219, 708
acrostic 533, 561, 842
act *imitate* 19
   physical 170
   - *of a play* 599
   personate 599
   voluntary 680
   statute 697
   in the – 680, 947
   - *a part feign* 544
   - *one's part* 625, 926
   - *upon*
      physical 170
      mental 615
      take steps 680
   - *up to* 772
   - *well one's part* 944
   - *without author-ity* 738
acting *deputy* 759
actinic 420
actinometer 445
action *physical* 170
   voluntary **680**
   battle 720
   law 969
   line of – 692
   put in – 677
   suit the – to the word 550
   thick of the – 682
activate 171
actionable 964
active *physical* 171

voluntary 682
- *service* 722
- *thought* 457
activity 682
actor
   impostor 548
   player 599
   agent 690
   affectation 855
Acts *record* 551
   Apostolic 985
actual *existing* 1
   present 118
   real 494
actuary 85, 811
actuate 176, 615
actum est 729
acu tetigisti, rem 465, 494
acuity 253
aculeated 253
acumen 498
acuminated 253
acupuncture 260
acustics 402
acute *energetic* 171
   physically violent 173
   pointed 253
   physically sensible 375
   musical tone 410
   perspicacious 498
   cunning 702
   strong feeling 821
   morally painful 830
   - *angle* 244
   - *ear* 418
   - *note* 410
acutely 31
acuteness 465
ad
   - *eundem* 27
   - *hominem* 79
   - *infinitum* 105
   - *instar* 82
   - *interim* 106
   - *lib* 705
   - *rem* 23
A.D. 106
adage 496
adagio *music* 415
   slow 275
Adam *sin* 945
   - *'s apple* 250
adamant 159, 323
adapt 23, 27
   - *oneself to* 82
adaptable
   conformable 82

useful 644
add *increase* 35
   join 37
   numerically 85
   - *up* 811
addendum 39
adder 913
addict *habit* 613
adding machine 85
additament 39
addition
   extrinsical 6
   increase 35
   adjunction **37**
   thing added 39
   arithmetical 85
addle *barren* 169
   incomplete 730
   abortive 732
   - *the wits,* 475, 503
addlehead 501
addleheaded 499
address
   residence 189
   direction 550
   speech 582
   speak to 586
   skill 698
   request 765
   - *oneself to* 673
addresses
   courtship 902
addressful 894
adduce
   bring to 288
   evidence 467
addulce 834
ademption 789
adenoid 250
adenology 329
adept 700
adequate *power* 157
   sufficient 639
   for a purpose 644
adhere *stick* 46
   - *to* 604a, 613
   - *to an obligation* 772
   - *to a duty* 926
adherent
   follower 711
adhesive, 46, 327, 352
adhibit 677
adhortation 695
adieu *departure* 293
   loss 776
adipocere 356
adipose 355
adit *orifice* 260
   conduit 350

passage 627
adjacent 197
adjection 37
adjective 39
adjoin 197, 199
adjourn 133
adjudge 480
adjudicate 480
adjunct
   thing added **39**
   accompaniment 88
   aid 707
   auxiliary 711
adjuration 535, 536
adjure 765, 768
adjust *adapt* 23
   equalize 27
   order 58
   prepare 673
   settle 723, 762
   - *differences* 774
adjutage 260, 350
adjutant
   auxiliary 711
   military 745
adjuvant *helping* 707
   auxiliary 711
admeasurement 466
adminicle 467
administer
   utilize 677
   conduct 693
   exercise authority 737
   distribute 786
   - *correction* 972
   - *oath* 768
   - *sacrament* 998
   - *to aid* 707
   give 784
administration of justice 965
administrative 737, 965
administrator 694
admirable 648, 744
admiral 745
Admiralty, court of – 966
admirari, nil – 871, 932
admiration
   wonder 870
   love 897
   respect 928
   approval 931
admired disorder 59
admirer 897
admissible

aery 317
Æsculapius 662
Æsop 846
æsthetic
　sensibility 375
　beauty 845
　taste 850
æstival 125
æternum　servans
　sub pectore vul-
　nus 919
ætiology [*see* etiol-
　ogy]
afar 196
affable 879, 894
affair *event* 151
　topic 454
　business 625
　battle 720
　love 902, 903
　– of honour 720
affaires, charge d' –
　758
affaire de coeur 897
affect *relate to* 9
　tend to 176
　qualify 469
　feign 544
　touch 824
　desire 865
　love 897
affectation **855**
affected with
　feeling 821
　disease 655
affectibility 822
affecting 830
affection 821, 897
affections **820**
affettuoso 415
affiance 768, 858
affianced 897, 903
affiche 531
affidation 769
affidavit
　affirmation 535
　record 551
　lawsuit 969
affiliation
　relation 9
　kindred 11
　attribution 155
affine 116
affinitive 9
affinity 9, 17
　mate 905
affirmation **535**, 488
affix *add* 37
　sequel 39
　fasten 43
　letter 561

afflation 349
afflatus 349,　597,
　985
afflict 830
　– with illness 655
affliction *pain* 828
　infliction 830
　adversity 735
affluence
　sufficiency 639
　prosperity 734
　wealth 803
affluent *river* 348
afflux 286
afford *supply* 784
　wealth 803
　yield 810
　sell for 812
　– aid &c. 707
afforestation 371
affranchise
　make free of 748
　liberate 750
affray 720
affreet 980
affriction 331
affright 860
affront *molest* 830
　provocation 900
　insult 929
　– danger 861
affuse 337
afield 186
afire 382
afloat *extant* 1
　unstable 149
　going on 151
　ship 273
　navigation 267
　ocean 341
　news 532
　preparing 673
　keep oneself – 734
　set – *publish* 531
afoot *on hand* 625
　preparing 673
　astir 682
afore 116
aforementioned 116
aforesaid
　preceding 62
　repeated 104
　prior 116
aforethought 611
aforetime 116
afraid 860
　be – *irresolute* 605
　– to say *uncertain*
　475
afresh 104, 123
Afric heat 382

Afrikander 57
afrite 980
aft 235
after *in order* 63
　in time 117
　too late 135
　rear 235
　pursuit 622
　be – *intention* 620
　pursuit 622
　go – *follow* 281
　– all *for all that* 30
　qualification 469
　on the whole 476
　– time 133
after acceptation
　516
after-age 124
after-clap 509
after-crop 65, 168
after-dinner 117
after-glow 40, 65,
　420
after-growth 65
after-life 152
aftermath
　sequel 65
　fertile 168
　profit 775
aftermost 235
afternoon 126
　– farmer 683
after-part 65, 235
after-piece 599
after-taste 65, 390
after-thought
　thought 451
　memory 505
　change of mind
　607
after-time 121
afterwards 117
age 745
agacerie 615
again 90, 104
　– and again 136
　come – *periodic* 138
　fall off – 661
　live – 660
against
　counteraction 179
　anteposition 237
　provision 673
　voluntary opposi-
　tion 708
　chances – 473
　declaim – 932
　false witness – 934
　go – 708
　set – *actively* 898
　set one's face –

764, 932
stand　up　–　*resist*
　719
raise &c. one's
　voice – 489
　– one's will 744
　–　one's　expecta-
　tion 508
　– the grain *difficult*
　704
　painful 830
　dislike 867
　– the stream 704
　–　the　time　when
　510
　– one's will 744
　– one's wishes 603
agamist 904
agape *open* 260
　curious 455
　expectant 507
　wonder 870
Agapemone 827,
　897
agate 847
age *time* 106
　period 108
　long time 110
　era 114
　present time 118
　oldness 124
　advanced life **128**
　of – 131
　from age to – 112
age quod agis! 682
agency
　physical **170**
　instrumentality
　631
　means 632
　employment 677
　voluntary action
　680
　direction 693
　commission 755
agenda 625, 626
agent *physical* 153
　intermediary 228
　voluntary **690**
　consignee 759
　– provocateur 615
agentship 755
ages: for – 110
　– ago 122
agglomerate 46, 72
agglutinate 46
aggrandize
　in degree 35
　in bulk 194
　honour 873
aggravate

increase 35
vehemence 173
exaggerate 549
render worse 659
distress 835
exasperate 900
aggravating 830
aggravation 835
aggregate 50, 72, 84
aggregation 46
aggression 716
aggressor 726
aggrieve 649, 830
aggroup 72
aghast
  disappointed 509
  fear 860
  wonder 870
agile 274, 682
agio 813
agiotage 794
agitate move 315
  inquire 461
  activity 682
  excite the feelings
   824
  – a question 476
agitation [see agi-
  tate]
  changeableness
   149
  energy 171
  motion 315
  in – preparing 673
agitator leader 694
aglet 554
agley, gang – 732
aglow 382, 420
agnate 11
agnition 762
agnomen 564
agnostic 487
agnosticism 984,
  989
agnus Dei 993, 998
ago 122
  not long – 123
agog expectant 507
  desire 865
  wonder 870
agoing 682
  set – 707
agonism 720
agonizing 824, 830
agony 378, 828
  – of death 360
  – of excitement
   825
agrarian 371
agree accord 23
  concur 178

assent 488
concord 714
consent 762
compact 769
compromise 774
– in opinion 488
– with salubrity
  656
agreeable
  comfortable 82
  physically 377
  mentally 829
agreeably to 82
agreement 23 [see
  agree]
  compact 769
agrestic 371
agriculture 371
agronomy 371
aground fixed 150
  in difficulty 704
  failure 732
ague-fit 860
aguets, aux –
  expectation 507
  ambush 530
aguish cold 383
ah me! 839
aha! rejoicing 838
ahead 234, 280
  go – progression
   282
  shoot – transcur-
   sion 303
  activity 682
  rock – 665, 667
Ahrimanes 987, 980
aid 707, 906
  by the – of 631,
   632
aide-de-camp 711,
  745
aidless 160
aigrette 847
aiguille 253
aiguillette 747, 847
aiglet 847
ail 655, 828
aileron 267, 273
ailment 655
aim 278, 620, 675
  – a blow at 716
aimable 894
  faire l' – 897
aimer éperdument
  897
aimless without
  motive 615a
  chance 621
air unsubstantial 4
  broach 66

lightness 320
gas 334
atmospheric 338
wind 349
tune 415
appearance 448
refresh 689
demeanour 692
fashionable 852
beat the – 645
fill the – 404
fine – salubrity 656
fish in the – 645
fowls of the – 366
in the – 527
rend the – 404
take – 531
air-balloon 273
air base 728
air-commodore 745
aircraft 273, 726
air-drawn 515
airdrome 273
air-force 726
air-gun 727
airing 266
air-mail 273
airman 269
airmanship 698
air-marshal 745
air-passage 351
air-pipe 351
airport 273, 292,
  728
air-pump 349
air-raid 716
airs affectation 855
  pride 878
  vanity 880
  arrogance 885
air-shaft 351
air service 267
airship 273, 726
air-tight 261
airways 267
airworthy 273, 664
airy [see air]
  windy 349
  unimportant 643
  gay 836
  – hopes 858, 859
  give to – nothing
  a local habita-
  tion &c. 515
aisle passage 260
  way 627
  in a church 1000
ait 346
ajar open 260
  discordant 713
ajee 217

ajutage 260, 350
akimbo angular 244
  stand – 715
akin related 9
  consanguineous11
  similar 17
al fresco 220
alabaster white 430
alack! 839
alacrity willing 602
  active 682
  cheerful 836
Aladdin's lamp 993
alar 267
alarm warning 668
  notice of danger
   669
  fear 860
  cause for – 665
  give an – indicate
   550
alarmist 862
alarum 114, 550, 669
alas! 839
alate 267
alb 999
albeit 30
albert
  chain 847
albification 430
albinescence 430
albinism 430
albino 443
album 593, 596
albumen
  semi-liquid 352
  protein 357
Alcaic 597
alcaid 745
alcalde 745
alcazar 189
alchemy 144
alcohol 995
Alcoran 986
alcove 191, 252
Aldebaran 423
alderman 745
ale 298
alea, jacta est – 601
aleatory 665
Alecto 173
alectromancy 511
alehouse 189
  go to the – 959
alembic
  conversion 144
  vessel 191
  furnace 386
  laboratory 691
alentours 197
alert watchful 457,

459
active 682
alerte 669
aleuromancy 511
Alexandrine
  ornate style 577
  verse 597
alexandrite 848
alexipharmic 662
alexiteric 662
algebra 85
algid 383
algology 369
algorithm 85
alguazil 965
alias
  otherwise 18
  pseudonym 565
alibi 187
alien *irrelevant* 10
  foreign 57
  transfer 783
  gentile 989
alienable 783
alienate
  transfer 783
  estrange 44, 889
  set against 898
alienation
  mental – 503
alieni appetens
  grasping 865
  envious 921
  selfish 943
alienism 54
align 278
alight *stop* 265
  arrive 292
  descend 306
  on fire 382
alike 17
  share and share –
  778
aliment *food* 298
alimentary 662
– canal 350
alimentation
  aid 707
alimony
  property 780
  provision 803
  income 810
aliquot 51, 84
aliter visum, diis –
  601
alive
  living 359
  intelligent 498
  active 682
  cheerful 836
  be – with 102

keep – *continue*
  143
keep the memory
  – 505
look – 684
– to *attention* 457
  cognizant 490
  informed 527
  able 698
  sensible 822
alkahest 335
all *whole* 50
  complete 52
  generality 78
– absorbing 642
in – ages 112
– aboard 495
– agog 865
– in all 50
– along 106
– along of 154
– but 32
– colours 440
– considered 451,
  480
– day long 110
– devouring 190
in – directions 278
– engrossing 190
at – events *com-*
  pensation 30
  qualification 469
  true 494
  resolve 604
– fours *easy* 705
  cards 840
– in good time 152
– hail! *welcome* 292
  honour to 873
  celebration 883
  courtesy 894
– hands *everybody*
  78
on – hands 488
– of a dither 824
– of a heap 72
– knowing 976
– manner of *differ-*
  ence 15
  multiform 81
with – one's might
  686
– at once 113
– one 27, 866
– out 52
– over *end* 67
  universal 78
  destruction 162
  space 180
at – points 52
– in one's power

686
– powerful
  mighty 159
  God 976
in – quarters 180
with – respect 928
in – respects 52,
  494
– right! 922
– Saints' day 998
– searching 461
– seeing 976
on – sides 227
– sorts *diverse* 16a
  mixed 41
  multiform 81
– talk 4
– things to all
  men 894
– the time 106
at – times 136
– together 50
– ways 243, 279
– wise 976
– the world and
  his wife 78
of – work
  useful 644
  maid - 746
Allah 979
allay
  moderate 174
  pacify 723
  relieve 834
– *excitability* 826
allective 615
allege *evidence* 467
  assert 535
  plea 617
allegiance 743, 926
allegory 464, 521,
  594
allegro *music* 415
  cheerful 836
allelujah 990
allemande 840
all-embracing 76
alleviate 174, 834
alley *court* 189
  passage 26
  way 627
alliance *relation* 9
  kindred 11
  physical co-opera-
  tion 178
  voluntary co-oper-
  ation 709
  party 712
  union 714
allied to *like* 17
alligation 43

allign 278
alliteration
  similarity 17
  style in writing
  577
  poetry 597
allocation 60, 786
allocution 586
allodium *free* 748
  property 780
allopathy 662
alloquy 586
allot *arrange* 60
  distribute 786
  due 924
allow *assent* 488
  admit 529
  permit 760
  consent 762
  give 784
  – to have one's
  own way 740
allowable 760, 924
allowance
  qualification 469
  gift 784
  allotment 786
  discount 813
  salary 973
  with grains of –
  485
  make – for *forgive*
  918
  vindicate 937
alloy *mixture* 41
  combination 48
  debase 659
allude *hint* 514
  mean 516
  refer to 521
  latent 526
  inform 527
allure *move* 615
  create desire 865
alluring 829
allusive
  relative 9
alluvial *level* 213
  land 342
  plain 344
alluvium
  deposit 40
  land 342
  soil 653
ally *combine* 48
  auxiliary 711
  friend 891
alma mater 542
almanac
  list 86
  chronometry 114

record 551
almighty 157
Almighty, the – 976
almoner
  treasurer 801
  giver 784
  church officer 996
almonry 802
almost *nearly* 32
  not quite 651
  – all 50
  – *immediately* 132
alms *gift* 784
  benevolence 906
  worship 990
almshouse 189, 666
almsman 785
Alnaschar's dream
  515, 858
aloes 395
aloft 206
alogy 497
alone *single* 87
  unaided 706
  let – *not use* 678
  not restrain 748
along 200
  get – *progress* 282
  go – *depart* 293
  go – with *concur*
  178
  assent 488
  co-operate 709
  – of *caused by* 154
  – with *added* 37
  together 88
  by means of 631
alongside *near* 197
  parallel 216
  laterally 236
aloof *distant* 196
  high 206
  secluded 893
  stand – *inaction*
  681
  refuse 764
  cautious 864
alopecia 226
aloud 404
  think – 589
  naïveté 703
Alp 206
alpenstock 215
Alpha 66
  – and Omega 50
alphabet
  beginning 66
  letters 561
alphabetarian 541
alphabeticize 60
alphitomancy 511

alpine *high* 206
Alpine Club 268, 305
already
  antecedently 116
  even now 118
  past time 122
Alsatia 791, 945
also 37
altar 903, 1000
alter 140
  – the case 468
  – one's course 279
alter ego *similar* 17
  auxiliary 711
  deputy 759
  friend 890
alterable 149
alteram partem,
  audire – 468, 922
alterative
  substitute 634
  remedy 662
altercation 713
altered *worn* 688
  – for the worse 659
alternate
  reciprocal 12
  sequence 63
  discontinuous 70
  periodic 138
  changeable 149
  oscillate 314
alternative
  substitute 147
  choice 609
  plan 626
although
  compensation 30
  counteraction 179
  unless 469
altiloquence 577
altimetry
  height 206
  angle 244
  measurement 466
altitude *height* 206
  – and azimuth 466
alto 410, 416
  – part 415
alto-rilievo 250, 557
altogether 50, 51
  nude 226
altruism 910, 942
altruist 906
alum 397
alumnus 541
alveolus 252
always
  uniformly 16
  generally 78
  during 106

perpetually 112
  habitually 613
a.m. 114, 125
amability 829, 894
amah 753
amain 173, 684
amalgam, -ate 41,
  48
amalgamation 709
Amalthæa's horn
  639
amantium iræ 918
amanuensis 553,
  590
amaranthine 112
amari aliquid
  bad 649
  imperfect 651
  painful 830
amaritude 395
amass *whole* 50
  collect 72
  store 636
amateur *volunteer*
  602
  layman 699
  taste 850
  votary 865
amatory 897
amaurosis 442
amaze 870
amazingly 31
Amazon
  woman 374
  warrior 726
  courage 861
ambages
  convolutions 248
  circumlocution
  573
  circuit 629
ambagious 573
ambassador
  messenger 534
  representative 758
  recall of – s 713
amber 356*a*
  – colour 436
ambidexter
  right and left 238
  fickle 607
  clever 698
ambient 227
ambigu 41
ambiguas spargere
  voces
  uncertain 475
  misteach 538
  false 544
  cunning 702
ambiguous

uncertain 475
  unintelligible 519
  equivocal 520
  obscure 571
ambiloquy 520
ambit 230
ambition 620, 865
ambivalence 605,
  708
amble 266
ambo *school* 542
  pulpit 1000
ambo, Arcades –
  alike 17
  friends 890
  bad men 949
ambrosia 298
ambrosial 394, 490
ambulance
  vehicle 272
  hospital 662
ambulation 266
ambuscade 530
ambush **530,** 667
  lie in – 528
âme – **de boue** 949
  – damnée
  catspaw 711
  servant 746
  servile 886
  bad man 949
  – qui vive 101, 187
ameer 875
ameliorate 658
amen *assent* 488
  submission 725
  content 831
amenable 177, 602,
  926
  not – to reason 608
amend 658
amendatory 20
amende honorable
  952
amends
  compensation 50
  atonement 952
  reward 973
amenity 829, 894
amentia 503
amerce 974
American organ 417
Americanism 563
amethyst
  purple 437
  jewel 847
amiable
  courteous 894
  loving 897
  kind 906
amicable 707, 888

moral 828
angular 244
  – velocity 264
angularity 244
angusta domi, res
  – 804
angustation 203
anhelation 688
anhydrate 340
anhydrous 340
aniline dyes 437
anility 128, 499
animadvert
  consider 451
  attend to 457
  reprehend 932
animal 366
  female – 374
  – cries 412
  – economy 359
  – gratification 377
  – life 364
  – physiology 368
  – spirits 836
  – and vegetable
    kingdom 357
animalcule 193, 366
animalism
  sensuality 954
animality 364
animate
  induce 615
  excite 824
  enliven 836
animation
  life 359
  animality 364
  activity 682
  vivacity 836
  suspended – 823
animism 984
animo, ex – 602
  quo – 620
animosity
  dislike 867
  enmity 889
  hatred 898
  anger 900
animus
  willingness 602
  intention 620
  desire 865
ankle 244
  – deep 208, 209
anklet 847
ankylosis 150
annalist 114, 553
annals
  chronology 114
  record 551
  account 594

anneal 673
annex
  addition 37
  adjunct 39
  junction 43
  acquire 775
Annie Oakley 815
annihilate 2, 162
anniversary 138
anno 106
Anno Domini
  era 106
  old age 124
annotation 522, 550
annotator 524
  scholar 492
  interpreter 524
  editor 595
annotto 434
announce
  predict 511
  inform 527
  publish 531
  assert 535
announcer 527
annoy
  molest 649, 907
  disquiet 830
annoyance 828
  source of – 830
annual *periodic* 138
  plant 367
  book 593
annuity 810
annul 162, 750
annular 247
annunciate 527
annus magnus 108
anodyne
  lenitive 174
  remedial 662
  relief 834
anoint *coat* 223
  lubricate 332
  oil 355
anointed
  deity 976
  king 745
anomaly 59, 83
  disorder 59
  irregularity 83
anon 132
anonymous 565
anopsia 442
anorexy 866
another
  different 15
  repetition 104
  – story 468, 526
  go upon – tack 607
  – time 119

answer
  to an inquiry **462**
  confute 479
  solution 522
  succeed 731
  pecuniary profit
    775
  pleadings 969
  require an – 461
  – for *deputy* 759
  promise 768
  go bail 806
  I'll – for it 535
  – the helm 745
  – the purpose 731
  – to *correspond* 9
  – one's turn 644
answerable
  agreement 23
  liable 177
  bail 806
  duty 926
  censurable 932
ant 690
Antæus 159, 192
antagonism
  difference 14
  physical 179
  voluntary 708
  enmity 889
antagonist 710, 891
antagonistic 24
antarctic 237
antecedence 62, 116
antecedent 64
antechamber 191
ante Christum 106
antedate 115
antediluvian 124
antelope 274
antemundane 124
antenna 379
anteposition 62
anterior
  in order 62
  in time 116
  in place 234
  – to *reason* 477
anteroom 191
antevert 706
anthem 990
anthemion 847
anthology
  book 533
  collection 596
  poem 597
anthracite 388
anthropoid 372
anthropology
  zoology 368
  mankind 372

anthropomancy 511
anthropophagi 913
anthroposcopy 511
anthroposophy 372
antic 840
anti-aircraft gun
  564, 727
antichambre,
  faire – 133
antichristian 984,
  989
antichronism 115
anticipate
  anachronism 115
  priority 116
  future 121
  early 132
  expect 507
  foresee 510
  prepare 673
  hope 858
  in – 116
anticlimax
  decrease 36
  bathos 497, 853
anticlinal 217
anticyclone 265
antidote 662
antigropelos 225
antilogarithm 84
antilogy 477
antimony 663
Antinomian 984
antinomy 964
Antinous 845
antiparallel 217
antipathy 867, 898
antiphon *music* 415
  answer 462
  worship 990
antiphrasis 563
antipodes
  difference 14
  distance 196
  contraposition
    237
antipoison 660
antiquary
  past times 122
  scholar 492
  historian 553
antiquas vias,
  stare super –
  613, 670
antiquated 128
antique 124
antiquity 122
antiscriptural 984
antiseptic 652, 662
antisocial 911
antistrophe 597

relation 9
relevancy 23
closeness 199
paraphrase 522
appraise 466, 812
appreciate
 realize 450, 451
 measure 466
 judge 480
 know 490
 taste 850
 approve 931
apprehend
 believe 484
 know 490
 fear 860
 seize 789
apprehension
 idea 453
 taking 789
apprentice 541
 – *oneself* 676
apprenticeship 539, 673
apprise 527
apprised of 490
approach
 of time 121
 impend 152
 nearness 197
 move **286**
 path 627
approaching 9
approbation **931**
appropinquation 286
appropriate *fit* 23
 peculiar 79
 expedient 646
 assign 786
 take 789
 steal 791
approval 488, 931
 on – 609
approximate
 related to 9
 resemble 17
 in mathematics 85
 nearness 197
 approach 286
appulse *meeting* 199
 collision 276
 approach 286
 convergence 290
appurtenance
 part 51
 component 56
 belongings 780
 accompaniment 88
appurtenant 9

après nous le
 déluge 943
apricot *colour* 439
April
 – *fool* 547, 857
 make an – *fool of* 545
 – *showers* 149
apron *extension* 39
 clothing 225
 defence 717
 canonicals 999
àpropos [*see* à]
aprotype 591
apse 1000
apt *consonant* 23
 tendency 176, 177
 docile 539
 willing 602
 clever 698
aqua-fortis 335
aquamarine 435
aquarium 370
Aquarius 348, 636
aquatic *water* 337
aquatics 267
aquatinta 558
aqueduct 350
aqueous 337
aquiline 244
A.R. 106
Arab *wanderer* 268
 horse 271
 street – 876
araba 272
arabesque 847
Arabian
 – *perfumes* 400
 – *nights* 515
arable 371
arbalest 727
arbiter *critic* 480
 director 694
 adviser 695
 judge 967
 – *elegantiarum*
 revels 840
 taste 850
 fashion 852
arbitrage 794
arbitrament 480
 judgment 480
 – *of the sword* 722
arbitrary
 without relation 10
 irregular 83
 wilful 606
 capricious 608
 authoritative 737
 severe 739

insolent 885
 lawless 964
 – *power* 739
arbitrate
 adjudicate 480
 mediate 724
arbitration
 court of – 966
 submit to – 774
arbitrium, ad – 600
arbor 215, 312
arborescent
 ramifying 242
 rough 256
 trees 367
arboriculture 371
arbour *abode* 189
 summer-house 191
 plaisance 840
arc 245
 heat 382
arcade *street* 189
 curve 245
 gateway 260
Arcades ambo
 alike 17
 friends 890
 bad men 949
Arcadia 827, 981
Arcadian 703, 946
arcanum 533
arch *great* 31
 support 215
 curve 245
 convex 250
 concave 252
 clever 498
 cunning 702
 triumphal – 733, 883
archæologist
 pastimes 122
 scholar 492
archæology 122
archaic *old* 124
archaism 122, 563
archangel 977
archbishop 996
archbishopric 995
archdeacon 996
archduchy 181
archduke 745
archegenesis 161
archer 726
archery 840
Arches, court of – 966, 995
archetype 22
archetypal 20
Archeus 359

archfiend 978
archiater 695
archiepiscopal 995
archimandrite 996
archipelago 346
architect 164, 690
architectonic 161
architecture
 arrangement 60
 construction 161
 fabric 329
 ornament 847
architrave 210
archive 551
archlute 417
archon *ruler* 745
 deputy 759
 judge 967
archtraitor 941
arctic *northern* 237
 cold 383
arctics 225
arcuation 245
ardent *fiery* 382
 eager 682
 feeling 821
 loving 897
 – *expectation* 507
 – *imagination* 515
ardet, proximus – 665, 667
ardour *vigour* 574
 activity 821
 feeling 821
 desire 865
arduous 704
area 181, 182
arefaction 340
arena *space* 180
 region 181
 field of view 441
 field of battle **728**
arenaceous 330
areola 247
areolar 219
areometer 321
Areopagus 966
arête 253
aretinism 961
aretology 926
Argand lamp 423
argent 430
argillaceous 324
argosy 273
argot 563
argonaut 269
argue *evidence* 467
 reason 476
 indicate 550
 dissection 595
argument *disagree-*

give 784
allot 786
– as cause 155
– a duty 926
– places 60
assignat 800
assignation 892
place of – 74
assignee *donee* 785
assimilate
uniform 16
resemble 17
imitate 19
agree 23
transmute 144
assist 707
– at 186
assistant 711
assister *be present*
186
assize *measure* 466
tribunal 966
justice of – 967
associate *mix* 41
unite 43
collect 72
accompany 88
colleague 690
auxiliary 711
friend 890
– with 892
association
[*see* associate]
relation 9
combination 48
co-operation 709
partnership 712
– of ideas
intellect 450
thought 451
intuition 477
hint 514
– football 840
assoil *acquit* 970
assonance
music 413
poetry 597
assort *arrange* 60
assortment 72, 75
assuage 174, 834
assuetude 613
assume *believe* 484
suppose 514
falsehood 544
take 789
insolent 885
right 924
– authority 737
– a character 554
– command 741
– a form 144

– the offensive 716
assumed name 565
assumption
[*see* assume]
severity 739
hope 858
usurpation 925
assurance
speculation 156
certainty 474
belief 484
assertion 535
promise 768
security 771
hope 858
vanity 880
insolence 885
make – double
sure *safe* 664
caution 864
assuredly
assent 488
assythment 973
astatic 320
asterisk 550
astern 235
put the engines –
275
fall – 283
asteroid 318
Asteroth 979
asthenia 160
astigmatism 443
astir 682
set – 824
astonish 870
astonished
– at nothing 871
astonishing
great 31
astound *excite* 824
fear 860
surprise 870
astra, sic itur ad –
360, 873
Astræa 922
astraddle 215
astragal 847
astral 318
– body 717, 992
– influence 601
– plane 317
astray 475, 495
go – *deviate* 279
sin 945
astriction 43
astride 215
astringent 195
astrolabe 466
astrologer 994

astrology 511
astromancy 511
astronomy 318
astute 498, 702
asunder 44, 196
as poles – 237
asylum *hospital* 663
retreat 666
defence 717
asymptote 290
at, be – 620
up and – them!
716
ataghan 727
atavism 144, 163
ataxia 158
atelier 556, 691
athanasia 112
Athanasian creed
983a
athanor 386
atheism 989
atheist 487
Athenae 979
Athens, owls to –
641
athirst 865
athlete *strong* 159
gladiator 726
athletic *strong* 159
strenuous 686
– sports
contest 720
games 840
athwart
oblique 217
crossing 219
opposing 708
Atkins, Tommy 726
Atlantis 515
Atlas *arrangement*
60
list 86
strength 159
support 215
maps 554
atmosphere
circumambience
227
air 338
painting 556
atmospheric blue
438
atoll 346
atom *small* 32, 193
atomic energy 157
atomizer 336
atoms
crush to – 162
atomy 193

atonement
restitution 790
expiation **952**
amends 973
religious 976
atony 160
atrabilious 837
atramentous 431
atrium 191
atrocity
malevolence 907
vice 945
guilt 947
atrophy
shrinking 195
disease 655
decay 659
atropos 601
attach *join* 43
love 897
legal 969
– importance to
642
attaché
employé 746
diplomatic 758
– case 191
attack *singing* 580
disease 655
assault **716**
debauch 961
attaghan 727
attain *arrive* 292
succeed 731
– majority 131
attainable 470
attainder
taint 651
at law 971
attainment
knowledge 490
learning 539
skill 698
attar 400
attempter 41, 174
attempered 820
attempt 675
vain – 732
– impossibilities
471
attend
accompany 88
be present 186
follow 281
apply the mind
457
medically 662
aid 707
serve 746
– to business 625
– to orders 743

attendance on
dance – 886
attendant
[*see* attend]
attention 457
care 459
respect 928
attract – 882
call to – 457
call – to 550
give – 418
pay –s to 894
pay one's –s to
902
attenuate
decrease 36
weaken 158
reduce 195
rarefy 322
attenuated 203
attest
bear testimony 467
affirm 535
adjure 768
attested copy 771
attic *simple* 42
garret 191
summit 210
style 578
wit 842
taste 850
Attila 913
attire 225
attitude
circumstance 8
situation 183
posture 240
attitudinarian 882
attitudinize 855
attollent 307
attorney
consignee 758
at law 968
power of – 755
attract
bring towards 288
induce 615
allure 865
excite love 897
– the attention
457
visible 446
attraction
[*see* attract]
natural power 157
bring towards
288
attractive
[*see* attract]
pleasing 829
beautiful 845

attrahent 288
attribute
speciality 79
accompaniment
88
power 157
–s of the Deity 976
– to 155
attribution 155
attrite 330
attrition 330, 331
attroupement 72
attune *music* 415
prepare 673
attuned to
habit 613
attunement 23
auburn 433
A.U.C. 106
auction 796, 840
auctioneer 758, 796
auctorial 599
audacity
courage 861
rashness 863
insolence 885
audible 402
become – 418
scarcely – 405
audience
hearing 418
conversation 588
before an – 599
audire alteram
partem
counter-evidence
468
right 922
justice 939
audit
numeration 85
examination 461
accounts 811
auditive 418
auditor
hearer 418
accountant 811
auditorium 189, 588
auditory
sound 402
hearing 418
theatre 599
– *apparatus* 418
au fait 698
au fond 5
auf wiedersehen
293
Augean
– stable 653
– task 704
auger 262

aught 51
for – one cares
unimportant 643
indifferent 866
for – one knows
ignorance 491
conjecture 514
augment
increase 35
thing added 39
expand 194
augur 513
– well 858
augurate 511
augury 512
august 873
Augustinian 996
auk 366
auld lang syne 122
aulic council 696
aumbry 1000
aunt 11
aura *wind* 349
sensation 380
aurea mediocritas
628
aureate 436
aureola 420
aureole 420, 873
aureolin 436
auribus, arrectis –
418
auricular *hearing*
418
clandestine 528
– confession 998
auri sacra fames
819
aurist 662
aurora
dawn 125
light 420, 423
twilight 422
– *australes* 423
– *borealis* 423
Auroral 236
auscultation 418
auspice *omen* 512
auspices
influence 175
prediction 511
protection 664
direction 693
aid 707
under the – of 693,
737
auspicious
opportune 134
prosperous 734
hopeful 858
austerity

harsh taste 395
severe 739
discourteous 895
ascetic 955
pietism 988
austral 237
austromancy 511
authentic 467
certain 474
true 494
authentication
evidence 467
security 771
author 164, 593
projector 626
dramatic – 599
– of our being 976
– of evil 978
– 's proof 591
authoritative 474,
741
authority
testimony 467
sage 500
informant 527
power **737**
permission 760
right 924
ensign of – 747
person in – 745
do upon one's own
– 600
authorized *due* 924
legalized 963
authorship
production 161
style 569
writing 590
autobiography 594
autocar 272
autochthonous 188
autocracy 737, 739
autocrat 745
autocratic 600, 737
auto-da-fe 384, 972
autograph 550, 590
Autolycus *thief* 792
pedlar 797
automaniac 504
automatic 601, 633
- pistol 727
- writing 992
automaton 554, 601
automobile 272
automobilist 268
automotive 266
autonomasia 521
autonomy 737, 748
autopsy
post-mortem 363
vision 441

autoptical 446, 535
autotype 558
autumn 126
auxiliary **711**
  additional 34
  helpful 707
  – forces 726
avail *benefit* 618
  useful 644
  succeed 731
  of no – 645
  – oneself of 677
avalanche *fall* 306
  snow 383
  redundance 641
avaler les couleu-
  vres 725, 886
avant-courier 64,
  673
avant-propos 64
avarice 819
avast! *stop* 142, 265
  desist 624
  forbid 761
avatar *change* 140
  deity 976
  idol 991
avaunt! 297, 449
ave! *honour* 873
  courtesy 894
Ave maria 990
avenge 919
avenue
  plantation 371
  way 627
aver 535
average *mean* 29,
  628
  médiocre 651
  – circumstances
  736
  take an – 466
Averni, facilis de-
  scensus – 217,
  665
Avernus 982
averruncate 297,
  301
aversion *unwilling-
  ness* 603
  dislike 867
  hate 898
avert 706
  – the eyes 442
aviary 370
aviation 267
aviator 269
avidity *avarice* 819
  desire 865
airette 273
avile 932, 934

avion 273
aviso 532
avocation 625
avoidance **623**
avoidless 474, 601
avoirdupois 319
avolation 623, 671
avouch 535, 768
avow *assent* 488
  disclose 529
  assert 535
avulsion 44, 301
avuncular 11
await *future* 121
  be kept waiting
  133
  impend 152
  expect 507
awake *attentive* 457
  careful 459
  intelligent 498
  active 682
  – to life *immortal*
  360
awaken *inform* 527
  excite 824
  – the attention 457
  – the memory 505
award *adjudge* 480
  give 784
aware 490
away 187, 196
  break – 623
  fly – 293
  move – 287
  take – from 789
  get &c. – 671
  throw &c. –
  eject 297
  reject 610
  waste 638
  relinquish 782
  – from *unrelated* 10
  – with! 930, 932
  do – with *undo* 681
  abrogate 756
awe *fear* 860
  wonder 870
  respect 928
aweless *fearless* 861
  insolent 885
  disrespectful 329
awful 31, 860
  – silence 403
awhile 111
awkward
  inelegant 579
  inexpedient 647
  unskilful 699
  difficult 704
  painful 830

  ugly 846
  vulgar 851
  ridiculous 853
  – squad 701
awl 262
awn 253
awning 223, 424
awry *oblique* 217
  distorted 243
  evil 619
axe *edge tool* 253
  impulse 276
  weapon 727
  for beheading 975
  have an – to grind
  702
Axinomancy 511
axiom 496
axiomatic 474
axis *support* 215
  centre 222
  rotation 312
axle 312
  wheel and – 633
axle load 466
axletree 215
ay 488
ayah 746, 753
aye *ever* 112
  yes 488
azimuth
  horizontal 213
  direction 278
  measurement 466
  – circle 212
azoic 358
azote 663
azotic 657
azure 438
azygous *single* 87

B

Baal 979, 986
Babbittry 851
babble *rivulet* 348
  faint sound 405
  unmeaning 517
  talk 584, 588
babbler 501
babbling
  foolish 499
babe 129
  innocent as the –
  unborn 946
Babel *confusion* 59
  discord 414
  tongues 560
  jargon 563
  loquacity 584

baboon 846
baby *infant* 129
  fool 501
  – linen 225
babyhood 127
babyish 499
baccarat 840
bacchanals 959
Bacchus 979
  drink 959
bachelor 904
  – of arts 492
  – girl 374
bacillus 193
back *rear* 235
  shoulder 250
  aid 707
  behind one's –
  latent 526
  hidden 528
  come – 292
  give – 790
  fall – *relapse* 661
  go – 283
  go – from *retract*
  773
  have at one's – 215
  hold – *avoid* 623
  keep – *reserve* 636
  look – 505
  on one's – *impo-
  tent* 158
  horizontal 213
  failure 732
  pat on the –
  incite 615
  encourage 861
  approve 931
  pay – *retaliate* 718
  put – *deteriorate*
  659
  restore 660
  send – 764
  take – again 790
  carry one's
  thoughts – 505
  some time – 122
  spring – 277
  trace – 505
  turn – 283
  turn one's – 283
  turn one's – upon
  repel 289
  inattention 458
  avoid 623
  oppose 508
  seclusion 893
  discourtesy 895
  disrespect 929
  contempt 930
  set one's – against

worse than bite 885
barker 767
barleycorn
little 193
Barleycorn, Sir John - 298
barm *leaven* 320
bubbles 353
Barmecide feast 956
barmy 320, 503
barn 189
barnacles 445
barndoor fowl 366
barograph 206, 338
barometer *air* 338
measure 466
consult the - 463
baron *peer* 875
husband 903
court - 966
- of the Exchequer 967
baronet 875
baronial 878
baroque 853
baroscope 338
barouche 272
barque 273
barrack 189
barracoon 717
barrage 407, 717
barratry 940
barred 219, 440
barrel 191, 249
- *organ* 417
barren 169, 645
barricade *fence* 232
obstacle 706
defence 717
prison 752
barrier [*see* barricade]
barring *save* 38
excluding 55
except 83
- out *resist* 719
disobey 742
barrister 968
revising - 967
barrow
mound 206
vehicle 272
grave 363
barter
reciprocate 12
interchange 148
commerce **794**
barytone 408
basal 215

bas-bleu
scholar 492
affectation 855
base
site 183
lowest part **211**
support 215
bad 649
cowardly 862
shameful 874
servile 886
dishonourable 940
vicious 945
- ball 840
- born 876
- coin 800
- note 408
- of operations
plan 626
attack 716
- viol 417
baseball diamond 213
baseboard 211
based on *ground of belief* 467
baseless 2, 4
basement *cellar* 191
lowest part 207, 211
bash 276
bashaw 739, 745
bashful 881
bashi bazouk 726
basilica 1000
basilisk *sight* 441
cannon 737
serpent 949
basin *dock* 189
vessel 191
hollow 252
plain 344
basinet 717
basis
lowest part 211
support 215
preparation 673
bask *physical enjoyment* 377
warmth 382
prosperity 734
moral enjoyment 827
basket 191
- of 190
bas-relief 250, 557
bass *music* 415
- note 408
- viol 417
basset horn 417
bassinet 191, 215

bassoon 417
basso-profondo 408
basso-rilievo 250, 557
bastard 545, 925
baste *beat* 276
punish 972
Bastille 752
bastinado 972
bastion 717
bat 276, 727
batch 25, 72
bate *diminish* 36
subtract 38
reduce price 813
bated breath
with - *faint sound* 405
expecting 507
hiding 528
whisper 581
humble 879
bath 337, 652
public -s 652
warm - 386
- room 191, 652
Bath chair 272
bathe *immerse* 300
plunge 310
vater 337
bathos 497
bathysphere 208
batik 440
batman 637
bâton *support* 215
sceptre 747
batrachian 366
betta 973
battalion 726
batten
feed 298
stage lighting 599
- down the hatches 261
- on 886
batter *destroy* 162
beat 276
battered 659, 688
battering-ram 276
battering-train 727
battery *electric* 153
artillery 726
guns 727
floating - 726
plant a - 716
battle 720, 722
half the - 642
win the - 731
- array *order* 60
prepare 673
war 722

- axe 727
- cruiser 726
- cry 550, 722
- field *arena* 728
- ground *discord* 713
- ship 726
- with *oppose* 708
battledore and shuttlecock
interchange 148
game 840
battlement 257, 717
battre
- la campagne
nonsense 497
diffuse style 573
excitable 825
- l'eau avec un bâton 645
- le fer sur l'enclume 134
- la générale 669
se - contre des moulins 645
ne - que d'une aile 683
battology
repeat 104
diffuse style 373
battue *pursuit* 622
attack 716
kill 361
bauble 643, 840
bavardage 517, 584
bawd 962
bawdy, - house 961
bawl 411
bawn 189
bay *concave* 252
gulf 343
cry 412
brown 433
at - *danger* 665
difficulty 704
defence 717, **719**
bring to - 716
- the moon 645
- window 260
bayadére 599
bayard 271
bayonet *kill* 361
attack 716
weapon 727
crossed -s 708
at the point of the - *war* 722
severity 739
coercion 744
bays *trophy* 733
crown 877

Column 1 (BAZ)

bazaar 799
B.C. 106
be 1
  – all and end all
    whole 50
    intention 620
    importance 642
  – off *depart* 293
    eject 297
    retract 773
  – it so 488
  – that as it may 30
beach 231, 342
beach comber 268
beacon 550, 663
bead 249
beadle *janitor* 263
  law officer 965
  church 996
beadledom 737
beadroll *list* 86
  prayers 990
  ritual 998
beads
  ornament 847
  tell one's – 990,
    998
beadsman
  servant 746
  clergy 996
beagle 366
beak *face* 234
  nose 250
  magistrate 967
beaker 161
beam *support* 215
  plank 236
  weigh 319
  light 420
  on – ends
  powerless 158
  horizontal 213
  side 236
  fail 732
  wonder 870
beaming
  beautiful 845
bean 276
beanfeast 840
bear *produce* 161
  sustain 215
  carry 270
  admit of 470
  suffer 821
  endure 826
  bring to – 677
  more than flesh
    and blood can –
    824
  unable to –
    excited 825

Column 2 (BEA)

dislike 867
– away 789
– away the bell
  648, 731
– the brunt 704,
  717
– the burden 625
– the cross 828
– company 88
– down 173, 885
– down upon 716
– false witness 544
– fruit *produce* 161
  useful 644
  success 731
  prosper 734
– a hand 680
– hard upon 649
– harmless 717
– ill 825
– off *deviate* 279
– on 215
– oneself 692
– out *evidence* 467
  vindicate 937
– pain 828
– the palm 33
– a sense 516
– through 707
– up *approach* 286
  persevere 604a
  relieve 834
  cheerful 836
– up against 719,
  861
– upon
  relevant 9, 23
  influence 175
– with
  tolerate 740
  permit 760
  take coolly 826
  forgive 918
bear
  savage 907
  surly 895
  had it been a – it
    would have bit-
    ten you 458
– garden
  disorder 59
  discord 713
  arena 728
– leader 540
– pit 370
– skin *cap* 225
  helmet 717
– with a sore back
  901
bearable 651
beard *hair* 205

Column 3 (BEA)

prickles 253
rough 256
defy 715
brave 861
insolence 885
pluck by the –
  disrespect 929
– the lion 604
beardless 127, 226
bearer 271, 363
bearing *relation* 9
  support 215
  direction 278
  meaning 516
  demeanour 692
– rein 706, 752
bearings
  circumstances 8
  situation 183
  armorial – 550
beast *animal* 366
  unclean 653
  discourteous 895
– of burden 271,
  690
beat *be superior* 33
  periodic 138
  region 181
  impulse 276
  surpass 303
  oscillate 314
  agitation 315
  crush 330
  sound 407
  line of pursuit 625
  path 627
  overcome 731
  strike 972
– about
  circuit 629
– the air 645
– against 708
– one's breast 839
– about the bush
  try for 463
  evade the point 477
  prevaricate 544
  diffuse style 573
– down *destroy* 162
  cheapen 794, 819
  insolent 885
– of drum
  music 416
  publish 531
  alarm 669
  wear 722
  command 741
  pomp 882
without – of
  drum 528
– into *teach* 537

Column 4 (BEC)

– off 717
– a retreat
  retire 283
  avoid 623
  submit 725
– time *clock* 114
  music 416
– up *churn* 352
– up against
  oppose 708
– up for *cater* 637
– up one's quarters
  seek 461
  visit 892
– up for recruits
  prepare 673
  aid 707
beaten track
  habit 613
  way 627
  leave the – 83
  tread the – 82
beatic 827
beatific 829, 981
beatification 827,
  987
beating high
  the heart – 824
beatitude 827
beau *man* 373
  fop 854
  admirer 897
– idéal 650, 845
– monde 852
beautify 845, 847
beautiless 846
beauty 845
beaver *hat* 225
becalm 265
because *cause* 153
  attribution 155
  answer 462
  reasoning 476
  motive 615
bechance 151
beck *rill* 348
  sign 550
  mandate 741
  at one's – *aid* 707
  obey 743
beckon *sign* 550
  motive 615
  call 741
becloud *dark* 421
  hide 528
become
  change to 144
  accord with 23
  behove 926
– of 151
becoming

accordant 23
proper 646
beautiful 845, 847
due 924
becripple 158
bed *lodgment* 191
    layer 204
    support 215
    garden 371
    marriage 903
    brought to – 161
    death – 360
    smooth the – of
        death 707
    go to – 265, 683
    keep one's – 655
    – of down 687
    – gown 255
    – maker 746
    – out 371
    – ridden 655
    – room 191
    – of roses 377, 734
    put to – with a
        shovel 363
    – time 126
bedarken 421
bedaub 223, 653
bedazzle 420
bedding 215
bedeck 847
bedel 965
bedesman
    [*see* beadsman]
bedevil *derange* 61
    sorcery 992
bedew 339
bedight 847
bedim 421, 422
bedizen *clothe* 225
    ornament 847
    vulgar 851
Bedlam
    – broke loose 59
    candidate for –
        504
be-dog 281
Bedouin 792
bedraggled 59
bedwarf 195
bee 690
    busy – 682
    swarm like –s 102
    – in one's bonnet
        503
    – in a bottle 407
    – line 246, 278
    –'s wax 352
beef-eater 726
beef-headed 499
beehive 250

Beelzebub 978
beer 298
beery 959
beetle *overhang* 206,
    214
    project 250
    blind as a – 442
    Colorado – 913
    – head 501
befall 151
befit *agree* 23
    expedient 646
    due 924, 926
befog 353, 528
befool *mad* 503
    deceive 545
befooled
    victimized 732
before *in order* 62
    in time 116
    presence 186
    in space 234
    precession 280
    preference 609
    set – one 525
    – Christ 106
    – long 132
    – mentioned 62,
        116
    – now 122
    – one's eyes 446,
        525
    – one's time 132
    – you could –turn
        round, – say
        Jack Robinson
        113
beforehand
    prior 116
    early 132
    foresight 510
    resolve – 611
befoul 653
befriend 707, 888
befuddlement 959
beg *Turk* 745
    ask 765
    – one's bread 765
    poor 804
    – leave 760
    – one's life 914
    – pardon 952
    – the question 477
beget 161
begetter 164, 166
beggar *idler* 683
    petitioner 767
    poor 804
    degrade 874
    low person 876
    sturdy – 792

– description 83,
    870
– my neighbour
    840
– on horseback 885
beggared
    bankrupt 808
beggarly *mean* 643
    vile 874
    vulgar 876
    servile 886
    – account of
        empty boxes
        640, 804
begging
    go a –
    too much 641
    useless 645
    offered 763
    free 748
    – letter 765
begilt 847
begin 66
    – again 104
beginner 541
beginning 66
begird 227, 229
beglerbeg 745
begone
    depart 293
    ejection 297
    abrogate 756
    – dull care 836
Begotten, the only
    – 976
begrime 653
begrudge
    unwilling 603
    refuse 764
    stingy 819
beguile *mislead* 495
    deceive 545
    reconcile 831
    – the time
    inaction 681
    amusement 840
beguine 996
begum 745, 875
behalf 618, 707
    in – of 759
behave oneself
    conduct 692
    fashion 852
    courtesy 894
behaviour 692
    on one's good –
        894, 944
behead 361, 972
behemoth 192
behest 741
behind

in order 63
in space 235
sequence 281
– the age 124, 491
– one's back 187
speak ill of – one's
    back 934
– the bars 751
– the scenes
    cause 153
    unseen 447
    cognizant 490
    latent 526
    hidden 528
    playhouse 599
    – time 133
behindhand
    late 133
    shortcoming 304
    adversity 735
    insolvent 808
behold 441, 457
beholden 916, 926
beholder 444
behoof 618
behoove 926
being 1, 3
    created – 366
    human – 372
    time – 106
Bel 979
belabour 276, 972
belated *late* 133
    ignorant 491
belaud 931
belay *join* 43
    restrain 706
belch 297
beldam 130, 913
beldame 173
beleaguer 716
bel esprit 844
belfry 206, 1000
Belial 978, 980
    sons of – 988
belie *deny* 536
    falsify 544
    contradict 708
belief **484**, 983
    easy of – 472
    hug a – 606
believe
    [*see* belief]
    suppose 514
    reason to – 472
    – who may 485
    not – one's senses
        870
believer
    religious 987
    true – 983*a*

belike 472
belittle
  decrease 36
  underestimate 482
  disparage 934
bell 417, 550
  alarm − 669
  bear away the −
  goodness 648
  success 731
  repute 873
  church − 350
  cracked − 408a
  passing − 363
  − book and candle
  swear 535
  curse 908
  spell 993
  rite 998
  − the cat 861
  − shape 249, 252
belladonna 663
belle 374, 854
  a la − étoile 220, 845
belles-lettres 560
belli, casus − 824
bellicose 720, 722
bellied 250
belligerent
  contentious 720
  warlike 722
  combatant 726
belling 412
bellman 354
bello, flagrante − 722
Bellona 722
bellow *loud* 404
  cry 411
  animal cry 412
  wail 839
bellows 349, 580
bells, peal of − 407
bellwether 64, 694
belly *receptacle* 191
  inside 221
  convex 250
  −ful 52, 639
  − god 957
  − timber 298
belomancy 511
belong to *related* 9
  component 56
  included 76
  attribute 157
  property 777, 780
  duty 926
beloved 897
below 207
  here − 318

[410]

− the mark 32
− par 34, 207
  bad 649
  indifferent 651
  discount 813
  ignoble 876
− its full strength 651
− stairs 207
belt *outline* 230
  ring 247
  strait 343
  swimming − 666
belting 633
Belus 979
belvedere 441
bemask 528
bemingle 41
bemire 653
bemoan 839
bemused 458
bench *support* 215
  council 696
  tribunal 966
Bench, King's − 752
bencher 968
bend *oblique* 217
  angle 244
  curve 245
  incline 278
  deviate 279
  depression 308
  circuit 311
  give 324
  submit 725
− backwards 235
− the bow 686
− the brows 932
− one's course 27
− the knee
  bow down 308
  submit 725
  humble 879
  servile 886
  courtesy 894
  respect 928
  worship 990
− one's looks upon 441
− the mind 457
− over 250
− to rules &c. 82
− sinister 874
− one's steps 622
− to *tend* 176
− towards 278
− to one's will 737
beneath 207
− one 940
− notice 643

Benedick 903
Benedictine 996
benediction
  gratitude 916
  approval 931
  worship 990
  nuptial − 903
benefaction 784
benefactor 816, **912**
benefice 995
beneficent 906
beneficial 648
− interest 780
beneficiary
  possessor 779
  receive 785
  clergy 996
benefit *good* 618
  use 644
  do good 648
  aid 707
  acquisition 775
  property 780
  benevolence 906
  reap the − of 131
benefits forgot 917
bene gesserit, quamdiu se − 926
benet 545
benevolence
  tax 812
  love 897
  kindness **906**
  universal − 910
Bengal heat 382
benighted
  dark 421
  ignorant 491
benign 656, 906
benignant 906
benison 618, 931
Benjamin's mess 33, 50
Benshie 979
bent *tendency* 176
  angle 244
  turn of mind 820
  desire 865
  fool to the top of one's − 856
− on *willing* 602
  resolved 604
  intention 620
  desirous 865
Benthamite 910
ben trovato
  likely 472
  imagination 515
  untruth 546
  wit 842

benumb
  insensible 376
  cold 385
  deaden affections 823
beplaster 933
bepraise 931
bequest 270
  gift 784
bereavement
  death 360
  loss 776
  take away 789
bereft *poor* 804
− of life 360
− of reason 503
béret 225
berg, ice − 383
bergamot 400
berlin 272
berth *lodging* 189
  bed 215
  office 625
beryl *green* 435
  jewel 847
beseech 765, 990
beseem 926
berserk 173, 503
beset *surround* 227
  follow 281
  attack 716
  entreat 765
  annoy 830
  haunt 860
− with difficulties 704
besetting 78, 613
− sin 945
beshrew 908
beside *except* 83
  near 197
  alongside 236
− the mark 10, 495
− oneself 503, 824
besides 37
besiege
  surround 227
  attack 716
  solicit 765
bésique 840
beslaver 933
beslime 653
beslubber 933
besmear 233, 653
besom 652
besotted 481
bespangle 847
bespatter *dirt* 653
  disapprove 932
  flatter 933
  detract 934

bespeak *early* 132
  evidence 467
  indicate 516
  engage 755
  ask for 765
bespeckle 440
bespot 440
besprinkle 41, 440
best 648, 650
  all for the –
  good 618
  prosper 734
  content 831
  hope 858
  bad is the – 649
  do one's –
  care 459
  try 675
  activity 682
  exertion 686
  have the – of it 731
  make the – of it
  over-estimate 482
  use 677
  submit 725
  compromise 774
  take easily 826
  hope 858
  the – 800
  to the – of one's
  belief 484
  – bib and tucker
  prepared 673
  ornament 847
  ostentation 882
  – friends 890
  – intentions 906
  – man 903
  – part 31, 50
  – seller 731
  make the – of
  one's time 684
bestead 644
bestial 954, 961
bestir oneself
  activity 682
  haste 684
  exertion 686
bestow 784
  – one's hand 903
  – thought 451
bestraddle 215
bestrew 73
bestride 206, 215
bet 621
betake oneself to
  journey 266
  business 625
  use 677
bête, pas si – 498
bête noire *bane* 663

fear 860
hate 898
bethel 1000
bethink 451, 505
bethral 749, 751
betide 151
betimes 132
betoken
  evidence 467
  predict 511
  indicate 550
betray *disclose* 529
  deceive 545
  dishonour 940
  – *itself visible* 446
betrayer 941
betrim 673
betroth 768, 903
betrothed 897
better *good* 648
  improve 658
  appeal to one's –
  feelings 914
  get – *health* 654
  improve 658
  refreshment 689
  restoration 660
  get the – of, 479,
  702, 731
  think – of 658, 950
  seen – days
  deteriorate 659
  adversity 735
  poor 804
  – half 903
  only – than noth-
  ing 651
  – sort 875
  for – for worse
  choice 609
  marriage 903
between 228
  – cup and lip 111
  far – 198
  lie – 228
  – the lines 526
  vibrate – two ex-
  tremes 149
  – ourselves 528
  – two fires 665
  – maid 746
betwixt 228
bevel 217
  – gearing 653
bever 298
beverage 298
bévue 732
bevy 72, 102
bewail *regret* 833
  lament 839
beware 665, 668

bewilder
  put out 458
  uncertainty 475
  astonish 870
bewitch
  fascinate 615
  please 829
  excite love 897
  exorcise 992
bey 745
beyond *superior* 33
  distance 196
  go – 303
  – compare 31, 33
  – control 471
  – one's depth 208,
  519
  – expression 31
  – one's grasp 471
  – hope 731, 534
  – the mark 303,
  641
  – measure 641
  – possibility 471
  – praise
  perfect 650
  approbation 931
  virtue 944
  – price 814
  – question 474, 494
  – reason 471
  – remedy 859
  – seas 57
bezel 217
bhang 663
bias *influence* 175
  tendency 176
  slope 217
  prepossession 481
  disposition 820
bib *pinafore* 225
  drink 959
bibber *weep* 839
  tope 959
bibble-babble 584
bibelot 847
**bibendum, nunc
est** – 959
Bible 895
  – oath 535
biblioclasm 162
bibliography 593
bibliolatry
  learning 490
  heterodoxy 984
  idolatry 991
bibliomancy 511
bibliomania 490
bibliomaniac 492
bibliophile 492
bibliopole 593

bibliotheca 593
bibulous 298, 959
bicameral 90
bicapital 90
bice 435, 438
bicentenary 98,
  138, 883
bicker *flutter* 315
  quarrel 713
bicolour 440
biconjugate 91
bicuspid 91
bicycle 272
bid *order* 741
  offer 763
  – the banns 903
  – defiance 715
  – fair *tend* 176
  probable 472
  promise 511
  hope 858
  – a long farewell
  624
  – for *intend* 620
  offer 763
  request 765
  bargain 794
bidder 767
bide *wait* 133
  remain 141
  take coolly 806
  – one's time 133
  watch 507
  inactive 681
bidet 271
biennial
  periodic 138
  plant 367
bienséance 852, 894
bier 363
bifacial 90
bifarious 90
bifid 91
bifold 90
biform 90
bifurcate 91, 244
big *in degree* 31
  in size 192
  wide 194
  look – *defy* 715
  proud 878
  insolent 885
  talk – 885, 909
  – sounding
  loud 404
  words 577
  affected 855
  – swollen 194
  – with 161
  – with the fate of
  511

bigamy 903
biggin 191
bight 343
bigot *positive* 474
  prejudice 481
  obstinate 606
  heterodox 984
  impious 988
bigotry 907
bigwig *scholar* 492
  sage 500
  nobility 875
bijou *goodness* 648
  beauty 845
  ornament 847
bilander 273
bilateral 90, 236
bilbao 727
bilboes 752
  put into − 751
bile 900
bilge *base* 211
  convex 250
  yawn 260
  − water 653
bilious 837
bilingual 560
bilk
  disappoint 509
  cheat 545
  steal 791
bill *list* 86
  hatchet 253
  placard 531
  ticket 550
  paper 593
  plan 626
  weapon 727
  money order 800
  money account
  811
  charge 812
  in law 969
  true − 969
  − and coo 902
  − of exchange 771
  − of fare *food* 298
  plan 626
  − of indictment
  938
  −s of mortality 360
  − of sale 771
billet *locate* 184
  ticket 550
  apportion 786
billet *epistle* 592
  − doux 902
billfold 191
billhook 253
billiard − ball 249
  − room 191

− table *flat* 213
billiards 840
Billingsgate 563,
  908
billion 98
billow *sea* 348
  river 341
billy-cock 225
billy-goat 373
bimetallism 800
bin 191
binary 89
bind *connect* 43
  cover 223
  compel 744
  condition 770
  obligation 926
  − hand and foot
  751
  − oneself 768
  − over 744
  − up wounds 660
binding 681, 744
bine 367
binnacle 693
binocular 445
binomial 89
biogenesis 161
biograph 448
biography 594
biology 357, 359
bioscope 448
biota 357
biparous 89
bipartite 44, 91
biplane 273
biplicity 89
biquadrate 96
birch *flog* 972
  − rod 975
bird 366
  kill two −s with
  one stone 682
  −'s eye view 441,
  448
  −s of a feather 17
  the − has flown
  187, 671
  − in hand 777, 781
  − of ill omen
  omen 512
  warning 668
  hopeless 859
  − of passage 268
  − of prey 739
  a little − told me
  527
birdcage 370
birdlime *glue* 45
  trap 545
biretta 999

birth *beginning* 66
  production 161
  paternity 166
  nobility 875
  − place 153
  − right 924
birthday 138, 883
  − suit 226
birthmark 848
bis *repeat* 104
  approval 931
biscuits, s'embar-
  quer sans − 674
bise 349
bisection 68, **91**
bishop *punch* 298
  clergy 996
  −'s palace 1000
  −'s purple 437
bishopric 995
bisque 33
bissextile 138
bistoury 253
bistre 433
bisulcate 259
bit
  small quantity 32
  part 51
  interval 106
  curb 752
  just a − 26
  − by bit
  by degrees 26
  by instalments 51
  in detail 79
  slowly 275
  − between the
  teeth 600, 719
bitch *animal* 366
  female 374
  clumsy 699
  fail 732
  impure 962
bite *eat* 298
  physical pain 378
  cold 385
  cheat 545
  dupe 547
  etch 558
  mental pain 830
  − the dust 725
  − in 259
  − the thumb 900,
  929
  − the tongue 392
biter bit 718
biting *pain* 378
  cold 383
  pungent 392
  painful 830
  discourteous 895

censorious 932
bitten 897
bitter *beer* 298
  cold 383
  taste 392, 395
  painful 830
  acrimonious 895
  hate 898
  angry 900
  malevolent 907
  − end 67
  − ender 606, 710,
  832
  − pill 735
  − words 932
bitterly *greatly* 31
bitterness
  [see bitter]
  pain 828
  regret 833
bitumen 356a
bituminous coal
  388
bivouac
  encamp 184
  camp 189
  repose 265
  watch 668
bi-weekly 138
bizarre 83, 853
blab 529
blabber 584
black *colour* 431
  crime 945
  look − *feeling* 821
  discontent 832
  angry 900
  − art 992
  − and blue
  beat 972
  − board 590
  − book 938
  − eye 848, 972
  − in the face
  swear 535
  excitement 821,
  824
  − flag 722
  − hole *crowd* 72
  prison 752
  − lead 556
  − letter *old* 124
  barbarism 563
  print 591
  − list 932
  − looks
  discourteous 895
  sullen 901a
  disapprove 932
  magic 998
  − mail *theft* 791

[413]

severe 739
hands in − *cruel*
    907
in the − 5
life − 359
new − 658, 824
spill − *war* 722
− for blood 919
− boil *excite* 824,
    825
    anger 900
− run cold 830,
    860
− heat 382
− horse 271
− hound 913
− letting 297, 662
− poisoning 655
− red 434
− stained 361
− sucker 789, 913
− thirsty
    murderous 361
    cruel 907
− up *excited* 824
    angry 900
bloodless 160
    peace 721
    virtue 946
bloody [*see* blood]
    red 434
    unclean 653
    cruel 907
bloom *youth* 127
    flower 367
    blue 438
    health 654
    prosperity 734
bloomer 495
bloomers 225
blooming 654, 845
blossom
    flower 154, 161,
    367
    prosperity 734
blot *blacken* 431
    error 495
    obliterate 552
    dirty 653
    blemish 848
    disgrace 874
    guilt 947
− out *destroy* 162
    forgive 918
blotch 848
blouse 225
blow *expand* 194
    knock 276
    wind 349
    unexpected 508

disappointment
    509
evil 619
action 680
get wind 688
failure 732
prosper 734
pain 828, 830
come to −s 720, 722
deal a − at 716
deal a − to 972
death − 360, 361
− for blow 718
− one's brains out
    361
− the coals 824
− down 162
− the fire 384
− the gaff 529
− hole 351
− the horn 416
− hot and cold
    lie 544
    irresolute 605
    tergiversation 607
    caprice 608
− a kiss 902
− off *disperse* 73
− out *food* 298
    darken 421
    gorge 957
− over *past* 122
− pipe 349, 727
− the trumpet 873
− one's own
    trumpet 882
− up *destroy* 162
    eruption 173
    inflate 194
    wind 349
    excite 824
    objurgate 932,
    934
blower 349
blowhard 884
blown [*see* blow]
    fatigued 688
    proud 878
storm − over 664,
    721
− upon 874, 932
blow-out 406
blowzy *swollen* 194
    red 434
blubber *fat* 356
    cry 839
Blucher boot 225
bludgeon 727
− man 726, 913
blue *sky* 338
    colour 438

learned 490
bit of − hope 858
look −
    disappointed 509
    feeling 821
    discontent 832
    disrepute 874
out of the − 508
swear till all's −
    535
true − 543, 939
− book 86, 551
− blood 875
− devils 837
− jacket 269
− light 550, 669
− pencil 174, 596
− moon 110
− Peter 293, 550
− and red 437
− ribbon 733, 877
− ruin 959
− stocking
    scholar 492
    affectation 855
− and yellow 435
Bluebeard
    marriage 903
    libertine 962
blueness 438
blues 837, 840
bluff *violent* 173
    high cliff 206
    blunt 254
    deceive 545
    boasting 884
    insolent 885
    discourteous 895
blunder *error* 495
    absurdity 497
    awkward 699
    failure 732
− upon 156
blunderbuss 727
blunderhead 701
blunderheaded 499
blunt *weaken* 160
    inert 172
    moderate v. 174
    obtuse 254
    benumb 376
    damp v. 616
    plain-spoken 703
    cash 800
    deaden 823
    discourteous 895
− tool 645
− witted 499
bluntness 254
blur
    imperfect vision

443
dirt 653
blemish 848
stigma 874
blurb 931
blurred
    invisible 447
blurt out 529, 582
blush *flush* 382
    redden 434
    feel 821
    humbled 879
    modest 881
at first − *see* 441
    appear 448
    manifest 525
put to the −
    humble 897
    browbeat 885
    discourtesy 895
blushing honours
    873, 881
bluster *violent* 173
    defiant 715
    boasting 884
    insolent 885
    threaten 909
blusterer **887**
blustering [*see*
    bluster]
    windy 349
Bo to a goose, not
    say − 862
boa 225
boanerges 540
boar 366, 373
board *layer* 204
    support 215
    food 298
    hard 323
    council 696
    attack 716
    tribunal 966
festive − 892
go by the − 158,
    162
go on − 293
on − 186, 273
preside at the −
    693
− of trade 621
− school 542
boarding-house 189
boarder 188
boards 599, 728
boast 884
not much to − of
    651
boasting **884**
boaston 840
boat 273

bonzer 648
booby 501
– trap 545
boodle 793
book *register* 86
publication 531
  record 551
  volume **593**
  script 599
  enter accounts 811
  at one's –s 539
  bring to –
    evidence 467
    account 811
    reprove 932
  mind one's – 539
  school – 542
  without –
    by heart 505
  – of Books 985
  – club 593
  – of fate 601
  – learning 490
  – shop 593
book-case 191
booked *dying* 360
bookish 490
bookkeeper 553
bookkeeping 811
bookless
  unlearned 493
bookmaking 156
bookseller 593
bookworm 492, 593
boom
  support 215
  sail 267
  rush 274
  impulse 276
  sound 404
  obstacle 706
  defence 717
boomerang
  recoil 277
  retribution 718
  weapon 727
boon 784
  beg a – 765
  – companion 890
boor *clown* 876
boorish 851, 895
boost 276, 482, 931
booster 935
boot *box* 191
  dress 225
  advantage 618
  punishment 975
  to – *added* 37
  – legging 964
booted and spurred
  673

booth 189, 799
bootless 645, 732
boots *dress* 225
  servant 746
  low person 876
  what – it? 643
booty 793
booze 959
bo-peep 441, 528
bordel 961
border *edge* 231
  limit 233
  flower bed 371
  ornament 847
  – upon 197, 199
bore *diameter* 202
  hole 260
  tide 348, 667
  fatigue 688
  trouble 828
  plague 830
  weary 841
bored 456
boreal
  Northern 237
  cold 383
Boreas 349
boredom 841
borer 262
born 359
  – so 5
  – under an evil
    star 735
  – under a lucky
    star 734
borne 826
  – down *failure* 732
  defection 837
borné 499
borough 181, 189
  rotten – 893
  – council 696
borrow 19, 788
  – of Peter &c. 147
borrowed plumes
  deception 545
borrower 806
borrowing 788
bosh *absurdity* 497
  unmeaning 517
  untrue 546
  trifling 643
bosky 959
bosom *breast* 221
  mind 450
  affections 820
  in the – of 229
  – of one's family
    221
  – friend 890

boss 250, 694, 737
  straw – 694
boston 840
botanic garden 369,
  371
Botanomancy 511
Botany 367, **369**
botch *bungle* 59
  mend 660
  unskilful 699
  difficulty 704
  fail 732
both 89
  listen with – ears
    418
  burn the candle at
    – ends 641
  butter one's bread
    on – sides 641
bother
  uncertainty 475
  bustle 682
  difficulty 704
  trouble 828
  harass 830
bothy 189
bottle
  receptacle 191
  preserve 670
  bee in a – 407
  crack a – 298
  pass the – 959
  smelling – 400
  – green 435
  – holder
    auxiliary 177
    mediator 724
  – up *remember* 505
    hide 528
    restrain 751
bottom
  lowest part 211
  support 215
  posterior 235
  combe 252
  ship 273
  pluck 604a
  courage 861
  at – 5
  at the – of
    cause 153
  go to the – 310
  probe to the – 461
  from the – of one's
    heart *veracity*
    543
  feeling 821
  – upwards 218
  – land 180, 207
bottomless 208
  – pit 982

angel of the – pit
  978
bottomry 771
botulism 663
bouche:
  bonne – *end* 67
  savoury 394
  saving 636
  pleasant 829
  – à feu 727
bouderie 901a
boudoir 191
bouffe, opera 599
bouge 250
bough *part* 51
  curve 245
  tree 367
bought *flexure* 245
bougie 423
boulder 249
boulevards 227
bouleversement
  revolution 146
  destruction 162
  excite 824
bouillabaise 298
bouillon 298
bounce *violence* 173
  jump 309
  lie 546
  boast 884
  insolence 885
  – upon 292, 508
bouncing *large* 192
bound
  circumscribe 229
  swift 274
  leap 309
  certain 474
  I'll be – 535
  – back *recoil* 277
  – by 926
  – for *direction* 278
  destination 620
  – to *promise* 768
  responsible 926
boundary 233
bounden duty 926
bounder 851
boundless 105, 180
bounds 230, 233
  keep within –
    moderation 174
    shortcoming 304
    restrain 751
    prohibit 761
  – of possibility 470
bountiful 816, 906
  Lady – 816
bounty *gift* 784
bouquet

cards 840
bridle *restrain* 751
  rein 752
– road 627
– one's tongue
  585, 864
– up 900
brief *time* 111
  space 201
  concise 572
  compendium 596
  hold a – for 759
– case 191
briefly *anon* 132
brier
  sharp 253
  pipe 390
  bane 663
brig 273
brigade 726
brigadier 745
brigand 792
brigandage 791
brigandine 717
brigantine 273
bright *shine* 420
  colour 428
  intelligent 498
  cheery 836
  beauty 845
  glory 873
– days 734
– eyed 845
– prospect 858
– side 829
  look at the – side
  836, 858
– thought
  sharp 498
  good stroke 626
  wit 842
brighten up
  furbish 658
brigue 712, 720
brilliant
  shining 420
  good 648
  wit 842
  beautiful 845
  gem 847
  glorious 873
– idea 842
brilliantine 356
brim 231
– over 641
brimful 52
brimstone 388
brindled 440
brine 341, 392
bring 270
– about 153, 729

– back 790
– back to the
  memory 505
– to bear upon
  relation 9
  action 170
– into being 161
– to a crisis 604
– forth 161
– forward
  evidence 467
  manifest 525
  teach 537
  improve 658
– grey hairs to the
  grave 735, 830
– grist to the mill
  644
– home 775
– home to 155
– in *receive* 296
  income 810
  price 812
– to life 359
– to light 480*a*
– low 874
– to maturity 673,
  729
– to mind 505
– under one's
  notice 457
– off 672
– out
  discover 480*a*
  manifest 525
  publish 591
– over
  persuade 484
– to perfection
  677
– into play 677
– to a point 74
– in question 461
– up the rear 235
– round
  persuade 615
  restore 660
– to terms 723
– to *convert* 144
  halt 265
– together 72
– in its train 88
– to trial 969
– up *develop* 161
  vomit 297
  educate 537
– in a verdict 480
– word 527
brink 231
  on the –
  almost 32

coming 121
  near 197
– of the grave 360
briny 392
– ocean 341
brio *music* 415
  active 682
brisk *prompt* 111
  energetic 171
  active 682
  cheery 836
bristle 253
– up *stick up* 250
  angry 900
– with 639, 641
– with arms 722
bristly 256
Britannia metal
  545
Briticism 563
British 188
– lion 604
Briton, true – 939
  work like a – 686
brittleness 328
britzska 272
broach *begin* 66
  found 153
  reamer 262
  tap 297
  publish 531
  assert 535
broad *general* 78
  space 202
  lake 343
  emphatic 535
  indelicate 961,
  962
– accent 580
– awake 459, 682
– daylight 420,
  525
– farce 842
– grin 838
– highway 627
– hint 527
– meaning 516
– minded 498
broadcast
  disperse 73
  spread 78
  publish 531
  sow – 818
broadcloth 219
broadhearted 906
broadsheet 593
broad-shouldered
  159
broadside 236
  publication 531
  cannonade 716

broadsword 727
Brobdingnagian
  192
brocade 847
brochure 593
Brocken, spectre of
  the 443
broder 549
brogue *boot* 225
  dialect 563
broidery 847
broil *heat* 382
  fry 384
  fray 713, 720
broke *poor* 804
broken
  discontinuous 70
  weak 160
– colour 428
– down
  decrepit 659
  failing 732
  dejected 837
– English 563
– fortune 735, **804**
– heart 828, 837
  hopeless 859
– reed 160, 665
– meat 645
– voice 581, 583
– winded
  disease 655
  fatigue 688
broker 758, 797
brokerage *pay* 812
brokery 794
bromidic 613
bronchia 351
bronze *alloy* 41
  brown 433
  sculpture 557
brooch 847
brood 102, 167
– over 451, 847
brooding
  preparing 673
brook *stream* 348
  bear 821, 826
broom 652
broth 298
brothel 961
brother *kin* 11
  similar 17
  equal 27
brotherhood 712
brotherly
  friendship 888
  love 897
  benevolence 906
brougham 272
brought to bed 161

brouillerie 713
brouillon 626
brow *top* 210
  edge 231
  front 234
browbeat
  intimidate 860
  swagger 885
  disrespect 929
  —en *humbled* 879
brown 433
  — Bess 727
  — *study* 451, 458
Brown, Jones and
  Robinson 876
brownie 980
browse 298
bruin 895
bruise *powder* 330
  hurt 619
  injure 649
  blemish 848
bruiser 726
bruit
  report 531, 532
brumal 126, 383
brumous 353
Brummagem 545
brunette 433
brunt *beginning* 66
  impulse 276
  bear the —
  difficulty 704
  defence 717
  endure 821, 826
brush *rough* 256
  rapid motion 274
  graze 379
  clean 652
  fight 720
  paint — 556
  — away *reject* 297
  abrogate 756
  — up *clean* 652
  furbish 658
  prepare 673
brushwood 367
brusque *violent* 173
  haste 684
  discourtesy 895
brutal *vulgar* 851
  rude 895
  savage 907
brutalize
  [*see* brutal]
  corrupt 659
  deaden 823
  vice 945
brute *animal* 366
  rude 895
  maleficent 913

— force
  strength 159
  violence 173
  animal 450a
  severe 739
  compulsion 744
  lawless 964
— matter 316, 358
Brute, et tu 917
brutish [*see* brute]
  vulgar 851
  ignoble 876
  intemperate 954
brutum fulmen
  impotent 158
  failure 732
  lax 738
  boast 884
bubble
  unsubstantial 4
  transient 111
  little 193
  convexity 250
  light 320
  water 348
  air 353
  error 495
  deceit 545
  trifle 643
— burst
  fall short 304
  disappoint 509
  fail 732
— reputation 873
— and squeak 298
— up *agitation* 315
buccaneer 791, 792
bucentaur 273
Bucephalus 271
buck *stag* 366
  male 373
  wash 652
  money 800
  fop 854
— basket 191
— jump 309
— up 684
bucket 191
  kick the — 360
  drop — in empty
    well 645
  like —s in well 314
buckle *tie* 43
  fastening 45
  distort 243
  curl 248
— on one's armour
    673
— to 604, 686
— with *grapple* 720
buckler 717

buckram 855, 878
  men in — 549
bucolic
  pastoral 370
  poem 597
bud 367
  beginning 66
  germ 153
  expand 194
  graft 300
— from 154
Buddha 979, 986
Buddhism 984
budding *young* 127
buddy 711, 890
budge 264
budget *heap* 72
  bag 191
  store 636
  finance 811
— of news 532
buff 436
  blind man's — 840
  native — 226
buffer
  hindrance 706
  defence 717
buffet 191
  strike 276
  agitate 315
  evil 619
  bad 649
  affront 900
  smite 972
— the waves 704,
    708
  bar 189
buffo 599
buffoon *actor* 599
  humorist 844
  butt 857
buffoonery 840, 842
bug 653
bugaboo 669, 860
bugbear
  imaginary 155
  bane 663
  alarm 669
  fear 860
buggy 272
bugle
  instrument 417
  war-cry 722
  ornament 847
— call 550, 741
build *construct* 161
  form 240
— anew 658
— upon a rock 150
— up *compose* 54
— upon *belief* 484

builder 626, 690
building material
  635
buildings 189
built on *basis* 211
bulb 249, 250
bulge 250
bulk 50, 192
— large 31
bulkhead 228, 706
bull *animal* 366
  male 373
  error 495
  absurdity 497
  solecism 568
  police 664
  ordinance 741
— in a china shop
    59
  like a — at a gate
    173
  take the — by the
    horns 604, 861
Bull, John — 188
bullcalf 501
bulldog *animal* 366
  pluck 604, 604a
  courage 861
bulldoze 885
bullet *ball* 249
  arms 727
  missile 284
bulletin 532, 592
— board 551
bullfight 720
bullhead 501
bullion 800
bullseye *centre* 222
  lantern 423
  aim 620
bully *fighter* 726
  maltreat 830
  frighten 860
  courage 861
  rashness 863
  bluster 885
  blusterer 887
  threaten 909
  evil doer 913
  bad man 949
bulrush
  worthless 643
bulwark 706, 717
bum 876
bumbailiff 965
bumbledom 737,
  965
bumboat 273
bump 250, 276
— off 361
bumper 52

[420]

bumpkin 876
bumptious
  proud 878
  insolent 885
  contemptuous 930
bun 298
bunch *collection* 72
  protuberance 250
  – light 599
bunchbacked 243
Buncombe
  [*see* bunkum]
Bund 712
bundle *packet* 72
  go 266
  – on 275, 684
  – out 297
bung 263
  – up 261
bungalow 189
bungle 59, 699
bungler **701**
bunion 259
bunk 186, 215
bunker 181
bunkie 890
bunkum *lie* 544
  style 577
  boast 884
  flattery 933
bunting 550
buoy *raise* 307
  float 320
  hope 858
buoyant
  floating 305
  light 320
  elastic 325
  prosperous 734
  cheerful 836
  hopeful 858
bur *clinging* 46
  sharp 253
  rough 256
  in engraving 558
burden *lading* 190
  weight 319
  melody 413
  poetry 597
  too much 641
  clog 706
  oppress 828
  care 830
  – the memory 505
  – of a song
  repetition 104
burdensome
  [*see* burden]
  hurtful 649
  labouring 686
bureau *chest* 191

office 691
shop 799
tribunal 960
bureaucracy 737
bureaucrat 694
burgee 550
burgeon
  [*see* bourgeon]
burgess 188
burgh 189
burgher 188
burghmote 966
burglar 792
  – alarm 669
burglary 791
burgomaster 745
burgrave 745
burial 363
buried *deep* 208
  imbedded 229
  hidden 528
  – in a napkin 460
  – in oblivion 506
burin 558
burke 361
burlesque
  imitation 19
  travesty 21
  absurdity 497
  misrepresent 555
  drama 599
  comic 853
  ridicule 856
burletta 599
burly 192
burn *near* 197
  rivulet 348
  hot 382
  consume 384
  near the truth
    480a
  excited 825
  love 897
  punish 972
  – the candle at
    both ends
  waste 638
  exertion 686
  prodigal 818
  – daylight 683
  – one's bridges 604
  – one's fingers 699
  – in 384
  – out 385
  – to 865
burner 423
burning [*see* burn]
  passion 821
  angry 900
  – glass 445
  – with curiosity

455
  – pain 378
  – shame 874
burnish *polish* 255
  shine 420
  beautify 845
burnous 225
burnt [*see* burn]
  red 434
  – offering 952, 990
burr 410
burrock 706
burrow *lodge* 184
  excavate 252
bursar 801
bursary 802
burst *disjoin* 44
  instantaneous 113
  explosion 173
  brittle 328
  sound 406
  paroxysm 825
  bubble –
  disclosure 529
  all over 729
  ready to –
  replete 641
  excited 824
  – of anger 900
  – away 623
  – of eloquence 582
  – of envy 921
  – into a flame 825
  – forth *begin* 66
  expand 194
  be seen 446
  –ing with health
    654
  – with grief 839
  – in 294
  – of laughter 838
  – out 295
  – upon *arrive* 292
  unexpected 508
  – into tears 839
burthen
  [*see* burden]
bury *enclose* 229
  inter 363
  conceal 528
  – the hatchet 918
  – one's talent 528
busboy 746
busby 225
bush *branch* 51
  jungle 344
  shrub 367
  beat about the –
    629
bushel *much* 31
  multitude 102

receptacle 191
size 192
hid under a – 460
not hide light un-
  der a – 878
bush-fighting 720
bushing 224
bushranger 792
bushy 256
business *event* 151
  topic 454
  occupation **625**
  commerce 794
  full of – 682
  man of –
  proficient 700
  consignee 758
  mind one's –
  incurious 456
  attentive 457
  careful 459
  let alone 748
  send about one's –
    297
  stage – 599
business-like
  orderly 58
  business 625
  active 682
  practical 692
  skilful 698
buskin *dress* 225
  drama 599
buss *boat* 273
  courtesy 894
  endearment 902
bust 554
bustle *energy* 171
  dress 225
  agitation 315
  activity 682
  haste 684
  difficulty 704
bustling
  [*see* bustle]
  eventful 151
busy 682
busybody 532, 682
but
  on the other hand
    30
  except 83
  limit 233
  qualifying 469
  – now 118
butcher *kill* 361
  provisions 637
  evil-doer 913
butler 746
butt *cask* 191
  push 276

caravan 266, 272
caravansary 189
caravel 273
carbine 727
carbohydrates 298
carbon 388
– dioxide 663
– monoxide 663
carbonaro 742
carbonization 384
carboy 191
carbuncle *red* 434
abscess 655
jewel 847
carcanet 847
carcass
structure 329
corpse 362
bomb 727
carcelage 973
carcinoma 655
card *unravel* 60
ticket 550
plan 626
address – 550
by the – 82
great – 873
house of –s 328
leave a – 892
on the –s 152, 177, 470
play one's – 692
play one's best – 686
play one's –s well 698
playing –s 840
shuffle the –s
begin again 66
change 140
chance 621
prepare 673
speak by the –
care 459
veracity 543
phrase 566
throw up the –s 757
ticklish – 704
trump – 626
– index 60, 86, 551
–s to play 632
cardcase 191
cardiac 836
cardigan 225
cardinal *intrinsic* 5
dress 225
red 434
important 642
excellent 648
priest 995, 996

–'s hat 747
– points 278
– virtues 944
cardioid 245
card-sharper 792
card-sharping 545
care *attention* **459**
business 625
adversity 735
custody 751
economy 817
pain 828
fear 860
for aught one –s 643, 866
begone dull – 836
drive – away 840
have the – of 693
take – 665, 864
take – of 459
– for *important* 642
desire 865
love 897
careen *slope* 217
repair 660
career 625, 692
careless
inattentive 458
neglectful 460, 927
feeble 575
insensible 823
indifferent 866
caress 897, 902
caret *incomplete* 53
want 640
careworn 828, 837
cargo 270
large quantity 31
contents 190
property 780
goods 798
– boat 273
caricature
likeness 19
copy 21
exaggerate 549
misrepresent 555
ridicule 856
caricaturist 844
caries 49, 653, 655
carillon 417
cariole 272
carious 563
carking 828
– care 830
carle 876
Carlist 925
car-load 31
carman 694

Carmelite 996
carminative 662
carmine 434
carnage 361
carnal 364
intemperate 954
impure 961
irreligious 989
carnation 434
carnival 840
carnivorous 298
carol
music 415, 416
cheerful 836
rejoice 838
caro sposo 897
carouse *feast* 298
festivity 840
intemperance 954
drinking 959
carousel 840
carp at 932
carpe diem 134
carpenter 690
carper 936
carpet 211
on the –
topic 454
project 626
– bag 191
– knight *fop* 854
servile 886
sybarite 954a
– sweeper 652
carrefour 627
carriage *gait* 264
transference 270
vehicle 272
aspect 448
conduct 692
keep one's – 852
carried
– by acclamation &c. 488
– away by passion 824
carrier **271**
– pigeon 534
carrion 362, 653
carronade 727
carroty 434
carry
conduce to 176
support 215
transfer 270
induce 615
reap and – 775
– all before one 731
– coals 879
– conviction 484

– into execution 729, 772
– with a high hand
authority 737
pride 878
insolence 885
– in the mind 505
– off *take* 789
steal 791
– on [*see below*]
– oneself 692
– out *conduct* 692
complete 729
– over
transfer 270
accounts 811
– a point 731
– by storm 731
– through 692, 729
– weight
influence 175
evidence 467
importance 642
carry on
continue 143
pursue 622
do 680
conduct 692
undertake 326
– an argument 476
– business 625
– an enquiry 461
– a trade 794
– war 722
cart 272
– away 185
– before the horse
disorder 59
inversion 218
bungling 699
– horse 271
work like a –
horse 686
– load 31, 190
cartage 270
carte *list* 86
à la – 298
– blanche 760, 816
– du pays 626
– and tierce 716
– de visite 550
photograph 554
cartel
combination 709
defiance 715
truce 723
compact 769
cartelize 709
carter 268

cartes sur table
525, 543
**Carthago, delenda
est** – 908
Carthusian 996
cartilage
dense 321
hard 323
tough 327
cartography 466,
554
cartoon 21, 556
cartoonist 559
cartouche
ammunition 727
ornament 847
cartridge 727
cartulary 86, 551
caruncle 250
carve *cut* 44
make 161
form 240
sculpture 557
apportion 786
– one's way 282
carvel 273
carver 559
caryatides 215
**Cary's chickens,
Mother** – 668
cascade 348
case *state* 7
box 191
sheath 223
topic 454
argument 476
specification 527
grammar 567
affair 625
patient 655
law-suit 969
be the – 1, 494
in good – 654, 734
in –
circumstance 8
event 151
supposition 514
make out a – 467,
924
– in point 23, 82
caseation 321
caseharden
strengthen 159
habituate 613
case-hardened
callous 376, 823
obstinate 606
casemate 189, 717
casement 260
casern 189
cash *money* 800

pay 807
in – 803
pay – for 795
– account 811
– book 551
– box 802
– down 807
– register 85, 553,
802
cashier *dismiss* 756
treasurer 801
casing 223
casino 712; 840
cask 191
casket 191
casque 717
Cassandra 513, 668
cassation 552
casserole 191
Cassiopeia's chair
318
cassock 999
cast *mould* 21
small quantity 32
spread 73
tendency 176
form 240
throw 284
tinge 428
aspect 448
drama 599
reject 610
plan 626
company 712
give 784
allot 786
condemn 971
give one a – 707
set on a – 621
– about for 463
– accounts 811
– adrift *disperse* 73
eject 297
liberate 750
dismiss 756
– anchor 265, 292
– aside 460
– aspersions 934
– away 610, 638
lost 732
– behind one
forget 506
refuse 764
relinquish 782
– away care 836
– off clothes 645
– of countenance
448
– of the dice 156
– in a different

mould 18
– dishonour &c.
upon 874
– to the dogs 162
– down 308, 837
– in the eye 443
– the eyes back
122
– eyes on 441
– the eyes over
457
– a gloom 837
– off a habit 614
– iron 323
resolute 604
– in one's lot with
609
– lots 621
– lustre upon 420
– of mind 820
– a nativity 511,
992
– one's net 463
– off *divest* 226
disused 678
dismiss 756
relinquish 782
– over-board 678
– the parts 60
– reflection upon
932
– in the same
mould 17
– a shade 421
– the skin 226
– a slur 874
accuse 938
– a spell 992
– off trammels 750
– up *add* 85
happen 151
eject 297
castanet 417
castaway *exile* 893
reprobate 949
caste 75, 873
lose – 940
castellan 746, 753
castellated 717
caster *cruet* 191
wheel 312
castigate 932, 972
castigator 936
casting 21
casting – *vote* 480
– *weight* 28, 30
castle *at chess* 148
abode 189
defence 717
– in the air
impossible 471

imagination 515
hope 858
Castle of Indolence
683
castor *hat* 225
Castor and Pollux
89, 890
castrametation
189, 722
castrate *subduct* 38
impotent 158
casual *extrinsic* 6
chance 156
uncertain 475
lax 773
casualty *event* 151
killed 361
evil 619
misfortune 735
casuist 476
casuistry
sophistry 477
falsehood 544
duty 926
casus belli
quarrel 713
irritation 824,
900
casus fœderis 770
cat *nine lives* 359
animal 366
keen sight 441
fall on one's feet
734
cross 901
gib –, tom – *male*
373
rain –s and dogs
348
let – out of bag
529
– boat 273
– burglar 792
– call *whistle* 417
disapproval 932
–'s cradle 219
– and dog life 713
as the – jumps
event 151
see how the –
jumps 510
fickleness 607
caution 864
– o' nine tails 975
– in pattens 652
–'s paw *dupe* 547
instrumental 631
use 677
auxiliary 711
catabasis 36
catachresis 521, 523

concord 714
cemetery 363
cenobite 893, 996
cenotaph 363
censer 998
censor
moderate 174
critic 480
ban 761
detractor 936
censorious 480, 932
censurable 947
censure 932
censurer 936
census 85, 86
record 551
centaur 83, 366
centenarian 130
centenary
hundred 98
period 138
celebration 883
centesimal 99
cento 597
centrality 222
centralize
combine 48
centre 68, 222
– round 72, 290
centrifugal 291
centripetal 290
centroidal 222
centuple 98
centurion 745
century
hundred 98
period 108
long time 110
money 800
ceramic
bake 384
– ware 557
cerate 662
Cerberus
janitor 263
custodian 664
hades 932
sop for – 615
cereal 298
cerebration 451
cerebrum 450
cere-cloth 363
cerement
covering 223
wax 356
burial 363
ceremonious 928
ceremony
parade 882
courtesy 894
rite 998

Ceres 979
cerise 434
cerography 558, 590
Ceromancy 511
ceroplastic 557
certain *special* 79
indefinite number 100
sure 474
belief 484
true 494
make – of 480a
of a – age 128
to a – degree 32
certainly *yes* 488
certainness 474
certainty **474**
certes 474, 488
certificate
evidence 467
record 551
security 771
certify 467, 535
certiorari 969
certitude 474
cerulean 438
cess *tax* 812
sewer 653
cessation **142**
cession
surrender 725
of property 782
gift 784
cesspool 653
cestui-que trust 779
cestus 45, 247
chafe
physical pain 378
warm 384
irritate 825
mental pain 828, 830
discontent 832
incense 900
chaff *trash* 643
ridicule 856
vulgar 876
not to be caught with – 698, 702
winnow – from wheat 609
chaffer 794
chafing-dish 386
chagrin 828
chain *fasten* 43
vinculum 45
series 69
measure 200
interlinking 219
measure 466

gearing 633
imprison 752
ornament 847
drag a – 749
drag a lengthened – 686
in –s 754
chain gang 752, 972
chain-shot 727
chair *support* 215
vehicle 272
professorship 542
throne 747
celebration 883
president 694
in the – 693
chairman 694
chaise 272
chalcography 558
chalet 189
chalice 191, 998
chalk *earth* 342
white 430
mark 550
drawing 556
– from cheese 14, 491
– out *plan* 626
challenge
question 461
doubt 485
claim 924
defy 715
accuse 938
– comparison 648
cham 745
chamber *room* 191
council 696
mart 799
sick – 655
chamberlain 746
chambermaid 746
chameleon 149, 440
chamfer 259
chamois 309
champ 298
– the bit *disobedient* 742
chafe 825
angry 900
champagne 298
champaign 344
champain 874
Champ de Mars 728
champêtre, fête – 840
champion
best 648
auxiliary 711
defence 717

combatant 726
representative 759
sympathizer 914
championship 707
chance 156, **621**
be one's – 151
game of – 840
great – 472
small – 473
stand a – 177, 470
take one's – 675
–s against one 665
whirligig of – 156
as – would have it 152
chancel 1000
chancellor
president 745
deputy 759
judge 967
– of the exchequer 801
chancery
court of – 966
– suit *delay* 133
chandelier 214, 423
chandelle, le jeu n'en vaut pas la – 638, 643
dear 814
chandler 797
change
alteration **140**
mart 799
small coin 800
inter– 148
radical – 146
sudden – 146
– about 149
– colour 821
– for 147
– hands 783
– of mind 607
– of opinion 485
– of place 264
changeableness **149,** 605
changeful
fickle 607
changeling
substitute 147
fool 501
changeless 16
changer 797
channel
furrow 259
opening 260
conduit 350
way 627
chant *song* 415
sing 416

worship 990
chant du cygne 360
chanter 416
chanticleer 366
chantry 1000
chaomancy 511
chaos 59
chap *crack* 198
  jaw 231
  fellow 373
  – book 593
chapel 1000
chaperon
  accompany 88
  watch 459
  protect 664
chapfallen 878
chaplain 995, 996
chaplet *circle* 247
  garland 550
  trophy 733
  ornament 847
chapman 797
chapter *part* 51
  topic 454
  book 593
  council 696
  church 995
  – of accidents
    156, 621
  – house 1000
  – and verse 467,
    494
char *burn* 384
  serve 746
char-à-banc 272
character
  nature 5
  state 7
  class 75
  oddity 83
  letter 561
  drama 599
  disposition 820
  reputation 873
characteristic
  intrinsic 5
  special 79
  tendency 176
  mark 550
characterize 564,
  594
characterized 820
charade 533, 599
charcoal *fuel* 384,
  388
  black 431
  drawing 556
charge *fill* 52
  contents 190
  business 625

requisition 630
direction 693
advice 695
precept 697
attack 716
order 741
custody 751
commission 755
bargain for 794
price 812
accusation 938
in – prisoner 754
justifiable – 937
take – of 664
take in – 751
– on *attribute* 155
– with 155, 777
chargé d'affaires
  758
chargeable *debt* 806
  – on *duty* 926
charger
  carrier 271
  fighter 726
Charing Cross, pro-
  claim at – 531
chariot 272
  drag at one's –
    wheels 749
charioteer 268, 694
charity *give* 784
  liberal 816
  beneficent 906
  pity 914
  Christian – 906
  cold as – 823
  – that begins at
    home 943
charivari 404, 407
charlatan
  ignoramus 493
  imposter 548
  mountebank 844
  boaster 884
charlatanism
  ignorance 491
  falsehood 544
  affectation 855
Charles's wain 318
Charleston 840
Charley 753
charm *motive* 615
  please 829
  beauty 845
  love 897
  conjure 992
  spell 993
  bear a –ed life 644,
    734
charmer 994
  voice of the – 933

not listen to voice
  of – 604
charnel-house 363
Charon 982
chart 527, 554
charter
  commission 755
  permit 760
  compact 769
  security 771
  privilege 924
chartered
  legal 963
  – accountant 801,
    811
  – libertine 962
Chartist 742
charwoman 690,
  746
chary
  economical 817
  stingy 819
  cautious 864
Charybdis 312, 665
chase *emboss* 250
  furrow 259
  drive away 289
  killing 361
  forest 367
  pursue 622
  ornament 847
  wild goose – 645
chaser 559
chasm *interval* 198
  opening 260
chassé 840
chassemarée 273
chassepot 727
chasser 297
  – balancer 605
chasseur 726
chassis 215
chaste
  shapely 242
  language 576, 578
  simple 849
  good taste 850
  pure 960
chasten
  moderate 174
  punish 972
chastened
  subdued spirit
    826
  penitent 950
chastise 932, 972
  – with scorpions
    739
chasuble 999
chat 588
chat qui dort 667,

668
château 189
  – en Espagne 858
chatelaine 847
chatoyant 440
chattels 633, 789
chatter 314, 584
chatterbox 584
chattering of teeth
  cold 383
chatty 584, 892
chauffeur 268
chaunt
  song 415
  sing 416
  worship 990
chaussé 225
Chauvinism 884,
  885
chawbacon 876
cheap 643, 815
  hold – 930
  – jack 797
cheapen *haggle* 794
  begrudge 819
cheapness **815**
cheat 545, 548
check
  numerical 85
  stop 142
  moderate 174
  counteract 179
  slacken 275
  plaid 440
  experiment 463
  measure 466
  evidence 468
  ticket 550
  dissuade 616
  hinder 706
  misfortune 735
  restrain 751
  money order 800
  – the growth 201
  – oneself 826
checkered 149
checkers 440, 840
checkmate
  stop 142
  success 731
  failure 732
check-roll 86
check-string
  pull the – 142
cheek *side* 236
  impertinence 885
  – by jowl *with* 88
  near 197
cheeks *dual* 89
cheep 412
cheer *repast* 298

unanimity 488
poetry 597
opera 599
concord 714
– girl 599
chose
– in action 780
– in possession 777
chouse 545
choux gras, faire ses – 377
chrestomathy 560
chrism 998
Christ 976
 Church of – 893*a*
 receive – 987
Christ-cross-row 561
christen 564, 998
Christendom 983*a*, 995
Christian 983*a*, 987
– charity 906
– science 662, 984
Christmas 138, 998
Christmas-box 784
chromatic
 colour 428
 – scale *music* 413
chromato-pseudoblepsis 443
chromatrope 445
chrome 436
chromolithograph 558
chromosphere 318
chronic 110
chronicle
 measure time 114
 annals 551
chronicler 553
chronography
 measure time 114
 description 594
chronology 114
chronometry 114
Chrononhotontho-logos 887
chrysalis 129
chrysoprase 847
chrysolite 847
 perfection 650
chrysology 800
chubby 192
chuck *throw* 284
 animal cry 412
 – it 142
 – under chin 902
chuck-farthing 621
chuckle

animal cry 412
laugh 838
exult 884
chuff 876
chum 711, 890
chunk 51
Church
 infallible 474
 orthodox 983*a*
 Christendom 995
 temple 1000
 dignitaries of – 996
 go to – 990
 High –, Low – &c. 984
 – of Christ 983*a*
 – bell 550
 – house 1000
churchdom **995**
churching 998
churchman 996
churchwarden 996
 pipe 392
churchyard 363, 1000
 – cough 655
churl *boor* 876
churlish
 niggard 819
 rude 895
 sulky 901*a*
 malevolent 907
churn 315, 352
chut! *silent* 403
 taciturn 585
chute 348
chutney 393
chypre 400
cibarious 298
cicatrix 551
 manet – 919
cicatrize 660
Cicero 582
cicerone 524, 527
ciceronian 578
cicisbeo 897
cicuration **370**
cider 298
cider squeezer 876
ci-devant 122
cigar 392
ci-git 363
cilia 205, 256
cimeter 727
Cimmerian 421
cinch 45
cincture 247
cinder
 combustion 384
 dirt 653

Cinderella
 servant 746
 commonalty 876
cinema 448, 599, 840
cinematograph 448
cinematographer 553
cinerary 363
cineration 384
cinereous 432
cingle 230
cinnabar 434
cinnamon 393, 433
cinque 98
cipher
 unsubstantial 4
 number 84
 compute 85
 zero 101
 concealment 528
 mark 550
 letter 561
 unimportant 643
 writing in – 590
Circe 615, 994
 –an cup 377, 954
circination 312
circle *region* 181
 embrace 227
 form 247
 party 712
 describe a – 311
 great – sailing 628
 – of acquaintance 892
 – of the sciences 490
circlet 247
circling 248
circuit *region* 181
 outline 230
 winding 248
 tour 266
 indirect path 311
 indirect course **629**
circuition **311**
circuitous 279, 311
– method 629
circular *round* 247
 publication 531
 letter 592
 pamphlet 593
 – note 805
circularity **247**
circularize 592
circulate
 circuit 311
 rotate 312
 publish 531

circulating medium 800
circulation
 [*see* circulate]
 in – *news* 532
 – of money 809
circumambient 227, 229, 311, 629
circumambulate
 travel 266
 go round 311, 629
circumaviate 311
circumbendibus 248, 629
circumcision 44, 998
circumduction 552
circumference 230
circumferential 227
circumflex 311
circumfluent
 lie round 227
 move round 311
circumforaneous
 travelling 266
 circuition 311
circumfuse 73
circumgyration 312
circumjacence **227**
circumlocution 573
circumnavigate
 navigation 267
 circuition 311
circumrotation 312
circumscribe
 surround 229
 limit 233, 761
circumscription **229**
circumspection
 attention 457
 care 459
 caution 459
circumstance
 phase 8
 event 151
circumstances
 property 780
 bad – 804
 depend on – 475
 good – 803
 under the – 8
circumstantial 8
 – account 594
 – evidence 467
 probability 472
circumstantiality 459
circumstantiate 467
circumvallation
 enclosure 229, 232

testament 771
codify 60, 963
codlin 129
cœcum 261
coefficient
  factor 84
  accompany 88
  co-operate 709
Cœlebs 904
coemption 795
coequal 27
coerce *compel* 744
  restrain 751
coetaneous 120
coeternal
  perpetual 112
  synchronous 120
cœur, à contre –
  603
coeval 120
  – with birth 5
coexist *exist* 1
  accompany 88
  synchronism 120
  contiguity 199
coextension
  equality 27
  parallelism 216
  symmetry 242
coffee 298
coffee-house 189
coffee-pot 191
coffer *chest* 191
  store 636
  money chest 802
cofferdam 55
coffin 363
  add a nail to one's
  – 830
cog *tooth* 253
  boat 273
  deceive 545
  flatter 933
cogent
  powerful 157
  – reasoning 476
cogitate 451
cogitative faculties
  450
cognate
  consanguineous
  11
  related 9
  similar 16
cognition 490
cognitive faculties
  450
cognizance 490
  take – of
  intellect 490
  attention 457

cognomen 564
cognoscence 490
cog-wheel 312
cohabitation
  location 184
  marriage 903
coheir 778
coherence *unite* **46**
  dense 321
cohesive 46
cohibit
  restrict 706
  restrain 751
  prohibit 761
cohobation 336
cohort 726
cohue 72
coif 225
coiffure 225
coign of vantage 33
coil *disorder* 59
  curve 245
  convolution 248
  circuition 311
  shuffle off this
    mortal – 360
coin *fabricate* 161
  imagine 515
  money 800
  – money 775
  – words 563
coincidence
  identity 13
  in time 120
  chance 156
  concurrence 178
  in place 199
  in opinion 488
coiner *thief* 792
coistril 862
coition 42
coke 388
colander 260
colature 652
cold *frigid* **383**
  colour 429, 438
  style 575
  insensible 823
  indifferent 866
  in – blood
    premeditated 611
    purposely 620
    unfeeling 823
    dispassionate 826
  – comfort 832
  – shoulder
    discourtesy 895
    contempt 930
  – steel 727
  – storage 387
  – sweat *fear* 860

dislike 867
  – water cure 662
  throw – water on
    dissuade 616
    hinder 706
    dull 843
cold feet 862
coldhearted
  unfeeling 823
  hostile 889
  malevolent 907
cold pack 670
Coliseum 189, 588,
  728
collaboration 178
collaborator 690,
  711
collapse
  prostration 158
  contract 195
  shortcoming 304
  deteriorate 659
  fatigue 688
  failure 732
collar *dress* 225
  circlet 247
  shackle 752
  seize 789
  slip the – 750
collate 464
collateral
  relation 9, 11
  parallel 216
  lateral 236
  security 771
  – evidence 467
collation
  repast 298
  comparison 464
colleague
  accompany 88
  co-worker 696
  co-operation 709
  auxiliary 711
  friend 890
collect
  assemble 72
  opine 480
  understand 518
  acquire 775
  prayer 990
  – evidence 467
  – knowledge 539
  – one's thoughts
    451
collectanea
  assemblage 72
  compendium 596
collected *calm* 826
collection
  assemblage 72

offertory 998
collectively
  whole 50
  generality 78
  together 88
collectivism 737,
  778
college 542
  go to – 539
  – of cardinals 996
  – education 537
colleen 129
colley 366
collide 276
collier 273
colligate 72
collimation 216,
  278
colliquate 335
collision *disagree-*
  ment 24
  clash 179
  percussion 276
  opposition 708
  encounter 720
collocate
  arrange 60
  assemble 72
  place 184
collocution 588
collogue 933
colloid 352
collop 51, 298
colloquial
  figure of speech
  521
  neology 563
  conversation 588
  – meaning 516
colluctation 720
collusion *deceit* 545
  conspiring 709
collusive 544
colluvies 653
collyrium 662
Cologne
  eau de – 398
colon 142
colonel 745
colonist 188
colonize 184, 294,
  295
colonnade
  series 69
  houses 189
colony 184, 188, 780
colophon 65
colophony 356*a*
Colorado beetle 913
coloration 428
coloratura 415, 416

comfit 396
comfort
  pleasure 377
  delight 827
  content 831
  relief 834
  give – 906
comfortable
  pleasing 829
comforter
  covering 223
Comforter 976
comfortless
  painful 830
  dejected 837
comic *wit* 842
  ridiculous 853
  – opera 599
  – strips 531
coming [*see* come]
  impending 152
  – events
  prediction 511
  – out 883
  – time 121
comitia 696
comity 894
comma 142
  inverted –s 550
command *high* 206
  requisition 630
  authority 737
  order 741
  possess 777
  at one's –
  obedient 743
  – belief 484
  – of language
  writing 574
  speaking 582
  – of money 803
  – one's passions
  944
  – respect 928
  – one's temper
  826
  – a view of 441
commandant 745
commander 269
commandeer 744,
  789
commanding
  [*see* command]
  important 642
commando 726
commandment 697
comme deux
  gouttes d'eau 17
comme il faut
  taste 850
  fashion 852

genteel 875
commemorate 883
commence 66
commencement de
  la fin *end* 67
  destruction 162
commend 931
  – the poisoned
  chalice 544
commendable 944
commensurate
  accordant 23
  numeral 85
  adequate 639
comment
  reason 476
  judgment 480
  interpretation 522
  criticize 595
commentary 595
commentator 492,
  524, 527
commerce
  conversation 588
  barter 794
  cards 840
commercial 811
  – arithmetic 811
  – traveller 758
commère 599
commination 908,
  909
commingle 41
comminute 330
commiserate 914
commissariat 637
commissary
  provisions 637
  consignee 758
commission
  task 625
  delegate 755, 759
  Royal – 696
  – of the peace 965
commissioner 758
commissionaire
  doorkeeper 263
  messenger 534
  consignee 758
commissure 43
commis-voyageur
  758
commit *do* 680
  delegate 755
  cards 840
  arrest 969
  – an absurdity 853
  – oneself to a
  course 609
  – to the flames
  384

– to memory 505
– oneself
  clumsy 699
  promise 768
  – to prison 751
  – sin 945
  – to writing 551
committee
  council 696
  consignee 758
  (*director* 694)
commix 41
commode 191
commodious 644
commodity 798
commodore 745
common
  general 78
  ordinary 82
  plain 344
  habitual 613
  trifling 643
  base 876
  in – *related* 9
  participate 778
  right of – 780
  short –s 640
  tenant in – 778
  make – cause 709
  – consent 488
  – council 966
  – course 613
  – herd 876
  – law *old* 124
  law 697, 963
  – measure 84
  – origin 153
  – parlance 576
  – place 82
  – place book
  record 551
  compendium 596
  – saying 496
  – sense 498
  – sewer 653
  – stock 778
  – weal
  mankind 372
  good 681
  utility 644
  philanthropy 910
Common Pleas
  Court of – 966
commonalty 876
commoner 876
commonplace
  usual 82
  known 490
  plain 576
  habit 613
  unimportant 643

dull 843
commons 298
commonwealth
  territory 181
  community 372
  authority 737
commorant 188
commotion 315
communalism 778
commune
  township 181
commune with 588
  – oneself 451
communibus annis
  29
communicant 990
communicate
  join 43
  tell 527
  correspond 592
  give 784
  sacrament 998
communication
  news 532
  of disease 657
  oral – 582, 588
communion
  discourse 588
  society 712
  participation 778
  sacrament 998
  hold – with 888
  – table 1000
communiqué 527
communism 737
communist
  party 712
  rebel 742
  participation 778
  philanthropy 910
  evil doer 913
community
  party 712
  – at large 372
  – of goods 778
commutation
  compensation 30
  substitution 147
  interchange 148
  compromise 774
  barter 794
commutual 12
compact
  joined 43
  united 87
  receptacle 191
  small 193
  compressed 195
  compendious 201
  dense 321
  bargain 769

compages
  whole 50
  structure 329
compagination 43
companion *match*
  17
  accompaniment
  88
  ladder 305
  friend 890
companionable 892
companionship 892
companionway 305
company
  assembly 72
  actors 599
  party, partner-
  ship 712
  troop 726
  sociality 892
  bear – 88
  in – with 88
comparable 9
comparative 464
  degree 26
  – anatomy 368
comparatively 32
compare 464
  – notes 695
comparison 464
compartition 44
compartment
  part 51
  region 181
  place 182
  cell 191
  carriage 272
compass
  degree 26
  space 180
  surround 227
  measure 466
  intend 620
  guidance 693
  achieve 729
  box the –
  azimuth 278
  rotation 312
  keep within –
  moderation 174
  fall short 304
  economy 817
  points of the – 236
  in a small – 193
  – about 229
  – of thought 498
compassion 914
  object of – 828
compatible
  consentaneous 23
  possible 470

compatriot
  inhabitant 188
  friend 890
compeer *equal* 27
  friend 890
compel 744
compellation 564
compendency 43
compendious 201
compendium 596
  book 593
compensate
  make up for 30
  requite 973
compensation 30
compère 599
competence
  power 157
  sufficiency 639
  skill 698
  wealth 803
competition
  opposition 708
  contention 720
competitor
  opponent 710
  combatant 726
  candidate 767
compilation
  collect 72
  book 593
  compendium 596
compile 54
complacent
  pleased 827
  content 831
  courteous 894
  kind 906
complain 839
complainant 938
complaint
  illness 655
  murmur 839
  lodge a – 938
  – without cause
  839
complaisant
  lenient 740
  courteous 894
  kind 906
complement
  adjunct 39
  remainder 40
  part 52
  arithmetic 84
complementary
  correlation 12
  colour 428
complete
  entire 52
  accomplish 729

compact 769
  – answer 479
  – circle 311
  in a – degree 31
completeness 52
completion 729
complex 59
complexion
  state 7
  colour 428
  appearance 448
compliance
  conformity 82
  obedience 743
  consent 762
  observance 772
complicate
  derange 61
complicated
  disorder 59
  convolution 248
complice 711
complicity 709
compliment
  courtesy 894, 896
  praise 931
  poor – 932
  –s of season 896
complimentary
  free 815
complot 626
comply [see compli-
  ance]
compo *coating* 223
  material 635
component 56
componere lites
  723, 724
comport
  – oneself 692
  – with 23
compos mentis 502
compose
  make up 54, 56
  produce 161
  moderate 174
  music 416
  write 590
  printing 591
  pacify 723
  assuage 826
composed
  self-possessed 826
composer
  music 413
composite 41
composition 54
  [see compose]
  combination 48
  piece of music 415
  picture 556

  style 569
  writing 590
  building material
  635
  compromise 774
  barter 794
  atonement 952
compositor
  printer 591
compost 653
composure 826, 871
compotation 959
compote 298
compound
  mix 41
  combination 48
  limited space 182
  enclosure 232
  compromise 774
  – arithmetic 466
  – for *substitute* 147
  barter 794
comprador 637
comprehend
  compose 54
  include 76
  know 490
  understand 518
comprehension [see
  comprehend]
  intelligence 498
comprehensive 76
  complete 50
  general 78
  wide 192
  – argument 476
compress
  contract 195
  curtail 201
  condense 321
  remedy 662
compressible 322
comprise 76
comprobation
  evidence 467
  demonstration 478
compromise
  dally with 605
  mid-course 628
  taint 659
  danger 665
  pacify 723
composed
  compact 769
  compound 774
  atone 952
compromised
  promised 768
compter 799
compte rendu
  record 551
  accounts 811

comptroller 694
compulsion **744**
compunction 833, 950
compurgation
  evidence 467
  acquittal 970
compute 85
comrade 890
comradeship 892
con *think* 451
  get by heart 505
  learn 539
conation 600
conatu magnas
  nugas, magno –
  waste 638
  unimportance 643
conatus 176
concamerate 245
concatenation
  junction 43
  continuity 69
concavity **252**
conceal
  invisible 447
  hide 528
  cunning 702
concealment **528**, 893
concede
  assent 488
  admit 529
  permit 760
  consent 762
  give 784
conceit *idea* 453
  folly 499
  supposition 514
  imagination 515
  wit 842
  affectation 855
  vanity 880
conceited
  dogmatic 481
conceivable 470
conceive *begin* 66
  beget 161
  teem 168
  believe 484
  understand 490
  imagine 515
  plan 626
concent 413
concentrate
  assemble 72
  centrality 222
  converge 290
concentric 216, 222
conception
  [*see* conceive]

intellect 450
idea 453
concern
  relation 9
  event 151
  business 625
  importance 642
  firm 797
  grief 828
  – oneself with 625
concert
  agreement 23
  synchronism 120
  music 415
  act in – 709
  in – *musical* 413
  concord 714
  – *measures* 626
concertina 417
concerto 415
concert-room 840
concession
  permission 760
  consent 762
  compromise 774
  giving 784
  discount 813
concesso, ex –
  reasoning 476
  assent 488
concetto 842
conchoid 245
conchology 223
concierge 163, 753
conciliate
  talk over 615
  pacify 723
  satisfy 831
  courtesy 894
  atonement 952
conciliatory [*see* conciliate]
  concord 714
  forgiving 918
conciliatrix 962
concinnity
  agreement 23
  style 578
  beauty 845
conciseness **572**
concision 201
conclave
  assembly 72
  council 696
  church 995
conclude
  end 67
  infer 480
  resolve 604
  complete 729
  compact 769

conclusion
  [*see* conclude]
  sequel 65
  germination 161
  judgment 480
  try –s 476
  forgone – 611
  hasty – 481
conclusive
  [*see* conclude]
  answer 462
  evidence 467
  certain 474
  proof 478
  – *reasoning* 476
concoct *lie* 544
  write 590
  plan 626
  prepare 673
concomitant
  accompany 88
  same time 120
  concurrent 178
concord *agree* 23
  music **413**
  assent 488
  harmony **714**
concordance 562
  book 593
concordant 173
concordat 769
concordia discors 24, 59
concours 720
concourse
  assemblage 72
  convergence 290
concremation 384
concrete *existent* 3
  mass 46
  definite 79
  density 321
  hardness 323
  materials 635
concubinage 961
concubine 926
concupiscence 865, 961
concur
  co-exist 120
  causation 178
  converge 290
  assent 488
  concert 709
concurrence **178**, 216
concussion 276
condemnation 932, **971**
condemned cell 752
condense

compress 195
dense 321
condensed
  concise 572
condescend 879
condign 924
condiment **393**
condisciple 541
condition *state* 7
  modification 469
  supposition 514
  term 770
  repute 873
  rank 875
  in – *plump* 192
  in good – 648
  on – 770
  in perfect – 650
  physical – 316
conditional 8
conditions **770**
condolence 914, **915**
condone 918
condottiere
  traveller 268
  fighter 726
conduce
  contribute 153
  tend 176
  concur 178
  avail 644
conducive 631
conduct
  transfer 270
  music 416
  procedure **692**
  lead 693
  safe –
  passport 631
  safety 664
  – a funeral 363
  – an inquiry 461
  – to 278
conduction 264
conductor 269
  conveyer 271
  director 694
  lightning – 666
conduit **350**
conduplicate 89
condyle 250
cone *round* 249
  pointed 253
confabulation 588
confection 396
  confectionary 396
confectioner 637
confederacy
  co-operation 709
  party 712
confederate 711

confer *advise* 695
  give 784
  – benefit 648
  – power 157
  – privilege 760
  – right 924
  – with 588
conference [*see*
  confer]
  council 696
confess *assent* 488
  avow 529
  penitence 950,
  998
  – and avoid 937
confession [*see*
  confess]
  auricular – 998
  – of faith 983
confessional 1000
confessions
  biography 594
confessor 996
confidant 711
confidante
  servant 746
  friend 890
confidence
  trust 484
  hope 858
  courage 861
  in – 528
  – trick 545
confident 535
configuration 240
confine
  region 182
  circumscribe 229
  limit 231, 233
  imprison 751
confined
  narrow judgment
  481
  ill 655
confinement
  childbed 161
confines of
  on the – 197
confirm
  corroborate 467
  assent 488
  consent 762
  compact 769
  rite 998
confirmed 150
  – habit 613
confiscate *take* 789
  condemn 971
  penalty 974
confiture 396
conflagration 382,

384
conflexure 245
conflict
  opposition 708
  discord 713
  contention 720
conflicting
  contrary 14
  counteracting 179
  – evidence 468
confluence
  junction 43
  convergence 290
  river 348
conflux
  assemblage 72
  convergence 290
conform *assent* 488
  – to rule 494
conformable 23,
  178
conformation 54,
  240
conformity 82, 178
confound
  disorder 61
  destroy 162
  not discriminate
  465a
  perplex 475
  defeat 731
  astonish 870
  curse 908
confounded
  great 31
  bad 649
confraternity
  party 712
  friendship 888
confrère
  colleague 711
  friend 890
confrication 331
confront *face* 234
  compare 464
  oppose 708
  resist 719
  – danger 861
  – witnesses 467
confucianism 984
Confucius 986
confuse *derange* 61
  perplex 458
  obscure 519
  not discriminate
  465a
  abash 879
confused *disorder*
  59
  invisible 447
  uncertain 475

style 571
confusion
  [*see* confuse]
  – seize 908
  – of tongues 560,
  563
  – of vision 443
  – worse-con-
  founded 59
confutation 479
congé 293, 756
  – d'élire 995
congeal *dense* 321
  cold 385
congeneric
  similar 17
  included 76
congenial
  related 9
  agreeing 23
  concord 714
  love 897
congenital 5, 820
congeries 72
congestion 641
conglaciation 385
conglobation 72
conglomerate
  cohere 46
  assemblage 72
  council 696
  dense 321
conglutinate 46
congratulate 896
  – oneself 838
congratulation 896
congregation
  assemblage 72
  worshippers 990
  laity 997
Congregationalist
  984
congress
  assembly 72
  convergence 290
  conference 588
  council 698
Congressional
  Medal 733
Congressional
  Record 551
congreve *fuel* 388
  – rocket 727
congruous
  agreeing 23
  (*expedient* 646)
conical *round* 249
  pointed 253
conjecture 475, 514
conjoin 43
conjoint 48

conjointly 37
conjugal 903
conjugate
  words 562
  grammar 567
  – in all its tenses
  &c. 104
conjugation
  junction 43
  pair 89
  phase 144
  grammar 567
conjunction 43
  in – with 37
conjuncture
  contingency 8
  occasion 134
conjure *deceive* 545
  entreat 765
  sorcery 992
  name to – with
  873
  – up *recall* 505
  – up a vision 505
conjuror
  deceiver 548
  sorcerer 994
connaître les des-
  sous des cartes
  490
connate
  intrinsic 5
  kindred 11
  cause 153
connatural
  uniform 16
  similar 17
connect *relate* 9
  link 43
connection
  [*see* connect]
  kin 11
  in – with 9
connections
  cards 840
connective 45
conned, well – 490
connive
  overlook 460
  co-operate 709
  allow 760
connoisseur
  critic 480
  scholar 492
  taste 850
connotate 550
connote 516, 550
  imply 526
connubial 903
connuted 9
conoscente 850

conquer 731
conquered
  (*failure* 732)
conquering hero
  comes 883
conqueror 731
consanguinity **11**
consciarecti, mens—
  pride 878
  innocence 946
conscience
  knowledge 490
  moral sense 926
  in all – *great* 31
  affirmation 535
  awakened – 950
  qualms of – 603
  clear – 946
  stricken – 950
  tender – 926
  honour 939
conscientious 926
  scrupulous 939
  – objector 489
conscious
  intuitive 450
  knowledge 490
  – of disgrace 874
  – of glory 873
conscript 726
conscription 744
consecrate *use* 677
  dedicate 873
  sanctify 987
  holy orders 995
consecration
  rite 998
consectory 478
  – reasoning 476
consecution 63
consecutive
  following 63
  continuous 69
  – fifth 414
consecutively
  slowly 275
consensus 488
  – of opinion 23
consent *assent* 488
  compliance **762**
  with one – 178
consentaneous
  agreeing 23
  (*expedient* 646)
consequence
  event 151
  effect 154
  importance 642
  in – 478
  of no – 643
  take the –s 154

consequent 63
consequential
  deducible 478
  arrogant 878
consequently
  reasoning 476
  effect 154
conservation
  permanence 141
  storage 636
  preservation 670
conservatism 141,
  670
conservative 141,
  712
  – policy 681
conservatoire 542
conservator
  of the peace 967
conservatory
  receptacle 191
  floriculture 371
  furnace 386
  store 636
conserve 396, 636
consider *think* 451
  attend to 457
  examine 461
  adjudge 480
  believe 484
considerable
  in degree 31
  in size 192
  important 642
considerate
  careful 459
  judicious 498
  benevolent 906
consideration
  purchase money
  147
  thought 451
  idea 453
  attention 457
  qualification 469
  inducement 615
  importance 642
  gift 784
  benevolence 906
  respect 928
  requital 973
  deserve – 642
  in – of
  compensation 30
  reasoning 476
  on – 658
  take into –
  thought 451
  attention 457
  under –
  topic 454

  inquiry 461
  plan 626
considered, all
  things –
  collectively 50
  judgment 480
  premeditation 611
  imperfection 651
consign
  transfer 270
  commission 755
  property 783
  give 784
  – to the flames 384
  – to oblivion 506
  – to the tomb 363
consignee **758**
consignor 796
consignment
  commission 755
  gift 784
  apportionment
  786
consilience 178
consist
  – in 1
  – of 54
consistence
  density 321
consistency
  uniformity 16
  agreement 23
consistently with
  82
consistory
  council 696
  church 995
consolation
  relief 834
  condole 915
  religious 976
console
  table 215
Consoler
  the – 976
consolidate
  unite 46, 48
  condense 321
consols 802
consommé 298
consonant
  agreeing 23
  musical 413
  letter 561
consort
  accompany 88
  associate 892
  spouse 903
  – with 23
consortium 23
consortship 892

conspection 441
conspectus 596
conspicuous
  visible 446
  famous 873
conspiracy 626
conspirator 626
  traitor 941
conspire
  concur 178
  co-operate 709
constable
  policeman 664
  governor 745
  officer 965
constant
  fixed 5
  uniform 16
  continuous 69
  regular 80
  continual 112
  frequent 136
  regular 138
  immutable 150
  exact 494
  persevering 604a
  obey 743
  faithful 939
  – flow 69
constellation
  stars 318
  luminary 423
  glory 873
consternation 860
constipation
  closure 261
  density 321
constituency 181,
  737
constituent 51, 56
constitute
  compose 54, 56
  produce 161
constitution
  nature 5
  state 7
  composition 54
  structure 329
  charter 924
  law 963
constitutional
  walk 226
  – government 737
constrain
  compel 744
  restrain 751
  abash 881
constraint 195
constrict 195, 706
constringe 195
construct 161

construction 161
 form 240
 structure 329
 meaning 522
 put a false – upon
  523
constructive
 latent 526
 – evidence 467
constructor 164
construe 522
consubstantiation
 998
consuetude 618
consul 758, 759
consulship 737
consult 695
 – one's pillow 133
 – one's own wishes
  943
 – the wishes of 707
consultant 662
consultation 695,
 696
consume
 destroy 162
 waste 638
 use 677
 – away 36
 – time
 time 106
 inactivity 683
consumere natus,
 fruges – 683
consuming 830
consummate
 great 31
 complete 52
 completed 729
 – skill 698
consummation
 end 67
 completion 729
 – devoutly to be
  wished
 good 618
 desire 865
consumption [*see*
 consume]
 decrease 36
 shrinking 195
 disease 655
contact 199
 come in –
 arrive 292
contagion
 transfer 270
 disease 655
 unhealthy 657
contain
 be composed of 54

include 76
container 191
contaminate
 soil 653
 spoil 659
contaminated
 diseased 655
contango 133, 813
contemn 930
contemper 174
contemplate
 view 441
 think 451
 expect 507
 purpose 620
contemporary 120
contemporation 174
contempt 930
 – of danger 861
contemptible
 unimportant 643
 dishonourable 940
contend
 reason 476
 assert 535
 fight 720
 – with difficulties
  704
 – for
 vindicate 937
content
 assenting 488
 willing 602
 calm 826
 satisfied **831**
 to one's heart's –
 sufficient 639
 success 731
contention 720
contentious 901
contents
 ingredients 56
 list 86
 components **190**
 synopsis 596
conterminate
 end 67
 limit 233
conterminous 199
contesseration 72
contest 709, 720
contestant 710
context 591
 from the – 516
contexture 329
contiguity 199
continence 960
continent
 land 342
continental 643
contingency

event 151
 uncertainty 475
 expectation 507
contingent
 conditional 8
 casual 156
 liable 177
 possible 470
 uncertain 475
 supply 635
 aid 707
 allotted 786
 donation 809
 unforeseen 508
 – duration **108a**
 – interest 780
continual
 perpetual 112
 frequent 136
continuance 143
continuation
 adjunct 39
 sequence 63
 sequel 65
 – school 542
continue
 endure 106, 110
 persist 143
 continued 69
 – success 731
continuity 69
 uniformity 16
contortion
 distortion 243
 convolution 248
contortionist 599,
 700
contour
 outline 230
 appearance 448
contra 14
 per – 708
 – bonos mores
 vulgar 851
 improper 925
 vice 945
contraband
 deceitful 545
 prohibited 761
 illicit 964
contrabasso 417
contraception 706
contract
 shrink 195
 narrow 203
 promise 768
 bargain 769
 bridge 840
 – a debt 806
 – a habit 613
 – an obligation

 768
contractility 195
contraction 195
 short-hand 590
 compendium 596
contractor 690
contradict
 contrary 14
 answer 462
 dissent 489
 deny 536
 oppose 708
contradictory
 disagreement 24
 evidence 468
 discord 713
contradistinction 15
contraindicate
 dissuade 616
 warning 668
contraire, tout au
 – 536
contralto 408, 416
contraposition
 inversion 218
 reversion **237**
contrapuntist 413
contrariety 14
contrary
 opposite 14
 antagonistic 179
 captious 608
 opposing 708
 quite the – 536
 – to expectation
 improbable 473
 unexpected 508
 – to reason 471
contrast
 contrariety 14
 difference 15
 comparison 464
contravallation 717
contravene
 contrary 14
 counterevidence
  468
 deny 536
 hinder 706
 oppose 708
contre cœur, à –
 603
contre-coup 277
contretemps
 ill-timed 135
 hindrance 706
 misfortune 735
contribute
 cause 153
 tend 176
 concus 178

coportion 778
copper *money* 800
  policeman 664
copper-coloured
  433, 439
copper-plate
  engraving 558
  writing 590
coppice 367
coprolite 653
copse 367
copula 45
copulation 43
copy
  imitate 19
  facsimile **21**
  prototype 22
  news 532
  record 551
  represent 554
  write 590
  for the press 591
  plan 626
  – *book* 22
copyhold 780
copyist
  imitator 19
  artist 559
  writer 590
copyright 780
coquet *lie* 544
  change the mind
  607
  affected 855
  endearment 902
  flattery 933
  – *with*
  irresolute 605
coquette
  affected 854, 855
  flirt 897
coquillage 847
coracle 273
coral 847
  – *reef* 667
coram judice
  jurisdiction 965
  lawsuit 969
cor Anglais 417
corbeille 191
corbel 215
cord *tie* 45
  filament 205
cordage 45
cordated 245
cordial
  pleasure 377
  dram 392
  willing 602
  remedy 662
  feeling 821

grateful 829
friendly 888
courteous 894
cordiform 245
cordite 727
cordon
  inclosure 232
  circularity 247
  decoration 877
  – *bleu* 733, 746
  – *sanitaire*
  safety 664
  preservation 670
corduroy 259
cordwainer
  shoemaker 225
  artificer 690
core *gist* 5
  source 153
  centre 222
  gist 642
  true to the – 939
coriaceous 327
Corinthian 850
co-rival
  [*see* corrival]
cork *plug* 263
  lightness 320
  – *jacket* 666
  – *up close* 261
  restrain 751
corking pin 45
corkscrew
  spiral 248
  perforator 262
  circuition 311
cormorant
  desire 865
  gluttony 957
corn
  projection 250
Cornaro 953
cornea 441
corned 959
cornelian 847
corneous 323
corner *place* 182
  receptacle 191
  angle 244
  monopoly 777
  – *creep into a* –
  893
  in a dark – 528
  drive into a – 706
  push into a – 874
  rub off –*s* 82
  – *turn a* – 311
  turn the – 658
  – *stone*
  support 215
  importance 642

defence 717
cornet *music* 417
  officer 745
cornice 210
corniculate 253
cornification 323
Cornish hug 545
corno 417
cornopean 417
cornucopia 639
cornute
  projecting 250
  sharp 253
corollary
  adjunct 39
  deduction 480
corona 247
coronach 839
coronation
  enthronement 755
  celebration 883
coroner 363, 965
  –'*s jury* 967
coronet *hoop* 247
  insignia 747
  title 877
corporal
  corporeal 316
  officer 745
corporate 43
  – *body* 712
corporation
  bulk 192
  convex 250
  association 712
  jurisdiction 965
corporeal 3, 316,
  364
  – *hereditaments*
  780
corporeity 316
corps *assemblage* 72
  troops 726
à – *perdu*
  haste 684
  rash 863
  – *de reserve* 636
corpse **362**
corpulence 192
corpus 316
  – *Christi* 998
  – *delicti*
  guilt 947
  lawsuit 969
  – *juris*
  precept 697
  law 963
corpuscle
  small 32
  little 193
corradiation

focus 74
convergence 290
corral 232, 370
correct
  orderly 58
  true 494
  inform 527
  disclose 529
  improve 658
  repair 660
  due 924
  censure 932
  honourable 939
  virtuous 944
  punish 972
  – *ear* 416, 418
  – *memory* 505
  – *reasoning* 476
  – *style*
  grammatical 567
  elegant 578
correction
  [*see* correct]
  house of – 752
  under – 879
corrective 662
corregidor 745
correlation
  relation 9
  reciprocity **12**
correspondence
  correlation 12
  similarity 17
  agreement 23
  writing **592**
  – *course* 537
correspondent
  messenger 534
  journalist 593
  consignee 758
corresponding
  similar 17
  agreeing 23
corridor *region* 181
  place 191
  passage 627
  – *train* 272
corrigendum 495
corrigible 658
corrival 726
corrivalry 720
corrivation 348
corroborant 662
corroboration
  evidence 467
  assent 488
corrode *burn* 384
  erode 659
  afflict 830
corrosive
  [*see* corrode]

creditable *right* 924
creditor 805
credo quia
  impossibile 486
credulity **486**
credulous person
  dupe 547
creed *belief* 484
  theology 983
  Apostles' – 983*a*
creek *interval* 198
  water 343
creel 191
creep *crawl* 275
  tingle 380
  (*inactivity* 683)
  – in 294
  – into a corner 893
  – into the good
    graces of 933
  – out 529
  – upon one 508
  – with
    multitude 102
    redundance 641
creeper 367
creeping
  sensation 380
  – thing 366
creese 727
cremation
  of corpses 363
  burning 384
crematorium 363,
  386
crematory 386
crème de la crème
  648
Cremona 417
crenate 257
crenelle 257
crenulate 257
creole 57
crêpé 248, 839
crepidam, ultra –
  471
crepitation 406
crepuscule
  dawn 125
  dusk 422
crescendo
  increase 35
  musical 415
crescent
  growing 35
  street 189
  curve 245
cresset 423, 550
crest *supremacy* 33
  summit 210
  pointed 253

tuft 256
sign 550
armorial 877
pride 878
on the – 33
crest-fallen
  dejected 837
  humble 879
crevasse 198, 667
crevice 198
crew *assemblage* 72
  inhabitants 188
  mariners 269
  party 712
crib *bed* 215
  key 522
  granary 636
  steal 791
  parsimony 819
cribbage 840
cribbed, confined,
  cabined – 751
cribble 260
cribriform 260
Crichton,
  Admirable –
  scholar 492
  perfect 650
  proficient 700
crick *pain* 378
cricket *game* 840
  not – 940
  – ground 213
crier 534
  send round the –
    531
crim. con. 961
crime 945, 947
criminal 923, 945
  culprit 949
  – law 963
  court of – appeal
    966
criminality 947
criminate 938
crimp *crinkle* 248
  notch 257
  brittle 328
  deceiver 548
  take 789
  steal 791
crimple 258
crimson 434, 821
cringe *submit* 725
  subject 749
  servility 886
crinite 256
crinkle *angle* 244
  convolution 248
  roughen 256
  fold 258

crinoline 225
cripple *disable* 158
  weaken 160
  injure 659
crippled
  disease 655
crisis
  conjuncture 8
  present time 118
  opportunity 134
  event 151
  strait 704
  excitement 824
  bring to a – 604
  come to a – 729
crisp *rumpled* 248
  rough 256
  brittle 328
  style 572
Crispin 225
criss-cross 219
cristallomantia 511
criterion *test* 463
  evidence 467
  indication 550
crithomancy 511
critic *judge* 480
  taste 850
  detractor 936
critical
  contingent 8
  opportune 134
  discriminating
    465
  important 642
  dangerous 665
  difficult 704
  censorious 932
criticism
  judgment 480
  dissertation 595
  disapprobation
    932
  detraction 934
critique
  [*see* criticism]
croak *cry* 412
  hoarseness 581
  stammer 583
  warning 668
  discontent 832
  lament 839
croaker 832, 837
Croat 726
crochet 847
crock 191
crockery 384
crocodile tears 544
crocus *yellow* 436
Crœsus 803
croft 189, 232

Croix de Guerre 733
cromlech 363, 551
crone *veteran* 130
  fool 501
crony *friend* 890
  favourite 899
crook *curve* 245
  deviation 279
  thief 792
crooked
  sloping 217
  distorted 243
  angular 244
  latent 526
  crafty 702
  ugly 846
  dishonourable 940
  – path 704
  – temper 901
  – ways 279
croon 580
crop
  stomach 191
  harvest 154
  shorten 201
  eat 298
  vegetable 367
  store 636
  gather 775
  take 789
  second – 167, 775
  – out *visible* 446
  disclose 529
  – up *begin* 66
  take place 151
  reproduction 163
cropper *fall* 306
croquet *game* 840
  – ground *level* 213
croquette 298
crosier 747, 999
cross *mix* 41
  across 219
  pass 302
  grave 363
  oppose 708
  failure 732
  disaster 735
  refuse 764
  pain 830
  decoration 877
  fretful 901
  punishment 975
  rites 998
  fiery – 722
  proclaim at the –
    roads 531
  red – 662
  –ed bayonets 708
  – breed 63
  – cut 628

Darby and Joan
secluded 893
married 903
dare *defy* 715
face danger 861
– *not* 860
– *say probable* 472
believe 484
suppose 514
dare-devil
courage 861
rash 863
bluster 887
daring 861
unreserved 525
– *imagination* 515
dark
obscure 421
dim 422
black 431
blind 442
invisible 447
unintelligible 519
latent 526
joyless 837
insidious 940
in the –
ignorant 491
leap in the –
experiment 463
chance 621
rash 863
keep – *hide* 528
– *ages* 491
– *cloud* 735
view with – eyes
932
– *lantern* 423
darkly
see through a
glass – 443
darkness [*see* dark]
421
children of – 988
love – better than
light 989
powers of – 978
darky 431
darling *beloved* 897
favourite 899
darn 660
dart *swift* 274
propel 284
missile 727
– to and fro 684
Dartmoor 752
Darwinism 357
dash
small quantity 32
mix 41
swift 276

fling 284
mark 550
courage 861
cut a – *repute* 873
display 882
– *at resolution* 604
attack 716
– board 666
– cup from lips 761
– down 308
– hopes
disappoint 509
fail 732
dejected 837
despair 859
– on 274
– off *paint* 556
write 590
active 682
haste 684
– of the pen 590
dashed [*see* dash]
humbled 879
dashing
fashionable 852
brave 861
ostentatious 882
dastard 862
data *evidence* 467
reasoning 476
supposition 514
date *time* 106
chronology 114
datum 673
daub *cover* 223
paint 428
misrepresent 555
dirt 653
daughter 167
daunt 860
dauntless 861
Dauphin 875
davenport 191, 215
davit 214
Davus sum non
Œdipus
unintelligent 499
artless 703
dull 843
Davy Jones' locker
310
dawdle *tardy* 133
slow 275
inactive 683
dawk 534
dawn
precursor 64
begin 66
priority 116
morning 125
light 420

dim 422
glimpse 490
dawplucker 936
day
period 108
present time 118
light 410
all – 110
clear as –
certain 474
intelligible 518
manifest 525
close of – 126
decline of – 126
denizens of the –
366
good old –'s 122
have had its – 124
one fine – 119
open as – 703
order of the – 613
red letter – 642
see the light of –
446
– after day
diuturnal 110
frequent 136
– by day
repeatedly 104
time 106
periodic 138
– after the fair
135
–s gone by 122
– of judgment 121
happy as the – is
long 827, 836
– and night
frequent 136
labour – and night
686
–s numbered
transient 111
death 360
– one's own 731
– of rest 686
– star 423
– after to-morrow
121
– before yesterday
122
–s of week 138
all in –'s work 625
daybed 215
daybook *record* 551
accounts 811
daybreak
morning 125
dim 422
day-dream
fancy 515

hope 858
day-labourer 690
daylight 125, 420
see – *intelligible*
518
– *saving* 114
daymare 859
daze 420
dazed 376
dazzle
light 420
blind 422, 443
put out 458
astonish 870
awe 928
dazzling
[*see* dazzle]
beautiful 845
de : – die in diem
time 106
periodic 138
– facto 1
– fond en comble
52
– novo 104
– omnibus rebus
81
– profundis 821
deacon 996
deaconry 995
dead *complete* 52
inert 172
colourless 429
lifeless 360
insensible 376
– against
contrary 14
oppose 708
more – than alive
688
– asleep 683
– beat
powerless 158
– certainty 474
– colour 556
– cut 893
– drunk 959
– failure 732
– flat 213
– heat 27
– languages 560
– letter
impotent 158
unmeaning 517
useless 645
laxity 738
exempt 927
illegal 964
– level 16
– lift *exertion* 686
difficulty 704, 706

- lock *cease* 142
stoppage 265
- march 363, 415
- of night
midnight 126
dark 421
- reckoning
numeration 85
measurement 466
- secret 533
- set against 708
- set at
attack 716
- shot 700
- silence 403
- sound 408a
- stop 142
- to 823
- wall
hindrance 706
defence 717
- weight 706
- water 343
deaden
weaken 158
moderate 174
sound 405
mute 408a
benumb 823
dead-house 363
deadlock 142, 704
deadly *killing* 361
pernicious 649
unhealthy 657
- sin 947
- weapon 727
deads 645
deaf 419
inattentive 458
- to advice 606
- and dumb 581
turn - ear to
neglect 460
unbelief 487
refuse 764
- to reason 901a
- to *insensible* 823
deafen *loud* 404
deafness **419**
deal *much* 31
arrange 60
bargain 768
allot 786
- a blow
injure 659
attack 716
punish 972
- board 323
- in 794
- out *scatter* 73

give 784
- with
treat of 595
handle 692
barter 794
dealer 797
dealings *action* 680
have - with
trade 794
friendly 888
dean 128, 694, 996
deanery *office* 995
house 1000
dear
high-priced 814
loved 897
favourite 899
Ō - ! *lament* 839
- at any price 646
- me *wonder* 870
pay - for whistle
647
dearest foe 936
dearness **814**
dearth 640
- of ideas 843
death **360**
house of - 363
in at the -
arrive 292
kill 361
persevere 604a
pale as -
colourless 429
fear 860
put to - 361, 972
still as - 265
violent - 361
be the - of one
amuse 480
-'s head 837
- in the pot
unhealthy 657
hidden danger
667
deathbed repent-
ance 950
death-blow
end 67
killing 361
failure 732
death-house 752
deathless
perpetual 112
fame 873
deathlike
silent 403
hideous 846
death-song 839
death-struggle 720
death-warrant 971

death-watch 668
débâcle 145
destruction 162
downfall 306
torrent 348
debar *hinder* 706
restrain 751
prohibit 761
debark 292
debase *depress* 308
foul 653
deteriorate 659
degrade 874
debased
lowered 207
dishonoured 940
debate *reason* 476
talk 588
hesitate 605
dispute 720
debatable 475
debauch
spoil 659
intemperance 954
impurity 961
debauchee 962
debenture
security 771
money 800
credit 805
debility 160
debit *debt* 806
accounts 811
debitor 806
débonnaire 836
debouch 293, 295
débris
fragments 51
crumbled 330
useless 645
debt **806**
out of - 803
get out of - 807
- of nature 360
debtor 806
- and creditor 811
debunk 529
début *beginning* 66
essay 675
celebration 883
débutant
learner 541
drama 599
decade *ten* 98
period 108
decadence 659
decagon 244
decalescence 382
decalogue 926
decamp
go away 293

run away 623
decant 270
decanter 191
decapitate *kill* 361
punish 972
decay *decrease* 36
decompose 49
shrivel 195
unclean 653
disease 655
spoil 659
adversity 735
natural - 360
- of memory 506
decayed
[*see* decay]
old 124
rotten 160
decease 360
deceit
falsehood 544
deception 545
cunning 702
deceived
in error 495
duped 547
deceiver **548**
gay - 962
decelerate 275
decennium 108
decent
mediocre 651
pure 960
decentralize 49
deceptio visûs 443
deception **545**
deceptive reason-
ing 477
decession 293
dechristianize 989
decide
turn the scale 153
judge 480
choose 609
decided *great* 31
ended 67
certain 474
resolved 604
take a - step 609
deciduous
transitory 111
falling 306
spoiled 659
decies repetita
placebit 829
decimal 84, 98, 99
decimate
subtract 38
tenth 99
few 103
weaken 160

712
defer 133
– to *assent* 488
submit 725
respect 928
deference
obedience 743
humility 879
courtesy 894
respect 928
defiance 715, 909
threat 909
in – *opposition* 708
set at – *disobey* 742
– of danger 861
deficiency
[*see* deficient]
vice 945
deficient
inferior 34
incomplete 53
shortcoming 304
insufficient 640
imperfect 651
deficit
incompleteness 53
debt 806
defigure 846
defile
interval 198
march 266
dirt 653
spoil 659
shame 874
impure 961
define
specify 79
limit 233
explain 522
name 564
definite
[*see* define]
visible 446
certain 474
exact 494
intelligible 518
manifest 525
perspicuous 570
definition
interpretation 521
definitive *final* 67
affirmative 535
decided 604
deflagration 384
deflate 195
deflation
currency 800
deflect
curve 245
deviate 279
deflower

spoil 659
violate 961
defluxion
egress 295
flowing 348
defœdation 653,
659
deform 241
deformity
distortion 243
ugliness 846
blemish 848
defraud *cheat* 545
swindle 791
defray 807
deft *suitable* 23
clever 698
defunct 360, 362
defy 715
disobey 742
threaten 909
– *danger* 861
dégagé *free* 748
fashion 852
degenerate 659
deglutition 298
degradation
deterioration 659
shame 874
dishonour 940
degree 26
term 71
honour 873
by –s 26
by slow –s 275
degustation 390
dehiscence 260
dehort
dissuade 616
advise 695
dehydrate 340
Dei gratiâ 924
deification 873, 981
deify
honour 873
idolatry 991
deign
condescend 762
consent 879
Deism
heterodoxy 984
irreligion 989
Deity 976
tutelary – 664
dejection
excretion 299
melancholy **837**
déjeûner 298
délabrement 162
delaceration 659
delation 938

delator 527
delay 133
dele 552
delectable
savoury 394
agreeable 829
delectation 827
delectus 562
delegate
transfer 270
commission 755
consignee 758
deputy 759
delenda est
Carthago
destroy 162
curse 908
delete 162
deleterious
pernicious 649
unwholesome 657
deletion 552
deletory
destructive 162
deliberate
slow 275
think 451
attentive 457
leisure 685
advise 695
cautious 864
deliberately
[*see* deliberate]
late 133
with premedi-
tation 611
delicacy *weak* 160
slender 203
dainty 298
brittleness 328
texture 329
savoury 394
colour 428
exact 494
scruple 603
ill health 655
difficult 704
pleasing 829
beauty 845
taste 850
fastidious 868
honour 939
pure 960
delicate ear 418
délice 377
delicious *taste* 394
pleasing 829
delicti, corpus –
guilt 947
lawsuit 969
delicto, in

flagrante – 947
delight
pleasure 827
pleasing 829
Delilah 962
delimit 233
delineate
outline 230
represent 554
describe 594
delineator 559
delineavit 556
delinquency 304,
947
delinquent 949
deliquation 335
deliquesce 36
deliquescence 335
deliquium
paralysis 158
fatigue 688
delirant reges
plectuntur
Achivi 739
delirium
raving 503
passion 825
– *tremens* 503,
959
delitescence
invisible 447
latency 526
seclusion 893
deliver
transfer 270
utter 580, 582
birth 662
rescue 672
liberate 750
give 784
relieve 834
– as one's act and
deed 467
– the goods 729
– judgment 480
– a speech 582
deliverance 672
delivery
[*see* deliver]
bring forth 161
cash on – 807
dell 252
Delphic oracle
prophetic 513
equivocal 520
latent 526
delta 342
delude *error* 495
deceive 545
deluge *crowd* 72
water 337

flood 348
redundance 641
delusion
  [*see* delude]
  insane 503
  self – *credulous*
  486
delve *dig* 252
  till 371
  – into *inquire* 461
demagogue
  director 694
  malcontent 710
  rebel 742
demagogy 737
demand
  inquire 461
  order 741
  ask 765
  price 812
  claim 924
  in – *require* 630
  desire 865
  saleable 796
demarcation 233
dematerialize 317
demean oneself
  conduct 692
  humble 879
  dishonour 940
demeanour
  aid 448
  conduct 692
  fashion 852
demency 503
dementia 503
demerit 945
demesne
  abode 189
  property 780
demi- 91
demigod *hero* 861
  angel 948
demigration 266
demijohn 191
demi-jour 422
demi-lune 717
demi-monde
  plebeian 876
  licentious 962
démenti 536
demirep 962
demise *death* 360
  transfer 783
  lease 787
demisemiquaver
  413
demission 756
demit 757
demiurge
  deity 979

demivolt 309
demobilize 73
democracy *rule* 737
  commonalty 876
Democrats
  party 712
Democritus 838
demoiselle 129
demolish 479
demon *violent* 173
  bane 663
  devil **980**
  – in human shape
  913, 949
  – worship 991
demoniacal
  malevolent 907
  furious 824
  wicked 945
demonology
  demons 980
  sorcery 992
demonstration
  number 85
  proof **478**
  manifest 525
  ostentation 882
  ocular – 441, 446
demonstrative
  manifest 525
  indicative 550
  vehement 825
demonstrator 524
demoralize
  unnerve 158
  spoil 659
  vicious 945
Demosthenes 582
demotic 590
demulcent
  mild 174
  soothing 662
demur
  disbelieve 485
  dissent 489
  unwilling 603
  hesitate 605
  without – 602
demure
  grave 826
  sad 837
  affected 855
  modest 881
demurrage 132
demurrer 969
den *abode* 189
  study 191, 893
  sty 653
  prison 752
  – of thieves 791

denary 98
denaturalize
  corrupt 659
denaturalized
  abnormal 83
dendriform 242, 367
dendrology 369
denial
  negation 536
  refusal 764
  self– 953
denigrate 431
denization 748
denizen
  inhabitant 188
  freeman 748
  –s of the air 979
  –s of the day 366
Denmark, rotten in
  the state of –
  526
denomination
  class 75
  name 564
  sect 712
  religious – 983
denominational
  dissent 489
  theological 983
  – education 537
denominator 84
denote
  specify 79
  mean 516
  indicate 550
dénouement
  end 67
  result 154
  disclosure 529
  completion 729
denounce
  curse 908
  disapprove 932
  accuse 938
dense
  crowded 72
  ignorant 493
density **321**
dent 252, 257
dental 561
denticulated 253,
  257
dentifrice 652
dentistry 662
denude 226
denuded *loss* 776
  – of
  insufficient 640
denunciation
  [*see* denounce]
deny *dissent* 489

negative 556
refuse 764
– oneself
  avoid 623
  seclude 893
  temperate 953
  ascetic 990
Deo volente 470,
  976
deobstruct 705
deodand 974
deodorize 399
  clean 652
deontology 926
deoppilation 705
deorganization 61
deosculation 902
depart 293
  – from
  deviate 15, 279
  relinquish 624
  – this life 360
departed
  non-existent 2
department
  class 75
  region 181
  business 625
departure 293
  new – 66
  point of – 293
depend *hang* 214
  contingent 475
  – upon
  be the effect of 154
  evidence 467
  trust 484
  – on circumstan-
  ces 475
depended on, to
  be –
  certain 474
  reliable 484
  honourable 939
dependency 777,
  780
dependent
  effect 154
  liable 177
  hanging 214
  puppet 711
  servant 746
  subject 749
deperdition 776
dephlegmation 340
depict 554, 556
  describe 594
depilation 226
depilatory 662
depletion 638, 640
deplorable *bad* 649

conduct 692
complete 729
command 741
happy – 972
– *case* 191
– *food* 298
– *rider* 534
desperado
  rash 863
  blusterer 887
  evil-doer 913
desperate *great* 31
  violent 173
  impossible 471
  resolved 604
  difficult 704
  excitable 825
  hopeless 859
  rash 863
  anger 900
despicable
  trifling 643
  shameful 874
  contemptible 930
despise 930
– *danger* 861
despite 30, 907
  in – 708
despoil *injure* 659
  take 789
  rob 791
despond 837, 860
despot 745
despotism
  authority 737
  severity 739
  arbitrary 964
despumate 652
desquamation 226
dessert 298
dessous des cartes
  cause 153
  latent 526
  secret 533
  connaître le – 490
dessus dessous
  sens – 218
destination *end* 67
  arrival 292
  intention 620
destiny *chance* **152**
  fate 601
  fight against – 606
destitute
  insufficient 640
  poor 804
  refuge for – 666
destrier 726
destroy
  demolish 162·
  injure 659·

– *hopes* 859
– *life* 361
destroyed
  [*see* destroy]
  inexistent 2
  failure 732
destroyer 165
  warship 726
  evil-doer 913
destructive
  bad 649
destructor 383
desuetude 614
  disuse 678
desultory
  disordered 59
  fitful 70
  multiform 81
  irregular in time 139
  changeable 149
  deviating 279
  agitated 315
desume 788
detach 44
detached
  irrelated 10
  loose 47
detachment
  part 51
  army 726
detail *describe* 594
  special portions 79
  allot 786
  ornament 847
  attention to – 457, 459
  in – 51
details
  minutiæ 32
  unimportant 643
detain 781
detect 480a
detective 527, 664
detention 133, 751, 781
  house of – 752
  in house of – 938
détenu 754
deter *dissuade* 616
  alarm 860
deterge *clean* 652
detergent
  remedy 662
deterioration 659
determinate
  special 79
  exact 474
  conclusive 480
  intended 620

determine *end* 67
  define 79
  cause 153
  direction 278
  satisfy 462
  make sure 474
  judge 480
  discover 480a
  resolve 604
determined
  resolute 604
determinism 601
deterration 529
detersion 652
detersive 662
detest *dislike* 867
  hate 898
detestable 649
dethronement
  anarchy 738
  abrogation 756
detonate
  explode 173
  sound 406
detortion *form* 243
  meaning 523
détour *curve* 245
  circuit 629
detract *subduct* 38
  underrate 483
  defame 934
  slander 938
detraction 934
detractor 936
detrain 292
detriment
  evil 619
  deterioration 659
detrimental 649
detrition 330
detritus
  fragments 51
  deposit 270
  powder 330
detrude
  cast out 297
  cut down 308
detruncate 38
deuce *two* 89
  devil 978
  play the – 825
  – is in him 608
deuced *great* 31
  painful 830
deus 976
– *ex machinâ*
  aid 707
  auxiliary 711
  deity 976
  sorcerer 994
deuterogamy 903

devastate
  destroy 162
  havoc 659
develop
  increase 35
  produce 161
  expand 194
  evolve 313
development 144, 154
devexity
  bending 217
  curvature 245
deviate *vary* 20a
  change 140
  turn 279
  diverge 291
  circuit 629
– *from* 15
– *from rectitude* 940
– *from virtue* 945
deviation 279
device *motto* 550
  expedient 626
  artifice 702
devil
  seasoned food **392**
  evil-doer 913
  bad man 949
  Satan 978
  demon 980
  fight like –s 722
  have a – 503
  machinations of the – 619
  play the – with
  injure 659
  malevolent 907
  printer's – 591
  raise the – 828
– *may care*
  rash 863
  indifferent 866
  insolent 885
  give the – his due
  right 922
  vindicate 937
  fair 939
– *in one*
  headstrong 863
  temper 901
– *to pay*
  disorder 59
  violence 173
  evil 619
  failure 732
  penalty 974
– *take* 908
– *take the hind-most*

run away 623
haste 684
cowardice 862
−'s tattoo 407
devilish *great* 31
bad 649
malevolent 907
devious *curved* 245
deviating 279
circuitous 311
devisable 270
devise *imagine* 515
plan 626
bequeath 784
devised by the
enemy 546
devisee *possess* 779
receive 785
deviser 164
devitalize 158
devoid *absent* 187
empty 640
not having 777a
devoir *courtesy* 894
respect 928
devolve 783
− *on* 926
devote *destine* 601
employ 677
consecrate 873
− to destruction
908
− the mind to 457
− oneself to 604
devoted
habit 613
ill-fated 735
obedient 743
undone 828
friendship 888
love 897
devotee
zealot 682
aspirant 865
pious 987
fanatic 988
devotion [*see* de-
votee, devoted]
love 897
piety 987
worship 990
self − 942
devour
destroy 162
eat 298
gluttony 957
devoured by
feeling 821
devouring element
382
devout 987, 990

devoutless 989
devoutly 821
dew 339
shake as −drops
from lion's
mane 483
dewy eve 126
dexterous 238, 698
dextrality **238**
dey 745
dhow 273
diable:
avoir le − au corps
503
− à quatre
disorder 59
violence 173
loud 404
excitement 825
tirer le − par la
queue 804
diablerie 978, 992
diabolic
bad 649
malevolent 907
wicked 945
Satanic 978
Diacoustics 402
diacritical 550
diadem 747, 847
diaeresis 49
diagnosis 465, 655
diagnostic
special 79
experiment 463
indication 550
(*intrinsic* 5)
diagonal 217
diagram 554
dial 114
as the − to the sun
veracious 543
faithful 772
dialect 563
dialectic
argument 476
language 560
dialogism 586
dialogue 588
diameter 202
diametrically
opposite
contrariety 14
contraposition
237
diamond
lozenge 244
type 591
goodness 648
ornament 847
rough − 703

− cut diamond
cunning 702
retaliation 718
− jubilee 883
− wedding 883
Diana *moon* 318
chaste 960
goddess 979
diapason 413
diaper 847
diaphanous 425
diaphonics 402
diaphoresis 299
diaphragm 68, 228
diaporesis 475
diarchy 737
diarrhœa 299
diary 114, 551
diastole 194
diatessaron 413
diathermancy 384
diathesis
nature 5
state 7
temperament 820
diatonic 413
diatribe 932
dibble
perforator 262
till 371
dibs *money* 800
dicacity 885
dice 156, 621
on the − 470
dicer 621
false as −'s oaths
546
dichotomy
bisect 91
angle 244
dichroism 440
dichromatic 443
dickens 978
dicker 794
dicky 215, 225
dictaphone 553
dictate
write 590
enjoin 615
advise 695
authority 737
command 741
dictator 694, 745
−'s of society 852
dictatorial
dogmatic 481
wilful 600
insolent 885
dictatorship 737,
739
diction 569

dictionary
list 86
words 562
book 593
dictum
judgment 480
maxim 496
affirmation 535
command 741
didactic 537
didder 383
diddle 545, 791
Diddler, Jeremy −
792
diduction 44
die *mould* 22
expire 360
engraving 558
hazard of the −
621
never say − 604a
not willingly let −
670
− away
vanish 4
decrease 36
cease 142
the − is cast 601
− with ennui 841
− for *desire* 865
endearment 902
− game 951
− hard
obstinate 606
resist 719
− in harness 143,
604a
− in the last ditch
604a
− with laughter
838
− from the mem-
ory 536
− and make no
sign 951
− out 2, 4
− of a rose in aro-
matic pain 822
− in one's shoes
972
− a violent death
361
− hard 710, 832
dies non *never* 107
rest 687
diet *food* 298
council 696
spare − 956
dietetics 662
differ 15
discord 713

agree to – 489
beg to – 439
– in opinion 489
– toto cœlo
contrary 14
dissimilar 18
dissent 489
difference 15
[*see* differ]
numerical 84
perception of –
465
split the – 774
– engine 85
different 15
multiform 81
– time **119**
differentia 15
differential 15, 84
– calculus 85
differentiate 79, 465
differentiation
calculation 85
discrimination
465
difficult 704
– to please 868
difficulties
poverty 804
in – 806
difficulty 704
question 461
diffide 485
diffident 860, 881
diffluent 348
diffraction 470
– grating 445
diffuse *mix* 41
disperse 73
publish 531
style 573
diffuseness 104, **573**
dig *deepen* 208
excavate 252
till 371
– out 461
– the foundations
673
– up 455, 480a
digamy 903
digest *arrange* 60
boil 384
think 451
compendium 596
plan 626
prepare 673
brook 826
diggings 189
dight *dress* 225
ornament 847
digit 84

digitate 44
digitated 253
digladiation 720
dignify 873
dignitary
clergy 996
dignity
glory 873
pride 878
honour 939
dignus vindice
nodus
unintelligible 519
difficulty 704
prodigy 872
digress
deviate 279
style 573
digression
circuit 629
dihedral 89
– angle 244
diis alitur visum
disappointment
509
necessity 601
dijudication 480
dike *gap* 198
fence 232
furrow 259
gulf 343
conduit 350
defence 717
dilaceration 44
dilapidation 659
dilate
increase 35
swell 194
widen 202
rarefy 322
expatiate 573
dilatory
slow 275
inactive 683
dilection 89
dilemma
uncertain 475
logic 476
choice 609
difficulty 704
dilettante 492, 850
dilettantism
knowledge 490
diligence
coach 272
diligent
active 682
– thought 457
dilly-dally
irresolution 605
inactivity 683

dilucidation 522
diluent 335
dilute *weaken* 160
water 337
diluvian 124
dim *dark* 421
faint 422
invisible 447
unintelligible 519
dime 800
dimension 192
dimidiate 91
diminish
lessen 36
contract 195
– the number 103
diminutive 32, 193
diminuendo
decreasingly 36
music 415
dimness 422
dimple 252, 257
dimsightedness 443
unwise 499
din 404
– in the ear
repeat 104
drum 407
loquacity 584
dine 298
– with Duke
Humphrey 87
ding 408
ding-dong
repeat 104
chime 407
dining-car 272
dining-room 191
dingle 252
dingy *boat* 273
dark 421, 422
colourless 429
black 431
gray 432
dinner 298
– jacket 225
– party 892
dint *power* 157
concavity 252
blow 276
by – of
instrumentality
631
dio, sub – 220, 338
diocesan 996
diocese 181, 995
Diogenes
recluse 893
cynic 911
lantern of –
inquiry 461

dioptrics 420
diorama *view* 448
painting 556
diorism 465
dip *slope* 217
concavity 252
ladle 270
direction 278
insert 300
descent 306
plunge 310
water 337
candle 423
baptize 998
– one's hands into
take 789
– into
glance at 457
inquire 461
learn 539
diphthong 561
diploma
evidence 467
commission **755**
diplomacy
artfulness 702
mediation 724
negotiation 769
diplomatist
messenger 534
expert 700
consignee 758
dipper 191
dipsomania
insanity 503
desire 865
drunkenness **959**
dipsomaniac 504
diptych 86, 551
dire *hateful* 649
disastrous 735
grievous 830
fearful 860
direct
straight 246
teach 537
artless 703
command 741
– attention to **457**
– one's course
motion 278
pursuit 622
– the eyes to 441
direction
[*see* direct]
tendency **278**
indication 550
management **693**
precept 697
directly *soon* 132
director

teacher 540
theatre 599
manager **694**
master 745
– of the budget 801
directorship 737
directory *list* 86
council 696
diremption 44
direption 791
dirge
funeral 363
song 415
lament 839
dirigible balloon 273, 726
dirk 727
dirt 653
throw –
defame 874
disrespect 929
– *cheap* 815
like – under one's feet 749
dirty *dim* 222
opaque 426
unclean 653
disreputable 874
dishonourable 940
– end of stick 699
– sky 353
– weather 349
do – work
servile 886
flatterer 935
diruption 162
disability
impotence 158
disable 158
weaken 160
disabuse 527, 529
disaccord 713
disadvantage
evil 619
inexpedience 647
at a – 34
lie under a – 651
disadvantageous 647, 649
disaffection
dissent 489
enmity 889
hate 898
disaffirm 536
disagreeable 830, 867
disagreement
difference 15
incongruity **24**
dissent 489

discord 713
disallow 761
disannul 756
disappearance **449**
disappointment
balk **509**
fail 732
discontent 832
disapprobation 706, **932**
disapprover 936
disarm *disable* 158
weaken 160
reconcile 831
propitiate 914
disarrange 61
disarray
disorder 59
undress 226
disaster *evil* 619
failure 732
adversity 735
calamity 830
disastrous *bad* 649
disavow 536
disband
separate 44
disperse 73
liberate 750
disbar
abrogate 756
punish 972
disbarment 55
disbelief 485, 487
religious 989
disbench 756, 972
disbowel 297
disbranch 44
disburden
facilitate 705
– one's mind 529
– oneself of 782
disburse 809
disc 220, 234
discard *eject* 297
relinquish 624
disuse 678
abrogate 756
refuse 764
repudiate 773
surrender 782
– from one's thoughts 458
discarded 495
disceptation 476
discern *see* 441
know 490
discernible 446
discernment 498, 868
discerption 44

discharge
violence 173
propel 284
emit 297
excrete 299
sound 406
acquit oneself 692
complete 729
liberate 750
abrogate 756
pay 807
exempt 927a
acquit 970
– a duty 926, 944
– a function
business 625
utility 644
– itself *egress* 295
river 348
– from the memory 506
– from the mind 458
– an obligation 772
discind 44
disciple *pupil* 541
votary 711
Christian 985
disciplinarian
master 540
martinet 739
discipline
order 58
teaching 537
training 673
restraint 751
punishment 972
religious 990
disclaim *deny* 536
repudiate 756
abjure 757
refuse 764
disclosure 480a, **529**
discoid *layer* 204
frontal 220
flat 251
discoloration 429
discoloured
shabby 659
ugly 846
blemish 848
discomfit 731
discomfiture 732
discomfort
physical 378
mental 828
discommend 932
discommode
hinder 706
annoy 830

discommodious 645, 647
discompose
derange 61
put out 458
hinder 706
pain 830
disconcert 874
anger 900
discomposure 828
disconcert
derange 61
distract 458
disappoint 509
hinder 706
discontent 832
confuse 879
disconcerted
hopeless 859
disconformity 83
discongruity 24
disconnected
style 575
disconnection
irrelation 19
disjunction 44
discontinuity 70
disconsolate 837
discontent **832**
discontinuance
cessation 142
relinquishment 624
discontinuity **70**
discord
difference 15
disagreement 24
of sound **414**
of colour **428**
dissension **713**
discount
decrease 36
decrement 40a
money **813**
at a –
disrepute 874
disapproved 932
discountenance
disfavour 706
refuse 764
discourage
dissuade 616
sadden 837
frighten 860
discourse
teach 537
speech 582
talk 588
dissert 595
sermon 998
discourtesy **895**

discous 202
discover
  perceive 441
  solve 462
  find 480a
  disclose 529
  – itself
  be seen 446
discovery 480a
discredit
  disbelief 485
  dishonour 874
discreditable
  vicious 945
discreet *careful* 459
  cautious 864
discrepancy 15
discrepant 24, 713
discrete
  separate 44, 70
  single 87
discretion *will* 600
  choice 609
  skill 698
  caution 864
  surrender at – 725
  use – 609
  years of – 131
discrétion à – 600
discrimination
  difference 15
  nice perception
  465
  wisdom 498
  taste 850
  fastidiousness 868
disculpate 937
discumbency 213
discursion 266
discursive
  moving 264
  migratory 266
  wandering 279
  argumentative 476
  diffuse style 573
  conversable 588
  disserting 595
discus 840
discuss *eat* 298
  reflect 451
  inquire 461
  reason 476
  dissert 595
discussion
  [see discuss]
  open to – 475
  under – 461
disdain
  indifference 866
  fastidious 868
  arrogance 885

  pride 878
  contempt 930
disease **655**
  occupational – 655
  –d mind 503
disembark 292
disembarrass 705
disembody
  decompose 49
  disperse 73
  spiritualize 317
disembogue
  emit 295
  eject 297
  flow out 348
disembowel 297,
  301
disembroil 60
disenable 158
disenchant
  discover 480a
  dissuade 616
  displease 830
disencumber 705
disendow 756
disengage
  detach 44
  facilitate 705
  liberate 750
disengaged
  to let 763
disentangle
  separate 44
  arrange 60
  unroll 313
  decipher 522
  facilitate 705
  liberate 750
disenthral 750
disenthrone 756
disentitle 925
disespouse 905
disestablish
  displace 185
  abrogate 756
disesteem 929, 932
disfavour
  oppose 708
  hate 898
  disrespect 929
  view with – 932
disfigure
  deface 241
  injure 659
  deform 846
  blemish 848
disfranchise 925
disgorge *emit* 297
  flow out 348
  restore 790
  pay 807

disgrace
  shame 874
  dishonour 940
  sense of – 879
disgraceful
  vice 945
disgruntle 509
disguise
  unlikeness 18
  conceal 528
  mask 530
  falsify 544
  untruth 546
disguised in drink
  959
disgust *taste* 395
  offensive 830
  weary 841
  dislike 867
  hatred 898
  – of life 837
dish *destroy* 162
  plate 191
  food 298
  – of tea 892
dishabille
  undress 225
  unprepared 674
dishearten
  dissuade 616
  pain 830
  discontent 832
  deject 837
dished 252, 732
disherison 789
dishevel
  loose 47
  untidy 59
  disorder 61
  disperse 73
  intermix 219
dishonest *false* 544
  base 940
dishonour
  disrepute 874
  disrespect 929
  baseness 940
  – bills 808
dish-water 653
disillusion 509
disincline
  dissuade 616
  dislike 867
disinclined 603
disinfect
  purify 652
  restore 660
disinfectant 662
disingenuous
  false 544
  dishonourable 940

disinherit
  relinquish 782
  transfer 783
  deprive 789
disintegrate
  separate 44
  decompose 49
  pulverize 330
disinter *exhume* 363
  discover 480a
disinterested **942**
disjecta membra
  separate 44
  disorder 59
  dispersed 73
  – poetæ 597
disjoin 44
disjointed
  disorder 59
  powerless 158
  style 575
disjunction **44**
disjunctive 70
diskindness 907
dislike **867**
  reluctance 603
  hate 898
dislocate
  separate 44
  put out of joint 61
dislocated
  disorder 59
dislodge
  displace 185
  eject 297
disloyal 940
dismal
  depressing 830
  dejected 837
dismantle
  destroy 162
  divest 226
  render useless 645
  injure 659
  disuse 678
dismask 529
dismast
  render useless 645
  injure 659
  disuse 678
dismay 860
dismember
  separate 44
  disperse 73
dismiss
  send away 289
  discharge 297
  discard 678
  liberate 750
  abrogate 756
  relinquish 782

punish 972
– from the mind
  452, 458
dismount
  arrive 292
  descend 306
  render useless 645
disnest 185
disobedience 742
  non-observance
  773
disoblige 907
disorder
  confusion **59**
  derange 61
  turbulent 173
  disease 655
  –ed intellect 503
disorderly
  unprincipled 945
disorganize
  derange 61
  destroy 162
  spoil 659
disorganized 59
disown 536
dispair 44
disparage
  underrate 483
  disrespect 929
  dispraise 932
  detract 934
disparity
  different 15
  dissimilar 18
  disagreeing 24
  unequal 28
  isolated 44
dispart 44
dispassionate 826
  – opinion 484
dispatch
  [*see* despatch]
dispel *scatter* 73
  destroy 162
  displace 185
  repel 289
dispensable
  useless 645
dispensary 662
dispensation
  [*see* dispense]
  command 741
  licence 760
  relinquishment
  782
  exemption 927a
  –s of Providence
  976
dispense
  disperse 73

give 784
apportion 786
retail 796
– with
  disuse 678
  permit 760
  exempt 927a
cannot be –d with
  630
dispeople
  eject 297
  expatriate 893
disperse
  separate 44
  scatter 73
  diverge 291
  waste 638
dispersion 73
– of light 420
chromatic – 428
dispirit
  discourage 616
  sadden 837
displacement
  derange 61
  remove **185**
  transfer 270
displacency
  dislike 867
  incivility 895
  disapprobation
  932
displant 185
display *appear* 448
  show 525
  parade 882
displease 830
displeasure 828
  anger 900
displosion 173
displume 789
disport 840
disposal
  [*see* dispose]
  at one's – 763, 777
dispose
  arrange 60
  tend 176
  induce 615
  – of *use* 677
  complete 729
  relinquish 782
  give 784
  sell 796
disposed 620
disposition
  nature 5
  order 58
  arrangement 60
  inclination 602
  mind 820

dispossess
  transfer 783
  take away 789
  – oneself of 782
dispraise 932
dispread 73
disprize 483
disproof
  counter-evidence
  468
  confutation 479
disproportion
  irrelation 10
  disagreement 24
disprove 479
disputable 475, 485
disputant 710, 726
disputatious 901
dispute
  discuss 476
  doubt 485
  deny 536
  discord 713
in – 461
disqualification
  incapacitate 158
  useless 645
  unprepared 674
  unskilful 699
  disentitle 925
disquiet
  changeable 149
  agitation 315
  excitement 825
  uneasiness 828
  give pain 830
disquietude
  apprehension 860
disquisition 539,
  595
disregard
  overlook 458
  neglect 460
  make light of 483
  insensible to 823,
  826
  disrespect **929**
  contempt 930
  – of time 115
disrelish 867, 898
disreputable 874
  vicious 945
disrepute 874, 929
disrespect 929
  despise 930
disrobe 226
disruption
  disjunction 44
  destruction 162
  discord 713
dissatisfaction

disappointment
  509
sorrow 828
discontent 832
dissect
  anatomize 44, 49
  investigate 461
dissemblance 18
dissemble 544
dissembler 548
disseminate
  scatter 73
  pervade 186
  publish 531
  teach 537
dissension 713
  sow – 898
dissent
  disagree **489**
  refuse 764
  heterodoxy 984
dissentient 15
dissentious 24
dissertation 595
disservice
  disadvantage 619
  useless 645
disserviceable 649
dissever 44
dissidence
  disagreement 24
  dissent 489
  discord 713
  discontent 832
  heterodoxy 984
dissilience 173
dissimilarity 18
dissimulate 544
dissipate *scatter* 73
  destroy 162
  pleasure 377
  prodigality 818
  amusement 840
  intemperance 954
  dissolute 961
dissocial 893
dissociate 44
dissociation
  irrelation 10
  separation 44
dissolute 961
  profligate 945
  intemperate 954
dissolution
  [*see* dissolve]
  decomposition 49
  destruction 162
  death 360
dissolve *vanish* 2, 4
  liquefy 335
  disappear 449

abrogate 756
dissolving views
448, 449
dissonance
disagreement 24
unmusical 414
discord 713
dissuasion **616**
dissyllable 561
distaff
– side 374
distain *dirty* 653
ugly 846
distal 196
distance **196**
overtake 282
go beyond 303
defeat 731
angular – 244
keep at a –
discourtesy 895
keep one's –
avoid 623
modest 881
respect 928
teach one his – 879
– of time
long time 110
past 122
distaste 867
distasteful 830
distemper 299, 428
colour 428
painting 556
disease 655
distend 194
distended 192
distich 89, 597
distil *come out* 295
extract 301
evaporate 336
drop 348
distinct
disjoined 44
audible 402
visible 446
intelligible 518
manifest 525
express 535
articulate 580
distinction
difference 15
discrimination
465
style 578
fame 873
rank 875
– without a differ-
ence 27
distinctive 15
– feature 79

distinctness 15
distingué 852, 873
distinguish
perceive 441
discriminate 465
– by the name of
564
distinguishable 15
distinguished
superior 33
repute 873
Distinguished
Service Cross
733
distortion
obliquity 217
twist **243**
of vision 443
misinterpret 523
falsehood 544
misrepresent 555
ugly 846
distract 458
distracted
confused 475
insane 503
excited 824
distraction
passion 825
love to – 897
distrain *take* 789
appraise 812
attach 969
distrait 458
distraught 824
distress
distraint 789
poverty 804
affliction 828
cause pain 830
signal of – 669
distressingly
excessively 31
distribute
arrange 60
disperse 44, 73
allot 786
district 181
– council 696
distrust
disbelief 485
fear 860
distrustful 487
disturb
derange 61
change 140
agitate 315
excite 824
distress 828, 830
disturbance 59
disunion

discord 24
separation 44
disorder 59
discord 713
disuse
desuetude 614
relinquish 624
unemploy **678**
disused
old 124
disvalue 932
ditch
inclosure 232
trench 259
water 343
conduit 350
defence 717
to the last – 606
ditch-water 653
ditheism 984
dither 315
dithyramb
music 415
poetry 597
dithyrambic 503
ditto 13, 104
say – to 488
ditty 415
– box 191
diurnal 138
diuturnity **110**
diva 416
divagate 279, 629
divan *sofa* 215
council 696
throne 747
tribunal 966
divaricate *differ* 15
bifurcate 91
diverge 291
dive *swim* 267
fly 267
plunge 306, 310
– into *inquire* 461
divellicate 44
diver 208
divergence
difference 15
variation 20a
disagreement 24
deviation 279
separation **291**
divers *different* 15
multiform 81
many 102
– coloured 440
diverse 15
diversify
very 20a
change 140
diversion

change 140
deviation 279
pleasure 377
amusement 840
diversity
difference 15
irregular 16a
dissimilar 18
multiform 81
– of opinion 489
divert *turn* 279
deceive 545
amuse 840
– the mind 452,
458
divertissement
diversion 377
drama 599
amusement 840
Dives 803
divest *denude* 226
take 789
– oneself of
abrogate 756
relinquish 782
divestment **226**
divide *differ* 15
separate 44
part 51
arrange 60
arithmetic 85
bisect 91
vote 609
apportion 786
dividend *part* 51
number 84
portion 786
divina particula
auræ 450
divination
prediction 511
sorcery 992
divine *predict* 511
guess 514
perfect 650
of God 976, 983,
983a
clergyman 996
divine afflatus 515
– right
authority 737
due 924
– service 990
diving 840
diving-bell 208
divining-rod 550,
993
Divinity *God* 976
theology 983
divisible
number 84

[465]

division
[*see* divide]
part 51
class 75
arithmetic 85
discord 713
military 726
divisor 84
divorce
separation 44
relinquish 782
matrimonial **905**
Divorce Court 966
divulge 529
divulsion 44
divvy 786
dixi 535
dizen 847
dizzard 501
dizzy
dimsighted 443
confused 458
vertigo 503
– *height* 206
– *round* 312
djerrid 727
djinn 980
do *fare* 7
suit 23
produce 161
cheat 545
act 680
complete 729
succeed 731
I beg 765
all one can – 686
plenty to – 682
thing to – 625
– away with
destroy 162
eject 297
abrogate 756
– battle 722
– one's bidding
743
– business 625
– to death 361
– as done by 906,
942
– for *destroy* 162
kill 361
conquer 731
serve 746
punish 972
– good 906
– harm 907
– honour 873
– into
translate 522
– justice to 595
– like 19

– little 683
– no harm 648
– nothing 681
– nothing but 136
– one's office 772
– as others do 82
– over 223
– as one pleases
748
– a service
useful 644
aid 707
– up 660
have to – with
680, 692
– without 678
– the work 686
– wrong 923
**docere, pisces na-
tare** – 641
docile *domesticated*
370
learning 539
willing 602
docimastic 463
dock *diminish* 36
cut off 38
port 189
shorten 201
edge 231
store 636
tribunal 966
docked
incomplete 53
docker 690
docket
list 86
evidence 467
note 550
record 551
security 771
dockyard 691
doctor
learned man 492
restore 660
remedy 662
after death the –
135
– *accounts* 811
when –s disagree
475
doctrinaire
positive 474
pedant 492
affectation 855
blusterer 887
doctrinal 537
doctrinarian 514
doctrine *tenet* 484
knowledge 490
document 551

documentary
evidence 467
dodder 315
doddering 128
dodecahedron 244
dodge *change* 140
shift 264
deviate 279
oscillate 314
pursue 461
avoid 623
stratagem 702
dodger, artful – 792
dodo 366
extinct as the –
122
doe *swift* 274
deer 366
female 374
doer
originator 164
agent 690
doff 226
– the cap 894
dog *follow* 281
animal 366
male 373
pursue 622
wretch 949
cast to the –s
destroy 162
reject 610
disuse 678
abrogate 756
relinquish 782
fire – 386
go, to the –s
destruction 162
fail 732
adversity 735
poverty 804
sea – 269
watch –
safety 664
warning 668
keeper 753
hair of – that bit
you 959
let sleeping –s lie
141
– in manger 706,
943
–tired 686
–s of war 722
dog-cart 272
dog-cheap 815
dog-days 382
doge 745
dogged
obstinate 606
valour 861

sullen 901a
dogger 273
doggerel
verse 597
ridiculous 851,
853
dog-hole 189
dog-Latin 563
dogma *tenet* 484
theology 983
dogmatic
certain 474
positive 481
assertion 535
obstinate 606
dogmatist 887
dog's ear 258
dog robber 746
dog-sick 867
dog-star 423
dog-trot 275
dog-weary 688
doily 852
doing
up and – 682
what one is – 625
doings
events 151
actions 680
conduct 692
doit *trifle* 643
coin 800
dolce far niente 681
doldrums
dejection 837
sulks 901a
dole
small quantity 32
scant 640
give 784
allot 786
parsimony 819
grief 828
doleful 837
– *dumps* 901a
doll *small* 193
image 554
dollar 800
dolman 225
dolmen 363, 551
**dolorem, infandum
renovare** – 833
dolorous 830
dolour
physical 378
moral 828
dolphin 341
dolt 501
doltish 499
domain
class 75

region 181
property 780
Domdaniel 982
dome *high* 206
  roof 223
  curvature 245
  convex 250
Domesday book
  list 86
  record 551
domesman 967
domestic
  inhabitant 188
  home 189
  interior 221
  servant 746
  secluded 893
  – *animals* 366
domesticate
  locate 184
  acclimatize 613
  – *animals* 370
domicile 189
domiciled 186
domiciliary 188
  – *visit* 461
dominant 175
  note in music 413
domination 737
dominical 998
domineer
  tyrannize 739
  insolence 885
Domini, anno – 106
Dominican 996
Dominie 540
dominion 181, 737
domino *dress* 225
  mask 530
  game 840
domn 745
don *put on* 225
  scholar 492
  teacher 540
  noble 875
Don Juan 897
donation 784
done *finished* 729
  work – 729
  – *for spoilt* 659
  failure 732
  – *up*
    impotent 158
    tired 688
  have – *with*
    cease 142
    relinquish 624
    disuse 678
donee 785
donjon 717, 752
donkey *ass* 271

fool 501
  talk a –'*s hind leg*
    off 584
donna 374
Donnybrook Fair
  disorder 59
  discord 713
donor 784
donzel 746
doodle 501
doom *end* 67
  fate 152
  destruction 162
  death 360
  judgment 480
  necessity 601
  sentence 971
  – *sealed*
    death 360
    adversity 735
doomed 735, 828
doomsday
  end 67
  future 121
  till – 112
door *entrance* 66
  cover 223
  brink 231
  barrier 232
  opening 260
  passage 627
  at one's – 197
  beg from door to –
    765
  bolt the – 666
  close the – *upon*
    751
  death's – 360
  keep within –*s* 265
  lie at one's – 926
  lock the – 666
  open a – *to*
    liable 177
  open the – *to*
    receive 296
    facilitate 705
    permit 760
  show the – *to*
    eject 297
    discourtesy 895
  – *mat* 652
doorkeeper 263
doorway 260
dope 376, 545, 663
doquet
  security 771
Dorado, El – 803
Doric mode 413
dormant
  inert 172
  latent 526

asleep 683
dormer 260
dormeuse 272
dormir debout,
  conte à – 843
dormitive 841
dormitory 191
dormouse 683
dorp 189
dorsal 235
dorser 191
dorsum 235, 250
dory 273
dose *quantity* 25
  part 51
  medicine 662
  apportion 786
dosser 191
dossier *bundle* 72
  record 551
dossil 223, 263
dot *small* 32
  place 182
  little 193
  variegate 440
  mark 550
  dowry 780
  on the – 113
dotage 128, 499
dotard 130, 501
dotation 784
dottle 40, 645
dote *drivel* 499, 503
  – *upon* 897
douanier 965
double
  similar 17
  increase 35
  duplex 90
  substitute 147
  fold 258
  turn 283
  finesse 702
  march at the – 274
  see –
    dim sight 443
    drunk 959
  – *acrostic*
    letters 561
    wit 842
  – *dutch* 518
  – *entry* 811
  – *the fist* 909
  – *march* 684
  – *meaning* 520
  – *a point* 311
  in – *quick time*
    274
  – *reef topsails* 664
  – *sure* 474
  work – *tides* 686

– *up*
  render powerless
    158
double bar 747
double-bass 417
doublecross 545
double-dealing
  lie 544
  cunning 940
double-distilled 171
double-dyed 428
double-eagle 800
double-edged 90,
  171
double entendre
  ambiguity 520
  impure 961
double-faced
  lie 544
  cunning 702, 940
double-headed 90
double-minded 605
double-shotted 171
doublet 225
double-tongued
  lie 544
  cunning 702, 940
doubt
  uncertain 475
  disbelieve **485**
  sceptic 989
doubtful 475
  more than – 473
  – *meaning*
    unintelligible 519
doubtless
  certain 474
  belief 484
  assent 488
douceur 784, 973
douche 337
dough 324, 354, 800
doughty 861
dour 739
douse
  immerse 310
  splash 337
  blow 972
Dove
  Holy Ghost 976
dove
  innocent 946
  roar like sucking –
    174
dovecote 189
dovetail
  agree 23
  join 43
  intersect 219
  intervene 228
  angle 244

insert 300

dowager 374, 905
dowdy 653, 851
dower 780, 803, 810
dowerless 804
down
  below 207
  light 320
  bear – *upon* 716
  bed of –
  pleasure 377
  repose 687
  come – 306
  get – 306
  go –
  sink 306
  calm 826
  keep – 36
  money – 807
  take –
  lower 308
  rebuff 874
  humble 879
  – on one's mar-
   row-bones 886
  – in the mouth 837
  – and out 874
  – in price 815
  go – like a stone
   310
  be – upon
  attack 716
  severe 739
downcast 306, 837
  – eyes 879
downfall
  destruction 162
  fall 306
  failure 732
  misfortune 735
downhill 217, 306
  go –
  adversity 735
downpour 348
downright
  absolute 31
  manifest 525
  sincere 703
downs 206, 344
down-trodden
  submission 725
  vanquished 732
  subject 749
  dejected 837
  disrepute 874
  contempt 930
downwards 306
downy
  smooth 255
  plumose 256
  soft 324

dowry 780, 784
dowse 276
dowser 994
doxology 990
doxy 897
doyer 128
doyley 652
doze 683
dozen 98
drab *colour* 432
  slut 653
  hussy 962
drabble 653
drachm 319
Draco 694, 739
draff 653
draft [*see also*
  draught]
  multitude 102
  drawing 554, 556
  write 590
  abstract 596
  plan 626
  cheque 800
  credit 805
  – off *displace* 185
  transfer 270
draft-horse 271
drag *carriage* 272
  crawl 275
  traction 285
  impediment 706
  put on the – 275
  – a chain
  tedious 109, 110
  exertion 686
  subjection 749
  – into
  implicate 54
  compel 744
  – through mire
  disrepute 874
  disrespect 929
  – on *tedious* 110
  – into open day
   531
  – towards
  attract 288
  – slow length
  long 200
  weary 841
draggle 285, 653
  – tail 59
drag-net
  all sorts 78
dragoman 524
dragon *monster* 83
  violent 173
  animal 366
  irascible 901
dragonnade

  attack 716
  punish 972
dragoon
  soldier 726
  compel 744
  insolent 885
  worry 907
drain
  flow out 295
  empty 297
  dry 340
  conduit 350
  waste 638
  clean 652
  unclean 653
  exhaust 789
  dissipate 818
  – the cup
  drink 298
  drunken 959
  – the cup of
   misery 828
  – into 348
  – pipe 249
  – of resources 640
drake *male* 373
  fire – 423
dram *drink* 298
  pungent 392
  stimulus 615
  – drinking 959
drama 599
dramatic 599
  ostentation 882
  – author 599
  – critic 599
  – poetry 597
dramatis personæ
  mankind 372
  play 599
  agents 690
  party 712
drapery 225, 847
drast 645
drastic 171
draught
  [*see also* draft]
  depth 208
  traction 285
  drink 298
  stream of air 349
  delineation 554,
   556
  plan 626
  physic 662
  troops 726
  – off 73
draughts
  game 840
draughtsman
  artist 559

draw *equality* 27
  compose 54
  pull 285
  delineate 554, 556
  – aside 279
  – off the attention
   458
  – back
  deduction 40a
  regret 283
  avoid 623
  – breath
  refresh 689
  feeling 821
  relief 834
  – a cheque 800
  – a curtain 424
  – down 153
  – forth 677
  – from 810
  – on futurity 132
  – in one's horns
  tergiversation 607
  humility 879
  – in 195
  – an inference 480
  – the line 465
  – lots 621
  – near *time* 121
  approach 286
  – off *eject* 297
  hinder 706
  take 789
  – on *time* 121
  event 151
  induce 615
  – out
  protract 110
  late 133
  prolong 200
  extract 301
  discover 480a
  exhibit 525
  diffuse style 573
  – over *induce* 615
  – a parallel 9
  – the pen through
   552
  – a picture 594
  – profit 775
  – and quarter 972
  – the sword
  attack 716
  war 722
  – the teeth of 158
  – together
  assemble 72
  co-operate 709
  – towards 288
  – up *order* 58
  stop 265

write 590
- up a statement 594
- upon *money* 800
- the veil 528
drawback *evil* 619
  imperfection 651
  hindrance 706
  discount 813
drawbar 45
drawbridge
  way 627
  escape 671
  raise the - 666
drawcansir 887
drawee 800
drawer
  receptacle 191
  artist 559
  - of water 690
drawers
  dress 225
drawhead 45
drawing
  delineation 554, 556
  prize 810
drawing-room
  assembly 72
  room 191
  fashion 852
drawl *prolong* 200
  creep 275
  in speech 583
  sluggish 683
drawn *equated* 27
  - battle
  - irresistibly 601
  pacification 723
  incomplete 730
dray 272
  - horse 271
drayman 268
dread 860
dreadful *great* 31
  bad 649
  dire 830
  depressing 837
  fearful 860
dreadless 861
dreadnought
  warship 726
dream
  unsubstantial 4
  error 495
  fancy 515
  sleep 683
  golden - 858
  - of *think* 451
  intend 620
  - on other things

458
dreamer
  madman 504
  imaginative 515
dreamy
  unsubstantial 4
  inattentive 458
  sleepy 683
dreary
  monotonous 16
  solitary 87
  melancholy 830, 837
dredge *collect* 72
  extract 301
  raise 307
dregs
  remainder 40
  refuse 645
  dirt 653
  - of the people 876
  - of vice 945
drench *drink* 298
  water 337
  redundance 641
  - with physic 662
drencher 248
drenching rain 348
dress
  uniformity 16
  agree 23
  equalize 27
  clothes 225
  prepare 673
  ornament 847
  ostentation 882
  full - 852
  - circle 599
  - the ground 371
  - up *falsehood* 544
  represent 554
  - wounds 662
  - to advantage 847
dress-coat 225
dresser
  sideboard 215
  surgeon 662
dressing 932, 972
  - room 191, 599
dressing-gown 225
dressmaker 225
dribble 295, 348
driblet 25, 32
drift
  accumulate 72
  distance 196
  motion 264
  flying 267
  float 267
  transfer 270

direction 278
  deviation 279
  approach 286
  wind 349
  meaning 516
  intention 620
  snow - 383
drifter 273
drifting 605
driftless 621
drill *fabric* 219
  bore 260
  auger 262
  teach 537
  prepare 673
  - hall 191
drink
  swallow 296
  liquor 298
  tipple 959
  - one's fill
  enough 639
  - in *imbibe* 296, 298
  - in learning 539
  - to *celebrate* 883
  courtesy 894
drinking-bout 954
drink-money 784
drip 295, 348
dripping *wet* 330
  fat 356
drive *airing* 266
  impel 276
  propel 284
  break in 370
  urge 615
  haste 684
  direct 693
  attack 716
  compel 744
  - at *mean* 516
  intend 620
  - a bargain
  barter 794
  parsimony 819
  - care away 836
  - a coach and six through 83
  - into a corner
  difficult 704
  hinder 706
  defeat 731
  subjection 749
  - to despair 859
  - matters to an extremity 604
  - from *repel* 289
  - one hard 716
  - home 729
  - in 300

- to the last 133
- out 297
- trade
  business 625
  barter 794
drivel *slobber* 297
  imbecile 499
  mad 503
  rubbish 517
driveller 501, 584
driver 268
  director 694
driving rain 348
drizzle 348
droil 683
droit du plus fort 744
drôle *cards* 840
drole 949
  - de corps 844
drollery
  amusement 840
  wit 842
  ridiculous 853
dromedary 271
drone *slow* 275
  sound 407, 412, 413
  inactive 683
drool 297
droop
  weak 160
  hang 214
  sink 306
  disease 655
  decline 659
  flag 688
  sorrow 828
  dejection 837
drop *small quantity* 32
  discontinue 142
  powerless 158
  bring forth 161
  spherule 249
  emerge 295
  fall 306
  trickle 348
  relinquish 624
  discard 782
  gallows 975
  let - 308
  ready to -
  fatigue 688
  - asleep 683
  - astern 283
  - from the couds 508
  - dead 360
  - by drop
  by degrees 26

in parts 51
– in the bucket 32
– in upon 674
– into a good
 thing 734
– into the grave
 360
– a hint 527
– all idea of 624
– in *arrive* 292
 immerse 300
 sociality 892
– the mask 529
– off *decrease* 36
 die 360
 sleep 683
– in the ocean
 trifling 643
– the subject 458
– too much 959
dropping fire 70
drop-scene 599
dropsical 194, 641
droshki 272
dross
 remainder 40
 slag 384
 trash 643, 645
 dirt 653
drought
 dryness 340
 insufficiency 640
drouth *desire* 865
drove
 assemblage 72
 multitude 102
drover 370
drown
 affusion 337
 kill 361
 ruin 731, 732
 – care 840
 – the voice 581
drowsy *slow* 275
 sleepy 683
 weary 841
drub
 defeat 731, 732
 punish 972
drudge *labour* 686
 worker 682, 690
drug
 render insensible
 376
 superfluity 641
 trash 643
 remedy 662
 bane 663
 – in the market
 815
drugget

cover 223
clean 652
preserve 670
druggist 662
druid 996
drum
 repeat 104
 cylinder 249
 sound 407
 music 417
 party 892
 beat of –
 signal 550
 alarm 669
 war 722
 command 741
 parade 882
 ear – 418
 muffled –
 funeral 363
 non-resonance
 408a
– and fife band 417
– fire 407
– out 972
drum-head 964,
 966
drum-major 745
drummer 416
drunken 959
 reel like a – man
 315
drunkenness **959**
dry *arid* 340
 style 575, 576, 579
 hoarse 581
 scanty 640
 preserve 670
 exhaust 789
 tedious 841
 dull 842
 thirsty 865
 cynical 932
 teetotal 958
 run – 640
 with – eyes 823
 – dock 189
 – joke 842
 – land 342
 – the tears 834
 – up 340, 638
dryad 979
dry-as-dust
 antiquarian 122
 dull 843
dryness **340**
dry-nurse
 teach 537
 teacher 540
 aid 707
dry-point 558

dry-rot
 dirt 653
 decay 659
 bane 663
dualism 984
duality **89**
duarchy 737
dub 564
dubious 475
ducat 800
duce 745
duchess 745, 875
duchy 181
duck *stoop* 308
 plunge 310
 water 337
 darling 897, 899
 play –s and
 drakes
 recoil 277
 prodigality 818
 –'s egg
 zero 101
 – in thunder 870
ducking-stool 975
duckling 127
duck-pond 370
duct 350
ductile
 elastic 323
 flexible 324
 trimming 607
 easy 705
 docile 743
dud 158, 727
dude 854
duds 225
dudgeon
 dagger 727
 discontent 832
 churlishness 895
 hate 898
 anger 900
 sullenness 901a
due
 expedient 646
 owing 806
 proper 924, 926
 give his – to
 right 922
 vindication 937
 fair 939
 in – course 109
 occasion 134
 – respect 928
 – sense of 498
 – time
 soon 132
 – to
 cause and effect
 154, 155

give – weight 465
duel 720
duellist 726
dueness **924**
duenna
 teacher 540
 guardian 664
 keeper 753
dues 812
duet 415
duff 298
duffer
 bungler 701
 smuggler 792
dug 250
dug-out
 old man 130
 boat 273
 defence 717
duke *ruler* 745
 noble 875
dulce domum 189
dulcet
 sweet 396
 sound 405
 melodious 413
 agreeable 829
dulcify 174, 396
dulcimer 417
Dulcinea 897
dulcorate 396
dulia 990
dull *weak* 160
 inert 172
 moderate 174
 blunt 254
 insensible 376,
 381
 sound 405
 dim 422
 colourless 429
 ignorant 493
 stolid 499
 style 575
 inactive 683
 unapt 699
 callous 823
 dejected 837
 weary 841
 prosing 843
 simple 849
 – of hearing 419
 – sight 443
dullard 501
dullness **843**
duly 924
duma 696
dumb 581
 – animal 366
 – show 550
 – waiter 307

strike –
ignorant 493
astonish 870
humble 879
dumbfounder
disappoint 509
silence 581
astonish 870
humble 879
dummy
substitute 147
impotent 158
speechless 581
inactive 683
dump *music* 415
store 636
lament 839
undersell 796
dumpling 298
dumps
discontent 832
dejection 837
sulk 901*a*
dumpy *little* 193
short 201
thick 202
dun *dim* 422
colourless 429
grey 432
importune 765
creditor 805
dunce
ignoramus 493
fool 501
dunderhead 501
dune 206
dung 653
dungeon 752
dunghill
dirt 653
cowardly 862
baseborn 876
– *cock* 366
Dunker 984
dunt 716
duo 415
duodecimal 99
duodecimo
little 193
book 593
duodenary 98
duologue
interlocution 588
drama 599
dupe
credulous 486
deceive 545
deceived **547**
duplex 90, 189
duplicate
imitate 19

copy 21
double 90
tally 550
record 551
redundant 641
pawn 805
duplication
imitation 19
doubling **90**
repetition 104
duplicature
fold 258
duplicity
duality 89
falsehood 544
dura lex sed lex 926
durable
long time 110
stable 150
durance 141, 751
in – 754
duration 106
contingent – **108a**
infinite – 112
durbar
conference 588
council 696
tribunal 966
duress
compulsion 744
restraint 751
during 106
– *pleasure &c.*
108*a*
durity 323
dusk
evening 126
half-light 422
dusky
dark 421
black 431
dust *levity* 320
powder 330
corpse 362
trash 643
dirt 653
money 800
come to –
die 360
come down with
the – 807
humbled in the –
879
kick up a – 885
level with the –
162
lick the –
submit 725
fail 732
make to bite the –
731

turn to –
deorganized 358
die 360
– in the balance
643
throw – in the
eyes
blind 442
deceive 545
plead 617
– one's jacket 972
duster 652
dust-bin, dust-hole
191, 645
fit for the –
useless 645
dirty 653
spoilt 659
dustman
cleaner 652
dust-storm 330
dusty
powder 330
dirt 653
Dutch
double – 519
high – 519
– auction 796
– courage 862
Dutchman, flying
515
dutiful 944
duty
business 625
work 686
tax 812
courtesy 894
obligation **926**
respect 928
worship 990
rite 998
do one's –
virtue 944
on – 680, 682
duumvirate 737
Duval, Claude –
792
D.V. 470, 976
dwarf
lessen 36
small 193
elf 980
dwell
reside 186
abide 265
– upon
descant 573
dweller 188
dwelling 184, 189
dwindle *lessen* 36
shrink 195

dyad 89
dye 428
dying 360
dyke [*see* dike]
dynamic energy
157
dynamics 276
dynamitard 863
dynamite 727
dynamo 153
dynasty 737
dysentery 299
dyspepsia 655
dysphony 581

E

each 79
– to each 786
– other 12
– in his turn 148
eager
willing 602
active 682
ardent 821
desirous 865
– *expectation* 507
eagle
standard 550
money 800
– boat 726
– eye *sight* 441
intelligence 498
– winged *swift* 274
insignia 747
eagre 348
ean 161
ear 418
corn 154
come to one's –s
527
din in the –
loud 404
drum 407
all – 418
have the – of
belief 484
friendship 888
lend an –
hear 418
attend 457
meet the – 418
nice – 418
no – 419
offend the – 410
pick up the –s
attention 457
expectation 507
put about one's –s
308

quick – 418
reach one's –s 527
ring in the – 408
set by the –s
  discord 713
  hate 898
  resentment 900
split the –s 404
together by the –s
  discord 713
  contention 720
up to one's –s
  redundance 641
  active 680, 682
willing – 602
word in the – 586
– for music 416,
  418
in at one – out at
  the other
  inattention 458
  forget 506
not for –s polite
  961
make the –s tingle
  anger 900
– ache 378
ear-drum 418
earl 875
earless 419
earliness 132
early 132
get up – 682
earmark 550
earn 775
earnest *willing* 602
  determined 604
  emphatic 642
  pledge 771
  pay in advance
  809
  eager 821
in –
  affirmation 535
  veracious 543
  strenuous 682
ear-piercing 410
ear-ring 847
ear-shot 197
out of – 405
ear-splitting 404
earth *ground* 211
  world 318
  land 342
  corpse 362
what on –
  inquiry 461
  wonder 870
– closet 653
earthenware
  baked 384

sculpture 557
earthling 372
earthly 318
end of one's –
  career 360
of no – use 645
earthly-minded
  943, 989
earthquake 146,
  173
earthwork 717
earwig *flatter* 933,
  935
ear-witness 467
ease *bodily* 377
  style 578
  leisure 685
  facility 705
  mental 827
  content 831
at one's –
  prosperous 734
mind at –
  cheerful 836
set at – *relief* 834
take one's – 687
– off *deviate* 297
– one of *take* 789
easel *support* 215
  painting 556
  – picture 556
easement
  property 780
  relief 834
easily
  [see *easy*]
let one down – 918
– accomplished
  705
– deceived 486
– persuaded 602
East 236, 278
Easter *period* 138
  rite 998
– Monday
  holiday 840
– offering
  gift 784
– sepulchre 1000
easy *gentle* 275
  style 578
  facile 705
make oneself –
  about 484
take it –
  inactive 683
  inexcitable 826
– ascent 217
– of belief 472
– chair
  support 215

repose 687
– circumstances
  803
– going
  willing 602
  irresolute 605
  lenient 740
  inexcitable 826
  contented 831
  indifferent 866
– sail
  moderate 174
  slow 275
– temper 894
– terms 705
– to understand
  518
– virtue 961
eat *food* 298
  tolerate 826
– dirt 725, 879
– one's fill
  enough 639
  gorge 957
– heartily 298
– one's words 879
– out of house and
  home *take* 789
  prodigal 818
  gluttony 957
– of the same
  trencher 892
– one's words 607
eatables 298
eaten up with 820
eau, battre l' – 645
faire venir l' – à la
  bouche 865
mettre de l' – dans
  son vin 174
eaves 250
eavesdropper 455,
  527
eavesdropping 418,
  532
ébauche 626
ebb *decrease* 36
  contract 195
  regress 283
  recede 287
  waste 638
  spoil 659
low – 36
  low 207
  depression 308
  insufficient 640
– and flow 314
– of life 360
ebb-tide *low* 207
  dry 340
ebony 431

ebriety 959
ebullient
  violent 173
  hot 382
  excited 824
ebullition
  energy 171
  violence 173
  agitation 315
  heating 384
  excitation 825
  anger 900
écarté 840
ecce
– iterum Crispinus
  104
– signum 550
eccentric 220
  irregular 83
  foolish 499
  crazed 503, 504
  capricious 608
ecchymosis 299
ecclesiastic
  church 995
  clergy 996
ecclesiastical
  canonical 985
– court 966
– law 963
ecclesiolatry 991
écervelé 458
échafaudage 673
échappée 840
échapper belle 671
échelon 279
echo *imitate* 19
  copy 21
  repeat 104
  reflection 277
  resonance 408
  answer 462
  assent 488
applaud to the –
  931
awake –es 404
éclaircissement 522
éclat 873
eclectic 609
eclipse *surpass* 33
  disappearance
  449
  hide 528
  outshine 873, 874
partial – *dim* 422
total – *dark* 421
under an –
  invisible 447
  out of repute 874
ecliptic 318
eclogue 597

emboss *convex* 250
  ornament 847
embouchure 260
embowel 297
embrace
  cohere 46
  compose 54
  include 76
  enclose 227
  choose 609
  take 789
  friendship 888
  sociality 892
  courtesy 894
  endearment 902
  – an offer 760
embrangle 61
embranglement 713
embrasure 257, 260
embrocation 662
embroider
  variegate 440
  lie 544
  ornament 847
embroidery
  adjunct 39
  exaggeration 549
embroil *derange* 61
  discord 713
embroilment 59
embrown 433
embryo
  beginning 66
  cause 153
  in – *destined* 152
  preparing 673
embryology 357
embryonic 193, 674
embus 293
embusqué 603
emendation 658
emerald *green* 435
  jewel 847
emerge 295, 446
emergency
  circumstance 8
  event 151
  difficulty 704
emeritus 500, 928
emersion 295, 446
emery
  sharpener 253
  – paper
  smooth 255
emetic *remedy* 662
émeute 742
emication 420
emigrant 57, 268
emigrate 266, 295
emigré 268, 295
eminence

  height 206
  fame 873
  church dignitary
    996
eminent domain
  744
eminently 33
emir 745, 875
emissary
  messenger 534
  consignee 758
emission 297
emit *eject* 297
  publish 531
  voice 580
  – vapour 336
Emmanuel 976
emmet 193
emollient 662
emolument
  acquisition 775
  receipt 810
  remuneration 973
emotion 821
  –al appeal 824
  –al drama 599
empale 260, 972
empanel 86, 969
empathy 515
emperor 745
emphasis 580
emphatic 535, 642
emphatically 31
empierce
  perforate 260
  insert 300
empire 737, 789
  – day 840
empiric 548
empirical 463, 675
empiricism 463
emplane 293
employ
  business 625
  use 677
  servitude 749
  commission 755
  in one's – 746
  – one's capital in
    794
  – oneself 680
  – one's time in
    625
employé
  servant 746
  agent 758
employer 795
empoison 659
emporium 799
empower
  power 157

  commission 755
  accredit 759
  permit 760
empress 745
empressement
  activity 682
  emotion 821
  desire 865
emprise 676
emption 795
emptor 795
  caveat – 769
empty *clear* 185
  vacant 187
  deflate 195
  drain 297
  ignorant 491
  waste 638
  deficient 640
  useless 645
  beggarly account
    of – boxes
  poverty 804
  – one's glass 298
  – purse 804
  – sound 517
  – stomach 865
  – title *name* 564
  undue 925
  – words 546
empty-handed 640
empty-headed 4,
  491
empurple 437
empyrean *sky* 318
  blissful 829
empyreuma 41
empyrosis 384
emulate *imitate* 19
  goodness 648
  rival 708
  compete 720
  glory 873
emulsion 352
emunctory 350
en – bloc 50
  – masse 50
  – passant
  parenthetical 10
  transient 111
  à propos 134
  – rapport 9
  – règle *order* 58
  conformity 82
  – route
  journey 266
  progress 282
enable 157
enact *drama* 599
  action 680
  conduct 692

  complete 729
  order 741
  law 963
enallage 521
enamel *coating* 223
  painting 556
  ornament 847
enameller 559
enamour 897
encage 751
encamp 184, 189
encampment 184
encaustic 556
enceinte
  with child 161
  region 181
  inclosure 232
enchafe 830
enchain 751
enchant *please* 829
enchanted 827
enchanting 845,
  897
enchantment
  sorcery 992
enchase 43, 259
enchiridion 593
enchorial 188
encincture 229
encircle 76, 227,
  311
enclave *close* 181
  boundary 233
enclose 227, 229
enclosure
  region 181
  envelope 232
  fence 752
encomiast 935
encomium 931
encompass 227, 233
  –ed with difficul-
    ties 704
encore 104, 931
encounter
  undergo 151
  clash 276
  meet 292
  withstand 708
  contest 720
  – danger 665
  – risk 621
encourage
  animate 615
  aid 707
  comfort 834
  hope 858
  embolden 861
encroach
  transcursion 303
  do wrong 923

infringe 925
encumber 704, 706
encumbrance
 clear of − 807
encyclical 531
encyclopædia 490,
 593
 walking − 700
encyclopædical
 general 78
 − knowledge 490
encysted 229
end
 termination **67**
 effect 154
 object 620
 at an − 142
 come to its − 729
 one's journey's −
 292
 on − 212
 put an − to
 destroy 162
 kill 361
 begin at the
 wrong − 699
 − one's days 360
 −s of the earth 196
 − to end *space* 180
 touching 199
 length 200
 − of life 360
 − in smoke 732
 − of one's tether
 sophistry 477
 ignorant 491
 insufficient 640
 difficult 704
endamage 649
endanger 665
endear 897
endearment **902**
endeavour
 pursue 622
 attempt 675
 use one's best −
 686
 − after 620
endemic
 special 79
 interior 221
 disease 657
endimanché 847,
 882
endless
 multitudinous
 102
 infinite 105
 perpetual 112
endlessly 16
endlong 200

endocrine 221
endogenous 367
endorse
 evidence 467
 assent 488
 compact 769
 − *a bill* 800
 approve 931
endorsement 550
endosmose 302
endow
 confer power 157
endowed with
 possessed of 777
endowment
 intrinsic 5
 power 157
 talent 698
 gift 784
endrogynous 83
endue 157
endure *time* 106
 last 110
 persist 143
 continue 141
 undergo 151
 feel 821
 submit to 826
 unable to − 867
 − for ever 112
 − pain 828
enduring
 indelible 505
endwise 212
enemy *time* 841
 foe 891
 the common − 978
 thing devised by
 the − 546
 − to society 891
energumen 504
energy *power* 157
 strength 159
 physical **171**
 resolution 604
 activity 682
enervate 158, 160
enfant, bon − 906
 − gâté
 prosperity 734
 satiety 869
 favorite 899
 − perdu
 hopeless 859
 reckless 863
 − terrible
 curiosity 455
 artless 703
 object of fear 860
enfeeble 160
enfeoff 780, 783

Enfield rifle 727
enfilade
 lengthwise 200
 pierce 260
 pass through 302
enfold 229
enforce *urge* 615
 advise 695
 compel 744
 require 924
enfranchise
 free 748
 liberate 750
 permit 760
enfranchised 924
engage
 bespeak 132
 induce 615
 undertake 676
 do battle 722
 commission 755
 promise 768
 compact 769
 I'll −
 affirmation 535
 − the attention
 457
 − with 720
engaged
 marriage 903
 be − 135
 − in *attention* 457
engagement
 business 625
 battle 720
 betrothal 902
engaging
 pleasing 829
 amiable 897
engender 161
engine 153, 633
engine-driver 268
engineer 690, 694,
 726
engineering 633
engird 227
English 188
 broken − 563
 king's − 560
 murder the king's
 − 568
 plain −
 intelligible 518
 interpreted 522
 style 576
 − horn 417
engorge
 swallow 296
 gluttony 957
engorgement
 too much 641

engrail 256
engrave
 furrow 259
 mark 550
 − in the memory
 505
engraver 559
engraving 21, 22,
 558
engross *write* 590
 possess 777
 − the thoughts
 thought 451
 attention 457
engrossed in
 thought 451
engulf
 destroy 162
 plunge 310
 swallow up 296
enhance
 increase 35
 improve 658
enharmonic 413
enigma
 question 461
 secret 533
enigmatic
 uncertain 475
 unintelligible 517
 obscure 519
enigme, mot d' −
 522
enjoin *advise* 695
 command 741
 prescribe 926
enjoy
 physically 377
 possess 777
 morally 827
 − health 654
 − popularity 873
 − a state 7
enkindle *heat* 384
 excite 824
enlarge
 increase 35
 swell 194
 in writing 573
 liberate 750
 − the mind 537
enlarged views 498
enlighten
 illumine 420
 inform 527
 teach 537
enlightened
 knowledge 490
enlist *engage* 615
 war 722
 commission 755

under the ban-
ners of 707
– into the service
677
enliven
delight 829
cheer 836
amuse 840
enmity **889**
ennoble 873
ennui 841
enormity
crime 947
enormous *great* 31
big 192
– *number* 102
enough *much* 31
no more! 142
sufficient 639
moderately 651
satiety 869
know when one
has had – 953
– in all conscience
641
– to drive one
mad 830
– and to spare 639
enounce 535, 580
enrage 830, 900
enragé 865
enrapture
excite 824
beatify 829
love 897
enraptured 827
enravish 829
enravished 827
enravishment 824
enrich
improve 658
wealth 803
ornament 847
enrobe 225
enroll *list* 86
record 551
– *troops* 722
commission 755
ens *essence* 1
Ens Entium 976
ensample 22
ensanguined 361
ensconce
conceal 528
safety 664
ensconced
located 184
ensemble 50
enshrine
circumscribe 229
repute 873

sanctify 987
– in the memory
505
ensiform 253
ensign
standard 550
officer 726
master 745
– of authority 747
ensilage 637
enslave 749
ensnare 545
ensue *follow* 63, 117
happen 151
ensure 474
entablature 210
entail *cause* 153
tie up property
781
entangle
interlink 43
derange 61
ravel 219
entrap 545
embroil 713
entangled
disorder 59
– by difficulties
704
entend, cela s' – 613
entente
agreement 23
alliance 714
friendship 888
enter *go in* 294
appear 446
note 551
accounts 811
– into the compo-
sition of 56
– into details
special 79
describe 594
– into an engage-
ment 768
– into the feelings
of 914
– into the ideas of
understand 518
concord 714
– in *converge* 290
– the lists
attack 716
contention 720
– the mind 451
– a profession 625
– into the spirit of
feel 821
delight 827
– upon 66
– into one's views

488
enterprise
pursuit 622
undertaking 676
commercial – 794
enterprising
active 171, 682
courageous 861
entertain
bear in mind 457
support 707
amuse 840
sociality 892
– doubts 485
– feeling 821
– an idea 451
– an opinion 484
entertainment 840
pleasure 377
repast 298
entêté 481, 606
enthral
subjection 749
restraint 751
enthrone 873
enthronement 755
enthusiasm
language 574
willingness 602
feeling 821
hope 858
love 897
enthusiast
madman 504
obstinate 606
active 682
enthusiastic
imaginative 515
sensitive 822
excitable 825
sanguine 858
enthymeme 476
entice 615
enticing 829
entire *whole* 50
complete 52
continuous 69
– horse 373
entirely *much* 31
entitle *name* 564
give a right 924
entity 1
entoil 545
entomb *inter* 363
imprison 751
Entomology 368
entourage 88, 183,
227
entozoon 193
entrails 221
entrammel 751

entrance
beginning 66
ingress 294
way 627
enrapture 827,
829
magic 992
give – to 296
entranced 515
entrancement 824
entrap 545
entrain 293
entre nous 528
entreat 765
entrée
reception 296
dish 298
give the – 296
have the – 294
– dish 191
entremet 298
entrepôt 636, 799
entrepreneur 599
entre-sol 191
entrust
commission 755
give 784
credit 805
entry *beginning* 66
ingress 294
record 551
entwine *join* 43
intersect 219
convolve 248
enucleate 522
enumerate 85
– among 76
enumeration 86
enunciate
inform 527
affirm 535
voice 580
envelop 225
envelope 223, 232
envenom
deprave 659
exasperate 835
hate 898
anger 900
envenomed
bad 649
insalubrious 657
painful 830
malevolent 907
– tongue 934
environ 227
environment 183
environs 197
in such and such –
183
envisage 515, 861

envoy
 messenger 534
 consignee 758
envy **921**
enwrap 225
enzyme 320
Eolian harp 417
Eolus 349
eon 976
épanchement
 manifest 525
 artless 703
 endearment 902
epact 641
épaulette
 badge 550, 747
 ornament 847
 decoration 877
éperdu 824
épergne 191
ephemeral 111
ephemeris
 calendar 114
 record 551
 book 593
Ephesian letters
 993
ephialtes
 physical pain 378
 hindrance 706
 mental pain 828
ephod 999
ephor 967
epic 594, 597
epicedium 839
epicene 81, 83
épicier 876
epicure
 fastidious 868
 sybarite 954a
 glutton 957
epicurean 954
Epicurus, system
 of – 954
epicy-cle, -cloid
 247
epidemic
 general 78
 disease 655
 insalubrity 657
epidermis 223
epigenesis 161
epigram 496, 842
epigrammatic 572
epigrammatist 844
epigraph 550
epilepsy 315, 655
epilogue
 sequel 65
 end 67
 drama 599

èpingles, tiré à
 quatre – 855
Epiphany 998
episcopal 995
Episcopalian 984
episcopate 995
episode
 adjunct 39
 discontinuity 70
 interjacence 228
episodic
 irrelative 10
 style 573
epistle 592
Epistles 985
epistrophe 104
epistyle 210
epitaph 363
epithalamium 903
epithem 662
epithet 564
epitome
 miniature 193
 short 201
 concise 572
epizoötic 657
epoch *time* 106
 instant 113
 date 114
 present time 118
epode 597
eponym 564
epopœa 597
epos 594
epulation 298
epulotic 662
epuration 652
equable 16, 922
equal *even* 27
 equitable 922
 – chance 156
 – times 120
 – to *power* 157
equality 13, **27**
equalize 213
equanimity 826
equate 27, 30
equations 85
equator 68, 318
equatorial 68, 236
equerry 746
equestrian 268
equibalanced 27
equidistant 68
equilibration 27
equilibrist 599
equilibrium 27
equine *carrier* 271
 horse 366
equinox 125, 126
equip 225, 673

equipage
 vehicle 272
 instruments 633
 display 882
equiparent 27
equipment 633
equipoise &c. 27, 30
equiponderate 30
equitable *wise* 498
 just 922
 due 924
 honourable 939
 – interest 780
equitation 266
equity *right* 922
 honour 939
 law 963
 in – 922
 – draftsman 968
equivalent
 identical 13
 equal 27
 compensation 30
 substitute 147
 translation 522
equivocalness
 dubious 475
 double meaning
 520
 impure 961
equivocate
 sophistry 477
 palter 520
 lie 544
equivocation
 [*see* equivocate]
 without – 543
équivoque
 double meaning
 520
 impure 961
era *time* 106, 108
 date 114
eradicate
 destroy 162
 extract 301
erase *destroy* 162
 obliterate 331, 552
Erastian 984
erasure 552
Erato 416
ere 116
 – long 132
 – now 116
 past 122
Erebus *dark* 421
 hell 982
erect *build* 161
 vertical 212
 raise 307
 with head – 878

 – the scaffolding
 673
erewhile 116, 122
ergatocracy 737
ergo 476
ergotism 480
ergotize 485
eriometer 445
Erinys 900
Erl King 980
ermine
 badge of authority
 747
 ornament 847
erode 36, 659
Eros 897, 979
erosion 36
erotic 897, 961
err – *in opinion* 495
 – *morally* 945
errand
 message 532
 business 625
 commission 755
errand-boy 534
errant 279
erratic
 irregular 139
 changeable 149
 wandering 279
 capricious 608
erratum 495
erroneous 495
error *fallacy* **495**
 vice 945
 guilt 947
 court of – 966
 writ of – 969
ersatz 973
erst 122
erubescence 434
erubuit salva res
 est 95
eruct 297
eructate 297
erudition 490, 539
eruption
 upheaval 146
 violence 173
 egress 295, 297
 disease 655
 volcanic – 872
escadrille 726
escalade
 mounting 305
 attack 716
escalator 307
escalop 248
escapade
 absurdity 497
 freak 608

prank 840
escape
  flight **671**
  liberate 750
  evade 927
  means of − 664,
    666
  − the lips
  disclosure 529
  speech 582
  − the memory 506
  − notice &c.
  invisible 447
  inattention 458
  latent 526
escarp 717
escarpment
  stratum 204
  height 206
  oblique 217
escharotic
  caustic 171
  pungent 392
eschatology 67
escheat 144, 974
eschew
  avoid 623
  dislike 867
esclandre 828, 830
escort
  accompany 88
  safeguard 664
  keeper 753
escritoire 191
esculent 298
escutcheon 550
esoteric
  private 79
  concealed 528
Espagne, château
  en − *fancy* 515
  hope 858
espalier 232
especial 79
especially 33
espial 441
espiéglerie
  cunning 702
  fun 840
  wit 842
espionnage 441,
  461
esplanade
  houses 189
  flat 213
espouse
  choose 609
  marriage 903
  − a cause *aid* 707
  co-operate 709
esprit

shrewdness 498
wit 842
bel − 844
− de corps
bias 481
co-operation 709
sociality 892
(*party* 712)
− fort
thinker 500
irreligious 989
espy 441
esquire 875, 877
essay
  experiment 463
  dissertation 595
  endeavour **675**
essayist 593, 595
esse 1
essence
  nature 5
  scent 398
essential
  intrinsic 5
  great 31
  required 630
  important 642
essentially
  intrinsically 5
  substantially 3
essential stuff 5
establish
  settle 150
  create 161
  place 184
  evidence 467
  demonstrate 478
  − *equilibrium* 27
established
  permanent 141
  habit 613
  − church 983*a*
establishment
  party 712
  shop 799
estafette 534
estaminet 189
estate *condition* 7
  property 780
  come to man's −
    131
esteem
  believe 484
  repute 873
  approve 931
  in high − 928
estimable 648
estimate
  measure 466
  adjudge 480
  information 527

− too highly 482
estimation
  [*see* esteem,
  estimate]
estime
  succès d' − 873
estival 382
esto perpetua!
  perpetuity 112
  permanence 141
  desire 865
estop 706
estrade 213
estrange
  alienate 44, 889
  discord 713
  hate 898
estranged
  secluded 893
estrapade
  attack 716
  punishment 972
estreat 974
estuary 343
estuation 384
esurient 865
et − cætera
  add 37
  include 76
  plural 100
  − hoc genus omne
  similar 17
  include 76
  multiform 81
étalage 882
état major 745
etch *furrow* 259
  engraving 558
eternal 112
  − home 981
Eternal, the − 976
eterne 112
eternify 112
eternity 112
  an − 110
  launch into − 360,
    361
ether
  lightness 320
  rarity 322
  vapour 334
  anæsthetic 376
ethereal 4
ethicism 984
ethics 926
Ethiopian 431
  −'s skin 150
Ethiopian's skin
  unchangeable 150
ethnology 372
ethnic 984

ethology 926
ethos 5
etiolate 429, 430
etiology *causes* 155,
  359
  knowledge 490
  disease 655
etiquette
  custom 613
  fashion 832
  ceremony 882
étoile, à la belle −
  out of doors 220
  in the air 338
Eton jacket 225
étourderie
  inattention 458
  unskilfulness 699
etymological 560
etymology 562
etymon *origin* 153
  verbal 562
Eucharist 998
euchology 998
euchre 840
eudiometer
  air 338
  salubrity 656
euge! 931
eugenics 658
eulogist 935
eulogize 482
eulogy 931
Eumenides *fury*
  900
  evil-doers 913
  revenge 919
eunuch 158
eupepsia 654
euphemism
  metaphor 521
  style 577, 578
  flattery 933
euphemist
  man of taste 850
  flatterer 935
euphony 413, 578
Euphrosyne 836
euphuism
  metaphor 521
  elegant style 577
  affected style 579
  affectation 855
Eurasian 41
eureka! 462, 480*a*
Euripus 343
Eurus 349
eurythmics 537,
  840
eurythmy 242
Euterpe 416

euthanasia 360
euthenics 658
evacuate
  quit 293
  excrete 295
  emit 297
evacuation 299
evade *sophistry* 477
  avoid 623
  not observe 773
  exempt 927
evagation 279
evanescent
  small 32
  transient 111
  little 193
  disappearing 449
evangelical 983*a*,
  985
Evangelists 985
evanid 160
evaporable 334
evaporate
  unsubstantial 4
  transient 111
  vaporize 336
evaporation 340
evasion
  sophistry 477
  concealment 528
  falsehood 544
  untruth 546
  avoidance 623
  escape 671
  cunning 702
  non-observance
    773
  dereliction 927
eve 126
  on the – of
  transient 111
  prior 116
  future 121
evection 61
even
  uniform 16
  equal 27
  still more 33
  regular 138
  level 213
  straight 246
  flat 251
  smooth 255
  although 469
  in spite of 708
  – course 628
  – now 118
  – so
  for all that 30
  yes 488
  – temper 826

[480]

– terms 922
– tenor
  uniform 16
  order 58
  continuity 58
  pursue the –
    tenor
  continue 143
  avoid 623
  business 625
  be – with
  retaliate 718
  pay 807
  get – with 972
even-handed 922,
  939
evening **126**
  shades of – 422
  – classes 537
  – star 423
evenness 16
evensong 126, 990
event 151
  bout 720
  in the – of
  circumstance 8
  expectation 507
  supposition 514
  justified by the –
    937
eventful 151
  remarkable 642
  stirring 682
eventide 126
eventual 121
eventuality **151**
eventually
  effect 154
ever 16, 112
  did you – ? 870
  – and anon 136
  – changing 149
  – recurring 104
ever so 31
  – little 32
  – long 110
  – many 102
evergreen
  continuous 69
  lasting 110
  always 112
  fresh 123
everlasting 112
  – life 152
  – fire 982
evermore 112
eversion 218
evert 140
every 78
  – hand against
    one 891

– day
  conformity 82
  frequent 136
  habit 613
  – description 81
  – inch 50
  in – mouth
  assent 488
  news 532
  repute 873
  – other 138
  in – quarter 180
  in – respect 494
  on – side 227
  at – turn 186
  – whit 52
everybody 78
everyone 78
  – his due 922
  – in his turn 148
everywhere 180,
  186
evict 297
evidence **467**
  disclose 529
  ocular – 446
évidence, en – 446
evident
  concrete 3
  visible 446
  certain 474
  manifest 525
evidently 516
evil *harm* **619**
  badness 649
  impious 988
  – day
  prepare for – 673
  adversity 735
  – eye *vision* 441
  malevolence 907
  disapprobation
    932
  demon 980
  sorcery 992
  spell 993
  – favoured 846
  – fortune 735
  – genius 980
  – hour 135
  – one 978
  – plight 735
  through – report
    &c. 604*a*
  – star 649
evil-doer **913**
evil-doing 945
evil-minded 907,
  945
evil-speaking
  malediction 908

  censure 932
  detraction 934
evince *show* 467
  prove 478
  disclose 529
eviscerate 297, 301
eviscerated 4
evoke *cause* 153
  call upon 765
  excite 824
evolution
  numerical 85
  production 161
  motion 264
  extraction 301
  circuition 311
  turning out **313**
  organization 357
  training 673
  action 680
  military –s 722
evolve
  discover 480*a*
evolved from 154
  [*and see*
    evolution]
evulgate 531
evulsion 301
evivva! 931
ewe 366, 374
  – lamb 366
ewer 191
ex
  – animo 602
  – cathedra 542
  – officio 494, 924
  – parte 467
  – pede Herculem
    82
  – post facto 122,
    133
  – tempore
  instant 113
  occasion 134
exacerbate
  increase 35
  exasperate 173
  aggravate 659,
    835
exact *similar* 17
  special 79
  true 494
  style 572
  require 741
  tax 812
  insolence 885
  claim 924, 926
  – meaning 516
  – memory 505
  – observance 772
  – truth 494

exacting
severe 739
discontented 832
grasping 865
fastidious 868
exaction
[*see* exact]
undue 925
exactly
just so 488
exaggeration
increase 35
expand 194
overestimate 482
magnify **549**
misrepresent 555
exalt
increase 35
elevate 307
extol 931
– *one's horn* 873
exalté 504
tête –e 503
exalted *high* 206
repute 873
noble 875
magnanimous
942
examination
[*see* examine]
evidence 467
undergo – 461
examine 457, 461
example
pattern 22
instance 82
bad – 949
good – 948
make an – of 974
set a good – 944
exanimate
dead 360
supine 360
exarch 745
exasperate
exacerbate 173
aggravate 835
enrage 900
excavate 252
excecation 442
exceed *surpass* 33
remain 40
transgress 303
intemperance 954
excel *surpass* 33
– *in skilful* 698
excellence 648, 944
excellence, par –
642
excellency 877
excelsior 305

except *subduct* 38
exclude 55
reject 610
exception
unconformity 83
qualification 469
exemption 777a
disapproval 932
take –
qualify 469
resent 900
exceptionable
bad 649
guilty 947
exceptional
original 20
extraneous 57
unconformable 83
in an – degree 31
exceptious 901,
901a
exceptis
excipiendis 469
excern 297
excerpt 609
excerpta *parts* 51
compendium 596
selections 609
excerption 609
excess
remainder 40
redundance 641
intemperance 954
excessive 31
exchange
reciprocity 12
interchange 148
transfer 783
barter 794
mart 799
bill of – 771
rate of – 800
– *blows &c.*
retaliation 718
battle 720
Exchequer 802
Baron of – 967
Court of – 966
– bill 800
excise 812
exciseman 965
excision 38
excitability **825,**
901
excitation 824
excite *energy* 171
violence 173
– *morally* 824
– *attention* 457
– *desire* 865
– *hope* 811

– an impression
375
– love 897
excited fancy 515
excitement 824, 825
anger 900
exclaim 411
– *against* 932
exclamation 580
mark of – 550
exclude
leave out 42, 55
reject 610
prohibit 761
banish 893
exclusion **55, 57**
exclusive
simple 42
omitting 55
special 79
irregular 83
forbidding 761
– of 38
– *possession* 777
– *thought* 457
excogitate 451, 515
excommunicate
banish 893
curse 908
rite 998
excoriate 226
excrement
excretion 299
dirt 653
excrescence
projection 250
blemish 848
excreta
excretion 299
dirt 653
excretion 297, **299**
excruciating 378,
830
exculpate
forgive 918
vindicate 937
acquit 970
excursion 266, 311
excursionist 268
excursive
deviating 279
- *style* 573
excursus 595
excuse *plea* 617
forgive 918
exempt 927a
vindicate 793
execrable 649, 830
execrate 898, 908
execution
music 416

action 680
conduct 692
signing 771
observance 772
punishment 972
carry into –
complete 729
put in –
undertaking 676
executioner 975
executive
conduct 692
direction 693
authority 737
judicature 965
executor 690
to one and his –s
&c., *property*
780
exegetical 522
exemplar 22
exemplary 944
exemplify
quote 82
illustrate 522
exempt *free* 748
dispensation 927a
– from *absent* 187
unpossessed 777a
exemption
exception 83
qualification 469
deliverance 692
permission 760
non-possession
777a
non-liability **927a**
exenterate 297
exequatur 755
exequies 363
exercise
operation 170
teach 537
task 625
use 677
act 680
exert 686
– *authority* 737
– *discretion* 600
– *the intellect* 451
– *power* 157
exergue 231
exert *use* 677
– *authority* 737
– *oneself* 686
exertion 171, **686**
exfoliate 226
exhalation
ejection 297
excretion 299
vapour 336

186
up to one's –s
641
have one's –s
about one 459
– askance 860
–s draw straws 683
an – for an – 718,
919
– glistening 824
in the – of the law
963
– of the master
693
– of a needle 260
–s open
attention 457
care 459
intention 620
–s opened
disclosure 529
–s out 442
eye-ball 441
eyebrows 256
eyeglass 445
eyelashes 256
eyeless 442
eyelet 260
eyelid 223
eye-shade 443
eye-sight 441
eyesore 846, 848
eye-teeth
have cut one's –
adolescence 131
skill 698
cunning 702
eye-wash 544
eye-witness
spectator 444
evidence 467
eyot 346
eyre 966
eyry 189

F

Fabian policy
delay 133
inaction 681
caution 864
fable *error* 495
metaphor 521
fiction 546
description 590
fabric *state* 7
effect 154
texture 329
fabricate
composition 54

make 161
invent 515
falsify 544
fabrication *lie* 546
**fabula narratur, de
te** – *retaliate* 718
condemn 971
fabulist 594
fabulous
enormous 31
imaginary 515
untrue 546
exaggerated 549
faburden 413
façade 234
face *exterior* 220
covering 223
front 234
aspect 448
oppose 708
resist 719
brave 861
impudence 885
change the – of
146
fly in the – of
disobey 742
put a good – upon
sham 545
calm 826
cheerful 836
hope 858
pride 878
display 882
vindicate 93
in the – of
presence 186
opposite 708
look in the –
see 441
proud 878
make –s
distort 243
ugly 846
disrespect 929
on the – of
manifest 525
show –
present 186
visible 446
not show –
disreputable 874
bashful 879
to one's – 525
wry – 378
– about 279
set one's – against
708
– of the country
344
on the – of the

earth
space 180
world 318
– to face *front* 234
contraposition
237
manifest 525
– of the thing
appearance 448
facet 220
facetiæ 842
facetious 842
facia 234
facile *willing* 602
irresolute 605
easy 705
facile princeps 33
**facilis descensus
Averni**
sloping 217
danger 665
facilitate 705
facility *skill* 698
easy 705
facing *covering* 223
facinorous 945
façon de parler 521,
549
fac-simile 21, 554
fact *existence* 1
event 151
certainty 474
truth 494
in – 535
faction 712, 713
factious 24
factitious 545, 546
factor
numerical 84
director 694
consignee 758
factory 691
factotum
agent 690
manager 694
employé 758
facts *evidence* 467
summary of – 594
at variance with –
471
facula 420
faculties 450
in possession of
one's – 502
faculty
power 157
profession 625
skill 698
facundity 582
fad 481, 608
faddle 683

fade *vanish* 4
transient 111
become old 124
droop 160
grow dim 422
lose colour 429
disappear 449
spoil 659
– from the
memory 506
fade 391
fadge 23
fæces 299, 653
fæx populi 876
fag *cigarette* 392
labour 686
fatigue 688
drudge 690, 746
– end
remainder 40
end 67
faggot 72, 388
fagots et fagots 15,
465
faïence 557
fail *droop* 160
shortcoming 304
be confuted 479
illness 655
not succeed 732
not observe 773
not pay 808
dereliction 927
failing [see **fail**]
incomplete 53
insufficient 640
vice 945
guilt 947
– heart 837
– luck 735
– memory 506
– sight 443
– strength 160
failure **732**
heart – 360
fain *willing* 602
compulsive 744
wish 865
fainéant 683
faint
small in degree 32
impotent 158
weak 160
sound 405
dim 422
colour 429
swoon 688
– heart *fear* 860
cowardice 862
damn with –
praise 930, 932,

934
faintness 405
fair *in degree* 31
  pale 429
  white 430
  wise 498
  important 643
  good 648
  moderate 651
  mart 799
  beautiful 845
  just 922
  honourable 939
  – chance 472
  – copy *copy* 21
  writing 590
  – field
  occasion 134
  – game 857
  by – means 631,
    940
  – name 873
  – play 922, 923
  – question 461
  – sex 374
  in a – way
  tending 176
  probable 472
  convalescent 658
  prosperous 734
  hopeful 858
  – weather 734
  – weather sailor
    701
  – wind 705
  – words 894
fairing 784
fairly
  intrinsically 5
  get on – 736
  – well 643
fair-spoken
  courtesy 894
  flattery 933
fairy *fanciful* 515
  fay 979
  imp 980
  – godmother 711,
    784, 912
  – tale 545, 594
fairy-land 515
fait: au –
  knowledge 490
  skilful 698
  – accompli
  certain 474
  complete 729
faith *belief* 484
  hope 858
  honour 939
  piety 987

declaration of –
  983
bad – 544
i' – 535
keep – with
  observe 772
plight –
  promise 768
  love 902
true –
  orthodox 983a
want of –
  incredulity 487
  irreligious 989
– healing 662
faithful [*see* faith]
  like 17
  copy 21
  exact 494
  obedient 743
  – memory 505
  – to 772
faithless *false* 544
  dishonourable 940
  sceptical 989
fake 544, 545
fakir 996
falcate 244, 245
falchion 727
falciform
  [*see* falcate]
falcon 792
falconet 727
faldstool 215
fall *autumn* 126
  happen 151
  perish 162
  slope 217
  regression 283
  descend 306
  die 360
  fail 732
  adversity 73
  vice 945
  let – *lower* 308
  inform 527
  water– 348
  – asleep 683
  – astern 235, 283
  – away 105
  – back *return* 283
  recede 287
  relapse 661
  – back upon 677,
    717
  have to – back
    upon 637
  – a cursing 908
  – of the curtain 67
  – into a custom 82
  – of day 125

– dead 360
– into decay 659
– down 990
– down before 928
– upon the ear 418
– flat on the ear
  843
– at one's feet 725
– foul of *blow* 276
  hinder 706
  oppose 708
  discord 713
  attack 716
  contention 720
  censure 932
– for 897
– to the ground
  be confuted 479
  fail 732
– into a habit 613
– from one's high
  estate
  adversity 735
  disrepute 874
– in *order* 58
  continuity 69
  event 151
– into
  conversion 144
  river 348
– in with *agree* 23
  conform 82
  converge 2
  discover 480a
  concord 714
  consent 762
– on one's knees
  submit 725
  servile 886
  gratitude 916
  worship 990
– of the leaf 126
– from the lips 582
– in love with 897
– to one's lot
  event 151
  chance 156
  receive 785
  duty 926
– under one's
  notice 457
– into oblivion 506
– off *decrease* 36
  deteriorate 659
– off again 661
– out *happen* 151
  quarrel 713
  enmity 889
– into a passion
  900
– to pieces

disjunction 44
destruction 162
brittle 328
– a prey to 732,
  749
– in price 815
– into raptures
  827
– short *inferior* 32
  contract 195
  shortcoming 304
– of snow 383
– through *fail* 734
– to *eat* 298
  take in hand 676
  do battle 722
– into a trap 547
– under
  inclusion 76
  subjection 749
– upon
  discover 480a
  unexpected 508
  devise 626
  attack 716
– in the way of 186
– to work 686
fallacy *sophistry*
  477
  error 495
  show the – of 497
fallen angel 949,
  978
fallible 475, 477
falling-out 24
falling star 318, 423
fallow
  unproductive 169
  yellow 436
  unready 674
  inactive 681
false *imitation* 10
  sophistry 477
  error 495
  untrue 544, 546
  spurious 925
  dishonourable 940
– alarm 669
– colouring
  misinterpretation
  523
  falsehood 544
– construction
  523, 544
– doctrine 984
– expectation 509
– hearted 940
– impression 495
– light *vision* 443
– money 800
– ornament 851

ornament 847
decoration 877
in full –
  prepared 673
  prosperous 734
  rich 803
hear a – drop 403
in high –
  health 654
  cheerful 884
pleased with a –
  840
– in one's cap
  honour 873
  decoration 877
- one's nest
  prepare 673
  prosperity 734
  wealth 803
  economy 817
  selfish 943
– the oar 698
– in the scale 643
feather-bed 324
feathered tribes
  366
feathery 256
featly 682
feature
  character 5
  component 56
  form 240
  appearance 448
  press 531
  lineament 550
– in 56
features
  face 234
febrifuge 662
febrile 382, 825
fecal 653
fecit 556
feckless 866
feculence 653
fecund 168
fecundate 161
federal council 696
– penitentiary 752
federalism 737
federation 48, 709,
  712
fee *possession* 777
  property 780
  pay 809
  reward 973
feeble *weak* 160
  illogical 477
feeble-minded 497,
  605
feebleness
  style **575**

feed *eat* 298
  supply 637
– the flame 707
fee-faw-fum
  bugbear 860
  spell 993
feel *sense* 375
  touch 379
  emotion 821
– for *try* 463
  benevolence 906
  pity 914
  condole with 915
– the pulse 461
– the want of 865
– one's way
  essay 675
  caution 864
feeler 379
  inquiry 461
  experiment 463
feeling 698, **821**
feet *low* 207
  walkers 266
at one's –
  near 197
  subjection 749
  humility 879
fall at one's –
  submit 725
fall on one's –
  prosper 734
lick the – of
  servile 886
light upon one's –
  safe 664
spring to one's –
  307
throw oneself at
  the – of
  entreat 765
feign 544, 546
feigned 545
feint 545
felicitas, curiosa –
  698
felicitate 896
felicitous
  agreeing 23
- *style* 578
  skilful 698
  successful 731
  pleasant 829
felicity 827
feline *cat* 366
  stealthy 528
  cunning 702
fell *destroy* 162
  mountain 206
  lay flat 21
  skin 223

lay low 308
moor 344
dire 860
malevolent 907
fellah 876
felloe 231
fellow *similar* 17
  equal 27
  companion 88
  dual 89
  man 373
  scholar 492, 541
fellow-commoner
  541
fellow-companion
  890
fellow-countryman
  890
fellow-creature 372
fellow-feeling
  friendship 888
  love 897
  benevolence 906
  pity 914
fellowship
  partnership 712
  distinction 873
  friendship 888
  companionship
  890
  good – 892
fellow-student 541
fellow-worker 690
felly 231
felo-de-se 361
felon 949
felonious 945
felony 947
felt *texture* 219
  heart– 821
felucca 273
female 374
feme coverte 903
feme sole 904
feminality
  weakness 160
  woman 374
feminine 374
feminism 374
femme de chambre
  746
fen 345
fence *enclose* 232
  evade 544
  defence 717
  fight 720
  prison 752
  thief 792
– round 229
– with a question
  528

fenced 770
fenceless 665
fencible 726
fencing 840
feneration 787
fend 717
fender 717
Fenian 710, 742
fenum habet in
  cornu 668, 913
feodal 780
feodality 737, 777
feoff *property* 780
feoffee 779, 785
feoffer 784
feræ naturæ 366
feral 907
ferine 907
ferment
  disorder 59
  energy 171
  violence 173
  agitation 315
  lightness 320
  effervesce 353
  emotion 821
  excitement 824,
  825
  anger 900
fermentation,
  acetous – 397
fern 367
ferocity 173, 907
Ferrara
  sword 727
ferret out 461, 480*a*
ferro-concrete 635
ferrule 223
ferry 270, 627
ferry-boat 273
ferry-man 269
fertile 161, 168
– *imagination* 515
ferule 975
  come under the –
  932
fervent *hot* 382
  desirous 865
– *hope* 858
fervid *hot* 382
  heartfelt 821
  excited 824
fervour *heat* 382
  animation 821
  love 897
festal *eating* 298
  social 892
fester 653, 655
festina lente 864
festival
  music 416

filigree 219
filings 330
fill *complete* 52
  occupy 186
  contents 190
  stuff 224
  provision 637
  eat one's – 957
  have one's –
    enough 639
    satiety 869
  – the bill 229
  – an office
    business 625
    government 737
  – out
    expand 194
  –ed to overflow-
    ing 641
  – one's pocket 803
  – time 106
  – up *compensate*
    30
  compose 54
  close 261
  restore 660
  – up the time
    inaction 681
fille
  – de chambre 746
  – de joie 962
filled
  – to overflowing
    641
filler 532
fillet *band* 45
  filament 205
  circle 247
  insignia 550
  ornament 847
fillibeg 225
filling 224
fillip
  impulse 276
  propulsion 284
  stimulus 615
  excite 824
filly 271
film *layer* 204
  opaque 426
  semitransparent
    427
  – over the eyes
    dim sight 443
  cinema 448
  ignorant 491
filmy *texture* 329
filter *percolate* 295
  clean 652
filth 653
  –y lucre 800

filtrate 652
fimbriated 256
fin 267
final *ending* 67
  conclusive 474
  completing 729
  court of – appeal
    474
  – cause 620
  – stroke 729
  – touch 729
finale *end* 67
  completion 729
finality 67, 729
finally
  for good 141
  on the whole 476
finance 800, 811
  minister of – 801
financier 801
finch 366
find
  eventuality 151
  adjudge 480
  discover 480a
  acquire 775
  – one's account in
    644
  – the cause of 522
  – a clue to 480a
  – to one's cost 509
  – credence 484
  – it in one's heart
    602
  – in *provide* 637
  – the key of 522
  – the meaning 522
  – means 632
  – oneself *be* 1
    present 186
  – out 480a
  – vent 671
  – one's way 731
  – one's way into
    294
finding
  judgment 480
fine *small* 32
  large 192
  thin 203
  rare 322
  not raining 340
  exact 494
  good 648
  beautiful 845
  adorned 847
  proud 878
  mulct 974
  in – *end* 67
  after all 476
  – air 656

  – arts 554
  – feather 159, 654
  – feeling 850
  – frenzy 515
  – gentleman
    fop 854
    proud 878
  – grain 329
  – lady 854, 878
  one – morning 106
  some – morning
    119
  – powder 330
  – talking
    overrate 482
    boast 884
  – writing 577
  – time of it 734
  – voice 580
fine-draw 660
fine-fingered 698
fine-spoken 894,
  933
fine-spun *thin* 203
  sophistry 477
fine-toned 413
finem, respicere –
  510
finery 847, 851
finesse *tact* 698
  artifice 702
  taste 850
finger *touch* 379
  hold 781
  lay the – on
    point out 457
    discover 480a
  lift a – 680
  not lift a – 681
  point the – at 457
  turn round one's
    little – 737
  –'s breadth 203
  at one's –s' end
    near 197
    know 490
    remember 505
  – on the lips
    aphony 581
    taciturnity 585
  – in the pie
    cause 153
    interfere 228
    act 680
    active 682
    co-operate 709
fingerling 193
finger-post 550
finger-print 467
finger-stall 223
fingle-fangle 643

finical
  trifling 643
  affected 855
  fastidious 868
finicky 855, 868
finikin 643
finis 67
  – coronat opus
    729
finish *lend* 67
  symmetry 242
  complete 729
  skill 698
finished
  absolute 31
  perfect 650
  skilled 698
finishing
  – stroke 361
  – touch 729
finite 32
fiord 343
fire *energy* 171
  heat 382
  make hot 384
  stoke 388
  vigour 574
  discharge 756
  enthusiasm 821
  excite 824, 825
  catch – 384
  hell – 982
  on – 382
  open – *begin* 66
  play with – 863
  signal – 550
  take –
    excitable 825
    angry 900
  between two –s
    665
  under – 665, 722
  – at 716
  – the blood 824
  – and fury 900
  – the first shot 716
  – of genius 498
  – off 284
  – a salute 883
  – and sword 162
  – up *excite* 825
    anger 900
  – a volley 716
  go through – and
    water
    resolution 604
    perseverance 604a
    courage 861
fire-alarm 669
fire-annihilator 385
fire-arms 727

fire-ball *fuel* 388
  arms 727
fire-balloon 273
fire-barrel 388
fire-bell 669
fire-boat 726
fire-brand
  fuel 388
  instigator 615
  dangerous man
    667
  incendiary 913
fire-brigade 385
fire-curtain 599
fire-drake 423
fire-eater
  fighter 726
  blusterer 887
fire-eating
  rashness 863
  insolence 885
fire-engine 348
fire-escape 671
fire-extinguisher
  385
fire-fly 423
fireless cooker 386
fire-light 422
firelock 727
fireman *stoker* 268
  extinguisher 385
fire-place 386
fire-proof 385, 644
fireside 189
firewood 388
firework
  fire 382
  luminary 423
  celebration 883
  amusement 840
fire-worship 991
fire-worshipper 984
firing *fuel* 388
  explosion 406
firkin 191
firm
  junction 43
  stable 150
  hard 323
  resolute 604
  partnership 712
  merchant 797
  brave 861
  stand – 719
  – as a rock 604
  – belief 484
  – hold 781
firmament 318
firman 741, 760
first 66
  – blush

morning 125
leading 280
vision 441
appearance 448
manifest 525
– blow 716
– cause 976
– that comes 609a
– fiddle
  importance 642
  proficient 700
  authority 737
– come first
  served 609a
– and foremost 66
– impression 66
– and last 87
– line 234
come back to –
  love 607
– move 66
– opportunity 132
at – sight 448
– stage 66
– stone
  preparation 673
  attack 716
on the – summons
  741
of the – water
  best 648
  repute 873
first-born 124, 128
first-fruits 154
first-hand 20, 467
firstlings 128, 154
first-rate
  important 642
  excellent 648
  man-of-war 726
firth 343
fisc 802
fiscal 800
fish *food* 298
  sport 361, 622
  animal 366
  food for –es 362
  other – to fry
  ill-timed 135
  busy 682
  queer – 857
  – in the air 645
  – for compliments
    880
  – for *seek* 4
  experiment 463
  desire 865
  – hatchery 370
  – out *inquire* 461
  discover 480a
  – in troubled

  waters
  difficult 704
  discord 713
– up *raise* 307
  find 480a
– out of water
  disagree 24
  unconformable 83
  displaced 185
  bungler 701
fisherman 361
fishery 370
fishing *kill* 361
  pursue 622
fishing-boat 273
fishpond 343, 370
fish-trail 267
fishy transaction
  940
fisk 266, 274
fissile 328
fission 44
fissure 44
  chink 198
fist
  handwriting 590
  grip 781
shake the –
  defy 515
  threat 909
fisticuffs 720
fistula 260
fit *state* 7
  agreeing 23
  equal 27
  paroxysm 173
  agitation 315
  caprice 608
  expedient 646
  healthy 654
  disease 655
  excitement 825
  anger 900
  right 922
  due 924
  duty 926
  in –s 315
  think – 600
  – of abstraction
    458
  – of crying 839
  – for 698
  – out *dress* 225
  prepare 673
  – to be seen 845
  by –s and starts
  irregular 59
  discontinuous 70
  agitated 315
  capricious 608
  haste 684

fitful
  irregular 139
  changeable 149
  capricious 608
fittings 633
five 98
  division by – 99
  – act play 599
  – and twenty 98
Five Year Plan 626
fiver 800
fives *game* 840
fix *join* 43
  arrange 60
  establish 150
  place 184
  immovable 265
  solidify 321
  resolve 604
  difficulty 704
  – the eyes upon
    441
  – the foundations
    673
  – the memory 505
  – the time 114
  – the thoughts
    457
  – up 774
  – upon *discover*
    480a
  choose 609
fixed *intrinsic* 5
  permanent 141
  stable 150
  quiescent 265
  habitual 613
  – idea 481
  – opinion 484
  – periods 138
fixity 141
fixity of purpose
  141
fixture
  appointment 741
  property 780
fizgig 423
fizz 409
fizzle 353
  – out 304
flabelliform 194
flabbergast 870,
  879
flabby 324
flabbiness 324
flaccid *weak* 160
  soft 324
  empty 640
flag *weak* 160
  flat stone 204
  floor 211

way of all – 360
weakness of the –
945
– and blood
substance 3
materiality 316
animality 364
affections 820
make the – creep
pain 830
fear 860
flesh-colour 434
flesh-pots 298
– of Egypt 734,
803
fleshly 316
fleur-de-lis 847
fleuron 847
flexible 324, 705
flexion
curvature 245
fold 258
deviation 279
flexuous 248
flexure 245, 258
flibbertigibbet 980
flicker
changing 149
waver 314
flutter 315
light 420
dim 422
flickering 139
flier 621
flies theatre 599
flight flock 102
volitation 267
swiftness 274
departure 293
avoidance 623
escape 671
– lieutenant 745
put to –
propel 284
repel 717
vanquish 731
– of fancy 515
– of stairs 305,
627
– of time 109
flighty inattentive
458
mad 503
fanciful 515
flim-flam 544, 608
flimsy unsubstan-
tial 4
weak 160
rarity 322
soft 324
sophistical 477

trifling 643
flinch swerve 607
avoid 623
fear 860
cowardice 862
fling propel 284
jig 840
jeer 929
have one's –
active 682
laxity 738
freedom 748
amusement 840
– aside 782
have a – at
attack 716
resent 900
disrespect 929
censure 932
– away reject 610
waste 638
relinquish 782
– down 308
– to the winds
destroy 162
not observe 773
flint hard 323
flint-hearted 907
flintlock 727
flip beverage 298
flippant fluent 584
pert 885
flipper paddle 267
flirt propel 284
coquet 607, 854
love 897
endearment 902
– a fan 855
flit elapse 109
changeable 149
move 264
travel 266
swift 274
depart 293
run away 623
flitter
small part 32
changeable 149
flutter 315
flitting 111
float establish 150
navigate 267
boat 273
buoy up 305
lightness 320
before the –s
on the stage 599
– on the air 405
– before the eyes
446
– bonds 788

– in the mind
thought 451
imagination 515
floater 683
floating
[see float]
rumoured 532
– battery 726
– capital 805
– debt 806
– dock 189
flocculent
woolly 256
soft 324
pulverulent 330
flock
assemblage 72
multitude 102
laity 997
–s and herds 366
– together 72
floe ice 383
flog 972
hasten 684
flood much 31
crowd 72
river 348
abundance 639
redundance 641
prosperity 734
stem the – 708
– of light 420
– of tears 839
flood-gate
limit 233
egress 295
conduit 350
open the –s
eject 297
permit 760
flood-light 423,
599
flood-mark 466
flood-tide
increase 35
complete 52
height 206
advance 282
water 337
floor level 204
base 211
horizontal 213
support 215
overthrow 731
ground – 191
flop 315
Flora 369
floral 367
florescence 154
floriculture 371
florid colour 428

red 434
– style 577
health 654
florist 371
floss 256
flotilla 273, 726
flotsam and jetsam
73
flounce
trimming 231
jump 309
agitation 315
flounder
change 149
toss 315
uncertain 475
bungle 699
difficulty 704
fail 732
flour 330
flourish
brandish 314, 315
exaggerate 549
language 577
speech 582
prosper 618
healthy 654
prosperous 734
ornament 847
repute 873
display 882
boast 884
– of trumpets
loud 404
cheerfulness 836
publish 531
ostentation 882
celebrate 883
boast 884
flout 929, 936
flow course 109
hang 214
motion 264
stream 348
murmur 405
abundance 639
– from
result 154
– of ideas 451
– in 294
– into river 348
– out 295
– over 641
– of soul
conversation 588
affections 820
cheerful 836
social 892
– with the tide
705
– of time 109

frankincense 400
frantic
  violent 173
  delirious 503
  excited 824
fraternal
  brother 11
  concord 714
  friendly 888
fraternity
  [*see* fraternal]
  party 712
fraternize
  co-operate 48, 709
  agree 714
  sympathize 888
  associate 892
fratricide 361
Frau 374
fraud
  falsehood 544
  deception 545
  pretender 548
  dishonour 940
  pious – 988
fraught *full* 52
  pregnant 161
  possessing 777
  – with danger 665
fray *rub* 331
  battle 720
  in the thick of
    the – 722
frayed 659
frazzle
  beaten to a – 732
freak 608, 872
  – of Nature 83
freckle 848
freckled 440
fredaine 840
free
  detached 44, 47
  unconditional 52
  liberate 672
  unobstructed 705
  at liberty 748, 750
  gratis 815
  liberal 816
  insolent 885
  exempt 927a
  impure 961
  – balloon 273
  – and easy
  cheerful 836
  adventurous 863
  vain 880
  insolent 885
  friendly 888
  sociable 892
  – fight 720

– from
  simple 42
  never – from 613
  – gift 784
  – from imperfec-
    tion 650
  – lance 726
  – land 748
  – liver 954a
  – love 961
  make – of 748
  – play 170, 748
  – quarters
  cheap 815
  hospitality 892
  – space 180
  – stage 748
  – trade
  commerce 794
  – translation 522
  – will 600
  make – with
  frank 703
  take 789
  sociable 892
  uncourteous 895
freebooter 792
freeborn 748
freedman 748
freedom 748
free-handed 816
freehold 780
freely
  willingly 602
freeman 748
freemasonry
  unintelligible 519
  secret 528
  sign 550
  co-operation 709
  party 712
free-spoken 703
freethinker 989
freeze
  benumb 381
  cold 385
  – the blood 830
freezing 383
  – mixture 387
freight *lade* 184
  cargo 190
  transfer 270
freightage 812
freighter 273
freight train 272
French
  peddler's – 563
  – and English 840
  – horn 417
  – leave *avoid* 623
  freedom 748

– polish 847
frenetic 503
frenzy
  madness 503
  imagination 515
  excitement 825
frequency 136
frequent
  in number 104
  in time 136
  in space 186
  habitual 613
  visit 892
fresco *cold* 383
  painting 556
  al –
  out of doors 220
  in the air 338
fresh *additional* 37
  new 123
  flood 348
  cold 383
  colour 428
  remembered 505
  unaccustomed 614
  good 648
  healthy 654
  impertinent 885
  tipsy 959
  – breeze 349
  – colour 434
  – news 532
freshen 658, 689
freshet 348
freshman 541
freshwater 851
freshwater sailor
  701
fret *suffer* 378
  grieve 828
  gall 830
  discontent 832
  sad 837
  ornament 847
  irritate 900
  – and fume 828
fretful 901
fret-work 219
friable 328, 330
friandise 868
friar 996
  –'s lantern 423
  – Rush 980
  Black –s 996
friary 1000
fribble
  slur over 460
  trifle 643
  dawdle 683
  fop 854
fricassee 298

frication 331
friction *force* 157
  obstacle 179
  rubbing **331**
  on – wheels 705
friend 711, **890**
  candid – 936
  next – 759
friendless 893
friendly 714, **894**
friends, be – 888
  see one's – 892
friendship 9, **888**
frieze 210
frigate 726
fright
  cards 840
  alarm 860
frightful 31, 830,
  846
frightfully 31
frightfulness 860
frigid
  cold 383
  – *style* 575
  callous 823
  indifferent 866
frigidarium 387
frigorific 385
frill 231, 248
  frills and furbe-
  lows 847
fringe
  border 231
  lace 256
  exaggeration 549
  ornament 847
frippery
  trifle 643
  ornament 847
  finery 851
  ridiculous 853
  ostentation 882
frisk *prance* 266
  leap 309
  search 461
  gay 836
  amusement 840
frisky 682, 836
frith *chasm* 198
  strait 343
  forest 367
fritinancy 412
fritter *small* 32
  – away *lessen* 36
  waste 638
  – away time 683
fritters 298
frivolous
  unreasonable 477
  foolish 499

capricious 608
trivial 643
frizz *curve* 245, 248
  fold 258
frock *dress* 225
  canonicals 999
  – coat 225
frog *fastening* 45
  leaper 309
  ornament 847
frolic 827, 840
frolicsome 836
from *motive* 615
  – this cause 155
  – day to day 106,
    138
  – end to end 52
  – that time 117
  – time imme-
    morial 122
  – time to time 136
frond 367
fronder
  censure 932
frondeur
  disobey 742
front *foremost* 66
  wig 225
  fore part **234**
  resist 719
  insolence 885
  bring to the –
  manifest 525
  come to the –
  surpass 303
  important 642
  repute 873
  in – 280
  present a – 719
  – danger 861
  – to front 708
  – of the house 599
  – rank 234
  in the – rank
  important 642
  repute 873
frontage 234
frontal 220
fronti nulla fides
  doubt 485
  deception 545
frontier 199, 233
fronting 237
frontispiece 64
frosh 541
frost 283
frosted 430
  – glass 427
frostbite 383
froth
  bubble 353

trifle 643
dirt 653
  – up *angry* 900
frothy 320, 353
  - *style* 573, 577
  irresolute 605
frounce 258
frouzy 401
froward 901*a*
frown *lower* 837
  scowl 839
  discourteous 895
  angry 900
  sulky 901*a*
  disapprove 932
  – down
  abash 879
  –s of fortune 735
frozen 383, 385
fructify
  produce 161
  be productive 168
  improve 658
  prosper 734
frugal 817, 953
  – to excess 819
fruges consumere
  natus *drone* 683
  peasant 876
frugivorus 298
fruit *result* 154
  produce 161
  food 298
  profit 775
  forbidden – 615
  reap the –s
  succeed 731
  reward 973
  – tree 367
fruitful 168
fruition 161, 827
fruitless
  unproductive 169
  useless 645
  failure 732
frump 851, 895
frumpish 901*a*
frustrate 179, 706
frustrated 732
frustum 51
fry *shoal* 102
  child 129
  heat 384
  small –
  unimportant 643
  commonalty 876
frying-pan 386
  out of – into fire
  worse 659
  clumsy 699
  failure 732

misfortune 735
aggravation 835
fuddled 959
fudge 517, 643
fuel **388,** 638
  add – to the flame
    835
  – oil 388
  increase 35
  heat 384
  aggravate 835
  anger 900
fugaces labuntur
  anni 111
fugacious 111
fugitive
  transient 111
  emigrant 268
  avoiding 623
  – writings 596
fugleman
  pattern 22
  director 694
fugue 415
fulciment 215
fulcrum 215
fulfil
  complete 729
  – a duty 926
  – an obligation
    772
fulgent 420
fuliginous
  dim 422
  opaque 426
  black 431
full *much* 31
  complete 52
  large 192
  loud 404
  abundant 639
  cleanse 652
  hands –
  active 682
  receipt in – 807
  – blooded 641
  – bloom 131
  health 654
  beauty 845
  – blown 131
  expanded 194
  glorious 873
  – of business 682
  – coloured 428
  – cry *loud* 404
  bark 412
  pursuit 622
  – dinner pail 734
  dress 225
  ornament 847
  fashion 852

show 882
  – drive 274
  – feather
  prepared 673
  – force 159
  – gallop 274
  – heart 820
  – of incident 151
  – many 102
  – of meaning 516
  – measure 639
  – of people 186
  – play
  facility 705
  freedom 748
  – of point 842
  – scope 748
  – score 415
  – size 912
  – of sound and
    fury &c.
  unmeaning 517
  – speech 274
  – stop
  cease 142
  rest 265
  – swing
  strong 159
  active 682
  successful 731
  free 748
  – as a tick 52
  – tide 348
  – tilt *active* 682
  haste 684
  – view 446
  – of whims 608
full-fashioned 240
full-fed 954
full-flavoured 392
full-grown 131, 192
full-handed 816,
  818
full-length 556
full-mouthed 412
full-toned 413
fully 31
fulminate
  violent 173
  propel 284
  loud 404
  malediction 908
  threat 909
  – against
  accuse 932
fulness
  [*see* full]
  in the – of time
    109
fulsome
  nauseous 395

occupant 188
safety 664
defence 717
soldiers 726
garrotte
render powerless
158
kill 361
punishment 972
garrulity 584
garter
fastening 45
decoration 877
– blue 438
garth 181
gas 334
talk 482
fuel 388
boasting 883
– balloon 273
– stove 386
– bomb 727
– fitter 690
– mask 717
– projector 727
gasconade 884
gaseity 334
gaselier 214
gash cut 44
interval 198
wound 619
gasification 334,
336
gaskins 225
gas-light 423
gasoline 388
gasometer 636
gasp blow 349
droop 655
fatigue 688
at the last – 360
– for desire 865
gasper 392
gastriloquism 580
Gastromancy 511
gastronomy 298,
957
gate beginning 66
inclosure 232
mouth 260
barrier 706
water – 350
–way way 627
– keeper 263
gâté, enfant – 734
Gath, tell it not in –
conceal 528
disapprove 932
gather collect 72
expand 194
fold 258

conclude 480
acquire 775
take 789
– breath 689
– flesh 194
– from one
information 527
– fruits 731
gathered
– to one's fathers
360
gathering
assemblage 72
abscess 655
– clouds dark 421
shade 424
omen 512
danger 665
warning 668
adversity 735
gathering-place 74
gauche clumsy 699
gaucherie 699, 851
gaud 847
gaudery 880
gaudy colour 428
vulgar 851
showy 882
gauge 466
rain– 348
wind– 349
gauger 965
gaunt bulky 192
lean 203
ugly 846
gauntlet glove 225
armour 717
fling down the –
715
take up the – 720
gauntry 627
Gautama 986
gauze shade 424
semitransparent
427
gavel 72, 812
gavelkind 778
gavelock 633
gavot 840
gawky
awkward 699
ugly 846
(ridiculous 853)
gay colour 428
cheerful 836
adorned 847
showy 882
dissipated 961
– deceiver 962
– world 852
gaze 441

gazebo 441
gazelle swift 274
gazette
publication 531
record 551
in the –
bankrupt 808
gazetteer
list 86
information 527
record 551
gazing-stock
ridiculous 857
wondrous 872
géant, à pas de –
274
gear clothes 225
harness 633
high – 274
in – 673
low – 275
out of –
disjoin 44
derange 61
useless 645
unprepared 674
– wheel 633
geese are swans,
all his – 482
gehenna 982
geisha 599
Geist 498
gel 352
gelatin 352
gelatinify 352
geld 38, 158
gelding 271, 373
gelid 383
Geloscopy 511
gem 648, 847
geminate 90
Gemini twins 89
O – ! 870
gemote 72
gendarme 726, 965
gender 75
genealogy 69, 166
general
generic 78
habitual 613
officer 745
the –
commonalty 876
things in – 151
– breaking up 655
– favourite 899
– information 490
– meaning 516
– public 372
– run 613
– servant 690, 746

generalissimo 745
generality
mean 29
universal **78**
generalize 476
generally speaking
613
generalship 692,
722
generate 161, 168
generation
consanguinity 11
period 108
production 161
mankind 372
rising – 167
spontaneous – 161
wise in one's – 498
generator 164
generic 78
generosity
giving 784
liberality 816
benevolence 906
disinterestedness
942
genesis
beginning 66
production 161
genet 271
Genethliacs 511
genetics 161
Geneva gown 996
genial
productive 161
sensuous 377
warm 382
willing 602
delightful 829
affable 894
geniality 836
geniculated 244
genie 980
genital 161
genitor 166
geniture 161
genius
intellect 450
talent 498
skill 698
proficient 700
prodigy 872
evil – 980
good –
friend 898
benefactor 912
spirit 979
tutelary – 711
– for 698
– of a language
560

gill 348
gillie 746
gilt 436, 847
– edged 648
gimbals 312
gimcrack
  weak 160
  brittle 328
  trifling 643
  ornament 847
  ridiculous 853
gimlet 262
gimp
  clean 652
  pretty 845
  decoration 847
gin trap 545
  instrument 633
  intoxicating 959
  demon 980
gin mill 189
gin palace 189
gingerbread
  weak 160
  vulgar 851
gingerly 174, 459,
  864
gingle 408
gipsy
  wanderer 268
  wag 844
– lingo 563
giraffe 206
girandole 423
girasol 847
gird bind 43
  strengthen 159
  surround 227
  jeer 929
– up one's loins
  brace 159
  prepare 673
girder 45, 215
girdle bond 45
  encircle 227
  circumference 230
  circle 247
  put a – round the
  earth 311
girl 129, 374
girlhood 127
girt 45
girth
  bond 45
  circumference 230
gisarm 727
gist essence 5
  meaning 516
  important 642
gît, ci – 363
gittern 417

give yield 324
  melt 382
  bestow 784
  discount 813
– away 782, 784
  in marriage 903
– back 790
– birth to 161
– with both hands
  816
– in charge
  restrain 751
– chase 622
– consent 762
– one credit for
  484
– in custody 751
– expression to
  566
– forth 531
– the go by 623
– a horse his head
  748
– in submit 725
– into consent 762
– light 420
– the mind to 457
– notice
  inform 527
  warn 668
– it one
  censure 932
  punish 972
– out emit 297
  publish 531
  bestow 784
– over cease 142
  relinquish 624
  lose hope 859
– place to
  substitute 147
  avoid 623
– play to the im-
  agination 515
– points to 27
– quarter 740
– rise to 153
– one the slip 671
– security 771
– and take
  reciprocate 12
  compensation 30
  interchange 148
  retaliation 718
  compromise 774
  barter 794
  equity 922
  honour 939
– tongue 531
– a turn to 140
– one to under-

stand 527
– up
  not understand
  519
  unwilling 603
  reject 610
  relinquish 624
  submit 725
  resign 757
  surrender 782
  restore 790
  hopeless 859
– up the ghost 360
– way weak 160
  brittle 328
  submit 725
  pine 828
  despond 837
  modest 881
given [see give]
  circumstances 8
  supposition 514
  received 785
– over dying 360
– time 134
– to 613
giving 784
gizzard 191
  stick in one's –
  900
glabrous 225
glacial 383
glaciate 385
glacier 383
glacis 217, 717
glad 827, 829
  give the – eye 441
  would be – of 865
– tidings 532
gladden 834, 836
glade hollow 252
  opening 260
  shade 424
gladiator 726
gladiatorial 361,
  713, 720
gladsome 827, 829
Gladstone bag 191
glair 352
glaive 727
glamour 992
glance look 441
  sign 550
  see at a – 498
– at
  take notice of 457
  allude to 527
  censure 932
– off deviate 279
  diverge 291
gland 221

glare light 420
  stare 441
  imperfect vision
  443
  visible 446
glaring
  [see glare]
  great 31
  colour 428
  visible 446
  manifest 525
glass vessel 191
  smooth 255
  brittle 328
  transparent 425
  lens 445
  musical –es 47
  see through a –
  darkly 491
– of fashion 852
  live in a – house
  brittle 328
  visible 446
  danger 665
– too much 959
glass-coach 272
glasshouse 191, 371
Glassite 984
glassy [see glass]
  shining 420
  colourless 429
glaucous 435
glave 727
glaver 933
glaze 255
gleam small 32
  light 420
glean 609, 775
gleanings 636
glebe land 342
  ecclesiastical 995
  church 1000
glee music 415
  satisfaction 827
  merriment 836
gleek 929
glen 252
glengarry 225
glib voluble 584
  facile 705
glide lapse 109
  move 264
  travel 266
  fly 267
– into
  conversion 144
glider 273
glimmer
  light 420
  dim 422
  visible 446

slight knowledge
490, 491
glimpse 441, 490
glint 420
glissade 306
glisten 420
glitter
  shine 420
  appear 446
  illustrious 882
glittering
  ornament 847
  display 882
gloam 901*a*
gloaming 126, 422
gloar *look* 441
  wonder 970
gloat 884
  – on *look* 441
  – over 441
  pleasure 377
  delight 827
globated 249
globe
  sphere 249
  world 318
on the face of the
  – 318
  – trotter 268
globule 32, 249
glomeration 72
gloom 421, 827, 837
gloomy horizon 859
glorification 884
glorify
  honour 873
  approve 931
  worship 990
glorious
  illustrious 873
  tipsy 959
glory
  light 420
  honour 873
  heaven 981
King of – 976
  – in 878, 884
  – be to God 990
gloss *smooth* 255
  sheen 420
  interpretation 522
  falsehood 546
  plea 617
  beauty 845
  – of novelty 123
  – over
  neglect 460
  sophistry 477
  falsehood 544
  vindicate 937
glossary 86, 562

glossographer 492
glossologist 492
glossology 560, 562
glossy [*see* gloss]
glottology 560
glout 901*a*
glove 225
  take up the – 720
  throw down the –
  715
glow *warm* 382
  shine 420
  appear 446
  colour 428
  style 574
  passion 821
glower
  glare 443
  discourteous 895
  sullen 901*a*
glowing
  [*see* glow]
  orange 439
  excited 824
  beautiful 845
  – terms 574
glow-worm 423
gloze 933, 937
glucose 396
glue *cement* 45
  cementing 46
  semiliquid 352
glum
  discontented 832
  dejected 837
  sulky 901*a*
glut
  redundance 641
  satiety 869
gluttony 957
glutinous 352
glutton 954*a*, 957
gluttony **957**
glycerine 332, 356
glyphography 558
glyptography 558
glyptotheca 557
gnarl *protuberance*
  250
  anger 900
  threat 909
gnarled 256, 321
gnash one's teeth
  839, 900
gnat *little* 193
  strain at a – &c.
  caprice 608
gnaw *eat* 298
  rub 331
  injure 659
gnawing

  – grief 828, 830
  – pain 378
gnome 496, 980
gnomic 496
gnomon 114
Gnostic 984
go
  cease to exist 2
  energy 171, 682
  move 264
  recede 287
  depart 293
  fade 429
  disappear 449
  fashion 852
come and – 314
as things – 613
  – about
  turn round 311
  published 531
  undertake 676
  – across 302
  – after
  in time 117
  in motion 281
  – ahead
  energetic 171
  precede 280
  advance 282
  active 682
  – against 708
  – astray 495
  – away 293
  – back 283, 624
  – bad 659
  – bail 771
  – before 280
  – between
  interjacent 228
  instrumental 631
  mediate 631, 724
  – beyond 303
  – by the board
  158
  – about your
  business
  ejection 297
  dismissal 756
  – by
  conform to 82
  elapse 109
  past 122
  outrun 303
  subterfuge 702
give the – by to
  neglect 460
  deceive 545
  avoid 623
  – by the name of
  564

  – deep into 461
  – down *sink* 306
  decline 659
  – down with
  believed 484
  tolerated 826
  content 831
  – farther and fare
  worse 659
  – forth *depart* 293
  publish 531
  – halves 91
  – hand in hand
  accompany 88
  same time 120
  – hard 704
  – on ill 735
  – in 294
  – in for
  resolution 604
  pursuit 622
  – into
  ingress 294
  inquire 461
  dissert 595
  – all lengths
  complete 52
  resolve 604
  exertion 686
  – mad 503
  – near 286
  – no further
  keep secret 528
  – for nothing
  sophistry 477
  unimportant 643
  – off *explode* 173
  depart 293
  die 360
  wither 659
  marry 903
  – on *time* 106
  continue 143
  advance 282
  – on for ever 112
  – one better 303
  – out
  cease 142
  egress 295
  extinct 385
  – out of one's
  head 506
  – over
  passage 302
  explore 461
  apostate 607
  faithless 940
  – to pieces 162
  – on record 551
  – round 311
  – shares 778

– to sleep 683
– through
 meet with 151
 pass 302
 explore 461
 perform 599
 conduct 692
 complete 729
 endure 826
– to *extend* 196
 travel 266
 direction 278
 remonstrance 695
– up 305
– to war 722
– with
 assent 488
 concord 714
– with the stream
 conform 82
 servile 886
– from one's word
 773
goad 615
 hasten 684
goal *end* 67
 reach 292
 object 620
 reach the –
 complete 729
goat *substitute* 147
 jumper 309
 lecher 962
 he – *male* 373
 play the – 499
gob 269
gobang 840
gobbet
 small piece 32
 food 298
gobble *cry* 412
 gormandize 957
 eat 298
gobemouche 501,
 547
go-between 758
goblet 191
goblin 980
go-cart 272
GOD 976
 house of – 1000
 kingdom of – 981
 sons of – 977
 –'s acre 363
 – bless me! 870
 – bless you
 farewell 293
 – forbid 766
 –'s grace 906
 – grant 990
 – knows 491

–'s love 906
 for –'s sake 765
 –'s will 601
– willing 470
god 979
 household –s 189
 tutelary – 664
goddess *love* 897
 good woman 948
 heathen 979
Godhead 976
godlike 987
godly 944
godsend *good* 618
 prosperity 734
Godspeed
 farewell 293
 hope 858
 courtesy 894
 benevolence 906
 approbation 931
goer *horse* 271
goes [*see* go]
 as one – 270
 here – 676
Gog and Magog 192
goggle 441
 – *eyes* 443
goggles 445
going [*see* go]
 general 78
 rumour 532
 – to happen 152
 – on
 incomplete 53,
 730
 current 151
 transacting 625
goitre 250
Golconda 803
gold *yellow* 436
 orange 439
 money 800
 write in letters
 of – 642
 worth its weight
 in – 648
gold certificate 800
golden [*see* gold]
 – age
 prosperity 734
 pleasure 827
 – apple 615
 – calf
 wealth 803
 idol 985
 idolatry 991
 – dream
 imagination 515
 hope 858
 – mean

 moderation 174
 mid-course 628
 – opinions 931
 – opportunity 134
 – rule
 precept 697
 – season of life
 127
 – wedding 883
golf 840
Golgotha 363, 1000
Goliath 159, 192
goloshes 225
gondola 273
gondolier 269
gone [*see* go]
 past 122
 absent 187
 dead 360
 – bad 653
 – by
 antiquated 124
 – out of one's rec-
 ollection 506
gonfalon 550
gong 417
goniometer 244,
 466
good
 complete 52
 palatable 394
 assent 488
 benefit 618
 beneficial 648
 right 922
 virtuous 944
 pious 987
 as – as 197
 be so – as 765
 do – 906
 for –
 diuturnal 110
 permanent 141
 make –
 evidence 467
 provide 637
 restore 660
 complete 729
 substantiate 924
 vindicate 937
 atone for 952
 so far so – 931
 think – 931
 to the – 780
 turn to – account
 731
 what's the – 645
 – actions 944
 – at 698
 – auspices 858
 – behaviour

 contingent 108*a*
 duty 926
 virtue 944
 in one's – books
 888
 – bye 293
 in – case 192
 – chance 472
 – cheer *food* 298
 cheerful 826
 – circumstances
 803
 – condition 192
 – day
 arrival 292
 departure 293
 courtesy 894
 – effect
 goodness 648
 beauty 845
 – enough
 not perfect 651
 be – enough 765
 put a – face upon
 cheerful 836
 proud 878
 – fellow 892
 – fight *war* 722
 virtue 944
 – for
 useful 644
 salubrious 656
 – fortune 734
 – Friday 998
 – genius
 friend 890
 benefactor 912
 god 979
 in one's – graces
 888
 – hand 700
 – humour
 concord 714
 cheerfulness 836
 amuse 840
 courtesy 894
 kindly 906
 – intention 906
 – judgment 498
 – lack! 870
 – living
 food 298
 gluttony 957
 – look-out 459
 – looks 845
 – luck 734
 – man *man* 373
 husband 903
 worthy 948
 – manners 894
 much – may it do

gully *gorge* 198
  hollow 252
  opening 260
  conduit 350
gulosity 957
gulp *swallow* 296
  take food 298
  – down
  credulity 486
  submit 725
gum *fastening* 45
  fasten 46
  resin 356a
  – elastic 325
  – tree 367
gumbo 298
gummy 352
gumption 498
gun *report* 406
  weapon 727
  great – 626
  blow great –s 349
  sure as a – 474
gunboat 726
gunfire 404
gunman 361
gunner 776
gunnery
  warfare 722
  cannon 727
gunlayer 284
gunpowder
  warfare 722
  ammunition 727
  not invent – 665
  sit on barrel of –
  501
gunroom 193
gun-shot 197
gunwale 232
gurge 312, 348
gurgle
  flow 348
  bubble 353
  faint sound 405
  resonance 408
gurgoyle 350
gush
  flow out 295
  flood 348
  exaggeration 482
  talk 584
gushing
  emotional 821
  impressible 822
gusset 43
gust *wind* 349
  physical taste 390
  passion 825
  moral taste 850
gustation 390

gustful 394
gustless 391
gusto [*see* gust]
  physical pleasure
  377
  emotion 821
gut *destroy* 162
  opening 260
  strait 343
  eviscerate 297
  sack 789
  steal 791
gutling 954a
guts *inside* 221
guttapercha 325
gutter *groove* 259
  conduit 350
  vulgarity 851
guttersnipe 876
guttle 957
guttural
  letter 561
  inarticulate 583
guy
  fastening 45, 752
  fellow 373
  disrespect 929
  grotesque 853
guzzle
  gluttony 957
  drunkenness 959
gybe [*see* jibe]
gymkhana 720, 840
gymnasium 191
  school 542
  arena 728, 840
gymnast 159
gymnastics
  training 537
  exercise 686
  contention 720
  sport 840
gymnosophist
  abstainer 953
  sectarian 984
gynander 83
gynarchy 727
gynecæum 374
gynecology 662
gyniatrics 374
gynics 374
gyp 545, 746
gyre 311
gyrate 312
gyrfalcon 913
gyromancy 511
gyrostat 312
gysart 599
gyve 752

H

habeas corpus 963, 969
haberdasher 225
habergeon 717
habiliment 225
habilitation 698
habit
  essence 5
  coat 225
  custom **613**
  want of – 614
  –s of business 682
  – of mind 820
habitant 188
habitat 189
habitation 189
habit-maker 225
habitual
  unvariable 16
  orderly 58
  ordinary 82
  customary 613
habituate 537, 613
habitude
  state 7
  habit 613
habitué 613
hacienda 189, 780
hack *cut* 44
  shorten 201
  horse 271
  writer 594
  worker 690
  literary – 593
hackle 44
hackney-coach 272
hackneyed
  known 490
  trite 496
  habitual 613
Hades 982
Hadji
  traveller 268
  priest 996
hæ tibi erunt artes
  627
hæret lateri lethalis
  arundo
  displeasure 828
  anger 900
haft 633
hag *age* 128
  ugly 846
  wretch 913
  witch 994
haggard
  insane 503
  tired 688
  wild 824

ugly 846
haggis 298
haggle *cut* 44
  chaffer 794
Hagiographa 985
Hagiolatry 984
Hagiology 983, 985
haguebut 727
ha-ha *trench* 198, 719
haik 225
hail *welcome* 292
  ice 383
  call 586
  rejoicing 838
  honour to 873
  celebration 883
  courtesy 894
  salute 928
  approve 931
  –fellow well met
  friendship 888
  sociality 892
hailstone 383
hair *small* 32
  filament 205
  roughness 256
  to a – 494
  –'s breadth
  near 197
  narrow 203
  –breadth escape
  danger 665
  escape 671
  –s on the head
  multitude 102
  make one's –
  stand on end
  distressing 830
  fear 860
  wonder 870
hairless 226
hairy *rough* 256
halberd 727
halberdier 726
halcyon *calm* 174
  peace 721
  prosperous 734
  joyful 827, 829
hale 654
half 91
  – the battle
  important 642
  success 731
  – distance 68
  – a dozen *six* 98
  several 102
  see with – an **eye**
  intelligent 498
  intelligible 518
  manifest 525

– a gale 349
– and half
equal 27
mixed 41
incomplete 53
– a hundred 98
– light 422
– measures
incomplete 53
vacillating 605
mid-course 628
– moon 245
– price 815
– rations 640
– scholar 493
– seas over 959
– sight 443
– speed
moderate 174
slow 275
– truth 546
half-blind 443
half-blood
mixture 41
unconformity 83
imperfect 651
half-frozen 352
half-hearted
irresolute 605
insensible 823
indifferent 866
half-learned 491
half-melted 352
halfpenny
trifle 643
half-starved
insufficient 640
fasting 956
half-way
small 32
middle 68
between 228
go – *irresolute* 605
mid-course 628
meet –
willing 602
compromise 774
half-witted 499, 501
hall *chamber* 189
receptacle 191
mart 799
music – 599
– of audience 588
– mark 550
hallelujah 990
halliard 45
halloo *cry* 411
look here! 457
call 586
wonder 870
hallow

celebrate 883
respect 928
hallowed 976
hallucination
error 495
insanity 503
halo *light* 420
glory 873
Halomancy 511
halser 45
halt *cease* 142
weak 160
rest 265
go slowly 275
lame 655
fail 732
at the – 265
halter *rope* 45
restraint 752
punishment 975
wear a – 874
with a – round
one's neck 665
halting
style 579
– place 292
halve [*see* half]
halves
do by –
neglect 460
not complete 730
not do by – 729
go – 778
ham *house* 189
hamadryad 979
hammam 386, 652
hamlet 189
hammer
repeat 104
knock 276
stammer 583
under the –
auction 796
between the – and
the anvil 665
– at *think* 451
work 686
– out *form* 240
prepare 673
complete 729
hammock 215
hamper *basket* 191
obstruct 706
hamstring 158, 659
hanaper 802
hand
measure of
length 200
side 236
transfer 270
man 372

organ of touch
379
indicator 550
writing 590
medium 631
agent 690
grasp 781
transfer 783
at – *future* 121
destined 152
near 197
useful 644
bad – 590
bird in – 781
come to – 292, 785
fold one's –s 681
give one's – to
marry 903
good –
writing 590
skill 698
proficiency 700
helping – 707, 711
hold in – 737
hold out the – 894
hold up the –
vote 609
in –
incomplete 53
business 625
preparing 673
not finished 730
possessed 777
money 800
in the –s of
authority 737
subjection 749
lay –s on
discover 480a
use 677
take 789
rite 998
much on one's –s
682
on one's –s
business 625
redundant 641
not finished 730
for sale 796
on the other – 468
no – in 623
poor – 701
put into one's –s
784
put one's – to 676
ready to one's –
673
shake –s 918
stretch forth one's
– 680
take by the – 707

take in –
teach 537
undertake 676
time hanging on
one's –s
inaction 681
leisure 685
weary 841
try one's – 675
turn one's – 675
turn one's – to 625
under one's
in writing 590
promise 768
compact 769
– back 683
– cart 272
– of death 360
– down
record 551
transfer 783
have one's –s full
682
– gallop 274
– glass 445
– and glove 709,
888
– in hand
joined 43
accompanying 88
same time 120
concur 178
co-operate 709
party 712
concord 714
friend 888
social 892
– to hand
touching 199
transfer 270
fight 720, 722
– over head
inattention 458
neglect 460
reckless 863
have a – in
cause 153
act 680
co-operate 709
have one's – in
skill 698
keep one's – in
613
live from – to
mouth
insufficient 640
unprepared 674
poor 804
–s off! *avoid* 623
leave alone 681
prohibition 761

– over	handstaff 727	*concur* 178	– hunting grounds
transfer 783	handwriting	*co-operate* 709	981
give 784	*signature* 550	– upon	– returns of the
win –s down 731	*autograph* 590	*effect* 154	day 896
with the –s in the	– on the wall	*dependency* 749	– thought 842
pockets 681	*warning* 668	hangar 191, 273	– valley
hand-bag 191	handy	hang-dog look 901a	*imagination* 515
hand-barrow 272	*near* 197	hanged if, I'll be –	*delight* 827
handbook	*useful* 644, 646	489	harangue 582
travel 266	*ready* 673	hanger	hara-kiri 972
information 527	*dexterous* 698	*weapon* 727	harass
book 593	hang	*suspender* 45, 214	*fatigue* 688
handcuff 751, 752	*pendency* 214	pothooks and –s	*vex* 830
handfast 903	*kill* 361	590	*worry* 907
handful	*curse* 908	– on	harbinger
quantity 25	*execute* 972	*accompaniment*	*precursor* 64
small 32	– about 133, 197	88	*omen* 512
few 103	– back 133, 623	*servant* 746	*informant* 527
handicap	– in the balance	*servile* 886	harbour
equalize 27	133	hanging [*see* hang]	*abode* 189
inferiority 34	– in doubt 485	*elevated* 307	*haven* 292
encumber 706	– fire *late* 133	*ornament* 847	*refuge* 666
race 720	*cease* 142	– look 846	*cherish* 821
handicraft 625, 680	*unproductive* 169	hangman	natural – 343
handicraftsman 690	*inert* 172	*evil-doer* 913	– a design 620
effect 154	*slow* 275	*bad man* 949	in – 664
doing 680	*reluctance* 603	*executioner* 975	– an idea 451
handkerchief	*inactive* 683	hank *tie* 45	– revenge 919
clothes 225	*not finish* 730	hanker 865	harbourless 665
cleaner 652	*fail* 732	hanky-panky 545	hard *strong* 159
handle	*refuse* 764	Hansard 551	*dense* 323
feel, touch 379	*dullness* 843	hansom 272	*physically insen-*
name 565	– on hand 641	hap 156	*sible* 376
dissert 595	– down the head	haphazard	*sour* 397
plea 617	837	*chance* 156, 621	*difficult* 704
instrument 633	– over the head	hapless	*severe* 739
use 677	152	*unfortunate* 735	*morally insen-*
manage 693	– it! *regret* 833	(*miserable* 828)	*sible* 823
furnish a – 937	*contempt* 930	(*hopeless* 859)	*grievous* 830
make a – of 677	– out a light 420	haply	*impenitent* 951
– a case 693	– upon the lips of	*possibly* 470	blow – 349
– to one's name	418	(*by chance* 156)	go –
name 564	– on	happen 151	*difficult* 704
honour 877	*accompany* 88	– as it may	*failure* 732
handmaid	– out	*chance* 621	*adversity* 735
instrumentality	*display* 882	– what may	*pain* 828
631	*entertain* 892	*certain* 474	hit – 276
auxiliary 711	– over	*reckless* 863	look – at 441
servant 746	*destiny* 152	happening 151	not be too – upon
handpost 550	*height* 206	happiness	918
handsel	*project* 250	[*see* happy]	strike –
begin 66	– out a signal 550	the greatest – of	*energy* 171
security 771	– on the sleeve of	the greatest	*impulse* 276
gift 784	*servant* 746	number 910	try – 675
pay 809	*servility* 886	happy *fit* 23	work – 686
handsome	*flattery* 933	*opportune* 134	– at it 682
liberal 816	– in suspense 605	*style* 578	– bargain 819
beautiful 845	– by a thread 665	*glad* 827	– of belief 487
disinterested 942	– together	*cheerful* 836	– to believe 485
– fortune 803	*joined* 43	– despatch 972	– by 197
handspike 633	*cohere* 46	– go lucky 674	– case 735

– cash 800
– earned 704
– and fast rule 80
– fought 704
– frost 383
– of hearing 419
– heart
  malevolent 907
  vicious 945
  impenitent 951
– hit 732
– knocks 720
– life 735
– lines
  adversity 735
  severity 739
– liver 954*a*
– lot 735
– master 739
– measure 739
– names 932
– necessity 601
– nut to crack 704
– to please 868
– pressed
  haste 684
  difficulty 704
  hindrance 706
– put to it 704
– set 704
– tack 298
– task 703
– time 704
– up 704, 804
– upon
  attack 715
  severe 739
  censure 932
– winter 383
– words
  obscure 571
  rude 895
  censure 932
– work 686
– at work 682
harden [*see* hard]
  strengthen 159
  accustom 613
– the heart
  insensible 823
  enmity 889
  impenitence 951
hardened
  impious 988
– front
  insolent 885
hardening
  habit 613
hard-featured 846
hard-fisted 819
hard-headed 498,

739
hardihood 861, 885
hardly
  scarcely 32
  deal – with 739
– any *few* 103
– anything
  small 32
  unimportant 643
– ever 137
hard-mouthed 606
hardness 323
– of heart 914*a*
hardship 735
hardy
  strong 159
  healthy 654
  brave 861
hare 274
  hold with the –
  and run with
  the hounds
  fickle 607
  servile 886
hare-brained 458,
  863
harem 961
hariolation 511
hark 418, 457
– back 283
harl 205
harlequin
  changeable 149
  nimble 274
  motley 440
  pantomimic 599
  humorist 844
harlequinade 599
harlot 962
harlotry 961
harm
  evil 619
  badness 649
  malevolence 907
harmattan 349
harmless
  impotent 158
  good 648
  perfect 650
  salubrious 656
  safe 664
  innocent 946
  bear – 717
harmonica 417
harmonics 413
harmonist 413
harmonize 178, 416
harmonium 417
harmony
  agreement 23
  order 58

music 413
colour 428
concord 714
peace 721
friendship 888
harness
  fasten 43
  fastening 45
  accoutrement 225
  yoke 370
  instrument 633
  restraint 752
  in –
  prepared 673
  in action 680
  active 682
  subjection 749
– up 293
harp
  repeat 104
  musical instru-
  ment 417
  weary 841
Harpagon 819
harper 416
harpist 416
harpoon 727
harpsichord 417
harpy
  relentless 739
  thief 792
  miser 819
  evil-doer 913
  demon 980
harquebuss 727
harridan 846, 962
harrier 366
harrow
  agriculture 371
– up the soul 860
harrowing 830
harry *pain* 830
  attack 716
  persecute 907
Harry, old – 978
harsh
  acrid 171
  sound 410
  style 579
  discordant 713
  severe 739
  disagreeable 830
  morose 895
  malevolent 907
– voice 581
hart 366, 373
hartal 142, 489
harum-scarum 59,
  458
haruspice 513
Haruspicy 511

harvest
  effect 154
  profit 618
  store 636
  acquisition 775
  get in the –
  complete 729
  succeed 731
– home
  celebration 883
– time
  autumn 126
  exertion 686
has been 122
hash *mix* 41
  cut 44
  confusion 59
  food 298
  make a – 699
hashish 863
hasp 43, 45
hassock 215
hastate 253
haste
  velocity 274
  activity 682
  hurry **684**
hasten
  promote 707
hasty
  transient 113
  hurried 684
  impatient 825
  irritable 901
– pudding 298
hat 225
  cardinal's – 999
  send round the –
  765
  shovel – 999
– in hand 886
hatch
  produce 161
  gate 232
  opening 260
  chickens 370
  fabricate 544
  shading 556
  plan 626
  prepare 673
– a plot 626
hatches, under –
  restraint 751
  prisoner 754
  poor 804
hatchet
  cutting 253
  bury the – 918
  dig up the – 722
  throw the helve
  after the – 818

hatchet-faced 203
hatchment
  funeral 363
  arms 550
  record 551
hatchway 260
hate 867, **898**
hateful 649, 830
hath been, the
  time – 122
hatrack 215
hatter 225
  mad as a – 503
hatti-sheriff 741
hatred [*see* hate]
  object of – 898
hauberk 717
haud passibus
  æquis 28, 275
haugh 344
haughty
  proud 878
  insolent 885
  contemptuous 930
haul *drag* 285
  catch of fish &c.
  789
– down one's flag
  725
– in 10
haunch 236
haunt *focus* 74
  presence 186
  abode 189
  alarm 860
  persecute 907
– the memory
  remember 505
  trouble 830
haunted 980
haut
  traiter de –
  insolence 885
  contempt 930
hautboy 417
haut-goût 392
haut-monde 875
hauteur 878
have *confute* 479
  ken 49
  possess 777
– the advantage
  28, 33
– at 716
– no choice 609*a*
– done! 142
– to do with 9
– no end 112
– other fish to fry
  135
– it

discover 480*a*
believe 484
– one to know 527
– some knowledge
  of 490
– nothing to do
  with 10
– for one's own
  780
– rather 609
– one's rights 924
– the start 116
– in store 152, 637
– to 620
– up 638
– it your own way
  submission 725
haven 292, 666
haversack 191
havoc
  destruction 162
  cry – *war* 722
  play – *spoil* 659
haw 583
hawk *spit* 297
  stammer 583
  eye of a – 498
– about
  publish 531
  offer 763
  sell 796
– at 716
between – and
  buzzard 315,
  828
know a – from a
  handsaw 465,
  698
hawker 796
hawk-eyed 441
hawking *chase* 622
hawser 45
hay while the sun
  shines, make –
  134
haycock 72
hazard
  chance 156, 621
  danger 665
  at all –s 604
– a conjecture 514
– a proposition
  477
haze *mist* 353
  uncertainty 475
  in a –
  hidden 528
hazel 433
hazy *opaque* 426
he 373
head *precedence* 62

beginning 66
class 75
summit 210
coiffure 225
lead 280
froth 353
person 372
intellect 450
topic 454
wisdom 498
picture 556
nomenclature 564
chapter 593
direct 693
director 694
master 745
at the – of
  direction 693
  authority 737
  repute 873
bow the – 308
bring to a – 729
come into one's –
  451
come to a – 729
drive into one's –
  505
gain – 175
get into one's –
  thought 451
  learn 505
  belief 484
  intoxicate 959
give a horse his –
  748
hang one's – 879
have in one's – 490
from – to heels 52,
  200
hit on the – 912
knock on the –
  361
knock one's –
  against
  impulse 276
  unskilful 699
  fail 732
lie on one's – 926
lift up one's – 878
make – against
  oppose 708
  resistance 719
  success 731
never entered
  into one's – 458
have no – 506
on one's – 218
off one's – 503
can't get out of
  one's – 505
over – and ears

deep 641
debt 806
love 897
put into one's –
  supposition 514
  information 527
put out of one's –
  458
run in the – 505
not know whether
  one stands on –
  or heels
  uncertain 475
  wonder 870
take into one's –
  thought 451
  caprice 608
  intention 620
turn the – 824
trouble one's –
  about 457
as one's – shall
  answer for 768
with – erect 878
from – to foot 200
– and front
  important 642
– and front of
  one's offending
  provocation 830
  charge 938
– over heels
  inversion 218
  rotation 312
– light 423
– line 591
– and shoulders
  irrelevant 10
  complete 52
  haste 684
make neither – nor
  tail of 519
hold one's – up
  307
– above water
  safe 664
  prosperous 743
  wealth 803
with a – on 353
headache 378
head-dress 225
header 310
head-foremost
  violent 173
  rash 863
head-gear 225
heading *prefix* 64
  beginning 66
  indication 550
  title 564
headland

height 206
projection 250
headlong
hurry 684
rush 863
rush –
violence 173
headman 694
headmost
front 234
precession 280
head-piece
summit 210
intellect 450
helmet 717
ornament 847
head-quarters
focus 74
abode 189
authority 737
head-race 350
head-stone 363
heads
compendium 596
– or tails 156, 621
lay – together
advice 695
co-operate 709
– I win tails you
lose
unfair 940
headship 737
headsman 975
headstrong
violent 173
obstinate 606
rash 863
headway *space* 180
navigation 267
progression 282
headwind 708
headwork 451
heady 606
heal *restore* 660
remedy 662
let the wound –
forgive 918
– the breach
pacify 723
healing art 662
health 654
picture of – 654
healthiness 655
health resort 189
healthy 656
heap *quantity* 31
collection 72
store 636
too many 641
heaps 102
rubbish – 645

hear
audition 418
be informed 527
not – of (refuse)
764
– a cause
adjudge 480
lawsuit 969
– hear! 931
– and obey 743
– out 457
hearer 418
hearing 418, 696
[*see* hear]
gain a – 175
give a – 418
hard of – 419
out of – 196
within – 197
hearken 457
hearsay 532
– evidence 467
hearse 363
heart
intrinsicality 5
interior 221
centre 222
mind 450
willingness 602
essential 642
affections 820
courage 861
love 897
man after one's
own – 899
with all one's –
438, 602
at – 820, 821
from bottom of –
543
beating – 821, 824
break the – 830
by –
memory 505
go to one's – 824
in good – 858
with a heavy –
603
know by – 490
lay to – 837
learn by – 539
lift up the – 990
lose – 837
lose one's – 897
nearest to one's –
897
not find it in one's
– 603
have a place in
the – 897
put one's – into

604
set one's – upon
604
take –
content 831
hope 858
courage 861
take to –
sensibility 822
discontent 832
dejection 837
anger 900
warm – 822
wind round the –
897
– bleeding for 914
to one's –'s con-
tent
willing 602
enough 639
success 731
pleasure 829
–'s core
mind 450
affections 820
– expanding 821
– failing one 837,
860
do one's – good
829
– of grace 858
– in hand 602
– leaping with joy
827, 838
– leaping into
one's mouth 824
– of oak
strong 159
hard 323
– in right place
906
– sinking *fear* 860
– and soul
completely 52
willing 602
resolute 604
exertion 686
feeling 821
– of stone 823, 907
– swelling 824
heartache 828
heart-breaking 821,
830
heart-broken 828
heartburning
discontent 832
regret 833
enmity 889
anger 900
jealousy 920
hearten 858, 861

heartfelt 821, 829
hearth
home 189
fireplace 386
heartless 823, 945
heart-rending 830
heartsease 831
heart-shaped 245
heart-sick
dejection 837
dislike 867
satiety 869
heart-stricken 828
**heart-strings, tear
the –** 830
hearty
willing 602
healthy 654
feeling 821
cheerful 836
friendly 888
social 892
– laugh 838
– meal 298
– reception 892
heat *warmth* **382**
make hot 384
contest 720
excitement 824,
825
dead – 27
– of passion 900
– wave 382
heated imagination
515
heater 386
heath *moor* 344
plant 367
heathen 984, 989
– mythology 979
heathenish 851
heather *moor* 344
plant 367
heaume 717
**heautontimoru-
menos** 837, 955
heave *raise* 307
emotion 821
– the lead 208,
466
– a sigh 839
– in sight 446
– to 265
heaven 827, **981**
call – to witness
535
in the face of –
525
light of – 420
move – and earth
686

hemispheric 250
hemlock 663
hemorrhage 299
hemp 205
hen 366, 374
 female 374
 – with one chicken
  busy 682
henbane 663
hence
 arising from 155
 departure 293
 deduction 476
 – loathed mel-
  ancholy 836
henceforth 121
henchman 746
hencoop 370
hendiadis 91
henna 433
henpecked 743, 749
heptagon 244
heptarchy 98
Heraclitus 839
 rideret – 853
herald
 precursor 64
 precession 280
 predict 511
 forerunner 512
 proclaim 531
 messenger 534
heraldry 550
herb 367
herbage 365
herbal 369
herbivorous 298
herborize 369
herculean
 strong 159
 exertion 686
 difficult 704
Herculem, ex pede
 – 550
Hercules 159, 215
 pillars of – 233,
  550
herd 72, 102
herdsman 746
here
 situation 183
 presence 186
 arrival 292
 come –! 286
 – below 318
 – goes 676
 – and there
  dispersed 73
 few 103
 place 182, 183
 – there and

everywhere
 diversity 16a
 space 180
 omnipresence 186
 – to-day and gone
  to-morrow 111
hereabouts 183,
 197
hereafter 121, 152
hereby 631
hereditament 780
hereditary
 intrinsic 5
 derivative 154,
  167
heredity 167
herein 221
heresy 495, 984
heretic 984
heretofore 122
hereupon 106
herewith 88, 632
heritage
 futurity 121
 possession 777
 property 780
heritor 779
hermaphrodite 83
 – brig 273
hermeneutics 522
Hermes 534, 582
hermetically 261
hermit 893, 955
hermitage
 house 189
 cell 191
 seclusion 893
hero *brave* 861
 glory 873
 good man 948
 – worship 931, 991
Herod, out-Herod
 – 549
heroic [*see* hero]
 magnanimous
  942
 mock – 853
heroics 884
heroin 663
heroine 861
herpetology 368
Herr 373
herring
 pungent 392
 – pond 341
 draw a – across
  the trail 545
 trail of a red –
  615, 706
herring-gutted 203
hesitate

uncertain 475
sceptical 485
stammer 583
reluctant 603
irresolute 605
fearful 860
Hesperian 236
Hesperides, garden
 of the – 981
Hesperus 423
Hessian boot 225
hest 741
hesterni quirites
 876
heterarchy 737
heteroclite 83
heterodoxy 489,
 984
heterogeneous
 unrelated 10
 different 15
 mixed 41
 multiform 81
 exceptional 83
heterogeneity 15,
 16a
heteromorphism
 16a
hetman 745
hew *cut* 44
 shorten 201
 fashion 240
 – down 308
hewers of wood
 workers 690
 commonalty 876
hexagon 98, 244
hexahedron 244
hexameter 98, 597
hey! 586
heyday
 exultation 838
 festivity 840
 wonder 870
 – of the blood 820
 – of youth 127
hiation 260
hiatus 198
hibernal 383
hibernate 683
Hibernicism 497,
 563
hic:
 – jacet 363
 – labor hoc opus
  704
hick 701, 851, 876
hiccup 349
hid under a bushel
 460

hidalgo 875
hidden 528
 – meaning 526
hide *skin* 223
 conceal 528
 – diminished **head**
 inferior 34
 decrease 36
 humility 879
 – one's face
 modesty 881
 – and seek
 deception 545
 avoid 623
 game 840
hide-bound 751,
 819
hideous 846
hide-out 893
hiding-place
 abode 189
 ambush 530
 refuge 666
hie 264, 274
 – to 266
hiemal 126
hierarch 996
hierarchy 995
hieratic 590
hieroglyphic
 representation
  554
 letter 561
 writing 590
hierographa 985
hieromancy 511
hierophant 996
hieroscopy 511
higgle 794
higgledy piggledy
 59
higgler 797
high *much* 31
 lofty 206
 fetid 401
 treble 410
 foul 653
 noted 873
 proud 878
 from on – 981
 on – 206
 think –ly of 931
 – art 556
 – celebration 998
 – colour
 colour 428
 red 434
 exaggerate 549
 – commissioner
  745
 – days and holi-

H.M.S. 726
hoar *aged* 128
　white 430
　– frost 383
hoard 636
hoarse
　husky 405
　harsh 410
　voiceless 581
　talk oneself – 584
hoary [*see* hoar]
hoax 545
hob *support* 215
　stove 386
　– and nob
　celebration 883
　courtesy 894
hobble
　limp 275
　awkward 699
　difficulty 704
　fail 732
　shackle 751
　– skirt 225
hobbledehoy 129
hobby
　crotchet 481
　pursuit 622
　desire 865
hobby-horse 272
hobgoblin
　fearful 860
　demon 980
hobo 268
hobnail 876
Hobson's choice
　necessity 601
　no choice 609a
　compulsion 744
hoc genus omne
　876
hock 771
hock shop 787
hockey 840
hockey rink 213
hocus 545
hocus-pocus
　interchange 148
　unmeaning 517
　cheat 545
　conjuration 992
　spell 993
hod
　receptacle 191
　support 215
　vehicle 272
hoddy-doddy 501
hodge-podge 41, 59
hoe 272, 371
hog *animal* 366
　sensualist 954a

glutton 957
/greedy as a – 865
　go the whole – 604
hog's back 206
hogmanay 998
hogshead 191
hog-wash 653
hoist 307
　– the black flag
　722
　– a flag 550
　– on one's own
　petard
　retaliation 718
　failure 732
hoity-toity! 815,
　870
hold *cohere* 46
　contain 54
　remain 141
　cease 142
　go on 143
　happen 151
　receptacle 191
　cellar 207
　base 211
　support 215
　halt 265
　believe 484
　be passive 681
　defend 717
　power 737
　restrain 751
　prison 752
　prohibit 761
　possess 777
　retain 781
　enough! 869
have a firm – 781
have a – upon 175
gain a – upon 737
get – of 789
quit one's – 782
take – 175
– aloof
　stay away 187
　distrust 487
　avoid 623
– an argument
　476
– authority 737
– back *avoid* 623
　store 636
　hinder 706
　restrain 751
　retain 781
　miserly 819
– one's breath
　wonder 870
– converse 588
– a council 695

– fast 751, 781
– forth *teach* 537
　speak 582
– good 478, 494
– one's ground
　141
– in hand 737
– one's hand
　cease 142
　relinquish 624
– hard 265
– up one's head
　861
– a lease 771
– a meeting 72
– off 623
– office 693
– on
　continue 141, 143
　persevere 604a
– out [*see below*]
– one's own
　preserve 670
　defend 717
　resist 719
– oneself in readi-
　ness 673
– in remembrance
　505
– both one's sides
　838
– a situation 625
– in solution 335
– to 602
– together 43, 709
– one's tongue
　403, 585
– up [*see below*]
– oneself up 307
hold out
　endure 106
　affirm 535
　persevere 604a
　resist 719
　offer 763
　brave 861
– expectation
　predict 511
　promise 768
– temptation 865
hold up
　continue 143
　support 215
　not rain 340
　aid 707
　rob 791
　display 882
　extol 931
– one's hand
　sign 550
　threat 609

– to execration
　cures 908
　censure 932
– the mirror 525
– to scorn 930
– to shame 874
– to view 525
holder 779
holdfast 45
holding
　tenancy 777
　property 780
hole *place* 182
　hovel 189
　receptacle 191
　opening 260
　ambush 530
– in one's coat 651
– and corner
　place 182
　peer into – 461
　hiding 528, 530
– to creep out of
　plea 617
　escape 671
　facility 705
holiday *leisure* 685
　repose 687
　amusement 840
– task *easy* 705
holiness *God* 976
　piety 987
holloa 411
– before one is out
　of the wood 884
hollow
　unsubstantial 4
　completely 52
　incomplete 53
　depth 208
　concavity 252
　channel 350
　- sound 408
　specious 477
　false 544
　voiceless 581
　beat – 731
　– truce 723
holm 346
holocaust
　kill 361
　sacrifice 991
　(*destruction* 162)
holograph 590
holster 191
holt 367
holus bolus 684
Holy *of God* 976
　pious 987
　keep – 987
　– breathing 990

– Church 983a
– City 981
– day 998
– Ghost 976
temple of the –
   Ghost 983a
– men of old 985
– orders 995
– place 1000
– Scriptures 985
– Spirit 976
– water 998
– week 998
holystone 652
homage
   submission 725
   fealty 743
   reverence 928
   approbation 931
   worship 990
home *focus* 74
   habitation 189
   near 197
   interior 221
   arrival 292
   refuge 666
at – *party* 72
   present 186
   within 221
   at ease 705
   social gathering
   892
be at –
– *to visitors* 892
feel at –
   freedom 748
   pleasure 827
   content 831
look at –
   accusation 938
make oneself at –
   free 748
   sociable 892
not be at – 764
stay at – 265
at – in
   knowledge 490
   skill 698
at – with
   friendship 888
bring – to
   evidence 467
   belief 484
   accuse 938
   condemn 971
come – 292
eternal – 98
from – 187
get – 292
go – 283
go from – 293

long – 363
strike –
   energy 171
   attack 716
– stroke 170
– thrust
   attack 716
   censure 932
home-bred 851
home-felt 821, 824
home-rule 737, 748
homeless
   unhoused 185
   banished 893
homely
   language 576
   unadorned 849
   common 851, 876
Homeric
– *laughter* 838
home-sick 833
home-spun
   texture 329
home-stall 189
homestead 189
homeward bound
   292
homicidal maniac
   913
homicide 361
homiletical 892
homily
   teaching 537
   advice 595
   sermon 998
hominem, argu-
   mentum ad –
   938
homœpathic
   small 32
   little 193
Homœpathy 662
homogeneity
   relation 9
   identity 13
   uniformity 16
   simplicity 42
homogenesis 161
homologous 23
homology
   relation 9
   uniformity 16
   equality 27
   concord 714
homonym
   equivocal 520
   vocal sound 580
homophony 413
homunculus 193
Hon. 817
hone 253

honest
   veracious 543
   honourable 939
   pure 960
– *meaning* 516
turn an – penny
   775
– truth 494
honey
   sweet 396
   favourite 899
milk and – 734
honeycomb
   concave 252
   opening 260
   deterioration 659
honeyed
– *phrases* 894
– *words*
   allurement 615
   flattery 933
honeymoon
   pleasure 827
   endearment 902
   marriage 903
honey-mouthed
   894, 933
honeysuckle 396
honorarium 784, 973
honorary 815
honour
   demesne 780
   glory 873
   title 877
   respect 928
   approbation 931
   probity 939
affair of – 720
do – to 883
do the –s
   sociality 892
   courtesy 894
   respect 928
his – *judge* 967
in – of 883
man of – 939
upon my – 535,
   768
word of – 768
– be to 873
– a bill 807
– in the breach
   923
– bright
   veracity 543
   probity 939
honte, mauvaise –
   881
hood 225, 999
hooded 223
hoodlum 887

hoodoo 649
hoodwink
   ignore 491
   blind 442
   hide 528
   deceive 545
hoof 211
cloven – 907
hook *fasten* 43
   fastening 45
   hang 214
   curve 245
   deceive 545
   retain 781
   take 789
by – or by crook
   631
hookah 392
hooker *ship* 273
hookey, blind – 840
hooks, go off the
   360
hooligan 887, 913
hoop *circle* 247
   cry 411
hoot *cry* 411, 412
   deride 929
   contempt 930
   censure 932
hop *leap* 309
   dance 840, 892
– off 293
– skip and jump
   leap 309
   agitation 315
   haste 684
   game 840
– the twig 360
hope 858
band of – 958
beyond – 658, 734
dash one's –s 837
excite – 511
foster – 858
well-grounded –
   472
– against hope 859
– for the best 858
– deferred
   dejection 837
   lamentation 859
– for *expect* 507
   desire 865
hope chest 858
hopeful *infant* 129
   probable 472
   hope 858
hopelessness 471,
   859
Hop-o'-my-thumb
   193

hopper 191
horary 108
horde
  assemblage 72
  party 712
  commonalty 876
horizon
  distance 196
  view 441
  expectation 507
  appear on the –
    525
  gloomy – 859
horizontality 213
horn
  receptacle 191
  sharp 253
  music 417
  draw in one's –s
  recant 607
  submit 725
  humility 879
  exalt one's – 873
  wear the –s 905
  –s of a dilemma
  reasoning 476
  difficulty 704
  – in 294
  – mad 920
  – of plenty 639
hornbook 542
hornet
  evil-doer 913
  –'s nest
  pitfall 667
  difficulty 704
  adversity 735
  painful 830
  resentment 900
  censure 932
hornpipe 840
hornwork 717
horny 323
Horny, old – 978
horology 114
horoscope 511, 992
horresco referens
  860
horrible *great* 31
  noxious 649
  dire 830
  ugly 846
  fearful 860
horrid [*see* horrible]
  vulgar 851
horrida bella 722
horrific [*see*
  horrible]
horrified 828, 860
horrify 830, 860
horripilation 383

[522]

horrisonous 410
horror 860, 867
  view with – 898
horrors 837
  sup full of – 828
horror-stricken 828
hors de combat
  impotent 158
  useless 645
  tired out 688
  put – 731
hors-d'œuvre 298
horse *hang on* 214
  stand 215
  carrier 271
  animal 366
  male 373
  cavalry 726
  ride the high –
    885
  put the –s to 673
  put up one's –s at
    184
  put up one's –s
    together
  concord 714
  friendship 888
  take – 266
  to – 293
  war – 726
  work like a – 686
  – artillery 726
  – of another colour
    15
  – doctor 370
  – and foot 726
  – laugh 838
  – marine 701
  like a – in a mill
    613
  – racing
  pastime 840
  contention 720
  – soldier 726
  – track 627
horseback 266
horse-cloth 225
horseman 268
horsemanship
  riding 266
  skill 698
horseplay 856
horse power 466
horse-shoe 245
horse-whip 972
hortation 615, 695
hortative 537
horticulture 371
hortus siccus 369
hosanna 931, 990
hose

stockings 225
pipe 348, 350
extinguisher 385
hosier 225
hospice 189, 662
hospitable 816, 892
hospital 189, 662
  in – 655
hospitality
  [*see* hospitable]
hospodar 745
host *collection* 72
  multitude 102
  army 726
  friend 890
  rite 998
  reckon without
    one's –
  error 495
  unskilful 699
  rash 863
  – of heaven 977
  – in himself 175
hostage 771
hostel 189
hostelry 189
hostile
  disagreeing 24
  opposed 708
  enmity 889
  in – array 708
  – meeting 720
hostilities 722
hostility 889
hostler 746
hot *violent* 173
  warm 382
  pungent 392
  red 434
  orange 439
  excited 824
  irascible 901
  make – 384
  – air 482, 884
  – bath 386
  – blood *rash* 863
  angry 900
  irascible 901
  blow – and cold
  inconsistent 477
  falsehood 544
  tergiversation 607
  caprice 608
  in – haste 684
  in – pursuit 622
  – water
  difficulty 704
  quarrel 713
  painful 830
  – water bottle 386
hot air merchant

884
hot-bed *cause* 153
  centre 222
  workshop 691
Hotchkiss gun 727
hotchpotch
  mixture 41
  confusion 59
  participation 778
hotel 189
hot-headed 684,
  825
hothouse
  conservatory 371,
    636
  furnace 386
  workshop 691
hot-press 255
Hotspur 863
Hottentot 876
hough 659
hound *animal* 366
  hunt 622
  persecute 907
  wretch 949
  hold with the hare
    but run with the
    –s 607
  – on 615
houppelande 225
hour *period* 108
  point of time 113
  present time 118
  improve the shin-
    ing – 682
  one's – is come
  occasion 134
  death 360
  – after hour 110
hour-glass
  chronometer 114
  contraction 195
  narrow 203
Houri 845
hourly *time* 106
  frequent 136
  periodical 138
house *family* 166
  locate 184
  abode 189
  theatre 599
  make safe 664
  council 696
  firm 712
  before the – 454
  keep – 184
  eat out of – and
    home
  prodigal 818
  gluttony 957
  turn out of – and

the same a – years
hence 460
hundredth 99
hundredweight 319
hunger 865
hunger-strike 956
hunks 819
hunt *inquiry* 461
　pursuit 622
　– after 622
　– in couples 709
　– down 907
　– out *inquiry* 461
　discover 480a
　– slipper 840
hunter *horse* 271
　killer 361
　pursuer 622
　place &c. – 767
hunting 361, 622
hunting-ground 840
　happy – 981
hurdle 272
hurdy-gurdy 417
hurl 284
　– against 716
　– defiance 715
hurler avec les
　loups 82, 714
Hurlothrumbo 860
hurly-burly 315
hurrah 411, 836,
　838
hurricane 349, 667
　– deck 210
hurry *haste* 684
　excite 825
　– forward 684
　– off with 789
　– on 615
　– of spirits 821
　– up 684
hurst 367
hurt
　physical pain 378
　evil 619
　maltreat 649
　injure 659
　more frightened
　　than – 860
　– the feelings
　pain 830
　anger 900
hurtful 649
hurtle 276
hurtless 648
husband
　store 636
　director 694
　spouse 903
husbandman 371

husbandry
　agriculture 371
　conduct 692
　economy 817
hush *moderate* 174
　stop 265
　silence 403
　taciturn 585
　– up
　conceal 528
　pacify 723
hush-money 30,
　973
husk 223, 226
husky *strong* 159
　dry 340
　faint sound 405
　hoarse 581
hussar 726
hussy 962
hustings
　school 542
　arena 728
　tribunal 966
hustle
　perturb 61
　push 276
　agitate 315
　activity 682
　hinder 706
hustler 682, 962
hut 189
hutch 189
huzza 838
hyacinth
　jewel 847
hyæna 913
hyaline 425
hybrid
　mixture 41
　exception 83
hydra
　monster 83, 366
　productive 168
　– headed 163
hydrant 348, 385
hydraulics 333, 348
hydro-aeroplane
　273
hydrodynamics
　333, 348
hydrography 341
hydrology 333
hydrolysis 49
hydromancy 511
hydromel 396
hydropathy 662
hydrophobia 867
hydroplane 273
hydrostatics 333
hyemal 383

hyetology 348
hygeian 656
hygiantics 670
hygienic 656, 670
hygre 348
hygrometry 339
hyle 316
hylism 316
hylotheism 984,
　989
Hymen 903
hymeneal 903
hymn *song* 415
　worship 990
　– of hate 898
hymn-book 998
hyoscine 663
hypallage 218
hyperbation 218
hyperbola 245
hyperbole 549
hyperborean
　far 196
　cold 383
hypercriticism
　misjudgment 481
　discontent 832
　fastidiousness 868
　censure 932
hyperdulia 990
Hyperion 423, 845
　– to a satyr 14
hyperorthodoxy 984
hyperphysical 976
hypertrophy 194
hyphen 45
hypnology 683
hypnotic
　remedy 662
　sleep 683
hypnotize 376
hypocaust 386
hypochondriac
　madman 504
　low spirits 837
hypochondriasis
　837
hypocrisy
　falsehood 544
　religious – 988
hypocrite 548, 855
　play the – 544
hypostasis 1, 3
Hypostatic union
　976
hypothecate 771
hypothenuse 217
hypothesis 514
hypothesize 514
hypothetical 475,
　514

hypped *insane* 503
　dejected 837
hypsometer 206
Hyrcynian wood
　533
hysteria
　insanity 503
hysteric *violent* 173
hysterical
　spasmodic 608
　emotional 821
　excitable 825
hysterics 173
　in – *excited* 824
　frightened 860
hysteron proteron
　218

I

I 79
iambic 597
ibidem 13
Icarus
　navigator 269
　rash 863
　fate of – 306
ice *cold* 383
　refrigerate 385
iceberg 383
ice-bound 383
　restraint 751
ice-chest 385
ice-house 387
ice-yacht 273
Ichabod 874
ichnography 554
ichor 333
ichthyology 368
ichthyomancy 511
ichthyophagous 298
icicle 383
icon 554
iconoclasm 983a,
　984
iconoclast 165, 913
iconography 554
icosahedron 244
id est 522
idea
　small quantity 32
　notion **453**
　give an – of 537
ideal *unreal* 2
　completeness 52
　erroneous 495
　imaginary 515
　perfect 650
ideality 450, 515
idée fixe 481

identification
identity 13
comparison 464
discovery 480a
identity 13
– book 206
Ideology 450
Ides of March 601
idiocrasy
essence 5
tendency 176
idiocy 499
idiom 560, 566
idiomatic 79
idiosyncrasy
essence 5
speciality 79
unconformity 83
tendency 176
temperament 820
idiot 501
tale told by an –
517
idiotic
foolish 499
idiotism
folly 499
phrase 566
idle *foolish* 499
trivial 643
slothful 683
lie – *inaction* 681
– conceit 842
– hours 681
be an – man
leisure 685
– talk 588
– time away 683
idler 683
Ido 560
idol *desire* 865
favourite 899
fetich 991
– of the people
899
idolater 984
idolatry 897, **991**
idolize *love* 897
impiety 988
idoneous 23
idyl 597
if *circumstance* 8
qualification 469
supposition 514
– you please 765
– possible 470
igloo 189
igneous 382
ignis fatuus
luminary 423
phantom 443

ignite 384
ignoble 876
ignominy 874, 940
ignoramus 493
ignorance 491
keep in – 528
plead – 937
ignoratio elenchi
477
ignore
neglect 460
incredulity 487
not known 491
repudiate 756,
773
ignotum per
ignotius 477
ilk 13
ill *evil* 619
badness 649
sick 655
go on – *fail* 732
adversity 735
look – 846
take –
discontent 832
anger 900
– betide 908
– blood *hate* 898
malevolence 907
– at ease *pain* 828
dejection 837
house of – fame
961
–s that flesh is
heir to *evil* 619
disease 655
– humour
anger 900
sullenness 901a
– luck 735
as – luck would
have it 135
– off
insufficient 640
adversity 735
poor 804
do an – office to
907
bird of – omen
668
– repute 874
– turn *evil* 619
spiteful 907
– usage 907
– will 907
wind *bad* 649
hindrance 706
adversity 735
ill-adapted 24
ill-advised

foolish 499
inexpedient 647
unskilful 699
ill-affected 901a
illapse
conversion 144
ingress 294
illaqueate 545
ill-assorted 24
illation 480
illaudable 947
ill-balanced 28
ill-bred 851, 895
ill-conditioned
bad 649
difficult 704
discourteous 895
malevolent 907
vicious 945
ill-conducted 699
ill-contrived
inexpedient 647
bad 649
unskilful 699
malevolent 907
ill-defined 447
ill-devised 499, 699
ill-digested 674
ill-disposed 901a,
907
illegality 964
illegible 519
render – 552
– hand 590
illegitimate
deceitful 545
undue 925
illegal 964
ill-fated 735
ill-flavoured 395
ill-furnished 640
illiberal
narrow-minded
481
stingy 819
uncourteous 895
selfish 943
illicit 925, 964
ill-imagined 499,
699
illimited 105
ill-intentioned 907
illiterate 491, 493
ill-judged 499, 699
ill-judging 481
ill-made 243, 846
ill-mannered 851,
895
ill-marked 447
ill-matched 24
ill-mated 24

ill-natured 907
illogical 477, 495
ill-omened 605, 859
ill-proportioned 243
ill-provided 640
ill-qualified 699
ill-requited 917
ill-spent 646
ill-tempered 901
ill-timed 135
ill-treat *bad* 649
severe 739
malevolent 907
illuminant 388
illuminate
enlighten 420
colour 428
excite 824
ornament 847
illuminati 492
illumination
[see illuminate]
book-illustration
558
celebration 883
ill-use 907
ill-used 828
illusion
fallacy of vision
443
error 495
illusive, illusory
sophistical 477
erroneous 495
deceitful 545, 546
illustrate
exemplify 82
interpret 522
represent 554
engravings 558
ornament 847
illustrious 873
image
likeness 17
copy 21
appearance 448
idea 453
metaphor 521
representation
554
graven – *idol* 991
imagery *fancy* 515
metaphor 521
representation
554
imaginable 470
imaginary
non-existing 2
fancied 515
– quantity 84
imagination 515

imaum 745, 996
imbecile 158, 499
imbécile 501
imbecility **499**
imbed [see embed]
imbedded 229
imbibe 296
 – learning 539
imbrangle 61
imbricated 223
imbroglio
  disorder 59
  difficulty 704
  discord 713
imbrue
  impregnate 300
  moisten 339
 – one's hands in
   blood
  killing 361
  war 722
 – the soul 824
imbue *mix* 41
  impregnate 300
  moisten 339
  tinge 428
  teach 537
imbued
  affections 820
 – with
  belief 484
  habit 613
  feeling 821
imburse 803
imitation
  copying **19**
  copy 21
  representation
   554
immaculate
  perfect 650
  clean 652
  innocent 946
immanent 5, 132
immanity 907
Immanuel 976
immaterial
  unsubstantial 4
immateriality
  spiritual **317**
  trifling 643
immature 123, 674
immeasurable 31,
  105
immediate
  continuous 69
immediately 113,
  132
immedicabile
  vulnus 619
immedicable 859

immelodious 414
immemorial 124
  from time – 122
  ‑ usage 613
immense *great* 31
  infinite 105
  - *size* 192
immerge⟩
immerse⟩
  introduce 300
  dip 337
immersed in 229
immethodical 59
immigrant
  alien 57
  entering 294
immigration 266,
  294
imminent 152, 286
immiscible 47
immission 296
immitigable
  hopeless 859
  revenge 919
immix 41
immobility 150, 265
immoderately 31
immodest 961
immolation
  killing 361
  giving 784
  sacrifice 991
immoral 923, 945
immortal
  perpetual 112
  glorious 873
  celebrated 883
immotile 265
immovable
  stable 150
  quiescent 265
  obstinate 606
immundicity 653
immunity
  health 656
  freedom 748
  right 924
  exemption 777a,
   927a
immure 751
immutable
  stable 150
  deity 976
imo pectore, ab –
  821
imp 980
impact *contact* 43
  impulse 276
  insertion 300
impair 659
impale *transfix* 260

execute 972
impalpable
  small 193
  powder 330
  intangible 381
impanation 998
impar sibi 608
imparity 28
impart *inform* 527
  give 784
impartial
  judicious 498
  neutral 628
  just 922
  honourable 939
 – opinion 484
impassable
  closed 261
  impossible 471
impasse 706
impassible 823
impassion 824
impassionable 822
impassioned
  - *language* 574
  excited 825
impassive 823
impatient 825
 – of control 742
impawn 771
impeach
  censure 932
  accuse 938
  go to law 969
impeachment,
  soft – 902
impeccability 650,
  946
impecunious 804
impede 706
impediment 706
 – in speech 583
impedimenta 633,
  780
impel *push* 276
  induce 615
impend
  future 121
  imminent 132
  destiny 152
  overhang 206
impenetrable
  closed 261
  solid 321
  unintelligible 519
  latent 526
impenitence **951**
imperative
  require 630
  command 737,
   741

severe 739
  duty 926
imperator 745
imperceptible
  small 32
  minute 193
  slow 275
  invisible 447
  latent 526
impercipient 376
imperdible 664
imperfect
  incomplete 53
  failing 651
  vicious 945
imperfection **651**
  inferiority 34
  vice 945
imperfectly 32
imperforate 261
imperial
  trunk 191
  beard 256
  authority 737
imperil 665
imperious
  command 737
  proud 878
  arrogant 885
 – necessity 601
imperishable 112
  stable 150
  glorious 873
imperium in
  imperio 737
impermanent 111
impermeable
  closed 261
  dense 321
impersonal
  general 78
  neuter 316
impersonate 19,
  554
impersonator 19
imperspicuity 519
impersuasible 606
impertinent
  irrelevant 10
  insolent 885
imperturbable 823,
  826
impervious
  closed 261
  impossible 471
  insensible 823
 – to light 426
 – to reason 606
impetiginous 653
impetrate 765
impetuous

ingress 294
receipt 810
incommensurable 10
– quantity 84, 85
incommode 706
hinder 706
incommunicable
unmeaning 517
unintelligible 519
retention 781
incommunicado 528
incommutable 150
incomparable 33
incompassionate 914a
incompatible 24
incompatibility 15
incompetence
inability 158
incapacity 499
unskilful 699
dereliction 927
incompleteness 53
non-completion 730
incompliance 764
incomprehensible
infinite 105
unintelligible 519
incomprehension 491
incompressible 321
inconcealable 525
inconceivable
unthinkable 452
impossible 471
improbable 473
incredible 485
unintelligible 519
wonder 870
inconceptible 519
inconcinnity
disagreement 24
ugliness 846
inconclusive 477
inconcoction 674
incondite 851
incongruous
differing 15
disagreeing 24
illogical 477
ungrammatical 568
discordant 713
inconnection 10, 44
inconsequence
irrelation 10
inconsequential 477
inconsiderable 32,

643
inconsiderate
thoughtless 452
inattentive 458
neglectful 460
foolish 699
inconsistent
contrary 14
disagreeing 24
illogical 477
absurd 497
foolish 499
capricious 608
discord 713
inconsolable 837
inconsonant
disagreeing 24
fitful 149
inconspicuous 447
inconstant 149
incontestable 159, 474, 525
incontiguous 196
incontinent 961
incontinently 132
incontrollable 173
incontrovertible 150, 474
inconvenience 647
put to – 706
inconversable 585, 893
inconvertible 143
inconvincible 487
incorporate 48
combine 48
include 76
materialize 316
incorporation 761
incorporeal 317
– hereditaments 780
incorrect
illogical 477
erroneous 495
solecism 568
vicious 945
incorrigible
obstinate 606
hopeless 859
vicious 945
impenitent 951
incorruption
probity 939
innocence 946
incrassate
increase 194
density 321
– *fluids* 352
increase
– *in degree* **35**

– *in number* 102
– *in size* 194
incredible
great 31
impossible 471
improbable 473
doubtful 485
wonderful 870
incredulity 487, 989
increment
increase 35
addition 37
adjunct 39
expansion 194
increpation 932
incriminate 938
incrust 223, 224
incubate 370
incubation 673
incubus
hindrance 706
pain 828
demon 980
inculcate 6, 537
inculpable 946
inculpate 938
inculture 674
incumbency
business 625
churchdom 995
incumbent
inhabitant 188
high 206
weight 319
duty 926
clergyman 996
incumber 706
incumbered 806
incunabula 66, 127
incur 177
– blame 932
– danger 665
– a debt 806
– disgrace 874
– a loss 776
– the risk 621
incurable
ingrained 5
disease 655
hopeless 859
incuriam, per – 458, 460
incuriosity 456
incursion 294, 716
incurvation 245
indagation 461
indebted
owing 806
gratitude 916
duty 926
indecent 961

indeciduous 150
indecipherable 519
indecision 475, 605
indecisive 475
indeclinable 150
indecorous
vulgar 851
vicious 945
impure 961
indeed *existing* 1
very 31
assent 488
truly 494
assertion 535
wonder 870
indefatigable
persevering 604a
active 682
indefeasible
stable 150, 474
due 924
indefectible 650
indefensible
powerless 158
submission 725
accusable 938
wrong 945
indeficient 650
indefinite
great 31
unspecified 78
infinite 105
misty 447
uncertain 475
inexact 495
vague 519
indeliberate 612
indelible *stable* 150
memory 505
mark 550
feeling 821
indelicate 961
indemnity
compensation 30
restitution 790
forgiveness 918
atonement 952
reward 973
deed of – 771
indenizen 184
indent *scollop* 248
list 86
indentation 252, 257
indenture 769, 771
independence
irrelation 10
freedom 748
wealth 803
Independent 984
indescribable 31,

dull 840
insipidity
　tasteless **391**
　indifferent 866
insist *argue* 476
　command 741
　– upon *affirm* 535
　dwell on 573
　be determined 604
　contend 720
　compel 744
　conditions 770
　due 924
insnare 545
insobriety 959
insolation 382, 384
insolence 878, 885
insoluble *dense* 321
　unintelligible 519
insolvable 519
insolvent
　poverty 804
　debt 806
　non-payment 808
insomnia 682
insouciance
　thoughtlessness 458
　supineness 823
　indifference 866
inspan 293
inspect 441, 457
inspector 444
　inquisitor 461
　judge 480
　director 694
inspiration
　wisdom 498
　imagination 515
　poetry 577
　impulse 612
　motive 615
　feeling 821
　Deity 976
　revelation 985
　religious - 987
inspire *improve* 658
　prompt 615
　animate 824
　cheer 836
　– courage 861
　– hope 858
　– respect 928
inspirit *incite* 615
　animate 824
　encourage 861
inspiriting
　hopeful 858
inspissate 321, 352
instability 149
install *locate* 184

commission 755
celebrate 883
instalment
　portion 51
　payment 807, 809
instance
　example 82
　motive 615
　solicitation 765
instant *moment* 113
　present 118
　destiny 152
　required 630
　importance 642
　active 682
　lose not an – 684
　on the – 132
instantaneity 113
instanter 113, 132
instar omnium 17, 82
instate 883
instauration 660
instead 147
instep 245
instigate 615
instil *extrinsic* 6
　mix 41
　insert 300
　teach 537
instinct
　intellect 450
　intuition 477
　impulse 601
　– with *motive* 615
　possession 777
　brute – *450a*
instinctive
　inborn 5
institute *begin* 66
　cause 153
　produce 161
　academy 542
　society 712
　– an inquiry 461
institution
　academy 542
　society 712
　political - 963
　church 995
institutor 540
instruct *teach* 537
　advise 695
　precept 697
　order 741
instructed 490
instructor 540
instrument
　implement **633**
　security 771
　musical – 417

optical – 445
　recording – 553
instrumental 631
　– music 415
instrumentalist 416
instrumentality 631
insuavity 895
insubordinate 742
insubstantial 4
　– pageant 882
insufferable
　painful 830
　dislike 867
insufficiency 640
insufflation 349
insular *unrelated* 10
　detached 44
　single 87
　local 181
　island 346
　prejudice 481
insulate 44
insulse 499, 843
insult *rudeness* 895
　offence 900
　disrespect 929
insulting 898
insuperable 471
　– obstacle 706
insupportable 830
insuppressible 173
insurance 768, 771
insure
　make sure 474
　obtain security 771
insurgent 742
insurmountable 471
insurrection 719, 742
insusceptible 823
　– of change 150
inswept 195
intact
　permanent 141
　perfect 650
　preserved 670
intaglio *mould* 22
　concave 252
　sculpture 557
　engraving 558
intangible *little* 193
　numb 381
integer 50, 84
integer vitæ sceleriasque purus 939
integral 50
　– calculus 85
　– part 56
integrate 50

integrity *whole* 50
　probity 939
　virtue 944
integument 223
intellect 450
　absence of – **450a**
　exercise of the – 451
intellectual 450
intelligence
　mind 450
　capacity 498
　news 532
intelligencer 527
intelligentsia 492
intelligibility 518
intemperance 954
　drunkenness 959
intempestivity 135
intend 620
intendant 694
intended *will* 600
　predetermined 611
intense *great* 31
　energetic 171
　– colour 428
　– thought 457
intensification 35
intensify
　increase 35
　stimulate 171
intensity *degree* 26
　greatness 31
　energy 171
intensive culture 371
intent *attention* 457
　will 600
　design 620
　active 682
　– upon *desire* 865
　resolved 604
intention 620
　bad – 607
　good – 906
intently, look – 441
intents and purposes, to all – 27, 52
inter 363
interact 12
inter: – alia 82
　– nos 528
interaction 170
interbreeding 41
intercalate 228
intercalation 300
intercede
　mediate 724
　deprecate 766

prejudice 481
dissent 489
obstinacy 606
impatience 825
insolence 885
malevolence 907
intomb 363
intonation
  sound 402
  musical 313
  voice 580
intone 416, 992
intort 248
intoxicant 663
intoxication
  excitement 824,
    825
  inebriation 959
intra, ab − 221
intractable
  obstinate 606
  difficult 704
  sullen 901a
intramural 221
intransient 110
intransigeance 604
intransitive 110
intransmutable
  110, 150
intrap 545
intraregarding 221
intrench 717
  − on 303
intrepid 861
intricate
  confused 59
  convoluted 248
  difficult 704
intrigant
  meddlesome 682
  cunning 702
  libertine 962
intrigue *fascinate*
  615, 897
  plot 626
  activity 682
  cunning 702
  excite 824
  interest 829
  licentiousness 961
intrinsic 5
  − evidence 467
  − habit 613
  − truth 494
intrinsicality 5
introception 296
introduce *lead* 62
  interpose 228
  precede 280
  insert 300
  − new blood 140

− new conditions
  469
− to 888
introduction
  [*see* introduce]
  preface 64
  reception 296
  drama 599
  friendship 888
  courtesy 894
introductory
  precursor 64
  beginning 66
  priority 116
introgression 294
introit 998
intromission 228
intromit
  discontinue 142
  receive 296
introspection 441,
  457
introspective 451
introvert 218
intrude
  interfere 24
  inopportune 135
  intervene 228
  enter 294
  encroach 303
intruder 57
intrusiveness 682
intrust 755, 787
intuition *mind* 450
  unreasoning **477**
  knowledge 490
intumescence 194,
  250
intwine 43, 243
inunction 223
inundate
  effusion 337
  flow 348
  redundance 641
inunderstanding
  452
inurbanity 895
inure 613, 673
inured
  insensible 823
inusitation 614
inutility 645
invade *ingress* 294
  encroach 303
  attack 716
invalid
  powerless 158
  illogical 477
  diseased 655
  undue 925
invalidate

disable 158
weaken 160
confute 479
invaluable 648
invariable
  intrinsic 5
  uniform 16
  conformable 82
  stable 150
invasion
  ingress 294
  attack 716
invective 932
inveigh 932
inveigle 545, 615
invent
  discover 480a
  imagine 515
  lie 544
  devise 626
invented
  untrue 546
invention 480a
inventive
  skilful 698
inventor 164
inventory 86
inverse 14, 218
inversion
  derangement 61
  change 140
  of position **218**
  contraposition
    237
  reversion 145
  language 577
invertebrate 158
invest
  empower 157
  clothe 225
  besiege 227, 716
  commission 755
  give 784
  lend 787
  expend 809
  − in *locate* 184
  purchase 795
  − money 817
  − with *ascribe* 155
investigate 461
investment 225
  − trust 712
  make −s 673
inveterate *old* 124
  established 150
  inborn 820
  − belief 484
  − habit 613
invidious
  painful 830
  hatred 898

spite 907
envy 921
invigorate
  strengthen 159
invigorating
  . *healthy* 656
invincible 159
inviolable
  secret 528
  right 924
  honour 939
inviolate
  permanent 141
  secret 528
  honourable 939
invious *closed* 261
  pathless 704
invisibility 447
invisible *small* 193
  not to be seen 447
  concealed 526
  − ink 528
  become − 4
invitâ Minervâ 603,
  704
invite *induce* 615
  offer 763
  ask 765
  − the attention
    457
inviting
  [*see* invite]
  pleasing 829
invoice 86
invoke *address* 586
  implore 765
  pray 990
  − curses 908
  − saints 998
involucrum 223
involuntary
  necessary 601
  unwilling 603
  − servitude 749
involution [*see*
  involve]
  algebra 85
involve *include* 54
  derange 61
  wrap 225
  evince 467
  mean 516
  latency 526
involved
  disorder 59
  convoluted 248
  obscure style 571
  in debt 806
involvement 704
invulnerable 664
inward *intrinsic* 5

itinerary 266, 527
itur ad astra, sic –
  360
ivory 430
Ixion 312

J

jab 276
jabber
  unmeaning 517
  stammer 583
  chatter 584
jacent 213
jacet, hic – 363
jacinth 847
jack
  rotation 312
  ensign 550
  instrument 633
  money 800
Jack – Cade 742
  – Ketch 975
  – o' lantern 423
  – in office
  director 694
  bully 887
  – at a pinch 711
  – Pudding
  actor 599
  humorist 844
  boaster 884
before one can say
  ' – Robinson'
  132
  – tar 269
  – of all trades 700
jack-a-dandy 844,
  854
jackal
  auxiliary 711
  servility 886
jackanapes 854,
  887
Jackass 271
jack-boot 225
jackdaw in pea-
  cock's feathers
  701
jacket 225
  cork – 666
Jacobin 710
Jacquerie 716, 719
jacta est alea 601
jactitation
  tossing 315
  boasting 884
jaculation 284
jade *horse* 271
  fatigue 688

low woman 876
  scamp 949
  drab 962
jag 257
jagged 244
jail 752
  – bird
  prisoner 754
  bad man 949
jailer 753, 975
jakes 653
jalousie de métier
  921
jam *squeeze* 43
  crowd 72
  food 298
  pulp 354
  sweet 396
  scrape 732
  – *in interpose* 228
jamb 215
jamboree 840
jammed in 751
jangle
  harsh sound 410
  quarrel 713
janissary 726
janitor 263
janty *gay* 836
  pretty 845
  stylish 852
  showy 882
  insolent 885
January 138
januis clausis 528
Janus *deceiver* 607
  tergiversation 607
close the temple
  of – 723
Janus-faced 544
japan *coat* 223
  resin 356a
  ornament 847
jar *clash* 24
  vessel 191
  agitation 315
  stridor 410
  discord 713
  – upon the feel-
  ings 830
jardinière 191
jargon
  absurdity 497
  no meaning 517
  unintelligible 519
  neology 563
jarvey 694
jasper 847
jaundiced
  yellow 436
  prejudiced 481

dejected 837
  jealous 920
view with – eyes
  disapprove 932
jaunt 266
jaunting car 272
jaunty [*see* janty]
javelin 727
jaw *chatter* 584
  scold 932
jaw-fallen 837
jaws *mouth* 231
  eating 298
  – of death 360
jay 584
jaywalker 701
jazz 415, 840
  – band 417
jealous of honour
  939
jealousy 920
  suspicion 485
jecur, difficili bile –
  900
jeer 929
Jehovah 976
Jehu 268, 694
jejune *insipid* 391
  style 575
  scanty 640
  dull 843
jell 352
jelly 298, 352
  beat to a – 972
jemidar 745
jemmy *lever* 633
  dandy 854
je ne sais quoi
  exceptional 83
  what d'ye call 'em
  563
  beauty 845
jennet 271
jeopardy 665
jerboa 309
jeremiad
  lament 839
  invective 932
Jericho, send to –
  297
jerk *start* 146
  throw 284
  pull 285
  agitate 315
jerkin 225
jerks, by – 70
Jerry Sneak 862,
  941
jersey 225
Jerusalem
  the new – 981

Jessamy, Jemmy –
  854
jesse 1000
jest *trifle* 643
  wit 842
jest-book 842
jester 844
jesting-stock 857
Jesuit *deceiver* 548
  priest 996
jesuitical 477, 544
Jesus 976
jet *stream* 348
  – black 431
jetsam 73, 782
jettison 782
jetty *protection* 250
  harbour 666
jeu
le – n'en vaut pas
  la chandelle
  waste 638
  unimportant 643
  dear 814
  – d'esprit 842
  – de mots 842
  – de théâtre 599
jeune
  – premier 599
  – veuve 599
Jew *cunning* 702
  lender 787
  rich 803
  extortioner 819
  heretic 984
worth a –'s eye
  648, 814
  –'s harp 417
jewel *gem* 648
  ornament 847
  favourite 899
jewellery, false –
  545
Jezebel *wicked* 913
  wretch 949
  courtesan 962
jib *front* 234
  regression 283
cut of one's –
  form 240
  appearance 448
jibe 140
jiffy 113
jig 840
jig-saw puzzle 840
jilt *disappoint* 509
  deceive 545
  deceiver 548
  cast off 756
  dishonour 940
jilted 898

jimp 845
jingal 727
jingle 408
jingo 887
jingoism 884
jinks, high – 840
jinriksha 272
jinx 649, 735
Joan of Arc 861
job *business* 625
  action 680
  unfair 940
  tough – 704
Job:
  patience of – 826,
    830
  poor as – 804
  –'s comforter
    dejection 837
    hopeless 859
jobation 932
jobber
  deceiver 548
  tactician 700
  merchant 797
  trickster 943
jobbernowl 501
jobbery 702, 940
jobbing *barter* 794
jockey *rider* 268
  deceive 545
  deceiver 548
  servant 746
jocose 836, 842
jocoseness *fun* 840
jocular 836, 842
jocund 836, 840
jocundity 829
Joe Miller 842, 844
jog *push* 276
  shake 315
  – the memory 505
  – on *continue* 143
  trudge 266
  slow 275
  advance 282
  mediocrity 736
joggle 315
jog-trot
  trudge 266
  slow 275
  habit 613
John Doe and
  Richard Roe 4
Johnny 894
John's 653
Johnsonian 577
joie, feu de – 883
join *connect* 43
  assemble 72
  contiguous 199

arrive 292
party 712
sociality 892
marry 903
– battle 722
– in the chorus 488
– forces, hands,
  709
– in 778
– issue *discuss* 476
  deny 536
  quarrel 713
  contend 720
  lawsuit 969
– the majority 360
– up
  enlist 723
  – with 709
joint *junction* 43
  part 51
  accompanying 88
  concurrent 178
  meat 298
  – *concern* 721
joint-stock 709, 778
joint-tenancy 778
jointure 780
joist 215
joke *absurdity* 497
  trifle 643
  wit 842
  ridicule 856
  in – 842
  mere – 643
  no – *existing* 1
  important 642
  practical –
    deception 545
    ridicule 856
    disrespect 929
  take a – 498
joker 844
jokesmith 844
joking apart 535,
  604
jole 236
jollification
  amusement 840
  intemperance 954
jollity 840, 892
jolly *plump* 192
  marine 269
  gay 836
  ridicule 856
  – boat 273
  – fellow 892
jolt 276, 315
jolthead 501
Jonah 649
Jones
  Davy –' locker 360

Paul – 792
jorum 191
Joseph 960
  –'s coat 440
joss 991
  – house 1000
jostle *rush* 276
  jog 315
  clash 713
jot 32, 643
jotting 550, 551
jounce 315
journal *annals* 114
  newspaper 531
  record 551
  magazine 593
  narrative 594
  accounts 811
journalist
  messenger 534
  recorder 553
  author 593
journey 266
journeyman
  artisan 690
  servant 746
joust 720
Jove 979
  by – 870
  sub –
    out of doors 220
    air 338
jovial *gay* 836
  amusement 840
  social 892
jowl 236
joy 827
  give one – 896
joyful 836
joyless *painful* 830
  sad 837
joy stick 693
J.P. 967
Juan, Don – 962
jube 1000
jubeo, sic volo sic –
  741
jubilant *gay* 836
  rejoicing 838
  boastful 884
jubilee 138, 883
jubilitate 884
Judæus Apella,
  credat –
    disbelief 485
    absurdity 497
Judaism 984
Judas *deceiver* 548
  knave 941
  – kiss
    hypocrisy 544

base 940
judge *decide* 480
  master 745
  taste 850
  magistrate **967**
Judge *deity* 976
Judgment
  Day of – 67
judgment
  intellect 450
  discrimination
    465
  decision **480**
  wisdom 498
  sentence 972
judgment-seat 966
judicata, res –
  certain 574
  judgment 480
judication 480
judicatory 965, 966
judicature 965
Judicature, High
  Court of – 966
judice: coram –
  jurisdiction 965
  lawsuit 969
  me – 481
  sub – *inquiry* 461
    lawsuit 969
judicial 965
  – Astrology 511
  – murder 361
  – separation 905
judicious 498
jug 191, 752
juggernaut
  kill 361
  god 979
  idolatry 991
juggle *deceive* 545
  cunning 702
juggler 548, 599
jugulate 361
juice 333
juiceless 340
juicy 339
jujitsu 718
jujube 396
julep 396
jumble *mixture* 41
  confusion 59
  derange 61
  indiscriminate
    465a
jument 271
jump
  sudden change
    146
  leap 309
  neglect 460

at one – 113
– about 315
– at *willing* 602
　pursue 622
　hasten 684
　consent 762
　seize 789
　desire 865
– to a conclusion
　misjudge 481
　credulous 486
– over 460
– up 307, 309
jumper 225
junction 43
juncture
　circumstance 8
　junction 43
　period 134
jungle *disorder* 59
　vegetation 367
junior 127, 541
– counsel 968
junk 273
junket *dish* 298
　merry-making
　840
Juno 920, 979
junta 696
junto 712
jupe 225
Jupiter 979
jurare in verba ma-
　gistri 481, 486
jurat 967
jure: de – *due* 924
　legal 963
– *divino due* 924
　God 976
juridical 965
jurisconsult 968
jurisdiction 965
　authority 737
Jurisprudence 963
jurist 480, 968
jury 967
　empanel a – 969
– box 966
– mast
　substitute 147
　refuge 666
jus: summum –
　922
– civile
– gentium 963
– nocendi 737
– et norma
　loquendi 567
jussive 741
just *accurate* 494
　right 922

equitable 939
pious 987
– as *similar* 17
　same time 120
– do 639
– now 118
– out 123
– reasoning 476
– so 488
– then 113
– the thing
　agreement 23
　exact 494
– in time 134
juste milieu
　middle 68
　moderation 174
　mid-course 628
justice
　right 922
　honour 939
　magistrate 967
　administration of
　– 965
　bring to – 969
　court of – 966
　do – to *eat* 298
　duty 926
　praise 931
　vindicate 937
　not do – to 483
　retributive – 922,
　972
– seat 966
justifiable 922, 937
justification
　vindication 937
　religious 987
justle *push* 276
　contend 720
jut out 250
jute 205
jutty 250
juvenile 127
– lead 599
juxtaposition 199
j'y suis j'y reste
　141

K

kadi 967
kail 840
kaiser 745
kaleidoscope 149,
　445
καλόν, τὸ – 845
kangaroo 309
κατ᾽ ἐξοχήν
　greatness 31

superiority 33
importance 642
Katerfelto 994
kavass 965
K.C. 968
keck 297
kedge *navigate* 267
　anchor 666
keek 527
keel 211
– upwards 21
keelhaul 972
keen *energetic* 171
　sharp 253
　sensible 375
　cold 383
　intelligent 498
　poignant 821
　lament 839
　witty 842
　eager 865
– blast 349
keener 839
keen-eyed 441
keep *do often* 136
　persist 141
　continue 143
　food 298
　store 636
　provision 637
　refuge 666
　preserve 670
　citadel 717
　custody 751
　prison 752
　observe 772
　retain 781
　celebrate 883
– alive 359, 670
– aloof 196, 623
– accounts 811
– an account with
　805
– apart 44
– at it 143
– away 187
– back *late* 133
　conceal 528
　dissuade 616
　not use 678
　restrain 751
　retain 781
– the ball rolling
　143
– one's bed 655
– body and soul
　together *life* 359
　health 654
– within bounds
　304
– close 781

– company 88
– one in counte-
　nance
　conformity 82
　induce 615
　aid 707
　encourage 861
– one's counte-
　nance
　unexcitable 826
　sad 837
– one's course 282
– an eye upon 459
– the field 722
– firm 150
– on foot
　continuance 143
　support 215
　preparation 673
– from *conceal* 528
　refrain 623
　not do 681
　restrain 751
– going
　continue 143
　move 264
– one's ground 141
– one's hand in 613
– one's head above
　water 731, 817
– hold 150
– holy 987
– house 184
– in ignorance 528
– in *restrain* 751
　prohibit 761
– on one's legs 654
– a good look out
　for 507
– in mind 505
– moving 682
– off *avoid* 623
　hinder 706
　defend 717
　resist 719
　prohibition 761
– on *do often* 136
　continue 143
　persevere 604a
– to oneself 528
– in order 693
– out
　- *of the way* 187
　- *of harm's way*
　　864
– pace with 27,
　120
– the peace 714
– posted 527
– the pot boiling
　143

bill 800
fly a – *credit* 805
  insolvency 808
  – balloon 273, 726
kith 11
kithless 87
kitten *animal* 366
  young 129
  bring forth 161
  playful as a – 836,
    840
kleptomania
  insanity 502
  stealing 791
  desire 865
kleptomaniac 504
knack 698
  get into the – 613
knacker 361
knag 706
knaggy 901*a*
knap 206
knapsack 191
knave 548, **941**
  – of hearts 897
knavery
  deception 545
  cunning 702
  improbity 940
  vice 945
knead *mix* 41
  mould 240
  soften 324
  stroke 379
knee *angle* 244
  bend the –
  stoop 30
  submission 725
  down on one's –s
  humble 879
  on one's –s
  beg 765
  respect 928
  atone 952
  on the –s of the
    gods 121, 152
knee-deep 208, 209
kneel *stoop* 308
  submit 725
  beg 765
  servility 886
  courtesy 894
  ask mercy 914
  respect 928
  worship 990
knell 363
  strike the death –
    361
knickerbockers 225
knicknack 643, 847
knife 253

play a good – and
  fork *eat* 298
  appetite 865
  war to the – 708
knight 875
  – errant
  madman 504
  defender 717
  rash 863
  philanthropist
    910
  –'s move 279
  – service 777
  – of the road 792
  – Templar 71
knit 43
  well – 159
  – the brow
  discontent 832
  anger 900
  disapprobation
    932
knitting 847
knob *pendency* 214
  ball 249
  protuberance 250
knock *blow* 276
  sound 406
  hard –s 720
  – at the door
  death 360
  request 765
  – down
  destroy 162
  lay flat 213
  lower 308
  injure 659
  dishearten 837
  – on the head
  kill 361
  – one's head
    against 699
  – off *complete* 729
  – out 162
  – over 162
  – under 725
  – up 688
knock-down argu-
  ment 479
knocked
  – to atoms 162
  – on the head
  failure 732
knocker 936
knock-kneed 243,
  244
knoll 206
knot *ligature* 45
  entanglement 59
  group 72
  intersection 219

round 249
dense 321
difficulty 704
hindrance 706
junto 712
ornament 847
marriage 903
true lover's – *love*
  897
endearment 902
tie the nuptial –
  903
knotted *rough* 256
knout 975
know *believe* 484
  knowledge 490
  friendly 888
  associate 892
  I'd have you to –
    457, 535
  not that one –s
    491
  – what one is
    about 698
  – all 474
  I – better 536
  – no bounds
  great 31
  infinite 105
  redundance 641
  – for certain 484
  – by heart 505
  – one's own mind
    604
  – one's stuff 465
  – one's way about
    465
  – nothing of 491
  – what's what 698
  – which is which
    465
knowing 702
knowingly 620
knowledge 490
  [*and see* know]
  acquire – 539
  come to one's –
    527
  practical – 698
  – of the world 698
known:
  become – 529
  make – *inform* 527
  publish 531
  well – 490
  habitual 613
  – as 564
  – by 550
knuckle 244
  – down 725
knuckle-duster 727

knurl 256
knurr and spell 840
kobold 980
Koh-i-noor 650
kopje 206
Koran 986
kowtow *bow* 308
  submission 725
  courtesy 894
  respect 928
kraal 189, 232
kraken 83
kris 727
Krishna 979
kudos 931
Ku klux klan 712
kursaal 840
kyanize 670
kyles 343

L

laager 717
labarum 550
labefy 659
label 39, 550
labent 306
labial *lip* 231
  letter 561
labitur et labetur
  112, 143
labor hoc opus, hic
  – 704
laboratory 691
laborious
  active 682
  exertion 686
  difficult 704
labour
  parturition 161
  work 680
  exertion 686
  hard –
  punishment 972
  mountain in – 638
  – for 620
  – of love
  willing 602
  amusement 840
  disinterested 942
  – party 712
  – under *state* 7
  disease 655
  difficulty 704
  feeling 821
  affliction 828
  – in vain
  fall short 304
  useless 645
  – in one's voca-

tion 625
– unrest 832
laboured - *style* 579
  prepared 673
  – *study* 457
labourer 690
labouring
  – man 690
  – oar 686
labyrinth
  disorder 59
  convolution 248
  secret 533
lac *number* 98
  resin 356a
  – of rupees 800
lace *stitch* 43
  netting 219
  ornament 847
  – one's jacket 972
lacerable 328
lacerate 44
  – the heart 830
laches 460, 773
Lachesis 601
lachrymæ, hinc
  illæ – 830
lachrymatory gas
  727
lachrymis, quis
  temperet a – 914
lachrymose 837
lack *require* 630
  insufficient 640
  destitute 804
  desire 865
  – faith 989
  – harmony 708
  – preparation 674
  – wit 501
lackadaisical
  inactive 683
  melancholy 837
  indifferent 866
lackadaisy! 839,
  870
lack-brain 499, 501
lacker [*see* lacquer]
lackey 746
lack-lustre 422, 429
laconic 572
lacquer
  covering 223
  resin 356a
  adorn 847
lacrosse 840
lacteal 352
lacuna 198, 252
lacustrine 343
lad 129
ladder 305, 627

  kick down the –
  604
lade *load* 184
  transfer 185
  contents 190
  dip 270
  – out 297
laden 52
  heavy – 828
  – with 777
ladies' man 897
lading 190, 780
  bill of – *list* 86
ladle *receptacle* 191
  transfer 270
  vehicle 272
lady *woman* 374
  rank 875
  wife 903
  our – 977
  – day 138
  – help 746
  –'s maid 746
lady chapel 1000
ladylike
  womanly 374
  fashionable 852
lady-love 897
lag *linger* 275
  follow 281
  dawdle 683
  – behind 133
laggard 603, 683
lager *beer* 298
lagoon 343
laical 997
laid: – on one's
  back 158
  – by the heels 751
  – low 160
  – up 655
lair 189, 653
laird *master* 745
  proprietor 779
  nobility 875
Lais 962
laisse manger, cela
  se – 394
laisser: – aller,
  – faire
  permanence 141
  neglect 460
  inaction 681
  laxity 738
  freedom 748
  inexcitable 826
laity 997
lake *water* 343
  pink 434
  – of fire and brim-
  stone 982

Lama 745, 996
Lamaism 984
Lamarkism 357
lamb *infant* 129
  animal 366
  gentle 826
  innocent 946
go out like a – 174
lion lies down
  with – 721
Lamb of God 976
lambent
  touching 379
  – flame *heat* 382
  light 420
Lambeth 1000
lame *incomplete* 53
  impotent 158
  weak 160
  imperfect 651
  disease 655
  injury 659
  failing 732
  – conclusion
  illogical 477
  failure 732
help a – dog over
  a stile *aid* 707
  vindicate 937
  – duck 808
  – excuse 617
lamellar 204
lamentable *bad* 649
  painful 830
  sad 837
lamentably *very* 31
lamentation **839**
lamia 980, 994
lamina 51, 204
lamination 204
Lammas 998
lamp 423
rub the – 992
safety – 666
smell of the –
  style 577
  prepared 673
lamplighter
  quick 682
lampoon 932, 934
lampooner 936
lanâ caprinâ, de –
  643
lanary 636
lanate 25, 256
lance *pierce* 260
  throw 284
  spear 727
break a – with
  attack 716
  warfare 722

couch one's – 720
  – corporal 745
lancer 726
  –'s *dance* 340
lancet 253, 262
lancinate 378, 830
land *arrive* 292
  ground **342**
  estate 780
gone to a better –
  360
hug the – 286
make the – 286
on – 342
see – 858
  – covered with
  water 343
  – flowing with
  milk and honey
  168
how the – lies
  circumstances 8
  experiment 463
  foresight 510
in the – of the
  living 359
landamman 745
landau 272
landed
  – gentry 779
  – estate 780
landgrave 745
landholder 779
landing field 273
landing-place 215,
  292
landlady 779
land-locked 229,
  343
landloper 268
landlord 779
land-lubber 343,
  701
landmark
  limit 233
  indication 550
land-mine 727
landreeve 694
landscape
  prospect 448
  – gardening
  agriculture 71
  beauty 845
  – painting 556
  – painter 559
land-shark 792
land-slip 306
landsman 342
Landsturm 726
land-surveying 466
Landwehr 726

pioneer 64
influence 175
tend 176
soundings 208
- *in motion* 280
heavy 319
rôle 599
induce 615
direct 693
authority 737
heave the – 466
red – 434
take the –
influence 175
importance 642
authority 737
white – 420
- to the altar 903
- astray 495
- captive
subject 749
restraint 751
- a merry chase
623
- the choir 990
- a dance
run away 623
circuit 629
difficulty 704
disrespect 929
- the dance 280
- one to expect
511
- a life 692
- on 693
- to no end 645
- by the nose 737
- off 62
- the way
precedence 62
begin 66
precession 280
importance 642
direction 693
repute 873
leaden *dim* 422
colourless 429
grey 432
inactive 683
leader
precursor 64
dissertation 595
director 694
counsel 968
- writer 593
leading
beginning 66
important 642
- article 595
- lady 599
- note *music* 413

- part 175
- question 461
- seaman 745
- strings
childhood 127
child 129
pupil 541
subject 749
restraint 751, 752
leads 223
leaf *part* 51
layer 204
plant 367
- *of a book* 593
turn over a new –
658
- green 435
leafless 226
leaflet 531
leafy 256
league *length* 200
co-operation 709
party 712
- of Nations 696
leak *crack* 198
dribble 295
waste 638
spring a –
injury 659
- out
disclosure 529
leaky *imperfect* 651
leal 743
lean *thin* 203
oblique 217
- on 215
- to *shed* 191
willing 602
- towards 923
- upon *belief* 484
subjection 749
hope 858
leaning
tendency 176
willingness 602
desire 865
friendship 888
favouritism 923
leap
sudden change
146
ascent 305
jump **309**
–s and bounds 274
make a – at 622
- in the dark
experiment 463
uncertain 475
chance 621
rash 863
- with joy 838

- year 138
leap-frog 840
learn 490, 539
- by experience
950
- by heart 505
learned 490
learner **541**
learning 490, **539**
lease *property* 780
lending 787
grant a – 771
take a new – of
life 654
- and release 783
leasehold 780
leash *lie* 43
three 92
hold in – 751
least
- *in quantity* 34
- *in size* 193
at the – 32
leather *skin* 223
tough 327
beat 972
nothing like – 481
- bottle 191
- or prunello 643
leave *remainder* 40
part company 44
relinquish 624
permission 760
bequeathe 784
French – 623
take – *depart* 293
freedom 748
- alone
inaction 681
freedom 748
permit 760
- the beaten track
83
- to chance 621
- an inference 526
- a loophole 705
- in the lurch
pass 303
decisive 545
- no trace
be no more 2
disappear 449
obliterate 552
- it to one 76
- to oneself 748
- off *cease* 142
desuetude 614
relinquish 624
disuse 678
- out 55
- out of one's cal-

culation 460
- a place 293
- ad referendum
605
give me – to say
535
- undecided 609a
- undone 730
- a void *regret* 833
- word 527
leaven
component 56
cause 153
lighten 320
qualify 469
unclean 653
deterioration 659
bane 663
leavings
remainder 40
useless 645
lecher 962
lechery 961
lectern 1000
lection *special* 79
interpretation 522
lectionary 998
lecture *teach* 537
speak 582
dissertation 595
censure 932
sermon 998
- room 542
lecturer
teacher 540
preacher 996
lectureship 542
led – *captain*
follower 746
servile 886
favourite 899
- by the nose 749
ledge *height* 206
horizontal 213
shelf 215
projection 250
ledger *list* 86
record 551
accounts 811
lee 236
leech 662, 695
leef 829
leek eat the –
recant 607
submit 725
Lee-Metford
rifle 727
leer *stare* 441
dumb-show 550
leery 702, 864
lees 653

– slip	*smooth* 255	liberalism	lid 223
miss an oppor-	*lower* 308	*freedom* 748	lie *situation* 183
tunity 135	– at *direct* 278	liberality	*presence* 186
neglect 460	*intend* 620	*giving* 784	*recline* 213
not complete 730	*attack* 716	*generosity* **816**	*falsehood* 544
lose 776	– best 686	liberate 672	*untruth* 546
relinquish 782	– headed 826	liberation **750**	give the – to 536
– the matter stand	– off 27	liberavi animam	white – 617
over 133	– with the ground	meam 703	– abed 683
– things take their	207	libertinage 961	– in ambush 528
course 143	lever *cause* 153	libertine **962**	– by 681
– well alone	*instrument* 633	libertinism 961	– at one's door
content 831	– de rideau 599	liberty *freedom* 748	926
caution 864	leverage 175	*permission* 760	– down *flat* 213
lethal 361	leviathan 192	*right* 924	*rest* 687
– chamber 975	levigate 255, 330	*exemption* 927*a*	– fallow 674
lethalis arundo,	levitate 320	gain one's – 750	– hid 528
hæret lateri –	Levite 996	set at – *free* 750	– in *be* 1
900	levity *lightness* **320**	*exempt* 927*a*	*give birth* 161
lethargy 683, 823	*irresolution* 605	take a –	– low 528
Lethe 982	*trifle* 643	*arrogate* 739	– under a neces-
waters of – 506	*jocularity* 836	*make free* 748	sity 601
lethiferous 361	*rashness* 863	*insolence* 885	– in a nutshell 32
letter *mark* 550	levy *muster* 72	*discourtesy* 895	– on 215
character **561**	*military* 726	libidinous 961	– over *defer* 133
epistle 592	*distrain* 789	libitum, ad –	*destiny* 152
to the – 494	*demand* 812	*at will* 600	– in one's power
– card 524	lewd 961	*enough* 639	157
– of credit 805	Lewis gun 727	*freely* 748	– at the root of
– of the law 494	lex – mercatoria	librarian 593, 694	153
– writer 592	963	library *room* 191,	– still 265
letter-bag 534	– scripta 697	593	– to
letter-carrier 534	– scripta et non-	*books* 593	*quiescence* 265
lettered 490	scripta 963	*storehouse* 636	*inaction* 681
letterpress 591	– talionis	librate 314	– under 177
letters	*retaliation* 718	libretto 593, 599	– in wait for
knowledge 490	*right* 922	licence *laxity* 738	*expect* 507
language 560	lexicography 562	*permission* 760	*inaction* 681
description 594	lexicology 562	*right* 924	lief *pleasant* 829
in large – 642	lexicon 86, 562	*exemption* 927*a*	as – *willing* 602
man of – 492	ley 344	– to plunder 791	*choice* 609
– of marque 791	liability **177**	licentiate 492	liege 745
lettres de cachet	*debt* 806	licentious *lax* 738	liegeman 746
751	*duty* 926	*dissolute* 954	lien 771, 805
leucophlegmatic	liaison 961	*debauched* 961	lienteria 653
823	liar 548	lichgate 363	lieu 182
leucorrhea 299	libation	lichen 367	in – of 147
Levant *east* 236	*potation* 298	licit 760, 924	lieutenant 745, 759
levant *abscond* 623	*drunkenness* 959	lick *lap* 298	lord – 965
levanter *wind* 349	*worship* 990	*conquer* 731	life *essence* 5
defaulter 808	libel 934, 938	*punish* 972	*events* 151
levée *assemblage* 72	libelant 989	– the dust 933	*vitality* **359**
sociality 892	libeller 936	– into shape 240	*biography* 594
– en masse 719	liberal *ample* 639	lickerish	*activity* 682
level *uniform* 16	– party 712	*savoury* 394	*conduct* 692
equal 27	*generous* 816	*desirous* 865	*cheerful* 836
destroy 162	*disinterested* 942	*fastidious* 868	animal – 364
horizontal 213	over – 818	*licentious* 961	battle of – 682
instrument 213,	– education	lickpenny 819	come to – 660
217	*knowledge* 490	lickspittle 886	infuse into
flat 251	*teaching* 537	lictor 965	*excite* 824

mitigate 174
silence 403
– to sleep 265
lullaby
  moderate 174
  song 415
  verses 597
  inactivity 683
  relief 834
lumbago 378
lumbar 235
lumbar *disorder* 59
  slow 275
  store 636
  useless 645
  hindrance 706
lumbering 647, 846
lumber-room 191
lumbriciform 249
luminary *star* 318
  light **423**
  sage 500
luminescence 420
luminous *light* 420
  intelligible 518
  – paint 423
lump *whole* 50
  chief part 51
  amass 72
  mass 192
  projection 250
  weight 319
  density 321
  in the – 50
  – of affectation
    855
  – sum 800
  – together *join* 43
  combine 48
  assemble 72
lumpish [*see* lump]
  inactive 683
  ugly 846
Luna 318
lunacy 503
lunar 318
  – caustic 384
lunatic 503, 504
luncheon 298
lune avec les dents,
  prendre la –
  158, 471
lunette 717
lunge 276, 716
lungs *wind* 349
  loudness 404
  shout 411
  voice 580
luniform &c. 245
lupanar 961
lurch *incline* 217

sink 306
oscillation 314
failure 732
leave in the –
  outstrip 303
  deceive 545
  relinquish 624
left in the –
  defeated 732
lure *attraction* 288,
  865
  deceive 545
  entice 615
lurid *dark* 421
  dim 422
  red 434
lurk *unseen* 447
  latent 526
  hidden 528
lurking-place 530
luscious 394, 829
lush *vegetation* 365
  drunkenness 959
lushy 959
lusk 683
lusory 840
lust 865, 961
  – after 921
lustily 404, 686
  cry out – 839
lustless 158
lustration 652, 952
lustre
  brightness 420
  chandelier 423
  glory 873
lustrum 108
lusty 159, 192
lusus naturæ 80
lute *cement* 45, 46
  guitar 417
luteous 436
Lutheran 984
luxation 44
luxuriant 168, 639
luxuriate in 377,
  827
luxurious
  pleasant 377
  delightful 829
  intemperate 954
luxury
  physical - 377
  redundance 641
  enjoyment 827
  sensuality 954
lycanthropy 503
Lyceum 542
Lydford law 964
Lydian measure
  415

lyddite 727
lying
  decumbent 213
  deceptive 544
  faithless 986
Ly-king 986
lymph *fluid* 333
  water 337
  transparent 425
lymphatic 337
lynch 972
  – law 964
lyncher 975
lynching 361
lynx-eyed 441, 498
lyre 417
lyric 415
  – poetry 597
lyrist 597

M

Mab 979
macadamize 255,
  635
Macaire, Robert –
  792
macaroni 854
macaronic
  absurdity 497
  neology 563
  verses 597
Macchiavel [*see*
  Machiavelism]
mace
  weapon 727
  sceptre 747
mace-bearer 965
maceration
  saturation 337
  atonement 952
  asceticism 955
  rite 998
Macheath 792
Machiavelism
  falsehood 544
  cunning 702
  dishonesty 940
machicolation 257,
  717
machination
  trick 545
  plan 626
  cunning 702
  –s of the devil 619
machinator 626
machine 633
  like a – 698
  – gun 407, 727
  be a mere – 749

machinist
  theatrical - 599
  workman 690
macilent 203
mackerel
  mottled 440
  procuress 962
  – sky 349, 353
mackintosh 225
macrobiotic 110
macrocosm 318
macrography 441
macrology 577
mac Sycophant,
  Sir Pertinax –
  886, 935
mactation 991
macte virtute 931
macula 848
maculate
  unclean 653
maculation 440, 848
mad *insane* 503
  excited 824
  drive one – 900
  go – 825
  – after 865
  – with rage 900
madam 374
mad-brained 503
madcap
  violent 173
  lunatic 504
  excitable 825
  buffoon 844
  rash 863
madder *colour* 434
made
  – to one's hand
    673
  – man 734
  – to order 673
madefaction 339
madman **504**
Madonna
  good 948
  angel 977
  pious 987
madrigal *music* 415
  verses 597
Mæcenas 492, 890
Maelstrom
  whirl 312
  water 348
  pitfall 667
maestro 415
maffick 883
magazine
  periodical 53
  record 551
  book 593

- of 902
- off 623, 671
- off with 791
- out *see* 441
  evidence 467
  demonstrate 478
  discover 480a
  know 490
  intelligible 518
  interpret 522
  due 924
- over 658, 783, 784
- peace 723, 724
- a piece of work 832
- things pleasant 702
- a present 784
- public 531
- a push 682
- ready 673
- a requisition 741, 765
- a speech 582
- a sucker of 853
- sure 150, 673
- terms 769
- time 110
- tracks 293
- towards 278
- up [*see below*]
- use of 677
- way 282
- one's way 302, 734
- way for 147, 623
- a wry face 867
make up
  complete 52
  compose 54
- accounts 811
- for 30
- matters 952
- one's mind
  judgment 480
  belief 484
  resolve 604
- a quarrel 723
- a sum 809
- to *approach* 286
  address 586
maker *artificer* 690
Maker, the - 976
makeshift 147, 617
make-weight
  inequality 28
  compensation 30
  completeness 52
making of, be the -
  utility 644

goodness 648
aid 707
mal du pays 833
mala fides 940
malachite 435
malacology 368
malade imaginaire 837
maladie du pays 833
maladministration 699
maladroit 699
malady 655
malaise 378, 828
malapert 885, 887
Malaprop, Mrs. - 565
malapropism 495
mal à propos 24, 135
malaria 657, 663
malconformation 243
malcontent 710, 832
male 159, 373
- animal 373
malediction 908
malefaction 947
malefactor 949
malefic 649
maleficent 907
- being 913
malevolence 907
malfeasance 647
malformed 241
malformation 243
malgré 179
- soi 603
malice *hate* 898
  spite 907
  bear - *revenge* 919
- aforethought 907
- prepense 907
malign *bad* 649
  malevolent 907
  detract 934
malignant 649, 907
malignity
  violence 173
malinger 544, 655
malison 908
malkin 653
mall *walk* 189
  club 276
malleable 324
mallet 276
malnutrition 655
mal-odour 401

malpractice 947
malt liquor 298
maltreat
  injure 649
  aggrieve 830
  molest 907
malum
- prohibitum 925
- in se 923
malversation 818, 947
Mameluke 726
mamelon 250
mamma 166
mammal 366
mammiform 250
mammilla 250
Mammon 803, 978
  serve - 989
mammoth 192
man *adult* 131
  mankind 372
  male **373**
  prepare 673
  workman 690
  servant 746
  courage 861
  husband 903
  make a - of 648, 861
  Son of - 976
  straight - 599
  to a - 488
  -at-arms 726
  one's - of business 758
  -'s estate 131
- in office 745
- in the street 876
  -of-war 273, 726
  -of-war's man 269
- at the wheel 694
- and wife 903
manacle 751, 752
manage 693
- to *succeed* 731
manageable 705
management
  conduct 692
  skill 698
manager
  stage - 599
  director 694
managery 693
manche après la cognée, jeter le - 859
mancible 637
mancipation 751
mandamus 741
mandarin 745

mandate 630, 741
mandible 298
mandolin 417
mandragora 174
mandrel 312
manducation 298
mane 256
man-eater 361
manége 266, 370
manes 362
manet: - altâmente
  repostum 505
- cicatrix 919
manful *strong* 159
  resolute 604
  brave 861
manger 191
manger:
  cela se laisse - 394
- son blé en herbe 818
mangle
  separate 44
  smooth 255
  injure 659
mangled 53
mangy 655
man-hater 911
manhood 131, 861
mania *insanity* 503
  desire 865
maniac 504
manibus pedibus-que 686
manic 503
manic-depressive 503
manicure 847
manicheism 978
manichord 417
manie 865
maniéré 855
manifest
  list 86
  visible 446
  obvious 525
  disclose 529
manifestation 525
manifesto 531
manifold 81, 102
manikin *dwarf* 193
  image 554
maniple 103
manipulate
  handle 379
  use 677
  conduct 692
manipulator 621
mankind 372
manly
  adolescent 131

strong 159
male 373
brave 861
honest 939
manna *food* 396
 – in the wilderness
  aid 707
  pleasing 829
manner *kind* 75
 style 569
 way 627
 conduct 692
 in a – 32
 by all – of means
  536
 by no – of means
  602
 to the – born 5
mannered 579
mannerism
 special 79
 unconformity 83
 affectation 855
 vanity 880
mannerly 894
manners 852, 894
manœuvre 680, 702
manor 780
 lord of the – 779
 – house 189
manorial 780
Mansard roof 223
manse 1000
mansion 189
manslaughter 361
mansuetude 894
mantelpiece 215
mantilla 225
mantle *spread* 194
 dress 225
 foam 353
 shade 424
 redden 434
 robes 747
 flush 821, 824
 anger 900
mantlet *cloak* 225
 defence 717
Mantology 511
manual *guide* 527
 schoolbook 542
 book 593
 advice 695
 – labour 686
manubial 793
manufactory 691
manufacture 161,
  680
manufacturer 690
manumission 750
manure

agriculture 371
dirt 653
aid 707
manuscript 22, 590
many 102
 the – 876
 for – a day 110
 – irons in the fire
  682
 – men many
  minds 489
 – times
  repeated 104
  frequent 136
many-coloured 440
many-sided 81, 236
many-tongued 532
map 234, 527, 554
 – out 626
mar 659, 706
marabou 83
marabout 1000
maranatha 908
marasmus
 shrinking 195
 atrophy 655
 deterioration 659
maraud 791
marauder 792
marble *ball* 249
 hard 323
 sculpture 557
 tablet 590
 insensible 823
marble 440
marble-hearted 907
march *region* 181
 journey 266
 progression 282
 music 415
 dead – 363
 forced – 684
 on the – 264
 steal a –
  advance 280
  go beyond 303
  deceive 545
  active 682
  cunning 702
 – against 716
 – of events 151
 – of intellect
  knowledge 490
  improvement 658
 – off 293
 – on a point 278
 – past 882
 – of time 109
 – with 199
March, Ides of – 601
marches 233

marchioness 875
marcid 203
marconigram 523
marcor 203
mare *horse* 271
 female 374
 –'s nest 497, 546
 –'s tail *wind* 349
 cloud 353
marechal 745
margarine 356
margin *space* 180
 edge 231
 redundance 641
 latitude 748
margravate 780
margrave 745, 875
marimba 417
marine *fleet* 273
 sailor 269
 oceanic 341
 soldier 726
 tell it to the –s
  489, 497
 – painter 559
 – painting 556
mariner 269
Mariolatry 991
marionnette
 representation
  554
 drama 599
 amusement 840
marish 345
marital 903
maritime 267, 341
mark *degree* 26
 term 71
 take cognizance
  of 450
 attend to 457
 indication 550
 record 551
 writing 590
 object 620
 importance 642
 repute 873
 beyond the – 303
 leave one's – 873
 man of – 873, 875
 near the – 197
 overshoot the –
  699
 put a – upon 457
 save the – 870
 up to the –
  enough 639
  good 648
  skill 698
  due 924
 wide of the – 196,

  495
 within the – 304
 – down 813
 – off 551
 – out *choose* 609
  plan 626
  command 741
 – of recognition
  894
 – with a red letter
  883
 – time
  chronometry 114
  halt 265
  wait 507
 – with a white
  stone 931
marked [*see* mark]
 great 31
 affirmed 535
 well– 446
 in a – degree 31
 play with – cards
  545
 – down 815
marker 550
market *buy* 795
 mart 799
 bring to – 796
 buy in the cheap-
  est &c. – 794
 in the –
  offered 763
  barter 794
  sale 796
 rig the – 794
 – garden 371
 – overt
  manifest 525
  mart 799
 – place *street* 189
  mart 799
 – price 812
 – woman 797
marketable 794,
  796
marksman 700
marksmanship 698
marl 342
marmalade 396
marmot 683
maroon
 colour 433, 434
 abandon 782, 893
marplot
 bungler 701
 obstacle 706
 malicious 913
marque, letters of –
  791
marquee 223

marquetry 440
marquis 875
marriage **903**
  companionate –
    903
  ill-assorted – 904
  – bells 836
  – portion 780
marriageable 131,
  903
marrow *essence* 5
  interior 221
  central 222
  chill to the – 385
marrow-bones, on
  one's –
  submit 725
  beg 765
  humble 879
  servile 886
  atonement 952
marrowless 158
marry *combine* 48
  assertion 535
  wed 903
  – come up
  defiance 715
  anger 900
  censure 932
Mars 722, 979
  – orange 439
marsh **345**
marshal
  arrange 60
  messenger 534
  auxiliary 711
  officer 745
Marshalsea 752
marsupial 191, 366
mart 799
Marte, suo –
  exertion 686
  skill 698
martello tower 717
martial 722
  court– 966
  – law 737, 739
  compulsory 744
  illegal 964
  – music 415
martinet 739
martingale 752
Martinmas 998
martyr
  bodily pain 378
  mental pain 828
  ascetic 955
  – to disease 655
martyrdom
  killing 361
  agony 378, 828

unselfish 942
punishment 972
marvel 870, 872
– whether 514
marvellous 31, 870
  deal in the – 549
Masaniello 742
mascaro 847
mascot 993
masculine 159, 373
mash *mix* 41
  disorder 59
  soft 324
  semiliquid 253
  pulpify 354
masher 854
mask *dress* 225
  shade 424
  concealment 528
  ambush 530
  deceit 545
  shield 717
  put on the – 544
mason 690
Masorah 985
masque 599
masqué, bal – 840
masquerade
  dress 225
  concealment 528
  disguise 530
  frolic 840
mass *quantity* 25
  much 31
  whole 50
  heap 72
  size 192
  gravity 319
  density 321
  worship 990
  rite 998
  attend – 990
  in the – 50
  – book 998
  – of society 876
massacre 361
massage 33, 379,
  662
masse, en – 712
masses, the – 876
massive *large* 31
  huge 192
  heavy 319
  dense 321
mast 206
master
  boy 129
  influence 175
  man 373
  know 490
  understand 518

learn 539
teacher 540
director 694
proficient 698,
  700
succeed, conquer
  731
ruler **745**
possession 777
possessor 779
title 877
eye of the – 693
hard – 739
past – 700
– of Arts 492
– one's feelings
  826
– hand 700
– key *open* 260
instrument 631
– mariner 269
– mind *sage* 500
proficient 700
– passion 820
– one's passions
  944
– of the position
  731
– of the revels 840
– of the Rolls 553,
  967
– of self 604
– of the situation
  731, 737
– spirit of the age
  500, 873
– of one's time 685
masterdom 737
masterpiece
  good 648
  perfect 650
  skill 698
master-stroke 626,
  731
mastery 731, 737
  get the – over 175
masthead
  punish 972
mastic *viscid* 352
  resin 356a
masticate 298
mastiff 366
mat *support* 215
  woven 219
  misty 427
  cover 652
matador 361
match *coincide* 13
  similar 17
  copy 19
  equal 27

fuel 388
contest 720
marriage 903
matchless
  supreme 33
  excellent 648
  virtuous 944
matchlock 727
mate *similar* 17
  equal 27
  duplicate 89
  mariner 269
  auxiliary 711
  master 745
  friend 890
  wife 903
  check– 732
maté 298
mater alma – 542
  –familias 166
materia medica 662
material
  substance 316
  stuff 635
  important 642
  – for thought 454
  – point 32
materialism
  matter 316
  heterodoxy 984
  irreligion 989
materiality **316**
materialize 446
materials **635**
matériel 633
maternal
  parental 166
  benevolent 906
  – love 897
maternity 166
mathematical
  precise 494
  – point 193
mathematics 25
mathesis 25
matin 125
matinée 892
matins 990
matrass 191
matriarch 11, 166
matriarchate 737
matriculate 86
matriculation 539
matrilinear 11, 166
matrimony
  mixture 41
  wedlock 903
matrix *mould* 22
  workshop 691
matron 374, 903
matronly 128, 131

matross 726
matter *substance* 3
 material world
   316
 topic 454
 meaning 516
 type 591
 business 625
 importance 642
 pus 653
 no – 460
 what – 643
 what's the – 455,
   461
 – of course
  conformity 82
  certain 474
  habitual 613
 – in dispute 461
 – of fact *event* 151
  certainty 474
  truth 494
  language 576
  artless 703
  dull 843
 – in hand 454, 625
 – of indifference
   866
 – nothing 643
mattock 253
mattress 215
mature *old* 124
 adolescent 131
 conversion 144
 scheme 626
 perfect 650
 improve 658
 prepare 673
 complete 729
 – thought 451
maturely consid-
   ered 611
maturine 996
maturity [*see*
   mature]
 bring to – 729
matutinal 125
matzoon 298
maudlin
 inactive 683
 drunk 959
maugre 30
maukin 562
maul *hammer* 276
 hurt 649
maulstick 215
maund *basket* 191
 mumble 583
maunder
 diffuse style 573
 mumble 583

talk 584
lament 839
maundy
 – money 784
 – Thursday 988
Mauser rifle 727
mausoleum 363
mauvais
 – goût 851
 – quart d'heure
   828
 – sujet 949
 – ton 851
mauvaise:
 – honte
  affectation 855
  modesty 881
 – plaisanterie 851
mauve 437
maw 191
mawkish 391
Mawworm
 deceiver 548
 sham piety 988
maxim 80, **496**
Maxim gun 727
maximal 33
maximalist 742
maximum 33, 210
maxixe 840
may be 470
 as it – 156
May-day 138, 840
May-fly 111
mayhap 470
mayor 745, 965
maypole 206
mayonnaise 298
May-queen 847
mazard 298
maze
 disorder 59
 convolution 248
 enigma 533
 difficulty 704
 in a –
  uncertain 475
mazed 503
mazurka 840
me 317
me judice 484
meâ culpâ 950
mead *plain* 344
 sweet 396
meadow *plain* 344
 grass 367
 – land 371
meagre *small* 32
 incomplete 53
 thin 203
 – *style* 575

scanty 640
poor 643
 – diet 956
meal *repast* 298
 powder 330
mealy-mouthed
 falsehood 544
 servile 886
 flattering 933
mean *average* **29**
 small 32
 middle 68, 228
 signify 516
 intend 620
 contemptible 643
 stingy 819
 shabby 874
 ignoble 876
 sneaking 886
 base 940
 selfish 943
 golden – 174
 take the – 774
 – nothing 517
 – parentage 876
 – time 114
 – wretch 949
meander
 convolution 248
 deviate 279
 circuition 311
 river 348
 – around Robin
   Hood's barn 279
meandering
 diffuse 573
meanest capacity
   499
 intelligible to the
   – 518
meaning **516**
meaningless 517
means
 appliances **632**
 property 780
 wealth 803
 by all – 602
 by any – 632
 by no – 536
 – of access 627
meantime 106
meanwhile 106
measurable 466
 within – distance
   470
measure *extent* 25
 degree 26
 moderation 174
 music 413
 compute 466
 verse 597

proceeding 626
action 680
apportion 786
angular – 244
full – 629
out of – 641
without – 641
 – of inclination
   217
measured
 moderate 174
 sufficient 639
 temperate 953
measureless 105
measurement 25,
   466
measures
 have no – with 713
 take – *plan* 626
  prepare 673
  conduct 692
 – of length 200
meat 298
 broken – 645
 one man's – is
  another man's
  poison 15
mechanic 690
mechanical 601,
   633
 – warfare 722
 – powers 633
mechanician 690
mechanism 633
medal
 record 551
 sculpture 557
 palm 733
 decoration 877
 – of Honor 733
medallion 557
medallist 700
meddle 682
médecin tant pis
   837
médecine expec-
   tante 133, 662
Medes and Per-
   sians, law of the
   – 80, 141
mediæval 124
mediævalism 122
medial 29, 68
median 228
mediant 413
medias res, in – 68
 plunge – 300, 576
mediation—*instru-
   mentality* 631
 intercession **724**
 deprecation 766

Christ 976
mediator 711
Mediator
  Saviour 976
medical 662
medicament 662
medicaster 548
medicate
  compound 41
  heal 660
medicine 662
  – *man* 994
medico 662
mediety 68
mediis rebus, in –
  682
medio tutissimus,
  in – 864
mediocritas,
  aurea – 628
mediocrity
  average 29
  smallness 32
  imperfect 651
  - *of fortune* **736**
meditate *think* 451
  purpose 620
mediterranean 68,
  228
medium *mean* 29
  middle 68
  atmosphere 227
  intermediary 228
  colour 428
  oracle 513
  impostor 548
  instrument 631
  seer 994
  transparent – 425
medley 41, 59
  music 415
  chance – 156
medullary 324
Medusa 860
meed
  apportion 786
  reward 973
  – of praise 931
meek 826, 879
meerschaum 392
meet *agreement* 23
  assemble 72
  touch 199
  converge 290
  arrive 292
  expedient 646
  fulfil 772
  proper 924
  make both ends –
  wealth 803
  economy 817

unable to make
  both ends –
  poverty 804
  not pay 808
  – with attention
  457
  – one's death 360
  – the ear 418
  – one at every
  turn
  present 186
  redundant 641
  – one's expenses
  817
  – the eye 446
  – in front 861
  – half way
  willing 602
  concord 714
  pacification 723
  mediation 724
  compromise 774
  friendship 888
  benevolence 906
  – hand to hand
  720
  – one's wishes
  consent 762
  pleasurable 829
  – with *event* 151
  find 480a
meeting [*see* meet]
  junction 43
  hostile – 720
  place of – 74
meeting-house
  hall 189
  chapel 1000
megacosm 318
megalomania 482,
  504
megaphone 404,
  418
megascope 445
megatherium 124
Megæra 173, 900
megrims *fits* 315
  melancholy 837
mehari 271
Mein Herr 877
meister-singer 597
melancholia
  insanity 503
  dejection 837
melancholy 830,
  837
  away with – 836
mélange 41
mêlée *disorder* 59
  contention 720
melinite 727

meliora, spero –
  858
meliorate 658
meliorism 658
melius inquiren-
  dum, ad – 658
melliferous
  sweet 396
mellifluous
  music 413
  - *language* 578
mellow
  old 128
  grow into 144
  soft 324
  sound 413
  colour 428
  improve 658
  prepare 673
  tipsy 959
melodeon 417
melodious 413
melodist 416
melodrama 599,
  824
melody **413**
Melpomene 599
melt *convert* 144
  liquefy 335
  fuse 384
  pity 914
  – in the air 405
  – away
  cease to exist 2
  unsubstantial 4
  decrease 36
  disappear 111,
  449
  waste 638
  – the heart 914
  – into one 48
  – into tears 839
melting-pot 691
member *part* 51
  component 56
  councillor 696
membrane 204
même, quand – 708
memento 505
  – mori 363, 837
meminisse juvabit
  505
memoir 594, 595
memorabilia
  reminiscences 505
  important 642
memorable 642
memorandum
  memory 505
  record 551
  plan 626

– book 505, 551
  compendium 596
memorial
  record 551
memorialist 553
memorialize 505
memorials 594
memoriam, in –
  363, 505
memory **505**
  fame 873
  failing – 506
  short – 506
  in the – of man
  122
  – runneth not to
  the contrary
  124
mem-sahib 374
menace 909
ménage 692
menagerie
  collection 72
  animals 370
  store 636
mend 658, 660
  – one's manners
  894
mendacity 544
mendicancy 765,
  804
mendicant
  beggar 767
  poor 804
  monk 996
menhir 363
menial 746, 876
meniscus 245, 445
mens sana 502
  – in corpore sano
  827
mens sibi conscia
  recti 878
mensâ et thoro,
  separatio a –
  905
menses 299
menstrual 138
menstruum 335
mensuration 466
mental 450
  – calm 826
  – excitement 824
  – pabulum 454
  – philosophy 450
  – reservation 528
  – suffering 828
menteur à triple
  étage 548
menticulture 658
mention 527

[560]

disregard distinc-
tion between –
791
mew *moult* 226
cry 412
– up 751
mewed up 229
mewl 412
mews 189
mezzanine floor
191, 599
mezzo rilievo
convex 250
sculpture 557
mezzo termine
middle 68
mid-course 628
compromise 774
Mezzofanti 492
mezzosoprano 416
mezzotint 420, 558
miasm 663
mica 425
micacious 204
mi-carême 840
Micawber 460
Michael 977
Michaelmas 998
microbe 163, 193
microcosm 193
micrography 193,
441
micrometer 193
micro-organism
193
microphone 418
microscope 193, 445
microscopic 32, 193
mid 68
Midas 803
mid-course 628
mid-day 125
midden 653
middle – *in degree*
29
– *in order* **68**
– *in space* 222,
228
– classes 736
– constriction 203
– course 29, 628
– man *director* 694
agent 758
– point 29
– term 68
compromise 774
middlemost 222
middling 29, 32, 68,
651
middy 225, 269

midge 193
midget 193
midland 342
midnight *night* 126
dark 421
– oil 539, 689
mid-progress 282
midriff 68, 228
midshipman 269,
745
midships 68
midst – *in order* 68
central 222
interjacent 228
in the – of
mixed with 41
doing 680
midsummer 125
– day 138
midway 68
midwife
instrument 631
remedy 662
auxiliary 711
midwifery 161, 662
mien 448, 692
miff 900
might *power* 157
violence 173
energy 686
mightily 31
mighty *much* 31
strong 159
large 192
haughty 878
migraine 378
migrate 266, 295
mikado 745
milch cow
productive 168
animal 366
store 636
mild *moderate* 174
warm 382
insipid 391
lenient 740
calm 826
courteous 894
mildew 653, 663
mildewed
spoiled 659
mile 200
milestone 550
whistle jigs to a –
645
milieu, juste – 174,
628
militant 722
church – 983*a*
military
warfare 722

soldiers 726
– authorities 745
– band 417
– power 737
– time 132
– train 726
militate against 708
militia 726
milk *moderate* 174
semiliquid 352
cows &c. 370
white 430
mild 740
– a he-goat into a
sieve 471
flow with – and
honey *plenty*
639
prosperity 734
pleasant 829
– of human kind-
ness 906
– the ram 645
– and water
weak 160
insipid 391
unimportant 643
imperfect 651
milk-livered 862
milksop
incapable 158
fool 501
coward 862
milky [*see* milk]
semitransparent
427
whiteness 430
– way 318
mill 330
notch 257
machine 633
workshop 691
fight 720
like a horse in a –
312
millennium
number 98
period 108
futurity 121
utopia 515
hope 858
millesimal 99
millet seed 193
milliard 98
milliner 225
man – 854
millinery *dress* 225
ornament 847
display 882
man – 855
million 98

multitude 102
people 372
populace 876
for the –
intelligible 518
easy 705
–s *money* 800
millionaire 803
mill-pond *level* 213
pond 343
store 636
mime 19, 599, 844
mimeograph 19
mimeotype 19
mimic 19
mimodrama 599
minacity 909
minaret 206
minatory 668
minauderie 855
mince *cut up* 44
slow 275
food 298
stammer 583
affected 855
extenuate 937
– the matter 868
not – the matter
affirm 525
artless 703
– the truth 544
mincemeat of
make – 162
mincing 855
– steps 275
mind *intellect* 450
attend to 457
take care 459
believe 484
remember 505
will 600
willing 602
purpose 620
warning 668
desire 865
dislike 867
bear in – 451, 457
bit of one's – 527
food for the – 454
give the – to 457
have a – 602, 865
in the –
thought 451
topic 454
willing 602
make up one's –
484, 604
never – *neglect* 46(?)
unimportant 643
not – 866
out of – 506

set one's – upon 604
speak one's – 582, 703
to one's – *taste* 850
love 897
willing – 602
– one's book 539
– one's business 456, 457
– at ease 827
make one's – easy 826
–'s eye 515
– what one is about 864
minded 602, 620
mindful 457, 505
mindless
inattentive 458
imbecile 499
forgetful 506
insensible 823
mine
sap 162
hollow 252
open 260
snare 545
store 636
abundance 639
damage 659
attack 716
defence 717
explosive 727
·dig a – *plan* 626
prepare 673
spring a –
unexpected 508
attack 716
– of information 700
–layer 726
–sweeper 726
–thrower 727
– of wealth 803
miner 252
sapper and – 726
mineral 358
– oil 356
mineralogy 358
Minerva 979
– invita 603, 709
– press 577, 594
mingle 41
miniature *small* 193
portrait 556
– painter 559
Minié rifle 727
minikin 193
minim *small* 32
music 413

minimize 36, 483, 934
minimum *small* 32
inferior 34
minion 899
type 591
minister *instru-mentality* 631
remedy 662
director 694
aid 707
deputy 759
give 784
clergy 996
rites 998
– to 746
ministerial
clerical 995
ministering spirit 977
ministration
direction 693
aid 707
rite 998
ministry
direction 693
aid 707
church 995
clergy 996
miniver 223
minnesinger 597
minnow 193
minor *inferior* 34
infant 129
– key 413
Minorites 996
minority *few* 103
youth 127
Minos 694
minotaur 83
minster 1000
minstrel 416, 597
minstrelsy 415
mint *mould* 22
workshop 691
wealth 803
– of money 800
minuend 38
minuet 415, 840
minus *less* 34
subtracted 38
absent 187
deficient 304
loss 776
in debt 806
non-payment 808
minusculæ 561
minute
– *in degree* 32
– *of time* 108
instant 113

– *in size* 193
record 551
compendium 596
to the – 132
– account 594
– attention 457
minuteness
care 459
minutiæ 32, 79, 643
minx 887, 962
mirabile
– dictu &c. 870
mirabilis, annus – 872
miracle 83, 872
– play 599
miraculous 870
mirage 443
mire 653
mirror *imitate* 19
reflector 445
perfection 650
glory 873
hold up the – 525
hold the – up to nature 554
magic – 443
mirth 836
misacceptation 235
misadventure 735
misadvised 699
misanthropy **911**
misapply
misinterpret 523
misuse 679
mismanage 699
misapprehend 495, 523
misappropriate 679
misarrange 61
misbecome 925
misbegotten 243, 945
misbehave 851, 945
misbehaviour 895, 947
misbelief 485
misbeliever 487, 984
miscalculate
misjudge 481
err 495
disappoint 509
miscall 565
miscarry 732
miscegenation 41
miscellany
mixture 41
collection 72
generality 78
compendium 596

mischance 619, 735
mischief 619
do – 649
make – 649
mischief-maker 913, 941
miscible 41
miscite 544
miscompute 481, 495
misconceive 495, 523
misconduct 699, 947
– oneself 945
misconjecture 481
misconstrue 523
miscorrect 538
miscount 495
miscreance 485
miscreant 949
miscreated 945
misdate 115
misdeed 947
misdemean 945
misdemeanant 949
misdemeanour 947
misdevotion 988
misdirect 538, 699
misdo 945
misdoing 947
misdoubt 485, 523
mise en scène
appearance 448
drama 599
display 882
misemploy 679
miser 819
–'s hoard 800
miserabile dictu 839
miserable *small* 32
contemptible 943
unhappy 828
miserably *very* 31
miserere 215
sing – 950
misericordiam, argumentum ad – 914
miseries of human life 828
miseris succurrere disco 914
miserly 819
misery 828
put out of one's – 914
misestimate
misjudge 481
misfeasance 699, 947

misfit 24
misfortune
  adversity 735
  unhappiness 830
misgiving 485, 860
misgovern 699
misguide 495, 538
misguided 699
mishap *evil* 619
  failure 732
  misfortune 735
  painful 830
Mishna 985
misinform 538
misinformed 491
misinstruct 538
misintelligence 538
misinterpretation
  523
misjoined 24
misjudgment
  sophistry 477
  misjudge **481**
  misinterpretation
  523
mislay *derange* 61
  lose 776
mislead *error* 495
  misteach 538
  deceive 545
mislike 867
mismanage 699
mismatch 15, 24
misname 565
misnomer **565**
misogamist 904,
  911
misogyny 904
mispersuasion 538
misplace
  derange 61
misplaced
  intrusive 24
  unconformable 83
  displaced 185
misprint 495
misprision
  concealment 528
  guilt 947
  – of treason 742
misprize 483, 929
mispronounce 583
misproportioned
  243, 846
misquote 544
misreckon 481, 495
misrelish 867
misreport 495, 544
misrepresent
  misinterpret 523
  misteach 538

lie 544
misrepresentation
  555
  untruth 544, 546
misrule
  misconduct 699
  laxity 738
  Lord of – 701
miss *girl* 19
  neglect 460
  error 495
  unintelligible 519
  fail 732
  lose 776
  want 865
  courtesan 962
  – one's aim 732
  – fire 732
  – stays 304
  – one's way
    uncertain 475
    unskilful 699
missa cantata 998
missal 998
missay 563, 583
missend 699
misshapen 243, 846
missile 727
missing
  non-existent 2
  absent 187
  disappear 449
  – link 53, 83, 729
mission 625, 755
missionary 540, 996
missive 592
misspell 523
misspend 818
misstate 495, 544
misstatement 495,
  546
mist 353, 424
  in a – 528
  seen through a –
    519
  –s of error 495
  – before the eyes
    443
mistake *error* 495
  misconstrue 523
  mismanage 699
  failure 732
  never was a
    greater – 536
misteaching **538**
mister 373
misterm 565
misthink 481
mistime 135
mistral 349
mistranslate 523

mistress *lady* 374
  master 745
  possessor 779
  title 877
  love 897
  concubine 962
mistrust 485
misty [*see* mist]
  semi-transparent
    427
misunderstand
  misinterpret 523
misunderstanding
  495, 713
misuse **679**
mite *bit* 32
  small 193
  insufficiency 649
  money 800
  little – 129
Mithridate 662
mitigate *abate* 174
  improve 658
  relieve 834
mitigation
  [*see* mitigate]
  extenuation 937
mitraille 727
mitrailleur 727
mitre *junction* 43
  angle 244
  crown 747, 999
mitten 225
mittimus 741
mix 41
  – oneself up with
    meddle 682
  co-operate 709
  – with 720
mixen 653
mixture **41**
  mere – 59
mix-up 59
mizzen 235
mizzle 348
mnemonics 505
Mnemosyne 505
moa 366
moan 405
  cry 411
  lament 839
moat *enclosure* 232
  ditch 259
  canal 350
  defence 717
mob *crowd* 72
  multitude 102
  vulgar 876
  hustle 929
  scold 932
  king – 876

– cap 225
– law
  authority 737
  illegality 964
mobile
  inconstant 149
  movable 264
  sensitive 822
mobility, the – 876
mobilize
  assemblage 72
  render movable
    264
  – troops 722
mobocracy 737
mobster 361
moccasin 225
mock *imitate* 17, 19
  repeat 104
  erroneous 495
  deceptive 545
  chuckle 838
  ridicule 856
  disrespect 929
  – danger 861
  – modesty 855
  – sun 423
mockery
  [*see* mock]
  unsubstantial 4
  solemn – 882
  – delusion and
    snare
  sophistry 477
  deception 545
mocking-bird 19
modal 6, 7, 8
mode *state* 7
  music 413
  habit 613
  method 627
  fashion 852
  – of expression 569
mode, à la – 852
model *copy* 21
  prototype 22
  rule 80
  form 240
  representation
    554
  sculpture 557
  perfection 650
  good man 948
  new – 658
  – after 19
  – condition 80
modeller 559
moderate
  average 29
  small 32
  allay **174**

ugly 846
vulgar 851
ridiculous 853
wonderful 870
mont-de-piété 787
montagne russe
  slope 217
  sport 840
monté *cards* 840
Montgolfier 273
month 108
monthly 138
  magazine 531
  – nurse 662
monticle 206
monument *tall* 206
  tomb 363
  record 551
monumentum ære
  perennius 733
moo 412
mood *nature* 5
  state 7
  change 140
  tendency 176
  willingness 602
  temper 820
moods and tenses
  15, 20*a*
moody *furious* 825
  sad 837
  sullen 901*a*
moodish 895, 901
moon *changes* 149
  world 318
  luminary 423
  bay the – 645
  jump over the –
    309
  man in the – 515
  – of green cheese
    credulity 486
moonbeam 420, 422
mooncalf 501
moon-eyed 443
moonshee 493, 540
moonshine
  unsubstantial 4
  dim 422
  absurdity 497
  unmeaning 517
  untrue 546
  excuse 617
moonstone 847
moonstruck 503,
  870
moor *fasten* 43
  open space 180
  locate 184
  highland 206
  plain 344

Moore, Old – 513
moored *firm* 150
mooring mast 184
moorings 45, 184
moorish 345
moorland 180, 206
moot *inquire* 461
  argue 476
  – point *topic* 454
  question 461
  discuss 514
mooted 514
mop 243, 652
mope 837
mope-eyed 443
moppet 899
mopsy 962
mopus *dreamer* 515
  drone 683
  money 800
  sad 837
mora nec requies,
  nec – 682
moral *judgment* 480
  maxim 496
  right 922
  duty 926
  virtuous 944
  point a – 537
  – *certainty* 474
  – courage 604
  – education 537
  – obligation 926
  – support 707
  – tuition 537
  – turpitude 940
moral philosophy
  mind 450
  duty 926
morality play 599
moralize 476
morals *duty* 926
  virtue 944
morass 345
moratorium 133
morbid 655
morbific 657
mordacity 907
mordant *keen* 171
  pungent 392
  colour 428
  language 574
more *superior* 33
  added 37
  – than enough 641
  – than flesh and
    blood can bear
    830
  – last words 65
  – or less
    quantity 25

small 32
inexact 495
– than a match
  for 33, 159
– than meets the
  eye 526
– than one 100
more:
– majorum 82
– solito
  conformable 82
  habitual 613
– suo 613
moreover 37
mores, O – 932
Morgana, Fata –
  423
morganatic mar-
  riage 903
morgue 363
– littéraire 569
mori, memento –
  363
moribund 369, 655
  dying 360
  sick 655
morient 360
morion 717
morisco 840
mormo 860
Mormon 984
Mormonism 903,
  984
morning 125
– coat 225
– dress 225
– noon and night
  repetition 104
  diuturnal 110
  frequent 136
– star 423, 977
morocco 223
moron 493, 501
moronic 499
morose 895, 901*a*
morosis 503
Morpheus 683
morphew 653
morphia 381, 663
morphology
  form 240
  zoology 368
morra 840
morris
  nine men's – 840
morris-dance 840
morrow 121
morse 45
morsel *small* 32
  portion 51
  food 298

mors aux dents,
  prendre le – 719
mort, guerre à –
  722
mortal
  transient 111
  fatal 361
  man 372
  wearisome 841
  – antipathy 867
  – blow 619
  – coil 362
  – funk 860
  – remains 362
  – sin 947
mortality
  evanescence 111
  death 360
  mankind 372
  bills of – 360
mortar *cement* 45
  pulverizer 330
  cannon 727
mortem, post – 360,
  363
mortgage
  security 771
  lend 787
  sale 796
  credit 805
mortgagee 779, 805
mortgagor 779, 806
mortician 363
mortiferous 361
mortification
  disease 655
  pain 828
  vexation 830
  discontent 832
  humiliation 879
  asceticism 955
mortise *unite* 43
  intersect 219
  interjacence 228
mortmain 748
  in – 781
Morton's fork 475
mortuary 360, 363
mosaic *mixture* 41
  multiform 81
  variegation 440
  painting 556
Moslem 984
mosque 1000
moss *tuft* 256
  marsh 345
  vegetation 367
moss-grown 659
moss-trooper 726,
  792
most 31

at – 32
make the – of
 over-estimate 482
 exaggerate 549
 improve 658
 use 677
 skill 698
the – 33
– often 136
for the – part 78,
 613
make the – of
 one's time 682
mot 496
– de l'énigme 522
– du guet 550
– à mot 19
– d'ordre 741
– de passe 550
– pour rire 842
mote *small* 32
 light 320
– in the eye
 dim-sighted 443
 misjudging 481
motet 990
moth *bane* 663
moth-eaten 124,
 653, 659
mother *parent* 166
 mould 653
– country 189
– of-pearl 440
– superior 996
– tongue 560
– wit 498
motherly *love* 897
 kind 906
motif 415, 847
motile 264
motion
 change of place
 264
 topic 454
 plan 626
 proposal 763
 request 765
make a – 763
put in – 284
put oneself in –
 680
set in – 677
– downwards 306
– from
 recession 287
 repulsion 289
– into *ingress* 294
 reception 296
– out of 295
– through 302
– towards

approach 286
attraction 288
– upwards 305
motionless 265
motive **615**
 absence of – **615a**
 – power 264
motivity 264
motley 81, 440
 wearer of the – 844
motor 153, 266
 vehicle 271, 272
 instrument 633
 –boat 273
 –car &c. 272
 –driver 268
 –man 694
motorist 268
motory 264
mottled 440
motto *maxim* 496
 device 550
 phrase 566
motu: ex mero –
 737
suo – 600
mouchard 527
mould *condition* 7
 matrix 22
 convert 144
 form 240
 structure 329
 earth 342
 vegetation 367
 model 554
 carve 557
 decay 653
 turn to account
 677
moulded 820
– on 19
moulder 653, 659
moulding 847
mouldy 653, 659
moulin:
 se battre contre
  des –s 645
– à paroles 584
moult 226
mound *large* 192
 hill 206
 defence 717
mount *increase* 35
 hill 206
 horse 271
 ascend 305
 raise 307
 display 882
– guard *care* 459
 safety 664
– up to *money* 800

price 812
mountain *large* 192
 hill 206
 weight 319
– artillery 726
– in labour
 waste 638
make –s of mole-
 hills 482
– brought forth
 mouse
 disappoint 509
mountaineer 268
mountainous 206
mountebank
 quack 548
 drama 599
 buffoon 844
mounted rifles 726
mourn 828, 839
mourner 363
mournful
 afflicting 830
 sad 837
 lamentable 839
mourning *dress* 225
in – *black* 431
 lament 839
mouse *little* 193
 search 461
 mountain brought
 forth – 509
 not a – stirring
 265
mouse-coloured
 432
mousehole 260
mouser 366
mousetrap 545
mousseux 353
moustache 256
mouth *entrance* 66
 receptacle 191
 brink 231
 opening 260
 eat 298
 estuary 343
 enunciate 580
 drawl 583
deep –ed
 resonant 408
 bark 412
down in the – 879
make –s 929
open one's – 582
stop one's – 581
word of – 582
– honour
 falsehood 544
 show 882
 flattery 933

pass from – to
 mouth 531
– wash 652
– watering 865
mouthful
 quantity 25
 small 32
 food 298
mouthpiece
 speaker 524
 information 527
 speech 582
mouthy *style* 577
moutonné 250
moutons, revenons
 à nos – 660
movable 264, 270
movables 780
move *begin* 66
 motion 264
 propose 514
 induce 615
 undertake 676
 act 680
 offer 763
 excite 824
get a – on 684
good – 626
on the – 293
– forward 282
– from 287
– in a groove 82
– heaven and
 earth 686
– off 293
– on *progress* 282
 activity 682
– out of 295
– quickly 274
– slowly 275
– to 894
moveless 265
movement
 motion 264
 music 415
 action 680
 activity 682
moved with 821
mover 164
movies 448, 599,
 840
movie star 899
moving
 keep – 682
 self – 266
 – pictures 448
mow *shorten* 201
 smooth 255
 agriculture 371
 store 636
– down

destroy 162
moxa 384
M.P. 696
Mr. 373, 877
Mrs. 374
MS. 22, 590
much 31
  make – of
    importance 642
    friends 888
    love 897
    endearment 902
    approval 931
  not say – for 932
  think – of 928, 931
  – ado *exertion* 686
    difficulty 704
  – ado about noth-
    ing
    over-estimate 482
    exaggerate 549
    unimportant 643
    unskilful 699
  – cry and little
    wool 884
  – the same
    identity 13
    similarity 17
    equality 27
  – speaking 584
mucid 352, 653
mucilage 352
muck 653
  run a – *kill* 361
    attack 716
    excitement 825
muckle 31
muckworm 819,
  876
mucor 653
mucosity 352
mucronate 253
muculent 352
mud *marsh* 345
  semiliquid 352
  dirt 653
  clear as – 519
  stick in the – 704
  – guard 666
muddle *disorder* 59
  derange 61
  inattention 458
  absurd 497
  difficulty 704
  failure 732
  – one's brains 475
muddled 959
muddle-headed 499
muddy *moist* 339
  dim 422
  opaque 426

colour 429
stupid 499
mudlark *dirty* 653
  commonalty 876
muezzin 550, 996
muff *incapable* 158
  dress 225
  bungle 699
  bungler 701
muffettee 225
muffle *wrap* 225
  silent 403
  deaden 408a
  conceal 528
  voiceless 581
  stammer 583
muffled *faint* 405
  latent 526
  – drums
    funeral 363
    non-resonance
    408a
muffler 225, 384
mufti *undress* 225
  judge 967
  priest 996
mug *cup* 191
  face 234, 448
  pottery 384
  dupe 547
mug-house 189
muggy *moist* 339
  dim 422
  opaque 426
mugient 412
mugwump 607
mulatto
  mixture 41
  exception 83
mulct *steal* 791
  fine 974
mule *mongrel* 83
  beast of burden
  271
  obstinate 606
muleteer 694
muliebrity 374
mull
  prominence 250
  sweeten 396
mullah 967, 996
muller 330
mullion 215
mullioned 219
multifarious
  irrelevant 10
  diverse 16a
  multiform 81
multiferous 102
multifid
  divided 51

multifold 81
multiformity **81**
multigenerous 81
multilateral 236,
  244
multilocular 191
multiloquence 582,
  584
multinomial 102
multiparous 168
multipartite 44
multiple 84, 102
multiplex 81
multiplicand 84
multiplicate 81
multiplication
  increase 35
  arithmetic 85
  multitude 102
  reproduction 163
  productiveness
  168
multiplicator 84
multiplicity 102
multiplier 84
multiply 35
multipotent 157
multisonous 404
multitude 72, **102**
  the – 876
multum in parvo
  596
multure 330
mum 581, 585
  –'s the word 403
mumble *chew* 298
  mutter 583
Mumbo Jumbo
  979, 993
mummer 599
mummery
  absurdity 497
  imposture 545
  masquerade 840
  parade 882
mummify 363
mummy *dry* 340
  corpse 362
  beat to a – 972
mump *mutter* 583
  beg 765
mumper 767, 804
mumpish *sad* 837
mumps 837, 901a
munch 298
Munchausen 549
mundane
  world 318
  selfish 943
  irreligious 989
mundation 652

mundivagant 266
munerary 973
munerate 973
municipal 965
municipality 737
munificent 816
muniment
  evidence 465
  record 551
  defence 717
  security 771
munition
  materials 635
  defence 717
mural 717
murder 361
  – the King's Eng-
    lish
    solecism 568
    stammering 583
  the – is out 529
murderer 361
muricated 253
murky *dark* 421
  opaque 426
  black 431
  gloomy 837
murmur *purl* 348
  sound 405
  voice 580
  complain 839
murmurer 832
murrain 655
Murray *travel* 266
  Lindley – 542
murrey 434
murrion 717
mus, nascitur ridi-
  culus – 509, 643
muscadine 400
muscle 159
muscular 159
muse 451
  [*and see* musing]
Muse *poetry* 597
  historic – 594
  unlettered – 579
musette 417
Muses, the – 416
museum
  collection 72
  store 636
mush 354
mushroom
  new 123
  fungus 367
  upstart 734
  low-born 876
  spring up like –s
  163
  – anchor 666

narrow-minded 481, 943
narrowness 203
narrows 343
nasal accent 583
nascent 66
nascitur: – ridiculus mus 509
– a sociis 82
naso, omnia suspendens – 868
nasty
unsavoury 395
foul 653
offensive 830
cheap and – 815
natâ, pro re – 770
natal *birth* 66
indigenous 188
natation 267
natatorium 652
nathless 30
nation 372
national 188, 372
– guard 726
nationality 372, 910
nations, law of 963
native
inhabitant 188
artless 703
– accent 580
– land 189
– soil 189
– tongue 560
nativity *birth* 66
cast a –
predict 511
sorcery 992
natty 845
natura il fece e po
roppe la stampa 87
naturæ, vis medicatrix – 662
natural *intrinsic* 5
musical note 413
true 494
fool 501
- *style* 576, 578
spontaneous 621
not prepared 674
artless 703
simple 849
– course of things 613
– death *death* 360
completion 729
– impulse 601
– meaning 516
– order of things 82

– state 90
– turn 820
Natural – History 357
– Philosophy 316
– Theology 983
naturalist 357
naturalization
conformity 82
conversion 144
location 184
naturalize
habit 613
naturalized
inhabitant 188
naturally 154
nature *essence* 5
rule 80
tendency 176
world 318
reality 494
artlessness 703
affections 820
animated – 357
organized – 357
second – 613
state of –
naked 226
raw 674
in –'s garb 226
naught *nothing* 4
zero 101
bring to – 732
set at –
make light of 483
opposition 708
disobey 742
not observe 773
disrespect 929
contempt 930
naughty 945
naumachia 720
nausea 841, 867
nauseate 395, 830
nauseous
unsavoury 395
unpleasant 830
disgusting 867
nautch dancer 840
nautical 267
naval 267
– authorities 745
– engagement 720
– forces 726
nave *middle* 68
centre 222
church 1000
navel 68, 222
navigation 267
navigator 269
navvy 673, 690

navy 273, 726
– blue 438
nay 536
– rather 14
Nazarene 989
naze 250
N.C.O. 745
ne plus ultra
supreme 33
complete 52
distance 196
summit 210
limit 233
perfection 650
completion 729
neaf 781
neap 195, 207
– tide 36, 340
near *like* 17
- *in space* 197
- *in time* 121
soon 132
impending 152
approach 286
stingy 819
bring – 17
draw – 197
come – 286
– one's end 360
– at hand 132
– the mark 32
– run 32
– side 239
– sight 443
– the truth 480a
– upon 3
sail – the wind
skilful 698
rash 863
nearly 32
nearness 197
neat *simple* 42
order 58
in writing 572, 576, 578
clean 652
spruce 845
–'s foot oil 356
– as a pin 58
neat-handed 698
neatherd 370
neb 250
nebula *stars* 318
mist 353
nebular *dim* 422
nebulous *misty* 353
obscure 519
necessarian 601
necessaries 630
necessarily 154
necessitate 630

necessity *fate* **601**
requirement 630
compulsion 744
indigence 804
make a virtue of – 698
neck
contraction 195
narrow 203
make love 902
break one's – 360
– and crop
completely 52
turn out - 297
– of land 342
– and neck 27
– or nothing
resolute 604
rash 863
neckcloth 225
necklace 247, 847
necks 980
necrology 360, 594
necromancer 548, 994
necromancy 992
necropsy 363
necroscopic 363
necrosis 49
nectar 394, 396
need *necessity* 601
requirement 637
insufficiency 640
indigence 804
desire 865
friend in – 711
in one's utmost – 735
needful
necessary 601
requisite 630
money 800
do the – *pay* 807
needle *sharp* 253
perforator 262
compass 693
as the – to the pole
veracity 543
observance 772
honour 939
– in a bottle of hay 475
needle-gun 727
needle-shaped 253
needless 641
needle-witted 498
needlewoman 690
needlework 847
ne'er-do-well 949
nefarious 945

contrary 14	nodus, dignus vin-	lex – scripta 963	– of one's hopes
dissimilar 18	dice – 704	– semper erit	509
– surrender 606,	Noel 998	æstas 111	**non-imitation 20**
717	noggin 191	– sequitur 477	**non-interference**
– thank you 764	noise 402, 404	– sum qualis eram	*inaction* 681
at – time 107	– abroad 531	140, 160·	*freedom* 748
– wonder 871	make a – in the	**non-addition** 38	nonius 466
Noah's ark 41, 72	world 873	**non-admission** 55	**non-juror** 489, 984
nob 210	noiseless 403	nonage 127	**non-naturals** 657
nobilitate 873	noisome	nonagenarian 98	nonny 501
nobility 875	*fetid* 401	**non-appearance**	**non-observance**
noble *great* 31	*bad* 649	447	*inattention* 458
important 642	*unhealthy* 657	**non-assemblage 73**	*desuetude* 614
rank 873	nolens volens 601	**non-attendance** 187	*infraction* **773**
peer 875	noli me tangere	nonce 118	*dereliction* 927
disinterested 942	*defiance* 715	for the – 118, 134	**nonpareil** 648
virtuous 944	*excitable* 825	**nonchalance**	*type* 591
noblesse 875	*fastidious* 868	*neglect* 460	**non-payment 808**
nobody	nolition 603	*insensibility* 823	**non-performance**
unsubstantial 4	nolle prosequi 624	*indifference* 866	*non-completion*
zero 101	nolumus leges	**non-coincidence** 14	730
absence 187	Angliæ mutari	**non-cohesive** 47	*dereliction* 927
low-born 876	*permanence* 141	**non-com.** 726	**non-plus**
– knows	*continuance* 143	**non-commissioned**	*uncertain* 475
ignorance 491	*preservation* 670	**officer** 745	*difficulty* 704
– knows where	nom de: – guerre	**non-committal** 528,	*conquer* 731
distance 196	565	864	**non-preparation**
– present 187	– plume 565	**non-completion 730**	**674**
– would think 508	nomad 268	**non-compliance**	**non-prevalence** 614
noctambulation 266	nomadic 266	742, 764	**non-residence** 187
noctivagant	Nomancy 511	**nonconformity**	**non-resistance** 725,
travel 266	**nomenclature 564**	*difference* 15	743
dark 421	**nominal**	*exception* 83	**non-resonance**
noctograph 421	*unsubstantial* 4	*dissent* 489	**408a**
noctuary 421, 551	*word* 562	*sectarianism* 984	**nonsense**
nocturnal	*name* 564	**non-content** 489	*absurdity* 497
night 126	– price 815	**non-cooperation**	*unmeaning* 517
dark 421	**nomination** 564,	489, 927	*trash* 643
black 431	755	**nondescript** 83	talk – *folly* 499
nocturne 415	nominee 758	**none** 101	**non-subsistence** 2
nocuous 649	nominis umbra 4	– else 87	**non-success** 732
nod *wag* 314	Nomology 963	– to spare 640	**nonsuch** [*see* none]
assent 488	**non:**	– such	**nonsuit** *defeat* 731
signal 550	– compos mentis	*superior* 33	*fail* 732
sleep 683	503	*exceptional* 83	*condemn* 971
command 741	– constat 477	*very good* 648	**nonum prematur in**
bow 894	– deficit alter 100	– in the world 4	**annum** 133
– of approbation	– est in ventus 187	– the worse 660	**non-uniformity** 16a
931	– hæc in fœdera	**non-endurance** 825	**noodle** 501
– of assent 488	536, 610	**nonentity**	**nook** *place* 182
nodding to its fall	– nobis Domine	*inexistence* 2	*receptacle* 191
162, 306	990	*unsubstantial* 4	*corner* 244
noddle 210, 450	– obstante 707	*unimportant* 643	**noology** 450
noddy 501	– placet 489	**non esse** 2	**noon** *mid-day* 125
node 250	– possumus	**non-essential** 6,	**noon-day** *light* 420
nodosity 250, 256	*impossible* 471	643	clear as –
nods and becks and	*obstinate* 606	**non-existence** 2	*intelligible* 518
wreathed smiles	*refusal* 764	**non-expectance** 508	*manifest* 525
894	– nostrum tantas	**non-extension** 180a	**nooscopic** 450
nodule 250	componere lites	**non-fulfilment** 730,	**noose** *ligature* 45
nodular 256	471, 713	732	*loop* 247

snare 545
gallows 975
norma loquendi 567
normal
  intrinsic 5
  mean 29
  regular 82
  perpendicular 212
  – condition
  rule 80
normality 80, 502
Normand, répon-
  dre en – 544
Norns 601
North 278
  – and South 237
Northern 237
  – light 423
  – star
  constant 939
North-west
  passage 311
nose *prominence*
  250
  smell 398
  with one's – in
    the air 878
  lead by the – 615,
    737
  led by the – 749
  not see beyond
    one's –
  misjudge 481
  folly 499
  unskilful 699
  speak through
    the – 583
  thrust one's – in
  interjacence 228
  busy 682
  under one's –
  present 186
  near 197
  manifest 525
  defy 715
  put one's – out of
    joint *defeat* 731
  disrepute 874
  – ring 847
nose-dive 306
nosegay 400, 847
nosey 455
Nosology 655
nostalgia 833
nostril 351
  breath of one's –s
    359
  stink in the –s 401
nostrum 626, 662
not *negation* 536
  what is – 546

what ought – 923
– at all 32
– allowed 964
– amiss 618, 651,
  845
– any 101
– bad 651
– bargain for 508
– a bit 536
– to be borne 830
– a Chinaman's
  chance 471
– come up to 34
– cricket 923
– to be despised
  642
it will – do 923
– of the earth 987
– expect 508
– fail 939
– far from 197
– a few 102
– fit to be seen 846
– following 477
– grant 764
– guilty 946
– to be had 471,
  640
– having 187, 777a
– hardened 950
– hear of 764
– included 55
– know what to
  make of 519
– a leg to stand
  on 158
– likely 473
– a little 31
– matter 643
– to mention 37
– mind 823, 930
– often 137
– on your life 489
– one 101
– a particle 4
– particular 831
– pay 808
– a pin to choose
  27
– playing the
  game 923
– within previous
  experience 137
– to be put down
  604
– quite 32
– reach 304
– right 503
– sorry 827
– a soul 101
– on speaking

terms 889
– the thing 925
– to be thought of
  incogitancy 452
  impossible 471
  refusal 764
  hopeless 859
  undue 925
  disapprobation
    932
– trouble oneself
  about 460
– understand 519
– vote 609a
– wonder 871
– for the world
  603, 764
– worth
  trifling 643
  useless 645
nota bene 457
notabilia 642
notabilities 875
notable
  manifest 525
  important 642
  active 682
  distinguished 873
notables 875
notably 31
notary 553, 968
notation 85
notch 198, **257**, 550
note *cry* 412
  music 413
  take cognizance
    450
  remark 457
  explanation 522
  sign 550
  record 551
  printing 591
  epistle 592
  minute 596
  money 800
  fame 873
  change one's – 607
  make a – of 551
  of – 873
  take – of 457
  – of admiration
    870
  – of alarm 669
  – of preparation
    673
note-book
  memorandum 505
  record 551
  compendium 569
  writing 590
noted 490, 873

noteworthy
  great 31
  exceptional 83
  important 642
nothing *nihility* 4
  zero 101
  trifle 643
  come to – 304, 732
  do – 681
  for – 815
  go for – 643
  good for – 646
  make – of
    under-estimate
    483
  fail 732
  take – by 732
  think of – 930
  worse than – 808
  – comes amiss 831
  – to do 681
  – to do with 764
  – doing 681
  – to go upon 471
  – in it 4
  – of the kind 18,
    536
  – loth 602
  – on 226
  – more to be said
    478
  – to signify 643
nothingness 2
notice *intellect* 450
  observe 457
  review 480
  information 527
  warning 668
  bring into – 525
  deserve – 642
  give –
    manifest 525
    inform 527
    indicate 550
  short – 111
  take – of 450
  this is to give –
    457
  worthy of – 642
  – is hereby given
    publication 531
  – to quit 782
noticeable 31
notification 527
notion *idea* 453
notional 515
notoriety 531, 873
notorious
  known 490
  public 531
  famous 873

infamous 874
notturno 415
notwithstanding 30
nought
  [*see* naught]
noun 564
nourish 707
nourishment
  food 298
nous 498
nous avons changé
  tout cela 140
nouveau riche 123,
  734, 876
Nova Zembla 383
novation 609
novel
  dissimilar 18
  new 123
  unknown 491
  tale 594
novelette 594
novelist 594
novice
  ignoramus 493
  learner 541
  bungler 701
  religious 996
novitiate 539, 673
novocaine 376, 381
novus homo 57,
  876
now 118
  – and then 136
  – or never 134
noways 32
nowhere 187
nowise 32, 536
noxious 649, 657
noyade 361, 972
noyerait dans une
  goutte d'eau, il
  se – 699
nozzle
  projection 250
  opening 260
  air-pipe 351
nuance 15, 465
nubibus, in – 2, 515
nubiferous 353, 426
nubile 131, 903
nucleus *middle* 68
  cause 153
  centre 222
  kernel 642
nuda veritas 494
nude 226, 849
nudge 550
nudity 226
nugacity 499, 645
nugæ canoræ 517,

842
nugas, magno co-
  natu magnas –
  643
nugatory 158
  unimportant 643
nuggar 273
nugget *mass* 192
  money 800
nuisance 619, 830
null 4
  – and void
  inexistence 2
  powerless 158
  unproductive 169
  illegal 964
  dec'are – and void
  abrogation 756
  non-observance
  773
nulla dies sine
  lineâ 682
nullah 198
nullâ pallescere
  culpâ, nil con-
  scire sibi – 946
nulli secundus 33
nullibiety 187
nullify *inexistence* 2
  compensate 30
  destroy 162
  abrogate 756
  not observe 773
  not pay 808
nullity 2, 4
nullius jurare in
  verba magistri
  487
numb
  physically insen-
  sible 376, 381
  morally insensible
  823
  –skull 493
number
  part 51
  abstract - **84**
  count 85
  plural 100
  - *of a magazine*
    &c. 593
  – *among* 76
  take care of – one
    943
  – of times 104
numbered: days –
  kill 361
  necessity 601
  hopeless 859
  – with the dead
  360

numberless 105
numbers *many* 102
  verse 597
numbness 375, **381**
numerable 85
numeral 84, 85
numeration 85
numerator 84
numerical 85
numerose
  many 102
numerous 102
numismatics 800
numps 501
numskull 501
nun 996
nunc dimittis 990
nuncio 534, 758
nuncupation
  naming 564
nuncupatory
  informing 527
nunindation 794
nunnery 1000
nuptials 903
nurse *remedy* 662
  preserve 670
  help.707
  servant 746
  custodian 753
  fondle 902
  put to – 537
nurseling 129
nursery *infancy* 127
  nest 153
  room 191
  garden 371
  school 542
  workshop 691
  – *rhymes* 597
  – *tale* 546, 594
nursing home 493
nurture *feed* 298
  educate 537
  prepare 673
  aid 707
  – a belief 484
  – an idea 451
nut
  – to crack
  fanatic 504
  riddle 533
  difficulty 704
  – oil 365
nut-brown 433
nutmeg 393
nutmeg-grater 330
nuts 618, 829
nutshell *small* 32
  lie in a – 572
  little 193

compendium 596
nutation 314
nutriment 298
nutrition 707
nutritious *food* 298
  healthy 656
  remedy 662
nutty 499
nuzzle 902
nyctalopy 443
nymph *girl* 129
  woman 374
  mythology 979
  sea – 341
nystagmus 443

O

O! *wonder* 870
  discontent 932
  – *for desire* 865
oaf *fool* 501
  bungler 701
  changeling 980
oak *strong* 159
  heart of –
  hard 323
  brave 861
oakum 205
oar *paddle* 267
  oarsman 269
  instrument 633
  labouring – 686
  lie upon one's –s
    681
  ply the –
  navigate 267
  exert 686
  pull an – 680
  put in an – 228,
    682
  rest on one's –
  cease 142
  quiescence 265
  repose 687
  stroke – 693
oarsman 269
oasis *separate* 44
  exceptional 83
  land 342
oast-house 386
oath
  assertion 535
  bad language 908
  on – 543
  rap out –s 885
  upon – 768
oatmeal 298
obbligato 88, 415
obduction 223

obdurate
obstinate 606
severe 739
malevolent 907
graceless 945
impenitent 951
obedience 743
obeisance *bow* 308
submission 725
courtesy 894
reverence 928
obelisk 206, 551
Oberon 979
obese 194
obesity 192
obey 743
be subject to 749
− *a call* 615
− *the helm* 705
− *rules* 82
obfuscate 421, 426
obfuscated
drunk 959
obit 360, 363
post − 360, 363
obiter dictum
irrelevant 10
occasion 134
interjacent 228
obituary 360, 594
object *thing* 3
matter 316
take exception 469
intention 620
ugly 846
disapprove 932
be an −
important 642
− *to dislike* 867
− *lesson* 82
objection 706, 932
no − 762
objectionable
inexpedient 647
wrong 923, 947
objective
extrinsic 6
material 316
objector
conscientious −
710
objurgate 932
oblate 201
− *spheroid* 249
oblation *gift* 784
religious − 990
oblectation 827
obligation
necessity 601
promise 768
conditions 770

debt 806
confer an − 648
feeling of − 916
under an − 916,
926
oblige *benefit* 707
compel 744
duty 926
oblige, bien −
refusal 764
obliged
necessity 601
grateful 916
duty 926
obligee 800
obliging
helping 707
courteous 894
kind 906
obliquation 279
obliquity
slope **217**
vice 945
− of judgment 481
− of vision 443
obliteration 552
− of the past 506
oblivion 506
nothingness 2
pardon 506
forgiveness 918
redeem from − 505
− of benefits 917
− of time 115
oblivious 506
oblong 200
− spheroid 249
obloquy
disrepute 874
disapprobation
932
detraction 934
obmutescence 581,
585
obnoxious
pernicious 649
unpleasing 830
hateful 898
− *to liable* 177
obnubilated 422
oboe 417
obreption 528
obscene 653, 961
obscurantist 421,
519, 710
obscure *dark* 421
dim 422
unseen 447
uncertain 475
unintelligible 519
eclipse 874

ignoble 876
obscurity *style* **571**
obscurum per
obscurius 519
obsecration 765
obsequies 363
obsequious
subject 749
servile 886
courteous 894
respectful 928
flattery 932
observance *rule* 82
attention 457
habit 613
practice 692
fulfilment **772**
duty 926
rite 998
observant
friar 996
observation
intellect 450
idea 453
attention 457
assertion 535
− *car* 272
observatory 318
observe [*see observ-*
ance, observa-
tion]
remark 535
− *a duty* 926
− *rules* 82
observer 444
obsess 860, 992
obsession 716
obsidional 716
obsolete *old* 124
words 563
effete 645
obstacle 179, 706
obstant, Fata − 601
obstetrician 631
obstetrics 161, 662
obstinacy 606
prejudice 481
obstipation 261
obstreperous 173,
404
obstruct *close* 261
hinder 706
− *the passage of*
light 426
− *the view* 424
obstructive
opponent 710
obstruent 706
obstupefaction 823
obstupui steterunt-
que comæ 860

obtain *exist* 1
prevail 78
get 775
− *under false*
pretences 791
obtainable 470
obtenebration 421
obtestation 765
obtrectation 934
obtrude
interfere 228
insert 300
meddle 682
obtruncate 201
obtrusion 228, 706
obtrusive
interfering 228
vulgar 851
rude 895
obtund *mitigate* 174
blunt 254
deaden 376
paralyze 823
obturate 261
obturator 263
obtuse *blunt* 253
insensible 376
imbecile 499
dull 823
− *angle* 244
obtuseness 456*a*
obumbrate 421
obverse 234
obviate 706
obvious *visible* 446
evident 474
clear 518
manifest 525
ocarina 417
occasion
juncture 8
opportunity **134**
cause 153
befit the − 646
have − *for* 630
on the present −
118
on the spur of −
612
occasional 475
occasionally 136
occidental 236, 560
occiput 235
occision 361
occlusion 261
unintelligible 919
latent 526
hidden 528
− *art* 992
occultism 984
occultation 449, 528

occupancy 186, 777
occupant 188, 779
occupation
  business 625
  in the – of 188
  – road 627
occupied 682
  – by 188
  – with 457, 625
occupier 188, 779
occupy 186, 777
  – the chair 693
  – oneself with 457, 625
  – the mind 451, 457
  – a post 737
  – time 106
occur 1, 151
  – to the mind 451
  – in a place 186
occurrence 151
  of daily – 613
occursion 276
ocean 341
  plough the – 267
oceanography 341
ochlocracy 737
ochre 433, 439
  yellow – 436
o'clock 114
  know what's – 698
octagon 244
octahedron 244
Octateuch 895
octave
  eight 98
  music 413
  period 108
octavo 593
octet 98
octifid 99
octodecimo 593
octogenarian 98, 130
octoroon 41
octroi 812
octuple 98
ocular 441
  – demonstration *see* 441
  visible 446
  – inspection 441
oculis subjecta
  fidelibus 446
oculist 662
od force 992
odalisque 746
odd *remaining* 40
  exception 83

single 87
insane 503
vulgar 851
ridiculous 853
– fellows 712
– fish 857
oddity 857
oddments 51
odds *inequality* 28
  superiority 33
  chance 156
  discord 713
  at – 24, 713
  long – 704
  what's the – 643
  – against one 665
  the – are 472
  – and ends
    remainder 40
    mixture 41
    part 51
    useless 645
ode 597
odi profanum
  vulgus 878
Odin 979
odious
  disagreeable 830
  ugly 846
  hateful 898
odium *disgrace* 874
  hatred 898
  blame 932
odium theologicum
  481, 988
  church 995
odograph 200
odometer 200
odontoid 250, 253
odour **398**
  in bad – 932
  – of sanctity 897
odylic force 992
odzookens 870
œcumenical 78
œdematous 194, 324
Œdipus 462, 524
  – complex 897
  Davus sum non – 703
œil de maître 459
o'er [*see* over]
œsophagus 260
œuvre 161
of: – all things 33
  – course 82, 154
  – late 123
  – one mind 23
  – no effect 169
  – old 122

– a piece
  uniform 16
  similar 17
  agreeing 23
off 196
  be – 623
  keep – 623
  make – with 791
  move – 287
  sheer – 287
  stand – 287
  start – 293
  – one's balance 605
  throw – one's
    centre 874
  – one's guard 260, 508
  – one's hands 776
  take – one's hands 785
  – one's head 503
  – one's legs 284, 309
  – one's mind 452
  – and on
    periodical 138
    changeable 149
    irresolute 605
  throw – the scent
    uncertain 475
    avoid 623
  – side 238
  – with you 297
offal 653
offence *attack* 716
  anger 900
  guilt 947
offend 830, 945
  – against the law 964
offensive
  unsavoury 395
  fetid 401
  foul 653
  aggressive 716
  displeasing 830
  distasteful 867
  obnoxious 898
  – and defensive
    alliance 712
  – to ears polite 579
offer *proposal* **763**
  – the alternative 609
  – a choice 609
  – of marriage 902
  – oneself 763
  – up prayers 990
  – sacrifice 990
  – for sale 796

offering *gift* 784
  burnt – 990
  sin – 952
offertory *gift* 784
  worship 990
  rite 998
off-hand *soon* 132
  inattentive 458
  careless 460
  spontaneous 612
office *doing* 170
  room 191
  business 625
  mart 799
  worship 900
  do one's – 772
  good –s 724, 906
  hold – 693
  kind –s 906
  do an ill – 907
  man in – 694
officer *director* 694
  commander 745
  constable 965
offices
  kitchen &c. 191
official *certain* 474
  true 494
  business 625
  man in office 694
  authoritative 737
  master 745
  servant 746
officialism 739
officiate
  business 625
  act 680
  conduct 692
  religious 998
officio ex –
  officer 694
  authority 737
  duly 924
officinal 613
officious 682
offing 196, 341
offscourings 645, 653
offset
  compensation 30
  offspring 167
offshoot *adjunct* 39
  part 51
  effect 154
  offspring 167
offspring *effect* 154
  posterity 167
offuscate 121, 426
often *repeated* 104
  frequent 136
  most – 613

- to be met with 136
ogee 847
Ogham 590
ogive 215
ogle *look* 441
  desire 865
  rude 895
  endearment 902
ogpu 696
ogre *bugbear* 860
  evil-doer 913
  demon 980
oil *lubricate* 332
  grease 355, **356**
pour – on
  relieve 834
– on the troubled
  waters 174, 714
– lamp 423
– stove 386
oiled *drunk* 959
oilcloth 223
oilskin 386
oil-painting 556
oily *smooth* 255
  greasy 355
  servile 886
  courteous 894
  flattery 933
oinomania 959
ointment
  grease 356
  remedy 662
O.K. 58
old 124
of – 122
– age 128
die of – age 729
– bachelor 904
– clothes 225
– fashioned 851
– fogey 501, 857
– joke 842
– maid *cards* 840
  spinster 904
– man *veteran* 130
  husband 903
– man of the sea 706
– Nick 978
– school 124
  obstinate 606
  habit 613
pay off – scores 718
– song
  repetition 104
  trifle 643
  cheap 815
– stager

veteran 130
actor 599
proficient 700
– story
  repetition 104
  stale news 532
  love 897
– times 122
one's – way 613
– woman *fool* 501
  wife 903
Oldbuck 122
olden 124
older 128
oldest inhabitant
  not in memory of
  – 137
old-fashioned 124, 851
oldness **124**
oleagine 356
oleaginous 355
oleomargarine 356
oleum addere
  camino 35, 173
olfactory 398
olid 401
oligarch 745
oligarchy 737
olio 41
olive-branch
  infant 129
  offspring 167
  pacification 723
olive-green 435
olla podrida 41
Olympiad 720
Olympus 981
ombre 840
ombres chinoises 448
omega *end* 67
omelet 298
omen **512**
ominate 511
ominous
  predicting 511
  indicating 550
  danger 665
  hopeless 859
omission
  incomplete 53
  exclusion 55
  neglect 460
  failure 732
  non-observance 773
  guilt 947
omitted 2, 187
omne tulit
  punctum 731

omnibus 272
omnifarious 81
omnific 168
omniform 81
omnigenous 81
omnipotence 157, 976
omnipresence 186, 976
omniscience 490, 976
omnium gatherum
  mixture 41
  confusion 59
  assemblage 72
omnivorous
  eating 298
  desire 865
  gluttony 957
omphalos 68
on *forwards* 282
– account of 155
– all accounts 52
– that account 155
– approval 463
– an average 29
– the brink of 32
– the cards 152
– foot *duration* 106
  event 151
  doing 170
– the fire 730
– all fours 13, 23
– the other hand 30
– one's head 218
– the increase 35
– a large scale 31
– these lines 627
– the move 264
– the nail 118
– no account 32
– no occasion 107
– a par 27
– the part of 9
– the point of 111
– the present oc-
  casion 118
– trial 463
– the whole 50
on dit 532, 588
once *past* 119, 122
  seldom 137
at – 113, 132
– for all *final* 67
  infrequency 137
  tell one - 527
  determine - 604
  choose 609
– in a blue moon 137

– more 90, 104
– over 457
– upon a time
  time 106
  different time 119
  formerly 122
– in a way 137
Ondine 979
one *identical* 13
  whole 50
  unity 87
  somebody 372
  married 903
all – to 823
at – with *agree* 23
  concur 178
  concord 714
make – of 186
neither – nor the
  other 610
of – accord 488
– and all
  whole 50
  general 78
  unanimous 488
from – to another
  transfer 783
– thing with
  another 476
– of the best 948
– bone and one
  flesh 903
– consent 178, 488
– of these days 121
– fell swoop 113, 173
– fine morning 106
– and a half 87
– horse 643
– idea 481
– jump 113
– leg in the grave 160
as – man 488, 709
– mind 178, 488
– by one
  separately 44
  respectively 79
  unity 87
both the – and
  the other 89
the – or the other 609
– over the eight 959
– and the same 13
on – side 217, 236
– step 840
– in ten thousand
  648, 948
– at a time 87

– or two 100
with – voice 488
– in a way 83
– way or another 627
at – with
  agree 23
  concur 178
  concord 174
one-eyed 443
oneirocritic 524
oneiromancy 511
oneness 13
onerous *bad* 649
  difficult 704
  burdensome 706
  troublesome 830
oneself 13
have all to – 777
kill – 361
take merit to – 884
take upon –
  will 600
  undertake 676
talk to – 589
true to – 604*a*
be – again 660
one-sided
  misjudging 481
  wrong 923
  dishonourable 940
onion 393
onlooker 444
only *small* 32
  simple 42
  single 87
  imperfect 651
if – 865
– think 870
– yesterday 123
only-begotten 87
onomancy 511
onomatopœia 560, 564
onset *beginning* 66
  attack 716
onslaught 716
ontology 1
onus *burden* 706
  duty 926
– probandi
  uncertainty 475
  doubt 485
onward 282
onychomancy 511
onyx 847
oof 800
ooze *emerge* 295
  flow 348
  semiliquid 352

– out
  disclosure 529
opacity **426**
opal 847
opalescent 427, 440
opaque 426
open *begin* 66
  expand 194
  unclose 260
  manifest 525
  reveal 529
  frank 543
  artless 703
break – 173
lay – 226
lay oneself – to 177
leave the matter – 705
pry – 173
throw – 296
– and above board 703, 939
– air 220, 338
– arms *willing* 602
  friendship 888
  social 892
  courtesy 894
– the ball 62, 66
– a case 476
– country 344
in – court 525, 531
– a discussion 476
– to discussion 475
– the door to
  cause 153
  facilitate 705
  permit 760
with – doors 531
– enemy 891
– eyes *see* 441
  attention 457
  discovery 480*a*
  expectation 507
  inform 527
  undeceive 529
  teach 537
  predetermination 611
  wonder 870
– fire 716
– house 892
– into
  conversion 144
  river 348
– the lips 529
– the lock 480*a*
– market 799
– one's mind 529
– order 194
– one's purse-

strings 809
– question 461, 475
– rupture 713
– sesame 631, 993
– the sluices 297
– space 180
– to suspicion 485
– to *liable* 177
  facile 705
– the trenches 716
– up *begin* 66
  disclose 529
– to the view 446
– war 722, 889
– warfare 722
– the wound 824
opening
  beginning 66
  opportunity 134
  space 180
  gap 198
  aperture **260**
open-handed 809, 816
open-hearted
  veracious 543
  artless 703
  liberal 816
  honourable 939
open-mouthed
  cry 411
  expectation 507
  speak 582
  loquacious 584
  desire 865
  wonder 870
opera *music* 415
  poetry 597
  drama 599
– glass 445
– hat 225
– house 599
opéra bouffe 599
operculum 261
operæ pretium est 646
operandi, modus 627, 692
operate *cause* 153
  produce 161
  act 170
  work 680
– upon *motive* 615
operation
  [*see* operate]
arithmetical – 85
in – 680
put in – 677
surgical – 662
operative

acting 170
workman 690
operator
  surgeon 662
  doer 690
operculated 261
operculum 223
operetta 415
operose 686, 704
ophicleide 417
ophiology 368
ophiomancy 511
ophthalmia 443
ophthalmic 441
opiate 174
opine 484
opiniative 481
opiniator 606
opinion 484
give an – 480
have too high an – of oneself 880
popular – 488
system of –s 484
wedded to an – 606
opinionate 481, 606
opinionated 474
self– 880
opiniâtre 481
opinionist 474, 606
opitulation 707
opium *soothe* 174
  deaden sense 376
  bane 663
opium-eater 683
oppidan 188
oppilation 706
opponent **710**, 891
opportune
  well-timed 134
  expedient 646
opportunism 605, 646
opportunity 134
lose an – 135
oppose *contrary* 14
  counteract 179
  evidence 468
  clash 708
opposite 14
– scale 30
– side 237
opposition
  [*see* oppose] **708**
the – 710
oppositionist 710
oppress *molest* 649
  severe 739
  malevolence 907
oppressed with

melancholy 837
oppressive *hot* 382
 painful 830
oppressor 739, 913
opprobrium 874
oppugnation 708,
 719
optative 865
optical 441
 – instruments **445**
 – lantern 448
optician 445
optics *light* 420, 445
optics *sight* 441
optimacy 875
optimates 875
optime! 931
optimism 482, 858
optimist 858
 flatterer 935
option 609
optional 600
optometer 443
optometry 445
opulence 803
opuscule 593
or *yellow* 436
 orange 439
 alternative 609
oracle 500, **513**
Oracle, Sir –
 positive 474
 vanity 880
 blusterer 887
oracular
 answering 462
 ambiguous 475
 wise 498
 prediction 511
oral *information*
 527
 voice 580
 speech 582
 – communication
  588
 – evidence 467
orange *round* 249
 colour **439**
orangery 371
orarium 999
oration 582
 funeral – 363
orator 582
oratoric 415
oratory
 speaking 582
 place of prayer
  1000
orb *region* 181
 circle 247
 luminary 423

eye 441
sphere of action
 625
– of day *sun* 318
 luminary 423
– of night 318
orbicular 247
orbit *circle* 247
 heavens 318
 path 627
orchard 371
orchestra
 music 415
 musicians 416
 instruments 417
 theatre 599
orchestral 415
orchestrate 60, 413,
 416
orchestration 413
orchestrelle 417
ordain
 command 741
 commission 755
 due 924
 legal 963
 God 976
 church 995
ordained *due* 924
 clergy 996
ordeal
 experiment 463
 trouble 828
 sorcery 992
 – of battle 722
order
 regularity **58**
 arrangement 60
 class 75
 record 551
 requisition 630
 direct 693
 command 741
 money 800
 rank 873
 quality 875
 decoration 877
 law 963
 at one's – 743
 call to – 932
 in – 620
 keep in – 693
 money – 800
 out of – 651
 put in – 60
 recur in regular –
  138
 set in – 60
 set one's house
  in – 673
 standing – 613

in working – 673
– of the day
 conformity 82
 events 151
 habit 613
 plan 626
 command 741
 pass to the – of
  the day 624
orderless 59
orderly
 regular 58, 80
 arrange 60
 conformable 82
 servant 746
 – of succession 63
 – of things 80
orders, holy – 995
 in – 996
ordinal 998
ordinance
 command 741
 law 963
 rite 998
ordinary *usual* 82
 meal 298
 habitual 613
 imperfect 651
 ugly 846
 simple 849
 in – *store* 636
 lie in – 681
 – condition
  rule 80
 – course of things
  613
ordinate 466
ordination
 measurement 466
 command 741
 commission 755
 church 995
 rite 998
ordnance 727
ordonnance 963
ordure 653
ore 635
ore rotundo 577
oread 979
orectic 865
organ *music* 417
 voice 580
 instrument 633
 internal –s 221
 – point 413
organic *state* 7
 structural 329
 protoplastic 357
 – change 146
 – chemistry 357
 – remains 357

dead 329
organism 329
organist 416
organization 60
 production 161
 structure 329
 animated nature
  357
organize
 arrange 60
 produce 161
 plan 626
organized hypoc-
 risy 544
organology 329
orgasm 173
orgies 954
oriel *recess* 191
 corner 244
 window 260
 chapel 1000
Orient 236, 420
orifice
 beginning 66
 opening 260
oriflamme 550
Origenism 984
origin 66, 153
 derive its – 154
original
 dissimilar 18
 not imitated 20
 model 22
 initial 66
 individual 79
 exceptional 83
 cause 153
 invented 515
 unaccustomed 614
 laughing-stock
  857
 return to – state
  660
originality 600
 want of – 843
originate *begin* 66
 cause 153
 invent 515
 – in 154
originator 164
originative 168
Orion's belt 318
orismology 562, 564
orison *request* 765
 worship 990
orlop deck 211
ormoln
 sham 545
 ornament 847
Ormuzd 979
ornament

palatial *palace* 189
  ostentatious 882
palatinate 181
palatine 745
Palatine Court 966
palaver
  unmeaning 517
  speech 582
  loquacity 584
  colloquy 588
  council 696
pale *stake* 45
  region 181
  inclosure 232
  limit 233
  dim 422
  colourless 429
  emotion 821
  frightened 860
  turn –
  lose colour 429
  emotion 821
  fear 860
  – of the church
    995
  – its ineffectual
    fire
  dim 422
  out of repute 874
pale-faced 429
paleography
  past 122
  philology 560
paleology *past* 122
  language 160
paleontology 368
paleozoic 124
palestric 686, 720
paletot 225
palette 556
palfrey 271
palimpsest 147, 528
palindrone
  inversion 218
  neology 563
paling 232, 752
palingenesia 163
palingenesis 660
palinode 597
palinody 607
palisade
  wall 212
  defence 717
  prison 752
pall *covering* 223
  mantle 225
  funeral 363
  disgust 395
  insignia 747
  weary 841
  dislike 867

satiety 869
  canonicals 999
palladium
  safety 664
Pallas 979
pall-bearer 363
pallet *support* 215
  painter's – 556
palliament 225
palliate
  moderate 174
  mind 658
  relieve 834
  extenuate 937
palliative 174
  remedy 662
pallid 429
pallium 999
pall-mall 840
pallone 840
pallor 429
palm
  measure of length
    200
  trophy 733
  steal 791
  laurel 877
  bear the – 873
  grease the –
    induce 615
    give 784
  itching – 865
  win the – 731
  – off, – upon 545
  – tree 367
palmated 257
palmer
  traveller 268
  clergy 996
palmist 513
palmistry 511
palmy
  prosperous 734
  pleasant 829
  – days
  prosperous 734
  pleasure 827
palpable
  material 316
  tactile 379
  obvious 446
  manifest 525
  – obscure 421
palpation 379
palpitate
  tremble 315
  colour 440
  emotion 821
  fear 860
palsy
  impotence 158

physical insensi-
  bility 376
  disease 655
  mental insensi-
    bility 823
palter
  falsehood 544
  shift 605
  elude 773
paltry *small* 32
  unimportant 643
  mean 940
paludal 345
pampas 344
pamper 902, 954,
  957
pamphlet 531, 593
pamphleteer 595
Pan 979
pan 191
panacea 662
panache 256, 847
panama *hat* 225
panary 636
pancake 298
pandar [*see* pander]
Pandean pipes 417
pandect
  knowledge 490
  dissertation 595
  compendium 596
  code 963
pandemonium 59,
  404, 982
  inhabitants of –
    978
pandemic 657
pander *pimp* 962
  – to *instrument*
    631
  help 707
  flatter 933
pandiculation
  expansion 194
  opening 260
  sleepy 683
Pandoor 726
Pandora's box 619
  bottom of 858
paned 440
panegyric 931
panegyrize 482
panel *list* 86
  layer 204
  partition 228
  accused 938
  jury 967
  sliding – 545
panelling 847
pang 378, 828
Pangloss 492

panguid 355
panhandle 765, 767,
  876
panic 860
panier 225
Panjandrum 875
pannel 213
pannikin 191
pannier 191
panoply 717, 727
panopticon 752
panorama 448, 556
panoramic 78, 446
  – view 441
pansophy 490
pant *heat* 382
  fatigue 688
  emotion 821
  – for 865
pantaloon
  old man 130
  pantomimist 599
  buffoon 844
pantaloons 225
pantechnicon 272,
  636
pantheism 984
Pantheon 979, 1000
panther 861
pantile 223, 350
pantologist 492, 700
pantology 490
pantomime 550, 599
pantry 191, 636
pants 225
panurgy 698
pap 250, 354
papa *father* 166
Papa *pope* 996
papacy 984, 995
papal 995
paper *cover* 223
  white 430
  writing 590
  book 593
  security 771
  exist only on – 4
  – credit 805
  – money 800
  – pellet 643
  – war 476, 720
Paphian 954, 961
papilla 250
papistry 984
papoose 129
pappous 256
papula 250
papulose 250
papyrus 590
par 27
  above – 648

below – *low* 207
imperfect 651
– excellence 33
– nobile fratrum
alike 17
friends 890
de – le roi 737
– parenthèse 134
– pari refero 718
– value 812
parable
metaphor 521
teaching 537
description 594
parabola *curve* 245
parabolic
metaphorical 521
paracentesis 297
parachronism 115
parachute
balloon 273
means of safety
666
– light 423
Paraclete 976
parade *procession*
69, 266
walk 189
ostentation 882
paradigm 22, 567
Paradise *bliss* 827
heaven 981
in – 827
parados 717
paradox
absurdity 497
obscurity 519
difficulty 704
paradoxical 475,
519
paraffine 356
paragon
perfect 650
glory 873
good man 948
paragram
ambiguous 520
neology 563
paragraph *part* 51
phrase 566
article 593
paraleipsis 460
parallax 196
parallel
similarity 17
imitate 19
harmonious 178
- *position* 216
symmetry 242
draw a – 464
none but himself

can be his – 873
run – 178
parallelism 216
agreement 23
parallelogram 244
parallelopiped 244
paralogism 477
paralogize 477
paralysis
impotence 158
physical insensi-
bility 376
disease 655
moral insensi-
bility 823
paralyze 158, 376,
823
paramount
supreme 33
important 642
authority 737
lord – *master* 745
possessor 779
– *estate* 780
paramour 897
paranoia 503, 504
parapet 717
paraph 550
paraphernalia
machinery 633
belonging 780
paraphrase
imitation 19
copy 21
synonym 522
phrase 566
paraphrast 524
paraphrastic 19,
522
parasite *auxiliary*
711
servile 886
flatterer 935
parasitic
subjection 749
grasping 789
servile 886
parasol *covering* 223
shade 424
paratus:
in utrumque –
resolved 604
ready 673
semper – 673
parboil 384
parbuckle 633
Parcæ 601
parcel *part* 51
group 72
part and – 56
– out *arrange* 60

allot 786
parcels
property 780
parcere subjectis
740, 914
parch *dry* 340
heat 382
bake 384
parched with thirst
865
parchment
writing 590
security 771
parcity 819
pardi 535
pardon 506, 918
beg – 952
– me 489
pardonable 937
pare *cut* 38
reduce 195
peel 204
divest 226
– down
shorten 201
paregoric 662
parenchyma 316,
329
parent 166
– ship 726
parentage 11, 166
parenthesis
discontinuity 70
inversion 218
interjacence 228
by way of – 134
parenthetical
irrelative 10
pargeting 847
parhelion 423
pari passu 27, 120
Pariah
outlaw 83
commonalty 876
outcast 893
parian
sculpture 557
parietal 236
parietes 224
paring 32
parish 181
bring to the – 804
come upon the –
804
– council 696
parishioner 997
paritor 965
parity 17, 27
park *house* 189
plain 344
trees 367

artillery 727
pleasure ground
840
– paling 232
parkway 627
parlance 582
in common – 576
parlante 415
parlementaire 534,
723
parler:
façon de – 521
– a tort et à
travers
illogical 477
nonsense 497
parley *talk* 588
conference 695
mediation 724
parliament 696
parliamentary
securities 802
parlour 191
parlour-maid 746
parlous 665
Parnassus 597
parochial 181, 189
prejudiced 48
parody
imitation 19
copy 21
misinterpret 523
misrepresent 555
travesty 865
parole *speech* 582
on – *restraint* 751
prisoner 754
promise 763
Parolles 887
paronomasia
neology 563
ornament 577
paronymous 562
paroxysm
violence 173
agitation 315
emotion 825
anger 900
parquetry 440
Parr, Old – 130
parricide 361
parrot
imitation 19
repetition 104
loquacity 584
repeat as a – 505
parry *confute* 479
avert 623
defend 717
pars magna fui,
quorum – 690

parse 461, 567
Parsee 984
parsimony **819**
parson 996
parsonage 1000
part *divide* 44
  portion **51**
  diverge 291
  music 413
  book 593
  rôle 599
  function 625
  duty 926
act a – *action* 680
take an active –
  682
bear – in 709
component – 56
fractional – 100*a*
in – *a little* 32
for my – 79
on the – of 707
play a – in 175
principal – 642
take the – of 709
take – with 709
take a – in 680
take no – in 623
– company
  disjunction 44
  avoid 623
  quarrel 713
– and parcel 56
– by part 51
–song 415
– of speech 567
– with 782, 784
partake 778
– of the sacrament
  998
parte, ex – 481
parterre *level* 213
  cultivation 371
Parthis mendacior
  544
parti pris 611
partial *unequal* 28
  incomplete 51
  special 79
  misjudging 481
  unjust 923
– shadow 422
partiality
  preponderance 33
  desire 865
  friendship 888
  love 897
partially 32, 51
partible 44
particeps criminis
  690, 711

participote 709, 778
– in *be a doer* 680
participation **778**
participator 690
particle 32, 330
parti-coloured 440
particular *item* 51
  event 151
  attentive 457
  careful 459
  exact 494
  capricious 608
  odd 851
  fastidious **868**
in – 79
– account 594
– estate 780
particularize
  special 79
  describe 594
particularly 31, 33
particulars 79, 594
partie carrée 892
parting 44
partisan
  auxiliary 711
  weapon 727
  friend 890
  sympathizer 914
partisanship
  warped judgment
  481
  co-operation 709
  partiality 923
partition *wall* 228
  allot 786
partlet 366
partly 51
partner
  companion 88
  auxiliary 711
  sharer 778
  friend 890
  spouse 903
sleeping – 683
partnership
  party 712
join – with 709
parts *intellect* 450
  skill 698
  wisdom 498
parturition 161
parturiunt montes
  482, 509
party *assemblage* 72
  special 79
  person 372
  association **712**
  sociality 892
– spirit
  warped judgment

481
  cooperation 709
  wrong 923
– to *action* 680
  agent 690
  co-operate 709
– to a suit 969
– wall 228
parva componere
  magnis 464
parvenu
  new 123
  successful 734
  vulgar 851
  low-born 876
parvitude 193
pas *precedence* 62
  term 71
  precession 280
  rank 873
– de quatre 840
– seul 840
pas si bête 498
paschal 998
pasha 875
pashalic 737
pashaw 745
pasigraphie 560
pasigraphy 590
pasquinade 934
pass *conjuncture* 8
  be superior 33
  course 109
  lapse 122
  happen 151
  interval 198
  defile 203
  move 264
  transfer 270
  move through 302
  exceed 303
  vanish 449
  way 627
  difficulty 704
  thrust 716
  passport 760
  gratuity 815
- *as property* 783,
  784
barely – 651
let it – 460
make a – at 716
pretty – 704
– away
  cease to exist 2
  end 67
  transient 111
  past 122
  cease 142
  die 360
– by *course* 109

inattention 458
neglect 460
disrespectful 929
– comprehension
  519
– current 484
– an examination
  648, 873
– the eyes over
  457
– the fingers over
  379
– into one's hand
  785
– through one's
  hands 625
– into 144
– judgment 480
– a law 963
– in the mind 451
– muster
  conform to 82
  sufficient 639
  good 648
  approbation 931
barely – muster
  651
– under the name
  of 564
– off *be past* 122
  egress 295
– off for 544
– on 282
– an opinion 480
– to the order of
  the day 624
– out of 295
– over
  exclude 55
  cross 302
  give 784
  forgive 918
  exemption 927*a*
– over to 709
– and repass 302,
  314
– in review 457,
  461
– the Rubicon 609
– sentence on **971**
– time *exist* 1
  time 106
  do nothing 681
– one's time in
  625
– to 144
– through
  event 151
  motion 302
– one's word **768**
passable *small* 32

unimportant 643
imperfect 651
pretty 845
passado 716
passage [*see* pass]
  part 51
  conversion 144
  street 189
  corridor 191
  opening 260
  navigation 267
  moving through
    302
  music 413
  - *in a book* 593
  action 680
  cut a – 260
  force a – 302
  – of arms 720
passant, en –
  transit 270
  incidentally 621
pass-book 811
passe: mot de –
  550
passé
  antiquated 124
  aged 128
  spoiled 659
passed away 122
passementerie 847
passenger 268
  – train 272
passe-partout
  key 260
  instrument 631
passer by 444
passer le temps,
  pour – 681
passerout pas, il ne
  717
passe-temps 840
passim
  dispersed 73
  place 182
  situation 183
passing *very* 31
  transient 111
  – bell 363
  – strange 870
  – word 527
pass-key 631
passion
  emotion 820, 821
  excitability 825
  pain 828
  desire 865
  love 897
  anger 900
  ruling – 606
Passion-week 998

passionate
  warm 825
  irascible 901
passionless 823
passive *inert* 172
  inaction 681
  obedient 743
  inexcitable 826
  – *resister* 489
passivity 172, 989
Passover 998
passport
  indication 550
  instrumentality
    631
  order 741
  permission 760
pass-word
  answer 462
  sign 550
  military 722
past 122
  danger – 664
  insensibility to
    the – 506
  obliteration of
    the – 506
  thing of the – 124
  – bearing 830
  – comprehension
    519
  – cure 859
  – dispute 474
  – praying for 945
  – one's prime 128
  – recollection 506
  – work
    useless 645
    impaired 659
paste *attach* 43
  cement 45
  to cement 46
  pulp 354
  sham 545
  tinsel 847
  scissors and – 609
pastel 556
pasteurize 652
pasticcio 21, 41
pastil 400
pastime 840
pastor 996
pastoral
  bucolic 370
  music 415
  poem 597
  religious 995
  sermon 998
pastorale 415
pastry *food* 298
  sweets 396

pasturage
  meadow 344
  herbage 367
pasture *food* 298
pasty *tart* 298
  like paste 352
pat *pertinent* 23
  strike 276
  (*expedient* 646)
  – on the back
  induce 615
  comfort 834
  encourage 861
  approve 931
  – on the cheek 902
  – on the head
  endearment 902
Patagonian 206
patch *small* 32
  change 140
  region 181
  blemish 848
  – up *restore* 660
  compromise 774
patchwork
  mixture 41
  discontinuous 70
  variegation 440
pate *summit* 210
  brain 450
patefaction 260
patella 191
paten 191
patent *open* 260
  manifest 525
  licence 760
  property 780
  – *medicine* 662
pater 166
  – *patriæ* 912
patera *cup* 191
  sacramental 998
paterfamilias 166
paternal
  father 166
  benevolent 906
  – *domicile* 189
paternity **166**
paternoster 990
path *direction* 278
  way 627
  cross the – 706
  secret – 530
pathetic 830
pathless
  spacious 180
  closed 261
  difficult 704
pathognomonic 550
pathology 655, 662
pathos 821

pathoscopic 820
pathway 627
patience
  perseverance 604a
  endurance 826
  cards 840
patient *sick* 655
patisserie 298
patois 563
patriæ: amor – 910
  pater – 912
patriarch
  family 11
  veteran 130
  ancestors 166
  priest 996
patriarchal
  ancient 124
  ancestral 166
patriarchate 737
patrician 875
patrilineal 11, 166
patrimony 780
patriot 910
patrol *walk* 266
  safeguard 664
  (*warning* 668)
patrolman 664
patron
  auxiliary 711
  customer 795
  friend 890
  benefactor 912
patronage
  influence 175
  aid 707
  authority 737
patronize 693, 707
patronymic 564
patten 225, 998
patter *strike* 276
  sound 407
  meaningless 417
  talk 584
  stage 599
patterer 582
pattern *model* 22
  perfection 650
  ornament 847
  – after 20
patte de
  – *mouche* 590
  – *velours* 544, 545
patulous 194
patty 298
pauciloquy 585
paucity *small* 32
  few 103
  scanty 640
paughty 878
Paul Jones 792

Paul Pry
curious 455
prattle 588
paulo post futurum
121
paunch 191, 250
pauper 804
pause
discontinue 70
cease 142
quiescence 265
doubt 485
irresolution 605
repose 687
pauvre diable 804
pavanne 840
pave 223
– the way 705
pavé, on the – 961
pavement *base* 211
covering 223
path 627
pavilion 189
paving 211
paviour 673
pavor 859
paw *touch* 379
retention 781
– the ivories 416
pawky 702
pawl 45
pawn 771
pawnbroker 787
pax *hush!* 403
– in bellow 723
– *vobiscum* 894
pay *paint* 223
profitable 775
defray 807
expend 809
income 810
punish 972
remunerate 973
in one's –
servant 746
hired 795
– in advance 809
– attention to 457
– back 718
– down 807
– dues 924
– in full 807
– homage
submission 725
worship 990
– the debt of
nature 360
– no attention &c.
to 458, 460
– through the

nose 814
– off 718
– off old scores 919
– old debts 807
– out 200, 972
– in one's own
coin 718
– the penalty 952
– the piper 707
– regard to 484
– one's respects
894
– too much 814
– a visit 892, 894
– one's way
defray 807
economy 817
paymaster 801
payment **807**
remuneration 973
paynim 984
pays, mal du –
regret 833
sociality 892
pea 249
peace
silence 403
concord 714
amity **721**
at – 714
commission of
the – 965
justice of the –
967
keep the –
moderation 174
concord 714
make – 723
make – with 831
Prince of – 976
speak – 831
peaceable
moderate 174
peaceably, get on –
736
peaceful
inexcitable 826
peace-maker 714
mediator 724
contented 831
peace-offering
pacification 723
mediation 724
gift 784
atonement 952
peach 529
peach-coloured 434
peacock
variegation 440
beauty 845
proud 878

vain 880
gaudy 882
jackdaw in –'s
feathers 701
pea-green 435
pea-jacket 225
peak *height* 206
summit 210
sharp 253
sicken 655
peaked 253
peaky 203
peal *loud* 404
roll 407
music 415
– of bells 407, 417
– of laughter 838
pearl *type* 591
goodness 648
ornament 847
glory 873
mother-of– 440
cast –s before
swine 638
pearly
semitransparent
427
colour 428
white 430
grey 432
variegated 440
pear-shape 249
peasant 876
peat 388
pebble *little* 193
hard 323
– dash 223
peccability 945
peccable 947
peccadillo 947
peccant *bad* 649
unclean 653
diseased 655
– *humour* 653, 655
peccavi 950
peck *much* 31
multitude 102
eat 298
– at *censure* 932
– of troubles
difficulty 704
adversity 735
pain 828
peckish 865
Pecksniff 548
pectinated 253
peculate 791
peculator 792
peculiar 79, 83
peculiarly 31, 33
pecuniary 800

pecunious 803
pedagogic 537
pedagogue
scholar 492
teacher 540
pedantic 855
pedagogy 537
pedal 633
– note 408
– point 416
pedant *scholar* 492
pedantic
half-learned 491
- *style* 577
affected 855
pedantry 481
peddle *meddle* 683
hawk 796
peddler 796, 797
peddling
trifling 643
miserly 819
pederero 727
pedestal 215
place on a – 307,
931
pedestrian 268
pedicel 215
pedicle 215
pedigree 69, 166
pediment 210, 215
pedlar 797
–'s French 563
pedometer 200
peduncle 215
peek 441
peel *layer* 204
skin 223
uncover 226
– off *separate* 44
peeler 664
peel-house 717
peep 441
– behind the cur-
tain 461
– of day 125
– into the future
510
– out 446, 529
peep-hole 260
peep-show 448, 840
peer *equal* 27
pry 441
inquire 461
lord 875
– out 446
peerless *supreme* 33
first rate 648
glorious 873
virtuous 944
peeved 900

firm 604
authoritative 737
rigorous 739
compulsory 744
duty 926
– denial 536
– refusal 764
perennial
continuous 69
diuturnal 110
– *plants* 367
perennius, ære –
873
pererration 266
perfect
great 31
entire 52
excellent 650
complete 729
perfection 650
bring to – 729
perfervidum in-
genium 682
perfidy 874, 940
perflate 349
perforate 260
perforator 262
perforce 601, 744
perform
produce 161
do 170
– *music* 416
action 680
achieve 729
fulfil 772
– a circuit 629
– a duty 926
– the duties of 625
– a function 644
– an obligation
772
– a part 599, 680
– a service 998
performable 470
performance
[*see* perform]
effect 154
performer
musician 416
stage-player 599
agent 690
affectation 855
perfume 400
perfunctory 53, 460
pergola 191
perhaps 470, 514
peri 845, 979
periapt 993
pericranium 450
periculous 665
peridot 847

perihelion 197
peril 665
at your – 909
take heed at
one's – 668
perilepsis 476
perimeter 230
period *end* 67
point 71
– *of time* 106, **108**
recurrence 138
at fixed –s 138
well rounded –s
577, 578
periodical
recurring 138
book 593
periodicity 138
peripatetic 266, 268
periphery 230
periphrase 566, 573
periplus 267
periscope 441, 445
periscopic 446
– *lens* 445
perish
cease to exist 2
be destroyed 162
die 360
decay 659
– *with cold* 383
– *with hunger* 956
perishable 111
perissology 573
peristaltic 248
peristyle 189
periwig 225
perjured 940
perjurer 548
perjury 544
perk *dress* 225
– *up elevate* 307
revive 689
perked up
proud 878
perky 880
perlustration 441
permanence
durability 110
unchanging **141**
unchangeable 150
permanent
habitual 613
permeable 260
permeate
insinuate 228
pervade 186
pass through 302
–d *with* 613
permissible 760
permission 760

permissive 760
permit 760
permitting
weather &c. – 469,
470
permutation
numerical – 84
change 140
interchange 148
pernicious 649
pernicity 274
perorate
diffuse style 573
peroration
sequel 65
end 67
speech 582
perpend *think* 451
perpendicular 212
perpension
attention 457
perpetrate 680
– a pun &c. 842
perpetrator 690
perpetua, esto –
928, 931
perpetual 112
frequent 136
– *curate* 996
– *motion* 467
perpetuate 112
continue 143
establish 150
perpetuity 69, **112**
perplex *derange* 61
distract 458
uncertainty 475
bother 830
perplexed 59, 248
perplexity
disorder 59
uncertainty 475
unintelligibility
519
difficulty 704
perquisite 775, 973
perquisition 461
perron 627
perscrutation 461
persecute
oppress 649
annoy 830
malevolence 907
perseverance 143,
604a
Persides 215
persiflage 842, 856
persifleur 844
persist *duration* 106
permanence 141
continue 143

persevere 604a
persistence
diuturnity 110
person 3, 372
without distinc-
tion of –s 922
persona grata 890,
899
personable 845
personæ, dramatis
– 599, 690
personage 372
personal
[*see* person]
special 79
subjective 317
– *narrative* 594
– *property* 780
– *remarks* 932
– *security* 771
personality
[*see* personal]
discourtesy 895
disrespect 929
censure 932
detraction 934
personalty 780
personate 19, 554
personify 521, 554
personnel 56, 590
perspective
view 448
expectation 507
painting 556
aerial – 428
in – 200
perspicacity
sight 441
intelligence 498
fastidiousness 868
perspicuity
intelligibility 518
style **570**
perspiration 295,
299
in a – 382
perstringe 457
persuadable 602
persuade *belief* 484
induce 615
persuasibility
willingness 602
persuasion
class 75
opinion 484
teaching 537
inducement 615
religious – 983
persuasive
reasoning 476
pert

photogravure 558
photolysis 49
photometer 445
photosphere 318
photostat 553
phrase *part* 51
  music 413
  language **566**
phrasemonger 577
phraseology 569
phrenetic 503
phrenitis 503
phrenology 450
phrenotypics 505
Phryne 962
phthisozoics 361
phylacteric
  sorcery 992
phylactery
  maxim 496
  spell 993
physic
  cure 660
  remedy 662
physical 316
  – education
  material 316
  teaching 537
  – force
  strength 159
  compulsion 744
  – nature 3
  – pleasure **377**
  – pain **378**
  – science 316
physician
  remedy 662
  advice 695
Physics 316
physiognomy
  face 234
  appearance 448
  interpret 522
Physiology
  organization 357
  life 359
  Vegetable – 369
physique
  strength 159
  animality 364
phytivorous 298
Phytology 369
pi 591
piacere, al – 600
piacular 952
pianino 417
pianissimo 415
pianist 416
piano *gentle* 174
  music 415
  – organ 417

– player 417
pianoforte 417
pianola 417
piazza 189, 191
pibroch *music* 415
  war 722
pica 591
picaresco, gusto –
  945
picaroon 792
piccolo 410, 417
pick *axe* 253
  eat 298
  select 609
  best 648
  clean 652
  gain 775
  – a-back 215
  – the brains of 461
  – holes
  censure 932, 934
  – the lock 480a
  – me up 662
  – out *extract* 301
  select 609
  – to pieces
  separate 44
  destroy 162
  find fault 932
  – a quarrel 713
  – one's steps 459
  – up *learn* 539
  get better 658
  gain 775
  – one's way 675
pickaninny 129
pickaxe 253
picked 648
  – men 700
pickeer 791
pickeerer 792
pickelhaube
  armour 717
picket *join* 43
  locate 184
  fence 229
  guard 668
  defence 717
  soldiers 726
  restrain 751
  imprison 752
  torture 972
  – boat 273
pickings 775, 793
pickle *condition* 7
  macerate 337
  pungent 392
  condiment 393
  preserve 670
  difficulty 704
  have a rod in – 673

pickle-herring 844
pickpocket 792
  abuse like a – 932
pickthank *busy* 682
  servile 886
  flatterer 937
picnic *food* 298
  participation 778
  amusement 840
picquet 840
pictorial
  painting 556
  beauty 845
picture
  appearance 448
  representation
  554
  painting 556
  description 594
  – to oneself 515
picture-gallery 556
picture-theatre 599
picturesque
  painting 556
  beauty 845
piddle *dawdle* 683
piddling *trivial* 643
pidgin **English** 563
pie *food* 298
  sweet 396
  printing 591
piebald 440
piece *adjunct* 59
  bit 31
  painting 556
  drama 599
  cannon 727
  coin 800
  courtesan 962
  fall to –s 162
  go to –s 162
  in –s 330
  of a – 42
  pull to –s 162
  give a – of advice
  695
  – of good fortune
  618
  – of music 415
  – of news 532
  – out 52
  – together 43
  – of work 713
  make a – of work
  about 642
pièce
  – justificative 467
  – de résistance 298
piecemeal 51
pied *variegated* 440
pied de la lettre,

au – 494
pie-poudre, **court**
  of – 966
pier 189, 666
pierce
  perforate 260
  bodily pain 378
  chill 385
  hurt 649
  wound 659
  affect 824
  mental pain 830
  – the head 410
  – the heart 830
piercer 262
piercing *cold* 383
  loud 404
  shrill 410
  intelligent 498
  feeling 821
  – eye 441
  – pain 378
pier-glass 445
Pierian spring 597
pierre fendre, à –
  383
Pierrot 599
pietas 998
piété, mont de –
  787
pietism 988
pietist 987, 988
piety **987**
pig *animal* 366
  sensual 954a
  – in a poke
  uncertain 475
  chance 621
  rash 863
  – together 72
pigeon
  dupe 547
  steal 791
  gorge de – 440
pigeon-hearted 862
pigeon-hole 191,
  260
piggin 191
piggish 954
pig-headed 499, 606
pigment 428
pigmy 193
pignoration 771
pignus 771
pig-sticking 361
pigsty 653
pigtail 214
pigwidgeon 193,
  980
pike *hill* 206
  sharp 253

pitched battle 720
pitcher 191
pitchfork 273, 284
  rain –s 348
pitch-pipe 417
piteous 830
piteously *much* 31
pitfall 545, **667**
pith *gist* 5
  strength 159
  interior 221
  centre 222
  meaning 516
  important part
  642
pithless 158
pithy *meaning* 516
  concise 572
  vigorous 574
pitiable *bad* 649
  painful 830
  contemptible 930
pitied, to be – 828
pitiful
  unimportant 643
  bad 649
  disrepute 874
  pity 914
pitiless **914a**
  revengeful 919
pittance
  quantity 25
  dole 640
  allotment 786
  income 810
pitted 848
pituitous 352
pity **914**
  express – 915
  what a –
  regret 833
  lament 839
  for –'s sake 914
pivot *junction* 43
  cause 153
  support 215
  axis 222, 312
pix *box* 191, 998
  assay 463
pixy 980
pizzicato 415
placable 918
placard 531
placate 723, 918
place
  circumstances 8
  order 58
  arrange 60
  term 71
  situation **182**, 183

locate 184
abode 189
office 625
rank 873
give – to 623
have – 1
in – 183
in – of 147
make a – for 184
out of – 185
take – 151
– to one's credit
  805
– itself 58
– in order 60
– upon record 551
– under
  include 76
placebit, decies re-
  petita – 829
placebo 933
place-hunter 767
placeman 758
placet 488, 741
placid 826
placket 260
plagiarism
  imitation 19
  borrowing 788
  theft 791
plagiarist 792
Plagiary, Sir
  Fretful – 901
plagiedral 217
plague *disease* 655
  pain 828
  worry 830
plague-spot 657
plaguy 704, 830
plaid *shawl* 225
  variegation 440
plaidoyer 476
plain
  horizontal 213
  country **344**
  obvious 446
  meaning 518
  manifest 525
  style 576
  artless 703
  ugly 846
  simple 849
speak –ly 576
tell one –ly 527
– English 576
– dealing 543
– interpretation
  522
– question 461
– sailing 705
– sense 498

– speaking 525,
  703
– terms
  intelligible 518
  interpreted 522
  language 576
  – truth 494
– words 703
plainness **576**
plainsong 990
plain-spoken 525,
  703
plaint 411, 839
plaintiff 938
plaintive 839
plaisance
  [*see* pleasance]
plaisanterie 842
plaister 223
plait 219, 258
plan *itinerary* 266
  information 527
  representation
  554
  scheme **626**
  according to – 82
planchette 992
plane *horizontal* 213
  flat 251
  smooth 255
  fly 267
  aeroplane 273
  soar 305
  inclined – 633
planet *world* 318
  luminary 423
  fate 601
planet-struck
  adversity 735
  wonder 870
planimeter 466
planish 255
plank *board* 204
  programme 626
  path 627
  safety 666
plant *place* 184
  insert 300
  vegetable 367
  agriculture 371
  trick 545
  tools 633
  property 780
– a battery 716
– a dagger in the
  breast 830
– oneself 184
– a thorn in the
  side 830
plantation
  location 184

agriculture 371
estate 780
planter 188
planter ses choux,
  aller – 893
plaque 204
plash *lake* 343
  stream 348
  sound 405, 408
plashy 345
plasm 22
plasma 847
plasmic 240
plaster *cement* 45
  covering 223
  remedy 662
– up *repair* 660
plastered 959
plastic *alterable* 149
  form 240
  soft 324
– arts 557
plastron 717
plat *weave* 219
  ground 344
plate *dish* 191
  layer 204
  covering 223
  flat 251
  food 298
  engraving 558
  – layer 690
  – printing 558,
  591
plateau 213, 344
plated 545
platform
  horizontal 213
  support 215
  stage 542
  scheme 626
  arena 728
– orator 582
platinum-blond 430
platitude 517, 843
Platonic
  contemplative 451
  inexcitable 826
  chaste 960
  – bodies 244
Platonism 451
platoon 726
– fire 716
platter 191
  layer 204
  flat 251
clean the outside
  of the – 544
plaudit 931
plausible
  probable 472

porch *entrance* 66
lobby 191
mouth 231
opening 260
church 1000
porcupine 253, 901
pore *opening* 260
egress 295
conduit 350
– over *look* 441
apply the mind 457
learn 539
porism 461, 480
pornographic 961
porous 260
porpoise 192
porridge 298
porringer 191
port *abode* 189
sinistral 239
gait 264
arrival 292
carriage 448
harbour 666
in – 664
make – 666
– admiral 745
– fire 388
– wine 959
portable *small* 193
transferable 270
light 320
portage 270
portal *entrance* 66
mouth 231
opening 260
portative 193, 270
portcullis 706, 717
let down the – 666
porte-monnaie 802
portend 511
portent 512
portentous
prophetic 511
fearful 860
porter *janitor* 263
carrier 271, 690
porterage 270
portfolio *case* 191
book 593
magazine 636
direction 693
insignia 747
porthole 260
portico 66, 191
portion 51, 786
– out 786
portly 192
portmanteau 191

– word 116
portrait 554
portrait painting 556
portrait painter 559
portraiture 554, 556
portray 19, 554
portreeve 745, 965
posada 189
pose *situation* 183
form 240
puzzle 475
difficulty 704
affectation 855
– as 554
strike a – 855
posited 184
position
circumstances 8
term 71
situation 183
proposition 514
assertion 535
– in society 873
positive *real* 1
great 31
strict 82
certain 474
narrow-minded 481
belief 484
unequivocal 518
assertion 535
obstinate 606
absolute 739
Philosophie – 316
– colour 428
– degree 31
– fact 474
– quantity 84
positivism 984, 989
posnet 191
posology 662
posse 72, 712
in – 470
– comitatûs
collection 72
army 726
authority 737
jurisdiction 965
possess 777
– knowledge 490
– the mind 484
– oneself of 789
– the soul 824
– a state 7
possessed with a devil 503
possession 777, 780
sorcery 992
come into – 775,

783
in one's – 777
person in – 779
put one in – of 527
remain in – of the field 731
possessor 779
posset 298
possibility
chance 156
liability 177
may be 470
property 780
– upon a possibility 475
possidetis, uti –
possession 777
retention 781
post *fastening* 45
situation 183
location 184
support 215
transmit 270
swift 274
publish 531
mail 534
beacon 550
record 551
employment 625
accounts 811
stigmatize 874
punish 972
at one's –
persist 604a
prepared 673
on duty 926
sign – 550
stand like a – 265
– hoc ergo propter hoc 477
drive from – to pillar 704
postal order 800
postboy 268
post-card 592
postcenal 117
post-chaise 272
postcibal 117
post-date 115
post-diluvial 117
postfix 37
postprandial 117
post-war 116
poster 531
posterior
in order 63
in time 117
in space 235
posteriority 117
posterity 121, 167
hand down to –

551, 873
postern *portal* 66
back 235
opening 260
post-existence 152
post-graduate 492
– student 541
post-haste
swift 274
haste 864
rash 863
post-horse 271
posthumous 117, 133
– fame 873
postilion 268, 694
postliminious 117, 133
postman 534
post-meridiem 126
post-mortem 360, 363
postnate 117
post-obit 360, 363
post-office 534
– order 800
– red 434
postpone 133
postscript 39, 65
postulant
asking 765
petitioner 767
nun 996
postulate 496
reasoning 476
supposition 514
postulation
supposition 514
request 765
posture
circumstance 8
situation 183
form 240
posture-master 599, 844
posy *motto* 550
poem 597
flowers 847
pot *much* 31
mug 191
heat 384
saucepan 386
preserve 670
death in the – 657
go to – 162, 732
keep the – boiling 143, 682
make the – boil 775
le – au lait
imagination 515

hope 858	*bruise* 330	*loud* 404	*medical* - 662
potable 298	*imprison* 752	- *of style* 574	*doer* 690
potage 298	– together 41	*authority* 737	**præcognita** 467
potager 191	**poundage** 813	do all in one's –	**prænomen** 564
potation 298, 959	**pounds, shillings,**	686	**prætor** 967
pot-bellied 194	**and pence** 800	give – 760	**Pragmatic**
pot-companion 890	**pour** *emerge* 295	in the – of	**Sanction** 769
potency 157	*stream* 348	*authority* 737	**pragmatical** 855,
potent 157, 159	*sufficient* 639	*subjection* 749	880
potentate 745	it never rains but	literary – 569	**pragmatism** 677
potential	it –s 641	- of attorney 755	**prahu** 273
inexistent 2	– out blood like	– behind the	**prairie** *space* 180
potentiality 157,	water 361	throne 694	*plain* 344
470	– a broadside into	- of money 800	*vegetation* 367
pother *disorder* 59	716	**powerful** 159, 171	**praise** *thanks* 916
feeling 821	– forth *eject* 297	– voice 580	*commendation*
excitement 825	*speak* 582	**powerless** 158, 160	931
annoyance 830	*loquacity* 584	**powers that be** 745	*worship* 990
pot-herbs 393	– forth like water	**pow-wow** 588, 696	**praiseworthy** 931,
pot-hooks 590	818	**pox** 655	944
pot-house 189	– in *converge* 290	**praam** 273	**prame** 273
pot-hunter 767	*ingress* 294	**practicable** 470, 644	**prance** 266, 315
potion	*sufficiency* 639	**practical**	**prandial** 298
beverage 298	– on *lavish* 784	*acting* 170	**prank** *caprice* 608
medicine 662	– with rain 348	*expedient* 646	*amusement* 840
cordial 992	– water into a	*executive* 692	*adorn* 847
pot-luck *eating* 298	sieve 638, 818	– joke	**prate** 584
chance 621	– out 295, 297	*absurdity* 497	**prattle** 582, 584
non-preparation	**pourboire** 784	*deception* 545	**pravity** 945
674	**pourparler**	*ridicule* 856	**praxis**
take – with 892	*interlocution* 588	*disrespect* 929	*grammar* 567
Potosi 803	*advice* 695	– knowledge 698	*action* 680
pot-pourri	*council* 696	**practically**	**Praxiteles** 559
mixture 41	**pout** *project* 250	*intrinsically* 5	**pray** 765, 990
fragrance 400	*sad* 837	**practice**	**prayer** 765, 990
music 415	*discourteous* 895	*arithmetic* 85	house of – 1000
pottage 298	*irate* 900	*training* 537	**prayer-book** 998
pottering 682, 683	*sulky* 901a	*habit* 613	**preach** *teach* 537
pottery *baked* 384	**poverty**	*conduct* 692	*speak* 582
art 557	*insufficiency* 640	in – *prepared* 673	*predication* 998
pottle 191	*unimportance* 643	*skilled* 698	– to the winds 645
potulent 298, 959	*indigence* **804**	put in – *use* 677	– to the wise 538
pot-valiant 959	- of intellect 499	*action* 680	**preacher**
potwalloper 876	**powder** 330	*conduct* 692	*teacher* 540
pouch 191	*cosmetics* 847	*complete* 729	*priest* 996
poudre:	food for – 726	out of – 699	**preachment** 998
qui n'a pas	gun– 727	- of medicine 662	**preadamite** 124,
inventé la –	smell – 722	**practise** *train* 537	130
501, 701	keep one's – dry	*use* 677	**preamble** 64
jeter de la – aux	673	*act* 680	**preapprehension**
yeux 442	– and shot 727	– at the bar 968	481
poultice *pulp* 354	waste – 638	– on one's credu-	**prebend** 995
remedy 662	not worth – 645	lity 545	**prebendary** 996
relief 834	**powdered**	– upon	**precarious**
poultry 298, 366	*variegated* 440	*experiment* 463	*transient* 111
pounce upon	**powdering**	*deceive* 545	*uncertain* 475
unexpected 508	*ornament* 847	**practised**	*dangerous* 665
attack 716	**power**	*skilled* 698	**precatory** 765
seize 789	*much* 31, 102	– eye 700	**precaution**
pound *inclose* 232	*numerical* 84	– hand 700	*care* 459
weight 319	*efficacy* **157**	**practitioner**	*expedient* 626

prepossessing 829
prepossession
  prejudice 481
  possession 777
preposterous
  great 31
  absurd 497
  exaggerated 549
  ridiculous 853
  undue 925
prepotency 157
pre-Raphaelite 122, 124, 556
pre-require 630
pre-resolve 611
prerogative 737, 924
presage 511, 512
presbyopia 443
presbyter 996
Presbyterian 984
presbytery 995, 996, 1000
prescience 510
prescious 511
prescribe *direct* 693
  advice 695
  order 741
  entitle 924
  enjoin 926
prescript 697, 741
prescription
  remedy 662
prescriptive *old* 124
  unchanged 141
  habitual 613
  due 924
presence
  in space **186**
  appearance 448
  breeding 894
  in the – of
  near 197
  real – 998
  saving one's – 928
  – of God 981
  – of mind 826, 864
presence-chamber 191
present
  - *in time* 118
  - *in space* 186
  offer 763
  give 784
  church prefer-ment 995
  at – 118
  these –s 590, 592
  – arms 894, 928
  – a bold front 861

– a front 719
– itself *event* 151
  visible 446
  thought 451
– oneself
  presence 186
  offer 763
  courtesy 894
– to the mind 457, 505
– *time* **118**
  instant 113
– to the view 448
presentable 852
presentation 883, 894
presentiment
  instinct 477
  prejudgment 481
  foresight 510
presently 132
presentment
  information 527
  law proceeding 969
preservation
  continuance 141
  conservation **670**
  Divine attributes 976
preserve *sweets* 396
preserver 664
preshow 511
preside 693, 737
presidency 737
president 694, 745
press *crowd* 72
  closet 191
  weight 319
  public - 531
  printing 591
  book 593
  move 615
  compel 744
  offer 763
  solicit 765
  go to – 591
  under – of 744
  writer for the – 593
  – of business 682
  – one hard 716
  – in 300
  – on *course* 109
  progression 282
  haste 684
  – into the service 677, 707
  – out 301
press-agent 599
pressed: hard – 704

– for time 684
press-gang 965
pressing *need* 630
  urgent 642
pressure *power* 157
  influence 175
  weight 319
  urgency 642
  exertion 686
  adversity 735
  centre of – 222
  high – 824
  work under – 684
Prester John 515
prestidigitation 545
prestidigitator 548
prestige *bias* 481
  authority 737
  fascination 865
  fame 873
prestigiation 545
prestissimo 415
presto
  instantly 113
  music 415
prestriction 442
presumable 472
presume
  misjudge 481
  believe 484
  suppose 514
  hope 858
  pride 878
presumption
  [*see* presume]
  probability 472
  expectation 507
  rashness 863
  arrogance 885
  unlawfulness 925
presumptive
  probable 472
  supposed 514
  due 924
  heir – 779
  – evidence
  evidence 467
  probability 472
presumptuous 885
presuppose
  misjudge 481
  suppose 514
presurmise 510, 514
pretence
  imitation 19
  falsehood 544
  untruth 546
  excuse 617
  ostentation 882
  boast 884

pretend *assert* 535
  simulate 544, 546
pretended 545
pretender
  deceiver 548
  braggart 884
  unentitled 925
pretending 544
pretension
  ornament 577
  affectation 855
  due 924
pretentious
  affected 855
  vain 880
  ostentatious 882
  boasting 884
  undue 925
preterite 121
preterition **122**
preterlapsed 122
pretermit 460
preternatural 83
preterperfect 122
pretext 546, 617
pretty
  much 31
  imperfectly 651
  beautiful 845
  – fellow 501
  – good 651
  – kettle of fish, pass &c. 59, 704
  – well *much* 31
  little 32
  trifling 643
preux chevalier 939
prevail *exist* 1
  superior 33
  general 78
  influence 175
  habit 613
  succeed 731
  – upon 615
prevailing 78
  – taste 852
prevalence
  [*see* prevail]
prevaricate 544
prévenance 894
prevenient 62, 132
prevention
  prejudice 481
  hindrance 706
  – of waste 817
preventive 55
preventorium 656
previous 116
  move the – question 624
  not within –

experience 137
prevision 510
pre-war 116
prewarn 668
prey *food* 298
  quarry 620
  booty 793
  victim 732, 828
  fall a – to
  be defeated 732
  subjection 749
  – to grief 828
  – to melancholy
   837
  – on the mind
  excite 824
  regret 833
  fear 860
  – on the spirits
   837
price
  consideration 147
  value 648
  money **812**
  reward 973
  at any – 604*a*
  beyond – 814
  cheap at the – 815
  of great –
  good 648
  dear 814
  have one's – 812
price-current 812
priceless
  valueless 645
  dear 814
prick *sharp* 253
  hole 260
  sting 378
  sensation of touch
   380
  incite 615
  mental suffering
   830
  kick against the –s
  useless 645
  resistance 719
  – up one's ears
  hear 418
  curiosity 455
  attention 457
  expect 707
prickle 253, 380
pride
  ornament 847
  loftiness **878**
  take a – in 878
prie-dieu 211
priest 996
priestcraft 995
priesthood 995, 996

priest-ridden 988,
  995
prig *steal* 791
  puppy 854
  affected 855
  blusterer 887
priggish 855, 880
prim *affected* 855
  fastidious 868
  proud 878
prima: – donna
  actress 599
  important 642
  proficient 700
  – facie *sight* 441
  appearance 448
  probable 472
  - *meaning* 516
  manifest 525
primacy
  superiority 33
  celebrity 873
  church 995
primary
  original 20
  cause 153
  important 642
  – *colour* 428
  – *education* 537
primarily 66
primate 996
primates 875
prime
  primeval 124
  early 132
  teach 537
  important 642
  excellent 648
  prepare 673
  in one's – 131
  in the – of man-
   hood 159
  – cost *price* 812
  cheap 815
  – of life *youth* 127
  adolescence 131
  – and load 673
  – minister 694
  – of the morning
   125
  – mover 153
  – number 84
prime constituent 1
primed
  skilled 698
  tipsy 959
primer 542
primeval 124
  – forest 367
primigenous 124
primitive 124, 153

– colour 428
primogenial 66
primogeniture
  old 124
  age 128
  posterity 167
primordial 20, 124,
  153
primordinate 124
primrose-coloured
  436
primum:
  – mobile 153, 615
primus inter pares
  33
prince
  perfection 650
  master 745
  nobility 875
  – of darkness 978
princely
  authoritative 737
  liberal 816
  famous 873
  noble 875
  generous 942
princeps
  facile – 33
princess 745, 875
principal
  important 642
  director 694
  – part 31, 50
principality 181,
  780
principally 33
principia 66, 496
principiis obstare
  673
principle
  intrinsic 5
  rule 80
  cause 153
  element 316
  idea 453
  reasoning 476
  tenet 484
  maxim 496
  motive 615
  probity 939
  on – 615
  want of – 945
principled, high-
  939
prink 847, 882
print *copy* 21
  mark 550
  engraving 558
  letter-press 591
  out of – 552
printer 591

printing 531, **591**
  – telegraph 553
prior
  - *in order* 62
  - *in time* 116
  clergy 996
priori reasoning,
  a – 476
priority 116, 234
priory 1000
Priscian's head,
  break – 568
prism
  angularity 244
  optical 445
  see through a –
   443
prismatic
  colour 428
  variegated 440
prison **752**
  cast into – 751
  in – 754
prisoner **754**, 938
  take – 751, 789
prison-house
  secrets of the –
   529, 533
pristine 20, 122
prithee 765
prittle-prattle 588
private *special* 79
  hidden 528
  secluded 893
  to gain some –
   ends 943
  in – 528
  keep – 881
  talk to in – 586,
   588
  – road 627
  – soldier 726
privateer 726, 792
privateering 791
privately 881
privation 776, 804
privative 789
privilege
  freedom 748
  permission 760
  exemption 777*a*
  due 924
privity 490
privy *hidden* 528
  latrines 653
  – to 490
Privy Council 966
prize *good* 618
  palm 733
  gain 775
  booty 793

receipt 810
love 897
approve 931
reward 973
win the – 731
– open 173
prizer 767
prize-fighter 726
prize-fighting 720
prizeman 700
pro: – and con
　476, 615
– formâ 82
– hâc vice
　special 79
　present time 118
　occasion 134
　seldom 137
– rata 23
– re natâ
　circumstances 8
　relation 9
　special 79
　occasion 134
　conditions 770
– tanto 26, 32
– tempore 111
proa 273
probability 156, **472**
probable 858
probate 771
Probate Court 966
probation
　trial 463
　demonstration
　478
probationary 463,
　675
probationer 541
probative 478
probatum est 478,
　931
probe *depth* 208
　perforator 262
　investigate 461
　measure 466
probity **939**
problem *topic* 454
　question 461
　enigma 533
problematical 475
proboscis 250
procacity
　insolence 885
　rudeness 895
　irascibility 901
procedure
　method 627
　action 680
　conduct 692
proceed *time* 109

advance 282
– from 154
– with 692
proceeding
　incomplete 53
　event 151
　action 680
　not finished 730
　course of – 692
proceedings 551
proceeds *gain* 775
　money 800
　receipts 810
procerity 206
procès-verbal
　record 551
　law proceeding
　969
process
　projection 250
　conduct 692
　legal – 963
– engraving 558
– of time 109
in – of time 117
procession
　continuity 69
　march 266
　ceremony 882
processional
　rite 998
prochronism 115
proclaim 531
proclivity 176, 820
proconsul 759
proconsulship 737
procrastination 133,
　460, 683
procreant 168
procreate 161, 168
procreator 166
procrustean 82
– law 80
Procrustes:
　stretch on the bed
　of – 27
proctor *teacher* 540
　officer 694, 965
　consignee 758
　lawyer 968
proctorship 693
procumbent 213
procurator 694
procuration 170,
　755
procure *cause* 153
　induce 615
　get 775
　buy 795
procuress 962
procurement 170

prod 276
prodigal 641, 816
prodigality **818**
prodigious 31, 870
prodigy 83, **872**
– of learning 700
prodition 940
prodrome 64
produce
　increase 35
　cause 153
　effect 154
　create 161
　prolong 200
　show 525
　stage 599
　fru t 775
　merchandise 798
– itself 446
producer **164**
product
　multiple 85
　effect 154
　harvest 636
　gain 775
　finished – 154
production 54, **161**
　[*and see* pro-
　duce]
productive
　cause 153
　power 157
　inventive 515
　profitable 775
productiveness **168**
proem 64
proemial
　preceding in order
　62
　beginning 66
profane
　desecrate 679
　impious 988
　laical 997
– swearing 908
profanum vulgus
　876
profession
　assertion 535
　pretence 546
　business 625
　promise 768
　enter a – 625
– of faith 484, 983
professional 700
– mourner 363,
　839
professor 492, 540,
　700
professorship 542
proffer 763

proficient
　knowledge 490
　skill 698
　adept **700**
proficuous 644
profile
　outline 230
　side 236
　appearance 448
　portraiture 556
profit
　increase 35
　advantage 618
　utility 644
　acquisition 775
– by *use* 677
– sharing 778
profitable
　useful 644
　good 648
　gainful 775
profitless 646
profligacy 945
profluent
　progressive 282
　stream 348
profound
　great 31
　deep 208
　learned 490
　wise 498
　sagacious 702
　feeling 821
– attention 457
– knowledge 490
– secret 533
profundis, de –
　839, 950
profuse
　diffuse style 573
　redundant 641
　prodigal 818
profusion 102, 639
prog 298
progenerate 161
progenitive 163
progenitor 166
progeny 167
prognosis 510, 511,
　522, 655
prognostic 511, 512
prognosticate 511
prognostication 507
programme
　catalogue 86
　publication 531
　plan 626
progress
　growth 144
　motion 264
　advance 282

agreement 23
elegance 578
expedience 646
fashion 852
right 922
duty 926
proprio motu 600
props 599
propter hoc 155
propugn
resist 717
vindicate 937
propulsion 284
propylon 66
prore 234
prorogue 133
proruption 295
prosaic usual 82
- style 575, 576
dull 843
prosaism prose 598
proscenium
front 234
theatre 599
proscribe
interdict 761
banish 893
curse 908
condemn 971
prose
diffuse style 573
prate 584
not verse **598**
– run mad 517, 597
– writer 598
prosecute
pursue 622
act 680
accuse 938
arraign 969
– an inquiry 461
prosecutor 938
proselyte
convert 144, 607
learner 541
proselytism 537
proser 841
prosody 597
prosopopœia 521
prospect
futurity 121
view 448
probability 472
expectation 507
landscape paint-
ing 556
good – 858
in – intended 620
prospective 121
prospector 463
prospectus list 86

foresight 510
compendium 596
scheme 626
prosper 618
prosperity 734
prospicience 510
prosternation
dejection 837
servility 886
prostitute
corrupt 659
misuse 679
impure 961
courtesan 962
prostrate
powerless 158
destroyed 162
low 207
horizontal 213
depress 308
laid up 655
exhausted 688
dejected 837
servile 886
fall – 306
– oneself
servile 886
obeisance 928
worship 990, 991
prostration
[see prostrate]
submission 725
pain 828
prosy 841, 843
prosyllogism 476
protagonist
actor 599
proficient 700
protasis
precursor 64
beginning 66
maxim 496
protean 149
protect safe 664
protective 717
protection
influence 175
defence 717
restrain 751
protected cruiser
726
protector 664, 717
master 745
keeper 753
protectorate 737,
780
protégé servant 746
friend 890
proteiform 149
protein 298
semiliquid 352

organic 357
protervity 901
protest dissent 489
assert 535
deny 536
refuse 764
deprecate 766
not observe 773
not pay 808
counter – 468
enter a – 766
under – 603, 744
– against 708, 932
protestant 489, 764
Protestant 984
protested bills 808
Proteus 149
prothesis 1000
prothonotary 553
protocol scheme 626
compact 769
protogram 572
protoplasm
prototype 22
material 316
organization 357
protoplast 22
prototype 22
prediction 511
prototypal 20
protozoon 366
protract time 110
late 133
lengthen 200
diffuse style 573
protreptical 615
protrude 250
protuberance 250
protypify 511
proud 873, 878
– flesh 250
prove
arithmetic 85
turn out 151
try 463
demonstrate 478
affect 821
– one's case
vindication 937
– true 494
provender 298, 637
proverb 496
proverbe acting 599
proverbial 490
provide
furnish 637
– against
prepare 673
– against a rainy
day 817
provided

conditionally 8
qualification 469
supposition 514
well – 639
– for 803
providence
foresight 510
preparation 673
divine govern-
ment 976
Providence 976
special – 711
waiter on – 683,
831
provident
careful 459
wise 498
prepared 673
providential
opportune 134
fortunate 734
province
department 75
region 181
abode 189
office 625
provincial
[see province]
prejudiced 481
vulgar 851
provincialism
neology 563
provision food 298
supply **637**
preparation 673
wealth 803
– merchant 637
provisional
uncertain 475
circumstances 8
temporary 111
preparing 673
provisions
conditions 770
proviso 469, 770
provisory 111
provoke cause 153
incite 615
excite 824
vex 830
anger 900
– desire 865
– hatred 898
provoquant 824
provost master 745
deputy 759
prow 234
prowess 861
prowl walk 266
lurk 528
– after 622

proximate
  next 63
  near 197
  – *cause* 153
proximity *near* 197
  adjacent 199
proximo 121
proximus ardet
  danger 665, 667
proxy 634, 759
prude *affected* 855
  chaste 960
prudent
  careful 459
  wise 498
  economical 817
  cautious 864
prudery 855, 868
prudish 739
prune
  take away 38
  lop 201, 371
  repair 658
prunes and prisms
  855
prunello, leather
  or – 643
prurience 865, 961
Prussian blue 438
Prussic acid 663
pry *look* 441
  curiosity 455
  inquire 461
  – into the future
  510
Prytaneum 931
psalm 415, 990
psalm-book 998
psalmody 415, 998
psalter 998
psaltery 417
psephomancy 511
pseudo 17, 545
pseudoblepsis 443
pseudonym 565
pseudo-revelation
  986
pseudoscope 445
pshaw
  trifling 643
  excitement 825
psychiatry 662
psychical 450
psycho-analysis
  662
psychological
  moment 824
Psychology 450
Psychomancy 511
psycho-therapy 662
ptisan 662

ptomaine poisoning
  663
ptyalism 229
puberty 127
pubescent 131
public, general –
  372
make – 531
– enemy 891
– good 644
– opinion 488
– press 531
– school 542
– spirit 910
– welfare 910
publican 637
publication **531**
  production 161
  book 593
public-house 189
go to the – 959
publicist 593, 595,
  968
publicity 531
publicly rumoured
  532
publico, pro bono –
  644, 910
publish 531
– the banns 765
publisher 593
puce 433, 437
pucelage *youth* 127
  celibacy 904
  purity 960
Puck 980
play – 699
pucker *fold* 258
  anger 900
in a – 824
pudder
  disorder 59
pudding *food* 298
  soft 324
  pulpy 354
  sweets 396
in – time 132
Pudding, Jack –
  599
puddle 343
pudicity 960
pudor, proh –
  874
puerile *boyish* 129
  foolish 499
  feeble 575
  trifling 643
puerperal 161
puff *inflate* 194
  wind 349
  tartlet 396

exaggerate 482
  advertisement 531
  pant 688
  boast 884
  praise 931
  flatter 933
– of smoke 330
– out 194
– up *vanity* 880
puffed up
  exaggerated 482
  pride 878
puffer 935
puffery 884
puffy 194
pug *short* 201
  dog 366
  pugilist 726
pugh! 643
pugilism 720
pugilist 726
pugilistic 720
pugnacity 720, 901
puisné
  posterior 117
  young 127
puissant 157, 159
puke 297
pukka 494
pulchritude 845
pulcinella 599, 844
pule *cry* 411, 412
  weep 839
pull *superiority* 33
  influence 175
  row 267
  draw 285
  printing 591
a long and a
  strong – 709
strong – 636
– the check string
  142
– different ways
  713
– down 162, 308
– about one's ears
  308
– in 751
– an oar 680
– out 301
– to pieces
  separate 44
  destroy 162
  censure 932
  detract 934
– upon the purse
  814
– by the sleeve
  505
– the strings 631

– through 660,
  707
– together 709
– towards 288
– up *stop* 142
  rest 265
  root out 301
  reprimand 932
  accuse 969
– the wires 693
pulled down 160,
  688
pullet 129
pulley 633
Pullman car 272
pullulate
  produce 161
  multiply 168
  grow 194
pulmonary 349
pulmotor 349
pulp 354
pulpiness **354**
pulpit *rostrum* 542
  church 1000
the – 996
pulsate
  periodic 138
  oscillate 314
  agitate 315
pulsation
  feeling 821
pulse [see pulsate]
  vegetable 367
feel the –
  inquire 461
  test 463
pulsion 276
pultaceous 354
pulverize 330
  destroy 162
  dust 358
pulverulence **330**
pulvil 400
pummel
  [see pommel]
pump *shoe* 225
  water supply 348
  inquire 461
– up 349
pump-room
  house 189
  remedy 662
pun *similarity* 17
  absurdity 497
  ambiguity 520
  wit 842
punce 276
punch *mould* 22
  perforate 260
  perforator 262

end 67
stop 142
destroy 162
- *oneself* 361
– in force
complete 729
compel 744
– forth
expand 194
suggest 514
publish 531
assert 535
- *a question* 461
- *strength* 686
– forward
suggest 514
publish 531
ostentation 882
– one's hand to
  676
– the horses to 673
– in [*see below*]
– to inconvenience
  647
– a mark upon 457
– one's nose out of
  joint 33
– off *late* 133
divest 226
depart 293
plea 617
– on *clothe* 225
deceive 544
hasten 684
affect 855
– out [*see below*]
– on paper 551
– over 484, 731
– a question 461
– right 660
– the saddle on
  the right horse
  155
– the seal to 729,
  769
– to [*see below*]
– together *join* 43
combine 48
assemble 161
– one's trust in
  484
– up [*see below*]
– upon 545, 649
put in *arrive* 292
insert 300
– an affidavit 535
– hand 676
– one's head 514
– mind 505
– motion 264
– order 60

– the place of 147
– one's pocket 785
– practice 692
– remembrance
  505
– shape 60
– trim 60, 673
– the way of 470
– a word 582, 588
put out
destroy 162
outside 220
extinguish 385
darken 421
distract the atten-
  tion 458
uncertain 475
difficult 704
discontent 832
– of countenance
  874
oneself – of court
sophistry 477
bungling 699
– of gear 158
– of one's head
  458
– of joint 61
– of one's misery
  914
– to nurse 707
– of order 59
put to *attribute* 155
request 765
– the blush 879
– death 361
– the door 261
– it 704
– one's oath 768
– press 591
– the proof 463
– the question 830
– the rack 830
– rights 60
– sea 293
– shame 874
– silence 581
– the sword 361
– task 677
– use 677
– the vote 609
put up *assemble* 72
locate 184
store 636
– to auction 796
– for 865
– a petition ⎱ 765
– a prayer ⎰ 990
– for sale 796
– a shutter 424
– the sword 723

– to 615
– with 147, 826
putative
attributed 155
believed 484
supposed 514
putid 643
putrefy 653
putrescence 49
putrid 653
putsch 742
puttee 225
putter 683
putting the weight
  840
putty 45
puzzle *uncertain*
  475
conceal 528
enigma 533
– out 522
puzzled 475, 533
puzzle-headed 499
puzzling 519
pyæmia 655
pyjamas 225
Pylades and
  Orestes 890
pylon 206
pyramid *heap* 72
height 206
point 253
pyramids
billiards 840
pyre 363
pyriform 249
pyrology 282
pyromaniac 384,
  504, 913
pyromancy 511
pyrometer 389
pyrotechnics 423
pyrotechny 382
Pyrrhic victory 814
pyrrhonism 487,
  989
Pythagorean 953
Pythia *oracle* 513
Python, -ess 513
pyx *vessel* 191, 998
temple 1000

Q

Q-boat 726
Q.C. 968
Q.E.D. 478
quack *cry* 412
imposter 548

quackery
falsehood 544
want of skill 699
affectation 855
quacksalver 548
quad 189
quadragesima 956
quadrangle
four-sided 95
precinct 182
house 189
angular 244
quadrant 244, 247
quadrate with 23
quadratic 95
quadrature
four 95
angle 244
quadrennial 95
quadrible 96
quadrifid 97
quadriga 95, 272
quadrilateral
sides 236
angles 244
quadrille 840
quadripartition 97
quadrisection **97**
quadrivalent 95
quadroon 41
quadruped 366
quadruplet 96
quadruplex 96
quadruplication **96**
quære 461
quaff 298
– the bitter cup
  828
quaggy 345
quagmire
marsh 345
dirty 653
difficult 704
quail 860, 862
quaint *odd* 83
pretty 845
ridiculous 853
quake *oscillate* 314
shake 315
cold 383
fear 860
quakerish 826, 855
Quakerism 984
qualification
  [*see* qualify]
power 157
modification **469**
skill 698
discount 813
qualify *change* 140
modify 469

– upon the fretful
   porcupine 256
quilt *covering* 223
   variegated 440
quinary 98
quincunx 98
quinquarticular 99
quinquennium 108
quinquesection **99**
quinquifid 99
quint 98
quintain 620, 840
quintal 319
quinteron 41
quintessence 5
quintet 98, 415
quintuple 98
quinze 840
quip
   amusement 840
   wit 842
   ridicule 856
   disrespect 929
quire *singers* 516
   paper 593
   church 1000
quirk
   sophistry 477
   misjudgment 481
   caprice 608
   amusement 840
   wit 842
quirt 975
quis custodiet istos
   custodes? 459
quit *depart* 293
   relinquish 624
   pay 807
   – claim 927a
   – one's hold 782
   – of 776, 782
   – scores 807
qui-tam 969
quite 52
   – another thing
     10, 18
   – the reverse 14
   – the thing 23
quits *equal* 27
   atonement 952
be – with
   retaliation 718
   pay 807
quittance
   security 771
   payment 807
   forgiveness 918
   atonement 952
   reward 973
quiver
   receptacle 191

[610]

oscillation 314
agitation 315
shiver 383
store 636
feeling 821
fear 860
in a – 821, 824
– with rage 900
qui-vive 669
   on the – 459
Quixote, Don –
   504, 863
Quixotic 515, 863
Quixotism 825
quiz 856, 857
quizzical 853
quo animo 620
quoad minus 30
quod *prison* 752
   in – 754
quodlibet
   inquiry 461
   sophism 477
   wit 842
quoits 840
quondam 122
quorum 696
quot homines tot
   sententiæ 489,
   713
quota
   quantity 25
   contingent 786
   expenditure 809
   furnish its – 784
quotation
   imitation 19
   conformity 82
   price 812
   – marks 550
quote 82
   evidence 467
quoth 535, 582
quotidian 138
quotient 84
quotum 25

R

Ra 423, 979
R's, three – 537
rabbet 43
Rabbi 996
Rabbist 984
rabbit
   productive 168
rabble 72, 876
rabid *insane* 502
   emotion 821
   eager 865

angry 900
rabies 503
raccroc 156
race *relation* 11
   sequence 69
   kind 75
   lineage 166
   run 274
   stream 348
   conduit 350
   pungency 392
   course 622
   business 625
   haste 684
   career 692
   opposition 708
   contention 720
run a – 720
run in a – 680
run one's – 729
one's – is run 360
   – prejudice 479
race-course 728
racehorse
   horse 271
   swift 274
racing car 272
rack *receptacle* 191
   frame 215
   cloud 353
   physical pain 378
   purify 652
   moral pain 828
   torture 830
   punish 972
   instrument of
    torture 975
on the – 507
   – one's brains
    thought 451
    imagination 515
   –rent 810
go to – and ruin
   735
racket
   agitation 315
   loud 404
   roll 407
   scheme 626
   discord 713
racket-court 840
racketeer 913
racketeering 361,
   792
racketing 682, 840
rackets 840
rackety *loud* 404
raconteur 594
racy *strong* 171
   pungent 392
   - *style* 574

feeling 821
raddle *weave* 219
raddled *tipsy* 959
radiance *light* 420
   beauty 845
radiant
   diverging 291
   glorious 873
   – heat 420
radiate 73, 291
radiation 420
radiator 386
radical
   essential 5
   complete 52
   algebraic root 84
   cause 153
   important 642
   reformer 658
   party 712
   – change 146
   – cure 662
   – reform 658
radically 31
radication 613
radio 532
radio-active 171
radio-activity 420
radio-graph 421,
   554
radiogram
   wireless 532
   X-ray 554
radiometer 420, 445
radiomicrometer
   389
radiophone 418
radio star 899
radiotelegraph 534
radiotelephone 534
radium 423
radius 200, 202
radix 153
radoter 499
radoteur 501
raff 653, 876
raffle 156
Raffles
   thief 792
raft 273
rafter 215
rag 32
   tease 830, 856,
    929
ragamuffin 876
rage *violence* 173
   influence 175
   excitement 824,
    825
   fashion 852
   desire 865

angry 900
censure 932
punish 972
– out *affirm* 535
voice 580
speak 582
– out oaths 885, 908
rapacity
taking 789
stealing 791
avarice 819
greed 865
rape 791, 961
– oil 356
rapid 274
– slope 217
– strides
progress 282
velocity 274
– *succession* 136
rapids 348
rapier 727
rapine 791
rapparee 792
rappel 722
rapping, spirit –
992
rapport 9
rapports, sous tous
les – 494
rapprochement
714, 888
rapscallion 949
rapt *attention* 457
inattention 458
emotion 821
– in thought 451
raptorial 789, 791
rapture 827, 897
rapturous 827
rara avis
exceptional 83
good 648
famous 873
rare *exceptional* 83
few 103
infrequent 137
light 322
excellent 648
raree show 448, 840
rarefaction 194, 322
rari nantes 103
rarity 322
rasa, tabula – 552
rascal 941, 949
rascality 940
rase *obliterate* 552
rash
skin disease 655
reckless 863

rasher 204
rashness **863**
rasp 330, 331
rasper *difficult* 704
rasure 552
rat *recant* 607
smell a –
discover 480a
doubt 485
rataplan 407
rat-a-tat 407
ratchet 253
rate *degree* 26
motion 264
measure 466
estimation 480
price, tax 812
abuse 932
at a great – 274
rath *early* 132
fort 717
rather 32, 643
have – 609
– good 651
have – not 867
ratification
confirm 467
affirm 488
consent 762
compact 769
ratio *relation* 9
degree 26
proportion 84
apportionment
786
ratiocination 476
ration *quantity* 25
food 298
provisions 637
allotment 786
short –s 956
rational
– *quantity* 84
intellectual 450
judicious 498
sane 502
rationale *cause* 153
attribution 155
answer 462
interpretation 322
rationalism 476, 989
rationalization 60
rats in the upper
story 503
rattan 975
ratten 158
rattle *noise* 407
music 417
prattle 584
death – 360

watchman's – 669
– on 584
rattle-snake 913
rattle-traps 780
rattling 836
– pace 274
raucity 405, 410
raucous *hoarse* 581
ravage 162, 659
ravages of time 659
rave *madness* 503
excitement 824, 825
– against 932
ravel *untwist* 60
derange 61
entangle 219
difficulty 704
ravelin 717
ravelled 59
raven *black* 431
hoarse 581
gorge 957
– for 865
ravening 173, 865
ravenous 789, 865
raver 504
ravine *interval* 198
narrow 203
dike 259
channel 350
raving *mad* 503
feeling 821
excitement 824, 825
ravish *seize* 789
please 829
ravished
pleased 827
ravishment 824
raw *immature* 123
sensitive 378
cold 383
colour 428
unprepared 674
unskilled 699
– head and bloody
bones 860
– levies 726
– material 635
raw-boned 203
ray 420
– of comfort 831
rayah 745
rayless 421
raze 162
– to the ground
308
razor 253
cut a whetstone
with a – 638

misuse 679
unskilful 699
keen as a – 821
razzia
destruction 162
attack 716
plunder 791
re, in – 9
reabsorb 296
reach *degree* 26
equal 27
distance 196
fetch 270
arrive at 292
river 348
deceive 545
grasp 737
take 789
within – *near* 197
possible 470
– the ear
hearing 418
information 527
– of thought 498
– to *distance* 196
length 200
reach-me-down
673
reaction
compensation 30
reversion 145
counteraction 179
recoil 277
restoration 660
reactionary 145, 607
reactionist 710
read 522, 539
well – 490
– a lecture 537
readable 578
reader *teacher* 540
printer 591
clergyman 996
readership 542
readily 705
reading
speciality 79
knowledge 490
interpretation 522
learning 539
– glass 445
– in 995
reading-desk 1000
readjust 23, 27
readmit 296
ready
expecting 507
willing 602
useful 644
prepare 673

assent 488
concord 714
retaliate 718
re**c**iprocity 709
recision 38
recital 415
recitativo 415
recite
　enumerate 85
　speak 582
　narrate 594
reck 459
reckless
　careless 460
　defiant 715
　rash 863
recklessly profuse
　818
reckon *count* 85
　– among 76
　– upon 484, 507
　– with 807
　– without one's
　　host
　unskilful 699
　fail 732
　rash 863
reckoning
　numeration 85
　measure 466
　expectation 507
　payment 807
　accounts 811
　reward 973
　day of – 919
　out of one's – 704
reclaim *restore* 660
　command 741
　due 924
　atonement 952
reclaimed
　penitent 950
recline *lie flat* 213
　depress 308
　repose 687
　– on 215
recluse 893
recognition
　[*see* recognize]
　courtesy 894
　thanks 916
　means of – 550
recognizable 446,
　518
　– by 550
recognizance 771
recognize *see* 441
　attention 457
　discover 480a
　assent 488
　know 490

remember 505
understand 518
permit 760
recognized
　influential 175
　customary 613
　– maxim 496
recoil *reaction* 179
　repercussion **277**
　reluctance 603
　shun 623
　from which
　　reason –s 471
　– at *hate* 898
　– from *dislike* 867
recollect 505
recommence 66
recommend 695,
　931
　– itself
　approbation 931
recompense 790,
　973
reconcile *agree* 23
　pacify 723
　content 831
　forgive 918
　– oneself to 826
recondite 519, 528
recondition 660,
　790
reconnaissance 441
reconnoitre 441,
　461
reconsideration 451
　on – 658
reconstitute 660
reconstruct 660
reconvert 660
record **551**
　break the – 33
　court of – 966
　gramophone – 551
recorder **553**
　judge 967
recount 594
recoup 30, 790
recourse 677
recovery
　improvement 658
　reinstatement 660
　getting back 775
　restitution 790
　– of strength 689
recreant
　coward 862
　base 940
　knave 941
　vicious 945
　bad man 949
recreation 840

recrement 653
recriminate 932
recrimination 938
recrudescence 661
recruit *strength* 159
　learner 541
　provision 637
　health 654
　repair 658
　reinstate 660
　refresh 689
　aid 707
　auxiliary 711
　soldier 726
　beat up for –s
　　673, 707
rectangle 244
rectangular 214,
　244
rectify
　straighten 246
　improve 658
　re-establish 660
rectilinear 346
rectitude 939, 944
rector 694, 996
rectorship 995
rectory 1000
rectus in curiâ 946
reculer pour mieux
　sauter 673, 702
reculons, à – 283
recumbent 213, 217
recuperation 790
recuperative 660
recur
　repeat 104
　frequent 136
　periodic 138
　– to the mind 505
　– to 677
recure 660
recursion 292
recurvity 245
recusant
　dissenting 489
　denying 536
　disobedient 742
　refusing 764
　impenitent 951
　heterodox 984
red 434
　paint the town –
　　840
　turn – *feeling* 821
　– book *list* 86
　– coat 726
　– cross 662
　– flag 668
　– hot *great* 31
　violent 173

hot 382
emotion 821
excited **824**
　– letter 550, 883
　–letter day
　important 642
　rest 687
　amusement 840
　celebration 883
　– light 669
　– rag to a bull 900
　– republican 742
　– tape 613
　– tapist 694
　– and yellow 439
redact 590, 658
redan 717
redargue 479
red cap 271
redden *colour* 434
　humble 879
　angry 900
reddition
　interpretation 522
　restitution 790
redeem
　compensate 30
　substitute 147
　reinstate 660
　deliver 672
　regain 775
　restore 790
　pay 807
　atone 952
　– from oblivion
　　505
　– one's pledge
　　772, 926
Redeemer 976
redemption
　[*see* redeem]
　liberation 750
　duty 926
　salvation 976
red-handed
　murder 361
　in the act 680
　guilty 947
redict 905
redingote 225
redintegrate 660
redintegratio
　amoris 607
redivivus 660
redness **434**
redolence
　odour 398
　fragrance 400
redouble
　increase 35
　duplication 90

reliquary 191, 998
reliquiæ 362
relish *pleasure* 377
  savour 390
  condiment 393
  savoury 394
  delight 827
  desire 865
relive 660
relucent 420
reluct 720
reluctance
  dissuasion 616
  unwilling 603
  dislike 867
reluctation 719
relume 384, 420
rely 484, 858
rem acu tetigisti 23
remain *be left* 40
  endure 106
  long time 110
  continue 141
  be present 186
  stand 265
  – firm 150
  – on one's hands
    641
  – in one's mind
    505
  – neuter 605
  – in possession of
    the field 731
remainder 40
  estate 780
  in – *posterior* 117
remainder-man 779
remains
  remainder 40
  corpse 362
  vestige 551
  organic – 357
remand *defer* 133
  order 741
remanet 40
remark *observe* 457
  affirmation 535
  worthy of – 642
remarkable
  great 31
  exceptional 83
  important 642
remarry 903
Rembrandtesque
  160
remediable, reme-
  dial 660, 662
remediless 859
remedy 660, **662**
remembrance 505
remembrances 894

rememoration 505
remigration
  regression 283
  arrival 292
  egress 295
remind 505
  that –s me 134
reminiscence 505
remise 927*a*
remiss
  neglectful 460
  reluctant 603
  idle 683
  lax 738
remission
  cessation 142
  moderation 174
  laxity 738
  forgiveness 918
  exemption 927*a*
remit
  [*see* remission]
  – one's efforts 681
remittance 807
remittent
  periodic 138
remitter 790
remnant 40
remodel
  convert 144
  revolutionize 146
  improve 658
remonstrance 615,
  766, 932
remora *cohere* 46
  hindrance 706
remorse 950
remorseless 919
remote 10, 196
  – age 122
  – cause 153
  – future 121
remotest idea, not
  have – 491
remotion 270
remount 147
remove *subduct* 38
  term 71
  displace 185
  transfer 270
  recede 287
  depart 293
  dinner 298
  extract 301
  school 541
  – the mask 529
removedness
  distance 196
remugient 412
remunerate 973
remunerative 644,

775
renaissance 660
renascence 660
renascent 163
rencounter
  contact 199
  meeting 292
  fight 720
rend 44
  – the air 404, 411,
    839
  – the heart-strings
    830
render *convert* 144
  interpret 522
  give 784
  restore 790
  – an account
    inform 527
    describe 594
  – *hors de combat* 645
  – a service 644
rendering
  covering 223
rendezvous 72, 74
rendition
  interpretation 522
  restore 790
renegade
  convert 144
  turncoat 607
  fugitive 623
  apostate 941
renew *twice* 90
  repeat 104
  reproduce 163
  recollect 505
  improve 658
  restore 660
  – one's strength
    689
reniform 245
renitence
  counteraction 179
  hardness 323
  elasticity 325
  unwillingness 603
  resistance 719
renitency
  light 420
renounce
  recant 607
  relinquish 624
  resign 757
  abnegate 764
  - *property* 782
  repudiate 927
renovare dolorem,
  infandum – 833
renovate 160, 660
renovated *new* 123

renown 873
renownless 874
rent *tear* 44
  fissure 198
  hire 788
  purchase 795
rental 810
renter 188, 779
rent-free 815
rent-roll 780, 810
rents *houses* 189
renunciation
  [*see* renounce]
  exemption 927*a*
reorganize
  order 60
  convert 144
  improve 658
  restore 660
repair
  mend 658
  make good 660
  refresh 689
  out of – 659
  – to 266
reparation
  [*see* repair]
  compensation 30
  restitution 790
  atonement 952
  reward 973
repartee 462, 842
reparteeist 844
repartition 786
repass, pass and –
  314
repast 298
repatriation 790
repay 790, 807, 973
repeal 756
repeat *imitate* 19
  duplication 90
  iterate 104
  reproduce 163
  affirm 535
  – by rote 505
repeated 104, 136
repeater
  watch 114
  fire-arm 727
repel *repulse* 289
  deter 616
  defend 717
  resist 719
  refuse 764
  give pain 830
  disincline 867
  banish 893
  excite hate 898
repent 950
repercussion 277

répertoire 599
repertory 636
repetend
  arithmetical 84
  iteration 104
repetition 19, **104**
repine
  pain 828
  discontent 832
  regret 833
  sad 837
replace
  substitute 147
  locate 184
  restore 660
replenish 52, 637
repletion
  filling 639
  redundance 641
  satiety 869
replevin
  recovery 775
  borrow 788
  restore 790
replica 21
replication
  answer 462
  law pleadings 969
reply 462, 937
répondre en
  Normand 544
report *noise* 406
  judgment 480
  inform 527
  publish 531
  news 532
  rumour 532
  record 551
  statement 594
  good – 873
  through evil re-
    port and good –
    604a
  – progress 527
reporter
  informant 527
  messenger 534
  recorder 553
  journalist 593,
    758
reports *law* 969
repose
  quiescence 265
  leisure 685
  rest **687**
  – confidence in
    484
  – on *support* 215
  evidence 467
  – on one's laurels
    142

reposit 184
repository 636
repostum, manet
  alta mente –
  919
repoussé 250
reprehend 932
reprehensible 945,
  947
represent *similar* 17
  imitate 19
  exhibit 525
  intimate 527
  declare 535
  denote 550
  delineate 554
  commission 755
  deputy 759
  – to oneself 515
representation
  [*see* represent]
  copy 21
  portrait **554**
  drama 599
representative
  typical 79
  commissioner 758
  deputy 759
  – government 737
  – of the people 696
  – of the press
  messenger 534
  writer 593
repress 751
  – one's feelings
    826
  – a smile 837
reprieve
  respite 133, 970
  deliverance 672
  release 750
  pardon 918
reprimand 932
reprint
  copy 21
  repetition 104
  reproduce 183
reprisal
  retaliation 718
  resumption 789
reprise 40a
reproach
  disgrace 874
  blame 932
  accusation 938
reprobate
  disapproved 932
  vicious 945
  bad man 949
  sinner 988

reprobation 932,
  988
reproduce
  imitate 19
  repeat 104
  renovate 163
reproduction [*see*
  reproduce] 21,
  163
reproductive 163
reproof 932
reprover 936
reptile
  animal 366
  servile 886
  knave 941
  miscreant 949
republic
  country 181
  people 372
  government 737
  – of letters 560
republican
  party 712
  government 737
  commonalty 876
republicanism 737
repudiate
  exclude 55
  deny 489
  reject 610
  abrogate 756
  violate 773
  not pay 808
  evade 927
repugn 719
repugnance
  incongruity 24
  resistance 719
  dislike 867
  hate 898
repulse *recoil* 277
  repel 289
  resist 719
  failure 732
  refusal 764
repulsion 157, **289**
repulsive
  [*see* repulse]
  unsavoury 395
  painful 830
  ugly 846
  disliked 867
  discourteous 895
  hateful 898
repurchase 795
reputable 873, 939
reputation 873
repute **873**
request **765**
  in – 630

– permission 760
requiem 839
requies, nec mora
  nec – 682
requiescat in pace
  363, 723
require
  need 630
  insufficient 640
  exact 741
  compel 744
  price 812
  due 924
  duty 926
  – explanation 519
requirement **630**
requisite 630
requisition 741, 765
  put in – *use* 677
  order 741
requital
  retaliation 918
  gratitude 916
  punishment 972
  reward 973
reredos 1000
res ipsa loquitur
  525
rescind *cut off* 44
  abrogate 756
  refuse 746
rescission 44, 756
rescript *answer* 462
  transcript 590
  letter 592
  order 741, 963
rescriptive 761
rescue *preserve* 670
  deliver 672
  aid 707
research 461
  – student 541
reseat 660
resection 44
reseda 435
resemblance 17, 21
resent 900
resentful 901
resentment **900**
reservation
  location 184
  concealment 528
  mental – 477, 528
  equivocation 520
  untruth 546
  with a – 38, 770
reservatory 191,
  636
reserve
  concealment 528
  silence 585

resuscitate
reproduce 163
reinstate 660
retable 215
retail *distribute* 73
inform 527
barter 794
sell 796
retailer 797
retain *stand* 150
keep 781
– the memory of 505
– one's reason 502
retainer 746
retake 789
retaliation 718, 919
retard *later* 133
slower 275
hinder 706
retch 297
retection 529
retention 781
retentive 781
– memory 505
reticence 528
reticle 219
reticulation 219, 248
reticule 191
retiform 219
retina 441
retinue *followers* 65
series 69
servants 746
retire *move back* 283
recede 287
resign 757
modest 881
seclusion 893
-- into the shade
inferior 34
decrease 36
– from sight
disappear 449
hide 528
retiring
concave 252
- *colour* 438
retold 104
retort
receptacle 191
vaporizer 336
boiler 386
answer 462
confutation 479
retaliation 718
wit 842
retouch *restore* 660
retoucher 559
retrace 505

– one's steps 607
retract
recant 607
annul 756
abjure 757
violate 773
retreat
resort 74
withdraw 187
abode 189
regression 283
recede 287
ambush 530
refuge 666
escape 671
give way 725
beat a – 623
retreating
concave 252
retrench *subduct* 38
shorten 201
lose 789
economize 817
retribution
retaliation 718
payment 807
punishment 972
reward 973
retrieve *restore* 660
acquire 775
retriever *dog* 366
retroaction
counteraction 179
recoil 277
regression 283
retroactive
past 122
retrocession
regression 283
recession 287
retrograde
moving back 283
deteriorated 659
relapsing 661
retrogression
regression 283
deterioration 659
relapse 661
retrospection
past 122
thought 451
memory 505
retroussé 245
retroversion 218
retrude 289
return *list* 86
repeat 104
periodic 138
reverse 145
recoil 277
regression 283

arrival 292
answer 462
report 551
relapse 661
appoint 755
profit 775
restore 790
proceeds 810
reward 973
in –
compensation 30
– the compliment
interchange 148
retaliate 718
– to the original
state 660
–ed prodigal 950
– thanks 916, 990
return game 104
return match 104
reunion *junction* 43
réunion
assemblage 72
concord 714
lieu de – 74
point de – 74
social – 892
revamp 140
revanche, en – 718
reveal 529
– itself 446
reveille 550
**réveiller le chat qui
dort, ne pas** –
668, 864
revel 840, 954
– in *enjoy* 377
revelation
disclosure 480a, 529
theological 985
Revelations 985
reveller 840
drunkard 959
revelling 59, 838
revendicate
claim 741
acquisition 775
due 924
revenge 919
breathe – 900
**revenons à nos
moutons** 283, 660
revenue 632, 810
reverberate 277, 408
reverberatory 386
revere *love* 897
respect 928
piety 987

reverence *title* 877
respect 928
piety 987
clergy 996
reverenced 500
reverend 877, 996
reverent 987, 990
reverential 928
reverie
train of thought 451
inattention 458
imagination 515
reversal 218, 607
reverse *contrary* 14
inversion 218
- of a medal 235
anteposition 237
adversity 735
abrogate 756
cards 840
– of the shield 468
reverseless 150
reversible 605
reversion
[*see* reverse]
posterity 117
return **145**
possession 777
property 780
succession 783
remitter 790
reversioner 779
revert *repeat* 104
return 145
turn back 283
revest 790
– to 457
revest 790
revet 223
reviction 660
review *consider* 457
inquiry 461
judge 480
recall 505
periodical 531
dissertation 595
compendium 596
entertainment 599
revise 658
parade 882
reviewer 480, 595
revile 932, 988
reviler 936
revise *copy* 21
consider 457
printing 591
plan 626
improve 658
revising barrister 967

RIG

– and left 180, 227, 236
– line 246
– man in the right place 23
in one's – mind 498, 502
hit the – nail on the head 480*a*, 698
– owner 779
keep the – path 944
in the – place 646
– thing to do 926
– as a trivet 650
– word in the right place 578
right about: to the – 283
go to the – 311, 607
send to the –
  eject 297
  reject 610
  refuse 764
turn to the – 218, 279
right hand
  power 157
  dextrality 238
  help 711
not let the – know what the left is doing 528
– of friendship 888
righteous 944
the – 987
– overmuch 988
Righteousness:
Lord our – 976
Sun of – 976
rightful 922
– owner 779
rightly served, be – 972
right-minded 939, 944
rights 748
put to – 660
set to – 60
stand on one's – 748
rigid *regular* 82
  hard 323
  exact 494
  severe 739
rigmarole 517, 573
rigor 383
– mortis 360
rigorous *exact* 494

RIO

severe 739
revengeful 919
rigour 494, 739
Rigsdag 696
rigueur
de – 744
rile *annoy* 830
  hate 898
  anger 900
rilievo *convex* 250
  sculpture 557
rill 348
rim 231
rime *chink* 198
  frost 283
rimer 262
rimple 258
rind 223
ring
  fastening 45
  pendency 214
  circle 247
  loud 404
  resonance 408
  test 463
  combination 709
  clique 712
  arena 728, 840
  badge 747
rub the – 992
have the true – 494
– the changes
  repeat 104
  change 140
  changeable 149
– in the ear 408
in a – fence 229, 232
– with the praises of 931
– the tocsin 669
– up 527
ringleader
  director 694
  mutineer 742
ringlet 247, 256
rink 840
rinse 652
rinsings 653
riot *confusion* 59
  derangement 61
  violence 173
  discord 713
  resist 719
  mutiny 742
run – *activity* 682
  excitement 825
  intemperance 954
– in *pleasure* 742
rioter 742

RIT

riotous 173
rip 949, 962
– open 260
– up *tear* 44
  recall the past 505
  excite 824
Rip van Winkle 130
riparian 342
ripe 673
– age *old* 128
ripen *perfect* 650
  improve 658
  prepare 673
  complete 729
– into 144
rippet 713
riposte 462
ripple *ruffle* 256
  shake 315
  water 348
  murmur 405
ripuarian 342
rire, pour – 853
rise *grow* 35
  begin 66
  slope 217
  progress 282
  ascend 305
  stir 682
  revolt 742
– again 660
– in arms 722
– from 154
– to the occasion 612
– in price 814
– up *elevation* 307
– in the world 734
risible 838, 853
rising [*see* rise]
– of the curtain 66, 448
– generation 127, 167
– ground
  height 206
  slope 217
worship the – sun 886
risk *chance* 621
  danger 665
  invest 787
at any – 604
risqué 961
rissole 298
risum teneatis amici? 853
rite 963, **998**
funeral – 363
ritornello 64, 104

ROA

ritual
  ostentation 882
  rite 998
ritualism 984
rival
  emulate 648
  oppose 708
  opponent 710
  compete 720
  combatant 726
  outshine 873
rivalry *envy* 921
rive 44
rivel 258
river 348
rivet 43, 45
– the attention 457, 824
– the eyes upon 441
– in the memory 505
– the yoke 739
riveted *firm* 150
rivulet 348
rixation 713
Ro 560
road *street* 189
  direction 278
  way 627
on the –
  transference 270
  progression 282
  approach 286
on the high – to 278
– to ruin
  destruction 162
  danger 665
  adversity 735
road-book 266
roads *lake* 343
roadstead 154
  abode 189
  refuge 666
roadster 271
roadway 627
roam 266
roan *horse* 271
  colour 433
roar *violence* 173
  wind 349
  sound 404, 407
  bellow 411, 412
  laugh 838
  weep 839
roaring *great* 31
– trade 731, 734
roast *heat* 384
  ridicule 856
rib – 972

– and boiled 298	*worship* 990	– stock 272	**root** *algebraic* - 84
– an ox 883	**rogue** *cheat* 548	– stone 312	*cause* 153
rob 354, 791	*knave* 941	**Rolls: Master of**	*place* 184
robber 792	*scamp* 949	the –	*abide* 186
robbery 791	–'s march 297	*recorder* 553	*base* 211
robe 225, 999	**roguery** 940	*judge* 967	*etymon* 562
robes – of state 747	**roguish**	– Court 966	lie at the – of 642
Robin Goodfellow	*playful* 840	**Roman candle** 840	pluck up by the
980	**Roi le veut, le** –	**Roman Catholic**	–s 301
Robinson	741	984	strike at the – of
say Jack – 132	**roister** 885	**romance**	716
Robot 554	**roisterer** 887	*music* 415	take –
robust *strong* 159,	**Roland for an**	*absurdity* 697	*influence* 175
654	**Oliver**	*imagination* 515	*locate* 184
roc 83	*retaliation* 716	*untruth* 546	*habit* 613
rocaille 853	*revenge* 719	*fable* 594	– and branch 52
rock *firm* 150	*barter* 794	**Romanism** 984	cut up – and
oscillate 314	**rôle** *drama* 599	**romantic**	branch 162
hard 323	*business* 625	*imaginative* 515	– out *eject* 297
land 342	*plan* 626	*art* 556	*extract* 301
safety 664	*conduct* 692	*sensitive* 822	*discover* 480a
danger 667	**roll** *list* 86	**romanticism** 515	**rooted**
build on a – 150	*fillet* 205	**Romanus sum,**	*old* 124
founded on a –	*convolution* 248	civis – 924	*firm* 150
664	*rotundity* 249	**Romany** 563	*located* 184
split upon a – 732	*make smooth* 255	**Rome: Church of**	*habit* 613
– ahead 665	*move* 264	984	deep – 820
–bound coast 342	*fly* 267	do at – as the	– antipathy 867
– oil 356	*rotate* 312	Romans do 82	– belief 484
rocket *rapid* 274	*rock* 314	**romp** *violent* 173	**rope** *fastening* 45
rise 305	*flow* 384	*game* 840	cord 205
light 423	*sound* **407**	**rondeau** *music* 415	*freedom* 749
signal 550	*record* 551	*poem* 597	*scourge* 975
arms 727	*money* 800	**rondel** 597	give – enough 738
fireworks 840	strike off the –	**rondolette** 597	–'s end 975
go up like a – and	756, 972	**rood** *area* 180	– of sand
come down like	– along 312	*cross* 998	*incoherence* 47
the stick 732	– in the dust 731	– loft 1000	*weakness* 160
rocking–chair 215	– on the ground	**roof** 189, 223	*impossible* 471
rococo 124, 853	839	**roofless** 226	– way 627
rod *support* 215	– of honour 86	**rook** 791, 792	**rope–dancer** 700
measure 466	– in 639, 641	**rookie** 726	**rope–dancing** 698
scourge 975	– on 109	**rookery** *nests* 189	**ropy** 352
divining 993	– into one 43	*dirt* 653	**roquelaure** 225
kiss the – 725	– in riches 803	**room** *occasion* 134	**roric** 339
sounding – 208	– up 312	*space* 180	**rosâ, sub** – 528
– of empire 747	– up in 225	*lodge* 186	**rosary** 990, 998
– in pickle	– in wealth 803	*chamber* 191	**Roscius** 599
prepared 673	**roll–call** 85	*plea* 617	**rose** *pipe* 350
accusation 938	**roller** *fillet* 45	assembly – 840	*fragrant* 400
punishment 972	*round* 249	in the – of 147	*red* 434
scourge 975	*clothing* 255	make – for	*beauty* 845
rodeo 720, 840	*rotate* 312	*opening* 260	bed of –s 377, **734**
rodomontade	**roller–coaster** 840	*respect* 928	couleur de –
exaggeration 482	**rollers** *billows* 348	**roommate** 890	*red* 434
unmeaning 517	**rollick** 836	**rooms**	*good* 648
boast 884	**rollicker** 838	*lodgings* 189	*prosperity* 734
roe 366, 374	**rollicking**	**roomy** 180	*hope* 858
Roentgen rays 420	*frolicsome* 836	**roost** 189	under the – 528
rogation	*blustering* 885	rule the – 737	welcome as the –s
request 765	**rolling:** – pin 249	**rooster** 366	in May 829, 892

roseate *red* 434
　hopeful 858
rose-coloured
　hope 858
Rosetta stone 522
rosette 847
rose-water
　moderation 174
　flattery 933
　not made with –
　　704
Rosicrucian
　sect 984
　sorcerer 994
rosin *rub* 331
　resin 356a
Rosinante 271
roster 86
rostrum *beak* 234
　pulpit 542
rosy 434
　– wine 959
rosy-cheeked 845
rot *decompose* 49
　absurdity 497
　rubbish 517
　putrefy 653
　disease 655
　decay 659
rota 86, 138
Rotarian 892
rotate 138
rotation **312**
　periodicity 138
rote, by – 505
　know – 490
　learn – 539
rôti 298
rôtisserie 189
rotogravure 531,
　558
rotten *weak* 160
　bad 649
　foul 653
　decayed 659
　– at the core
　deceptive 545
　diseased 655
　– borough 893
rotulorum, custos –
　553
rotund 249
rotunda 189
rotundity **249**
roturier 876
roué 949
rouge 434, 847
rouge-et-noir 621
rough *violent* 173
　shapeless 241
　uneven 256

pungent 392
unsavoury 395
sour 397
sound 410
unprepared 674
fighter 726
ugly 846
low fellow 876
bully 887
churlish 895
evil-doer 913
bad man 949
cut up – 900
– copy *writing* 590
unprepared 674
– diamond
uncouth 241
unprepared 674
artless 703
vulgar 851
commonalty 876
good man 948
– draft 626
– guess 514
– it 686
– sea 348
– side of the
　tongue 932
– and tumble 59
– weather 173, 349
rough-cast 256
　covering 223
　shape 240
　scheme 626
　unpolished 674
rough-hew 240, 673
roughly
　nearly 197
rough-neck 876,
　887
roughness **256**
rough-rider 268
roughshod over,
　ride – 739
roulade 415
rouleau
　assemblage 72
　cylinder 249
　money 800
roulette 621, 840
round *series* 69
　revolution 138
　– of a *ladder* 215
　curve 245
　circle 247
　rotund 249
　music 415
　fight 720
all – 227
bring – 660
come –

periodic 138
　recant 607
　persuade 615
dizzy – 312
get – 660
go – 311
go one's –s 266
go the –
　publication 531
make the – of 311
run the – of 682
go the same – 104
turn – *invert* 218
　retreat 283
　revolve 311
– assertion 535
– a corner 311
– dance 840
– game 840
– hand 590
– like a horse in a
　mill 613
– of the ladder 71
– number 84, 102
in – numbers 29,
　197
– pace 274
– of pleasures
　377, 840
– robin
　information 527
　petition 765
　censure 932
– and round 138,
　312
– sum 800
– terms 566
– trot 274
– up 370
– of visits 892
round about
　circumjacent 227
　deviation 279
　circuit 311
　amusement 840
– phrases 573
– way 729
rounded periods
　577, 578
roundelay 597
rounders 840
round-house 752
roundlet 247
round-shouldered
　243
roup 796
rouse 615, 824
– oneself 682
rousing 171
rout *crowd* 72
　agitation 315

overcome 731
discomfit 732
rabble 876
assembly 892
put to the – 731
– out 652
route 627
en – 270
en – for 282
routine
　uniform 16
　order 58
　rule 80
　periodic 138
　custom 613
　business 625
rove *travel* 266
　deviate 279
rover *traveller* 268
　pirate 792
roving commission
　475
row *disorder* 59
　series 69
　violence 173
　street 189
　navigate 267
　discord 713
– in the same
　boat 88
rowdy *vulgar* 851,
　876
　blusterer 887
　bad man 949
rowel 253, 615
rower 269
rowlock 215
royal 737
– blue 438
– highness 877
– road 627, 705
Royal Academician
　559
royalist 737
royaliste que le roi,
　plus 33
royalty 737
Rt. Hon. 877
ruade *impulse* 276
　attack 716
ruat cœlum 908
rub *friction* 331
　touch 379
　difficulty 704
　adversity 735
　painful 830
– off corners 82
– down *lessen* 195
　powder 330
– down with an
　oaken towel 972

sandal 225
sand-blind 442
Sandemanian 984
sand-paper 255
sands *danger* 667
– on the seashore
  multitude 102
sand-storm 330
sandwich-wise 228
sandy *yellow* 436
sane 502
sangar 717
sang-froid
  insensibility 823
  inexcitability 826
  presence of mind
  864
sangrail 998
sanguinary 361
sanguine *red* 434
  hopeful 858
  – expectation 507,
  858
  – imagination 515
sanhedrim 696, 995
sanies 333
sanitaire, cordon –
  670
sanitarian 656
sanitarium 656, 662
sanitary 656
sanity *mental* **502**
  bodily - 654
sans 187
  – cérémonie 888,
  892
  – façon
  simple 849
  modest 881
  social 892
  – pareil 33
  – peur et sans
  reproche
  perfect 650
  heroic 873
  honourable 939
  – souci
  insensible 823
  pleasure 827
  content 831
sans-culotte 742,
  876
Santa Claus 784
santé, maison de –
  662
santon 893, 996
sap *essence* 5
  destroy 162
  excavate 252
  juice 333
  damage 659

attack 716
  – the foundations
  162, 659
sapid 390
sapient 498
sapless 160, 340
sapling 129, 367
saponaceous 355
saporific 390
sapper 252, 726
sappers and miners
  preparers. 673
Sapphic 597
sapphire *blue* 438
  gem 847
sappy
  young 127
  juicy 333
  foolish 499
sarà sarà, che – 601
saraband 840
sarcasm
  disrespect 929
  censure 932
  detraction 934
sarcastic 856, 895
sarcoma 250
sarcophagus 363
sarculation 103
sard 847
Sardanapalus 954a
sardonic 932, 934
  – grin
  laughter 838
  ridicule 856
  discontent 932
sardonyx 847
sark 225
sartorial 225
Sarum, old – 893
sash 247
Satan **978**
satanic
  malevolent 907
  vicious 945
  diabolic 978
satchel 191
sate 869
satellite
  companion 88
  follower 281
  heavenly body 318
  auxiliary 711
  servant 746
satiate 957
satiety
  sufficient 639
  pleasant 829
  cloy **869**
satin 255
satire 521, 856, 932

satirical 546, 932
  detraction 934
satirist 936
satis: jam – 869
  – superque 641
satisfaction
  [*see* satisfy]
  duel 720
  pleasure 827
  atonement 952
hail with – 931
satisfactorily 618
satisfactory 648
satisfy *answer* 462
  convince 484
  sufficient 639
  consent 762
  observance 772
  pay 807
  gratify 829
  content 831
  satiate 869
  reward 973
  – an obligation
  926
  – oneself 484
satrap 745
saturate *fill* 52
  moisten 339
  satiate 869
Saturn 979
saturnalia
  disorder 59
  games 840
  intemperance 954
Saturnian 829, 946
  – age 734
Saturnia regna 734,
  827
saturnine 837
satyr *ugly* 846
  libertine 962
  demon 980
sauce *adjunct* 39
  mixture 41
  food 298
  condiment 393
  impertinence 885
  abuse 908
  – boat 191
pay – for all 807
sauce piquante 829
sauce-box 887
saucer 191
  – eyes 441
saucepan 191
saucy 885, 895
saunter 133, 266,
  275
sausage 298
saute aux yeux,

cela – 525
sauvage 893
sauve qui peut
  run away 623
  alarm 669
  haste 684
  cowardice 862
savage *violent* 173
  vulgar 851
  brave 861
  boorish 876
  angry 900
  malevolent 907
  evil-doer 913
savanna 344
savant 490, 492
save *subduct* 38
  exclude 55
  except 83
  store 636
  preserve 670
  deliver 672
  economize 817
God – 990
  – one's bacon 671
  – and except 83
  – money 817
  – the necessity
  927a
  – us 707
save-all 817
saving 817
  – clause 469
  – one's presence
  928
savings 636, 817
saviour 912
Saviour 976
savoir: – faire
  698, 852
  – gré 916
  – vivre *skill* 698
  fashion 852
  sociality 892
savour 390
  – of *resemble* 17
  – of the reality
  780
savouriness **394**
savourless 391
savoury 394
saw *cut* 44
  jagged 257
  maxim 496
  – the air
  gesture 550
sawbuck 800
sawder, soft –
  flattery 933
sawdust 330
sawney 501

sax-horn 417
Saxon
style 576, 578
saxophone 417
say *nearly* 32
assert 535
speak 560, 582
you don't – so 870
go without –ing
525
have one's – 535,
582
that is to – 522
what do you – to
that 870
– by heart 505
– no 489
– nothing 585
– to oneself 589
– one's prayers
990
– what comes up-
permost 612
saying 496, 535
sbirro 965
scabbard 191
throw away the –
resolution 604
war 722
scabby 940
scabrous 256
scaffold
support 215
preparation 673
execution 975
scagliola 545
scalawag 193
scald *burn* 384
poet 597
scale *transcend* 31
portion 51
series 69
term 71
slice 204
skin 223
mount 305
weigh 319
gamut 413
measure 466
hold the –s 480
turn the –
reversion 145
influence 175
counter evidence
468
motive 615
hold the –s even
922
–s of justice 922
– the heights 305
– the walls 716

–s falling from the
eyes 441, 529
scalene 243
scallop 248, 257
scalp 226
scalpel 253
scamble 44
scamp *neglect* 460
shirk 603
rascal 949
scamped *sham* 545
scamper *speed* 274
– off 623
scampish 945
scan *see* 441
attend to 457
inquire 461
know 490
prosody 597
scandal *news* 532
obloquy 934
scandaleuse, chro-
nique – 934
scandalize 932
scandal-monger
532
scandalous 874, 945
scandalum magna-
tum
infamy 874
detraction 934
accusation 938
scandent 305
scansion 597
scant *small* 32
few 103
little 193
narrow 203
insufficient 640
scantling *model* 22
scrap 32
dimensions 192
scanty [*see* scant]
scape 671
scapegoat 147, 952
scapegrace 863, 949
Scapin 548, 941
scapulary 999
scar *shore* 342
record 551
blemish 848
scarab 993
scaramouch 844
scarce
few 103, 137, 640
make oneself –
187, 623
scarcely 32
– any 103
– anything 643
– ever 137

scarcity 103
scare 860
scarecrow 846, 860
scarf 225, 999
scarfskin 223
scarify *notch* 257
torment 830
scarlet 434
– Lady 984
scarp *oblique* 217
defence 717
scathe 649, 659
scatheless 650
scatter *derange* 61
disperse 73
diverge 291
– to the winds
destroy 162
confute 479
scatterbrained 458,
503
scattering 268
scavenger 652
scenario 594, 626
scene
appearance 448
painting 556
drama 599
excitement 825
– of action 728
look behind the
–s 461
scene-painter 559
scene-painting 556
scenery 448, 559
scenic 599, 882
– railway 840
scenography 556
scent *smell* 398
discovery 480a
disbelieve 485
knowledge 490
sign 550
trail 551
get – of 527
put on a new –
279
on the – 622
throw off the –
623
on the right – 462
– from afar 510
scent-bag 400
scent-bottle 400
scented 400
scentless 399
sceptre **747**
sway the – 737
schedule 86
schematist 626
scheme *draft* 554

plan 626
schemer 626
scherif 745, 875
scherzo 415
schesis 7
schism *dissent* 489
discord 713
heterodoxy 984
schismless 983a
schistose 204
scholar 492, 541
scholarly 539
scholarship
knowledge 490
learning 539
distinction 873
scholastic
knowledge 490
teaching 537
learning 539
school 542
scholiast 496, 522
scholium 496, 522
school
herd 72
multitude 102
system of
opinions 484
knowledge 490
teaching 537
academy **542**
painting 556
go to – 539
send to – 537
schoolboy 129, 541
familiar to every –
490
schooldays 127
schoolfellow 541
schoolgirl 129, 541
schoolman 492, 983
schoolmaster 540
– abroad 490, 537
schoolroom 191
schooner 273
schottische 840
sciatica 378
science 490, 698
scientific *exact* 494
scientist 476, 492
scimitar 727
scintilla *small* 32
spark 420, 423
scintillate 446, 873
scintillation
heat 382
light 420
wit 842
scintillula forsan,
latet – 858
sciolism 491

sciolist 493
sciomachy 497
Sciomancy 511
scion *part* 51
  child 129
  posterity 167
scire: – facias 461
– quid valeant
  humeri 698
scission 44
scissors 253
– and paste 609
scissure 198
sclerotics 195
scobs 330
scoff *ridicule* 856
  deride 929
  impiety 988
– at *despise* 930
  censure 932
scold *shrew* 901
  malediction 908
  censure 932
scollop 248, 257
sconce *top* 210
  candlestick 423
  brain 450
  defence 717
  mulct 974
scone 298
scoop
  depression 252
  perforator 262
scooter 272
scope *degree* 26
  opportunity 134
  extent 180
  meaning 516
  freedom 748
scorch
  rush 274
  heat 382, 384
scorching
  violent 173
score
  music 60, 415
  count 85
  list 86
  twenty 98
  notch 257
  furrow 259
  mark 550
  success 731
  credit 805
  debt 806
  accounts 811
on the – of
  relation 9
  motive 615
scores *many* 102
scoriæ *ash* 384

dirt 653
scorify 384
scoring board 551
scorn 930
scorpion
  painful 830
  evil-doer 913
  (*bane* 663)
  chastise with –s
  739
scorse 794
scot *reward* 973
scot free *free* 748
  cheap 815
  exempt 927a
escape –
  escape 671
let off – 970
scotch *notch* 257
  injure 659
– the snake
  maim 158
  insufficient 640
  non-completion
  730
– the wheel 706
Scotsman
  canny 702
Scotticism 563
scotomy 443
scoundrel 913, 949
scour *run* 274
  rub 331
  clean 652
– the country 266
– the plain 274
scourge *bane* 663
  painful 830
  punish 972
  instrument of
    punishment **975**
– of the human
  race 913
scourings 645
scout 234
  observer 444
  feeler 463
  messenger 534
  reject 610
  warship 726
  servant 746
  watch 664
  warning 668
  disrespect 929
  disdain 930
  (*looker* 444)
  (*underrate* 483)
  (*ridicule* 856)
scow 273
scowl
  complain 839

frown 895
  anger 900
  sullen 901a
  disapprobation
  932
scrabble
  unmeaning 517
  scribble 590
scrag 32, 203
scraggy *lean* 193,
  203
  rough 256
scramble
  confusion 59
  climb 305
  pursue 622
  haste 684
  difficulty 704
  contend 720
  seize 789
scranch 330
scrannel 643
scrap 32, 720
-- of paper 158, 940
scrap-book 596
scrape *subduct* 38
  reduce 195
  pulverize 330
  abrade 331
  mezzotint 558
  difficulty 704
  mischance 732
  bow 894
– together
  assemble 72
  acquire 775
scraper 652
scratch *groove* 259
  abrade 331
  mark 550
  daub 555
  draw 556
  write 590
  hurt 619
  wound 649
come to the –
  720, 861
mere – 209
old – 978
up to the – 861
without a – 654,
  670
– the head 461
– out 552
scrawl 590
scrawny 203
screak 411
scream *cry* 411, 839
screech 411, 412
screech owl 412
screed 582, 593

screen *sift* 60
  sieve 260
  shade 424
  cinema 448
  hide 528
  hider 530
  side-scene 599
  clean 562
  safety 664
  shelter 666
  defence 717
– from sight 442
screw *fasten* 43
  fastening 45
  distort 243
  oar 267
  rotation 312
  instrument 633
  miser 819
put on the – 739,
  744
– one's courage to
  the sticking
  place 861
– loose *insane* 503
  imperfect 651
  unskilful 699
  hindrance 706
  attack 713
– up *fasten* 43
  strengthen 159
  prepare 673
– up the eyes 443
screwed
  drunk 959
screw-driver 633
screw-steamer 273
scribble 517, 590
scribbler 593
scribe *recorder* 553
  writer 590, 593
  priest 996
–s and Pharisees
  988
scribendi, ca-
  coëthes – 580
scrimshanker 603
scrimmage 713, 720
scrimp *short* 201
  insufficient 640
  stingy 819
scrip 191
script 590, 599
scripta, lex – 963
scriptæ, literæ – 590
scriptural 983a
Scripture
  certain 474
  revelation 985
scrivener *writer* 590
  lawyer 968

in the – 490
keep a – 585
– motive 615
– passage 627, 671
– place 530
– writing 590
secrétaire 191
secretary
  recorder 553
  writer 590
  director 694
  auxiliary 711
  servant 746
  consignee 758
  – of state 694
  – of the treasury
    801
secrete *excrete* 297
  conceal 528
secretion 299
secretive 528
sect 75
  religious – 983,
    984
sectarian
  dissent 489
  ally 711
  heterodox 984
sectary 489
section *division* 44
  part 51
  class 75
  chapter 593
  troops 726
sector *part* 51
  circle 247
secula seculorum,
  in – 112
secular
  centenary 98
  periodic 138
  laity 997
  – education 537
secularism 984
secundum artem
  82, 698
secure *fasten* 43
  bespeak 132
  belief 484
  safe 664
  restrain 751
  engage 768
  gain 775
  confident 858
  – an object 731
securities 802–805
security *safety* 664
  pledge **771**
  hope 858
lend on – 787
Sedan

disaster 162
sedan chair 272
sedate
  thoughtful 451
  calm 826
  grave 837
sedative 174, 662
sedentary 265
sedge 367
sedile 1000
sediment *dregs* 653
sedimentary 40
sedition 742
seduce *entice* 615
  love 897
  debauch 961
seducer 962
seduction 829, 865
sedulous 682, 865
see *view* 441
  look 457
  believe 484
  know 490
  bishopric 995
we shall – 507
– after 459
– daylight 480*a*
– double 959
– fit 600, 602
– at a glance 498
– justice done 922
– life 840
– the light
  born 359
  published 531
– service 722
– sights 455
– through 480*a*,
  498
– to *attention* 457
  care 459
  direction 693
– one's way
  foresight 510
  intelligible 518
  skill 698
  easy 705
seed *small* 32
  cause 153
  posterity 167
  grain 330
run to – *age* 128
  lose health 659
sow the – 673
seedling 129
seed-plot 168, 371
seed-time of life
  127
seedy *weak* 160
  disease 655
  deteriorated 659

exhausted 688
  needy 804
seeing that 8, 476
seek *inquire* 461
  pursue 622
  offer 763
  request 765
  – safety 664
seek-sorrow 837
seel 217
seem 448
as it –s good to
  600
seeming 488
seemingly 472
seemless 846, 925
seemliness 926
seemly
  expedient 646
  handsome 845
  due 924
seep 295
seer *veteran* 130
  madman 504
  oracle 513
  sorcerer 994
see-saw 12, 314
seethe *wet* 339
  hot 382
  make hot 384
  excitement 824
seething caldron
  386
segar 392
segment 44, 51
segnitude 683
s'égosiller 411
segregate
  not related 10
  separate 44
  exclude 55
segregated
  incoherent 47
seigneur, grand –
  pride 878
  insolence 885
seignior 745, 875
seigniority
  authority 737
  possession 777
  property 780
seigniory 737
seine net 232
seisin 777, 780
seismic 314
seismograph 553
seismometer 276,
  314
seize 789, 791
– an opportunity
  134

seized with
  disease 655
  feeling 821
seizure 925
sejunction 44
seldom 137
select *choose* 609
  good 648
self 13, 79
–abasement 879
–accusing 950
–admiration 880
–applause 880
–appointed task
  602
–assertion 885
–called 565
–command 604,
  864
–communing 451
–complacency
  836, 880
–confidence 880
–conquest 604
–conscious 855
–consultation 451
–contained 52
–control 604
–conviction
  belief 484
  penitent 950
  condemned 971
–counsel 451
–deceit *error* 495
–deception 486
–defence 717
–delusion 486
–denial
  disinterested 942
  temperance 953
  penance 990
–discipline 990
–effacement 879,
  942
–esteem 880
–evident 474, 525
–examination 990
–existing 1
–government 748
–help 698
–immolation 991
–indulgence
  selfishness 943
  intemperance 954
–interest 943
–knowledge 881
–love 943
–luminous 423
–mastery 604
–opinioned 481
–possession

– right	setaceous 256	– times 104	eye – 443
inform 527	seton 662	severalize 465	in the – 528, 874
disclose 529	setose 256	severally 44, 79	shadow of a – 32,
teach 537	sett *lease* 771, 787	severalty 44	422
reinstate 660	settee 215	severance 38	throw into the –
vindicate 937	setter 366	severe	*surpass* 303
– to rights 60	settle *regulate* 60	*energetic* 171	*conceal* 528
– sail 293	*establish* 150	*symmetry* 242	*glory* 873
– the seal on 729	*be located* 184	*exact* 494	throw all else into
– one's seal to 467	*bench* 215	- *style* 576	the – 642
– store by 642	*come to rest* 265	*harsh* 739	thrown into the –
– straight 246, 723	*subside* 306	*painful* 830	34, 874
– the table in a	*kill* 361	*simple* 849	under the – of 664
roar 840	*decide* 480	*critical* 932	without a – of
– one's teeth 604	*choose* 609	severely *very* 31	doubt 474
– terms	*vanquish* 731	severity **739**	shades:
manifest 525	*consent* 762	sew 43	– below 982
phrase 566	*compact* 769	sewage 299, 653	– of death 360
style 574	*pay* 807	sewed up	– of difference 15
– a trap for 545	– accounts 807,	*drunk* 959	– of evening 422
– to 720, 722	811	sewer 350, 653	shading 421
– in towards 286	– down 133	sewerage 652, 653	– off 26
– up	*stability* 150	sewer-gas 663	shadow
printing 54	*moderate* 174	sewing-silk 205	*unsubstantial* 4
originate 153	*locate oneself* 184	sex *kind* 75	*copy* 21
strengthen 159	– into 144	*women* 374	*small* 32
produce 161	– matters 723	fair – 374	*accompaniment*
upright 212	– preliminaries	sexagenarian 98,	88
raise 307	673	130	*thin* 203
successful 731	– property 781	sexagenary 99	*be behind* 235
prosperous 734	– the question 478	sextant 217, 244,	*sequence* 281
– up shop 676	– to sleep 683	247	*dark* 421
– upon	– upon *give* 784	sextet 98	*shade* 424
resolved 604	– with 807, 992	sextodecimo 593	*pursue* 461, 622
attack 716	settled [*see* settle]	sexton 363, 996	*dream* 515
desirous 865	*characteristic* 5	sextuple 98	*demon* 980
– too high a value	*ended* 67	seyyid 745	fight with a – 699
upon 482	account – 811	sforzando 415	follow as a – 281
– watch 459	– opinion 484	shabbiness 34	partial – 422
– one's wits to	– purpose 620	shabby *trifling* 643	without a – of
work *think* 451	settlement [*see*	*deteriorated* 659	turning 141
imagine 515	settle]	*stingy* 819	worn to a –
plan 626	*location* 184	*mean* 874	*thin* 203
– to work	*colony* 188	*disgraceful* 940	*worse for wear*
undertake 676	*dregs* 653	shabby-genteel 851	659
impose 741	*compact* 769	shack 189	– of coming
set-back 735	*deed* 771	shackle	events 511
set down	*property* 780	*fastening* 45	– forth *dim* 422
record 551	strict – 781	*hinder* 706	*predict* 511
unseat 756	settler 188	*restrain* 751	*metaphor* 521
humiliate 879	settlor 784	*fetter* 752	*represent* 554
slight 929	seven 98	shade *degree* 26	may your – never
censure 932	–league boots 274,	*small quantity* 32	be less
give one a –	992	*manes* 362	*courtesy* 894
confute 479	wake the –	*darkness* 421	*respect* 928
– as 484	sleepers 404	*shadow* **424**	*approbation* 931
– for 484	seventy 98	*colour* 428	take the – for the
– a cause for	sever 38, 44	*conceal* 528	substance
hearing 969	several *special* 79	*screen* 530	*credulous* 486
– to 155	*plural* 100	*paint* 556	*mistake* 495
– in writing 551	*many* 102	*ghost* 980	*unskilful* 699

[635]

under the – of
one's wing 664
shadowy 4, 447
shady 874
shaft *deep* 208
frame 215
pit 260
missile 284
axis 312
air-pipe 351
handle 633
weapon 727
shaggy 256
shagreen 223
shah 745
shake *totter* 149
weak 160
vibrate 314
agitation 315
shiver 383
trill 407
music 416
dissuade 616
injure 659
impress 821
excited 824
fear 860
– one's faith 485
– hands
pacification 723
friendship 888
courtesy 894
forgive 918
– the head
dissent 489
deny 536
refuse 764
disapprove 932
– off 297
– off the yoke 759
– to pieces 162
– one's sides 838
– up 315
shakedown *bed* 215
shakes, no great –
643, 651
shako 225, 717
shaky *weak* 160
in danger 665
fearful 860
shallop 273
shallow
not deep 32, 209
ignorant 491
ignoramus 493
foolish 499
trifling 643
– pretext 617
– profundity 855
shallow-brain 501
shallowness 209

shallow-pated 499
shallows
danger 667
sham *imitation* 19
falsehood 544
deception 545,
546
– fight 720
shaman 994
shamanism 992
shamble 275, 315
shambles 361
shame
disrepute 874
wrong 923
censure 932
chastity 960
cry – *upon* 932
false – 855
for – 874
sense of – 879
– the devil 939
to one's – *be it*
spoken 874
shamefaced 881
shameful
disgraceful 874
profligate 945
shameless
bold 525
impudent 885
profligate 945
indecent 961
shampoo 652
shandredhan 272
shanghai 791
shank *support* 215
instrument 633
Shanks's mare 266
shanty 189
shape 240, 448
– one's course
direction 278
pursuit 622
conduct 692
– out a course 626
shapeless 241, 846
shapely 242, 845
shard 51
share
part 51
participate 778
allotted portion
786
– and share alike
778
shareholder 778
shark 792
sharp
energetic 171
violent 173

acute 253
sensible 375
pungent 392
– *sound* 410
musical tone 413
intelligent 498
active 682
clever 698
cunning 702
feeling 821
painful 830
rude 895
censorious 932
look – 459, 682
– *appetite* 865
– *contest* 720
– *ear* 418
– *eye* 441
– *fellow* 682, 700
– *frost* 383
– *look-out* 459,
507
– *pain* 378
– *practice*
cunning 702
severity 739
improbity 940
– *set* 865
sharpen
[*see* sharp]
excite 824
– one's tools 673
– one's wits 537
sharpener 253
sharper 792
sharpness 253
sharpshooter 726
sharpshooting 716
Shaster 986
shatter *disjoin* 44
disperse 73
render powerless
158
destroy 162
shatter-brained 503
shattered 160, 688
shave *reduce* 195
shorten 201
layer 204
smooth 255
grate 330
lie 546
close – 671
shaved 226
shaving *small* 32
layer 204
filament 205
shave-tail 726, 745
shawl 225
shawm 417
shay 272

she 374
sheaf 72
shear *reduce* 195
shorten 201
sheep 370
take 789
shears 253
sheath 191, 223
sheathe 225
moderate 174
– the sword 723
sheathing 223
sheave 633
shed *scatter* 73
building 189
divest 226
emit 297
give 784
– *blood* 361
– *light upon* 420
– *a lustre on* 873
– *tears* 839
Shedim 980
sheen 420
sheep 366
sheep-dog 366
sheep-fold 232
sheepish 881
sheep's eye, cast a –
desire 865
modest 881
endearment 902
sheer *simple* 42
complete 52
deviate 279
– *off avoid* 623
sheet *layer* 204
covering 223
paper 593
come down in –s
rain 348
white – 952
winding – 363
– *of fire* 382
– *of water* 343
sheet-anchor
safety 664, 666
hope 858
sheet-lightning 423
sheik *ruler* 745, 875
lover 897
priest 996
shelf 215, 667
on the –
powerless 158
disused 678
inaction 681
shell *cover* 223
coffin 363
bombard 716
bomb 727

–burst 404
–shock 655
– out 784, 807, 809
shellac 356a
shellback 269
shell-fish 366
shelter 664, 666
– oneself under plea of 617
sheltie 271
shelve *defer* 133
  locate 184
  slope 217
  neglect 460
  disuse 678
shelving beach 217
shend 659
shepherd *tender of sheep* 370
  director 694
  pastor 996
Shepherd, the Good – 976
shepherd's dog 366
Sheppard, Jack – 792
shere 32
sheriff 745, 965
Shetland pony 271
shew [*see* show]
shibboleth 550
shield
  heraldry 550
  safety 664
  buckler 666
  defend 717
  scutcheon 877
  look only at one side of the – 481
  reverse of the – 235, 468
  under the – of 664
shift *change* 140
  convert 144
  substitute 147
  changeable 149
  chemise 225
  move 264
  transfer 270
  deviate 279
  prevaricate 546
  plea 617
  cunning 702
  last – 601
  make a – with 147, 677
  put to one's –s 704, 804
  – one's ground 607

– off *defer* 133
– for oneself 692, 748
  left to – for one-self 893
– one's quarters 264
– the scene 140
– to and fro 149
shifting [*see* shift]
  transient 111
– sands 149
– trust or use 783
shiftless 674, 699
shillelagh 727
shilling 800
  cut off with a – 789
– shocker 594
shilly-shally 605
shimmer 420
shimmy
  dance 840
shindy 720
shine *light* 420
  beauty 845
  glory 873
  take the – out of 874
– in conversation 588
– forth 873
– upon
  illumine 420
  aid 707
shingle 330
shingled
  hair 53
shingles 223
shining [*see* shine]
– light *sage* 500
Shintoism 984
shiny 420
ship *lade* 190
  transfer 270
  vessel **273**
  take – 267, 293
  one's – coming in 803
– of the line 726
shipboard, on – 273
ship-load 31, 190
shipman 269
shipmate 890
shipment
  contents 190
  transfer 270
shippen 189
shipping 273
shipshape *order* 58
  conformity 82

skill 698
shipwreck
  destruction 162
  vanquish 731
  failure 732
shire 181
shirk 603, 623, 742
shirker 862
shirt 225
Shiva 979
shive 22, 204
shiver
  small piece 32
  divide 44
  destroy 162
  filament 205
  shake 315
  brittle 328
  cold 383
  fear 860
  go to –s 162
– in one's shoes 860
shivery *brittle* 328
  powdery 330
shoal
  assemblage 72
  multitude 102
  shallow 209
shoals *danger* 667
  surrounded by – *difficulty* 704
shoat 366
shock *sheaf* 72
  violence 173
  concussion 276
  agitation 315
  unexpected 508
  disease 655
  discord 713
  affect 821
  move 824
  pain 828
  give pain 830
  dislike 867
  scandalize 932
shocking *bad* 649
  painful 830
  ugly 846
  vulgar 851
  fearful 860
  disreputable 874
  hateful 898
  in a – temper 901a
shockingly *much* 31
shod 225
shoddy 645
shoe *support* 215
  dress 225
  hindrance 706
  stand in the –s of

commission **755**
  deputy 759
  where the – pinches
  badness 649
  difficulty 704
  opposition 708
  sensibility 822
  painful 830
shoemaker 225
shofle 272
shoful 792
shog 173
shoneen 855
shoot
  offspring 167
  expand 194
  dart 274
  propel 284
  kill 361
  sprout 365, 367
  pain 378
  execute 972
  teach the young idea to – 537
– ahead 282
– ahead of 303
– at 716
– out beams 420
– up *increase* 35
  prominent 250
shooting
  [*see* shoot]
  chase 622
– pain 378
– star 318, 423
shooting-coat 225
shop 795, 799
  keep a – 625, 794
  shut up – *end* 67
  cease 142
  relinquish 624
  rest 687
  smell of the – 851
shopkeeper 797
shoplifter 792
shoplifting 791
shopman 797
shopmate 890
shopping 794, 795
shore
  support 215
  border 231
  land 342
  buttress 717
  hug the – 286
  on – 342
– up 215, 670
shoreless 180
shorn *cut short* 21
  deprived 776

– of its beams
422, 874
– lamb 828
short
not long 201
brittle 328
concise 572
uncivil 895
come – of, fall – of
inferior 34
shortcoming 304
insufficient 640
in – 572, 596
– allowance 640
– answer 895
– breath 688
– by 201
– of cash 804
– commons
insufficiency 640
fasting 956
– circuit 279, 628
– cut *straight* 246
mid-course 628
– distance 197
– life and merry
840
– measure 53
at – notice 111,
132
– of *small* 32
inferior 34
subtraction 38
incomplete 53
shortcoming 304
insufficient 640
– sea 348
make – work of
destroy 162
active 682
haste 684
complete 729
conquer 731
punish 972
shortage 53
shortcoming
inequality 28
inferiority 34
motion short of
304
non-completion
730
deficiency 945
shorten 201
– sail 275
shorthand 590
short-handed 651
shorthorn 366
short-lived 111
shortly *soon* 132
shortness 201

for – sake 572
shorts 225
short-sighted
myopic 443
misjudging 481
foolish 499
short-story 594
short-winded 160,
688
short-witted 499
shot *missile* 284
report 406
variegated 440
guess 514
war material 722,
727
price 812
reward 973
bad – 701
exchange –s 720
good – 700
have a – at 716
like a – 113
off like a – 623
pistol – 406
random – 463, 621
round – 727
– in the locker 632
not have a – in
one's locker 804
– and shell 722
shot-free 815
shot-gun 727
should be:
no better than
she – 961
what – 922
shoulder
support 215
projection 250
shove 276
broad –ed 159
cold – 289
have on one's –s
625
on the –s of
high 206
elevated 307
instrumentality
631
shrug the –s
[*see* shrug]
rest on the –s of
926
rub –s with no-
bility 852
take upon one's –s
676
– arms 673
– a musket 722
– to shoulder 709,

712
– to the wheel
604, 676
shoulder-knot 847
shoulder-strap 747
shout
loud 404
cry 411
rejoice 838
shove 276
give a – to
aid 707
shovel
receptacle 191
transfer 270
vehicle 272
fire-iron 386
cleanness 652
put to bed with
a – 363
– away 297
shovel-hat 999
show *visible* 446
appear 448
draw attention
457
evidence 467
demonstrate 478
manifest 525
entertainment 599
parade 882
dumb – 550
make a – 544
mere – 544
peep– 840
– off 525
– one's cards 529
– cause 527
– one's colours,
550
– one's face
presence 186
manifest 525
disclose 529
– fight *defy* 715
attack 716
defend 717
brave 861
– forth 525
– in front 303
– one's cards 529
– one's hand 529
– a light pair of
heels 623
– itself 446
– of 17, 472
– off 882, 884
– one's teeth 715
– up *visible* 446
manifest 525
ridicule 856

degrade 874
censure 932
accuse 938
shower
assemblage 72
rain 348
– bath 386
– down
abundance 639
– down upon 784,
816
showman 524
showy *colour* 428
beauty 845
ornament 847
fashion 852
vulgar 851
ostentatious 882
shrapnel 727
shred 32, 205
shredder 260
shrew 901
shrewd
knowing 490
wise 498
cunning 702
shriek 410, 411
shrievalty 965
shrieve 965
shrift
confession 529
absolution 952
shriftless 951
shrill 410, 411
shrimp 193
shrine 363, 1000
receptacle 191
shrink
decrease 36
shrivel 195
go back 283, 287
unwilling 603
avoid 623
sensitive 822
– from *fear* 860
dislike 867
hate 898
shrive 952, 998
shrivel 195
shrivelled *thin* 203
shroud *cover* 225
funeral 363
hide 528
safety 664
defend 717
–ed in mystery
519
shrouds 45
Shrove Tuesday
998
shrub *plant* 367

plantation 371
shrug *sign* 550
 – the shoulders
  dissent 489
  submit 725
  discontent 832
  dislike 867
  contempt 930
  disapprobation
  932
shrunk 193, 195
shudder *cold* 383
 fear 860
 make one –
  painful 830
 – at *aversion* 867
  hate 898
shuffle *mix* 41
 derange 61
 change 140
 interchange 148
 changeable 149
 move slowly 275
 agitate 315
 falsehood 544
 untruth 546
 irresolute 605
 recant 607
 dance 840
 improbity 940
 – the cards
  begin again 66
  change 140
  chance 621
  prepare 673
 patience and –
  the cards 826
 – off *run away* 623
 – off this mortal
  coil 360
 – on 266
shuffler 548
shun 623, 867
shunt 270, 279
shunted
 shelved 460
shut 261
 – the door 761
 – the door in one's
  face 764
 – the door upon
  893
 – one's ears 419,
  487
 – the eyes 442
 – one's eyes to
  not attend to 458
  neglect 460
  not believe 487
  permit 760
  not observe 773

– the gates of
 mercy 914*a*
– in 751
– oneself up 893
– out 55, 761
– up shop *end* 67
 cease 142
 silence 403
 relinquish 624
 repose 687
– up *close* 261
 confute 479
 imprison 751
shutter 424
shuttle 314
shuttlecock 605
shy *deviate* 279
 draw back 283
 propel 284
 avoid 623
 fearful 860
 cowardly 862
 modest 881
 fight – of 623
 have a – at 716
 – of belief 487
 – cock 862
 – of *doubtful* 485
 unwilling 603
 cautious 864
 dislike 867
Shylock 787
Siamese twins 89
sib 11
Siberia 383
sibi gladio hunc
 jugulo, suo–718
sibilation *hiss* **409**
 disrespect 929
 disapprobation
 932
Sibyl *oracle* 513
 ugly 846
Sibylline 511
 – leaves 513
sic *imitation* 19
 exact 494
si – omnes! 948
 – transit gloria
  mundi 111
 – volo sic jubeo
  600
 – vos non vobis
  791
siccity 340
sick *ill* 655
 make one – 830,
  867
 visitation of the –
  998
 – at heart 837

– of *weary* 841
 dislike 867
 satiated 869
in –ness and in
 health 604
sick-chamber 655
sicken *nauseate* 395
 disease 655
 pain 830
 weary 841
 disgust 867
sickener
 too much 641
sickle 244, 253
sickly *weak* 160
sick-room 655
side
 consanguinity 11
 edge 231
 laterality 236
 party 712
 ostentation 882
 at one's – 197
 on every – 227
 on one – 243
 on one's – 714
 look only at one –
  of the shield 481
 pass from one – to
  another 607
 take up a – 476
 wrong – up 218
 – by side
  accompaniment
  88
  near 197
  laterality 236
  party 712
 from – to side 314
 – with *aid* 707
  co-operate 709
  concord 714
side-arms 727
side-blow 702
sideboard 191
side-car 272
side-dish 298
side-drum 417
side-kick 890
side issue 643
sideling 279
sidelong 236
sideration 158
sidereal 318
 – time 114
siderite 288
Sideromancy 511
side-saddle 215
side-scene 599
sideslip 267
sidesman 996

side-track 287
sidewalk 627
sideways 217, 236
side-wind
 oblique 217
 circuit 629
 cunning 702
sidle *oblique* 217
 lateral 236
 deviate 279
siege 716
 lay – to 716
 state of – 722
siege-train 727
siesta 683
sieve *sort* 60
 perforate 260
 clean 652
 memory like a –
  506
 pour water into
  a – 638, 818
 stop one hole in
  a – 819
sift *simplify* 42
 sort 60
 inquire 461
 discriminate 465
 clean 652
 – the chaff from
  the wheat 609
sigh 405, 839
 – for 865
sighing like
 furnace 902
sight *much* 31
 multitude 102
 vision 441
 appearance 448
 ugly 846
 prodigy 872
 at – 132, 441
 dim – 443
 in – 446
 in – of 197, 441
 in plain – 525
 keep in – 457
 within – of shore
  858
sightless
 blind 442
 invisible 447
 ugly 846
sightly 845
sights, see – 455
sightseeing 441
sightseer 444, 455
sigil *seal* 550
 evidence 769
sigmoidal 248
sign *attest* 467

left-handed 239
sullen 901a
sink *disappear* 4
destroy 162
descend 306
lower 308
submerge 310
neglect 460
conceal 528
cloaca 653
fatigue 688
vanquish 731
fail 732
adversity 735
invest 787
pain 828
depressed 837
– back 661
– of corruption
653
– into the grave
360
– of iniquity 945
– in the mind
thought 451
memory 505
excite 824
– money 809
– into oblivion 506
– or swim
certainty 474
perseverance 604a
sinking
heart – 837
– fund 802
sinless 946
**sinned against than
sinning, more –**
946
sinner 949
Sinn Fein 742
sin-offering 952
sinuous 243, 248
sinus 252
sip *small* 32
drink 298
siphon 350
sippet 298
sir *man* 373
title 877
– Oracle 887
sirdar 745
sire 166
siren
sea-nymph 341
loud sound 404
musician 416
seducing 615
warning 668
alarm 669
evil-doer 913

demon 980
sorcerer 994
song of the –s 615
– strains 415
sirene *musical
instrument* 417
siriasis 503
sirius 423
sirocco *wind* 349
heat 382
sirrah! 949
sister *kin* 11
likeness 17
nurse 662
nun 996
sisterhood
party 712
frail – 962
sisterly 906
sisters:
weird – 994
– three 601
sistrum 417
Sisyphus, task of –
useless 645
difficult 704
sit 308
– down *settle* 184
lie 213
stoop 308
– in judgment
adjudge 480
jurisdiction 965
lawsuit 969
– on 215
– on thorns
annoyance 828
fear 860
site 183, 780
sith 476
sitting [*see* sit]
incubation 673
convocation 696
– up *late* 133
work 686
sitting-room 191
situ, in – 183, 265
situation
circumstances 8
place **183**
location 184
business 625
out of a – 185
Siva 979
six 98
– of one and half-
a-dozen of the
other 27
**sixes and sevens,
at** – 59, 713
sixty 98

sizar 746
size *degree* 26
magnitude 31
glue 45
arrange 60
dimensions **192**
viscid 352
– up 480
sizzle 409
sjambok 975
skat 840
skate
locomotion 266
vehicle 272
skating 840
skean 727
skedaddle 623
skeel 191
skein 219
tangled – 59
skeleton
remains 40
essential part 30
thin 203
support 215
corpse 362
plan 626
reduced to a – 659
– in the closet
649, 830
– at the feast 836
skelter 276
skepticism
doubt 485
incredulity 487
irreligion 989
sketch
form 240
represent 554
paint 556
describe 594
plan 626
sketcher 559
sketchy
incomplete 53
feeble 575
unfinished 730
skew 217
–bald 440
skewer 45
ski 266, 272
–running 840
–joring 840
–jumping 840
skiagraphy 421,
554, 556
skid *support* 215
hindrance 706
skies:
exalt to the – 873
praise to the – 933

skiff 273
skill **698**
acquisition of –
539
game of – 840
skillet 191
skilly 293
skim *move* 266
navigate 267
rapid 274
neglect 460
summarize 596
skimp 460, 819
skimpy 640
skin *outside* 220
tegument 223
peel 226
swindle 791
fleece 814
wet to the – 339
with a whole – 670
without – 822
mere – and bone
203
– a flint 471, 819
– over 660
skin-deep
shallow 32, 209
external 220
skinned: thick– 376
thin– 375
skinny 203, 223
skip *jump* 309
neglect 460
rejoice 838
skipjack
prosperous 734
low-born 876
skipper
sea captain 269
captain 745
skippingly 70
skips, by – 70
skirmish 720
skirmisher 726
skirt
appendix 39
pendent 214
dress 225
surrounding 227
edge 231
side 236
– dance 840
skirting 231
skirts of:
hang upon the –
sequence 281
on the –
near 197
skit *ridicule* 856
detraction 934

fail 732
slipper 225
 hunt the – 840
slippery
 transient 111
 smooth 255
 greasy 355
 uncertain 475
 vacillating 607
 dangerous 665
 facile 705
 faithless 940
 – *ground* 667
slipshod 575
slipslop
 absurdity 497
 solecism 568
 weak language 575
slit *divide* 44
 chink 198
 furrow 259
slither 264
sliver 51
slobber *drivel* 297
 slop 337
 dirt 653
sloe *black* 431
slog 143
slogan 722
sloop 273
 –of-war 726
slop *spill* 297
 water 337
 dirt 653
slope *oblique* 217
 run away 623
sloppy *moist* 339
 marsh 345
 - *style* 575
slops *clothes* 225
slosh 337, 653
slot 44, 260
sloth 683
slouch *low* 207
 oblique 217
 move slowly 275
 inactive 683
slouching *ugly* 846
slough
 quagmire 345
 dirt 653
 difficulty 704
 adversity 735
 – of Despond 859
sloven *untidy* 59
 bungler 701
slovenly *untidy* 59
 careless 460
 - *style* 575
 dirty 653

awkward 699
vulgar 851
slow *tardy* 133
 inert 172
 moderate 174
 motion 275
 inactive 683
 wearisome 841
 dull 843
by – degrees 26
– *movement*
 music 415
march in – time 275
– as molasses in January 275
be – to
 unwilling 603
 not finish 730
 refuse 764
slow-coach 701
slowness 275
sloyd 537
slubber 653
slubberdegullion 876
sludge 653
slug *slow* 275
 inaction 681
 inactivity 683
 bullet 727
sluggard 275, 683
sluggish 172, 823, 843
sluice *limit* 233
 egress 295
 river 348
 conduit 350
 open the –s 297
slum 653
slumber 683
slump 304
slur *blemish* 847
 stigma 874
 gloss over 937
 reproach 938
 – over *neglect* 460
 slight 483
slush *marsh* 345
 semiliquid 352
 dirt 653
slut *untidy* 59
 female 374
 dirty 653
 unchaste 962
sly *stealthy* 528
 cunning 702
smack
 small quantity 32
 mixture 41
 boat 273

impulse 276
taste 390
thud 406
kiss 902
strike 972
– the lips
 pleasure 377
taste 390
savoury 394
rejoice 838
– of *resemble* 17
small
 – *in degree* 32
 – *in size* 193
 become – 195
 feel – 879
 of – *account* 643
 esteem of –
  account 930
 – arms 727
 – beer 643, 880, 930
 – coin 800
 – chance 473
 – fry 193, 643, 876
 – matter 643
 – number 103
 – part 51
 – pica 591
 in the – hours 125
 on a – scale 32, 193
 – talk 588
small-bore 727
small-clothes 225
smaller 34, 195
smallness 32
smalls 225
smalt 438
smart *pain* 378
 active 682
 clever 698
 feel 821
 grief 828
 witty 842
 pretty 845
 ornamental **847**
 – *pace* 274
 – *saying* 842
 – under 821
smarten 847
smart-money 973
smash 162, 732
smasher 792
smatch 390
smatterer 493
smattering 491
smear *cover* 223
 soil 653
 blemish 848
smell 398

bad – 401
– of the lamp
 ornate style 577
 prepared 673
– powder 722
smell-feast 886
smelling-bottle 400
smelt *heat* 384
 prepare 673
smicker 838
smile 836, 838
 raise a – 840
 – at 856
 – of contempt 930
 – of fortune 734
 – upon *aid* 707
 courtesy 894
 endearment 902
smirch 431, 653
smirk 838
smite *maltreat* 649
 excite 824
 afflict 830
 punish 972
smith 690
smithereens 161
smitten *love* 897
 – with *moved* 615
smock 225, 258
smock-faced 862
smock-frock 225
smoke
 dust 330
 vapour 336
 heat 382
 tobacco 392
 discover 480a
 suspect 485
 unimportant 643
 dirt 653
 cure 670
 disrespect 929
 end in –
  shortcoming 304
  failure 732
 – the calumet of peace 723
 –ed glasses 424
 – screen 424
 – stack 260
smoking hot 382
smoking-jacket 225
smoking-room 191
smoky *opaque* 426
 dirty 653
smooth *uniform* 16
 calm 174
 flattery 213, 251
 not rough 255
 easy 705
 – the bed of death

sobriety **958**
sobriquet 565
sob sister 534
so-called 545, 565
soc *jurisdiction* 965
socage 777
soccer 840
sociable
  carriage 272
  sociality 892
social *mankind* 372
  sociable 892
  – circle 892
  – evil 961
  – gathering 892
  – science 910
socialism
  government 737
  participation 778
  philanthropy 910
socialist 712
sociality **892**
society
  mankind 372
  party 712
  fashion 852
  sociality 892
  position in – 873
Socinianism 984
sociology 712
sock *hosiery* 225
  drama 599
socket 191, 252
socle 215
Socratic method
  461
sod 344
  beneath the – 363
sodality 712, 888
sodden 339, 384
sofa 215
Sofi 984, 996
soft *stop!* 142
  weak 160
  moderate 174
  smooth 255
  not hard 324
  moist 339
  marsh 345
  silence! 403
  - sound 405
  dulcet 413
  credulous 486
  silly 499
  lenient 740
  tender 822
  timid 862
  own to the – im-
    peachment 529
  – music 415
  – pedal 405

– sawder 617, 933
– soap 356, 933
– tongue, – words
  894
soften [*see* soft]
  moderate 174
  relieve 834
  pity 914
  palliate 937
softening of the
  brain 158
softer sex 374
soft-hearted 914
softling 160
softness **324**
  persuasibility 615
soft-spoken 894
soggy 339
soho
  attention 457
  parley 586
  hunting 622
soi-disant
  asserting 535
  pretender 548
  misnomer 565
  vain 880
  boastful 884
soil *region* 18
  land 342
  dirt 653
  deface 846
  till the – 371, 673
soirée 892
sojourn 186, 189
sojourner 188
soke 181
solace *relief* 834
  recreation 840
  – oneself with
    pleasure 827
solar 318
  – system 318
  – time 114
solatium 973
sold to the devil 949
soldan [*see* sultan]
solder *join* 43
  cement 45
  cohere 46
soldier 726
soldier-like 722,
  861
sole *alone* 87
  base 211
  support 215
  feme – 904
solecism **568**
soleil, coup de –
  hot 384
  mad 503

solemn
  affirmation 535
  important 642
  grave 837
  glorious 873
  ostentatious 882
  religious 987
  worship 990
  – mockery 882
  – silence 403
solemnity *rite* 998
solemnization 883
sol-fa 416
solfeggio 415
solicit *induce* 615
  request 765
  desire 865
  – the attention
    457
solicitor *agent* 758
  petitioner 767
  lawyer 968
solicitous 865
solicitude *care* 459
  pain 828
  anxiety 860
  desire 865
solid *complete* 52
  dense 321
  certain 474
  learned 490
  exact 494
  wise 498
  persevering 604a
  solvent 803
  – angle 244
solidarity
  party 712
solidify 321
soliloquy **589**
solitaire *game* 840
  hermit 893
solitary   } *alone*
solitude   }   87
  secluded 893
solmization 416
solo 87, 415
  – dance 840
Solomon } *wise*
Solon   }   498
  sage 500
solstice 125, 126
soluble *fluid* 333
  liquefy 335
solus 87
solution
  liquefaction 335
  answer 462
  explanation 522
  – of continuity 70
solve *liquefy* 335

  discover 480a
  unriddle 522
solvent
  liquefier 335
  monied 803
somatics 316
sombre *dark* 421
  black 431
  grey 432
  sad 837
sombrero 225
some *indefinite*
  quantity 25
  small quantity 32
  more than one
    100
  –body *person* 372
  important or dis-
    tinguished 642
  in – degree
    degree 26
    small 32
  at – other time 119
  in – place 182
  – ten or a dozen
    102
  – time ago 122
  – time or other
    119
somehow or other
  cause 155
  instrument 631
somersault 218
something *thing* 3
  small degree 32
  matter 316
  – else 15
  – like 17
  – or other 475
sometimes 136
somewhat
  a little 32
  a trifle 643
somewhere 182
  – about 32
somnambulism
  walking 266
  trance 515
somnambulist
  walker 268
  dreamer 515
somniferous
  sleepy 683
  weary 841
somnolence 683
son 167
Son, God the – 976
sonant 402
  letter 561
sonata 415
Sonderbund 769

song *music* 415
  poem 597
  death – 360, 839
  love– 597
  for a mere – 815
  no – no supper 812
  old – 643
songster 416
soniferous 402
sonnet 597
sonneteer 597
sonorous *sound* 402
  loud 404
  language 577
sons of:
  – Belial 988
  – God 977
Soofeeism 984
soon *transient* 111
  future 121
  early 132
  too – for 135
sooner: – or later
  another time 119
  future 121
  – said than done
    704
soot 431, 653
sooth 511
  in good – 543
soothe
  allay 174
  relieve 834
  flatter 933
soothing
  faint sound 405
  – syrup 174
soothsay 511
soothsayer 513, 994
soothsaying 511
sop
  small quantity 32
  food 298
  fool 501
  inducement 615
  reward 973
  – to Cerberus 458
  – in the pan 615
soph 492, 541
Sophi 745, 996
sophism 477, 497
sophist *scholar* 492
  dissembler 548
sophister 492
  student 541
sophistical 477
sophisticate *mix* 41
  debase 659
sophisticated
  spurious 545
sophistry 477

sophomore 541
soporific 683, 841
soporous 683
soprano 410, 416
sorbet 298
sorcerer 994
sorcery 992
sordes 653
sordet 417
sordid *stingy* 819
  covetous 865
sordine 417
sore
  bodily pain 378
  disease 655
  mental suffering
    828, 830
  discontent 832
  anger 900
  – as a boil 901*a*
  – place 822
  – subject 830, 900
sorely *very* 31
s'orienter 278
sorites 476
sorority 712
sorrel 433, 434
sorrow 828
  give – words 839
sorry *trifling* 643
  grieved 828
  mean 876
  make a – face 874
  cut a – figure 874
  be – for 750, 914
  in a – plight 732
  – sight 830, 837
sort *degree* 26
  arrange 60
  kind 75
  – with
    sociality 892
sortable ⎫
sortance ⎭
  agreement 23
sortes
  chance 156, 621
  – Virgilianæ
    sorcery 992
sortie 716
sortilege
  prediction 511
  sorcery 992
sortilegy 621
sortition 621
sorts, out of –
  ill-health 655
  sulky 901*a*
S.O.S. 669, 707
so-so *small* 32
  trifling 643

imperfect 651
sostenuto 415
sot *fool* 501
  drunkard 959
sot à triple étage
  501
sotto voce
  faint sound 405
  conceal 528
  voiceless 581
sou *money* 800
  qui n'a pas le –
    804
soubrette 599, 746
sough *conduit* 350
  noise 405
  cloaca 653
soul *essence* 5
  person 372
  intellect 450
  genius 498
  affections 820
  cure of –s 995
  flow of – 588
  not a – 187
  not dare to say
    one's – is his
    own *subjection*
    749
  fear 860
  – of wit 572
  have one's whole
    – in his work
    686
soulless 683, 823
soul-mate 905
soul-sick 837
soul-stirring 821,
  824
sound *great* 31
  conformable 82
  stable 150
  strong 159
  fathom 208
  bay 343
  noise 402
  investigate 461
  measure 466
  true 494
  wise 498
  sane 502
  good 648
  perfect 650
  healthy 654
  solvent 803
  orthodox 983*a*
  catch a – 418
  safe and – 654,
    670
  – the alarm
    indication 550

warning 668
  alarm 669
  fear 860
  – asleep 683
  full of – and fury
    unmeaning 517
    insolent 885
  – the horn 416
  – of limb 654
  – locator 726
  – mind 502
  – the praises of
    931
  – the note of prep-
    aration 673
  – reasoning 476
  – a retreat 283
  – sleep 683
  – a trumpet
    publish 531
    alarm 669
  – of wind 654
sounding: big –
  577
  – brass 517
sounding-board 417
soundings 208
soundless
  unfathomable 208
  silent 403
soup 298, 352
soupçon 32, 41
souplé 298
sour *acid* 397
  discontented 832
  embitter 835
  uncivil 895
  sulky 901
  – grapes
    impossible 471
    excuse 617
  – the temper 830
source *beginning* 66
  cause 153
sourdet 417
sourdine 417
  à la – *noiseless* 405
  concealed 528
sourdough 463
soured 832
sourness 397
sous tous les
  rapports 52
souse 310, 337
South *direction* 278
  North and –
    opposite 237
Southern
  antipodes 237
  – Cross 318
souvenir 505

optical instru-
  ment 445
spectrum
  colour 428
  variegation 440
  optical illusion
  443
speculate
  view 441
  think 451
  suppose 514
  chance 621
  essay 675
  traffic 794
speculation
  experiment 463
  cards 840
speculative 463, 514
speculum 445
  veluti in – 446
sped *completed* 729
speech 582
  figure of – 521
  parts of – 567
speechify 582
speechless 403, 581
speechmaker 582
speed
  velocity 274
  activity 682
  haste 684
  help 707
  succeed 731
  with breathless –
  684
  God – 731, 906
speedily *soon* 132
speedometer 200,
  274, 553
speedway 840
speer 455, 461
spell *period* 106
  influence 175
  read 539
  letter 561
  necessity 601
  motive 615
  exertion 686
  charm **993**
  cast a – 992
  wonder 870
  knurr and – 840
  – for 865
  – out *interpret* 522
spell-bound 601,
  615
spence 636
spencer 225
spend *effuse* 297
  waste 638
  give 784

purchase 795
expend 809
– freely 816
– time 106
– time in 683
– one's time in
  625
spender 818
spendthrift 818
spent 160, 688
spermaceti 356
spermatic 168
spermatize 168
spero, dum spiro –
  858
spes sibi quisque
  604
spew 297
sphacelus 655
sphere *rank* 26
  domain 74
  space 180
  region 181
  ball 249
  world 318
  business 625
  – of influence 181,
  780
spheroid 249
spherule 249
sphery 318
sphinx *monster* 83
  oracle 513
  ambiguous 520
  riddle 533
spial 668
spice
  small quantity 32
  mixture 41
  pungent 392
  condiment 393
spiced 390
spicilegium 72, 596
spick and span 123
spiculate 253
spiculum 253
spicy 400, 824
spigot 263
spike *sharp* 253
  pierce 260
  plug 263
  – *guns* 158, 645
spikebit 262
spikenard 356
spill *filament* 205
  stopper 263
  shed 297
  splash 348
  match 388
  waste 638
  lavish 818

– blood 722
– and pelt 59
spin *flying* 267
  rotate 312
  pluck 610
  – out *protract* 110
  late 133
  prolong 200
  diffuse style 573
  – the wheel 140
  – a long yarn 549
spindle 312
spindling 203
spindle-shanks 203
spindle-shaped 253
spindrift 353
spine 222, 253
spinel 847
spinet *copse* 367
  harpsichord 417
spinney 367
spinner of yarns
  594
spinosity
  unintelligible 519
  discourtesy 895
  sullenness 901a
spinous *prickly* 253
spinster 374, 904
spiracle 351
spiral 248
spire *height* 206
  convolution 248
  peak 253
  soar 305
spirit *essence* 5
  immateriality 317
  fuel 388
  intellect 450
  meaning 516
  vigorous language
  574
  activity 682
  affections 820
  courage 861
  ghost 980
  bad – 980
  keep one's – up
  hope 858
  with life and – 682
  unclean – 978
  – away 791
  – up 615, 824
Spirit, the Holy –
  976
spirited
  language 574
  active 682
  sensitive 822
  cheerful 836
  brave 861

generous 942
spiritless
  insensible 823
  sad 837
  cowardly 862
spirit-level 213
spiritoso *music* 415
spirit-rapping 992
spirits *drink* 298,
  959
  cheer 836
spirit-stirring 824
spiritual
  immaterial 317
  psychical 450
  heterodoxy 984
  divine 976
  pious 987
  – director 996
  – existence 987
spiritualism
  immateriality 317
  intellect 450
  sorcery 992
spiritualize 317
  reasoning 476
spirituel 842
spirt *eject* 297
  stream 348
  haste 684
  exertion 686
spirtle *disperse* 73
  splash 348
spissitude 321, 352
spit *pointed* 253
  perforate 260
  eject 297
  rotate 312
  rain 348
  – fire *irascible* 901
spite 907
  in – of
  disagreement 24
  notwithstanding
  30
  counteraction 179
  opposition 708
  in – of one's teeth
  unwilling 603
  compulsion 744
spiteful 898, 907
  hating 898
spittle 299
spittoon 191
splanchnology 329
splash *affuse* 337
  stream 348
  spatter 653
  parade 882
  make a –
  fame 873

silent 403
– less 467
– life matter 316
painting 556
– more
superior 33
evidence 467
– small voice 405
in – water 714
still-born 360, 732
stillroom 636
stillicidium 348
stilted
elevated 307
- style 577
ridiculous 853
affected 855
boasting 884
stilts support 215
on – high 206
elevated 307
hyperbolical 549
proud 878
boasting 884
stimulant 662
stimulate
energy 171
violence 173
incite 615
excite 824
stimulating
suggestive 514
stimulus 615
sting pain 378
tingle 380
poison 663
excite 824
mental suffering
830
anger 900
stinging
pungent 392
stingo 298
stingy 819
stink 401
– in the nostrils
unpleasant 830
dislike 867
hate 898
stink-bomb 727
stink-pot 401
stint degree 26
limit 233
scanty 640
begrudge 819
stintless 639
stipend salary 973
stipendiary
subject 749
receiving 785
magistrate 967

stipple
variegate 440
painting 556
engraving 558
stipulate 769, 770
– for 720
stipule 51
stir energy 171
move 264
agitation 315
excite 375
activity 682
jail 752
emotion 824
make a – 642, 682
– about 682
– the blood 824,
900
– up dissension
713
– the embers 163,
824
– the feelings 824
– the fire 384
– a question 461,
476
– one's stumps
266, 682
– up mix 41
violent 173
excite 824
stirps kin 11
source 153
paternity 166
stirring events 151
important 642
active 682
– news 532
stirrup
support 215
with a foot in the
– 293
stirrup-cup 293, 959
stitch junction 43
pain 378
work 680
– in time 132
– of work 686
stive 384
stiver 800
stoat 401
stoccado 717
stock kinship 11
quantity 25
origin 153
paternity 166
collar 225
soup 298
fool 501
habitual 613
materials 635

store 636
property 780
merchandise 798
money 800
in – 777
laughing – 857
lay in a – 637
take – inspect 457
accounts 811
– exchange 799
– still 265
– in trade
means 632
store 636
property 780
merchandise 798
– with 637
stockade 717
stocked, well – 639
stock exchange 621
stock-farm 370
stocking 225
hoard 800
stock-jobbing 794
stock operator 621
stocks prison 752
funds 802
punishment 975
on the –
business 625
preparation 673
incomplete 730
– and stones 316,
823
stocky 201
stodge 957
stoicism
insensibility 823
inexcitability 826
disinterested 942
temperance 953
stoke 388
stoker 268
stole 999
stolen: – away 671
– goods 793
stolid 499, 843
stomach pouch 191
taste 390
brook 826
desire 865
not have the – to
603
turn the – 830
– of an ostrich 957
stomacher 225
stone heavy 319
dense 321
hard 323
kill 361
lithography 558

material 635
attack 716
weapon 727
punish 972
corner – 642
go down like a –
310
cast the first – at
938
heart of – 823, 907
key– 642
musical –s 417
no – unturned
461, 686
philosopher's –
662
precious – 648
stepping – 627
throw a – at
attack 716
censure 932
accuse 938
throw –s at 907
tomb– 363
mark with a
white – 642
throw a – in one's
own garden 699
– dead 360
– of Sisyphus 645
stone-blind 442
stone-coloured 432
stone-deaf 419
stone's throw 197
stoneware 384
stony 323
stony-hearted 907,
919
stooge 711, 746, 886
stook 72
stool 215
between two –s
704
– of repentance
950
– pigeon 527, 548
stoop slope 217
lower 308
humble 879
servile 886
dishonourable 940
– to conquer 702
stop end 67
cease 142
close 261
rest 265
silent 403
danger 665
inaction 681
hinder 706
prohibit 761

put a – to 142
– the breath 361
– the ears 419
– a flow 348
– a gap 660
– the mouth 479, 581
– payment 808
– press news 532
– short 142, 265
– short of 304
– the sound 408*a*
– up 261
– the way 706
stopcock 263
stopgap
  substitute 147
  stopper 263
stoppage
  cessation 142
  hindrance 706
stopper 263
stopping place 292
store *store* 184
  stock **636**
  shop 799
  in – *destiny* 152
  preparing 673
  lay in a – 637
  set – by 642, 931
  set no – 483
  – of knowledge 490
  – in the memory 505
store-house 636
store-keeper 636
store-ship 273, 726
storied 594
storm *crowd* 72
  convulsion 146
  violence 173
  agitation 315
  wind 349
  danger 667
  attack 716
  passion 825
  anger 900
  ride the – 267
  take by –
  conquer 731
  seize 789
  – brewing 665
  – in a teacup
  overrate 482
  exaggerate 549
  unimportance 643
storthing 696
story *rooms* 191
  layer 204
  news 532

lie 546
  history 594
  the old – 897
  as the – goes 532
story-teller 548, 594
stot 366
stound 870
stoup *cup* 191
  altar 1000
stour 59
stout *strong* 159
  large 192
  drink 298
stout-hearted 861
stove *fireplace* 386
  – in 252
stow *locate* 184
  pack close 195
  store 636
stowage 180, 184
stowaway 528, 673
strabism 443
straddle 266, 607
Stradivarius 417
strafe 972
straggle 266, 279
straggler 268
straggling 44, 59
straight
  vertical 212
  rectilinear 246
  direction 278
  all – *rich* 803
  solvent 807
  – course 628
  – descent 167
  – face 837
  – sailing 705
straighten 246
  – up 60
straightforward 278
  truthful 543
  artless 703
  honourable 939
straightness 246
straight shot 278
straightway 132
strain *race* 11
  weaken 160
  operation 170
  violence 173
  percolate 295
  transgress 303
  sound 402
  melody 415
  overrate 482
  exaggerate 549
  style 569
  poetry 597
  voice 580
  clean 652

effort 686
  fatigue 688
  – in the arms 902
  – one's eyes 441, 507
  – at a gnat and swallow a camel 608
  – one's invention 515
  – the meaning 523
  – every nerve 686
  – a point
  go beyond 303
  exaggerate 549
  not observe 773
  undue 925
  – the throat 411
strait
  interval 198
  water 343
  difficulty 704
straitened
  poor 804
strait-handed 819
strait-jacket 752
strait-laced
  severe 739
  restraint 751
  fastidious 868
  haughty 878
strait-waistcoat 751, 752
strake 205
stramash 720
strand *thread* 205
  shore 231, 342
stranded
  stuck fast 150
  in difficulty 704
  failure 732
  pain 828
strange
  unrelated 10
  exceptional 83
  ridiculous 853
  wonderful 870
  – bedfellows 713
  – to say 870
strangely *much* 31
stranger 57
  a – to 491
strangle
  render powerless 158
  contract 195
  kill 361
strap *fasten* 43
  fastening 45
  restraint 752
  punish 972

instrument of punishment 975
strappado 972
strapping
  mighty 31
  strong 159
  pace 272
  big 192
strapwork 847
stratagem
  deception 545
  plan 626
  artifice 702
strategic *plan* 626
  artifice 702
strategist
  planner 626
  director 694
  proficient 700
strategy 692, 722
strath 252
strathspey 840
stratification 204, 329
stratocracy 737
stratosphere 338
stratum 204
stratus 353
straw *scatter* 73
  light 320
  unimportant 643
  care not a – 866, 930
  catch at –s
  overrate 482
  credulous 486
  misuse 679
  unskilful 699
  hope 858
  rash 863
  the eyes drawing –s 683
  in the – 161
  man of –
  unsubstantial 4
  cheat 525
  insolvent 808
  low person 876
  not worth a – 643, 645
  – to show the wind 463
straw-coloured 436
straw-hat 225
stray *dispersion* 73
  exceptional 83
  random 156
  wanderer 268
  deviate 279
streak *intrinsicality* 5

strong *great* 31
  powerful 159
  energetic 171
  tough 327
  taste 390
  pungent 392
  fetid 401
  healthy 654
  feeling 821
  wonderful! 870
  smell – of 398
  – accent 580
  – argument 476
  by a – arm 744
  – box 802
  with a – hand
  resolution 604
  exertion 686
  severity 739
  – language 574
  – pull 686
  – point 476
strong-headed 498
stronghold
  refuge 666
  defence 717
  prison 752
strong-minded 498,
  861
strong-scented 398
strong-willed 604
strop 253
strophe 597
strow 73
struck [*see*
  stricken, strike]
  awe– 860
  – down 732
  – all of a heap
  emotion 821
  wonder 870
  humbled 879
  – with *love* 897
structural *state* 7
structure
  production 161
  form 240
  texture 329
  organization 357
struggle *exert* 686
  difficulty 704
  contend 720
strum 416, 517
strumpet 962
strung
  highly – 825
strut *walk* 266
  pride 878
  parade 882
  boast 884
  – and fret one's

hour upon a
  stage 359, 599
strychnine 663
stub 40, 550
stubbed 201
stubble *remains* 40
  useless 645
stubborn
  strong 159
  hard 323
  obstinate 606
  resistance 719
stubby 201
stucco 45, 223
stuck [*see* stick]
  – fast 150, 704
  be – on 897
stuck-up 878
stud *hanging-peg*
  214
  knob 250
  horses 271
studded *many* 102
  spiked 253
  variegated 440
student 541
stud-farm 370
studied
  predetermined
  611
studio *room* 191
  painting 556
  workshop 691
studious
  thoughtful 451
  docile 539
  intending 620
study *copy* 21
  room 191
  thought 451
  attention 457
  research 461
  learning 539
  painting 556
  intention 620
  retreat 893
  brown – 515
stuff *substance* 3
  contents 190
  expand 194
  line 224
  matter 316
  texture 329
  absurdity 497
  unmeaning 517
  material 635
  trifle 643
  overeat 957
  such – as dreams
  are made of 515
  – gown 968

– in 300
  – the memory
  with 505
  – and nonsense
  unsubstantial 4
  absurdity 497
  unmeaning 517
  – up *close* 261
  hoax 545
stuffed
  redundancy 641
stuffing *contents* 190
  lining 224
  stopper 263
stuffy 321, 382
stultified 732
stultify oneself 699
stultiloquy 497
stumble *fall* 306
  flounder 315
  error 495
  unskilful 699
  failure 732
  – on *chance* 156
  discover 480a
stumbling-block
  difficulty 704
  hindrance 706
stump
  remainder 40
  trunk 51
  walk 266
  drawing 556
  speak 582
  stir your –s
  active 682
  worn to the – 659
  – along *slow* 275
stump orator 582,
  887
stumpy *short* 201
stun *physically*
  insensible 376
  loud 404
  deafen 419
  unexpected 508
  morally insen-
  sible 823
  affect 824
  astonish 870
stung [*see* sting]
  – to the quick 824
stunt *shorten* 201
  performance 680
stunted 193, 195
  insufficient 640
stupe 834
stupefaction 826
stupefy
  - *physically* 376
  - *morally* 823

astonish 870
stupendous
  great 31
  large 192
  wonderful 870
stupid
  unsubstantial 4
  misjudging 481
  credulous 486
  unintelligent 499
  tiresome 841
  dull 843
stupor
  insensibility 823
  wonder 870
stupration 961
sturdy *strong* 159
  persevering 604a
  – beggar 767, 792
stutter 583
sty *house* 189
  enclosure 232
  dirt 653
Stygian *dark* 421
  diabolic 945
  infernal 982
cross the – ferry
  die 360
  – shore
  death 360
style *state* 7
  time 114
  painting 556
  graver 558
  name 564
  diction **569**
  writing 590
  beauty 845
  fashion 852
stylet
  awl 262
  dagger 727
stylist 578
Stylites, Simon –
  893
stylographic pen
  590
stylography 590
stylus 590
styptic 397
Styx 982
suasible 602
suasion 615
suave mari magno
  664
suaviter in modo
  826, 894
suavity 894
sub 34
  – spe rati 475
subacid 397

subaction 330
subahdar 745
subalpine 206
subaltern
　inferior 34
　soldier 726
　officer 745
　servant 746
　plebeian 876
subaqueous 208
subastral 318
subaudition 527
subcommittee 696
subconscious 317
subcontrary 237
subcutaneous 221
subdean 996
subdichotomy 91
subdititious 147
subdivide 44
subdivision
　part 51
　class 75
　military 726
　realty 780
subdolous 702
subdominant 413
subdual 731
subduction **38**
subdue *calm* 174
　succeed 731
subdued
　morally 826
sub-editor 593
subitaneous 113
subito 113
subjacent 207
subject *dominate*
　175
　liable 177
　topic 454
　meaning 516
　servant 746
　enthral 749
　- of dispute 713
　- to examination
　461
　- of inquiry 461
　- of thought 454
　- to 469, 475
subjection **749**
subjective
　intrinsic 5
　immaterial 317
　intellectual 450
subjoin 37
subjugate 731, 749
subjugation 732,
　824
subjunctive 37
sublapsarian 984

sublation 38
sublevation 307
sub-lieutenant 745
sublimate
　elevate 307
　lighten 320
　vaporize 336
sublime *high* 206
　language 574
　beauty 845
　glory 873
　magnanimous
　942
from the - to the
　ridiculous 853
subliminal 317
sublineation 550
sublunary 318
submarine
　deep 208
　ship 272
　warship 726
　- chaser 726
　- warfare 722
submediant 413
submerge
　destroy 162
　immerse 300
　plunge 310
　steep 337
submersible 273,
　726
submersion 208
subministration
　707
submission **725**
　obedience 743
submissive
　tractable 705
　enduring 826
　humble 879
submit to arbitra-
　tion 774
submonish 695
submultiple 84
subordinate
　inferior 34
　unimportant 643
　subject 749
subordination 58
suborn 615, 795
subpœna 741, 969
subreption
　falsehood 544
　acquisition 775
subrogation 147
subscribe
　assent 488
　aid 707
　agree to 769
　give 784

subscript 39, 65
subscription
　gift 784
subsequent
　- *in order* 63
　- *in time* 117
subserviency
　servility 886
subservient
　instrumental 631
　aid 707
　subject 749
subside 36, 306
subsidiary *aid* 707
　servant 746
subsidy
　assistance 707
　gift 784
　pay 809
subsist *exist* 1
　continue 141
　live 359
subsistence 298
subsoil 221, 342
substance
　existence 1
　thing 3
　quantity 25
　inside 221
　matter 316
　texture 329
　important part
　642
　wealth 803
in - 596
man of - 803
substantial
　existing 1
　hypostatic 3
　material 316
　dense 321
　true 494
　- *meaning* 516
substantiality **3**
substantially
　intrinsically 5
　- *true* 494
substantiate 467,
　924
substantive 1, 3
substitute
　inferior 34
　change 147
　means **634**
　deputy 759
substitution **147**
substratum
　substance 3
　layer 204
　base 211
　support 215

　interior 221
　materiality 316
substructure 211
subsultory 315
subsume 54
subtend 237
subterfuge 617
　sophistry 477
　lie 546
　cunning 702
subterranean 208
subtile *light* 320
　rare 322
　- *texture* 329
subtilize *rarefy* 322
　sophistry 477
subtle *slight* 32
　light 320
　cunning 702
　- point 704
　- reasoning 476
subtlety 477, 498
subtraction
　subduction 38
　arithmetic 85
　taking 789
subtrahend 38, 84
suburb *town* 189
　near 197
　environs 227
subvention
　support 215
　aid 707
　gift 784
subversion 146
subvert *destroy* 162
　invert 218
　depress 308
subway 627
　- train 272
succedaneum 147
succeed *follow* 63
　posterior 117
　success 731
　transfer 783
　- to *acquire* 775
succès d'estime 873
success **731**
succession
　sequence 63
　continuity 69
　repetition 104
　posteriority 117
　transfer 783
in quick - 136
in regular - 138
　- of ideas 451
　- of time 109
successless 732
successor 65, 117
succinct 572

succour 707
succubus 980
succulent
  nutritive 298
  juicy 333
  semiliquid 352
succumb
  fatigue 688
  yield 725
  fail 732
succussion 315
such: – as 17
  – being the case 8
  – like 17
  – a one 372
suchwise 8
suck
  draw off 297
  drink 298
  take 789
  – in 296
  – the blood of 789
sucker 260, 547
suckle 707
suckling *infant* 129
suction *force* 157
  reception 296
sudary 652
sudation 299
sudatory 386
sudden
  transient 111
  instantaneous 113
  soon 132
  unexpected 508
  – burst 508
  – death 360
  – and quick in
    quarrel 901
  – thought 612
sudorific 382
suds *froth* 353
  in the – 704, 837
sue *demand* 765
  go to law 969
suet 356
suffer *physical pain*
  378
  disease 655
  allow 760
  feel 821
  endure 826
  moral pain 828
  – for 972
  – punishment 972
sufferance, tenant
  on – 779
suffice 639
sufficiency 639
suffix *adjunct* 39
  sequence 63

sequel 65
letter 561
suffiation 349
suffocate *kill* 361
  excess 641
suffocating 382, 401
suffocation 361
suffragan 996
suffrage 609
suffragette 742
suffusion
  mixture 41
  feeling 821
  blush 879
sugar 396
sugar-loaf 253
suggest *suppose* 514
  inform 527
  influence 615
  advise 695
  – itself 451, 515
  – a question 461
suggestio falsi 546
suggestion 626, 695
suggestive
  reminder 505
  significant 516
  descriptive 594
  bawdy 961
sui generis 83
suicidal 162
suicide *killing* 361
suisse *beadle* 996
Suisse, point d'ar-
  gent point de –
  812
suit *accord* 23
  series 69
  class 75
  clothes 225
  expedient 646
  petition 765
  courtship 902
  follow – 19
  law– 969
  love– 897
  – the action to the
    word 550
  – the occasion 646
  do – and service
    743
suit case 191
suitable 23, 646
  – season 134
suite *sequel* 65
  series 69
  escort 88
  retinue 746
  – of rooms 189, 191
suitor
  petitioner 767

lover 897
lawsuit 969
sulcated 259
sulky *carriage* 272
  obstinate 606
  discontented 832
  dejected 837
  sullen 901a
sullen
  obstinate 606
  gloomy 837
  discourteous 895
  sulky 901a
sullenness 901a
sully 653, 874
sulphur 388
  – coloured 436
sultan 745
sultry 382
sum *number* 84
  money 800
  – and substance
  meaning 516
  synopsis 596
  important part
    642
  – total 800
  – up *reckon* 85
  description 594
  compendium 596
sumless 105
summation 37, 85
summary
  transient 111
  early 132
  short 201
  concise 572
  compendious 596
  illegal 964
  – of facts 594
summer *season* 125
  support 215
  heat 382
  Indian – 125
  St. Luke's – 125
  St. Martin's – 125
  – lightning 423
  – time 114
summer-house 191
summerset 218
summit *top* **210**
summon 741, 969
  – up 505, 824
  – up courage 861
summum:
  – bonum 618, 827
  – jus 922
sump *base* 211
  pool 343
  slough 345
  store 636

cess 653
sumpter-horse 271
sumptuary 800, 809
sumptuous 882
sum-total 50
sun 318
  luminary 423
  glory 873
  bask in the – 377
  going down of
    the – 126
  farthing candle to
    the – 645
  under the – 180,
    318
  as the – at noon-
    day *bright* 420
  certain 474
  plain 525
  – oneself 384
Sun:
  – of Righteousness
    976
sunbeam 420
  –s from cucumbers
    471
sunburn *heat* 384
sunburnt *brown* 433
Sunday:
  – Monday &c. 138
  –'s best 847, 882
  – school 542
sunder 44
sundial 114
sundown 126
sundry 102
sunk [*see* sink]
  deep 208
  – fence 717
  – in iniquity 945
  – in oblivion 508
sunken rocks 667
sunless 421
sunlight 420
sunny *warm* 382
  luminous 420
  cheerful 836
sunny side 829
  view the – 858
  – of the hedge 734
sun-painting 556
sunrise 125
sunset 126
  at – 133
sunshade 223, 424
sunshine *light* 420
  prosperity 734
  happy 827
  cheerful 836
sunstroke 384, 503
sun-up 125

- wine 396
- words 894
sweeten 396, 829
sweetheart 897
sweetmeat 396
sweetness 396
sweets 298, 396
sweet-scented 400
swell *increase* 35
　expand 194
　wave 348
　sound 404
　emotion 821
　fop 854
　nobility 875
　swagger 885
　extol 931
　ground – 315
　– over 250
　– with rage 900
　– the ranks of 37
　– out
　diffuse style 573
swelling
　expansion 194
　prominence 250
　- *style* 577
　excitement 824
swell-mob 792
swelter 382
swerve *change* 140
　deviate 279
　demur 603
　tergiversation 607
swift 274
swig 298, 959
swill *dirt* 653
　drink 298
　intemperance 954
　drunkenness 959
swim *navigate* 267
　float 305
　light 320
　– against the
　　stream 704
　– in *pleasure* 377
　abundance 639
　– with the stream
　　82, 683
　– with the tide
　　734
swimming 840
　- *eyes* 443
　- *head* 503
　– belt 666
　– pool 652, 840
swimmingly
　easily 705
　success 731
　prosperity 734
swindle 545, 791

swindler 548, 792
swine 366
　cast pearls
　　before – 638
　– of Epicurus
　　954*a*
swineherd 746
swing
　operation 170
　space 180
　hang 214
　oscillate 314
　freedom 748
　amusement 840
　full – 682, 731
　give full – 705
　have one's – 738
　– the lead 544
swinge 972
swinging *great* 31
swinish 954, 957
　– multitude 876
swink 686
swipe 276
swirl 312
swish 409
switch *shunt* 279
　flog 972
　rod 975
switchback 840
Swithin, reign of
　St. – 348
swivel *hinge* 312
　cannon 727
swivel-eye 443
swollen 194, 878
swoon 158, 688
swoop 274
　descend 306
　seize 789
　at one fell – 173
swop 794
sword *weapon* 727
　draw the – ⎫
　flesh one's– ⎬ 722
　measure –s 720, ⎭
　　722
　at the point of
　　the – 722, 889,
　　898
　severity 739
　compulsion 744
　subjection 749
　put to the – 361
　– of Damocles 667
　– in hand
　prepare 673
　war 722
　turn –s into
　　ploughshares
　　723

- of state 747
swordsman 726
Sybarite 954*a*
sybaritism 954
sycophancy 933
sycophant 886, 935
syenite *blue* 438
syllable 561
　breathe not a –
　　528
syllabus 86, 596
syllogism 476
sylph 979
sylvan 367
symbol
　copy 21
　*mathematica*ι - 84
　sign 550
symbolize 526, 550
　represent 554
symmetrical 80
symmetry
　equality 27
　order 58
　conformity 82
　centrality 222
　regular form **242**
　style 578
　beauty 845
　want of – 846
sympathizer
　partisan 890
sympathy
　concord 714
　friendship 888
　love 897
　kindness 906
　pity 914
　condolence 915
symphonious 413
symphony
　overture 64
　music 415
　concord 714
symphysis 43
symposium 72, 840,
　　892
symptom 550, 668
symptomatology
　　522
synagogue 1000
synchronism 120
synchysis 218
syncopation 415
syncope
　impotence 158
　musical 413
　rhetoric 572
　fatigue 688
syncretic 61
syncretism 24, 984

syndic 745, 967
syndicate 696, 712
synecdoche 521
synod 696, 995
synonym
　identity 13
　meaning 516
　interpretation 522
　term 564
synonymous 13
synopsis
　arrangement 60
　list 86
　compendium 596
synovia 332, 356
syntagma 60
syntax 567
synthesis
　combination 48
　composition 54
　reasoning 476
synthesize 54
syntony 23, 120
syringe 337, 348
syrup 352, 396
system *order* 58
　rule 79
　plan 626
　– of knowledge
　　490
　– of opinions 484
systematize 60, 626
systole 195
syzygy 199

T

T, to a – 494
tab 39, 550, 747
tabard 225
tabby *mottled* 440
　gossip 588
tabefaction 195
tabernacle 189,
　　1000
　house 189
　temple 1000
tabid *shrunk* 195
　thin 203
　disease 655
　deteriorated 659
table
　arrangement 60
　list 86
　defer 133
　layer 204
　support 215
　flat 251
　repast 298
　writing 590

on the – 626, 673
turn the –s 218, 468
under the –
  hidden 528
  drunk 959
– of the Lord 1000
– the motion 624
tableau *list* 86
  appearance 448
  painting 556
  theatrical 599
table-cloth 652
table d'hôte 298
table-land 213, 344
tabescent 195
tablet *layer* 204
  flat 251
  record 551
  writing 590
  remedy 662
table-talk 532, 588
tablets of the
  memory 505
table-turning 992
tabloid 531, 662
taboo 762, 992
tabor 417
tabouret 215
tabret 417
tabula rasa
  inexistence 2
  absence 187
  ignorance 491
  obliterated 552
  facility 705
tabulate 60, 69
tabulation 551
tachometer 274
tachygraphy 590
tachy case 191
tacit 526
taciturnity 585
Tacitus
  concise style 572
tack *join* 43
  nails 45
  change course 140
  sharp 253
  direction 278
  turn 279
  food 289
  way 627
  go upon another – 607
  wrong – 732
  – to *add* 37
tackle
  fastening 45
  gear 633
  try 675

undertake 676
manage 693
tacky 352
tact *touch* 379
  discrimination 465
  wisdom 498
  skill 698
  taste 850
  want of – 851
tactful 894
tactician 700
tactics 692, 722
tactless 895
tactile &c. 379
tadpole 129
tædium vitæ 837, 841
tag *small* 32
  addition 37
  adjunct 39
  fastening 45
  sequel 65
  end 67
  point 253
  sheep 366
  – after 281
tagrag and bobtail 876
tail *sequel* 65
  end 67
  pendent 214
  back 235
  aircraft 273
  estate – 780
  turn – 623
  – off *decrease* 36
tail-coat 225
tailor 225, 690
tailoring 225, 882
tail-piece *sequel* 65
  rear 235
  engraving 558
  ornament 847
tail-race 350
taint
  imperfection 651
  dirt 653
  decay 659
  disgrace 874
tainted 401, 655
taintless 652
taj 225
take *eat* 298
  believe 484
  know 490
  understand 518
  succeed 731
  receive 785
  appropriate 789
  captivate 829

give and – 718
– a back 508, 870
– an account of 85
– action 680
– advice 695
– after 17
– aside 586
– away
  annihilate 2
  subtract 38
  remove 185
  seize 789
– back again 790
– a back seat 34
– by [*see below*]
– the cake 33
– care 668, 864
– care of 459, 664
– no care of 460
– off 293
– one's chance 621, 675
– one's choice 609
– things as they come 683, 826
– comfort 831, 834
– the consequences 154
– coolly 826
– a course 692
– its course 143, 151
– no denial 606, 744
– a disease 655
– down
  swallow 298
  depress 308
  record 551
  write 590
  dismantle 681
  humiliate 874
  censure 932
– easily 826
– effect 151, 170
– an ell 885
– exception 932
– one's fancy 829, 865
– fire 384
– flight 623
– from 38, 789
– for [*see below*]
– the good the gods provide 831
– heart 831, 836
– to heart 828, 832
– heed 864
– a hint 498
– hold of 46, 789

– hold of the mind 484
– ill 832
– in [*see below*]
– an infection 655
– no interest in 823
– into [*see below*]
– it 484, 514
– the lead 62
– a leaf out of another's book 19
– a lease 788
– leave of 624
– a liberty 748
– away life 361
– a likeness 554
– measures 626
– money 810
– no note of 460
– no note of time 115
– notice 457
– one's oath 535
– off [*see below*]
– oneself off 293
– on [*see below*]
– one with another 29
– out 301, 552
– over 783
– part with 709
– pattern by 19
– a peep 441
– pen in hand 590
– to pieces 44, 681
– place 151
– the place of 147
– possession of 589
– precedence 33, 62
– its rise 66, 154
– root 150, 184
– the shine out of 33
– ship 267
– steps 673, 680
– stock 85
– time
  duration 106
  late 133
  leisure 685
– time by the forelock 132
– to *habit* 613
  pursuit 622
  use 677
  like 827
  desire 865
  love 897
– on trust 484

tape *string* 205
  measure 466
  – machine 553
taper *contract* 195
  narrow 203
  candle 423
  – to a point 253
tapestry 556, 847
tapinois, en – 528
tapis: on the –
  event 151
  topic 454
  intention 620
  plan 626
tap-root 153
taps 550
tapster 746
tar *cover* 223
  sailor 269
  pitch 356a
  – and feather 929, 972
taradiddle 546
tarantass 272
tarantella 840
tarboosh 225
tardiloquence 583
tardy 133, 275
tare 40a
  – and tret 813
tares 645
targe 717
target 620
  shield 717
tariff 812
tarmac 635
tarn 343
tarnish
  discoloration 429
  soil 653
  deface 848
  disgrace 874
tarpaulin 223
tarry *remain* 110, 265
  later 133
  continue 141
  – for *expect* 507
tart *pastry* 298, 396
  acid 397
  rude 895
  irascible 901
  harlot 962
tartan 440
tartane 273
Tartar *choleric* 901
  catch a – *dupe* 547
  unskilful 699
  retaliation 718
tartar *dirt* 653
  – emetic 663

Tartarus 982
Tartufe
  hypocrisy 544
  deceiver 548
  impiety 988
task *lesson* 537
  business 625
  put to use 677
  fatigue 688
  command 741
  hard – 704
  set a – 741
  take to – 932
  – the memory 505
taskmaster 694
tass 191
tassel 847
taste *sapidity* **390**
  experience 821
  good taste **850**
  man of – 850
  to one's – *savoury* 394
  pleasant 829
  love 897
tasteful 850
tasteless *insipid* 391
tasty 394, 850
tâtonner 463
tatter
  small quantity 32
tatterdemalion 876
Tattersalls 799
tatters *garments* 225
  tear to – 162
tatting 847
tattle 588
tattler 532, 588
tattoo
  drumming 407
  mottled 440
  summons 741
taught [*see* teach]
  fastened 43
taunt 929, 938
tauromachy 720
taut 43
tautology 104, 573
tavern 189
tawdry 851
tawny 433, 436
tax *inquire* 461
  employ 677
  fatigue 688
  command 741
  compel 744
  request 765
  accounts 811
  impost 812

discount 813
accuse 938
– one's energies 686
– the memory 505
taxi 266
taxi-cab 272
taxi-driver 268
taxidermy 368
taxis 60
taxonomy 60
tazza 191
Te Deum 990
te fabula narratur, de – *retaliate* 718
  condemn 971
tea 298
teach 537
  – one's grand- mother 641, 885
  – one his place 879
teachable 539
teacher **540**, 673
teaching **537**
  false – 538
teacup, storm in a –
  overrate 482, 549
  exaggerate 549
teagown 225
team *assemblage* 69, 72
teamster 694
tea-party 892
tea-pot 191
tear *separate* 44
  violence 173
  move rapidly 274
  excite 825
  weeping 839
  – away from 789
  – oneself away 623
  – asunder one's bonds 750
  – one's hair 839
  – out 301
  – to pieces
    separate 44
    destroy 162
  – up *destroy* 162
tear-gas 663, 727
tearful 839
tearing passion 839
tears: draw – 830
  shed – 839
  – in one's eyes
    excited 824
    sad 837
tease *annoy* 830
  spite 907
teaser *difficult* 704

teasing 830
teat 250
tea-table talk 588
technic 698
technica, memoria – 505
technical
  conformable 82
  workmanlike 698
  – college 542
  – education 537
  – knowledge 698
  – school 542
  – term 564
technicality
  special 79
  cant term 563
  formulary 697
technique 556, 698
technocracy 698
technology 698
techy 901
tedious 841
  while away the – hours 681
tedium 841
teem
  produce 161
  productive 168
  abound 639
  – with *multitude* 102
teemful 168
teeming *crowd* 72
teemless 169
'teens 98
  in one's – 127, 129
teeter 314
teeth 330, 781
  armed to the – 673, 717, 722
  between the – 405
  cast in one's – 938
  chattering of – 383
  have cut one's eye – 698
  in the – of 704, 708
  grind one's – 900
  the run of one's – 815
  set one's – 604
  show one's – 900
  in spite of one's – 708, 744
  make one's – chatter 385, 860
  set the – on edge
    scrape 331
    saw 397
    stridor 410
    pain the feelings

627
thorough-going 52
thoroughly, do – 729
thorough-paced 31
thorp 189
though
 compensation 30
 qualification 469
 opposition 708
thought *little* 32
 reflection **451**
 idea 453
 give a – to 457
 not to be – of 610, 761
 organ of – 450
 quick as – 274
 seat of – 450
 subject of – 454
 want of – 458
 who could have – it? 508
 – of 454
thoughtful 451, 498
thoughtless
 incogitant 452
 inattentive 458
 careless 460
 improvident 674
thoughts:
 – that breathe 574
 – elsewhere 458
thousand 98, 102
 one in a – 648, 948
thraldom 749, 750
thrash 972
Thraso 887
Thrasonic 884, 885
thread
 arrange 60
 series 69
 weak 160
 filament 205
 pass through 302
 not have a dry – 339
 hang by a – 665
 life hangs by a – 360
 worn to a – 659
 – one's way 266, 302
threadbare 226, 659
threadpaper 203
threat **909**
threaten
 future 121
 destiny 152
 danger 665

threatening
 warning 668
 unhopeful 859
three 93
 – in one and one in – 976
 sisters – 601
 go through – hundred and sixty degrees 311
 – sheets in the wind 959
 – times three
 number 98
 approbation 931
threefold 93
three-score 98
 – years and ten 128
three-tailed bashaw
 master 745
 nobility 875
threne 938
threnody 839
thresh 972
 – out 461
threshold
 beginning 66
 edge 231
 at the – *near* 197
 – of an inquiry 461
thrice 93
 – happy 827
 –told tale 573
thrid 302
thrift
 prosperity 734
 gain 775
 economy 817
thriftless 818
thrill
 physical pain 378
 touch 380
 feeling 821
 excitation 824
thrilling
 pleasing 829
 painful 830
thrive 734
throat *opening* 260
 pipe 350, 351
 cut the – 361
 force down the – 739
 stick in one's – 581, 585
 take by the – 789
throb 315, 821
throbbing: – heart 860

 – pain 378
throe
 revolution 146
 violence 173
 agitation 315
 physical pain 378
 agony 828
 birth– 161
throne *abode* 189
 seat 215
 emblem of authority 747
 ascend the – 737
 occupy the – 737
 power behind the – 526
 – of God 981
throng 72
throttle
 render powerless 158
 close 261
 kill 361
 seize 789
 – down 275
through
 owing to 154
 viâ 278
 by means of 631
 get – 729
 go – one 824
 wet – 339
 – thick and thin
 complete 52
 violence 173
 perseverance 604a
throughout 50, 52
 – the world 180
throw *impel* 276
 propel 284
 exertion 686
 – oneself into the arms of 664
 – away *reject* 610
 waste 638
 relinquish 782
 – back 144
 – cold water on 616
 – of the dice 156
 – doubt upon 485
 – down 162, 308
 – oneself at the feet of 725
 – good money after bad 818
 – in 228
 – off [*see below*]
 – open 260, 296
 – out [*see below*]
 – over *destroy* 162

 – overboard
 exclude 55
 destroy 162
 eject 297
 abrogate 756
 – on paper 590
 – away the scabbard 722
 – into the shade
 superior 33
 lessen 36
 surpass 303
 important 642
 – a tub to catch a whale 545
 – up [*see below*]
 – a veil over 528
throw off 297
 – all disguise 529
 – one's guard 508
 – the mask 529
 – the scent
 misdirect 538
 avoid 623
throw out 284, 297
 eject 297
 – a feeler 379
 – of gear
 disjoin 44
 derange 61
 – a hint 527
 – a suggestion 514
throwing stick 727
thrown out 704
throw up *eject* 297
 resign 757
 – one's cap 884
 – the game 624
thrum 416
thrush 416
thrust *push* 276
 attack 716
 – in *insert* 300
 (*interpose*) 228
 – one's nose in 682
 – out 55
 – down one's throat 744
 – upon 784
thud 406, 408a
thug *murderer* 361
 thief 792
thumb *touch* 379
 bite the – 929
 one's fingers all –s 699
 rule of –
 experiment 463
 unreasoning 477
 essay 675
twiddle one's –

inaction 681
leisure 685
weariness 841
– immemorial 122
– of life
  duration 106
  now 118
  age 128
– out of mind 122
– to spare 685
– after time 104
– up 111, 134
– was 122
there being –s
  when 136
timeful 134
time-honoured
  old 124
  repute 873
  respected 928
time-keeper 114
time-recorder 553
timeless 135
timelessness 112
timely 132, 134
timeo Danaos 485,
  864
timeous 134
time-piece 114
time-pleaser 607
timetable 605
times *present* 118
  events 151
  hard – 735
  many – 136
  – out of number
    104
time-serving
  tergiversation 607
  cunning 702
  servility 886
  improbity 940
  selfishness 943
time-worn *old* 124
  age 128
  deteriorated 659
timid *fearful* 860
  cowardly 862
  humble 881
timist 607
Timocracy 803
Timon of Athens
  wealth 803
  seclusion 893
  misanthrope 911
timorous [*see* timid]
tin *preserve* 670
  money 800
  – hat 717
tinct 428
tinctorial 428

tincture
  small quantity 32
  mixture 41
  colour 428
tinctured
  disposition 820
tinder *fuel* 388
  irascible 901
tine 253
tinge
  small quantity 32
  mix 41
  colour 428
tingent 428
tingle *pain* 378
  touch 380
  emotion 821
  make the ears –
    900
tink 408
tinker
  repair 660
tinkle
  faint sound 405
  resonance 408
tinkling cymbal 517
tinnient 408
tinsel *glitter* 420
  sham 545
  ornament 847
  frippery 851
tinsmith 690
tint 428
tintamarre 404
tintinnabulary 408
tiny 32, 193
  – bit 32
tip *end* 67
  summit 210
  cover 223
  give 784
  reward 973
  on –toe *high* 206
  expect 507
  – off 527
  – the wink 550
tip-cat 840
tippet 214, 225
tipple 298, 959
tippler 959
tipstaff 965
tipsy 959
tip-top 210, 648
tirade 582, 932
tire *dress* 225
  fatigue 688
  worry 830
  weary 841
tiré à quatre épin-
  gles 850
tirer d'affaire 672

se – 731
Tiresias 513
tiresome [*see* tire]
Tisiphone 173, 900
tissue *whole* 50
  assemblage 72
  matted 219
  texture 329
tit *small* 193
  pony 271
tit for tat 718
Titan 159, 980
Titania 979
titanic 192
titbit 291, 394, 829
tithe *tenth* 99
  tax 812
tithing 181
titillate 840, 865
titillation 377, 380
titivate 847
title
  indication 550
  name 564
  printing 590
  right to property
    780
  distinction **877**
  right 924
titled 875
title-deed 771
title-page 66
titter 838
tittle 32
  to a – 494
tittle-tattle 532, 588
titubancy 583
titubate 306, 732
titular 562, 564
tmesis 218
T.N.T. 727
to *direction* 278
  lie – 681
  – all intents and
    purposes 27, 52
  – a certain degree
    32
  – come 121, 152
  – the credit of 805
  – crown all 33, 642
  – do 59
  – the end of the
    chapter 52
  – the end of time
    112
  – and fro 12, 314
  – the full 52
  – a great extent
    31
  – the letter 19
  – a man 78

– the point 23
– the purpose 23
– a small extent 32
– some extent 26
– be sure 488
– this day 118
– wit 79
toad 649, 846
  – under a harrow
    378
toad-eater 886, 935
toad-eating
  flattery 933
toadstool 367
toady 886
toast *roast* 384
  celebrate 883
tobacco 392
toboggan 272, 840
toby *jug* 191
toccata 415
tocsin 669
tod 319
to-day 118
toddle 266, 275
toddy 298
toe 211
  on the light fan-
    tastic 309, 840
  toes turn up the –
    die 360
toff 854
toffee 396
toga 225, 747
  assume the –
    virilis 131
together 88, 120
  come – 290
  get – 72
  hang – 709
  lay heads – 695
  – with 37, 88
toggery 225
toil
  activity 682
  exertion 686
  – of a pleasure 682
  –s *trap* 545
toilet 225
  – water 4C0
toilette 225
  en grande – 847
toilsome 686, 704
toilworn 688
token 550
  give – 525
  – of remembrance
    505
told, do what one
  is – 743
tolderolloll 838

Toledo 727
tolerable
  a little 32
  trifling 643
  pretty good 648
  not perfect 651
  satisfactory 831
tolerably, get on –
  736
toleration
  laxity 738
  lenity 740
  permission 760
  feeling 821
  calmness 826
  benevolence 906
toll *sound* 407
  tax 812
  – the knell 363
tollbooth
  prison 752
  market 799
tomahawk 727
tomb 363
  lay in the – 363
  – of the Capulets
   506
tombé des nues 83,
  870
tombola 156
tomboy 129, 851
tombstone 363
tom-cat 373
tome 593
tomentous 256
tomfool 501
tomfoolery
  absurdity 497
  amusement 840
  wit 842
  ostentation 882
Tom Noddy 501
Tommy Atkins 726
tommy-gun 727
to-morrow 121
  – and to-morrow
   104, 109
tompion 263
tomtit 193
Tom Thumb 193
tom-tom 417, 722
ton *weight* 319
  fashion 852
  –s of money 800
tonality 413, 420
tone *state* 7
  strength 159
  tendency 176
  sound 402
  music 413
  colour 428

blackness 431
painting 556
method 627
disposition 820
give a – to 852
– down
  moderate 174
  darken 421
  discolour 429
– in with 714
– of voice 580
tone poem 415
toney 852
tongs
  fire-irons 386
  retention 781
tongue
  projection 250
  taste 390
  language 560
  bite the – 392
  bridle one's – 585
  give – 404, 580
  hold one's – 403
  slip of the –
   error 495
   solecism 568
   stammering 583
  on the tip of
   one's –
   near 197
   forget 506
   latent 526
   speech 582
  wag the – 582
  – cleave to the
   roof of one's
   mouth 870
  have a – in one's
   head 582
  – of land 342
  – running loose
   584
  keep one's – be-
   tween one's
   teeth 585
tongueless 581
tongue-tied 581
tonic
  musical note 413
  healthy 656
  medicine 662
  – sol fa 415
tonicity 159
tonnage 192
tonsillectomy 662
tonsils 351
tonsure 999
tonsured 226
tontine 810
tony 501

Tony Lumpkin 876
too
  also 37
  excess 641
  – bad
   disreputable 874
   wrong 923
   censure 932
  – clever by half
   702
  in a – great degree
   31
  – far 641
  – hot to hold one
   830
  – late 133
  – late for 135
  – little 640
  – many 641
  – much [*see below*]
  – soon 132
  – soon for 135
  – true 833 839
too much
  redundance 641
  intemperance 954
  have – of 869
  make – of 482
  – for 471
  – of a good thing
   869
tool *instrument* 633
  steer 693
  catspaw 711
  ornament 847
  servile 886
  edge – 253
  mere – 690
toot 406
tooth *fastening* 45
  projection 250
  sharp 253
  roughness 256
  notch 257
  texture 329
  taste 390
  sweet –
   desire 865
   fastidious 868
  – and nail
   violence 173
   exertion 686
   attack 716
  – paste &c. 652
toothache 378
toothed 253
toothsome 394
top *supreme* 33
  summit 210
  roof 223
  spin 312

sleep like a – 683
fool to the – of
  one's bent 545
go over the – 861
– to bottom 52
– coat 225
– hat 225
at the – of the
  heap 210
– of the ladder 873
at the – of one's
  speed 274
from – to toe 200
at the – of the
  tree 210, 873
at the – of one's
  voice 404, 411
toparchy 737
topaz 436, 847
top-boot 225
tope *tomb* 363
  trees 367
  drink 959
  temple 1000
topee 225
toper 959
top-full 52
top-gallant mast,
  206, 210
top-heavy
  unbalanced 28
  inverted 218
  dangerous 665
  tipsy 959
Tophet 982
topiary 847
topic 454
  – of the day 532
topical 183
top-mast 206
topmost 210
topography 183
topographer 466
topple
  unbalanced 28
  perish 162
  decay 659
  – down *fall* 306
  – over 28, 306
topsail schooner
  273
topsawyer 642, 700
top sergeant 745
topsy-turvy 14, 218
toque 225
tor 206
torch 388, 423
  apply the – 824
  light the – of war
   722
  – of Hymen 903

Tories 712
torment
  physical 378
  moral 828, 830
  place of – 982
Tormes, Lazarillo
  de – 941
torn [*see* tear]
  discord 713
tornado 312, 349
torpedo *bane* 663
  sluggish 683
  weapon 727
  evil-doer 913
  – boat 726
  – boat destroyer
  726
  – plane 276
torpid, torpor
  inert 172
  inactive 683
  insensible 823
torque 847
  torrefy 384
torrent
  violence 173
  rapid 274
  flow 348
  rain in –s 348
torrid 382
torsion 248
torso 50
tort 925, 947
tort et à travers, à –
  disagreement 24
  absurdity 497
  resolution 604
tortious 925
tortile 248
tortive 248
tortoise 275
tortoise-shell 440
tortuous
  twisted 248
  dishonourable 940
torture
  physical 378
  moral 828, 830
  cruelty 907
  punishment 972
  – a question 476
torvity 901*a*
toss *derange* 61
  throw 284
  oscillate 314
  agitate 315
  – in a blanket 929
  – the caber 840
  – the head
  pride 878
  insolence 885

contempt 930
– off *drink* 298
– overboard 610
– on one's pillow
  825
– up 156, 621
tosspot 959
tot *child* 129
tot homines, tot
  sententiæ 15
total 50, 84
  sum – 800
  – abstinence 953,
  955
  – eclipse 421
totalisator 621
totality 52
totally 52
totidem verbis 19,
  494
totient 84
toties quoties 136
totis viribus 686
totitive 84
toto: in – 52
  – cœlo 52
totter
  changeable 149
  weak 160
  limp 275
  oscillate 314
  agitate 315
  decay 659
  danger 665
  – to its fall 162
touch *relate to* 9
  small quantity 32
  mixture 41
  contact 199
  sensation **379,**
  380
  music 416
  test 463
  indication 550
  act 680
  receive 785
  excite 824
  pity 914
  – and go
  instant 113
  soon 132
  changeable 149
  easy 705
  – the guitar 416
  – the hat 894
  – the heart 824
  – on 516
  – to the quick 822
  – up 658
  – upon 595
  in – with 9

touched *crazy* 503
  tainted 653
  compassion 914
  – in the wind 655
  – with *feeling* 821
touching 830
touchstone 463
touchwood
  fuel 388
  irascible 901
touchy 901
tough *coherent* 46
  tenacious 327
  difficult 704
toujours perdrix
  repetition 104
  weary 841
  satiety 869
toupee 256
tour 266
tour de force
  skill 698
  stratagem 702
  display 882
touring car 272
tourist 268
tournament 720
tourniquet 263
tournure 230, 448
  belle – 845
tous les rapports,
  sous – 494
tousle 61
tout *solicit* 765
tout: – au contraire
  14
  – court 265
  – ensemble 50
  – le monde 78
touter *agent* 758
  solicitor 767
  eulogist 935
tow 285
  take in – *aid* 707
towage 812
towardly 705
towards 278
  draw – 288
  move – 286
towel *clean* 652
  flog 972
tower
  stability 150
  edifice 161
  abode 189
  height 206
  soar 305
  defence 717
  – of strength
  strong 159
  influential 175

safety 664
towering *great* 31
  furious 173
  large 192
  high 206
  – passion 900
  – rage 900
town *city* 189
  fashion 852
  man about – 854
  on the – 961
  all over the – 532
  talk of the – 873
  – council 696
town-hall 189, 966
township 181
townsman 188
  fellow – 892
town-talk 532, 588
toxic 657
toxicology 663
toxophilite 284
toy *trifle* 643
  amusement 840
  fondle 902
toy-dog 366
toy-shop 840
trabant 717
tracasserie 713
trace *inquire* 461
  discover 480*a*
  mark 550
  record 551
  delineate 554
  – back 122
  – out 480*a*
  – to 155
  – up 461
tracery
  lattice 219
  curve 245
  ornament 847
traces *harness* 45
trachea 351
tracing 21
track *trace* 461
  record 551
  way 627
  cover up one's –s
  528
  in one's –s 113
  racing – 840
  – meet 840
  – racing 728
trackless
  space 180
  difficult 704
  – trolley 272
tract *region* 181
  book 593
  dissertation 595

– of time 109
tractable
  malleable 324
  willing 602
  easy 705
tractarian 984
tractile
  traction **285**
  soft 324
traction 285
tractor 271
trade *exchange* 148
  business 625
  traffic 794
  drive a – 625
  learn one's – 539
  tricks of the – 702
  two of a – 708
  – with 794
trader 797
trade-mark 550
tradesman 797
trade-publication
  531
trade-union 712
trade-wind 349
tradition *old* 124
  description 594
  custom 613
traduce 934
traducer 936
traffic 794
tragedian 599
tragedy
  drama 599
  evil 619
tragic *drama* 599
tragical 830
tragi-comedy 599
tragi-comic 853
trail *sequel* 65
  pendent 214
  slow 275
  follow 281
  traction 285
  odour 398
  inquiry 461
  record 551
  highway 627
  follow in the – of
  281
  – of a red herring
  615, 706
train *sequel* 65
  series 69
  pendent 214
  vehicle 272
  sequence 281
  traction 285
  - *animals* 370
  teach 537

accustom 613
  prepare 673
  bring in its – 615
  in – 673
  in the – of 281,
  746
  lay a – 626, 673
  put in – 673
  siege – 727
  – de luxe 272
  – of reasoning 476
  – of thought 451
train-band 726
train-bearer 746
train-ferry 272
trained 698
trainer
  - *of horses* 268
  - *of animals* 370
  teacher 540
training
  education 537
  – college 542
train-oil 356
traipse 275
trait *speciality* 79
  appearance 448
  mark 550
  description 594
traitor
  disobedient 742
  knave 941
  enemy 891
trajection 297
trajectory 627
tra-la-la 838
tralatitious 521
tralineate 279
tralucent 425
tram 272
trammel *hinder* 706
  restrain 751
  fetter 752
  cast –s off 750
tramontane
  foreign 57
  distant 196
  wind 349
  outlandish 851
tramp *stroll* 266
  stroller 268
  idler 683
  vagabond 867
  on the – 264
trample
  – in the dust
  destroy 162
  prostrate 308
  – out 162
  – under foot
  vanquish 731

not observe 773
  disrepute 874
  insolence 885
  dereliction 927
  contempt 930
  – upon 649, 739
tramway 627
trance *insensibility*
  376
  dream 515
  sleep 683
  lethargy 823
tranquil *calm* 174
  quiet 265
  peaceful 721
  calmness 871
  – mind 826
tranquillize
  moderate 174
  pacify 723
  soothe 826
transact *act* 680
  conduct 692
  – business 625
  – business with
  794
transaction 151,
  625, 680, 769
transactions 551
transalpine 196
transanimation 140
transatlantic 196
transcalency 384
transcend *great* 31
  superior 33
  go beyond 303
transcendency 641
transcendent 33,
  873
transcendental 78,
  519
transcendentalism
  450
transcolate 295
transcribe 19, 590
transcript 21, 590
transcursion 303
transept 1000
transfer
  copy 21
  displace 185
  - *of things* 270
  - *of property* **783**
transference 270
transfiguration
  change 140
  divine - 998
transfix 260
transfixed *firm* 150
transform 140
transformation

scene 599
transfuse 41, 270
  – the sense of 522
transgress
  go beyond 303
  infringe 773
  violate 927
  sin 945
transgression 947
transi de froid 383
transient 111, 149
transientness 111
transilience 146,
  303
transit
  conversion 144
  motion 264
  transference 270
  - *circle* 244
transit gloria
  mundi, sic –
  735, 874
transition 144, 270
transitional 140
transitory 111
transitu, in –
  transient 111
  journey 266
  transference 270
translate
  interpret 522
  promote 955
translator 524
translation
  transference 270
  resurrection 981
translocation 270
translucence 425
transmarine 196
transmigration 140,
  144
transmission
  moving 270
  passage 302
  - *of property* 783
transmit light 425
transmogrify 140
transmutation 140,
  144
transom 215
transparency 425
transparent
  transmitting
  light 425
  obvious 518
transpicuous
  transmitting
  light 425
  obvious 518
transpierce 260
transpire

148, 149
- turtle 218
- and twist 248
- under 258
- up [see below]
- upon
  depend upon 154
  retaliate 718
turn over give 784
  invert 218
  entrust 755
- the leaves 457,
  539
- in the mind 451
- a new leaf
  change 140
  improve 658
  repent 950
- to 270
turn up happen 151
  chance 156
  visible 446
  unexpected 508
- one's eyes
  wonder 870
  hypocrisy 988
- one's nose at
  aversion 867
  fastidious 868
  contempt 930
turn-coat 605, 607
turnover 298
turned of 128
turning-point
  crisis 8
  end 67
  occasion 134
  reversion 145
  cause 153
  summit 210
  limit 233
turnkey 753
turnpike 706
- road 627
turnscrew 633
turnspit 366
turnstile 553, 706
turpentine and
  beeswax 255
Turpin, Dick - 792
turpitude 874, 940
turquoise blue 438
  jewel 847
turret 206
turret-ship 726
turtle savoury 394
turtle-doves 897
tush silence 403
  taciturn 585
  trifling 643
tusk 253

tussle 720
tussock 256
tut [see tush]
  censure 932
tutelage
  teaching 537
  learning 539
  safety 664
  subjection 749
tutelary safety 664
- genius
  auxiliary 711
  god 979
- god 664
- saint 890, 912
tutor cultivate 375
  teach 537
  teacher 540
tutus, cavendo -
  664
tuyère 386
twaddle
  absurd 497
  unmeaning 517
  diffuseness 573
  talk 584
twain 89
in - 44
twang taste 390
  pungency 392
  sound 402
  stridor 410
  music 416
  voice 583
twattle
  [see twaddle]
tweak 378
- the nose 830
tweed 219
tweedle touch 379
  music 416
tweedledum and
  tweedledee 415
tweeny 746
tweezers 781
twelfth 99
twelve 98
twentieth century
  118
twenty &c. 98
- shillings in the
  pound 803
twice 90
twice-told tale 104,
  841
twiddle 379
twig 51
hop the - 360
twilight
  morning 125
  evening 126

dusk 422
- sleep 376
twill crossing 219
  convolution 248
  fold 258
twin similar 17
  accompanying 88
  two 89
  duplicate 90
twine string 205
  intersect 219
  convolution 248
- round 43, 227
twinge 378, 828
twinkle
  instantaneous 113
  light 420
  dimness 422
twinkling of an eye,
  in the - 113
twins 11
twire 315
twirl convolute 248
  revolve 311
  rotate 312
twist join 43
  thread 205
  oblique 217
  crossing 219
  distort 243
  convolution 248
  deviate 279
  bend 311
  prejudice 481
  insanity 503
  fault 651
  appetite 865
twit deride 856
  disrespect 929
  censure 932
  accuse 938
twitch pull 285
  shake 315
  pain 378
  mental - 828
twitter
  agitation 315
  cry 412
  music 416
  emotion 821
  excitement 824
'twixt 228
two 89
kill - birds with
  one stone 682
make - bites of a
  cherry 629, 956
- dozen 98
- meanings 520
in - places at once
  471

game at which -
  can play 718
- score 98
fall between -
  stools 732
- strings to one's
  bow 632
- or three 100
- of a trade 708
unable to put -
  words together
  583
two-bits 800
two-edged 253
two-faced 544
twofold 90
twopenny-haif-
  penny 643
two-sided 90
two-step 840
Tyburn tree 975
tycoon 745
tyg 191
tyke 876
tymbal 417
tympani 417
tympanum 210, 218
tympany 194
type essential 5
  similarity 17
  pattern 22
  class 75
  form 240
  prediction 511
  metaphor 521
  indication 550
  letter 561
  printing 591
heavy - 550
- script 21
- writing 590
typhoon 349
typical special 79
  conformable 82
  metaphorical 521
  significant 550
typist 590
typify 511
typography 591
tyranny 739
tyrant severe 739
  ruler 745
  evil-doer 913
tyre 230
tyro ignoramus 493
  learner 541

U

uberrima fides 484
uberty 168
ubiety 186

unbesought 766
unbetrayed 939
unbewailed 932
unbiassed 498, 748
unbidden 600, 742
unbigoted 498
unbind 44, 750
unblamable 946
unblamed 946
unblemished 650,
946
unblenching 861
unblended 42
unblest 735, 932
– with 777a
unblown 674
uncommenced 67
unblushing
proud 878
vain 880
imprudent 885
unboastful 881
unbodied 317
unboiled 674
unbolt 750
unbookish 491
unborn 2, 152
unborrowed 787,
788
unbosom oneself
529
unbought
not bought 796
honorary 815
honourable 939
unselfish 942
unbound 748, 927a
unbounded 105
unbrace 160, 655
unbreathed 526
unbred 895
unbribed 939, 942
unbridled
violent 173
lax 738
free 748
unbroken
entire 50
continuous 69
preserved 670
unviolated 939
unbruised 50
unbuckle 44
unburden
– one's mind 529
unburdened 705
unburied 362
unbusinesslike 699
unbuttoned 748
uncalculating 863
uncalled for

redundant 641
useless 645
not used 678
uncandid 544, 907
uncanny 846, 980
uncanonical 984
uncared for
neglected 460
indifference 866
disliked 867
hated 898
uncase 226
uncaught 748
uncaused 156
unceasing 112
uncensured 931
unceremonious
880, 895
uncertain
irregular 139
not certain 475
doubtful 485
in an – degree 32
uncertainty **475**
unchain 44, 750
unchained 748
unchallenged 488,
924
unchangeable 150,
604a
unchanged 16, 141
unchanging 5
uncharitable 907
unchartered 925,
964
unchaste 961
unchastised 970
unchecked 748
uncheckered 141
uncheerful 837
unchivalric 940
unchristian 984,
989
uncial 590
uncinated 244
uncircumscribed
180
uncircumspect 460
uncivil 851, 895
uncivilized 876, 895
unclaimed 748
unclassical 851
uncle *kin* 11
my –'s
pawnshop 787
unclean 653
– spirit 978, 980
uncleanness **653**
unclipped 50
unclog 705, 750
unclose 260, 750

unclothe 226
unclouded 420, 446
unclubbable 893
unclutch 790
uncoif 226
uncoil 313
uncoloured
achromatic 429
true 494
uncombed 653, 851
uncombined
simple 42
incoherent 47
uncomeatable 471
uncomely 846
uncomfortable 828,
830
uncommenced 67
uncommendable
blamable 932
bad 945
guilt 947
uncommensurable
24
uncommon 31, 83,
137
uncommonly 31
uncommunicated
781
uncommunicative
528
uncompact 322
uncompassionate
914a
uncompelled 748
uncomplaisant 764
uncompleted
incomplete 53
unfinished 730
failure 732
uncomplying 742,
764
uncompounded 42
uncompressed 320,
322
uncompromising
conformable 82
severe 739
unconcealable 525
unconceived
uncreated 12
unintelligible 519
unconcern 823, 866
unconcocted 674
uncondemned 970
unconditional
complete 52
free 748
permission 760
consent 762
release 768a

unconducive 175a
unconfined 748
unconfirmed 475
unconformity
disagreement 24
irregularity **83**
unconfused
methodical 58
clear 518
unconfuted 478,
494
uncongealed 333
uncongenial 24, 657
unconnected
irrelative 10
disjointed 44
discontinuous 70
illogical 477
unconquerable
strong 159
persevering 604a
– will 604
unconquered 719
unconscientious
940
unconscionable
excessive 31
unprincipled 945
unconscious
ignorant 491
insensible 823
unconsenting 603,
764
unconsidered 452
unconsolable 837
unconsolidated 47
unconsonant 24
unconspicuous 447
unconstitutional
925, 964
unconstrained 748,
880
unconsumed 40
uncontested 474
uncontradicted 488
uncontrite 951
uncontrollable
violent 173
necessity 601
emotion 825
uncontrolled
free 748
excitability 825
uncontroverted 488
unconventional 83,
614
unconversant 491,
699
unconverted
dissenting 489
irreligious 989

unconvinced 489
uncooked 674
uncopied 20
uncork 750
uncorrupted 939
uncounted 475
uncouple 44
uncourteous 895
uncourtly 851, 895
uncouth
- *style* 579
ugly 846
vulgar 851
uncover
denude 226
open 260
disclose 529
bow 894
uncreated 2
uncritical 931
uncropped 50
uncrown 756
unction
emotion 821, 824
divine functions 976
piety 987
extreme - 998
lay the flattering
- to one's soul
834, 858
unctuous *oily* 355, 894
flattering 933
hypocritical 988
unctuousness **355**
unculled
unused 678
relinquished 782
unculpable 946
uncultivated
vulgar 85
ignorant 491
unprepared 674
uncurbed 748
uncurl 246
uncustomary 83
uncut 50
undamaged (648)
undamped 340
undated
without date 115
waving 248
undaunted 861
undazzled 498
undebauched 939
undeceive 527, 529
undeceived 490
undecided
inquiring 461
uncertain 475

irresolute 605
leave - 609*a*
undecipherable 519
undecked 849
undecomposed 42
undefaced 845
undefended 725
undefiled
honest 939
innocent 946
chaste 960
undefinable
uncertain 475
unmeaning 517
unintelligible 519
undefined
invisible 447
uncertain 475
undeformed 845
undemolished 50
undemonstrable
485
undemonstrated
475
undemonstrative
826
undeniable 474, 478
undeplored 898
undepraved 939
undeprived 781
under *less* 34
below 207
subject to 749
range - 76
- advisement 454
- age 127
- agent 758
- arrest 751
- breath 405
- the conditions 8
- one's control 743
- cover
covered 223
hidden 528
safe 664
- the domination
of 737
- one's eyes 446
- foot [*see below*]
- full strength 651
- the head of 9
- lock and key 664
- the mark 34
- press of 744
- protest 489, 744
- restraint 751
- the rule of 737
- seal 467
- subjection 749
- the sun 1
- way 282

underbid 794
underbreath 405
underbred 851
underclothing 225
undercurrent
cause 153
stream 348, 349
latent 526
opposing 708
underestimation
483
underfed 640
underfoot 207
tread - 739
undergo 151
- a change 144
- pain 828
undergraduate 541
underground
low 207
deep 208
latent 526
hidden 528
underhand 526, 528
- dealing 528
underhung 250
underived 20
underlessee 779
underlet 787
underlie 207, 526
underline
mark 550
emphatic 642
underling
servant 746
clown 876
undermine
weaken 158
burrow 252
damage 659
stratagem 702
hinder 706
undermost 211
underneath 207
undernourished
640
underpaid 817
underpin 215
underplot 626
underprop 215
underrate 483
underreckon 483
undersell 796
underset 215
undershot 250
undersign 467
undersized 193
understand
know 490
intelligible 518
latent 526

be informed 527
give one to - 572
- by 516, 522
- one another
709, 714
understanding
agreement 23
intellect 450
intelligence 498
come to an - 488
intelligible 518
agree 714
pacification 723
compact 769
good - 714, 888
by a mutual - 526
with the - 469
understate 489
understood
meaning 516
implied 526
customary 613
understrapper 746
understudy 134
undertake
endeavour 676
promise 768
undertaker 363
undertaking 625,
676
undertone 405
undertow 348
undervalue 483
underwood 367
underwrite
promise 768
compact 769
insurance 771
underwriter 758
undescribed 83
undeserved 925
undeserving of be-
lief 485
undesigned 621
undesigning 703
undesirable 647,
830
undesired 830, 866
undesirous 866
undespairing 858
undestroyed
existing 1
whole 50
persisting 141
undetermined
chance 156
inquiry 461
uncertain 475
unintelligible 519
irresolute 605
undeveloped 526

unopened 261
unopposed 709
unorganized 674
 – matter 358
unornamental 846
unornamented
 - *style* 576
 simple 849
unorthodox 984
unostentatious 881
unowed 807
unowned 782
unpacific 713, 722
unpacified 713
unpack
 unfasten 44
 take out 297
unpaid *debt* 806
 honorary 815
 the great –
 magistracy 967
 – worker 602
unpalatable 395,
 830
unparagoned
 supreme 33
 best 648
 perfect 650
unparalleled
 unimitated 20
 supreme 33
 exceptional 83
unpardonable 938,
 945
unparliamentary
 language 895,
 908
unpassable 261
unpassionate 826
unpatriotic 911
unpeaceful 720, 722
unpeople
 emigration 297
 banishment 893
unperceived
 neglected 460
 unknown 491
unperformed 730
unperjured 543,
 939
unperplexed 498
unpersuadable 606
unpersuaded 616
unperturbed 826
unphilosophical 499
unpierced 261
unpin (44)
unpitied 932
unpitying 914a
unplaced 185
unplagued 831

unpleasant 830
unpleasing 830
unpoetical 598, 703
unpolished
 rough 256
 inelegant 579
 unprepared 674
 vulgar 851, 876
 rude 895
unpolite 895
unpolluted
 good 648
 perfect 650
unpopular 830, 867
unpopularity 898
unportioned 804
unpossessed 777a
unpractical 699
unprecedented 83,
 137
unprejudiced 498,
 748
unpremeditated
 impulsive 612
 undesigned 621
 unprepared 674
unprepared 508,
 674
unprepossessed 498
unprepossessing
 846
unpresentable 851
unpretending 881
unprevented 748
unprincipled 945
unprivileged 925
unprized 483
unproclaimed 526
unproduced 2
unproductive 645
unproductiveness
 169
unproficiency 699
unprofitable
 unproductive 169
 useless 645
 inexpedient 647
 bad 649
unprolific 169
unpromising 859
unprompted 612
unpronounceable
 519
unpronounced 526
unpropitious
 ill-timed 135
 opposed 708
 hopeless 859
unproportioned 24
unprosperous 735
unprotected 665

unproved 477
unprovided
 scanty 640
 unprepared 674
unprovoked (616)
unpublished 526
unpunctual
 tardy 133
 untimely 135
 irregular 139
unpunished 970
unpurchased 796
unpurified 653
unpurposed 621
unpursued 624
unqualified
 incomplete 52
 impotent 158
 certain 474
 unprepared 674
 inexpert 699
 unentitled 925
 – truth 494
unquelled 173
unquenchable
 strong 159
 desire 865
unquenched
 violence 173
 heat 382
unquestionable 474
unquestionably 488
unquestioned 474,
 488
unquiet
 motion 264
 agitation 315
 excitable 825
unravel *untie* 44
 arrange 60
 straighten 246
 evolve 313
 discover 480a
 interpret 522
 disembarrass 705
unreached 304
unread 491
unready 674
unreal
 not existing 2
 erroneous 495
 imaginary 515
unreasonable
 impossible 471
 illogical 477
 misjudging 481
 foolish 499
 exorbitant 814
 unjust 923
unreclaimed 951
unrecognizable 146

unreconciled 713
unrecorded 552
unrecounted 55
unreduced 31
unrefined 851
unreflecting 458
unreformed 951
unrefreshed 688
unrefuted 478, 494
unregarded
 neglected 460
 unrespected 929
unregenerate 988
unregistered 552
unreined 748
unrelated 10
unrelenting 914a,
 919
unreliable
 uncertain 475
 irresolute 605
 dangerous 665
unrelieved 835
unremarked 460
unremembered 506
unremitting
 continuous 69
 continuing 110
 unvarying 143
 persevering 604a
unremoved 184
unremunerated 808
unrenewed 141
unrepealed 141
unrepeated 87, 103
unrepentant 951
unrepining 831
unreplenished 640
unrepressed 173
unreproached 946
unreproved 946
unrequited 806, 917
unresented 918
unresenting 826
unreserved
 manifest 525
 veracious 543
 artless 703
unresisted 743
unresisting 725
unresolved 605
unrespected 929
unrest 149, 264
unrestored 688
unrestrained
 capricious 608
 unencumbered
 705
 free 748
unrestricted
 undiminished 31

free 748
unretracted 535
unrevenged 918
unreversed 143
unrevoked 143
unrewarded 806,
  917
unrhymed 598
unriddle 480a, 529
unrig 645
unrighteous 945
unrip 260
unripe
  young 127
  sour 397
  immature 674
unrivalled 33
unroll *evolve* 313
  display 525
unromantic 494
unroot 301
unruffled
  calm 174
  quiet 265
  unaffected 823
  placid 826
unruly *violent* 173
  obstinate 606
  disobedient 742
unsaddle 756
unsafe 665
unsaid 526
unsaleable
  useless 645
  selling 796
  cheap 815
unsaluted 929
unsanctified 988,
  989
unsanctioned 925
unsated 865
unsatisfactory
  inexpedient 647
  bad 649
  displeasing 830
  discontent 832
unsatisfied 832, 865
unsavouriness **395**
unsay *recant* 607
unscanned 460
unscathed 654
unschooled 491
unscientific 477
unscoured 653
unscriptural 984
unscrupulous 940
unseal 529
unsearched 460
unseasonable 24,
  135
unseasoned 614,

674
unseat 756
unseemly
  inexpedient 647
  ugly 846
  vulgar 851
  undue 925
  vicious 945
unseen
  invisible 447
  neglected 460
  latent 526
unseldom 136
unselfish 942
unseparated 46
unserviceable 645
unsettle *derange* 61
unsettled
  mutable 149
  displaced 185
  uncertain 475
  – in one's mind
  503
unsevered 50
unsex 146
unshaded 525
unshaken 159
  – belief 484
unshapely 846
unshapen 241
unshared 777
unsheathe
  – the sword 722
unsheltered 665
unshielded 665
unshifting 143
unship 185, 297
unshocked 823
unshorn 50
unshortened 200
unshrinking 604,
  861
unsifted 460
unsightly 846
unsinged 670
unskilfulness **699**
unslaked 865
unsleeping 604a,
  682
unsmooth 256
unsociable 893
unsocial 893
unsoiled 652
unsold 777
unsoldierlike 862
unsolicitous 866
unsolved 526
unsophisticated
  simple 42
  genuine 494
  artless 703

unsorted 59
unsought
  avoided 623
  unrequested 766
unsound
  illogical 477
  erroneous 495
  deceptive 545
  imperfect 651
  – mind 503
unsown 674
unsparing
  abundant 639
  severe 739
  liberal 816
  with an – hand
  818
unspeakable 31,
  870
unspecified 78
unspent 678
unspied 526
unspiritual 316, 989
unspoiled 648
unspotted
  clean 652
  beautiful 845
  innocent 946
unstable 218
  changeable 149
  uncertain 475
  irresolute 605
  precarious 665
  – equilibrium 149
unstaid 149
unstained
  clean 652
  honourable 939
unstatesmanlike
  699
unsteadfast 605
unsteady
  mutable 149
  irresolute 605
  in danger 665
unstinted 639
unstinting 816
unstirred 823, 826
unstopped
  continuing 143
  open 260
unstored 640
unstrained
  turbid 653
  relaxed 687
  – meaning 516
unstrengthened 160
unstruck 823
unstrung 160
unstudied 460
unsubject 748

unsubmissive 742
unsubservient
  useless 645
  inexpedient 647
unsubstantial 4
  weak 160
  rare 322
  erroneous 495
  imaginary 515
unsubstantiality **4**
unsuccessful 732
unsuccessive 70
unsuitable
  incongruous 24
  (*inexpedient* **647)**
  – time 135
unsullied *clean* 652
  honourable 939
  (*guiltless* 946)
unsung 526
unsupplied 640
unsupported
  weak 160
  (*unassisted* 706)
  – by evidence **468**
unsuppressed 141
unsurmountable
  471
unsurpassed 33
unsusceptible 823
unsuspected
  belief 484
  latent 526
unsuspecting
  hopeful 858
unsuspicious
  belief 484
  artless 703
  hope 858
unsustainable 495
unsweet 395
unswept 653
unswerving
  straight 246
  direct 278
  persevering 604a
unsymmetric 83
unsymmetrical 59,
  243
unsystematic 59
untainted *pure* 652
  healthy 654
  honourable 939
untalked of 526
untamed 851, 907
untarnished 939
untasted 391
untaught 491, 674
untaxed 815
unteach 538
unteachable 499,

699
untenable
  powerless 158
  illogical 477
  undefended 725
untenanted 187,
  893
unthanked 917
unthankful 917
unthawed 321, 383
unthinkable 471
unthinking
  unconsidered 452
  involuntary 601
unthought of 452,
  460
unthreatened 664
unthrifty
  unprepared 674
  prodigal 818
unthrone 756
untidy 59, 653
untie 44, 750
  – the knot 705
until 106
  – now 118
untilled 674
untimely 135
  – end 360
untinged 42
untired 689
untiring 604*a*
untitled 876
untold
  countless 105
  uncertain 475
  latent 526
  secret 528
untouched
  disused 678
  insensible 823
untoward
  ill-timed 135
  bad 649
  unprosperous 735
  unpleasant 830
untraced 526
untracked 526
untractable 606,
  699
untrained
  unaccustomed 614
  unprepared 674
  unskilled 699
untrammelled 705,
  748
untranslatable 523
untranslated 523
untravelled 265
untreasured 640
untried *new* 123

not decided 461
untrimmed 674,
  849
untrodden *new* 123
  impervious 261
  not used 678
untroubled 174, 721
untrue 495, 546
untrustworthy
  uncertain 475
  erroneous 495
  danger 665
  dishonourable 940
untruth 544, **546**
untunable 414
unturned 246
untutored
  ignorant 491
  unprepared 674
  artless 703
untwine 313
untwist 313
unused
  new 123
  unaccustomed 614
  unskilful 699
unusual 83
unusually *very* 31
unutterable 31,
  519, 870
unvalued
  underrated 483
  undesired 866
  disliked 898
unvanquished 748
unvaried
  continuing 143
  - *style* 575, 576
unvarnished
  true 494
  - *style* 576
  unreserved 703
  simple 849
  – *tale* 494, 543
unvarying 16, 143
unveil 525, 529
unventilated 261
unveracious 544
unversed 491
unvexed 831
unviolated 939
unvisited 893
unwakened 683
unwarlike 862
unwarmed 383
unwarned 508, 665
**unwarped judg-
  ment** 498
unwarrantable 923
unwarranted
  illogical 477

undue 925
  illegal 964
unwary 460
unwashed 653
  great – 876
unwatchful 460
unwavering 604*a*
unweakened 159
unwearied
  persevering 604*a*
  indefatigable 682
  refreshed 689
unwedded 904
unweeded garden
  674
unweeting 491
unweighed 460
unwelcome 830,
  893
unwell 655
unwept 831
unwholesome 657
unwieldy
  large 192
  heavy 319
  cumbersome 647
  difficult 704
  ugly 846
unwilling 489
unwillingness 603
unwind *evolve* 313
unwiped 653
unwise 499
unwished 866
unwithered 159
unwitting
  ignorant 491
  involuntary 601
unwittingly 621
unwomanly 373
unwonted 83, 614
unworldly 939
unworn 159
unworshipped 929
unworthy
  shameful 874
  vicious 945
  – of belief 485
  – of notice 643
unwrap 246
unwrinkled 255
unwritten
  latent 526
  obliterated 552
  spoken 582
  – law 697, 963
unwrought 674
unyielding
  tough 323
  resolute 604
  obstinate 606

resisting 719
up
  aloft 206
  vertical 212
  effervescing 353
  excited 824
  the game is – 735
  prices looking –
    814
  time – 111
  – in arms
    prepared 673
    active 682
    opposition 708
    attack 716
    resistance 719
    warfare 722
  – and at them 716
  – and doing 682
  – and down 314
  – on end 212
  – in 698
  – to [*see below*]
  all – with
    destruction 162
    failure 732
    adversity 735
up to
  time 106
  power 157
  knowing 490
  skilful 698
  brave 861
  – the brim 52
  – date 123
  – one's ears 641
  – one's eyes 641
  – the mark
    equal 27
    sufficient 639
    good 648
    due 924
  – snuff 702
  – this time
    time 106
    past 122
Upas tree 663
upbear 215, 307
upbraid 932
upcast 307
upgrow 206
upgrowth 194, 305
upheaval 146
upheave 307
uphill
  acclivity 217
  ascent 305
  laborious 686
  difficult 704
uphoist 307
uphold

deviating 279
vague
  unsubstantial 4
  uncertain 475
  unreasoning 477
  unmeaning 517
  obscure 519
  - *language* 571
  - suggestion 514
vail *panel* 228
  donation 784
  reward 973
vain *unreal* 2
  unprofitable 645
  unvalued 866
  conceited 880
  in - *failure* 732
  labour in -
  come *short* 304
  useless 645
  fail 732
  take a name in -
    895
  - attempt 732
  use - efforts 645
  - expectation 509
vainglorious
  haughty 878
  vain 880
  boasting 884
vaivode 745
valance 231
vale 252
  - of years 128
valeat quantum 467
valediction 293, 894
valedictory 293
valentine 902
valet 631, 746
valet
  - de chambre 746
  - de place 524, 527
valetudinarian 655,
  656
Valhalla 981
valiant 861
valid *confirmed* 150
  powerful 157
  strong 159
  true 494
  sufficient 639
  - reasoning 476
valise 191
valley 252
  - of the shadow of
  death 360
vallum 717
valoir, se faire -
  884
valorem, ad - 812
valour 861

valuable 644, 648
value *colour* 423
  measure 466
  estimate 480
  importance 642
  utility 644
  goodness 648
  price 812
  approbation 931
  of priceless - 814
  set a - upon 482
  - received 810
  -s *painting* 556
valueless 645
valve *stop* 263
  conduit 350
  safety - *safety* 664
  refuge 666
  escape 671
vamp *change* 140
  music 463
  - up *improve* 658
  restore 660
  prepare 673
vampire 913, 980
vampirism 789, 992
van *beginning* 66
  front 234
  wagon 272
  in the - 234
  precession 280
van-courier 64
Vandal
  destroyer 165
  vulgar 851
  commonalty 876
  evil-doer 913
vandalism 851
vandyke 257
Vandyke brown 433
vane *wind* 349
  indication 550
vanguard 234
vanish
  unsubstantial 4
  transient 111
  disappear 449
vanishing 32, 193
vanity *useless* 645
  conceit **880**
  - bag 191
Vanity Fair 852
vanquish 731
vantage ground
  superiority 33
  power 157
  influence 175
  height 206
vapid *insipid* 391
  - *style* 575
vaporization **336**

vaporous
  imaginary 515
  opaque 426
vapour *gas* 334
  bubbles 353
  fancy 515
  boast 884
  insolence 885
  - bath 386, 652
vapourer 887
vapours
  dejection 837
variable 149, 605
variance
  difference 15
  disagreement 24
  discord 713
  at - *enmity* 889
  at - with 489
variant 15
variation
  difference 15
  diverseness **20a**
  number 84
  chance 140
  music 415
varied 15
variegated 16a, 440
variegation **440**
variety
  difference 15
  class 75
  multiformity 81
  exception 83
  entertainment 599
variform 81
various 15, 102
  - places 182
  - times 119
varlet 949
varnish
  overlay 223
  resin 356a
  sophistry 477
  falsehood 544
  painting 556
  decorate 847
  excuse 937
vary *differ* 15
  dissimilar 18
  variation 20a
  change 140
  fluctuate 149
vascular *cells* 191
  holes 260
  pipes 350
vase 191
vassal 746
vassalage 749
vast *great* 31
  spacious 180

large 192
- learning 490
vasty deep 341
vat 191
Vatican 995, 1000
  thunders of the -
  908
vaticination 511
vatum, genus irri-
  tabile - 597
vaudeville 599, 840
vault
  cellar 191
  curve 245
  leap 309
  tomb 363
  store 636
  - of heaven 318
vaulted 245, 252
vaulting 33, 865
vaunt 884
vaurien 949
vavasour
  possessor 779
  nobleman 875
V.C. 733
vection 270
Vedas 986
vedette 668
Vedidad 986
veer
  change 140
  deviate 279
  go back 283
  change intention
  607
vegetability **365**
vegetable **367**
  - kingdom 367
  - life 386
  - oil 356
  - physiology 369
vegetarian 298, 953
vegetate 365
  exist 1
  grow 194
  stagnate 265
  inactive 681, 683
  insensible 823
vegetation 365
vehemence
  violence 173
  feeling 821
  emotion 825
vehement
  - *language* 574
vehicle
  carriage **272**
  instrument 631
veil *covering* 225
  shade 424

concealment 526, 527
conceal 528
ambush 530
behind the − 360
draw aside the − 529
take the − 893, 995
veiled
uncertain 475
invisible 447
concealed 528
vein *temper* 5
tendency 176
thin 203
thread 205
channel 350
humour 602
mine 636
affections 820
in the − 602
not in the − 603
veined 440
veld 344
velis et remis 274
velitation 720
velleity 600
vellicate 315
vellicating 392
vellum 590
veloce *music* 415
velocipede 272
velocity 264, **274**
angular − 244
veluti in speculum 17
velvet 255, 256
pleasure 377
on − *easy* 705
venal *price* 812
stingy 819
dishonest 940
selfish 943
venation 622
vend 796
vendee 795
vender 796
vendetta 919
vendible 796
venditation 884
vendor 796
veneer 204, 223
venenation 659
venerable *old* 124
aged 128
sage 500
respected 928
veneration
respect 928
piety 987

venereal disease 655
venery *killing* 361
hunting 622
impurity 961
venesection
ejection 297
remedy 662
Venetian blinds 351
vengeance 919
cry to heaven for − 923
with a − 31, 173
vengeful 919
veni vidi vici 731
venial 937
veniam petimusque damusque vicissim 918
venienti occurrere morbo 673
venison 394
venom 663, 907
venomous *bad* 649
poisonous 657
rude 895
maleficent 907
vent *opening* 260
egress 295
air-pipe 351
disclose 529
escape 671
sale 796
find − *egress* 295
passage 302
publish 531
escape 671
give − to 297, 529
− one's rage 900
− one's spleen 900
venter 191
ventiduct 351
ventilate
begin 66
air 338
wind 349
discuss 595
− a question 461, 476
ventilator 349, 351
ventosity 349
vent-peg
stopper 263
safety 666
escape 671
ventre
− à terre 274
danse du − 840
ventricle 191
ventriloquism 580

venture
chance 621
danger 665
try 675
courage 861
I'll − to say 535
venturesome
undertaking 677
brave 861
rash 863
venue 74, 183
Venus *woman* 374
planet 423
beauty 845
love 897
goddess 919
veracity **543**
verandah 191
verbal 562
− *intercourse* 582, 588
− *quibble* 497, 842
verbatim
imitation 19
exact 494
words 562
verbiage
unmeaning 517
words 562
diffuse 573
verbis:
totidem − 494
− ad verbera 720
verborum, copia −
diffuse 573
eloquence 582
loquacious 584
verbosity
words 562
diffuse 573
loquacity 584
verboten 761
verbum sapienti 527
verdant 367, 435
verd-antique 435
verdict
opinion 480
lawsuit 969
snatch a − 545, 702
verdigris 435
verditer 435
verdure 367, 435
verecundiam, argumentum ad − 874, 939
verecundity 879, 881
veredical 543
Verein 712

verge
tendency 176
near 197
edge 231
limit 233
direction 278
verger 996
veriest 31
verification 463, 771
verify 463
evidence 467
demonstrate 478
find out 480a
verily *truly* 494
verisimilitude 472
veritable 494
veritas, nuda − 494
vérité, palais de − 703
verity 494
verjuice 397
vermicular
convoluted 248
worm 366
vermiform 248
vermilion 434
vermin
animal 366
unclean 653
base 876
vernacular
native 188
internal 221
language 560
habitual 613
vernal 123, 125
vernier
minuteness 193
− *scale* 466
vero, vitam impendere − 535, 939
verrons, nous − 507
versatile 149
verse *division* 51
poetry 597
versed in 490
versicolour 440
versify 597
version *change* 140
special 79
interpretation 522
versus 278, 708
vert 435
vertebral 222
vertebrate 366
vertex 210
verticality **212**
verticity 312
vertigo
rotation 312

delirium 503
verve
  imagination 515
  vigorous language 574
  energy 682
  feeling 821
very 31
  – best 648
  – image 554
  – many 102
  – minute 113
  – much 31
  – picture 17
  – small 32
  – thing
  identity 13
  agreement 23
  exact 494
  – true 488
  – well 831
Véry light 423
vesicle *cell* 191
  covering 223
  globe 249
vesicular 191, 260
vespers 126, 990
vespertine 126
vessel
  receptacle 191
  tube 260
  ship 273
vest *place* 184
  dress 225
  – in *belong to* 777
  give 784
Vesta 979
vesta *match* 388
vestal 960
vested *fixed* 150
  legal 963
  – in *located* 184
  – interest
  given 780
  due 924
vestibule 66, 191
vestige 551
vestigia:
  veteris – flammæ 505, 613
  – nulla retrorsum 282, 604*a*
vestment 225, 999
vestry *council* 696
  churchdom 995
  church 1000
vesture 225
vesuvian
  match 388
veteran *old* **130**
  adept 700

warrior 726
veterinary art 370
veteris vestigia
  flammæ 505, 613
veto 761
vetturino 694
vex 830, 898
vexata quæstio 704, 713
vexation 828, 830
  – of spirit 828
  discontent 832
  resentment 900
vexatious 830
vexed question 704, 713
vi et armis
  violence 173
  exertion 686
  compulsion 744
viâ 278, 627
viable 359
via lactea 318
viaduct 627
vial 191
vials:
  – of hate 898
  – of wrath 900
viands 298
viaticum
  provision 637
  rite 998
vibrate 314
  – between two extremes 149
vibrato 415
vibratory 149
vibroscope 314
vicar *deputy* 759
  clergyman 996
  – of Bray 607, 886
vicarage 1000
vicariate 995
vicarious 147
vicarship 995
vice *deputy* 759
  holder 781
  wickedness **945**
vice versâ
  reciprocal 12
  contrary 14
  interchange 148
vice-admiral 745
Vice-Chancellor 967
  –'s Court 966
vicegerency 755
vicegerent 758, 759
vice-president 694
vice-regal 759

viceroy
  governor 745
  deputy 759
vicesimal 98
vicinage 197
vicinism 145
vicinity 197, 227
vicious 173, 945
  render – 659
  – reasoning 477
vicissitude 149
Vickers gun 727
victim *dupe* 547
  defeated 732
  sufferer 828
victimize *kill* 361
  deceive 545
  injure 649
  baffle 731
victis, væ – 722, 909
victor 731
victoria
  carriage 272
Victoria Cross 733
victory 731
victual *provide* 637
victuals 298
videlicet 79, 522
viduage 905
viduity 905
vie *good* 648
  – with 720
vielle 417
view
  sight 441
  appearance 448
  attend to 457
  opinion 484
  landscape painting 556
  intention 620
  bring into – 525
  come into – 446
  commanding – 441
  in – *visible* 446
  intended 420
  expected 507
  keep in – 457
  on – 448
  present to the – 448
  with a – to 620
  – as 484
  – in a new light 658
viewer 444
viewless 447
view-point 441
vigesimal 98
vigil *care* 459
vigilance *care* 459

wisdom 498
  activity 682
  caution 864
vigils *worship* 990
vignette 558, 594, 847
vigour *strength* 159
  energy 171
  style **574**
  resolution 604
  health 654
  activity 682
viking 792
vile *valueless* 643
  bad 649
  painful 830
  disgraceful 874
  plebeian 876
  dishonourable 940
  vicious 945
vilify *shame* 874
  malediction 908
  censure 932
  detract 934
vilipend
  disrespect 929
  censure 932
  detract 934
vilipendency 930
villa 189
village 189
  – talk 588
villager 188
villain
  servant 746
  serf 876
  knave 941
  rascal 949
villainous 649, 945
  – saltpetre 727
villainy 940
villein [*see* villain]
villenage 749, 777
villi 256
villous 256
vim 171
vin: – d'honneur 292, 894
  not think – ordinaire of oneself 880
vinaigrette 400
vincible 158
vincture 43
vinculo matrimonii, separatio a – 905
vinculum **45**
  – matrimonii 903
vindicate 467, 937
  – a right 924
vindication **937**

vindicator 919
vindictive 901, 919
vine 367
  – grower 371
vinegar 397
  – aspect 846
vinery 191
vineyard 371, 691
vingt et un 840
vintage 371, 636
vintner 637
viol 417
violate
  disobey 742
  non-observance
    773
  undue 925
  dereliction 927
  ravish 961
  – a law 83
  – the law 964
  – a usage 614
violence **173**
  arbitrary 964
  do – to *bad* 649
  non-observance
    773
  undue 925
violent 173
  excitable 825
  – death 360, 361
  in a – degree 31
  lay – hands on 789
violet 437
violin 417
violinist 416
violoncello 417
viper *snake* 366
  bane 663
  evil-doer 913
  bad man 949
  – in one's bosom
    667
virago 901
virent 435
vires acquirit
  eundo
  increase 35
  energy 171
  velocity 274
virescence 435
Virgilianæ, sortes –
  621
virgin *new* 123
  girl 129
  woman 374
  spinster 904
  good 948
  pure 960
  – forest 367
  – soil

ignorance 491
  untilled 674
  the – Mary 976
virginals 417
virginibus
  puerisque 960
viribus, totis – 686
viridity 435
virile
  adolescent 131
  strong 159
  manly 373
virtu 850
  article of – 847
virtual 2, 5
  – image 443
virtue *power* 157
  courage 861
  goodness **944**
  purity 960
  by – of 157, 631
  in – of 737
  make a – of neces-
    sity *no choice*
    609a
  skill 698
  submit 725
  compromise 774
  bear 826
virtueless 945
virtuoso 416, 850
virtuous 944, 960
virulence
  energy 171
  noxiousness 649
  insalubrity 657
  discourtesy 895
  anger 900
  malevolence 907
virulent 932
virum volitare per
  ora 531
virus 655, 663
vis:
  – comica 842
  – conservatrix 670
  – inertiæ
    power 157
    inertness 172
  insensibility 823
  – medicatrix 660,
    662
  – mortua 157
  – a tergo 284
  – viva 157
visa 488
visage 234, 448
vis-à-vis *front* 234
  opposite 237
  carriage 272
viscera 221

viscid 352
viscount 875
viscous 352
vise 781
Vishnu 979
visibility **446**
visible 446
  be – 448
  become – 448
  darkness – 421
  – radiation 420
vision *sight* **441**
  phantasm 443
  dream 515
  spectre 980
  organ of – 441
visionary
  inexistence 2
  unsubstantial 4
  impossible 471
  imaginary 515
  heterodox 984
visionless 442
visit *arrival* 292
  social 892
  courtesy 894
  – upon 972
  pay a surprise –
    647
visitation
  disease 655
  adversity 735
  suffering 828
  –s of Providence
    976
  – of the sick 998
visiting:
  – card 550
  on – terms 888,
    892
visitor *incomer* 294
  director 694
  friend 890
visor 530
vista
  convergence 260
  sight 441
  appearance 448
  expectation 507
visual 441
  – organ 441
vitability 359
vitæ, elixir – 662
vital *life* 359
  important 642
vitality
  stability 150
  strength 159
  life 359
vitalize 359
vitals 221

vitamin impendere
  vero 535, 939
vitamines 298
vitiate 659
vitiated 655
viticulture 371
vitreous 323, 425
vitrify 323
vituperate 908, 932
vituperator 936
viva! 873, 931
vivace *music* 415
vivacious
  active 682
  sensitive 822
  cheerful 836
vivamus, dum
  vivimus – 840
vivandière 797
vivarium 370
vivâ voce 582
vive *glory be to* 873
  on the qui – 824
vivendi
  modus – 723
  – causa 359
vivid *energetic* 171
  sensibility 375
  light 420
  colour 428
  distinct 518
  – memory 505
vivify 159, 359
vivisection 378
vixen *fox* 366
  female 374
  shrew 901
viz. [*see* videlicet]
vizier *director* 694
  mask 530
  shield 717
  deputy 759
vizor 530
vobis, sic vos non –
  791
vocable 562
vocabulary 562
vocal 415, 580
  – training 537
vocalist 416
vocalize 580
vocation 625
voce, sotto – 581
vociferation
  loud 404
  cry 411
  voice 580
vogue *custom* 613
  fashion 852
  fame 873
vogue la galère

wait 133, 681	**wall** *vertical* 212	wax and – 140	**wardrobe** 191, 225
lie in – for 530	*parietes* 224	**wangle** 943	**ward-room** 191
– for 507	*inclosure* 232	**want**	**war-drum** 417
– impatiently 133	*refuge* 666	*inferiority* 34	**wardship** 664
– on *accompany* 88	*obstacle* 706	*shortcoming* 304	**ware**
aid 707	*defence* 717	*requirement* 630	*warning* 668
– to see how the	*prison* 752	*insufficiency* 640	*merchandise* 798
wind blows 607	driven to the –	*poverty* 804	**warehouse** 636, 799
– upon *serve* 746	704	*desire* 865	**warfare** **722**
call on 894	go to the –	**wanted** 187	*discord* 713
waiter *servant* 746	*destruction* 162	**wanting**	**war-horse** 726
– on Providence	*die* 360	*incomplete* 53	**warlike** 722
neglect 460	*fail* 732	*absent* 187	**warlock** 994
inactive 683	pushed to the –	*imbecile* 499	**warm**
content 831	601	found –	*violent* 173
waiting 507	take the – 873,	*imperfect* 651	*hot* 382
be kept – 133	878	*disapproval* 932	*make hot* 384
waiting-maid 746	wooden –s 726	*guilt* 947	*red* 434
waitress 746	–eyed 442	**wantless** 639	*orange* 439
waits 416	– in 229, 751	**wanton**	*wealthy* 803
waive *defer* 133	**wallah** 746	*unconformable* 83	*ardent* 821
not choose 609a	**wallet** 191	*capricious* 608	*excited* 824
not use 678	**wallop** 315	*unrestrained* 748	*angry* 900
waiwode 745	**wallow** *low* 207	*amusement* 840	*irascible* 901
wake *sequel* 65	*plunge* 310	*rash* 863	*flog* 972
rear 235	*rotate* 312	*impure* 961	– bath 386
funeral 363	– in 377, 641	**wapentake** 181	– the blood 824
trace 551	– in the mire 653	**war** 722	– the cockles of
excite 824	– in riches 803	at – 24, 720	the heart 829
amusement 840	– in voluptuous-	at – with 708, 722	– imagination 515
in the – of 281	ness 954	declare – 713	– man 803
enough to – the	**wallsend** 388	man of – 727	– reception
dead 404	**Wall-street** 799	seat of – 728	*repel* 717
– the thoughts	– slang 563	– correspondent	*welcome* 892
457	**waltz** 415, 840	534, 593	– up 658, 660
– up 824	**wamble**	– of words 588,	– work 686
wakeful	*vacillate* 149	720	**warm-hearted**
careful 459	*oscillate* 314	**warble** 416	*feeling* 821
active 682	*dislike* 867	**war-cry** *alarm* 669	*sensibility* 822
Walhalla 981	**wampum** 800	*defiance* 715	*friendship* 888
walk *region* 181	**wan** 429, 837	*war* 722	*benevolence* 906
lane 189	**wand** *sceptre* 747	**ward** *part* 51	**warming** 384
move 266	*magic* 993	*parish* 181	**warming-pan**
business 625	wave a – 992	*safety* 664	*locum tenens* 147
way 627	**wander** *move* 264	*asylum* 666	*heater* 386
conduct 692	*journey* 266	*dependent* 746	*preparation* 673
arena 728	*deviate* 279	*restraint* 751	**warmth**
– one's chalks	*delirium* 503	watch and – 459,	*vigorous language*
293, 623	the attention –s	753	574
– the earth 359	458	– off 706, 717	**warn** *dissuade* 616
– of life 625	**wanderer** 268	**war-dance** 715	*caution* 668
–ed off one's legs	**wandering**	**warden**	– off 761
688	*exceptional* 83	*guardian* 664	**warning** *omen* 512
– off with 791	– Jew 268	*master* 745	*dissuasion* 616
– over the course	**wane**	*deputy* 759	*caution* **668**
705, 731	*decrease* 36	**warder**	give – *dismiss* 678
– in the shoes of	*age* 128	*perforator* 262	*relinquish* 782
19	*contract* 195	*porter* 263	– voice *alarm* 666
walker 268	*decay* 659	*guardian* 664	**warp** *change* 140
walking gentleman	one's star on the –	*keeper* 753	*tend* 176
599	735	**wardmote** 966	*contract* 195

inquiry 461
reasoning 476
where 186, 461
  – am I? 870
whereabouts 183, 197
whereas 9, 476
whereby 631
wherefore
  attribution 155
  inquiry 461
  reasoning 476
  motive 615
wherein 221
whereness 186
whereupon 106, 121
wherever 180, 182
wherewith 632, 800
wherret 830
wherry 273
whet *sharpen* 253
  meal 298
  incite 615
  excite 824
  take a –
  tipple 959
  – the appetite 865
  – the knife 673
whether or not 609
whetstone, cut a –
  with a razor 638
which:
  at – time 119
  know – is which 465
whiff 349, 825
whiffle 349
Whig 712
while *time* 106
  in a – 132
  worth – 646
  – away time
  inaction 681
  pastime 840
  – speaking of 9, 134
whilom 122
whilst 106
whim *fad* 481
  fancy 515
  caprice 608
  wit 842
  desire 865
whimper 839
whimsey 515, 865
whimsical [*see* whim] 853
whimwam 608, 643
whin 367
whine 411, 839
whinyard 727

whip *collect* 72
  coachman 268
  strike 276
  stir up 315
  urge 615
  hasten 684
  director 694
  flog 972
  scourge 975
  – and spur 274
  – away 293
  – hand 731, 737
  – in 300
  – on 684
  – off 293
  – up 789
whipcord 205
whipper-in 694
whippersnapper 129
whipping-post 975
whipster 129
whir *rotate* 312
  sound 407
whirl *rotate* 312
  flurry 825
whirligig 312
whirlpool *rotate* 312
  agitation 315
  water 348
  danger 667
whirlwind
  disorder 59
  agitation 315
  wind 349
  reap the –
  product 154
  fail 732
  ride the –
  resolution 604
  authority 737
whisk *rapid* 274
  circuition 311
  agitation 315
  – off 297
whisker 256
whisket 191
whisky
  vehicle 272
  drink 298
whisper
  faint sound 405
  tell 527
  conceal 528
  stammer 583
  stage – 580
  – about
  disclose 529
  publish 531
  – in the ear
  voice 580
whist *hush* 403

cards 840
whistle *wind* 349
  hiss 409
  play music 416
  *musical instru-
  ment* 417
  clean as a –
  thorough 52
  perfect 650
  neatly 652
  pay too dear for
  one's –
  inexpedient 647
  unskilful 699
  dear 814
  police – 669
  wet one's –
  drink 298
  tipple 959
  – at 930
  – for *request* 765
  desire 865
  – jigs to a mile-
  stone 645
  – for want of
  thought
  inaction 681
whit *small* 32
whit-leather 327
Whit-Monday 840
white 430
  – of the eye 41
  – feather 862
  – flag 723
  – frost 383
  – heat 382
  – horses 348
  – lie *equivocal* 520
  concealment 528
  untruth 546
  plea 617
  – liver 862
  – as a sheet 860
  – slave 962
  stand in a – sheet 952
  mark with a –
  stone 642, 931
whitechapel
  vehicle 272
Whitefriars 996
whiteness **430**
whitewash
  cover 223
  whiten 430
  cleanse 652
  ornament 847
  justify 937
  acquit 970
whitewashed
  get – 808

whitewasher 935
white wings 652
whitey-brown 433
whither
  tendency 176
  direction 278
  inquiry 461
whitlow 655
whittle 44, 253
whittled
  drunk 959
Whitsuntide 998
whiz 409
who 461
  – goes there? 669
  – would have
  thought? 508, 870
whoa! 265
whole *entire* **50**
  healthy 654
  make – 660
  as a – 50
  on the – 476, 480
  go the – hog 729
  the – time 106
  – truth
  truth 494
  disclosure 529
  veracity 543
wholesale
  large scale 31
  whole 50
  abundant 639
  trade 794
wholesome 656
wholly 50, 52
whoop 411
  war – 715, 722
whop *flog* 972
whoopee 840
whopper *lie* 546
whopping *huge* 192
whore 962
whoredom 961
whoremonger 962
whorl 248
why *cause* 153
  attribution 155
  inquiry 461
  indeed 535
  motive 615
  – not 868
wibble-wabble 314
wick 388, 423
wicked 945
  the – *bad men* 949
  impious 988
  the – one 978
wicker 219
wicket 66, 260

wide 202
  — apart 15
  —awake *hat* 225
  intelligent 498
  — away 196
  — berth 748
  — of the mark
  distance 196
  deviation 279
  error 495
  — of *distant* 196
  — open 194, 260
  — of the truth 495
  — world 180, 318
  in the — world 180
widen 194
  — the breach 713,
  900
wide-spread
  great 31
  dispersed 73
  space 180
  expanded 194
widow 905
widowhood 905
width 202
wield
  brandish 315
  handle 379
  use 677
  — authority 737
  — the sword 722
wieldy 705
wife 903
wig 225
wigging 932
wiggle 315
wight 373
wigwam 189
wild 851
  unproductive 169
  violent 173
  plain 344
  inattentive 458
  mad 503
  shy 623
  unskilled 699
  excited 824, 825
  untamed 851
  rash 863
  angry 900
  licentious 954
  run — 825
  — animals 366
  — beast *fierce* 173
  evil-doer 913
  — goose chase
  caprice 608
  useless 645
  unskilful 699
  — imagination 515

sow one's — oats
  grow up 131
  improve 658
  amusement 840
  vice 945
  intemperance 954
Wild, Jonathan —
  thief 792
  bad man 949
wilderness
  disorder 59
  unproductive 169
  space 180
  solitude 893
wild-fire 382
  spread like —
  violence 173
  influence 175
  expand 194
  publication 531
wile 545, 702
wilful
  voluntary 600
  obstinate 606
will
  volition **600**
  resolution 604
  testament 771
  gift 784
  at — 600
  at one's own
  sweet — 608
  have one's own —
  600, 748
  make one's — 360
  tenant at — 779
  — be 152
  — for the deed
  774, 937
  — of Heaven 601
  — he nil he 601
  — power 600
  — and will not 605
  — you 765
Will o' the wisp
  luminary 423
  imp 980
willing or unwilling
  601
willingness **602**
willow 839
willy-nilly 601, 744
wilted 659
wily 702
wimble 262
wimple 225
win 731, 775
  — the affections
  897
  — golden opinions
  931

— the heart 829
  — laurels 873
  — out 33
  — over *belief* 484
  induce 615
  content 831
wince
  bodily pain 378
  emotion 821
  excitement 825
  mental pain 828
  flinch 860
winch 307, 633
wind *convolution*
  [*see below*]
  velocity 274
  blast **349**
  life 359
  against the — 278,
  708
  before the — 278,
  734
  cast to the —s
  repudiate 610
  disuse 678
  not observe 773
  relinquish 782
  close to the — 278
  fair — 705
  to the four —s 180
  get — 531
  get the — up 860
  see how the —
  blows
  direction 278
  experiment 463
  foresight 510
  fickle 607
  in the — 151, 152
  lose — 688
  sail near the —
  direction 278
  skill 698
  sharp practice 940
  outstrip the — 274
  preach to the —s
  645
  raise the — 775
  scatter to the —s
  756
  see where the —
  lies 698
  short —ed 688
  sport of —s and
  waves 315
  sound of — and
  limb 654
  take the — out of
  one's sails
  render powerless
  158

hinder 706
  defeat 731
  touched in the —
  655
  what's in the — ?
  461
  — ahead 708
  — bag 584
  in the —'s eye 278
  — the horn 416
  hit between — and
  water 659
  — and weather
  permitting
  qualification 469
  possibility 470
wind *blast* [*see*
  above]
  convolution 248
  deviate 279
  circuition 311
  — round the heart
  897
  — up *strengthen* 159
  prepare 673
  complete 729
  - *accounts* 811
windbag 884
wind instruments
  417
wind-bound 706
windfall 618
wind-gauge 349
wind-gun 727
winding 248, 311
winding-sheet 363
windings and turn-
  ings 248
wind-jammer 273
windlass 307, 633
windless 688
windmill 312
  tilt at —s 638
window 260
  make the —s shake
  loud noise 404
  — dressing 544
wind-pipe 351
wind-up 67
windward, to - 236,
  278
windy 349
wine 298, 959
  put new — into old
  bottles 699
  look upon the —
  when it is red
  953
wine-bibbing 959
wine-cooler 387
wineglass 191

wing *extension* 39
  part 51
  side 236
  fly 267
  side-scene 599
  instrument 633
  refuge 666
  army 726
clip the –s 275
lend –s to 707
on the –
  motion 264
  flying 267
  transference 270
  departure 293
take – *journey* 266
  fly 267
  depart 293
under the – of
  safe 664
with –s *active* 682
– one's flight 293
– one's way 267
on the –s of the
  wind 274
wing-commander
  747
winged *swift* 274
wink 443, 550
  tip the – 550, 527
  – at
    be blind to 442
    disregard 458
    neglect 460
    permit 760
    forgive 918
  – of sleep 683
winning [*see* win]
  pleasing 829
  courteous 894
  lovable 897
winnings 775
winnow *sift* 42
  exclude 55
  inquire 461
  pick 609
  clean 652
  – the chaff from
    the wheat 465
winsome 829, 836
winter 126, 383
  – of our discon-
    tent 832
  – garden 840
  – sports 840
wintry 126
wipe *dry* 340
  clean 652
  disrespect 929
  flog 972
  give one a –

rebuke 932
– away 552
– the eyes
  relieve 834
– off old scores
  807, 952
– the tears 914
wire *ligature* 45
  filament 205
  telegraph 527, 534
  pull the –s 693
wire-drawn
  long 200
wireless 531
  – telegram 532
  – telegraph 534
  – telephone 534
wire-puller 526, 694
wire-worm 913
wiry *strong* 159
wis 514
wisdom **498**
  have cut one's –
    teeth 698
  worldly – 864
wise
  intelligent 498
  sage 500
  manner 627
  in such – 8
  word to the – 695
  – in one's own
    conceit 880
  – after the event
    135
  – man 500
  – maxim 496
  dine not –ly but
    too well 953
wiseacre 493, 500,
  wiser, nobody the –
  528
wish *will* 600
  intention 620
  desire 865
  do what one –es
    748
  – at the bottom of
    the Red Sea 832
  – the father to the
    thought
  misjudge 481
  credulous 486
  hope 858
  desire 865
  – joy 896
  – well 906
wishing-cap 993
wish-wash
  unmeaning 517

wishy-washy
  languid 160
  insipid 391
  feeble style 575
  unimportant 643
wisket 191
wisp 72
wistful
  thought 451
  care 459
  feeling 821
  desire 865
wit *intellect* 450
  wisdom 498
  humour **842**
  humorist 844
  mother – 498
  soul of – 572
  to – 522
  at one's –'s end
    475, 704
witch *oracle* 513
  ugly 846
  sorceress 994
  – doctor 994
witchcraft 992
witchery
  attraction 615
  pleasing 829
  sorcery 992
witching time 126,
  421
witenagemote 696
with *added* 37
  mixed 41
  ligature 45
  accompanying 88
  means 632
  go – 178
  – all its parts 52
  – regard to 9
  – a vengeance 31,
    52
  – a witness 31
withal
  in addition 37
  accompanying 88
  enough 639
withdraw
  subduct 38
  absent 187
  turn back 283
  recede 287
  depart 293
  – from
  recant 607
  relinquish 624
  dislike 867
withe 45
wither 195, 659
  – one's hopes 837

withered *weak* 160
  disease 655
withering
  harsh 739
  painful 830
  contempt 930
  censure 932
withers 250
  – unwrung 159,
    323
withhold *hide* 528
  restrain 751
  prohibit 761
  retain 781
  stint 819
  – one's assent 764
within 221
  derived from – 5
  place – 221
  keep – 221
  – an ace 32
  – bounds
    small 32
  shortcoming 304
  restraint 751
  – call 197
  – compass
  shortcoming 304
  temperate 953
  – the mark 304
  – one's memory
    505
  – reach 197, 705
without *unless* 8
  subduction 38
  exception 83
  absence 187
  exterior 220
  circumjacent 227
  exemption 777a
  derived from – 6
  not be able to do –
    630
  – alloy 827
  – ballast 605, 945
  – ceasing 136
  – ceremony 881
  – charge 815
  – fear of contra-
    diction 535
  – a dissentient
    voice 488
  – end 105, 112
  – exception 16, 79
  – excuse 945
  – fail 474, 604a
  – God 989
  – a leg to stand on
    158
  – limit 105
  – measure 105

complete 729
–room 191
– out one's salvation 990
– against time 684
– up [*see below*]
– upon
  influence 175
  incite 615
  excite 824
– one's way
  progress 282
  ascent 305
  exertion 686
  succeed 731
– well 705, 731
– wonders 682, 731
work up
  prepare 673
  use 677
  excite 824
– into *form* 240
– into a passion 900
workable 470
work-a-day 625, 682
worker 690
workhouse 691
working *acting* 170
  active 682
– bee 690
– man 690
– order 673
– towards 176
workman 690
workmanlike 698
workmanship 161, 680
works
  board of – 696
  good – 906
– of the mind 451
workshop 691
workwoman 690
world *great* 31
  events 151
  space 180
  universe **318**
  mankind 372
  fashion 852
  all the – over 180
  citizen of the – 910
  come into the – 359
  for all the – 615
  give to the – 531
  knowledge of the – 698
  man of the –

proficient 700
fashion 852
not for the – 489, 764
organized – 357
Prince of this – 978
rise in the – 734
throughout the – 180
– to come 152
follow to the –'s end 743
– forgetting by the world forgot 893
as the – goes 613
– of good 618, 648
a – of 102
– and his wife 102
– without end 112
worldling 943, 988
worldly 943, 989
world-wide
  great 31
  universal 78
  space 180
world-wisdom
  skill 698
  caution 864
  selfishness 943
worm *small* 193
  spiral 248
  animal 366
  bane 663
– in 228
– oneself
  ingress 294
  love 897
– out 480a
– that never dies 982
– one's way 275, 302
worm-eaten 659
worms, food for – 362
wormwood
  gall and – 395
worn *weak* 160
  damage 659
  fatigue 688
  well– *used* 677
– out 659, 841
worry
  vexation 828
  tease 830
  harass 907
worse 659, 835
– for wear 160
worship *title* 877
  servility 886

religious **990**
demon – 991
idol – 991
fire – 991
his – 967
place of – 1000
– Mammon 803
– the rising sun 886
worshipful 873
worst *defeat* 731
do one's – 659, 907
do your – 715, 909
have the – of it 732
make the – of 482
worst come to the – *certain* 474
  bad 649
  hopeless 859
worsted 205
worth *value* 644
  goodness 648
  possession 777
  price 812
  virtue 944
  penny – 814
  what one is – 780
– a great deal 803
– the money 815
– much 803
– one's salt 644
– while 646
worthless
  trifling 643
  useless 645
  profligate 945
worthy
  famous 873
  virtuous 944
  good 948
– of 924
– of belief 484
– of blame 932
– of notice 642
– of remark 642
wot 490
would: – fain 865
– that! 865
would-be *pert* 885
  usurping 925
wound *evil* 619
  injure 659
  pain 830
  anger 900
  keep the – green 919
– the feelings 830
– up 704
woven fabrics 219
wowser 988

wrack 162
  go to – and ruin
  perish 162
  fail 732
  bankrupt 804
wraith 980
wrangle
  disagreement 24
  reason 476
  quarrel 713
  contend 720
wrangler
  reasoner 476
  scholar 492
  opponent 710
wrap 223, 225
wrapped in
  attention 457
– clouds 528
– self 943
– thought 458
wrapper 223, 225
  inclosure 232
wraprascal 225
wrath 900
wreak *violent* 173
  harsh 739
– one's anger 919
– one's malice on 907
wreath *woven* 219
  circle 247
  trophy 733
  ornament 847
  honour 877
wreathe *weave* 219
wreathy 248
wreck
  remainder 40
  destruction 162
  damage 659
  defeat 732
wrecker 792
wrench *disjoin* 44
  draw 285
  extract 301
  twist 311
  tool 633
  seize 789
wrest *distort* 243
– from 789
– the sense 523
wrestle 720
wrestler 726
wretch *sufferer* 828
  sinner 949
wretched
  unimportant 643
  bad 649
  unhappy 828
wretchedly